Related Books of Interest

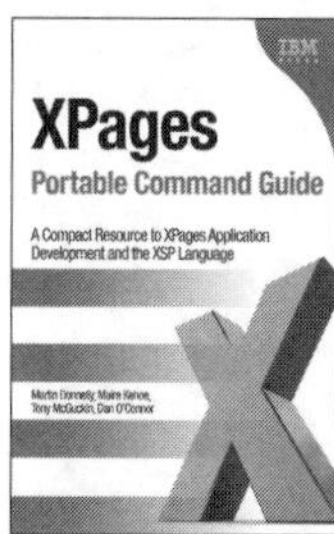

XPages Portable Command Guide

A Compact Resource to XPages Application Development and the XSP Language

By Martin Donnelly, Maire Kehoe, Tony McGuckin, Dan O'Connor

0-13-294305-0

A Practical Primer for XPages Application Development, Debugging, and Performance

Straight from the experts at IBM, this perfect portable XPages quick reference offers fast access to working code, tested solutions, expert tips, and example-driven best practices. Drawing on their unsurpassed experience as IBM XPages lead developers and customer consultants, the authors explore many lesser known facets of the XPages runtime, illuminating these capabilities with dozens of examples that solve specific XPages development problems. Using their easy-to-adapt code examples, you can develop XPages solutions with outstanding performance, scalability, flexibility, efficiency, reliability, and value.

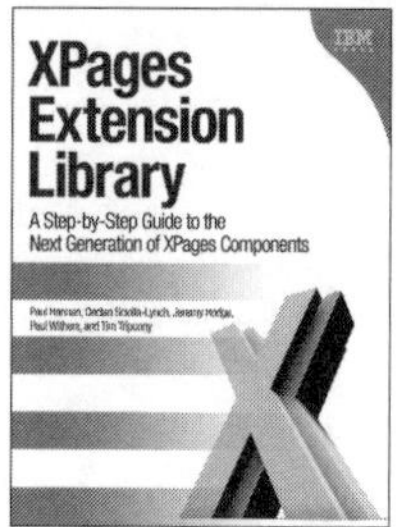

XPages Extension Library

A Step-by-Step Guide to the Next Generation of XPages Components

By Paul Hannan, Declan Sciolla-Lynch, Jeremy Hodge, Paul Withers, Tim Tripcony

0-13-290181-1

The first and only complete guide to Domino development with this library; it's the best manifestation yet of the underlying XPages Extensibility Framework. Complementing the popular *Mastering XPages*, it gives XPages developers complete information for taking full advantage of the new components from IBM.

Combining reference material and practical use cases, the authors offer step-by-step guidance for installing and configuring the XPages Extension Library and using its state-of-the-art applications infrastructure to quickly create rich web applications with outstanding user experiences.

Related Books of Interest

IBM Lotus Connections 2.5

Planning and Implementing Social Software for Your Enterprise

By Stephen Hardison, David Byrd, Gary Wood, Tim Speed, Michael Martin, Suzanne Livingston, Jason Moore, and Morten Kristiansen

ISBN: 0-13-700053-7

In *IBM Lotus Connections 2.5*, a team of IBM Lotus Connections 2.5 experts thoroughly introduces the newest product and covers every facet of planning, deploying, and using it successfully. The authors cover business and technical issues and present IBM's proven, best-practices methodology for successful implementation. The authors begin by helping managers and technical professionals identify opportunities to use social networking for competitive advantage–and by explaining how Lotus Connections 2.5 places full-fledged social networking tools at their fingertips. *IBM Lotus Connections 2.5* carefully describes each component of the product–including profiles, activities, blogs, communities, easy social bookmarking, personal home pages, and more.

Survival Guide for Lotus Notes and Domino Administrators

By Mark Elliott

ISBN: 0-13-715331-7

Mark Elliott has created a true encyclopedia of proven resolutions to common problems and has streamlined processes for infrastructure support. Elliott systematically addresses support solutions for all recent Lotus Notes and Domino environments.

Survival Guide for Lotus Notes and Domino Administrators is organized for rapid access to specific solutions in three key areas: client setup, technical support, and client software management. It brings together best practices for planning deployments, managing upgrades, addressing issues with mail and calendars, configuring settings based on corporate policies, and optimizing the entire support delivery process.

Listen to the author's podcast at:
ibmpressbooks.com/podcasts

Visit ibmpressbooks.com
for all product information

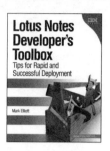

Mastering XPages

A Step-by-Step Guide to XPages Application Development and the XSP Language

2nd Edition

Martin Donnelly
Mark Wallace
Tony McGuckin

IBM Press
Pearson plc
Upper Saddle River, NJ • Boston • Indianapolis • San Francisco
New York • Toronto • Montreal • London • Munich • Paris •
Madrid

IBM Press Program Managers: Steven M. Stansel, Ellice Uffer
Cover design: IBM Corporation
Associate Publisher: Dave Dusthimer
Marketing Manager: Stephane Nakib
Executive Editor: Mary Beth Ray
Publicist: Heather Fox
Senior Development Editor: Christopher Cleveland
Editorial Assistant: Vanessa Evans
Managing Editor: Kristy Hart
Designer: Alan Clements
Senior Project Editor: Lori Lyons
Technical Reviewers: Dan O'Connor, Paul Stephen Withers
Copy Editor: Apostrophe Editing Services
Indexer: Larry Sweazy, Wordwise Publishing Services
Compositor: Nonie Ratcliff
Proofreaders: Kathy Ruiz, Sarah Kearns
Manufacturing Buyer: Dan Uhrig

Published by Pearson plc

Publishing as IBM Press

For information about buying this title in bulk quantities, or for special sales opportunities (which may include electronic versions; custom cover designs; and content particular to your business, training goals, marketing focus, or branding interests), please contact our corporate sales department at corpsales@pearsoned.com or (800) 382-3419.

For government sales inquiries, please contact governmentsales@pearsoned.com.

For questions about sales outside the U.S., please contact international@pearsoned.com.

Library of Congress Control Number: 2014930531

ISBN-13: 978-0-13-337337-0
ISBN-10: 0-13-337337-1

Text printed in the United States on recycled paper at Courier Westford, Inc. in Westford, Massachusetts.

First Printing: April 1014

For my wife and best friend Aileen, survivor of three XPages books ...
please don't let me write any more! Somehow "thanks"
can never say enough for all your help, advice, and patience.
—Martin

For Dee, Sam, and Becky. Second time around and a new set of challenges—
but the support, encouragement, and patience are still the same.
Go raibh míle maith agat, mo Ghrá.
—Mark

First, a big thank you to Martin and Eamon for giving leadership, motivation, time,
and most of all, understanding as we all made our journey through this second edition!
Second, sincere thanks and love to my parents for being truly the best parents—
and also to my extended family, thanks to all the in-laws and out-laws!
Finally, I dedicate this book to Paula and Anna-Rose—always live happy
and follow your dreams wherever they take you. All my love!
—Tony

Contents at a Glance

Part IV: Programmability

Part V: Application User Experience

Part VI: Performance, Scalability, and Security

Part VII: Appendixes

Contents

Foreword

Already three years have elapsed since we launched the first edition of this best seller. I say "best seller" because not only has it been a big hit with the community, but it also broke many IBM Press publishing records. I have seen it on a lot of desks while visiting customers, which is a real indicator of its true value! And there is a good reason for this: This book is an exhaustive reference for every XPages developer, from novice to expert. And this release is a worthy successor, with extensive information on all the major new features. Kudos to the gang of authors—it is most definitely an honor for me to be invited to take part in this adventure again.

Three years—even though it allowed my kids to grow by a couple of inches—it still seems like yesterday. But, in the IT space, it feels like decades. A lot of water has flowed under the bridge during this time. The IT landscape evolved toward social, mobile, and cloud development. Let's look at what happened over the course of this time and what's coming next.

The first edition of *Mastering XPages* was based on Notes®/Domino® 8.5.2. This was *before* the advent of the XPages Extension Library, an asset so important to XPages developers today that life without it seems unthinkable! Not only did this deliver a slew of new capabilities in and of itself, but it allowed us to offer a new application development paradigm to the community whereby XPages features could be delivered outside of the regular Notes/Domino product release cycle. In fact, we made good on this promise by delivering Upgrade Pack 1 for 8.5.3 in December 2011 (just a few months after 8.5.3 itself shipped). More goodies came in 9.0 with the release of a new server-side JavaScript™ debugger in Domino Designer. At the same time, we addressed performance issues with XPages for the Notes client and have continued to upgrade our key components such as Dojo, CKEditor, and XULRunner with each release. In 9.0.1 the XPages runtime has been updated to meet the latest and most stringent accessibility standards and achieve Section 508 compliance. It has also seen its support for mobile application development make significant strides—more on this a little later.

But in a sense, perhaps *the* biggest achievement for XPages over all this time has been its solidification. From a technical standpoint, we have made the code very robust, performant, and functional. These three intervening years have sealed the adoption of XPages by the community. We have seen many customers moving to XPages—not just to modernize existing applications, but also to create completely new applications from the ground up. I remember the early days when we were looking for successful implementations of XPages. It was a challenge as the technology was so new, but nowadays XPages is widely used for both mission-critical and situational applications. Because of great customer adoption, it now has a large and solid install base around the globe and in all types of organizations, from nonprofits to small and medium enterprises (SMEs) to Fortune 500 corporations. Japan has an "XPages Day" event; an XPages Code-A-Thon has just completed in India...and did you know that *Mastering XPages* has been translated to Chinese?

On the social side, we recently integrated the XPages runtime with the IBM Social Business® Toolkit SDK. This enables XPages applications to extend their reach beyond Notes/Domino and integrate with the broader ICS social platform. By leveraging this SDK, developers can easily integrate social features into their applications and move them to the next level. For example, it becomes easy to collaborate through a community, to query people profiles, to share files, and have a unified search mechanism. This opens up a world of new possibilities, particularly for organizations that have a mix of ICS technologies deployed. From a technical standpoint, because the SDK also targets regular J2EE platforms, the code is the same between all these platforms. This demonstrates one of the key capabilities of XPages for sharing and reusing code across the portfolio.

The XPages mobile story started on OpenNTF.org when a set of dedicated mobile controls was released in 2011. This mobile library was ultimately productized and released in 8.5.3 UP1, along with a "mobilized" version of the Discussion and Teamroom templates. Further improvements have arrived more recently in 9.0.1, including new server-side APIs to assist with device detection and resource management, new mobile debug enablers, and a new common mobile theme based on the IBM OneUI Dojo Extension stylekit (aka IBM IDX). Mobile will definitely be a key focus area in the future: We want XPages to be a technology of choice for writing web-based mobile applications, leveraging the latest and most popular libraries. Despite the proliferation of different devices, with different screen sizes and UI, we aim to ensure that the promise of our write-once-run-everywhere paradigm is a reality in this space. Furthermore, XPages now has the infrastructure to support responsive design—an essential building block for modern mobile applications—and you should expect to see more innovation in this area coming soon in both the core product and on OpenNTF.org. One such example is the recently released Twitter Bootstrap4XPages project on OpenNTF, which makes the great Twitter Bootstrap UI framework available to XPages developers.

To conclude, I would like to talk about increasing access to our application development platform. It is our constant goal to break down barriers to entry and to on-board more and more developers by making our development and deployment story quicker, lighter, and better for everyone. Think about how the cloud can help us here—for instance, what about a lightweight design-time experience provided via a web-based design tool? This would make XPages immediately available to *any* developer *anywhere*! Couple with this a simple facility for instantly deploying the resulting applications to the cloud, and you suddenly have a massively powerful and productive environment. Moreover, by adding tight and seamless integration with IBM SmartCloud® for Social Business, you have a compelling and valuable new model for your enterprise featuring XPages as its shining star.

So the XPages story continues apace, embracing all the new technologies and trends: social, mobile, and cloud computing. What is coming is exciting, and XPages aims to put all of it at your fingertips. Enjoy this book—it marks the gateway to the future.

Philippe Riand
IBM Senior Technical Staff Member
ICS Social Application Development Architect

Preface

XPages made its official public debut in Notes/Domino version 8.5, which went on general release in January 2009. In the intervening 5 years, there have been five more releases, and that's not including the XPages Upgrade Pack, which shipped for 8.5.3, or the many XPages Extension Library releases on OpenNTF.org. Even since the first edition of this book was published in 2011, two other XPages books have come to market; the *XPages Portable Command Guide* and the *XPages Extension Library*. XPages boasts a vibrant global development community that has adopted, extended, and innovated with the technology in so many different ways to build a veritable myriad of applications. Suffice to say it has been a rapid, eventful, and successful journey so far, and one which the authors of this book have at times struggled to keep pace with! But nonetheless, the goal of this new edition remains the same as before: to provide a single comprehensive guide that enables readers to confidently take on, or actively participate in, real-world XPages application-development projects.

Approach

The first edition of this book is based on XPages in Notes/Domino 8.5.2. This edition is based on XPages in Notes/Domino 9.0.1 and thus is a considerably larger volume than its predecessor, as it needs to cover a lot more ground. As well as wide-ranging updates to the material featured in the first edition, it also adds four new chapters and several hundred extra pages of content. Despite its considerable bulk, it is intended to be accessible to both novice and expert alike, and aims to provide all the help and information needed to get XPages projects built and delivered to the highest standard.

The authors seek to cover all aspects of the XPages development spectrum and to engage the reader with hands-on problems wherever possible. Most chapters come with one or more sample applications that provide plentiful exercises and examples aimed at enabling you to quickly and efficiently solve everyday development challenges. These resources are located on the web at www.ibmpressbooks.com/title/9780133373370, so waste no time in downloading before getting started!

Conventions

Any programming code, markup, or XSP keywords are illustrated in numbered listings using a fixed width font.

User-interface elements (menus, links, buttons, and so on) of the Notes client, Domino Designer, or any sample applications are referenced using a bold font.

Visual representations of the design-time experience or runtime features are typically captured as screen shots and written as numbered figures, using superimposed callouts where appropriate.

How This Book Is Organized

This book is divided into seven parts to separately address the many different aspects of XPages software development in as logical a manner as possible:

Part I, "Getting Started with XPages": This part gets you familiar with XPages at a conceptual level. It aims to have you up and running quickly on the basics of the design-time tooling and runtime framework, and to get you comfortable with the overall application development paradigm.

- **Chapter 1, "An Introduction to XPages":** Here, you are introduced to the history of XPages and given some high-level insights into its design principles in order to understand exactly what it is and what it is not. This is all about giving you the right context for XPages by defining the problems it solves, the technologies on which it is based, and where it might go in the future.
- **Chapter 2, "Getting Everything You Need":** This chapter concerns itself with the practical business of obtaining, installing, and configuring Domino Designer and successfully walking you through your first "Hello World" XPage! It also focuses on the XPages Extension Library and how best to integrate it into your XPages development environment.
- **Chapter 3, "Building Your First XPages Application":** This chapter aims to provide a breadth-first hands-on experience of building a simple web application using the XPages integrated development environment. This is really just an introductory practical to get your feet wet and ensure you are comfortable with the basics of the application development model before diving any deeper.

Part II, "XPages Development: First Principles": This part is mostly architectural in nature and aims to give you an appreciation of what's happening under the XPages hood. This is an essential prerequisite to some of the more advanced topics, like XPages performance and scalability.

- **Chapter 4, "Anatomy of an XPage":** This chapter examines the XSP markup language and gives a simple example of all the XPages core elements (controls and such) as well as the more important elements contributed to XPages via the XPages Extension Library. It provides a great broad-based view of XPages basics.
- **Chapter 5, "XPages and JavaServer Faces":** This chapter looks at JavaServer Faces (JSF), which is the web-application development framework on which XPages is based. It looks at some core JSF design points and how XPages leverages and extends the framework.
- **Chapter 6, "Building XPages Application Logic":** This chapter is a primer for XPages programmability. It introduces the various tools that can be used to implement XPages application logic so that you will be ready to work with the practical examples that are coming down the pike.

Part III, "Data Binding": This part is really about how XPages reads and writes Notes/Domino data. XPages comes with a library of visual controls that are populated at runtime using a process known as data binding. The mechanics of the data binding process is explored in depth for Notes views and documents.

- **Chapter 7, "Working with Domino Documents":** This chapter focuses on reading and writing Notes documents via XPages. Advanced use cases are explored and **every** design property on the Domino document data source is explained and put through its paces using practical examples.
- **Chapter 8, "Working with Domino Views":** In this chapter, the Domino view data source is dissected and examined, property by property. A section is also dedicated to Domino calendar views, including an in-depth look at how to use REST services to access calendar data. Again, practical exercises are used to drive home the material under discussion
- **Chapter 9, "Beyond the View Basics":** Working with Notes/Domino views is a large subject area, so much so that it demands a second chapter to cover all the details. This chapter looks at the various container controls that are available in the standard XPages control library, whose job is to display view data in different formats and layouts in order to support a myriad of customer use cases. This edition includes an in-depth look at the DataView control that was added to the XPages runtime in Notes/Domino 9.0.

Part IV, "Programmability": This part covers the black art of programming—essentially how to code your applications to do everything from the most basic user operation to writing your own controls that implement completely customized behaviors. This part includes a look at XPages in the Notes client and considers cross-platform application development issues. This edition adds two new chapters in this part focused on XPages debugging and mobile application development.

- **Chapter 10, "Custom Controls":** This chapter explains the "mini-XPage" design element that is the custom control. It explains how to leverage the custom control in order to "componentize" your application and then maximize the reuse of your XPages development artifacts.
- **Chapter 11, "Advanced Scripting":** Advanced scripting is an umbrella for many cool topics, like AJAX, Dojo, @Functions, agent integration, managed beans, and so forth. This edition includes a new, extensive field guide that looks at the practicalities of extending the functionality of the rich text editor. This is a must for anyone looking to add pizzazz to their XPages applications.
- **Chapter 12, "XPages Extensibility":** This chapter explains how to use the XPages extensibility APIs to build and/or consume new controls. This is an amazingly powerful feature that has only recently become available and is well worth exploring once you have mastered XPages fundamentals.
- **Chapter 13, "XPages in the Notes Client":** XPages in the Notes client initially explains how you can take your XPages web applications offline and then goes on to highlight how you can take advantage of powerful features of the client platform itself, and how to manage applications that run in both environments. The content of this chapter is considerably expanded in this edition to account for many new innovations in this space since Notes/Domino 8.5.2. In particular, it gives in-depth examinations to performance related enhancements.
- **Chapter 14, "XPages Mobile Application Development":** This new chapter explains how to build Domino mobile applications using XPages. It covers mobile application design patterns and best practices, as well as all the XPages mobile controls. It gives invaluable information as to how best to debug XPages mobile applications and also looks at the very latest XPages mobile extensions available on OpenNTF.org.
- **Chapter 15, "XPages Unplugged and Debugged":** This new chapter explains the many and varied means of debugging XPages applications—everything from basic printing and logging techniques right through to a thorough exploration of the Server-Side Java Script debugger which was added to Domino Designer 9.0. It also features sections on Java debugging and Client-Side JavaScript debugging.

Part V, "Application User Experience": This part is all about application look and feel. You learn not just how to make your apps look good and behave well, but how to do so for an international audience! It also includes a new chapter on the enhanced application layout features that were delivered as part of the 9.0 release.

- **Chapter 16, "XPages Theming":** This chapter teaches you how to manage the appearance and behavior of your application's user interface. It provides an in-depth look at ad-hoc XPages application styling using cascading style sheets, as well as the main features of the standard XPages UI themes, and explains how to create your own customized themes.
- **Chapter 17, "Application Layout":** This new chapter describes how to build slick user interfaces quickly using out-of-the-box controls, in particular the Application Layout control that gives the chapter its name.
- **Chapter 18, "Internationalization":** Read this chapter to learn how your XPages applications can be translated so that they look, feel, and behave as native applications in any geographical locale.

Part VI, "Performance, Scalability, and Security": Up to this point this book has concentrated on the skills and tools you need to know to develop state-of-the-art collaborative applications. Part VI shifts to deployment and what you need to do to make sure your applications meet customer expectations in terms of performance, scalability, and security.

- **Chapter 19, "A First Look at Performance and Scalability":** This chapter highlights various tips and tricks that will enable you to tune your XPages application for optimal performance and scalability in various deployment scenarios.
- **Chapter 20, "Advanced Performance Topics":** This voluminous chapter is new to the second edition and aims to impart all you ever need to know about XPages performance and scalability. Building on the previous chapter, it introduces you to the XPages Toolbox—an essential utility used to profile XPages applications and identify problem performance areas. It also explains key aspects of the XPages request processing lifecycle, and what you need to understand when using partial refresh, partial execute, dynamic content and so forth. This is essential reading for anyone putting XPages applications into production.
- **Chapter 21, "Security":** Learn about application security issues and considerations and see how XPages integrates with the Domino server and Notes client security models.

Part VII, "Appendixes"

- **Appendix A, "XSP Programming Reference":** This appendix points to a collection of definitive reference sources that describe all the details of the XSP tags, Java™ and JavaScript classes. It provides examples of how to use these resources to find the information you need.

- **Appendix B, "XSP Style Class Reference":** This appendix identifies all the standard XPages CSS files and style classes used to build XPages application user interfaces. It's an essential quick reference for Chapter 16.
- **Appendix C, "Useful XPages Sites on the Net":** A snapshot of the authors' favorite XPages websites at the time of writing. This list of sites should help you find whatever it is you need to know about XPages that isn't found in this book.

Acknowledgments

One might be forgiven for thinking that a second edition of any book is no major undertaking, but somehow or other the effort required on this occasion has proven every bit as challenging as the first time around! After a long haul, we have finally gotten over the line and we would like to take this opportunity to thank the many people who helped us stay the course.

It is only fitting that we start with our two technical reviewers, Dan O'Connor and Paul Withers. You two did a tremendous job and didn't just confine your feedback to the new content. Your keen insights and observations have made this a much better book.

A sincere thank you to Eamon Muldoon, whose support on this effort was critical to its success. In fact, most every member of the XPages and Domino Designer teams were leaned on for a bit of help at some stage of the process—so "muchas gracias" to Brian Gleeson, Carlos Parreno Bonano, Darin Egan, Dario Chimisso, Gary Marjoram, Jonathan Roche, Lisa Henry, Máire Kehoe, Padraic Edwards, Paul Hannan, Robert Dignam and Torsten Weigelt. A special mention also goes out to Pete Janzen, Scott Morris, John Woods, and Philippe Riand for their encouragement, support, and advocacy of all things XPages. And also to Jim Quill, whose contributions to the original book remain largely intact in this updated edition.

Needless to say, we remain indebted to all those who helped us with the first edition, namely: Azadeh Salehi, Bill Hume, Brian Bermingham, Brian Leonard, Dan O'Connor, Dave Connolly, Dave Kern, David Taieb, Edel Gleeson, Gearóid O'Treasaigh, Girish P. Baxi, Graham O'Keeffe, Ishfak Bhagat, Jaitirth Shirole, Jeff deRienzo, Jeff Eisen, Jim Cooper, Jim Quill, John Grosjean, John Mackey, Kathy Howard, Lorcan McDonald, Margaret Rora, Matthew Flaherty, Mike Kerrigan, Maureen Leland, Na Pei, Peter Rubinstein, Russ Holden, Santosh Kumar, Simon Butcher, Simon Hewett, Srinivas Rao, Steve Castledine, Steve Leland, Thomas Gumz, Tom Carriker, Willie Doran, Xi Pan Xiao, and Yao Zhang. Apologies to any IBMers accidentally omitted; let us know and we'll be sure to include you in the reprints!

To our friends at IBM Press—in particular Mary Beth Ray, Chris Cleveland, and the Production team—your patience for our many fits and starts over the course of this edition is gratefully appreciated! And on the IBM side of that relationship, we echo those sentiments to Steven Stansel and Ellice Uffer.

Finally, a great big THANK YOU, as always, to our customers and business partners! You are a fantastic community to whom we owe so much for the success of XPages. We hope you enjoy this book and that it helps you in a practical everyday way. Keep building those apps!

About the Authors

The authors of this book have a number of things in common. All three hail from Ireland, work for the IBM Ireland software lab, and have made significant contributions to the development of XPages over the past number of years.

Martin Donnelly is a software architect and technical lead for the Domino Designer and XPages teams in IBM Ireland. He has worked on all XPages releases to date and also on a precursor technology known as XFaces. Martin was also a development contributor to such products as the IBM Java Visual editor and IBM Rational® Application Developer. In the 1990s while living and working in Massachusetts, Martin was a lead developer on Domino Designer; this has now gone full circle as he rejoined the Domino Designer team in 2013 to head up the 9.0.1 release. Martin lives in Cork with his wife Aileen, daughters Alison, Aisling, and Maeve, and retired greyhounds Evie and Chelsea. Outside of work his main leisure time pursuits are soccer, fishing, and gardening.

Mark Wallace is a software architect in the IBM Ireland software lab. In the past, he worked on the XFaces runtime, which was developed for Lotus® Component Designer and subsequently evolved into the XPages runtime. He has a keen interest in programming models and improving developer productivity. Mark has worked in Lotus and IBM for more than 17 years on various products, and he is currently leading the Social Business Toolkit open source project. Mark lives in Dublin with his wife and two children and spends as much time as possible in the Ireland's sunny south east enjoying fishing and kayaking with his family.

Tony McGuckin is a senior software engineer in the IBM Ireland software lab. Having studied software engineering at the University of Ulster, he began his career with IBM in 2006 and joined the XPages core runtime team shortly thereafter. When not directly contributing to the core runtime, Tony is busy with software research and development for the next generation of application development tooling, most recently focusing on mobile and responsive design. Tony also spends a lot of time directly engaging with IBM customers as an XPages consultant, where he shows his flair for UI development and his deep understanding of application performance. Tony enjoys spending time with his wife and daughter, and getting out into the great outdoors for hill walking and the occasional chance to do some hunting in the surrounding hillsides of his native County Derry.

Contributing Author

Jim Quill is a development manager on the IBM Connections team in IBM Ireland. He has been with IBM for 5 years, and in this time he has managed to pack a lot in. He started on the XPages team and helped deliver several 8.5 releases. He then moved to the Connections Mail team where he was the technical lead role for the integration of Connections and Domino. He has most recently just taken up a new challenge—switching to development management. Previous to IBM, Jim enjoyed more than 13 years at Oracle Ireland. There, he worked in areas such as product development and database migration technology, and he was both principal software engineer and technical architect for a number of internal Oracle® support systems. Jim lives in the coastal village of Malahide, north County Dublin, with his wife and four children. When not acting as the kids' taxi, he continues to play competitive basketball...way past his retirement date.

PART I

Getting Started with XPages

CHAPTER 1

An Introduction to XPages

The first step on this journey is to learn what XPages is as a technology, to understand its objectives, and to recognize the strategic value it offers as an application development framework. This chapter is not just for XPages newbies—XPages is after all an ever-evolving work-in-progress, and thus it pays for even the most experienced XPages developers to take a fresh look at its core themes from time to time. So why not now?

XPages Fundamentals

XPages is a web-application development framework for the Notes/Domino platform. That is, from Notes/Domino 8.5 onward, XPages is *the* recommended approach for anyone writing a new web application or embarking on modernizing an existing application to the latest state-of-the-art. In a nutshell, XPages is a standards-based Java runtime environment that supports all the defining features of Web 2.0.

At the core of XPages is a technology known as JavaServer Faces (JSF). JSF is commonly used as a base technology across many other commercial web-application development offerings, such as IBM Rational Application Developer, Oracle JDeveloper, JBoss, and so on.

Rest assured however that even though JSF is an industry standard for Java developers engaged in J2EE™ application development, *you* do not have to be a Java/Java 2 Platform Enterprise Edition (J2EE) developer to use XPages. In fact there is no requirement whatsoever to write any Java code to build a "typical" XPages application because the presence of JSF as the foundation layer of XPages is completely transparent to the mainstream Domino application development experience. That said, the full power of JSF is right there in XPages and can be leveraged directly by advanced users as appropriate, and if you are a Java developer with some JSF experience, you will probably find many aspects of XPages to be very intuitive.

XPages is based on JSF version 1.1, although some important fixes and capabilities from JSF version 1.2 and 2.0 have been applied to the XPages foundation layer. This was done on a case-by-case basis to either solve a specific problem or take advantage of particular optimizations introduced to JSF after the 1.1 release. As a consequence, XPages, in reality, is roughly equivalent to the JSF 2.0 standard. However, XPages is unlikely to be *formally* rebased to a particular JSF release level in the future.

JSF 1.1 was developed through the Java Community Process (JCP) under Java Specifications Request (JSR) 127. So, what's all this JCP and JSR mumbo jumbo and why should you care? Well, according to Wikipedia, the JCP "is a formalized process that allows interested parties to get involved in the definition of future versions and features of the Java platform." The JSR, however, is the instrument used to describe the nitty-gritty details of an actual feature specification. Thus, JSF is not an IBM creation but the collective result of collaborations between many technical leaders in the industry to come up with an agreed-upon framework that enables all players to build better Java tools and applications. In that light, it's easy to argue that building XPages on top of a JSF platform can be only a good thing!

Among the many benefits XPages derives from JSF is the capability to target multiple platforms (for example, the web, the Notes client, and mobile devices), to maintain stateful applications, to adapt to and work with data from different sources, and so on. These particular JSF-centric topics are given in-depth treatment in Part II, "XPages Development: First Principles." Most important, however, is that the extensible nature of JSF is fully exposed in XPages. Without this, for example, there would be no XPages Extension Library—now there's a frightening thought! Indeed, extensibility is so critical to XPages that is has changed the way we do business: It governs how, where, and when features are delivered. This key point will be expanded upon a little later as the history and evolution of XPages in examined.

Onward and Upward: A Path of Continuous Improvement

As already mentioned, the initial release of XPages took place in January 2009. Since then, the runtime has gone through four further significant releases in as many years. With each revision came a slew of new features, continuous upgrades to core technologies (Dojo, CKEditor, XUL-Runner, and such), as well as a raft of enhanced application development tooling capabilities inside Domino Designer. Figure 1.1 summarizes the evolution of Domino Designer and XPages in terms of key features since 2009.

On reading about the official history of Notes/Domino, it was interesting to note that the provenance of the product was not simply traced back to Lotus Notes Release 1 in 1989, but as far back as work done by the founders of Iris Associates on PLATO Notes in the late 1970s! To some extent, similarities exist here with XPages. That is, although XPages first surfaced in Notes/Domino version 8.5, a precursor of the technology, called `XFaces`, appeared a few years earlier in a product called Lotus Component Designer (LCD). LCD was an Eclipse-based integrated development environment that used XFaces to build applications for IBM WebSphere® Application Server (WAS) and IBM WebSphere Portal Server. While Lotus Component Designer went into maintenance mode for a variety of reasons, its technology continued to receive development investment. The XFaces runtime was seen as a flexible technology that could quickly simplify, modernize, and standardize the Notes/Domino web-application development experience. It was quickly adapted and specialized for the Notes/Domino platform and evolved into what is now known as XPages. The Eclipse plug-ins that composed the LCD IDE were integrated into Domino Designer and updated and augmented from there to suit the new XPages runtime.

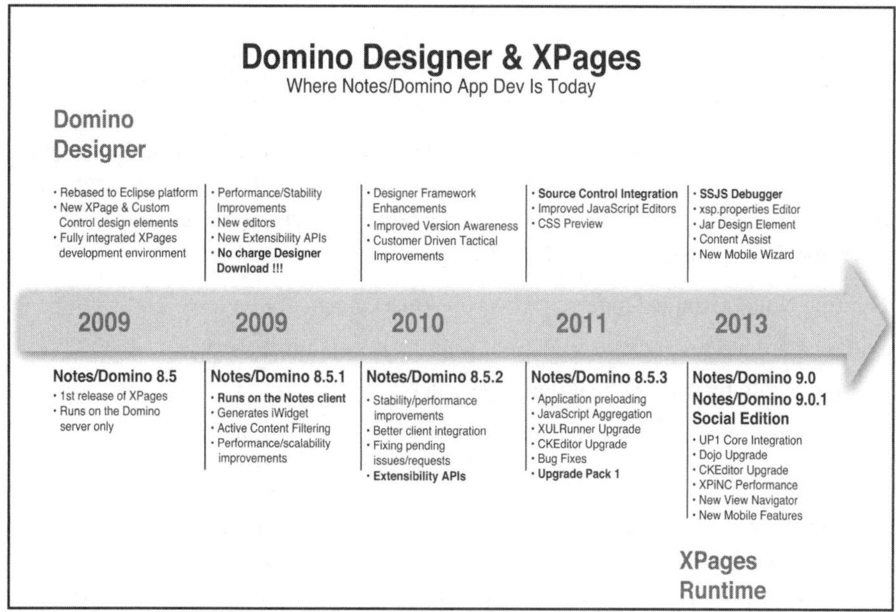

Figure 1.1 The Application Development Progress Curve for Notes Domino since 8.5

In its first release, XPages shipped as part of the Domino server and Domino Designer kits. Domino Designer was rebased to run on the Eclipse platform in that same 8.5 release, and with it, the application development experience for Domino web developers was utterly transformed. The new underlying Eclipse platform meant that an entire host of new tools could be built for or surfaced in Domino Designer. The XPages development experience suddenly featured all the tooling that had been requested for Designer in general for many a long day (such as a control and data palette, drag-and-drop components, property sheets, structural page outlines, specialized editors, and so on). A new design element called an `XPage`, along with a junior sidekick called a *custom control*, appeared on the navigator, and instances of these could be built up in an intuitive WSYISYG fashion, using a combination of all the aforementioned cool tools. When built, they could be immediately previewed or run directly on the Domino server from a web browser. Things had suddenly become more interesting and, as it happened, this was just the start.

XPages support for the Notes client was added in version 8.5.1, which was released just 9 months later in October 2009. It is a testament to the architecture of the XPages runtime environment that support for a major platform could be added in the course of such a quick-turnaround point release. Given the short development runway, the feature scope for XPages in the Notes client (abbreviated to XPiNC for convenience, which is pronounced "x-pink") was understandably restricted. In essence, its main goal was to enable customers to run their new XPages web applications offline. For any customer with an existing XPages application, the use case to run locally in the client had just two simple requirements:

1. Create a local replica of your application using standard NSF replication.
2. Select a new XPages client launch option in the local replica.

Of course, a new XPages client application can be created, just like it could be for the web, as long as the client launch option is selected in the Notes client or in Domino Designer. With some opportunistic exceptions, however, in its initial release, the client user experience was, to a large extent, a web user experience. Some of the notable exceptions included

- Integrating Notes client behaviors, such as bookmarking and failover
- Providing a limited set of client-side JavaScript-to-Java platform services
- Conforming with the Notes client security model
- Adding support for preemptive document saving
- Enabling XPages to fully participate in Composite Applications

Another hugely significant aspect of the 8.5.1 release was that Domino Designer became available as a no-charge download for the first time. This powerful initiative aimed to empower the Notes/Domino application development community by putting all the tools it needed into its hands at no expense. Finally, it was possible for newcomers to freely experiment with Notes/Domino as a development platform. As you will learn in the next chapter, getting up and running with XPages development is now just a matter of downloading and installing the Domino Designer image. You can be up and running in one-half an hour: win-win!

Within another year, Notes 8.5.2 was released, and it also broke new ground in several important ways. Most significant among these was that XPages now came with an official set of published extensibility APIs. On the face of it, this may not seem like a big deal, but it was a game changer for XPages development. Why? The extensibility APIs enabled XPages developers to create their own components, be they visual controls, data sources, validators, converters, simple actions—you name it. The community was now free to innovate and create new customized extensions as needed. For instance, a business partner could build new extensions and either share them with the community or include them as part of a commercial product offering. To get the ball rolling, a sample extension library was released on OpenNTF.org in September 2010. The intention was to provide useful and practical examples that demonstrated the power of the extensibility APIs. The outcome went far beyond that!

The XPages Extension Library (as it became known) contained a veritable slew of new components dotted right across the broad app dev landscape. It also continued to grow rapidly as new updates appeared on OpenNTF with quick-fire regularity, and it soon contained everything from iNotes control wrappers to OneUI application layout containers to RDBMS data sources. A slick sample application showed off its capabilities (see Figure 1.2), and the community grabbed this manna from heaven and used it with pioneering abandon. In essence, an extension library that had been intended as a demo implementation of the extensibility APIs had suddenly grown arms and legs and taken on a life of its own. Soon it was used in production applications, and questions inevitably arose about support and future directions.

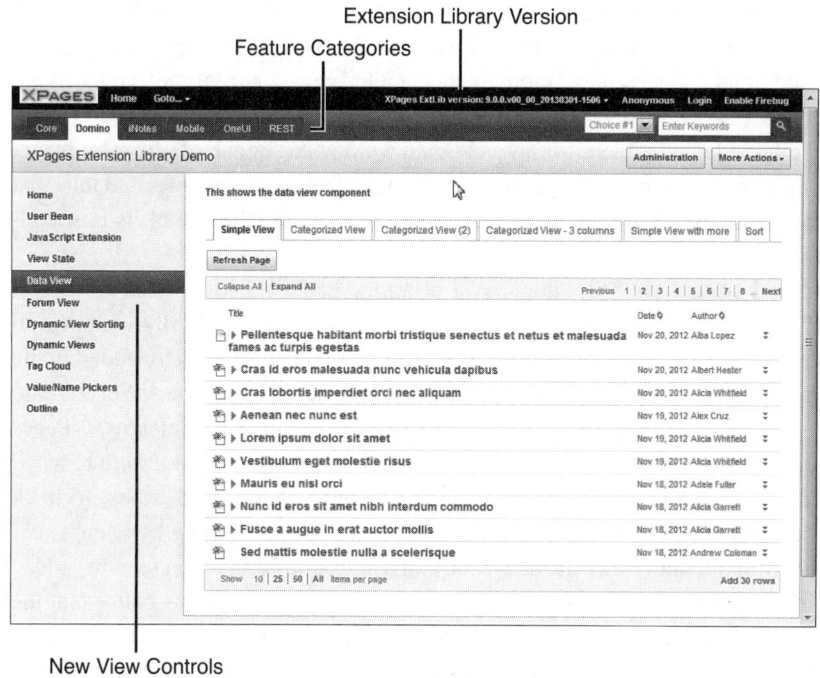

Figure 1.2 The Extension Library Sample Application: XPagesExt.nsf

The Extension Library posed an interesting dilemma for product management. The XPages core runtime is a fully supported IBM technology, whereas the XPages Extension Library is an open source technology provided by the OpenNTF community. What happens when a production application uses extension library components—is this configuration supported by IBM? Technically, the answer is no; although support for any issues arising with extended components are typically resolved either by IBMers or business partners through the OpenNTF forum (or through similar online resources such as Stack Overflow). The picture that emerged, however, was that although many organizations are willing to adopt open source software for production applications, others have a more conservative policy. The challenge was how to satisfy both constituencies.

A decision was taken to *productize*[1] large parts of the Extension Library and fold it back into the core XPages offering to make sure that customers could enjoy all the best newly added extensions in a fully supported manner. This was achieved by inventing a new software delivery instrument called an *Upgrade Pack*. As you can see referring to Figure 1.1, the 8.5.3 release featured an Upgrade Pack (UP1). An Upgrade Pack is a set of new features that depends on a given base version (8.5.3 in this example) and that can be installed on top of the base platform. 8.5.3 UP1 shipped in December 2011, just a few months after 8.5.3, and delivered a fully supported suite of components that originated from the Extension Library. For XSP markup, the content of UP1 amounted to more than 100 new tags...more than the underlying core runtime! This was the first time a significant set of new features was delivered outside the regular Notes/Domino product release cycle and heralded a new era for application development on the platform. It meant that it was now possible to deliver new XPages features as and when the need arose, and thus that application development deliverables need no longer be a slave to the schedule of its host container. Good news for developers!

When 2013 rolled around you, saw the arrival of a new major release: Notes 9.0 Social Edition and a 9.0.1 maintenance release later that year. This release automatically included all the 8.5.3 UP1 content as standard—plus any bug fixes and enhancements that were added in the intervening time. In terms of brand-new features, Domino Designer boasted a new Server-Side JavaScript (SSJS) debugger—a much requested capability. For all the 8.5.x releases, XPages developers had coded application logic primarily using SSJS but, for all that time, were reduced to using fairly primitive debugging methods (think `print()` and `_dump()` functions) to track down problems. The SSJS debugger filled a major gap in the tooling story and greatly enhances developer productivity. In the same vein, the new code assist and code completion features added to the XSP editor in the same release make life all the easier because it is in this editor that the XPages developer spends a large portion of the working day. On the runtime side, XPages delivered many new XPiNC performance enhancements as well as the latest updates to core technologies such as Dojo, CKEditor, Active Content Filtering, and so on.

At press time, both the XPages and Domino Designer development teams continue to work on cool new features for future releases. The improvement curve for application development on Notes/Domino continues onward and upward.

The XPages Development Paradigm

XPages brought along a new development paradigm that is quite different to what Domino web developers were used to up until version 8.5. With XPages, black magic practices, such as

1. The term "productize" was used by the XPages team to describe the processes that needed to be applied to make the Extension Library open source software compliant with IBM product guidelines and standards. For starters, this meant that all the runtime code included in UP1 had to be accessible and localized. It also meant that all the code had to be consistent with the XPages core model; for example, that tag semantics had to be made consistent across the whole runtime. A lot of work also went into ensuring that the extension library code was actually feature complete.

`$$Return` fields and strategically embedded pass-through HTML, are no longer the web dev modus operandi. Instead XPages development is driven by combining Cascading Style Sheets (CSS), JavaScript, HTML, and the XSP tag language. Although this is no doubt a superior model, and certainly one that is immediately more intuitive to web developers from a non-Domino background, an investment of time and energy in learning the ins and outs of XPages development cannot be avoided.

The term *XPages* (plural) usually refers to the entity that is the runtime as a whole. In its singular form, an *XPage* refers to a Notes/Domino design element, just like a traditional form or view. It is the basic unit of currency for XPages development. Developers create individual XPage elements to present information, accept user input, execute application logic, and then link them to form an end user application. If you look under the covers at an XPage in Domino Designer, you see an XML document composed of various tags and attributes, and the XPages engine ultimately transforms this XML document into an HMTL page.

Any developer familiar with JSF will already notice a departure here with XPages. The default markup layer for JSF is provided using a technology known as JavaServer Pages (JSP). As indicated previously, this layer in XPages has been replaced with a pure XML markup, which greatly simplifies the programming model. In other words, all the visual controls, application logic, and layout information that comprise an XPage are encapsulated in a well-defined, well-formed tag syntax that is easier for developers to work with. Even at that, however, this raw XML file is not the default developer interface. Domino Designer provides a design-time visualization of the XPage that the developer can work with interactively by dragging and dropping controls and data objects, setting attributes using simple gestures in property panels, or by simply using direct keyboard input. All such activity causes the appropriate XPages XML markup to be generated on behalf of the user. The XML markup can be viewed or further modified manually via a specialized XPages source editor in Domino Designer (often referred to as the XSP editor).

Thus, Designer provides different entry levels for the application developer working at the XPages frontlines. Newcomers typically begin by working with the visual XPage canvas and then may start to work more directly with the source markup as they become more familiar with the technology, depending of course on what they are trying to achieve in a given scenario. At the end of the day, however, regardless of how it is edited or viewed, it is worth remembering that an XPage is just a text file made up of an orderly bunch of tags.

It is also important to realize that any *controls* defined by these XPages tags are user-interface objects only. Associating data with such controls is a separate step that is achieved by explicitly binding a control to a data source object. This differs from the traditional Notes/Domino paradigm where display fields and data items are tightly coupled. (For example, when a field is created on a form, a data item of the same name is automatically created after a document instance of that form is saved.) This schema-less approach has always been "the Notes way" and is useful for putting an application together quickly, but it also has some serious downsides. For example, when data fields are defined purely within a particular form, what happens if and when this data needs to be accessed or updated from somewhere else in the application? It may well be that reusing the same form is not appropriate in that user interface (UI) context. Clever use of subforms can alleviate that problem to some degree, but metadata often ends up being duplicated across forms and subforms to get around this issue.

The problem becomes more egregious when dealing with heavyweight design elements, such as views. A view, like a form, contains all the presentation layout details and the content definition in one big blob. After a view is defined, it is difficult to customize it for reuse elsewhere in the application. Duplicating views to achieve what are often minor UI customizations inevitably results in bloatware. It negatively affects the final application by producing a larger NSF footprint, adversely impacting performance, and results in a longer list of design elements that the application developer must then somehow manage. As a consequence, separation of presentation and data has been a long-requested feature of the Notes/Domino application development community. The good news is that with XPages, this is exactly what you get.

XPages controls are typically bound to data contained in Domino documents or views. The XPages runtime comes equipped with standard Domino data source objects that automate the data connection and retrieval process, and Domino Designer provides various assistants that simplify the procedure of matching controls with items of metadata. Thus, the extra data-binding overhead imposed on the developer is reduced to some simple point-and-click operations at design time. This is a small price to pay for the extra design flexibility brought about by decoupling the presentation and data. Under this model, for example, a single XPage can work with multiple document data sources (such as read/write documents, where the data is defined in more than one form), and XPages view controls can effectively "join" data stored in different Domino views—even across different databases. Part III, "Data Binding," explores the many and varied details of data binding, but at this stage it is important to recognize that the XPages data model is fundamentally different to the traditional Notes/Domino model.

The More Things Change, the More Things Stay the Same

Having just stressed some advantages of the new XPages development model, it does not imply that traditional Domino development skills are any less valuable. Quite the contrary. For example, if you have already gained experience with the Domino object programming model by using the LotusScript® or Java backend classes, these skills enormously benefit you in building XPages applications because a parallel set of JavaScript classes are available in XPages. This means that, albeit with a slightly different class nomenclature, the usual suspects, such as `Session`, `Database`, and `Document`, are all present and accounted for when it comes to coding the application logic.

Similarly, the time you may have spent learning your Notes/Domino `@Functions` through the years continues to pay dividends. An extensive set of the procedures you already know and love, such as `@DbColumn()`, `@DbLookup()`, and so on, have been implemented in the XPages runtime as JavaScript functions and can thus be called directly in any XPage. For Domino developers familiar with using Notes canned actions to perform simple common tasks, XPages offers a similar concept in the form of Simple Actions. Effectively these are a collection of parameterized functions that execute common applications tasks such as `Open Page`, `Send Mail`, `Modify Field`, `Save Document`, and so forth. Beyond Simple Actions and `@Functions`, the next level of sophistication for building XPages application logic is through JavaScript coding, on both the client and server side. Finally, at the advanced end of the scale, XPages enables other programming methods such as XPath and Java...so, no shortage of tools to choose from.

When using XPages to modernize an existing Notes/Domino application, many original assets can be automatically leveraged. Web agents, for example, can be executed directly from within an XPage. Existing design resources, such as style sheets, images, and JavaScript library files, are also consumable, whereas existing forms and views can be used as XPages metadata resources.

New Horizons

The Extension Library has made the world of difference to XPages development. Not only does it enable you to build your own components, but it also enables the XPages team to deliver innovative technology as open source on OpenNTF.org and to strategically fold in the most useful and successful features to the core runtime. Thus, a lot of XPages development takes place on a twin track. You have the OpenNTF.org continuum where open source XPages features are regularly released and updated. In parallel with this, you have the core XPages runtime along with the productized features of the open source components. These two parallel paths can be synchronized periodically at chosen milestones according as it makes tactical sense—8.5.3 UP1 being one example, but there could be other upgrade packs in the future according as needs arise. Figure 1.3 shows a graphical representation of the new XPages development model.

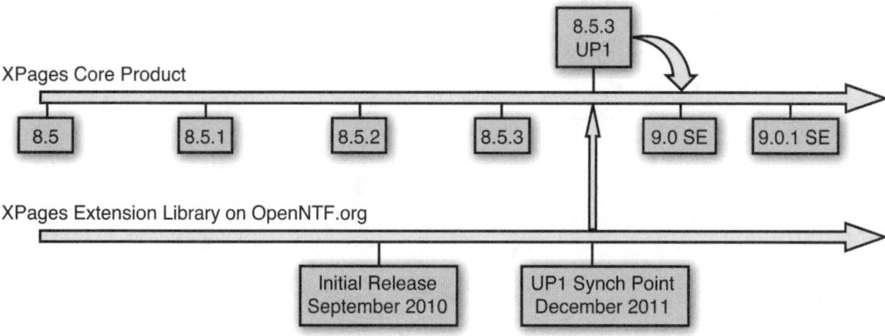

Figure 1.3 The XPages Development Model

Conclusion

This chapter introduced you to XPages at a high and general level. It looked at its provenance and history, revisited the initial goals of the technology, provided a broad view of the development paradigm it offers, and took a look at the extensible nature of the framework and how that can be used to provide technology updates to customers on a dynamic basis. Hopefully, you will find it both interesting and useful to have this big-picture context as you prepare to dive headfirst into the voluminous technical details ahead. The next step is to start with the practical aspects of the technology by installing XPages and Domino Designer and work through some simple examples. You also see how the XPages Extension Library can be seamlessly installed on top of an existing XPages core installation to leverage new runtime capabilities. Let the fun begin!

CHAPTER 2

Getting Everything You Need

This chapter provides a guide for getting the software you need to start working with XPages. The main tool you need is, of course, IBM Domino Designer. The good news is that this tool is available as a no-charge download today! The other free asset you require is the XPages Extension Library. You learn here how to make the XPages core runtime and Extension Library work together in a seamless manner.

Downloads, Versions, and Locations

The second edition of this book is based on Domino Designer 9.0.1, so ideally, you need to obtain this version of the product or something more recent, if available. Domino Designer can be downloaded from the IBM developerWorks® site (`www.ibm.com/developerworks/`).

Follow these steps to get the latest Domino Designer release:

1. Navigate to `http://tinyurl.com/DominoDesignerDownload`. You are automatically brought to the Domino Designer section in developerWorks. The IBM Domino Designer no-charge download should be right there, but if it's not, go to the Downloads area.
2. If you follow the links to download IBM Domino Designer, you are prompted to sign in using your universal IBM user ID. If you don't already have one, you must register first. You just need a valid email address to register.
3. You can select the language version of the client you want to install. Currently, IBM Domino Designer is available in 26 different languages and runs on Windows 7 Enterprise, Windows 7 Professional, Windows 8 Enterprise, Windows 8 Professional, and Windows XP Professional editions.
4. Before downloading the client, you need to accept the license agreement. This agreement allows you to use IBM Domino Designer only for the development of applications on an individual system that is not connected to an IBM Domino Server and to use such

applications on the same system on which the Domino Designer is installed. An additional license is required to deploy these applications to an IBM Domino Server. Read the license agreement carefully so you are aware of the specific terms for the download you are installing.

5. After you accept the license agreement, you are redirected to a page where you can download IBM Domino Designer and any fix packs that apply to that version. It is strongly recommended that you download and install any available fix packs. Your download is approximately 600–700MB.

Congratulations! You are now in possession of the latest release of IBM Domino Designer. The next step is to install the program.

Installing Domino Designer

The Domino Designer download (and any fix packs) is an executable file. Follow these steps to install the program:

1. Launch the executable you downloaded from the developerWorks site. This executable unpacks all the files needed to install the program on your machine. You can select to have the install files automatically cleaned up after the install completes or keep them around for reuse later. You need approximately 2GB of free disk space to perform the install.
2. The install wizard guides you through the process of installing Domino Designer. You need to specify your name and the location where you want to install the program.
3. On the screen where you select the program features you want installed, make sure that the following are selected (at a minimum):
   a. Notes Client
   b. Domino Designer
   c. Composite Application Editor (required for some rich client samples in this book)
4. Select the install option to start the installation of the selected program features.

When the install completes, two icons appear on your desktop: one for Domino Designer and one for the Notes client. Just a few more short steps before you can create your first XPage!

Installing Client Fix Packs

The download site might list fix packs for the version of Domino Designer you are downloading. As the name suggests, a *fix pack* contains fixes that have been made to the product since it was originally released. You are strongly encouraged to download and apply any available fix packs. Installing the fix pack couldn't be simpler:

1. Launch the fix-pack executable you downloaded from the developerWorks site. As before, the executable unpacks all the files needed to install the fix pack onto your machine in a location of your choosing, with the option to remove the unpacked files.
2. The wizard guides you through the process of installing the Domino Designer fix pack. You should not need to provide any settings.

Client Configuration

If you are using the no-charge download version of Domino Designer, you will not be connecting to a Domino server. You can follow the majority of exercises in this book without being connected to a Domino server. Follow these steps to configure your client:

1. Launch Domino Designer by clicking the icon on your desktop.
2. For the user information, fill out your name and unselect the option to connect to a Domino Server.
3. You don't need to configure any of the additional services.
4. When the client configuration completes, you are presented with a welcome screen that provides some useful information about the version of Domino Designer you just installed.
5. Restart your computer.

To optimize Domino Designer performance, you should check the default JVM settings before launching the program. The relevant settings are stored in this file: **<Notes_root_dir>/framework/rcp/deploy/jvm.properties**. A system with at least 2 GB of physical RAM should apply the following three recommended property values. More information on this topic can be found at http://tinyurl.com/DominoDesignerVMSettings:

- **vmarg.Xmx=-Xmx1024m**
- **vmarg.Xms=-Xms512m**
- **vmarg.Xmca=-Xmca512k**

Although these settings may be optimal for a *standalone* installation of Domino Designer, they can have side effects when the Notes client is also used for every day work—particularly if Notes is installed with the embedded Sametime client. For this configuration, the most optimal 9.0.1 settings were:

- **vmarg.Xmx=-Xmx512m**
- **vmarg.Xms=-Xms48m**
- **vmarg.Xmca=-Xmca512k**

Quick Tour of Domino Designer

When you start Domino Designer, you are presented with a welcome page that provides some useful information about the version you have installed. If this is the first time you have used Domino Designer since it was rebased to the Eclipse platform, or if you are not familiar with Eclipse-based Integrated Development Environments (IDE), the following sidebar provides a brief background on Eclipse.

A Brief History of Eclipse

In the late 1990s, IBM began developing an integrated development environment platform in IBM's Object Technology International (OTI) labs. This later formed the basis of the Eclipse project. The main goal was to develop a platform that could be used within IBM for its many IDE projects—and specifically for a new Java IDE. IBM recognized that developing a community of third parties who would use and contribute to this new platform was critical to its success. So, in November 2001, this new platform and the associated Java tooling was used to seed the Eclipse open source project, and the Eclipse consortium was founded. Since its inception, Eclipse.org has experienced huge success and rapid growth. IBM has been developing Eclipse-based product offerings for 13 years now, and the platform has evolved to include not only IDE products but also end-user products. Both IBM Sametime and Notes are now Eclipse Rich Client Platform (RCP) applications. RCP is an Eclipse platform for building end-user desktop applications. As Eclipse evolved, its IDE-specific parts were abstracted out to provide a generic windowing framework that could be used to create general-purpose applications. A great advantage of RCP is that the GUI end product is native to the particular target platform, be it Windows, Linux, or MAC.

What does it mean that Domino Designer is now an Eclipse-based product?

- If you are not familiar with Eclipse-based tools, you need to familiarize yourself with the basic concepts, such as perspectives, editors, and views (nothing to do with Notes views). Visit www.eclipse.org for more information. The URL http://eclipsetutorial.sourceforge.net/workbench.html takes you to a tutorial that teaches you how to use the features of the Eclipse workbench.
- Eclipse is a highly productive environment to work in, largely because there are so many add-ons available that allow the developer to customize his work environment to exactly meet his needs.
- Existing Eclipse-based tooling (such as Java source editors) now becomes available directly within Domino Designer.
- Because of its open source heritage, Eclipse is widely used in academia, particularly in the fields of computer science and information technology. Consequently, lots of new and recent graduates are already familiar with using Eclipse-based IDEs.
- Eclipse provides Domino developers with the opportunity to extend Domino Designer in ways that had never been possible. In fact, a slew of extensibility APIs were added

in V8.5.3 that enable tools to be added to Domino Designer, which tightly integrate into the core tooling interface. XPages provides similarly expansive APIs for the runtime, and this is described in detail in Chapter 12, "XPages Extensibility." See the following websites for more information on this topic:

www-10.lotus.com/ldd/ddwiki.nsf/dx/Domino_Designer_Extensibility_APIs_Javadoc_8.5.3
www-10.lotus.com/ldd/ddwiki.nsf/dx/xpages_extensibility_api_documentation

Whichever way you look at it, taking a popular development tool with a 20-year history and a unique set of development artifacts and moving it to a new Java-based IDE platform has got to be a risky proposition, right? If the approach was to rewrite all the existing tools (for example, editors for Forms, Views, and so on), the answer is a most definite yes. In release 8.5, the Domino Designer team took to the approach of hosting some of the preexisting Domino Designer tools (such as the Form and View editors) within the Eclipse IDE and developing brand-new native Eclipse tooling (such as the new JavaScript editor). So, for most traditional Domino design elements, it was business as usual insofar as the design-time experience remained the same. This is also the approach that was adopted and proven in moving the Notes Client to the Eclipse RCP; however, that's only the first part of the story. In addition to having all the old tools without the risk of a rewrite, developers now have lots of new stuff (such as new editors for style sheets, Java, and JavaScript). All the tools for XPages were developed specifically for Eclipse and, as such, take full advantage of the platform. The new Domino Designer also includes a virtual file system that allows Eclipse to view an NSF file as if it were a hierarchical collection of files.

I've been using Eclipse for many years, but I'm still learning new things all the time. When I sit with a colleague to do some pair programming, I often find that he has a slightly different way of doing something or a cool shortcut that I haven't seen. We share our favorite tips with you throughout this book.

Domino Designer Home Page

When you launch Domino Designer, you are presented with the Home Page (see Figure 2.1). This book is based on Domino Designer 9.0.1, so if you have installed another version, there may be some differing information on the Home Page about other cool features.

Domino Designer Perspective

The Domino Designer perspective is where you do the majority of your work, as shown in Figure 2.2. This provides a Domino-centric view on all the projects that you have open. The Application Navigator lists all the Domino applications you are working on and enables you to expand and explore all the design elements and resources contained therein. Start by creating a new application and creating your first XPage. The Domino Designer home page provides a shortcut that allows you to quickly create a new application.

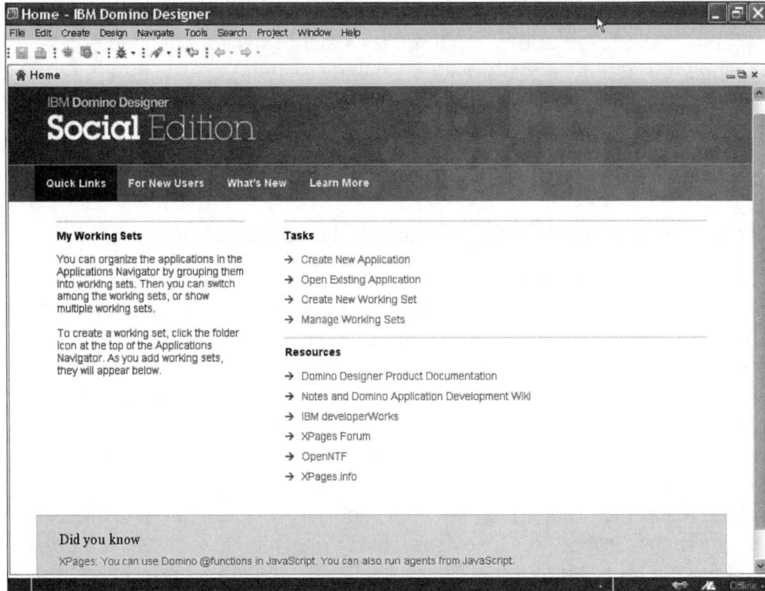

Figure 2.1 Domino Designer Home Page

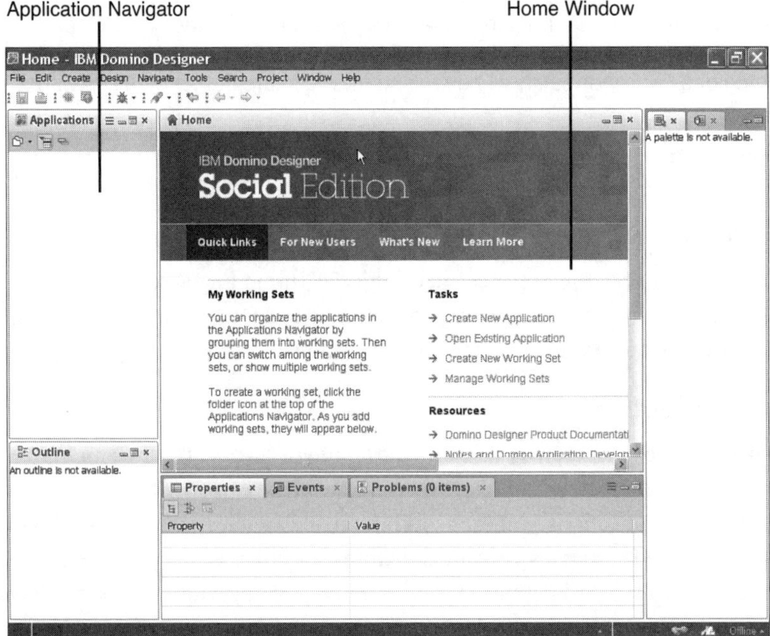

Figure 2.2 Domino Designer Perspective with the Home window

In the event that you get lost in Eclipse, and it can happen when you start to explore, you can always get back to the Domino Designer perspective by using **Window > Open Perspective > Domino Designer**. You can also reset your Domino Designer perspective to the defaults by using **Window > Reset Perspective**.

Creating a New Application

Following the time-honored tradition, your first step is to create a "Hello World" application. Here are the steps to create a new application:

1. Choose **File > New > Application**.
2. In the New Application dialog (see Figure 2.3), enter the file name of the application (for example, HelloWorld.nsf) and choose **OK**.

Figure 2.3 New Application dialog

A new application is created and appears in the Applications navigator (see Figure 2.4 and the next section).

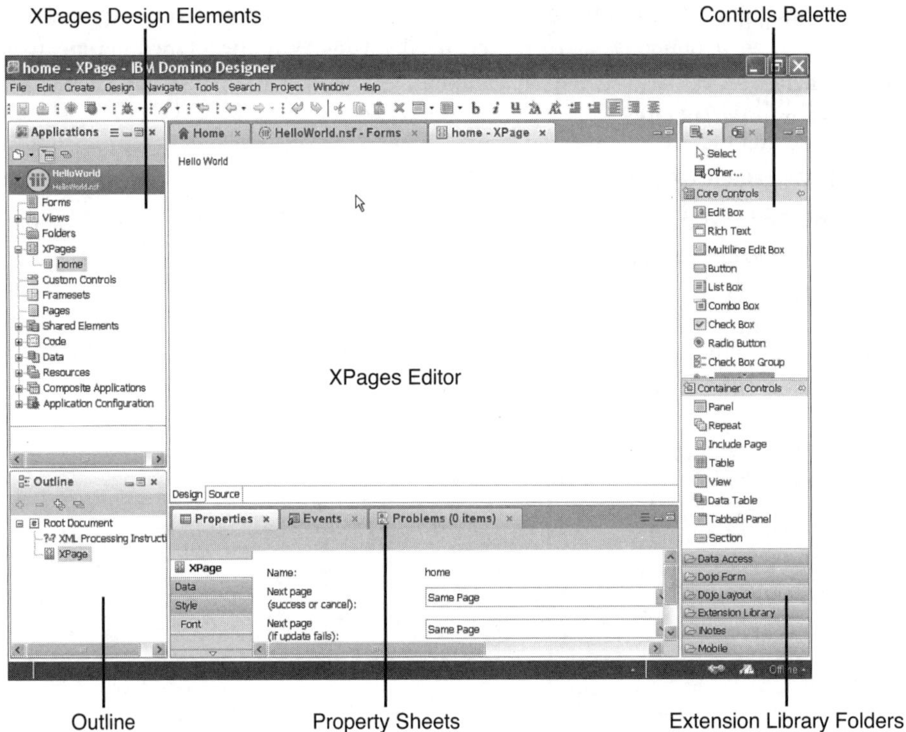

Figure 2.4 XPages Editor

Creating an XPage

Next, create your first XPage design element:

1. With the newly created application selected in the Applications navigator, choose **File > New > XPage**.
2. In the New XPage dialog, enter the name for the XPage (for example, home) and choose **OK**.
3. Type the text **"Hello World"** into the new XPage Editor Panel and save the XPage.

After you create and open an XPage design element, the Domino perspective fills with all the appropriate tools for you to work on that design element, as shown in Figure 2.4.

The default tools that are provided are as follows:

- **XPages Design Elements:** All the application XPages design elements are listed here. Double-click the XPages entry in the Designer Database Navigator to bring up the

XPages design list. This lists all the application XPages and some summary information about each item.

- **XPages Editor:** An XPages-specific editor supports two modes of operation:
  - The default mode of operation is visual editing; that is, you can type directly in the editor to add text, drag-and-drop new controls into the editor, and change the attributes of the page or elements within the page using the property panels.
  - Source-mode editing is also provided; each XPage is just an XML file and, in source mode, you can directly edit the tags.
- **Controls Palette:** Lists all the UI controls that you can add to an XPage to create your application user interface. This includes all the core XPages controls plus any controls that have been contributed via an extension library. The palette also gets automatically expanded to include any custom controls you create. Custom controls are explained in Chapter 10, "Custom Controls."
- **Property Sheets:** Contain tabs for the selected item's Properties, Events, and Problems:
  - The Properties tab allows you to visually configure the properties for the currently selected item (for example, the XPage or a selected item within the page).
  - The Events tab lists all the events for the currently selected item and allows you to add application logic, which executes when that event is triggered.
  - The Problems tab lists any errors or warnings for the current XPage.
- **Outline:** Provides a hierarchical outline that shows all the elements in the current XPage.
- **Data:** Shows all the data sources associated with the current XPage and allows you to define new data sources (not shown in Figure 2.4). Data sources are covered in more detail in Chapters 7 and 8.

The "Hello World" application is complete. The next step is to run it and see it working. Domino Designer provides options to preview an XPage in the Notes Client or a web browser.

Previewing in the Notes Client

Previewing an XPage design element in the Notes Client couldn't be simpler:

1. Choose **Design > Preview in Notes**.
2. The Notes Client starts and the XPage is displayed, as shown in Figure 2.5.

> **TIP**
>
> The Preview in Notes option is available in the context menu when you right-click in an XPage design element. It's also available on the toolbar under the Design top-level menu, and by right-clicking the XPage in the navigator.

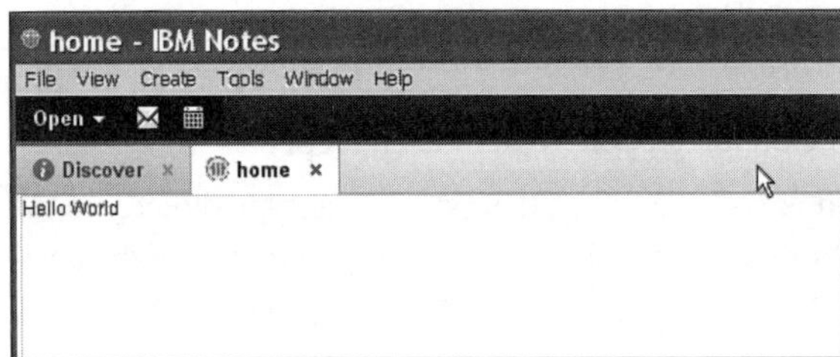

Figure 2.5 XPages Preview in Notes

Previewing in a Web Browser

If you try to preview the XPage in a web browser, you see the following error message:

> To successfully preview this element in a Web Browser, please add (or modify) the ACL entry for Anonymous (or the default ACL) to have at least Author access with the ability to create documents.

The security aspects of Notes and Domino are covered in depth later in this book; however, for now, it suffices to say that access to every application is controlled using an access control list (ACL). By default, anonymous access is prevented, but this is the access level used when previewing a local application for the web.

Here is how you allow anonymous access to the Notes application:

1. Choose **File > Application > Access Control**.
2. The Default entry is selected in the **Access Control List**.
3. Change the **Access** level from **No Access** to **Author**.
4. Select the option to **Create documents** (see Figure 2.6) and choose **OK**.

Now the application is configured to allow you to preview in a web browser. The next step is to configure your application to use the XPage that you just created as the design element when the application is launched:

1. Choose **File > Application > Properties**.
2. Choose the **Launch** tab.
3. Under **Web Browser Launch**, select **Open designated XPage** from the **Launch** drop-down.
4. Select the **home** XPage from the list the **XPage** drop-down, as shown in Figure 2.7.

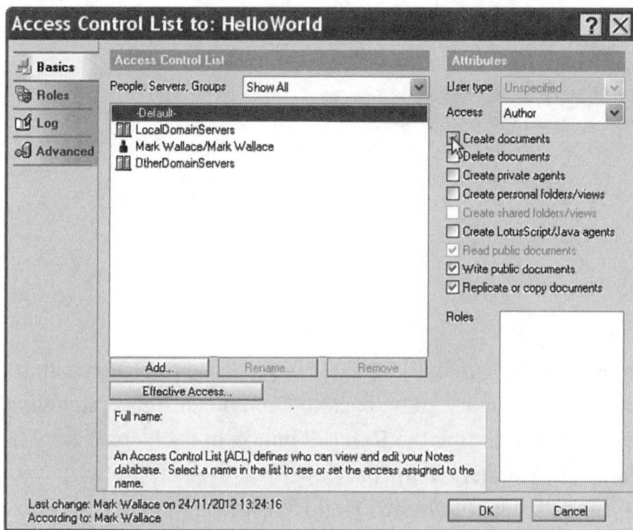

Figure 2.6 ACL for the Hello World application

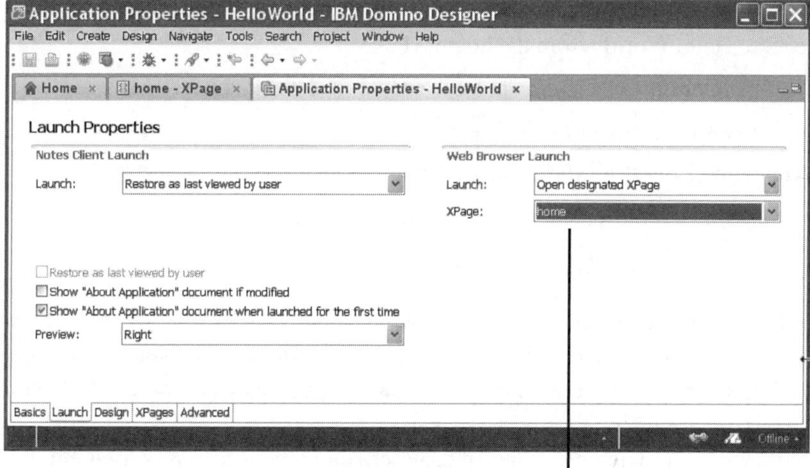

Figure 2.7 Web browser Launch Properties

5. Choose **File > Save** to apply these new application properties.
6. Choose **Design > Preview in Web Browser > Select either of the default browsers as specific browser to use when previewing**.

7. Your preferred web browser starts and the XPage appears, as shown in Figure 2.8.

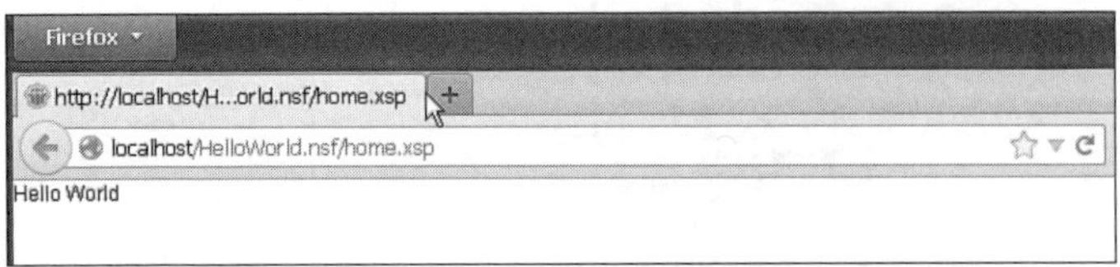

Figure 2.8 XPage Preview in a web browser

Preview in Notes and the web browser dynamically updates in response to changes in the XPage being previewed. You can see this working by going back to Domino Designer, changing and saving the XPage, and then going back and hitting the **Refresh** button in the Notes Client or web browser. Your changes are updated immediately in the preview.

So far, you've seen how easy it is to create the basic "Hello World" application and preview your work. Next, you complete this application by adding a customized greeting.

Adding a Control to an XPage

You now change "World" to a Computed Field (possible theme song for this book):

1. Delete the text "Hello World" from the home XPage.
2. Drag-and-drop a **Computed Field** from the **Controls palette** to the XPage.
3. In the **Properties** sheet, choose the **Value** tab.
4. Select **JavaScript** as the **Bind data using** option.
5. Enter the following JavaScript and save the XPage (see Figure 2.9):

```
"Hello " + context.getUser().getFullName()
```

You just added a control that computes its value, and you configured it to retrieve the common name of the current user and prefixed this with the static text "Hello." Chapter 6, "Building XPages Application Logic," covers data binding and the JavaScript classes in more detail. You should now preview this XPage again.

As you saw earlier when previewing in a web browser, anonymous access is used. So, it's no surprise how the greeting appears in the browser preview (see Figure 2.10).

> **TIP**
>
> Change the computed expression to "Hello "+session.getCommonUserName() and you get a proper username when previewing in a web browser.

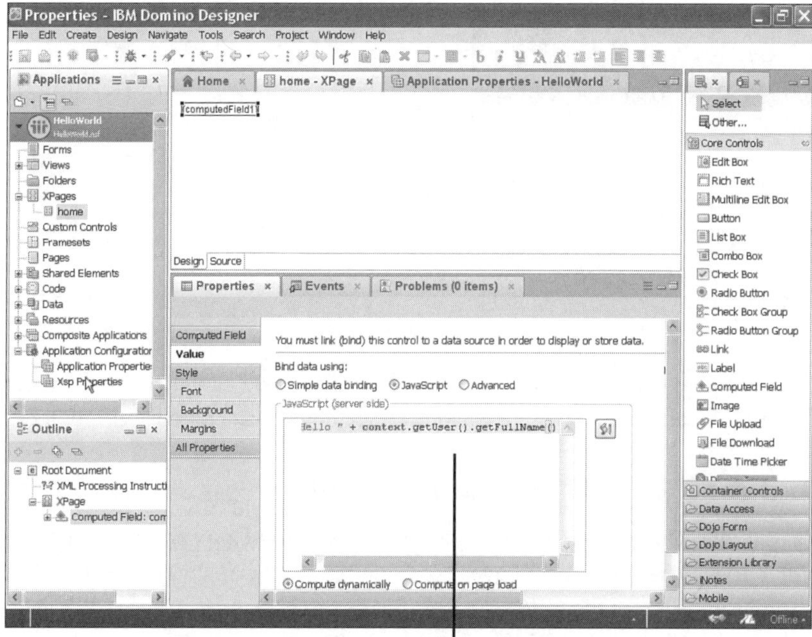

Figure 2.9 Adding a Computed Field

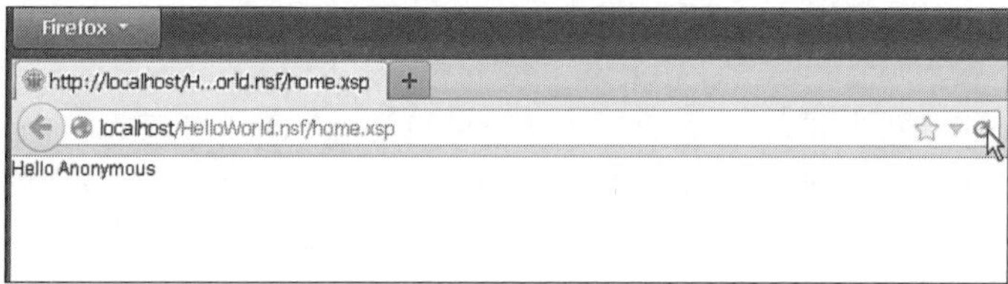

Figure 2.10 Preview in a web browser

If you repeat the Notes Client preview, you see that the name comes from the Notes ID that was used when you logged into Domino Designer (see Figure 2.11).

> **TIP**
>
> If you are using the no-charge download, you may see "Hello null" when you do this test. This is because the full name may not be set on the Notes user ID that was created.

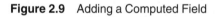

Figure 2.11 Preview in Notes

Well done! You are now up and running with core XPages development in Domino Designer. Next, you need to learn how to integrate and leverage the XPages Extension Library.

Working with the XPages Extension Library

As previously discussed, the XPages Extension Library is an open source set of assets that can be installed on top of a given version of the XPages core runtime. You can always get the latest version of the Extension Library from the following website: `extlib.openntf.org`. When on the landing page, simply click the **Download latest release** button, and save the zip file to your local computer.

Note that there are separate releases of the Extension Library for each official revision of XPages. That is, there is a set of Extension Library releases based on XPages 8.5.2, 8.5.3, 9.0, 9.0.1, and so forth. Actually, on the same OpenNTF web page, you can see a **Downloads/Releases** link to a page that includes all the individual Extension Library releases from the first drop made September 2010. Figure 2.12 shows a snapshot of the list.

You should take note of the format of the unique identifier used for all OpenNTF releases targeting 9.0 and beyond. All releases are made available in zip format and start with an ExtensionLibraryOpenNTF prefix; for example, ExtensionLibraryOpenNTF-900v00_02.20130515-2200.zip. Figure 2.13 explains how the canonical unique id is composed:

For the purpose of this section, it is assumed that you work with an Extension Library build based on a Notes/Domino 9.0 release or later. After you complete a download of the Extension Library, you should expand the archive into a temporary folder. The zip file contains many artifacts, including licenses, documentation, samples, source code, and various update sites for the Extension Library. The file most of interest here is **updateSiteOpenNTF-designer.zip** because it contains both the runtime and tooling plug-ins that you need. The next step is to install the plug-ins contained in that archive into Domino Designer.

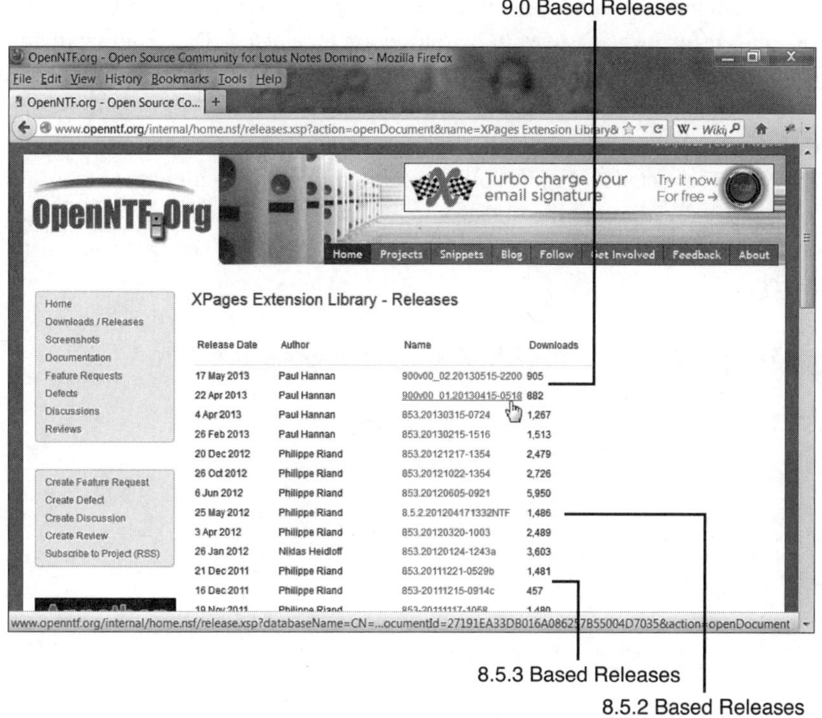

Figure 2.12 A snapshot of XPages Extension Library Releases

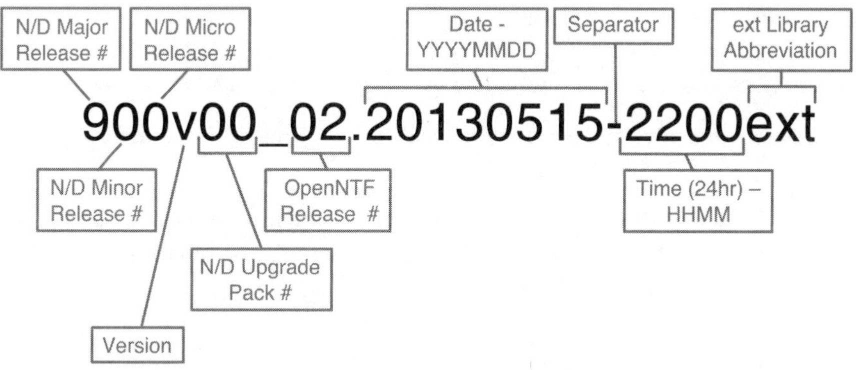

Figure 2.13 Extension Library Unique IDs for Notes/Domino 9

To begin the process, you need to ensure that a required preference has been selected in Domino Designer. To do so, click **File > Preferences > Domino Designer** and ensure that the **Enable Eclipse plug-in install** check box is selected. This will ensure that the

File > Application > Install menu is enabled in Designer. You should now invoke that menu and click **Next** when the **Search for new features to install** option is selected. The resulting dialog allows you to select applications to install from various locations, and you can point it at the **updateSiteOpenNTF-designer.zip** file by clicking **Add Zip/Jar Location**. An Eclipse update site is just a zip file that contains special metadata—the curious reader can view the **site.xml** file at the root level of the zip. The metadata exposes all the features contained within this Extension Library offering. To install everything in the update site, which is the recommended approach, then you need to select only the root level entry, as shown in Figure 2.14, and doing so automatically selects all child items.

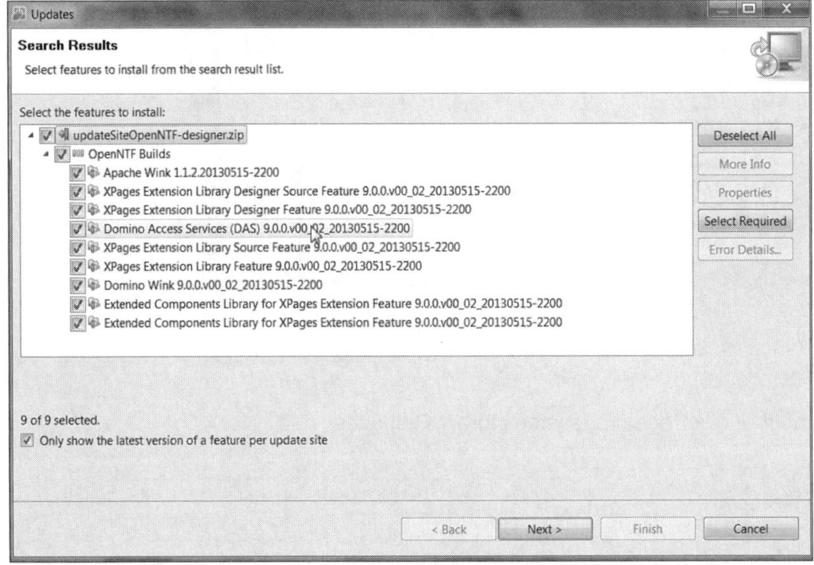

Figure 2.14 Features included in an OpenNTF Extension Library Release for XPages 9.0

When you see the dialog shown in Figure 2.14, click **Next** and then read and accept the license terms presented on the following dialog. This leads you to the **Installation** dialog box, which lists the features to be installed. (An Eclipse feature is made up of a collection of one or more plug-ins.) To proceed, you must click the **Finish** button.

Each of the Extension Library plug-ins is then installed one by one. You must explicitly accept each feature by clicking the **Install this plug-in** option, as shown in Figure 2.15.

After you have cycled through the collection of features, you will be prompted to restart Domino Designer so that all the newly installed plug-ins can be properly loaded into your Designer session. There are a couple of interesting points to note after restart is complete. First, you should look at your new Designer plug-in configuration by selecting the **File > Application**

> **Application Management** menu. When you expand the **worskspace\applications\eclipse** folder in the dialog box, you should see an entry for the update site you have just installed, as shown in Figure 2.16.

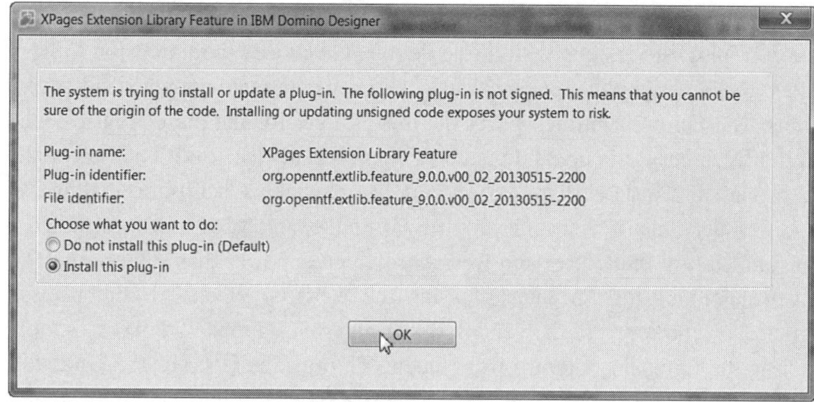

Figure 2.15 Accepting Extension Library Features for Installation to Domino Designer

Extension Library Feature

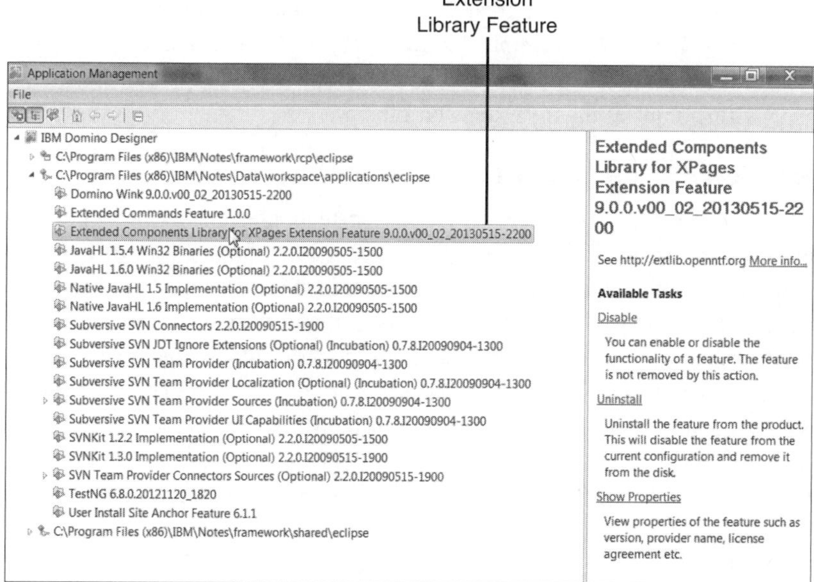

Figure 2.16 Application Management Features in Notes/Designer

As you can observe, the core Notes Java plug-ins are installed in the **rcp** and **shared** folders under the Notes framework folder, while third-party features and plug-ins are installed to the Notes applications workspace. In Notes 9.0, many Extension Library features were included in the core release, such as the XPages mobile library, iNotes controls, and so forth. Thus, from 9.0 onwards, by installing a newer release of the Extension Library from OpenNTF, you are effectively overriding the core plug-in versions with later releases. Given that the Extension Library plug-ins are installed to the Notes applications workspace, however, they do not physically overwrite the core versions. The Eclipse runtime figures out that two versions of these plug-ins exist when Notes or Domino Designer starts up, and the latest version is always used. That's why the naming convention explained a little earlier is so important—it enables Eclipse to distinguish between older and newer versions of the same plug-ins. In this example, you have installed a version of the Extension Library into Notes and Designer, which is newer than the original 9.0 core release for a given set of plug-ins. The latest plug-ins (the ones from OpenNTF) will be used by Notes and Designer. You can revert to the version of the plug-ins shipped with 9.0 by simply uninstalling or disabling the Extension Library from OpenNTF.org. The **Disable** and **Uninstall** links are also shown in Figure 2.16. This is how the standard XPages runtime can co-exist with open source releases from OpenNTF.org. This was *not* possible in releases prior to 9.0.

If you use an older version of Notes/Domino (specifically, less than 8.5.3 UP1), and this is the first time you have installed the Extension Library, you will notice that your control palette in Domino Designer has suddenly expanded greatly. Many new folders containing Extension Library controls are now in evidence; for example, the **Data Access**, **Dojo Form**, **Dojo Layout**, **Extension Library**, **iNotes**, and **Mobile** folders shown in the bottom-right corner of Figure 2.4 were all contributed by virtue of installing the Extension Library.

Some Quick Notes on Extension Library Structure

The XPages Extension Library is not a single behemoth encapsulating an avalanche of plug-ins but rather an organized layered structure. The productized layer of the library sits directly on top of the XPages core, whereas another experimental collection of features sits on top of that again. Experimental features such as XPages RDBMS connectivity do not ship as part of the Notes/Domino core (at least at this point in time) but instead are made available via the Extension Library on OpenNTF.org. The plug-ins and features in each layer of the XPages runtime follow a naming convention that enables you to discern the part of the stack to which they belong, as illustrated in Figure 2.17.

A real-world snapshot of the XPages can be viewed at any time by selecting the **Help > About IBM Domino Designer > Plug-in Details** menu in Domino Designer and then sorting the table of plug-ins displayed in the resulting dialog using the **Plug-in Id** column. Figure 2.18 shows a sample of the runtime stack in an inverted manner.

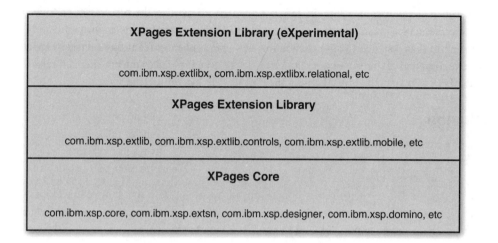

XPages Extension Library (eXperimental)

com.ibm.xsp.extlibx, com.ibm.xsp.extlibx.relational, etc

XPages Extension Library

com.ibm.xsp.extlib, com.ibm.xsp.extlib.controls, com.ibm.xsp.extlib.mobile, etc

XPages Core

com.ibm.xsp.core, com.ibm.xsp.extsn, com.ibm.xsp.designer, com.ibm.xsp.domino, etc

Figure 2.17 The XPages runtime stack

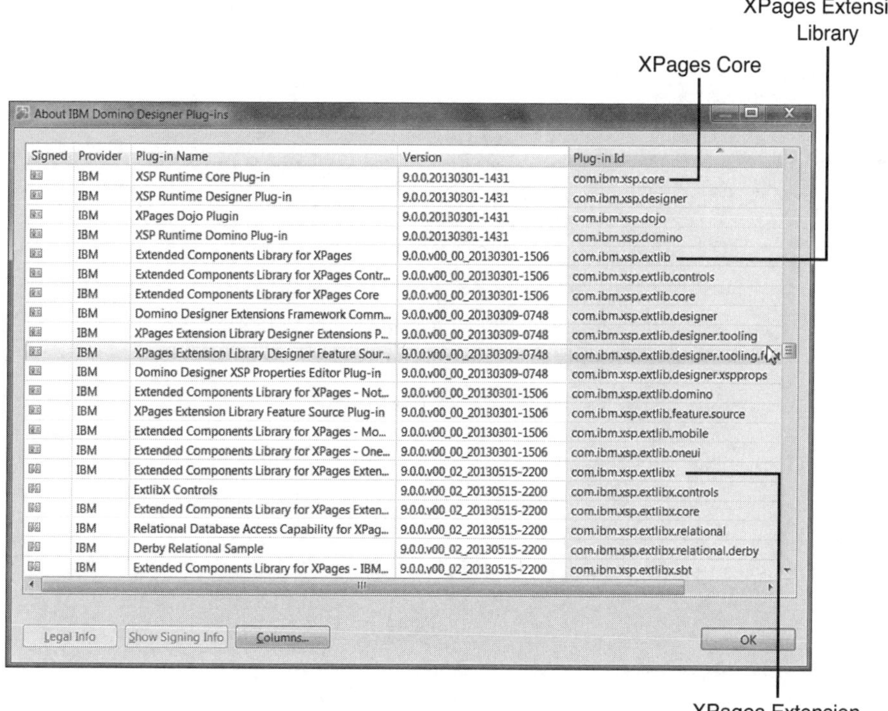

Signed	Provider	Plug-in Name	Version	Plug-in Id
	IBM	XSP Runtime Core Plug-in	9.0.0.20130301-1431	com.ibm.xsp.core
	IBM	XSP Runtime Designer Plug-in	9.0.0.20130301-1431	com.ibm.xsp.designer
	IBM	XPages Dojo Plugin	9.0.0.20130301-1431	com.ibm.xsp.dojo
	IBM	XSP Runtime Domino Plug-in	9.0.0.20130301-1431	com.ibm.xsp.domino
	IBM	Extended Components Library for XPages	9.0.0.v00_00_20130301-1506	com.ibm.xsp.extlib
	IBM	Extended Components Library for XPages Contr...	9.0.0.v00_00_20130301-1506	com.ibm.xsp.extlib.controls
	IBM	Extended Components Library for XPages Core	9.0.0.v00_00_20130301-1506	com.ibm.xsp.extlib.core
	IBM	Domino Designer Extensions Framework Comm...	9.0.0.v00_00_20130309-0748	com.ibm.xsp.extlib.designer
	IBM	XPages Extension Library Designer Extensions P...	9.0.0.v00_00_20130309-0748	com.ibm.xsp.extlib.designer.tooling
	IBM	XPages Extension Library Designer Feature Sour...	9.0.0.v00_00_20130309-0748	com.ibm.xsp.extlib.designer.tooling.f...
	IBM	Domino Designer XSP Properties Editor Plug-in	9.0.0.v00_00_20130309-0748	com.ibm.xsp.extlib.designer.xspprops
	IBM	Extended Components Library for XPages - Not...	9.0.0.v00_00_20130301-1506	com.ibm.xsp.extlib.domino
	IBM	XPages Extension Library Feature Source Plug-in	9.0.0.v00_00_20130301-1506	com.ibm.xsp.extlib.feature.source
	IBM	Extended Components Library for XPages - Mo...	9.0.0.v00_00_20130301-1506	com.ibm.xsp.extlib.mobile
	IBM	Extended Components Library for XPages - One...	9.0.0.v00_00_20130301-1506	com.ibm.xsp.extlib.oneui
	IBM	Extended Components Library for XPages Exten...	9.0.0.v00_02_20130515-2200	com.ibm.xsp.extlibx
		ExtlibX Controls	9.0.0.v00_02_20130515-2200	com.ibm.xsp.extlibx.controls
	IBM	Extended Components Library for XPages Exten...	9.0.0.v00_02_20130515-2200	com.ibm.xsp.extlibx.core
	IBM	Relational Database Access Capability for XPag...	9.0.0.v00_02_20130515-2200	com.ibm.xsp.extlibx.relational
	IBM	Derby Relational Sample	9.0.0.v00_02_20130515-2200	com.ibm.xsp.extlibx.relational.derby
	IBM	Extended Components Library for XPages - IBM...	9.0.0.v00_02_20130515-2200	com.ibm.xsp.extlibx.sbt

Figure 2.18 A listing of XPages plug-ins installed in Designer

Experimental features can "graduate" to fully fledged production features over time if demand from the market place is sufficient. Even though the names of the plug-ins and features would change in that instance (losing the extlibx tag) any application that has been developed using the experimental features would continue to run when upgraded to the productized release because the Java package names used within the plug-ins always remain the same.

Conclusion

Now you have everything you need to start exploring the world of XPages. There is a sample Notes application associated with each chapter of the book, which includes the XPages discussed in the chapter (you can access these files at `www.ibmpressbooks.com/title/9780133373370`). The best way to get the most from this book is to follow along with the samples in Domino Designer and to install the Extension Library if you use an older release that does not include it automatically. In the next chapter, you build your first XPages application.

CHAPTER 3

Building Your First XPages Application

Now that the setup details are squared away, it's time to roll up your sleeves and start some real-world XPages application development. Development technologies are best absorbed by working through practical examples and solving everyday concrete problems. For this, you need a reference application to work with, and the standard Notes Discussion template is an ideal candidate. Pretty much all the topics covered in this book are already implemented in one way or another in the Discussion template, and you will disassemble and rebuild this application as a way of developing your XPages expertise! This is also convenient for you insofar as the Discussion template ships out-of-the-box with Domino Designer, so you automatically obtained this application template as part of the installation work performed in Chapter 2, "Getting Everything You Need." Furthermore, although it is not explicitly covered in this book, the Teamroom application template now also comes with an XPages implementation as standard—it was first included in 8.5.3 Upgrade Pack 1 release and in all subsequent releases since then. This template provides even more advanced examples of XPages features and capabilities and is well worth exploring.

A different instance of the reference application is provided for each chapter. Be sure to download these resources so that you can work through the exercises in Domino Designer according as you read your way through this book. This will undoubtedly be the most effective approach from a learning point of view. Typically, the name of a given reference application instance is derived from the chapter with which it is associated. For example, for this chapter, open **Chp03Ed2.nsf** in Designer. The NSF resources can be downloaded from this website:

`www.ibmpressbooks.com/title/9780133373370`

This chapter provides a general breadth of information covering both Designer and XPages. It gets you accustomed to building simple XPages that read and write Notes data and implement standard application features. In summary, you will learn the following:

- How to define application metadata using forms and views
- How Notes stores real application data using documents and views
- How XPages can access that data for reading and writing

- How XPages elements can be linked to form a cohesive entity
- How to implement simple application logic without writing any code

This is an ambitious undertaking for one chapter! Obviously, some details will need to be glossed over to achieve this goal in such a short time, but any such details will be explored in depth in the remainder of this book.

Laying the Foundations

You should start by creating an instance of the Discussion application and play around with it to get a feel for its features and functionality. Whatever new XPages you create in this new application instance have already been created in for you in **Chp03Ed2.nsf**, but it would be good to create your own XPages based on the instructions set out over the course of the chapter, and then compare your results when complete. As you learned in the previous chapter, you can create a new application by simply selecting the **File > New** main menu option or type **Control-N** in your Designer workspace. Many application templates are shipped with Notes (mail, discussion, teamroom, doc library, and so on), and you should select **discussion9.ntf** to create your new application based on the latest Discussion design. Figure 3.1 shows all the relevant selections.

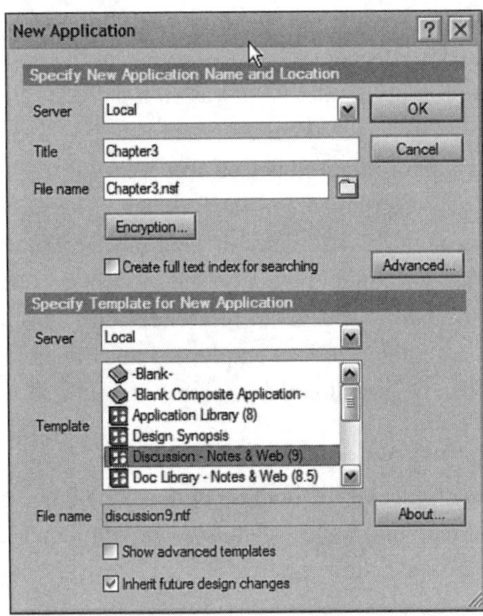

Figure 3.1 Creating a new Discussion application in Domino Designer

To experiment with the application, simply open its main page, **allDocuments.xsp**, and choose to preview it using a web browser or the Notes client. To enable web preview, you need to tweak the application's access control list (ACL), as you learned in Chapter 2; however, this time assign **Editor** level access as a minimum, as this is required to complete all the exercises in this chapter. To save yourself some time, you should also enable the `Anonymous` user to delete documents, because you will need this capability for a later exercise. Once opened in preview mode, the application is fully functional, so you can create new documents, categorize them into different groupings, navigate between different views, and so on. Figure 3.2 outlines the anatomy of a Discussion application populated with some sample data and running in the Notes client.

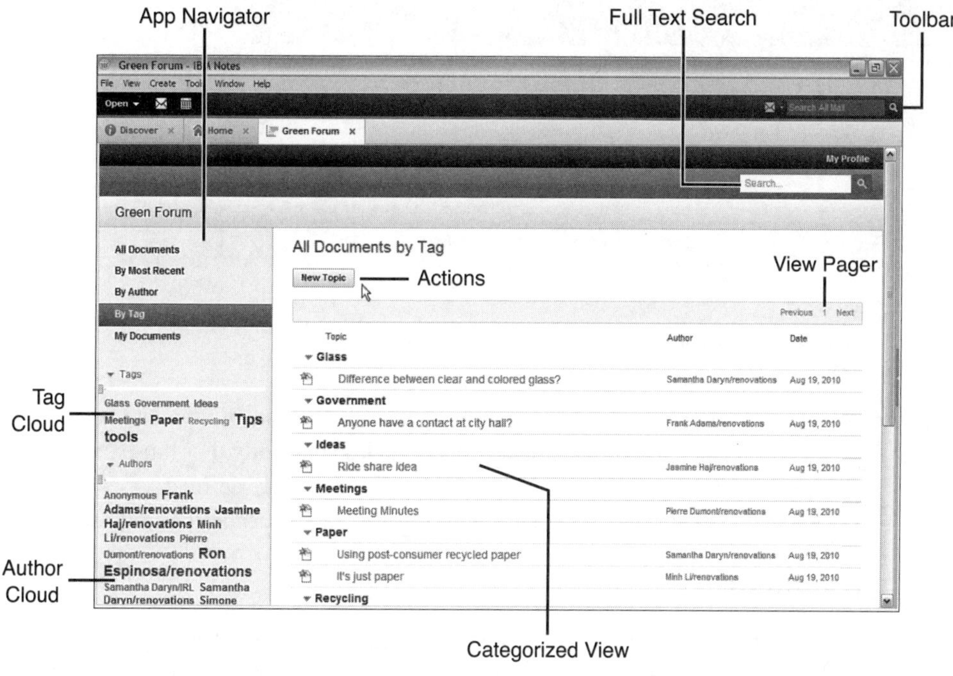

Figure 3.2 Sample Discussion application and its component parts

As you explore the template more fully over the course of this book, you will discover that it is a feature-rich Web 2.0 and mobile application, making full use of AJAX, Dojo, JavaScript, and Cascading Style Sheets (CSS). This is what makes it so useful as a learning vehicle. At this point, however, you might need to start with the basics, such as learning how documents are defined, created, and stored in an application.

Figure 3.3 shows a sample new topic under composition in the XPages Discussion app. At this point, you can use the **New Topic** button to create some sample documents. The text you enter in the **Subject** field is displayed in the summary document view, the **Tags** field categorizes your documents (it supports multiple categories if you use comma-separated entries), and the third field is the main document body and is fully rich-text enabled. When you enter data in all three fields, click **Save** to store the document. As you navigate around the application, you can also edit and delete these documents. Doing so gives you a feel for the application's features and behaviors.

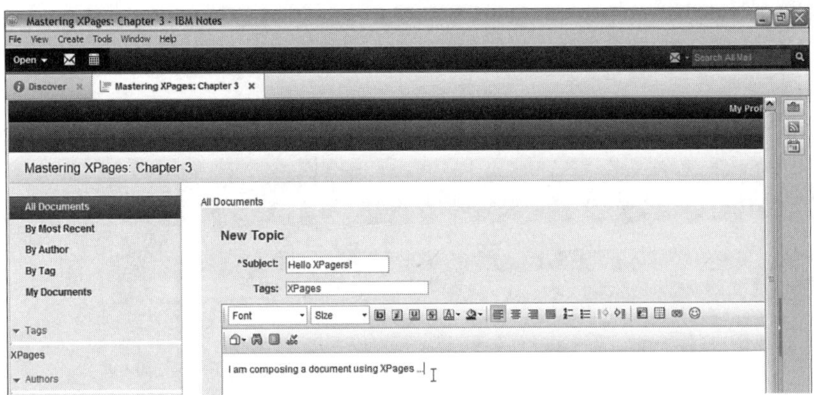

Figure 3.3 Sample topic document

A cursory glance at Figure 3.3 tells you that any new document, from a data standpoint, must contain at least three data items: say **Subject**, **Categories**, and **Body**. For those of you new to XPages and Notes, the question is how and where these data items are defined.

Save the sample document shown here, because it is used in the upcoming exercises.

Forms and Views

Although you have just been playing with the Discussion template as an XPages application, it is also, of course, a native Notes application that runs independently of XPages in the basic Notes client itself. In fact, the XPages interface was only added to the template in version 8.5, while the Discussion app itself was first introduced over a decade before that! The original Discussion application was built using traditional Domino design elements, such as forms and views. To see the native application in operation, simply expand the **Forms** entry in the Designer navigator, double-click the **Main Topic** form to open it, and perform a client design preview using the same **Preview** toolbar button used when previewing any XPage. After the form loads, enter some text. Compare the XPage interface shown in Figure 3.3 to the traditional form shown in Figure 3.4—different renderings but the same data! For the purpose of the exercises in this chapter, there is no need to save the document shown here.

Return to Domino Designer and, this time, open the **Views** entry in the navigator. (It is recommended that you work your way through this chapter and actually perform the various tasks in

Designer while you read them here.) Locate and select the **All Documents** view in the navigator and click the **Preview in Notes** toolbar button. When the view opens in the Notes client, you see that the document you just created is presented.

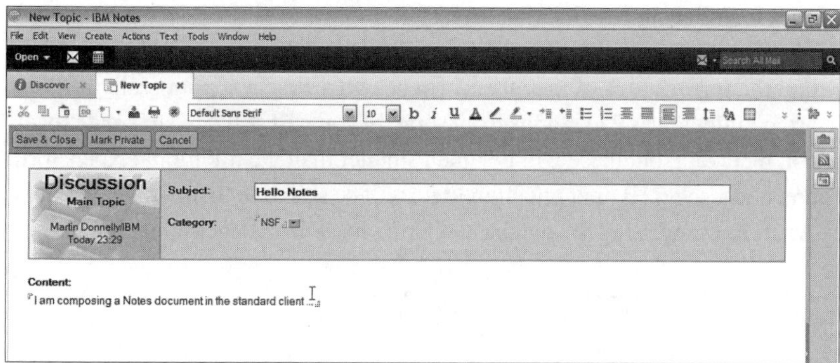

Figure 3.4 Preview of the Main Topic form

Now, you should reopen the sample document, right-click anywhere in the view window, and select **Document Properties** from the context menu. A nonmodal floating dialog box, commonly known as an *infobox* in Notes/Domino, is presented, and this can inspect the data stored within the document. Choose the second (**Fields**) tab on the infobox and click any of the fields presented in the listbox. As you do so, the data stored in those fields is displayed in the adjacent text box—for example, the XPages category text appears to be stored in a **WebCategories** field, as shown in Figure 3.5.

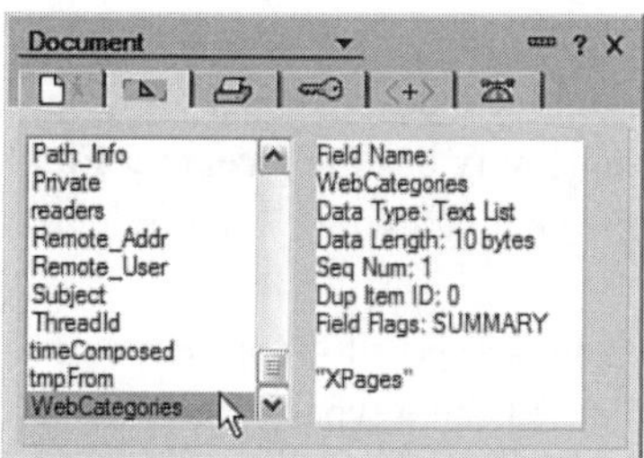

Figure 3.5 Infobox listing the field properties of a sample Notes document

All the fields you see listed in the infobox are defined using a form design element. In Notes, a document is simply an instance of a form. All the fields or items defined on any given form can be assigned values after a document is composed and then saved. For traditional Notes applications, the form design element is the container for both the metadata (for example, data design and structure definitions) and the user interface (controls, layout, and so on). The key point for you to understand is that an XPage allows you to create a Notes document based on the metadata defined within a form, but entirely ignores the form's presentation layer. In other words, XPages gets the data definition of any given document directly from one or more forms, but provides its own user interface and application logic.

Reopen the **Main Topic** form in Designer. Figure 3.6 shows the three fields mentioned earlier as defined within the form. Much of the other form design artifacts are not really relevant to XPages. As you start to build new XPages apps from scratch, you will still need to create forms to define the application metadata, but these will be much smaller than the traditional Notes form definitions you see here, because no UI or application logic will be stored in them. In other words, think of these Notes forms as comprising the database schema for your XPages application.

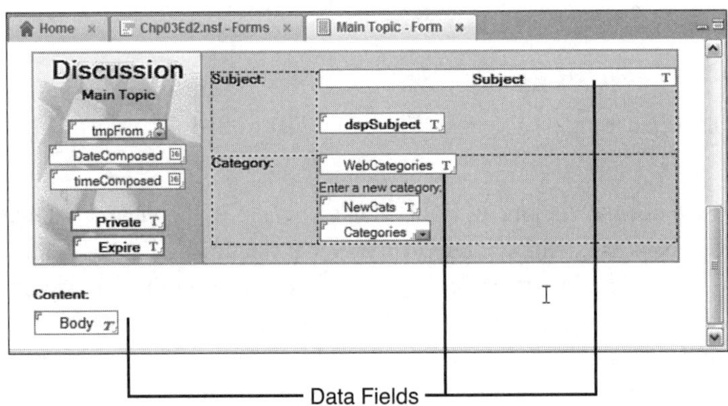

Figure 3.6 Field definitions in Main Topic form

From an XPages perspective, there is not a lot to learn about form design because XPages only really uses them as metadata containers. On any form, you simply use the **Create > Field** option on the main menu to add a field and then enter the name and data type via the infobox. Figure 3.7 shows a sample field infobox.

The types displayed in Figure 3.7 are interesting, because they appear to represent a mixture of data and presentation concepts. It is easy to think of the first three types (`Text`, `Date/Time`, `Number`) purely in data terms; however, many of other types are usually thought of only as UI widgets, rather than as data types per se (for example, `Radio button`, `Listbox`, and `Combobox`). For example, if a field is defined as a `Radio button` in Notes, what type of data is stored in the document when the user makes a selection at runtime? The answer is perhaps not clear cut. If you are working with forms designed by other developers (such as a legacy application that you inherited), it is always useful to inspect some document instances using the infobox and reconcile the metadata definitions with the actual document field data.

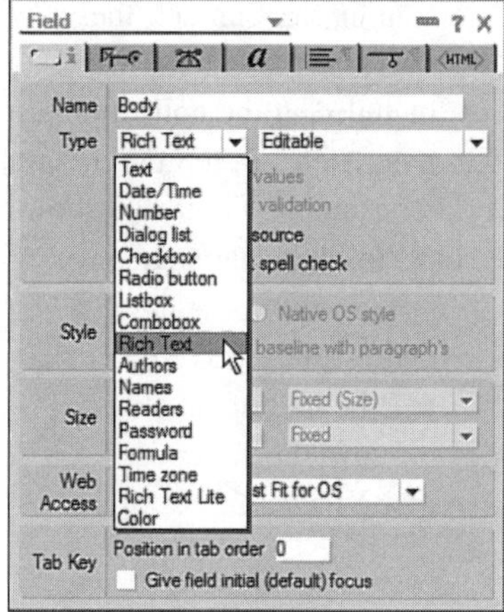

Figure 3.7 Inspecting field definitions in Domino Designer

Note that other important fields are created and stored automatically by Notes, over and above those that are explicitly defined in an application's forms. Every document, for example, automatically contains a document id (also referred to as a note id) and universal id (UNID). These items will prove useful in your development tasks later on, and examples of these fields are shown in Figure 3.8.

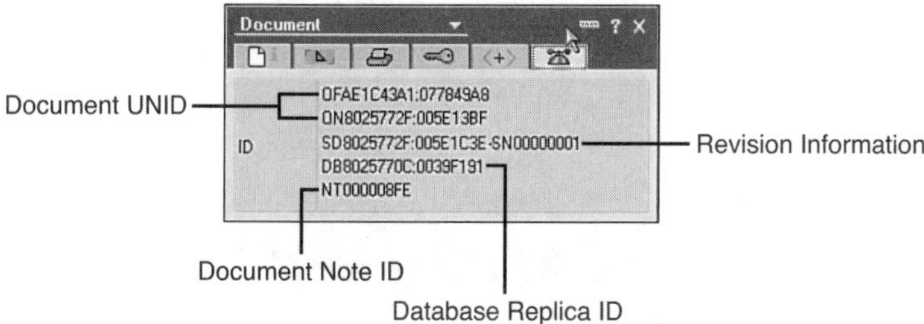

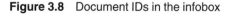

Figure 3.8 Document IDs in the infobox

TIP

Other tools are available to inspect Notes data. A long-time favorite in the community is Notespeek, which provides an explorer-like interface for NSF files and the elements contained within them. This utility can be downloaded from an IBM developerWorks sandbox using this URL: http://tinyurl.com/NotesPeek.

Although the form design element is used to define the content of a document, the view design element is what Notes uses to manage collections of documents. A Notes view presents summary data for a collection of documents, and the documents included in the collection are chosen using some type of selection query. Explore some of the many views in the Discussion template. You see that they all contain a `View Selection` query. For example, Figure 3.9 shows the **($xpCategorized)** view in design mode, including a simple Notes formula language `query`:

```
SELECT (form = "Main Topic")
```

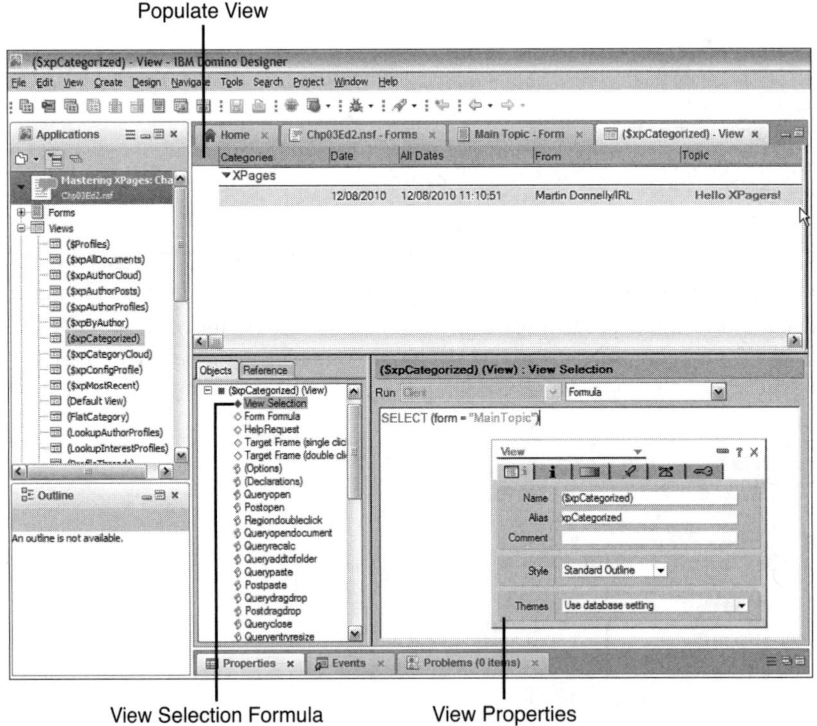

Figure 3.9 View design

Basically, every Notes document is automatically assigned a `Form` field that identifies the form used to compose it, and this particular view includes all documents contained within the NSF that were created using the **Main Topic** form.

The view itself is comprised of an array of columns. A column can simply be the name of a field contained in the selected documents or a computed value. The top-left corner of the view contains a **Refresh** button that allows you to populate the view at design time, which comes in handy if you are building a view from scratch and want to periodically validate your content.

Again, for Notes/Domino neophytes, there's not a lot to figure out with Notes view design—certainly at this basic level. New view instances are typically created using the helper dialog invoked from the **Create > Design > View** menu or by copying and modifying an existing view of a similar design to what you want. Columns are added to a view via the main menu or view context menu, and configured using the infobox—just like fields in a form.

The form and view you will work with in this chapter already exist, namely **Main Topic** and **All Documents**, respectively. Thus, at this juncture, there is no need to delve any deeper into how these elements are created. The key thing to understand is that XPages uses a Notes view to work with a document collection. Again, XPages is not interested in the presentational aspect of the Notes view, but just its content. The presentation of the view data is performed by XPages; this concept will become clearer when you build a sample view in the next section.

TIP

If you are new to the Notes/Domino document-centric data model, but understand the basic relational data model, the following analogy might add clarity. Think of the documents as records, the document items as fields, and the views as tables.

In any case, it's time to create some new XPages and put what you just learned about Notes forms, documents, and views to good use!

Building an XPages View

The Discussion template offers the user numerous ways to view the documents contained in the application (for example, **By Author**, **By Tag**, and so on). In this section, you learn to build a view just like these. To jump in, create a new XPage, call it **myView**, accept all other dialog default values, and click **OK.** Start by finding the View control within the **Container Controls** section of the **Controls** palette and dropping it anywhere on the blank page (aesthetics are not important at this point). Figure 3.10 identifies the required control for you.

As the drag-and-drop gesture is executed, Domino Designer presents a helper dialog that allows you to bind this XPages View control to a Notes/Domino view data source. Confused? Hope not—this is where you bind the XPages UI View control to the backend Domino view data (remember the concept of presentation/data separation previously discussed). A binding can be thought of as a direct connection or tie between a visual control and a data element: the former is drawn on the user's display and the latter is the content used to populate it. So here, the View control picked from the palette is the presentation layer object that will display data, and you can bind it to the Notes `All Documents` view, which contains the actual data. Figure 3.11 shows the binding dialog.

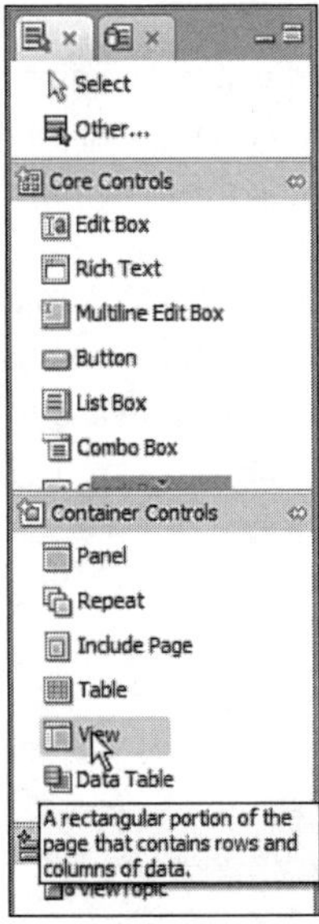

Figure 3.10 View control in Container Controls palette

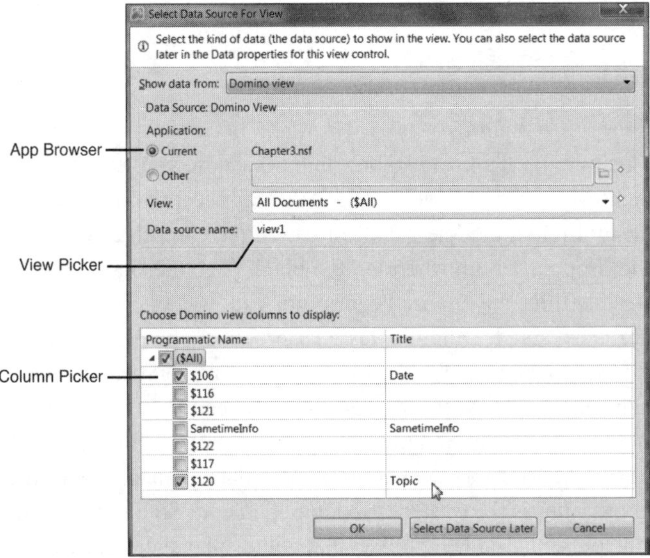

Figure 3.11 View data binding helper dialog

After **All Documents** is selected, a list of its constituent columns are dynamically retrieved and displayed. Thus, you are not compelled to select all columns from the Notes view chosen as the data source. If you do not want to display a particular column in your XPage, simply deselect it by unchecking the checkbox that is located alongside its name. To keep it simple in this instance, select just two columns—**Date** and **Topic**—and click **OK**.

The result is perhaps surprising! I think you'll agree that this helper dialog has done a lot of work on your behalf. A View control has been defined on the XPage based on the dialog choices provided, and some default settings have been applied, such as the maximum number of rows to display in the View control at any one time (30 by default).

Domino Designer provides at least three interesting ways to look at the View control. Obviously, there is the WYSIWYG design pane representation, which gives a rough sketch of how the view will look at runtime. Then, there is the outline viewer, which may be more instructive in this instance. The fully expanded outline shown in the bottom-left corner of Figure 3.12 encapsulates the hierarchical structure of the control that's been created. You can see that the View control has many parts, including a default pager wrapped up in something called a facet (more on facets in Part II, "XPages Development: First Principles"), a view data source reference, and two columns, each of which contain `header` elements. The full markup is also available in the **Source** pane and included in Listing 3.1.

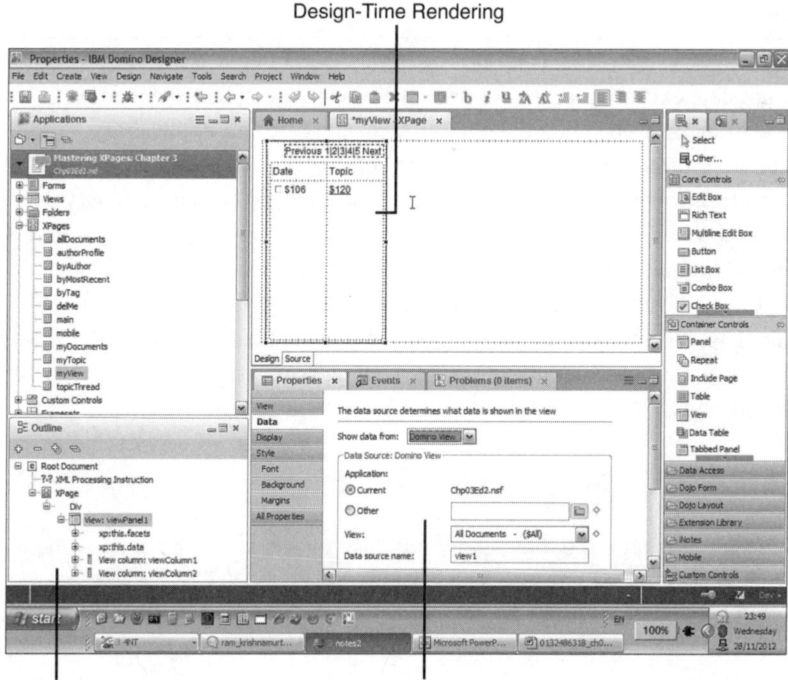

Figure 3.12 View drag-and-drop results

Listing 3.1 View Control XSP Markup

```
<xp:viewPanel rows="30" id="viewPanel1">
     <xp:this.facets>
          <xp:pager partialRefresh="true" layout="Previous Group Next"
               xp:key="headerPager" id="pager1">
          </xp:pager>
     </xp:this.facets>
     <xp:this.data>
          <xp:dominoView var="view1"
               viewName="($All)"></xp:dominoView>
     </xp:this.data>
     <xp:viewColumn columnName="$106" id="viewColumn1">
          <xp:viewColumnHeader value="Date"
               id="viewColumnHeader1">
          </xp:viewColumnHeader>
     </xp:viewColumn>
     <xp:viewColumn columnName="$120" id="viewColumn2">
          <xp:viewColumnHeader value="Topic"
               id="viewColumnHeader2">
          </xp:viewColumnHeader>
     </xp:viewColumn>
</xp:viewPanel>
```

With the possible exception of the pager element, which will be expanded on in later sections, it can be reasonably argued that the markup semantics are self-explanatory—for the most part, just a descriptive summary of the information collected in the data binding helper dialog. Save the page and then, when you preview it, you will see that the correct summary data is now displayed in your view, as shown in Figure 3.13. Note that the empty parentheses in the **Topic** column entry would normally display the name of the document author. This document has been created using `Anonymous` access and, for simplicity, the XPage did not create a **From** field in the underlying **Main Topic** form, so no author information is available for display. You learn how to compute and save an author field in the section, "Executing Form Logic" in Chapter 7, "Working with Domino Documents."

TIP

Starting in Domino Designer 9.0, hovering the mouse over a tag or attribute name in the XPages source pane provides useful descriptive information about that item.

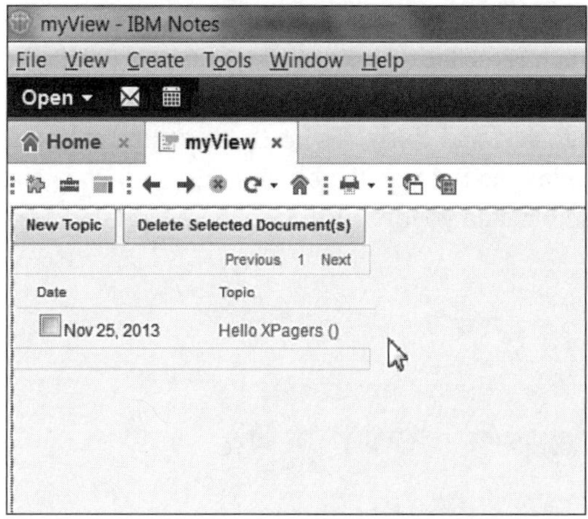

Figure 3.13 View control preview

So far, so good, but how do you work directly with individual documents as opposed to viewing document collections? To do this, you need another XPage. Call this new XPage **myTopic**, because it will be used to create, read, and edit documents created using the **Main Topic** form. The first thing you do in this new XPage is create a new document data source. Again, this is a simple point-and-click procedure:

1. Select the **Data** property sheet on the new blank XPage.
2. Choose **Domino Document** from the **Add** drop-down button.
3. In the **Form** combo box, select the **Main Topic** form.

This is all you need to do to create a new basic document data source. There are, of course, a host of other options that can be used to configure the data source (see Chapter 7 for all the details), but simply nominating a form is sufficient to gain access to all of its metadata, and that's all you need to do at this stage.

TIP

From Notes/Domino version 8.5.1 onward, you can create the Domino document data source while creating the XPage. There is a new option on the New XPage dialog to add the data source at the same time. This is a useful shortcut. Alternatively, you can also create a new data source from the Data Palette, which you can find in the tab adjoining the Controls palette by default.

The contents of the document data source (all the fields defined in the **Main Topic** form) can be viewed by activating the **Data** palette, which is the tab adjacent to the **Controls** palette in the top right of the Designer perspective. You will see many fields listed there, but you are just interested in three of them: **Subject**, **WebCategories**, and **Body**. These fields can be selected by control-clicking each member, and then dragging the fields to the blank XPage, which again saves you a lot of work. Figure 3.14 should closely match your results. Save the XPage and preview it to see how it looks at runtime.

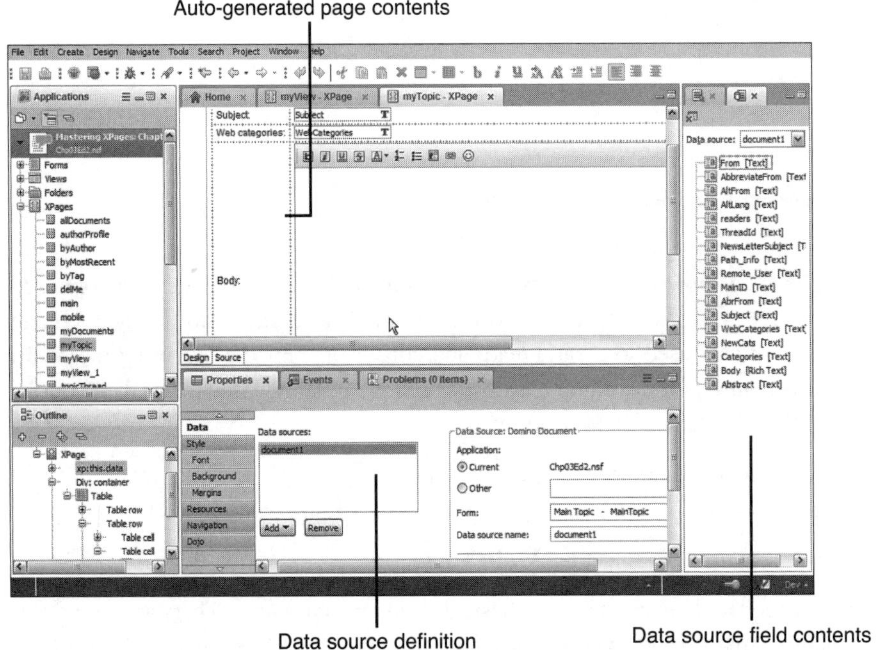

Figure 3.14 Document drag-and-drop results

Now for the missing link—quite literally! It would be natural in any view to be able to open one of its entries by simply clicking it. The view control supports this feature in a simple way. Track back to the **myView** XPage and select the **View** control to activate its property sheet. There is a combo box with the label "**At runtime, open selected document using:**", and here is where you can bridge **myView** to **myTopic** by simply selecting the latter as the target XPage.

After you mark the View control column as a link column, XPages opens the associated document using **myTopic.xsp** when the column entry is selected by an end user at runtime. So, to finish this task, select the **Topic** column in the View control and move to the **Display** property sheet. This property sheet provides the option to wrap the column's data as an HTML link, so check the appropriate checkbox, as shown in Figure 3.15.

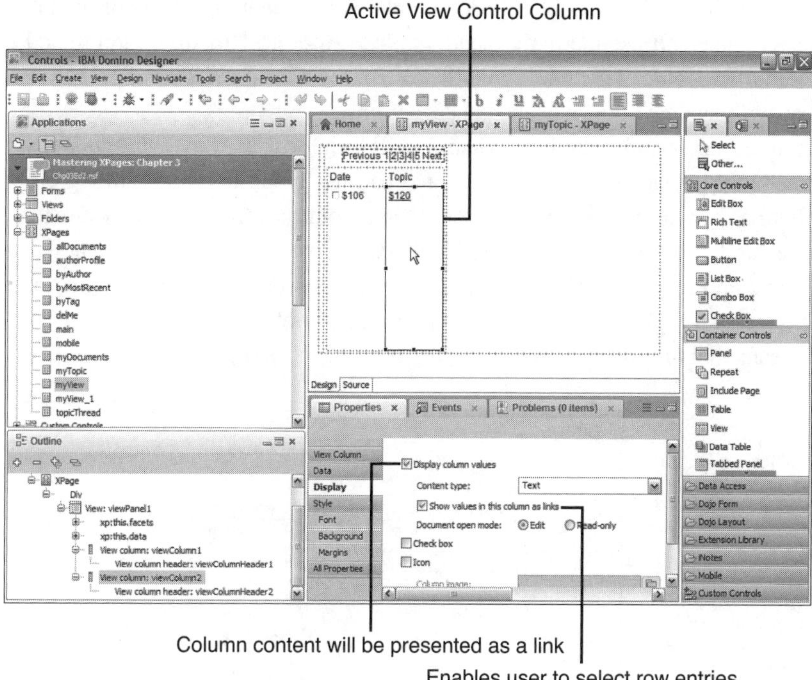

Figure 3.15 Display view column as link property

It's save and preview time again—as long you're making progress, you'll never tire of this feature! This time, your XPage renders the "Hello XPagers!" text as a link, and following this link opens the XPage that contains all the full document details. Here, you can read and edit the details. You could even save your changes if the XPage allowed you to, and navigate back to the original XPage. Hmmm...I guess it's obvious what needs to be done next!

Completing the CRUD

Most any application you have ever used is required to **c**reate, **r**ead, **u**pdate, and **d**elete records—or perform CRUD operations, as it is commonly known. To fully support CRUD operations in the current example, there are a few things left to do.

First, **myTopic.xsp** needs a way to save new or edited documents, or cancel such edits and navigate back to the view. Second, you need to enable the user to create new documents and delete existing documents. You can do this by adding actions to **myView.xsp**. Start with **myTopic**.

The drag-and-drop action of the Domino document data source in **myTopic** neatly wrapped all the generated controls into a HTML table. Select a table cell in the bottom row of the table presented in the Design pane and use the main menu **Table > Append Row(s)** option to add a new row to the bottom of the table. Then, drag-and-drop a Button from the **Control** palette into each table cell. These will become your save and cancel actions.

Start by clicking the left-hand button and changing its label text to "Save" in the **Button** property sheet. Immediately adjacent to this label is an **Options** group box that, among other things, allows the button type to be set. Make this a `Submit` button. This simply means that, when this button is clicked, the entire page is submitted to the server, and once that occurs, any data sources contained therein will be saved (assuming no validation failures). Thus, in this case, there is no need to perform an explicit document save operation. Simply designating the button to be of type `Submit` means that this happens automatically (see Figure 3.16). Nice!

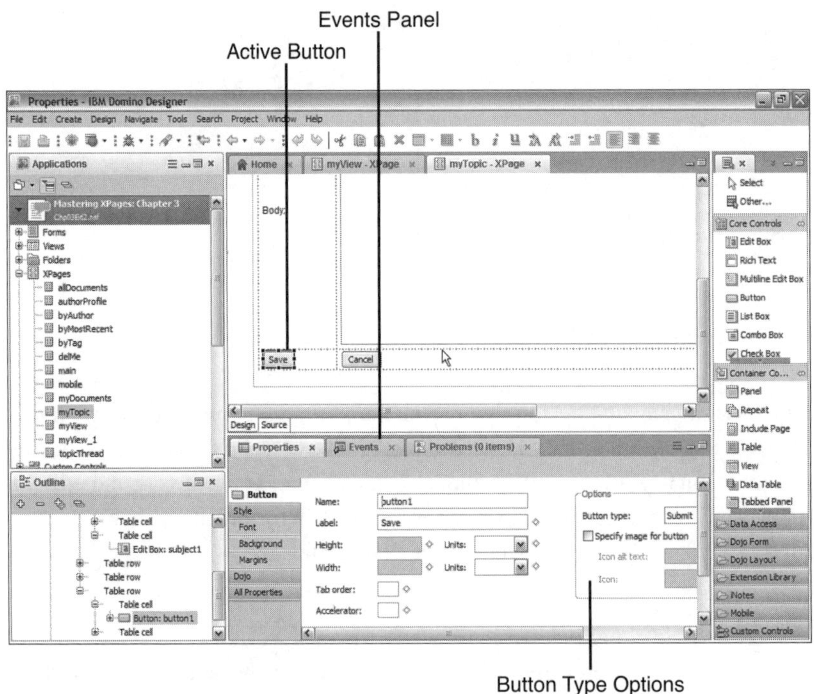

Figure 3.16 Adding action buttons

Taking care of the cancel action is even easier. Again, you must first change the label, although this time, let's do it a little differently to show off another Designer feature. When you select the second Button control, hit function key **F2** on your keyboard; this allows you to change the label using in-place editing (for example, you can type the new text directly into the control). This update is immediately reflected in the property sheet and, on the same sheet, you should set the Button type to Cancel. Save your sheet and view the markup generated for these two controls in the source pane. If all goes well, your source-code snippet should be identical to Listing 3.2.

Listing 3.2 XSP Button Markup

```
<xp:tr>
    <xp:td>
        <xp:button id="button1" value="Save">
            <xp:eventHandler
                        event="onclick"
                        submit="true"
                        refreshMode="complete"
                        immediate="false"
                        save="true">
                  </xp:eventHandler>
        </xp:button>
      </xp:td>
    <xp:td>
        <xp:button value="Cancel" id="button2">
            <xp:eventHandler
                        event="onclick"
                        submit="true"
                         refreshMode="complete"
                        immediate="true"
                        save="false">
                  </xp:eventHandler>
        </xp:button>
    </xp:td>
</xp:tr>
```

Although you are not required in this chapter to directly enter any XSP markup in the Source pane, it is nevertheless interesting to see what is automatically generated by selecting a few simple UI options. The event handlers you see here define the runtime behavior that occurs when the buttons are clicked. Ignoring some of the more subtle attributes for the moment, you can see that the first button requests a save and the second button does not.

> **TIP**
>
> If you don't like the way some tags are autoformatted in the source pane window, you can quickly reformat or "pretty print" the tags in question by highlighting them with the mouse and typing Control-Shift-F on your keyboard. Try it!

The last thing you need to do with **myTopic.xsp** is to define some simple navigation rules to control where the user ends up after these actions are performed. The XPage itself has **Next Page** properties that you can use. Simply click anywhere outside the main table so that the XPage itself becomes the selected object, or select the XPage root node in the **Outline** pane and choose **myView** from the Next Page combo boxes on the property sheet, as shown in Figure 3.17. Thus, the user returns to **myView** after the **myTopic** is submitted. In fact, in Figure 3.17, the **myView** page navigation is also selected in the case where there is an update failure, so you will end up in **myView.xsp** one way or another.

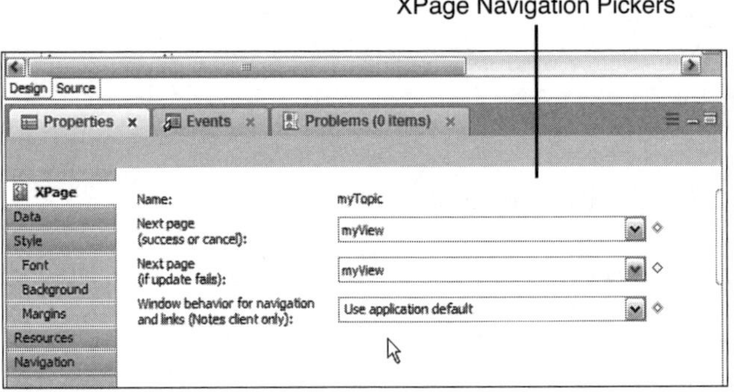

Figure 3.17 XPage navigation properties

The second part of your current task is to revisit **myView.xsp** and introduce CREATE and DELETE operations. After the **myView** XPage is activated in Designer, add two new Button controls anywhere on the page. Being a dab hand with buttons at this stage, you can quickly change their titles to "New Topic" and "Delete Selected Document(s)," respectively. Once complete, use what are known as `Simple Actions` to execute the operations.

To create a new topic document, select the Button on the **Design** pane and activate the **Events** tab that is located alongside the **Properties** tab. Front and central on this property sheet is an **Add Action** button. Assuming that `Simple Actions` is the currently selected action type (it is by default), click this button and you see the helper dialog presented in Figure 3.18. In summary, the steps are as follows:

1. Select the **New Topic** button.
2. Activate the **Events** tab.
3. Be sure that both the **onclick** event and **Server** tab are selected.
4. Click the **Add Action** button to launch the Simple Action helper dialog.
5. Choose the **Open Page** as your action.
6. Choose **myTopic** as the name XPage to open action.
7. Choose **New Document** as the target document.
8. Click **OK** to complete the operation.

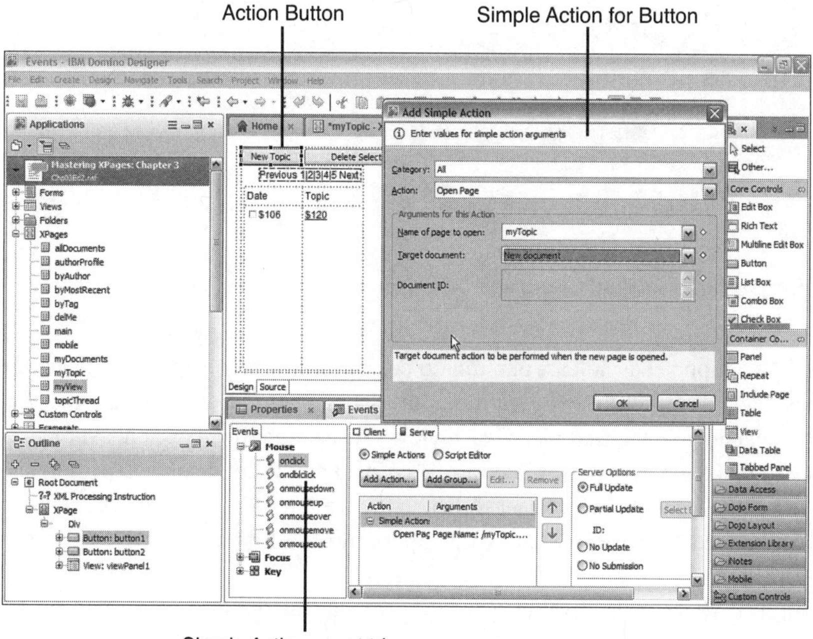

Figure 3.18 Add Simple Action dialog: open page

You do not need to enter or compute a document ID in the helper dialog because your action is creating a new document, so the ID is automatically created by Notes at runtime. If you were using this simple action to open an existing document, you would need to provide an identifier. In later chapters, you will see examples of how these IDs can be obtained programmatically.

Similarly, with the second button, you need to add another simple action. This time, it is a `Delete Selected Documents` action, and it's safe to say that, as a best practice, you need to add some text to warn the user that this action will remove data from the database! You also need to add the id of the view control because this is a required parameter. Figure 3.19 shows an example of a full completed dialog for this simple action.

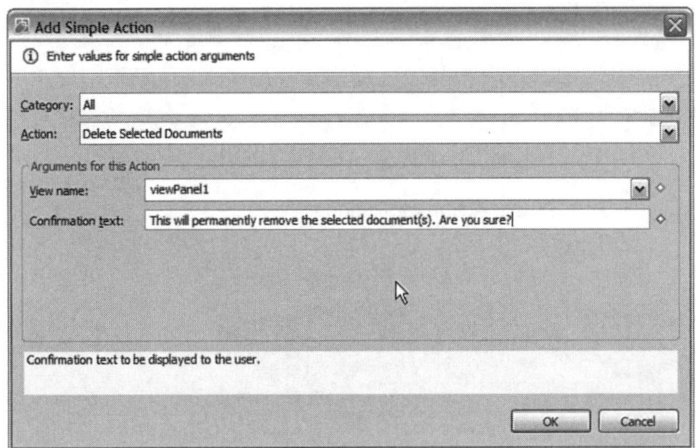

Figure 3.19 Add Simple Action dialog: delete selected documents

Be aware that the action needs at least one row to be selected to have something to act on (that is, the user must have the capability of identifying the document to be deleted). In order for rows in a view to be selectable in the first place, each view row needs to display a checkbox that enables the end user to make the necessary selection. This checkbox is not displayed by default, but it can be enabled via the same property sheet shown in Figure 3.15. Yes, you guessed it—it's the checkbox property called **Check box**. Select this option for the first column (**Date**) in the view control.

All that remains is to preview the **myView** page to verify that everything works as intended. You should now be able to carry out a full CRUD operation in preview mode. Test this scenario as follows:

1. Use the **New Topic** button to create a new "throw away" document.
2. Enter some arbitrary details and click **Save**.
3. Once returned to the view, click the link to your new document and edit its details.
4. Save your modifications and verify that those changes are saved.
5. Once returned to the view for the last time, select the checkbox for the newly created document and click **Delete Selected Document(s)**.

6. Verify that a warning dialog is presented (see Figure 3.20). Click **OK** to proceed.
7. Verify that your new "throw away" document has indeed been thrown away, meaning that it is no longer displayed in the view (it has been deleted from the NSF).

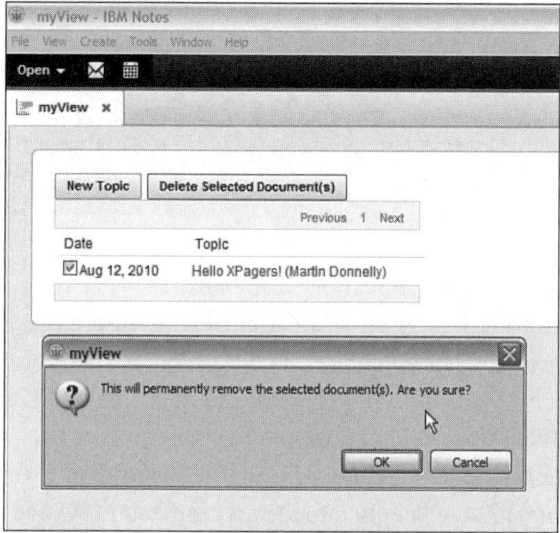

Figure 3.20 Confirmation dialog for Delete Selected Documents action

If all the preceding steps execute as described, then congratulations are justifiably in order, as you have succeeded in building a functional XPages CRUD application in no time at all. You have followed the same basic procedures that are used in the template itself, although these would not be clearly evident to you at this stage because the real XPages contain so many other features. In having walked through this scenario in the course of umpteen XPages demonstrations, this author can assure you that this whole CRUD app dev scenario can be completed from scratch in about ten minutes. Rapid application development indeed!

Conclusion

Although you made great progress in a short time, there's obviously a long way to go with building the XPages applications. Remember that this chapter gave you some breadth on XPages application development—all the depth comes later. You learned to build a basic view similar to those you see in the standard Discussion template. You learned to perform CRUD operations on Notes documents using only point-and-click operations. You linked XPages to create an application flow, and you implemented simple application logic without writing a line of code.

Going forward, clearly more advanced features need to be added; for example, input validations need to be applied to manage end-user data entry, rich objects need to be handled, uploading and downloading must be supported, security enforced, a sleeker and more dynamic user interface built, and so on! You will do all those things and more over the course of this book.

Tip

If you are new to XPages and want to work on other introductory examples before continuing, study the XPages Site Finder tutorial under Domino Designer User Guide in Designer Help.

Now that you have gotten your feet wet in XPages application development, it is perhaps the most appropriate time to take a brief sojourn from the Discussion template, and instead take a more holistic look at the technology that underpins what you have just built. Part II, therefore, provides an architectural view of XPages, which hopefully will prove all the more meaningful now that you have done some introductory practical work with the technology here in Part I.

Thus armed with both experience and deeper understanding, you will return to hands-on XPages application development in Part III. You will dive deeply into the great spread of XPages features and look at how they can be applied when building more sophisticated application solutions. Sound like a plan?

PART II

XPages Development: First Principles

CHAPTER 4

Anatomy of an XPage

Several years ago, I participated in a study that set out to identify steps to help increase the use of Eclipse in universities and colleges around the world. One aspect of the study involved conducting a series of interviews with lecturers of computer and information technology–related courses. During the interviews, I heard the same message being repeated, and it was something that initially took me by surprise. Most lecturers actively discouraged or even disallowed the use of Integrated Development Environments (IDEs) when teaching a programming language course. For example, when teaching Java, a common practice was to have students write their code in a plain text editor and then compile and run it from the command line. The value in this approach was that students learned the fundamentals of the language (how to write code without the benefit of content assistance and other tools that would help them write code and prevent them from making obvious mistakes).

This is the primary reason that this chapter is important to you:

You will learn to create an XPage by hand so that you understand what is actually happening under the covers to an XPage when you use Domino Designer.

You might even find that you prefer to create XPages this way. More importantly, you won't be bound to the editors and wizards of Domino Designer. Depending on your preference and/or the task you are performing, you can switch between visual and source code editing. In particular, when you need to modify an existing XPage, using the source mode allows you to see the full page in one go and can be quicker than navigating through the relevant editors.

That said, using Domino Designer's editors and properties panels typically remains the fastest way to create an XPage for even experienced developers. In the real world, professional developers need tools to help increase their productivity and make performing simple, routine tasks quick and easy. However, there is one drawback with using a graphical editor tool: It can be difficult to understand how an XPage actually works. If you weren't the person who created a particular XPage, it's often difficult to quickly understand what the XPage is doing and where the application logic is embedded. This is because the XPage, as presented in the graphical editor, can be dramatically different from what is presented at runtime, especially when there is heavy use of custom controls and Cascading Style Sheets. The XPage graphical editor has some great features to help you see where the application logic is specified (such as the computed diamond to overview all properties of a particular element in the page or within the **All Properties** view). Although you can do everything with the WYSIWYG editor in Domino Designer, an important skill to develop is the ability to read and understand the markup of an actual XPage. This is the secondary reason that this chapter is important to you:

You will learn how to read the XPage source (XSP markup) and understand how the different elements work together at runtime.

This chapter teaches you to write and read XSP markup and helps you understand the first principles of the XPages programming model. This chapter is written to allow you to skim for now if you are happy to rely on the graphical editor and to come back later to dive into particular concepts as they get introduced. This chapter contains many sample XPages that demonstrate different syntaxes and the behavior of different tags. To get the most out of this chapter, preview each sample so you can see how they behave and experiment by modifying the samples. You can use these samples as a source of snippets of XSP markup for reuse within your own applications.

With these thoughts in mind, let's dispense with the WYSIWYG editor in Domino Designer and work primarily in the Source editor. Even when working in source mode, the graphical tools are useful for inspecting the properties of a tag you are editing or providing a starting point when creating the user interface. Be sure to download the **Chp04Ed2.nsf** file provided online for this book to run through the exercises throughout the chapter. You can access these files at `www.ibmpressbooks.com/title/9780133373370`.

What Exactly Is an XPage?

The definition of an XPage will grow the more you learn about the XPages programming model. For now, an XPage is

> "A Notes database design element that is used to present content in either a web or mobile browser or the Notes client."

Each Notes database design element performs a specific job, such as a Notes Form is used to create, edit, and view Notes documents, and a Notes View is used to view collections of Notes documents. An XPage is a powerful Notes design element because it can do the same types of content presentation that a Notes Form and a Notes View can do—and more. Also, the XPages programming model supports the capability to use XPages to extend itself. Later in this book, you see that a special kind of XPage can be created, called a Custom Control, which allows you to extend the set of controls available for use in your applications. This is a powerful concept; if you need to extend XPages, firstly you can do so easily, and secondly, you don't need to learn something new to do it.

You will learn more about the architectural heritage of the XPages programming model later in Chapter 5, "XPages and Java Server Faces," and this will increase your understanding of XPages' capabilities.

Understanding XSP Tag Markup

XPages uses XML as its file format. The XPages XML syntax is called XSP. This acronym doesn't stand for anything but was used for historical reasons. If you are new to XML, we strongly urge you to read one of the many XML primers available on the Internet or, if you're feeling brave, look at the specification (www.w3.org/XML/). For now, the following XML primer provides the basics.

Getting Started with XML

XML is a text-based data format that has been defined by the World Wide Web Consortium (W3C). It is widely used for many applications, including electronic publishing, data exchange, document file formats, and more. The primary characteristics of XML are

- XML is a markup language and similar to HTML.
- XML is a standard widely used in the industry.
- XML is a general-purpose data format with strict rules in how the data is formatted.
- XML does not include any definition of tags.

HTML is probably the most widely known markup language; however, HTML differs from XML in the last two points in the preceding list.

First, the formatting of HTML is not strict, and web browsers still render HTML that doesn't have properly terminated tags or properly defined attributes. Listing 4.1 shows an example of some badly formed HTML that will nevertheless work in a browser. In this example, notice that the tags are not properly terminated and the attribute is not inside quotes. This is one of the strengths of HTML—it's easy for anyone to create an HTML page that displays correctly.

Listing 4.1 Sample HTML

```
<html>
        <table BORDER=1>
                 <td>First Cell
                 <td><b>Second Cell
</html>
```

By contrast, XML must be well formed, which means that, at a minimum, all tags must be properly terminated and all attributes correctly defined. So, taking the same example, to be well-formed XML, it must look like Listing 4.2.

Listing 4.2 Sample XML

```
<html>
    <table BORDER="1">
        <tr>
            <td>First Cell</td>
            <td><b>Second Cell</b></td>
        </tr>
    </table>
</html>
```

XML is general purpose and does not define any tags. Instead, XML can be used as the basis for the definition of many different languages. The language definition has its own rules; these rules can be defined in a Document Type Definition (DTD) or an XML schema. XML DTDs and schema are two ways to define an XML-based language—they define the rules to which the language must adhere. The rules define the tags that are permissible in that language, what attributes can be used with these tags, and the relationship between the tags. One such language definition is Extensible Hypertext Markup Language (XHTML), which is an XML-based version of HTML. So, considering the previous example one more time, the XHTML version looks like Listing 4.3.

Listing 4.3 Sample XHTML

```
<!DOCTYPE html PUBLIC "-//W3C//DTD XHTML 1.0 Strict//EN"
"http://www.w3.org/TR/xhtml1/DTD/xhtml1-strict.dtd">
<html xmlns="http://www.w3.org/1999/xhtml">
        <head>
                <title>Title goes here</title>
        </head>
        <body>
                <table border="1">
                        <tr>
                                <td>First Cell</td>
                                <td><b>Second Cell</b></td>
                        </tr>
                </table>
        </body>
</html>
```

If you are familiar with HTML, the majority of the markup in Listing 4.3 should be readily understood. As you can see, XHTML is strict: All of your tags must be lowercase and correctly terminated—attribute values must also be quoted. The `<html>` tag is the root of this XML document and the rest of the document forms a tree, which starts at this root tag. The root `<html>` tag contains the head and body tags, the relationship is described in terms of parents and children. So, the <html> tag has two children—the <head> and <body> tags—and the parent of the <head> tag is the <html> tag.

What's more, there's no cheating in XHTML; a page that doesn't obey the rules is not processed. The DOCTYPE declaration at the beginning of the markup declares what the markup contains and is used by whatever browser processes the markup to make sure that the rules are obeyed. The DOCTYPE is not mandatory and is not declared within XPages markup, but it is emitted in the generated HTML response. So, it is useful to understand this declaration because you have ways to change the default DOCTYPE that XPages uses.

One other thing might be new to you in this sample, and that is the `xmlns` attribute. The `xmlns` attribute is a reserved XML attribute and is used to define an XML namespace. An *XML namespace* qualifies the tags and attributes in an XML document, meaning that it declares that these specific tags belong to a specific XML language. So, the `xmlns` attribute in the previous example specifies that all the associated tags belong to the declared XHTML namespace. The usefulness of XML namespaces is not immediately obvious; however, consider the following problem: What if you want to create an XML document that contains tags from two different XML languages? Different languages have different tags, and the XML author needs to be able to specify which language specific tags belong to. Different languages might use the same tag name, so it is critical to differentiate one from another. This is where XML namespaces are your friend; in the previous example, we used an abbreviated form of the `xmlns` attribute. The following form, which includes a namespace prefix, can also be used:

```
xmlns:xhtml="http://www.w3.org/1999/xhtml"
```

This form of the `xmlns` attribute allows you to specify a prefix, and all tags that use this prefix belong to the associated namespace. An XML document that contains multiple namespaces is referred to as a *compound document*. Listing 4.4 shows an XML document that contains multiple namespaces.

Listing 4.4 XML Document with XHTML and XForms

```
<?xml version="1.0" encoding="UTF-8"?>
<xhtml:html
xmlns:xhtml=http://www.w3.org/1999/xhtml xmlns:xf="http://www.
w3.org/2002/xforms">
        <xhtml:head>
                <xf:model>
                        <xf:instance id="person">
                                <person xmlns="">
                                        <firstName>How</firstName>
                                        <lastName>Bloggs</lastName>
                                </person>
                        </xf:instance>
```

```
            </xf:model>
    </xhtml:head>
    <xhtml:body>
            <xhtml:p>
                    First name:
                    <xf:input ref="instance('person')/firstName" />
                    <xhtml:br />
                    Last name:
                    <xf:input ref="instance('person')/lastName" />
            </xhtml:p>
    </xhtml:body>
</xhtml:html>
```

This example starts with an XML processing instruction:

```
<?xml version="1.0" encoding="UTF-8"?>
```

This defines the version and encoding of the XML document. All XPages contain this same instruction and are encoded as UTF-8, which means Unicode is used by default.

Chapter 10, "Custom Controls," shows you how useful XML namespaces can be.

This ends a brief tour of XML. More XML tips are provided throughout this chapter, but for now, let's look at the XPages application of XML.

XPages XML Syntax

By now, you know that XML can be used to define new applications. In XPages, XML is used to define a declarative programming model—a way to program where you define what you want done but not how to do it. You already saw how a basic application can be created using XPages without the need to write a single line of code. You won't always be able to do that, but you'll be pleasantly surprised by how much you can achieve without writing code.

So, the XPages markup allows you to

1. Create the user interface for your application.
2. Define the data that will be manipulated and displayed.
3. Define the application logic to be executed in response to events that occur.

Therefore, you need tags that represent the building blocks for an application. Each tag in XSP markup corresponds to a user interface control, a data source, predefined application logic, or a property used by one of these components. There is a well-defined interaction between the user interface, data, and application logic components. You must learn how the various components interact to program using XSP. Each component can be configured to provide a variety of behaviors. In XSP, you program by creating a hierarchy of tags and setting the attributes of these different tags. This process allows you to describe a user interface, its data, and what happens when the user interacts with this user interface. So, you are telling XSP what to do in your application rather than how to do it. This is the power of declarative programming; applications repeat a lot of the same behaviors and all this logic is implemented, tested, and debugged just once for each and reused many times. If that was all XPages supported, people would quickly run into limits; however, because of its extensible architecture, you can also add your own custom application logic and create your own components to extend the programming model.

Let's start by creating a new XPage and then switching to the Source view, as shown in Figure 4.1.

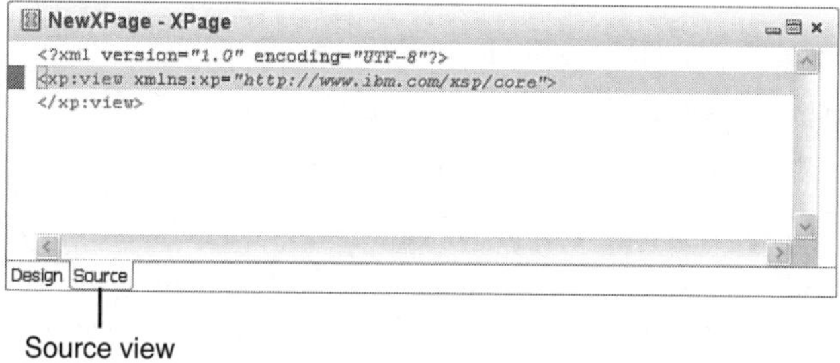

Figure 4.1 New XPage

Each new XPage is an XML document, and every XML document must have a root tag. The root tag for every XPage is the `<xp:view>` tag (not to be confused with a Notes view). Why view? Here, you begin to see the XPages heritage emerging, the root of a JavaServer Faces (JSF) component hierarchy is the `<view>` tag, and this convention has been adopted in XPages. (The relationship between XPages and JSF is discussed in Chapter 5.) XPages markup allows you to create a view that is displayed as HTML and the `<view>` tag represents the component that is root of this HTML document—effectively, this notion of a view maps directly to the HTML `<body>` tag.

The XPages namespace is www.ibm.com/xsp/core (no, there is nothing at this URL) and the default prefix is `xp`. This namespace is reserved for use by IBM, because all namespaces beginning with www.ibm.com are. When you need to define your own namespace, the convention is to use a URL that starts with your company's web address to ensure that there are no collisions.

Simple Properties

The first thing you will learn is how to alter the behavior of the `<view>` tag by changing its properties. XML allows you to set attributes on a tag, and this is one way you can set the properties of the component associated with that tag. To get a list of all the properties associated with a particular tag, perform the following steps:

1. Expand the XPage outline and select the tag (in this case, the tag labeled XPage).
2. Select the **All Properties** tab from the **Properties** page.

All the properties for that tag are listed, and they are categorized based on function:

- **Accessibility:** Properties used to make your application more readily interpreted by assistive technologies.
- **Basics:** General category of properties.
- **Dojo:** Properties that are used by Dojo (this use of Dojo in XPages is covered in Chapter 11, "Advanced Scripting").
- **Data:** Optional properties that allow data to be associated with the tag and its children.
- **Events:** Properties that are events to which the component can respond.
- **Styling:** Properties that control the visual appearance of the component.

To set the value of a property, you can select the cell in the Value column and directly type in the value. For example, to set the background color of the XPage to a shade of light gray, edit the style property. The style property allows you to use Cascading Style Sheets (CSS) syntax to change the appearance of the XPage. Select the style property and type in the following value:

```
background-color:rgb(0,0,255)
```

When you do this, the markup changes as you type, and you see the style attribute being added to the view tag, as shown in Figure 4.2.

When you select a cell in the value column of the All Properties tab, you might see a button to the right of the editable value area. This button allows you to launch an external property editor if one exists for the property you are currently editing. An external property editor provides a GUI that simplifies the editing of a specific property type for well-known property types. (You learn how to work with property editors in Chapter 10.) So, if you are not a CSS expert, you can open the property editor and have a user-friendly interface that allows you to set the style property, as shown in Figure 4.3.

If you switch back to the Design tab for this XPage, you see that the page now has a blue background.

Complex Properties

XML attributes can be used to set properties that have primitive data types (such as strings, integers, and so on); however, not all the properties of a component are primitive types. Non-primitive properties are referred to as *complex properties*. Complex properties are represented as their own tags in the XPages XML vocabulary. Listing 4.5 shows an example of how to set the data property.

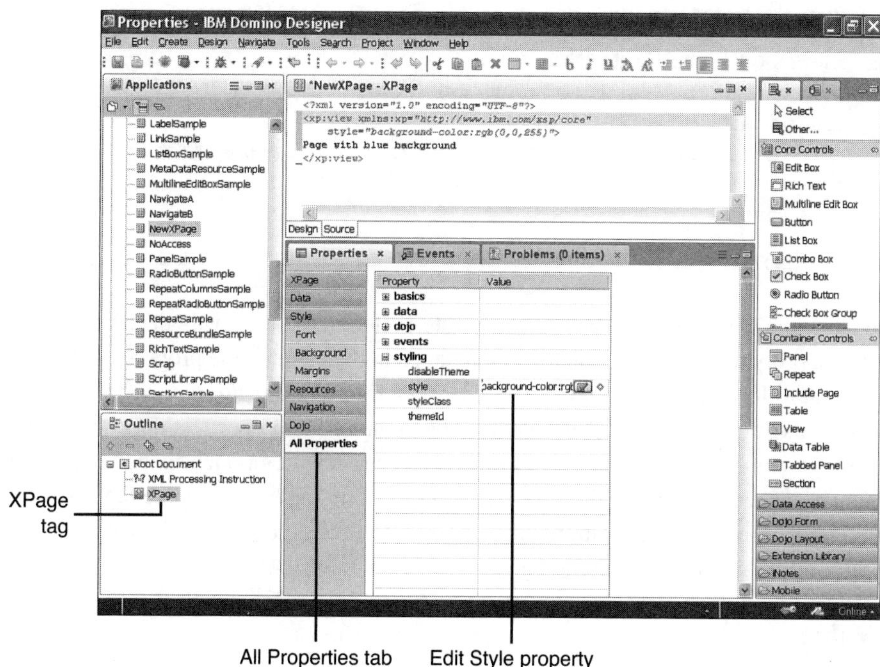

Figure 4.2 Editing a tag property

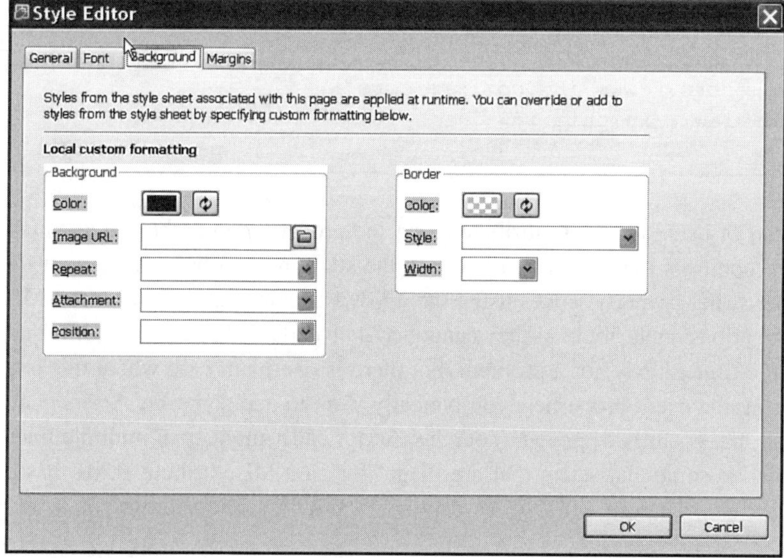

Figure 4.3 Style Editor

Listing 4.5 Setting the Data Property

```
<?xml version="1.0" encoding="UTF-8"?>
<xp:view xmlns:xp="http://www.ibm.com/xsp/core">
      <xp:this.data>
            <xp:dominoDocument var="document1" forumName="Topic"></
xp:dominoDocument>
      </xp:this.data>
</xp:view>
```

A tag that begins with the prefix `xp:this.` is interpreted in a special way in XPages. This tag indicates that a property is being set on the parent tag, and the name of the property is the part of the tag name that follows the `this.` prefix. These tags are referred to as *this* tags and the syntax is referred to as the `xp:this.` (or just *this*) syntax. The value of the property is the child of the `this` tag. In the previous example, the `data` property of the view component is being set to a Domino document (as represented by the `xp:dominoDocument` tag). Data source tags are discussed in detail later in the section, "Data Sources." To summarize, the `xp:this.` syntax allows you to set complex properties on the parent tag.

Complex Values

The `this` tag syntax is generic and can be used to set any property of an XPages component. Listing 4.6 demonstrates how you set the `id` property using `xp:this.id`. This is for educational purposes only; it's not recommend for use in practice.

Listing 4.6 Setting the ID Property Using the xp:this. Syntax

```
<?xml version="1.0" encoding="UTF-8"?>
<xp:view xmlns:xp="http://www.ibm.com/xsp/core">
      <xp:this.id>view1</xp:this.id>
</xp:view>
```

This time, instead of using an XML attribute to set the property value, the `this` syntax and the value of the property is the text nested between the start and end tags. As previously mentioned, you can set string property values using the XML attribute syntax; however, XML imposes numerous limitations on attributes—they cannot contain certain characters (<, >, ") and line breaks. Most of the time, this is not a problem, but there is one main case where this is a major issue. When using the event properties, you typically want to add some JavaScript code that will execute when that event is triggered. Your JavaScript code might span multiple lines and might need to include some characters that are illegal for an XML attribute. XML has a solution to this problem: *character data (CDATA)* section. A CDATA section allows you to add content to an XML document that an XML parser interprets as character data and not markup. A CDATA section starts with the following sequence of characters:

```
<![CDATA[
```

and ends with this sequence:

```
]]>
```

> **TIP**
>
> The delimiters used in a CDATA section are intentionally meant to be obscure—something that would not normally appear in an XML document and, as such, are easily forgotten. By default, when you use the XPages Editor to add JavaScript, it is included in a CDATA section. So, if you forget the exact syntax of a CDATA section, using the Script Editor is a quick way to generate one.

Listing 4.7 shows how to add some JavaScript that executes on the server after the XPage loads. This example uses the XPage `afterPageLoad` event property; this event is triggered after the XPage first loads and the associated application logic is executed.

Listing 4.7 Using a CDATA Section with the xp:this. Syntax

```
<?xml version="1.0" encoding="UTF-8"?>
<xp:view xmlns:xp="http://www.ibm.com/xsp/core">
      <xp:this.afterPageLoad>
            <![CDATA[#{javascript:var msg = "Page loaded successfully";
println(msg);}]]>
      </xp:this.afterPageLoad>
</xp:view>
```

> **TIP**
>
> When you preview this page in the Notes client, you can see the message that was printed using this JavaScript by viewing the trace (Help > Support > View Trace). This trace file contains all server logging and XPages server print statements.

Computed Properties

So far, you have seen how to set static property values (values that are fixed to a specific value that is known at the time the XPage is created). But, what happens if you need to compute the value of a property dynamically? For example, the value is not known when the page is created, but it needs to be computed based on some data that will be available at the time the XPage executes, such as the current username or current time. A good example of this is deciding when to display some part of the user interface. XPages uses the `rendered` property to control when user interface controls are emitted to the output HTML. This is a Boolean property, so the valid values are either true or false (in the UI, this property is called Visible). If you go to the All Properties tab and edit this property, you are presented with a drop-down that lists the valid values, but also notice a small blue diamond. By default, this diamond is empty, which means that the property value is not being computed. If you add application logic to compute the property value, the diamond changes to a solid blue diamond. This convention is used throughout the user interface to allow you to easily determine where application logic is being used. Select this diamond and you are presented with an option to compute the property value, as shown in Figure 4.4.

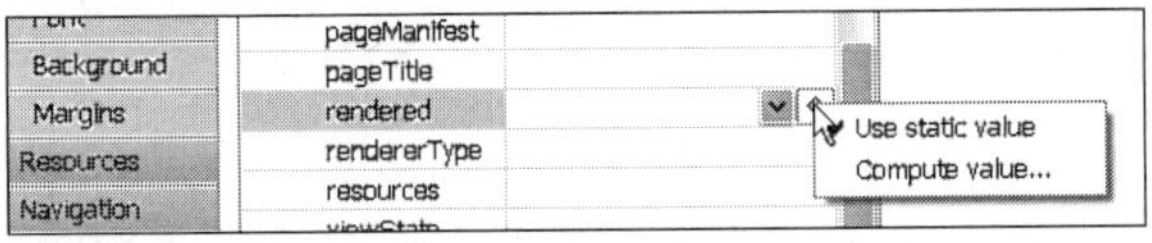

Figure 4.4 Computing a property value

The Script Editor is opened to allow you to add your own JavaScript application logic to compute the property value, as shown in Figure 4.5.

The Script Editor is discussed later in this book, but for now, let's look at how computed values are presented in the XPages markup. Listing 4.8 uses a Computed Field control that displays the computed value and a `submit` button, which is labeled `"Refresh"`, to cause the page to be redrawn.

Listing 4.8 Computing a Value Dynamically

```
<?xml version="1.0" encoding="UTF-8"?>
<xp:view xmlns:xp="http://www.ibm.com/xsp/core">
      <xp:text escape="true"
           value="#{javascript:new Date().getSeconds()}">
      </xp:text>
      <xp:button value="Refresh" id="button1">
            <xp:eventHandler event="onclick" submit="true"
                  refreshMode="complete" immediate="false" save="true">
            </xp:eventHandler>
      </xp:button>
</xp:view>
```

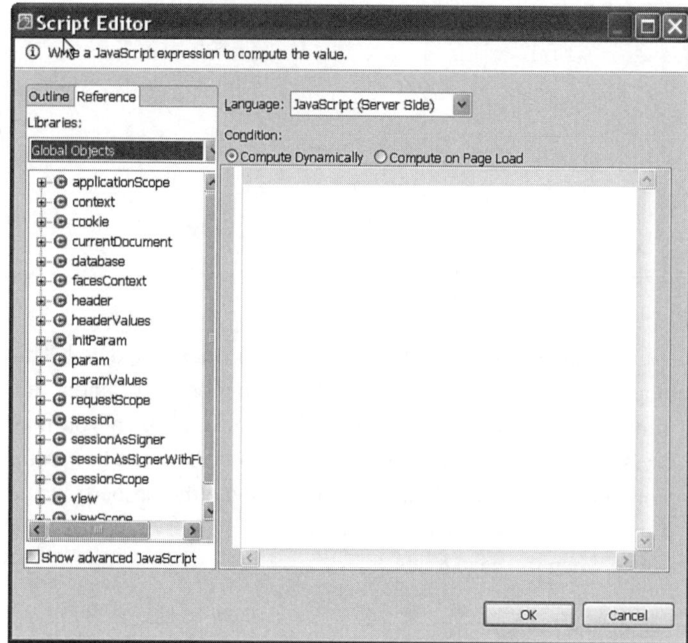

Figure 4.5 Script Editor

> **TIP**
>
> Controls that can display HTML or XML (such as a Computed Field or rich text editor) support a property called escape. This property indicates that the contents need to be encoded before being displayed so that characters sensitive in HTML or XML (such as <,>) are escaped and display correctly.

A dynamically computed expression starts with the `#{` character sequence, followed by the programming language (for example, `javascript`), then a `:` character, then the computed expression, and it ends with the `}` character. Here is the generic syntax of a dynamically computed expression:

```
propertyName="#{<language>:<expression>}"
```

Preview the page in the Notes client and the number of seconds is displayed, as shown in Figure 4.6.

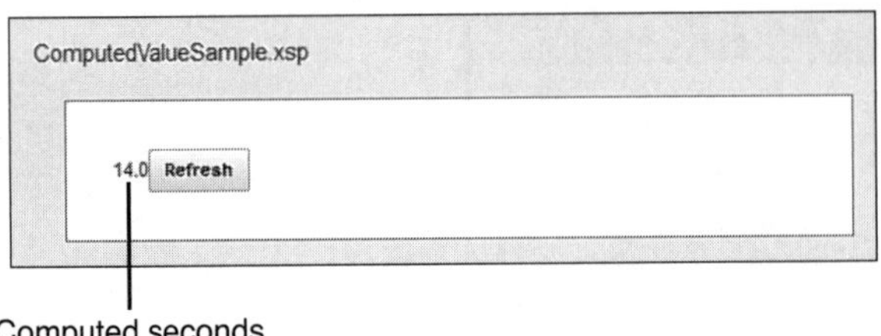

Figure 4.6 Preview a computed value

Select the `Refresh` button, the page refreshes, and the number of seconds is updated. This is because the value is being computed every time it is accessed. It is important to know that the property is computed each time it is accessed, which might be more often than you may expect. The property might be accessed multiple times as a page is being processed, so be careful if you're performing expensive computations. Another option is to compute the property value once, when the page is loaded. Listing 4.9 shows a modified version of the previous example, where the value is computed just once when the page loads.

Listing 4.9 Computing a Value when the Page Loads

```
<?xml version="1.0" encoding="UTF-8"?>
<xp:view xmlns:xp="http://www.ibm.com/xsp/core">
      <xp:text escape="true"
            value="${javascript:new Date().getSeconds()}">
      </xp:text>
      <xp:button value="Refresh" id="button1">
            <xp:eventHandler event="onclick" submit="true"
                  refreshMode="complete" immediate="false" save="true">
            </xp:eventHandler>
      </xp:button>
</xp:view>
```

Computed expressions are evaluated either every time they are accessed, dynamically or just once when the XPage loads. The only difference between a dynamically computed expression and one that is computed when the page loads is the start delimiter. The start delimiter for a computed expression that is only evaluated when the page loads is the `${` character sequence. Here is the generic syntax of a computed expression that is evaluated when the page is loaded:

```
propertyName="${<language>:<expression>}"
```

With that one small change, refreshing the page no longer changes the computed value, because it does not get reevaluated after the initial page load.

Listing 4.10 shows XPages markup for a more complete sample, which shows dynamically computed and computed-on-page-load values side by side. When you preview this sample, initially both values should be the same (or at least within 1 second of each other), but each time you click the submit button, only the dynamically computed value changes.

Listing 4.10 Complete Computed Values Sample

```
<?xml version="1.0" encoding="UTF-8"?>
<xp:view xmlns:xp="http://www.ibm.com/xsp/core">
      <xp:table>
            <xp:tr>
                  <xp:td>Compute dynamically:</xp:td>
                  <xp:td>
                        <xp:text escape="true" id="computedField1"
                        value="#{javascript:new Date().getSeconds()}">
                        </xp:text>
                  </xp:td>
            </xp:tr>
            <xp:tr>
                  <xp:td>Compute on page load:</xp:td>
                  <xp:td>
                        <xp:text escape="true" id="computedField2"
                        value="${javascript:new Date().getSeconds()}">
                        </xp:text>
                  </xp:td>
            </xp:tr>
            <xp:tr>
                  <xp:td>
                        <xp:button value="Submit" id="button1">
                              <xp:eventHandler event="onclick"
                                   submit="true"
                                   refreshMode="complete"
                                   immediate="false"
                                   save="true">
                              </xp:eventHandler>
                        </xp:button>
                  </xp:td>
                  <xp:td></xp:td>
            </xp:tr>
      </xp:table>
</xp:view>
```

Data Binding

The computed values you saw in the previous section are read only. But, what if you want to bind a control to a value and allow the control to read and update that value? You already saw an example of this in Chapter 3, "Building Your First XPages Application," where an edit box was used to edit the value in a Notes document. Listing 4.11 shows the basic syntax of how to bind an edit box to a field in a Domino document so that the edit box can be used to read and write the field value.

Listing 4.11 Data Binding to a Notes Document Field

```
<?xml version="1.0" encoding="UTF-8"?>
<xp:view xmlns:xp="http://www.ibm.com/xsp/core">
	<xp:this.data>
		<xp:dominoDocument var="document1" formName="Document">
		</xp:dominoDocument>
	</xp:this.data>
	<xp:inputText id="inputText1" value="#{document1.TextField}">
	</xp:inputText>
</xp:view>
```

Notice that, again, the #{ and } delimiters have been used around the value to which the control is bound. In this case, no programming language is specified. When no language is specified, the default Expression Language (EL) is used. EL is a scripting language that provides access to Java objects, and it is discussed in Chapter 5. Here again, you see XPages' JSF heritage emerging, because EL is what JSF uses by default for data binding. EL allows you to bind the edit box value to a property of some object (in this case, a field named TextField in a Domino document). This data binding is bidirectional (it can be used to read and write the property value). EL is discussed in more detail in Chapters 5 and 6.

XPages Tags

Now that we've covered the basics of the XPages syntax, let's look at the different types of tags that XPages supports. There are nine categories of tags:

- Data sources
- Controls
- Containers
- View resources
- Converters
- Validators

- Simple actions
- Client-side scripting
- HTML

All the tags are listed by category, and we look closely at what the tags in each category are used for and the specialized behavior of each type of tag.

The XPages core controls cover the basic set of controls you need to build an application. There is also a set controls available for creating mobile applications, which are covered in Chapter 14, "XPages Mobile Application Development." In addition to the controls provided as part of Domino, there is an extensive collection of controls available in the XPages Extension Library. In fact, there is a separate book dedicated to and named after the XPages Extension Library.

Data Sources

The data source tags represent the data that users of your application can read and possibly create, update, and delete. A data source can be set as the property of the main `xp:view` tag, and this makes the data available to the entire XPage. Domino applications are inherently a special type of database that allows you to store application data as Domino documents. A Domino document stores the data as a collection of fields, each with its own data type. The structure of the data in a Domino document can be specified by creating a *form*, which acts as a schema for the fields, when a document is created using that form. A Domino document also contains special reserved fields that contain information about the document (metadata), such as when the document was last modified. Domino documents are discussed in Chapter 7, "Working with Domino Documents." The data from a collection of Domino documents can be read using a Domino view. When a Domino view is created, you must specify the types of documents it will contain (such as documents created with a particular form) and what data from those documents is displayed in the view (specific fields or event values computed from multiple fields). Domino views are discussed in Chapter 8, "Working with Domino Views." Not surprisingly, data source tags correspond to Domino documents and Domino views, as described in the following sections.

Domino Document

An `xp:dominoDocument` tag can be added to an XPage when you want to use that page to create a new document, edit an existing document, read an existing document, or any combination of these actions. Always specify the `var` and `formName` properties. The `var` property defines a variable name by which the Domino document can be referenced by other tags in the XPage. For example, when binding a control to a Domino document, the value of the `var` property is the first part of the value binding expression (normally set to document1). The `formName` property defines the form associated with the Domino document. As previously mentioned, the form defines the structure of a document created with that form, and the XPages editor uses the information when creating binding controls to the Domino document. By default, the Domino document being operated on is contained in the same Domino database as the XPage; however, you can specify another database on the same or even another server by using the `databaseName` property. Listing 4.12 demonstrates how to edit the first Domino document in the Countries view.

Listing 4.12 Domino Document Sample

```
<?xml version="1.0" encoding="UTF-8"?>
<xp:view xmlns:xp="http://www.ibm.com/xsp/core">
      <xp:this.data>
            <xp:dominoDocument var="document1" formName="Country"
            documentId="#{javascript:database.getView('Countries')
            .getNthDocument(1).getNoteID()}"action="editDocument">
            </xp:dominoDocument>
      </xp:this.data>
      Country name:
      <xp:inputText value="#{document1.CountryName}" id="countryName1">
      </xp:inputText>
      <xp:br></xp:br>
      Country code:
      <xp:inputText value="#{document1.CountryCode}" id="countryCode1">
      </xp:inputText>
      <xp:br></xp:br>
      <xp:button value="Save" id="button1">
            <xp:eventHandler event="onclick" submit="true"
                  refreshMode="complete" immediate="false" save="true">
            </xp:eventHandler>
      </xp:button>
</xp:view>
```

Domino View

A `xp:dominoView` tag can provide access to the collection of documents associated with a Domino view. Listing 4.13 shows how a Domino view data source, which is configured on the top-level `xp:view` tag, can be accessed by a data table control and a Computed Field. The data table control iterates over the data to which it is bound (in this case, each entry or row in the view). The data table makes the row data available by using the variable name specified by the `var` property (for example, country). The row data can then be accessed, and values from the current row are displayed by a Computed Field. The example shows how to access the column value using JavaScript and EL. The data table control is discussed in more detail in the section,

"Containers." The Domino view data source is most often used with the view control, and Chapter 8 gives a detailed explanation.

Listing 4.13 Domino View Sample

```
<?xml version="1.0" encoding="UTF-8"?>
<xp:view xmlns:xp="http://www.ibm.com/xsp/core">
      <xp:this.data>
            <xp:dominoView var="countries" viewName="Countries">
            </xp:dominoView>
      </xp:this.data>
      <xp:dataTable rows="30" id="dataTable1" value="#{countries}"
            var="country">
            <xp:column id="column1">
                  <xp:text escape="true" id="computedField1"
                  value="#{javascript:country.getColumnValue('Country
➥Code')}">
                  </xp:text>
            </xp:column>
            <xp:column id="column2">
                  <xp:text escape="true" id="computedField2"
                        value="#{country['Country Name']}">
                  </xp:text>
            </xp:column>
      </xp:dataTable>
      <xp:text escape="true" id="computedField3"
            value="#{javascript:'Entries Count: ' + countries.
getAllEntries().getCount()}">
      </xp:text>
</xp:view>
```

Data Context

The `xp:dataContext` tag provides access to data values within an XPage. Strictly speaking, this tag is not a data source because there is no underlying data store; however, it is used in a similar way. A data context can be used compute a value. (If you needed to compute a value based on some fields in a Domino document, you could compute the value once using a data context and then make the result available through a variable that can be referenced throughout the XPage.) Listing 4.14 demonstrates how a data context can be used to compute a date value and then how the value is referenced by a Computed Field.

Listing 4.14 Data Context Sample

```
<?xml version="1.0" encoding="UTF-8"?>
<xp:view xmlns:xp="http://www.ibm.com/xsp/core">
      <xp:this.dataContexts>
            <xp:dataContext
                  var="SeventeenMar2013"
                  value="${javascript:new Date(2013,2,17,0,0,0,0)}">
            </xp:dataContext>
      </xp:this.dataContexts>
      <xp:text value="#{ SeventeenMar2013}">
      </xp:text>
</xp:view>
```

Controls

The control tags represent the user interface widgets that you can use to create your application interface. There are five broad categories of controls:

- Controls that support both the display and modification of a data value.
- Controls that provide a way for a user to trigger some action in the application (these include buttons and hyperlinks).
- Controls that allow the user to select one or more predefined values.
- Controls that are used to display purposes only (for example, the user cannot interact with these controls to directly modify the data).
- Controls that are used to upload and download files.

Each group of controls shares common properties, and the behavior of those properties is basically the same across the group. If you can understand how a property applies to one control, you can apply that knowledge to other controls of the same type. Control properties belong to the following categories:

- **Styling:** Controls the appearance and some behavior of the control. All styling in XPages is performed using CSS, which is an industry standard.
- **Events:** Provide a way to add logic that will be executed when an event associated with a control is triggered. All controls support a set client-side JavaScript event, which can be scripted.
- **Data:** Most, but not all, controls can be bound to data, either to display/modify the data or manage the data for their child controls.

- **Dojo:** Adds Dojo functionality to a control.
- **Basics:** All controls have some shared basic properties (such as control ID, flag indicating if the control should be rendered, and so on).
- **Accessibility:** Provides more information about a control for use by assistive technologies.

This section helps you to learn how to read the markup for the XPages control and understand what that control does. Most controls are represented by a single tag in the markup, which makes understanding them straightforward. Some controls are represented by a collection of tags (such as a data table control). Other controls are normally used together in standard patterns. This section takes you through some of the most common patterns for the different types of controls.

Editing Controls

Editing controls are used to edit data values in your application. Each control can be bound to a data value and used to display and modify that value. This section reviews the following controls:

- Edit box
- Multiline edit box
- Rich text
- Date time picker

Here are some other things that you can do with editing controls:

- One or more validators can be applied, which checks that the value entered by the user adheres to certain constraints.
- A single converter can be applied, which converts the user-entered string into another data type (such as an Integer or Date value).
- Application logic can be written, which executes when the value bound to the control changes.
- Type ahead can be enabled for an edit box, which provides a list of suggestions as the user types a value.

Converters and validators are covered later in this chapter in the sections, "Converters" and "Validators," respectively.

Edit Box

The edit box `xp:inputText` tag adds a text edit control to the page. Listing 4.15 demonstrates the most common use case where the edit box is bound to text field in a Notes document.

Listing 4.15 Edit Box Bound to a Notes Document Field

```
<?xml version="1.0" encoding="UTF-8"?>
<xp:view xmlns:xp="http://www.ibm.com/xsp/core">
	<xp:this.data>
		<xp:dominoDocument var="document1" formName="Document">
		</xp:dominoDocument>
	</xp:this.data>
	<xp:inputText id="inputText1" value="#{document1.TextField}">
	</xp:inputText>
</xp:view>
```

To enable type ahead, add the `xp:typeAhead` tag as a child of the edit box. The type ahead is responsible for adding new behavior to the edit box, which displays the appropriate list of suggestions as the user types. Listing 4.16 demonstrates a fixed list of suggestions that is provided using a comma-separated list, but you can also dynamically compute the list of suggestions (for example, using a column from a Notes view). Preview the associated sample and type the letter A in the text field to see the type ahead in action.

Listing 4.16 Adding Type Ahead to an Edit Box

```
<?xml version="1.0" encoding="UTF-8"?>
<xp:view xmlns:xp="http://www.ibm.com/xsp/core">
	<xp:this.data>
		<xp:dominoDocument var="document1" formName="Document">
		</xp:dominoDocument>
	</xp:this.data>
	<xp:inputText id="inputText1" value="#{document1.TextField}">
		<xp:typeAhead mode="full" minChars="1"
valueList="Australia,Austria,Canada,China,Estonia,
Ethiopia,Germany,Ghana,Iceland,Ireland"
valueListSeparator="," ignoreCase="true">
		</xp:typeAhead>
	</xp:inputText>
</xp:view>
```

Multiline Edit Box

Listing 4.17 shows the markup for a multiline edit box that has been configured to display a specific size. The size is based on the number of rows and columns of text to display and, therefore, resizes itself if the default font changes. Type ahead is not supported for multiline edit boxes.

Listing 4.17 Multiline Edit Box Bound to a Notes Document Field

```
<?xml version="1.0" encoding="UTF-8"?>
<xp:view xmlns:xp="http://www.ibm.com/xsp/core">
      <xp:this.data>
            <xp:dominoDocument var="document1" formName="Document">
            </xp:dominoDocument>
      </xp:this.data>
      <xp:inputTextarea id="inputTextarea1" value="#{document1.
➥TextField}"
            rows="4" cols="40">
      </xp:inputTextarea>
</xp:view>
```

Rich Text

A rich text edit `xp:inputRichText` tag allows the user to enter text with some basic rich formatting using HTML syntax. Listing 4.18 shows a rich text control being used to edit a rich text Notes field. The sample also has a Computed Field that displays the contents of the Notes field, and a `submit` button so you can add rich text, submit, and then see what the rich text looks like. The rich text content is stored in MIME format and is rendered to HTML for display. The Computed Field is configured to escape the rich text, which will display the rich text markup. You can experiment with changing this escape property to false, and you will see that the Computed Field now displays the rich text instead of the markup.

Listing 4.18 Rich Text Control Bound to a Notes Document Field

```
<?xml version="1.0" encoding="UTF-8"?>
<xp:view xmlns:xp="http://www.ibm.com/xsp/core">
      <xp:this.data>
            <xp:dominoDocument var="document1" formName="Document">
      </xp:dominoDocument>
      </xp:this.data>
      <xp:inputRichText id="inputRichText1"
            value="#{document1.RichTextField}">
      </xp:inputRichText>
      <xp:text escape="true" id="computedField1"
             value="#{document1.RichTextField}">
      </xp:text>
      <xp:br></xp:br>
      <xp:button value="Submit" id="button1">
            <xp:eventHandler event="onclick" submit="true"
                  refreshMode="complete"
```

```
                    immediate="false" save="false">
              </xp:eventHandler>
       </xp:button>
</xp:view>
```

Figure 4.7 shows this sample previewed in a browser client. You see that the rich text markup is displayed in the Computed Field.

Figure 4.7 Rich text sample

Date Time Picker

The date/time picker `xp:dataTimeHelper` tag is a helper that adds some behavior to an edit box that helps the end user enter date and time values in the correct format. Components that add behavior to another control are typically nested as children of the control they are enhancing. This is the case for the date/time picker. Listing 4.19 demonstrates the default date/time picker settings.

Listing 4.19 Date/Time Picker Sample

```
<?xml version="1.0" encoding="UTF-8"?>
<xp:view xmlns:xp="http://www.ibm.com/xsp/core">
       <xp:inputText id="inputText1">
              <xp:this.converter>
```

```
                <xp:convertDateTime type="date">
                </xp:convertDateTime>
            </xp:this.converter>
            <xp:dateTimeHelper id="dateTimeHelper1">
            </xp:dateTimeHelper>
        </xp:inputText>
</xp:view>
```

A date/time picker is constructed from an edit box with two children: a date/time converter `xp:convertDateTime` and the date/time helper `xp:dataTimeHelper`. The data being entered is stored in a date format, and the converter is required to handle data conversion. The date/time helper displays a button beside the edit box that can be used to open a date or time or date and time picker user interface. Listing 4.20 shows how to use the date/time picker to enter the date only, time only, and date plus time.

Listing 4.20 Date Only, Time Only, and Date Plus Time Sample

```
<?xml version="1.0" encoding="UTF-8"?>
<xp:view xmlns:xp="http://www.ibm.com/xsp/core">
        <xp:inputText id="inputText1" style="width:150px">
            <xp:dateTimeHelper id="dateTimeHelper1">
            </xp:dateTimeHelper>
            <xp:this.converter>
                <xp:convertDateTime type="date">
                </xp:convertDateTime>
            </xp:this.converter>
        </xp:inputText>
        <xp:inputText id="inputText2" style="width:150px">
            <xp:dateTimeHelper id="dateTimeHelper2">
            </xp:dateTimeHelper>
            <xp:this.converter>
                <xp:convertDateTime type="time">
                </xp:convertDateTime>
            </xp:this.converter>
        </xp:inputText>
        <xp:inputText id="inputText3" style="width:150px">
            <xp:dateTimeHelper id="dateTimeHelper3">
            </xp:dateTimeHelper>
            <xp:this.converter>
                <xp:convertDateTime type="dateTime">
                </xp:convertDateTime>
            </xp:this.converter>
        </xp:inputText>
</xp:view>
```

When you preview this example, you see buttons beside each edit box and, when you click a button, the appropriate picker control is displayed to allow you to enter either a date, time, or both, as shown in Figure 4.8.

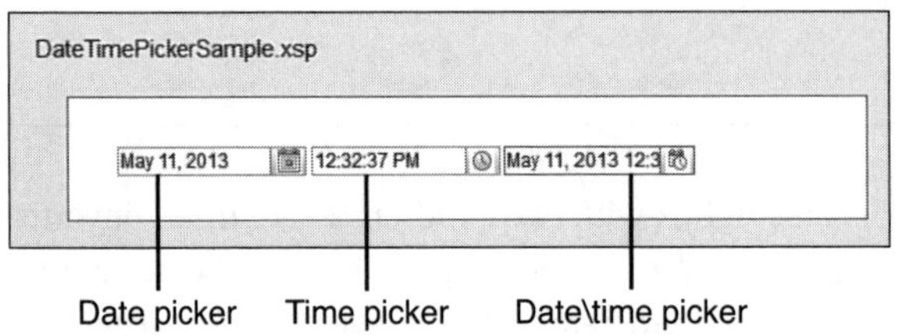

Figure 4.8 Date picker, time picker, and date/time picker

Command Controls

Command controls provide one way for the user to trigger some logic within your application. The following controls can trigger the execution of server-side application logic in response to a user action:

- Event handler
- Button
- Link

Event Handler

Chapter 3 presented some examples where buttons were used to save a document or cancel the editing of a document. In those examples, an `xp:eventHandler` tag was automatically added as a child of the button to submit the page and optionally save the document. The event handler is not displayed on the rendered page. Instead, it is added as the child to another control, which is visible on the page, and then it listens for client-side JavaScript events coming from its parent and will submit the page. Listing 4.21 shows how an `xp:eventHandler` tag can be added to a Computed Field control to force a page submit when the Computed Field is clicked.

Listing 4.21 Using an Event Handler to Submit an XPage When a Computed Field Is Clicked

```
<?xml version="1.0" encoding="UTF-8"?>
<xp:view xmlns:xp="http://www.ibm.com/xsp/core">
      <xp:text id="computedField1"
            style="border-color:rgb(0,0,0);border-style:double"
            value="#{javascript:new Date().getSeconds()}">
            <xp:eventHandler event="onclick" submit="true"
```

```
                    refreshMode="complete" immediate="true" save="false">
            </xp:eventHandler>
      </xp:text>
</xp:view>
```

The event handler is normally used in conjunction with a button; however, as you can see from the previous example, it can be used with any control. The event handler has built-in functionality that allows you to automatically save all documents associated with the XPage. Setting its `save` property to `true` automatically saves document updates. The event handler is also used when you want to cancel editing and move to another page. In this case, the `immediate` property needs to be set to `true`; this causes all processing of the submitted data to be ignored. The event handler is covered in Chapter 6, "Building XPages Application Logic."

Button

The `xp:button` tag is normally used in conjunction with an event handler. It is a command control, and it can directly invoke server-side JavaScript application logic. Listing 4.22 demonstrates using a button click to execute some server-side JavaScript that manipulates the label displayed in the button. The server-side JavaScript code gets the component associated with the button control and then sets the value (which is used as the button label) to indicate the button has been clicked. When you run this sample, you see that, initially, the label of the button is *Click Me*. Clicking the button submits the page and, when it is redisplayed, the label of the button is *Clicked*.

Listing 4.22 Executing Server-Side JavaScript Application Logic in Response to a Button Click

```
<?xml version="1.0" encoding="UTF-8"?>
<xp:view xmlns:xp="http://www.ibm.com/xsp/core">
      <xp:button id="button1" immediate="true" type="submit"
value="Click Me">
            <xp:this.action><![CDATA[#{javascript:
                  getComponent("button1").setValue("Clicked");
            }]]></xp:this.action>
      </xp:button>
      <xp:br></xp:br>
</xp:view>
```

Link

The `xp:link` tag displays a hyperlink on the rendered page. The link control is normally used to navigate to another XPage, open a URL, or jump to another part of the current page (specified by an anchor). A link can also be used in conjunction with an event handler to submit the XPage and execute server-side JavaScript application logic. Listing 4.23 demonstrates the most common usages of the link control. The value property of the link control can be set to either a location of an XPage within the current application or any URL link. From Domino Designer, you can specify the link type as being any one of the following:

- **Open Page** allows you to specify the page to open.
- **URL** allows you to open HTTP URL.
- **Anchor** allows you to navigate to another part of the current page.

Listing 4.23 Opening Another XPage, Web Page, and Submitting the Current Page with a Link

```
<?xml version="1.0" encoding="UTF-8"?>
<xp:view xmlns:xp="http://www.ibm.com/xsp/core">
      <xp:link escape="true" text="Open the Button Sample" id="link1"
            value="/IncludeSample.xsp?xpage=ButtonSample.xsp">
      </xp:link>
      <xp:br></xp:br>
      <xp:link escape="true" text="xpagesblog.com" id="link2"
            value="http://xpagesblog.com/">
      </xp:link>
      <xp:br></xp:br>
      <xp:link escape="true"  id="link3"
            text="#{javascript:new Date().getSeconds()}">
            <xp:eventHandler event="onclick" submit="true"
                  refreshMode="complete" immediate="false" save="false">
            </xp:eventHandler>
      </xp:link>
</xp:view>
```

> **TIP**
>
> Often, you might want to navigate to a different XPage after performing some application logic. The next XPage may differ, depending on the outcome of the application logic. You can use the `xp:navigationRule` tag to associate an XPage with an outcome. The application logic can return an outcome value and change which page is displayed next. Listing 4.24 contains the source code for two XPages that use navigation rules to navigate from one to the other. The action associated with the button is coded to the string outcome value in the navigation rule, and this is sufficient to trigger the navigation to the specified page.

Listing 4.24 Navigation Rule Sample

```
<?xml version="1.0" encoding="UTF-8"?>
<xp:view xmlns:xp="http://www.ibm.com/xsp/core">
      <xp:this.navigationRules>
            <xp:navigationRule
                  outcome="NavigateB"
                  viewId="/IncludeSample.xsp?xpage=NavigateB.xsp"/>
      </xp:this.navigationRules>
      Navigate A
      <xp:br/>
      <xp:button
            value="Navigate B" id="button1"
            type="submit" action="NavigateB">
      </xp:button>
</xp:view>
```

```
<?xml version="1.0" encoding="UTF-8"?>
<xp:view xmlns:xp="http://www.ibm.com/xsp/core">
      <xp:this.navigationRules>
            <xp:navigationRule
                  outcome="NavigateA"
                  viewId="/ IncludeSample.xsp?xpage=NavigateA.xsp"/>
      </xp:this.navigationRules>
      Navigate B
      <xp:br/>
      <xp:button
            value="Navigate A" id="button1"
            type="submit" action="NavigateA">
      </xp:button>
</xp:view>
```

Selection Controls

Selection controls allow the user to enter data by selecting one or more values from an available list of options. So, the data that can be entered is constrained by the options that you present to the user. In this section, you see how to specify what options are available to the user for each control. Each example shows the control bound to a field in a Notes document, a Computed Field, and a `submit` button. When you run the example, you can submit the page and see how changing the selection in the control impacts the values that are saved to the document. This section reviews the following controls:

- Listbox
- Combo box
- Checkbox
- Radio button
- Checkbox group
- Radio button group

Listbox

The `xp:listBox` tag presents a list of options to the user, and the user can select either a single value or multiple values, depending on how the listbox is configured.

The listbox example in Listing 4.25 shows a single selection listbox and contains a fixed list of values that are coded into the XPage using `xp:selectItem` tags (which represent the listbox items). Each item has a label, which is what is displayed to the user, and a value, which is what is saved to the document. When you preview this sample, select a language, and submit the page, you see that the current value is set to the item value instead of the item label.

Listing 4.25 Listbox Sample

```
<?xml version="1.0" encoding="UTF-8"?>
<xp:view xmlns:xp="http://www.ibm.com/xsp/core">
      <xp:this.data>
            <xp:dominoDocument var="document1" formName="Document">
            </xp:dominoDocument>
      </xp:this.data>
      <xp:listBox id="listBox1" value="#{document1.TextField}">
            <xp:selectItem itemLabel="Irish" itemValue="ga">
            </xp:selectItem>
            <xp:selectItem itemLabel="English" itemValue="en">
            </xp:selectItem>
            <xp:selectItem itemLabel="French" itemValue="fr">
            </xp:selectItem>
            <xp:selectItem itemLabel="German" itemValue="de">
            </xp:selectItem>
      </xp:listBox>
      <xp:br></xp:br>
      Current value:
      <xp:text escape="true" id="computedField1"
            value="#{document1.TextField}">
      </xp:text>
      <xp:br></xp:br>
      <xp:button value="Submit" id="button1">
            <xp:eventHandler event="onclick" submit="true"
```

```
                        refreshMode="complete" immediate="false"
save="false">
                </xp:eventHandler>
        </xp:button>
</xp:view>
```

The listbox example shown in Listing 4.26 shows a multiple selection listbox and how the options are computed using server-side JavaScript. The server-side JavaScript expression returns an array of strings, where each string is a label/value pair delimited by the | (pipe) character. These strings are then automatically converted into a collection of select items by the XPages runtime. Note that the computed expression is computed only once, when the page is loaded as indicated by the initial $ in the computed expression. This makes sense, because the list of options shouldn't change every time the page is submitted. When you preview this sample, notice that you can select multiple items from the listbox. When you submit the page, you see that the current value is set to a comma-delimited string that contains the item values of the selected items.

Listing 4.26 Computed Listbox Sample

```
<?xml version="1.0" encoding="UTF-8"?>
<xp:view xmlns:xp="http://www.ibm.com/xsp/core">
        <xp:this.data>
                <xp:dominoDocument var="document1" formName="Document">
                </xp:dominoDocument>
        </xp:this.data>
        Computed List
        <xp:br></xp:br>
        <xp:listBox id="listBox1" value="#{document1.TextField}"
                multiple="true">
                <xp:selectItems>
                        <xp:this.value><![CDATA[${javascript:
                                var languages = new Array()
                                languages[0]="Irish|ga";
                                languages[1]="English|en";
                                languages[2]="French|fr";
                                languages[3]="German|de";
                                return languages;
                                }]]>
                        </xp:this.value>
                </xp:selectItems>
        </xp:listBox>
        <xp:br></xp:br>
        Current value:
        <xp:text escape="true" id="computedField1"
                value="#{document1.TextField}">
```

```
        </xp:text>
        <xp:br></xp:br>
        <xp:button value="Submit" id="button1">
                <xp:eventHandler event="onclick" submit="true"
                        refreshMode="complete" immediate="false"
                        save="false">
                </xp:eventHandler>
        </xp:button>
</xp:view>
```

Combo Box

The `xp:comboBox` tag is a visually more compact form of a single-selection listbox control. It presents a list of options to the user, and the user can select a single item. Listing 4.27 demonstrates a combo box with a fixed list of options.

Listing 4.27 Combo Box Sample

```
<?xml version="1.0" encoding="UTF-8"?>
<xp:view xmlns:xp="http://www.ibm.com/xsp/core">
        <xp:this.data>
                <xp:dominoDocument var="document1" formName="Document">
                </xp:dominoDocument>
        </xp:this.data>
        <xp:comboBox id="comboBox1" value="#{document1.TextField}">
                <xp:selectItem itemLabel="Ireland" itemValue="IE">
                </xp:selectItem>
                <xp:selectItem itemLabel="United Kingdom" itemValue="GB">
                </xp:selectItem>
                <xp:selectItem itemLabel="France" itemValue="FR">
                </xp:selectItem>
                <xp:selectItem itemLabel="Germany" itemValue="DE">
                </xp:selectItem>
        </xp:comboBox>
        <xp:br></xp:br>
        Current value:
        <xp:text escape="true" id="computedField1"
                value="#{document1.TextField}">
        </xp:text>
        <xp:br></xp:br>
        <xp:button value="Submit" id="button1">
                <xp:eventHandler event="onclick" submit="true"
                        refreshMode="complete" immediate="false"
                        save="false">
```

```
            </xp:eventHandler>
        </xp:button>
</xp:view>
```

Figure 4.9 shows a Notes view that is used to populate the values in the combo box sample shown in Listing 4.28. The third column of the Notes view contains the options to be displayed. The lookup column contains the values needed for each select item that will be added to the combo box. Each value in the third column contains the label and value for the select item that will be created.

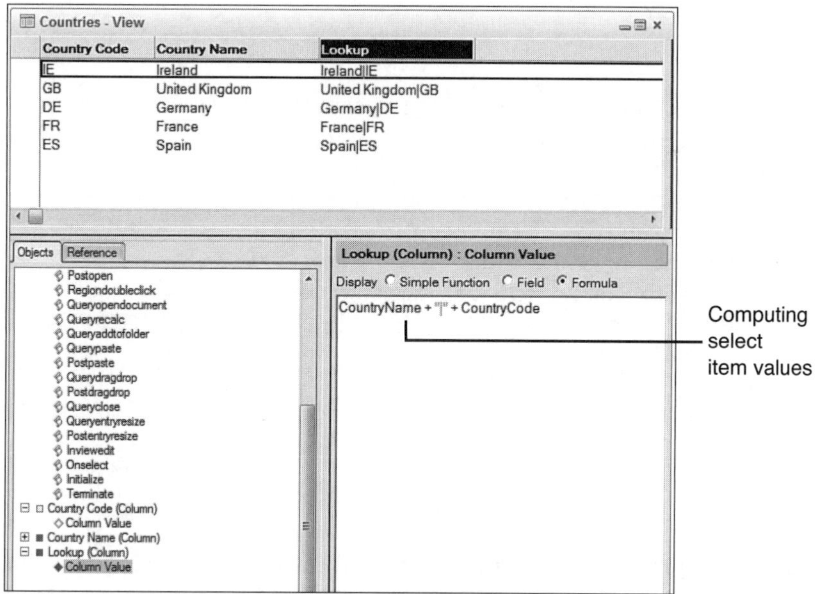

Figure 4.9 Countries view

Instead of using `<xp:selectItem>` tags, the `value` property of the `xp:comboBox` tag has a JavaScript expression that reads the third column of the Countries view. When this JavaScript expression is evaluated, the combo box selections are automatically added. This JavaScript expression uses a server-side JavaScript @function to access the database column (using `@DbColumn()`, in fact) and the current database (`@DbName()`). Server-side JavaScript @ functions are covered in Chapter 6. You can see from Listing 4.28 that it is easy to populate a combo box from the contents of a view. Readers familiar with Notes programming know that this means that, as your application supports more countries, the combo box automatically displays the new options after the corresponding Notes document is added to the Countries view.

Listing 4.28 Computed Combo Box Sample

```
<?xml version="1.0" encoding="UTF-8"?>
<xp:view xmlns:xp="http://www.ibm.com/xsp/core">
      <xp:this.data>
            <xp:dominoDocument var="document1" formName="Document">
            </xp:dominoDocument>
      </xp:this.data>
      <xp:comboBox id="comboBox1" value="#{document1.TextField}">
            <xp:selectItems
            value="#{javascript:@DbColumn(@DbName(), 'Countries', 3)}">
            </xp:selectItems>
      </xp:comboBox>
      <xp:br></xp:br>
      Current value:
      <xp:text escape="true" id="computedField1"
            value="#{document1.TextField}">
      </xp:text>
      <xp:br></xp:br>
      <xp:button value="Submit" id="button1">
            <xp:eventHandler event="onclick" submit="true"
                  refreshMode="complete" immediate="false"
                  save="false">
            </xp:eventHandler>
      </xp:button>
</xp:view>
```

Checkbox

A `xp:checkBox` tag allows the user to select or unselect a particular option. Depending on the option the user selects, the checkbox returns a different value. The default values for a checkbox are `true` and `false`. The checked and unchecked values can be set to any arbitrary value that is appropriate for your application. In Listing 4.29, the check and unchecked values are set to `CHECKED` and `UNCHECKED`, respectively.

Listing 4.29 Checkbox Sample

```
<?xml version="1.0" encoding="UTF-8"?>
<xp:view xmlns:xp="http://www.ibm.com/xsp/core">
      <xp:this.data>
            <xp:dominoDocument var="document1"
                  formName="Document">
            </xp:dominoDocument>
      </xp:this.data>
      <xp:checkBox text="I am a checkbox" id="checkBox1"
```

```
            defaultChecked="true"
            value="#{document1.TextField}" checkedValue="CHECKED"
            uncheckedValue="UNCHECKED">
      </xp:checkBox>
      <xp:br></xp:br>
      Current value:
      <xp:text escape="true" id="computedField1"
            value="#{document1.TextField}">
      </xp:text>
      <xp:br></xp:br>
      <xp:button value="Submit" id="button1">
            <xp:eventHandler event="onclick" submit="true"
                 refreshMode="complete" immediate="false" save="false">
            </xp:eventHandler>
      </xp:button>
</xp:view>
```

Radio Button

A `xp:radio` tag allows the user to select only one option from a list of selections (the options are all mutually exclusive). Radio buttons are always created in a group, because it doesn't make sense to have a single radio button on an XPage. When one radio button in a group is selected, all the other radio buttons are automatically unselected. You can also specify which radio button is selected by default. Listing 4.30 provides three options (Red, Green, and Blue, with Red being selected by default). The label displayed to the user differs from the value saved when the user selects that radio button. For example, the first radio button will have a label of `Red` (as denoted by the `text` property), but the saved value will be RED (as denoted by the `selectedValue` property).

Listing 4.30 Radio Button Sample

```
<?xml version="1.0" encoding="UTF-8"?>
<xp:view xmlns:xp="http://www.ibm.com/xsp/core">
      <xp:this.data>
            <xp:dominoDocument var="document1" formName="Document">
</xp:dominoDocument>
      </xp:this.data>
      <xp:radio text="Red" id="radio1" groupName="PrimaryColours"
            defaultSelected="true" selectedValue="RED"
            value="#{document1.TextField}">
      </xp:radio>
      <xp:radio id="radio2" text="Green" groupName="PrimaryColours"
            selectedValue="GREEN" value="#{document1.TextField}">
      </xp:radio>
```

```
        <xp:radio id="radio3" text="Blue" groupName="PrimaryColours"
              selectedValue="BLUE" value="#{document1.TextField}">
        </xp:radio>
        <xp:br></xp:br>
        Current value:
        <xp:text escape="true" id="computedField1"
             value="#{document1.TextField}">
        </xp:text>
        <xp:br></xp:br>
        <xp:button value="Submit" id="button1">
              <xp:eventHandler event="onclick" submit="true"
                    refreshMode="complete" immediate="false"
                    save="false">
              </xp:eventHandler>
        </xp:button
</xp:view>
```

Checkbox Group

A `xp:checkBoxGroup` tag allows the user to select or unselect from a list of options. Depending on the options the user selects, the checkbox group returns a different value. The value is a comma-delimited string made up of the item values for all the selected items. In Listing 4.31, the item values are 1,2,3 and, when all three items are selected, the value stored on the document will be 1,2,3.

Listing 4.31 Checkbox Group Sample

```
<?xml version="1.0" encoding="UTF-8"?>
<xp:view xmlns:xp="http://www.ibm.com/xsp/core">
        <xp:this.data>
              <xp:dominoDocument var="document1" formName="Document">
              </xp:dominoDocument>
        </xp:this.data>
        <xp:checkBoxGroup id="checkBoxGroup1" value="#{document1.TextField}">
              <xp:selectItem itemLabel="First" itemValue="1">
              </xp:selectItem>
              <xp:selectItem itemLabel="Second" itemValue="2">
              </xp:selectItem>
              <xp:selectItem itemLabel="Third" itemValue="3">
              </xp:selectItem>
        </xp:checkBoxGroup>
        <xp:br></xp:br>
        Current value:
        <xp:text escape="true" id="computedField1"
```

```
            value="#{document1.TextField}">
        </xp:text>
        <xp:br></xp:br>
        <xp:button value="Submit" id="button1">
              <xp:eventHandler event="onclick" submit="true"
                    refreshMode="complete" immediate="false" save="false">
              </xp:eventHandler>
        </xp:button
</xp:view>
```

Radio Button Group

A xp:radioGroup tag allows the user to select only one option from a list of items (the options are all mutually exclusive). You use a radio button group in preference to individual groups when all the items are at the same level in the hierarchy and are being grouped together without any other controls or text between them. Listing 4.32 shows an example of this, which is functionally equivalent to the earlier example that used individual radio buttons.

Listing 4.32 Radio Button Group Sample

```
<?xml version="1.0" encoding="UTF-8"?>
<xp:view xmlns:xp="http://www.ibm.com/xsp/core">
      <xp:this.data>
            <xp:dominoDocument var="document1" formName="Document">
            </xp:dominoDocument>
      </xp:this.data>
      <xp:radioGroup id="radioGroup1" value="#{document1.TextField}"
            defaultValue="RED">
            <xp:selectItem itemLabel="Red" itemValue="RED">
            </xp:selectItem>
            <xp:selectItem itemLabel="Green" itemValue="GREEN">
            </xp:selectItem>
            <xp:selectItem itemLabel="Blue" itemValue="BLUE">
            </xp:selectItem>
      </xp:radioGroup>
      <xp:br></xp:br>
      Current value:
      <xp:text escape="true" id="computedField1"
            value="#{document1.TextField}">
      </xp:text>
      <xp:br></xp:br>
      <xp:button value="Submit" id="button1">
            <xp:eventHandler event="onclick" submit="true"
                  refreshMode="complete" immediate="false"
```

```
save="false">
            </xp:eventHandler>
      </xp:button
<xp:view>
```

Display Controls

Display controls present data to the user. These controls do not support any editing features. The following controls are reviewed in this section:

- Label
- Computed Field
- Image

Label

The label `xp:label` tag provides a way for you to specify information about another control, typically the data to be entered for an input control (such as an edit box). Labels can be specified by entering text next to the input control; however, doing this causes a problem for screen readers. For example, when a visually impaired user sets focus on an edit box, his screen reader looks for the label associated with that control and reads out the label text. If you do not associate a label control with its corresponding input field control, a screen reader will not have the critical hint and your application is not fully accessible. Listing 4.33 demonstrates how to associate a label control with an edit box.

Listing 4.33 Label Sample

```
<?xml version="1.0" encoding="UTF-8"?>
<xp:view xmlns:xp="http://www.ibm.com/xsp/core">
      <xp:label value="Label for inputText1" id="label1"
            for="inputText1">
      </xp:label>
      <xp:inputText id="inputText1">
      </xp:inputText>
</xp:view>
```

Computed Field

An `xp:text` tag presents the value of some computed expression to the user. The value can be computed dynamically each time the page is displayed or alternatively when the page is first loaded. Listing 4.34 demonstrates two Computed Fields, both of which have the same computed value: <b>Bold</b>. The first Computed Field presents the computed value as typed in the previous sentence. The second Computed Field presents the computed value in Bold format. This is because the second Computed Field has its escape property set to false so that the computed value is not encoded for presentation as HTML.

Listing 4.34 Computed Field Sample

```
<?xml version="1.0" encoding="UTF-8"?>
<xp:view xmlns:xp="http://www.ibm.com/xsp/core">
      <xp:text escape="true" id="computedField1">
            <xp:this.value><![CDATA[#{javascript:'<b>Bold</b>'}]]>
            </xp:this.value>
      </xp:text>
      <xp:br></xp:br>
      <xp:text escape="false" id="computedField2">
            <xp:this.value><![CDATA[#{javascript:'<b>Bold</b>'}]]>
            </xp:this.value>
      </xp:text>
</xp:view>
```

Image

The xp:image tag allows you to add graphics to an XPage, as shown in Listing 4.35. Images can be imported and stored as part of your Domino application as image resource design elements. When you add an image control to an XPage, you can select from the images that have been imported into your application. You can find the images under Resources > Images in the application navigator.

Listing 4.35 Image Sample

```
<?xml version="1.0" encoding="UTF-8"?>
<xp:view xmlns:xp="http://www.ibm.com/xsp/core">
      <xp:image url="/mxpd.jpg" id="image1">
      </xp:image>
</xp:view>
```

File-Handling Controls

The file-handling controls allow you to upload and download files. When used with the Domino document data store, the files are saved as attachments to the current Domino document. You can also use server-side JavaScript to retrieve the files and implement your own logic to store them. The following controls are reviewed in this section:

- File Upload
- Filed Download

File Upload

Listing 4.36 demonstrates how to use the File Upload control to attach a file to a Domino document. The `xp:fileUpload` tag is bound to a rich text field in the Domino document and, when the Domino document is saved, the file specified by the user is attached to the field in the document.

Listing 4.36 File Upload Sample

```
<?xml version="1.0" encoding="UTF-8"?>
<xp:view xmlns:xp="http://www.ibm.com/xsp/core">
	<xp:this.data>
		<xp:dominoDocument var="document1" formName="PersonPhoto">
		</xp:dominoDocument>
	</xp:this.data>
	<xp:table>
		<xp:tr>
			<xp:td>
				<xp:label value="Person name:"
					id="personName_Label1" for="personName1">
				</xp:label>
			</xp:td>
			<xp:td>
				<xp:inputText value="#{document1.personName}"
					id="personName1">
				</xp:inputText>
			</xp:td>
		</xp:tr>
		<xp:tr>
			<xp:td>
				<xp:label value="Person photo:"
					id="personPhoto_Label1"
					for="personPhoto1">
				</xp:label>
			</xp:td>
			<xp:td>
				<xp:fileUpload
					value="#{document1.personPhoto}"
					id="personPhoto1">
				</xp:fileUpload>
			</xp:td>
		</xp:tr>
```

```
    </xp:table>
    <xp:button value="Save" id="button1">
        <xp:eventHandler event="onclick" submit="true"
            refreshMode="complete" immediate="false" save="true">
        </xp:eventHandler>
    </xp:button>
</xp:view>
```

File Download

Listing 4.37 shows how to use the File Download control to download an image attached to the first document from the PeoplePhotos view. The `xp:fileDownload` tag is bound to the rich text field in the Domino document and displays all files that are attached to this field. The File Download control presents a list of the files that can be downloaded by the user and are retrievable by clicking the associated link within this control.

Listing 4.37 File Download Sample

```
<?xml version="1.0" encoding="UTF-8"?>
<xp:view xmlns:xp="http://www.ibm.com/xsp/core">
    <xp:this.data>
        <xp:dominoDocument var="document1" formName="PersonPhoto"
documentId="#{javascript:database.getView('PeoplePhotos').
➥getNthDocument(1).getNoteID()}"
            action="openDocument">
        </xp:dominoDocument>
    </xp:this.data>
    <xp:table>
        <xp:tr>
            <xp:td>
                <xp:label value="Person name:"
                    id="personName_Label1"
                    for="personName1">
                </xp:label>
            </xp:td>
            <xp:td>
                <xp:text value="#{document1.personName}"
                    id="personName1">
                </xp:text>
            </xp:td>
        </xp:tr>
        <xp:tr>
            <xp:td>
                <xp:label value="Person photo:"
```

```
                                        id="personPhoto_Label1"
                                        for="personPhoto1">
                              </xp:label>
                    </xp:td>
                    <xp:td>
                              <xp:fileDownload
                                        value="#{document1.personPhoto}"
                                        id="personPhoto1">
                              </xp:fileDownload>
                    </xp:td>
          </xp:tr>
     </xp:table>
</xp:view>
```

Containers

Containers are a specialized group of controls that can contain other controls. Some containers are used for layout purposes, but some can be used to provide additional behavior to the controls they contain. Several containers are designed for use with collections of data (such as the view, data table, and repeat controls). Other containers allow you to more efficiently use the real estate within your XPage (the tabbed panel and section controls). The following containers are available for use within XPages:

- Panel
- Table
- View
- Data table
- Repeat
- Include page
- Tabbed panel
- Section

The following sections describe these containers in detail.

Panel

The panel container is used to layout its children within a rectangular area of an XPage. A panel allows you to manipulate its children as a group. In Listing 4.38, the `background-color` for the panel is set, and this changes the background for the Computed Fields contained within the panel. You could also show or hide a group of controls by changing the `rendered` property of their parent panel, please refer to Chapter 20, "Advanced Performance Topics," for information on how to do this in performant manner. Another powerful feature is the ability to scope data using panels. In Listing 4.38, there are two document data sources—one associated with the XPage and one associated with a Panel within the XPage. Both document sources use the same variable name: `document`. Three Computed Fields reference the document variable and, at first glance, you might expect that they will reference the same data source. When you run this example, you see that the first and third Computed Field reference the document data source associated with the XPage. The second Computed Field, however, references the data source associated with the panel. So, the document data source is different for controls within the panel as opposed to those outside the panel, because the data source associated with the panel is scoped to the children of the panel and is not made available to controls outside the panel.

Listing 4.38 Panel Sample

```
<?xml version="1.0" encoding="UTF-8"?>
<xp:view xmlns:xp="http://www.ibm.com/xsp/core">
      <xp:this.data>
            <xp:dominoDocument var="document" formName="Document">
            </xp:dominoDocument>
      </xp:this.data>
      <xp:text escape="true" id="computedField1"
            value="#{javascript:document.getNoteID()}">
      </xp:text>
      <xp:panel id="panel1" style="background-color:rgb(215,215,255)">
             <xp:this.data>
                   <xp:dominoDocument var="document"
                                                  formName="Document">
                   </xp:dominoDocument>
            </xp:this.data>
            <xp:text escape="true" id="computedField2"
                  value="#{javascript:document.getNoteID()}">
            </xp:text>
      </xp:panel>
      <xp:text escape="true" id="computedField3"
             value="#{javascript:document.getNoteID()}">
      </xp:text>
</xp:view>
```

Another useful feature of the panel container is the ability to assign access control to a panel. This allows you to do the following:

- Prevent certain users or groups of users from accessing part of an XPage
- Provide read-only access to part of an XPage for certain users or groups of users

Listing 4.39 includes four panels, each with an associated access control list (ACL). An ACL (<xp:acl> tag) determines what access a user or group has to the associated content (the contents of the panel). An ACL contains a list of entries (<xp:aclEntry> tag), and each entry has a type, access rights, and optionally the name of the user or group. In Listing 4.39, the access is set as follows:

- The first panel defaults to no access, so when you run the sample, you cannot see the contents.
- The second panel provides reader access, so you can only read the contents; editing is disabled.
- The third panel provides editor access, so you can edit the value.
- The fourth panel appears to provide multiple conflicting access but, in fact, the user gets the highest access available. This is because a user might be in a user group (who might have read-only access) and an administrators group (who might have editor access) and, in this case, the user gets higher access rights.

> **TIP**
>
> The `tagName` attribute can also be used with the panel when you need it to render as a `<span>` element rather than a `<div>` element.

Listing 4.39 Access Control List Sample

```
<?xml version="1.0" encoding="UTF-8"?>
<xp:view xmlns:xp="http://www.ibm.com/xsp/core">
      <xp:text value="Default: No Access " />
      <xp:panel style="border-style: double; padding: 4;">
            <xp:this.acl>
                  <xp:acl>
                        <xp:aclEntry type="DEFAULT" right="NOACCESS" />
                  </xp:acl>
            </xp:this.acl>
            <xp:inputText value="Some Value" />
      </xp:panel>
      <xp:br />
      <xp:br />
      <xp:text value="Default: Reader " />
      <xp:panel style="border-style: double; padding: 4;">
            <xp:this.acl>
                  <xp:acl>
```

```
                <xp:aclEntry type="DEFAULT" right="READER" />
            </xp:acl>
        </xp:this.acl>
        <xp:inputText value="Some Value" />
    </xp:panel>
    <xp:br />
    <xp:br />
    <xp:text value="Default: Editor " style="width:200px;" />
    <xp:panel style="border-style: double; padding: 4;">
        <xp:this.acl>
            <xp:acl>
                <xp:aclEntry type="DEFAULT" right="EDITOR" />
            </xp:acl>
        </xp:this.acl>
        <xp:inputText value="Some Value" />
    </xp:panel>
    <xp:br />
    <xp:br />
    <xp:text value="Default: Editor, Reader, No Access "
        style="width:200px;" />
    <xp:panel style="border-style: double; padding: 4;">
        <xp:this.acl>
            <xp:acl>
                <xp:aclEntry type="DEFAULT" right="EDITOR" />
                <xp:aclEntry type="DEFAULT" right="READER" />
                <xp:aclEntry type="DEFAULT" right="NOACCESS" />
            </xp:acl>
        </xp:this.acl>
        <xp:inputText value="Some Value" />
    </xp:panel>
    <xp:messages showDetail="true" />
</xp:view>
```

> **TIP**
>
> The `<xp:acl>` tag can also be used with the XPage view. ACLs are covered in detail in Chapter 21, "Security."

Table

A table container provides a way to lay out controls in an HTML table. The table is made up of one or more rows with each row containing one or more cells. Cells can span multiple rows or multiple columns. The style can be set for an individual cell or the entire row. The vertical and horizontal alignment for rows and cells can also be set. Listing 4.40 includes a table with some cells spanning multiple columns and rows. You can see that the syntax is similar to that used for a regular HTML table. The reason XPages provides its own table tags is so that the associated components can be manipulated in JavaScript like all the other XPages controls.

Listing 4.40 Table Sample

```
<?xml version="1.0" encoding="UTF-8"?>
<xp:view xmlns:xp="http://www.ibm.com/xsp/core">
	<xp:table border="2">
		<xp:tr>
			<xp:td style="background-color:yellow">1</xp:td>
			<xp:td>2</xp:td>
			<xp:td>3</xp:td>
			<xp:td rowspan="2" valign="top">4&amp;8</xp:td>
		</xp:tr>
		<xp:tr>
			<xp:td colspan="2">5&amp;6</xp:td>
			<xp:td>7</xp:td>
		</xp:tr>
	</xp:table>
</xp:view>
```

View

The view control (aka, view panel) provides a way to display collections of Domino documents. An entire chapter is dedicated to the view control, so for now, the basic functionality is introduced. Listing 4.41 shows the default markup that is generated when you drag a view onto an XPage and configure it to display data from an existing Notes view. The default view control has the following features:

- A pager is displayed at the top of the view control to allow users to page over all the documents in the view. Only the contents of the view control are retrieved and modified during paging.
- A view column is created for each column of data. Each column has a header that displays the column title. The view column displays the contents of the Domino view column with the same name.
- The associated view data source is defined within the view control and scoped to that control.

Listing 4.41 View Sample

```
<?xml version="1.0" encoding="UTF-8"?>
<xp:view xmlns:xp="http://www.ibm.com/xsp/core">
      <xp:viewPanel rows="30" id="viewPanel1">
            <xp:this.facets>
                  <xp:pager partialRefresh="true"
                        layout="Previous Group Next"
                        xp:key="headerPager" id="pager1">
                  </xp:pager>
            </xp:this.facets>
            <xp:this.data>
                  <xp:dominoView var="countries" viewName="Countries">
                  </xp:dominoView>
            </xp:this.data>
            <xp:viewColumn columnName="Country Code" id="viewColumn1">
                  <xp:viewColumnHeader value="Country Code"
                        id="viewColumnHeader1">
                  </xp:viewColumnHeader>
            </xp:viewColumn>
            <xp:viewColumn columnName="Country Name" id="viewColumn2">
                  <xp:viewColumnHeader value="Country Name"
                        id="viewColumnHeader2">
                  </xp:viewColumnHeader>
            </xp:viewColumn>
      </xp:viewPanel>
</xp:view>
```

Facets

In Listing 4.41, notice that the view has a property called facets (the value being set is a complex property so the `this.facets` syntax is used). Also notice that the pager tag has an attribute called `xp:key`. These two constructs work together to provide a mechanism that allows child controls to be placed in a specific place within their container. When you preview the view sample, you see that the pager is displayed at the top of the view. This is because the view has a reserved area at the top, and the pager is configured to be placed within that region. This reserved area within a container is called a facet. Each facet has a name. To place a control within a facet, you must add that control to the facet's property and use the `xp:key` attribute to specify the name of the facet. Facets are stored using a map with the facet name being the key. The special `xp:key` attribute is used by the XPages page loader to assign a complex property to a map. The order that the controls appear in the facets property is irrelevant; only the value of the `xp:key` attribute is important. Listing 4.42 shows a view with two pagers: the first is placed in the footer of the view and the second in the header area. Each control has defined facet key values that correspond to specific areas where a facet can be displayed.

Listing 4.42 View with Two Pagers

```
<?xml version="1.0" encoding="UTF-8"?>
<xp:view xmlns:xp="http://www.ibm.com/xsp/core">
      <xp:viewPanel rows="30" id="viewPanel1">
            <xp:this.facets>
                  <xp:pager partialRefresh="true"
                        layout="Previous Group Next"
                        xp:key="footerPager" id="pager2"
                        style="background-color:rgb(255,206,255)">
                  </xp:pager>
                  <xp:pager partialRefresh="true"
                        layout="Previous Group Next"
                        xp:key="headerPager" id="pager1"
                        style="background-color:rgb(255,255,206)">
                  </xp:pager>
            </xp:this.facets>
            <xp:this.data>
                  <xp:dominoView var="countries" viewName="Countries">
                  </xp:dominoView>
            </xp:this.data>
            <xp:viewColumn columnName="Country Code" id="viewColumn1">
                  <xp:viewColumnHeader value="Country Code"
                        id="viewColumnHeader1">
                  </xp:viewColumnHeader>
            </xp:viewColumn>
            <xp:viewColumn columnName="Country Name" id="viewColumn2">
                  <xp:viewColumnHeader value="Country Name"
                        id="viewColumnHeader2">
                  </xp:viewColumnHeader>
            </xp:viewColumn>
      </xp:viewPanel>
</xp:view>
```

Tip

In Chapter 10, you learn how to extend XPages by creating your own custom controls. When you create a custom control, you need a way to specify the location of its facets. The `xp:callback` tag provides a way for custom controls to specify the location of a facet.

Data Table

The data table provides the same functionality as the view control, but without the adaptations to make it work seamlessly with a Domino view data source. In fact, the view control extends the data table control and adds these adaptations. It is possible to create the same behavior using a data table, and this is a good way to demonstrate what data tables can do and to improve your understanding of what a view control does under the covers. Listing 4.43 shows a data table configured with the same functionality as a standard view. The contents of the data table are defined using `xp:column` tags. Each column can contain an arbitrary control, including other containers. A column header can be specified using the `header` facet. The data table is bound to a collection data value (in this case, a Domino view). It iterates over a dataset and renders the contents of each column once for each entry. The value of the entry (such as the row data) is made available to the children in the columns using the name specified in the `var` property. The children in the column can extract values from the row data by using computed expressions. In Listing 4.43, you see that the Computed Fields are configured to display the value of a specific column in the corresponding row of the Domino view. The data table provides much more flexibility than the view control, but as you can see, it requires more work to configure.

Listing 4.43 Data Table Sample

```
<?xml version="1.0" encoding="UTF-8"?>
<xp:view xmlns:xp="http://www.ibm.com/xsp/core">
	<xp:this.data>
		<xp:dominoView var="countries" viewName="Countries">
		</xp:dominoView>
	</xp:this.data>
	<xp:dataTable rows="30" id="dataTable1" value="#{countries}"
		var="country" style="width:auto">
		<xp:this.facets>
			<xp:pager partialRefresh="true"
				layout="Previous Group Next"
				xp:key="header" id="pager1">
			</xp:pager>
		</xp:this.facets>
		<xp:column id="column1">
			<xp:this.facets>
				<xp:text escape="true" xp:key="header"
					id="computedField1" value="Country Code"
					style="font-weight:bold;color:blue">
				</xp:text>
			</xp:this.facets>
			<xp:text escape="true" id="computedField2"
		value="#{javascript:country.getColumnValue('Country Code')}">
			</xp:text>
```

```
            </xp:column>
            <xp:column id="column2">
                  <xp:this.facets>
                        <xp:text escape="true" xp:key="header"
                              id="computedField3" value="Country Name"
                              style="color:blue;font-weight:bold">
                        </xp:text>
                  </xp:this.facets>
                  <xp:text escape="true" id="computedField4"
            value="#{javascript:country.getColumnValue('Country Name')}">
                  </xp:text>
            </xp:column>
      </xp:dataTable>
</xp:view>
```

Repeat

The repeat control is the last in the family of containers that provide a way to iterate a dataset. The repeat is useful when building modern style user interfaces. Unlike the view and data table, the repeat does not limit you to displaying multiple columns of data and controls. The first repeat example shows how to display multiple values using a Computed Field and have the values display in a row. In Listing 4.44, you can see that the repeat does not impose any layout restrictions on its children.

Listing 4.44 Repeat Sample

```
<?xml version="1.0" encoding="UTF-8"?>
<xp:view xmlns:xp="http://www.ibm.com/xsp/core">
      <xp:this.data>
            <xp:dominoView var="countries" viewName="Countries">
            </xp:dominoView>
      </xp:this.data>
      <xp:repeat id="repeat1" value="#{countries}" var="country"
            indexVar="index">
            <xp:text id="computedField1">
                  <xp:this.value><![CDATA[#{javascript:
var text = country.getColumnValue("Country Name");
var count = countries.getAllEntries().getCount();
if (index + 1 < count) {
      text += ",";
}
return text;
}]]></xp:this.value>
```

```
            </xp:text>
        </xp:repeat>
</xp:view>
```

The repeat control can also be used to create controls. Consider the data table example in Listing 4.43 again. What if you don't know how many columns are needed in the data table when you are designing the XPage (for example, if the dataset varies depending on who the user is)? The repeat control can be used to create the correct number of columns and then it can remove itself from the XPage after its job is done. Listing 4.45 shows how to do this and introduces a new way to work with computed expressions. Setting the `repeatControls` property to `true` instructs the repeat control to create a new copy of its children for each iteration over the dataset. The `removeRepeat` property tells the repeat control to remove itself after the XPage is built. It is important to remove the repeat in this example because, for the data table to work correctly, its children must be `xp:column` tags. So, after the repeat creates the correct number of columns, it needs to be removed to allow the data table to its job. The data table is bound to a two-dimensional array with three columns of data and ten rows of data. The repeat is bound to an array, the size of which defines the number of columns that will be created (such as three columns), and the contents of this array are used as the titles of the columns (for example, A, B, C). The Computed Field in the header facet of each column is bound using a load time computed expression; this means that the title is computed once and remains static thereafter. The Computed Field, which displays the column value, needs to be a computed value bound to the row data that the data table makes available. A load time computed expression is used to compute the dynamic computed expression, which binds the Computed Field to the row data. Here's the sequence of computations for the Computed Field, which displays the data for each column:

1. During page load, the following expression is computed:

   ```
   '#{data['+rowIndex+']}'
   ```

2. This results in a dynamic computed expression; for example, the first column is:

   ```
   #{data[0]}
   ```

3. This expression extracts the appropriate value for the two-dimensional array.

Listing 4.45 Repeat Data Table Columns Sample

```
<?xml version="1.0" encoding="UTF-8"?>
<xp:view xmlns:xp="http://www.ibm.com/xsp/core">
    <xp:dataTable id="dataTable1" var="data">
        <xp:this.value><![CDATA[${javascript:
var rows = new Array(10)
for (i=0; i<10; i++)
    rows[i] = [ "A" + i, "B" + i, "C" + i ];
```

```
return rows;}]]>
            </xp:this.value>
            <xp:repeat id="repeat1" rows="30" repeatControls="true"
                  var="rowData" value="#{javascript:['A', 'B', 'C']}"
                  removeRepeat="true" indexVar="rowIndex">
                  <xp:column>
                        <xp:this.facets>
                              <xp:text xp:key="header"
                                    value="${rowData}"
                                   style="font-weight:bold" />
                        </xp:this.facets>
                        <xp:text escape="true" id="computedField1">
                              <xp:this.value>
                  <![CDATA[${javascript:'#{data['+rowIndex+']}'}]]>
                              </xp:this.value>
                        </xp:text>
                  </xp:column>
            </xp:repeat>
      </xp:dataTable>
</xp:view>
```

When you preview the example shown in Listing 4.45, you see a table that contains the three columns and ten rows of data with the headings A, B, C, as shown in Figure 4.10.

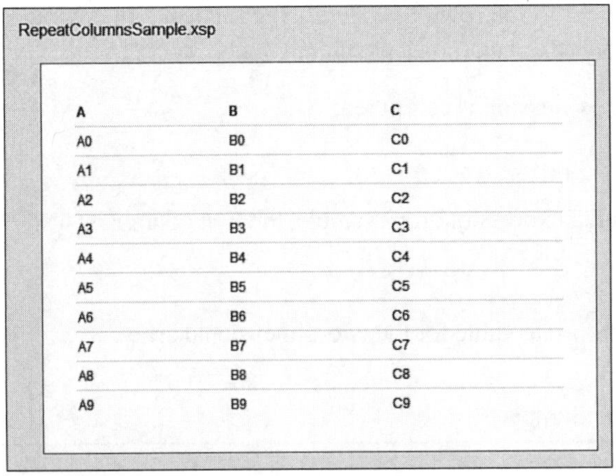

RepeatColumnsSample.xsp

A	B	C
A0	B0	C0
A1	B1	C1
A2	B2	C2
A3	B3	C3
A4	B4	C4
A5	B5	C5
A6	B6	C6
A7	B7	C7
A8	B8	C8
A9	B9	C9

Figure 4.10 Repeat columns sample

The final repeat example also shows how to create controls using a repeat; this time, radio buttons are created. Radio buttons allow the user to select one from a list of mutually exclusive options. Defining a group for the radio buttons ensures that only one button can be selected. When all the radio buttons are at the same level in the control hierarchy, this works fine; however, when radio buttons are nested inside different containers, this grouping behavior doesn't work as expected. You need to instruct the radio button to skip the correct number of containers for the groups to apply. Listing 4.46 demonstrates how the `skipContainers` property on the radio button is set to 1 to get the group behavior to work correctly. By setting the `skipContainers` -property to 1, each radio button behaves as if it was a separate control in the containing XPage and, because they appear at the same level in the page hierarchy and they have the same group name, they have a group behavior (only one can be selected at a time).

Listing 4.46 Repeat Radio Buttons Sample

```
<?xml version="1.0" encoding="UTF-8"?>
<xp:view xmlns:xp="http://www.ibm.com/xsp/core">
      <xp:this.data>
            <xp:dominoView var="countries" viewName="Countries">
            </xp:dominoView>
      </xp:this.data>
      <xp:repeat id="repeat1" var="country" removeRepeat="true"
            repeatControls="true"
    value="#{javascript:database.getView('Countries').getAllEntries()}"
            indexVar="index">
            <xp:radio id="radio1" groupName="countries"
    text="${javascript:country.getColumnValues().elementAt(1)}"
    selectedValue="${javascript:country.getColumnValues().elementAt(0)}"
                  defaultSelected="${javascript:index==0}"
                  skipContainers="1">
            </xp:radio>
      </xp:repeat>
</xp:view>
```

Include Page

This control allows you to embed the contents of one XPage into another XPage. Listing 4.47 includes the view sample and data table sample shown earlier, so you can see the two samples side by side. The page name to include can be computed, but only using an expression that is evaluated when the page loads.

Listing 4.47 Include Page Sample

```
<?xml version="1.0" encoding="UTF-8"?>
<xp:view xmlns:xp="http://www.ibm.com/xsp/core">
      <xp:include pageName="/ViewSample.xsp" id="include1">
     </xp:include>
      <xp:include pageName="/DataTableSample.xsp" id="include2">
      </xp:include>
</xp:view>
```

Tabbed Panel

This container allows you to organize its children across multiple tabs. This allows you to group related controls, which helps the user focus on a particular part of your XPage. Listing 4.48 extends the include page sample and adds each included page into a separate tab. It also shows how to use a button to navigate between the tabs; this is a common pattern in wizard-style interfaces.

Listing 4.48 Tabbed Panel Sample

```
<?xml version="1.0" encoding="UTF-8"?>
<xp:view xmlns:xp="http://www.ibm.com/xsp/core">
      <xp:tabbedPanel id="tabbedPanel1" selectedTab="tabPanel1">
            <xp:tabPanel label="View Sample" id="tabPanel1">
                  <xp:include
                        pageName="/ViewSample.xsp" id="include1">
                  </xp:include>
                  <xp:button value="Next" id="button1"
                        immediate="true" type="submit">
                        <xp:this.action><![CDATA[#{javascript:
                        var tabbedPanel = getComponent("tabbedPanel1");
                        tabbedPanel.setSelectedTab("tabPanel2");
                        }]]></xp:this.action>
                  </xp:button>
            </xp:tabPanel>
            <xp:tabPanel label="Data Table Sample" id="tabPanel2">
                  <xp:include
                        pageName="/DataTableSample.xsp" id="include2">
                  </xp:include>
                  <xp:button value="Previous" id="button2"
                        immediate="true" type="submit">
                        <xp:this.action><![CDATA[#{javascript:
                        var tabbedPanel = getComponent("tabbedPanel1");
                        tabbedPanel.setSelectedTab("tabPanel1");
```

```
                    }]]></xp:this.action>
                </xp:button>
            </xp:tabPanel>
        </xp:tabbedPanel>
</xp:view>
```

Section

The section container organizes its children in a region that can be toggled between an opened and closed state. In Listing 4.49, there are two sections: first, a default section that is closed by default; and second, a section that is surrounded by gray bars on all sides, which is initially open. It is also possible to disable the ability to expand and collapse a section, so if, in certain circumstances, it is not appropriate to allow this, that feature can be controlled.

Listing 4.49 Section Sample

```
<?xml version="1.0" encoding="UTF-8"?>
<xp:view xmlns:xp="http://www.ibm.com/xsp/core">
      <xp:section id="section1" header="View" initClosed="true">
            <xp:include pageName="/ViewSample.xsp" id="include1">
            </xp:include>
      </xp:section>
      <xp:section id="section2" header="Data Table" type="box">
            <xp:include pageName="/dataTableSample.xsp" id="include2">
            </xp:include>
      </xp:section>
</xp:view>
```

XPage Resources

For all the example XPages shown in this chapter, all the JavaScript has been included within the page, typically in CDATA sections. This procedure is acceptable when the JavaScript code is simple. However, as your XPages applications become more complex, the need arises to write JavaScript that might be broken into multiple methods and needs to be shared across multiple, different XPages. The same applies for styling; if you apply styles to each individual control in each XPage, it becomes difficult to maintain consistency across all of your XPages. For example, if you decide to change the standard look for your buttons, you have to change every XPage that contains a button control. These are the two most common examples of the need to associate resources with your XPage. To solve these problems, XPages supports the ability to link to external resource files. You have already seen an example of this, where the image control allows you to link to an image resource that was created in the application. Seven types of resources can be associated with an XPage:

- JavaScript Library
- Style Sheet
- Resource Bundle
- Dojo Module
- Dojo Module Path Resource
- Linked Resource
- Metadata

The sections that follow examine these resources in greater detail.

JavaScript Library

XPages supports linking to client-side or server-side JavaScript script libraries. To create a script library, follow these steps:

1. Choose **File > New > Script Library**.
2. In the New Script Library dialog (shown in Figure 4.11), enter a name (such as ServerJavaScriptSample), and change the type to **Server JavaScript**.

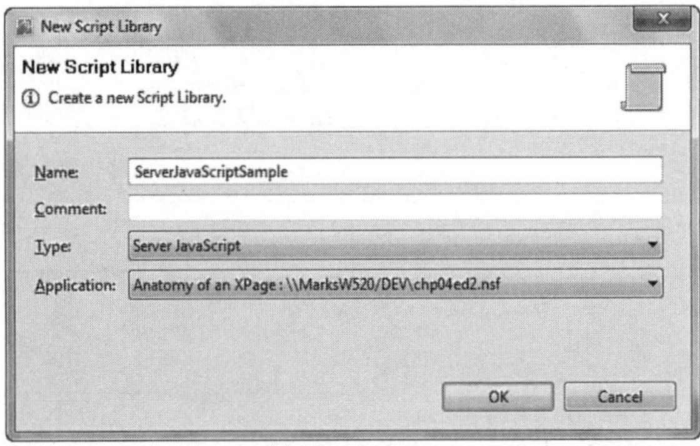

Figure 4.11 New Script Library dialog

3. Choose **OK**, and the new script library opens in the JavaScript™ editor (see Figure 4.12).

Next, create a simple JavaScript method that will be referenced later from an XPage:

1. Use the keyword `function` to start a new method (see Figure 4.12).

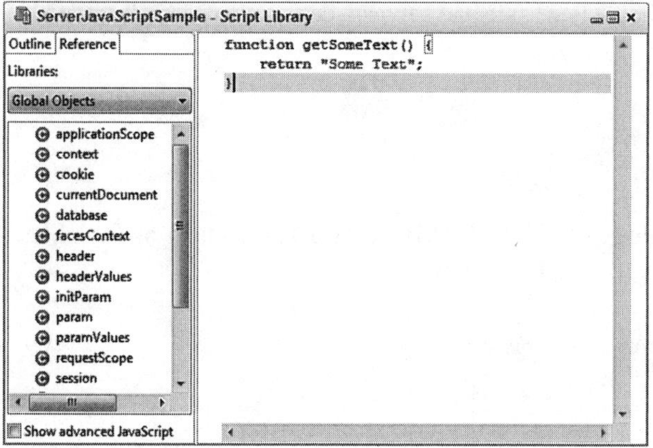

Figure 4.12 JavaScript editor

2. Give the method a name (such as getSomeText). This method does not take any parameters.
3. In the body of this new method, return a static string (such as Some Text).

Finally, the script library can be referenced in an XPage, and the method you created can be called (see Listing 4.50). The `xp:script` tag links to a script library. This tag can be added as a child to the resources property of the `xp:view` tag. This makes the contents of the script library available within the XPage. The script library can be created for either client-side or server-side scripting. If the script library is for client-side use, a link to the library will be created in the head section of the HTML page. The method that was defined can now be invoked from within the XPage. In Listing 4.50, you can see the method being used to set the `value` property of a Computed Field.

Listing 4.50 Script Library Sample

```
<?xml version="1.0" encoding="UTF-8"?>
<xp:view xmlns:xp="http://www.ibm.com/xsp/core">
      <xp:this.resources>
            <xp:script src="/ServerJavaScriptSample.jss"
                  clientSide="false">
            </xp:script>
      </xp:this.resources>
      <xp:text escape="true" id="computedField1"
            value="#{javascript:getSomeText()}">
      </xp:text>
</xp:view>
```

The use of JavaScript libraries, both client-side and server-side, is covered in Chapter 11.

Style Sheet

Follow these steps to create a style sheet:

1. Choose **File > New > Style Sheet Resource**.
2. In the New Style Sheet dialog (see Figure 4.13), enter a name (such as StyleSheet Sample).

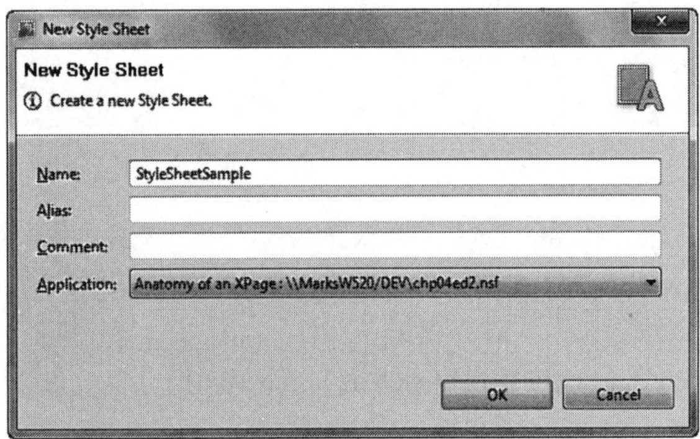

Figure 4.13 New Style Sheet dialog

3. Choose **OK**, and the new style sheet opens in the style sheet editor (see Figure 4.14).

Next, create a button style class that will be referenced later from an XPage:

1. Use the name `.sample` to indicate that this style only applies to all elements with style class set to sample (see Figure 4.14).
2. In the body of this new style class, set the various styles that you want to apply.

The style sheet can now be referenced from an XPage, and the style class you defined can be applied to controls. The `xp:styleSheet` tag links to a style sheet resource. This tag can be added as a child to the resources property of the `xp:view` tag. Listing 4.51 demonstrates how the style class you just defined can be applied to a button.

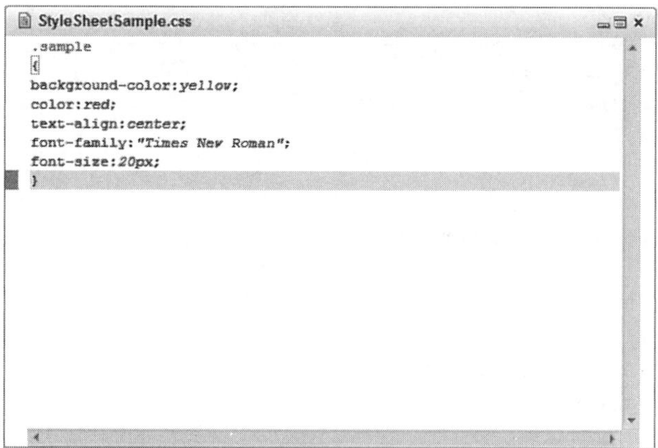

Figure 4.14 Style sheet editor

Listing 4.51 Style Sheet Sample

```
<?xml version="1.0" encoding="UTF-8"?>
<xp:view xmlns:xp="http://www.ibm.com/xsp/core">
      <xp:this.resources>
            <xp:styleSheet href="/StyleSheetSample.css">
            </xp:styleSheet>
      </xp:this.resources>
      <xp:button value="Button Sample" id="button1"
            styleClass="sample">
      </xp:button>
</xp:view>
```

The use of style sheets is covered in Chapter 16, "XPages Theming."

Resource Bundle

This complex property is used to load a resource bundle file and make its contents available within the XPage. A resource bundle file is a text file that contains name/value pairs and is the standard format used when localizing Java-based applications. XPages and the resource bundle are explained in Chapter 18, "Internationalization." Listing 4.52 demonstrates how to load a resource bundle where the source is a file associated with the Domino application. It also shows how to reference a value from within the properties bundle (run this to get a free Irish lesson). Chapter 11 covers the use of dojo with XPages in detail.

Listing 4.52 Resource Bundle Sample

```
<?xml version="1.0" encoding="UTF-8"?>
<xp:view xmlns:xp="http://www.ibm.com/xsp/core">
      <xp:this.resources>
            <xp:bundle
                  var="greetings"
                  src="greetings.properties">
            </xp:bundle>
      </xp:this.resources>
      <xp:text
            escape="true" id="computedField1"
            value="${greetings.hello}">
      </xp:text>
</xp:view>
```

Dojo Module and Dojo Module Path

These complex properties are used to load Dojo Modules. The Dojo Module resource is used to conditionally load Dojo modules. The Dojo Module Path is used to specify the location from which modules with a specific prefix are loaded. Although XPages already provides a nice set of controls, you might want to use some of the additional controls in the Dojo library in your application. In this case, you need to add the appropriate module to your page. Listing 4.53 demonstrates a sample of the `<xp:dojoModule>` and `<xp:dojoModulePath>` tags. Chapter 11 covers the use of Dojo with XPages.

Listing 4.53 Dojo Module Sample

```
<?xml version="1.0" encoding="UTF-8"?>
<xp:view xmlns:xp="http://www.ibm.com/xsp/core">
      <xp:this.resources>
                <xp:dojoModulePath prefix="some"
➥url="http://server.com/modules">
                </xp:dojoModulePath>
            <xp:dojoModule
                  condition="dojo.isBrowser" name="some.Module">
            </xp:dojoModule>
      </xp:this.resources>
</xp:view>
```

Generic Head Resource

This complex property provides a way to link to any external resource. (For example, you can output a HTML `<link>` tag into the HTML page generated for an XPage.) HTML authors typically use this for linking to style sheets. Listing 4.54 demonstrates how to use the `<xp:linkResource>` tag to link to a style sheet. As you can see, this is a lot less intuitive than using the `<xp:styleSheet>` tag.

Listing 4.54 Generic Head Resource Sample

```
<?xml version="1.0" encoding="UTF-8"?>
<xp:view xmlns:xp="http://www.ibm.com/xsp/core">
	<xp:this.resources>
		<xp:linkResource
			rel="stylesheet"
			type="text/css"
			href="/xsp/chp04ed2.nsf/xsp/StyleSheetSample.css">
		</xp:linkResource>
	</xp:this.resources>
	<xp:button value="Button Sample" id="button1"
		styleClass="sample">
	</xp:button>
</xp:view>
```

Metadata Resource

This complex property provides a way to output an HTML `<meta>` tag in the head section of the HTML page generated for an XPage. Meta tags provide information about the page (such as a page description, keywords, author name, and other metadata). The meta tag is added inside of the HTML `<head>` tag. Listing 4.55 shows how to use the `<xp:metaData>` tag to provide description metadata about an XPage. The meta tag is used to provide search engines with information about your site. If you preview this sample and view the page source, you see the following HTML tag within the generated HTML:

```
<meta name="description" content="Meta-Data Resource Sample">
```

Listing 4.55 Metadata Resource Sample

```
<?xml version="1.0" encoding="UTF-8"?>
<xp:view xmlns:xp="http://www.ibm.com/xsp/core">
	<xp:this.resources>
		<xp:metaData
			name="description"
			content="Meta-Data Resource Sample">
		</xp:metaData>
	</xp:this.resources>
	Meta-Data Resource Sample
</xp:view>
```

Converters

Every control that has an associated value optionally needs to be able to convert that value into a format that's suitable for display to the application users. Additionally, if the control allows the user to enter a new value, the control optionally needs to be able to convert the value the user entered into the appropriate data type. Controls with an associated value use string values by default, but even if the underlying data value is a string, conversion might still be needed because users should see the data by using the appropriate conventions for their locale. When the underlying data type is not a string, conversion must be performed both when the initial values are presented to the user and before the user-inputted value is processed by the application logic. Converters perform these conversions. You have already seen converters being used in the date/time picker example—a date/time converter is set on the edit box to handle the date/time conversion. Table 4.1 lists all the converter tags, the converter name, and a short description.

Table 4.1 Converters

Tag	Converter ID	Description
`xp:convertDateTime`	Date Time	Converts to and from date values.
`xp:convertList`	List	Converts between to and from list values. The string representation of the list is the string value of each list item separated by the specified delimiter.
`xp:convertMask`	Mask	Masks the local value.
`xp:convertNumber`	Number	Converts to and from numeric values, including currency and percent values.
`xp:customConverter`	Custom	Provides a way to provide your own logic to convert the data value to and from its string representation. Used with `xp:converter`.
`xp:convertBoolean`	Boolean	Converts to and from boolean values.
`xp:converter`		Allows the converter type to be dynamically specified or a custom converter to be used.

Listing 4.56 demonstrates how to use each of the converters with a Computed Field:

- The Date Time converter is set to the German/Germany locale and displays the long representation of the date and time. The `xp:converter` tag allows another converter to be loaded using its converter ID.
- The List converter is shown converting a JavaScript array to a | delimited string.
- The Mask converter masks out the first three uppercase characters for the string value.

- The Number converter converts a random number (between 1 and 100) with two decimal places.
- The Custom converter converts the string value 1 to the string representation One. A custom converter allows you to provide your own conversion logic.
- The Boolean converter converts the boolean value true/false to the string representation "true"/"false".

Listing 4.56 Converter Sample

```
<?xml version="1.0" encoding="UTF-8"?>
<xp:view xmlns:xp="http://www.ibm.com/xsp/core">
      <xp:this.afterPageLoad>
            <xp:actionGroup>
                  <xp:setValue binding="#{viewScope.date}"
                        value="#{javascript:new Date()}" />
                  <xp:setValue binding="#{viewScope.number}"
                        value="#{javascript:Math.random()*100}" />
                  <xp:setValue binding="#{viewScope.boolean}"
                        value="#{javascript:Math.random()>0.5}" />
            </xp:actionGroup>
      </xp:this.afterPageLoad>
      <xp:text escape="true" id="computedField1"
            value="#{viewScope.date}">
            <xp:this.converter>
                  <xp:convertDateTime locale="de_DE"
                        dateStyle="long"
                        timeStyle="long"
                        type="both">
                  </xp:convertDateTime>
            </xp:this.converter>
      </xp:text>
      <xp:br/>
      <xp:text escape="true" id="computedField2"
            value="#{viewScope.date}">
            <xp:this.converter>
                  <xp:converter
                        converterId="com.ibm.xsp.DateTime">
                  </xp:converter>
            </xp:this.converter>
      </xp:text>
      <xp:br/>
      <xp:text escape="true" id="computedField3"
            value="#{javascript:['One','Two','Three']}">
            <xp:this.converter>
```

```
                <xp:convertList delimiter="|">
                </xp:convertList>
            </xp:this.converter>
        </xp:text>
        <xp:br/>
        <xp:text escape="true" id="computedField4"
            value="AbCdEf">
            <xp:this.converter>
                <xp:convertMask
                    mask="UUU">
                </xp:convertMask>
            </xp:this.converter>
        </xp:text>
        <xp:br/>
        <xp:text escape="true" id="computedField5"
            value="#{viewScope.number}">
            <xp:this.converter>
                <xp:convertNumber
                    maxFractionDigits="2">
                </xp:convertNumber>
            </xp:this.converter>
        </xp:text>
        <xp:br/>
        <xp:text escape="true" id="computedField6"
            value="1">
            <xp:this.converter>
                <xp:customConverter
                getAsObject="#{javascript:if(value=='One') return '1'}"
                getAsString="#{javascript:if(value=='1') return 'One'}">
                </xp:customConverter>
            </xp:this.converter>
        </xp:text>
        <xp:br/>
        <xp:text escape="true" id="computedField7"
            value="#{viewScope.boolean}">
            <xp:this.converter>
                <xp:convertBoolean>
                </xp:convertBoolean>
            </xp:this.converter>
        </xp:text>
</xp:view>
```

Validators

Every control that can be used to edit a value must have a way to allow the inputted value to be checked for correctness. This is the purpose of a validator—you can optionally associate one or more validators with an input control to check that the value the user entered meets certain criteria. The validation can be performed as the XPage is submitted and, if the values are invalid, the submit operation is cancelled. This saves unnecessary round trips to the server and improves the user experience. When validation fails, an error message is presented to the user, allowing him to take corrective action. XPages supports special output controls for displaying either the error messages associated with a single control or all the error messages for the entire XPage. Table 4.2 lists all the validator tags, the validator name, and a short description.

Table 4.2 Validators

Tag	Name	Description
`xp:validateRequired`	Required	Used when a value must be provided.
`xp:validateConstraint`	Constraint	Used when the value must adhere to a convention as defined by the associated regular expression.
`xp:validateDateTimeRange`	Date Time Range	Used when a date value must lie within a specified range.
`xp:validateDoubleRange`	Double Range	Used when a double value must lie within a specified range.
`xp:validateExpression`	Expression	Used when the value must adhere to a convention as defined by the associated computed expression.
`xp:validateLength`	Length	Used when the length of a string value must be constrained to a certain size.
`xp:validateLongRange`	Long Range	Used when a long value must lie within a specified range.
`xp:validateModulusSelfCheck`	Modulus Self Check	Used for numbers with a self-check digit (such as a credit-card number).
`xp:customValidator`	Custom	Used when custom application logic needs to be provided to validate the value.

Listing 4.57 demonstrates usage for each validator listed in Table 4.2. Notice that there is no data source associated with this page, but you can still run this sample and see the validators in action. If you preview this page and select the Submit button without entering any values, you

are prompted with an error message saying, "Value is required," and the page is not submitted. This is because the first validator requires that you enter a valid in the first edit box. This is an example of client-side validation in action (that is, the value is validated on the client-side and the page won't be submitted with invalid values). Performing the validation on the client-side is good from the user perspective, because she doesn't have to wait for a server round trip before finding out that she hasn't entered a value correctly. It is also good from the server perspective, because valuable server cycles are not taken up processing pages that need to be returned to the user. Entering a value allows you to submit the page because only this first edit box is a required value. To see the other validators in action, you must enter a value. Try entering various values to see how each validator behaves. The only validator that does not support client-side validation is the modulus self-check validator. When you enter an invalid value into the associated edit box, the page is submitted and the error is displayed when the page is redrawn. The `xp:message` tag displays any error messages associated with a specific control. To see all the error messages for the entire page, the `xp:messages` tag is used.

Listing 4.57 Validator Sample

```
<?xml version="1.0" encoding="UTF-8"?>
<xp:view xmlns:xp="http://www.ibm.com/xsp/core">
      <xp:table>
            <xp:tr>
                  <xp:td>
                        <xp:label value="Required:" id="label1">
                        </xp:label>
                  </xp:td>
                  <xp:td>
                        <xp:inputText id="inputText1">
                              <xp:this.validators>
                                    <xp:validateRequired
                                          message="Value is required.">
                                    </xp:validateRequired>
                              </xp:this.validators>
                        </xp:inputText>
                  </xp:td>
                  <xp:td>
                        <xp:message id="message1" for="inputText1">
                        </xp:message>
                  </xp:td>
            </xp:tr>
            <xp:tr>
                  <xp:td>
                        <xp:label value="Constraint ('foo'):"
                              id="label2">
                        </xp:label>
```

```
        </xp:td>
        <xp:td>
              <xp:inputText id="inputText2">
                    <xp:this.validators>
                          <xp:validateConstraint
                          message="Value must be set to 'foo'"
                                regex="foo">
                          </xp:validateConstraint>
                    </xp:this.validators>
              </xp:inputText>
        </xp:td>
        <xp:td>
              <xp:message id="message2" for="inputText2">
              </xp:message>
        </xp:td>
  </xp:tr>
  <xp:tr>
        <xp:td>
              <xp:label value="Date Range (after 31 Dec 2010):"
                    id="label3">
              </xp:label>
        </xp:td>
        <xp:td>
              <xp:inputText id="inputText3">
                    <xp:this.validators>
                          <xp:validateDateTimeRange
                    message="Earliest date is 1 Jan 2011"
minimum="#{javascript:new Date(2011,0,1,0,0,0,0)}">
                          </xp:validateDateTimeRange>
                    </xp:this.validators>
                    <xp:dateTimeHelper id="dateTimeHelper1">
                    </xp:dateTimeHelper>
                    <xp:this.converter>
                          <xp:convertDateTime type="date">
                          </xp:convertDateTime>
                    </xp:this.converter>
              </xp:inputText>
        </xp:td>
        <xp:td>
              <xp:message id="message3" for="inputText3">
              </xp:message>
        </xp:td>
  </xp:tr>
  <xp:tr>
        <xp:td>
```

```
                    <xp:label value="Double Range (1-100):"
                         id="label4">
                    </xp:label>
               </xp:td>
               <xp:td>
                    <xp:inputText id="inputText4">
                         <xp:this.validators>
                         <xp:validateDoubleRange
                          maximum="100"
                          minimum="1"
                          message="Enter value between 1-100">
                               </xp:validateDoubleRange>
                         </xp:this.validators>
                    </xp:inputText>
               </xp:td>
               <xp:td>
                    <xp:message id="message4" for="inputText4">
                    </xp:message>
               </xp:td>
          </xp:tr>
          <xp:tr>
               <xp:td>
                    <xp:label value="Expression ('bar'):"
                         id="label5">
                    </xp:label>
               </xp:td>
               <xp:td>
                    <xp:inputText id="inputText5">
                         <xp:this.validators>
                            <xp:validateExpression
➥clientScript="value=='bar'"   expression="#{javascript:value=='bar'}"
                              message="Value must be set to 'bar'">
                                </xp:validateExpression>
                         </xp:this.validators>
                    </xp:inputText>
               </xp:td>
               <xp:td>
                    <xp:message id="message5" for="inputText5">
                    </xp:message>
               </xp:td>
          </xp:tr>
          <xp:tr>
               <xp:td>
                    <xp:label value="Length (min. 5 chars.):"
                         id="label6">
```

```
                <//xp:label>
            </xp:td>
            <xp:td>
                <xp:inputText id="inputText6">
                    <xp:this.validators>
                        <xp:validateLength minimum="5"
                         message="Enter min. 5 characters">
                        </xp:validateLength>
                    </xp:this.validators>
                </xp:inputText>
            </xp:td>
            <xp:td>
                <xp:message id="message6" for="inputText6">
                </xp:message>
            </xp:td>
        </xp:tr>
        <xp:tr>
            <xp:td>
                <xp:label value="Long Range (1-100):"
                    id="label7">
                </xp:label>
            </xp:td>
            <xp:td>
                <xp:inputText id="inputText7">
                    <xp:this.validators>
                        <xp:validateLongRange
                         minimum="1"
                         maximum="100"
                         message="Enter value between 1-100">
                        </xp:validateLongRange>
                    </xp:this.validators>
                </xp:inputText>
            </xp:td>
            <xp:td>
                <xp:message id="message7" for="inputText7">
                </xp:message>
            </xp:td>
        </xp:tr>
        <xp:tr>
            <xp:td>
                <xp:label value="Modulus Self Check (964387):"
                    id="label9">
                </xp:label>
            </xp:td>
            <xp:td>
```

```
                    <xp:inputText id="inputText9">
                        <xp:this.validators>
                            <xp:validateModulusSelfCheck
                             modulus="10"
                             message="Value must be modulus 10">
                            </xp:validateModulusSelfCheck>
                        </xp:this.validators>
                    </xp:inputText>
                </xp:td>
                <xp:td>
                    <xp:message id="message9" for="inputText9">
                    </xp:message>
                </xp:td>
            </xp:tr>
            <xp:tr>
                <xp:td>
                    <xp:label value="Custom Validator ('baz'):"
                        id="label10">
                    </xp:label>
                </xp:td>
                <xp:td>
                    <xp:inputText id="inputText10">
                        <xp:this.validators>
                            <xp:customValidator>
                                <xp:this.validate>
<![CDATA[#{javascript:
if (value != "baz") {
    return new javax.faces.application.FacesMessage("Value must be set to
➥'baz'");
}
}]]>
                                </xp:this.validate>
                            </xp:customValidator>
                        </xp:this.validators>
                    </xp:inputText>
                </xp:td>
                <xp:td>
                    <xp:message id="message10" for="inputText10">
                    </xp:message>
                </xp:td>
            </xp:tr>
```

```
            <xp:tr>
                  <xp:td colspan="3">
                        <xp:messages id="messages1" layout="table">
                        </xp:messages>
                  </xp:td>
            </xp:tr>
            <xp:tr>
                  <xp:td colspan="3">
                        <xp:button value="Submit"
                              id="button1">
                              <xp:eventHandler
                                    event="onclick"
                                    submit="true"
                                    refreshMode="complete"
                                    immediate="false"
                                    id="eventHandler1">
                              </xp:eventHandler>
                        </xp:button>
                  </xp:td>
            </xp:tr>
      </xp:table>
</xp:view>
```

TIP

There are occasions where using client-side validation is not what you want. So you can disable this for a particular edit control using the `disableClientSideValidation` property, set this to true to disable client-side validation. To disable client-side validation for the entire page, don't use the `xp:eventHandler` tag to submit the page—if using a button to submit, change its type to submit. To disable client-side validation for the entire application, go to the XSP properties and in the Page Generation tab, set Client Validation to off. To disable client-side validation for the entire server, change the server xsp.properties file. Figure 4.15 shows how the page behaves when client-side validation is not being used.

For your interest, to get the page to submit with no errors using the values shown, see Figure 4.16.

ValidatorSample.xsp
Required:
Value is required.
Constraint ('foo'):
bad
Value must be set to 'foo'
Date Range (after 31 Dec 2012):
May 11, 2013
Earliest date is 1 Jan 2013
Double Range (1-100):
101
Enter value between 1-100
Expression ('bar'):
bad
Value must be set to 'bar'
Length (min. 5 chars.):
123
Enter min. 5 characters
Long Range (1-100):
101
Enter value between 1-100
Modulus Self Check (964387):
123
Value must be modulus 10
Custom Validator ('baz'):
bad
Value must be set to 'baz'
Enter value between 1-100
Value must be set to 'bar'
Enter min. 5 characters
Value must be set to 'baz'
Enter value between 1-100
Value must be modulus 10
Value is required.
Value must be set to 'foo'
Earliest date is 1 Jan 2013
Submit

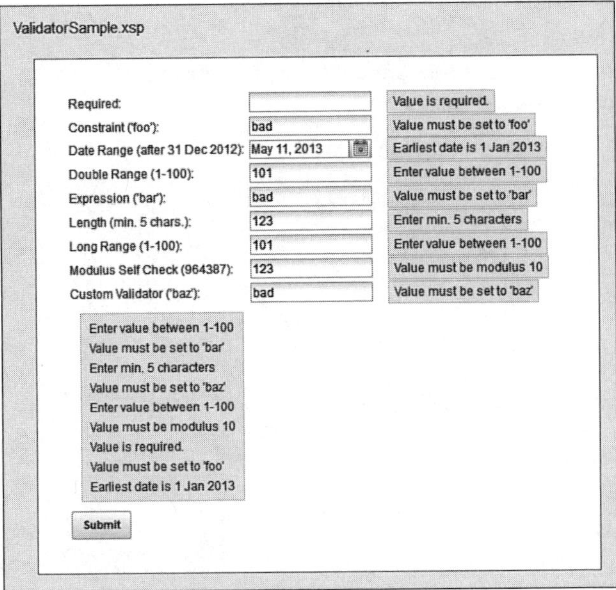

Figure 4.15 Validation failing

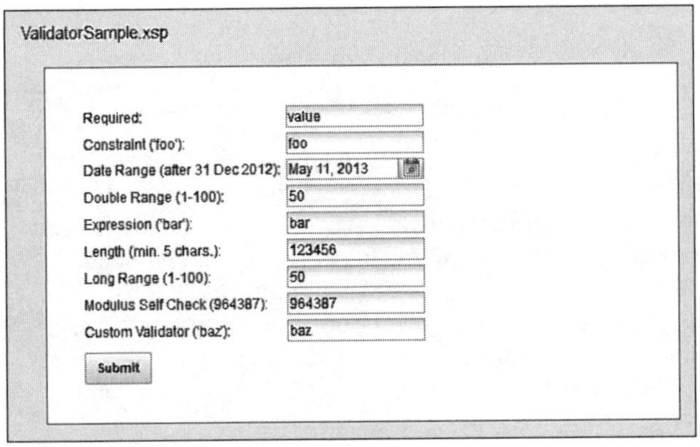

ValidatorSample.xsp
Required:
value
Constraint ('foo'):
foo
Date Range (after 31 Dec 2012):
May 11, 2013
Double Range (1-100):
50
Expression ('bar'):
bar
Length (min. 5 chars.):
123456
Long Range (1-100):
50
Modulus Self Check (964387):
964387
Custom Validator ('baz'):
baz
Submit

Figure 4.16 Validation passing

Simple Actions

Simple actions provide a simple way to add application logic to an XPage without the need to write any code. They perform common actions, such as opening a page, setting a value, deleting a document, and so on. Their behavior can be simply configured by changing their parameters.

Simple actions are covered in Chapter 6. In this section, the tags are listed with a brief description, and the syntax for using simple actions is shown and explained.

Table 4.3 lists all the simple action tags and briefly describes their purposes.

Table 4.3 Simple Action Tags

Tag	Name	Type	Description
`xp:changeDocumentMode`	Change Document Mode	server	Changes the access mode for the document to one of: read only, edit, auto edit (i.e., edit mode if user has sufficient rights) and toggle (if in edit mode, change to read-only and vice versa).
`xp:confirm`	Confirm Action	server	Presents the user with a message and options to allow execution to continue or stop.
`xp:createResponse`	Create Response Document	server	Creates a response document and opens the specified page to edit it.
`xp:deleteDocument`	Delete Document	server	Deletes the current document and opens the current page.
`xp:deleteSelectedDocuments`	Delete Selected Documents	server	Deletes the documents selected in a view after first prompting the user to confirm this action.
`xp:executeClientScript`	Execute Client Script	client	Executes a client-side script.
`xp:executeScript`	Execute Script	server	Executes a server-side script.
`xp:modifyField`	Modify Field	server	Modifies a field in the current document.
`xp:openPage`	Open Page	server	Navigates to a specific page where you can set the document ID of an existing document that can be opened for reading or editing.
`xp:publishValue`	Publish Component Property	client	Publishes the value for a component event.
`xp:publishViewColumn`	Publish View Column	client	Publishes the value of a view column as a component event.
`xp:save`	Save Data Sources	server	Saves all the data sources in the current page and optionally navigates to another page.
`xp:saveDocument`	Save Document	server	Saves the current document.

Tag	Name	Type	Description
xp:sendMail	Send Mail	server	Send Mail action sends an email and optionally embeds content in the email.
xp:setComponentMode	Set Component Mode Action	server	Changes the mode of a component to either view, edit, or help mode.
xp:setValue	Set Value	server	Sets the value of a computed expression.
xp:actionGroup	Action Groups	server	Executes a group of simple actions.

Some of the simple actions refer to the current document, which means the nearest Domino document to the action. You saw earlier in this chapter that an XPage can contain multiple Domino documents, and each can be referenced by name using the value of its `var` property. The current document can be referenced by an implicit variable called `currentDocument`. Listing 4.58 contains two Domino documents: one associated with the view and one associated with a panel. Two Computed Fields are both bound to the variable `currentDocument`, which displays a string representation of the value of that variable. (In this case, it is the Java class name and hash code of the associated Java object.) When you run this sample, you see that the values displayed by each Computed Field is different, which means that the Domino document being referenced changes. In this case, the Domino document referenced by the first Computed Field is the document associated with the view. The second Computed Field references the document associated with the panel.

Listing 4.58 Current Document Sample

```
<?xml version="1.0" encoding="UTF-8"?>
<xp:view xmlns:xp="http://www.ibm.com/xsp/core">
      <xp:this.data>
            <xp:dominoDocument var="document1"
                  formName="Document">
            </xp:dominoDocument>
      </xp:this.data>
      <xp:text escape="true" id="computedField1"
            value="#{currentDocument}">
      </xp:text>
      <xp:br/>
      <xp:panel>
            <xp:this.data>
                  <xp:dominoDocument var="document2"
                        formName="Document">
                  </xp:dominoDocument>
```

```
            </xp:this.data>
            <xp:text escape="true" id="computedField2"
                  value="#{currentDocument}">
            </xp:text>
      </xp:panel>
</xp:view>
```

Simple actions are associated with the event properties of a control, which means that, when the corresponding event is triggered, the simple action is executed. Listing 4.59 demonstrates the set value simple action being used to set a view scope (limited to the lifetime of the XPages view) variable to the value Some Value. The simple action is executed once, after the page loads. A Computed Field on the XPage is also bound to the same variable and displays the value. When you run this sample, you see the string Some Value displayed on the page.

Listing 4.59 Simple Action Sample

```
<?xml version="1.0" encoding="UTF-8"?>
<xp:view xmlns:xp="http://www.ibm.com/xsp/core">
      <xp:this.afterPageLoad>
            <xp:setValue
                  binding="#{viewScope.someValue}"
                  value="Some Value" />
      </xp:this.afterPageLoad>
      <xp:text escape="true" id="computedField1"
            value="#{viewScope.someValue}">
      </xp:text>
</xp:view>
```

Multiple simple actions can be grouped and executed together by using action groups. Action groups can be nested and have conditions that allow you to build up an execution hierarchy. Listing 4.60 demonstrates using action groups to create a simple calculator that can perform addition and subtraction. The sample contains edit boxes that allow you to enter the values to use in the calculation and buttons to specify the operation you want to execute. When you select the = button, the action group that executes will execute one of two child action groups. The first is used when the operation is subtraction, and the second when the operation is addition.

Listing 4.60 Action Group Sample

```
<?xml version="1.0" encoding="UTF-8"?>
<xp:view xmlns:xp="http://www.ibm.com/xsp/core">
      <xp:this.afterPageLoad>
            <xp:actionGroup>
                  <xp:setValue
                        binding="#{viewScope.first}"
```

```
                    value="0" />
                <xp:setValue
                    binding="#{viewScope.second}"
                    value="0" />
                <xp:setValue
                    binding="#{viewScope.operation}"
                    value="+" />
            </xp:actionGroup>
        </xp:this.afterPageLoad>
        <xp:table>
            <xp:tr>
                <xp:td>
                    <xp:inputText id="inputText1" style="width:50px"
                        value="#{viewScope.first}">
                        <xp:this.converter>
                            <xp:convertNumber type="number">
                            </xp:convertNumber>
                        </xp:this.converter>
                    </xp:inputText>
                </xp:td>
                <xp:td>
                    <xp:button value="+" id="button1"
                        style="width:25px;height:25.0px"
                        type="submit">
                        <xp:this.action>
                            <xp:setValue
                            binding="#{viewScope.operation}"
                                value="+" />
                        </xp:this.action>
                    </xp:button>
                </xp:td>
                <xp:td></xp:td>
                <xp:td></xp:td>
            </xp:tr>
            <xp:tr>
                <xp:td>
                    <xp:inputText id="inputText2" style="width:50px"
                        value="#{viewScope.second}">
                        <xp:this.converter>
                            <xp:convertNumber type="number">
                            </xp:convertNumber>
                        </xp:this.converter>
                    </xp:inputText>
                </xp:td>
                <xp:td>
```

```
                        <xp:button value="-" id="button2"
                              style="width:25px;height:25.0px"
                              type="submit">
                              <xp:this.action>
                                    <xp:setValue
                                    binding="#{viewScope.operation}"
                                          value="-" />
                              </xp:this.action>
                        </xp:button>
                  </xp:td>
                  <xp:td>
                        <xp:button value="=" id="button3"
                              style="width:25px;height:25.0px"
                              type="submit">
                              <xp:this.action>
                                    <xp:actionGroup>
                                          <xp:actionGroup
                              condition="#{viewScope.operation=='-'}">
                                                <xp:setValuebinding=
"#{viewScope.result}"
      value="#{viewScope.first - viewScope.second}" />
                                          </xp:actionGroup>
                                          <xp:actionGroup

     condition="#{viewScope.operation=='+'}">
                                                <xp:setValue
     binding="#{viewScope.result}"
     value="#{viewScope.first + viewScope.second}" />
                                          </xp:actionGroup>
                                    </xp:actionGroup>
                              </xp:this.action>
                        </xp:button>
                  </xp:td>
                  <xp:td>
                        <xp:inputText id="inputText3" style="width:50px"
                              value="#{viewScope.result}">
                              <xp:this.converter>
                                    <xp:convertNumber type="number">
                                    </xp:convertNumber>
                              </xp:this.converter>
                        </xp:inputText>
                  </xp:td>
            </xp:tr>
      </xp:table>
</xp:view>
```

As well as making execution conditional based on some computed value, you can also make execution conditional on the user agreeing to proceed. The confirm simple action can prompt the user before proceeding with an execution. In Listing 4.61, the confirm simple action is used within an action group. This causes some client-side JavaScript to execute when the user clicks the button. The specified message, such as "Add some more?," displays with OK and Cancel options. If the user chooses OK, the page is submitted, the next action executes, and otherwise no further action occurs. The simple actions for deleting a single document or multiple documents have this confirmation built in.

Listing 4.61 Confirm Sample

```
<?xml version="1.0" encoding="UTF-8"?>
<xp:view xmlns:xp="http://www.ibm.com/xsp/core">
	<xp:this.afterPageLoad>
		<xp:setValue
			binding="#{viewScope.someValue}"
			value="Some Value" />
	</xp:this.afterPageLoad>
	<xp:text escape="true" id="computedField1"
		value="#{viewScope.someValue}">
	</xp:text>
	<xp:br></xp:br>
	<xp:button value="Add More?" id="button2">
		<xp:eventHandler event="onclick"
			submit="true" refreshMode="complete">
			<xp:this.action>
				<xp:actionGroup>
					<xp:confirm
						message="Add some more?">
					</xp:confirm>
					<xp:setValue
						binding="#{viewScope.someValue}"
						value="#{viewScope.someValue} More">
					</xp:setValue>
				</xp:actionGroup>
			</xp:this.action>
		</xp:eventHandler>
	</xp:button>
</xp:view>
```

Client-Side Scripting

Earlier, you saw how to add a script library to an XPage, which is the most common approach to including client-side JavaScript. Two additional tags can be used for client-side scripting:

- The `xp:scriptBlock` tag (Script Block) can be used to include a block of JavaScript code at a specified location in the page.
- The `xp:handler` tag (Event Handler) is used to add an event handler to a control. This tag is used in conjunction with the `xp:eventHandler` to set its handlers property, meaning that you must create an `xp:this.handlers` tag as a child of `xp:eventHandler` and make the `xp:handler` a child of this, as shown in Listing 4.62.

Listing 4.62 demonstrates how to include two JavaScript functions in a script block and how to call those functions in response to the onclick event from a button. (Chapter 11 covers client-side JavaScript scripting in depth.)

Listing 4.62 Client-Side Scripting Sample

```
<?xml version="1.0" encoding="UTF-8"?>
<xp:view xmlns:xp="http://www.ibm.com/xsp/core">
	<xp:scriptBlock type="text/javascript">
		<xp:this.value>
		<![CDATA[
			function doSomething() {
				alert("Did Something");
			}
			function doSomethingElse() {
				alert("Did Something Else");
			}
		]]>
		</xp:this.value>
	</xp:scriptBlock>
	<xp:button value="Do Something" id="button1">
		<xp:eventHandler event="onclick">
			<xp:this.handlers>
				<xp:handler
					type="text/javascript"
					script="doSomething()">
				</xp:handler>
			</xp:this.handlers>
		</xp:eventHandler>
	</xp:button>
	<xp:br/>
	<xp:button value="Do Something Else" id="button2">
		<xp:eventHandler event="onclick">
			<xp:this.handlers>
				<xp:handler
					type="text/javascript"
					script="doSomethingElse()">
```

```
                        </xp:handler>
                    </xp:this.handlers>
                </xp:eventHandler>
        </xp:button>
</xp:view>
```

HTML Tags

The next group of tags adds some fundamental HTML tags to the displayed page. Table 4.4 lists the tags, their name, and a short description. You can also type text and HTML directly into the source view of an XPage to add arbitrary markup to an XPage.

Table 4.4 HTML Tags

Tag	Name	Description
<xp:br>	Line Break	Inserts a line break at the specified point in the XPage
<xp:span>	Span Content	Inserts an HTML span at the specified point in the XPage
<xp:paragraph>	Paragraph	Inserts an HTML paragraph at the specified point in the XPage

Listing 4.63 demonstrates the use of these tags and how to add the equivalent markup directly to an XPage. One of the main reasons that you might favor the XSP tags or plain pass-through HTML is that you can manipulate the XSP tags by using server JavaScript. (In the example shown, the `rendered` property is being set using a JavaScript-computed expression. This allows you to easily show/hide the XSP tags using server logic.)

Listing 4.63 HTML Sample

```
<?xml version="1.0" encoding="UTF-8"?>
<xp:view xmlns:xp="http://www.ibm.com/xsp/core">
        <xp:span id="span1" rendered="#{javascript:true}">
                This is an XSP span
        </xp:span>
        <xp:br></xp:br>
        <xp:paragraph id="paragraph1" rendered="#{javascript:true}">
                This is an XSP paragraph
        </xp:paragraph>
        <span>This is a HTML span</span>
        <br></br>
        <p>This is a HTML paragraph</p>
</xp:view>
```

Extension Library

Artifacts from the XPages Extension Library (see http://extlib.openntf.org/) were contributed to the core XPages runtime in the 8.5.3 Upgrade Pack 1 release. This update moved the Extension Library from an optional add-on to part of the product and provided a major enhancement to the palette of components available for an XPages developer. There is an entire book *XPages Extension Library: A Step-by-Step Guide to the Next Generation of XPages Components* dedicated to this topic. This chapter introduces you to a few of the important controls from the Extension Library. We are also going to cover more of the Extension Library later in this book. Chapter 9, "Beyond the View Basics," provides in-depth coverage of the Data View and Calendar. Chapter 17, "Application Layout," and Chapter 14, "XPages Mobile Application Development," were added in the second edition of this book and all include content from the Extension Library.

The start of this book introduced the prototypical CRUD application, which was developed using a traditional approach where there were separate views for displaying a collection of documents and for editing or creating a new document. This style of application is somewhat outdated because modern applications tend to feature few if any context switches. For example, it is more typical in a modern web application to have a single page used to perform multiple-related operations. So the theme for this section is how to use some components from the Extension Library to build a single page CRUD application. There are a variety of patterns in use in modern web applications and the Extension Library provides controls:

- **Partial refresh:** The idea here is to update parts of the page using an XML Http Request rather than a full page refresh. Support for partial refresh in XPages is not new, but the Extension Library adds some new components to make using this technique even simpler and keeps the design of your XPages elegant and easy to read.
- **In place editing:** Here instead of switching parts of the page, you simply insert a new section to perform a specific operation and then dismiss it when you finish. This technique is highly effective when used to allow the user to see a summary view and then to bring up an additional user interface to perform an operation and dismiss it when done. It allows you to build user interfaces that lack clutter but still provide rich functionality.

The following controls are reviewed in this section:

- Dynamic Content
- Change Dynamic Content Action
- In Place Form
- Dialog
- Dialog Context
- Dialog Button Bar
- Tooltip Dialog
- Json RPC Service

Dynamic Content

The Dynamic Content container (`xe:dynamicContent` tag) is used to dynamically show different content. Each group of content you want to display is added to a different facet of the Dynamic Content container. A common pattern is to use custom controls to define each facet. Only one facet at a time is displayed, and you can programmatically switch between facets at any time in response to some event, for example, use clicking a button or link. The Dynamic Content container is efficient in managing its facets, so if you have different data sources associated with each facet, only the data sources associated with the currently shown facet are loaded. In fact, only the component tree for the currently displayed facet is loaded, which means you do not have a performance penalty for hidden facets. This optimization is shared by all the components with the dynamic behavior and is an important factor in allowing a highly performant single page application to be developed. Listing 4.64 demonstrates how to use the Dynamic Content `xe:dynamicContent` tag to provide basic CRUD support. The Dynamic Content control contains two facets (not shown in the listing), one each to display a view of a set of documents and one to allow a new document to be created. A default facet can be specified to display when the Dynamic Content is first rendered, or when there is no explicit default, the first facet will be shown. The listing also shows three ways to change the dynamic content:

- **Client-side JavaScript**—Use the `XSP.showContent` to switch the currently displayed facet in a Dynamic Content container.
- **Server-side JavaScript**—The Dynamic Content component has a `show` function that provides programmatic access to set the displayed facet from server-side JavaScript.
- **Simple Action**—There is also a new simple action to change the dynamic content, which is described later in this section.

The sample also includes a check box to allow the use hash feature (useHash) of the Dynamic Content container to be toggled on and off. The useHash feature enables you to keep track of the current facet being displayed and also any parameters by automatically encoding these parameters into the browser URL. The # part of the URL is used for these values because this can prevent a page refresh being triggered. The Dynamic Content container can manage all this, so all you need to do is set useHash to true. Users of your application can bookmark the page, and when they return the correct facet is displayed and the correct parameters are passed to that facet.

Listing 4.64 Dynamic Content Sample

```
<?xml version="1.0" encoding="UTF-8"?>
<xp:view xmlns:xp="http://www.ibm.com/xsp/core"
        xmlns:xe="http://www.ibm.com/xsp/coreex">
      <xe:dynamicContent id="dynamicContent1" defaultFacet="people"
            useHash="#{javascript:viewScope.useHash == 'true'}"
            partialEvents="true">
```

```
                <xp:this.facets>
                        <xp:panel xp:key="people">
                        [This facet contains a view of people]
                        </xp:panel>
                        <xp:panel xp:key="newPerson">
                        [This facet contains a form to create a new person]
                        </xp:panel>
                </xp:this.facets>
        </xe:dynamicContent>
        <xp:panel style="font-size:x-small;margin-top:2.0em">
                <xp:link text="Add Person" value="#content=newPerson"
                        title="Switch to newPerson facet using client-side
➥JavaScript">
                        <xp:eventHandler event="onclick" submit="false"
                                id="eventHandler3">
                                <xp:this.script><![CDATA[
XSP.showContent("#{id:dynamicContent1}","newPerson")
]]></xp:this.script>
                        </xp:eventHandler>
                </xp:link>
                <xp:label value=" | "></xp:label>
                <xp:link text="Add Person" value="#content=newPerson"
                        title="Switch to newPerson facet using server-side
➥JavaScript">
                        <xp:eventHandler event="onclick" submit="true"
                                refreshMode="partial"
refreshId="dynamicContent1"
                                id="eventHandler4">
                                <xp:this.action><![CDATA[
#{javascript:getComponent("dynamicContent1").show("newPerson")}
]]></xp:this.action>
                        </xp:eventHandler>
                </xp:link>
                <xp:label value=" | "></xp:label>
                <xp:link text="Add Person" value="#content=newPerson"
                title="Switch to newPerson facet using a server-side simple
➥action">
                <xp:eventHandler event="onclick" submit="true"
                                refreshMode="partial"
refreshId="dynamicContent1"
                                id="eventHandler5">
                                <xp:this.action>
                                        <xe:changeDynamicContentAction
                                                for="dynamicContent1"
                                                facetName="newPerson">
```

```
                                </xe:changeDynamicContentAction>
                            </xp:this.action>
                        </xp:eventHandler>
                </xp:link>
                <xp:br></xp:br>
                <xp:checkBox
text="Use Hash" id="checkBox1" value="#{viewScope.useHash}">
                </xp:checkBox>
        </xp:panel>
</xp:view>
```

The Dynamic Content container has proven to be tremendously useful and is now a widely adopted control in most XPages applications. As always, improvements are made based on feedback from the development community, and in 9.0.1 a new xsp.properties setting was introduced that allows you to fine-tune the behavior of the control. This modification aims to enable the Dynamic Content container to play well with web crawlers or bots—programs that systematically navigate websites and index their content for use by web search engines. In an XPages application, when the Dynamic Content control needs to swap facets, an AJAX request is used to dynamically fetch the content for the newly activated facet. Unfortunately, bots cannot execute JavaScript, so the AJAX requests used to fetch the facet content cannot be resolved; thus, the page information cannot be indexed for web search engines. As you can imagine, depending on the type of application you are building, this can be a big issue.

The solution has two fundamental requirements:

- XPages recognizes when a request originates from a bot and not a regular web user.
- The Dynamic Content control can issue either AJAX or plain old GET requests to retrieve facet content.

...the idea being that if XPages could distinguish between bots and humans, it would be possible to switch the mechanism used to retrieve facet content (from AJAX requests to regular GET requests). Identifying bots comes down to looking for well-known user agent signatures on the request sent to initiate an XPages session. There are several popular bots in common use that XPages supports by default, namely Google, Bing, and Yahoo!. You can control what and how bots are identified through Domino Designer by navigating to **Application Configuration > Xsp Properties > Page Generation** and using the newly added **Search Engine Robot User Agents** section, as shown in Figure 4.17.

The options referred to in Figure 4.17 use a new xsp.properties setting mentioned a little earlier. (You can see these property settings directly by selecting the **Source** pane.) This particular setting is defined as `xsp.search.bot.id.list` and is assigned a value of `<auto>` by default, which is a keyword representing the three bots that are automatically supported. You can add in support for other bots by using the Designer UI to add the user agent keyword or by simply manually adding the key word to the xsp.properties list directly. For example, the following setting in the xsp.properties file adds the Blekkobot web crawler to the list of supported bots:

```
xsp.search.bot.id.list=<auto>,blekkobot
```

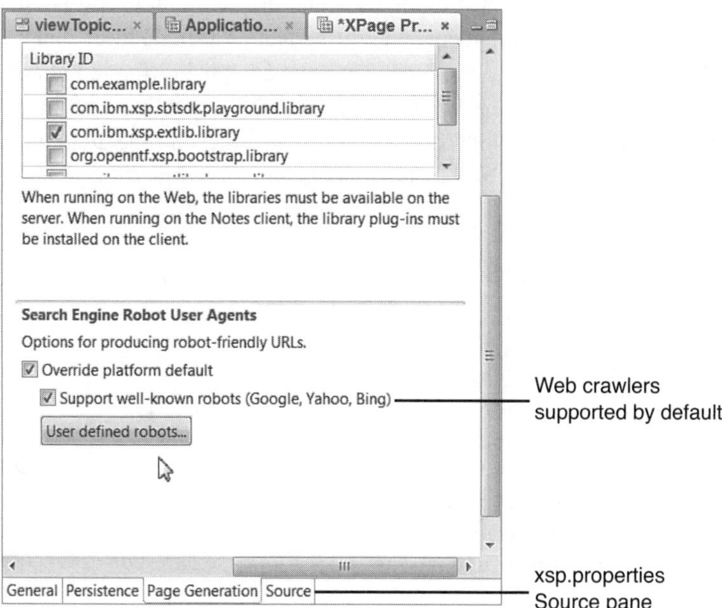

Figure 4.17 Designer Options to Identify Bots

This means that when a new XPages session is created that the user agent value in the request is inspected to see if it matches any of the supported bots. If it does, then a session variable is set to indicate that the user is in fact a bot, and the Dynamic Content control renderer adjusts its markup to generate *non*-AJAX URLs for each facet. Effectively, this means using '?' or '&' characters in the facet URLs in place of the '#' characters described earlier. The bot can then follow these web URLs and index the relevant content, whereas the human end user still has a completely dynamic experience. Also, because the agent detection is carried out just *once* when the session is initiated, performance impact to the end user is minimal.

It is possible to disable this feature completely by assigning an `<empty>` value to the xsp.properties setting, like this:

```
xsp.search.bot.id.list=<empty>
```

Change Dynamic Content Action

The Change Dynamic Content `xe:changeDynamicContentAction` tag represents a simple action that can be used to change the facet displayed in a Dynamic Content container. Listing 4.65 shows how to pass parameters from the Change Dynamic Content Action to the facet that is about to display. In this sample, a URL is passed to the facet and this allows it to display the correct photo. In this sample, the Dynamic Content container just contains a single facet, and we are using it to reload the content that is shown to the users. As users click the different buttons, the photo associated with the corresponding item is shown by reloading the dynamic content. The Dynamic Content container is configured with `useHash` to `true`, so each time a button is clicked, the URL is rewritten so that the page can be bookmarked and the correct image loads when users revisit the page.

Listing 4.65 Change Dynamic Content Action Sample

```
<?xml version="1.0" encoding="UTF-8"?>
<xp:view xmlns:xp="http://www.ibm.com/xsp/core"
➥xmlns:xe="http://www.ibm.com/xsp/coreex">
        <xe:dynamicContent id="dynamicContent1" defaultFacet="Image"
                partialEvents="true" useHash="true">
                <xp:this.facets>
                        <xp:panel xp:key="Image"
➥style="width:500px;text-align:center;">
                                <xp:image style="height:200px;width:200px">
                                        <xp:this.url>
<![CDATA[#{javascript:requestScope.get("photoUrl") || param.photoUrl}]]>
                                        </xp:this.url>
                                </xp:image>
                                <xp:br />
                                <xp:text escape="true" id="computedField1">
                                         <xp:this.value>
<![CDATA[#{javascript:"Photo Url: " + (requestScope.get("photoUrl" ||
➥param.photoUrl))}]]>
                                        </xp:this.value>
                                </xp:text>
                        </xp:panel>
                </xp:this.facets>
        </xe:dynamicContent>
        <xp:panel style="width:500px;text-align:center;">
                <xp:this.data>
                        <xp:dominoView var="view1" viewName="PeoplePhotos">
                        </xp:dominoView>
                </xp:this.data>
                <xp:repeat id="btnRepeat" rows="4" value="#{view1}"
➥var="row">
```

```
                    <xp:button value="#{row.personName}" id="button1">
                        <xp:eventHandler event="onclick" submit="true"
                            refreshMode="partial"
                            refreshId="dynamicContent1">
                            <xp:this.action>
                            <xe:changeDynamicContentAction
                                facetName="Image"
                                 for="dynamicContent1">
                                <xe:this.parameters>
                                <xp:parameter
                                    name="photoUrl"
                                    value="#{row.photoUrl}">
                                </xp:parameter>
                                </xe:this.parameters>
                            </xe:changeDynamicContentAction>
                            </xp:this.action>
                        </xp:eventHandler>
                    </xp:button>
                </xp:repeat>
        </xp:panel>
</xp:view>
```

Figure 4.18 shows where the facet name and a Change Dynamic Content Action parameter are encoded in the browser URL.

TIP

When running this sample, you need to access the sample page directly (and not via the IncludeSample.xsp page); that is, using a URL like this: http://localhost/chp04ed2.nsf/ChangeDynamicContentSample.xsp.

In Place Form

A further refinement on the use of dynamic content is to insert the dynamic content at the specific location within the current page. (If you get the sense that you are just scratching the surface of this control, you are correct. Many aspects of Dynamic Content are explored in more detail in Chapter 20, "Advanced Performance Topics." Look for the section titled "Using Dynamic Content.") A common use case for this pattern is in place editing; that is, the ability for the user to see a collection of entries and then edit the data for one of the entries. Typically, in place editing is used to support editing a subset of the data associated with an entry or even to add comments to an entry. The In Place Form `xe:inPlaceForm` tag can be used to perform this task. The In Place Form can be included anywhere in the page and by default will be hidden. You can use server-side JavaScript to toggle the In Place Form, and when it is displayed, the form contents are dynamically built and displayed within the page using a partial refresh of the overall page. Listing 4.66 shows a page that uses a Repeat control to display data from a view, and for each row a link is displayed, which is used to toggle the display of an In Place Form.

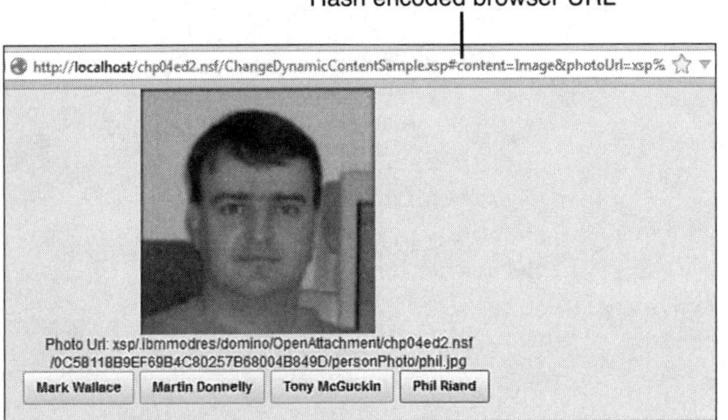

Figure 4.18 Encoding hash in browser URL

Listing 4.66 In Place Form Sample

```
<?xml version="1.0" encoding="UTF-8"?>
<xp:view xmlns:xp="http://www.ibm.com/xsp/core" xmlns:xe="http://www.ibm.
com/xsp/coreex">
        <xp:this.data>
                <xp:dominoView var="view1" viewName="PeoplePhotos">
</xp:dominoView>
        </xp:this.data>
        <xp:table id="table1">
                <xp:repeat id="repeat1" rows="30" value="#{view1}" var="row">
                        <xp:tr>
                                <xp:td>
                                        <xp:image url="#{row.photoUrl}">
                                        </xp:image>
                                </xp:td>
                                <xp:td>
                                        <h4>
                                                <xp:text value="#{row.
➥personName}">
                                                </xp:text>
```

```
                                    </h4>
                                    <xp:label value="Last Modified: ">
                                    </xp:label>
                                          <xp:text value="#{row.
➥lastModified}">
                                    </xp:text>
                                    <xp:label value=" | ">
                                    </xp:label>
                                    <xp:link text="Edit" id="editLink">
                                          <xp:eventHandler event="onclick"
                                                submit="true"
                                                refreshMode="partial"
                                                refreshId="inPlaceForm1">
                                                <xp:this.action>
      <![CDATA[#{javascript:getComponent("inPlaceForm1").toggle()}]]>
                                                </xp:this.action>
                                          </xp:eventHandler>
                                    </xp:link>
                              </xp:td>
                        </xp:tr>
                        <xp:tr>
                              <xp:td>
                              </xp:td>
                              <xp:td>
                                    [In Place Form Goes Here]
                              </xp:td>
                        </xp:tr>
                  </xp:repeat>
      </xp:table>
</xp:view>
```

Listing 4.67 shows the markup for the In Place Form. It is basically a panel with an associated document and the controls to edit some of the data associated with that document. When the document is saved, an additional action is triggered to hide the In Place Form.

Listing 4.67 In Place Form Sample

```
<?xml version="1.0" encoding="UTF-8"?>
...
<xe:inPlaceForm id="inPlaceForm1"
            partialEvents="true">
      <xp:panel style="font-size:x-small">
            <xp:this.data>
                  <xp:dominoDocument var="document1"
```

```
                        formName="PersonPhoto" action="editDocument"
                        documentId="#{javascript:row.getNoteID()}"
                        ignoreRequestParams="true">
                </xp:dominoDocument>
        </xp:this.data>
        <xp:table>
                <xp:tr>
                        <xp:td>
                                <xp:label value="Person name:"
                                        id="personName_Label1"
                                        for="personName1">
                                </xp:label>
                        </xp:td>
                        <xp:td>
                                <xp:inputText value="#{document1.
➥personName}"
                                        id="personName1">
                                </xp:inputText>
                        </xp:td>
                </xp:tr>
                <xp:tr>
                        <xp:td>
                        </xp:td>
                                <xp:td>
                <xp:link text="Save"      id="link2">
                        <xp:eventHandler event="onclick"
➥submit="true"
                                refreshMode="partial"
➥refreshId="table1">
                                <xp:this.action>
                                        <xp:actionGroup>
                                                <xp:saveDocument>
➥</xp:saveDocument>
                                                <xp:executeScript>
                                                        <xp:this.script>
                <![CDATA[#{javascript:getComponent(
➥"inPlaceForm1").hide()}]]>
                                                        </xp:this.script>
                                                </xp:executeScript>
                                        </xp:actionGroup>
                                </xp:this.action>
                        </xp:eventHandler>
                </xp:link>
                                </xp:td>
                        </xp:tr>
```

```
                    </xp:table>
              </xp:panel>
        </xe:inPlaceForm>
...
</xp:view>
```

Figure 4.19 shows an example where an In Place Form has been opened to edit the name for a person.

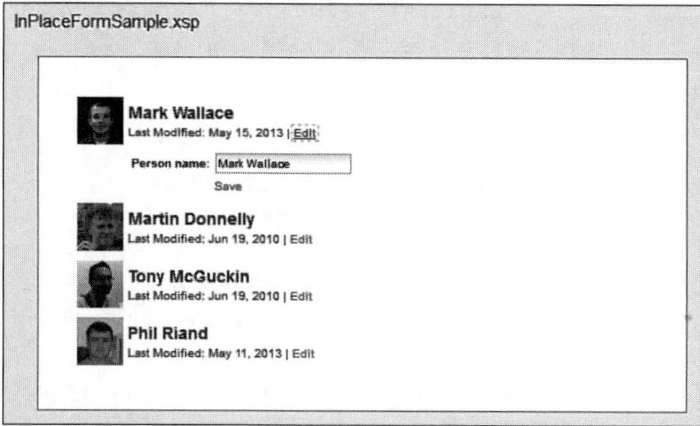

Figure 4.19 In Place Editing

Dialog, Dialog Context, and Dialog Button Bar

There are three containers provided to allow you to build modal dialogs. The dialog is displayed using the Dojo library, but it is recommended you use the XPages tags when you need to display a dialog. The XPages controls encapsulate the logic to make sure that the Dojo dialog plays well with the XPages processing model and also makes sure the code works well in the Notes Client. Listing 4.68 shows the section of the page that displays a table containing data from a Notes view. Each row contains a link that uses the client-side JavaScript XSP.openDialog to open a modal dialog. The client id of xe:dialog tag is used to identify the dialog to be opened.

Listing 4.68 Dialog Sample – Opening the Dialog

```
<?xml version="1.0" encoding="UTF-8"?>
<xp:view xmlns:xp="http://www.ibm.com/xsp/core" xmlns:xe="http://www.ibm.
com/xsp/coreex">
      <xp:this.data>
            <xp:dominoView var="view1" viewName="PeoplePhotos">
➥</xp:dominoView>
      </xp:this.data>
```

```
    <xp:table id="table1">
        <xp:repeat id="repeat1" rows="30" value="#{view1}" var="row">
            <xp:tr>
                <xp:td>
                    <xp:image url="#{row.photoUrl}"
                        style="height:40px;width:40px">
                    </xp:image>
                </xp:td>
                <xp:td>
                    <h4>
                        <xp:text value="#{row.personName}"
                    style="font-weight:bold;color:
➥rgb(0,64,128)">
                        </xp:text>
                    </h4>
                    <xp:label value="Last Modified: "
                        style="font-size:x-small">
                    </xp:label>
                    <xp:text value="#{row.lastModified}"
                        style="font-size:x-small">
                    </xp:text>
                    <xp:label value=" | " style="font-size:x-
➥small">
                    </xp:label>
                    <xp:link id="editLink" text="Edit"
                        style="font-size:x-small">
                        <xp:eventHandler
                            event="onclick"
➥submit="false">
                            <xp:this.script>
    <![CDATA[XSP.openDialog('#{id:inPlaceDialog1}')]]>
                            </xp:this.script>
                        </xp:eventHandler>
                    </xp:link>
                </xp:td>
            </xp:tr>
            <xp:tr>
                <xp:td>
                [Dialog Goes Here]
                </xp:td>
            </xp:tr>
        </xp:repeat>
    </xp:table>
</xp:view>
```

Listing 4.69 shows the xe:dialog container that includes the xe:dialogContent tag and the xe:dialogButtonBar tag. The dialog content contains the body for the dialog; that is, the content between the title and button bar. The dialog button bar contains the dialog buttons, which will typically be OK and Cancel actions. Each of these actions needs to close the dialog, which can be done using server-side, as shown in Listing 4.69, or client-side JavaScript using the XSP.closeDialog method.

Listing 4.69 Dialog Sample – xe:dialog Tag

```
<?xml version="1.0" encoding="UTF-8"?>
...
<xe:dialog id="inPlaceDialog1" title="Edit Person Name">
        <xp:panel>
                <xp:this.data>
                        <xp:dominoDocument var="document1"
➥formName="PersonPhoto"
                                action="editDocument"
                                documentId="#{javascript:row.getNoteID()}"
                                ignoreRequestParams="true">
                        </xp:dominoDocument>
                </xp:this.data>
                <xe:dialogContent>
                        <xp:table>
                                <xp:tr>
                                        <xp:td>
                                                <xp:label value="Person name:"
                                                        id="personName_Label1"
                                                        for="personName1">
                                                </xp:label>
                                        </xp:td>
                                        <xp:td>
                                                <xp:inputText
                                                      value="#{document1.
➥personName}"
                                                        id="personName1">
                                                </xp:inputText>
                                        </xp:td>
                                </xp:tr>
                        </xp:table>
                </xe:dialogContent>
                <xe:dialogButtonBar>
                        <xp:button value="OK" id="button1"
                                  styleClass="lotusFormButton">
                                <xp:eventHandler event="onclick" submit="true"
```

```
                                        refreshMode="partial"
➥refreshId="table1">
                                        <xp:this.action>
                                              <xp:actionGroup>
                                                    <xp:saveDocument>
➥</xp:saveDocument>
                                                    <xp:executeScript>
                                                          <xp:this.script>
     <![CDATA[#{javascript:getComponent("inPlaceDialog1").
➥hide("table1")}]]>
                                                          </xp:this.script>
                                                    </xp:executeScript>
                                              </xp:actionGroup>
                                        </xp:this.action>
                                  </xp:eventHandler>
                            </xp:button>
                            <xp:link id="button2" text="Cancel"
➥styleClass="lotusAction">
                                  <xp:eventHandler event="onclick" submit="true"
                                        immediate="true">
                                        <xp:this.action>
                                              <xp:actionGroup>
                                                    <xp:executeScript>
                                                          <xp:this.script>
     <![CDATA[#{javascript:getComponent("inPlaceDialog1").hide()}]]>
                                                          </xp:this.script>
                                                    </xp:executeScript>
                                              </xp:actionGroup>
                                        </xp:this.action>
                                  </xp:eventHandler>
                            </xp:link>
                      </xe:dialogButtonBar>
     </xp:panel>
</xe:dialog>
...
</xp:view>
```

Figure 4.20 shows the resulting dialog opened to edit the content for a specific row.

Tooltip Dialog

The tooltip dialog combines tooltip and dialog behavior and allows you to present a nonmodal dialog and anchor it on another control within the page. Because it is anchored, you cannot drag it around the page, but it does allow you to associate the dialog with part of the main page. This is a useful pattern if you want to allow editing of different parts of data in isolation and without overwhelming users with a complex form. Listing 4.70 shows a tooltip dialog that uses a HTML table to lay out the content.

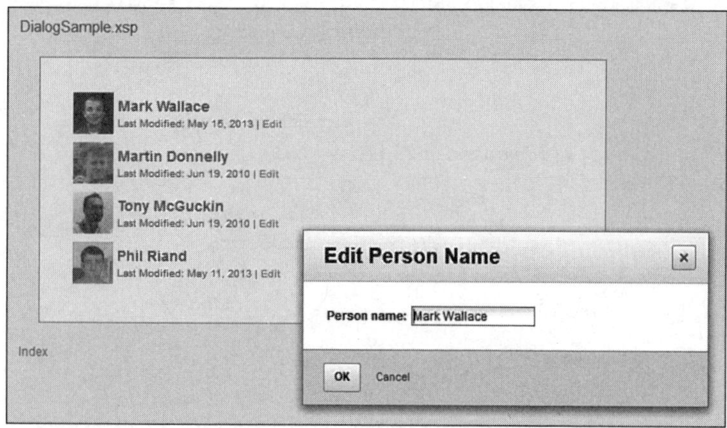

Figure 4.20 Modal Dialog

Listing 4.70 Tooltip Dialog Sample

```
<?xml version="1.0" encoding="UTF-8"?>
<xp:view xmlns:xp="http://www.ibm.com/xsp/core" xmlns:xe="http://www.ibm.
com/xsp/coreex">
        <xp:this.data>
                <xp:dominoView var="view1" viewName="PeoplePhotos">
</xp:dominoView>
        </xp:this.data>
        <xp:table id="table1">
                <xp:repeat id="repeat1" rows="30" value="#{view1}" var="row">
                        <xp:tr>
                                <xp:td>
                                        <xp:image url="#{row.photoUrl}">
                                        </xp:image>
                                </xp:td>
                                <xp:td>
                                        <h4>
                                                <xp:text value="#{row.
➥personName}">
                                                </xp:text>
                                        </h4>
                                        <xp:label value="Last Modified: ">
                                        </xp:label>
```

```
                                        <xp:text value="#{row.lastModified}">
➥</xp:text>
                                        <xp:label value=" | "></xp:label>
                                        <xp:link id="editLink" text="Edit">
                                              <xp:eventHandler
                                                    event="onclick"
➥submit="false">
                                                    <xp:this.script>
<![CDATA[XSP.openTooltipDialog('#{id:tooltipDialog1}',
➥'#{id:computedField1}')]]>
                                                    </xp:this.script>
                                              </xp:eventHandler>
                                        </xp:link>
                                  </xp:td>
                            </xp:tr>
                            <xp:tr>
                                  <xp:td>
                                        <xe:tooltipDialog id="tooltipDialog1"
                                                    title="Edit Person
➥Name">
                                              [Dialog Content Goes Here]
                                        </xe:tooltipDialog>
                                  </xp:td>
                            </xp:tr>
                      </xp:repeat>
                </xp:table>
 </xp:view>
```

Listing 4.71 shows the Tooltip Dialog that uses the Dialog Content and Dialog Button Bar. The logic to close the dialog is the same as for the normal dialog case.

Listing 4.71 Tooltip Dialog Content

```
<?xml version="1.0" encoding="UTF-8"?>
...
<xe:tooltipDialog id="tooltipDialog1" title="Edit Person Name">
      <xp:panel>
            <xe:dialogContent>
                  [Dialog Content Goes Here]
            </xe:dialogContent>
            <xe:dialogButtonBar>
                  <xp:button value="OK" id="button1">
```

```
                                <xp:eventHandler event="onclick" submit="true"
                                            refreshMode="partial"
➥refreshId="table1">
                                      <xp:this.action>
                                            <xp:actionGroup>
                                                  <xp:saveDocument>
➥</xp:saveDocument>
                                                  <xp:executeScript>
                                                        <xp:this.script>
      <![CDATA[#{javascript:getComponent("tooltipDialog1").
➥hide("table1")}]]>
                                                        </xp:this.script>
                                                  </xp:executeScript>
                                            </xp:actionGroup>
                                      </xp:this.action>
                                </xp:eventHandler>
                          </xp:button>
                          <xp:link id="button2" text="Cancel"
➥styleClass="lotusAction">
                                <xp:eventHandler event="onclick" submit="true"
                                      immediate="true">
                                      <xp:this.action>
                                            <xp:actionGroup>
                                                  <xp:executeScript>
                                                        <xp:this.script>
      <![CDATA[#{javascript:getComponent("tooltipDialog1").hide()}]]>
                                                        </xp:this.script>
                                                  </xp:executeScript>
                                            </xp:actionGroup>
                                      </xp:this.action>
                                </xp:eventHandler>
                          </xp:link>
                    </xe:dialogButtonBar>
      </xp:panel>
</xe:tooltipDialog>
...
 </xp:view>
```

Figure 4.21 shows the resulting dialog opened to edit the content for a specific row and anchored to a control within the row.

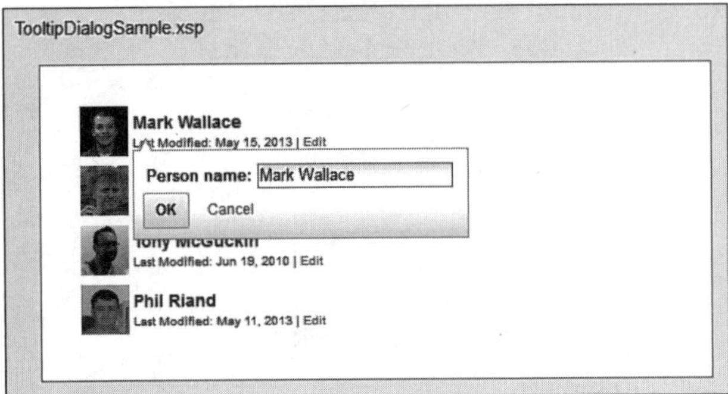

Figure 4.21 Tooltip Dialog

JSON RPC Service (Remote Service)

The final dynamic pattern you're going to look at is how to dynamically invoke server-side logic from the client. Listing 4.72 shows the JSON RPC Service `xp:jsonRpcService` tag used to define a client-side JavaScript API to allow access to a managed bean. The JSON RPC Service defines a new service named Book that has getTitle, getAuthors, getISBN, getAuthorCount, and getAuthor methods. These methods correspond to equivalent methods on the managed bean, and when you call these methods from client-side Javascript, the equivalent method on the managed bean is invoked and its return value is returned. What happens when you call one of the remote methods is that an XML Http Request is issued to the server, which will result in invoking the server-side JavaScript associated with the method. Because of the asynchronous nature of the remote call, the client-side JavaScript must create a callback function, which will be invoked when the result is available. Listing 4.72 shows that the getAuthorCount method is invoked followed by multiple calls to the getAuthor method. The order in which the authors are returned will change, which is caused by the asynchronous nature of the calls. You must exercise caution when using asynchronous calls because the thread of execution changes and assumptions about parameter values may not be valid. Chapter 6, "Building XPages Application Logic," includes further samples using the JSON RPC Service.

Listing 4.72 JSON RPC Service Sample

```
<?xml version="1.0" encoding="UTF-8"?>
<xp:view xmlns:xp="http://www.ibm.com/xsp/core"
xmlns:xe="http://www.ibm.com/xsp/coreex">
	<xe:jsonRpcService id="jsonRpcService1" serviceName="Book"
		state="false">
		<xe:this.methods>
```

```
                    <xe:remoteMethod name="getTitle">
                        <xe:this.script><![CDATA[return bookBean.
➥getTitle();]]>
                        </xe:this.script>
                    </xe:remoteMethod>
                    <xe:remoteMethod name="getAuthors">
                        <xe:this.script>
                        <![CDATA[return bookBean.getAuthors();]]>
                        </xe:this.script>
                    </xe:remoteMethod>
                    <xe:remoteMethod name="getISBN">
                        <xe:this.script><![CDATA[return bookBean.
➥getIsbn();]]>
                        </xe:this.script>
                    </xe:remoteMethod>
                    <xe:remoteMethod name="getAuthorCount">
                        <xe:this.script>
                        <![CDATA[return bookBean.getAuthorCount();]]>
                        </xe:this.script>
                    </xe:remoteMethod>
                    <xe:remoteMethod name="getAuthor">
                        <xe:this.arguments>
                            <xe:remoteMethodArg name="index"
➥type="number">
                            </xe:remoteMethodArg>
                        </xe:this.arguments>
                        <xe:this.script>
                        <![CDATA[return bookBean.getAuthor(index);]]>
                        </xe:this.script>
                    </xe:remoteMethod>
                </xe:this.methods>
        </xe:jsonRpcService>
        <xp:button value="Get Title" id="button1" style="font-size:x-small">
            <xp:eventHandler event="onclick" submit="false">
                <xp:this.script>
<![CDATA[var deferred = Book.getTitle();
deferred.addCallback(function(title) {
        alert(title);
});]]>
                </xp:this.script>
            </xp:eventHandler>
        </xp:button>
        <xp:button value="Get Authors" id="button2" style="font-size:
➥x-small">
            <xp:eventHandler event="onclick" submit="false">
```

```
                    <xp:this.script>
<![CDATA[var deferred = Book.getAuthorCount();
deferred.addCallback(function(count) {
        for (var i=0; i<count; i++) {
                Book.getAuthor(i).addCallback(function (author) {
                        alert(author);
                });
        }
});]]>
                    </xp:this.script>
                </xp:eventHandler>
        </xp:button>
</xp:view>
```

Conclusion

This concludes your lesson on the basics of the XSP language. Don't worry if you haven't fully mastered all the tags covered; at this point, the important thing is to look at the source for a simple XPage (like the samples provided in this chapter) and to read the source and begin to understand what the page will do. Being able to use source mode to read and write XSP is a key skill that you need to master XPages and the XSP programming language. In the next chapter, XPages is explored at a deeper level, and you learn about its JSF foundations. If you want to stick with pure XPages programming for now, feel free to temporarily skip the next chapter. But, you are strongly urged to read at least the section on the JSF processing model in the next chapter before moving on, because it provides some critical insight into how XPages are processed on the server.

CHAPTER 5

XPages and JavaServer Faces

As mentioned in the beginning of this book, XPages evolved from a previous runtime technology called XFaces. XFaces was conceived as a way for IBM to provide a universal user-interface programming model that could be adopted across its diverse portfolio of application development platforms. As a runtime technology, it needed to cater to developers of differing skill sets, such as Java/J2EE developers, Domino developers, and so forth. These categorizations are not mutually exclusive, and many organizations contain developers with both sets of skills who might be working on the same projects. In fact, many such developers want to choose which tools to use based on the task they need to accomplish at any given time. (For example, they might need to rapidly create a user interface using a WYSIWYG tool and then switch to using Java to add some complex application logic.)

What IBM set out to achieve with XFaces was to define a programming model that would be suitable for a so-called script-level developer, such as someone who knows how to program using a markup language and JavaScript. This programming model was intended to allow developers to target multiple platforms, such as web and the Eclipse Rich Client Platform (RCP). Also, this programming model was based on the JavaServer Faces (JSF) standard-based web application development framework. Achieving this goal would provide the following benefits to application developers:

- **Learn Once, Write Anywhere:** Developers need only learn one model for development across these platforms. The model must be flexible and powerful to allow programmers to fully exploit and optimize the UI for any particular platform.
- **Write Once, Run Anywhere™:** Developers can create a single set of artifacts that can run across multiple platforms.
- **Provide a script-based programming model:** A model that would be familiar for developers with a Domino Designer (or similar) and dynamic HTML programming background (no Java skills required).

- **Allow artifacts to be shared between Java and Script developers who work on the same project:** For example, script developers create the frontend user interface and Java developers create the backend application logic.
- **Flexibility:** Allows developers to use the most appropriate tool for the task they perform.

As XFaces morphed into XPages, these design points were all retained. This chapter examines the relationship between XPages and JSF. Although one of the goals in XPages is to hide all the Java and J2EE-centric aspects of the JSF programming model, having an understanding of the underlying technology is a major asset for any XPages developer. By understanding how JSF works, and especially the workings of the JSF lifecycle, you learn how your XPages are processed as your application executes. This helps understanding why your application behaves in a particular fashion. Also, both XPages and JSF are designed to be extended. For the Domino Developer, you are no longer restricted to what is provided within the platform as delivered by IBM; it's now possible to extend the platform either to solve a particular problem or as a way to start a new business. Please refer to Chapter 12, "XPages Extensibility," for more information on the options available to extend the XPages runtime.

This chapter is aimed at developers who are interested in extending the XPages runtime using Java by creating new XSP components or developers who are coming from a J2EE background and want to understand how XPages extends JavaServer Faces. This chapter uses the standard JSF terminology when explaining how JSF works and the relationship between JSF and XPages. In JSF parlance, a component is a UI element or what has been previously referred to as a UI control (an edit box or button). JSF uses the terms view and component tree interchangeably. XPages also uses view (remember the root tag of every XPage is the `xp:view` tag) and an XPages' view is, in fact, a component tree. Knowing this means the working definition of XPages can be extended to this: XPages is an XML-based language that can be used to define JSF views, and an XPage is a static representation of a JSF component tree.

Be sure to download the **Chp05Ed2.nsf** files provided online for this book to run through the exercises throughout this chapter. You can access these files at `www.ibmpressbooks.com/title/9780133373370`.

What Is JavaServer Faces?

JSF is a component-based, user interface framework for building Java-based web applications. The framework provides the following capabilities:

- A set of reusable user-interface components that can be used to easily create an application frontend or can be used as the starting point to create new custom user interface components
- A Model-View-Controller (MVC) programming model that supports event-driven programming

- A state-full server representation of the user interface that can be synchronized with the client representation
- A mechanism to allow data flow to and from the user interface, including the capability to perform data conversion and data validation
- A framework that can be extended using Java programming techniques

Using the JSF framework as the starting point when creating a web application frees the application developer from having to deal with the stateless nature of HTTP—without the use of a framework, no application state is maintained on the server between requests. The developer can create the required user interface using the standard UI components (a.k.a controls) provided by JSF. Then, the developer can bind these controls to the application data (in the form of Java beans) and then trigger server-side application logic in response to user actions on the application user interface. A Java bean is a reusable Java-based software component (see `http://docs.oracle.com/javase/tutorial/javabeans/` for more details). This type of programming model is familiar to developers of rich client-based applications using technologies such as the Standard Widget Toolkit (SWT); however, at the time JSF was introduced, it was pretty much a new concept for web developers.

The following JSF Primer sidebar provides a basic introduction to JSF and is written with the assumption that you have no knowledge of Java2 Enterprise Edition (J2EE). The relevant J2EE concepts are briefly explained in this sidebar. The JSF lifecycle is also explained in the sidebar; this is a key concept that all XPages developers should understand. For a detailed look at the JSF technology, the authors recommend the following resources:

- JavaServer Faces Specification, version 1.1 (`http://docs.oracle.com/cd/E17802_01/j2ee/j2ee/javaserverfaces/1.1/docs/api/`)
- *JavaServer Faces* (O'Reilly)
- *Mastering JavaServer Faces* (Wiley)

JSF Primer

To run a JSF-based application, you need a Java web container, such as an Apache Tomcat server, and an implementation of the JSF specification. A Java web container is a Java-based server for running Java web applications. JSF 1.1 (which is the version used in the XPages runtime) requires a web container that implements, at a minimum, the Servlet 2.3 and JavaServer Pages 1.2 specifications. (XPages requires support for the Servlet 2.4 specification.) IBM WebSphere Application Server (WAS) and Portal Server support the Servlet and JSP specifications.

A servlet is a Java class that runs in the web container, processes client requests, and generates responses. A servlet is passed parameters that represent the request and response and, in simple cases, all the processing logic can be included within the servlet. Typically, a servlet is defined as the entry point or front controller for a web application. A servlet typically delegates to request handlers to process the client requests and a presentation tier to generate the responses. Listing 5.1 shows the source code for a simple HTTP servlet. This servlet handles an HTTP GET request and responds with a HTML page that displays the text Hello World. The code to handle the request has access to a request object, which can be used to retrieve information about the request being processed and a response object, which can be used to write the response that is returned to the client.

Listing 5.1 Sample HTTP Servlet

```
package mxp.chap05;

import java.io.IOException;
import java.io.PrintWriter;

import javax.servlet.ServletException;
import javax.servlet.http.HttpServlet;
import javax.servlet.http.HttpServletRequest;
import javax.servlet.http.HttpServletResponse;

/**
 * Sample Servlet
 */
public class SampleServlet extends HttpServlet {

      /**
       * Handle a HTTP GET request.
       */
      protected void doGet(HttpServletRequest request,
                           HttpServletResponse response)
                 throws ServletException, IOException {

        response.setContentType("text/html");
        PrintWriter out = response.getWriter();

        out.println("<HTML>");
        out.println("<HEAD>");
        out.println("<TITLE>Hello World</TITLE>");
        out.println("</HEAD>");
        out.println("<BODY>");
        out.println("Hello World");
        out.println("</BODY>");
        out.println("</HTML>");
      }
}
```

JavaServer Pages (JSP) is a presentation logic layer that can generate HTML pages in response to client requests. A JSP page looks like a HTML page, but it contains a mix of static HTML and JSP directives, which can be used to generate dynamic content or performing some processing associated with generating the client response. JSP uses tag libraries to allow special tags to be declared, which can then be invoked by the JSP engine. A JSP implementation comes with a standard tag library called the JavaServer Pages Standard Tag Library (JSTL).

Listing 5.2 shows a sample JSP page that uses the JSF tag library to embed JSF components within an HTML page. Based on what you have learned so far about XSP markup, this sample should be readable. It contains a mix of HTML and JSF tags. The JSF tags cause JSF components to be created and results in a HTML form being created, which contains an edit box that can be used to enter a value and a button that can be used to submit the form.

Listing 5.2 Sample JSP with JSF Tags

```
<%@ taglib uri="http://java.sun.com/jsf/html" prefix="h" %>
<%@ taglib uri="http://java.sun.com/jsf/core" prefix="f" %>
<BODY>
  <f:view>
    <h:form id="form1">
      Enter some value:
      <h:inputText
          id="inputText1" value="#{ModelBean.someValue}"/>
      <h:commandButton
          id="commandButton1" action="success" value="Submit"/>
    </h:form>
  </f:view>
</BODY>
```

JSP is the default presentation tier used by the JSF reference implementation. The presentation tier is the layer in an application framework that is responsible for displaying the application data in a human-readable format. The presentation tier defines the JSF component tree (also known as the JSF view), which is the hierarchy of controls that is presented in the user interface. A typical starting point for a JSF-based application is where a user requests a JSP, such as typing a URL like this into a browser:

```
http://somehost/jsfapp/somepage.jsp
```

This causes the JSP engine to load and execute the specified JSP. If this page contains JSF components (using the standard JSF tag library), a JSF component tree is also created in addition to the regular JSP processing (the JSF tags are responsible for creating the JSF component tree). The JSF components generate the HTML markup that is presented to the user and the view is cached for the user (see section 2.1.1 of the JSF 1.1. specification, "Non-Faces Request Generates Faces Response").

Now, if the same page is submitted back to the server, it is handled by the JSF servlet. This servlet is part of the JSF implementation and acts as a front controller for all JSF-based applications. JSF requests are processed in accordance with the rules defined by the JSF request processing lifecycle. The JSF request processing lifecycle consists of a number of well-defined phases that describe how each request is handled and, of course, these phases also apply to XPages. The phases on the standard request processing lifecycle are as follows:

1. Restore View
2. Apply Request Values
3. Process Validations
4. Update Model Values
5. Invoke Application
6. Render Response

Figure 5.1 illustrates how the processing lifecycle operates.

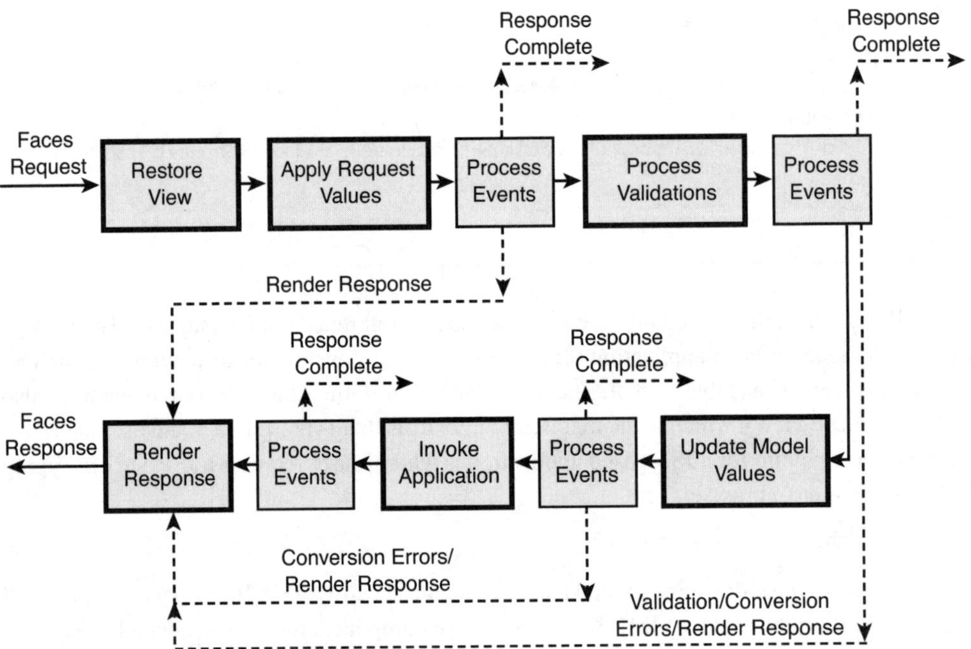

Figure 5.1 JSF request processing lifecycle

The *Restore View* phase retrieves the JSF view for the request. If no JSF view exists, a new one is created and cached for later use. Maintaining a consistent representation of the JSF view between requests simplifies the programming task for the application developer by simplifying the application logic to focus on the business problem and not having to maintain information about the state of the view.

The *Apply Request Values* phase is used to allow the JSF components to update their state based on the values from the current request; for example, if the component represents an editable value, the component stores the current value. Action and editable components have a special behavior during this phase. If the component `immediate` property is set to `true`, the JSF lifecyle is short circuited. For an action component, the action processing happens at the end of this phase instead of during the lifecycle. For an editable component, the validation processing happens immediately.

The *Process Validations* phase allows any validators associated with components in the view and any built-in server side validation associated with a specific component to be executed. All components that can be used to edit a value and support validation, have an associated property (aptly named `valid`) to indicate whether the current value is valid. When validation errors occur, messages are queued and the `valid` property of the associated component is set to `false`. Validation error messages can be displayed to the end user using the `xp:message` or `xp:messages` tags as described in Chapter 4, "Anatomy of an XPage." Validation errors typically cause the lifecycle processing to terminate and result in a response being immediately sent back to the end user.

If the *Update Model Values* phase is reached, it is assumed that the values provided in the request are valid (as defined by any validators specified in the view). The current values are stored in the `localValue` property of the associated component. During this phase, the application data is updated with the new values. In the case of an XPages application, the values are written to the Domino document during this phase.

If the *Invoke Application* phase is reached, it is assumed that the application data has been updated. The relevant application logic specified in the view is executed during this phase. In an XPages application, if application logic is associated with a button and that button caused the page to be submitted, it is now that the logic is executed.

The *Render Response* phase generates the response and saves the state of the view. In the XPages case, the response is an HTML page and the rendering is performed using a platform-specific renderkits, and the application developer has control over the state saving (for example, to optimize server performance, he can decide not to save any state). The JSF response rendering model is flexible and is discussed further.

From Figure 5.1, you see that, after certain phases, there is an event-processing operation that can result in the lifecycle being short circuited and the response being rendered. This typically happens if there is a conversion or validation error, which means that data specified by the end user is not valid, so it doesn't make sense to update the application data or to execute any application logic.

Numerous other key concepts in JSF are important to understand before looking at how XPages builds on top of this foundation:

1. Integration with JSP
2. User Interface Component Model
3. Value Binding and Method Binding Expression Evaluation
4. Per-Request State Model
5. Application Integration
6. Rendering Model
7. JSF APIs

JSF implementations must support JSP as the page-description language (the mechanism for defining the JSF component tree). This allows J2EE developers to start creating JSF-based applications using a well-known technology. When JSF tags are added to a JSP page, they cause the JSF component tree to be created when the page is executed.

A JSF user interface is created as a tree of components (known as *controls* in XPages). Components typically are rendered to the user as HTML markup, which produces the application interface. However, not all components render as visual elements in the UI; they can render no markup or just client-side JavaScript and thereby add behavior to the UI. Components can be manipulated on the server, and this can result in changes to the application UI (the Button sample in Chapter 4 shows an example of this). Components can have different types, such as have the ability to trigger application logic, can be a container for other components, can have an associated value, or can edit its associated value. A well-defined data conversion model associated with components allows application data to be converted between the underlying data types and string values and back again. This is essential as data is going to be represented as string values in the HTML markup. There is also a well-defined validation model that allows multiple checks to be performed on user input and prevents application logic executing on invalid data. JSF implementations provide a standard set of user interface components, and these form the basis for the controls you can add to an XPage. Finally, a standard set of data model classes can be used with the standard controls; refer to the JSF Java documentation for the `javax.faces.model` package for more information.

Binding expressions are how application logic and data binding is performed in JSF. Value bindings are used when you need to compute a component property or when you want to bind application data to a component for display and\or editing. JSF uses Expression Language (EL) to specify value binding expressions. EL is fully defined in the JavaServer Pages specification (version 2.0) and the JSF usage only differs in the delimiters used, such as `#{` and `}` instead of `${` and `}` and the fact that EL functions are not supported. EL can be used in XPages applications, as demonstrated in examples in Chapter 4.

Method-binding expressions are a variation on value bindings where parameters can be passed to the method being invoked and the result can be returned. Method bindings invoke application logic, which in JSF applications is code in Java. XPages additionally supports application logic written in JavaScript. JSF supports an extensible mechanism for resolving binding expression variables and properties. By default, JSF supports Java beans-based property resolution and a well-defined set of variables. This Java-centric approach has been extended in XPages to better support the use of JavaScript and Domino.

During the JSF request processing lifecycle, the request state is represented by a set of JSF objects, such as `FacesContext`, `FacesMessage`, `ResponseStream`, `ResponseWriter`, and `FacesContextFactory`. JSF provides a mechanism to allow built-in request related objects to be available during request processing.

The JSF programming model is Java-based, and there is a well-defined model for the execution of the JSF-based application. XPages provides a dynamic HTML-like programming model (combination of JavaScript and Markup Language) on top of JSF. This can be achieved because JSF provides an extensible mechanism to modify the execution of a JSF application. The application integration APIs in JSF provide access to modify the behavior of how JSF-based applications are executed.

During the execution of a JSF request, the incoming request values need to be decoded at the start of the lifecycle during the *Apply Request Values* phase and subsequently encoded when the response is generated. JSF allows each component to handle the decoding and encoding processes directly. One disadvantage with this approach is that it can tie a component to a particular platform or rendering technology, such as a component that decodes HTTP requests and encodes HTML responses that can't be used with a VoiceML client. To address this problem, JSF supports a model where each component can delegate the encoding and decoding processes to an associated *renderer*. Now, different renderer implementations can be provided for different client types, and JSF provides a simple mechanism to group these renders into a *renderkit* along with the ability to switch between renderkits. This keeps the components platform independent. JSF provides a default HTML renderkit.

The JSF reference implementation comes in two parts:

1. JSF API
2. JSF Implementation

The JSF API is a Java API that consists of interfaces and abstract classes that define the abstractions that make up the JSF engine. JSF allows key parts of the implementation to be extended while still preserving the default behavior. This is achieved by means of a delegation model, where the new extension has the option to execute first and then delegate to the default implementation when appropriate. The JSF API provides abstract Java classes for the modules, which can be extended. JSF also has an XML configuration file format and a mechanism for loading multiple instances of this file. To override a module in the JSF engine, you need to provide your custom implementation and a Faces configuration XML file that specifies that your implementation should be loaded and used instead of the default one. Consider the following quote from the JavaServer Faces specification:

> "JSF's core architecture is designed to be independent of specific protocols and markup. However it is also aimed directly at solving many of the common problems encountered when writing applications for HTML clients that communicate via HTTP to a Java application server that supports servlets and JavaServer Pages (JSP) based applications."

Although JSF is Java-centric and J2EE-based, the API provides sufficient flexibility to allow the JSF framework to be used in other contexts. So, it is possible to create a non Java-centric programming model on top of JSF and still maintain the benefits of providing a standards-based solution, and this is what has been achieved in XPages.

How Does XPages Extend JSF?

As previously mentioned, JSF provides a delegation model whereby key modules in the JSF engine can be replaced. To do this, you need to create your own Java class that extends the base class, which defines the module you want to extend. This class must have a constructor that takes a single argument, which is an instance of the class defining the module you are extending. A concrete example of this would be the custom variable resolver that is provided in XPages. The default variable resolver in JSF provides access to a number of built-in variables (see Table 5.1).

Table 5.1 JSF Default Variables

Name	Value
`applicationScope`	Map containing the application scope values
`cookie`	Map containing the cookies for the current request
`facesContext`	The `FacesContext` instance for the current request
`header`	Map containing the HTTP header values for the current request
`headerValues`	Map containing arrays that contain the header values for the HTTP headers for the current request
`initParam`	Map containing the initialization parameters for the web application
`param`	Map containing the request parameters for the current request
`paramValues`	Map containing arrays that contain the parameter values for request parameters for the current request
`requestScope`	Map containing the request attributes for the current request
`sessionScope`	Map containing the session attributes for the current request
`view`	UIViewRoot of the current component tree

XPages extends these variables to include some additional ones, which are relevant for a Domino application developer, such as the current database. JSF provides a pluggable mechanism to allow what is called a *variable resolver* to be configured for a JSF application. This variable resolver must provide the default behavior as defined in the JSF specification but can provide additional functionality. To do this, the following two steps are required:

1. An implementation of `javax.faces.el.VariableResolver` must be provided. It either must implement the default behavior or else delegate to the default implementation.
2. The `faces-config.xml` file for the JSF application must be edited to specify the new variable resolver implementation.

The `faces-config.xml` file is the main configuration file for a JSF-based application. It is used to configure the behavior of the application and the JSF runtime. You need to switch to the Java perspective in Domino Designer to perform both of these steps. The `faces-config.xml` file is located in the `\WebContent\WEB-INF` folder. Starting in Domino Designer 9.0, you can show the `faces-config.xml` file in the Applications navigator by editing the Domino Designer navigator preferences.

Listing 5.3 shows the Java code for a variable resolver, which adds support for an additional variable called "magic," which resolves to a string value "Abracadabra." This class provides a constructor that takes a single variable, which is an instance of `VariableResolver`; this delegate provides the default behavior. The custom implementation can delegate to this and still provide the default behavior and be compliant with the JSF specification.

Listing 5.3 Sample Variable Resolver

```
package mxp.chap05;


import javax.faces.context.FacesContext;
import javax.faces.el.EvaluationException;
import javax.faces.el.VariableResolver;

/**
 * Sample variable resolver
 */
public class SampleVariableResolver extends VariableResolver {

	private VariableResolver delegate;

	/**
	 * Constructor which takes delegate VariableResolver
	 */
	public SampleVariableResolver(VariableResolver resolver) {
		delegate = resolver;
	}
```

```
    /**
     * Return the object associated with the specified variable name.
     */
    public Object resolveVariable(FacesContext context, String name)
                throws EvaluationException {
            if ("magic".equals(name)) {
                    return "Abracadabra";
            }
            return delegate.resolveVariable(context, name);
    }
}
```

To get this instance to load, an entry must be added to the `faces-config.xml` specifying that this class as the variable resolver. Listing 5.4 shows what this entry looks like in the `faces-config.xml`.

Listing 5.4 Variable Resolver Configuration

```
<?xml version="1.0" encoding="UTF-8"?>
<faces-config>
  <application><variable-resolver>
       mxp.chap05.SampleVariableResolver
    </variable-resolver>
  </application>
  <!--AUTOGEN-START-BUILDER: Automatically generated by IBM Lotus Domino
Designer. Do not modify.-->
  <!--AUTOGEN-END-BUILDER: End of automatically generated section-->
</faces-config>
```

After these two changes are made, you can now reference the "magic" variable from the `SampleVariableResolver` XPage. Listing 5.5 shows the XSP markup that contains Computed Fields that reference the new "magic" variable.

Listing 5.5 Variable Resolver Sample XPage

```
<?xml version="1.0" encoding="UTF-8"?>
<xp:view xmlns:xp="http://www.ibm.com/xsp/core">
      <xp:text escape="true" id="computedField1" value="#{magic}">
      </xp:text>
</xp:view>
```

When you preview this page, you see the results illustrated in Figure 5.2.

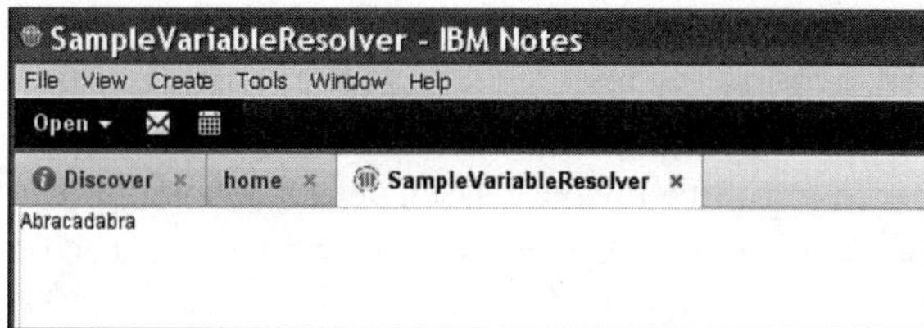

Figure 5.2 Variable resolver sample preview

XML-Based Presentation Tier

As mentioned earlier, the default presentation tier in JSF version 1.1 is JSP. There are well-known issues with using JSP and JSF, but the biggest hurdle from the Domino developer perspective is that JSP is a Java-based technology, and not all Domino developers are familiar with Java. Domino developers are, however, familiar with creating HTML markup and, therefore, it was decided to create a new markup-based presentation for JSF. Additionally, JSF developers use the `faces-config.xml` file to configure certain aspects of their application, such as navigation rules and managed beans. In designing the new presentation tier, it was decided to allow the developer to perform most of the application configuration within the XPage itself including page navigation, the configuration of data sources, and the inclusion of application logic. This new presentation tier became the XSP language.

JSF provides the capability for a custom implementation to be provided for the Render Response and Restore View phases of the JSF lifecycle. An abstract Java class called `ViewHandler` can be extended and then this new implementation configured to be the view handler for the JSF application (as demonstrated previously with the custom navigation handler). This mechanism is used in XPages to provide the XSP markup-based presentation tier. So, the first and most important enhancement that XPages provides on top of JSF is the capability to create the JSF view using a markup language. Additionally, XPages provides some custom options for the Restore View phase. The default behavior for saving the state of the JSF view is to walk the component tree and request that each component save its state. The state data is then either stored on the server or serialized into the HTML response and stored on the client. Saving view state on the server has performance implications for the server. Saving state in the response increases the size of the response and, therefore, increases the network traffic. In some cases, there is no need to store the full state of the view (for example, when the page is being used for display only).

Request Processing Lifecycle

XPages allows you to execute the JSF request processing lifecycle on a portion of the component tree. To do this, use the `execMode` and `execId` properties of the event handler. The `execMode` property allows you to specify that either the complete or partial execution of the lifecycle. When partial execution is specified by setting `execMode="partial"`, only a portion of the component tree is used when executing the lifecycle. Components that are not part of this subtree are not processed during the lifecycle. The `execId` property specifies the component ID of a control within the pages component tree, which is the root of the subtree to be used when executing in the lifecycle. This allows you to optimize the execution of the lifecycle as a much smaller number of components need to be processed. This is something you will want to do to decrease the load on your server and to improve the performance of your XPages.

XPages also provides an optimization for the Render Response phase of the lifecycle, which either limits or eliminates the response. The event handler has two properties—`refreshMode` and `refreshId`—which specify and control partial refresh (partial or no rendering of the response). When partial refresh is specified by setting `refreshMode="partial"`, only a portion of the component tree contributes to the generated response. The response can also be completely eliminated by setting `refreshMode="norefresh"`. The `refreshId` is used in conjunction with a partial refresh to specify the portion of the component tree, which is used to generate the response, the specified control ID, which should be the root of the subtree that is used. Partial or no refresh is another optimization technique. The responsiveness of your XPages and the end user's experience can be significantly improved by using partial refresh to update just a part of the page and to reduce the number of page reloads.

User Interface Component Model

JSF uses the term *component* to refer to user interface components or what are known as *controls* in XPages. These components are the user interface elements used to create the application user interface. JSF provides the following:

- A fundamental API for user interface components
- Component behavioral interfaces that allow components to provide specific functionality, such as access to a data model
- A facility to convert data values (for example, to string representation for use in the presentation tier)
- A facility for validating user input

XPages builds on top of the JSF user interface component model to provide the following:

- XPages behavioral interfaces that allow components to contribute to the XPages-specific pages
- XPages converters, which extend the default conversion facility provided by JSF
- XPages validators, which extend the default user validation provided by JSF

XPages Behavioral Interfaces

The behavioral interfaces are implemented by user-interface components that support XPages-specific behavior. For example, in regular JSF, you must add a tag corresponding to a form component in the view definition to have a HTML form rendered in the response. For convenience, the standard XPages view root component automatically adds a form to each XPages view. But, what happens now if you want to manually add the form yourself? When you do this, the standard XPages form component automatically disables the automatic form creation by finding the parent, which creates the form and tells it not to automatically create a form. This list describes the XPages behavioral interfaces:

- **`FacesAjaxComponent`:** Implemented by user-interface components that can handle an AJAX request and return a valid response. The type-ahead component implements this interface and returns the list of suggestions in XML format as the response to an AJAX request.
- **`FacesAttrsObject`:** Implemented by user-interface components that allow arbitrary extra attributes to be output on their base tag. This is also used to allow attributes to be specified, which are passed through and emitted on the page. All the XPages controls implement this interface. This allows controls to be forward-compatible as attributes, such as Dojo attributes, can be added later without requiring updates to the controls or their renderers.
- **`FacesAutoForm`:** Implemented by user-interface components that automatically create a form component and is used to ensure that when a form is manually inserted into the view that an automatic form is not created. The XPages view root component implements this interface and normally automatically creates a form for each XPage.
- **`FacesComponent`:** Implemented by user-interface components that need to perform some initialization before and/or after their children are created or want to build their own children. The repeat component implements this because it builds its own children. The repeat container component (which is the parent for each row of children in a repeat) also implements this interface to ensure the correct row data is available to its children as they are being created.
- **`FacesDataIterator`:** Implemented by user-interface components that iterate over a value and is used to get information about the data model being used and the rows of data that is displayed. The repeat component implements this.
- **`FacesDataProvider`:** Implemented by user-interface components that can be configured with a data source. The view root and panel control, among others, implement this and can be configured with a Domino document or view data source.
- **`FacesInputComponent`:** Implemented by input components and is used to disable validation and to disable the behavior in the Notes client where the user gets prompted if a value is modified and might need to be saved before closing an XPage. The XPages standard input component (described in the next section) implements this interface.

- **`FacesInputFiltering:`** Implemented by input components that support input filtering and find the correct input filter to be applied. The XPages standard input component implements this interface and supports the filtering of active content.
- **`FacesNestedDataTable:`** Implemented by user-interface components that render using multiple tables and is used to support AJAX requests that replaces the component rendering. The XPages standard view panel component (described in the next section) implements this interface.
- **`FacesOutputFiltering:`** Implemented by output components that support output filtering and is used to find the correct output filter to be applied. The XPages standard output component (described in the next section) implements this interface and supports the filtering of active content.
- **`FacesPageIncluder:`** Implemented by user-interface components that include another XPage and need to perform some initialization before and/or after their children are created or want to build their own children. The **include** component implements this interface because it is used to include another XPage. The standard **include** composite component (described in the next section) also implements this interface because including a Custom Control is a special case of including another XPage.
- **`FacesPageProvider:`** Implemented by user-interface components that act as the root of a page during the create view phase of the JSF lifecycle. This is only intended for internal use by the XPages page-loading mechanism and must never be implemented by a third party.
- **`FacesParentReliantComponent:`** Implemented by user-interface components that have a strict child/parent relationship and does not behave correctly if an additional container is inserted between them, and their parent and is used with Custom Controls to force the **include** composite component to remove itself when the children of the Custom Control all rely on the parent. The XPages select item component implements this because it depends on its parent to render the selection it represents.
- **`FacesPropertyProvider:`** Implemented by the **include** composite component and used in the publishing of composite data. This must not be implemented by third parties.
- **`FacesRefreshableComponent:`** Implemented by user-interface components that can be refreshed by one of its children in response to an AJAX request. If the component changes its client ID while rendering its children (this is allowed for a `NamingContainer`), the child uses the wrong client ID and the refresh fails. This interface allows the child to get the correct client ID for use in a partial refresh. The XPages standard data component implements this interface.
- **`FacesRowAttrsComponent:`** Implemented by user-interface components that output an HTML TABLE and TR elements. The attributes (provided via `FacesAttrsObject`) are output on the TABLE element and the row attributes are output on each TR element.

- **`FacesRowIndex:`** Implemented by user-interface components that support a row index and is used by data sources to compute the components bean ID. The XPages standard data component implements this interface.
- **`FacesSaveBehavior:`** Implemented by action components which support the save property and is used to check if the data sources on the page should be saved after the corresponding action is performed. The XPages standard command component (described in the next section) implements this interface.
- **`FacesThemeHandler:`** Implemented by user-interface components that handle setting their own default styles. The XPages standard file download component implements this interface.
- **`FacesDojoComponent:`** Implemented by user-interface components that support Dojo attributes. The XPages type-ahead component implements this interface.
- **`FacesDojoComponentDelegate:`** Implemented by user-interface components that support Dojo attributes on behalf of another component. The XPages date time helper component implements this interface.
- **`ThemeControl:`** Implemented by user-interface components that support style kits. The majority of the XPages components support this.

You could use the behavioral interfaces if you decide to extend XPages (for example, by building your own Java components for XPages). This subject is covered in Chapter 12, "XPages Extensibility."

XPages Converters

JSF defines a mechanism to perform conversion to and from the string representation of the data model value. Model values need to be converted to a string representation to be displayed for the user and, when the user edits a value, it is received as a string value and needs to be converted to the correct type for the underlying data model. The `javax.faces.convert.Converter` interface defines the converter behavior. JSF provides a standard set of converters for common data types: various number formats and date\time values. XPages extends two of the standard converters and provides one new converter implementation:

- **`DateTimeConverter:`** The XPages data/time converter extends the standard JSF date/time converter, but it uses the International Components for Unicode (ICU) libraries for the conversions. For more information on ICU, visit http://site.icu-project.org.
- **`MaskConverter:`** The XPages mask converter applies the specified mask to the string representation of the value being converted. Table 5.2 shows a table listing the supported mask characters.
- **`NumberConverter:`** The XPages number converter handles the fractional part of integers and can handle the result of XPath.

Table 5.2 Mask Characters

Mask Character	Description
#	Any valid decimal digit number (uses `Character.isDigit`)
'	Used to escape any of the special formatting characters
U	All lowercase letters are mapped to uppercase (uses `Character.isLetter`)
L	All lowercase letters are mapped to lowercase (uses `Character.isLetter`)
A	Any valid decimal digit or letter (uses `Character.isDigit` and `Character.isLetter`)
?	Any letter
*	Anything
H	Any valid hex character (0–9, a–f, or A–F)

XPages Validators

JSF defines a mechanism to provide the validation (checks) of user inputted values. Although only a single converter may be associated with an input control, multiple validators can be assigned to a control. The reason for this is that the data might need to pass several validation checks before being persisted;, for example, the value is required (not empty), the value is a number, or the value is a credit card number. The `javax.faces.validator.Validator` interface defines the validator behavior. Again, JSF provides some standard validators for checking that numbers or strings lie within a specific range. XPages provides some additional validators and some additional interfaces to customize the validator behavior. The following list describes the XPages validators in detail:

- **`ClientSideValidator:`** Implemented by validators that support client-side validation. Validators that support client-side validation are asked to provide a single line of JavaScript to be included in the rendered response. For XPages validators, this Java Script references the xspClientDojo.js library and emits a call to the appropriate validator method. Listing 5.6 shows the JavaScript that gets included in a page that contains an edit box with a length validator and a `submit` button. Note the call to attach the length validator to the input control in the HTML page; this associates the length validator with the edit box whose contents it needs to validate.

Listing 5.6 Length Validator Client-Side JavaScript

```
<script type="text/javascript">
XSP.addOnLoad(function() {
XSP.attachValidator("view:_id1:inputText1",null,null,new
```

```
XSP.LengthValidator(0,5,"Incorrect length"));
XSP.attachEvent("view:_id1:_id4", "view:_id1:button1", "onclick", null,
true, false);
});
</script>
```

- **FacesRequiredValidator:** Implemented by the required validator and used by the XPages standard input component to identify if a required validator has been added to its list of validators.
- **ConstraintValidator:** Validates using the specified regular expression or, if the regular expression is set to one of the predefined keywords, performs the associated standard validation. Table 5.3 shows the predefined keywords the constraint validator supports.

Table 5.3 Predefined Constraint Checks

Regex	Description
AlphabetOnly	Checks if the value contain only letter characters
DigitOnly	Checks if the value contain only number characters
AlnumOnly	Checks if the value contain only letter and number characters

- **DateTimeRangeValidator:** Validates that a date value lies within the specified time period. Client-side validation and computed properties are supported.
- **DoubleRangeValidatorEx2:** Extends the standard JSF validator to support client-side validation and computed properties.
- **ExpressionValidator:** Enables you to provide custom logic for the client-side and server-side validation.
- **LengthValidatorEx and LongRangeValidatorEx2:** The XPages version of these validators extends the standard JSF validator to support client-side validation and computed properties.
- **ModulusSelfCheckValidator:** Performs a modulus self check (for modulus 10 and 11 only). Client-side validation is not supported. A modulus self check is a standard mechanism for validating identification numbers; for example, modulus 10 (or Luhn algorithm) is a single checksum formula used to validate credit-card numbers.
- **RequiredValidator:** Checks that a value has been specified.

Standard User-Interface Components

JSF provides a standard set of user interface components which cover the standard control types. Each of these components has a well-defined behavior which is platform independent. The intention is that the JSF standard components would be extended to provide specific implementations for different client platforms. In fact, JSF extends these standard components to provide HTML-specific components. XPages extends the standard components to add XPages-specific behavior and also defines its own completely new standard components. XPages then extends these components to provide the specialized XPages user interface components that are used in Domino Designer and supports the browser and IBM Notes clients. Figure 5.3 shows the hierarchy of user interface components. If you are going to create your own user interface components, you will normally be extending one of the JSF or XPages standard components.

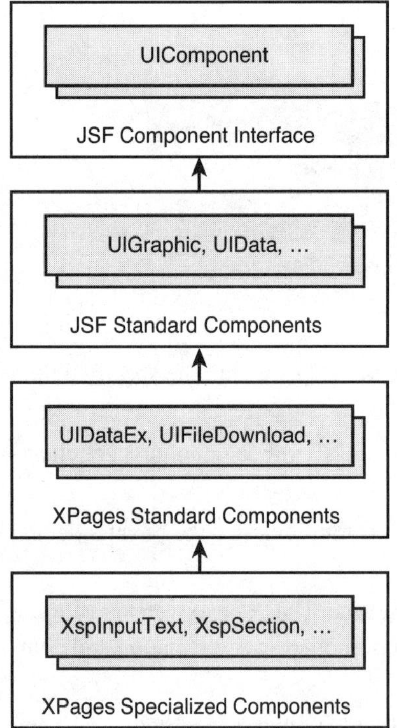

Figure 5.3 XPages user interface component hierarchy

The following list briefly describes each of the standard user interface components:

- **`UICallback`:** Represents an area in Custom Control where the user of the Custom Control can add additional content. This component builds its own contents and, after its children are added, it checks if they are all instances of `NamingContainer` and, if they are, it removes itself from the component hierarchy.

- **`UIColumnEx:`** Represents a single column of data and expects to have a parent `UIData`. `UIColumnEx` implements `FacesParentRelientComponent` to signal this dependency on its parent.
- **`UICommandButton:`** Represents a button that, when clicked by the user, can trigger some application logic.
- **`UICommandEx2:`** Represents a control that, when activated by the user, can trigger some application logic. `UICommandEx2` implements `FacesSaveBehavior`, which means that, when triggered, it can cause the saving of all data sources on the XPage.
- **`UIComponentTag:`** An abstract component that is extended by specialized XPages components which represent a tag, such as a div, span, table, and so on.
- **`UIDataColumn:`** Extends `UIColumnEx`, but currently does not add any new behavior.
- **`UIDataEx:`** Represents a multirow data model. The only allowed children are instances of `UIColumnEx`, which collectively define the presentation a row of data from the model.
- **`UIDataIterator:`** Like `UIDataEx`, this component represents a multirow data model, but does not have any restriction on what type of children it will have. The children process multiple rows of data, but in a free format rather than the tabular format that `UIData` uses.
- **`UIDataPanelBase:`** Represents a component that organizes the layout of its children and provides data (it implements `FacesDataProvider`) that is scoped to its children.
- **`UIDateTimeHelper:`** Used to transform an edit box into a date time picker.
- **`UIEventHandler:`** Used to handle events on behalf of its parent. It can be configured to handle both client-side events or server-side actions for the component that is its direct parent.
- **`UIFileDownload:`** Represents a control that can be used to download one or more files.
- **`UIFileuploadEx:`** Represents a control and can be used to upload a file from a user to the server.
- **`UIFormEx:`** Represents a HTML form and ensures an XPage doesn't contain nested forms because of the automatic creation of a form elsewhere in the component hierarchy.
- **`UIGraphicEx:`** Represents a control that displays a graphical image to the user. Currently, the XPages version does not add any new behavior, but it might do so in the future.
- **`UIInclude:`** Used to support including one XPage within another.
- **`UIIncludeComposite:`** Used to support including a Custom Control within an XPage.
- **`UIInputCheckbox:`** Represents a checkbox control.

- **`UIInputEx`:** Used for controls that display a value and allow that value to be edited. `UIInputEx` adds support for HTML filtering, disabling the validation, and Dojo.
- **`UIInputRadio`:** Represents a radio button control.
- **`UIInputRichText`:** Represents a rich text edit control.
- **`UIInputText`:** Represents an edit box control.
- **`UIMessageEx`:** Supports the display of error messages for a specific component and adds style kit support.
- **`UIMessagesEx`:** Supports the display of error messages not related to a specific component and adds theme support.
- **`UIOutputEx`:** Used to display data model values to the user and adds HTML filtering support.
- **`UIOutputLink`:** Represents a HTML link.
- **`UIOutputText`:** Displays a computed value.
- **`UIPager`:** Used to display a pager control to allow paging through the rows of data associated with the `UIData` or `UIDataIterator` component.
- **`UIPagerControl`:** Used to display one of the buttons in a pager control, such as first, previous, next, or last buttons.
- **`UIPanelEx`:** Used as a base component for the controls that are used include an XPage.
- **`UIPassThroughTag`:** Used whenever a non-xsp tag is added to an XPage. There is no associated xsp tag for this component, but it is used by the page-loading mechanism and appears in the XPages page-translation source code.
- **`UIPassThroughText`:** Used whenever text added to an XPage. There is no associated xsp tag for this component, but it is used by the page-loading mechanism and appears in the XPages page translation source code.
- **`UIPlatformEvent`:** Represents a control that can handle a platform event. When the specified platform event occurs, the associated script is executed.
- **`UIRepeat`:** This component is a `FacesDataIterator` and has two modes of operation: It can either use either a single instances of its children (like a `UIData` component) or it can create one instance of its children for every row of data.
- **`UIRepeatContainer`:** Used by the `UIRepeat` component when it is creating multiple instances of its children. Each instance of `UIRepeats` children are nested inside a `UIRepeatContainer`, and the container provides access to the row data and index.
- **`UIScriptCollector`:** Automatically added to the root of an XPages component tree. Its job is to aggregate all the JavaScript code that needs to be included in the generated HTML and to include it within a single script tag at the bottom of the page.

- **UISection:** Represents a container control that displays as a section and can be expanded and collapsed.
- **UISelectItemEx:** Represents a single selection option for a control that allows the user to select from a number of choices, such as a listbox.
- **UISelectItemsEx:** Represents multiple section options for a control that allows the user to select from a number of choices, such as a listbox.
- **UISelectListbox:** A listbox control, which will have nested `UISelectItemEx` or `UISelectIvtemsEx`, representing the available choices. Depending on whether the listbox is configured for multiple selection, a different specialized XPages component is used, either `XspSelectManyListbox` or `XspSelectOneListbox`.
- **UISelectManyEx:** Represents a control that allows the user to select multiple values from a number of choices.
- **UISelectOneEx:** Represents a control that allows the user to select one value from a number of choices.
- **UITabbedPanel:** Represents a control that contains children which are instances of `UITabPanel` and displays the children as a series of tabs.
- **UITabPanel:** Represents a single tab in a tabbed panel control.
- **UITypeAhead:** A helper component that is used with an edit box to provide type-ahead functionality, such as the ability for the user to start typing in the edit box and see a list of suggestions.
- **UIViewColumn:** Represents a single column in a view control.
- **UIViewColumnHeader:** Represents the header for a single column in a view control.
- **UIViewPager:** Represents a pager in a view control.
- **UIViewPanel:** Represents a view control that can be bound to the data in a Domino view.
- **UIViewRootEx2:** The root component of all XPages component hierarchies.
- **UIViewTitle:** Represents the title of a view control.

You could use one the standard user interface components as the base class if you were building your own Java components for XPages. This subject is covered in Chapter 12.

Value Binding and Method Binding Expression Evaluation

JSF supports two types of binding expressions:

- **Value binding:** Computes a value for a property and can support both reading and writing a value
- **Method binding:** Executes some logic

Binding expressions are identified using the `#{` and `}` expression delimiters. JSF supports Expression Language (EL) for value and method bindings. JSF defines the `javax.faces.el.ValueBinding` abstract class to represent a value binding expression and `javax.faces.el.MethodBinding` to represent a method binding. The JSF application object is responsible for creating instances of these for use in the JSF processing. XPages extends support for expression binding to include the following:

- Using JavaScript
- Using a special syntax to resolve client IDs
- Support for multipart expressions
- Simple actions

JavaScript Binding Expressions

A JavaScript binding expression is delimited using `#{javascript:` and `}`. Listing 5.7 shows an example of a JavaScript value binding expression being used to compute the value for a Computed Field. When this code is executed, a string representation of the database property is displayed in the Computed Field. This value binding expression is computed each time the property is accessed. There is an alternative syntax that starts with `${`, which gets evaluated just once when the page is loaded.

Listing 5.7 JavaScript Value Binding Expression

```
<xp:text escape="true"
         id="computedField2"
         value="#{javascript:database}">
</xp:text>
```

Listing 5.8 shows the syntax for the JavaScript method binding. When the button is clicked, the XPage is submitted and the JavaScript executes. The output from the `print` statement can be seen in the Domino console or Notes trace file.

Listing 5.8 JavaScript Method Binding Expression

```
<xp:button value="Execute JavaScript" id="button1" type="submit">
      <xp:this.action>
            <![CDATA[#{javascript:print("Executed JavaScript")}]]>
      </xp:this.action>
</xp:button>
```

Client ID Binding Expressions

An ID binding expression is delimited using `#{id:` and `}`. The ID of the user component whose client ID you want to compute is specified in the content of the computed expression, as shown in Listing 5.9. ID expressions are typically used as part of a multipart expression.

Listing 5.9 Client ID Binding Expression

```
<xp:text escape="true"
         id="computedField3"
         value="#{id:computedField3}">
</xp:text>
```

Multipart Binding Expressions

A multipart expression allows static and dynamic content to be mixed. In Listing 5.10, the value of the Computed Field combines static text, a client ID computed expression, and a JavaScript computed expression.

Listing 5.10 Multipart Value Binding Expression

```
<xp:text escape="true"
         id="computedField4"
         value="ID: #{id:computedField4} DB: #{javascript:database}">
</xp:text>
```

Simple Actions

A simple action is a special type of method binding which is represented by a tag in the XPage and its behavior can be configured using properties. Listing 5.11 shows how to configure a simple ExecuteScript action, which, in turn, invokes a JavaScript method binding.

Listing 5.11 Simple Action Method Binding Expression

```
<xp:button value="Execute Simple Action" id="button2" type="submit">
      <xp:this.action>
            <xp:executeScript
            script="#{javascript:print('Executed Simple Action')}">
            </xp:executeScript>
      </xp:this.action>
</xp:button>
```

XPages Default Variables

Earlier in this chapter, the default JSF variables were listed (see Table 5.1). XPages provides some additional default variables for the Domino application developer. Table 5.4 shows a listing of all the default variables, their values, and a short description of each variable. Refer to the XPage named DefaultVariables in **Chp05Ed2.nsf** to see how this table was generated. At the end of the list, the six new XPages default variables are listed:

- **`viewScope`:** Map containing the view scope values
- **`context`:** XspContext instance for the current request
- **`database`:** Database instance for the current request
- **`session`:** Session instance for the current request
- **`sessionAsSigner`:** Session instance with the credentials of the XPage signer
- **`sessionAsSignerWithFullAccess`:** Session instance with the credentials based on those of the XPager signer and with fill administrative access

Table 5.4 Table of Default Variables

Name	String Value	Description
`applicationScope`	{com.sun.faces.OneTimeInitialization=com.sun.faces.OneTimeInitialization, com.sun.faces.ApplicationAssociate=com.sun.faces.application.ApplicationAssociate@51a551a5 com.sun.faces.HTML_BASIC=com.ibm.xsp.renderkit.ReadOnlyRenderKit@45f045f0 javax.servlet.context.tempdir=C:\Users\Mark\AppData\Local\Temp\notes0E3C5E\xsp\chp05ed2.nsf}	Map containing the application scope values
`cookie`	{SessionID=javax.servlet.http.Cookie@63a863a8}	Map containing the cookies for the current request
`facesContext`	com.ibm.xsp.domino.context.DominoFacesContext@6d346d34	The FacesContext instance for the current request

Name	String Value	Description
header	{Cookie=SessionID=81A74A5C8161D376B0373C275 603E4BB8E12AE5B Accept-Encoding=gzip, deflate Accept=text/html,application/xhtml+xml,application/ xml;q=0.9*/*;q=0.8 Accept-Language=en-ie,en;q=0.7 en-us;q=0.3 User-Agent=Mozilla/5.0 (Windows NT 6.1; WOW64; rv:23.0) Gecko/20100101 Firefox/23.0 Referer=http://localhost/chp05ed2.nsf Connection=keep-alive, Host=localhost}	Map containing the HTTP header values for the current request
headerValues	{Accept=com.ibm.domino.xsp.bridge.http.util. SingleValueEnumeration@43d843d8 Referer=com.ibm.domino.xsp.bridge.http.util. SingleValueEnumeration@443c443c Accept-Encoding=com.ibm.domino.xsp.bridge.http. util.SingleValueEnumeration@441c441c Connection=com.ibm.domino.xsp.bridge.http.util. SingleValueEnumeration@44eb44eb Accept-Language=com.ibm.domino.xsp.bridge.http. util.SingleValueEnumeration@43fa43fa User-Agent=com.ibm.domino.xsp.bridge.http.util. SingleValueEnumeration@43b843b8 Cookie=com.ibm.domino.xsp.bridge.http.util. SingleValueEnumeration@44ca44ca Host=com.ibm.domino.xsp.bridge.http.util.SingleValue Enumeration@43974397}	Map containing arrays which contain the header values for the HTTP headers for the current request
initParam	{com.sun.faces.forceLoadConfiguration=true com.ibm.xsp.SHARED_CONFIG=true com.sun.faces.verifyObjects=false}	Map containing the initialization parameters for the web application
param	{}	Map containing the request parameters for the current request

Name	String Value	Description
paramValues	{}	Map containing arrays which contain the parameter values for request parameters for the current request
requestScope	{com.ibm.xsp.SESSION_ID=81A74A5C8161D376B0373C275603E4BB8E12AE5B __xspconvid=null database=chp05ed2.nsf session=CN=MarksW520/O=DEV com.sun.faces.FORM_CLIENT_ID_ATTR=view:_id1 context=com.ibm.xsp.designer.context.ServletXSPContext@f450f45 com.sun.faces.INVOCATION_PATH=.xsp cookie={SessionID=javax.servlet.http.Cookie@63a863a8} componentParameters=com.ibm.xsp.application.ComponentParameters@ff80ff8}	Map containing the request attributes for the current request
sessionScope	{__XSP_STATE_BASIC=com.ibm.xsp.application.BasicStateManagerImpl$ViewHolder@44f444f4 VIEW LIST: !dnms5mob49!/Index __notescontext_publicaccess=com.ibm.domino.xsp.module.nsf.NotesContext$AccessPrivileges@47544754 xspIsBot=false xsp.sessionData=com.ibm.xsp.designer.context.PersistentSessionData@fb90fb9}	Map containing the session attributes for the current request
view	com.ibm.xsp.component.UIViewRootEx2@753f753f	UIViewRoot of the current component tree
viewScope	{}	Map containing the view scope values
context	com.ibm.xsp.designer.context.ServletXSPContext@f450f45	The XspContext instance for the current request
database	chp05ed2.nsf	The Database instance for the current request

Name	String Value	Description
session	CN=MarksW520/O=DEV	The Session instance for the current request
sessionAsSigner	CN=MarksW520/O=DEV	The Session instance with the credentials of the XPage signer
sessionAsSigner-WithFullAccess	CN=MarksW520/O=DEV	The Session instance with the credentials of the XPage signer and with full administrative access

Chapter 6, "Building XPages Application Logic," covers XPages default variables and examples of their usage in more detail. A short description of each of the XPages default variables is provided next.

viewScope

XPages introduces this new scoped variable to supplement the default scoped variables: `requestScope`, `sessionScope`, and `applicationScope`. The `viewScope` variable allows you to scope your own variables to the lifetime of the associated view, such as XPage. As previously mentioned, the state of a view can be cached between requests so that multiple requests act on the same state of the XPage. The view is restored at the beginning and saved at the end of each request and any view scope variables are saved and restored as part of this process. The `viewScope` object is a map, so you can add your own variables keyed by name. By default, this map is empty, so you can select whatever names you want without concern for name clashes. The variables you add must be serializable for their state to be saved.

context

The `context` variable provides access to the XPages `XSPContext` object, which is an instance of `com.ibm.xsp.designer.context.XSPContext`. The context object provides XPages-specific contextual information about the current request, such as access to the associated user, timezone, locale, and so on. It also provides numerous utility methods that can be used within your application logic, such as page navigation, HTML filtering, and so on.

database

The `database` variable provides access to the `Database` object, which is an instance of `lotus.domino.Database`. The database object provides access to the current Domino database and supports a wide range of database centric operations. The complete documentation for the

`Database` class is available in the Java/CORBA Classes section of the IBM Domino Designer Basic User Guide and Reference help document, which is part of the Domino Designer help. Use **Help > Help Contents** to access this documentation.

session

The `session` variable provides access to the `Session` object, which is an instance of `lotus.domino.Session`. The session is assigned credentials based on those of the current user. The session is restricted by the application's ACL and the security tab of the server's Domino Directory entry. The complete documentation for the `Session` class is available in the Java/CORBA Classes section of the IBM Domino Designer Basic User Guide and Reference help document.

sessionAsSigner

The `session` variable provides access to the `Session` object, which is an instance of `lotus.domino.Session`. The session is assigned credentials based on those of the signer of the XPages' design element. The session is restricted by the application's ACL and the Security tab of the server's Domino Directory entry. The complete documentation for the `Session` class is available in the Java/CORBA Classes section of the IBM Domino Designer Basic User Guide and Reference help document.

sessionAsSignerWithFullAccess

The session variable provides access to the `Session` object, which is an instance of `lotus.domino.Session`. The session is assigned credentials based on those of the signer of the XPages' design element and allows full administrative access to the application's data. The signer must have permission for full administrative access or this session is not created and will not be available. The complete documentation for the `Session` class is available in the Java/CORBA Classes section of the IBM Domino Designer Basic User Guide and Reference help document.

Conclusion

This concludes the overview of how XPages is built on top of JSF. You learned how XPages extends JSF to add new capabilities and enhanced behaviors while maintaining the JSF standard. As previously mentioned, XPages is currently built with JSF version 1.1, so if you plan to read more about JSF, this is the version to reference.

CHAPTER 6

Building XPages Application Logic

This is the first of two chapters where you learn about adding application logic to your XPages application. This chapter introduces the fundamental principles: how to add your application logic, simple actions, and using JavaScript with XPages. This chapter explores the differences between creating server and client-side application logic and explains the Script Editor tool. You also learn about some of the common objects that you can use from within your application logic. Be sure to download the **Chp06Ed2.nsf** file provided online for this book to run through the exercises throughout this chapter. You can access these files at `www.ibmpressbooks.com/title/9780132486316`.

> **SIGNING THE SAMPLE APPLICATIONS**
>
> In this and the subsequent chapter, you preview samples that contain application logic, so it is recommended that you sign the sample database to avoid receiving execution control list (ECL) alerts. You can assign each database from Designer by right-clicking it in the application navigator and selecting Application > Sign Design.

Adding Application Logic

Your application logic is normally executed in response to a user action, such as when a user clicks a button to submit a page, you might want to process the data that has been inputted. To achieve this, when editing an XPage in Designer, use the Events tab to add application logic to the `onclick` event for the respective button. There are two main options for adding your application logic: Server or Client. Server logic executes in the XPages runtime and has access to the XSP representation of the page and the associated XSP runtime artifacts. Client logic is running in a browser context and has access to the browser Document Object Model (DOM) and some additional artifacts when running in the Notes client (more on this in Chapter 13, "XPages in the

Notes Client”). Figure 6.1 shows the Events tab with the Server subtab selected. This is your starting point for adding application logic that executes on the server. When Server is selected, you see a Server Options section available. This is only available when adding server-side application logic, and these options are discussed in Chapter 11, “Advanced Scripting.”

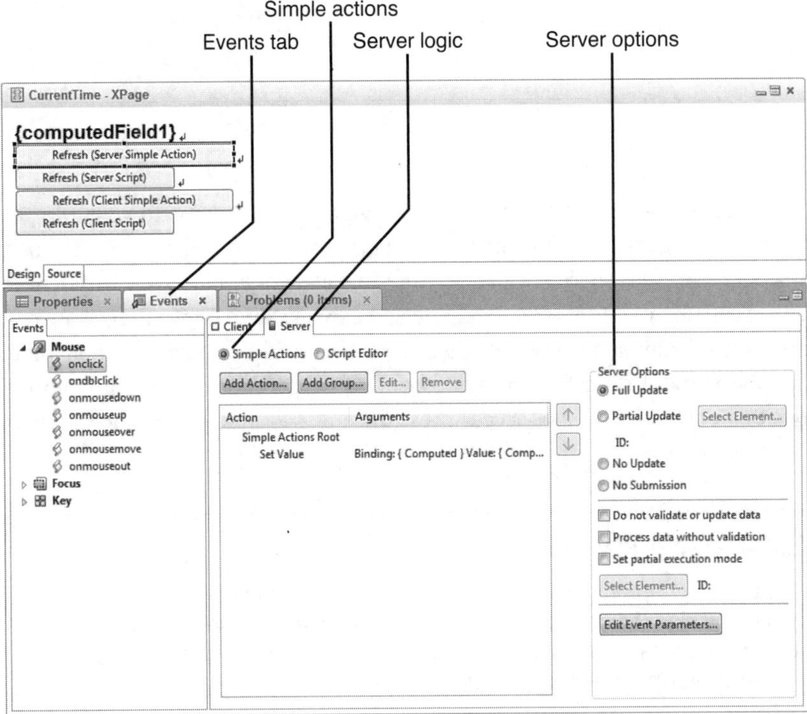

Figure 6.1 Events tab with Server and Simple Actions selected

Within both the **Client** and **Server** subtabs, there are options to use **Simple Actions** or the **Script Editor**. A simple action represents some standard application logic, such as creating a response document that can be configured by simply just changing its properties. The intent is to free the application developer from having to write (and debug) code for common actions. Figure 6.2 shows the **Events** tab with the **Client** subtab selected and the **Script Editor** option selected. This allows you to view the client-side JavaScript expression, which executes when the specified event occurs. You can also open the **Script Editor** dialog from here, which provides additional features to help you add scripting logic.

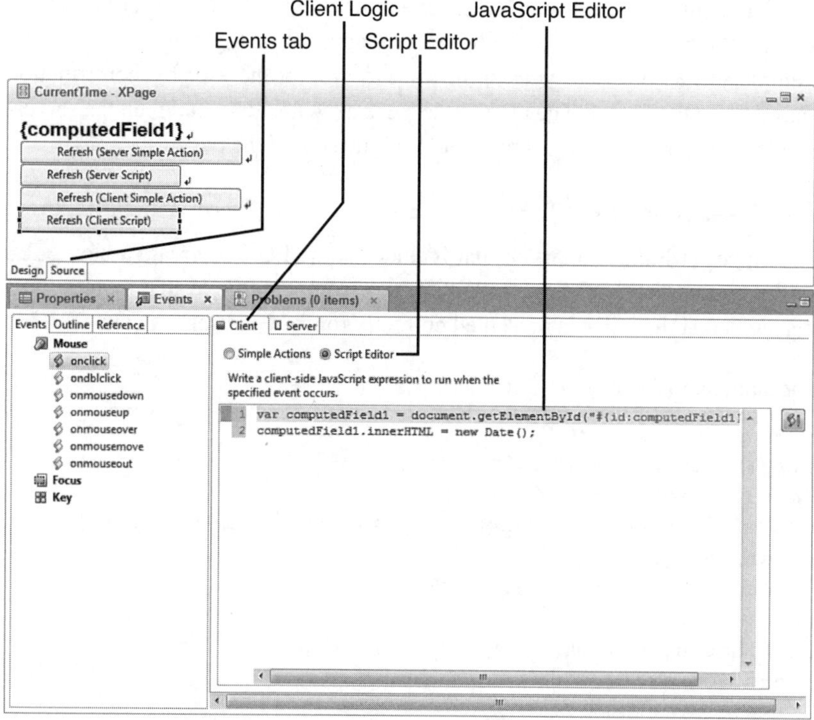

Figure 6.2 Events tab with Client and Script Editor selected

So, what happens in your XPage when you use one of these options to add some application logic? There are four possible options:

- Server simple action
- Server script
- Client simple action
- Client script

The good news is that in the XPages markup there is a single syntax that can be used for all four options, so there is only one thing you need to learn: the `xp:eventHandler` tag.

The `xp:eventHandler` tag is a component that associates application logic with any control in an XPage. You have seen this pattern before (`xp:dataTimeHelper`) where XPages uses a child tag to add new behavior to its parent. So, the `xp:eventHandler` tag can be nested inside any control tag when you want to trigger application logic in response to an event fired from the control, and that application logic can be server and/or client-side simple actions and/or JavaScript. Yes, you can combine client-side and server-side application logic in response to the same event! An example of this is where you might want to prompt the user for confirmation before deleting documents on the server. The client-side logic executes first, and then the server-side logic executes unless the client-side logic prevented submission of the page.

Using the xp:eventHandler Tag

Listing 6.1 shows a snippet of XPages markup that includes some logic to create a new `Date` object that contains the current date and time, followed by a Computed Field that displays this value. A converter ensures that the value is presented correctly for the end user's locale.

Listing 6.1 XPages Sample to Display the Current Date/Time

```
<?xml version="1.0" encoding="UTF-8"?>
<xp:view xmlns:xp="http://www.ibm.com/xsp/core">
    <xp:this.beforePageLoad>
        <![CDATA[#{javascript:viewScope.put("now", new Date())}]]>
    </xp:this.beforePageLoad>
    <xp:text escape="true" id="computedField1"
        value="#{viewScope.now}"
        style="font-size:16pt;font-weight:bold">
        <xp:this.converter>
            <xp:convertDateTime type="both">
            </xp:convertDateTime>
        </xp:this.converter>
    </xp:text>
    <xp:br></xp:br>
</xp:view>
```

This view scope value is created as the page is being loaded, using the `beforePageLoad` event, and can subsequently be updated using server or client-side simple actions or JavaScript.

Refreshing Using a Server-Side Simple Action

Use the following steps to add logic that allows the value in the Computed Field to be updated using a server-side simple action (the completed sample is available in XPage named CurrentTime):

1. Add a button to the XPage.
2. Go to the Event tab and select **Server** and **Simple Actions** (this should be the default).
3. Select **Add Action**, and then select the **Set Value** simple action.
4. Set **Binding** to be a computed value, select Expression Language, and enter `viewScope.now`.

5. Set Value to be a computed value, select JavaScript (Server Side) and enter `new Date()`.
6. Save the XPage.

Listing 6.2 shows the markup that is generated for you. An `xp:eventHandler` tag is added as a child of the button control and is configured as follows:

1. The `event` property is set to `onclick`, which means the event handler is triggered in response to the user clicking the button.
2. The `submit` property is to `true`, which causes the page to be submitted.
3. The `refreshMode` is set to `complete`, which means the entire page will be redrawn.
4. The `action` property is set to the `xp:setValue` tag, which represents the single action to be invoked.

Listing 6.2 Server Simple Action to Update the Current Date/Time

```
<xp:button value="Refresh (Server Simple Action)" id="button1">
     <xp:eventHandler event="onclick" submit="true"
          refreshMode="complete">
          <xp:this.action>
               <xp:setValue
                         binding="#{viewScope.now}"
                         value="#{javascript:new Date()}">
               </xp:setValue>
          </xp:this.action>
     </xp:eventHandler>
</xp:button>
```

The `xp:eventHandler` causes the runtime to add some client-side JavaScript to the rendered page. This JavaScript adds a listener to the button, which responds to the `onclick` event by submitting the page. This is the line of code in the rendered page, which causes this to happen:

```
XSP.attachEvent("view:_id1:_id3", "view:_id1:button1", "onclick", null,
true, false);
```

If you preview this page, you can click this button and see the page being submitted and the current date/time being refreshed when the page is redisplayed. If you do a view source on the previewed page, you can see the preceding script in the generated markup.

Refreshing Using Server-Side JavaScript

Refreshing using server-side JavaScript is similar to the previous simple action example except, in this case, the supplied JavaScript expression is executed. Here are the steps:

1. Add a button to the XPage.
2. Go to the Event tab and select **Server** and **Script Editor**.
3. Enter the expression `viewScope.put("now", new Date())`.
4. Save the XPage.

Listing 6.3 shows the markup that is generated for you. The only difference in how the `xp:eventHandler` tag is configured is that now the action property contains a computed expression that contains the JavaScript to be executed.

Listing 6.3 Server JavaScript to Update the Current Date/Time

```
<xp:eventHandler event="onclick" submit="true" refreshMode="complete">
	<xp:this.action>
	<![CDATA[#{javascript:viewScope.put("now", new Date())}]]>
	</xp:this.action>
</xp:eventHandler>
```

Refreshing Using a Client-Side Simple Action

The steps to add a client-side simple action are similar to the ones you used earlier to add a server-side simple action. As you would expect, the available simple actions differ between client and server because the environment where the simple actions execute is different, more on this later in the section, "Simple Actions." Follow these steps:

1. Add a button to the XPage.
2. Go to the Event tab and select **Client** and **Simple Actions**.
3. Select **Add Action** and select the **Execute Client Script** simple action.
4. Set **Language** to be a JavaScript (Client Side).
5. Set **Condition** to be the following JavaScript expression:
   ```
   var computedField1 = document.getElementById
   ("#{id:computedField1}");
   computedField1.innerHTML = new Date();
   ```
6. Save the XPage.

This time, the `xp:eventHandler` tag has the `script` property set. The `script` property is used when a client-side simple action or JavaScript is to be executed. The script in this sample gets the DOM element corresponding to `computedField1` using the `getElementById` method and then updates the contents of the element by setting the `innerHTML` property to the current time. As you saw earlier, the `action` property is used for server-side simple actions and Java Script. An `xp:executeClientScript` tag is set as the value for the `script` property. This represents the client-side simple action. An `xp:executeClientScript` tag has its own `script` property, which is set to the client-side JavaScript to be executed. In the generated markup, notice that the submit property is set to true. If you preview the page and click this button, you see that the current date/time changes momentarily and then changes back to the previous value. This is because the page is being submitted in response to the button click and then redrawn with the only server value. To prevent the submit from happening, you need to make sure the `submit` property on the `xp:eventHandler` is set to `false`. Now, if you preview the page, notice that the date/time value does change and the page is no longer submitted. Also, notice that the format of the date/time string is different. This is because a pure client-side operation has been executed and the value is not being set in the view scope and converted for display using the configured converter. The client-side script is just updating the HTML within the browser or Notes client. Listing 6.4 shows the XSP markup for this example.

Listing 6.4 Client Simple Action to Update the Current Date/Time

```
<xp:eventHandler event="onclick" submit="false"
      refreshMode="complete">
      <xp:this.script>
            <xp:executeClientScript>
                  <xp:this.script>
<![CDATA[var computedField1 = document.getElementById
➥("#{id:computedField1}");
computedField1.innerHTML = new Date();]]>
                  </xp:this.script>
            </xp:executeClientScript>
      </xp:this.script>
</xp:eventHandler>
```

Listing 6.5 shows the client-side script that the `xp:executeClientScript` caused to be included in the rendered page. The `xp:eventHandler` also includes client-side script that causes this method to be invoked when the associated button is clicked.

Listing 6.5 JavaScript Rendered by xp:executeClientScript

```
function view__id1__id7_clientSide_onclick(thisEvent) {
var computedField1 = document.getElementById
➥ ("view:_id1:computedField1");
computedField1.innerHTML = new Date();
}
```

Refreshing Using Client-Side JavaScript

Refreshing with client-side JavaScript uses the same script as the previous example. Here are the steps:

1. Add a button to the XPage.
2. Go to the **Event** tab and select **Client** and **Script Editor**.
3. Enter the following expression:

   ```
   var computedField1 = document.getElementById
   ("#{id:computedField1}");
   computedField1.innerHTML = new Date();
   ```

4. Save the XPage.

Listing 6.6 shows the markup that is generated for you. You can see that now the script expression is associated with the script property on the `xp:eventHandler` tag and, this time, the submit property is set to `false`, so no manual update of the XPage is required.

Listing 6.6 Client JavaScript to Update the Current Date/Time

```
<xp:eventHandler event="onclick" submit="false">
     <xp:this.script>
     <![CDATA[var computedField1 =
     document.getElementById("#{id:computedField1}");
     computedField1.innerHTML = new Date();]]>
     </xp:this.script>
</xp:eventHandler>
```

As you expect, the rendered JavaScript is almost identical to the previous case where the `xp:executeClientScript` was used and the behavior when clicking the button is the same.

Event Handler Properties

This section describes the properties associated with the `xp:eventHandler` tag. Numerous properties are relevant when using the event handler to make an AJAX request, such as for a partial refresh of the page. These properties are described in Chapter 11 and elsewhere.

- **`event:`** Name of the event, which triggers the associated server action or client script.
- **`execId:`** ID of the control, which is the root of the branch used for the partial execution of the JSF lifecycle.
- **`execMode:`** Execution mode for the event handler. Valid values are
  - **`complete:`** Lifecycle is executed on the complete control hierarchy (default).
  - **`partial:`** Lifecycle is executed on the part of the branch of the control hierarchy specified by the execId.

> **NOTE**
>
> Chapter 11 covers the uses of the `execMode` property in detail.

- **`handlers:`** Collection of client event handlers. Each handler has the following properties:
  - **`type:`** Currently only `text/javascript` is supported.
  - **`script:`** The client script that is executed.
  - **`renderkit:`** Use `HTML_BASIC` if this script is for the web only and `HTML_RCP` if this script is for the Notes client.

Listing 6.7 shows how to have different client scripts for the browser and Notes clients. Other examples of web and Notes platform differentiation are covered in Chapter 13.

Listing 6.7 Renderkit-Specific Client Script Handlers

```
<?xml version="1.0" encoding="UTF-8"?>
<xp:view xmlns:xp="http://www.ibm.com/xsp/core">
     <xp:button id="button1" value="Click Me">
          <xp:eventHandler event="onclick" submit="false">
               <xp:this.handlers>
                    <xp:handler
                         type="text/javascript"
                         script="alert('Browser')"
                         renderkit="HTML_BASIC">
                    </xp:handler>
                    <xp:handler
                         type="text/javascript"
                         script="alert('Notes')"
                         renderkit="HTML_RCP">
                    </xp:handler>
               </xp:this.handlers>
          </xp:eventHandler>
     </xp:button>
</xp:view>
```

- **`loaded:`** A boolean flag that indicates if the event handler should be included in the control hierarchy when the page is loaded. Set this to false if you want the event handler to be omitted when the page is loaded. The default value is `true`, and one example where you would use this is if there was application logic didn't apply to a particular user based on their application roles.

- **navigate:** A boolean flag that indicates if navigation should be performed when the event associated with the event handler is being processed.
- **refreshId:** ID of the control, which is the root of the branch to be refreshed when partial refresh has been specified.
- **refreshMode:** The refresh mode for the event handler. Valid values are
  - **complete:** Entire page is refreshed (default).
  - **partial:** Part of the page specified by the `refreshId` is refreshed.
  - **norefresh:** No part of the page is refreshed.
- **rendered:** Boolean flag that indicates in the event handler should be rendered as part of the page. Set this to `false` if you want the event handler to be omitted when the page is rendered.
- **save:** Boolean flag that indicates if a save operation should be performed when the event handler is processed. Set to `true` to automatically save the data sources on the page.
- **submit:** Boolean flag that indicates if the page should be submitted when the event associated with this event handler is triggered. Set to `true` to submit the page.
- **parameters:** Collection of parameters and name/value pairs, which are made available when the action associated with the event handler is executed.
- **action:** The server action that executes when this event handler is triggered. This can be a simple action, a JavaScript expression, or a Java method.
- **immediate:** Boolean flag that indicates that processing of the server action associated with the event handler should proceed after the apply-request-values phase of the JSF lifecycle and before the inputted values are validated. If the action causes a navigation to another XPage or causes the page to be redrawn, the remaining phases of the lifecycle are not executed. The `immediate` property is set to true when you specify a button type is `Cancel` (as shown in Listing 6.8) because this allows the operation to proceed even if the inputted values are not valid. Because the update-model phase has not executed when the action is processed, the latest values are not available in the model. If the update-model phase doesn't execute (which is the norm with `immediate` set to `true`), the values entered by the user are discarded. If, during the processing of an immediate action, the inputted values need to be referenced, one option is to reference them directly from the control. Be aware that, if you do this, the values are available in string format only; they have not been converted to the correct type or validated.
- **disableValidators:** Boolean flags that indicate whether to execute the associated validators. By default this is set to true and the valuators are executed. You may want to disable this when the page is being submitted, but editing isn't complete, so you don't want the validation to be performed yet.

Listing 6.8 Using the immediate Property for a Cancel Button

```
<xp:button value="Cancel" id="button1">
     <xp:eventHandler
event="onclick" submit="true"
          refreshMode="complete" immediate="true"
save="false">
</xp:eventHandler>
</xp:button>
```

> **USING IMMEDIATE WITH AN INPUT CONTROL**
>
> The `immediate` property is also supported for input controls. When set to true, the inputted value is validated during the apply-request-values phase of the JSF lifecycle. If validation fails on a control marked as immediate, the response is rendered and the validation errors are available in the response.
>
> Non-immediate controls may not be validated if a validation error in an immediate control caused the response to be rendered. Non-immediate controls only validate in the process-validations phase of the lifecycle.

- **`onComplete`:** Used when the event handler triggers an AJAX request. This property is the client script to be executed after the AJAX request is executed.
- **`onError`:** Used when the event handler will trigger an AJAX request. This property is the client script to be executed if there is an error executing the AJAX request.
- **`onStart`:** Used when the event handler will trigger an AJAX request. This property is the client script to be executed before the AJAX request is executed.
- **`script`:** The client script to be executed when the associated event associated with the event handler is triggered.

> **USING ON*XXX* PROPERTIES**
>
> The `onComplete`, `onError`, and `onStart` properties can be accessed by selecting the event handler in the Outline view and using All Properties or by typing them directly into the XPage in source mode.

Simple Actions

Previously, you saw how some examples of simple actions that execute in the client and on the server. Simple actions are represented by tags in the XPage and provide reusable application logic that can be configured by setting the tag properties. In this section, you learn how to use all the simple actions and you find descriptions of their properties. Required properties are identified; if you save an XPage without specifying a value for the required properties, the XPage has errors (which you can see in the Problems panel). Localizable properties are also identified; these properties can be localized using the built-in localization features, which you learn about in Chapter 18, "Internationalization." The following sections describe each of the simple actions, its properties, and sample usage.

Change Document Mode

The change document mode simple action changes the access mode, read-only or editable, for the specified document.

Tag:

`xp:changeDocumentMode`

Properties:

- **`var:`** The variable name of the document whose mode is to be changed. If not specified, this defaults to `currentDocument` (the closest available Domino Document).
- **`mode:`** The access mode to set for the document. This is a required property.

The mode can be set to one of the following values:

- **`edit:`** Changes the document mode to edit mode so its contents can be modified.
- **`readOnly:`** Changes the document mode to read only; editing is not possible.
- **`autoEdit:`** Changes the document mode to edit if the current user has permission to edit the document; otherwise, set mode to read only.
- **`toggle:`** Toggles the document mode between read-only and edit mode (for example, if document is currently read-only, toggle to edit mode and vice versa).

Sample:

Listing 6.9 shows the change document mode simple action being used to set the mode of the Domino document referenced by `document` to editable. Note that the button that triggers the simple action is displayed only when the document is not already editable.

> **TIP**
>
> If you were to test the sample shown in Listing 6.9 using Preview in Browser with the normal Anonymous as Author access, you find it doesn't work. When you click the button, the document stays in read mode. This is because you need to change Anonymous access to Editor to allow users to edit a document. This can trip you up during development, but it's reassuring to know that users with the incorrect access level cannot edit existing documents, even if the application puts them in a position to do so.

Listing 6.9 Change Document Mode to Editable

```
<xp:button value="Edit" id="button2"
     rendered="#{javascript:!currentDocument.isEditable()}">
     <xp:eventHandler event="onclick" submit="true"
          refreshMode="complete">
          <xp:this.action>
               <xp:changeDocumentMode
                    var="document"
                    mode="edit">
               </xp:changeDocumentMode>
          </xp:this.action>
     </xp:eventHandler>
</xp:button>
```

Confirm Action

The confirm simple action presents the user with a message and options to allow execution to continue or stop.

Tag:

```
xp:confirm
```

Properties:

- **`message`:** The message displayed to the user. This is a required property.

Sample:

Listing 6.10 uses three simple actions, namely the action group, delete document, and confirm actions. The action group and delete document actions are covered later in this section. The confirm action causes a JavaScript function to be included in the rendered page. This function is called after the Delete button is clicked, but before the page is submitted, and prompts the user with the specified message and provides her the opportunity to either proceed or cancel.

TIP

You need to ensure that Anonymous access is allowed to delete documents before this sample works.

Listing 6.10 Confirm Before Deleting a Document

```
<xp:button value="Delete" id="button4"
     rendered="#{javascript:!currentDocument.isNewNote()}">
     <xp:eventHandler event="onclick" submit="true"
          refreshMode="complete">
          <xp:this.action>
               <xp:actionGroup>
                    <xp:confirm
                message="Are you sure you want to delete this
➥document?">
                    </xp:confirm>
                    <xp:deleteDocument name="/AllCars.xsp">
                    </xp:deleteDocument>
               </xp:actionGroup>
          </xp:this.action>
     </xp:eventHandler>
</xp:button>
```

Create Response Document

The create response document simple action creates a response document and opens the specified page to edit it.

Tag:

`xp:createResponse`

Properties:

- **`name`:** The name of the XPage to open to create the response. This is a required property.
- **`parentId`:** The document ID of the parent document for the new response. This is a required property.

Sample:

Listing 6.11 shows the create response simple action being used to create a response with the current document as its parent and the `CarDetails.xsp` page being used to edit the new response.

Listing 6.11 Create Response Document

```
<xp:button value="Add Car Details" id="button5">
     <xp:eventHandler
          event="onclick" submit="true"
          refreshMode="complete">
          <xp:this.action>
               <xp:createResponse
               name="/CarDetails.xsp"
               parentId="#{javascript:currentDocument.getNoteID()}">
               </xp:createResponse>
          </xp:this.action>
     </xp:eventHandler>
</xp:button>
```

Delete Document

The delete document simple action, as the name implies, deletes a document and then opens the specified page. By default, the current document will be deleted.

Tag:

`xp:deleteDocument`

Properties:

- **`message`:** An optional message displayed to the user before the specified document is deleted. This is a localizable property.
- **`var`:** The variable name that references the document to be deleted; if not specified, this defaults to `currentDocument` (closest available Domino Document).
- **`name`:** The name or symbolic identifier of the XPage to be opened after the specified document has been deleted. This is a required property.

The name can be set to the name of an XPage or one of the following symbolic identifiers:

- **`$$PreviousPage`:** The previously opened page.
- **`$$HomePage`:** The launch page, as specified in the application properties.

Sample:

Listing 6.12 shows the delete document being used to delete the document, including allowing the user to confirm that the document should be deleted. If the document is deleted, navigation proceeds to the previous page. The Delete button is not displayed if the current document is new and has not yet been saved because there is nothing to delete in this case.

Listing 6.12 Delete the Current Document and Navigate to the Previous Page

```
<xp:button value="Delete" id="button4"
     rendered="#{javascript:!currentDocument.isNewNote()}">
     <xp:eventHandler event="onclick" submit="true"
          refreshMode="complete">
          <xp:this.action>
               <xp:deleteDocument name="$$PreviousPage"
          message="Are you sure you want to delete this document?">
               </xp:deleteDocument>
          </xp:this.action>
     </xp:eventHandler>
</xp:button>
```

Delete Selected Documents

The delete selected documents simple action deletes the documents selected in a view after first prompting the user to confirm this action.

Tag:

```
xp:deleteSelectedDocuments
```

Properties:

- **`message:`** A message displayed to the user before the specified documents are deleted. This is a localizable property.
- **`noFilesSelectedMessage:`** A message that will be displayed if no documents are selected in the specified view. This is a localizable property.
- **`view:`** The variable name of the view from which the selected documents will be deleted. This is a required property.

Sample:

Listing 6.13 shows a sample action that deletes documents from a view and the message that is displayed to the user before the documents are deleted and the message to use if no documents are selected.

> **TIP**
>
> For this simple action, the convention is to use the column display properties to display a checkbox in the first column of the specified view when you want users to be able to delete selected documents from that view.

Listing 6.13 Delete the Documents Selected in a View

```
<xp:button value="Delete Cars" id="button2">
     <xp:eventHandler
          event="onclick" submit="true"
          refreshMode="complete">
          <xp:this.action>
               <xp:deleteSelectedDocuments view="viewPanel1"
     message="Are you sure you want to delete this documents?"
     noFilesSelectedMessage="No documents are currently selected">
               </xp:deleteSelectedDocuments>
          </xp:this.action>
     </xp:eventHandler>
</xp:button>
```

Execute Client Script

The execute client script simple action executes a client-side JavaScript. This is a client simple action.

Tag:

```
xp:executeClientScript
```

Properties:

- **`script`:** The client script to be executed. This is a required property.

Sample:

Listing 6.14 shows the execute client script simple action being used to display an alert message to the end user. Note that the event handler tag is configured with submit set to false so that clicking the button does not cause the page to be submitted.

Listing 6.14 Executing a Client Script

```
<xp:button value="Execute Client Script" id="button1">
    <xp:eventHandler
        event="onclick" submit="false" refreshMode="complete">
        <xp:this.script>
            <xp:executeClientScript script="alert('Hello World')">
            </xp:executeClientScript>
        </xp:this.script>
    </xp:eventHandler>
</xp:button>
```

Execute Script

The execute script simple action executes a server-side JavaScript expression.

Tag:

`xp:executeScript`

Properties:

- **`script`:** The server script to be executed. This is a required property.

Sample:

Listing 6.15 shows the execute script simple action being used to display a message in the log file.

Listing 6.15 Executing a Server Script

```
<xp:button value="Execute Script" id="button1">
    <xp:eventHandler
        event="onclick" submit="true" refreshMode="complete">
        <xp:this.action>
            <xp:executeScript>
                <xp:this.script>
                <![CDATA[#{javascript:print("Hello World")}]]>
                </xp:this.script>
            </xp:executeScript>
        </xp:this.action>
    </xp:eventHandler>
</xp:button>
```

Modify Field

The modify field simple action modifies a field in the specified document or the current document if none is specified.

Tag:

`xp:modifyField`

Properties:

- **`var`:** The variable name that references the document to be modified, if not specified this defaults to `currentDocument` (closest available Domino Document).
- **`name`:** The name of the field to be modified. This is a required property.
- **`value`:** The new value to be set in the specified field. This property is required and localizable.

Sample:

Listing 6.16 shows how to use the modify field action to set a value in the current document after the page has loaded.

Listing 6.16 Modify Field Being Invoked After Page Has Loaded

```
<?xml version="1.0" encoding="UTF-8"?>
<xp:view xmlns:xp="http://www.ibm.com/xsp/core">
     <xp:this.data>
          <xp:dominoDocument var="dominoDocument1"
               formName="CarDetails">
          </xp:dominoDocument>
     </xp:this.data>
     <xp:this.afterPageLoad>
          <xp:modifyField name="carDescription">
               <xp:this.value>
<![CDATA[<Enter the car description here>]]>
               </xp:this.value>
          </xp:modifyField>
      </xp:this.afterPageLoad>
...
```

Open Page

The open page simple action navigates to a specific page; you can set the document ID of an existing document that can be opened for reading/editing or you can cause the creation of a new document.

Tag:

`xp:openPage`

Properties:

- **`var:`** The variable name that references a document whose ID is passed to the page about to be opened. This value is used if no document ID has been specified using the documentId parameter.
- **`documentId:`** A document ID that is passed to the page about to be opened.
- **`parameters:`** A collection of user defined parameters, name/value pairs, which is passed to the page that is about to be opened.
- **`name:`** The name of the page to be opened. This is a required property.
- **`target:`** The target action to be performed when the new page is opened.

The `target` property can be set to one of the following values:

- `openDocument`: Used when you want to open a page to read a document.
- `editDocument`: Used when you want to open a page to edit a document.
- `newDocument`: Used when you want to open a page to create a new document.

Sample:

Listing 6.17 shows how to use the open page action to open a specific document for editing.

Listing 6.17 Open Page Being Used to Open a Document for Editing

```
<?xml version="1.0" encoding="UTF-8"?>
<xp:view xmlns:xp="http://www.ibm.com/xsp/core">
    <xp:this.data>
         <xp:dominoView var="allCars" viewName="All Cars">
         </xp:dominoView>
    </xp:this.data>
    <xp:repeat id="repeat1" rows="30" var="car" value="#{allCars}">
         <xp:button value="#{javascript:car}" id="button3">
              <xp:eventHandler event="onclick" submit="true"
                   refreshMode="complete">
                   <xp:this.action>
                   <xp:openPage
                       name="/Car.xsp"
                       target="editDocument"
                       documentId="#{javascript:car.getUniversalID()}">
                   </xp:openPage>
                   </xp:this.action>
              </xp:eventHandler>
```

```
        </xp:button>
    </xp:repeat>
</xp:view>
```

Publish Component Property

The publish component property simple action publishes the value for a component event. This is a client simple action.

Tag:

`xp:publishValue`

Properties:

- **`name`:** The name of the property to be published. This is a required property.
- **`value`:** The value of the property to be published. This is a required property.
- **`type`:** The type of the value being published. The default value is text.

The `type` property can be set to one of the following values:

- **`string`:** Used when the component value is a string.
- **`boolean`:** Used when the component value is a boolean.
- **`number`:** Used when the component value is a number.
- **`json`:** Used when the component value is a JavaScript Object Notation (JSON) object. JSON is covered in more detail in Chapter 11.

Sample:

Listing 6.18 shows how to use the publish component property action to publish a value from a column value.

Listing 6.18 Publishing a Column Value as a Component Property

```
<?xml version="1.0" encoding="UTF-8"?>
<xp:view xmlns:xp="http://www.ibm.com/xsp/core">
    <xp:this.data>
        <xp:dominoView var="allCars" viewName="All Cars">
        </xp:dominoView>
    </xp:this.data>
    <xp:repeat id="repeat1" rows="30" var="car" value="#{allCars}">
        <xp:button value="#{javascript:car.getColumnValue('model')}"
            id="button3">
            <xp:eventHandler
                event="onclick" submit="true" refreshMode="complete">
```

```
                <xp:this.script>
                <xp:publishValue
                    name="model"
                    value="#{javascript:car.getColumnValue('model')}"
                    type="string">
                </xp:publishValue>
                </xp:this.script>
            </xp:eventHandler>
        </xp:button>
    </xp:repeat>
</xp:view>
```

TIP

Further examples of publishing component data are explored in the section, "XPages and Composite Applications" in Chapter 13.

Publish View Column

The publish view column simple action publishes the value of a view column as a component event.

Tag:

`xp:publishViewColumn`

Properties:

- **`name`:** The name of the property to be published. This is a required property.
- **`columnName`:** The name of the column whose value is used. This is a required property.
- **`type`:** The new value to be set in the specified field. The default value is text.

The `type` property can be set to one of the following values:

- **`string`:** Used when the component value is a string.
- **`boolean`:** Used when the component value is a boolean.
- **`number`:** Used when the component value is a number.
- **`json`:** Used when the component value is a JSON object.

Sample:

Listing 6.19 shows how to use the publish view column action to publish a value from a view column.

Listing 6.19 Publishing a Column Value as a Component Property

```
<?xml version="1.0" encoding="UTF-8"?>
<xp:view xmlns:xp="http://www.ibm.com/xsp/core">
     <xp:viewPanel rows="30" id="viewPanel1" viewStyle="width:100%">
          <xp:this.data>
               <xp:dominoView var="allCars" viewName="All Cars">
               </xp:dominoView>
          </xp:this.data>
          <xp:viewColumn columnName="Make" id="viewColumn1">
               <xp:viewColumnHeader
                    value="Make" id="viewColumnHeader1">
               </xp:viewColumnHeader>
          </xp:viewColumn>
          <xp:viewColumn
               columnName="Model" id="viewColumn2" displayAs="link">
               <xp:viewColumnHeader
                    value="Model" id="viewColumnHeader2">
               </xp:viewColumnHeader>
               <xp:eventHandler event="onclick" submit="true"
                    refreshMode="complete">
                    <xp:this.script>
                         <xp:publishViewColumn
                              name="model" columnName="Model"
                              type="string">
                         </xp:publishViewColumn>
                    </xp:this.script>
               </xp:eventHandler>
          </xp:viewColumn>
     </xp:viewPanel>
</xp:view>
```

Save Data Sources

The save data sources simple action saves all the data sources in the current page and optionally navigates to another page.

Tag:

`xp:save`

Properties:

- **`name:`** The name of the page to navigate to after the save operation has completed. The symbolic names `$$PreviousPage` and `$$HomePage` can also be used.

Sample:

Listing 6.20 shows how to use the save data sources action to save a Domino Document and navigate to another page with a view so you can see that the documents have been saved. The following page contains two panels, each of which has an associated Domino Document data source and edit controls that allow you to enter in values. Each Domino Document is updated by the corresponding edit controls and, when you click the Save All button, both documents are saved.

Listing 6.20 Saving Two Documents at the Same Time

```
<?xml version="1.0" encoding="UTF-8"?>
<xp:view xmlns:xp="http://www.ibm.com/xsp/core">
     <xp:panel>
          <xp:this.data>
               <xp:dominoDocument var="document1" formName="Car">
               </xp:dominoDocument>
          </xp:this.data>
          <xp:label value="First car make:" for="carMake1">
          </xp:label>
          <xp:inputText value="#{document1.carMake}" id="carMake1">
          </xp:inputText>
          <xp:label value="First car model:" for="carModel1">
          </xp:label>
          <xp:inputText value="#{document1.carModel}" id="carModel1">
          </xp:inputText>
          <xp:br></xp:br>
     </xp:panel>
     <xp:panel>
          <xp:this.data>
               <xp:dominoDocument var="document2" formName="Car">
               </xp:dominoDocument>
          </xp:this.data>
          <xp:label value="Second car make:" for="carMake2">
          </xp:label>
          <xp:inputText value="#{document2.carMake}" id="carMake2">
          </xp:inputText>
```

```
        <xp:label value="Second car model:" for="carModel2">
        </xp:label>
        <xp:inputText value="#{document2.carModel}" id="carModel2">
        </xp:inputText>
    </xp:panel>
    <xp:button value="Save All" id="button1">
        <xp:eventHandler event="onclick" submit="true"
            refreshMode="complete">
            <xp:this.action>
                <xp:save name="/AllCars.xsp"></xp:save>
            </xp:this.action>
        </xp:eventHandler>
    </xp:button>
</xp:view>
```

Save Document

The save document simple action saves the specified document or the current document if none is specified.

Tag:

`xp:saveDocument`

Properties:

- **`var:`** The variable name that references the document to be saved, if not specified this defaults to `currentDocument` (closest available Domino Document).

Sample:

Listing 6.21 shows how to use the save document action to save one of the Domino Documents on a page. The following page contains two panels, each of which has an associated Domino Document data source, edit controls, which allow you to enter in values, and a button to save the corresponding document. The page also contains a view control so you can see what gets saved when you click each button.

Listing 6.21 Save Documents One at a Time

```
<?xml version="1.0" encoding="UTF-8"?>
<xp:view xmlns:xp="http://www.ibm.com/xsp/core">
    <xp:panel>
        <xp:this.data>
            <xp:dominoDocument var="document1" formName="Car">
            </xp:dominoDocument>
```

```
        </xp:this.data>
        <xp:label value="First car make:" for="carMake1">
        </xp:label>
        <xp:inputText value="#{document1.carMake}" id="carMake1">
        </xp:inputText>
        <xp:label value="First car model:" for="carModel1">
        </xp:label>
        <xp:inputText value="#{document1.carModel}" id="carModel1">
        </xp:inputText>
        <xp:button value="Save First" id="button1">
            <xp:eventHandler event="onclick" submit="true"
                refreshMode="complete">
                <xp:this.action>
                    <xp:saveDocument>
                    </xp:saveDocument>
                </xp:this.action>
            </xp:eventHandler>
        </xp:button>
        <xp:br></xp:br>
    </xp:panel>
    <xp:panel>
        <xp:this.data>
            <xp:dominoDocument var="document2" formName="Car">
            </xp:dominoDocument>
        </xp:this.data>
        <xp:label value="Second car make:" for="carMake2">
        </xp:label>
        <xp:inputText value="#{document2.carMake}" id="carMake2">
        </xp:inputText>
        <xp:label value="Second car model:" for="carModel2">
        </xp:label>
        <xp:inputText value="#{document2.carModel}" id="carModel2">
        </xp:inputText>
        <xp:button value="Save Second" id="button2">
            <xp:eventHandler event="onclick" submit="true"
                refreshMode="complete">
                <xp:this.action>
                    <xp:saveDocument>
                    </xp:saveDocument>
                </xp:this.action>
            </xp:eventHandler>
        </xp:button>
    </xp:panel>
```

```
    <xp:viewPanel rows="30" id="viewPanel1" viewStyle="width:100%">
        <xp:this.data>
            <xp:dominoView var="allCars" viewName="All Cars">
            </xp:dominoView>
        </xp:this.data>
        <xp:viewColumn columnName="Make" id="viewColumn1"
            showCheckbox="true">
            <xp:viewColumnHeader
                value="Make" id="viewColumnHeader1">
            </xp:viewColumnHeader>
        </xp:viewColumn>
        <xp:viewColumn columnName="Model" id="viewColumn2"
            displayAs="link" openDocAsReadonly="true">
            <xp:viewColumnHeader
                value="Model" id="viewColumnHeader2">
            </xp:viewColumnHeader>
        </xp:viewColumn>
    </xp:viewPanel>
</xp:view>
```

Set Component Mode

The set component mode simple action is used in a composite application to change the mode of a component to view, edit, or help mode.

Tag:

xp:setComponentMode

Properties:

- **cancel:** Indicates whether the mode can be closed through a cancel button.
- **mode:** The new mode. The mode property can be set to one of the following values:
  - **view:** Used to set the component in view mode.
  - **edit:** Used to set the component in edit mode.
  - **help:** Used to set the component in help mode.

Sample:

Listing 6.22 shows examples of using the set component mode action to set the mode to edit mode and view mode.

Listing 6.22 Change Component Mode to Edit and View Mode

```
<?xml version="1.0" encoding="UTF-8"?>
<xp:view xmlns:xp="http://www.ibm.com/xsp/core">
     <xp:button value="Edit Mode" id="button1">
          <xp:eventHandler event="onclick" submit="true"
               refreshMode="complete">
               <xp:this.action>
                    <xp:setComponentMode cancel="false" mode="edit">
                    </xp:setComponentMode>
               </xp:this.action>
          </xp:eventHandler>
     </xp:button>
     <xp:button value="View Mode" id="button2">
          <xp:eventHandler event="onclick" submit="true"
               refreshMode="complete">
               <xp:this.action>
                    <xp:setComponentMode cancel="false" mode="view">
                    </xp:setComponentMode>
               </xp:this.action>
          </xp:eventHandler>
     </xp:button>
</xp:view>
```

Set Value

The set value simple action sets the value of a computed expression.

Tag:

`xp:setValue`

Properties:

- **`binding`:** A computed expression that points to the data to be updated. This is a required property.
- **`value`:** The value to be set. This is a required property.

Sample:

Listing 6.23 demonstrates how to use the set value action to set a value in View Scope after the page loads. This value is then accessed using a Computed Field in the page.

Listing 6.23 Setting a Value into the viewScope

```
<?xml version="1.0" encoding="UTF-8"?>
<xp:view xmlns:xp="http://www.ibm.com/xsp/core">
     <xp:this.afterPageLoad>
          <xp:setValue
               binding="#{viewScope.afterPageLoadTime}"
               value="#{javascript:new Date()}">
          </xp:setValue>
     </xp:this.afterPageLoad>
     <xp:text escape="true" id="computedField1"
          value="#{viewScope.afterPageLoadTime}">
          <xp:this.converter>
               <xp:convertDateTime
                    type="time" timeStyle="medium">
               </xp:convertDateTime>
          </xp:this.converter>
     </xp:text>
</xp:view>
```

Action Group

The action group simple action is used to execute multiple simple actions. Each action in the group is executed in turn until all actions are executed or one of the actions causes a response to be returned.

Tag:

`xp:actionGroup`

Properties:

- **`actions`:** A list of simple actions to be executed when this group is invoked. This is a required property.
- **`condition`:** A boolean value that must be set to `true` for the group of actions to be invoked. By default this value is true.

Sample:

Listing 6.24 shows how to use action groups to conditionally execute other simple actions. In this example, there are two radio buttons and, depending on which one is selected, a different set value action executes.

Listing 6.24 Using Action Groups to Conditionally Execute Simple Actions

```
<?xml version="1.0" encoding="UTF-8"?>
<xp:view xmlns:xp="http://www.ibm.com/xsp/core">
     <xp:radio text="Group 1" id="radio1" groupName="actionGroup"
          defaultSelected="true" value="#{viewScope.actionGroup}"
          selectedValue="group1">
     </xp:radio>
     <xp:radio text="Group 2" id="radio2" groupName="actionGroup"
          value="#{viewScope.actionGroup}" selectedValue="group2">
     </xp:radio>
     <xp:br></xp:br>
     <xp:text escape="true" id="computedField1"
          value="#{viewScope.executed}">
     </xp:text>
     <xp:br></xp:br>
     <xp:button value="Execute Selected Group" id="button1">
          <xp:eventHandler event="onclick" submit="true"
               refreshMode="complete">
               <xp:this.action>
                    <xp:actionGroup>
                         <xp:actionGroup>
                              <xp:this.condition>
          <![CDATA[#{javascript:viewScope.actionGroup == "group1"}]]>
                              </xp:this.condition>
                              <xp:setValue
                              binding="#{viewScope.executed}"
                              value="Execute Action Group 1">
                              </xp:setValue>
                         </xp:actionGroup>
                         <xp:actionGroup>
                              <xp:this.condition>
          <![CDATA[#{javascript:viewScope.actionGroup == "group2"}]]>
                              </xp:this.condition>
                              <xp:setValue
                              binding="#{viewScope.executed}"
                              value="Execute Action Group 2">
                              </xp:setValue>
                         </xp:actionGroup>
                    </xp:actionGroup>
               </xp:this.action>
          </xp:eventHandler>
     </xp:button>
</xp:view>
```

Send Mail

The send mail simple action allows you to send an e-mail. The standard email parameters—that is, to, from, subject, and so forth—are supported. There is also support for delivery options and embedded experiences. Details of the supported parameters are provided here.

Tag:

`xp:sendMail`

Properties:

- **`from:`** Display email address of the person sending the email. By default the email address of the current user is used. This email address displays for the email, but the actual sender is always the current user.
- **`to:`** Email address(es) of the recipients. (Multiple addresses are separated with commas.)
- **`cc:`** Email address(es) of the carbon copy recipients. (Multiple addresses are separated with commas.)
- **`bcc:`** Email address(es) of the blind carbon copy recipients. (Multiple addresses are separated with commas.)
- **`subject:`** Subject of the email.
- **`bodyHtml:`** Email body content in HTML format.
- **`bodyPlain:`** Email body content in plain text format.
- **`importance:`** Delivery importance, which can be low, medium, or high.
- **`deliveryPriority:`** Delivery priority, which can be low, medium, or high.
- **`deliveryReport:`** Delivery report, which can be none, onlyonfailure, confirmdelivery, or traceentirepath.
- **`preventCopying:`** When set to true will prevent a recipient from copying, printing, forwarding, or replying with history for the sent mail.
- **`markSubjectConfidential:`** When set to true adds a "Confidential" prefix to the subject.
- **`htmlUrl:`** HTML URL for the associated embedded experience.
- **`gadgetUrl:`** Gadget URL for the associated embedded experience.
- **`embeddedFormat:`** Format of the embedded experience MIME part, which can be json or xml.
- **`eeContext:`** A list of name/value pairs, which provides the context for the associated embedded experience.

Sample:

Listing 6.25 shows how to use the send mail simple action. In this example, there are input controls provided for the to, subject, and bodyPlain properties, and the from property is computed based on the current user.

Listing 6.25 Send Mail Simple Action

```
<?xml version="1.0" encoding="UTF-8"?>
    <xp:label value="To:" id="label1">
    </xp:label>
    <xp:br></xp:br>
    <xp:inputText id="inputText1" style="width:300px"
        value="#{viewScope.toInput}">
    </xp:inputText>
    <xp:br></xp:br>
    <xp:br></xp:br>
    <xp:label value="Subject:" id="label2">
    </xp:label>
    <xp:br></xp:br>
    <xp:inputText id="inputText2" style="width:300px"
        value="#{viewScope.subjectInput}">
    </xp:inputText>
    <xp:br></xp:br>
    <xp:br></xp:br>
    <xp:inputTextarea id="inputTextarea1" style="width:300.0px"
        value="#{viewScope.bodyInput}">
    </xp:inputTextarea>
    <xp:br></xp:br>
    <xp:br></xp:br>
    <xp:button value="Send Mail" id="button1">
    <xp:eventHandler event="onclick" submit="true"
➥refreshMode="complete">
    <xp:this.action>
        <xp:sendMail
            from="#{javascript:context.getUser().getMail()}"
            to="#{viewScope.toInput}"
            subject="#{viewScope.subjectInput}"
            bodyPlain="#{viewScope.bodyInput}">
        </xp:sendMail>
    </xp:this.action>
    </xp:eventHandler>
    </xp:button>
</xp:view>
```

Change Dynamic Content

The change dynamic content simple action allows you to change which facet of a dynamic content control displays.

Tag:

`xp:changeDynamicContentAction`

Properties:

- **`facetName:`** Name of the facet to be displayed or one of the following reserved values: -empty- displays nothing, -children- displays the children of the synamic content control, or-default- recomputes the default facet.
- **`for:`** Name of the dynamic content control whose content will be changed.
- **`loaded:`** When set to true (default) this tag is created when the page is loaded.
- **`parameters:`** A list of name/value pairs that are passed as parameters to the simple action.

Sample:

Listing 6.26 shows how to use the change dynamic content simple action to switch between three different facets of a dynamic content control.

Listing 6.26 Change Dynamic Simple Action

```
<?xml version="1.0" encoding="UTF-8"?>
<xp:view xmlns:xp="http://www.ibm.com/xsp/core"
➥xmlns:xe="http://www.ibm.com/xsp/coreex">
    <xe:dynamicContent id="dynamicContent1">
    <xp:this.facets>
        <xp:panel xp:key="first">First Panel</xp:panel>
        <xp:panel xp:key="second">Second Panel</xp:panel>
        <xp:panel xp:key="third">Third Panel</xp:panel>
    </xp:this.facets>
    </xe:dynamicContent>
    <xp:button value="First" id="button1">
        <xp:eventHandler event="onclick" submit="true"
            refreshMode="complete">
            <xp:this.action>
                <xe:changeDynamicContentAction for="dynamicContent1"
                    facetName="first">
                </xe:changeDynamicContentAction>
            </xp:this.action>
        </xp:eventHandler>
    </xp:button>
```

```
    <xp:button value="Second" id="button2">
        <xp:eventHandler event="onclick" submit="true"
            refreshMode="complete">
            <xp:this.action>
                <xe:changeDynamicContentAction for="dynamicContent1"
                    facetName="second">
                </xe:changeDynamicContentAction>
            </xp:this.action>
        </xp:eventHandler>
    </xp:button>
    <xp:button value="Third" id="button3">
        <xp:eventHandler event="onclick" submit="true"
            refreshMode="complete">
            <xp:this.action>
                <xe:changeDynamicContentAction for="dynamicContent1"
                    facetName="third">
                </xe:changeDynamicContentAction>
            </xp:this.action>
        </xp:eventHandler>
    </xp:button>
</xp:view>
```

Move to Application Page

The move to application page simple action allows you to switch to another page in a single page application. This simple action is typically used in mobile applications and is covered in Chapter 14, "XPages Mobile Application Development."

Using JavaScript with XPages

XPages also allows you to use JavaScript to add your own logic to an application. This can be JavaScript that executes within the client (in the browser itself). Alternatively, this can be Java Script that executes on the backend (executed in the Domino server or within Notes embedded web container). So, the first piece of good news is that a single programming language can be used for developing your client and server-side logic. The second piece of good news is that if you have experience developing client-side JavaScript for web applications, you need to learn only a few things to apply those skills to XPages. If you are not familiar with JavaScript, you will likely find it an easy language to learn, and many excellent resources are available on the web to help you. Depending on where the JavaScript executes, the following are different:

- **Object model:** Model used to represent the XPage
- **Global objects:** Implicit objects that can be referenced
- **System libraries:** Libraries of available classes that can be used

Server-Side JavaScript

In this section, you learn about the following topics:

- XPages object model
- Global objects and system libraries

XPages Object Model

The first thing you need to learn is that XPages provides its own object model for server-side JavaScript. This object model is a combination of the JavaServer Faces object model, the Domino object model, and some new objects that XPages provides to make the application developer's life easier. Using server-side JavaScript, you can

- Manipulate the elements of the XPage; that is, you can programmatically modify the component tree of your application.
- Read information about the current request such as parameters, current user, user's locale, and so on.
- Interact with the runtime state, such as determining if the response has been rendered.
- Get information about the current application state, such as associated database.
- Use the Domino backend classes to access the application data, such as Domino documents and views.

Scripting the Component Tree When you create an XPage and add controls, you are actually defining a hierarchical component tree. Each tag in an XPage corresponds to one or more components, and these components can be accessed programmatically and manipulated using JavaScript. Listing 6.27 shows one of the simplest XPages you can create: the "Hello World" sample. From looking at this, you might assume that the component tree consists of an object to represent the `xp:view` tag and another to represent the Hello World text. This is a good guess, but it doesn't tell the full story.

Listing 6.27 Hello World XPage

```
<?xml version="1.0" encoding="UTF-8"?>
<xp:view xmlns:xp="http://www.ibm.com/xsp/core">
    Hello World
</xp:view>
```

To help with the examination of the component trees in this section, the accompanying sample database includes a Custom Control called `ViewInspector`. Custom Controls are covered in Chapter 10, "Custom Controls." For now, it's enough to know that this Custom Control contains a Computed Field that displays a simple string representation of the component tree and can be reused in multiple places within this application. Figure 6.3 shows a preview of the Hello World page that includes the view inspector Custom Control. You can see a basic outline that shows all the components in the current page. For each component, the class name of the Java implementation is displayed along with the component ID and client ID (if these are available). The component ID is the identifier for the control in the XPage and the client ID is the identifier for the control in then generated markup. Client IDs are examined in more detail in the section on Client JavaScript. Notice that there are some unexpected components in the tree and the pass-through text is represented by a component. The Custom Control that displays the component tree is also not included in the outline but this is because the code to generate the outline explicitly ignores this component.

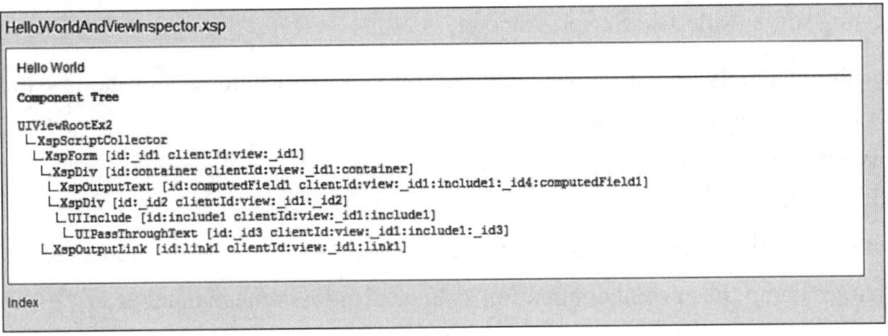

Figure 6.3 Hello World and View Inspector

The script collector and the form components in the hierarchy were automatically included by the component represented by the `xp:view` tag. The script collector's job is to aggregate all the client JavaScript that needs to be emitted as part of the HTML rendering and to emit it together at the end of the rendered page (this is done to optimize the generation of the client-side JavaScript). The form component is responsible for emitting an HTML form in the rendered page. In this case, an HTML form is not required because this page is never submitted. If you ever want to omit the form from the component tree, set the `createForm` property on the `xp:view` tag to `false` using the All Properties tab. Try this yourself and see that the component tree changes. You might want to do this to optimize XPages that are only ever used for presenting data and do not support entering or modifying data.

Listing 6.28 shows the JavaScript code that generates this component tree outline.

Listing 6.28 ViewUtils Script Library

```
function getViewAsString(exclude:string) {
      var retStr = "<hr/><b>Component Tree</b><pre>";
      retStr += getComponentAsString(view, 0, exclude);
      retStr += "</pre>";
      return retStr;
}

function getComponentAsString(component:javax.faces.component.
➥UIComponent, level:int, exclude:string) {
      var retStr = "";
      var id = component.getId();
      if (id == exclude) {
            return retStr;
      }
      for (i=0; i<level; i++) {
            retStr += "  ";
      }
      if (level > 0) {
            var filePath = database.getFilePath();
            retStr += "<img src='/" + filePath + "/descend.gif'>";
      }
      retStr += component.getClass().getName();
      if (id != null) {
            retStr += " [id:" + id;
            retStr += " clientId:" + getClientId(id);
            retStr += "]";
      }
      retStr += "<br/>"

      var children = component.getChildren();
      retStr += getComponentsAsString(children, level + 1, exclude);

      return retStr;
}

function getComponentsAsString(components:java.util.List, level:int,
                                exclude:string) {
      var retStr = "";
      for (component in components) {
```

```
        retStr += getComponentAsString(component, level, exclude)
    }
    return retStr;
}
```

The script library contains the following three methods:

- **`getViewAsString(exclude)`:** This function is passed the ID of a control to be excluded from the outline. It uses the view global object (explained in the section on global objects) as the starting point for creating the outline and adds a title and horizontal rule to the string that is generated. The string is treated as HTML and is emitted as is by the Computed Field in the ViewInspector Custom Control.
- **`getComponentAsString(component, level, exclude)`**: This function is passed the component to generate the outline for the level the component appears in the tree, and the ID of a component to exclude. If the current component is the component to exclude, the function just returns an empty string. Otherwise, it indents the text for this component using non breaking space characters; displays the descend image if the level is greater then zero; and adds the components class name, ID, and client ID to the outline. Finally, this method adds any children of the current component to the outline. Note children are added at a level higher in the outline.
- **`getComponentsAsString(components, level, exclude)`**: This function is passed a list of components to generate the outline for the level the components appears in the tree and the ID of a component to exclude. This function simply calls `getComponentAsString` for each component in the list and adds all the outlines together.

> **TIP**
>
> The view inspector Custom Control contains a Computed Field that calls the `getViewAsString` method and passes the ID of its parent (which is the Custom Control). To get the ID of its parent, the computed expression uses `this.getParent().getId()`. Here, `this` refers to the Computed Field component. This variable is automatically available for any of the component's properties that are computed expressions and it refers to the component itself.

This script library shows a good example of reading the elements in the component tree; however, you can also write logic that manipulates these elements. All the components in the tree extend the JSF defined component interface, `javax.faces.component.UIComponent`. If you want to see what methods are available for the specific component classes, refer to the

XPages Extensibility API Documentation, which is available on the Lotus Notes and Domino Application Development wiki (www-10.lotus.com/ldd/ddwiki.nsf).

> **EMBEDDING JAVA IN JAVASCRIPT**
>
> The previous example demonstrated an example of using Java classes from within Java Script. Any Java classes that are available as a shared library on the server (or within Domino Designer) can be used from within your JavaScript. The use of Java with XPages is covered in Chapter 12, "XPages Extensibility."

> **CONTROL DECLARATION SNIPPETS**
>
> Available since Domino Designer 8.5.2 is the ability to insert control declaration snippets into your server-side JavaScript. For example, if you have a page that contains a button (with control ID set to `"button1"`), you can insert a control -declaration snippet that provides a typed variable to access that control, such as `var button1:com.ibm.xsp.component.xp.XspCommandButton = getComponent ("button1");` To do this, use the **Reference** > **Libraries** > **Control Declaration Snippets** option in the Script Editor. This lists all the controls on the current XPage. By double-clicking a control, the appropriate declaration snippet is inserted for you. Specifying the type for the variable allows the Script Editor to provide the correct type-ahead options and improves your productivity.

From looking at the outline of the Hello World sample, there is a pass-through component with the ID of `_id2` and the class name of `com.ibm.xsp.component.UIPassThroughText`. By referring to the API documentation, you see that this class has methods to get and set the text for the component. So, you can write some server JavaScript that retrieves this component and changes the text. Listing 6.29 shows a sample XPage that does just that. There is a button on the page that, when clicked, invokes some server JavaScript that gets the pass-through component and changes the text.

Listing 6.29 Changing Pass-Through Text

```
<?xml version="1.0" encoding="UTF-8"?>
<xp:view xmlns:xp="http://www.ibm.com/xsp/core"
➥xmlns:xc="http://www.ibm.com/xsp/custom">
    Hello World
    <xp:br></xp:br>
    <xp:button value="Deutsch" id="button1">
        <xp:eventHandler event="onclick" submit="true"
            refreshMode="complete">
            <xp:this.action>
<![CDATA[#{javascript:getComponent("_id2").setText("Hallo Welt");}]]>
```

```
                </xp:this.action>
            </xp:eventHandler>
        </xp:button>
</xp:view>v
```

Figure 6.4 shows the output for a page that includes a view panel control and the view inspector Custom Control. Notice that the pager doesn't appear in the view hierarchy. Looking at the source for the page shows you why this is the case, the pager is added as a facet of the view panel. Facets are used when the parent component has some predefined areas within it that can be used to position children. In this case, the pager is added into the `headerPager` position within the view panel.

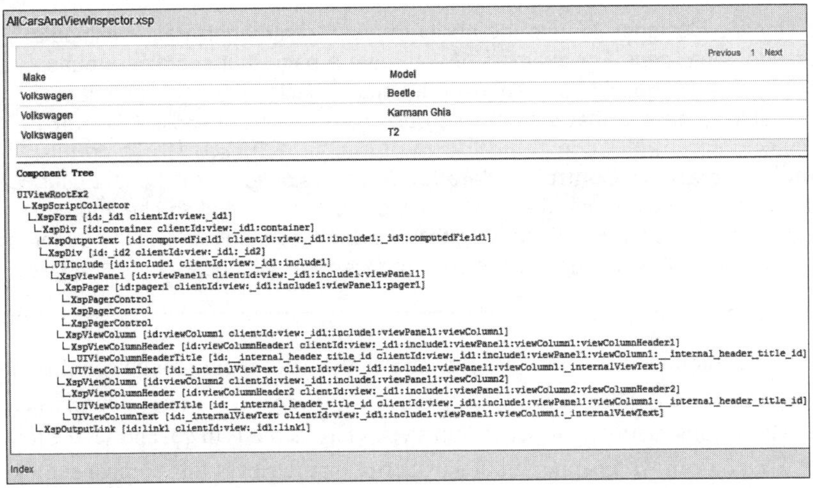

Figure 6.4 Hello World and View Inspector

Displaying facets in the view inspector outline requires some small changes to the Java Script library as demonstrated in Listing 6.30, with some walk-though explanation in the list following.

Listing 6.30 Including Facets in the View Inspector Outline

```
if (id != null) {
    retStr += " [id:" + id;
    try {
            retStr += " clientId:" + getClientId(id);
  }
  catch (e) {
```

```
28.   }
29.   retStr += "]";
30. }
31. retStr += "<br/>"
32.
33. var facetsAndChildren = component.getFacetsAndChildren();
34. retStr += getComponentsAsString(facetsAndChildren, level + 1,
    exclude);
35.
36. return retStr;
37. }
38.
39. function getComponentsAsString(children:java.util.Iterator,
    level:int, exclude:string) {
40. var retStr = "";
41. while (facetsAndChildren.hasNext()) {
42.   retStr += getComponentAsString(facetsAndChildren.next(), level,
      exclude)
43. }
44. return retStr;
45. }
```

- **Lines 24–28:** The method `getClientId` is a built-in function that returns the client ID for the specified component (explained more in section "Global Objects and Functions"). A try-catch block is placed around the call to get the client ID. This is because calling this method for a facet causes an exception to be thrown.
- **Lines 33–24:** The method `getFacetsAndChildren` is a standard JSF method that returns all the child and fact components for the specified component. Call the method `getFacetsAndChildren` to include the facets in the outline. This method returns an instance of `java.util.Iterator`.
- **Lines 39–42:** Handle the iterator to access the facets and children rather than just the list of children. The code calls methods on the iterator to iterate over all the facet and child components.

Global Objects and System Libraries

The Reference tab in the JavaScript editor, shown in Figure 6.5, provides access to the list of available global objects and methods plus the system libraries. By default, most classes and methods are displayed; however, you can select the Show advanced JavaScript option to display the complete list. You can also double-click any entry to add that element to your script.

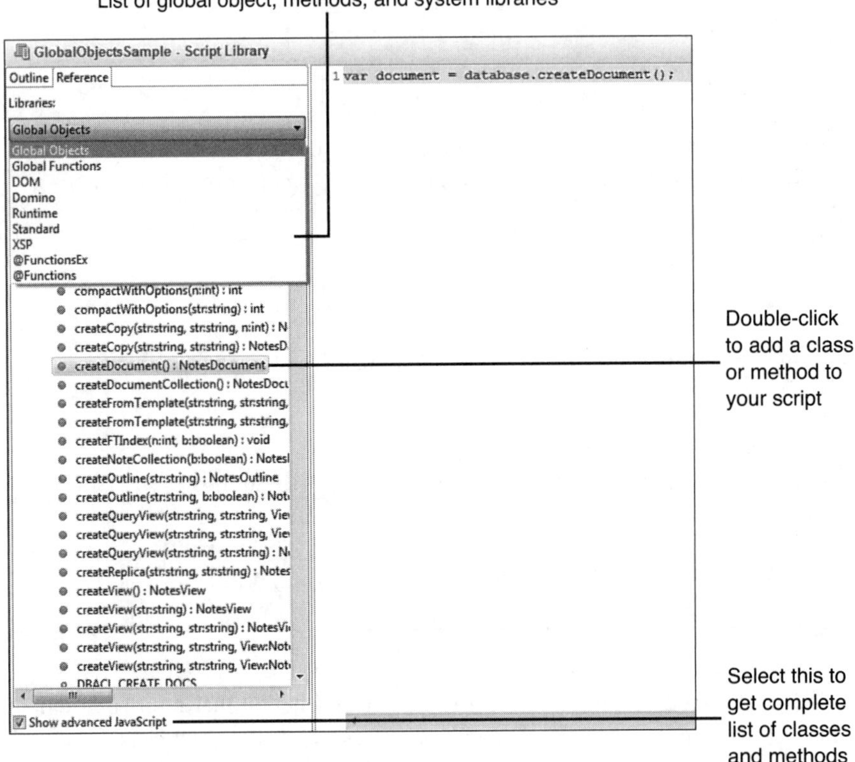

Figure 6.5 JavaScript editor Reference tab

The remainder of this section introduces the different groups of classes and methods and provides some guidance on their usage.

Global Objects and Functions The global objects and functions are available to all server-side JavaScript and provide a way to easily get access to the application objects and perform common actions. This section overviews these objects and functions and provides examples of their use.

Global Object Maps `requestScope`, `applicationScope`, `sessionScope` and `viewScope` are maps of objects, each of which has its own well-defined lifetime. Objects in the `requestScope` map last for the duration of a single request. Objects in the `viewScope` map last for the duration of the page, until the page is discarded by the server. Objects in the `sessionScope` map last for the duration of the user's session, until the user session timeout or the user logs out. Objects in the `applicationScope` map last for the duration of the application. Listing 6.31 uses some server JavaScript to populate a variable in each scope. It also includes `Computed`

Fields to display each of the variables. You can use this sample to learn when variables in each scope become unavailable.

Listing 6.31 Scope Sample

```
<?xml version="1.0" encoding="UTF-8"?>
<xp:view xmlns:xp="http://www.ibm.com/xsp/core">
    <xp:this.afterPageLoad><![CDATA[#{javascript:var now = new Date();
now = now.toString() + ":" + now.getSeconds();
if (!requestScope.containsKey("requestVar")) {
    requestScope.put("requestVar", "Request scope variable added: "+now);
}
if (!viewScope.containsKey("viewVar")) {
    viewScope.put("viewVar", "View scope variable added: "+now);
}
if (!sessionScope.containsKey("sessionVar")) {
    sessionScope.put("sessionVar", "Session scope variable added: "+now);
}
if (!applicationScope.containsKey("applicationVar")) {
    applicationScope.put("applicationVar", "Application scope variable
➥added: "+now);
}}]]></xp:this.afterPageLoad>
    <xp:table>
        <xp:tr>
            <xp:td>Request scope variable:</xp:td>
            <xp:td>
                <xp:text escape="true" id="computedField1"
                value="#{requestScope.requestVar}">
                </xp:text>
            </xp:td>
        </xp:tr>
        <xp:tr>
            <xp:td>View scope variable:</xp:td>
            <xp:td>
                <xp:text escape="true" id="computedField2"
                value="#{viewScope.viewVar}">
                </xp:text>
            </xp:td>
        </xp:tr>
        <xp:tr>
            <xp:td>Session scope variable:</xp:td>
            <xp:td>
                <xp:text escape="true" id="computedField3"
                value="#{sessionScope.sessionVar}">
                </xp:text>
```

```
                </xp:td>
            </xp:tr>
            <xp:tr>
                <xp:td>Application scope variable:</xp:td>
                <xp:td>
                    <xp:text escape="true" id="computedField4"
                    value="#{applicationScope.applicationVar}">
                    </xp:text>
                </xp:td>
            </xp:tr>
        </xp:table>
        <xp:button value="Refresh" id="button1">
            <xp:eventHandler event="onclick" submit="true"
                refreshMode="complete" immediate="false" save="true">
            </xp:eventHandler>
        </xp:button>
        <xp:button value="Reload" id="button2">
            <xp:eventHandler event="onclick" submit="true"
                refreshMode="complete">
                <xp:this.action>
                <![CDATA[#{javascript:context.reloadPage()}]]>
                </xp:this.action>
            </xp:eventHandler>
        </xp:button>
</xp:view>
```

The `requestScope` variable becomes unavailable when you click the Refresh button; the typical use of request scope variables is to pass parameters from one page to another. The `viewScope` variable changes when you click the reload button or reload the web page in your browser. The `requestScope` and `viewScope` variables are useful when you want to compute a value once and then make it available to use in multiple places within a page. The `sessionScope` variable becomes unavailable when the user session expires (if you are previewing you can restart the browser, the typical use is to store some information about a user). The `applicationScope` is still there and unmodified. To get rid of it, you need to restart Domino Designer or, if your application is running on a server, you need to restart the server or you can wait for it to timeout. (It expires after a period of inactivity greater than the xsp.application.timeout setting.) Application scope variables are for things you need to compute once and share across all the XPages in the entire application; all users see the value, so be careful about the security and multithreading implications of using these variables. For example, because application scope variables are visible to all users, avoid storing information that is sensitive for a single user in this scope. Also, because application scope is globally visible and could be updated by multiple users, you need to be careful about using it to store data that could be modified by multiple users at the same time. As a general rule, application scope should be used to store information that applicable for all users and doesn't need to be modified often.

Context Global Object The context global object is an instance of `com.ibm.xsp.designer.context.XSPContext` and represents the XPages runtime. Using this object, you can get and set the state of the runtime and also perform some useful operations such as

- Reloading the current XPage (`context.reloadPage()`)
- Redirecting to another XPage, such as the application home page, the previous page, or a specified page, like `context.redirectToPage(pageName)`
- Accessing the current user (`context.getUser()`)

Session and Database Global Objects The `session` and `database` objects provide access to the user's `NotesSession` and the application's `NotesDatabase`, respectively. These provide a way to perform Domino-related operations, and you see some examples in the next section on Domino classes.

View Global Object The `view` object provides access to the root of the component tree. You saw an example of how you can use this to access any component from the current XPage earlier. You can also use this object to change the state of the view (change the page orientation).

Many global functions are also provided for use within your server-side JavaScript. These global functions provide a convenient way to perform common operations and thereby simplify the code you need to write. The following global functions are provided:

- **`getComponent(id)`:** This allows you to retrieve the component with the specified ID. The origin of the starting point is either the view root or the component where the computed expression is being called from.
- **`getForm()`:** This method returns the `UIForm` instance that contains the component where the computed expression is being called from if one exists; otherwise, it returns null.
- **`getLabelFor(component)`:** Returns the label component associated with the specified component if one exists; otherwise, it returns null.
- **`getView()`:** Returns the view root component associated with the component where the computed expression is being called from.
- **`getClientId(id)`:** Returns the client ID for the specified component if it can be found; otherwise, it throws an exception with the message "Invalid component name." The client ID is the identifier for that component in the generated HTML.
- **`save()`:** Saves all data sources in the current page.

Domino This library provides access to the Domino backend classes. There are currently more than 50 classes in this library; however, if you are already familiar with the standard Notes Java or LotusScript classes, this script library represents a JavaScript interface to the same backend classes.

Listing 6.32 shows you how to use a profile document to store the date a user last visited your application and also how to display the number of days since they last visited.

Listing 6.32 User Profile Sample

```
<?xml version="1.0" encoding="UTF-8"?>
<xp:view xmlns:xp="http://www.ibm.com/xsp/core">
	<xp:this.afterPageLoad><![CDATA[#{javascript:var userName =
context.getUser().getDistinguishedName();
var profileDoc = database.getProfileDocument("UserProfile", userName);
var currentDate = new java.util.Date();
if (!profileDoc.hasItem("lastVisit")) {
	viewScope.put("newUser", true);
	viewScope.put("elapsedDays", 0);
}
else {
	var lastVisit = profileDoc.getItemValueDateTimeArray("lastVisit");
	var lastVisitDateTime = lastVisit.get(0);
	var lastVisitDate = lastVisitDateTime.toJavaDate();
	var elapsedMillis = currentDate.getTime() -
	                    lastVisitDate.getTime();
	var elapsedDays = elapsedMillis / 8640000;
	viewScope.put("elapsedDays", elapsedDays);
	viewScope.put("newUser", false);
}
viewScope.put("lastVisit", currentDate);
var dateTime = session.createDateTime(currentDate);
profileDoc.replaceItemValue("lastVisit", dateTime);
profileDoc.save();}]]></xp:this.afterPageLoad>
	<xp:table>
		<xp:tr>
			<xp:td>New user:</xp:td>
			<xp:td>
				<xp:text escape="true" id="computedField1"
					value="#{viewScope.newUser}">
				</xp:text>
			</xp:td>
		</xp:tr>
		<xp:tr>
			<xp:td>Elapsed days:</xp:td>
			<xp:td>
				<xp:text escape="true" id="computedField2"
					value="#{viewScope.elapsedDays}">
				</xp:text>
			</xp:td>
```

```
            </xp:tr>
            <xp:tr>
                <xp:td>Last visit:</xp:td>
                <xp:td>
                    <xp:text escape="true" id="computedField3"
                        value="#{viewScope.lastVisit}">
                    </xp:text>
                </xp:td>
            </xp:tr>
        </xp:table>
</xp:view>
```

The JavaScript is invoked after the page first loads. The JavaScript code retrieves a user-specific profile document from the database and checks if it contains a field with the date of the user's last visit. If this field does not exist, the code assumes it's the user's first visit, and it puts a flag indicating a new user into the view scope map. If the field exists, the code reads the value and calculates the number of elapsed days and puts this value into the view scope map. Finally, the code updates the user's profile document with the current date and saves the document. Figure 6.6 shows how the page displays the first time it is previewed. Note the user is flagged as a new user and the elapsed days are set to zero. On the second preview, as shown in Figure 6.7, the user is now recognized as a returning user and the elapsed days is updated to reflect the time since the last visit.

Figure 6.6 First preview of the user profile sample

UserProfileSample.xsp
New user: false
Elapsed days: 0.0
Last visit: Jun 18, 2013
Index

Figure 6.7 Second preview of the user profile sample

Runtime The runtime script library provides access to three classes:

- `I18n`
- `Locale`
- `Timezone`

The `I18n` class provides utility methods that help you with the internationalization of your application. This class is discussed further in Chapter 15. The XPage shown in Listing 6.33 shows an example usage of the `Locale` and `Timezone` classes. These classes are standard Java classes, `java.util.Locale` and `java.util.TimeZone`.

Listing 6.33 Locale and TimeZone Sample

```
<?xml version="1.0" encoding="UTF-8"?>
<xp:view xmlns:xp="http://www.ibm.com/xsp/core">
     <xp:table>
          <xp:tr>
               <xp:td colspan="2" style="font-weight:bold">
                  Locale                    </xp:td>
          </xp:tr>
          <xp:tr>
               <xp:td>Country:</xp:td>
               <xp:td>
                    <xp:text escape="true" id="computedField1"
             value="#{javascript:context.getLocale()
                      .getDisplayCountry()}">
                    </xp:text>
               </xp:td>
          </xp:tr>
          <xp:tr>
               <xp:td>Language:</xp:td>
               <xp:td>
                    <xp:text escape="true" id="computedField2"
            value="#{javascript:context.getLocale()
                     .getDisplayLanguage()}">
                    </xp:text>
               </xp:td>
          </xp:tr>
          <xp:tr>
               <xp:td colspan="2" style="font-weight:bold">
                    Time Zone
               </xp:td>
          </xp:tr>
          <xp:tr>
               <xp:td>Name:</xp:td>
```

```
            <xp:td>
                <xp:text escape="true" id="computedField3"
        value="#{javascript:context.getTimeZone().getDisplayName()}">
                </xp:text>
            </xp:td>
        </xp:tr>
    </xp:table>
</xp:view>
```

Figure 6.8 shows a preview of the results from Listing 6.33 and what you see is the locale and time zone information for the current user being displayed in the page.

Figure 6.8 Preview of the Locale and TimeZone sample

Standard The standard library lists the classes that are provided as part of standard Java Script. The JavaScript language elements are based on the ECMAScript Language Specification Standard ECMA-262 (see www.ecma-international.org/publications/standards/Ecma-262.htm). This library is available for both client-side and server-side JavaScript. The standard script library provides access to these classes:

- **`Array`:** Used when working with arrays
- **`Boolean`:** Used when working with boolean values
- **`Date`:** Used when working with date and time values
- **`Math`:** Provides some common mathematical values and functions
- **`Number`:** Used when working with numeric values
- **`Object`:** Provides common methods that are available in all classes
- **`RegExp`:** Provides properties and functions that can be used when working with regular expressions
- **`String`:** Used when working with string values

XSP The XSP script library provides access to some XPages-specific runtime objects. These classes provide access to information and allow manipulation of the runtime context.

Additionally, these classes wrap some commonly used objects and provide additional/simpler access. This library includes the following classes:

- **DirectoryUser:** Represents a user entry in the server directory.
- **NotesXspDocument:** Represents a Notes document in the XPages runtime. This class provides methods to simplify access to a Notes document.
- **NotesXspViewEntry:** Represents an entry from a Notes view in the XPages runtime. This class provides methods to simplify access to a Notes view entry.
- **XSPContext:** The XPages runtime context object.
- **XSPUrl:** Represents a URL.
- **XSPUserAgent:** Represents the User-Agent request header field of the HTTP request sent from the browser.

The XPage shown in Listing 6.34 shows some sample usage of the `DirectoryUser`, `XSPUrl`, and `XSPUserAgent` classes to perform the following operations:

1. Get the distinguished name of the current user by using `context.getUser()` to retrieve a `DirectoryUser` instance for the current user and then using `getDistingushedName()`.
2. Check if the current user is anonymous by using `context.getUser()` to retrieve a `DirectoryUser` instance for the current user and then using `isAnonymous()`.
3. Get the URL of the current page by using `context.getUrl()`.
4. Get the browser name by using `context.getUserAgent()` to retrieve a `XSPuserAgent` instance and then using `getBrowser()`.
5. Get the browser version by using `context.getUserAgent()` to retrieve a `XSPuserAgent` instance and then using `getBrowserVersion()`.

Listing 6.34 DirectoryUser, XSPUrl, and XSPUserAgent Sample

```
<?xml version="1.0" encoding="UTF-8"?>
<xp:view xmlns:xp="http://www.ibm.com/xsp/core">
      <xp:table>
            <xp:tr>
                  <xp:td colspan="2" style="font-weight:bold">
                        DirectoryUser
                  </xp:td>
            </xp:tr>
            <xp:tr>
                  <xp:td>Distingushed Name:</xp:td>
                  <xp:td>
                        <xp:text escape="true" id="computedField1"
      value="#{javascript:context.getUser().getDistinguishedName()}">
```

```
                </xp:text>
            </xp:td>
        </xp:tr>
        <xp:tr>
            <xp:td>Anonymous:</xp:td>
            <xp:td>
                <xp:text escape="true" id="computedField2"
            value="#{javascript:context.getUser().isAnonymous()}">
                </xp:text>
            </xp:td>
        </xp:tr>
        <xp:tr>
            <xp:td colspan="2" style="font-weight:bold">
                 XSPUrl
            </xp:td>
        </xp:tr>
        <xp:tr>
            <xp:td>Url:</xp:td>
            <xp:td>
                <xp:text escape="true" id="computedField3"
                    value="#{javascript:context.getUrl()}">
                </xp:text>
            </xp:td>
        </xp:tr>
        <xp:tr>
            <xp:td colspan="2" style="font-weight:bold">
                XSPUserAgent
            </xp:td>
        </xp:tr>
        <xp:tr>
            <xp:td>Browser:</xp:td>
            <xp:td>
                <xp:text escape="true" id="computedField4"
        value="#{javascript:context.getUserAgent().getBrowser()}">
                </xp:text>
            </xp:td>
        </xp:tr>
        <xp:tr>
            <xp:td>Browser Version:</xp:td>
            <xp:td>
                <xp:text escape="true" id="computedField5"
    ➥value="#{javascript:context.getUserAgent().getBrowserVersion()}">
                </xp:text>
            </xp:td>
        </xp:tr>
    </xp:table>
</xp:view>
```

Figure 6.9 shows a preview of the results from Listing 6.34. The distinguished name for the current user and a flag indicating whether they are anonymous is displayed. The preview in Figure 6.9 is using the browser so the user is anonymous; however, in Figure 6.10, a Notes client is used so the user's Notes distinguished name is displayed. The URL for the page also differs between the browser and Notes preview, you can see that, in the Notes case, there is a request parameter that indicates XPages is running in a Notes context, `xspRunningContext` is set to the value `Notes`. The user agent information is really only useful when you are running in the Browser context.

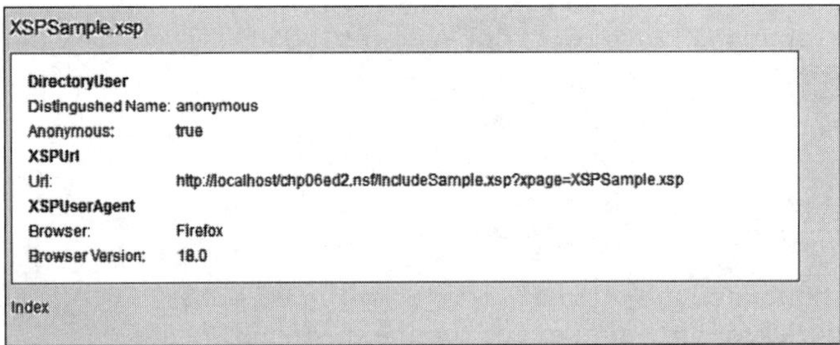

Figure 6.9 Browser preview of the DirectoryUser, XSPUrl, and XSPUserAgent sample

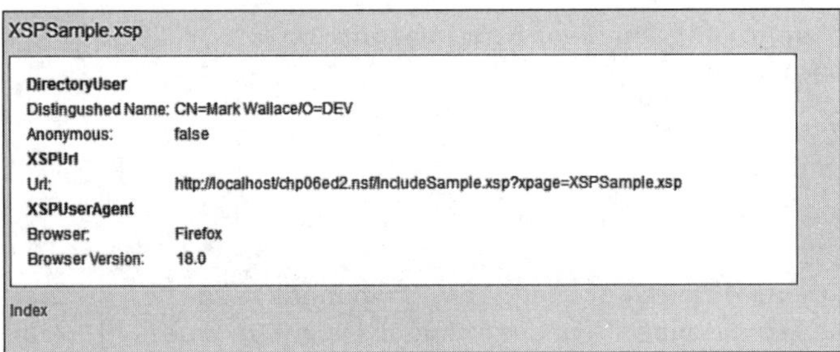

Figure 6.10 Notes preview of the DirectoryUser, XSPUrl, and XSPUserAgent sample

Earlier, you saw an example of how to use the `NotesDocument` class to read a date/time value from a profile document. It took three lines of code to do this. Using the `NotesXsp Document` simplifies the coding even further. The XPage shown in Listing 6.35 includes a computed expression that retrieves a date value from a Domino document data source. The Domino document data source makes the document available using the specified variable name, but also the default variable name `currentDocument`, which references a `NotesXspDocument` instance. The JavaScript in Listing 6.35 makes a call to the current document to get the date value and it returns an instance of `java.util.Date` directly.

Listing 6.35 NotesXspDocument Sample

```
<?xml version="1.0" encoding="UTF-8"?>
<xp:view xmlns:xp="http://www.ibm.com/xsp/core">
    <xp:this.data>
        <xp:dominoDocument var="dominoDocument1" formName="UserProfile"
             action="openDocument">
                <xp:this.documentId>
                <![CDATA[#{javascript:var userName =
➥context.getUser().getDistinguishedName();
var profileDoc = database.getProfileDocument("UserProfile", userName);
return profileDoc.getUniversalID();}]]>
                </xp:this.documentId>
        </xp:dominoDocument>
    </xp:this.data>
    <xp:text escape="true" id="computedField1">
        <xp:this.value>
        <![CDATA[#{javascript:currentDocument.getItemValueDate
                    ("lastVisit")}]]>
        </xp:this.value>
        <xp:this.converter>
             <xp:convertDateTime type="both"></xp:convertDateTime>
        </xp:this.converter>
    </xp:text>
</xp:view>
```

@Functions This library contains a collection of JavaScript methods that emulate the Lotus Notes @Functions. The @Functions provide a way for you to perform common Notes-related operations, like return the names of the authors for the current document or perform some string manipulation operations. For readers who are familiar with the traditional Notes programming model, this allows you to apply your existing knowledge to XPages. You need to be aware of some syntax differences: The JavaScript @Function method names are case sensitive and use commas as parameter separators, and not semicolons. The use of these methods is discussed in Chapter 11.

DOM This library contains a collection of classes that can be used to create and manipulate an XML document. The XPage shown in Listing 6.36 uses the DOM script library to dynamically create an XML document.

Listing 6.36 DOM Sample

```
<?xml version="1.0" encoding="UTF-8"?>
<xp:view xmlns:xp="http://www.ibm.com/xsp/core">
  <xp:this.beforePageLoad><![CDATA[#{javascript:
var document = DOMUtil.createDocument();
```

```
5. var person = document.createElement("person");
6. document.appendChild(person);
7. var firstName = document.createElement("firstName");
8. firstName.setStringValue("Joe");
9. person.appendChild(firstName);
10. var lastName = document.createElement("lastName");
11. person.appendChild(lastName);
12. lastName.setStringValue("Bloggs");
13. requestScope.put("document", document);
14. }]]></xp:this.beforePageLoad>
15.    <xp:text escape="true" id="computedField1"
16.          value="${xpath:document:/person/firstName}">
17. </xp:text>
18.    <xp:text escape="true" id="computedField2"
19. value="${xpath:document:/person/lastName}">
20. </xp:text>
21. </xp:view>
```

- **Lines 4–13:** This server script creates an XML document with a root element named person, which has two child elements named firstName and lastName, respectively. Each child element contains a string value, such as Joe and Bloggs, respectively. Finally the XML document is placed in the `requestScope` map.
- **Lines 15–20:** Two Computed Fields use an XPath value binding to display the values from the XML document. XPath, the XML Path Language, is a query language that allows you to select nodes from an XML document. Here, it is being used to extract values from the XML document that was created before the page was loaded and made available using the document variable.

Client JavaScript

In general, developing client JavaScript in XPages is the same as developing client JavaScript for a web application; however, you need to consider some factors:

- Control IDs versus client IDs
- Including server data in your client JavaScript
- Adding client and server logic to the same event
- Using the XSP client script library

Control IDs Versus Client IDs

The ID you specify in the XPage markup is not the same as the ID that is used on the corresponding element in the HTML DOM. This is because the JSF engine creates different IDs for use in the generated markup. You can use the view inspector Custom Control mentioned earlier to see the client IDs that are assigned to the controls in your XPage. The XPage shown in Listing 6.37 includes three button controls. The first button is added directly to the page. The second button is nested inside a Repeat control, which repeat twice. The third button is nested inside a Repeat control, which creates its contents three times.

Listing 6.37 Client ID Sample

```
<?xml version="1.0" encoding="UTF-8"?>
<xp:view xmlns:xp="http://www.ibm.com/xsp/core"
     xmlns:xc="http://www.ibm.com/xsp/custom">
     <xp:button value="Button1" id="button1">
     </xp:button>
     <xp:repeat id="repeat1" value="2">
          <xp:button value="Button2" id="button2">
          </xp:button>
     </xp:repeat>
     <xp:repeat id="repeat2" value="3"
           repeatControls="true">
          <xp:button value="Button3" id="button3">
          </xp:button>
     </xp:repeat>
     <xc:ViewInspector></xc:ViewInspector>
</xp:view>
```

Figure 6.11 shows a browser preview of this client IDs sample. You can see the control ID and client ID of each button because the view inspector is included on the page. The reason that the client ID is not the same as the control ID is because of a behavior defined as part of JavaServer Faces. Certain JSF components provide a namespace for the IDs of their child components. These components are instances of `javax.faces.component.NamingContainer`, which is the interface that identifies that this component provides a new namespace. In JSF, component ID uniqueness is only required between all children of a `NamingContainer`. XPages enforces control ID unique for the entire page, which is more restrictive than JSF requires, but this helps avoid logic errors in your applications. This `NamingContainer` behavior is important for Custom Controls and when including XPages within XPages. In a Custom Control, there is no 100 percent reliable way to guarantee uniqueness, so the component used to include a Custom Control is a `NamingContainer` and, hence, provides a new namespace. Other controls in XPages also include this behavior, and you can check which ones do by referring to the API documentation. So, the client ID for the first button in the sample is `view:_id1:button1`, and you can see that this is made up of the control ID prefixed with the control IDs of the `NamingContainer` ascendants of the button control. Moving a control within the page—such as inside a repeat—changes the client ID. The repeat includes the row index in each client ID, so the client ID is unique for each iteration of the repeat. Also, changing the properties of a repeat changes the client ID. So, you can see that hard-coding these client IDs is a recipe for constantly tweaking your client script and constant heartache.

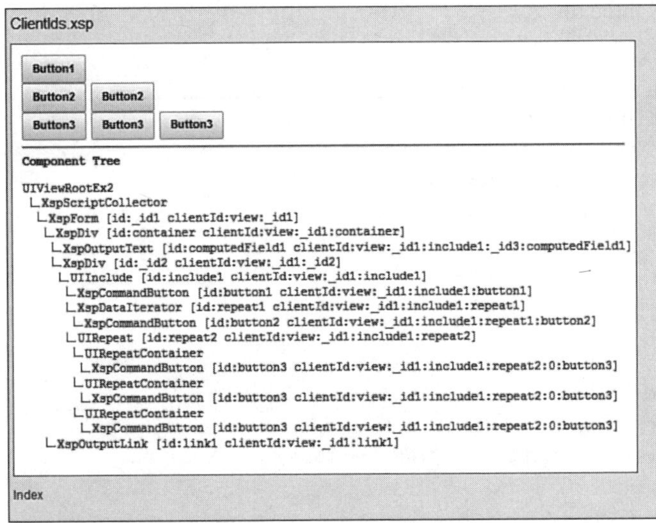

Figure 6.11 Browser preview of client ID sample

Thankfully, there are a couple of ways to compute the client ID. The Custom Control that generates the client ID uses the `getClientId()` global function, which is ideal when using server JavaScript. You can also use an ID computed expression when you are writing client JavaScript, as shown in Listing 6.38. If you preview this sample and click the button, an alert box is displayed containing the button's client ID.

Listing 6.38 Using an ID Computed Expression to Compute a Control's Client ID

```
<?xml version="1.0" encoding="UTF-8"?>
<xp:view xmlns:xp="http://www.ibm.com/xsp/core">
     <xp:button value="What is my Client Id?" id="button1">
          <xp:eventHandler event="onclick" submit="false">
               <xp:this.script>
<![CDATA[alert("#{id:button1}")]]>
</xp:this.script>
          </xp:eventHandler>
     </xp:button>
</xp:view>
```

Including Server Data in Your Client JavaScript

You just saw how to use an ID value binding to dynamically compute a control's client ID, and this is the first example of how to use the results of a server computation in your client script. Listing 6.39 shows an XPage that displays some data returned from a server JavaScript. You can see that a JavaScript computed expression is included in the client JavaScript. This works because a computed expression can be made up of static and dynamic parts. In this example, the computed expression is made up of the following three parts:

- `alert("`
- `#{javascript:getDatabaseDetails()`
- `")`

When this expression gets evaluated, it returns the following `alert("<string returned by getDatabaseDetails >")`, and this is what is included in the generated markup.

Listing 6.39 Using Output from a JavaScript-Computed Expression in Client JavaScript

```
<?xml version="1.0" encoding="UTF-8"?>
<xp:view xmlns:xp="http://www.ibm.com/xsp/core">
     <xp:this.resources>
          <xp:script src="/DatabaseDetails.jss" clientSide="false">
          </xp:script>
     </xp:this.resources>
     <xp:button value="Show Database Details" id="button1">
          <xp:eventHandler event="onclick" submit="false">
               <xp:this.script>
          <![CDATA[alert("#{javascript:getDatabaseDetails()}")]]>
               </xp:this.script>
          </xp:eventHandler>
     </xp:button>
</xp:view>
```

For completeness, Listing 6.40 provides the server JavaScript used in Listing 6.39.

Listing 6.40 Server JavaScript to Return Some Database Details

```
function getDatabaseDetails() {
     var serverName = session.getServerName();
     var onServer = session.isOnServer();
     var filePath = database.getFilePath();
     var creationDate = database.getCreated().toJavaDate();
     var managers = database.getManagers();
```

```
    var retStr = "Server name: "+serverName;
    retStr += " On server:"+onServer;
    retStr += " Database file path:"+filePath;
    retStr += " Creation date:"+creationDate;
    retStr += " Managers:";
    for (manager in managers) {
        retStr += manager + ";";
    }
    return retStr;
}
```

Adding Client and Server Logic to the Same Event

You can add client and server logic that is triggered by the same event, such as a button click, as shown in Listing 6.41. Here, the user is asked for confirmation before the execution of the server logic associated with a button click. If you run the sample, you are asked if you are sure you want to refresh the page, and clicking Cancel prevents the page from being submitted and updated.

Listing 6.41 Confirming Execution of the Server Logic by Prompting the User

```
<?xml version="1.0" encoding="UTF-8"?>
<xp:view xmlns:xp="http://www.ibm.com/xsp/core">
    <xp:this.afterPageLoad>
    <![CDATA[#{javascript:viewScope.put("currentTime",
➥java.lang.System.currentTimeMillis())}]]>
    </xp:this.afterPageLoad>
    <xp:text escape="true" id="computedField1"
        value="#{javascript: return new
➥Date(viewScope.currentTime);}"
        style="font-size:12pt;font-weight:bold">
    <xp:this.converter>
        <xp:convertDateTime type="both"></xp:convertDateTime>
    </xp:this.converter>
    </xp:text>
    <xp:br></xp:br>
    <xp:button value="Refresh" id="button1">
        <xp:eventHandler event="onclick" submit="true">
            <xp:this.script>
<![CDATA[if(window.confirm("Are you sure you want to refresh this
➥page?") != true) return false;]]>
            </xp:this.script>
            <xp:this.action>
<![CDATA[#{javascript:viewScope.put("currentTime",
➥java.lang.System.currentTimeMillis())}]]>
```

```
            </xp:this.action>
        </xp:eventHandler>
    </xp:button>
</xp:view>
```

Using the XSP Client Script Library

XPages provides a client JavaScript library that you can reference from within your client logic.

Useful XSP Properties The following three properties are the most useful of the available properties in the XSP client script library:

- **`validateAllFields`:** Normally, when submitting a page, the input values are validated, but the validation processes after the first failure. When the first validation failure occurs, the function `validationError` is invoked and, by default, this displays a message to the user containing the reason validation failed. This behavior of stopping after the first validation failure is controlled by the `validateAllFields` property, which has the default value of false. You can override the `validationError` function if desired and, if you want to validate all values irrespective of failures, you can change the `validateAllFields` property to true.
- **`lastSubmit`:** The property contains the timestamp of the last time this page was submitted. This property set when the method `XSP.canSubmit()` is invoked prior to submitting the page. It is recommended you use `XSP.canSubmit()` rather than modifying this value directly.
- **`submitLatency`:** This property contains the minimum number of milliseconds allowed between page submissions. The default value is 20,000 (20 seconds).

Useful XSP Functions The following functions are the most useful of the available properties in the XSP client script library:

- **`alert`**, **`error`**, **`confirm`**, **`prompt`**: When running in a browser, these methods simply wrap the standard JavaScript methods for invoking pop-up boxes. So, to display a message to the user, you can use `XSP.alert("Hello")`. When running in the Notes client, the implementation changes to display a native Notes dialog. It is recommended you use these methods if your application is going to be used from the Notes client.
- **`partialRefreshGet`**, **`partialRefreshPost`**: Used to invoke an AJAX GET or POST request to refresh part of the current page. Sample uses of these methods are provided in Chapter 11.
- **`publishEvent`:** Publishes a component event when running in the Notes client. Again, a sample usage of this method is provided in Chapter 13.
- **`showSection`:** Shows/hides a section of the current page.

- **`findForm`**, **`findParentByTag`**, **`getElementById`**: These useful DOM functions can find elements in the current page.
- **`trim`**, **`startsWith`**, **`endsWith`**: These useful string utility methods can help with string manipulation.
- **`log`**: Creates a logging message that is displayed in the JavaScript console.

Using the JSON RPC Service

XPages provides a way to invoke server-side application logic from the client. There are a number of scenarios in which this is a useful tool:

- Define a client interface based on some legacy application logic; for example, existing Java libraries.
- Solution to cross-domain policy issues.
- Developing dynamic web interfaces.

The Java code shown in Listing 6.42 shows how to use the Apache HttpClient component to make a HTTP GET request against a URL and to return the response body. The code can be used to provide a simple Ajax Proxy within an application to avoid same origin policy issues. The same origin policy is a browser security restriction which prevents script running in a web page from accessing different sites; that is, you cannot make an XML Http Request to a different site.

Listing 6.42 Simple Ajax Proxy

```
public class AjaxProxy implements Serializable {

       private static final long serialVersionUID = 1L;

       public String get(String url) {
            HttpClient httpClient = new DefaultHttpClient();
        try {
            HttpGet httpGet = new HttpGet(url);
            ResponseHandler<String> responseHandler = new
➥BasicResponseHandler();
            return httpClient.execute(httpGet, responseHandler);
        } catch (Exception e) {
              return e.getMessage();
        } finally {
            httpClient.getConnectionManager().shutdown();
        }
       }
}
```

To use the Apache Components in an XPages application, you need to first import the appropriate Jar files into your application. Figure 6.12 shows the Apache Jars used in the sample associated with this chapter.

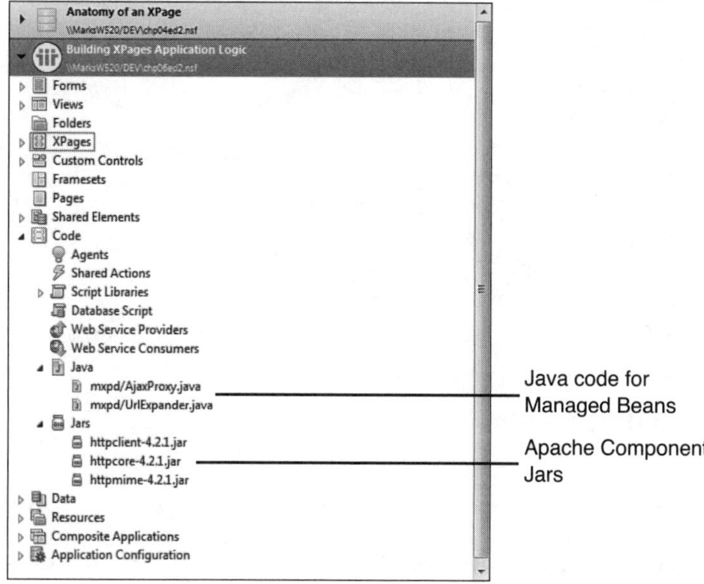

Figure 6.12 Application Jars

The simple Ajax Proxy code can be added to an XPages application as a managed bean as described in Chapter 11. The XPage shown in Listing 6.43 shows how to use the JSON RPC Service to invoke the simple Ajax Proxy and display the return value in a JavaScript alert.

Listing 6.43 Simple Ajax Proxy Sample

```
<?xml version="1.0" encoding="UTF-8"?>
<xp:view xmlns:xp="http://www.ibm.com/xsp/core"
        xmlns:xe="http://www.ibm.com/xsp/coreex">
      <xe:jsonRpcService id="jsonRpcService1" serviceName="ajaxProxy"
            state="false">
            <xe:this.methods>
                  <xe:remoteMethod name="get">
                        <xe:this.arguments>
                              <xe:remoteMethodArg
                                  name="url" type="string">
                              </xe:remoteMethodArg>
```

```
                            </xe:this.arguments>
                            <xe:this.script><![CDATA[return
➥ajaxProxy.get(url);]]>
                            </xe:this.script>
                    </xe:remoteMethod>
            </xe:this.methods>
      </xe:jsonRpcService>
      <xp:inputText id="inputText1"
  defaultValue="http://www.google.com">
      </xp:inputText>
       <xp:button value="Get" id="button1">
            <xp:eventHandler event="onclick" submit="false">
                  <xp:this.script><![CDATA[var inputText1 =
➥document.getElementById("#{id:inputText1}");
var deferred = ajaxProxy.get(inputText1.value);
deferred.addCallback(function(response) {
      alert(response);
});]]></xp:this.script>
            </xp:eventHandler>
      </xp:button>
</xp:view>
```

This idea can be extended to develop a service that wraps a specific REST API; for example, the Google URL shortener API (see http://goo.gl/). The Java code shown in Listing 6.44 shows how to use the Apache HttpClient to invoke the Google URL Shortener API to expand a shortened URL. This code could optionally retrieve an API key to use when invoking the Google REST API or other data OAuth keys if that were required.

Listing 6.44 URL Expander

```
<?xml version="1.0" encoding="UTF-8"?>
public class UrlExpander implements Serializable {

      private static final long serialVersionUID = 1L;

      public String expandUrl(String url) {
            HttpClient httpClient = createHttpClient();
        try {
            url = URLEncoder.encode(url, "UTF-8");
            HttpGet httpGet = new HttpGet("https://www.googleapis.com/
➥urlshortener/v1/url?shortUrl=" + url);
            ResponseHandler<String> responseHandler = new
➥BasicResponseHandler();
            return httpClient.execute(httpGet, responseHandler);
        } catch (HttpResponseException hre) {
```

```
            return hre.getStatusCode() + " " + hre.getMessage();
        } catch (Exception e) {
            e.printStackTrace();
            return "Error: " + e.getMessage();
        } finally {
            httpClient.getConnectionManager().shutdown();
        }
    }
}
```

The XPage shown in Listing 6.45 shows how to use the JSON RPC Service to invoke the URL expander and to display the expanded URL in a JavaScript alert.

Listing 6.45 URL Expander Sample

```
<?xml version="1.0" encoding="UTF-8"?>
<xp:view xmlns:xp="http://www.ibm.com/xsp/core"
xmlns:xe="http://www.ibm.com/xsp/coreex">
	<xe:jsonRpcService id="jsonRpcService1" serviceName="urlExpander"
		state="false">
		<xe:this.methods>
			<xe:remoteMethod name="expandUrl">
				<xe:this.arguments>
					<xe:remoteMethodArg
name="url" type="string">
</xe:remoteMethodArg>
				</xe:this.arguments>
				<xe:this.script><![CDATA[return
urlExpander.expandUrl(url);]]>
				</xe:this.script>
			</xe:remoteMethod>
		</xe:this.methods>
	</xe:jsonRpcService>
	<xp:inputText id="inputText1" defaultValue="http://goo.gl/IFb9C">
</xp:inputText>
	 <xp:button value="Expand URL" id="button1">
		<xp:eventHandler event="onclick" submit="false">
			<xp:this.script><![CDATA[var inputText1 =
➥document.getElementById("#{id:inputText1}");
var deferred = urlExpander.expandUrl(inputText1.value);
deferred.addCallback(function(response) {
	var computedField1 = document.getElementById
➥("#{id:computedField1}");
	computedField1.innerHTML = response;
});]]></xp:this.script>
```

```
            </xp:eventHandler>
        </xp:button>
        <xp:br/><xp:br/>
        <pre>
            <xp:text escape="true" id="computedField1"></xp:text>
        </pre>
</xp:view>
```

Figure 6.13 shows the URL Expander XPage in action.

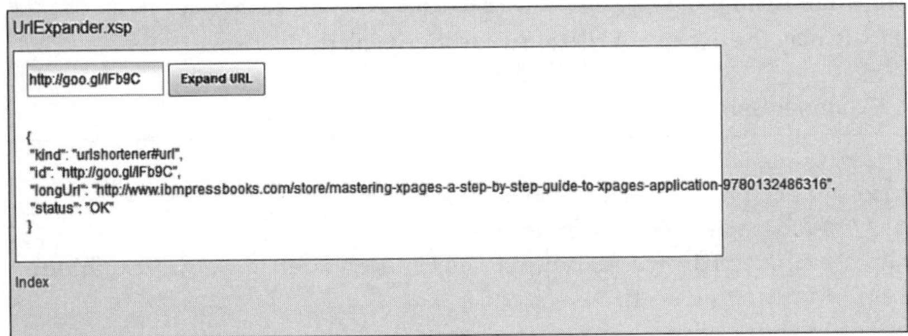

Figure 6.13 Using URL Expander

Conclusion

This concludes the first chapter of dealing with creating your own application logic within XPages. You learned the basic concepts that enable you to use simple actions, server, and client JavaScript. In Chapter 11, you learn advanced topics, such as AJAX, partial refresh, Dojo integration, and more.

Another great source of information is the introduction to the JavaScript and XPages reference that is part of the Notes/Domino Infocenter. The current version is available at `http://tinyurl.com/pk9cwlt`.

Part III

Data Binding

CHAPTER 7

Working with Domino Documents

Notes/Domino is often referred to as a distributed document-centric database system. Sometimes, this description is used as a convenient means of defining what Notes is not—as in, it is not a relational or object database, without actually attempting to identify what its key characteristics really are, so it might be useful to do so quickly here.

A Notes application or database is manifested on disk as a Notes Storage File (NSF). All information stored within an NSF is contained in a collection of data documents or design documents. Each document in turn contains fields or items (these terms can be used interchangeably) of different data types, from simple scalar types to multivalue fields and ultimately to rich text content. Documents are created based on a design element called a form, but do not require a strict schema per se. This loose and less formalized structure facilitates the quick and easy construction of collaborative applications and is at the heart of what makes IBM Notes a leader in this space. Notes provide many other core features that further underpin this document-centric collaborative system, like full-text indexing, document-level access control, and field-level data replication. In fact, the very name of the product, "Notes," can also be thought of as reference to a collection of documents! In the Notes/Domino world, the terms "note" and "document" are used interchangeably. (Note ID is synonymous with document ID, and so on.)

Suffice to say, therefore, that if you are to get very far with XPages development, you need to have a firm grasp of how XPages works with Notes documents. This is the focus of this chapter. Because the document as an entity is so central to everything Notes is and does, some document-related topics are given more expansive treatment in later chapters, and so forward references are included here as appropriate. In any case, the logical place to start is with a discussion of how XPages accesses and uses Notes documents—via the Domino document data source. You need a sample application to work through the examples covered in this chapter, so download **Chp07ed2.nsf** from the following website, `www.ibmpressbooks.com/title/9780133373370`, and open it in Domino Designer before getting started.

Domino Document Data Source

Chapter 3, "Building Your First XPages Application," introduced the concept of the data source, and you used a Domino document data source in the process of building a simple sample application, albeit in a basic manner. The document data source enables XPages controls to bind to the underlying Notes/Domino document data. There are four ways to create a document data source in Domino Designer:

- From the **New XPage** dialog box when creating a new XPage
- Through the **Data** property panel options for most XPages controls
- Through the **Define Data Source** option in the **Data** palette combo box
- By creating the `<xp:dominoDocument>` tag directly in the XSP markup via the Designer **Source** window

The user interface for creating a document data source contains the same options whether launched through the New XPage dialog box or anywhere else in Domino Designer. Figure 7.1 shows the UI options as laid out in the New XPage dialog. Note that custom controls may also contain document data sources, although the New Custom Control dialog does not provide the option.

Regardless of method, creating a document data source results in the creation of an `<xp:dominoDocument>` tag. For example, clicking the **OK** button in the dialog shown in Figure 7.1 generates the XSP markup shown in Listing 7.1, not including the comment!

Listing 7.1 Basic Document Data Source Markup

```
<?xml version="1.0" encoding="UTF-8"?>
<xp:view xmlns:xp="http://www.ibm.com/xsp/core">
  <!-- this data source is available to any control on the XPage -->
  <xp:this.data>
    <xp:dominoDocument formName="Main Topic" var="document1"/>
  </xp:this.data>
</xp:view>
```

In this example, the data source lists just two properties. The form specified as the `formName` makes any fields defined on that form (including those defined in its subforms) available for data binding on this XPage, which effectively means that the nominated form is the data schema for the XPage. The `var` property is the only mandatory document data source property, and without it, there would be no way for XPages controls to refer to the data source component! In other words, the `var` value is the reference variable used by controls elsewhere on the XPage to access the data source object. Table 7.1 gives the complete list of all Domino document data source properties along with a brief description of each one.

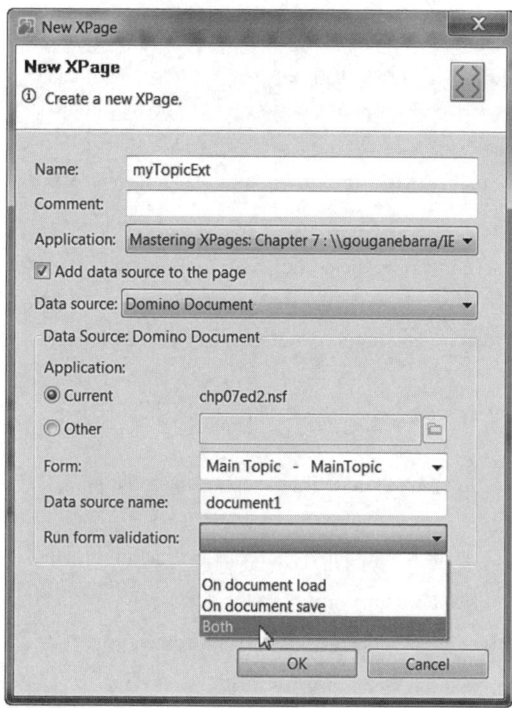

Figure 7.1 Creating a Domino document data source using the New XPage dialog

Some of these properties need further explanation. Others are best understood through the application of practical examples. In terms of examples, it is best to pick up where you left off in Chapter 3. To help you with this, the two XPages that you built there, **myView.xsp** and **myTopic.xsp**, have been copied into the sample application for this chapter, **Chp07ed2.nsf**. Okay, they have been tidied up just a wee bit!

Table 7.1 Domino Document Data Source Definition

Name	Description
`action`	The action to execute on the document. Takes "`newDocument`" or "`editDocument`" values to create a new document or edit an existing document, respectively.
`allowDeletedDocs`	Allows soft deleted documents to be accessed and opened.
`computeDocument`	Code applied to this property is called on document create, edit, and save events.
`computeWithForm`	A flag that controls when and if form logic on the associated document should be executed. Valid settings are `onload`, `onsave`, and `both`.

Name	Description
`concurrencyMode`	A flag that controls how concurrent updates are handled when the document is updated by more than one user at the same time. The four applicable flag settings are `createResponse`, `fail`, `exception`, and `force`.
`databaseName`	Name of the database containing the form, if not the current database.
`documentId`	A note ID or UNID used to uniquely identify the target document.
`formName`	The form name (or alias) containing the design definition for the document.
`ignoreRequestParams`	Ignores the value provided for any property in this list if specified as a URL parameter.
`loaded`	A boolean property that indicates whether the data source should be loaded.
`parentId`	A note ID or UNID used to uniquely identify the document's parent document.
`postNewDocument`	Any code applied to this event is called just *after* the document is created.
`postOpenDocument`	Any code applied to this event is called just *after* the document is opened.
`postSaveDocument`	Any code applied to this event is called just *after* the document is saved.
`queryNewDocument`	Any code applied to this event is called just *before* the document is created.
`queryOpenDocument`	Any code applied to this event is called just *before* the document is opened.
`querySaveDocument`	Any code applied to this event is called just *before* the document is saved.
`requestParamPrefix`	A string prepended to parameters to distinguish one data source instance from another.
`saveLinksAs`	The URL format used when links are saved in a document—that is, Notes or Domino format.
`scope`	`request`, `view`, `session`, or `application` scope applied to the data source.
`var`	Variable name that identifies the data source to other controls on the XPage.
`webQuerySaveAgent`	Name of a web agent to run when the document is about to be saved.

Creating and Editing Documents

If you inspect these two pages, you observe that **myTopic.xsp** has a document data source identical to that shown in Listing 7.2. When creating **myView.xsp**, you added a simple action to create a new topic, and also configured one of the View control columns to display links in order to enable end users to open any listed document. Reload **myView.xsp** in a web browser and click the **New Topic** button. The following URL appears in the browser's navigation bar (substitute your server home for local host, if appropriate):

```
http://localhost/Chp07ed2.nsf/myTopic.xsp?action=newDocument
```

Here, the `action=newDocument` URL parameter is passed to **myTopic.xsp** and the XPages runtime dynamically applies it to any document data sources found on that page. If you were to imagine this behavior in terms of XSP markup, it would be as shown in Listing 7.2.

Listing 7.2 Hard-Wired Document Data Source Markup for Creating New Discussion Topics

```
<xp:this.data>
    <xp:dominoDocument formName="Main Topic" var="document1"
      action="newDocument" />
      <!-- ignore for now any events or complex properties present in
the tag body -->
</xp:this.data>
```

Thus, **myTopic.xsp** opens a new document based on **Main Topic** when this action completes. When the page is submitted by the user (by clicking the **Save** button in this example), then documents are created for all document data sources defined on the page by default.

Perhaps more interesting for you to observe is that document data source properties can be specified directly in the XSP tag markup or passed in as URL parameters. Note that parameter values specified via the URL will override any values specified in the XSP markup. You see in the next example that property values can also be computed programmatically using JavaScript. This combination of options allows you to create flexible and dynamic applications!

So, to take this example further, return to **myView.xsp** and click one of the links in the **Topic** column. The URL generated on this occasion looks something like this:

```
http://localhost/Chp07Ed2.nsf/myTopic.xsp?documentId=1DAE4B29198F792F80
25778B004CD46B&action=editDocument
```

Because the link is designed to allow an end user to open an existing document, then **myTopic.xsp** needs a different action parameter, `editDocument` rather than `new Document`, and then some means of identifying the document to open, which is provided by the `documentId` parameter. The 32-character hexadecimal ID, known as the document universal ID (UNID), is automatically obtained for you by the XPages View Panel runtime logic and is guaranteed to uniquely identify the target document. The note ID or document ID (the shorter hexadecimal ID string) can also be used as a data source `documentId` property value—the note ID, however, is not guaranteed to be unique across database replica instances. In any case, these two simple examples show how both the `action` and `documentId` properties can be put to work when creating and opening Notes documents.

Controlling URL Parameter Usage

It might occur to you that, as flexible as these URL parameters are, they could potentially open up your application in ways you had not intended. If, for any such reason, you want to disable this feature, you can simply set the `ignoreRequestParams=`"`true`" on the document data source for any given XPage. For example, if you make this modification in **MyTopic.xsp** and then click a view column link in **myView.xsp** in the browser, you see that the selected document is not loaded—the `editDocument` action and `documentId` parameters are ignored. You can, of course, invent your own document parameters and add code to handle them, and these are *not* affected by the `ignoreRequestParams` setting.

Apart from security considerations, this feature can also help ensure graceful handling of bookmarks. For example, take the use case where an end user uses the web browser to bookmark an XPage and the resulting URL contains a document ID. Suppose that, by the time the user uses the bookmark again, the document has been deleted. This would inevitably end up in an error page in the browser when XPages fails to load the document. You can configure the application to disregard such bookmark parameters and avoid the failure using the `ignoreRequestParams` property. I'm sure you can think of many more use cases also!

Creating Response Documents

Now that you have learned how to create and open regular top-level documents, the next most logical follow-up is to learn how to create response documents. The example used to demonstrate this adds a simple extension to **myView.xsp**, and the required steps are described in the following exercise:

1. In **myView.xsp**, append a new column to the end of the View Panel using the **View > Append Column** main menu.
2. Specify an empty `value` for the column by entering a space in the **All Properties** panel. The resulting `viewColumn` tag markup in the source pane should look like this: `value=" "`
3. While in the Domino Designer **Source** pane, add `var="rowData"` to the `<xp:viewPanel>` tag.
4. Drag-and-drop a button control from the palette on to the XPage. You cannot drop this directly into the new View column, but it can be relocated there indirectly in the next step.

5. Activate the **Outline** view and drag-and-drop the new button over the newly added column, `viewColumn3`.
6. Select the button control in the **Outline** view, activate the **Events** panel, and click the **Add Action** button to define a new simple action.
7. In the **Add Simple Action** dialog, select the **Document > Create Response Document** simple action and choose **myTopic** as the XPage to open, as shown in Figure 7.2.
8. For the **Parent ID** field, click the little blue diamond adjacent to the text box, select **Compute value**, and simply enter `rowData.getUniversalID()` in the Script Editor. Click **OK** when done.
9. For aesthetics, while the button is still activated, select the **Properties** tab and change the label to Respond.
10. Similarly, if you select the new view column's header in Designer, you should change its label (or `value` if using the **All Properties** sheet) to the word Action.
11. Save **myView.xsp** and reload it in a web browser.

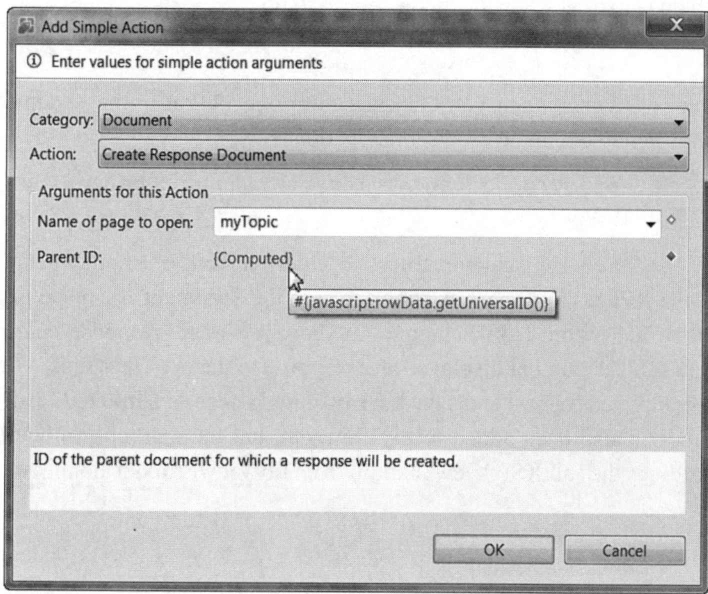

Figure 7.2 Simple action Create Response Document dialog

Although most of these steps are hopefully somewhat intuitive, it might also be challenging for a couple of reasons, explained as follows.

First, because you cannot drag-and-drop directly into a view column, the Domino Designer WYSIWYG editor does not visually reflect all of your changes in the design-time rendering of the View control. You must simply take it on trust that the controls are rendered correctly at runtime.

Second, steps 3 and 8 dabble just a little in server-side JavaScript (SSJS) and use concepts and objects that you might not be familiar with as yet; however, the JavaScript code is fairly trivial and can be explained right here. The `<xp:viewPanel>` `rowData` property defined in step 2 gives programmatic access to the each row in the view as the View control is being populated. The `rowData` property makes available a JavaScript `NotesXspViewEntry` object that exposes various API functions, one of which is `getUniversalID()`. Thus, for any given row, the action button can create a response document and retrieve the UNID of the current entry for use as the `parentId` of that new reply.

> **TIP**
>
> If you do not specify a var property value on the `<xp:viewPanel>` tag in step 3, then you can refer to the row in JavaScript using the default "viewEntry" variable name instead, as in `viewEntry.getUniversalID()`, and so on. This name is provided automatically by the XPages runtime when nothing is explicitly defined in the XSP markup.

The result of this becomes obvious when you click the `Respond` button in the updated XPage and view the URL that is generated in the browser navigation bar:

```
http://localhost/Chp07ed2.nsf/myTopic.xsp?action=newDocument&parentId=
1DAE4B29198F792F8025778B004CD46B
```

For **myTopic.xsp**, the URL `action` again instructs to create a `newDocument`, but a `parentId` is also specified—the XPages runtime thus knows to save the document as a response to the top-level document identified by the UNID. Figure 7.3 shows a sample response being composed, and Figure 7.4 shows this document displayed as a response in the **myView.xsp**.

This exercise has been completed for you and saved in **myViewExt.xsp** in **Chp07ed2.nsf**. Alternatively, the new column has also been added to **myView.xsp**, but the markup has been commented out. Listing 7.3 outlines the full XSP View markup from **myViewExt.xsp** along with some extra comments.

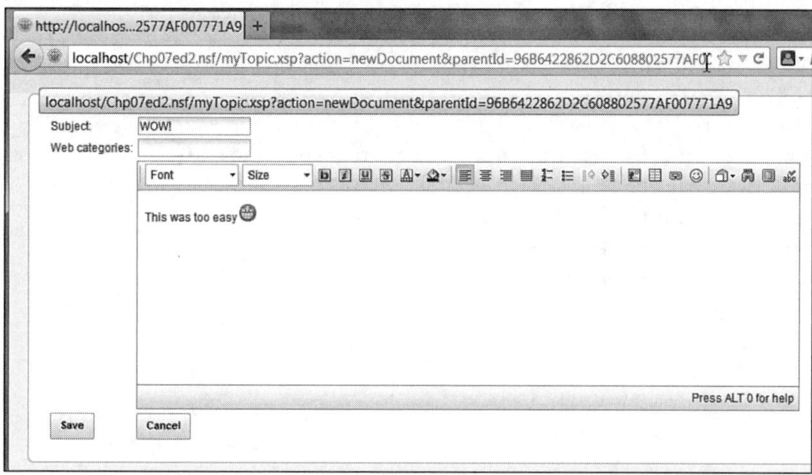

Figure 7.3 Creating a response document using simple actions and the document data source

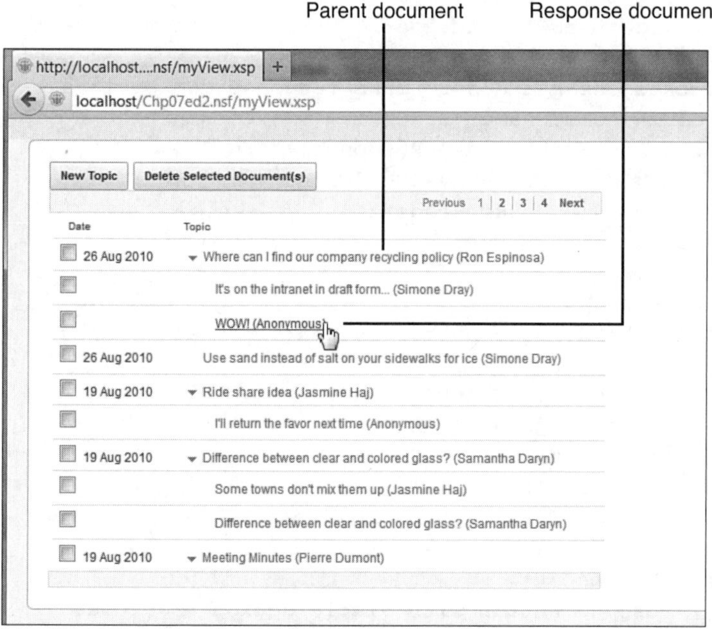

Figure 7.4 New Response document displayed in the View Panel

Listing 7.3 View Panel: Complete Source for Response Document Extension

```
<xp:viewPanel rows="10" id="viewPanel1"
      pageName="/myTopic.xsp"
      var="rowData">
      <!-- rowData property value set above on viewPanel -->
            <xp:this.facets>
            <xp:pager partialRefresh="true"
                  layout="Previous Group Next"
                  xp:key="headerPager" id="pager1">
            </xp:pager>
            </xp:this.facets>
            <xp:this.data>
                  <xp:dominoView var="view1"
                        viewName="($All)">
                  </xp:dominoView>
            </xp:this.data>
            <xp:viewColumn columnName="$106" id="viewColumn1"
                  showCheckbox="true">
                  <xp:viewColumnHeader value="Date"
                        id="viewColumnHeader1"></xp:viewColumnHeader>
            </xp:viewColumn>
            <!-- indentResponses added to make response doc obvious -->
            <xp:viewColumn columnName="$120" id="viewColumn2"
                  displayAs="link" indentResponses="true">
                  <xp:viewColumnHeader value="Topic"
                        id="viewColumnHeader2">
                  </xp:viewColumnHeader>
            </xp:viewColumn>
            <!-- New Column -->
            <!-- See how the Respond button is contained as a child -->

            <xp:viewColumn id="viewColumn3" value=" ">
                  <!-- "Action" header label -->
                  <xp:this.facets>
                        <xp:viewColumnHeader xp:key="header"
                              id="viewColumnHeader3" value="Action">
                        </xp:viewColumnHeader>
                  </xp:this.facets>
                  <!-- Respond button with simple action & JS code -->
                  <xp:button value="Respond" id="button3">
                   <xp:eventHandler event="onclick" submit="true"
                        refreshMode="complete">
                        <xp:this.action>
                              <xp:createResponse name="/myTopic.xsp"
                      parentId="#{javascript:rowData.
```

```
getUniversalID()}">
                    </xp:createResponse>
                   </xp:this.action>
                  </xp:eventHandler>
                </xp:button>
           </xp:viewColumn>
</xp:viewPanel>
```

Executing Form Logic

As well as providing all the metadata information for the documents you want to work with, the data source form can also contain application logic (LotusScript code, @Commands, and so on) that is executed at various times in the Notes document lifecycle, such as when a document is created, opened, saved, and so forth. This invariably holds true if you are building XPages functionality into a preexisting Notes application. If you are creating a new XPages application from scratch, however, as a general rule it is recommended that you create only form and view elements to define your metadata and not add any application logic to these elements. With the first use case, however, it might be beneficial and expedient to hook into the any preexisting form logic and leverage this code rather than reimplement it all using the equivalent XPages development technologies. The `computeWithForm` data source property can help you achieve this.

Refer to Figure 7.1, and look at the **Run form validation** control that is expanded at the bottom of the **New XPage** dialog. This UI control on the dialog box maps directly to the `computeWithForm` runtime property. Choosing **On document load** means that any underlying form logic designed to execute when the document is opened is executed when the document is opened by this XPage. Similarly, **On document save** causes any built-in form save logic to execute when the document is saved using this XPage, and there are no prizes for guessing what the **Both** option means! Although the underlying form logic is typically used to perform document validation, as the UI infers, it can obviously be completely arbitrary in nature. Because the Discussion template existed long before the advent of XPages, it is easy to find a suitable example within that application to further illustrate the point, as you now see!

Start by creating a new random topic from **myView.xsp** and save it with some data in all three fields. If you view the document fields using the infobox in Notes, you see a short listing like what's shown in Figure 7.5.

Now, open **myTopic.xsp** in Domino Designer and search for '`@UserName()`' in the source window. Uncomment the block of code encapsulating the table row that adds the **From** field to the XPage. The XPages `inputText` control is bound to the **From** field in the **Main Topic** form and has an XPages default value generated using the `@UserName()` @Function so that new documents are assigned an author once saved. Typically, this field would be hidden on an XPage so that the user would not see and could not change this value (for example, by assigning a `display:none` CSS rule to the control's style property). Creating a new topic now means that the username of the active user is saved in the **From** field when **myTopic.xsp** is submitted.

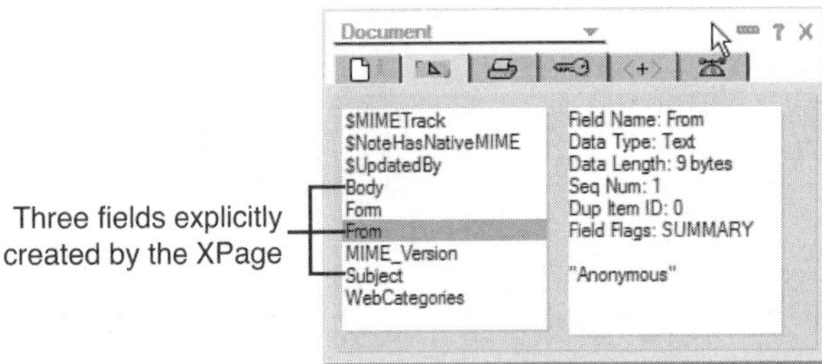

Figure 7.5 Infobox displaying document fields created using `myTopic.xsp`

However, an even simpler solution is available. Before proceeding, replace the comment block or simply remove the table row with the **From** field from **myTopic.xsp**. You can achieve the same results by just using the `computeWithForm` property. To begin to understand this alternative, open the **Main Topic** form in Designer and peruse all the hidden fields contained in the table at the top of the form, as shown in Figure 7.6.

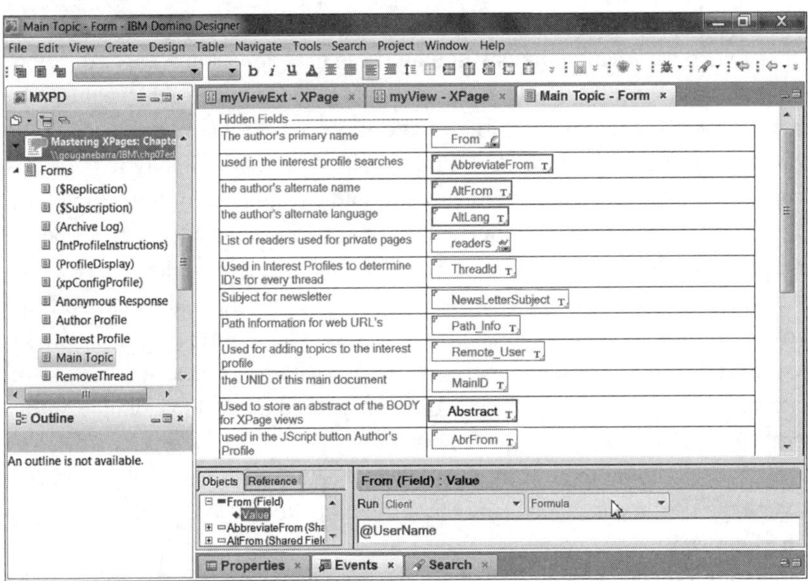

Figure 7.6 Hidden fields in the `Main Topic` form

A couple of interesting points arise. First, many of these hidden fields are automatically assigned values through Notes Formula Language or LotusScript code. This includes the **From** field, which is assigned a value using `@UserName` command. Thus, XPages does not have to compute the **From** value at all if the existing form logic is simply allowed to execute! To prove this out, return to **myTopic.xsp** and assign a value of `both` to the `computeWithForm` property either in the **Source** pane or **All Properties**. Save the XPage and create a new document from **myView.xsp**, again entering data in all three fields. As shown in Figure 7.7, the **From** field is still created in the new document, although it is the form logic that has performed the task on this occasion rather than XPages itself—because the data field is no longer accessed directly from the XPage itself as a result of commenting out the **From** control tags.

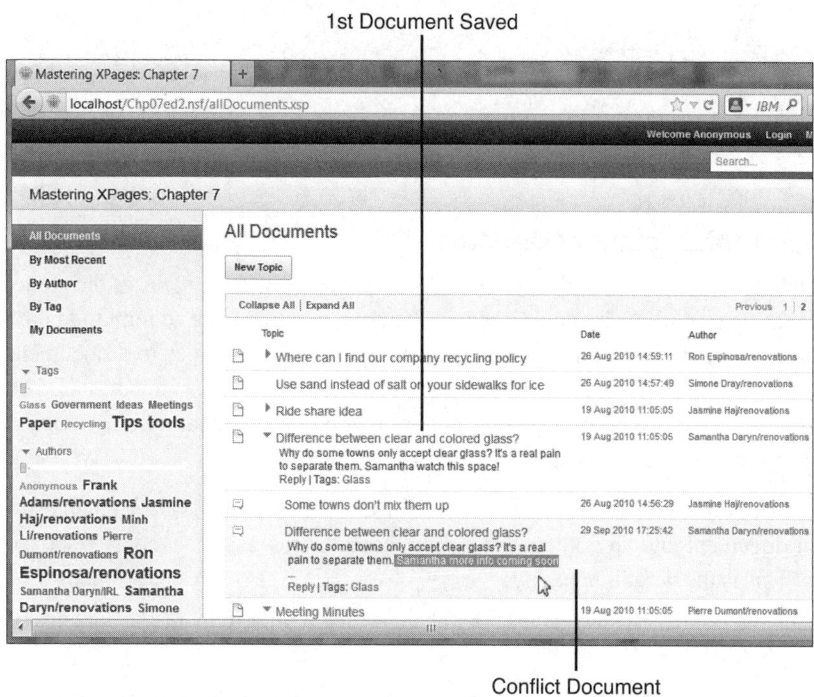

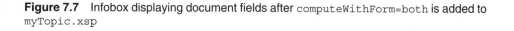

Figure 7.7 Infobox displaying document fields after `computeWithForm=both` is added to `myTopic.xsp`

Also note that lots more fields have been created than was the case with the previous version of the XPage. This ensures that any data needed by other functional parts of the application is created, which means that any new XPages documents retain compatibility with the original runtime environment—which might or might not be important for you, depending on your project requirements.

Although the `computeWithForm` property undoubtedly offers a convenient means of populating the underlying Notes document with all the computed fields defined on the form, there is also a potential performance cost to be considered. The core Notes function that implements this feature, `NSFNoteComputeWithForm`, is known to have performance issues—particularly if the computed form contains many subforms or other design artifacts. The Notes design cache is not optimally leveraged when accessing the subforms, resulting in additional network transactions when the form is located in an NSF on a remote server. This can be particularly problematical when running a remote XPages application in the Notes client. This issue, along with potential remedies, is discussed in more depth in Chapter 13, "XPages in the Notes Client."

> **TIP**
>
> To comment out XSP markup in the source pane, simply highlight the block of tags you want to disable and type `Ctrl-Shift-C`. This is a toggle command, so typing `Ctrl-Shift-C` also uncomments code if it is already commented out.

Managing Concurrent Document Updates

In a collaborative environment where information and document sharing is the name of the game, it is to be expected that save conflicts inevitably occur when two or more users attempt to update the same document around the same time. If one user attempts to save changes to a document when another user is also editing its contents, who wins? The document data source has a `concurrencyMode` property that can control behavior in this situation in accordance with your own preferences. The property offers four settings:

- `createResponse` means that the first user to perform the save writes their changes to the original document and any others that follow have their changes saved as response documents. This is the default behavior.
- `force` means the last user to save wins. Any changes made prior to that final concurrent save are simply lost!
- `fail` simply means that the save operation is not performed at all for any user involved in the document contention, and each is shown a warning message when attempting to save:

  ```
  "Document has been saved by another user - Save has not been performed"
  ```
- `exception` also means that the save is not performed, but a Java exception is thrown instead. This results in an error stack being displayed by default in the browser page, but gives the application developer the flexibility of providing their own handler for this particular exception.

Figure 7.8 shows an example of what happens when two simultaneous efforts were made to append information to the **Difference between clear and colored glass?** note, when the document data source in **myTopic.xsp** has `concurrencyMode="createResponse"`. Notice that a response document of the same subject exists, and the only difference between both is the trailing text shown in the abstract "watch this space!" versus "more info coming soon."

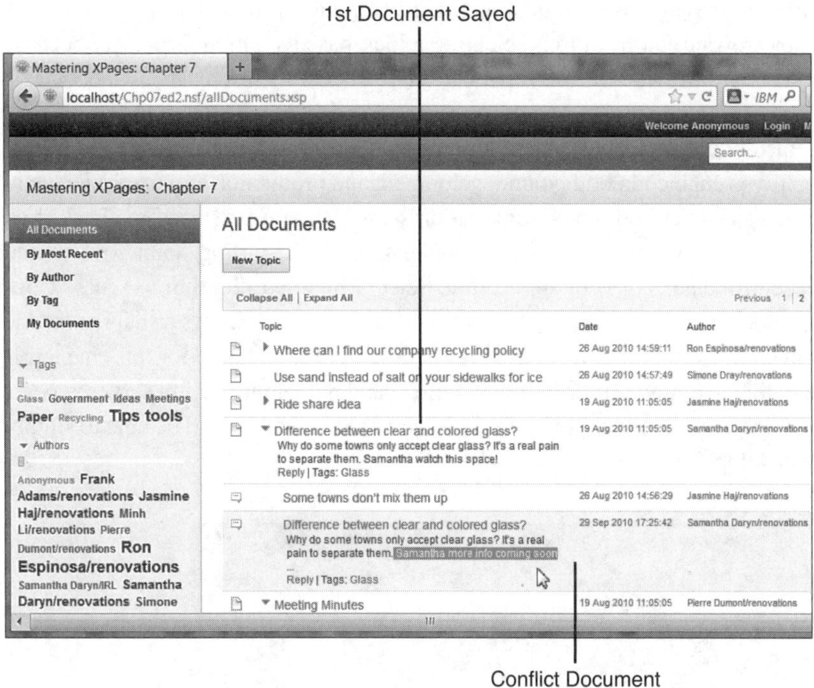

Figure 7.8 Response documents used to avoid data loss due to concurrent document updates

> **TIP**
>
> Apart altogether from multiuser document conflict scenarios, there are other use cases to account for when considering potential data loss scenarios. Chapter 13, "XPages in the Notes Client," has a section, "Introducing enableModifiedFlag and disableModifiedFlag." These properties were introduced in 8.5.1 to give the application developer granular control over what document data is saved and what document data may be thrown away. The implementation of these properties is more fully featured in an XPages Notes client environment, but most of the details are also applied to XPages on the web. It might be a good idea to read that section in conjunction with this material.

A topic closely related to managing concurrent document updates is document locking. In fact, a `lock` option could, and perhaps should, be available as a `concurrencyMode` choice. Such an option would instruct the runtime to lock a document when a user opens in edit mode, which would prevent concurrency conflicts altogether because only the user holding the lock would be in a position to update the document at any given point in time. The absence of this `lock` option does not prevent you from implementing a lock-based solution, however, because document-locking APIs are provided in the Java backend classes; therefore, it just becomes a small matter of some programming.

Before using the document-locking APIs in XPages, you first must ensure that the Notes/Domino locking facility is enabled in both your development and production environments. Document locking is managed by a Domino administration server, so you first need to check if an administration server is assigned to manage your application. As a starting point, you should examine the access control details of your application. Select **File > Application > Access Control > Advanced** and look at the administration server details. Figure 7.9 shows a snapshot of the ACL dialog when an administration server is assigned to a sample application for this chapter. If you use a local standalone Domino server for development and no administration server appears in your ACL dialog (that is, the **None** radio button is selected), then you should be able to simply assign your current development server as the administration server.

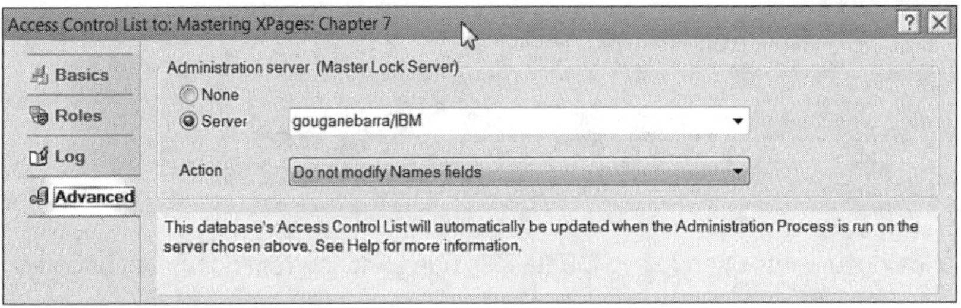

Figure 7.9 Advanced Access Control settings for Chp07ed2.nsf

You must also enable the **Allow document locking** option via the **Application Configuration > Application Properties > Basics** panel, as shown in Figure 7.10—not to be confused with the **Allow design locking** feature exposed in the neighboring **Design** panel.

When the document-locking capability is armed and ready, then the current View Panel sample can be modified to implement the feature. A sample XPage named **myViewLock.xsp** has been provided for you, and a screen shot of the page at runtime is displayed in Figure 7.11. Observe that the updated View Panel contains a new custom column that allows the user to explicitly lock and open the document associated with any row of the view. In addition, the lock status of currently open documents is also shown, identifying the lockholder and allowing users to unlock any documents that they may already have locked—for instance, in another application instance running in another browser.

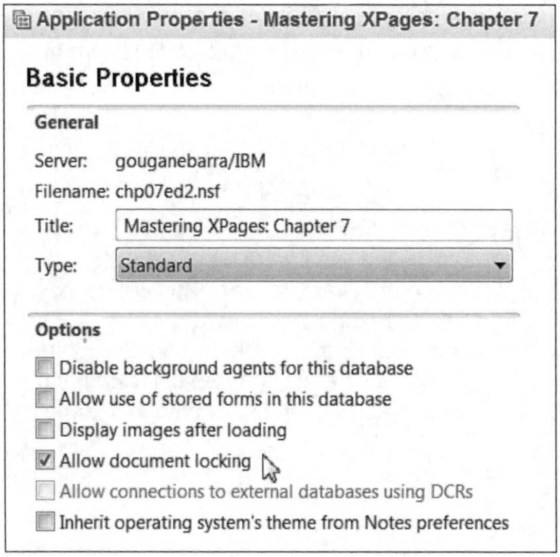

Figure 7.10 Allow Document Locking feature

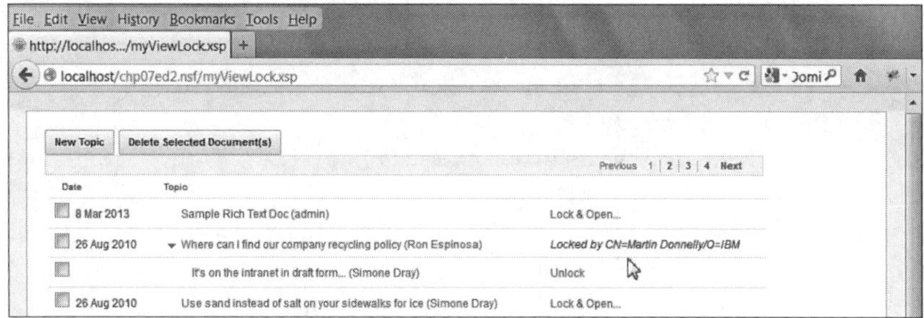

Figure 7.11 View Panel with Document Locking features

Although you won't deep dive on programmability topics until Part IV, "Programmability," of this book, the SSJS code that implements the locking features is not too complex to explore here because it is based around just four document-locking API calls that are self-explanatory:

- `database.isDocumentLockingEnabled`
- `document.getLockHolders`
- `document.lock`
- `document.unlock`

Listing 7.4 shows all the relevant document-locking code contained in the new custom column that has been added to **myViewLock.xsp**. Take a moment to review the code shown in the listing, or view it directly in the Domino Designer XPages source editor.

> **TIP**
>
> In the Domino Designer XPages source editor, you can make it easier to work with SSJS by highlighting the background color of the code area to distinguish it from other XSP markup. Bring up the **File > Preferences** dialog and type **XML** in the filter text area. This will expose a **Syntax Coloring** option for all XML file editors—remember that XSP markup is pure XML. Select this option and then select **CDATA Content** as the syntax element. (All SSJS code is wrapped in a CDATA section in the XSP markup.) Choose a background color from the color picker and apply this setting. You then see all your SSJS code highlighted in the chosen color in the source editor.

Listing 7.4 Custom View Column XSP Markup from myViewLock.xsp

```
<xp:viewColumn id="viewColumn3" displayAs="hidden">
   <xp:text escape="false" id="computedField1">
      <xp:this.rendered>
         <![CDATA[#{javascript:
            var lh = rowData.getDocument().getLockHolders();
            if(!lh.isEmpty()){
               if(lh.contains(@UserName())){
                  return false;
               }
               return true;
            }
            return false;
         }]]>
      </xp:this.rendered>
      <xp:this.value>
         <![CDATA[#{javascript:
            "<i>Locked by " + lh.toArray().toString() + "</i>"
            }]]>
      </xp:this.value>
      </xp:text>
      <xp:link escape="true" id="link1">
         <xp:this.rendered>
            <![CDATA[#{javascript:
               if(database.isDocumentLockingEnabled()){
                  if(!lh.isEmpty()){
                     if(lh.contains(@UserName())){
```

```
                              return true;
                          }
                          return false;
                      }
                      return true;
                  }
                  return false;
              }]]>
          </xp:this.rendered>
          <xp:this.text>
              <![CDATA[#{javascript:
                  if(!lh.isEmpty() && lh.contains(@UserName())){
                      viewScope[rowIndex] = {"lockState":1};
                      return "Unlock";
                  }
                  viewScope[rowIndex] = {"lockState":0};
                  return "Lock & Open...";
              }]]>
          </xp:this.text>
          <xp:eventHandler event="onclick" submit="true"
              refreshMode="complete" immediate="true">
              <xp:this.action>
                  <![CDATA[#{javascript:
                      if(viewScope[rowIndex].lockState == 0){
                          var doc = rowData.getDocument();
                          doc.lock(@UserName());
                          var x = new XSPUrl("myTopicLock");
                          x.setParameter("action", "editDocument");
                          x.setParameter("documentId",
➥doc.getUniversalID());
                          context.redirectToPage(x.toString());
                      }else{
                          rowData.getDocument().unlock();
                      }
                  }]]>
              </xp:this.action>
          </xp:eventHandler>
      </xp:link>
</xp:viewColumn>
```

As you can see from the XSP markup, the custom view column contains a simple computed text field and a link control. Observe that the boolean `rendered` property for both controls is computed based on document locking status information. That is, neither control is displayed if document locking is *not* enabled for the application.

Assuming document locking is enabled, the computed text field is displayed only when the current list of lock holders does *not* include the current user. The text field value shows the name or names of those who have the document locked at present—remember that in a clustered environment, it is possible to have more than one lock holder.

Conversely, because it is only possible to lock a document that is not already locked, a link control is displayed when the document is not locked or when the list of lock holders includes the current user. The link control enables the user to perform certain actions in this situation, like unlock a locked document or lock an unlocked one. Lines 78 to 83 manage the UI state of the application depending on whether the user is a member of the lock holder list.

Finally, there is the link event handler; or in other words, the action to perform when the link is clicked. The action depends on the lock state of the document on the given row. If the `lockstate` is zero (think false), then the link presents the option to open and lock the document. The link constructs an XSP URL (encapsulated in the SSJS XSPUrl object) to open the document by redirecting the browser to the new URL. However, if the document is locked (`lockstate==1`), then the option is to simply lock the document (see lines 90 to 99). Also look at **myTopicLock.xsp** to see how this page has been customized to reflect the document locking status.

One last thing to note is that the application logic on the **Delete Selected Document(s)** button needs to be updated in **myViewLock.xsp** to cater for a nuance introduced by the document locking feature. Basically, when document locking is enabled, documents cannot be deleted unless they are first locked by the end-user. You can look at the `Execute Script` action which has been added to the button in the sample application to see how this issue is addressed.

This sample proves a point—do not be overly concerned if the XPages runtime does not offer you a direct route to solving a problem. As demonstrated here, the Java backend API functions can often be exercised via SSJS to produce the desired outcome. Although this is just sample code, the idea is to show the "art of the possible" with XPages by leveraging long-standing Notes/Domino services to achieve a solution.

Multiple Document Data Sources

At this stage, it is apparent that a single XPage is not restricted to one document data source. Several document data sources can be included in an XPage and, thus, controls within an XPage can be bound to metadata defined in many forms. For example, an XPage in the Discussion template could include a data source that points to the **Main Topic** form and another that points to the **Author Profile** form. It might be desirable to do this in order to enable a contributor to update profile information while composing a discussion topic. More generally, an XPage might contain two data sources pointing to, say, a purchase order form and a supplier form—and these forms can even be located in different databases. Again, this allows supplier details to be displayed and/or edited on an XPage while an order entry is in progress. Although all this is eminently doable, it can require some careful stewarding to make sure that the separate data sources are correctly managed.

In the earlier section, "Creating and Editing Documents," you saw how URL parameters can be used to drive application behavior, such as passing a document ID as part of the URL to identify the document to edit. What happens in this scenario if the page contains more than one document data source? Which data source should the `documentId` parameter be applied to? The first one, or perhaps all data sources, or maybe none? The answer is that a `documentId` parameter would be applied to *all* document data sources on a given page, although if your page contains multiple data sources, this is probably *not* what you want!

The `requestParamPrefix` property is designed to manage URL parameters when multiple data sources exist. The concept is simple: You assign a prefix to each data source on the page and then prepend any URL parameters with this prefix to identify the target data source. To help demonstrate how this works, a new XPage has been created for you in **Chp07ed2.nsf**, namely **myTopicX2.xsp**. If you inspect this XPage, you see that it is really like two **myTopic** XPages rolled into one—hence, the name! The document data source has been duplicated except for the `var` and `requestParamPrefix` properties (see Listing 7.5), and the input controls have been copied so that two documents can be edited at once—a purely academic exercise to help illustrate the workings of this feature.

Listing 7.5 Data Source Snippet from myTopicX2.xsp

```
<!-- two data sources pointing to the same form -->
<xp:this.data>
      <!-- only requestParamPrefix and var properties differ -->
      <xp:dominoDocument var="document1" formName="MainTopic"
            computeWithForm="both" action="editDocument"
            requestParamPrefix="first">
      </xp:dominoDocument>
</xp:this.data>
<xp:this.data>
      <xp:dominoDocument var="document2" formName="MainTopic"
            computeWithForm="both" action="editDocument"
            requestParamPrefix="second">
      </xp:dominoDocument>
</xp:this.data>
```

In the regular client, you can use the infobox control to find the note IDs of the documents edited in the previous section, the updated "Difference between clear and colored glass?" note and the conflict document created as a response to it. Then, enter these note IDs as URL parameters to **myTopicX2.xsp** in the following fashion to edit both documents at once:

```
http://localhost/Chp07ed2.nsf/myTopicX2.xsp?firstdocumentId=9F2&secondd
ocumentId=96a
```

Basically, the `documendId` parameters has been prefixed with the `requestParamPrefix` properties specified for each data source on the page. This distinguishes which document ID is intended for which data source. Figure 7.12 shows the results in the browser—simple!

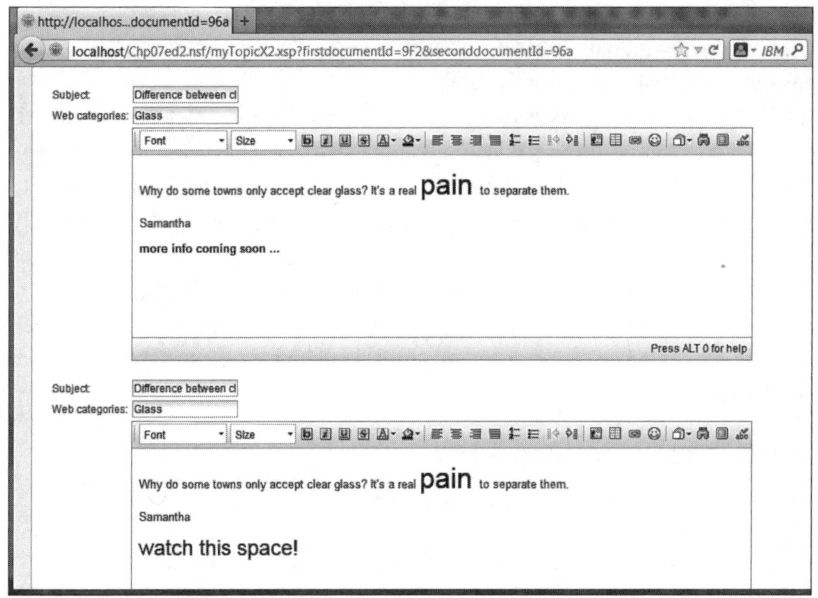

Figure 7.12 XPage editing two documents using `requestParamPrefix`

You could, of course, just assign a single `requestParamPrefix` to one of the data sources in this example, and then the nonprefixed data source would read the regular (nonprefixed) parameter arguments. Thus, if you only applied the "second" prefix parameter, the preceding URL could be rewritten like this:

```
http://localhost/Chp07ed2.nsf/myTopicX2.xsp?documentId=9F2&second
documentId=96a
```

The point is clear that, in order to address `n` document data sources, you need at least `n - 1` prefix parameters.

Document Data Source Events

Table 7.1 includes seven events that can be used to hook into the document lifecycle and execute code to perform tasks such as data initialization and validation. Three events can be hooked for a document data source: creating, opening, and saving a document. For each of these, a query event is called just before the event takes place and a post event that is fired immediately after the event occurs. Also, a single `computeDocument` event is fired for all three events. You can verify the timing of these events by inserting JavaScript `print` statements as the event handlers. Figure 7.13 shows how to access the data source events in Designer and a sample `print` statement for `queryOpenDocument`.

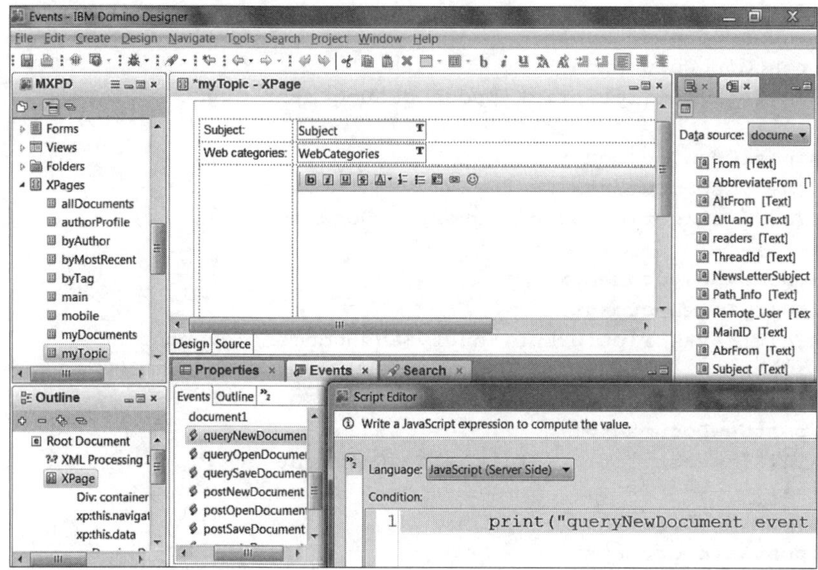

Figure 7.13 Document data source events in Domino Designer

When running on the web, JavaScript `print` statements are sent to the Domino server console, while on the Notes client, they are output to the trace log, which is viewable via **Help > Support > View Trace** menu. The **myTopic** XPage contains such `print` statements, but they have been commented out. Performing the following exercise helps you understand how and when these events are called:

1. Uncomment the data source event code in **myTopic.xsp** (same as lines 4 to 10 in Listing 7.6).
2. Create a new document from **myView.xsp**.
3. Enter some arbitrary data and save the document.
4. Open the new document again from **myView.xsp**.
5. Review the trace log or server console as appropriate.

Listing 7.6 Document Data Source SSJS Events

```
<xp:this.data>
 <xp:dominoDocument formName="Main Topic" var="document1"
   action="newDocument" />
    <xp:this.queryOpenDocument>
       <![CDATA[#{javascript:print("queryOpenDocument event
notification");}]]>
    </xp:this.queryOpenDocument>
    <xp:this.postOpenDocument>
       <![CDATA[#{javascript:print("postOpenDocument event
notification");}]]>
    </xp:this.postOpenDocument>
    <xp:this.queryNewDocument>
       <![CDATA[#{javascript:print("queryNewDocument event
notification");}]]>
    </xp:this.queryNewDocument>
    <xp:this.querySaveDocument>
       <![CDATA[#{javascript:print("querySaveDocument event
notification");}]]>
    </xp:this.querySaveDocument>
    <xp:this.postNewDocument>
       <![CDATA[#{javascript:print("postNewDocument event
notification");}]]>
    </xp:this.postNewDocument>
    <xp:this.postSaveDocument>
       <![CDATA[#{javascript:print("postSaveDocument event
notification");}]]>
    </xp:this.postSaveDocument>
    <xp:this.computeDocument>
       <![CDATA[#{javascript:print("computeDocument event
notification");}]]>
    </xp:this.computeDocument>
</xp:this.data>
```

Listing 7.7 shows the output you see when run on the web. Hopefully, the order of event execution is what you were expecting!

Listing 7.7 Output of Document Data Source Events on Domino Server Console

```
22:39:25   HTTP JVM: queryNewDocument event notification
22:39:25   HTTP JVM: postNewDocument event notification
22:39:25   HTTP JVM: computeDocument event notification
22:39:56   HTTP JVM: querySaveDocument event notification
22:39:56   HTTP JVM: postSaveDocument event notification
```

```
22:39:56    HTTP JVM: computeDocument event notification
22:40:20    HTTP JVM: queryOpenDocument event notification
22:40:20    HTTP JVM: postOpenDocument event notification
22:40:20    HTTP JVM: computeDocument event notification
```

TIP

In Domino Designer, if you do not see line numbers in the left gutter of the XPages source editor, then right-mouse click close to the left edge of the editor and select the **Show Line Numbers** context menu option.

Although this trivial example simply serves to show you how to access the events and verify the order in which they are executed, the Discussion template itself contains many examples of how these events are used to accomplish real application-development tasks. A good self-contained example can be seen in the **response.xsp** custom control. Open this design element and view the `postNewDocument` event in the JavaScript editor. A snippet of the code is shown in Listing 7.8.

Listing 7.8 postNewDocument Snippet from response.xsp

```
<!-- response docs do not automatically inherit data from parent doc -->
<xp:this.postNewDocument><![CDATA[#{javascript:
var parent:NotesDocument =
      database.getDocumentByID(responseDoc.getParentId());
var isResponse:boolean = parent.isResponse();

// Make subject and categories available to whole page as viewScope vars
viewScope.parentSubject = parent.getItemValue("Subject");
viewScope.parentTags = parent.getItemValue("Categories");

// inherit these items from the parent doc into the response doc
responseDoc.setValue("MainID", parent.getItemValue("MainID"));
responseDoc.setValue("ParentSubject", parent.getItemValue("Subject"));
responseDoc.setValue("Readers", parent.getItemValue("Readers"));
responseDoc.setValue("ParentForm", parent.getItemValue("Form"));
responseDoc.setValue("ThreadId", parent.getItemValue("ThreadId"));
responseDoc.setValue("ExpireDate", parent.getItemValue("ExpireDate"));
responseDoc.setValue("Categories", parent.getItemValue("Categories"));
responseDoc.setValue("ImmediateParentSubject",
                        parent.getItemValue("Subject"));
```

```
// this item below depends on the type of parent...
if (isResponse == false) {
      responseDoc.setValue("OriginalSubject",
                  parent.getItemValue("Subject"));
      } else {
      responseDoc.setValue("OriginalSubject",
                  parent.getItemValue("OriginalSubject"));
      }
}]]>
</xp:this.postNewDocument>
```

The code in Listing 7.8 can be explained as follows:

1. **response.xsp** is the XPage used to create a response document.
2. The `postNewDocument` is event is fired after the response document is created.
3. `responseDoc` is the `var` value assigned to the document data source, and this makes the response document available programmatically as an instance of standard Notes/Domino Java `Document` class. This Java class is wrapped by XPages and made available to JavaScript.
4. Standard `Document` class methods are used to read fields from the parent document and create fields of the same name and value in the response document.
5. It also makes the **Subject** and **Categories** field values from the parent available to the JavaScript elsewhere on the XPage by storing them as view scope variables.

This example provides a good insight into what's possible programmatically by hooking the document data source events. For example, the `querySaveDocument` and `postSaveDocument` events are commonly used in combination with the `Document` class to perform data validation when documents are being saved.

webQuerySaveAgent

This document data source property was added in 8.5.3. Traditional Notes/Domino web applications have a long established pattern of using WebQuerySave (WQS) agents to programmatically manage how documents are validated and saved. For anyone adding XPages to pre-existing Domino web applications, this property allows any WQS agents to be called directly from XPages, thus automatically leveraging tried and tested logic from the original application code base. All the XPages developer needs to do in this instance is assign the name of the WQS agent to the `webQuerySaveAgent` property.

The WQS agent can be a LotusScript or Java agent. If you are creating a new WQS agent, ensure that the following settings are applied on the agent's properties panel in Domino Designer:

- **Basics >Target** option is set to **None**.
- **Security > Run as Web user** is selected.

The sample chapter has a sample Java WQS agent included, namely `SampleWebQuery-Agent`. The source code for the agent is outlined in Listing 7.9.

Listing 7.9 Sample Java WebQuerySave Agent

```
import java.util.Vector;
import lotus.domino.*;

public class JavaAgent extends AgentBase {

    public void NotesMain() {
      try {
          Session session = getSession();
          AgentContext agentContext = session.getAgentContext();

          // Show that webQuerySaveAgent has been called
          System.out.println("webQuerySaveAgent event notification");

          // Get the doc and show all the available items
          Document doc = agentContext.getDocumentContext();
          Vector vItems = doc.getItems();
          System.out.println("Document Items:");
          for (int i=0; i < vItems.size(); i++) {
              System.out.println(vItems.get(i).toString());
          }

          // Only save if we have an identified author
          int saveOption = 1; // 0 = don't save, any other value = save
          String userName = doc.getItemValueString("From");
          if (userName == null || userName.length() == 0 ||
              userName.equalsIgnoreCase("anonymous")) {
              System.out.println("Document not saved: unidentified user!");
              saveOption = 0;
          }
          doc.replaceItemValue("SaveOptions",Integer.valueOf(saveOption));
      } catch(Exception e) {
          e.printStackTrace();
      }
    }
}
```

Although Java code may be a more advanced topic to some readers, the agent is straightforward and can be easily explained.

The entry point to the code is in the `NotesMain` function, and the first two lines within are automatically provided by Domino Designer to set up a session and an agent context in which the code can execute. Next, the agent simply prints a notification that it is being called, and this line is output by default to the client or server console. The document encapsulated by the Domino document data source is passed into the agent as an in-memory document by the XPages runtime and is retrieved by the agent calling the `getDocumentContext()` method. When retrieved, the collection of items in the in-memory document is read and printed to the console. Obviously, the agent can apply validation tests to any or all these fields. The item collection includes all fields explicitly bound to the XPage controls, as well as those computed when the document is loaded using the `computeWithForm` property.

Normally, the role of the WQS agent is to determine whether the active document should be saved. Actually, it has a special `SaveOptions` item that is used to tell Notes whether to save the document, and this is supported by the XPages `webQuerySaveAgent` feature. As the Java comments in Listing 7.9 indicate, a value of 0 (zero) means the document will not be saved, whereas any other value means the save will proceed. For simplicity, some arbitrarily trivial validation logic is applied in this sample: namely, do not save the document if the author is not identifiable—blank or "anonymous" document creators are not allowed. Note that if you use this special `SaveOptions` item and the agent logic prevents the submitted XPage from being saved, then the data entered on the XPage is lost when the page is submitted and would need to be re-entered by the user.

A new XPage called `myTopicExt.xsp` has been created to demonstrate this WQS agent in action, and `myViewExt.xsp` has been updated to call this XPage. Open `myTopicExt.xsp` in Domino Designer and review the source code. Observe that the `webQuerySaveAgent` property on the Domino document data source is set to `SampleWebQueryAgent`. Load the `myViewExt.xsp` in a web browser both as an anonymous and as a logged-in user, and create a new document each time. You will see that the new document is not saved when you are anonymous and vice versa. Listing 7.10 shows the agent output to the Domino console when run anonymously.

Listing 7.10 Output of Document Sample WQS Agent on Domino Server Console

```
22:49:55    HTTP JVM: querySaveDocument event notification
22:49:55    HTTP JVM: webQuerySaveAgent event notification
22:49:55    HTTP JVM: Document Items:
22:49:55    HTTP JVM: form
22:49:55    HTTP JVM: AbbreviateFrom
22:49:55    HTTP JVM: AltFrom
22:49:55    HTTP JVM: AltLang
```

```
22:49:55    HTTP JVM: ThreadId
22:49:55    HTTP JVM: Remote_User
22:49:55    HTTP JVM: MainID
22:49:55    HTTP JVM: AbrFrom
22:49:55    HTTP JVM: WebCategories
22:49:55    HTTP JVM: readers
22:49:55    HTTP JVM: NewsLetterSubject
22:49:55    HTTP JVM: Path_Info
22:49:55    HTTP JVM: Abstract
22:49:55    HTTP JVM: Subject
22:49:55    HTTP JVM: Categories
22:49:55    HTTP JVM: INetFrom
22:49:55    HTTP JVM: From
22:49:55    HTTP JVM: $MIMETrack
22:49:55    HTTP JVM: MIME_Version
22:49:55    HTTP JVM: $PaperColor
22:49:55    HTTP JVM: Body
22:49:55    HTTP JVM: Document not saved: unidentified user!
```

Notice from the output that the `querySaveDocument` is called just before the `webQuerySaveAgent`. Actually, you can readily emulate the `webQuerySaveAgent` behavior using SSJS within the `querySaveDocument` event. The SSJS code in Listing 7.11 would be analogous to the Java code executed using `webQuerySaveAgent`.

Listing 7.11 Snippet Showing WQS Agent Called via SSJS

```
var wsq = database.getAgent("SampleWebQuerySaveAgent");
    if (wsq != null) {
        wsq.runWithDocumentContext(currentDocument.getDocument());
    }
```

This code snippet is in fact included in `myTopicExt.xsp` but commented out by default. If you enable this code and remove `webQuerySaveAgent` property value, then you will see the same results at runtime. The `Agent.runWithDocumentContext()` API runs an agent passing in a saved or unsaved in-memory document. This document is retrievable inside the Java agent via the `AgentContext.getDocumentContext()` API, or via the `DocumentContext` property if running a LotusScript agent. Note that with LotusScript web agents, `Print` statements are not output to the web page when called from XPages, as is the case with the classic Domino web engine.

Common Data Source Properties

The document data source and the view data source share some common properties, namely `databaseName`, `ignoreRequestParams`, `loaded`, `parentId`, `requestParamPrefix`, `scope`, and `var`. The properties `ignoreRequestParams`, `parentId`, `requestParamPrefix`, and `var` have already been explained. The others are straightforward and briefly discussed in the following paragraphs.

The `databaseName` property allows you to specify a form that is not contained in the current database. The property value, in its simplest form, can just be the name of another database, or it can include a server name, full path, or replica ID. In Chapter 8, "Working with Domino Views," a section titled, "The databaseName Property," gives examples of all such usage, and all those examples are valid when applied to the document data source.

This leaves the `loaded` and `scope` properties. The former is a boolean property that determines whether or not to load the source document, and the latter simply dictates the scope in which any loaded document data is stored. Chapter 8 also contains a "Go Fetch! Or Maybe Not..." section, which briefly ruminates over some issues to consider when using these properties. Again, those points are equally valid in the context of the document data source, and you need to refer to them as necessary.

Miscellaneous Data Source Properties

The only two data source properties that have not been covered at this stage are `saveLinksAs` and `allowDeletedDocs`.

The `saveLinksAs` flag dictates the format to use when links (document, view, or database links) are saved in documents—Notes URL format, or Domino URL format. The property is designed to minimize any document incompatibility issues that can arise when documents are modified on different platforms. In Chapter 13, this property and broader compatibility topics are dealt with extensively in a section titled, "Notes Links Versus Domino Links." Refer to that section for details on `saveLinksAs`.

The `allowDeletedDocs` property determines whether soft deleted documents can be accessed and opened in XPages. This property is of interest to any developer who wants to undelete or restore documents that an end user has flagged for deletion, but which, as yet, have not been physically removed from the NSF. If your application offers a document trash folder feature, for example, `allowDeletedDocs`, could be useful in managing that. Soft deletions, of course, must be supported at the NSF layer itself, and this feature is enabled via another application level property, as shown in Figure 7.14.

This concludes the discussion of document data source properties and events.

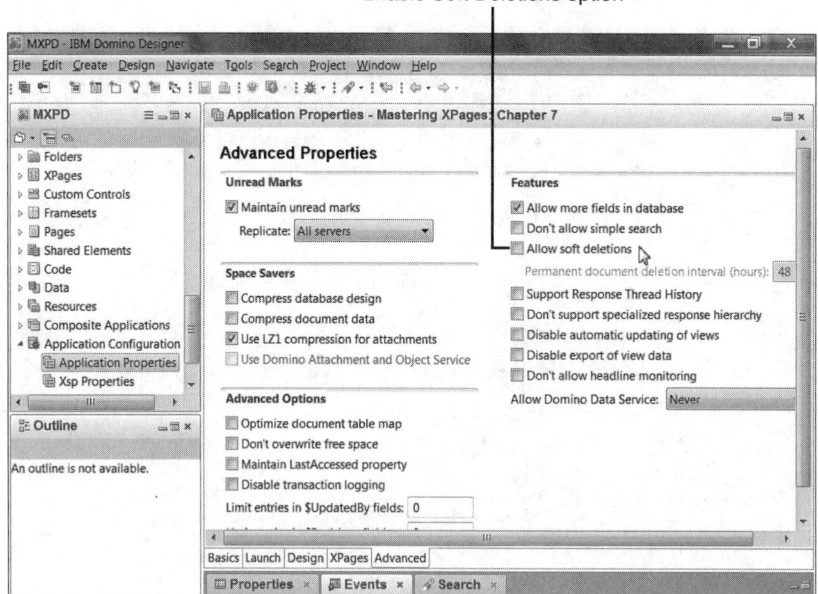

Figure 7.14 Allow Soft Deletions application property

Working with Domino Documents—Programmatically!

Almost all the use cases examined up to now involved manipulating the values of data source properties to invoke some particular runtime behavior. Dynamic access to these properties is generally achieved programmatically, typically using simple actions or server-side JavaScript. This section examines some of the specific tools at your disposal.

Simple Actions

The idea of simple actions is to automate everyday common actions without requiring any coding. "Simple" is the operative word in the title! These actions are designed to be dialog-driven so that the developer must merely choose a particular action from a menu and then pick any parameter values from helper controls. There are scenarios, of course, where parameter values must be computed to solve a particular problem. For example, in the section, "Creating Response Documents," you needed to enter a line of JavaScript to compute the parent ID for the new response document, but generally, convenience and simplicity are the order of the day.

Table 7.2 summarizes the simple actions that you are most likely to need when working with Domino documents and data sources.

Table 7.2 Domino Document Data Source Definition

Action	Description
Change Document Mode	Changes document between from edit and read mode and vice versa.
Create Response Document	Creates a document that is a child of another document; refer to the section "Creating Response Documents" and Figure 7.2.
Delete Document	Deletes a particular document from the NSF—the current document by default.
Delete Selected Documents	Deletes one or more documents from a view control.
Modify Field	Changes the value of a nominated field in a document.
Open Page	Navigates to another XPage, optionally opening one or more documents in the process.
Save Data Sources	Saves the document data source(s) on a given page. View data sources are read-only.
Save Document	Saves a specified document; uses the current document if no document is specified.

One or more examples of all these simple actions are available in Chapter 6, "Building XPages Application Logic."

JavaScript

If you already have experience with the Notes/Domino LotusScript or Java backend classes, you will no doubt be familiar with the `Document` class. A full description of all properties and methods along with examples is provided in the Domino Designer help pages, IBM Domino Designer Basic User Guide and Reference > Java/CORBA Classes > Classes A – Z > Document Class. There is also an XPages JavaScript class named `NotesXspDocument` that wraps the `Document` class, and an instance of this class is made available whenever you programmatically access a Notes document via the Domino document data source. The `NotesXspDocument` wrapper class is necessary so that XPages can keep track of any changes made to the actual document, cache and save its data, and so forth. `NotesXspDocument` exposes a reduced set of API methods, and this is the official XPages document scripting interface. However, the wrapped `Document` object is still available from the `NotesXspDocument` by simply calling its `getDocument()` method.

It is obviously important to know how to gain access to the document object when you want to apply some JavaScript logic to your page. Typically, as you have seen in the JavaScript examples in this chapter, the object reference is obtained from the `var` property defined on the data source—for example, `var="document1"`. For your convenience, the XPages runtime also provides an implicit global variable called `currentDocument`, which is always available and returns the document instance for the nearest document data source on the page. Remember, an XPage can have more than one data source! Data sources can be attached to the page itself or to container controls within the page. For example, if you are creating some JavaScript for a button within a panel on an XPage, and both the panel and the root XPage have declared a document data source, the `currentDocument` object uses the document instance associated with the panel, the closest data source in its document hierarchy path.

A document object can also be obtained programmatically from other classes. For example, in the section, "Creating Response Documents," you learned to extend a View control so that a response document could be created for any row entry. The `<xp:viewPanel> var` entry ("`rowData`" in your example) makes the current row available as an instance of the `Notes XspViewEntry` class. This enables you to call `rowData.getUniversalID()` on any row to pass the parent note ID to the `Create Response` simple action. If you needed access to the document itself, you could simply have called `rowData.getDocument()` and worked with that object as needed. Similarly, the `Database` class can return a document instance via the `get DocumentByID()` method, as shown back in Listing 7.8.

So, with all these access routes available, it should not be a problem to get your hands on a document instance and start experimenting with the extensive API it provides. Domino Designer puts all the API methods at your fingertips via the class browser and type-ahead facilities available in the JavaScript editor. (Simply type a dot after the variable name `currentDocument` or `doc1` in this case.) Since the 9.0 release of Domino Designer, typing **Control-Space** anywhere in the source pane will invoke content assist. Figure 7.15 shows an example of these utilities.

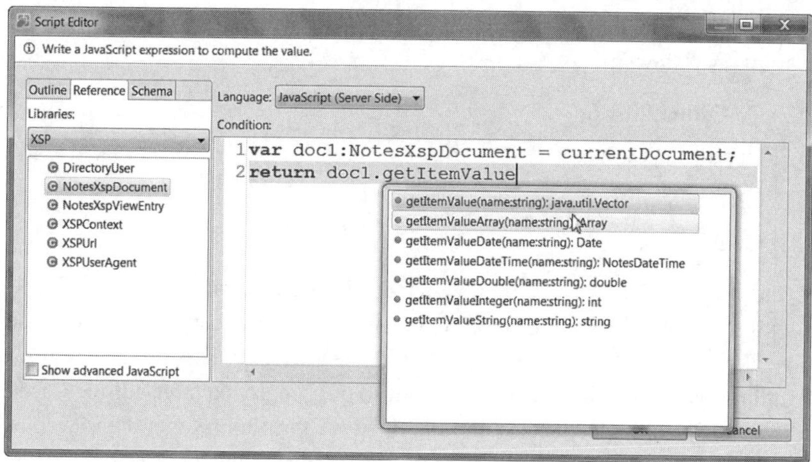

Figure 7.15 Document methods exposed using the JavaScript editor

TIP

A pertinent article titled, "XPages Straight Up," was contributed to the IBM developerWorks site in January 2010. One of its sections focuses on creating and updating Domino documents without using XPages Domino document data sources at all, but just pure JavaScript code. In other words, there is no Notes form providing the field metadata definitions—just dynamic SSJS code. Similarly, many XPages developers today use Java beans rather than forms as the data objects behind the XPages document. If you want to deep dive on script access to Domino documents and data, the URL is www.ibm.com/developerworks/lotus/library/domdes-xpages/index.html.

Rich Documents

Sooner or later, any discussion of Notes documents turns to the subject of rich text content! In Notes/Domino version 8.5.2, XPages made the CKEditor available as its default rich text control for the first time. Before that release, rich text fields within documents had been surfaced using the Dojo rich text editor, but the switch was made to the CKEditor as it provided a more expansive end-user feature set and was being adopted as a de facto standard across other products in the IBM Collaboration Solutions portfolio.

Apart from all the usual HTML text formatting options that one takes for granted with a modern rich text editor, CKEditor makes it easy to add tables, links, and emoticons to a rich text field, and to directly embed inline images. The latter in particular meant that the 8.5.2 release represented a big step forward for the both the Domino and XPages rich text experience. Fast-forward to Notes/Domino version 9.0.1, and the CKEditor revision included in XPages has gone through several revisions, as follows:

- XPages 8.5.2: CKEditor 3.2.1.6
- XPages 8.5.3: CKEditor 3.5.3.1
- XPages 9.0.0: CKEditor 3.6.6.1
- XPages 9.0.1: CKEditor 3.6.6.3

New features and fixes arrive with each new upgrade. If you compare the latest CKeditor included in 9.0 with the original included in 8.5.2, the stand-out new features would be the inclusion of a spellchecker on both Notes client and Domino server; auto-detection capabilities for enhanced link handling (Notes links, video content, and so on); improved table editing (drag-and-drop resizing of columns, tabbing between cells, and fixed width column support); as well as an autogrow feature which ensures that the toolbar always stays in view when large documents are being created. But there are many smaller improvements that add up to a much-improved overall rich text editing experience.

The **myTopic** XPage that you built features a CKEditor control. Open this page in Domino Designer and activate the control to take a closer look. The XSP markup for the rich text control is surprisingly minimal, as Listing 7.12 illustrates.

Listing 7.12 XSP Markup for Rich Text Control

```
<xp:inputRichText value="#{document1.Body}"
      id="body1">
</xp:inputRichText>
```

The control is highly configurable, however, so you can readily change its look and feel by defining more properties. The toolbar is often the first place people start with customizations. The CKEditor has three standard toolbar definitions, namely `Slim`, `Medium`, and `Large`, although these names don't do a lot in terms of describing functionality! However, the toolbars shown in Figure 7.16 might be more instructive.

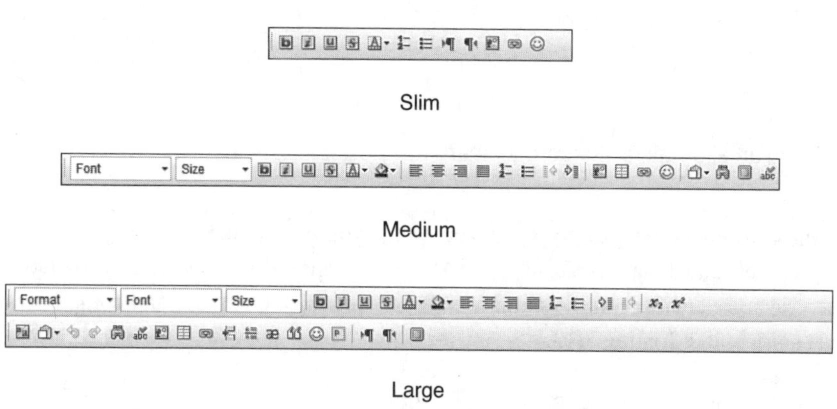

Figure 7.16 CKEditor slim, medium, and large toolbars

The `Medium` toolbar is the default setting, but if you want to change to another standard option, you can do so via the **Dojo** property sheet. Note that the CKEditor is not part of the Dojo library, but a completely separate JavaScript component. It is, however, integrated into XPages via a Dojo wrapper, and this allows XPages to maintain full compatibility with any historic XSP rich text markup generated previous releases, when the Dojo rich text editor was the default. Should you want to revert to the Dojo rich text editor, you simply have to set the `dojoType` property value to `ibm.xsp.widget.layout.RichText` in the **All Properties** sheet—but that's a slight aside! In any event, as Figure 7.17 shows, you can apply an alternative CKEditor standard toolbar setting by adding a `toolbarType` attribute to the **Dojo** property sheet and assigning a value of `Slim` or `Large`—note that these arguments are case sensitive.

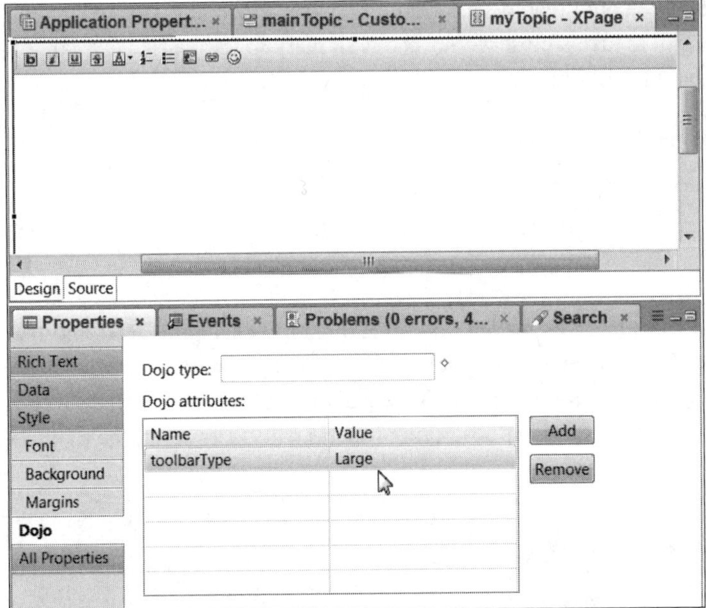

Figure 7.17 Defining an alternative standard toolbar

If none of these toolbars are exactly what you want, you can define your own customized toolbar using server-side JavaScript and a `toolbar` (as opposed to `toolbarType`) Dojo attribute. Add the `toolbar` attribute in the same way you added `toolbarType` and compute its value using a code snippet like Listing 7.13.

Listing 7.13 JavaScript Snippet for a Customized Toolbar

```
var myToolbar = "[['Font','FontSize'], \n"
      +"['Preview', 'Bold','TextColor','BGColor'], \n"
      +"['Italic','Underline','Strike','-
','Subscript','Superscript']]";
return myToolbar;
```

The resulting toolbar is populated only with the actions listed in the array. Note of course that a customized toolbar can also be an empty toolbar! Taking the snippet outlined in Listing 7.13, this would be achieved by returning an empty `myToolbar` array (`var myToolbar = "[]";`). Sometimes, this is desirable when an application has limited screen real estate and the area that can be afforded to the rich text control is much reduced. Removing the toolbar can free up a lot of pixel space, and users are still free to format rich content using the standard CKEditor hotkeys.

These are just simple customizations that can be achieved by changing property values or inserting a SSJS snippet. A more advanced customization of the CKEditor is explored in-depth in Chapter 11, "Advanced Scripting." The relevant section is named "A Real-World Use Case: Customizing the Rich Text Editor," and it shows how to support inline attachments and extend the UI to enable this feature.

Examples of other customization properties that can be applied using this same pattern are as follows:

- `language` defines the user interface language to use for translatable CKEditor UI artifacts using standard language codes, like `en`, `fr`, `pt`, and so on.
- `contentsLangDirection` defines the language orientation in the editor, such as `RTL`, `LTR`. This is just like the `dir` property exposed via JSF on other XPages controls.
- `enterMode` defines the behavior of the **enter** key and how it is recorded in the underlying HTML (for example, whether `<p>`, `<br>`, or `<div>` tags are used).
- `skin` is the name of a custom skin that can be provided here (as the CKEditor is a skinnable control).

Applying a custom skin is a nontrivial undertaking, but there are some patterns to follow. The Notes/Domino 9 releases come with two skins: a OneUI3 skin providing a general OneUI version 3 look and feel and a Lotus skin for backward compatibility. These skins are a useful reference point if you are interested in providing your own skin. You can find them in the `<data_folder>/domino/html/ckeditor/skins` directory on both the Notes client and Domino server. The CKEditor developer's guide also provides useful information on building skins at this location:

```
http://docs.cksource.com/FCKeditor_2.x/Developers_Guide/Customization/
Skins
```

Table 7.3 summarizes some of the other key features of the CKEditor.

Table 7.3 CKEditor Key Features

Action	Description
Maximize	Allows the editor area to be expanded to the full container window. This is particularly useful when creating and editing large documents.
Link	Provides a URL Link dialog that allows you to insert URLs into the document body.
Insert Image	Provides a dialog that allows you to browse your file system to select an image to insert into the current document. Alternatively, you can enter a URL to a remote image on the `Image Information` tab.

Action	Description
Insert Table	Provides a dialog that allows you to insert a table into the document. You can specify various table properties, such as number of rows, number of columns, width, height, and so on.
Insert Emoticons	Provides a dialog that gives numerous emoticons that you can select to insert into your document.
Paste	Provides a range of pasting options, including Paste Notes Document Link.
Check Spelling	Checks the current editor text for spelling errors using the Notes/Domino dictionaries. Provides a Replace/Suggestions dialog enabling the user to apply changes. Introduced in 9.0.

A sample rich text document has been created for you in **Chp07Ed2.nsf** using many of these features—see Sample Rich Text Doc, as shown in Figure 7.18.

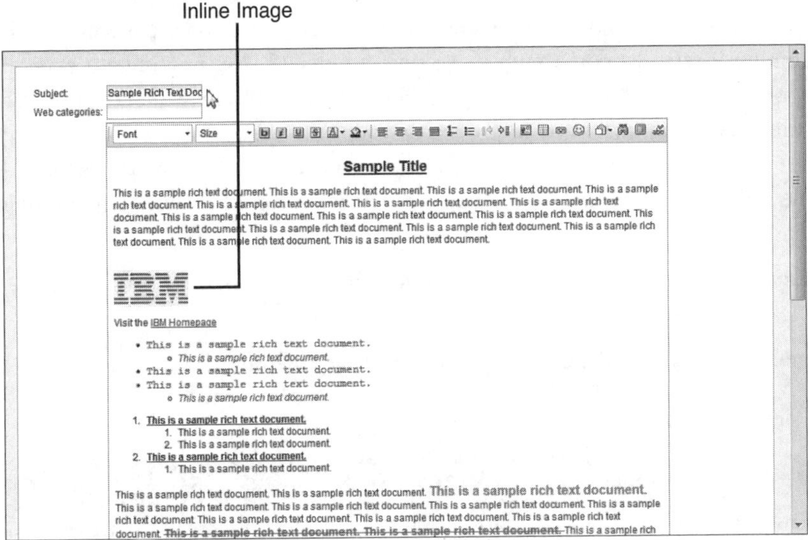

Figure 7.18 Rich text composed in the CKEditor

Experiment with the features and get an understanding of what can be achieved with rich text content.

Other CKEditor resources you may find useful are as follows:

```
http://docs.cksource.com/CKEditor_3.x/Developers_Guide
http://docs.cksource.com/ckeditor_api/
```

A final note regarding the creation of rich text and application security: It is theoretically possible to insert potentially malicious content into a rich text field by inserting inline executable script code. Chapter 17, "Application Layout," contains a section titled "Active Content Filtering," which explains how to deal with that issue.

Conclusion

This chapter explored *every* property of the Domino document data source and how they can be manipulated dynamically using URL parameters, simple actions, and SSJS. You have also been introduced to the CKEditor for creating and editing rich text content. Working with documents is a pervasive topic and you will find examples sprinkled throughout this book. Hopefully, this chapter provided a good grounding for you going forward.

CHAPTER 8

Working with Domino Views

This chapter looks at the Domino view data source. You already worked briefly with the view data source in Chapter 3, "Building Your First XPages Application," when you built a simple view panel, and Chapter 4, "Anatomy of an XPage," provided some further summary-level information. Now, it is time to explore the minutiae and learn all there is to know on this topic!

Before you dive in, download **Chp08ed2.nsf** and open it in Domino Designer so that you have all the examples and exercises that are covered here. As usual, the sample application is available from this website: `www.ibmpressbooks.com/title/9780133373370`

If you search **Chp08ed2.nsf** for the `<xp:dominoView>` tag, you will find many matches spread across various XPages and custom controls. For those of you wanting to jump right in, perform these steps:

1. Select the sample application in the Designer navigator panel.
2. Type **Control-H** to invoke the **Search** dialog.
3. Enter `xp:dominoView` in the **Containing Text** field.
4. Enter `*.xsp` as the file name pattern.
5. Click **Enclosing Project** to fix the search scope to just this application.
6. Click the **Search** button.

Results are listed in a **Search** tab located by default in the bottom pane of Designer, and you can double-click any matching tag to open the containing `.xsp` file. Then, moving to the **Properties > All Properties** panel, you will see a list of 24 view data source properties for the `<xp:dominoView>` tag, just like those listed and briefly described in Table 8.1.

Table 8.1 Developer Data Definition

Name	Description
`categoryFilter`	Identifies a category value in a categorized view and returns only the collection of documents found in that category.
`databaseName`	Name of the database containing the view, if not the current database.
`dataCache`	Identifier that controls how view data is cached between requests.
`expandLevel`	The depth of the document hierarchy to display for hierarchical collections.
`ignoreRequestParams`	Boolean property that, if set to true, indicates that any value provided for any property in this list should be ignored when specified as a URL parameter.
`keys`	One or more lookup values that are applied to the corresponding view columns, starting with the first column. Only matching documents are returned in the document collection.
`keysExactMatch`	Boolean property that indicates whether the full or partial key matches should be applied.
`loaded`	Boolean property that indicates whether the data source should be loaded.
`parentId`	Include only the children of the document identified by this document ID or UNID.
`postOpenView`	Code applied to this property is called after the view is opened.
`queryOpenView`	Code applied to this property is called before the view is opened.
`requestParameterPrefix`	A string prepended to parameters to distinguish one data source instance from another.
`scope`	`request, view, session`, or `application` scope applied to the data source.
`search`	Text string used as a full text `search` query on the view. Only matching documents are returned in the document collection.
`searchExactMatch`	A `true` value indicates that the full text query must find an exact case-sensitive match for the search term(s) for the view entry to be included in the result set.
`searchFuzzy`	A `true` value indicates that close words, like simple misspellings, can be considered a match for the search term(s).
`searchList`	One or more values combined to form a full text query. Multiple values are interpreted as OR criteria, that is, result set contains all documents containing any term.

Name	Description
searchMaxDocs	Constraint value applied to the search parameter (that is, include no more than this number of documents in the returned collection).
searchVariants	A true value indicates that word variants, like singular and plural forms, can be considered a match for the search term(s).
sortColumn	The document collection is sorted by the identified column, assuming the underlying Notes view column has this sorting capability.
sortOrder	The order in which to sort the sortColumn (for example, ascending, descending, or toggle). Again, assuming the underlying view column has such capability.
startKeys	Start the document collection at the document identified by this key.
var	Variable name used to identify this view source elsewhere on the XPage.
viewName	The name or alias of the Notes view to use as the view data source.

It is common to find just two properties in use with a typical <xp:dominoView> tag, namely viewName and var. The former is obviously required to identify which Notes view to target, while the latter is required as a reference so that other controls can bind to the data source. Thus, these are mandatory properties, and Designer will report an error if you do not include both in your view data source tag. You will now learn how to put all the others to good use through practical examples.

databaseName Property

The Notes view targeted by the view data source need not be in the current database. It can be in any other NSF that is locally accessible or in a database on a completely different server. If the databaseName property is not present or has a blank value (such as databaseName=""), the view is assumed to be in the current database. To specify a view in another database on the same server or local to your Notes client, just provide the name of the NSF, as Listing 8.1 demonstrates.

Listing 8.1 Simple DatabaseName Property

```
<xp:dominoView var="view1"
     databaseName="OtherDb.nsf"
     viewName="By Category">
 </xp:dominoView>
```

To specify another server, you need to use the same syntax as used in the Notes/Domino programming APIs: server_name!!database_name.nsf (see Listing 8.2).

Listing 8.2 Simple databaseName Property with Server Identifier

```
<xp:dominoView var="view1"
     databaseName="bigiron!!OtherDb.nsf"
     viewName="By Category">
</xp:dominoView>
```

If the database is located in a path relative to the data folder, simply enter the relative path as part of the `databaseName` value (such as `databaseName="subfolder\OtherDb.nsf"`). Absolute paths, such as `databaseName="C:\tmp\OtherDb.nsf"`, can be applied on the client; although this is generally considered not to be a best practice, particularly if portability is ever likely to become a requirement.

It is also possible to use the database replica ID as the `databaseName` property value, and the replica ID can include or exclude the middle colon character (for example, `databaseName="bigiron!! 8025775A:003A5264"`). Note, however, that you must not mix replica IDs with path information. It is up to the Domino server or Notes client to resolve the replica ID and locate the NSF, so combining any path information with the ID is invalid.

For the remainder of the chapter, "`localhost`" is used in URLs and as XSP properties wherever a server name is required. This is the reference name given to the loopback network interface and commonly resolves to the 127.0.0.1 IP address. It is used here to add clarity by employing a common server name throughout all the examples, and it should also be a valid name for those of you running the examples on a Domino server installed on your local computer.

> **TIP**
>
> From Domino Designer version 8.5 onward, you can simply copy/paste a database's replica ID from the Basics property panel. A strange boast, but it was previously not possible to copy/paste these 16 character IDs because they were embedded in an infobox dialog that was not clipboard-enabled. For any reader on an older version of Notes, if XPages itself does not make you want to upgrade, maybe this will.

View Data Source Filters

To date, any examples we have worked with have typically involved negligible volumes of data (for example, a dozen or so documents). With such small amounts of data, there is no real need to be concerned with filtering the result set by pruning the document collection returned by the data source. With real-world enterprise deployments, however, it is not uncommon for Domino applications to have views that contain tens of thousands of documents. For XPages applications to scale to the enterprise level and maintain performance, it is essential that the view data source be chopped and shaped according to various criteria that size the document collection into manageable proportions. Not just this, but having the ability to granularly refine the contents of any given view obviates the need to create specialized views for every query variation, and thus helps prevent the proliferation of view design elements in your application. A subset of the properties listed in Table 8.1 can be employed for this purpose—in particular, `categoryFilter`, `search`, `parentId`, and `keys`.

categoryFilter Property

The `categoryFilter` property is as good a place to start. Categorization is a traditional Domino mechanism for organizing data into logical groupings for interpretive analysis. Figure 8.1 shows an infobox definition for a selected column in a Notes/Domino view. Essentially, a categorized view is a view that contains one or more categorized columns.

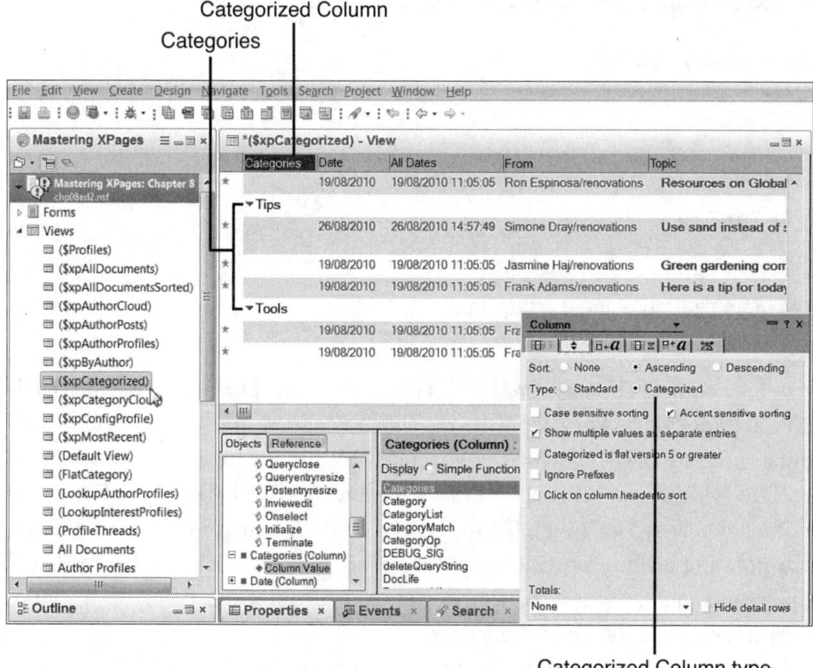

Figure 8.1 ($xpCategorized) view in Discussion template

In the presentation of the actual view data, you can see various categories, such as Tips and Tools, the contents of which can be expanded or collapsed using a "twistie" control (the little triangle that can be flipped, or "twisted," to open or close a category). The categories here correspond exactly with the elements shown in the tag cloud in the bottom-left corner of Figure 8.2. The tag cloud elements are simply sized in proportion to the number of documents found in each category, so categories containing a large number of documents are displayed in a bigger font than those with a lesser number. When you click an element in the tag cloud, you essentially filter a Notes categorized view so that just the content of the nominated category is displayed. In fact, when you open **Chp08ed2.nsf** in Designer and preview it in a web browser, notice that, when you click the largest tag cloud entry (**Tips**), the browser URL changes from

```
http://localhost/chp08ed2.nsf/allDocuments.xsp
```

to

```
http://localhost/chp08ed2.nsf/byTagViewPanel.xsp?categoryFilter=Tips
```

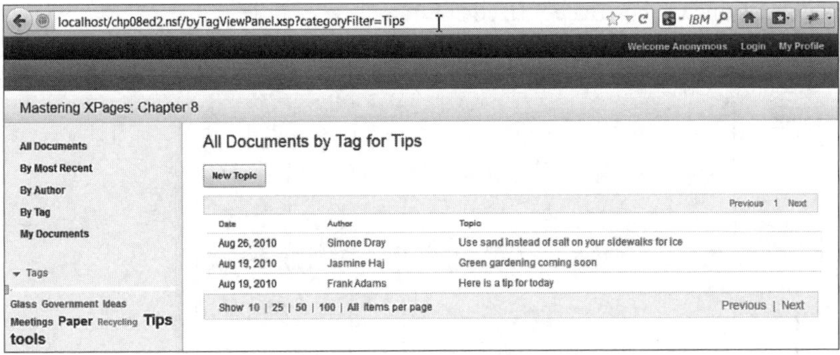

Figure 8.2 View category filtering using the tag cloud

What exactly is happening? The answer is simple: Clicking the **Tips** tag entry link navigates to the **byTagViewPanel.xsp** XPage, and the tag value is added as a `categoryFilter` parameter value to the navigation URL, which is generated by the tag cloud. The `category Filter` parameter value is then applied to the view data source on the **byTagViewPanel.xsp** XPage. This XPage includes a **byTagViewCC.xsp** custom control, which in turn has a Domino view data source pointing at the **($xpCategorized)** view. The view data source reads the `categoryFilter` parameter and returns a reduced document collection consisting of just those documents in the **Tips** category, as shown in Figure 8.2.

A different XPage is used in the *standard* Discussion template that ships with Notes/Domino (namely, **byTag.xsp** instead of **byTagViewPanel.xsp**). The latter is a customized page that is used in this chapter for instruction purposes; however, most examples work the same regardless of which XPage or template is used.

The ability to retrieve selective subsets of view data in this way is enormously beneficial in the context of scalability. In a hypothetical situation where a view has ten categories, each with a thousand documents, clearly the ability to request a small fraction of the entire data set (1/10th for those of you nodding off!) is quite efficient. Thus, if you structure your database views wisely and make good use of categorization, the `categoryFilter` property can help build efficient queries to populate your XPages view controls. If you are familiar with the Notes Java APIs, the results generated using the `categoryFilter` property is consistent with the view `createViewNavFromCategory()` method, as this is what is ultimately used by the XPages runtime to generate the result set. Experienced Domino developers might be aware of the `Show Single Category` formula that can be applied to an embedded view on a Notes form, which is basically the same concept. Similarly, with classic Domino web apps, the `RestrictToCategory` parameter is used on the `?OpenView` URL command to achieve the same results.

As you learned in Chapter 7, "Working with Domino Documents," many data source property values can be included as parameters as part of the XPages URL command that is entered in the browser. For example, any of the filter properties listed in Table 8.1 can be specified as URL parameters values in the way just demonstrated. This is an enormously powerful feature, and you will use this technique in this chapter's remaining examples. Incidentally, the instruction to preview these pages using a web browser rather than the Notes client was not an arbitrary one. Although the end results are the same, the Notes client does not display the URL address bar and, thus, you cannot see or modify the parameters.

TIP

In version 8.5.2, a long-standing issue was resolved in the Java API so that subcategories are properly supported. That is, if your Notes view is organized with multiple categories, you can now specify a subcategory as the `categoryFilter` value, such as "Europe\Ireland", "USA\MA", and so on. In other words, append the subcategory value to the category value and use the backslash character (\) as the argument delimiter. Although this has been a documented feature for many years, it did not work properly in previous releases because of shortcomings in the programming interfaces.

Full Text Search Properties

Next in the view filtering line are the various search properties, which allow you to perform full text queries on the associated view. Needless to say, your sample database needs to be full text indexed before proceeding with the next examples. You can verify this at a glance with the XPages discussion sample, because the **Search** toolbar does not display if the database is not indexed. (The Search toolbar is explicitly identified in the top-right corner of Figure 8.3.) If not, you can create a full text index in Designer, as follows:

1. Select the database itself in the Designer navigator panel.
2. Activate the **Index** property panel, located by default in the bottom pane of Designer.
3. Click the **Create Index** button.

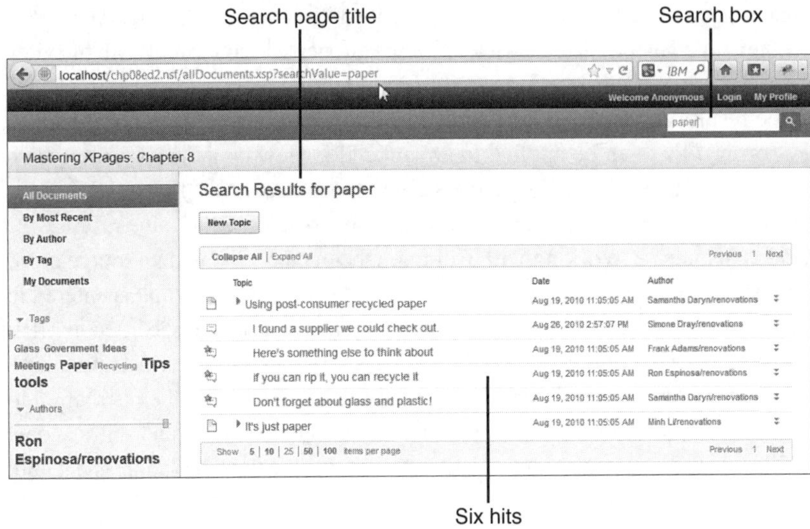

Figure 8.3 Results of a full text search

On the client, the full text index is created pretty much right away, whereas the request is put in a queue on the Domino server (executed every hour by default). If you have administration privileges on your server, you can force the indexer to kick in by using this command:

```
load Updall Chp08ed2.nsf -x
```

If you omit the NSF name, all databases are updated at once. To get all the options available on this command, enter the following:

```
load Updall -?
```

All these tasks assume that you are operating with your own development server, and are definitely not recommended practices to be carried out willy nilly in a production environment. In any case, assuming your database is ready, willing, and able to be searched, you can begin playing with the `search` property. The XPages implementation is straightforward, meaning that if a value is specified for the `search` property, it is applied as the full text query on the view and any matching documents are returned as the collection. The Discussion template includes a search box in its toolbar and, if you type "paper" as a query on the **allDocument.xsp** main page, six matching documents are returned as the result set, as shown in Figure 8.3.

You may well wonder why the parameter you see in the search URL is `searchValue` instead of just a plain `search` parameter. This is because the actual string value provided is also used for purposes besides just executing the full text search on the data source (for example, you can see that it is used as part of the title of the search results page). Thus, the text string is stored in a `searchValue` variable to cater for its various other uses, but for the view filter, it must ultimately be assigned to the `search` property, as so it is—seek out the snippet in Listing 8.3 in **allDocumentsView.xsp**. Note that this listing is the *actual* markup extracted from the application, so it contains other properties as well as JavaScript code that are not covered yet, but will be shortly. For the purposes of this example, properties like `dataCache` can be safely ignored for now, because they are described later. The important point is that you can see that the `searchValue` variable is ultimately assigned as the `search` property value—a different mechanism is used when running in a mobile context.

Listing 8.3 search Property Assigned the Value of the searchValue Parameter

```
<xp:dominoView var="dominoView" viewName="xpAllDocuments"
dataCache="full">
    <xp:this.search><![CDATA[#{javascript:
      if(isMobile()){
            requestScope.searchQuery;
      } else {
            param.searchValue; // * assign this as search prop value *
      }
    }]]></xp:this.search>
</xp:dominoView>
```

You could, therefore, modify the search URL shown previously in Figure 8.3 to just use the `search` property directly and get the same results, minus the page title update, of course:

```
http://localhost/chp08ed2.nsf/allDocuments.xsp?search=paper
```

To restrict the result set to a maximum number of documents, you can apply the `searchMaxDocs` property to the full text search query. Simply assign whatever number you want to use as the constraint:

```
http://localhost/chp08ed2.nsf/allDocuments.xsp?search=paper&search
MaxDocs=3
```

You will find that the result set of six hits is reduced to just three hits after this extra URL parameter is applied. In 8.5.3 even more options became available to help you further refine your searches. If you wanted to conduct a case-sensitive search for the previous query, for example, then you could do so as follows:

```
<ditto>/chp08ed2.nsf/allDocuments.xsp?search=PAPER&searchExactMatch=
true
```

This returns just one document in the result set, whereas the lowercase equivalent (as follows) returns six documents. This is because the document containing the search term PAPER also contains the search term paper:

```
<ditto>/chp08ed2.nsf/allDocuments.xsp?search=paper&searchExactMatch=
true
```

Note that for the `searchExactMatch` parameter to have any effect, the full text index must have been created with the `Enable case-sensitive searches` flag turned on. Figure 8.4 highlights the required option in the Notes **Create Full-Text Index** dialog box. (The terminology used in the dialog would suggest that `searchExactCase` might well have been a better choice of name for this property.)

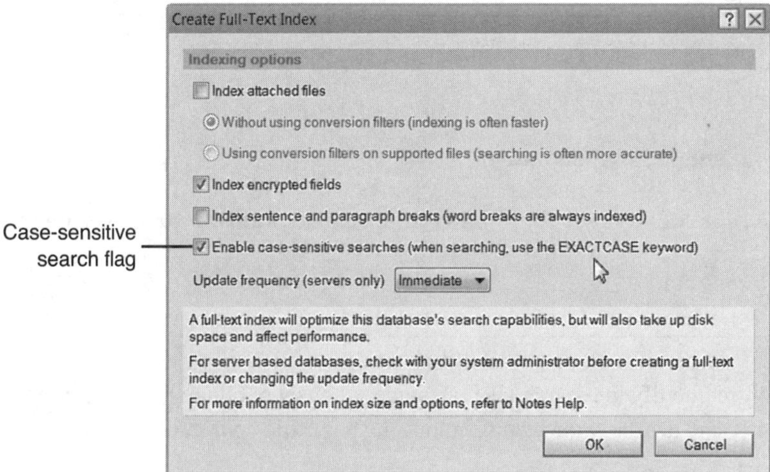

Figure 8.4 Create Full-Text Index dialog box invoked from Notes client

Two other parameters that add flexibility to full text queries are `searchVariants` and `searchFuzzy`. By way of example, start with a plain and simple search for the word "addendum" in the same manner as shown previously:

```
<ditto>/chp08ed2.nsf/allDocuments.xsp?search=addendum
```

With the sample application provided, this query will result in two hits. If you then change the search term to "addendums" and execute the query again, you will get no hits. This is correct, as the word cannot be found in any document. To account for the possibility of plurals however, you could refine your original search query as follows:

```
<ditto>/chp08ed2.nsf/allDocuments.xsp?search=addendums&searchVariants=true
```

When you execute this query, the original two documents are included in the result set again. (Although any good dictionary will inform you that the plural form is "addenda" ☺).

For resolving problems caused by any good old typos that may be present in the text, the `searchFuzzy` parameter is your best friend. Take this example:

```
<ditto>/chp08ed2.nsf/allDocuments.xsp?search=addendam&searchFuzzy=true
```

Execute the `searchFuzzy` query shown here and observe that it returns the two documents containing the term addendum despite the misspelling in the search term. This is because the matching algorithm will return words considered close to the search term.

The final new search parameter added in 8.5.3 is called `searchList`. This allows multiple search terms to be used in a query. Using a single value in the `searchList`, however, has the same effect as the `search` parameter and thus is fairly pointless. But, for instance, if you wanted to find all documents in a view that contain "paper" `OR` "recycle," then the `searchList` parameter is what you need. Note that the term `OR` is uppercased intentionally to indicate that the search terms provided are OR'd together such that any document containing any of the terms used is considered a match. In other words, any documents returned by this `searchList` query must contain at least one of the terms included.

A practical application of this feature would be to expand the search capability of the Discussion application to accept more than one search term. Listing 8.3 has markup that can be used to implement the simple search query. Listing 8.4 modifies the view data source markup so that the `search` query is replaced by a `searchList` query. This updated source is included in your sample NSF; see the **allDocumentsViewMultiTerm.xsp** Custom Control.

Listing 8.4 Building a Multiterm Full Text Query

```
<xp:dominoView var="dominoView" viewName="xpAllDocuments"
dataCache="full">
      <xp:this.searchList>
      <![CDATA[#{javascript: if (param.searchValue != null) {
         // create an array of args (from comma-separated input list)
         var args = param.searchValue.split(",");
            // Put items in a Vector to pass to Java API
            var v:java.util.Vector = new java.util.Vector();
            for (i = 0; i < args.length; i++) {
               v.addElement(args[i]);
            }
            return v;
      }]]>
      </xp:this.searchList>
      <!-- etc -->
</xp:dominoView>
```

The Server Side JavaScript (SSJS) code snippet is easy to interpret. The code expects a comma-separated list of search terms and splits up the input string into an array of arguments. The individual search terms are then added one by one to a Vector object (a Java class used to store a collection of items), which is assigned as the `searchList` property value. The XPages runtime ultimately passes this object to the Notes backend Java classes to execute the query. Figure 8.5 shows the results of a full text query run for "paper" or "glass" when the **allDocuments-MultiTerm.xsp** XPage is previewed in the Notes client from Domino Designer.

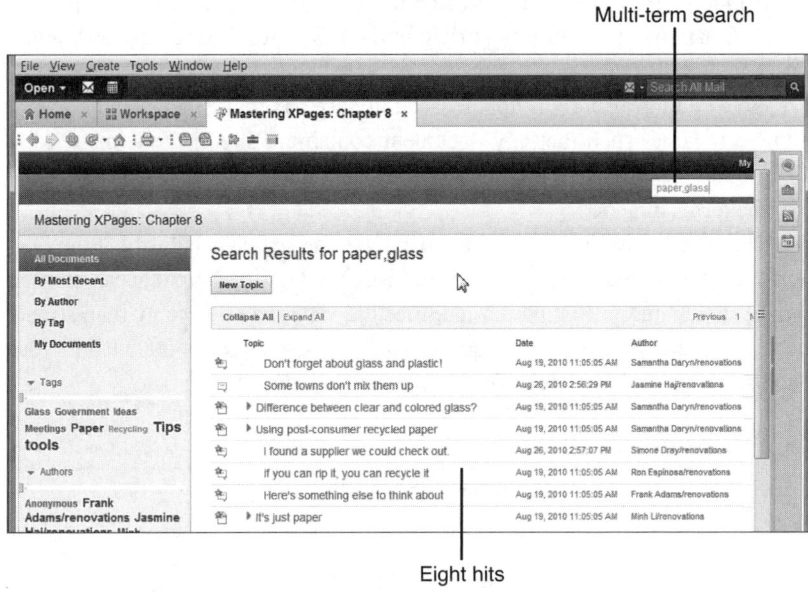

Figure 8.5 Results of a multiterm full text search

parentId Property

The `parentId` is an equally simple filter. A simple note ID or full UNID can be used as the `parentId` value. If a document with this ID is found in the view, all of its descendants, if any, are returned as the document collection. For example, the document titled "Meeting Minutes" has three response documents and a note ID of 942, as shown in Figure 8.6.

As you have come to expect at this stage, you can generate a filter URL that returns just the three documents in the response hierarchy, as follows:

```
http://localhost/chp08ed2.nsf/allDocuments.xsp?parentId=942
```

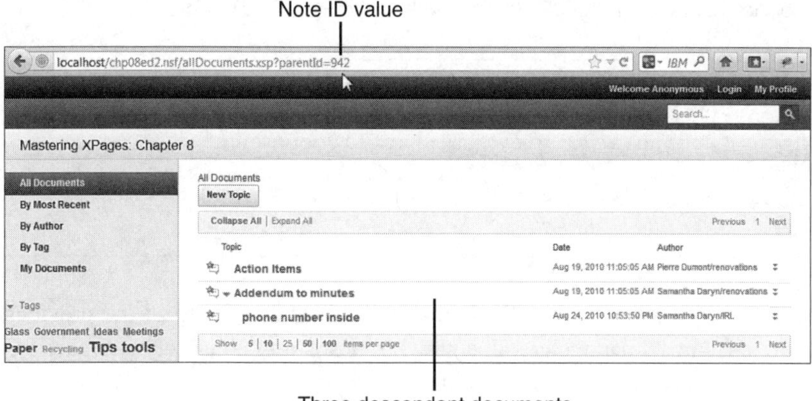

Figure 8.6 Response hierarchy to "Meeting Minutes" document

The results generated using the `parentId` filter are consistent with the `createViewNavFromDescendants()` method in the backend Java View class.

> **TIP**
>
> If you create new replicas or copies of the sample application, you may find that the parentId example shown here stops working or generates different results. This is because the short document ID (also known as the note ID) is not guaranteed to be consistent across database instances, whereas the 32 character universal ID (UNID) is. You can use either type of ID as the parentId property value.

Incidentally, if you have concerns that savvy users (sometimes referred to as hackers) could use URL parameters like these in an undesirable way on the web, the feature can be disabled by setting `ignoreRequestParams = "true"` on the view data source.

ignoreRequestParams Property

To prove this point, open the **allDocumentsView.xsp** custom control in Designer and add `ignoreRequestParams="true"` to the view data source tag, as shown in Listing 8.5. Remember that the fastest way to locate the view data source is to search for "`xp:dominoView`" in the **Source** pane.

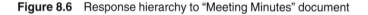

Listing 8.5 Domino View Data Source XSP Snippet with ignoreRequestParams Property Added

```
<!--View Data Source Snippet with ignoreRequestParams added to
byTagViewCc.xsp -->
<xp:dominoView var="dominoView" viewName="xpAllDocuments"
dataCache="full"
      ignoreRequestParams="true">
</xp:dominoView>
```

Save the custom control, preview the **allDocuments.xsp** again, and repeat the previous exercise. Note that the `parentId` parameter value now has absolutely no effect, as Figure 8.7 illustrates! You should undo this change before continuing.

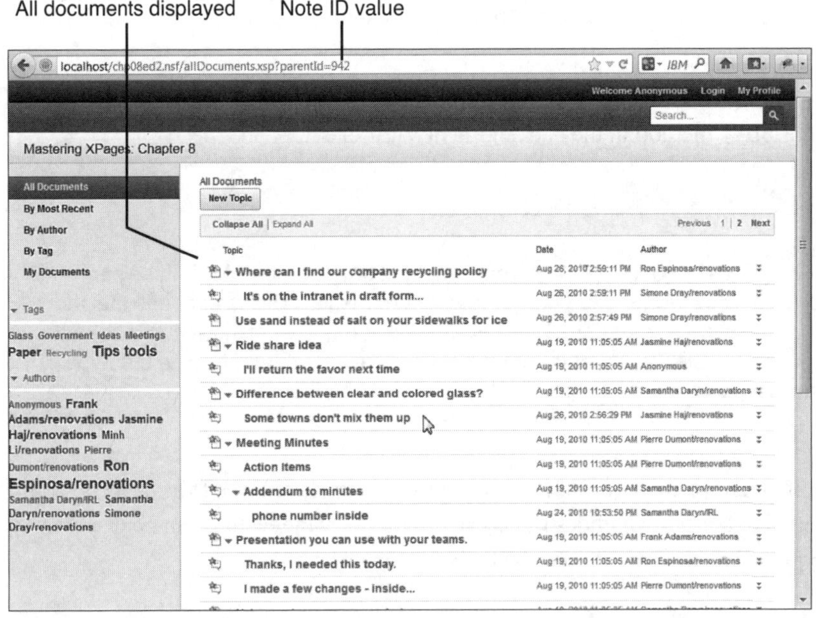

Figure 8.7 Disabling view filters using ignoreRequestParams

keys, keysExactMatch Properties

The final search filter to discuss is the `keys` property, which is a little trickier to use, because you must first understand some ground rules. A *key* is a search value applied to a column in a view. As the `keys` property name implies, this property value can be a single object, such as a text string or date, or a collection of such objects. When a single object is used as a key, it is applied as a lookup value against the *first* column of the Notes view, and that first column must be a sorted column. If a collection of two objects is provided as `keys`, the first object is used to search the first view column, and the second object is used to search the second view column. Again, both columns in the Notes view must be sorted. Ultimately, if a collection of *n* objects are provided as `keys`, they are applied against the first *n* columns of the Notes view, and all *n* columns must be sorted. If any of the *n* Notes view columns are not sorted, the key lookup fails.

The cumbersome nature of this filter means that it is less widely used than those discussed previously. The Discussion template, for example, does not employ any `keys` filters; it uses the `categoryFilter` and `search` properties instead. In fact, none of the views in the Discussion template are particularly suitable for `keys` filtering, so a new one has been added to **Chp08ed2.nsf** for your convenience, namely **keyView**, as shown in Figure 8.8.

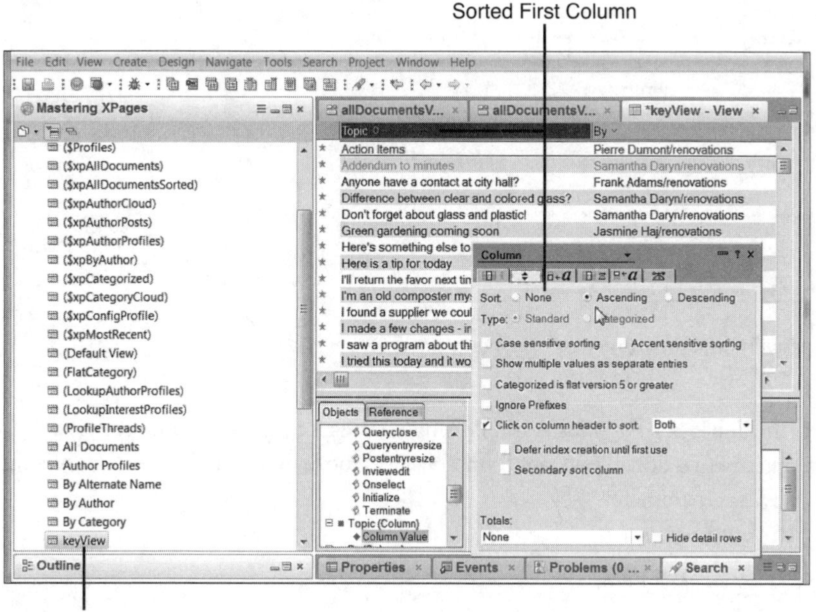

Figure 8.8 keyView featuring two sorted columns

To build a `keys` filter example, create a new XPage, called **byKeys.xsp**, and drag-and-drop a view control onto it. Bind this View control to the new **keyView** design element and include both columns (**Topic** and **By**) in the View control. Save the page and preview it in a web browser. Your page content should look like what's shown in Figure 8.9.

Now, simply add the keys properties as URL parameters, like this:

```
http://localhost/chp08ed2.nsf/byKeys.xsp?keys=thanks&keysExactMatch=false
```

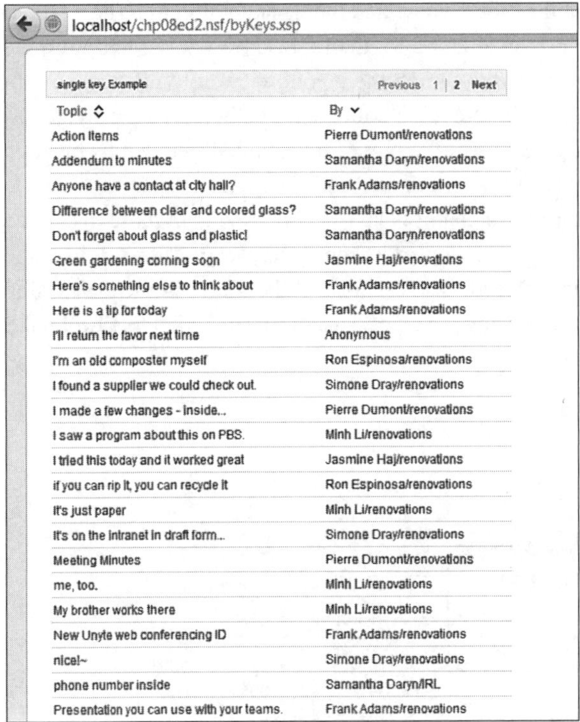

localhost/chp08ed2.nsf/byKeys.xsp

single key Example Previous 1 | 2 Next

Topic	By
Action Items	Pierre Dumont/renovations
Addendum to minutes	Samantha Daryn/renovations
Anyone have a contact at city hall?	Frank Adams/renovations
Difference between clear and colored glass?	Samantha Daryn/renovations
Don't forget about glass and plastic!	Samantha Daryn/renovations
Green gardening coming soon	Jasmine Haj/renovations
Here's something else to think about	Frank Adams/renovations
Here is a tip for today	Frank Adams/renovations
I'll return the favor next time	Anonymous
I'm an old composter myself	Ron Espinosa/renovations
I found a supplier we could check out.	Simone Dray/renovations
I made a few changes - inside...	Pierre Dumont/renovations
I saw a program about this on PBS.	Minh Li/renovations
I tried this today and it worked great	Jasmine Haj/renovations
if you can rip it, you can recycle it	Ron Espinosa/renovations
It's just paper	Minh Li/renovations
It's on the intranet in draft form...	Simone Dray/renovations
Meeting Minutes	Pierre Dumont/renovations
me, too.	Minh Li/renovations
My brother works there	Minh Li/renovations
New Unyte web conferencing ID	Frank Adams/renovations
nice!~	Simone Dray/renovations
phone number inside	Samantha Daryn/IRL
Presentation you can use with your teams.	Frank Adams/renovations

Figure 8.9 XPage with unfiltered keyView view content

The example in Figure 8.10 applies a simple single string key lookup value ("thanks") to the first view column, and two documents are found because loose matching is requested via the `keysExactMatch=false` parameter.

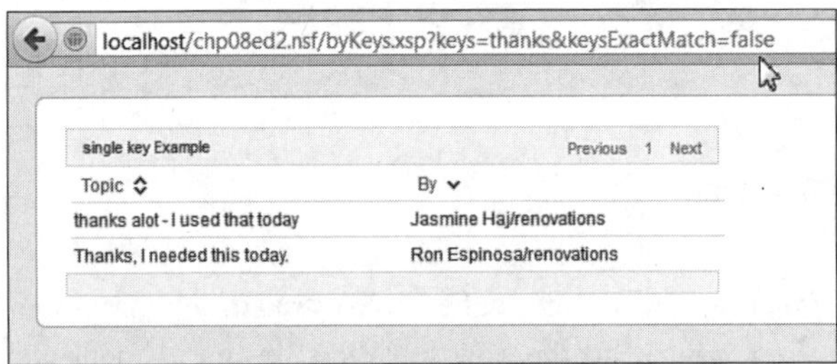

localhost/chp08ed2.nsf/byKeys.xsp?keys=thanks&keysExactMatch=false

single key Example Previous 1 Next

Topic	By
thanks alot - I used that today	Jasmine Haj/renovations
Thanks, I needed this today.	Ron Espinosa/renovations

Figure 8.10 XPage using single key filtering

Applying a collection of objects is not possible using URL parameters, but Listing 8.6 presents a simple example using some JavaScript code.

Listing 8.6 Filtering in Server Side JavaScript Using a Collection of Keys

```
<xp:dominoView var="view1" viewName="keyView" keysExactMatch="false">
      <xp:this.keys>
      <![CDATA[#{javascript:
            var v:java.util.Vector = new java.util.Vector();
            v.addElement("Ride share");
            v.addElement("Jasmine");
            return v;}
      ]]>
      </xp:this.keys>
</xp:dominoView>
```

Again a Java Vector is created to hold two key string objects, "Ride share" and "Jasmine" respectively, which are loosely applied to the first and second columns of **keyViews**. Because both columns are sorted and because one entry matches the `keys`, a single document is returned in the filtered document collection, as shown in Figure 8.11. A new XPage containing this code (**byManyKeys.xsp**) has been added to **Chp08ed2.nsf** for your convenience.

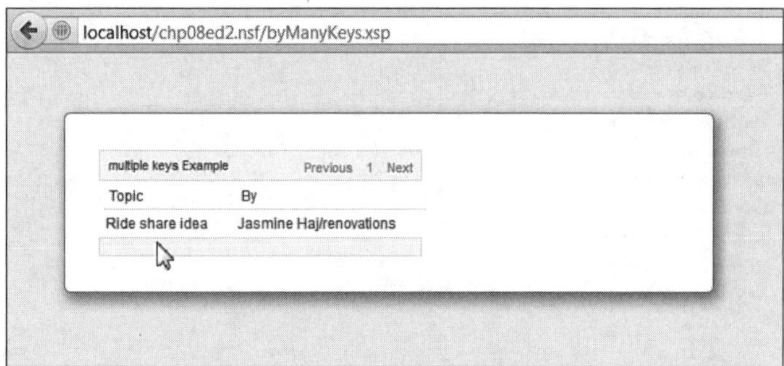

Figure 8.11 XPage multiple key filter results

The `keys` property runtime implementation uses the `getAllEntriesByKey()` method in the backend Java View class, so results are consistent with that API.

Other View Content Modifiers

This section describes some other properties, which, although not filters per se, can be used to alter the content of a view.

startKeys Property

The `startKeys` property does not parse the content of the view, filtering out documents that do not match certain criteria, but it sets a starting point in the view index, and the data collection is made up of all documents after that point.

A simple example can be shown by simply applying `startKeys=nice!~` as a URL parameter to the **byKeys.xsp** page provided in the sample application, as follows:

```
http://localhost/chp08ed2.nsf/byKeys.xsp?startKeys=nice!~
```

Compare the results shown in Figure 8.12 to Figure 8.9. As you can see, the document collection starts at the topic titled "nice!~" and continues to the end of the view. If you try imprecise matches, like `startKeys=ride` or `startKeys=phone!~`, notice that these also work. (In other words, the `startKeys` property uses loose matching automatically, and it is not related to the `keysExactMatch` property used earlier with the `keys` property.)

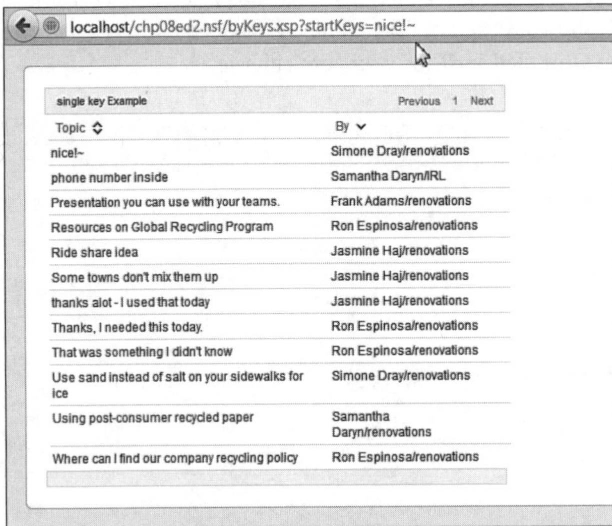

Figure 8.12 byKey view with startKeys property applied

You can also use a collection of objects for multiple `startKeys`, just like the SSJS example shown in Listing 8.6. The `startKeys` property was first introduced in the version 8.5.2 release of Notes/Domino and uses the `createViewNavFrom(viewEntry)` method defined in the backend Java View class.

expandLevel Property

Another property that gives fine-grained control over the set of documents obtained from the view data source is the `expandLevel` property. This property can only be applied to hierarchical document collections, such as categorized views or views containing response document chains. If you apply this property to a "flat" view, is it simply ignored. The `expandLevel` setting determines the maximum depth of document hierarchy to be retrieved from the target view. A setting of 1 means only top-level documents are included in the document collection retrieved from the data source, such as top-level categories in the case of categorized views or root documents for non-categorized views (no responses). This property is widely used in the Discussion template—if you navigate the main views of the sample application in a web browser at runtime, you notice how all the entries in **By Tag** page are displayed in a collapsed fashion, whereas the documents in the **All Documents, By Most Recent** and other pages are expanded. The application design uses the `expandLevel` property to drive this behavior. Listing 8.7 shows the `expandLevel` property setting used in **byTagViewCc.xsp**.

Listing 8.7 byTagViewCc.xsp expandLevel Setting Ensures Entries Are Displayed in a Collapsed State

```
<xp:dominoView
      var="xpCategorized"
      viewName="xpCategorized"
      expandLevel="1"
      dataCache="id">
</xp:dominoView>
```

You can experiment with the `expandLevel` setting by passing in an integer value as a URL parameter. Figure 8.13 shows the **By Tag** page with an `expandLevel` set to 2.

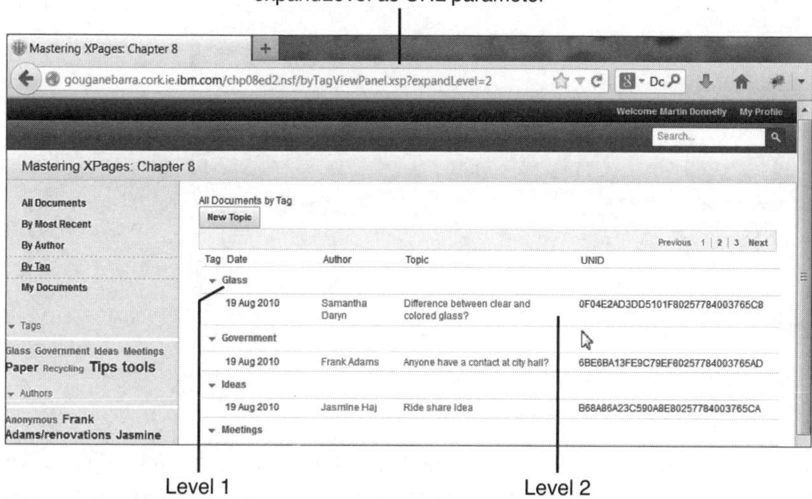

Figure 8.13 By Tag with a maximum document hierarchy depth set to 2 levels

A setting of 0 means that no `expandLevel` is applied and all entries are shown in full hierarchy. The maximum specific `expandLevel` value is 30.

A Page with Two Views

Because there is no restriction on the number of controls that can be contained within an XPage, and because each control obtains its data via an independently defined data source, there is nothing to stop you from placing two or more views in a single page. An example of this is provided with the sample application for this chapter in the aptly named **twoViews.xsp**. The **xpCategorized** view and the **($All)** views are the chosen ones. There is no magic associated with this, so if you want to create a similar page of your own, drag-and-drop some views onto an XPage and bind them to different Notes views as you go.

The `rows` property of the view control was set to 5 to help display the contents of both views more clearly within the confines of a single page. Figure 8.14 shows how it looks at runtime in a web browser. Note that the `rows` value does not discriminate between entry types, insofar as only the first five rows are displayed regardless of whether they are categories, documents, or responses.

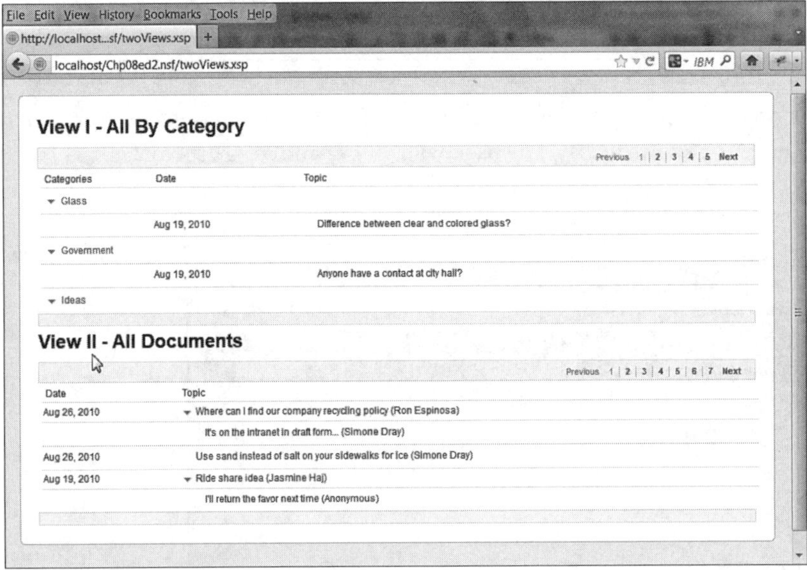

Figure 8.14 Two views in a single XPage

You can navigate both views separately by using the respective pagers and so forth. An interesting question, however, is this: What happens to any view data source parameters that you might pass into this page via the browser URL? By default, any property value is applied to all data sources in a given XPage, which may or may not be the behavior you require!

Suppose, for example, that you want all the entries in the categorized view to be collapsed, but all the entries in the second view to be expanded. How can this be achieved? Essentially, you need a way to address each data source separately so that the different settings can be applied individually. The mechanism for doing this is the `requestParamPrefix` property.

requestParamPrefix Property

If you open **twoViews.xsp** and inspect the markup, you see that both view data sources have the `requestParamPrefix` property applied. Listing 8.8 shows the relevant snippets.

Listing 8.8 View Data Source Snippets from twoViews.xsp Featuring requestParamPrefix Settings

```
<!-- Data Source for Categorized View -->
<xp:dominoView
      var="xpCategorized"
      viewName="xpCategorized"
      requestParamPrefix="cat">
</xp:dominoView>

<!-- ... -->

<!-- Data Source for All Documents View -->
<xp:dominoView
      var="all"
      viewName="($All)"
      requestParamPrefix="all">
</xp:dominoView>
```

The value specified as the `requestParamPrefix` property must be prepended to any parameter that is intended to be applied to that data source. Thus, the following URL sets different expand/collapse states for each view:

```
http://localhost/Chp08ed2.nsf/twoViews.xsp?catexpandLevel=1&allexpand
Level=2
```

Figure 8.15 shows the results of this request.

Passing in a regular `expandLevel` parameter now has no effect, because the data sources are primed to only accept values from prefixed parameters.

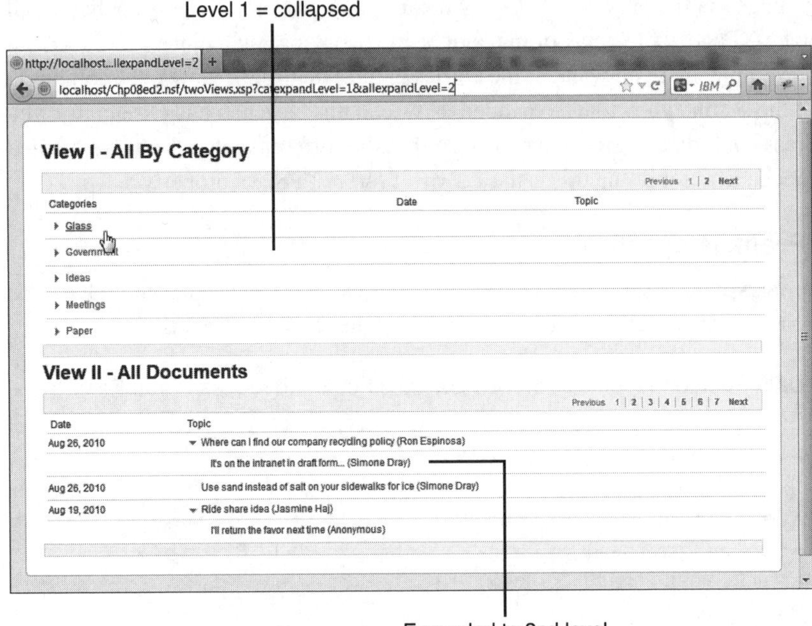

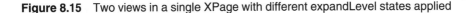

Figure 8.15 Two views in a single XPage with different expandLevel states applied

When Is a View Not a View?

Why, when it's a folder, of course! Although a view's contents are defined by a selection formula, a folder's contents are determined by whatever documents are arbitrarily placed in it by the end user. From a data source standpoint, however, a view and a folder are essentially the same thing. You can provide a folder name as the value for the `viewName` property and its contents are retrieved as if it were a view. The sample application for this chapter contains a **Follow Up** folder that is populated with some documents. Figure 8.16 shows this folder previewed in the Notes Client from Domino Designer.

If you drag-and-drop a View control to an XPage, the binding dialog presents both the views and the folders in its view list. You can select the columns in the usual way and then save and preview the XPage. Figure 8.17 shows an XPage called **folder.xsp**, which has been constructed just as described and is included in **Chp08ed2.nsf**. Note that Figures 8.16 and 8.17 are identical in terms of content.

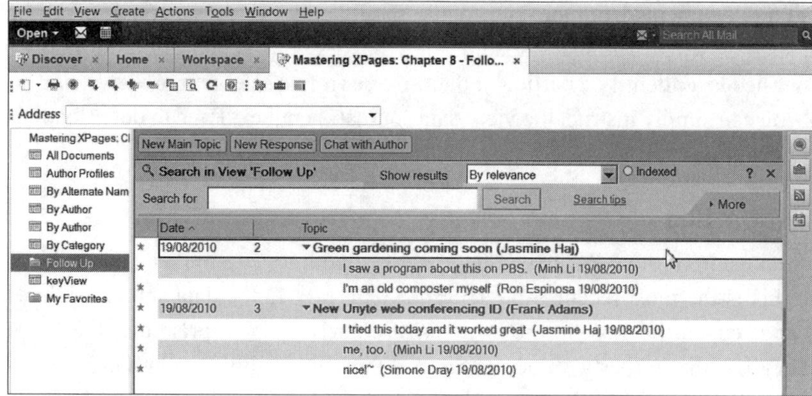

Figure 8.16 Contents of a Follow Up folder previewed in Notes

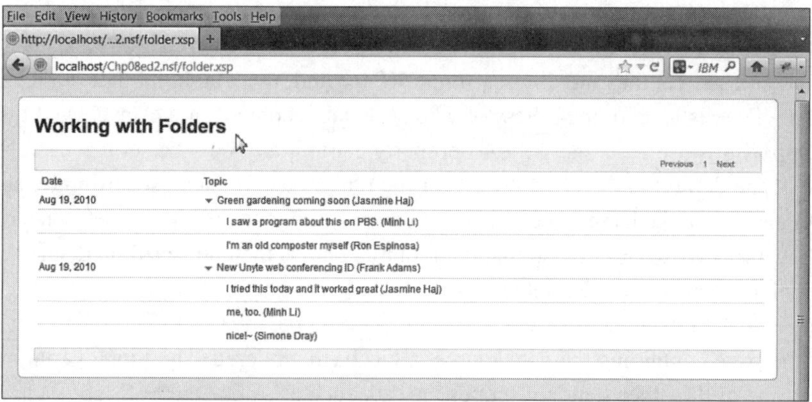

Figure 8.17 XPage displaying the contents of the Follow Up folder

Go Fetch! Or Maybe Not...

Retrieving the document collection for a folder or a view obviously comes at a cost. Depending on the volume of data stored in the view and the complexity of the query, fetching the document collection can be an expensive proposition. The mere presence of one or more data sources on an XPage causes the data retrieval process to automatically kick in when the page loads and, in the vast majority of use cases, this is the desired behavior. It is easy to imagine alternative situations, however, where loading documents from the data source should only occur as a consequence of an explicit request, such as where automatic loading may have a detrimental effect on performance, where the user needs to identify a particular data source from a selection of views, and so on. In this scenario, you can simply instruct the view data source(s) on the XPage to defer loading any data via the `loaded` property.

loaded, scope Properties

By way of example, take any of the XPages you have worked with to date in this chapter—say **folder.xsp**, because this is the most recent. Add `loaded="false"` to the data source declaration in the markup and reopen the page in the browser. It comes as no surprise that the View control is empty. Toggling the property value (`loaded="true"`) or simply removing it altogether restores the automatic data load behavior. For a real application, the `loaded` boolean value would most likely be set programmatically using SSJS in response to a user event or action. Think of an XPage that features a Tabbed Panel control, where each tab reveals different content when selected by the user at runtime. The data content of each tab could well emanate from a different data source, and it might be advantageous to load the required data only when and if a given tab is actually selected. After all, although there can be an arbitrary number of tabs, each with its own distinct data source, they are all on a *single* XPage and, by default, all data sources are loaded when the XPage is loaded, regardless of whether a tab's contents are ever viewed by the end user. To support this use case, the `loaded` property can initially only be set to `"true"` for the data source of the default tab, and `"false"` for the other inactive tabs. Accordingly, as other tabs on the XPage are clicked, the selection action can programmatically set the associated data source's `loaded` property to `"true"` so that the required data is then retrieved on demand. I'm sure you can think of many other relevant use cases!

After the data is loaded by an action, it is stored in `view` scope, meaning that it is no longer available after the page containing the data source(s) has been rendered. The scope variable allows you to select one of the other standard scopes instead, such as `application`, `session`, `view`, and `request`. The section, "Caching View Data," looks at how view data is managed.

postOpenView, queryOpenView Properties

Two other events are associated with the loading of the view data source: `postOpenView` and `queryOpenView`. If, for example, you want some logic to be executed just after the view is opened, you should attach this code to the `postOpenView` property. An example might be that you may want to capture the number of documents contained in the view and store that number for use elsewhere in the XPage. In the **All Properties** view, if you elect to compute the `postOpenView` property, you are automatically presented with the JavaScript editor. Listing 8.9 presents some sample code to store the total document count in a `viewScope` variable.

Listing 8.9 postOpenView Server-Side JavaScript Code

```
<xp:dominoView
      var="all"
      viewName="Follow Up">
      <xp:this.postOpenView><![CDATA[#{javascript:
            viewScope.count = all.getAllEntries().getCount();
            print(viewScope.count);
      }]]></xp:this.postOpenView>
</xp:dominoView>
```

The `var` property gives you an instance of the Notes/Domino View Java class, and you can call any of its methods in XPages via JavaScript. `viewScope.count` is assigned a value as soon as the view is opened and then other controls on the XPage can make use of that data.

> **TIP**
>
> For more information on the View class, look in Designer Help under the IBM Domino Designer Basic User Guide and Reference section. Select the **Java/CORBA Classes > Java Classes A – Z > ViewEntry**. All the available methods are described there, along with coding examples.

Any code applied to the `queryOpenView` property, on the other hand, is called just before the data source is opened. Perhaps the more logical property name is `preOpenView`, but `queryOpenView` is consistent with the traditional naming conventions used with the other design elements. Note that the View class is not available to you in the `queryOpenView` property because the `var` property is not yet in scope—the view is not yet open! Attempting to do something like `print(all.getAllEntries().getCount())` results in a runtime error, as shown in Figure 8.18.

The preceding code samples just illustrate an example of how to code the view data source events. Be aware that getting the view entry count of a large hierarchical view is an expensive operation, because the entire view needs to be navigated to calculate the count. In a real-world application, you need to consider the performance implications of using this method.

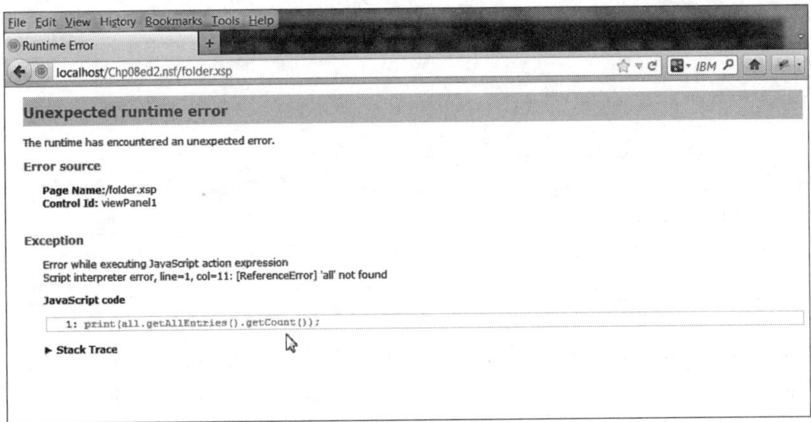

Figure 8.18 Runtime error reported for queryOpenView code

Caching View Data

No doubt, the `dataCache` property has caught your eye in some of the previous XSP markup illustrations, because it is used extensively in the Discussion template data sources. Having just discussed some of the properties associated with loading view data, now is an opportune time to examine what the `dataCache` property has to offer.

In simple terms, a view can be thought of as a collection of documents. Each document occupies a row in the view and the row in turn is made up of a collection of summary fields known as *columns*. When loading the data source, the XPages runtime iterates through each row within a selected range of entries and reads its data. The data associated with each row is not just the column values displayed in the control, but it includes other items, such as its position in the view, the note ID of the underlying document, its sibling count, descendant count, and so on.

After the view data is read and presented to the end user, the Notes view must be closed as the request/response cycle is completed. The problem is that users often want to perform actions on the data that is presented in the View control, such as open an entry, make a further calculation on a column value, and so on. Such actions often do *not* cause a new page to be displayed, but instead request that the current page be restored, albeit perhaps with some new details on display—this is called a postback request. For the current page to be restored and the action to succeed, the data that is presented to the user the first time around must be cached until the Invoke Application phase of the next request is completed; otherwise, the actions fail, because the required data is effectively gone. Refer to Chapter 5, "XPages and JavaServer Faces," for a refresher of the phases of the JSF request processing lifecycle.

Caching view information requires some careful thought for reasons of performance and scalability. Many of the properties associated with a view entry are scalar values (such as view position, indent level, child count, and so on) and are, therefore, not costly to maintain. On the other hand, the column values of a given row are arbitrarily large, and caching all the rows all the time just in case a user *might* want to perform a postback request could often be unnecessarily inefficient. Because it is the application developer who decides whether postback actions are provided on the page by virtue of designing and building it in the first place, the developer is the one who needs a way to configure the workings of the cache for each individual case. And that, in a nutshell, is why a view data source has a `dataCache` property—so the application developer can optimize the performance/scalability of the page based on the exact use case.

An example helps drive this point home. You will amend the **byTagViewCc** custom control in Designer, add a postback request, and see how the different `dataCache` settings impact application behavior. To do this, follow these steps:

1. Drag-and-drop a Computed Field to the **byTagViewCc XPage** (for example just below the view). Listing 8.10 has a snippet of the required markup.
2. Append a new fifth column to the **viewByTag** view.
3. Set its header label (column title) to “Abstract”.
4. In the **View Column > Data** property sheet, select **Computed value**.
5. Add the following line of code via the JavaScript editor (where `tagRow` is the `var` property value defined on the view control):

   ```
   return "[Get Entry " + tagRow.getPosition() + "]";
   ```

   The `tagRow` object is an instance of the `NotesXspViewEntry` JavaScript class and it provides full programmatic access to each view entry as it is being rendered in the View control. It is discussed more fully in Chapter 9, “Beyond the View Basics,” in the section, “Working with Categories.” The `getPosition()` method returns the position of the entry in the view hierarchy as a string (for example, “2.3” for the third document of the second category).
6. On the **Events** panel, select the `onclick` event and add this snippet of server-side JavaScript:

   ```
   var abs = tagRow.getColumnValue("Abstract");
   if (abs != null && abs != "" && abs != viewScope.abs) {
               viewScope.abs = abs;
         }
   ```
7. Define the `onclick` as a **Partial Update** event and select the Computed Field as the target, as shown in Figure 8.19
8. Select the **Value** tab on the computed field and add `viewScope.abs`, the data binding expression via the JavaScript editor.
9. Optionally, add some inline CSS as the style property value on the **All Properties** sheet for this control. The CSS used here is shown in Listing 8.10.

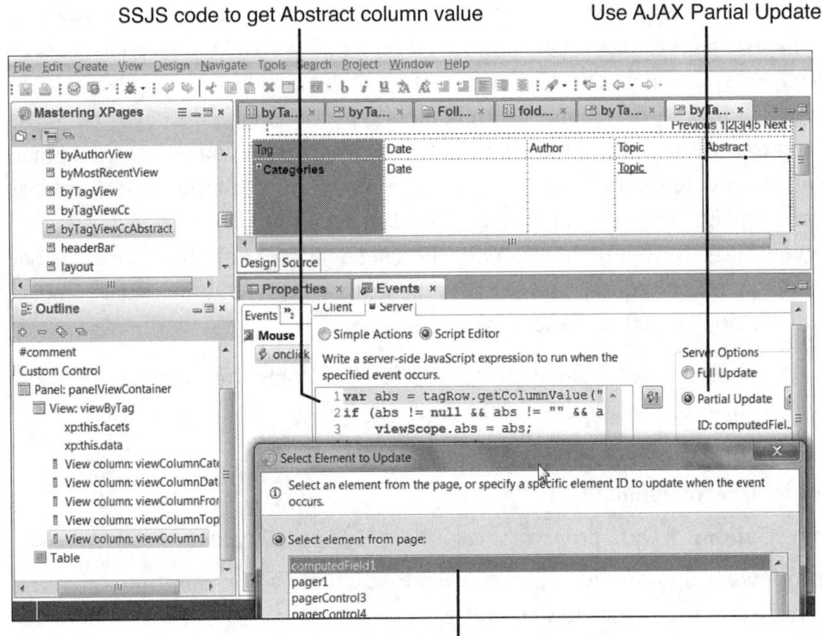

Figure 8.19 Updated byTagViewCcAbstract custom control in Domino Designer

10. Find the `<xp:dominoView>` tag on the page and change the `"dataCache"` value from "id" to "full."

With this ten-step program, you have added a new column called "Abstract". It displays its view row position as a link for each non-category row, and following the link fetches the `Abstract` column value from the Notes view and displays it in the computed field using AJAX partial refresh.

Listing 8.10 Markup for the Computed Field Added to byTagViewCc.xsp

```
<xp:table style="width:100%">
      <xp:tr>
            <xp:td style="width:20%"></xp:td>
            <xp:td>
                  <xp:text escape="true"
                        id="computedField1"
                        style="fontsize:14pt;color:rgb(255,128,255)"
                        value="#{javascript:viewScope.abs;}">
                  </xp:text>
```

```
            </xp:td>
            <xp:td style="width:20%"></xp:td>
        </xp:tr>
</xp:table>
```

If the markup for the Computed Field looks overly verbose, it is only because the field is wrapped in a three-column table to center it under the view control. This is purely for aesthetics and has no bearing on the functional aspect of this `dataCache` example. To insert the Computed Field under the View control, place this markup between the closing View control tag (`</xp:viewPanel>`) and the Panel control that houses it (`</xp:panel>`). A copy of the revised **byTagViewCc.xsp** has been provided with this **Chp08ed2.nsf**, so refer to **byTagViewAbstract.xsp** if you have any problems recreating this example.

If you inspect the data source view in Designer, you see that it contains an Abstract column that is not displayed in **byTagViewCc.xsp** by default. The `Abstract` column value can be up to 300 characters in length for any given row entry, so the decision to exclude it from the View control was probably driven by performance and scalability considerations. What you have done here is enable the user to fetch the `Abstract` column value on demand, but *not* routinely retrieve it for every row in the view (which would be an egregiously bad practice in terms of performance!).

Reload or preview the custom control's parent XPage (**byTagViewPanel.xsp**) to view the content and behavior of your new creation. If you have not updated **byTagViewCc.xsp** as part of the 10-step exercise just outlined, then you need to update **byTagViewPanel.xsp** to use in **byTagViewCcAbstract.xsp** rather than **byTagViewCc.xsp**. Again, this has been facilitated in the sample application—simply locate and uncomment the following line (by removing the enclosing <!-- and --> tags)

```
<!-- <xc: id="byTagViewControl1" rows="10" > </xc:byTagViewCcAbstract> -->
```

Then apply the comment tags to the markup that included the **byTagViewCc.xsp** custom control:

```
<xc:byTagViewCc id="byTagView" rows="10"> </xc:byTagViewCc>
```

Figure 8.20 shows the page after expanding the first category and clicking the [Get Entry 1.1] link.

The `onclick` event of the `Abstract` column is an example of a postback request mentioned a little earlier—the user can perform an action based on the data presented in the view, and the XPage is effectively posted back to itself. That is, the current XPage is restored after performing an action on it. In this instance, clicking the link calls `getColumnValue()` for the `Abstract` column. Given that the view instance used to retrieve the data was recycled after the original XPage was rendered, it is not possible to compute column values as part of the next request, unless, of course, those column values are cached temporarily to accommodate such requests. When the `dataCache` value is set to `full`, this is exactly what happens—all the column values are cached between the render phase of the first request/response and the post phase of the follow on request. After that phase is complete, the row entry data is discarded. If no `dataCache` value is specified, `full` is the default setting.

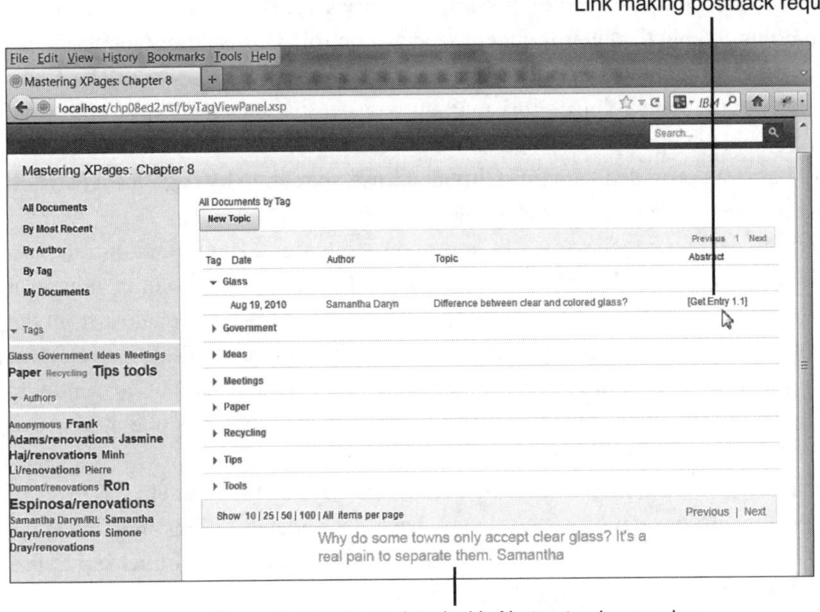

Figure 8.20 Updated byTagView custom control at runtime

The original **byTagViewCc.xsp** did not have any postback requests, so it is more efficient to set the `dataCache` property value to `id`, as is done in the default template. This means that column values are not maintained after the page is rendered, but the scalar IDs are. This ID data is cheap to maintain, and it means that simple postback requests automatically work. The third `dataCache` property value is `nodata`, which, as its name implies, does not cache any view data between requests at all.

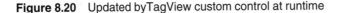

Now, go back to Domino Designer, reset the `dataCache` value to `id`, and reload the page. Figure 8.21 shows the result of clicking the first **Abstract** column entry. The error you see is, of course, the result of attempting to access data (in particular, the column values, which are only cached in `full` mode) that has not been cached and is, therefore, not available to the SSJS code.

This topic is explored further in Chapter 19, "A First Look at Performance and Scalability," but its salient points were covered here.

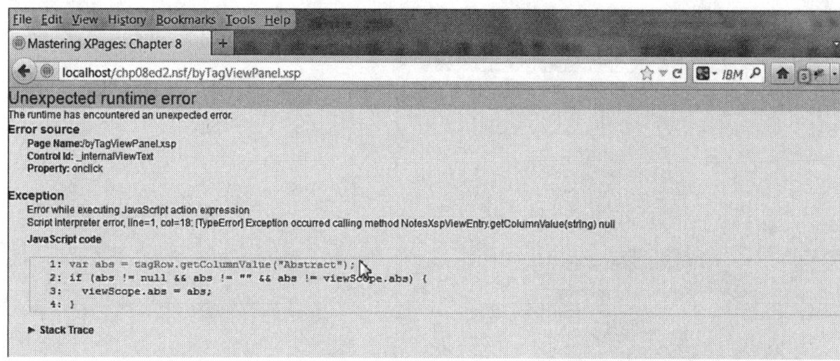

Figure 8.21 Result of a postback action attempting to use getColumnValues() with dataCache="id"

Sorting Columns

A new view, **keyView**, was introduced to the sample application to support examples that demonstrated the `keys` and `startKeys` properties. The first column of this view is defined as sortable in both ascending and descending order (refer to Figure 8.8).

Thus, the **byKeys.xsp** XPage built earlier can be leveraged here to show how the `sortColumn` and `sortOrder` properties work. Reload the page in a browser and pass `sortColumn=Topic` and `sortOrder=descending` as parameters in the URL, as shown in Figure 8.22. The order of documents displayed in the view is reversed. If you then change the second parameter value to `sortOrder=ascending` and reload the page, the original document order is restored.

These URL parameter values are ultimately used to feed the following backend Java API call:

```
View.resort(String columnName, boolean ascending);
```

This method was introduced in Notes/Domino version 8.5 to support user-driven column sorting. The view control offers user-driven columns via the `sortable` property on the view column header. You see that in action in the next chapter.

Combining Searching and Sorting

In version 8.5.3, another new Java API made it possible to use the `sortColumn` and `search` parameters in combination so that the results returned by full text query became fully sortable. This was not possible in any XPages release prior to 8.5.3. To quickly verify this new capability, amend the previous example to include a search criterion:

```
http://localhost/byKeys.xsp?sortColumn=Topic&sortOrder=
ascending&search=paper
```

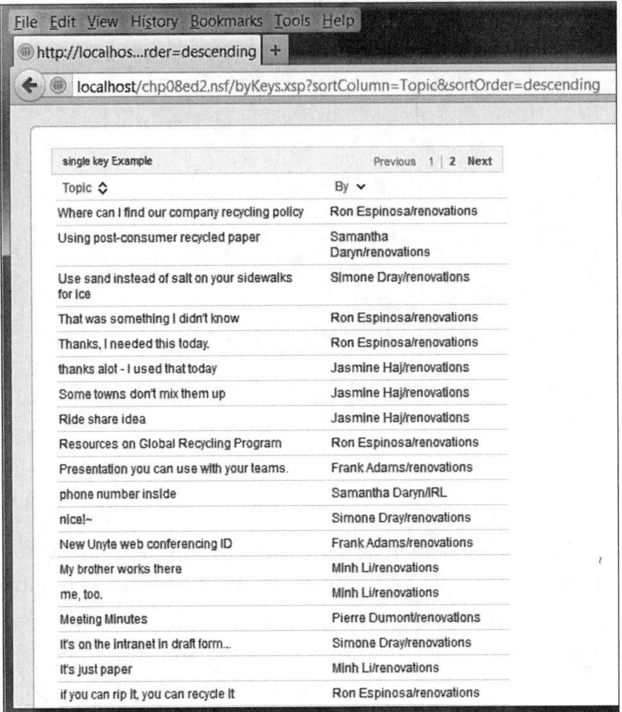

Figure 8.22 keyView documents sorted in descending order

Observe that the six entries returned are sorted in the requested ascending order, and the order can be inverted by simply reissuing the command with `sortOrder=descending`, as shown in Figure 8.23.

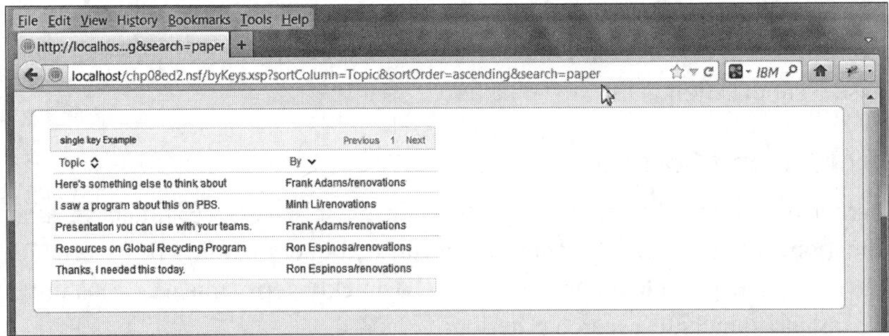

Figure 8.23 Full text query executed on keyView with results sorted in ascending order

The new Java API that made this possible is the `FTSearchSorted()` method added to the backend Java `View` class. Given that XPages uses the standard published APIs for its data access operations, you can emulate the results of the previous sorted search by creating a simple Java agent. Listing 8.11 shows the required agent code and should give you an insight into how XPages works with Domino view data, as it uses the same APIs:

Listing 8.11 Java agent FTSearchTest Used to Generate a Sorted Result Set for a Full Text Query

```
import lotus.domino.*;
public class JavaAgent extends AgentBase {
    public void NotesMain() {
      try {
          Session session = getSession();
          AgentContext agentContext = session.getAgentContext();
          // get the required view from the current NSF
          View view = session.getCurrentDatabase().getView("keyView");
          // get a document count for the view
          int docs = view.getEntryCount();
          String ftQuery = "paper";
          // run a sort full text query on the view and store the hit count
          int hits = view.FTSearchSorted(ftQuery, 100,
                      "Topic", false,
                      true, false, false);
          System.out.println(hits + " hits for \"" + ftQuery + "\" out of "
+ docs + " documents");
          // Iterate through the rows printing the topic field for each hit
          ViewEntryCollection results = view.getAllEntries();
          ViewEntry ve= results.getFirstEntry();
          int i = 0;
          while (ve != null) {
              // The Topic is stored in the 1st column (zero-based index)
              System.out.println(++i + ": " + ve.getColumnValues().get(0));
              ve = results.getNextEntry();
          }
      } catch(Exception e) {
          e.printStackTrace();
      }
    }
}
```

This Java agent has been provided for you in the sample NSF for this chapter. To view and run the code, select **Code > Agents > FTSearchTest** in the Domino Designer navigator and then double-click the JavaAgent.java entry shown in the **Agent Contents** section to view the Java source. To run the test agent, right-click the agent in the navigator and select **Run Agent** from the context menu. After the agent has completed execution, an Agent Log dialog displays. This can be dismissed and the results displayed by choosing **Tools > Show Java Debug Console** from the Designer main menu.

Figure 8.24 shows the results of running this particular agent. Note how the results correspond with those generated via XPages in Figure 8.23.

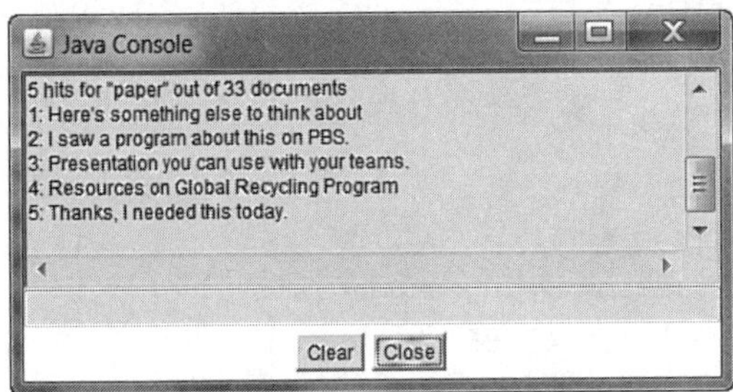

Figure 8.24 Java Debug Console showing output of FTSearchTest agent

Accessing Calendar Data

Another special type of Domino view is used to store calendar data. It is typically referred to as simply a calendar view, rather than the standard Domino view, and it has some unique characteristics that enable it to support calendar and scheduling functions. The distinguishing features of the calendar views used in the Notes client are listed as follows:

1. The view style must be of type `calendar` rather than `standard`.
2. The first column must be hidden, sorted ascending, and must be a Date/Time type.
3. The second column must be hidden and must map to a field or formula on the document that specifies, in minutes, the duration of the calendar entry.
4. A third column is required to indicate whether an entry should appear in a timed or untimed section of the Notes calendar. All day events and anniversaries are examples of events that do not have a specific time associated with them.

Although it is important to be aware of these special properties when creating a calendar view that will work well in Notes, the goal with XPages is really to read, display, and manipulate calendar data. To this end, XPages added support for calendar views in 8.5.3 UP1 by wrapping the iNotes calendar control as an XPages control and providing a REST service class capable of retrieving calendar data in the JSON format required by iNotes.

To experiment with the XPages calendar control, it is useful to have some sample calendar view data in place. Many Notes applications already contain calendar views. For example, the standard Notes mail application has a **($Calendar)** view, the XPages Extension Library sample application has a **TestCalendarOutline** calendar view, and the XPages Teamroom template has a **CalendarOutline** calendar view. You can experiment with any of these, but this chapter focuses on the Teamroom example. You can quickly create an instance of a Teamroom application within Domino Designer by following these steps:

1. Choose **File > New > Application** from the Domino Designer main menu.
2. Assign a name to your sample Teamroom application—"teamroom" is used in the upcoming examples.
3. Select **TeamRoom (9)** from the template list entry, and click **OK.**
4. Open your new "teamroom.nsf" sample application in a web browser.
5. Click the **Teamroom Setup** button, and configure the application. (Just selecting **Save** will suffice.)
6. Click the **Calendar** link in the Teamroom navigator to load the XPages calendar control.
7. Click the **New Meeting** button or simply double-click in a calendar slot to create one or more calendar entries.

This is enough to create the sample calendar entries you need for experimentation here. Figure 8.25 shows a screen shot of a Teamroom application instance created as previously described.

> **TIP**
>
> You can see from the CalendarOutline view in the Teamroom template that the special view properties stipulated for calendar views at the start of this section can be relaxed somewhat if the view does not need to be rendered in the native Notes client. The CalendarOutline, for example, does not contain a column with the duration data as the iNotes control computes this based on other view properties.

The XPages Calendar REST Service

The calendar data used to populate the calendar control is managed by the XPages calendar REST service. The XSP tag for this service is **<xe:calendarJsonLegacyService>**. The **xe** namespace indicates that the code originated from the Extension Library even though it is now part of the core runtime. It is *legacy* insofar as it is designed to return the specific JSON data format required for iNotes, and it should be noted that this REST service is an XPages artifact and not part of the standard Domino REST service APIs that ship independently as part of Domino Access Services (DAS). While you can also use DAS to work with calendar data (and much more beyond), the focus here is strictly on what is provided as part of the XPages runtime itself. If you are not familiar with REST, JSON, or DAS, then the following links may serve as good primers (in that order). Ideally, you should have a grasp of the basic concepts behind REST and JSON before continuing. Go to the following websites for more information:

```
http://www.ibm.com/developerworks/webservices/library/ws-restful/
http://www.w3schools./json/
http://tinyurl.com/DominoAccessServices
```

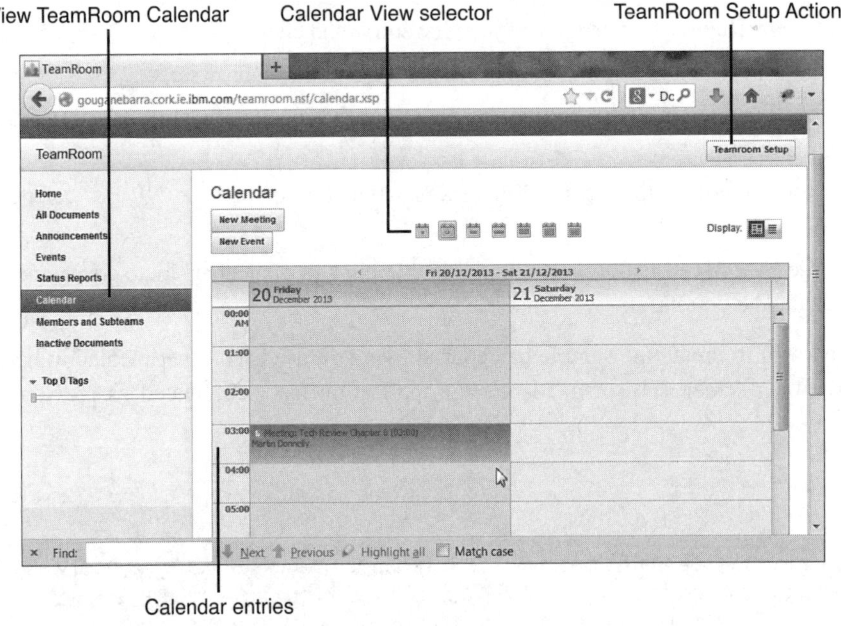

Figure 8.25 Sample TeamRoom application for calendar testing

The key to working with calendar data is to identify the columns within the calendar view that contain the data needed to display the entries in the wrapped iNotes control. Remember that a Domino developer is free to implement a calendar view in any number of ways, as long as the basic ground rules enumerated at the start of this section are followed. Thus, the items used to store the calendar entry data can vary arbitrarily from one calendar implementation to another. The XPages calendar REST service is designed in such a way as to allow you to identify the required calendar fields used in the particular application you are working with. Table 8.2 summarizes the properties of the XPages calendar REST service.

Table 8.2 Developer Data Definition

Name	Description
`colAltSubject`	Name of the alternative subject Column. Default is "$151".
`colCalendarDate`	Name of column containing the date of the calendar entries. Default is "$134".
`colChair`	Name of column containing the identity of the person responsible for the calendar entry. Default is "$153".
`colConfidential`	Name of column containing the confidential status of the entry. Returns an integer entry ID where 0 = nonconfidential and 1 = confidential. Default column name is "$154".
`colCustomData`	Name of column containing custom data. By Notes convention the custom data column contains whatever is found in a $UserData item in the calendar entry. Default is "$UserData".
`colEndTime`	Name of column containing the end time of the calendar entries. Default column name is "$146".
`colEntryIcon`	Name of column containing the calendar entry icon. The iNotes calendar has icons depicting the entry type (for example, meeting, anniversary and such) or entry status (for example, accepted). Returns an integer icon ID. Default column name is "$149".
`colEntryType`	Name of column containing the event type for the calendar entries. Returns an integer entry ID where 0 = appointment, 1 = anniversary, 2 = all day event, 3 = meeting, and such. Default column name is "$152".
`colStartTime`	Name of column containing the start time of the calendar entries. Default column name is "$144".
`colStatus`	Name of the column containing the status of the calendar entry. Returns status values like "Accepted", "Tentatively Accepted", "Draft", "Countered", and so on. Default column name is "$160".
`colSubject`	Name of column containing the subject field for the calendar entries. Default column name is "$147".
`compact`	Boolean property indicating with the JSON stream containing the calendar data should be compacted.
`contentType`	Response content type, typically "text/plain".
`databaseName`	Name of the database containing the view, if not the current database.
`dojoAttributes`	Specifies an optional list of Dojo attributes.
`dojoType`	Sets the default Dojo type. Not required.
`loaded`	Boolean property that indicates whether the data source should be loaded.
`var`	Variable name used to identify this view source elsewhere on the XPage.
`viewName`	The name or alias of the Notes view to use as the calendar view data source.

If you care to count, there are 11 properties containing a "**col**" prefix, which indicates that the value should be the name of a calendar view column. This is how the REST service is abstracted so that it can deal with any Notes calendar implementation because any arbitrary Notes application that supports calendaring must have some logical representation of these columns. If the cardinal column is not explicitly declared in your XSP markup (that is, the `colCalendarDate` property that maps to the first *magic* hidden column in any calendar view, as described earlier), then the default column names will be silently applied for all columns. These default column names map to those used in the view of the **($Calendar)** Notes mail template. Thus binding to an out-of-the-box Notes mail template is simple—you don't have to provide any column properties at all!

Listing 8.12 contains an XSP snippet taken from the XPages Teamroom template, specifically from the **calendarView.xsp** custom control. This application contains a custom calendar view, identified as **calendarOutline** in the markup, and a core set of column names are also declared. Thus this can be identified as a custom calendar and therefore *none* of the default column names are applied. The default column names are applied on an all or nothing basis—either you are dealing with a standard Notes mail calendar, or you are not.

Listing 8.12 XPages Calendar REST Service as Implemented in calendarView.xsp

```
< xe:restService id="restService2" pathInfo="/inoteslegacyjson"
                        preventDojoStore="false">
                        <xe:this.service>
                            <xe:calendarJsonLegacyService
                                viewName="calendarOutline"
                                var="entry"
                                contentType="text/plain"
                                colCalendarDate="CalDateTime"
                                colEntryIcon="Icon"
                                colStartTime="StartDateTime"
                                colEndTime="EndDateTime"
                                colSubject="For"
                                colChair="Chair">
                                <xe:this.compact>
                    <![CDATA[#{javascript:sessionScope.CompactJson2=="true"}]]>
                                </xe:this.compact>
                            </xe:calendarJsonLegacyService>
                        </xe:this.service>
</xe:restService >
```

The iNotes Calendar Control

XPages wraps a snapshot version of the iNotes calendar control. In Notes/Domino 9.0.1, the XPages wrapper does not contain the latest iNotes calendar control, but this is something that can be rebased in a future release depending on demand from customers. Nevertheless, the calendar control is a highly functional component capable of displaying calendar entries across a range of different timelines and supporting client-side events to create new entries, reschedule entries via drag and drop, and remove entries via the delete key.

The critical step is to bind the calendar control to the XPages Calendar REST service, and this part could not be simpler: Just refer to the id of the REST service in the **store ComponentId** property of the calendar control. Listing 8.13 is an outline snippet taken from the same **calendarView.xsp** custom control used in the Teamroom template.

Listing 8.13 XPages Calendar Control Wrapper for iNotes from calendarView.xsp

```
<xe:calendarView id="calendarView1"
    jsId="cview1"              type="#{javascript:sessionScope.
dateRangeActions_selectedValue}"
    storeComponentId="restService2"
      style="width:100%">
        <!-- Support Calendar Events via client-side JavaScript-->
            <xe:this.onNewEntry>
                <!--  CSJS code here -->
            </xe:this.onNewEntry>
            <xe:this.onOpenEntry>
                <!--  CSJS code here -->
            </xe:this.onOpenEntry>
            <xe:this.onRescheduleEntry>
                <!--  CSJS code here -->
            </xe:this.onRescheduleEntry>
            <xe:this.onDeleteEntry>
                <!--  CSJS code here -->
            </xe:this.onDeleteEntry>
</xe:calendarView>
```

You can see that the **storeComponentId** property value contains the id of the XPages Calendar REST service (`storeComponentId="restService2"`), as shown previously in Listing 8.12. When the XPage containing the iNotes calendar control is rendered, the markup for the calendar control container is emitted. After the page is loaded in the browser, *then* a REST request is sent to the Domino web server to populate the calendar control's data store, and the calendar entries appear in the browser after that (second) operation is complete. It is important to understand that this is a two-step process.

If you are comfortable with AJAX requests and JavaScript debuggers, it is easy to see what is going on. For example, if you load a sample Teamroom calendar containing at least one entry, then the process unfolds as follows.

The initial XPage request is sent to the Domino server. The browser URL will look like this:

```
http://localhost/teamroom.nsf/calendar.xsp
```

If you use a debugging tool like Firebug for the Firefox browser, you will see that various AJAX requests are fired in the course of loading the calendar page. The *last* such request is the one that requests the calendar entry data. Any browser debugger will show these requests to you; the calendar REST service request will look like this:

```
http://localhost/teamroom.nsf/calendar.xsp/inoteslegacyjson?startKey=20
130629T230000%2C00Z&untilKey=20130804T230000%2C00Z
```

The parameters are actually easy to decipher. The path identifier (`inoteslegacyjson`) points to the REST service that will handle this request, and it matches the `pathInfo` property value specified in the REST service markup (refer to Listing 8.12). After that two keys are provided to specify a date range for the calendar entries. In this example, the start date is specified as June 29, 2013 (`20130629`) and the end date is August 4, 2013 (`20130804`). The REST service then returns a collection of calendar entries in the required JSON format. Again, the JSON payload can be viewed in the browser debugger by looking at the response detail. A snapshot of this is shown in Figure 8.26 and the text content of a simple single calendar entry example is shown in Listing 8.14.

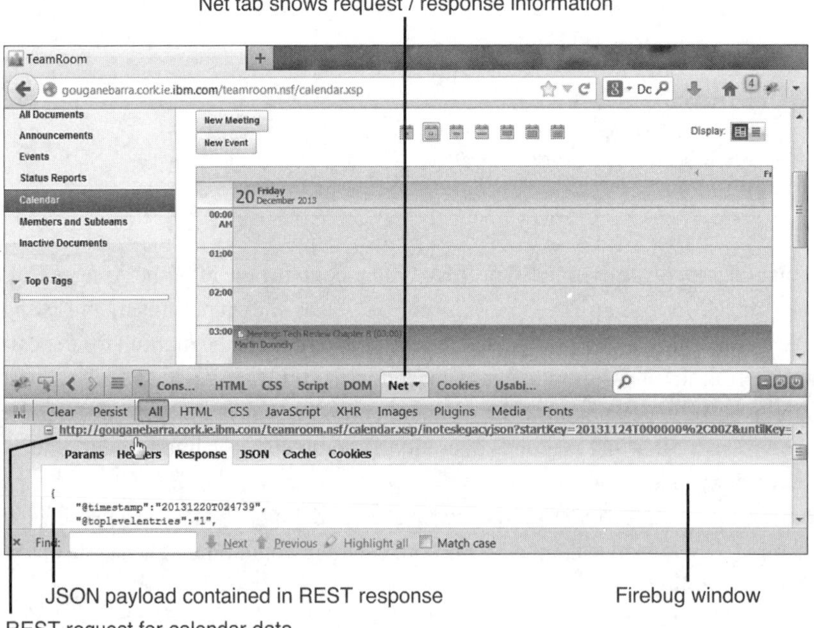

Figure 8.26 Viewing the calendar REST request/response using a browser debugger (Firebug)

Listing 8.14 Sample Response from XPages Calendar REST Service for a Single Calendar Entry


```
{
    "@timestamp":"20130712T142536",
    "@toplevelentries":"12",
    "viewentry":
    [
      {
          "@unid":"A6039ABD7C926DBD80257BA60049BA02",
          "@noteid":"125A",
          "@position":"12",
          "@read":"true",
          "@siblings":"12",
          "entrydata":
          [
            {
                "@columnnumber":"0",
                "@name":"$134",
                "datetime":
                {
                    "0":"20130712T150000"
                }
            },
            {
                "@columnnumber":"1",
                "@name":"$149",
                "number":
                {
                    "0":158
                }
            },
            {
                "@columnnumber":"2",
                "@name":"$144",
                "datetime":
                {
                    "0":"20130712T150000"
                }
            },
            {
                "@columnnumber":"3",
                "@name":"$146",
                "datetime":
                {
```

```
                    "0":"20130712T160000"
                }
            },
            {
                "@columnnumber":"4",
                "@name":"$147",
                "text":
                {
                    "0":"Meeting: Defect Triage Meeting (15:00)"
                }
            },
            {
                "@columnnumber":"5",
                "@name":"$153",
                "text":
                {
                    "0":"Martin Donnelly"
                }
            }
        ]
    }
  ]
}
```


You can see that the response contains the row data associated with all the columns requested in the REST service, as outlined in Listing 8.12. You should also note that the column names returned are the standardized default names and *not* the custom calendar view names that were actually used in the query. This mapping was performed automatically by the REST service so that the iNotes control parses the data correctly.

The last topic to discuss is the calendar control events. This may be an advanced topic for readers who are new to the client-side JavaScript model, in which case it is advisable to read Chapter 11, "Advanced Scripting," before proceeding. In the **calendarView.xsp** custom control example used thus far, you can see that four of these events are implemented. The `onDelete Entry` is discussed here, and a snippet of that event handler is shown in Listing 8.15:

Listing 8.15 onDeleteEntry Event Handler in calendarView.xsp

```
<xe:this.onDeleteEntry><![CDATA[
    var doIt = XSP.confirm("Are you sure you want to delete this
calendar entry?");
    if (doIt) {
        var sUnid = items[0].unid;
        var prOptions = {"unid" : sUnid, "action" : "deleteDocument"};
        XSP.partialRefreshGet("#{id:mainPanel}",
```

```
                {
                    params : prOptions
                }
            );
        }
]]>
</xe:this.onDeleteEntry >
```

When the user selects an entry in the calendar and hits the delete key, this JavaScript code is called to first check with the user if the entry should indeed be deleted. Once the action is confirmed, the universal id of the current calendar entry is obtained and assigned to an `unid` property in a JavaScript object called `prOptions`. Note that the `items` array seen in Listing 8.15 is automatically generated in the DOM by the iNotes calendar control and thus is automatically accessible to JavaScript code. The second item in the object is an action property that is assigned a `deleteDocument` instruction. Once these items have been gathered and aggregated into a JavaScript object, a partial refresh request is dispatched. This causes the main panel of the current page to be refreshed with `prOptions` passed in as a parameter object. As illustrated in Listing 8.16, this panel contains a hidden field that checks for a delete action request, and performs the action if an UNID is provided sufficient ACL privilege to allow the current user to perform such an operation.

Listing 8.16 Partial Refresh Handler for deleteDocument in calendarView.xsp

```
< xp:text escape="true" id="deleteDoc" style="display:none">
    <xp:this.loaded>
        <![CDATA[${javascript:(userBean.accessLevel >=
lotus.domino.ACL.LEVEL_AUTHOR) && userBean.canDeleteDocs}]]>
    </xp:this.loaded>
    <xp:this.value>
        <![CDATA[#{javascript:
        if(null != param && param.unid != null &&
                param.action == "deleteDocument") {
            var doc = database.getDocumentByUNID(param.unid);
            if (doc != null) {
                doc.remove(false); // DELETE THE DOC
            }
        }
}]]></xp:this.value>
</xp:text>>
```

Other techniques for performing server-side operations based on client-side JavaScript requests are also discussed in Chapter 11, but this mechanism works quite well with all releases of XPages. This snippet should also give a good insight into the art of bridging between client-side and server-side operations!

Conclusion

This chapter explored `every` property of the view data source and put them through their paces using either URL parameters, SSJS, or Java code samples. It also showed how the XPages runtime uses the standard Java backend classes to access and manipulate the view data. Beyond standard view data, you also learned to work with calendar views using XPages REST services (rather than the Domino view data source). Hopefully, you gained a thorough knowledge of how all sorts of view data may be extracted from Notes/Domino views and how the information can be filtered, shaped, and sized to meet your application needs.

CHAPTER 9

Beyond the View Basics

Because the preceding chapter concentrated exclusively on the gory details of data retrieval from Domino views, it's only fitting that this chapter focuses on the fine art of presenting view data in XPages. Once again, a modified version of the Discussion template is used as the sample application. In fact, for this chapter, you need two samples, namely **Chp09ed2.nsf** and **Chp09ed2a.nsf**. You need to download these resources now from the following website and load them up in Domino Designer so that you can work through all the examples provided: `www.ibmpressbooks.com/title/9780133373370`.

You see how the sample applications use various view controls to best effect when displaying Domino view data. You will also learn how to extend and modify the behaviors of the view controls using JavaScript, Cascading Style Sheets (CSS), and so on. If you work through all the examples as you read along, you will have consummate expertise on this topic by the end of this chapter!

XPages provides a wide range of controls for presenting Domino view data, such as the View panel, Repeat control, Data Table, Data View, Forum View, and so forth. You can find the first three of these controls on the **Container Controls** section of the palette in Designer, whereas the other two are located in the **Extension Library** drawer. You have already worked with some of these controls, mostly with the View control; although, you have used only the basic properties up until now. You see here how to put some of the lesser known properties to good use to solve some more advanced use cases. Perhaps it is best to start, however, with an explanation of why there are so many different view presentation controls in the first place.

Pick a View Control, Any View Control

When it comes to presenting view data, we all have our individual preferences! For some use cases, a view with a strictly tabular format where rows and columns crisscross to form a rigidly ordered grid layout is what's required. In other scenarios, a more free-form view layout of summary information that allows end users to dynamically dive deeper into the underlying data is the order of the day. In terms of providing off-the-shelf controls to meet these demands, no one-size-fits-all solution exists. In other words, separate specialized renderers are required to handle what are wildly different layout requirements, and each renderer has its own unique set of properties and behaviors that cater to those particular use cases.

Rather than simply describing various alternative view layouts, it is useful for you to see real-world use cases firsthand. As usual, the sample application can be readily called upon to demonstrate different view presentation examples. For example, explore the **All Documents** view on the main page of the application, and then compare its look and feel to one of the other views in the main navigator, such as **By Tag**, **By Author**, **By Most Recent**, and so on. Some key differences should come to your attention immediately. Chief among these is the interesting capability of the **All Documents** view to dynamically expand and collapse row content inline. That is, as you hover over any particular row, you are presented with a **Show details / Hide details** control, depending on the current state of the row content. If the row is collapsed, clicking the **Show details** option effectively injects an extra row of detail into your view, showing an abstract of the underlying document and presenting options to compose a reply or to switch to a view of documents that contain the same tags. Figure 9.1 summarizes this feature.

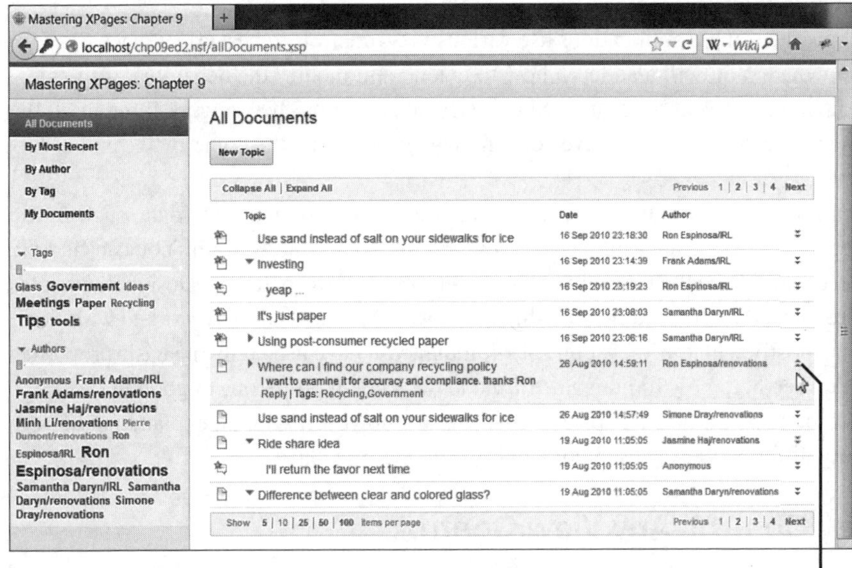

Figure 9.1 Sample application using the Data View to render the All Documents view

Other views do not provide this capability and instead display content on a strict one-document-per-row basis. The data in these views is typically organized according to a specific criterion, say by category, author, or date, and feature the standard document link navigators for some of the columns in each row.

The Data View control is used most commonly in the most recent versions of the standard templates, but you can find examples of the Repeat, Data Table, and View control in this chapter's sample. For example the **byTagView.xsp** custom control uses the View control in the sample (although in the latest 9.0.1 template, this page, too, is now driven by a Data View control), and you have already implemented a view sample similar to these in Chapter 3, "Building Your First XPages Application." That first sample demonstrated that you could build simple views using a View control in a matter of minutes. Although it also is possible to build sophisticated view renderings with the View control (as you'll soon see), there are some things it is simply not designed to do—dynamic inline row insertion/deletion being a case in point.

The fancy dynamics shown in Figure 9.1 are achieved using a Data View control. In previous releases, the same dynamic functionality was achieved using the Repeat control, but far more effort was required on the part of the developer to implement all the features. To a large extent, the Data View automates various common patterns that developers previously used Repeat controls to construct. That is, the Data View provides sophisticated high level behaviors that developers can enable simply by applying property values—no heavy lifting required. Similarly, the Forum View control also provides highly specialized view rendering. It aims to simplify the presentation of hierarchy of documents, enabling easy navigation and manipulations of root documents and responses. For collaborative applications, it gives a ready-made view of a discussion or forum that can be tweaked via properties to render in slightly different ways.

However, the Repeat control does little or nothing for the application developer—at least by default. This container control simply iterates over every row in the view data source to which it is bound. *Any* control that is added to the Repeat container (initially it is always empty) can be bound to a column in the backend view. The iterative read cycle that occurs at runtime then ensures that all contained controls display the appropriate column value *once* for every row in the view. Thus, you have a totally free-form means of laying out view data, where nothing is predefined but anything is possible. The presentation content is totally dependent on the controls you choose to add to the Repeat container. It is not required to be structured within an HTML table for example—something you are stuck with when using the View control or Data Table controls whether you like it or not. Also, Repeat controls can be nested within each other, meaning that different data sources can be navigated as part of one overall view presentation. The price you pay for all this power and flexibility is that *you* must define all the content and layout data yourself...which can be a lot of work depending on what you want to achieve.

The View control lies somewhere between the extremes of the high specialized Data View and Forum View versus the highly flexible but nothing-for-free Repeat control. A View control can be built quickly using easy point-and-click operations, but the end result is more restrictive than is the case with a Repeat control, and more general-purpose than the Data and Forum Views. Again, depending on what you want to achieve, the View control may be the correct instrument to use—a simple case of choosing the right tool for the right job!

The Data Table is probably the least used of all view controls. Its absence from most real-world XPages applications (at least in this author's experience) is because it is too basic in functionality—it does not offer the quick convenience of a View control, the flexibility of a Repeat control, or the sophistication of the Data and Forum Views. It is perhaps most useful for prototyping and for simple use cases. A practical example of a Data Table is nonetheless included in the sample application for this chapter.

To see how the various view controls have been employed in the sample application, you can search the NSF for the tags `xp:viewPanel`, `xp:repeat`, `xp:dataTable`, `xe:dataView`, and `xe:forumView` (in Designer, type `Ctrl-H` and specify the literal tags in the **File Search** tab, as shown in the previous chapter). First, however, it's time to take a closer look at the intricacies of the View control.

> **TIP**
>
> At this point you have no doubt noticed that XPages tags can have different namespace prefixes—the view controls listed here being a case in point. In summary, `xp:` indicates that the control in question is an XPages core control and `xe:` indicates that the control originated from the **X**Pages ***E***xtension Library and is thus always an open source component (regardless of whether it has been merged into core XPages). Finally, `xc:` indicates that the tag is the name of an ***X***Pages **C**ustom Control.

The View Control: Up Close and Personal

In this book, the *View control* is commonly referred to as the *View Panel*. This reference emanates from the markup tag used for the View control, `<xp:viewPanel>`, and it comes in handy when it's necessary to disambiguate the View control from the backend Domino view that serves as its data source. In any case, the terms "View control" and "View Panel" can be used interchangeably and refer to the visual control that renders the view data.

The View Panel is a rich control with an abundance of properties and subordinate elements, such as pagers, columns, data sources, converters, and so on. Some of its properties are generic insofar as they are also shared by other controls in the XPages library to support common features like accessibility, internationalization, and so forth. For the most part, this chapter concentrates on the other properties as they are more directly relevant to view presentation, while the generic properties are addressed separately in other chapters.

In any case, the View Panel properties used in the examples up to now have been few in number and basic in nature. The upcoming examples start to pull in more and more properties in order to tweak the look and feel of your views. As usual, you learn these by way of example, but before you dive in, it is useful to summarize the View Panel features that have already been covered and provide the necessary reference points should you need to recap. The forthcoming material assumes that you are proficient with the topics listed in Table 9.1, although more detailed information may be provided going forward.

Table 9.1 viewPanel Features Previously Discussed

Feature	Chapter Reference: Section	Description
viewPanel Designer: Drag & Drop	Chapter 3: Building an XPages View	Creating a View control from Controls palette Working with the View binding dialog
viewColumn property: `displayAs`	Chapter 3: Building an XPages View	Linking View control entries to underlying Notes/Domino documents
viewColumn property: `showCheckBox`	Chapter 3: Completing the CRUD	Making view entries selectable for executable actions
viewPanel`<xp:pager>`	Chapter 4: View	Basic description of View control with pager information
viewPanel property: `facets`	Chapter 4: Facets	General introduction to `facets` including simple examples using view pagers
viewPanel Designer: appending columns	Chapter 8: Caching View Data	Adding a new column to a View control and computing its value using server-side JavaScript

Column Data Like You've Never Seen Before

Start the next leg of this View Panel journey of discovery by creating a new XPage, say **myView.xsp**. Drop a View Panel from the control palette to view and bind it to the All Documents view when the helper dialog appears. Deselect all but three columns of the backend view—retain $106, $116, and $120. These are the programmatic names that have been assigned to the view columns; XPages allows you to use either the column's programmatic name *or* the view column title to identify the column you want to include in the View control. Not all view columns have titles, however! Click **OK** to create the View Panel.

When you preview this raw XPage, you see the **Date** and **Topic** fields as expected, along with what can best be described as some gobbledygook wedged in between those columns, as shown in Figure 9.2.

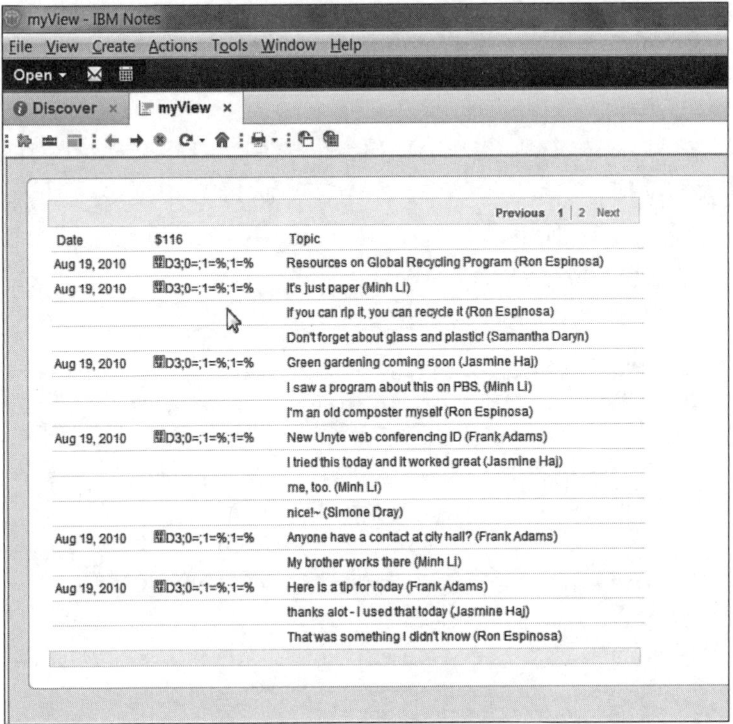

Figure 9.2 Columns from All Documents view displayed in a View Panel

It is not unreasonable to question what exactly this **$116** column represents. The formula behind the column in the backend view looks like this:

```
@If(!@IsResponseDoc;@DocDescendants(""; "%"; "%");"")
```

In the regular Notes client, this column displays the number of descendant documents for all root level documents. To decipher the code, the `@DocDescendants` function is only applied when `!@IsResponseDoc` evaluates to true, meaning when the current document is *not* a response document, or in other words, for top-level documents only. The `"%"` within the parameter strings is replaced with the actual number of descendant documents at runtime. According to the Help documentation, `@DocDescendants` is among a class of @Functions that are restricted in their applicability and cannot be run from web applications. The function is described as returning "special text," which is computed for client display only, not actually stored in the view, cannot be converted to a number, and so on. Other @Functions, such as `@DocNumber` and `@DocChildren`, present the same issues (you can find a more complete list in the Designer help pages). Designer itself attempts to preclude such columns from selection in the View Panel binding dialog, and the Java API `getColumnValues()` method, which is used to populate the View

Panel row data, also tries to "null out" any autogenerated values that are contained in a row. However, these @Functions can be embedded in conditional logic and thus can be difficult to detect in advance. As a result, you might occasionally see spurious results like this appearing in views you are working on. So, what to do?

Because you cannot always work with *all* types of data contained in Domino views, you might need to create a modified version of a view in order to match your design criteria. Remember that the root of this problem is that the data defined in such columns is not actually contained in the backend view, but it is possible that the underlying documents have fields that hold the required information or perhaps the information you need can be deduced using one or more fields. Thus, you could modify the backend view or create a new version that contains the column values you require based on fetching or computing the information by alternative means.

In the more immediate short term, however, you need to remove the offending column from the View Panel. This can be done in Designer in a number of different ways. You can highlight the column in the **Outline** panel or in the WYSIWYG editor, and use the right-mouse **Delete** menu to remove the column—you appended a new column back in Chapter 8, "Working with Domino Views," in much the same way. Alternatively, you can find the `<xp:viewColumn>` tag that is bound to **$116** in the source pane and delete the markup directly from there.

Simple View Panel Make Over

Many presentational issues can be taken care of directly at the XPages level without any modifications to underlying the Domino view! For example, you are not restricted to the column order defined in the Domino view. You can reorder the columns in a View Panel by simply cutting and pasting the `<xp:viewColumn>` tags in the source pane—try this now in myView.xsp. Also, the date format of what is now or soon to be the second column can be modified in the XPages layer using a component known as a *converter*—this is the same component you used in Chapter 4, "Anatomy of an XPage," when working with the Date Time Picker examples. To do this, click the Date ($106) column in the WYSIWYG editor, select the **Data** property sheet, and change the **Display type** from "String" to "Date/Time." Then, change the **Date style** from "default" to "full," as shown in Figure 9.3.

Listing 9.1 shows the markup generated from the cut/paste operation and the addition of the date converter.

Listing 9.1 viewPanel Markup with Reordered Columns and Alternative Date Formatting

```
<xp:viewPanel rows="30" id="viewPanel1">
      <xp:this.facets>
            <xp:pager partialRefresh="true"
                  layout="Previous Group Next"
                  xp:key="headerPager" id="pager1">
            </xp:pager>
      </xp:this.facets>
```

```
        <xp:this.data>
            <xp:dominoView
                var="view1"
                viewName="($All)">
            </xp:dominoView>
        </xp:this.data>
        <!-- Reordered columns so that Topic is first -->
        <xp:viewColumn columnName="$120" id="viewColumn7">
            <xp:viewColumnHeader value="Topic" id="viewColumnHeader7">
            </xp:viewColumnHeader>
        </xp:viewColumn>
        <xp:viewColumn columnName="$106" id="viewColumn1">
        <!-- Present full date like "Thursday, August 26, 2010" -->
            <xp:this.converter>
                <xp:convertDateTime type="date" dateStyle="full">
                </xp:convertDateTime>
            </xp:this.converter>
            <xp:viewColumnHeader value="Date" id="viewColumnHeader1">
            </xp:viewColumnHeader>
        </xp:viewColumn>
</xp:viewPanel>
```

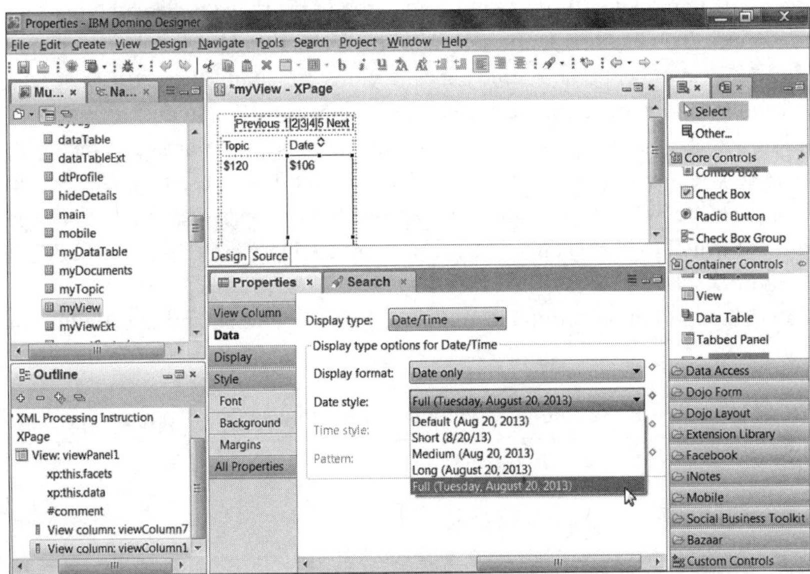

Figure 9.3 Applying a date converter in the View Panel

Now that you've turned the view presentation on its head, you might as well look at its run-time rendition. All going well, you see a View Panel like the one shown in Figure 9.4.

You're not done yet, however! Albeit a simple View Panel, it is still possible to dress this puppy up a little further and add some extra behaviors.

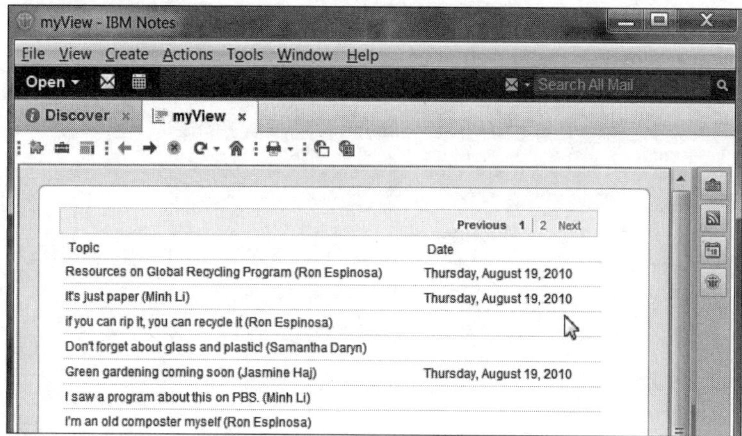

Figure 9.4 An alternative XPages view of All Documents

The World Is Flat???

An obvious limitation of the View Panel shown in Figure 9.4 is that the document hierarchy is not shown. The Topic column is just a flat list of entries that does not reflect their interrelationships in any way. To show the various threads in this view, all you need to do is click the Topic column in Domino Designer, select the **Display** property sheet, and check the Indent Responses control. Reload the page after doing this, and you find that all parent documents now have "twistie" controls that can be used to expand or collapse its own particular part of the document tree. If you don't like the standard blue twisties, feel free to add your own! Some extra images have been added as image resource elements to **Chp09Ed2.nsf**, so if you want to try this feature out, you can simply assign minus.gif and plus.gif from the list of image resources in the application as the alternative twisties, as shown in Figure 9.5, although I'm sure you can come up with more interesting ones than these! Whatever alternative images are specified in this property sheet would also be applied to the twistie controls used for expanding and collapsing category rows, if you were working with a categorized view. Category views are discussed in the section, "Working with Categories."

Linking the View Panel to Its Documents

In Chapter 3, you learned to use the Check box feature shown in Figure 9.5 to enable row selection by the end user. You also learned to display the contents of the Topic column as links and to bridge it to **myTopic.xsp** by explicitly nominating that XPage as `pageName` property for the View Panel itself. Select the **Show values in this column as links** feature for **Topic** column again now, but don't nominate **myTopic.xsp** as the target XPage this time. Preview the page and click any link. Do you know just why this happens to magically work?

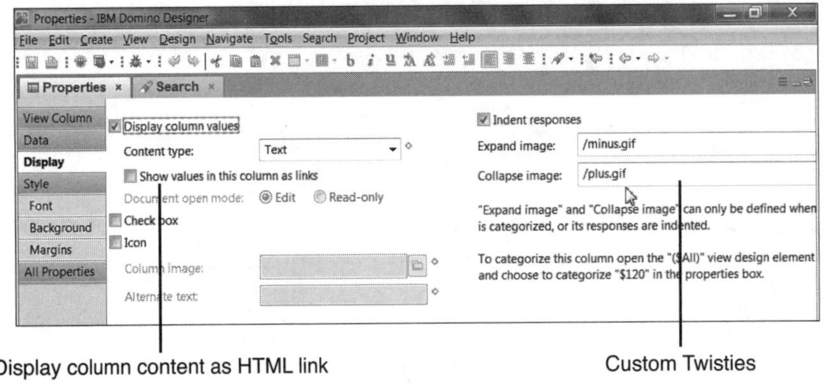

Figure 9.5 View Column Display Property sheet

The clue is in the View Panel's default link navigation option shown in Figure 9.6. When no page is explicitly nominated, XPages looks in the form used to create the underlying documents for a hint as to what XPage it should use. The form in question in this scenario is **Main Topic** and, if you open it in Designer and inspect its properties, you see a couple of interesting options, as highlighted in Figure 9.7.

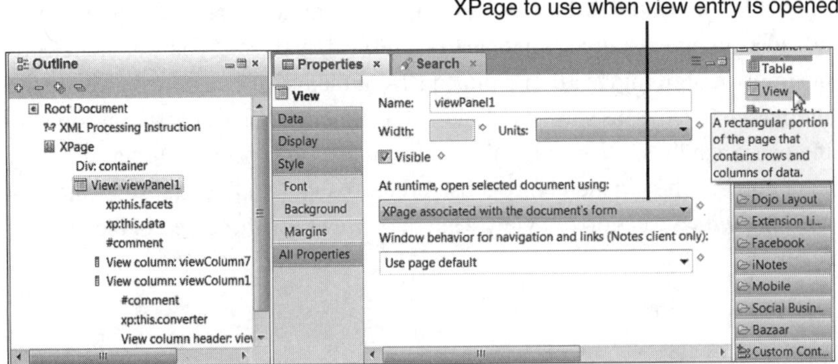

Figure 9.6 View Panel Basic Property panel

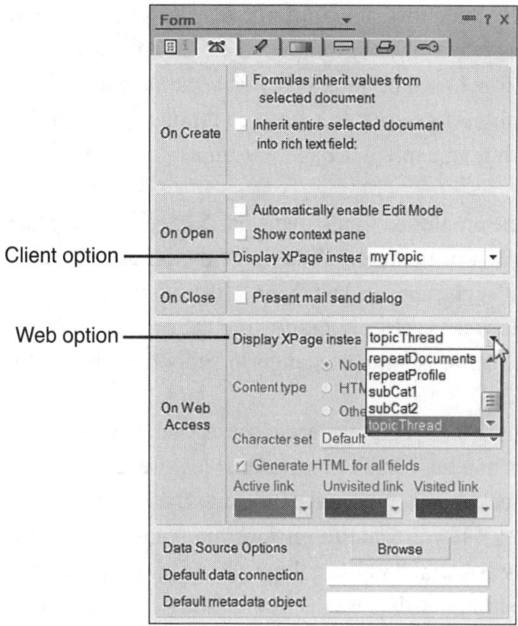

Figure 9.7 Form Properties Infobox: Display XPage Instead property

As you can see from the infobox, you can basically choose to override the form associated with a document on the web and on the client by opting to substitute an XPage instead in either or both environments. Any XPage that is capable of editing a document based on the **Main Topic** form can be nominated as the alternative XPage document editor. For example, the **Main Topic** form could be updated to use **myTopic.xsp** or **topicThread.xsp** as viable alternatives on both platforms. Whatever is declared as the alternative is resolved as the go-to XPage when a column is clicked in the View Panel at runtime.

> **TIP**
>
> **Display XPage instead** can be used to incrementally phase in XPages application implementations. If you are migrating an application to XPages, it might be possible to replace subsets of functionality that have been encapsulated in forms with XPages code, and then pull these blocks into your application on a piecemeal basis using this feature.

There was originally just one **Display XPage instead** property. Since XPages was first made available on the web before being released on the Notes client, many customers converted their application's web implementation to XPages, but still had the original client application in place. When running the application natively on the client, they did not want to suddenly start seeing XPages appearing in place of forms! This feature was revamped in 8.5.2 to allow XPages and non-XPages implementations of an application to run harmoniously on separate platforms.

Although **Display XPage instead** certainly has its uses, the more common practice in the app dev community would appear to favor having an explicit XPage `pageName` navigation setting on the View Panel itself.

There is, in fact, a third strategy that can be employed to resolve what XPage is used when opening a document, and it is perhaps the simplest of them all! If you give the XPage the same name as the form used to create the document, it is chosen as a last resort if the other two options come up blank. This can be a useful approach if you are closely mimicking the original application implementation in XPages and if the application is simple enough to support such one-to-one design element mappings.

But, what of the remaining features in Figure 9.5? You just learned a second way to handle the **Show values in this column as links** option, and the **Check box** feature was already explored in Chapter 3. The **Display column values** checkbox merely serves to hide the column value retrieved from the view. This is potentially useful if you want to retrieve the column value but display something else based on what's actually contained in the column. In my experience, this property is not widely used as there are other (perhaps easier) ways of computing column values. We work through some examples of this shortly in the course of this View Panel makeover. On the other hand, if you simply want to conceal a column, you need to deselect the **Visible** checkbox in its property sheet, which sets `rendered="false"` in the underlying `<xp:viewColumn>` tag.

This just leaves the **Icon** and **Content type** in the view column **Display** panel, so you can learn now how to further enhance this simple makeover by putting those properties to work.

Decorating Your Columns with Images

Any column in a View Panel can display an image as well as its column value. To add an image to a view column, you can simply check the Icon control (refer to Figure 9.5 to find the control, if needed) and type the name of the image resource or use the image browser dialog to locate it. It is good practice to enter some alternative text in case the image cannot be resolved at runtime and to facilitate screen readers and so on. The view column properties behind these two Designer choices are called `iconSrc` and `iconAlt`, respectively. You can implement a simple example as follows:

1. Insert a new column before the first column in the View Panel. You can use the **View > Insert Column** main menu when the **Topic** column is selected.
2. Check the **Icon** checkbox in the **Display** property sheet and add `/hash.gif` as the nominated image resource (you can also browse for this image resource). This image has already been added to **Chp09Ed2.nsf** for your convenience.
3. Add `Index` as the alternative text.

4. Add `indexVar="rowIndex"` to the `<xp:viewPanel>` tag in the **Source** pane. You can also do this via the View Panel's **Data** category in the **All Properties** sheet.
5. Add the following server-side JavaScript snippet to compute the column's value:

```
var i:Number = parseInt(rowIndex + 1);
return i.toPrecision(0);
```

In summary, you added an image to the new column and along with some alternative text. The `indexVar` property keeps a count of the rows in the View Panel as it is being populated. The `indexVar` property is used here as a simple row number to display in the UI. The JavaScript applied in step 5 simply increments each row index by 1 (it is a zero-based index) and ensures that no decimal places are displayed. Finally, to give the new column a title, click the view column header in the WYSIWYG editor and enter some text, say "Row", as the label. Now, you can preview or reload the page to see the results (all this has been done for you in myViewExt.xsp, if you want to look at the final creation), which should closely match Figure 9.8.

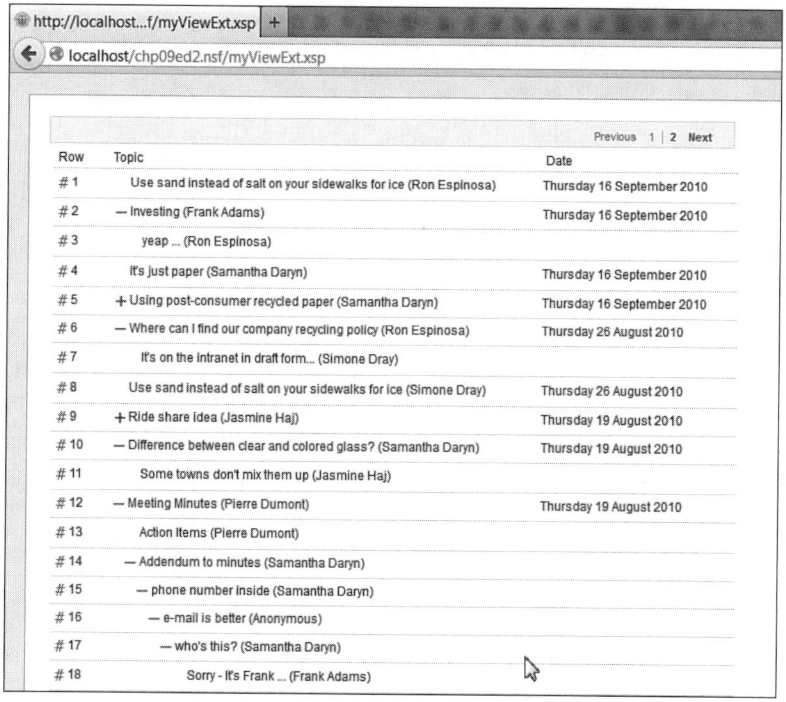

Row	Topic	Date
# 1	Use sand instead of salt on your sidewalks for ice (Ron Espinosa)	Thursday 16 September 2010
# 2	— Investing (Frank Adams)	Thursday 16 September 2010
# 3	yeap ... (Ron Espinosa)	
# 4	It's just paper (Samantha Daryn)	Thursday 16 September 2010
# 5	+ Using post-consumer recycled paper (Samantha Daryn)	Thursday 16 September 2010
# 6	— Where can I find our company recycling policy (Ron Espinosa)	Thursday 26 August 2010
# 7	It's on the intranet in draft form... (Simone Dray)	
# 8	Use sand instead of salt on your sidewalks for ice (Simone Dray)	Thursday 26 August 2010
# 9	+ Ride share idea (Jasmine Haj)	Thursday 19 August 2010
# 10	— Difference between clear and colored glass? (Samantha Daryn)	Thursday 19 August 2010
# 11	Some towns don't mix them up (Jasmine Haj)	
# 12	— Meeting Minutes (Pierre Dumont)	Thursday 19 August 2010
# 13	Action Items (Pierre Dumont)	
# 14	— Addendum to minutes (Samantha Daryn)	
# 15	— phone number inside (Samantha Daryn)	
# 16	— e-mail is better (Anonymous)	
# 17	— who's this? (Samantha Daryn)	
# 18	Sorry - It's Frank ... (Frank Adams)	

Figure 9.8 Computed View Panel column using iconSrc, iconAlt, and indexVar properties

This is all well and good except that the icon displayed is static in nature; observe that it is the same for each row (the hash symbol gif). Although it is a computable property, `iconSrc` does not have access to the View Panel `var` or `indexVar` properties, so it difficult to do something dynamic with it, such as select the image resource based on a particular row column value, for example. In any event a dynamic solution can still be provided by using the **Content type** option on the same **Display** panel. To implement an example of applying images based on row content, work through the following instructions:

1. Append a new column to the end of the View Panel using the **View > Append Column** main menu.
2. In the **Display** panel set the **Content type** to HTML.
3. In the **Source** pane, add `var="rowData"` to the `<xp:viewPanel>` tag to gain access to the current row via server-side JavaScript while the View Panel is being populated.
4. On the **Data** property sheet, add the following server-side JavaScript snippet to compute the column's `value` property:

```
var i:number = rowData.getDescendantCount();
if (i < 10) {
      return ("<img src=\"/Chp09Ed2.nsf/" + i
                  + ".gif\""+">");
} else {
      return ("<img src=\"/Chp09Ed2.nsf/n.gif\""+">");
}
```

5. Move to the **Events** tab for this column and for the only defined event, `onclick`, add another server-side JavaScript snippet:

```
if (rowData.getDescendantCount() > 0) {
      rowData.toggleExpanded();
}
```

As you can see, the column value is set using server-side JavaScript in step 4. An HTML image tag is returned with the `src` value determined by the number of documents in the row's document hierarchy, 1 descendant document means "1.gif" is used, 5 descendant documents means "5.gif" is used, and so on. Because you set the column's content type to HTML, the image tag is simply passed through to the browser as is. Moreover, the image is clickable (unlike the image added via the iconSrc property) and fires an expand/collapse event for any non-leaf entry, such as when the entry has any responses, thanks to the code you added in step 5.

The column header label should be set to Responses, and the content of the column can be quickly centered using the **Alignment** button on the column **Font** property panel. Reload the page and see the new runtime behavior for yourself. The rendering of this column is also shown in Figure 9.9. Note that the `expandLevel=1` data source setting discussed in the previous chapter was used here (via a URL parameter) to initially collapse all rows. Some were then expanded to create a good example.

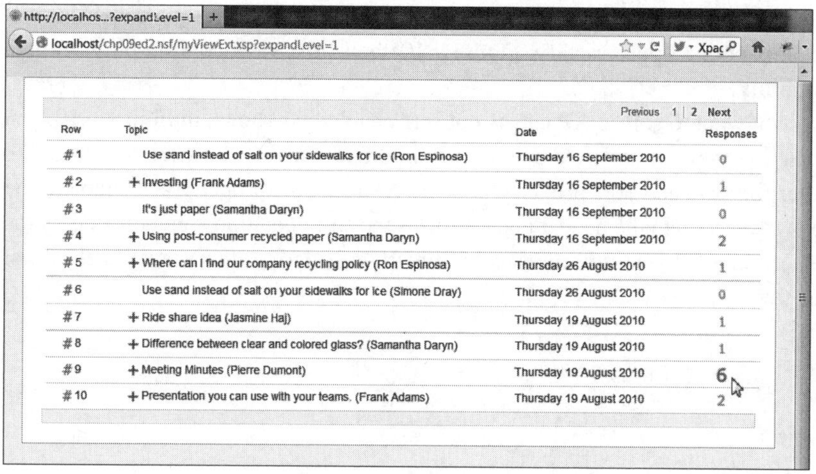

Figure 9.9 Computed View Panel column using computed pass-through HTML content

This time, the image resource in the **Responses** column indeed varies depending on the response count for each row entry. It might not be too evident in the printed screen shot, but the color of the images darken and increase in pixel size as the numbers increase. Thus, the rows with more responses get more emphasis in the UI (similar in concept to the tag cloud rendering) on the basis that they represent busier discussion threads and are, therefore, likely to be of more interest to forum participants. If the number of response documents exceeds nine, an ellipses image (`n.gif`) is shown instead. Add more documents yourself and create deep hierarchies to see how this View Panel rendering works in practice—interesting all the same to see what can be achieved by tweaking a few properties and adding some simple lines of JavaScript code!

Some Final Touches

Before completing our sample rendering of the All Documents view, there are some final miscellaneous features to apply and some other behaviors to observe. First, when used in native client mode, the backend All Documents view can be sorted by clicking the Date column. This sorting facility is not in evidence as yet in the XPages View Panel, so you must learn how to enable it.

The first thing to understand is that it is the backend view itself that performs the sorting. It is not performed client-side in XPages itself, and any attempt to do so is invariably inefficient and performs poorly as applications scale. Don't go there—leave the sorting operation to the view itself.

To enable the sort feature in the View Panel, you need to select the required view column header in the WYSIWYG editor and activate its property sheet. You see a **Sort column** checkbox that you need to check. If this is disabled, it means that the column as defined in the backend view does not have any sorting capability; Designer looks up the column design properties and enables or disables this option appropriately. Figure 9.10 shows the view column property that defines sorting capability.

If the column you want to sort in XPages is not sort-enabled, as shown in Figure 9.10, you need to either update the view design or create a new modified copy of the view to work with going forward. After the backend sort property *and* the XPages sort property are enabled, the View Panel displays a sort icon in the header and performs the sort operation when clicked by the user. Figure 9.11 shows the **All Documents** view after being resorted via the View Panel (oldest documents are now first).

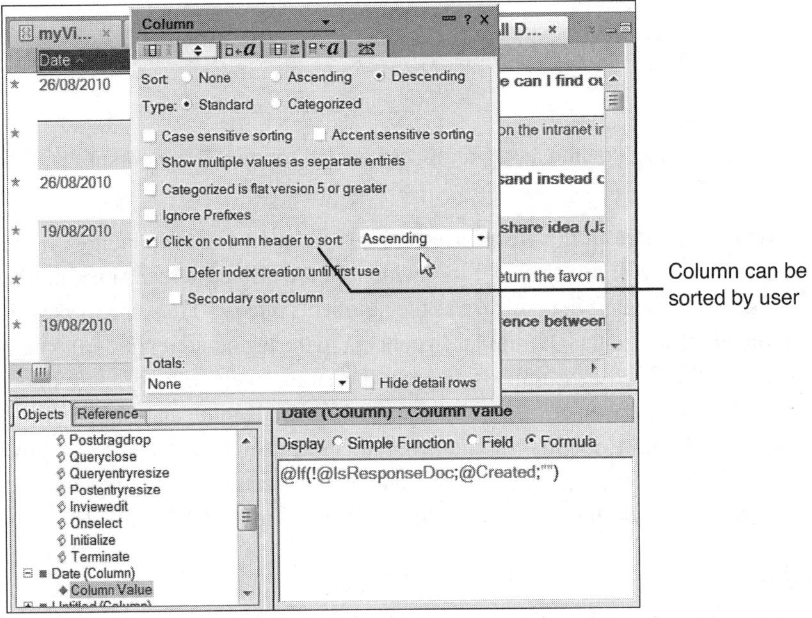

Figure 9.10 View Column infobox with sorting capability enabled

> **TIP**
>
> In 8.5.2, the View Panel sort icons are removed when it displays the results of a full text search as the result set was not sortable. Prior to 8.5.2 the icons remained enabled, thus implying that the result set was sortable when, in fact, it was not. In 8.5.3 this issue was addressed, and now the sort icons remain in the View Panel after a full text search is performed, with the result set being fully sortable. Refer to the "Combining Searching and Sorting" section in Chapter 8 for more details.

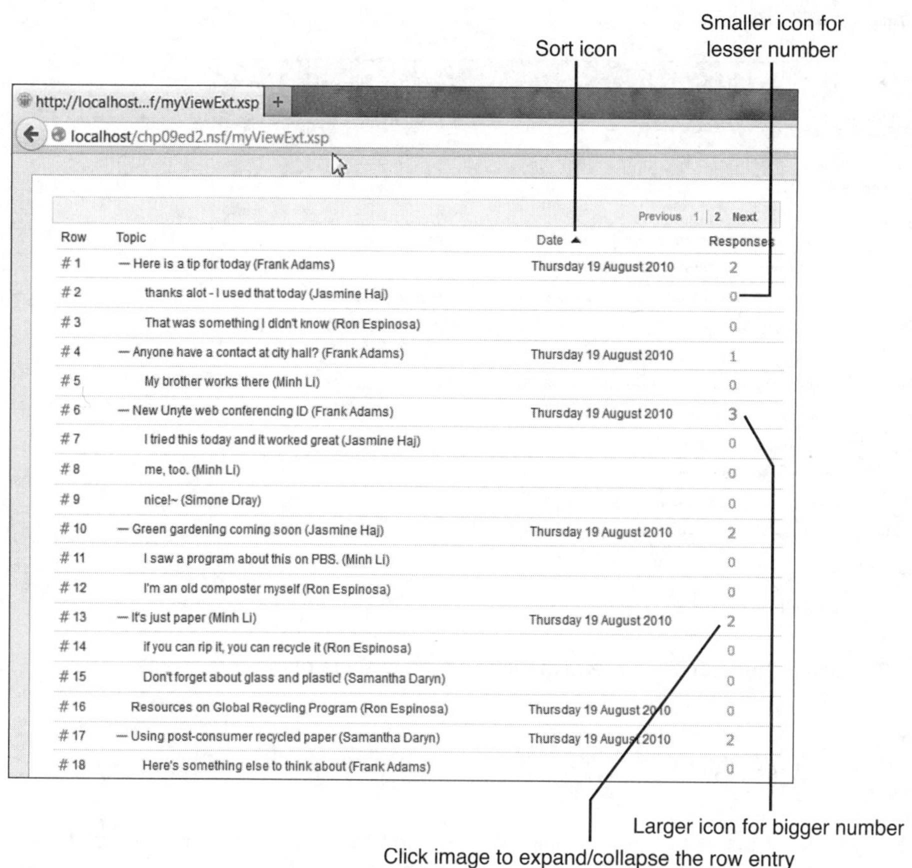

Figure 9.11 View Panel with all documents resorted by date in ascending order

Now complete this particular make-over by selecting the View Panel and selecting its **Display** property sheet. Check the **Show title** and **Show unread marks** controls, and change the number of maximum number of rows from the default of 30 to 10. Figure 9.12 shows the property sheet with these changes applied.

Clicking **Show title** places a View Title component into the header of the View Panel. You can now click this component directly in the WYSIWYG editor and then set its label and other properties via the component's property sheet. This results in a `<xp:viewTitle>` tag being inserted into the View Panel facets definition:

```
<xp:viewTitle xp:key="viewTitle" id="viewTitle1"
```

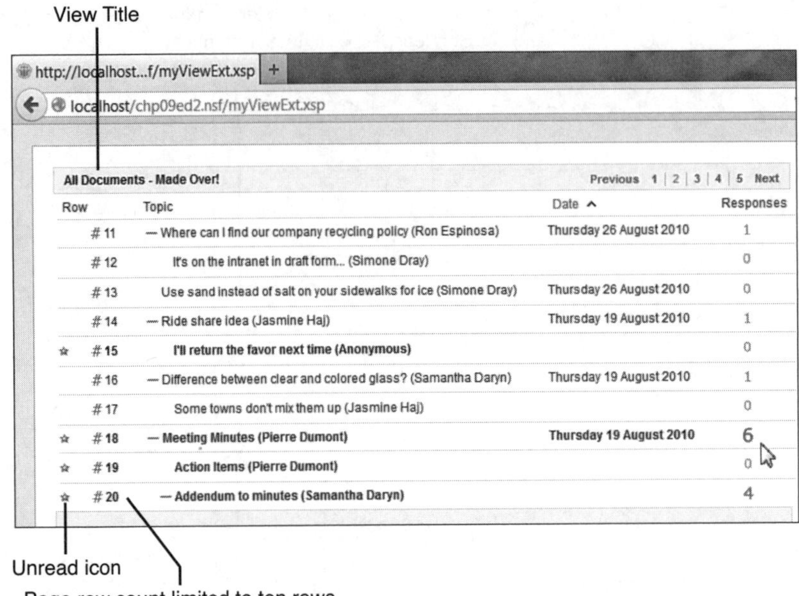

Figure 9.12 View Panel with title, unread marks, and a row count of ten documents

```
    value="All Documents - Make Over Complete!">
</xp:viewTitle>
```

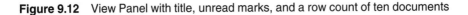

The View Panel also has a title property defined on the `<xp:viewPanel>` tag. This is merely exposing the `title` attribute of the underlying HTML table element that is used to construct the View Panel when rendered at runtime. If you enter a value for this property, it is passed through to the browser as part of the `<table>` HTML markup. For a visible view title, you need to use the **Show title** property and not this title property.

Secondly, if your unread view entries are not displayed as unread (no unread icon is displayed), this is most likely because the Domino server is not maintaining unread marks for the application—keeping track of read/unread documents is optional. You can ascertain the status of this feature in Designer via the **Application Properties > Advanced** property sheet. Look for the **Maintain unread marks** checkbox in the top-left corner.

The `rows` property that controls the maximum number of entries displayed in a view at any one time (set to 10) is exposed directly in the regular Discussion template UI. For example, the footer of the **All Documents**, **By Tag**, and **By Author** views conveniently *lets the user choose* the number of entries to display, as shown in Figure 9.13.

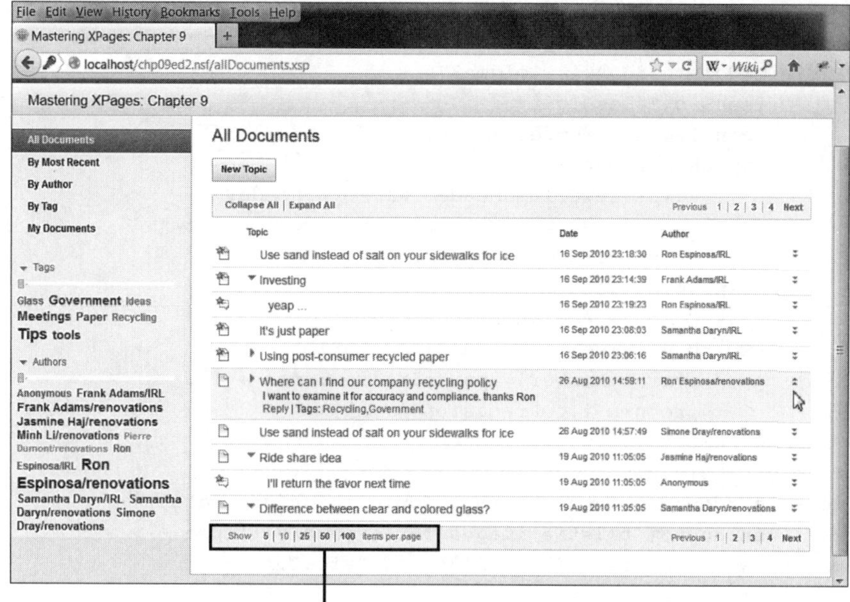

Figure 9.13 Rows property exposed as user option in view footer

Listing 9.2 provides the entire View Panel markup, along with comments in case you had difficulty applying any of the many and varied features discussed in this section. It is also included in **Chp09Ed2.nsf** in the **myViewExt.xsp** XPage.

Listing 9.2 View Panel: Complete Source for Make-Over Exercise

```
<xp:viewPanel rows="10" id="viewPanel1" var="rowData"
            indexVar="rowIndex" showUnreadMarks="true">
            <xp:this.facets>
                  <xp:pager partialRefresh="true"
                  layout="Previous Group Next"
                        xp:key="headerPager" id="pager1">
                  </xp:pager>
                  <!-- View Panel Title -->
                  <xp:viewTitle xp:key="viewTitle" id="viewTitle1"
                        value="All Documents - Made Over!">
                  </xp:viewTitle>
            </xp:this.facets>
            <xp:this.data>
                  <xp:dominoView var="view1" viewName="($All)">
                  </xp:dominoView>
```

```
</xp:this.data>
<!-- Static Column Image # -->
<xp:viewColumn id="viewColumn3"
      iconSrc="/hash.gif"
      iconAlt="Row Number Symbol">
      <xp:this.facets>
            <xp:viewColumnHeader xp:key="header"
                  id="viewColumnHeader3" value="Row">
            </xp:viewColumnHeader>
      </xp:this.facets>
      <!-- Compute Row Number -->
      <xp:this.value><![CDATA[#{javascript:
            var i:Number = parseInt(rowIndex + 1);
            return i.toPrecision(0);}]]>
      </xp:this.value>
</xp:viewColumn>
<!-- Reordered columns so that Topic is before Date -->
<!-- Use custom twistie images for expand/collapse -->
<xp:viewColumn columnName="$120" id="viewColumn7"
      indentResponses="true"
      collapsedImage="/plus.gif"
      expandedImage="/minus.gif">
      <xp:viewColumnHeader value="Topic"
             id="viewColumnHeader7">
      </xp:viewColumnHeader>
</xp:viewColumn>
<!-- Present full date like "Thursday, August 26, 2010" -->
<xp:viewColumn columnName="$106" id="viewColumn1">
            <xp:this.converter>
            <xp:convertDateTime type="date" dateStyle="full">
            </xp:convertDateTime>
      </xp:this.converter>
      <xp:viewColumnHeader value="Date"
            id="viewColumnHeader1"
            sortable="true">
      </xp:viewColumnHeader>
</xp:viewColumn>
<!-- Dynamic Column Images - 1.gif thru 9.gif -->
<!-- inline CSS to center img -->
<xp:viewColumn id="viewColumn2"
      contentType="HTML"
      style="text-align:center">
      <xp:this.facets>
            <xp:viewColumnHeader xp:key="header"
                  id="viewColumnHeader2" value="Responses">
```

```
                    </xp:viewColumnHeader>
                </xp:this.facets>
                <!-- Compute image name based on response count -->
                <xp:this.value><![CDATA[#{javascript:
                    var i:number = rowData.getDescendantCount();
                    if (i < 9) {
                        return ("<img class=\"xspImageViewColumn\"
src=\"/Chp09Ed2.nsf/" + i + ".gif\""+">");
                    } else {
                        return ("<img class=\"xspImageViewColumn\"
src=\"/Chp09Ed2.nsf/n.gif\""+">");
                    }
                    }]]></xp:this.value>
                <!-- Do collapse/expand for docs with responses -->
                <xp:eventHandler event="onclick" submit="true"
                    refreshMode="complete" id="eventHandler1">
                    <xp:this.action><![CDATA[#{javascript:
                        if (rowData.getDescendantCount() > 0) {
                            rowData.toggleExpanded();
                    }
                    }]]></xp:this.action>
                </xp:eventHandler>
            </xp:viewColumn>
</xp:viewPanel>
```

Working with Categories

Just like sorting, categorization is handled by the backend view itself and not by XPages. For a column to be treated as a category, the column type must be set to Categorized in the view column properties infobox; refer to the Type radio button option show in Figure 9.10, which allows columns to be defined as Standard or Categorized.

The View Panel merely presents category rows and columns and renders them so they can be expanded and collapsed as required. The expansion and contraction of category rows works the same as it does for indented responses. Note also that the state of both category rows and document hierarchies is maintained as you navigate through the view data. For example, as part of the final make over, you restricted the number of rows presented in the View Panel to ten elements (remember `rows="10"`). This caused more pages to be displayed in the view pager contained in the header. If you expand and collapse some categories or response hierarchies on any given View Panel page and then navigate forward and backward via the pager, you find that the display state of these rows is maintained and then redisplayed on your return exactly as you had left them. This statefulness is a great built-in feature of XPages and something often lacking in other web applications...try the same view navigation exercises using the classic Domino web engine.

In any case, categorization becomes more interesting when two or more category columns are in a view. To provide some working examples of this, a modified form and view were added to **Chp09Ed2.nsf**, namely the **Main Topic2** form and the **subCats** view. A small number of documents with multiple categories have also been created in the sample application so that examples can be quickly constructed. You do not see these documents in the **All Documents** view because the view selection formula on the **($All)** view only displays documents created using the **Main Topic** form, and thus excludes those created using **Main Topic2**. Figure 9.14 shows the sample multicategory documents when the **subCats** view is previewed in the client.

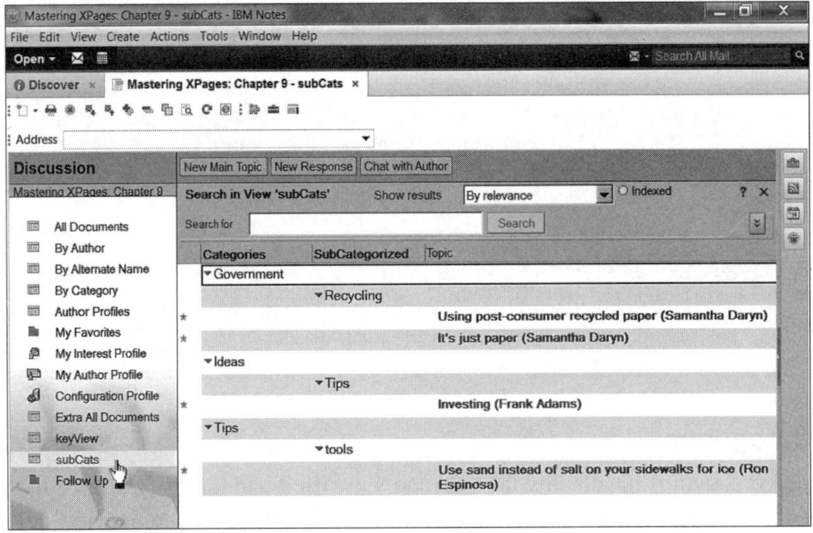

Figure 9.14 Domino view with subcategories

Figure 9.15 shows an XPage named **subCat1.xsp**, which is a default rendering of the **subCats** view. By "default rendering," I mean that a View Panel control was simply dropped on an XPage and all the columns in the **subCats** view were accepted for inclusion—nothing more than that.

> **TIP**
>
> A new control known as the Dynamic View Panel was introduced in 853 UP1 and is available as part of the XPages core from Notes/Domino 9.0 onward. This control is a simplified View Panel insofar as it uses the XPages View Panel renderer to display content, but it automatically includes *every* column defined in the Domino view to which it is bound.

This results in less XSP markup generated in the XPage, but you ultimately have less control over the content presented to the end user. For example, you cannot exclude columns contained in the Domino view definition, apply individual columns styles, rearrange column order, and such. Nonetheless, it is certainly useful for creating views quickly and may be enough to satisfy simple use cases. A sample XPage featuring this control is included in the **Chp09Ed2.nsf**—check out **dynamicViewPanel.xsp**.

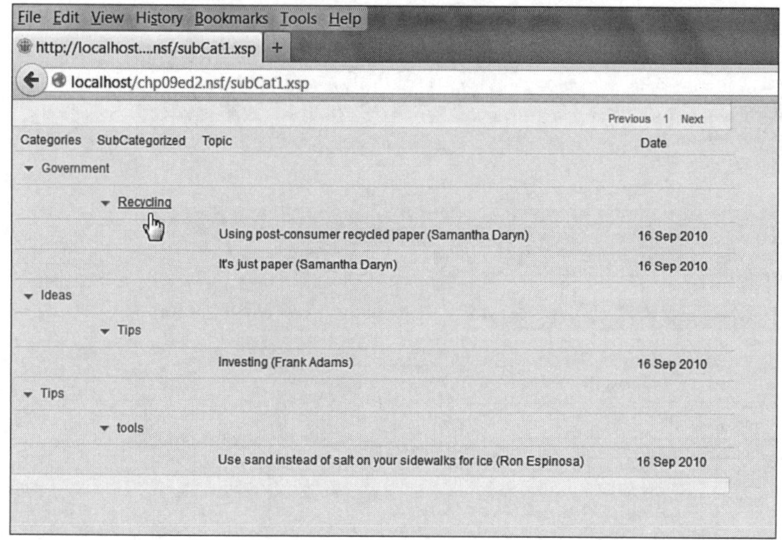

Figure 9.15 View Panel with subcategories

If you experiment with the XPages View Panel and the Notes view, you find that the presentation and behavior of both are identical. The category columns are automatically rendered as action links with twistie icons, both of which serve to expand and collapse the category row. Apart from this specialized behavior, all the regular column properties described thus far can also be applied to category columns. For example, category columns can be reordered within the View Panel just like plain columns. This is an important example to cite as many developers think that the XPage is stuck with column order defined in the backend Domino view.

Although adding two or more categorized columns to a view is one way of implementing subcategorization, there is an alternative method which seems to be a common practice. That is, instead of having multiple categorized columns in the view, which map to fields in the underlying form, the view has just one category column but it can support multiple categories through the use of a "category\subcategory" data-format notation. Thus, if a user enters something like

"Government" as a category value, this is interpreted as a top-level category. However, if "Government\Recycling" is entered by the user into the Categories field when creating a document, the document is categorized in a "Recycling" subcategory within the top-level "Government" category.

To provide an example of this, an alternative sample NSF is provided for this chapter, namely **Chp09Ed2a.nsf**. Some of the sample documents contained in **Chp09Ed2.nsf** have been recategorized in the manner just described (which is why you need a separate database). Figure 9.16 shows an example of a redefined category field as inspected in a Notes infobox and how these updated documents are displayed in the Notes client.

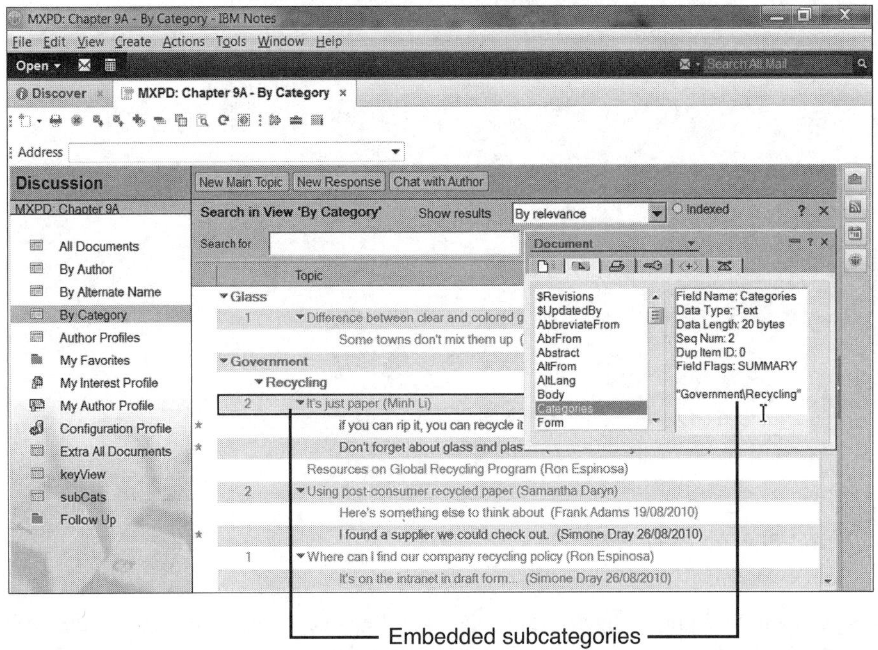

Figure 9.16 Category field containing hierarchical categories

Observe that the Notes client view indents the new subcategories tucked in under the main categories. You have little or no control over this particular rendering because it is built-in view behavior. However, if you repeat the exercise described for Figure 9.15 and create an XPages View Panel to do a default rendering of this view, you notice a problem (refer to **subCatsA.xsp** in **Chp09Ed2a.nsf** for convenience). As shown in Figure 9.17, XPages recognizes the entries as category columns, but the subcategories are not indented. The next section describes how this can be addressed within the design of an application.

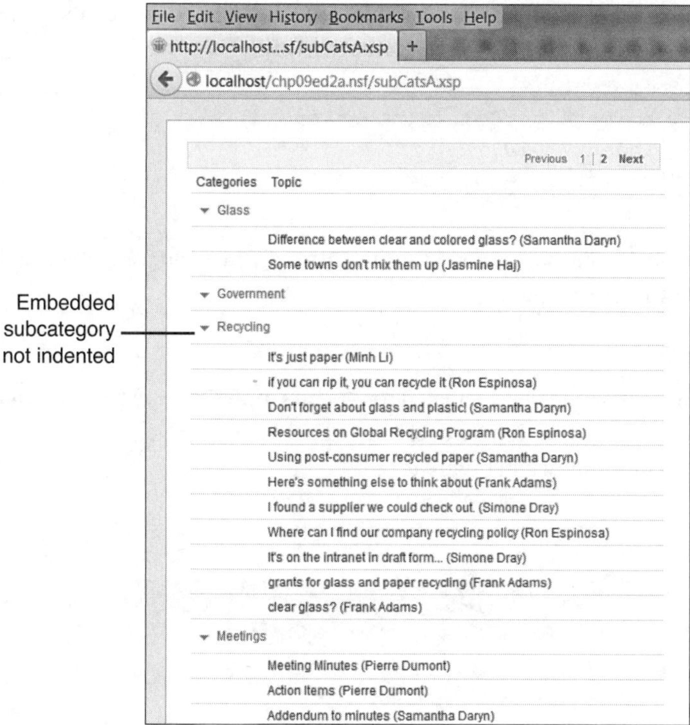

Figure 9.17 XPages View Panel default rendering of embedded subcategories

Making It Look Like Notes!

Building an XPage to emulate the Notes client rendering can be achieved in the following seven steps:

1. Create a new XPage called **subCatsB.xsp** and add a View Panel from the palette.
2. Bind to the **By Category** view but only include the **Topic** column.
3. As shown earlier, insert a new column before the **Topic** column and give it a title of "**Categories**" by updating the view column header.
4. In the **Display** panel set the **Content type** to HTML.
5. Add `var="rowData"` to the `<xp:viewPanel>` tag to gain access to the current row via server-side JavaScript while the View Panel is being populated.

6. Add the following server-side JavaScript snippet to compute the column's style property—**All Properties > Styling > Style > Compute value**:

```
if (rowData.isCategory()) {
    var indent = rowData.getColumnIndentLevel();
    var pixpad = indent * 10;
    return "padding-left:" + pixpad + "px";
}
```

7. Move to the **Events** tab for this column and for the only defined event, `onclick`, add another server-side JavaScript snippet:

```
rowData.toggleExpanded();
```

The **subCatsB.xsp** XPage has already been created for you in **Chp09Ed2a.nsf**, so you can load this or preview your own creation if you have worked through the steps above. In either case the results you see should match those shown in Figure 9.18.

Indented embedded subcategory

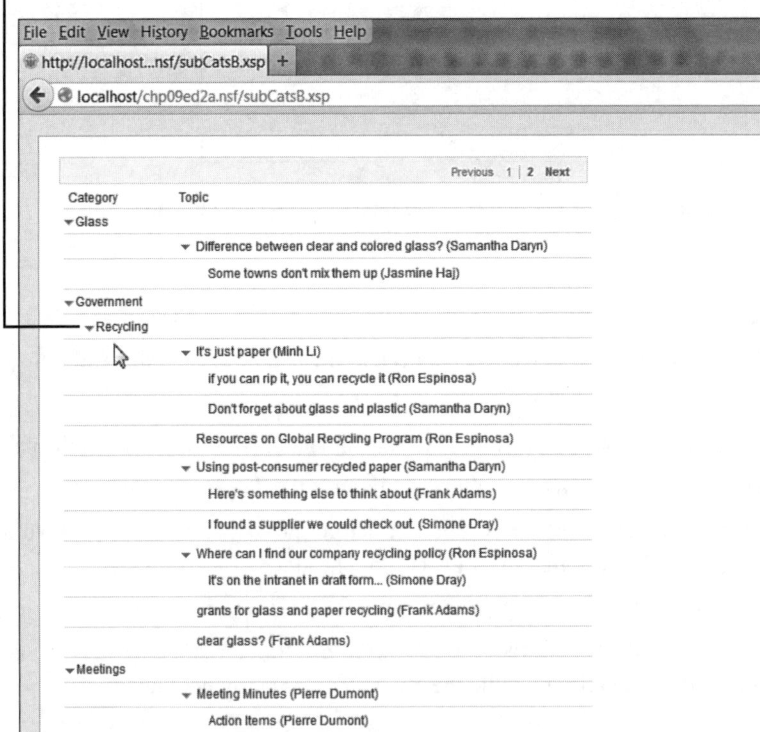

Figure 9.18 XPages View Panel displaying inline subcategories

You should note that the padding included in Step 6 assumes that the page direction is left to right (LTR). For much of the world, this is not the case, and applications with an international audience should be designed to support bidirectional text (bidi) by default. This can be achieved easily in this instance, however, by modifying the code snippet, as shown in Listing 9.3.

Listing 9.3 Indented Categorization with BiDi Support

```
if (rowData.isCategory()) {
    var rtl = context.isDirectionRTL();
    var paddingDir = rtl ? "padding-right:" : "padding-left:";
    var indent = rowData.getColumnIndentLevel();
    var pixpad = indent * 10;
    return paddingDir + pixpad + "px";
}
```

To test this code, you can change the language on your browser to one with a right-to-left (RTL) orientation—any of the Arabic languages will suffice—and refresh the XPage. You can see the View Panel and your categories adjust to an RTL orientation. You could also replace the `context.isDirectionRTL()` SSJS call with an alternative call to an XPages runtime API—namely, `com.ibm.xsp.util.DirLangUtil.isRTL(getComponent("viewPanel1"))`. This API gets the text direction for the part of the page containing your control, instead of just the HTML "dir" setting for the page itself. This enables you to properly support pages that have both LTR and RTL content. The sample application has been updated to contain these modifications, so you can uncomment and test this code.

At this point, you are no doubt seeing how SSJS is essential to tailoring XPages runtime behavior. Obviously, the `NotesXspViewEntry` class exposed via the `rowData` object is critical when working on view customizations as it gives full programmatic access to each view row as it is rendered. This JavaScript class is a pseudo class for the `DominoViewEntry` Java class defined in the XPages runtime, which, in turn, wraps the `ViewEntry` class defined in Notes Java API. JavaScript pseudo classes such as this one allow you to access the associated Java class without having to enter the entire package name, and have an automatic built-in type-ahead facility for method names when used in the JavaScript editor. In this example, for each row it allows you to

- Check if the row is a category: `rowData.isCategory()`
- Check for embedded categories: `rowData.getColumnIndentLevel()`
- Toggle the expand/collapse state of the row: `rowData.toggleExpanded()`

Appendix A, "XSP Programming Reference," includes documentation resources that provide a full outline of the `DominoViewEntry` XPages class, which `NotesXspViewEntry` uses under the covers. It is worthwhile to study this class in more detail to get to know the full set of tools you have at your disposal when working on view customizations. You can also resolve the mappings for any JavaScript/Java classes using a handy tool on the Domino Designer wiki:

www-10.lotus.com/ldd/ddwiki.nsf/dx/XPages_Domino_Object_Map_8.5.2

Tip

At press time, an enhancement has been made to the XPages runtime to automatically perform this subcategory column indentation. This enhancement is controlled by a setting in the **xsp.properties** file `xsp.domino.view.embeddedsubcategories.autoindent` and has a default value of `true`. Therefore, the plan is that all view controls that support categorized columns will auto-indent embedded subcategories in future releases (post 9.0.1), starting with some view controls provided via OpenNTF.org. Should you already have customized styles applied to category columns in your application, you can turn off the new XPages behavior *if* it interferes with the look and feel of your app by setting this property to `false`.

Incidentally, category view columns can be rendered inline ("tucked-in" under the parent category) as just shown *even* when they are defined as separate category columns, that is, as was the case with the **subCats** view used in **Chp09Ed2.nsf**, as shown in Figure 9.14. A **subCat2.xsp** XPage has been included in that sample application to illustrate how to reformat the column category display. Listing 9.4 shows the revised code that computes the column value and the style property.

Listing 9.4 Server-Side JavaScript for View Column Value and Style Properties

```
<xp:this.value>
      <![CDATA[#{javascript:if (rowData.isCategory()) {
      // Use the standard twistie icons
      var src = "/xsp/.ibmxspres/global/theme/common/images/expand.gif";
      // Look for the deepest subcategory first
      var colValue = rowData.getColumnValue("SubCategories")
      // If not found, keep looking back until back to top level cat
      if (colValue == null) {
        colValue = rowData.getColumnValue("Categories");
      }
      // Return "Not Categorized" for null or undefined data
      if (typeof colValue == 'undefined' || colValue == null) {
        colValue = "Not Categorized";
      }
      // Invert the twistie depending on row state
      if (rowData.isExpanded()) {
        src = "/xsp/.ibmxspres/global/theme/common/images/collapse.gif";
```

```
        }
        // return the <span> tag including the twistie & value
        return "<span style='cursor:pointer'><img src='" + src +
                        "' alt='' class='xspImageViewColumn'/>" + colValue +
                        "</span>";
                        }}]]>
</xp:this.value>
<xp:this.style>
        <![CDATA[#{javascript:
        if (rowData.isCategory()) {
           // Start at the deepest subcategory and work back to root
           var colValue = rowData.getColumnValue("SubCategories");
           // Insert padding for 10 pixel padding for 2nd column
           if (colValue != null && colValue != "") {
              return "padding-left:10px";
           // Insert more padding if needed back to the top level
            } else {
              return "padding-left:0px";
           }
        }}]]>
</xp:this.style>
```

As you can see from the code, the principle is exactly the same as previously, but the means of detecting the category columns has changed. No longer are the column values embedded in the Category\Subcategory fashion, so the `rowData.getColumnIndentLevel()` API is of no use here. Instead, the indentation is determined based on the structure of the backend view—the deepest subcategory columns are sought first, rewinding to the top level if no value is found. Load the **subCats2.xsp** page and compare the results to Figure 9.15.

The other interesting tidbit from this example is that it exposes the internal URLs used to locate embedded runtime resources like images, style sheets, and so on. The following URL, for example, points to the standard row expansion twistie that is part of the XPages runtime:

```
"/xsp/.ibmxspres/global/theme/common/images/expand.gif"
```

You see URLs just like this one whenever you view the source of a rendered XPage in a browser, and you can use these URLs as has been done in this example as part of your own customizations.

This tucked-in form of category styling seems popular in the community based on various Notes app dev forum postings and other customer feedback, so hopefully this section clarified how to achieve the Notes client look and feel in XPages.

View Properties and View Panel Properties

When working with views, any features to do with data structure and content are defined at the backend in the view design element itself—you have just seen this with the sorting and categorization examples, insofar as these capabilities needed to be enabled in the view. The view design element also contains properties that are purely related to presentation within the Notes client or classic web engine and, as such, do not apply to the XPages view controls. For example, the `Type` option in Figure 9.10 defines whether a categorization data is maintained for a particular column in the view, but the twistie options contained in the adjacent tab (see Figure 9.19) only apply to native Notes rendering and not to XPages.

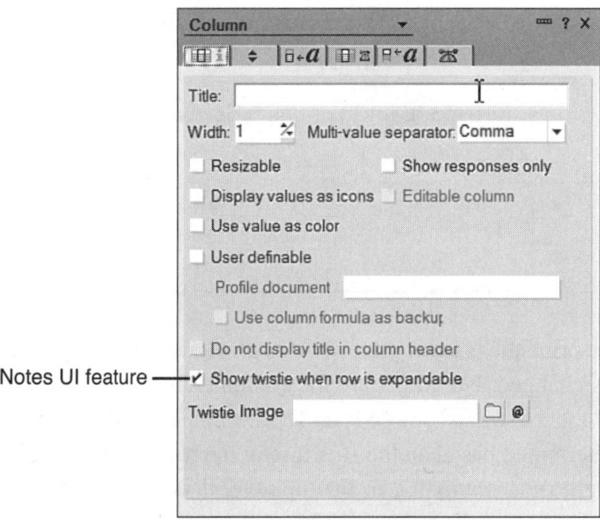

Figure 9.19 View Column Presentation properties

It is important to be able to distinguish the native view rendering features from the XPages View control presentation properties. In **Chp09Ed2.nsf** a new version of the **($xpByAuthor)** view, namely **($xpByAuthorExt)**, has been provided for use in an example that helps clarify this area. The extended view contains an extra column that totals the byte size of the documents for each category. These totals are shown in the Notes client for each category only, but can be displayed for each individual row entry if so desired. The hide/show nature of this data is determined using the **Hide Detail Rows** checkbox shown in Figure 9.20.

If you toggle the **Hide Detail Rows** checkbox value and refresh the view data from within Designer, you see the document byte size displayed for each entry. An agent has also been supplied in the sample application, which prints the column values for each view row entry using the Java API. The agent (`getViewEntryData`) details are shown in Listing 9.5.

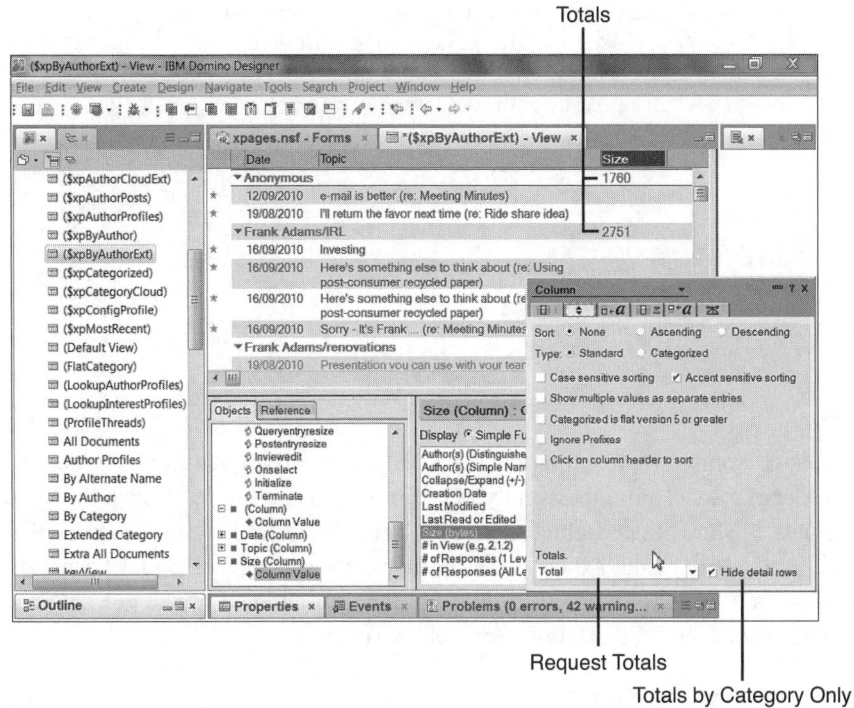

Figure 9.20 ($xpByAuthorExt) with document size totals for each category

Listing 9.5 Java Agent to Print View Column Data

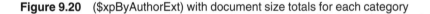

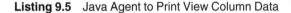

```
import lotus.domino.*;
public class JavaAgent extends AgentBase {
    public void NotesMain() {
      try {
          // Standard agent code to get session & context objects
          Session session = getSession();
          AgentContext agentContext = session.getAgentContext();
          // get the current db and the new ($xpByAuthorExt) view
          Database db = session.getCurrentDatabase();
          View view = db.getView("($xpByAuthorExt)");
          // iterate over each view entry and print the Topic & Size
          ViewEntryCollection vec = view.getAllEntries();
          if (vec != null) {
                for (int i = 0; i < vec.getCount(); i++) {
                      ViewEntry ve = vec.getNthEntry(i);
                      if (ve != null)
```

```
                        // just get the 3rd & 4th column values
                        // ViewEntry index is zero-based!
                          System.out.println(
                             ve.getColumnValues().get(2)
                             + " " +
                          ve.getColumnValues().get(3) );
                    }
               }
          } catch(Exception e) {
             e.printStackTrace();
          }
     }
}
```

Listing 9.6 shows some sample output generated when the **($xpByAuthorExt)** view is configured to hide detail rows. To run the agent yourself in Designer, you first launch the Java debug console (**Tools > Show Java Debug Console**), right-click **getViewEntryData** in the agent view, and select the **Run** menu. All the `println` output then appears in the Java console. As you can see, the detail totals rows are all included in the data returned by the `getColumnValues()` API call *regardless* of **Hide Details Rows** property setting.

Listing 9.6 Snippet of Java Agent Output

```
...
if you can rip it, you can recycle it (re: It's just paper) 573.0
It's just paper 618.0
Using post-consumer recycled paper 1045.0
who's this? (re: Meeting Minutes) 629.0
phone number inside (re: Meeting Minutes) 631.0
Difference between clear and colored glass? 927.0
...
```

Because XPages depends on the Java API to populate its View control, the detail rows appear in *any* XPages View control that includes the **Size** column. The **Hide Detail Rows** property is really just used in the core view rendering code and not honored in the programmability layer. Given the view customization tips and tricks you have learned thus far, you are now in a position to figure out how to emulate Notes **Hide Detail Rows** view display property in XPages! All you really need to do is not show the **Size** column value when the row is not a category. This is done for you in **hideDetails.xsp** page in **Chp09Ed2.nsf**, which contains a View Panel with four standard columns (**Name**, **Date**, **Topic**, and **Size**) plus a computed column. The SSJS code used to compute the column value is trivial, as demonstrated in Listing 9.7.

Listing 9.7 Server-Side JavaScript Snippet to Emulate Hide Detail Rows in a View Panel

```
<xp:this.value>
<![CDATA[#{javascript:
      // Only show the Total column value for category rows
      if (rowData.isCategory()) {
            return rowData.getColumnValue("Size");
}}]]></xp:this.value>
<!-- Also include a converter to display whole numbers only -->
<xp:this.converter>
      <xp:convertNumber type="number"
            integerOnly="true">
      </xp:convertNumber>
</xp:this.converter>
```

The converter just used was added via the same **Data** property panel used to add the Java Script code in Designer. Simply set the **Display type** to Number and check the **Integer only** control to eliminate the decimal points you see printed in the raw data in Listing 9.6. When loaded or previewed, the **hideDetails** XPage looks like Figure 9.21.

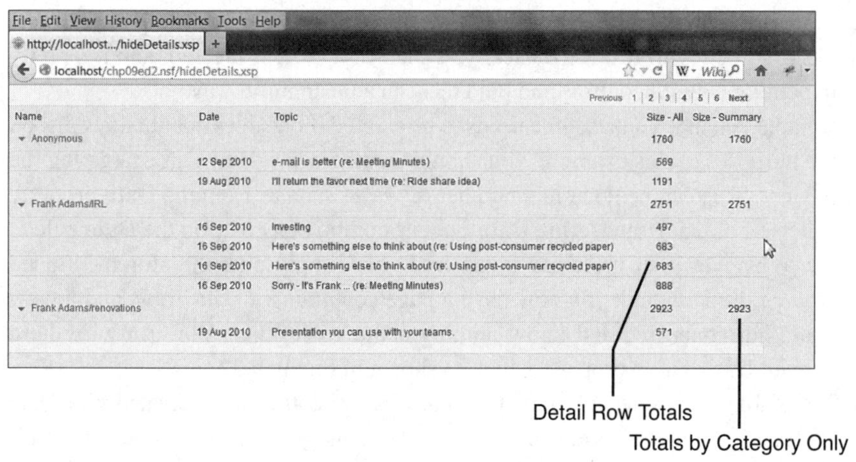

Figure 9.21 XPage with totals for detail and category-only rows

The discussion thus far covered all the main View Panel properties and dived into examples of how to customize View Panels using server-side JavaScript and other tools. The next most logical focus area for the View Panel would be styling. No doubt, as you have examined the View Panel properties, you noticed a slew of specialized style class properties (`rowClass`, `columnClass`, `viewClass`, and so on), which can modify its appearance. Rather than do that here in this chapter, it is covered in the section, "Working with Extended styleClass and style Properties," in Chapter 16, "XPages Theming." The discussion here instead shifts to the Data Table container control.

Data Table

The Data Table uses a simple table structure to display content. The table is configured to contain three row elements, such as a header, content row, and footer. The header and footer typically contain static elements, such as column titles, pagers, or just arbitrary one-off control instances.

The content row usually contains a collection of individual controls that are bound to elements of a data source, and this row is then rendered repeatedly for each entry in the data source (once for every row in a view) when the Data Table is invoked as part of a live application.

Unlike a View Panel, however, all the controls contained in the Data Table must be added and bound manually, and certain other capabilities are simply not available, e.g. categorization. In essence, it is like a dumbed-down View Panel control, but it can be useful if you need to display simple nonhierarchical data in a customized fashion. You see an example of a good use case in this section.

To start with, try to present a regular view using a Data Table to get familiar with its features and behaviors. You should create a new XPage, say **myDataTable.xsp**, and drag-and-drop a Data Table control from the palette. Compared to the View Panel drag-and-drop experience, you might be underwhelmed with results. Basically, a shell of a table is created, and it's pretty much up to you to populate it with controls and bind these in a meaningful way.

Designer prompts you that a data source needs to be created if one does not already exist on the page, so for the purposes of this example, you should create a view data source targeting the **xpAllDocuments** view. This can be done in a number of ways, such as from the **Data** property panel on the XPage itself or using the **Define Data Source** combo box entry on the **Data** palette data source picker. Whatever your preferred route might be, simply pick the aforementioned view as the data source. Even though you now have a page containing a Data Table and a view data source, they are not connected and know nothing about each other. You can wire these together using the main **Data Table** property panel, as shown in Figure 9.22.

With the Data Table entry selected in the **Outline** view, pick the newly created view data source instance ("view1") using the **Data source** combo box, and you also need to enter a **Collection name**. The collection name, "rowData" in this example, is used as the object to gain programmatic access to each row entry as it is being rendered—just as it was in the View Panel examples earlier. Rather than use server-side JavaScript in this case, however, you could just use simple Expression Language (EL) bindings. First, however, you need some controls to display the row data, so drag-and-drop a Computed Field from the **Core Controls** palette to the first cell in the middle row and then repeat the process for the adjacent table cell. These Computed Field instances can be selected and bound using EL expressions—or **Simple data binding**, as it is described in Designer's **Value** property panel and displayed in Figure 9.23. Bind the first field to the `_MainTopicsDate` column and the second field to the `_Topics` column.

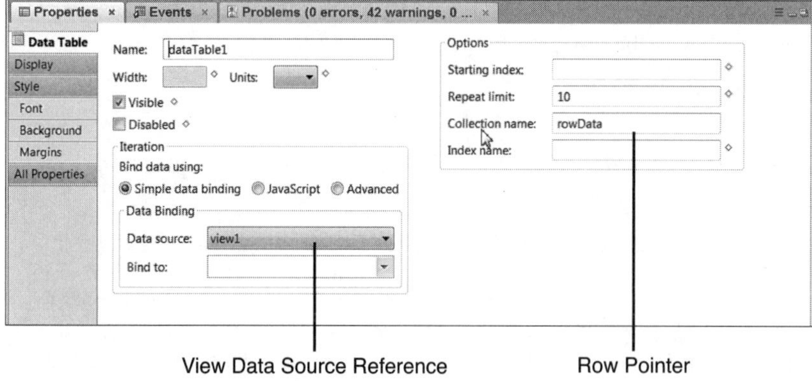

Figure 9.22 Connecting a Data Table to a view data source in Designer

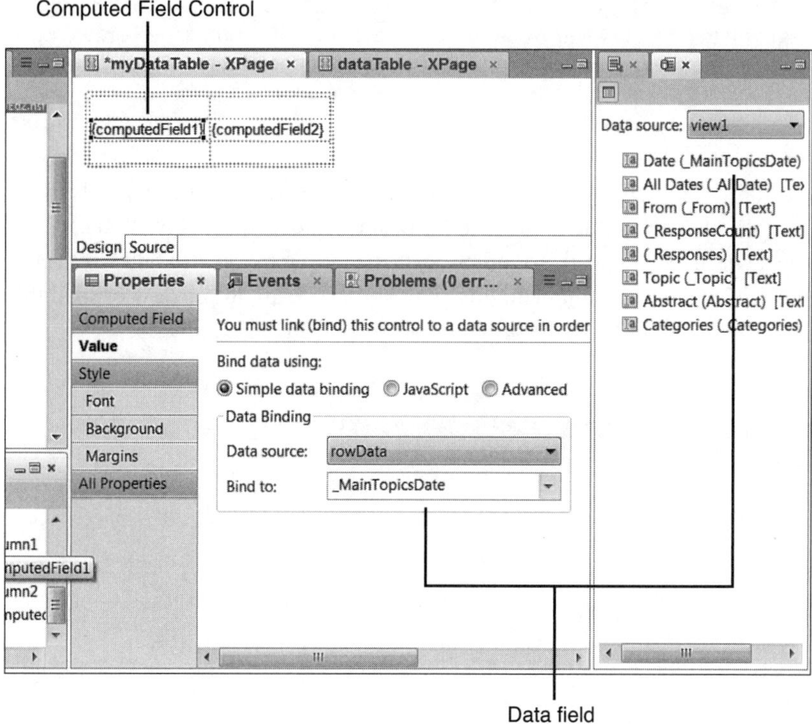

Figure 9.23 Binding a Computed Field to a view data source element in Designer

The EL data binding markup generated by Designer has the following form. The name of the column is provided as a key to the row data entry:

```
#{rowData['_MainTopicsDate']}
```

TIP

You can use EL expressions or Server-Side JavaScript for data binding. The EL expression `rowData['MainTopicsDate']` produces the same result as `rowData.getColumnValue("MainTopicsDate")` in SSJS. Some column names, however, are incompatible with the EL expression language and thus cannot be used at all. For example, many column names in the standard Domino templates begin with a dollar symbol, such as **$126**, **$150**, and so on. An EL expression like `rowData['$126']` would be expanded to a Java bean expression like `rowData.get$126()`, which is illegal in the Java language. It was precisely for this reason that this example uses the **xpAllDocuments** view rather than the **($All)** view. The former is essentially the same view as the latter, but with column names that are EL friendly. In this sense, JavaScript binding can be less problematical than EL binding, especially if you happen to have no control over the names of the data source elements. EL, however, is a powerful language that you can use to good effect in XPages development. For more information, visit this website: http://tinyurl.com/ExpressionLanguage.

You should also drop two Label controls from the palette directly into the two cells in the top row of the Data Table and change their values to Date and Topic, respectively. You can also assign the Data Table a width of 600 pixels for quick aesthetics using the **Width** and **Units** controls shown in Figure 9.22. After you complete this step, you are ready to preview or load this Data Table. The results should be just like the page you see displayed in Figure 9.24.

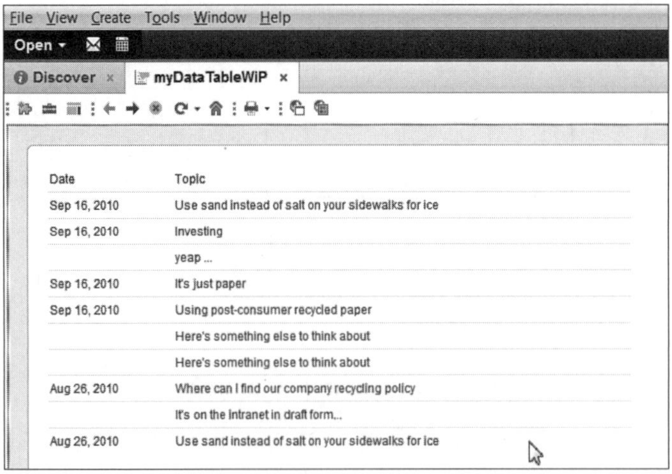

Figure 9.24 Data Table displaying data from xpAllDocuments view

The Data Table could do with a pager to split the rows into manageable chunks. The first step is to set the `rows` property of the Data Table to a smaller number than its default value of 30 (for example, 10). Interestingly, the pager you have worked with up to now in the View Panel is not an intrinsic part of that control, but an independent entity that can be used with any of the view controls. The View Panel just happens to include a pager instance by default. To add a pager to the Data Table, look for the Pager control in the **Core Controls** palette and drag it into one of the footer cells. Then, activate the **Pager** property panel and attach it to the Data Table by picking the ID of the Data Table from the **Attach to** combo box—where Designer kindly enumerates a list of eligible candidate controls for you! At the same time, turn on partial refresh so that paging updates are performed using AJAX. The various property panel selections are shown in Figure 9.25.

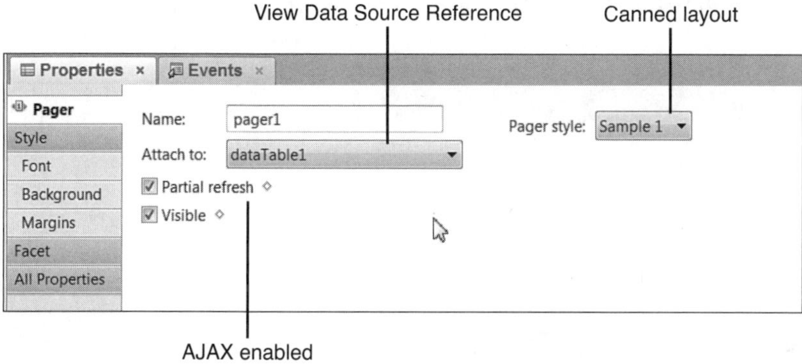

Figure 9.25 Pager property panel

Because the Pager is capable of working with any view control, you must nominate a target container. The **Partial refresh** checkbox selection instructs XPages to update just the targeted view control via an AJAX request when a pager action is executed. This means that only the view data in the Data Table is refreshed when the end user navigates from one page to the next, which is obviously more efficient than refreshing the entire page every time.

The only problem with the pager right now is that it resides in the wrong place. It has been dropped into the footer cell of a column when it really needs to be in the footer of the Data Table itself. Unfortunately, the footer of the Data Table is not an identifiable drag-and-drop target in Designer, so you must go to the **Source** pane to move the markup manually. Simply cut and paste the entire `<xp:pager>` tag from its current location so that it is a direct child of the Data Table. It should also be wrapped in a `<xp:this.facets>` tag—see the final markup in Listing 9.8.

To best illustrate the effect of the AJAX partial refresh, however, it is worthwhile adding two more Computed Fields to the XPage. Place the first Computed Field in one of the Data Table footer cells and then the second control can be dropped anywhere else on the page as long as it is outside the Data Table. Then, add the following server-side JavaScript as the computed value for both fields:

```
@Now().getMilliseconds();
```

Domino developers no doubt are familiar with the `@Now()` function, which returns the current date and time. The `getMilliseconds()` call expresses the time in milliseconds when the page is loaded. When you load or preview the page, both fields should display the same number. If you start navigating through the view data using the navigator, you notice that the Computed Field within the Data Table is updated with the current time in milliseconds value while the field external to the Data Table is not. This demonstrates the efficient behavior of the partial refresh feature.

Figure 9.26 shows the updated XPage in action. The full markup is done for you in the **dataTable.xsp** XPage in **Chp09Ed2.nsf** and is printed in Listing 9.8.

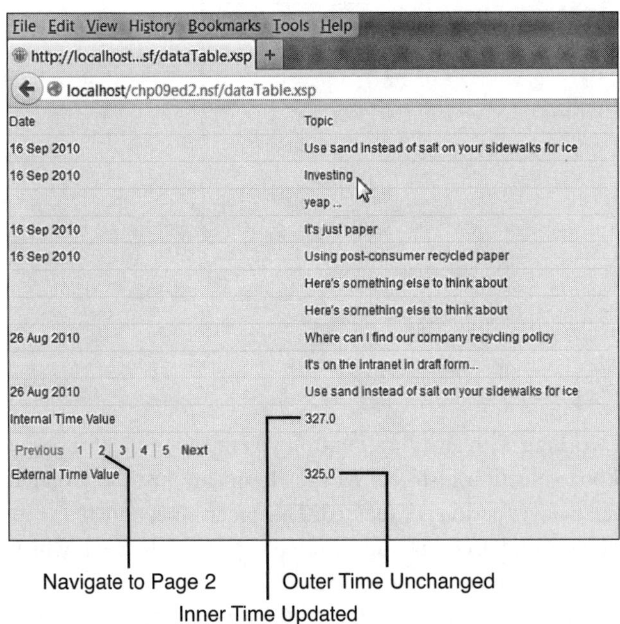

Figure 9.26 Data Table with partial refresh paging enabled

Listing 9.8 XSP Markup for Sample Data Table

```
<?xml version="1.0" encoding="UTF-8"?>
<xp:view xmlns:xp="http://www.ibm.com/xsp/core">
      <!-- The data source defined at root level -->
```

```
<xp:this.data>
      <xp:dominoView var="viewAll"
            viewName="xpAllDocuments"></xp:dominoView>
</xp:this.data>
<!-- The data table finds the data source using value prop -->
<xp:dataTable id="dataTable1" rows="10" var="rowData"
      value="#{viewAll}" style="width:600px">
      <xp:column id="column1">
            <!-- column header and footer entries -->
            <xp:this.facets>
                  <xp:label value="Date" id="label1"
                  xp:key="header"></xp:label>
                  <xp:label value="Internal Time Value"
                  id="label3" xp:key="footer"></xp:label>
            </xp:this.facets>
            <!-- Bound to the date field using EL -->
            <xp:text escape="true" id="computedField1"
                  value="#{rowData['_MainTopicsDate']}">
            </xp:text>
      </xp:column>
      <xp:column id="column2" style="width:300px">
            <xp:this.facets>
                  <!-- column header and footer entries -->
                  <xp:text escape="true" id="computedField3"
                  xp:key="footer"
                  value="#{javascript:@Now().getMilliseconds();}">
                  </xp:text>
                  <xp:label value="Topic" id="label2"
                  xp:key="header"></xp:label>
            </xp:this.facets>
            <!-- Bound to the Topic field using EL -->
            <xp:text escape="true" id="computedField2"
                  value="#{rowData._Topic}">
            </xp:text>
      </xp:column>
      <xp:this.facets>
            <xp:pager layout="Previous Group Next" id="pager1"
                  for="dataTable1"
                  xp:key="footer"
                  panelPosition="left"
                  partialRefresh="true">
            </xp:pager>
      </xp:this.facets>
</xp:dataTable>
<!-- Table only used for layout alignment -->
```

```
    <xp:table style="width:600px;text-align:left">
          <xp:tr><xp:td>
                <xp:label value="External Time Value"
                      id="label4">
                </xp:label></xp:td>
                <!-- external computed field -->
                <xp:td style="width:300px; text-align:left">
                      <xp:text escape="true" id="computedField4"
                      value="#{javascript:@Now().getMilliseconds();}"
                      style="text-align:left"></xp:text>
                </xp:td>
          </xp:tr>
    </xp:table>
</xp:view>
```

Although working with the Data Table may be vaguely interesting, it must occur to you that what you have just built could be achieved using a View Panel control in a fraction of the time with just a few point-and-click operations. So, why bother with the Data Table at all? The answer is that the Data Table can be useful when you want to build a small bare bones tabular view with a highly customized user interface. Perhaps these use cases are not commonplace but they do occur. The next exercise serves as a good example.

Building a Mini Embedded Profile View Using a Data Table

Carry out the following steps, drawing on what you learned in the current section up to this point:

1. Create a new XPage called **dtProfile.xsp** and add a Data Table from the palette.
2. Create a view data source targeting the **xpAuthorProfiles** view.
3. Connect the Data Table to the data source and set its **Collection name** to `"rowData"` in the Data Table property sheet. This should result in a `var="rowData"` attribute being created in the underlying `<xp:dataTable>` tag.
4. Append two new columns to the Data Table using the right mouse menu.
5. Add a Computed Field to the 1st content cell; that is, the first column, middle row.
6. Bind this field to the **From** column in the data source using JavaScript:

   ```
   rowData.getColumnValue("From")
   ```

7. Add a link control for the palette to both the 2nd and 3rd cells in the content row.
8. For the first link, activate the **Link** property panel and set the **Label** and **Link type** fields. For the label, enter "email" in the edit box, and then for the latter, add some

server-side JavaScript to compute a URL. This is a `mailto` URL, created by simply concatenating a `"mailto:"` to the **Email** column value, as follows:

```
"mailto:" + rowData.getColumnValue("Email")
```

9. Set the label for the second link to "Download" and compute its `value` in the same way as before, this time building a Domino resource image URL like this:

```
"/" + rowData.getUniversalID() + "/$FILE/" +
rowData.getColumnValue("FileUpFilename")
```

10. Drag-and-drop an image control to the fourth and final content row cell, using the **Use an image placeholder** radio button for now so that you can compute the image reference.
11. In the **Image** property panel, compute the **Image source** using *exactly the same* server-side JavaScript as previously shown.
12. For presentation purposes, select the **All > Style** cell in the property panel for each Data Table column and set this CSS rule:

```
text-align:center; vertical-align:middle
```

13. In the same way, set the **All > Style** property for the Data Table itself to this:

```
width:400px;
```

You already practiced most of the 13 steps in one way or another when working through View Panel or Data Table examples, so only a few steps need any further explanation.

Step 6 simply returns the name of the author of the document. This is in Notes canonical form, so it would be more natural to present the common user name in this column instead. Experienced Domino developers instinctively know to do this using the `@Name` @Function, which can reformat Notes names in a number of ways. Although @Functions and other traditional building blocks are covered in more detail in Chapter 11, "Advanced Scripting," in the section, "Working with @Functions, @Commands, and Formula Language," it is no harm to start dabbling with some simple use cases at this stage as the need arises. To do this, simply wrap the JavaScript binding command in with an `@Name()` call:

```
@Name("[CN]", rowData.getColumnValue("From"));
```

Step 8 uses JavaScript to build a "mailto" URL. Remember that you can just as easily use EL to fulfill this task. If EL is used, the XSP markup for the Computed Field value property is concise:

```
value="mailto:#{rowData.Email}"
```

As opposed to the more verbose SSJS form:

```
<xp:this.value>
<![CDATA[#{javascript:"mailto:"+rowData.getColumnValue("Email");}]]>
</xp:this.value>
```

As you can see, EL nicely facilitates simple string concatenation, and it is also efficient at retrieving the required view data. Although this means it is a good solution for Step 6 or Step 8, it cannot be used to build the Domino resource URL in Step 9 because this requires Java API calls to be made—not just simple data reads. The generic form of the Domino resource URL is

```
/UNID/$FILE/filename
```

where the first part is an ID to identify the document to use, the second part indicates that the URL represents a file attachment resource, and the third part is the name of the attachment. This form of URL has been used in classic Domino web development for a long time. Back in Chapter 3, you learned about special IDs that Notes maintains to manage its databases and documents. The universal ID (UNID) is a 32-character hexadecimal representation that uniquely identifies a document. The profile documents in the Discussion template each contain a single image (or placeholder image) of the author and the name of this image file can be obtained from the **FileUpFilename** column in the **xpAuthorProfiles** view. Thus, a resource URL can be dynamically constructed for all registered users and this URL resolves the image and retrieves it from the profile documents for display in the Data Table. An example of a real live resource URL is highlighted in the status bar of the browser in Figure 9.27.

You are now ready to preview or load the new XPage. **Chp09ed2.nsf** contains some sample profile documents, so you see these listed in the Data Table. The actual intention, however, is to display this Data Table as an embedded view in the **My Profile** page. To do this, you need to open the **authorProfileForm** custom control and copy/paste the markup from **dtProfile.xsp** to the bottom of the XPage, just before the final `</xp:view>` tag. Naturally, you do not copy the `<xp:view>` tag from **dtProfile.xsp** but just the Data Table and data source markup—everything you see in Listing 9.9. Figure 9.27 shows a snapshot of a **My Profile** page from **Chp09Ed2.nsf**.

Note that the copy/paste operations have also been done for you in the custom control **authorProfileFormExt.xsp**. This custom control is then referenced in the **authorProfileExt.xsp**. When using the sample application in a web browser, if you log in and click the **My Profile** link, you can then simply substitute **authorProfileExt.xsp** for **authorProfile.xsp** in the browser URL to see the new behavior. The idea is that the embedded Data Table enables users to view a summary of other application contributors while creating or editing their own profile information. Having an awareness of the conventions and styles used by other team members for profile information is potentially useful context data for new members of a discussion group.

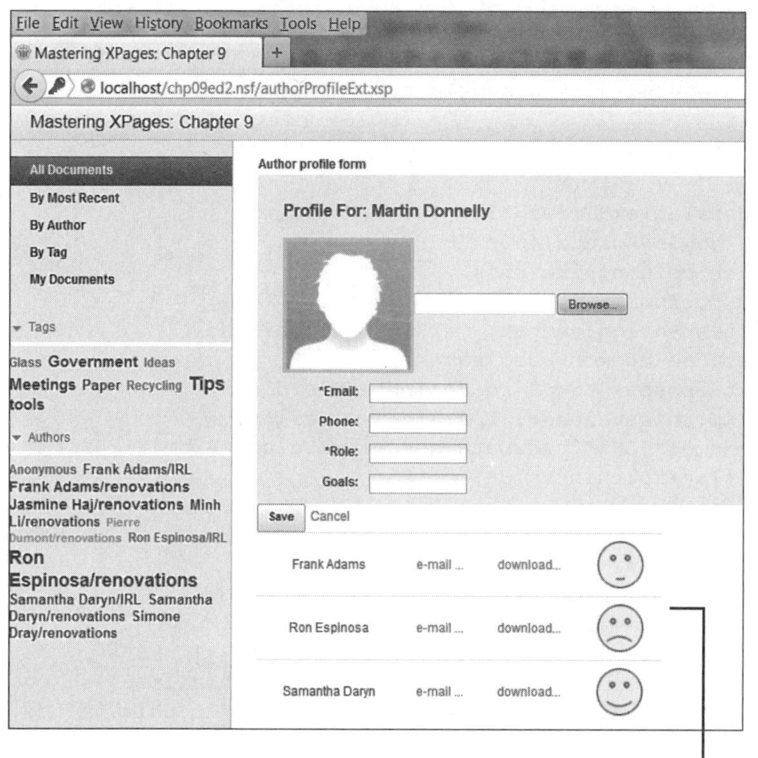

Figure 9.27 My Profile Page with Embedded Data Table

> **TIP**
>
> The next chapter introduces the XPage custom control and discusses all of its features in great detail. Suffice to say, at this stage that, it would have been a better design approach to create **dtProfile.xsp** as a custom control and drop it into **authorProfileForm.xsp** rather than copying and pasting the actual code. If you are already familiar with custom controls, it is trivial to rework this example accordingly. If not, perhaps it is worth revising this example to use a custom control after you read Chapter 10, "Custom Controls."

Listing 9.9 Data Table Displaying Profile Data

```
<xp:this.data>
      <xp:dominoView var="view1" viewName="xpAuthorProfiles">
      </xp:dominoView>
</xp:this.data>

<xp:dataTable id="dataTable1" rows="30" value="#{view1}"
      var="rowData" style="width:400px">
      <!-- style each column like this -->
      <xp:column id="column1"
            style="text-align:center; vertical-align:middle">
            <!-- get the common user name -->
            <xp:text escape="true" id="computedField1">
                  <xp:this.value><![CDATA[#{javascript:
                  @Name("[CN]", rowData.getColumnValue("From"));
                  }]]></xp:this.value>
            </xp:text>
      </xp:column>
      <xp:column id="column2"
            style="text-align:center;vertical-align:middle">
            <!-- return a mailto link -->
            <xp:link escape="true" text="e-mail ..." id="link2">
                  <xp:this.value><![CDATA[#{javascript:"mailto:" +
                  rowData.getColumnValue("Email");}]]></xp:this.value>
            </xp:link>
      </xp:column>
      <xp:column id="column3"
            style="text-align:center; vertical-align:middle">
            <!-- return Domino resource URL -->
            <xp:link escape="true" text="download..." id="link1">
                  <xp:this.value><![CDATA[#{javascript:
                  "/" + rowData.getUniversalID() + "/$FILE/" +
                  rowData.getColumnValue("FileUpFilename")}]]>
                  </xp:this.value>
            </xp:link>
      </xp:column>
      <xp:column id="column4"
            style="text-align:center; vertical-align:middle">
            <!-- use the same Domino resource URL for the image -->
            <xp:image id="image2" style="height:50px;width:50.0px">
                  <xp:this.url><![CDATA[#{javascript:"/" +
                  rowData.getUniversalID() + "/$FILE/" +
                  rowData.getColumnValue("FileUpFilename")}]]>
                  </xp:this.url>
            </xp:image>
      </xp:column>
</xp:dataTable>
```

Had you used a View Panel for this particular use case, you would have had to undo a lot of the features it gives you for free, such as pagers, column headers, and so on. You would also have had to customize the columns to display HTML and then return link and image HTML elements for three of the four columns. The Data Table actually simplifies the process by allowing you to drag-and-drop and arbitrary control into any content row cell and then just compute its value.

Another good example of Data Table usage is the File Download control. This out-of-the-box control is really a Data Table that has been adapted by the XPages runtime to display a simple table of any attachments contained in a nominated rich text field. Figure 9.28 shows the File Download control displaying some attachments in the Discussion application—it should be easy to see how this was built, given what you have just done to implement the embedded profile Data Table.

That is the Data Table, all done and dusted!

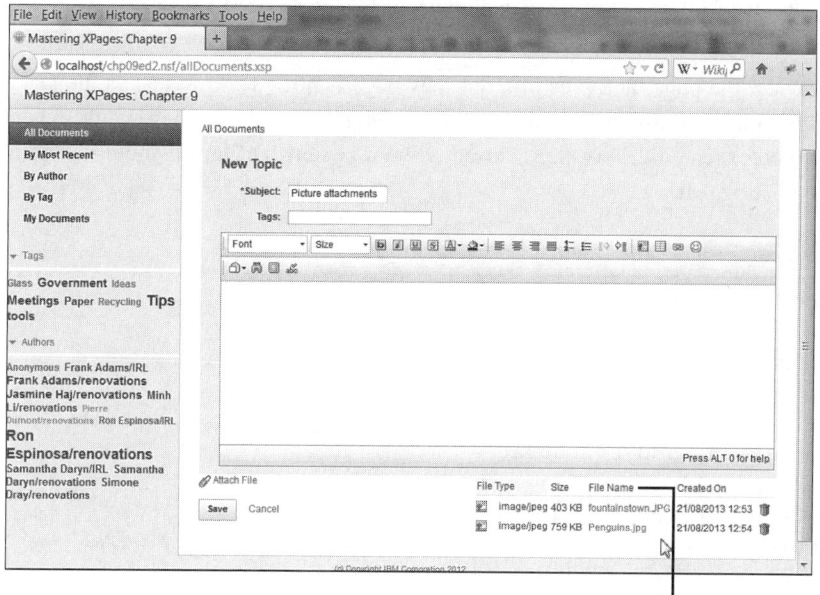

Figure 9.28 Example of the File Download control in the Discussion application

Repeat Control

The Repeat control is similar to the Data Table. The Repeat control does not have a table structure, but just like the Data Table, it can contain arbitrary controls that can be bound to elements of a collection object (like a Domino view or Java array). When the Repeat control is rendered, all child controls are repeated for each entry in the data source.

In fact, to prove just how similar the two controls are, do a quick exercise that involves rebuilding the previous Data Table as a Repeat. The steps are

1. In the Designer Navigator, copy and paste the **dtProfile.xsp** XPage.
2. Rename the new copy from **dtProfile_1** to **repeatProfile** and open it in Designer (the Designer right-mouse menu has a **Rename** option).
3. Use the Find/Replace dialog (`Ctrl-F`) to replace all occurrences of `dataTable` with `repeat`.
4. In the **Source** pane, delete all the `<xp:column ...>` and `</xp:column>` tags from **repeatProfile.xsp**.
5. Just before the closing repeat tag, `</xp:repeat>`, insert a line break using these tags `<xp:br></xp:br>`.
6. Move to the WYSIWYG editor and manually insert some spaces between the child controls so they are not touching each other.

Reload or preview the page, and presto! Your new page is now working just as the Data Table page did, although the individual elements do not align as neatly as they would when placed in a table. If you executed the six steps correctly, your **repeatProfile.xsp** should contain the same markup as Listing 9.10.

Listing 9.10 Displaying Profile Data Using a Repeat Control

```
<!-- data source has not changed. -->
<xp:this.data>
      <xp:dominoView var="view1" viewName="xpAuthorProfiles">
      </xp:dominoView>
</xp:this.data>
<!-- dataTable tag changed to repeat -->
<xp:repeat id="repeat1" rows="30"
      var="rowData" style="width:400px" value="#{view1}"> 
      <!-- removed columns but kept controls exactly as they were -->
      <xp:text escape="true" id="computedField1">
            <xp:this.value><![CDATA[#{javascript:
                  @Name("[CN]", rowData.getColumnValue("From"));}]]>
            </xp:this.value>
      </xp:text>
      <!-- spaces represented as HTML entities in markup:   -->
         
      <xp:link escape="true" text="e-mail ..." id="link1">
            <xp:this.value><![CDATA[#{javascript:"mailto:" +
                  rowData.getColumnValue("Email");}]]></xp:this.value>
```

```
        </xp:link>
          
        <xp:link escape="true" text="download ..." id="link2">
               <xp:this.value>
                       <![CDATA[#{javascript:"/" +
                              rowData.getUniversalID() + "/$FILE/" +
                              rowData.getColumnValue("FileUpFilename")}]]>
                       </xp:this.value>
        </xp:link>
          
        <xp:image id="image1" style="height:50px;width:50.0px">
               <xp:this.url>
               <![CDATA[#{javascript:"/" +
                      rowData.getUniversalID() + "/$FILE/" +
                      rowData.getColumnValue("FileUpFilename")}]]>
               </xp:this.url>
        </xp:image>
<xp:br></xp:br>
</xp:repeat>
```

This exercise shows that the bulk of the properties are shared across both controls and that the containment relationships are compatible—otherwise, your page would not build in Designer, let alone actually work at runtime.

A Repeat Control Design Pattern

Just because the Repeat control is not contained within a table does not mean it cannot use a tabular layout scheme. The **repeatDocuments.xsp** XPage in the sample application provides a great pattern for Repeat usage. This is a copy of the XPage that implemented the **All Documents** page in the 8.5.2 Discussion template. In the sample application, if you load **repeatDocuments.xsp** and **allDocuments.xsp** in adjacent browser tabs, you will find little difference between the two in terms of user experience—even though the former is based on the Repeat control and the latter has been updated to use a Data View (refer to Figure 9.1 for a screen shot of **allDocuments.xsp**). Both pages have a set of Collapse All | Expand All links and a pager at the top of the view—effectively, this is a header. The bottom of the view has a page size picker on the left side and a pager on the other—effectively, this is a footer. The data rows are repeated in between the header and footer using a Repeat control and make use of many other advanced features to generate dynamic content. Figure 9.29 features an outline view of the relevant parts of the **allDocumentViewCc.xsp**, a custom control used by the **repeatDocuments** XPage, with tags to identify various recognizable landmarks.

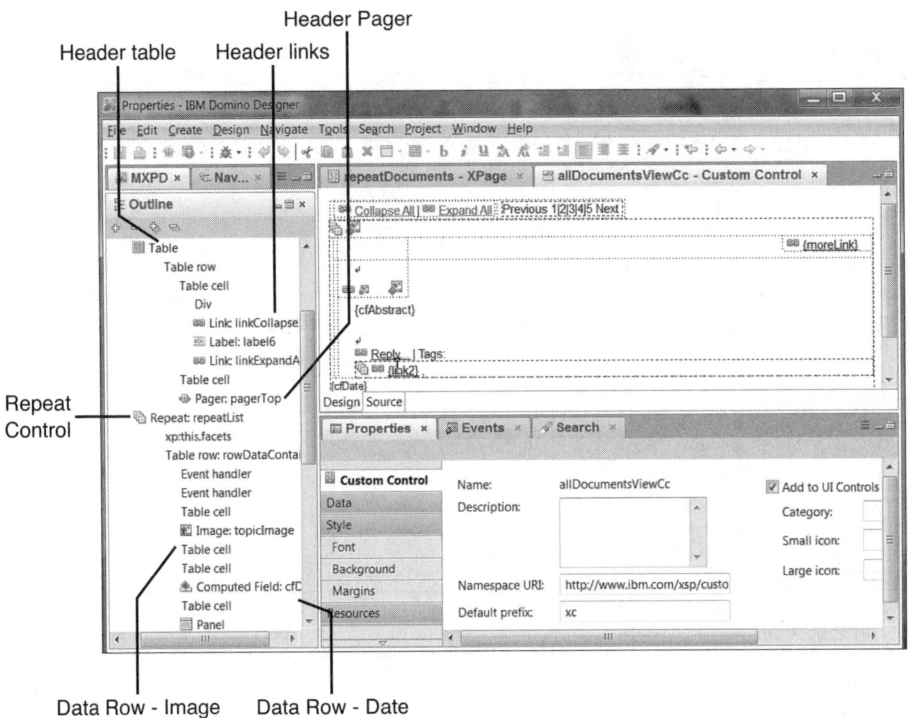

Figure 9.29 Outline structure of the all documents view

As you can see, the header and footer are encapsulated as HTML tables. This content is static, so an HTML table works fine for containment and layout. The middle section, which comprises all the data rows, is also contained in a HTML table, although this may not be immediately obvious. Note that the Repeat has a header facet, which emits an HTML `<table ...>` tag, and a footer facet, which closes the table tag with `</table>`. Again, header and footer facets are not repeated but just rendered once, so this sets up a middle table for the data rows. A table row is then repeated for each entry in the data source (**xpAllDocuments**) and the various table cells are populated with controls, and then bound, formatted, and scripted as required. The only element to be iterated over and repeated, therefore, is the HTML table row tags (`<tr>`), which makes the entire process efficient but, at the same time, well structured. This `Table | Repeat | Table` pattern is a recommended as a best practice for complex views of this nature.

Nested Repeats

Some of the tricks used in the data rows are definitely worth exploring. For example, when it was stated earlier that the Repeat control can contain arbitrary child controls, this does not exclude other Repeat control instances. There is a good example in the **allDocumentsViewCc.xsp** custom control of a nested Repeat being put to smart use. The particular snippet of XSP markup is displayed in Listing 9.11, with some comments added in bold script.

Listing 9.11 Nested Repeat Control Bound to a JavaScript Array

```
<!-- Nested Repeat control - note removeRepeat="true" -->
<xp:repeat id="repeatTags" rows="30" var="tagData"
      first="0" indexVar="tagIndex" repeatControls="false"
      removeRepeat="true"
      themeId="Repeat.Tags">
      <!-- Repeat is not bound to a View but to a Java array! -->
      <xp:this.value><![CDATA[#{javascript:
            // Category can be a single string or multi-text item
            var obj = rowData.getColumnValue("_Categories");
            var size = 0;
            var array = null;
            // must return an array regardless!
            if(typeof obj == "string"){
                  var str = obj.toString();
                  if(str != null){
                        array = new Array();
                        array[0] = str;
                        size = 1;
                  }
            }else if(typeof obj == "java.util.Vector"){
                  array = obj.toArray();
                  size = array.length;
            }
            return array;}]]>
      </xp:this.value>
      <!-- create a link for each item in the tagData array! -->
      <xp:link escape="true" id="link2" themeId="Link.person"
            text="#{javascript:tagData}" value="/byTag.xsp">
            <!-- set the ?categoryFilter param to the array item -->
            <xp:this.parameters>
                  <xp:parameter value="#{javascript:tagData;}"
                        name="categoryFilter">
                  </xp:parameter>
            </xp:this.parameters>
      </xp:link>
      <!-- only include a comma if multiple array items exist -->
      <xp:label value="," id="label5"
themeId="Text.commaSeparator">
<xp:this.rendered><![CDATA[#{javascript:
                  size > 1 && tagIndex < size - 1}]]>
                  </xp:this.rendered>
      </xp:label>
</xp:repeat>
```

This nested Repeat control is created on the fly, along with some other sibling controls, whenever the end-user expands a top level row using the **More** link. The Repeat control's value property does not in fact point to a view data source, as has been the norm up to now, but to a Java array that contains one or more tags, that is, tags are the contents of the **_Categories** multivalue field. You can also see this pattern used elsewhere in the sample application where Repeat controls are bound to attachment lists from rich text fields, and so forth. Anyway, within this particular nested Repeat, a Link control is created for each category found in the tag array. The link text is set to the tag text and the link value (URL) is set to the **byTag.xsp** XPage plus a `categoryFilter` parameter, which is also set to the tag text (for example, `/byTag.sp?categoryFilter=Government`). After all the links are generated, the Repeat removes itself from the component tree (`removeRepeat="true"`), because it is no longer required. Play with the sample application and see this feature in action. You can probably think of use cases for your own applications that would be well served using dynamic nested Repeats in this way.

The Rich Get Richer

One little amendment you could make to further enhance the rich nature of the Repeat control content is to insert the actual rich text into the dynamic row when the **More** link is clicked. Right now, it is the plain text stored in the **Abstract** column of the **xpAllDocuments** view that is displayed, but if you locate that value binding in the custom control (search `AllDocumentsViewCc.xsp` for *"cfAbstract"*), you could replace it, as shown in Listing 9.12.

Listing 9.12 Server-Side JavaScript Code to Extract HTML from Rich Text Fields Saved in MIME Format

```
// search for "Abstract" and comment out this next line of code
// return rowData.getColumnValue("Abstract");
// get the Notes document and body rich text field
var nd:NotesDocument = rowData.getDocument();
var mime = nd.getMIMEEntity("body");
// if it is MIME then you can passthrough as HTML
if (mime != null) {
      return mime.getContentAsText();
}
// Otherwise just return the plain text
else {
      return nd.getItemValueString("body");
}
```

You need to configure the **cfAbstract** Computed Field to have a content type of HTML. This has been done for you in the **allDocumentsViewCc** custom control, but the code is commented out. If you would like to see this feature in action, simply enable the code in Domino Designer. Figure 9.30 shows some sample rich content expanded in the repeated rows.

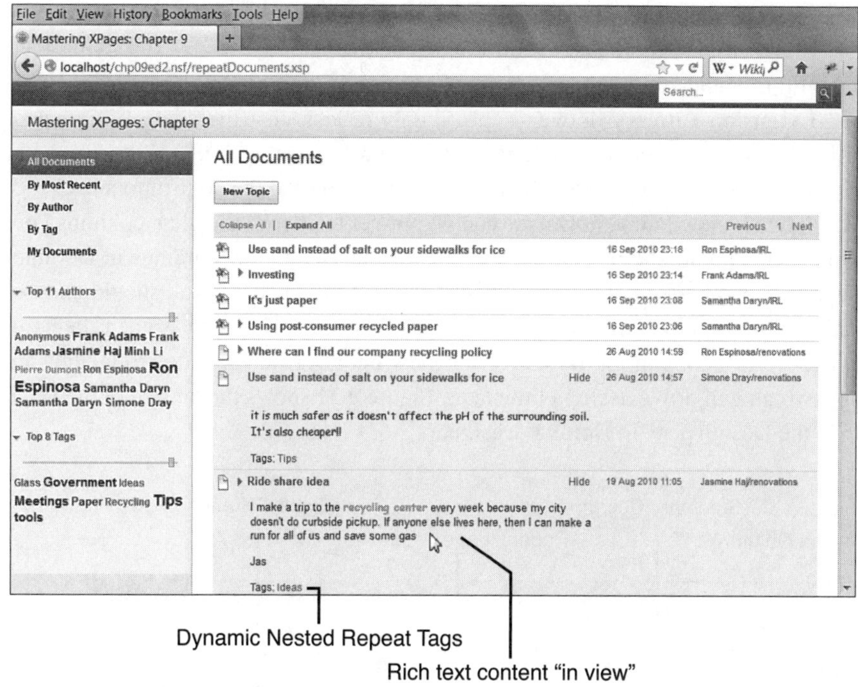

Figure 9.30 Expanded Rich Text Content in Repeat Control

Obviously, it is not efficient to open documents when building views, although this *only* occurs when the user clicks the **More** link, so the expense is only incurred on request and not for every repeated item. This example concludes our discussion of the Repeat Control.

Data View

The Data View control became an official part of the XPages runtime with the advent of 8.5.3 UP1 in December 2011. As of Notes/Domino 9.0.1 it has become the de facto view renderer control and features extensively in both the Discussion and Teamroom templates. Readers familiar with these templates will recognize that the sample application for this chapter, though based on the 9.0.1 template design, has various modifications. For instance, it has quite a few standalone XPages that serve as one-off examples of particular features, and it also has some pages whose design has been preserved from previous templates. These older pages are maintained so that examples used in various sections of this chapter remain valid. The **byTag.xsp.** XPage and its various custom controls for instance originate from the 8.5.3 Discussion template and are still used here to explain some interesting View Panel design capabilities. An interesting exercise would be to create a new **byTag** XPage using the Data View control and to compare that to the equivalent page in the latest template, which also uses the Data View. So, without further ado, you should roll up your sleeves and create a new XPage in Domino Designer.

The name used for this page in the sample application is **dataView.xsp**. After you create a new XPage, you need to find the Data View control on the palette. Perhaps surprisingly, it is not co-located with the other view controls in the **Container Controls** section—instead you can find it in the **Extension Library** drawer. (This simply reflects that the control originated from the Extension Library.) Simply drag and drop the control to the new XPage, and as with the View Panel, you will be provided with a helper dialog to help bind the control to a backend Domino view. Unlike the View Panel, however, you do not get to choose the view columns you want to work with at this point, and it's fair to say that working with view columns in Domino Designer can be a little cumbersome for this particular control. In any case, you should choose the **Extended Category** Domino view as the data source at this point. This view is not a standard part of the template—it is a copy of the **By Category** view but has been extended to include an **Abstract** column, which will prove useful a little later. Figure 9.31 shows the outline of the Data View, as shown in the Design pane in Domino Designer.

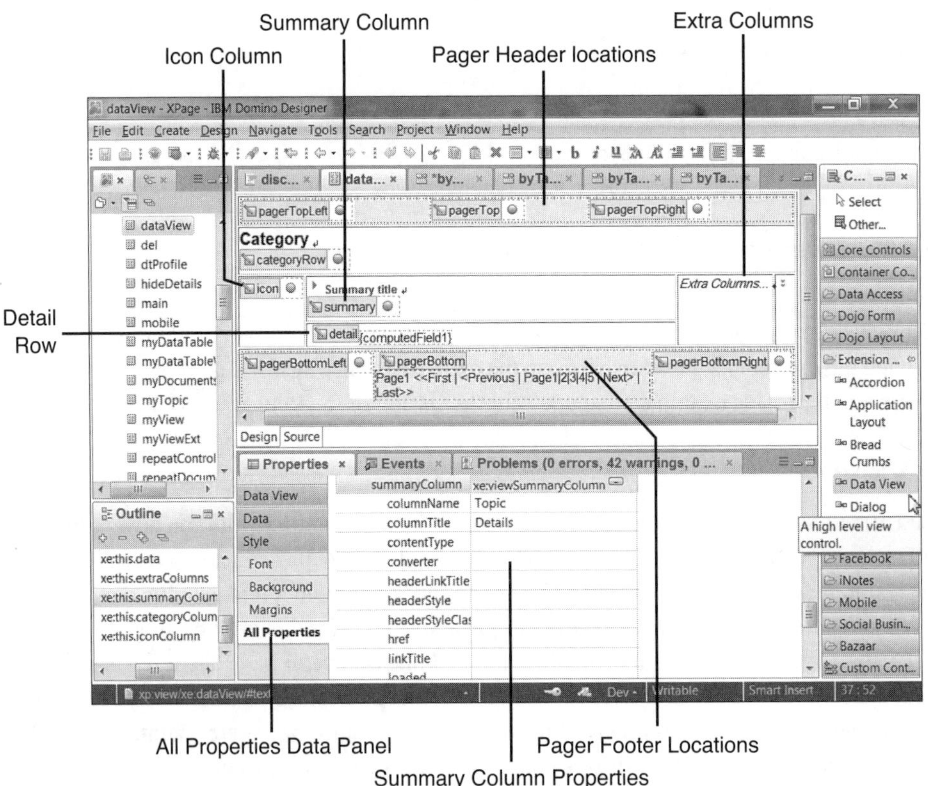

Figure 9.31 The Design Outline of the Data View in Domino Designer

The most significant properties of the Data View are shown in Figure 9.31 and summarized in Table 9.2. Although the Data View control has many other properties, you can build a powerful UI control using just these.

Table 9.2 Important Data View Properties

Name	Description
`summaryColumn`	The main column for display. This column is much front and central to the data view and should constitute the main theme of what you want to show.
`categoryColumn`	Name of the column to use for categorization. Must be defined as a categorized column in the Domino view.
`extraColumns`	A list of other columns to include in the rendered view.
`iconColumns`	A column used to display icons for any given row.
`detail`	A facet used to display the detailed information for any given row. This can be any arbitrary control, but computed fields are commonly used here.
`pagerTop*`	Three facets that enable pager controls to be optionally assigned to the header of the data view (`pagerTopLeft`, `pagerTop`, and `pagerTopRight`). Any arbitrary control can be used with this facet, but typical candidates would be the `<xp:Pager>` and `<xe:PagerSizes>`.
`pagerBottom*`	Ditto. Three facets that enable pager controls to be optionally assigned to the footer of the data view (`pagerBottomLeft`, `pagerBottom`, and `pagerBottomRight`). Any arbitrary control can be used with this facet, but typical candidates would be the `<xp:Pager>` and `<xe:PagerSizes>`.

Configuring a Basic Data View Control

If you were to preview the XPage immediately after the initial drag and drop, you would undoubtedly be underwhelmed (unless blank pages impress you) because all these important properties have yet to be assigned any meaningful values. So, the next task is to start filling in the blanks based on the properties referred to in Table 9.2.

Start by choosing a summary column because this forms the central plank of the view information you want to display. It represents the data item that will be of most prominence in the view—all other things will be subordinate to it. In this example, you should choose the **Topic** column in the Domino View as the Data View summary column. It is probably best to use the All Properties editor for this task (again, refer to Figure 9.31). You need to know the name of the Domino view column in advance because there is no metadata picker that will inspect the Domino view design and help you choose from a list. You can also specify other column properties at this time, like the `columnTitle` should you want to display titles as part of a view header.

Next, choose a category column in the same way. The **Extended Category** Domino view has one categorized column that defines your choice for you. To bind a Data View column to a Domino view column, simply specify the name of the Domino view column as the `columnName` property. If you want to dynamically compute a column instead, you can ignore the `columnName` property and focus on the `value` property. You can borrow from your previous View Panel adventures here and reuse some of the computed column logic in the Data View. Therefore, you can quickly come up with an initial rendition that includes summary, category, and extra columns, as summarized in Listing 9.13.

Listing 9.13 Data View Sample Based on Simple Column Definitions

```
<?xml version="1.0" encoding="UTF-8"?>
<xp:view xmlns:xp="http://www.ibm.com/xsp/core"
xmlns:xe="http://www.ibm.com/xsp/coreex">

    <xe:dataView id="dataView1" var="rowData"
        indexVar="rowIndex" rows="10" showCheckbox="true">
        <xe:this.data>
            <xp:dominoView var="view1"
                viewName="extCategory">
            </xp:dominoView>
        </xe:this.data>

        <xe:this.summaryColumn>
            <xe:viewSummaryColumn columnName="Topic"
                columnTitle="Details">
            </xe:viewSummaryColumn>
        </xe:this.summaryColumn>

        <xe:this.categoryColumn>
            <xe:viewCategoryColumn columnName="Categories">
            </xe:viewCategoryColumn>
        </xe:this.categoryColumn>

        <xe:this.extraColumns>
          <!-- Simple Binding -->
            <xe:viewExtraColumn columnName="$116"
                columnTitle="Date">
            </xe:viewExtraColumn>
          <!-- Computed Column -->
            <xe:viewExtraColumn columnTitle="Responses"
                style="text-align:center">
                <xe:this.value><![CDATA[#{javascript:
```

```
                var i:number = rowData.getDescendantCount();
                return i.toPrecision(0);}]]></xe:this.value>
        </xe:viewExtraColumn>
        <!-- Computed Column -->
        <xe:viewExtraColumn columnTitle="Row #"
            style="text-align:center">
            <xe:this.value><![CDATA[#{javascript:
                var i:number = rowIndex;
                return i.toPrecision(0);}]]></xe:this.value>
        </xe:viewExtraColumn>
    </xe:this.extraColumns>
  </xe:dataView>
</xp:view>
```

The markup in Listing 9.13 is saved as `dataViewWiP.xsp`. in the sample application and shows how a functional categorized Data View control can be created with just a few basic steps. On inspecting the source code, you already know the properties used on the `<xe:dominoView>` tag because they are already used with the View Panel. The view data source definition is basic, and after that there are just a number of Data View column definitions, which are self-explanatory—even the dynamic computed columns show how the logic created for previous View Panel examples can be simply re-applied here. Figure 9.32 show the results of reviewing the XPage.

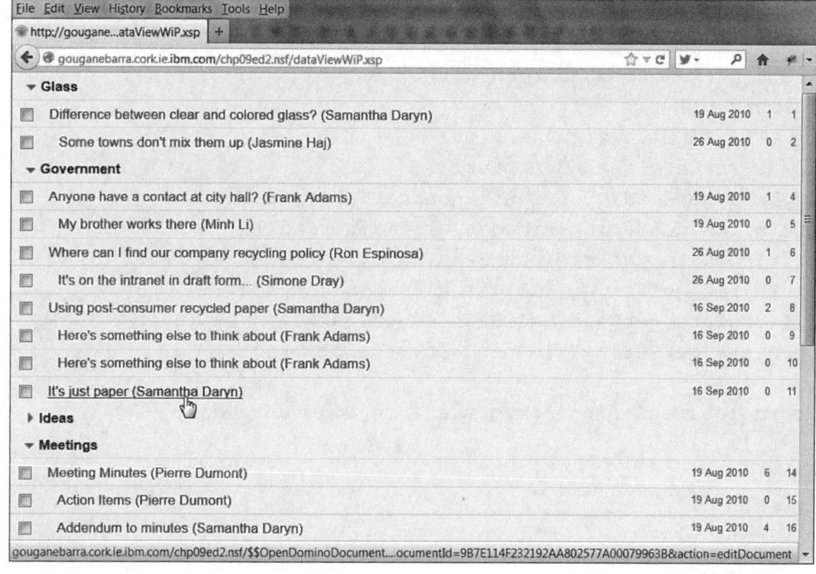

Figure 9.32 A Basic Data View Control

Using More Advanced Data View Control Features

To embellish the Data View you should start by adding an icon column. The purpose of this column is to visually identify a key characteristic of the row, and you've already used this technique in other views, whether it be displaying icons for read versus unread documents in a discussion application, message types in a mail application, and so forth. An icon column typically defines a number of icon entries and then displays a particular entry based on some characteristic of the row in question.

Listing 9.14 shows a powerful yet simple mechanism for displaying icons.. This snippet is taken directly from the 9.0.1 template and can be inserted directly into the current example as an immediate embellishment:

Listing 9.14 Data View Sample Based on Simple Column Definitions

```
<xe:this.iconColumn>
  <xe:viewIconColumn>
    <xe:this.icons>
      <xe:iconEntry>
        <xp:this.url><![CDATA[#{javascript:
          var level=rowData.getIndentLevel();
            if (rowData.getRead(userBean.canonicalName) && level == 0)
              {return "xpPostRead.gif";}
            else if(!rowData.getRead(userBean.canonicalName) && level == 0)
              {return "xpPostUnread.gif";}
            else if(rowData.getRead(userBean.canonicalName) && level > 0)
              {return "xpResponseRead.gif";}
            else
              {return "xpResponseUnread.gif";}
        }]]></xp:this.url>
        <xp:this.alt><![CDATA[#{javascript:
          var level=rowData.getIndentLevel();
          if (rowData.getRead(userBean.canonicalName) && level == 0)
            {return res.getString("images.alt.main.read");}
          else if(!rowData.getRead(userBean.canonicalName) && level == 0)
            {return res.getString("images.alt.main.unread");}
          else if(rowData.getRead(userBean.canonicalName) && level > 0)
            return res.getString("images.alt.repsone.read");}
          else
            {return res.getString("images.alt.repsone.unread");}
        }]]></xp:this.alt>
      </xe:iconEntry>
    </xe:this.icons>
  </xe:viewIconColumn>
</xe:this.iconColumn>
```

This snippet enables up to four different icons to be displayed per row. Any root level documents are regarded as postings, whereas everything else is a response to a posting. The Domino view entry API call `getIndentLevel()` is used to identify root level documents (those at the root or 0th level of the view) whereas the `getRead()` API is used to determine whether to display a read or unread icon. If you are puzzled by the userBean references, simply think of it as an automatic object that exists as part of the programming model that can be used at any time to retrieve information about the currently logged in user. You do not need to create this bean—it's created and populated for your programming convenience (more on this in Part IV, "Programmability"). These two API calls in concert with the userBean can determine which of the four icons to return as read/unread images for postings or response documents. The alternative text to display for these URLs is computed in an identical fashion. The strings that describe the images have been defined as resources, however, rather than literal strings, and therefore need to be extracted from a resource file. Resource files are used to enable application translation and that topic is dealt with in great detail in Chapter 18, "Internationalizaton." For now the resource file containing the string definitions must be imported into your XPage using a bundle tag like this under the resource section of the page:

```
<xp:bundle var="res" src="/strings.properties"></xp:bundle>
```

Perhaps the coolest feature of the Data View is its ability to dynamically inject detailed content for each row, so this should be the next job at hand now that you are finished with column definitions. To insert a detail row, drag and drop a control of your choice from the palette to the "detail" landing spot on the Design pane. Typically, you can use a Computed Field; although, it is not uncommon for developers to construct an aggregate control inside a panel and use that. This sample uses the former and simply binds it to the Abstract field in the Domino view using the following SSJS expression:

```
rowData.getColumnValue("Abstract")
```

Adding the dynamic detail is one thing, but to have it display, you must set the `collapsibleDetail` property on the Data View to `true`. This has the effect of introducing a twistie control to each row, which can show or hide the detail content. Think of the work needed to build this functionality using a Repeat control, whereas the Data View delivers it for free by simply enabling some properties. Note that if you want the dynamic detail to display by default when opening the XPage, you must set the `expandedDetails` property to `true`. Furthermore, you have the choice of serving up all the detail at one time when the page is rendered, meaning that no round-trip to the server is required when the detail row is expanded, or fetching the detail content on demand upon expansion via an AJAX request. The latter is the default, but you enforce the former by setting the `detailsOnClient` property to `true`.

Although the `collapsibleDetail` property must be set to `true` to introduce a twistie control for the detail row, two similarly named properties, `collapsibleRows` and `collapsibleCategory` if set to `false` will remove the standard twisties associated with response documents and category rows, respectively.

Finally, in much the same way as you dropped a Computed Field on the "detail" drop zone, you can drop a control like a pager on any of the six Pager hotspots shown in the Design pane for the Data View. You should experiment with this feature: Drop pagers on various locations and configure them differently to see what works best for your application (see next section). After completing these actions, if you inspect the generated source, you should observe that all the dropped controls end up in the facets section of the Data View markup, as shown in Listing 9.15.

Listing 9.15 Data View Facets

```
<xp:this.facets>
        <!-- Pager on bottom right -->
        <xp:pager layout="Previous Group Next" partialRefresh="true"
                id="pager1" xp:key="pagerBottomRight">
        </xp:pager>

        <!-- PagerSizes on bottom left -->
        <xe:pagerSizes id="pagerSizes1" sizes="5|10|25|50|100"
                xp:key="pagerBottomLeft">
        </xe:pagerSizes>

        <!-- detail row -->
        <xp:text escape="true" id="computedField1"
                xp:key="detail">
                <xp:this.value>
                <![CDATA[#{javascript:rowData.getColumnValue("Abstract");}]]>
                </xp:this.value>
        </xp:text>
</xp:this.facets>
```

The final version of this sample page is contained in **dataView.xsp** in the sample application, as shown in Figure 9.33.

> **TIP**
>
> The Notes In 9 site features two videos by Brad Balassaitis that explore the Data View in great detail. These great resources can be located at http://tinyurl.com/XPageDataViewEx1 and http://tinyurl.com/XPageDataViewEx2.

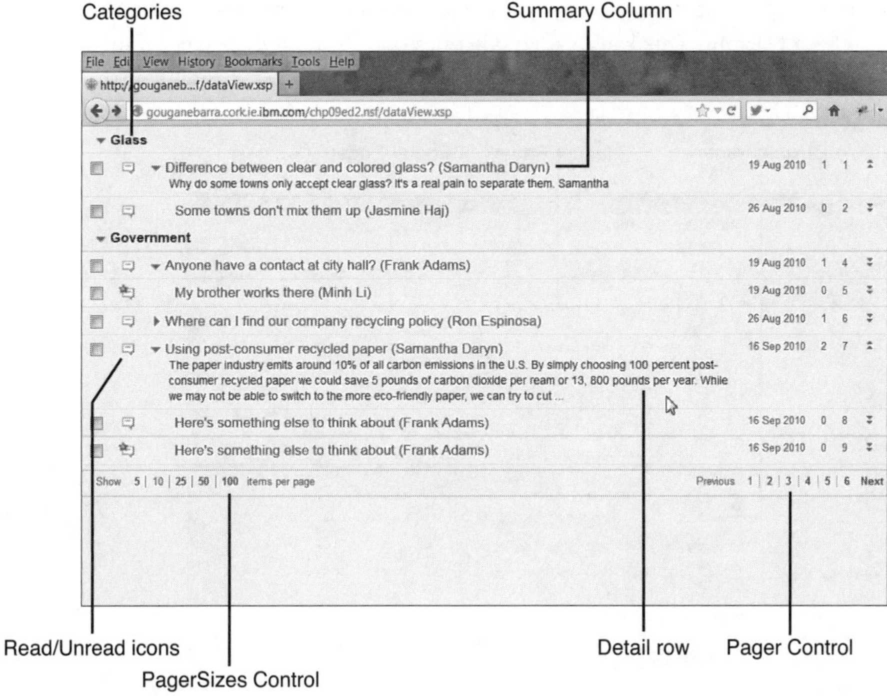

Figure 9.33 Data View Control Using Advanced Features

Some Fun with the Pager

After all the hard work done in this chapter, you might as well finish on a light note. The common view pager that you have worked with in various examples is actually a highly configurable control, even though it has only been used in its default state thus far. The next exercise shows how to transform the look and feel of your pager.

You should start by revisiting the **dataTable.xsp** XPage and making a new copy of this, called **dataTableExt.xsp**. In the new XPage, activate the **Source** pane and find the facets tag for the Data Table—careful not to accidentally pick the facets tag for one of the columns! Copy and paste the existing `<xp:pager>` tag that's already defined in the Data Table facets and then set `xp:key="header"` and `panelPosition="right"` on one of them. After completing this task, the Data Table should have two pagers: one on the right hand side of the header and one on the left hand side of the footer. Select the header pager in the **Outline** view and activate the WYSIWYG editor and **Pager** property panel.

The first thing you can do is apply different pager styles to the header pager (for example, Sample 1 through Sample 7), and preview or reload the XPage to see what features are exposed in the different canned styles. What's more interesting, however, is to play around with a custom layout. For this example, select the footer pager in the **Outline** view and change the **Pager style** combo box style to Custom. This causes a new list of controls to be displayed in the Property panel—select the ones shown in Figure 9.34.

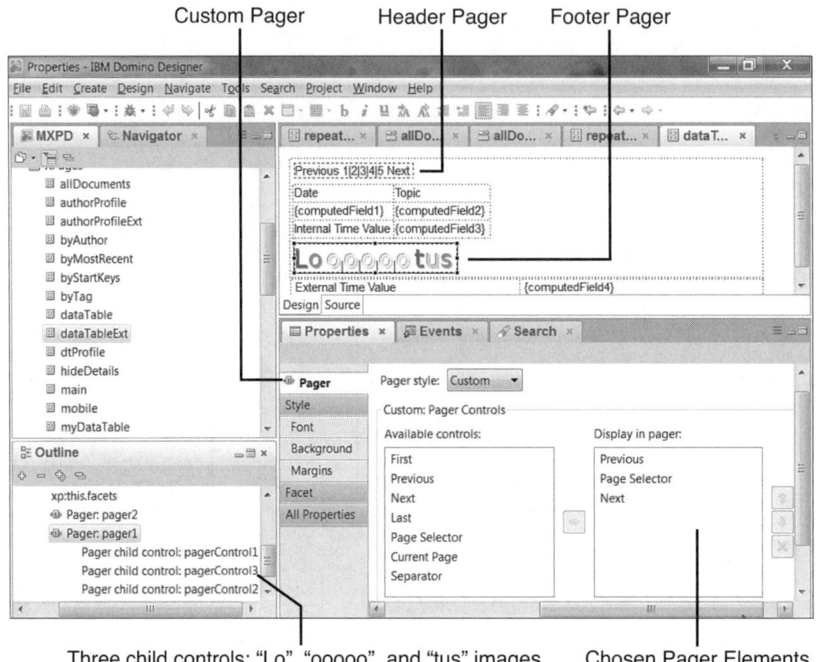

Figure 9.34 Working with a custom pager in Designer

In the **Outline** view, select each of the newly created three child controls in turn and assign images to them. The **Previous** control should be assigned "/Lo.gif", the **Group** control (Page Selector) should be assigned "/oooooo.gif", and the **Next** control should be assigned "/tus.gif". These image resources have been already added to **Chp09Ed2.nsf** for your convenience. In fact, a **dataTableExt.xsp** XPage is also included if you do not feel like building this example—it's been a long chapter! The updated markup for the Data Table facets tag should now look like Listing 9.16.

Listing 9.16 Custom Pager Definitions

```
<xp:this.facets>
    <xp:pager xp:key="header" id="pager2" for="dataTable1"
        partialRefresh="true" panelPosition="right">
    </xp:pager>
```

```
    <xp:pager xp:key="footer" id="pager1" for="dataTable1"
          partialRefresh="true" disableTheme="true">
          <xp:pagerControl id="pagerControl1" type="Previous"
                image="/Lo.gif">
          </xp:pagerControl>
          <xp:pagerControl id="pagerControl3" type="Group"
                image="/oooooo.gif">
          </xp:pagerControl>
          <xp:pagerControl id="pagerControl2" type="Next"
                image="/tus.gif">
          </xp:pagerControl>
    </xp:pager>
</xp:this.facets>
```

With this markup in place, preview the page. In Figure 9.35, observe that navigating on the footer pager updates the header pager state—as you would expect! So, even though the header and footer pagers no longer bear any visual resemblance to each other, their behaviors are identical.

Figure 9.35 Custom Loooooootus Pager

TIP

A new pager property was introduced in 8.5.2 called `alwaysCalculateLast`. Calculating the entry count in large categorized and/or hierarchical views can be expensive because the code has to navigate each view path to figure out the total count. Thus, the **Last** pager control was not always enabled in the Pager due to the cost associated with the calculation. If having a **Last** pager option is more important to you that any performance hits incurred as a result of calculating it, you should set `alwaysCalculateLast="true"` on the Pager control; you can find this property in the **basics** category of the **All Properties** sheet. This means that you always can jump to the end of the view no matter what!

Conclusion

This chapter extensively covered the main view container controls: the View Panel, Data Table, Repeat control, and Data View. You learned how to apply the lesser-used control properties, when to use one control over another, and how to customize the look and behavior in all cases. Hopefully, this material will help you build cool, slick, and efficient views that satisfy your own unique use cases. Go forth and view!

PART IV

Programmability

CHAPTER 10

Custom Controls

So far, you have been using the XPage design element as a container for all of your controls and other associated resources. In this chapter, you learn to refine this practice by using a slightly more specialized XPage design element—namely, the Custom Control. This chapter explains how to use Custom Controls effectively within your XPages applications and, as a result, save on development time by leveraging the reusable parts of your design.

Common design patterns can be identified in any strand of application development, regardless of the programming language, tool, or technology used to construct them. XPages application development is no different! As applications grow in size and complexity, development artifacts are often hurriedly duplicated or rehashed from one application to another. Custom Control helps eliminate such inefficient practices by promoting the encapsulation of common development assets into reusable components.

The concept underlying Custom Controls is by no means new! If you are a Domino developer, you are already familiar with the Domino form and subform design elements and how they work together. That is, reusable pieces of forms can be abstracted as subforms. And these little building blocks can then be reassembled in different ways to build many other forms and, thus, reduce bloat and increase maintainability in your application design. XPages and Custom Controls have a similar relationship, although it is not confined to simple containment.

If you are a Java developer, you can relate to similar concepts in various other Java development frameworks. For example, JSF actually extends the JavaServer Pages (JSP) framework, which allows developers to create application artifacts known as tag libraries. Such artifacts typically contain one or more tag declarations along with their constituent attribute declarations and associated Java classes—where the classes provide the implementation of the tag. Within JSP markup, this tag can be reused within a page or in any number of pages and across applications, depending on the deployment of the tag library. Custom Controls provide the same degree of reusability for XPages application, but do so in a more discrete manner (for example, the application developer does not need to know anything about tag libraries or Java programming). In fact, the process of creating a Custom Control is done within Domino Designer using the same WYSIWYG facilities used to create an XPage!

Perhaps the first question to explore is what exactly does a Custom Control provide that cannot be achieved directly with an XPage? The explanation will undoubtedly change the way you design and implement your XPages applications going forward. I say this based on my own personal experience of various web application-development technologies. As a fledging "XPager," I started by assembling numerous XPages and linking with them with some other resources to build my application. But then, I quickly discovered a degree of duplication and complexity was creeping into my early creations, making them difficult to maintain. When I learned about Custom Controls, I was able to redefine the structure of my XPages applications. Pretty quickly, just by looking at a screen mockup or whiteboard, I found myself zoning off areas of the design and designating them as Custom Control candidates. Life was never the same again!

Divide and Conquer

Simply put, Custom Controls allow you to design an application by dividing it up into little building blocks. By considering the "look and feel" elements of an application, you can quickly create numerous Custom Controls to represent these building blocks. The most beneficial characteristic of a Custom Control is the ability to use it in several places within the same XPage, across several XPages, or applications. This design element certainly lends itself well to modular design and implementation techniques in a team-based environment, where an entire application can be farmed out for development across the team in a loosely coupled manner. This team-based effort should, of course, be supported by a design specification from a User Interface design team. Such a specification would describe the inputs and outputs of the Custom Control as a form of contract similar to function or method specifications seen in several programming languages today.

The scoping rules for Custom Controls embodied within the XPages runtime are another powerful feature. Each time you include a Custom Control on an XPage, it is instantiated as a unique instance, and its constituent controls and scripting logic are sandboxed within that instance. This allows multiple instances of the same Custom Control to live on the same XPage at runtime without corrupting data or colliding with named controls within the Custom Control. You learn more on how these features can be exercised in the upcoming sections, "Using Property Definitions," and "Using the compositeData Object."

Before starting with some Custom Controls examples, it is important to understand that this design element can be used for two distinctly different purposes within an application. It is imperative to explain this early on to establish two distinct best practice design patterns that should be applied rigorously when creating Custom Controls in your applications:

- A Custom Control can be used as an "aggregate container" for the purpose of specialized control composition (such as bringing together several XPages controls into one place for a defined purpose). This allows assets to be developed once and reused extensively within an application or across applications. Production examples that I have seen include Tag Clouds, Menus, Search controls, and so on—the opportunities for encapsulation of generically reusable controls and application logic is endless and one of the biggest reasons to use Custom Controls in the first place! You learn more on this subject in the section "Aggregate Container Pattern."

- A Custom Control can be used as a "layout container" wherein structural elements such as `TABLE`, `SPAN`, or `DIV` elements and associated CSS style classes are defined. Including `Editable Areas` within this structure allows the addition of other arbitrary controls in this layout container at a later time. This function is highly reusable, and can save a lot of time in actually putting together the wire-frame of an application. You learn more on this subject in the section, "Layout Container Pattern."

Both of these best practice design patterns can benefit you in developing and maintaining an application. By clearly defining the purpose of a Custom Control and segregating "look" versus "feel" aspects into appropriate Custom Controls, your applications become highly reusable and easily maintained.

Getting Started with Custom Controls

Before you start, download the **Chp10Ed2.nsf** application provided online to run through the exercises throughout this chapter. You can access this file at `www.ibmpressbooks.com/title/9780133373370`. Now, create an XPage in Domino Designer within the **Chp10Ed2.nsf** application, name it **foo**, and save it. For now, leave this empty and open within Domino Designer. In the Applications navigator, select the **Custom Control**s navigator entry—this is the next direct sibling to the XPages design element. Right-click the Custom Controls design element and choose the **New Custom Control** option from the context menu. This invokes a dialog that allows you to name the Custom Control, as shown in Figure 10.1. Simply give it the name **bar** and click the **OK** button. (Note: The *Comment* field is optional, and the current database is already specified as a default.) After this is created, save it and leave it open in Domino Designer.

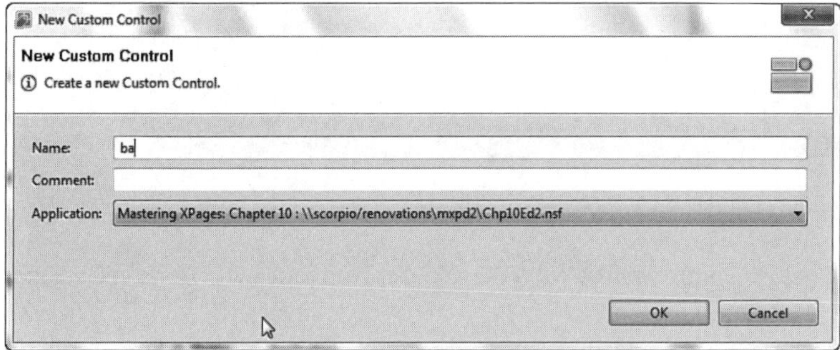

Figure 10.1 Create new Custom Control dialog for bar in Designer

As you can see in Domino Designer, a Custom Control is presented using the same WYSIWYG editor as provided for the XPage. A Custom Control does, in fact, share the same file extension under-the-hood as an XPage (**.xsp** extension). But, many key differences exist between an XPage and Custom Control for good reasons. One major difference is that, although both elements share the same file extension, a Custom Control cannot be viewed directly on the web or on the client in the same manner as a standalone XPage. As Figure 10.2 shows, by simply selecting the newly created **bar** Custom Control in the application navigator, the preview buttons become disabled within the main Designer toolbar. Note that hitting a Custom Control in a browser directly using an XSP URL also does not work—only a security exception is raised. Therefore, to preview a Custom Control, it must be embedded within an XPage. This holds true regardless of whether you are using a local preview server or deploying to a full-scale server.

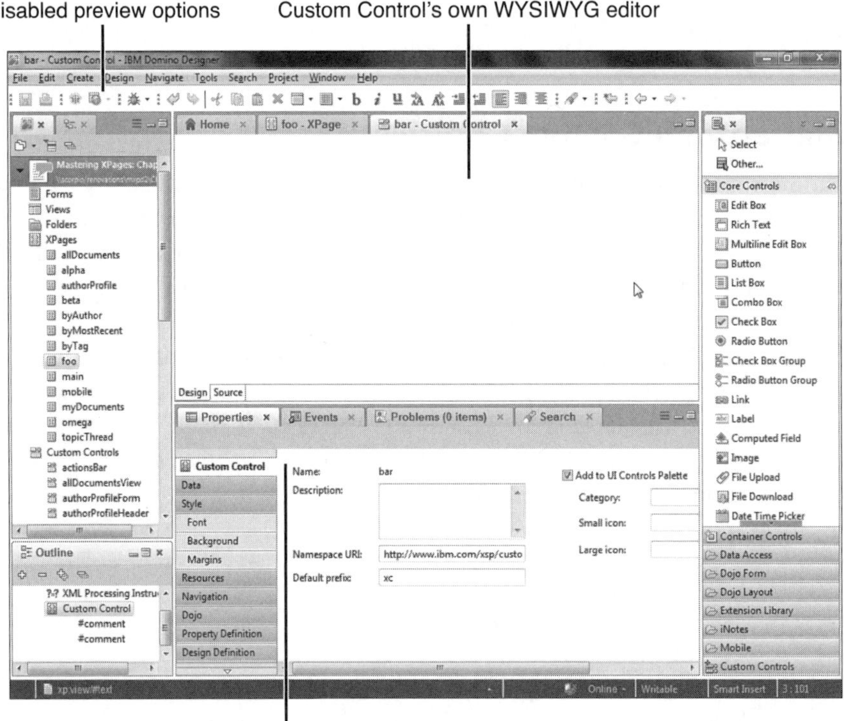

Figure 10.2 New bar Custom Control with WYSIWYG and disabled preview options in Designer

So, the next objective is to preview the **bar** Custom Control by using Designer's previewing capabilities. To do this, first of all, give focus to the **foo** XPage in Domino Designer by clicking in the editor. Now, you find a reference to **bar** within the Custom Control category in the control palette, as shown in Figure 10.3.

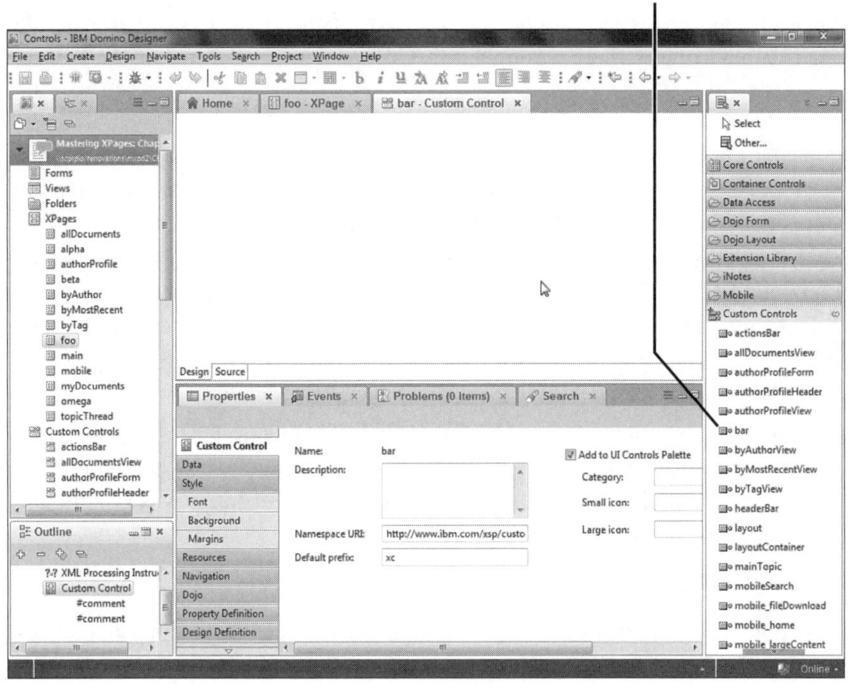

Figure 10.3 Bar Custom Control within the Custom Controls category in the control palette

Simply drag-and-drop the **bar** entry from the control palette to the **foo** XPage, and it is automatically inserted into the XPage. With the **bar** instance focused within the **foo** XPage, you see that the property sheet below the editor now contains properties associated with the newly created **bar** instance. The `name` property is blank by default, so for this example, specify one, such as *bar1*. As described in Chapter 3, "Building Your First XPages Application," the **Source** editor in Designer allows you to view the underlying XSP source markup—note that this is also the case for Custom Controls. If you activate the **Source** editor, you see a tag for **bar** inserted in the markup, as shown in Listing 10.1. (Note how the *name* is inserted as the *id* within the markup.)

Listing 10.1 XSP Markup of the foo XPage with the Bar Custom Control Tag Inserted

```
<?xml version="1.0" encoding="UTF-8"?>
<xp:view xmlns:xp="http://www.ibm.com/xsp/core"
xmlns:xc="http://www.ibm.com/xsp/custom">
<xc:bar id="bar1"></xc:bar>
</xp:view>
```

Another important aspect of the **Custom Control markup** is the declaration of two different XML namespaces on the `<xp:view>` tag, as shown in Listing 10.1. Prior to creating the instance of the **bar** Custom Control, there was only one XML namespace defined on the XPage:

```
xmlns:xp="http://www.ibm.com/xsp/core"
```

This default namespace declares the tag prefix `xp:` that you see before each XPage tag (for example, `<xp:view>`). Note, however, that the **bar** Custom Control tag now has its own distinct tag prefix of `xc:` (ie: `<xc:bar>`), and the namespace URI is different than that of the `xp:` prefix. It has also been automatically inserted onto the `<xp:view>` tag for you when you dropped the Custom Control on your XPage. These namespace declarations are a scoping mechanism of the underlying XML language to ensure that different tag definitions can be mixed within the same XPage without duplication. The benefit, therefore, is that different Custom Control tag declarations can coexist within the same XPage.

The independence that is granted to Custom Controls by this namespace feature is vital. Suppose that you develop a reusable Custom Control that you make publicly available for consumption within any XPages application. The name you assign to this control was **Gizmo**, and the prefix and namespace look like this:

```
xmlns:fb="http://www.foobar.com/gizmo"
```

Now, suppose that another XPages developer creates a different Custom Control, makes it publicly available, and names it the **Gizmo**...do you see a potential problem? If the two Custom Controls are ever included within the same application design, how can they be distinguished? The naming conflict is averted by specifying a unique prefix and namespace. For example, if the second Custom Control comes from the imaginatively named XYZ Corporation, and that name is used to scope the Custom Control, the tag definition should look like this:

```
xmlns:xyz="http://www.xyz.com/customcontrols"
```

In this example, an XPage application can reliably use both Custom Controls because of the uniqueness of the tag definitions. The resultant XPage markup is shown in Listing 10.2.

Listing 10.2 XPage Using Two Unique Versions of Custom Controls Named Gizmo

```
<?xml version="1.0" encoding="UTF-8"?>
<xp:view xmlns:xp="http://www.ibm.com/xsp/core"
xmlns:fb="http://www.foobar.com/gizmo"
xmlns:xyz="http://www.xyz.com/customcontrols">
<fb:Gizmo id="gizmo1"></fb:Gizmo>
<xyz:Gizmo id="gizmo2"></xyz:Gizmo>
</xp:view>
```

When you create a Custom Control, Domino Designer automatically applies the default prefix and namespace URI to your control, as shown in Figure 10.4. If you want to change these to your own settings, do so by specifying the values within the **Custom Control** property sheet, as shown in Figure 10.4.

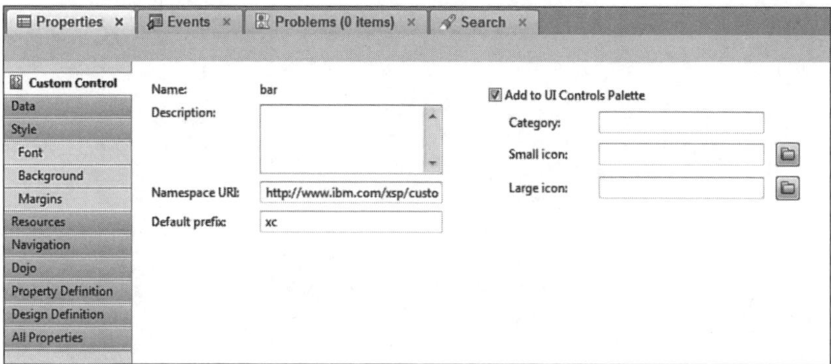

Figure 10.4 Custom Control property sheet, where you can apply a unique prefix and namespace URI

TIP

When specifying your own prefix and namespace URI values, try to make the prefix an acronym of your company name, the associated Custom Control, or a combination of both. Also, for the namespace URI, it is a recognized industry standard to always specify this value to be your company's Internet address. Categories beneath this can, of course, be represented by one or more trailing forward slashes to maintain uniqueness within your own Custom Control libraries. Note that this value only needs to be unique within the context of the application using it—it does not need to be resolvable on the Internet!

Moving on from this, before previewing the **foo** and **bar** example, it is useful to do a couple of extra things. First, add a text label to **bar** so that it is visible when previewed; otherwise, you will see a blank page! Click the Editor tab for the **bar** Custom Control to give it focus, and then drag-and-drop a `Label` control from the **Core Controls** category of the control palette. Within the **Properties** view below the editor, assign `Name` and `Label` values, say *label1* and *Hello World!*, respectively (see Figure 10.5).

You should also apply the following style definition to the `style` property of the <xp:view> tag by clicking the tag and selecting **All Properties > Styling > Style** from the properties panel:

```
margin:10px;padding:10px;width:300px;text-align:center;
```

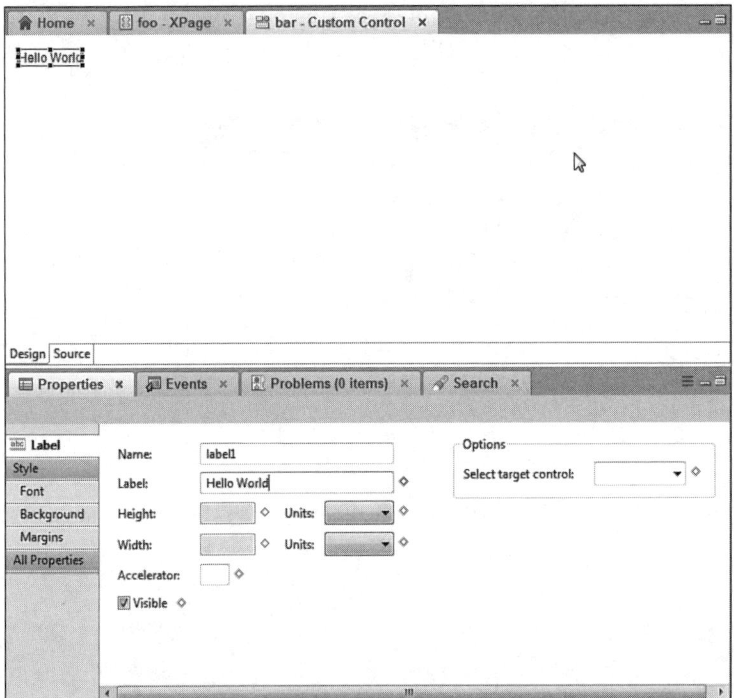

Figure 10.5 Applying the Label name and Label value within the Properties view in Designer

Also, apply the following style definition to the `style` property of the `Label` you just dropped:

```
font-weight:bold;font-style:italic;font-size:14pt;
```

Having saved your changes, you should have something similar to the XSP markup shown in Listing 10.3.

Listing 10.3 XSP Markup for Bar with the Label Name, Value, and Style, and View Style Applied

```
<?xml version="1.0" encoding="UTF-8"?>
<xp:view xmlns:xp="http://www.ibm.com/xsp/core"
style="margin:10px;padding:10px;width:300px;text-align:center;">
<xp:label value="Hello World!"
id="titleLabel"
style="font-weight:bold;font-style:italic;color:rgb(0,0,255);
➥font-size:14pt">
</xp:label>
</xp:view>
```

Next, reselect the **foo** XPage and drag-and-drop a second instance of the **bar** Custom Control onto the XPage—aim for just after the first instance with a couple of new lines in between. Name this instance *bar2* and save your changes. You can now preview **foo** as an XPage in its entirety within Domino Designer. The key point in previewing now is the fact that the **foo** XPage now includes two instances of the **bar** Custom Control, as shown in Figure 10.6.

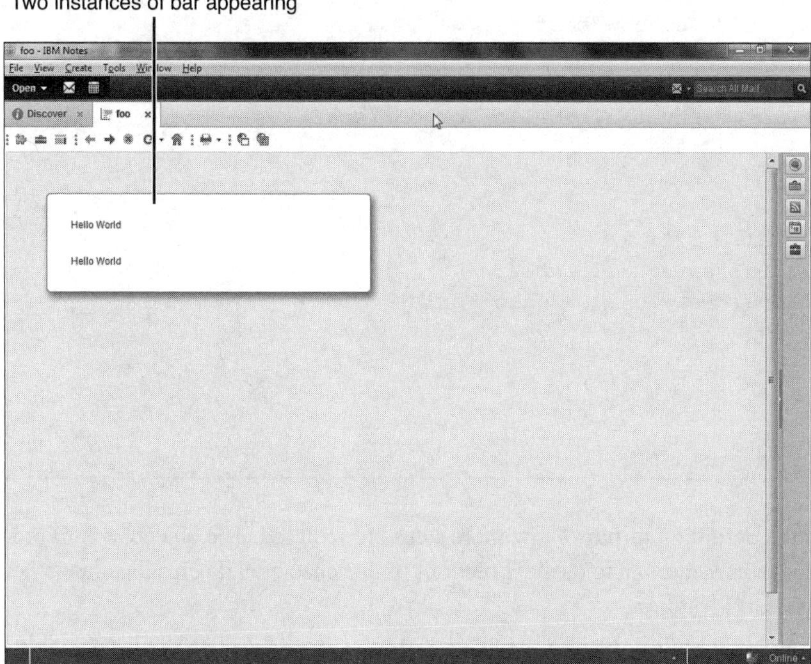

Figure 10.6 Previewing the foo XPage with two instances of the bar Custom Control

It is interesting to explore the emitted HTML markup for the **foo** XPage to gain an understanding of how the XPages runtime actually handles the naming of elements. Select the **View page source** option within the browser or client, and you should see something similar to Listing 10.4. Note that the `id` attributes emitted in the markup are expanded with fully namespaced identifiers. That is to say, for a given element, its `id` is resolvable from the root element through to itself. In this example, the root element has an `id` with the value **view:_id1**. This is then prefixed to all the child element `id` values. Nested children also maintain this convention of prefixing the parent `id` value. Therefore, the two instances of a Custom Control embedded in any XPage have unique, resolvable `id` attributes, as shown in Listing 10.4. This is an important feature of Custom Controls, and it ensures that an instance of any given Custom Control and its contained controls have unique identifiers. This is also especially important for HTML DOM programming using client-side JavaScript.

Listing 10.4 Browser Source Snippet for foo XPage with bar1 and bar2 in the Markup

```
<html>
      ...
<body ...>
<form id="view:_id1" method="post" ...>
<div id="view:_id1:bar1">
<span id="view:_id1:bar1:titleLabel"
class="xspTextLabel" style=...>Hello World!</span>
</div>
<br>
<br>
<div id="view:_id1:bar2">
<span id="view:_id1:bar2:titleLabel"
class="xspTextLabel" style=...>Hello World!</span>
</div>
                    ...
</form>
</body>
</html>
```

To complete the definition of **bar**, a few more steps are required. The objective is to produce an example that carries through to the next sections of this chapter and helps illustrate other important Custom Control features.

With the **bar** Custom Control focused within the editor, click the **Label** you placed on the Custom Control earlier and use the right-arrow key to move to the right-hand side of it. Now, hit ***Enter*** a few times to create two new line breaks. Drag-and-drop a `Computed Field` from the **Core Controls** category in the control palette. Repeat the same activity for the `Label` and give this control the name *messageField*. Again, create two new line breaks after this control and drag-and-drop an `Edit Box` at the current position after the line breaks. Give this control the name *messageText*. Again, create a few new line breaks, drag-and-drop a `Button`, and name this *replyButton*. After saving your additions, you end up with a **bar** Custom Control that's similar to Figure 10.7.

Upon completion of this exercise, you have created a Custom Control and added controls to it. You have worked with Custom Controls using both the WYSIWYG editor and the underlying source editor, and you have also added two instances of a Custom Control to an XPage. You have previewed the aggregated result and examined the emitted source code. ID resolution, tag prefixes, and namespaces have also been explained. Thus, you are now ready to explore some of the more advanced aspects of Custom Controls. Taking the example that you just constructed, you now learn how a Custom Control can be made into a configurable runtime object with *its own tag properties* using *Property Definitions* and how you can access these in JavaScript by using the `compositeData` object. You also learn how scripting objects and variables are protected from data corruption and object collisions.

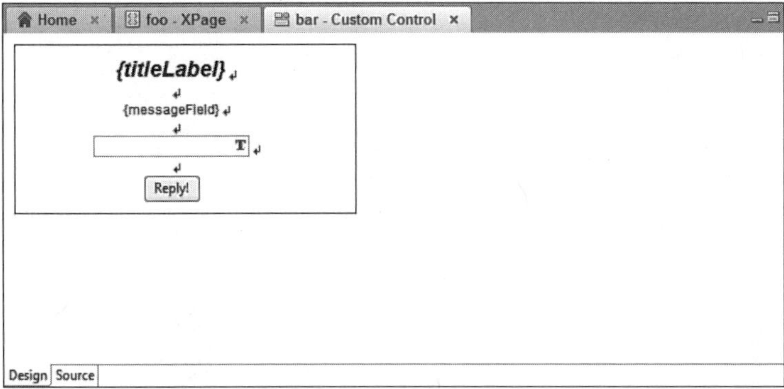

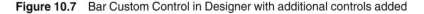

Figure 10.7 Bar Custom Control in Designer with additional controls added

Using Property Definitions

Property Definitions enhance the power of Custom Controls. They provide a means of assigning custom values and behaviors to individual Custom Control instances. In terms of design-time support, Domino Designer allows you to manage Property Definitions through the **Properties** view, and it provides a range of specialized property editors that help you pick everything from time-zone values to style classes rather than entering these values manually. You can also configure the design-time metadata of your Property Definitions so that the assignment of property values is restricted to the precise specification of the metadata definition. From a runtime perspective, you can use server-side JavaScript to dynamically manage the exposed properties on any given Custom Control. Scripting provides a communication mechanism across Custom Controls and establishes the need for the scoping rules mentioned earlier to protect and encapsulate data and objects within an instance of a Custom Control.

To begin an exploration of these concepts, open the **bar** Custom Control you created earlier within Domino Designer (if it is not already open). Ensure that the `<xp:view>` tag is the current context within the **Properties** view. You can use the **Outline** view to give focus to this tag by expanding the hierarchy of the Custom Control within the view and clicking the **Custom Control** node, as shown in Figure 10.8.

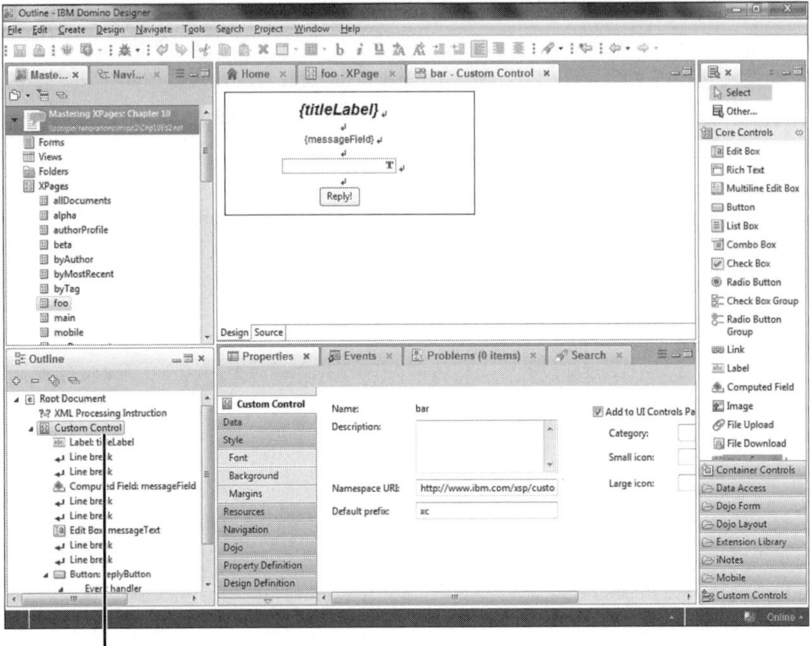

Using the Outline to focus the view root

Figure 10.8 Using the Outline view to select and give focus to the <xp:view> tag in bar

> **TIP**
>
> The Properties view is context-sensitive to whatever XPage markup tag is currently selected within the Outline view or the actual XPage source editor. The same applies to the WYSIWYG editor.

The **Properties** view is now populated with the supported properties of the Custom Control (or the `<xp:view>` tag, also referred to as the *root* tag). One of the property panels displayed within the **Properties** view is the **Property Definition** panel, and you should now click this panel. This UI element is unique to Custom Controls and allows you to manage any specialized properties associated with the control. These extended properties are an extra set supported by the Custom Control, above and beyond the standard properties that you can see in the **All Properties** panel and other panels, such as the Data and Style panels.

Every control and action on an XPage has a predefined and published set of properties, so this notion of being able to extend the runtime interface of your XPages application is a powerful one and one of the greatest application-development tools you can find within the XPages toolbox! Having clicked the **Property Definition** panel, you are presented with numerous actions to manage custom properties, some of which are disabled when no extended properties have been defined. The two actions of interest here are the **New Property** and **New Group** actions. The former enables you to specify a new property that is supported by the Custom Control (fairly obvious, based on its caption); however, the latter deserves more explanation.

The notion of custom properties is not only bound to simple properties with single instances, but in fact, allows the definition of simple and complex custom properties with single or multiple instances. The *New Group* action allows you to define a new group that contains one or more custom properties. Essentially, this action enables you to create a named group with several constituent subproperties and possibly more subgroups of properties. Within the XPages runtime, a property group is held within a `com.ibm.xsp.binding.PropertyMap` instance. Use cases for this type of property can be many-fold, where the most obvious uses are in defining options to drive the contents within a menu and submenus contained within the associated Custom Control, for example.

If you click the **New Property** action, the editor loads a new blank property for which you need to define a name and other attributes. The name defaults to *property_1*, but change this to the name *title* within the **name** field. Note this must be a single-string value and no special characters can be used; in fact, Domino Designer does not allow you to input any illegal characters into this particular field! Repeat this action two more times so you have three new properties declared on the **bar** Custom Control. Change the names of the last two you created to *message* and *senderId*, respectively. All three properties are now defined with the default type of `string` and without any other metadata set at this point, as shown in Figure 10.9.

Leaving the example in its current state, take a close look at the **Property Definition** panel to gain a better understanding of what it actually enables you to do. As Figure 10.10 illustrates, you can configure various design-time metadata for a custom property by using the **Property Definition** panel under the **Property** tab. Two other types of design-time metadata can also be set under the **Validation** and **Visible** tabs within the Property Definition panel. The **Property** tab manages the type-centric metadata. The **Validation** tab contains the rules for constraining the property value and requisite need of a property within Domino Designer at design-time. The **Visible** tab contains the settings that control exposure of the property within the Domino Designer editors at design-time, based on a given precondition within the XSP markup. Essentially, these three different categories of design-time metadata all manage the configuration of a custom property within the Domino Designer editors before an XPage or Custom Control even gets compiled. The following sections describe these three tabs for managing metadata in detail.

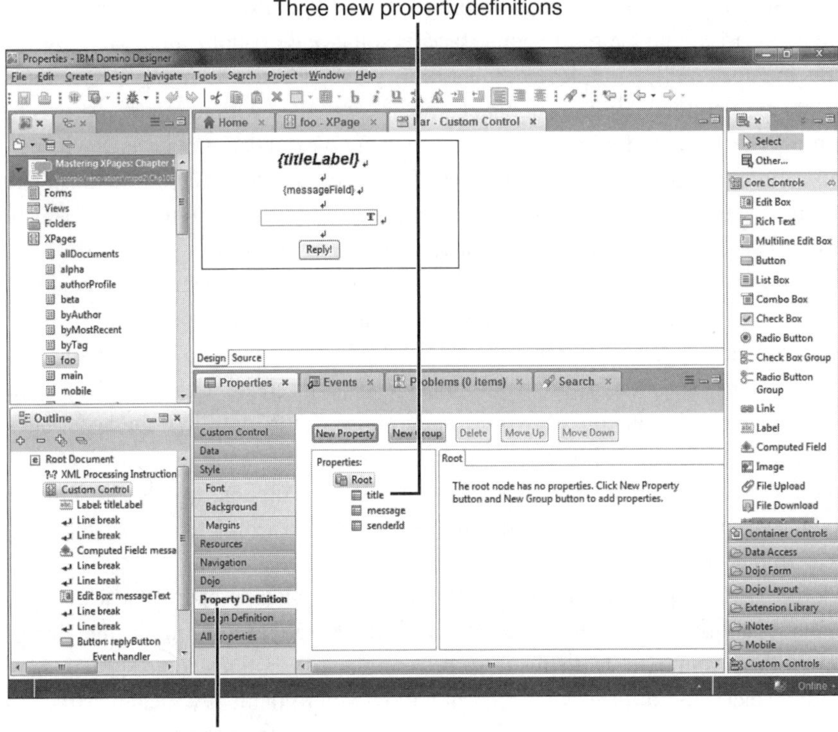

Figure 10.9 Three new properties defined on bar using the Property Definition panel

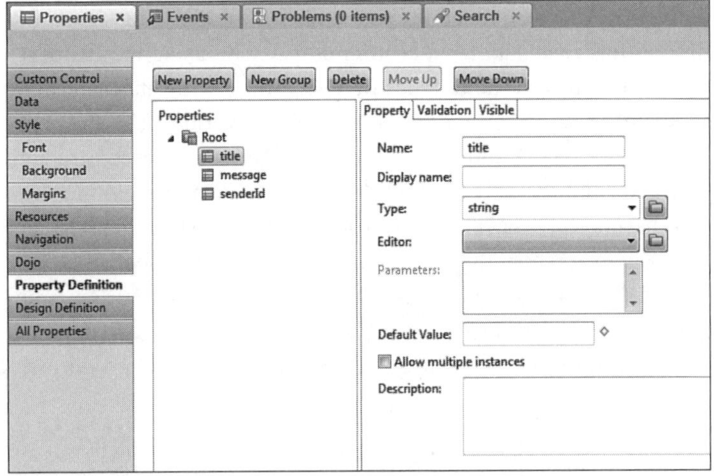

Figure 10.10 Property tab within the Property Definition panel

Property Tab

As shown in Figure 10.10, the **Property** tab contains a variety of settings applicable to a custom property. The **Name** field, as you have already learned, specifies a meaningful name for your property and must be declared as a single-string value with no special characters. The **Display name** is different in that it is only used to bubble a text value into the caption for the property in the **All Properties** panel for the Custom Control. You are free to give this a multivalued string value that can contain special characters. The **Type** field is where things get interesting. When you try to set a custom property on a Custom Control instance with a static value, the type of the static value is evaluated by Domino Designer to ensure that you are applying a value compatible with the data type specified in its **Property Definition** metadata. Setting a static value that does not successfully typecast to the data type specified for a property type results in the XPage or Custom Control not being compiled by Domino Designer and an error being raised within the **Problems** view indicating the error, as shown in Figure 10.11.

Error indicated within XSP markup

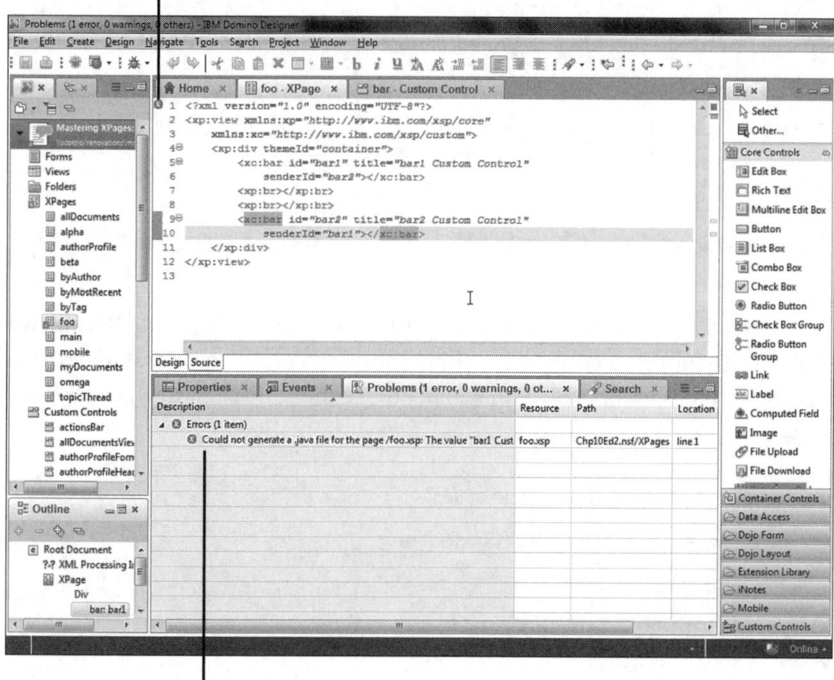

Error also logged in Problems view

Figure 10.11 Incorrectly set static boolean value applied to a custom property with a data type of string

Computed values do not get handled in this way as the computed expression typically contains logic that is evaluated on the server side when the application is running. (The value cannot be determined at design time and thus cannot be validated by Domino Designer.) Such computed values result in the successful design time compilation of the XPage or Custom Control, even if the result of the expression does not typecast to the specified custom property data type. Therefore, the onus is on you, as the developer of the application logic, to properly handle the result of such expressions within the context of the runtime environment.

The **Editor** field is typically used in conjunction with the **Type** and **Parameters** fields to specify the appropriate editor to use when choosing a value for a property of that type. For example, if you specify the **Type** of a property to be `boolean` and the **Editor** to be a *boolean checkbox*, when you set the value of this property on an instance of the Custom Control, you are presented with a checkbox control to assist you, as shown in Figure 10.12.

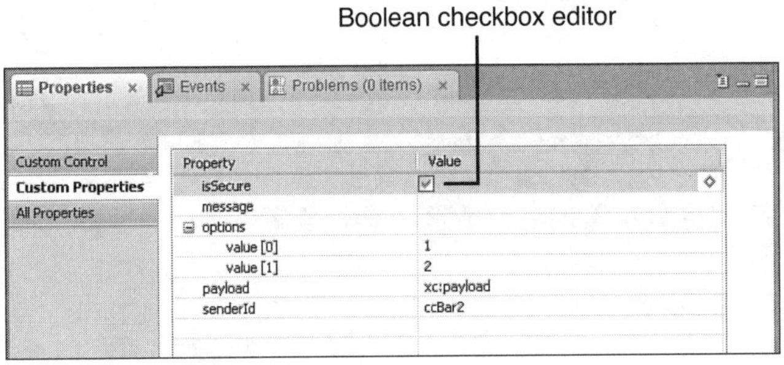

Boolean checkbox editor

Figure 10.12 Custom boolean property with its boolean checkbox editor displayed

Likewise, if you set the type to be `int`, and the **Editor** to be a *comboBox*, the **Parameters** field becomes enabled. If you then specify a multiline list of values for the **Parameters**, such as 0, 1, 2, 3... and so on, these will populate the combobox editor at design time, as shown in Figure 10.13.

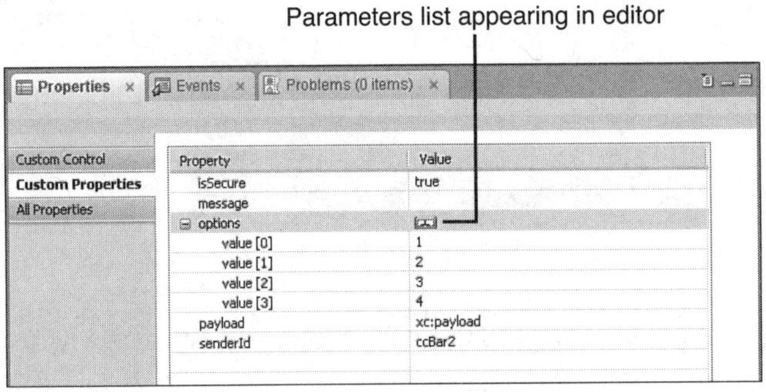

Parameters list appearing in editor

Figure 10.13 Custom int property with its combobox editor displayed with the Parameters list

One interesting type/editor combination that you can also leverage is the `java.lang.Object` type and the **Method Binding** editor. This combination enables you to assign the server-side JavaScript editor to the custom property as its design-time editor. You can then specify a server-side JavaScript expression for the property, or more importantly, use it to pass objects through the custom property `compositeData` object. A good example of using this approach is when you're working with a `NotesDocument` or `NotesView` object. Essentially, you can pass (*pass-by-reference*, in fact) an instance of either of these two classes into your Custom Control. Then, within the Custom Control, you can access the referenced object, as shown in Listing 10.5.

Listing 10.5 Accessing the Pass-By-Reference NotesView Instance Inside a Custom Control

```
<?xml version="1.0" encoding="UTF-8"?>
<xp:view xmlns:xp="http://www.ibm.com/xsp/core">
<xp:this.afterPageLoad>
<![CDATA[#{javascript:// get the pass-by-reference view...
if(null != compositeData.myView){
var ndc = compositeData.myView.getAllEntries();
if(null != ndc){
print("Count: " + ndc.getCount());
                        }
                  }
         }]]>
</xp:this.afterPageLoad>
</xp:view>
```

This same behavior follows through for any editor you select for a custom property. The important thing is to select an appropriate editor to correspond with the expected property type. The **Editor** and **Parameters** options are simply a specification for the type of assistance and are made available in Domino Designer when trying to set any custom properties on a Custom Control.

The **Default Value** field is self-explanatory and holds no secrets—the useful thing about it is its capability to be dynamically computed at runtime.

The **Allow multiple instances** option enables many instances of a custom property to be specified on its associated Custom Control. Within the XPages runtime, multiple instances of a custom property are held within a `java.lang.ArrayList` instance.

Finally, on this tab, the **Description** field is used in conjunction with the **Display Name** field described earlier to bubble information into the caption within the **All Properties** panel. You can specify an unrestricted multivalued string value for this field.

Validation Tab

Figure 10.14 shows the **Validation** tab contents applicable to a custom property. As described earlier, you can specify a requirement clause and validation rule on a custom property that is evaluated at design time within Domino Designer. The **Required field** checkbox within this tab enables you to specify the requirement clause. If this is checked, the custom property becomes a mandatory attribute that must be declared on the Custom Control tag, and a value must be applied or the containing XPage is not compiled. The default behavior is that custom properties are not required.

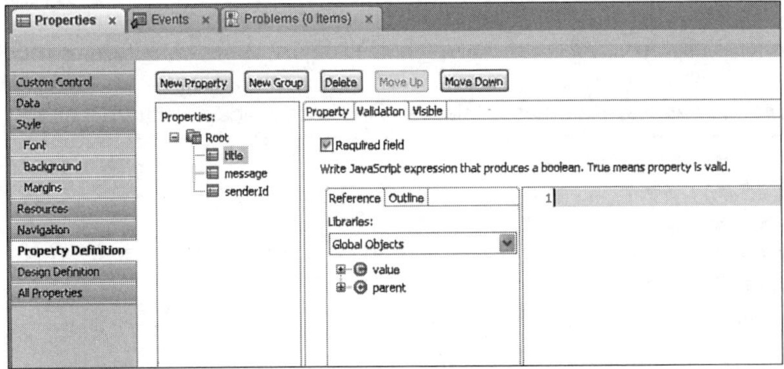

Figure 10.14 Validation tab within the Property Definition panel

Just below this is an editor that allows a Pseudo-Java language expression formulated to validate the design-time value of the custom property. This is a powerful feature of custom properties, because it gives a few ways to either check the value of the current property, any of its siblings, or parent properties of a property group within the design-time XSP markup. It is for these reasons that the `value` and `parent` object references exist in the **Reference** viewer, as shown in Figure 10.15. For example, a property named *serialCode*, of type `string`, is mandatory and needs to be exactly 20-characters long when specified. The design-time validation can use the `value` reference or, alternatively, use the property name directly within the validation expression to check the length, as shown in Figure 10.15.

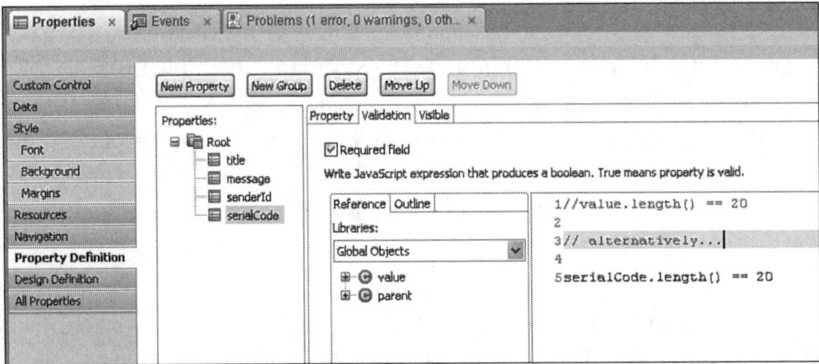

Figure 10.15 Using the property name directly within a validation expression

Note that the `parent` reference is only applicable while working within a property group, because it dereferences the property group parent tag. This is typically the actual Custom Control tag, but it can also be used to reference another property group and access a property of interest. As an example, assume that one custom property named *key* exists on a Custom Control tag along with one property group that allows multiple instances of another custom property named *code*. The premise here is that the *key* and any one of the given *code* property values are used together in some server-side application logic function. The *key* is of a restricted format, and the *code* is a combination of the *key* value as a prefix followed by a number. The validation cases hence require that the *key* has a validation expression checking its format; this can be done using the same technique explained in the previous example. (The `value` reference or direct use of the property name is used in the validation expression on the *key* property itself.) The *code* can check that the *key* exists on the parent tag by using the `parent` reference in the validation expression, as shown in Figure 10.16. Note that the `parent` and direct property name references are used in tandem to dereference the *key* value.

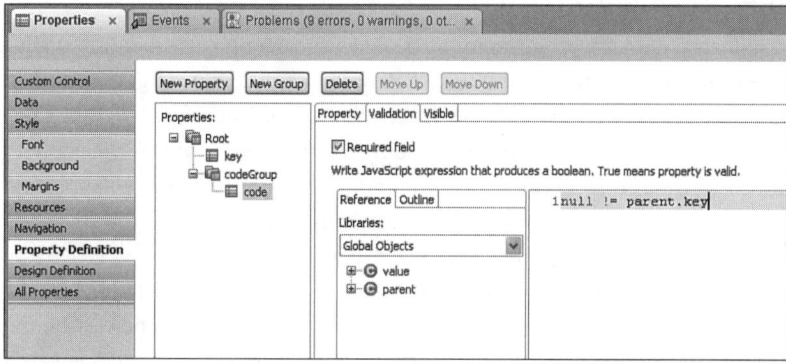

Figure 10.16 Using the parent and direct property name references within a group validation expression

Visible Tab

The last of the three design-time metadata categories is contained within the **Visible** tab, as shown in Figure 10.17. The term *visible* in this context literally means to make the custom property appear or not, as the case may be, within the **Properties** view for the Custom Control based on some precondition that's specified in the **Visible** expression. In Figure 10.17, the `value` and `parent` references are available to you when creating **Visible** expressions. Furthermore, the same semantics explained for **Validation** expressions using the `value` and `parent` references are applicable here. It is easy to imagine taking the previous *key* and *code* example and applying a **Visible** condition to the *code* custom property to hide it from the Domino Designer editors when the parent *key* custom property is not correctly specified.

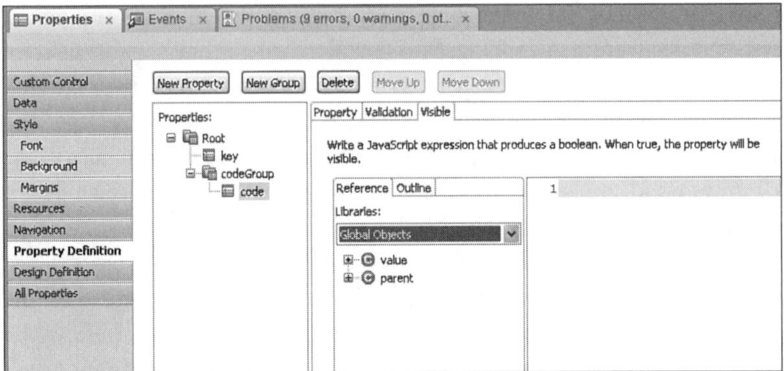

Figure 10.17 Visible tab within the Property Definition panel

Property Definitions Summary

You have seen the mechanisms available to manage the design-time data type, validation, inclusion, and exposure of the custom properties within the XSP markup before it even gets compiled into a runtime executable XPage! By applying these mechanisms when creating Custom Controls, you help other developers that reuse or need to maintain your Custom Controls to adhere to the expected format at design time in Domino Designer. Another benefit is that any supporting application logic requires less "policing" as the incoming runtime values are of the expected type, format, and so on, thus making your application a better performer.

Before leaving this section on **Property Definitions**, apply your new knowledge on custom properties to the previous example by modifying a couple of the custom properties on the **ccBar.xsp**. Remember that you created three new properties—*title*, *message*, and *senderId*—all of type `string`. Make the *title* and *senderId* properties mandatory by checking the **Required field** checkbox on the **Validation** tab for each of these two properties, but leave the *message* field with the default setting of non-mandatory. Also, set a **Visible** expression on the *message* property to always hide it in Domino Designer—simply add the keyword `false` into the expression editor and save all of your changes. The reason for setting this visibility expression becomes apparent in the next section.

TIP

Interested in knowing where all this design-time metadata is stored? Look inside the CustomControls folder within the current application under the Java Perspective in Domino Designer. You will find that every Custom Control in this folder is saved with an .xsp extension, but each also has a corresponding .xsp-config file. Inside this file, you find the metadata settings stored in XML format.

Using the compositeData Object

So far, you created the **bar** Custom Control, added numerous controls within it, and declared three custom properties. Now, the question is this: How can you use these properties? The answer lies with the `compositeData` object—a scripting class that XPages automatically provides that enables you to manipulate the properties of a Custom Control at runtime. Among other things, a Custom Control exposes its custom properties through getter and setter methods to its underlying custom property map. You learn about both of these in this section.

Sticking with the running example, on the **bar** Custom Control, select the **titleLabel** control within the editor or within the Outline view to make the **Properties** panel switch context to this control's properties. Earlier, you specified the label value to be *Hello World!* or something of your own choosing. Now, change this to be a computed value by clicking the blue diamond next to the **Label** field in the Properties view and selecting the **Compute value** option from the pop-up menu. This launches the **Script Editor**. Within the **Reference** viewer in the Script Editor, you now see a `compositeData` entry in the list of object references. If you expand this reference, you see three properties supported by this object—do you recognize them? Yes, here are the three custom properties that you specified on the **bar** Custom Control earlier. Double-click the `compositeData.title` reference, and this is automatically added into the Script Editor window as a line of code, as shown in Figure 10.18. Click **OK** to close the Script Editor and save your changes.

With the previous steps fresh in your mind, also give the **messageField** control a computed JavaScript value using the `compositeData` object, but this time, select the `message` property reference, as shown in Figure 10.19. As this is a Computed Field control, select the Value tab of the Properties panel to apply the value expression. In the Script Editor, type `compositeData.` and examine the content assist choices. Again, after setting this property, save your changes.

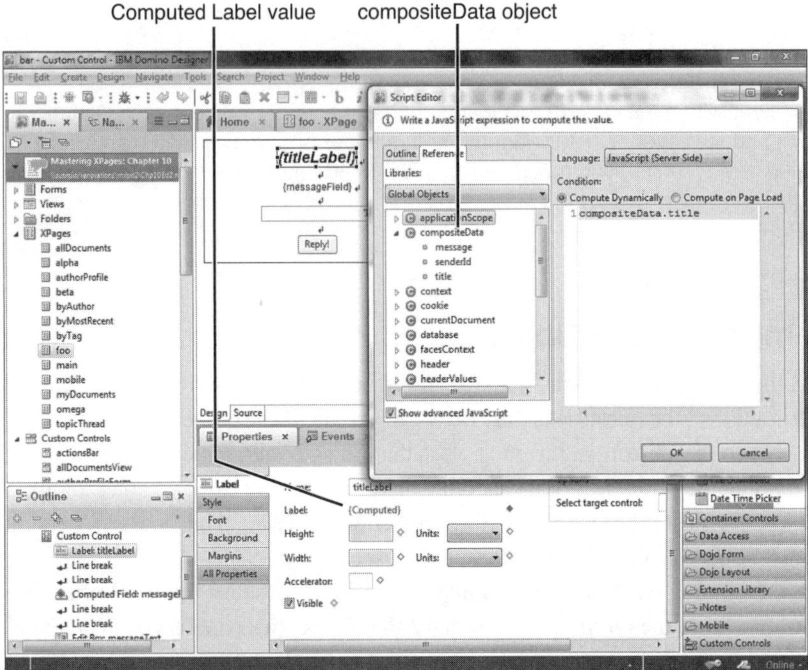

Figure 10.18 titleLabel computed label with the compositeData object and title property selected

In essence, you just bound `value` property of the **titleLabel** control to the `title` custom property by way of the `compositeData` object using server-side JavaScript. The same holds true for the `messageField`. The `compositeData` object is simply the bridge between the Custom Control properties and the server-side JavaScript context for the Custom Control. You learn more on this later, but for now, just complete this **titleLabel** example. Reopen the **foo** XPage and select the first of the two instances of **bar**, namely *bar1* so that the **Properties** view switches context to this control's properties. Within the **Properties** view, select the **Custom Properties** panel where you see the `title` and `senderId` properties listed in the editor. Remember, of course, that you set `visible` to `false` for the `message` property, hence its absence within this list in Domino Designer, even though it exists and you just used it in the computed value for the `messageField`—be patient, because you're getting close to finding out why! Now, enter a textual value for the `title` property and repeat the same steps on the second instance of **bar**, namely *bar2*, so that both instances of this Custom Control have their respective `title` properties configured with a static value, as shown in Figure 10.20.

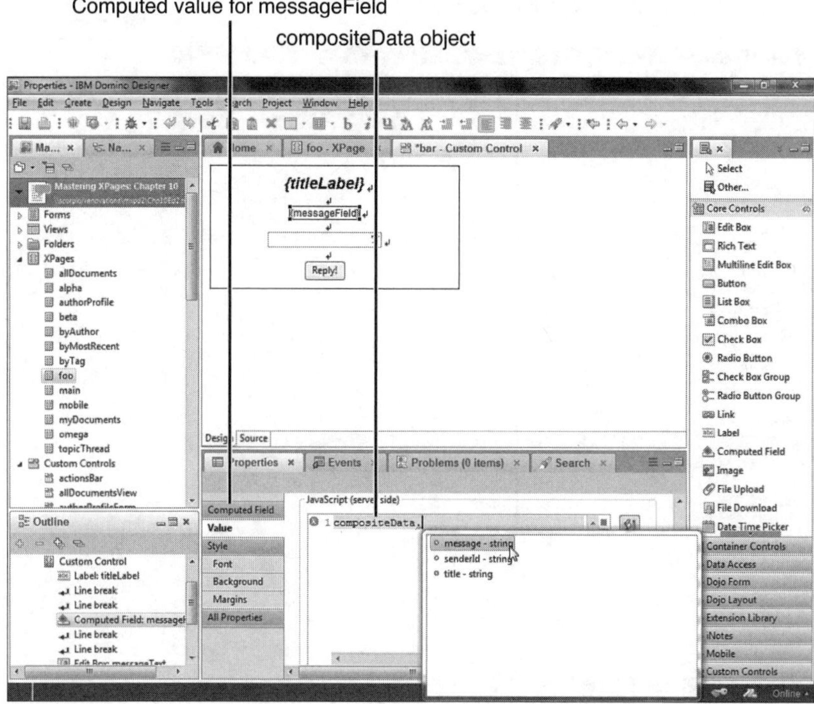

Figure 10.19 messageField's value computed using the compositeData.message property

Your natural instinct at this point is to save your changes, and this is always a wise thing to do! But, on this occasion, you find that the **foo** XPage, although correctly saved, has caused two new errors to appear within the **Problems** view. You can see more on this by switching to the **Source** editor for **foo**, whereupon you see the errors highlighted within the XSP markup, as shown in Figure 10.21.

As you probably already figured out, these errors are caused by the mandatory condition you set on the `senderId` property earlier when you checked the `Required` field on this property's **Validation** tab. This is a good example of Domino Designer actually enforcing the design-time metadata and throwing an error that indicates the cause. So, this requires two simple steps to rectify the errors—the purpose of the `senderId` property becomes apparent when you come to apply the logic on the **replyButton**. You can use the **Custom Properties** panel for each of the two **bar** instances and set the `senderId` to be the name of the other **bar** instance in each case. Therefore, for *bar1*, the `senderId` property should be the value *bar2* and, for *bar2*, the `senderId` property value should be *bar1*, as shown in Listing 10.6.

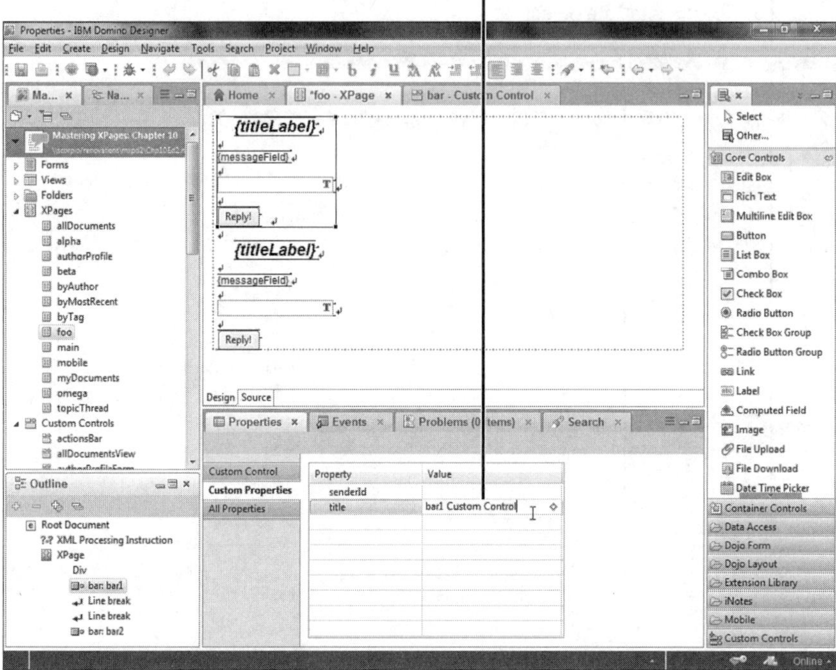

Figure 10.20 Title property with its value set within the Custom Properties panel on the **foo** XPage

Listing 10.6 Correctly Configured senderId and title Custom Properties

```
<?xml version="1.0" encoding="UTF-8"?>
<xp:view xmlns:xp="http://www.ibm.com/xsp/core"
xmlns:xc="http://www.ibm.com/xsp/custom">
<xp:div themeId="container">
<xc:bar id="bar1" title="bar1 Custom Control"
senderId="bar2">
</xc:bar>
<xp:br></xp:br>
<xp:br></xp:br>
<xc:bar id="bar2" title="bar2 Custom Control"
senderId="bar1">
</xc:bar>
</xp:div>
</xp:view>
```

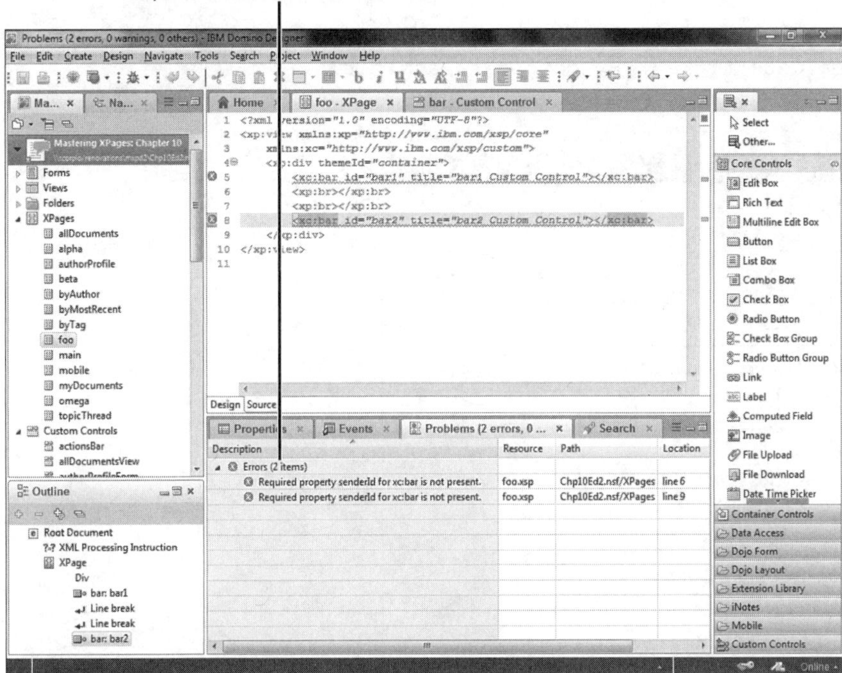

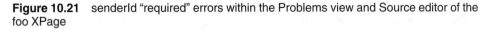

Figure 10.21 senderId "required" errors within the Problems view and Source editor of the foo XPage

Having applied these values, resave your changes. The previous two errors now disappear from the **Problems** view and the underlying **Source** editor for **foo**. The worked example now passes design-time validation so, if you once again preview the **foo** XPage, you should see something similar to that shown in Figure 10.22, where the title for each instance of **bar** is actually displayed by the **titleLabel** control.

The title values you see are a direct consequence of the binding you set up earlier by using the `compositeData.title` reference. The XPages runtime has evaluated this binding by taking the custom property values you set within Domino Designer on each of the two **bar** instances and pushed these into an instance of a `compositeData` object for each of the two Custom Control instances. If you are familiar with Java development, XPages essentially assigns a property map to each instance, and this object then contains a collection of name value pairs that represent the custom properties for that Custom Control instance. This map then becomes available within the context of the Custom Control instance, thus enabling the declared binding expression to be resolved:

```
compositeData.get("title") == compositeData.title
```

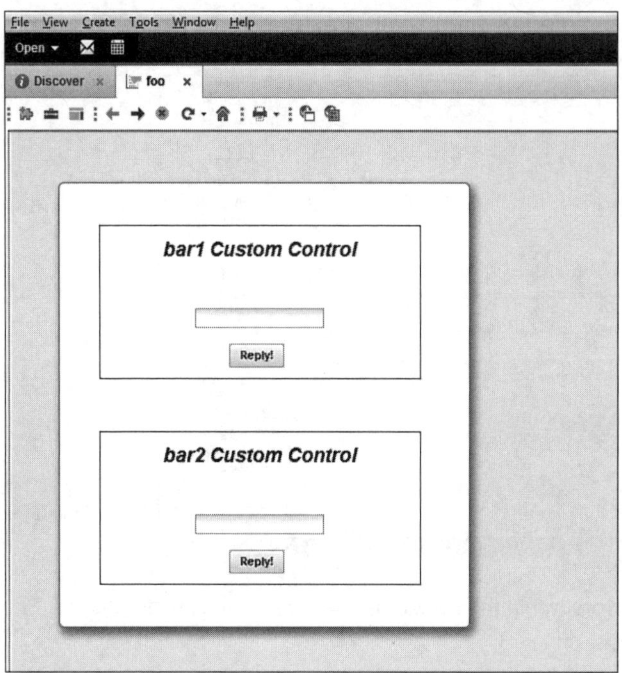

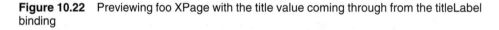

Figure 10.22 Previewing foo XPage with the title value coming through from the titleLabel binding

Note that every instance of any given Custom Control is instantiated with *its own copy* of a custom property map that is accessible in server-side JavaScript by using the `compositeData` reference. This map is also held within a private scope for its owning Custom Control to avoid data corruption across instances of any given Custom Control.

This is a useful mechanism for getting property values from the `compositeData` object, but it also enables you to set property values on the object using server-side JavaScript. This, of course, is all well and good within the context of the owning Custom Control, but what if you need to programmatically interact with other external Custom Controls' custom properties? This is achieved by obtaining the property map from that Custom Control directly and then using the getter/setter methods on the map to read and write the constituent custom properties. You see an example of this shortly with the **replyButton** logic.

The intent of the sample you've been building is to show that the two instances of the **bar** Custom Control should be able to communicate with one another in a send/receive manner. Essentially, when a user fills in a message within the **messageText** edit box and clicks the **replyButton**, the message should be sent to the other instance of the **bar** Custom Control on the **foo** XPage. To do this, you must have everything you need in the `compositeData` object and the getter/setter methods of the property map.

Send and You Shall Receive

To build this final part of the example, ensure that the **bar** Custom Control is open within Domino Designer, and then click the **replyButton** control within the WYSIWYG editor to prime the **Properties** view for this control. This time around, you do not need to set any properties supported by the **replyButton**, but you should click the **Events** view tab located beside the **Properties** view, as shown in Figure 10.23.

Figure 10.23 Events view for the replyButton control

You need to set an `onclick` server event for the **replyButton**, so ensure that the `onclick` event is selected within the **Events** list and then click the **Open Script Dialog** button to launch the **Script Editor**. Within the **Script Editor**, you can simply copy the fragment of server-side JavaScript (see Listing 10.7).

Listing 10.7 Fragment of Server-Side JavaScript for the replyButton onclick Event

```
1     if(null != compositeData.senderId){
2         var senderComponent = getComponent(compositeData.senderId);
3         var senderProps = senderComponent.getPropertyMap();
4         if(null != senderProps){
5             var messageText = getComponent("messageText");
6             if(null != messageText){
7                 var message = messageText.getValue();
8                 senderProps.setProperty("message", message);
9                 compositeData.message = null;
10            }
11        }
12    }
```

The code you just copied into the **Script Editor** does many interesting things involving the `compositeData` object and property map. Here is a line-by-line explanation:

1. On line 1, the existence of a `senderId` property value is checked, as this is crucial in enabling any outbound communication to the other Custom Control. That is why you were asked to specify the other **bar** instance's `name` value.
2. If this property exists, line 2 uses it in the `getComponent()` global function to retrieve a reference to that control. Here, you obtain a reference to the other **bar** Custom Control instance within the XPages runtime on the server side.
3. Line 3 asks the other **bar** instance for its property map, which contains its own copy of custom properties.
4. Line 4 simply ensures that the property map has been successfully retrieved.
5. Line 5 uses the `getComponent()` global method to retrieve the instance of the **messageText** control that lives within this same instance of the **bar** Custom Control.
6. It is considered best practice to always check dynamically retrieved objects for non-null values before attempting to use them.
7. Remember that the **messageText** field is an `Editbox` control and is not actually bound to any `compositeData` property, so its text value can simply be directly accessed here.
8. The retrieved value forms the outgoing message to be relayed to the other instance of the **bar** Custom Control, and it is explicitly set on its `message` custom property using the setter method on the other Custom Control's property map reference. After all this waiting, you can now understand why you made the `message` custom property's `Visible` metadata always `false`. This simply prevents it being set at design

time in Domino Designer's editors, as it is only set programmatically through the setter method on the property map—a small example of controlling what your Custom Control exposes within the Domino Designer editors based on what the underlying application logic is expected to do.

9. Line 9 nulls the current instance of the **bar** Custom Control's custom `message` property so that when the XPage redisplays after clicking the **replyButton**, the sending **bar** instance's **messageField** is cleared of any value.

Ensure that you saved all of your changes and then preview the **foo** XPage again. If everything has been correctly configured, after you press the first Reply button and type something into the second edit box, you see something similar to Figure 10.24.

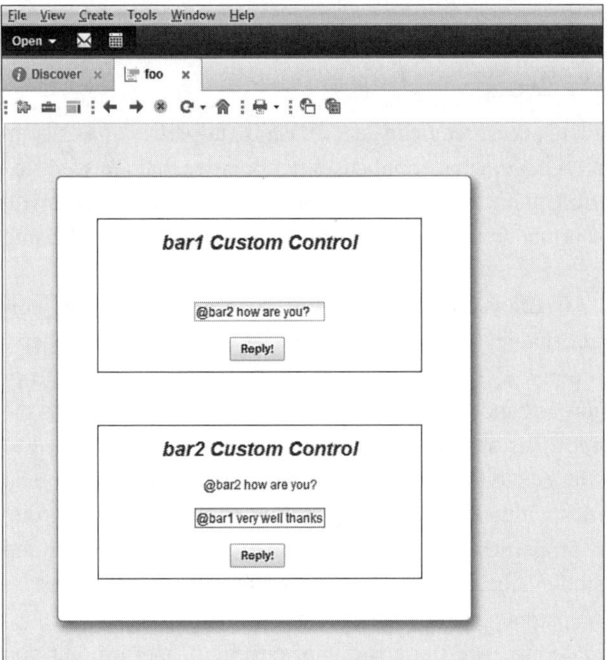

Figure 10.24 Completed foo XPage in preview mode in the Notes client

This time, when previewing, you should be able to type a message within the edit box and click the **Reply** button. The message should appear within the other **bar** Custom Control instance. Likewise, doing the same within the other **bar** Custom Control instance relays the message back to the first instance. If something does not appear to be working as expected, you can find the complete worked example within the **Chp10Ed2.nsf** application under the **foo** XPage and the **bar** Custom Control design elements.

Take a moment to review how all these scripting objects interact with each other in the **replyButton** logic and the `compositeData` bindings you have built. Think about the way in which the `getComponent()` global function returns the other Custom Control reference using the `senderId`—this is a relatively straightforward case, as the `senderId` explicitly refers to the other control, but then consider how the second call of this method on line 5 is only given the literal *messageText* ID as its parameter...the XPages runtime is still able to resolve this control without inconsistently returning an instance from the other Custom Control instance. Also, think about the fact that the **messageText** control and its value remain uncorrupted during the course of a message relay from one Custom Control to the other. Finally, consider the fact that the nullification of the `compositeData.message` property on line 9 affects only the current Custom Control's instance of that property. This firmly demonstrates that the private-scoping mechanism keeps the instance data and scripting objects safe during the execution of your XPages application.

Multiple Instances and Property Groups

Having used the `compositeData` object to access single instance custom properties of a Custom Control within your server-side JavaScript code, what about custom properties that are specified in the design-time metadata as **Allow multiple instances** or even property groups specified with the **New Group** action? The good news is that these are just as straightforward to deal with using the `compositeData` object.

First, if a custom property has its **Allow multiple instances** option checked, the editor within the **Custom Properties** panel enables you to add or subtract from a list of property instances for that particular custom property, as shown in Figure 10.25, where a custom property named `options` is shown. Note how instances of this property are actually written into the XSP markup as child nodes of the parent Custom Control tag. The same procedure is used to work with a property group, whereby the editor in the **All Properties** panel allows you to add a group and specify the custom properties within that group. Again Figure 10.25 shows a group named `payload` that has two custom properties specified within that group: `username` and `timestamp`. You should, once again, study the way such a group is written into the XSP markup as a subordinate complex property of the parent Custom Control tag.

The `compositeData` object can dereference these forms of custom properties, but you need to know the base type of each. Earlier, it was explained that a multiple instance custom property gets held within a `java.lang.ArrayList` instance and that a group of custom properties gets held within a `com.ibm.xsp.binding.PropertyMap` instance. Therefore, this establishes the basis handling for both, that is, the multiple instance case provides collection behavior where its elements can be iterated over, while the group case provides map behavior in that its elements are accessible by key name. For example, study the fragment of XSP markup shown in Listing 10.8, which relates to the custom property configuration shown in Figure 10.25.

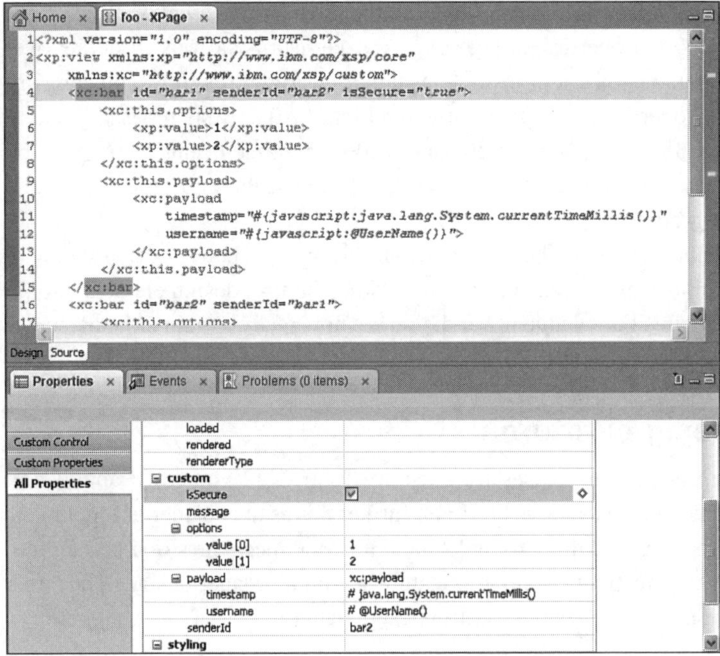

Figure 10.25 Options multiple instance and payload group custom properties shown in Designer

Listing 10.8 Dealing with a Multiple Instance and a Group Custom Property Using the compositeData Object

```
<!-- iterate over the options multiple instance property -->
<xp:repeat id="optionsRepeat" rows="30"
var="currentOption"
value="#{javascript:compositeData.options}">
<xp:text escape="true" id="computedField1"
value="#{javascript:currentOption}">
</xp:text>
</xp:repeat>
<!-- key into the payload group properties -->
<xp:text escape="true" id="timestamp"
value="#{javascript:compositeData.payload.timestamp}">
</xp:text>
<xp:text escape="true" id="username"
value="#{javascript:compositeData.payload.username}">
</xp:text>
```

It's a matter of using the `compositeData` object in the most suitable way for each case. For multiple instances of custom properties, a `<xp:repeat>` tag is a basic way to iterate over a collection, hence it is a suitable choice. For a single group of custom properties, you can simply dereference the group's properties directly, as shown in Listing 10.8. Remember, a property group can also be configured in its design-time metadata to allow multiple instances. Again, you are then simply dealing with a collection of property maps and can use the `<xp:repeat>` tag to iterate over the collection of groups.

This concludes this section on using the `compositeData` object. Up to this point, you've learned a lot about the capabilities and mechanics of the Custom Control design element at both design time and runtime. With this knowledge in hand, you are now ready to gain an understanding about the more holistic uses of Custom Controls.

Custom Control Design Patterns

Hopefully, you already see potential use cases for Custom Controls in your own application designs. Before beginning any conquests, there are some further things to consider before undertaking any application rework. It is one thing to understand how the mechanics of a certain feature works, but it is another to effectively apply the feature within a broader design. Thus, this section teaches you about best practice Custom Control design patterns.

Aggregate Container Pattern

The most typical approach to leveraging Custom Controls most likely focuses on generalizing functional parts of an application. An example might be taking a piece of code that is being used repeatedly to do something useful in numerous different places and separating it into a self-contained Custom Control. If you are thinking this way, you are already well on your way to becoming a skilled XPages developer! The *Aggregate Container* design pattern is the basis of this process—evaluating the viability of decomposing some part of an application into a loosely coupled reusable artifact based on the specialized task that it performs.

An aggregate container is a Custom Control that's composed of several parts that perform a well-defined task. Ideally, this container can be reused across different XPages or XPages applications in a loosely coupled manner with a minimum amount of integration. In fact, when you use Domino Designer to copy and paste a Custom Control from one application to another, Domino Designer automatically copies the corresponding `*.xsp-config` file for you (that's the metadata file managed in the background by Domino Designer for each Custom Control). This goes some way toward helping you easily reuse a Custom Control, but you need to manage other dependencies yourself, such as images, CSS, and JavaScript files, when performing the migration from one application to another.

Depending on your application architecture, you might want to leverage templates to inherit Custom Controls and their dependencies into multiple applications. Do this by setting up an inheritance chain. These are essentially deployment-related issues; however, the focus of this section is about the use of design patterns. For now, just keep in mind the fact that architecture exists within XPages to support a Custom Control reuse model.

You already learned about custom properties and their importance. Custom Controls would be of much less value without this feature, because they would be nonconfigurable within Domino Designer and equally difficult to interact with programmatically. Therefore, when considering the design of an aggregate container, give careful consideration as to what properties should be exposed to maximize the flexibility of a control. Always try to maintain a clean separation between external artifacts and those that are internally resident within the control. Ideally, aim to create aggregate containers that function as standalone objects (assuming some degree of custom property configuration) and, therefore, can be dropped into any XPage or application and made readily useable immediately. One highly productive and quality-oriented practice to adopt is using test harness XPages when developing and testing your aggregate containers. Simply dropping your Custom Control onto a blank XPage and configuring its custom properties within this context gives you a sanitized environment with the ability to quickly preview and test that control without actually embedding it within a fully blown and potentially complex XPage.

Also, try to establish a clear separation between resources used by an aggregate container, especially if you intend to make it publicly available. This is important and easy to achieve: Important because it reduces redundancy in that your control does not have logic embedded within a common JavaScript or CSS file that must be served down in any request for supporting resources. It's easy to achieve insofar as the corresponding CSS and JavaScript files for the control can be created in isolation, and only logic pertinent to that control should be kept within these resources. A straightforward naming convention that can be easily applied and followed is prefixing the name of a Custom Control itself across any dependencies for that Custom Control (for example, ***ccBar.xsp***, ***ccBar.jss***, ***ccBar.js***, ***ccBar.css***, and so forth). That way, when you actually copy or export such a control, it is easier to identify the artifacts on which it depends.

One other thing to bear in mind is the fact that nesting Custom Controls is supported and a useful thing to do, in some cases. It is really a matter of how many layers of decomposition can be represented by a functional part of an application. For example, if you want to represent something similar to an outline using Custom Controls, it is natural to conceptualize a single parent Custom Control used as the outline container, and then use one other Custom Control to represent the many child outline entries that may be needed. Therefore, a degree of Custom Control nesting is required. In the next section, you learn about **editable areas** within Custom Controls. These provide a different way to effectively achieve nesting of Custom Controls for a slightly different purpose.

Layout Container Pattern

The Layout Container design pattern complements the Aggregate Container design pattern by helping reduce duplication and redundancy across your XPages applications.

One control that is only available when working within the context of a Custom Control is the **Editable Area** control. This appears within the control palette under the *Core Controls* category, right at the bottom of the list, and note that it disappears when you switch over to work within an XPage! So, what is the reason for this phantom control? It all has to do with efficiency of presentation!

One of the biggest areas of duplication and redundancy within the code of any web-based application is in the presentation logic, regardless of the underpinning technology used to develop the application. XPages, albeit a client technology and a web technology, is driven by a web-based paradigm. Consequently, a typical application is constructed with artifacts, such as CSS, graphical images, JavaScript, and boilerplate HTML constructs sprinkled across many XPages. An interesting aspect of this is when an application's design demands several XPages to be used for navigation; there is inevitably a degree of duplication involved to try to achieve the same look and layout across all these XPages.

In this scenario, the developer typically creates an initial XPage that contains all the necessary code to define the structure of the XPage and includes any aggregate containers within this skeletal framework. It is then simply a matter of copying this boilerplate XPage code into any other required XPages and tweaking the resultant XPages independently of one another to suit the application design. At first glance, you might think that is not a bad strategy, and maybe it is expedient, but nonetheless, it actually introduces a costly flaw into the design of the application.

Consider the ramifications of the last step when it comes to making a change that must be reflected across the entire application. However small or large that change might be, every XPage spawned from the initial boilerplate code needs to be identified and modified on an individual basis, and then retested in the hope that no regressive behavior has been introduced. The same situation can occur to a greater extent if the application look or layout needs to be updated with new colors, images, or maybe even a complete change of positional placement of functional parts. The pain level here depends on what degree of externalization the CSS, images, and other resources have from the underlying source markup. If poorly implemented, a major application rewrite could be the only way forward; otherwise, it's a case of every single XPage needing costly rework!

The **Editable Area** control exists to facilitate the reduction of duplication and redundancy within an XPages application when using Custom Controls. The scenario described in the preceding paragraph highlights that a major flaw can easily creep into an application's design, either through bad planning or bad development practices. This situation can be averted by applying a simple technique—creating a Custom Control that contains the boilerplate look and layout code, plus one or more specially designated areas as placeholders or landing zones for the aggregate container Custom Controls. These specially designated areas are the *Editable Area*s of the Custom Control. In essence, the application implementation described in the example would be different in that there would still be the same number of XPages, but the boilerplate code would not be duplicated across all of them. Thus, a Custom Control containing all the boilerplate code and one or more **Editable Area** would be dropped onto each XPage. Each XPage can then be configured independently to use whatever aggregate containers are required on that XPage—by simply dragging and dropping aggregate containers' Custom Controls onto any given **Editable Area**.

The biggest benefit of applying this technique is that it is now extremely easy to modify the boilerplate code by changing the code of one single Custom Control. The changes are immediately reflected across the entire set of XPages that use the layout container Custom Control—without even having to open those XPages in Domino Designer!

A working example of this can be found within the supporting **Chp10Ed2.nsf** application. Open this application in Domino Designer. Then, open the **alpha**, **beta,** and **omega** XPages and, finally, open the **layoutContainer** Custom Control. Having opened each of these, turn to the **Source** editor for each. As a starting point to fully understanding how the layout container pattern has been applied in this example, study the XSP markup of the **alpha** XPage, as shown in Listing 10.9.

Listing 10.9 XSP Markup of the Alpha XPage

```
<?xml version="1.0" encoding="UTF-8"?>
<xp:view xmlns:xp="http://www.ibm.com/xsp/core"
    xmlns:xc="http://www.ibm.com/xsp/custom">
    <xc:layoutContainer showLeftColumn="true" showRightColumn="true">
          <xp:this.facets>
                <xp:panel id="panel1" xp:key="leftColumnAreaFacet">
                      <xp:label value="Alpha: Left Column Area"
                            id="label2"></xp:label>
                      <xp:br></xp:br>
                      <xp:link escape="true" text="Beta" id="link2"
                            value="/beta.xsp">
                      </xp:link>
                      <xp:br></xp:br>
                      <xp:link escape="true" text="Omega" id="link3"
                            value="/omega.xsp">
                      </xp:link>
                </xp:panel>
                <xp:label id="label1" xp:key="contentAreaFacet"
                      value="Alpha: Content Area">
                </xp:label>
          </xp:this.facets>
    </xc:layoutContainer>
</xp:view>
```

As you can see, there is a single declaration for the **layoutContainer** Custom Control within this XPage. This Custom Control has two custom properties configured, namely `showLeftColumn` and `showRightColumn`, both `boolean` types respectively with default values of true. There is a declaration referring to `<xp:this.facets>`, for which you need to study the XSP markup of the **layoutContainer** Custom Control to understand what this complex tag is doing. Listing 10.10 shows the XSP markup for this Custom Control. On lines 37 and 44, there are two instances of an <xp:callback> tag, each having an attribute called facetName set. Effectively, the complex tag <xp:this.facets>, shown in Listing 10.9 for the **alpha** XPage, refers to a collection of such <xp:callback>, or facets, that might exist on a Custom Control. In this particular case for the layoutContainer Custom Control, there are two facets: **leftColumnAreaFacet** and **contentAreaFacet**, respectively.

Listing 10.10 XSP Markup of the layoutContainer Custom Control

```
<?xml version="1.0" encoding="UTF-8"?>
<xp:view xmlns:xp="http://www.ibm.com/xsp/core"
    <xp:this.resources>
        <xp:styleSheet>
            <xp:this.contents>
                <![CDATA[
                    .container{
                        background-color:#fff;
                        padding:30px;
                        -moz-border-radius: 5px;
                        -moz-box-shadow: 3px 5px 10px #888888;
                        width:350px;
                        border: 1px solid #757575;
                        margin: 50px 0px 20px 50px;
                        height:80px;
                    }
                    .leftColumn{
                        border-right:1px solid #ccc;
                        display:inline-block;
                        float:left;
                        padding:10px
                    }
                    .content{
                        display:inline-block;
                        float:left;
                        padding:10px
                    }
                ]]>
            </xp:this.contents>
        </xp:styleSheet>
    </xp:this.resources>
    <xp:panel id="container" styleClass="container">
        <xp:panel id="body">
            <xp:panel id="columnLeft"
                styleClass="leftColumn"
                loaded="${javascript:compositeData.showLeftColumn}">
                <xp:callback id="leftColumnAreaFacet"
```

```
                    facetName="leftColumnAreaFacet">
                </xp:callback>
            </xp:panel>
            <xp:panel id="content"
                styleClass="content"
                loaded="${javascript:compositeData.showRightColumn}">
                <xp:callback id="contentAreaFacet"
                    facetName="contentAreaFacet">
                </xp:callback>
            </xp:panel>
        </xp:panel>
    </xp:panel>
</xp:view>
```

Note that the `<xp:callback>` tag represents the **Editable Area** control described earlier in this section. This control is effectively a drop zone, or injection point, for other controls at design time in that the layout container exposes one or more of these **Editable Area** controls, and each one accepts any other content to be included in that area. Note that an Editable Area can be used on any XPage or Custom Control under any context, not just for use as an enabler of a Layout Container. It also only accepts one control as its root content—this can be a single button control or even a Panel with lots of nested child controls inside of it. Typically, such content is provided by a Custom Control that contains several other controls, such as an aggregate container, or can simply be other core controls from the control palette. This is the case shown in Listing 10.9, where both `label1` and `panel1` are standard controls dropped into the two different **Editable Area** controls: `leftColumnAreaFacet` and `contentAreaFacet`. The facet/control association has been made using the special prefix and attribute `xp:key`:

```
<xp:label id="label1" xp:key="contentAreaFacet"...
<xp:panel id="panel1" xp:key="leftColumnAreaFacet"...
```

The value of this attribute must be the name of the target **Editable Area** exposed by the underlying layout container and, for both of these cases, shown in Listing 10.10:

```
<xp:callback id="leftColumnAreaFacet" facetName=
"leftColumnAreaFacet"...
<xp:callback id="contentAreaFacet" facetName="contentAreaFacet"...
```

Editable Areas on a Custom Control surface themselves at design time in the WYSIWYG editor of Domino Designer as gray-shaded rectangular areas when used within an XPage. You can then drag-and-drop other Custom Controls or standard controls onto these areas. In Figure 10.26, the **alpha** XPage is shown at design time with the **Editable Areas** exposed by the **layoutContainer**, which is also visible.

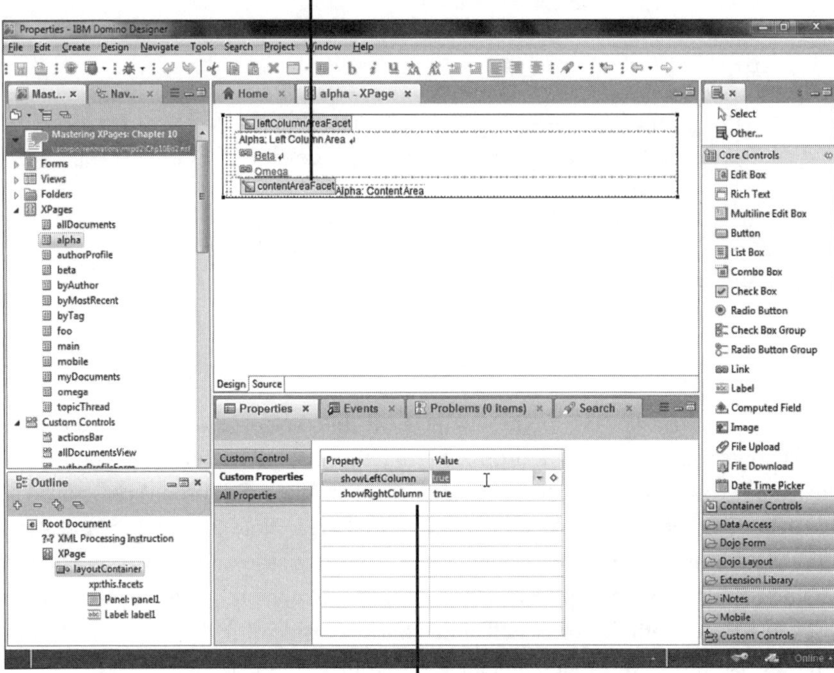

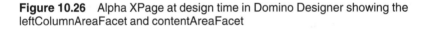

Figure 10.26 Alpha XPage at design time in Domino Designer showing the leftColumnAreaFacet and contentAreaFacet

The **beta** and **omega** XPages also use the same **layoutContainer** Custom Control for their contents. A couple of key differences can be examined in how they each use this Custom Control; first, the setting of the `showLeftColumn` and `showRightColumn` custom properties is different on each XPage. Second, the contents associated with each facet are different. Study the XSP markup of both these XPages to identify these differences. Listing 10.11 details the XSP markup for the **beta** XPage, and Listing 10.12 details the same for the **omega** XPage.

Listing 10.11 XSP Markup of the beta XPage

```
<?xml version="1.0" encoding="UTF-8"?>
<xp:view xmlns:xp="http://www.ibm.com/xsp/core"
    xmlns:xc="http://www.ibm.com/xsp/custom">
    <xc:layoutContainer showLeftColumn="true" showRightColumn="false">
          <xp:this.facets>
                <xp:panel id="panel1" xp:key="leftColumnAreaFacet">
                      <xp:label value="Beta: Left Column Area"
```

```
                    id="label2"></xp:label>
                <xp:br></xp:br>
                <xp:link escape="true" text="Alpha" id="link2"
                    value="/alpha.xsp">
                </xp:link>
                <xp:br></xp:br>
                <xp:link escape="true" text="Omega" id="link3"
                    value="/omega.xsp">
                </xp:link>
            </xp:panel>
            <xp:label id="label1" xp:key="contentAreaFacet"
                value="Beta: Content Area">
            </xp:label>
        </xp:this.facets>
    </xc:layoutContainer>
</xp:view>
```

Listing 10.12 XSP Markup of the omega XPage

```
<?xml version="1.0" encoding="UTF-8"?>
<xp:view xmlns:xp="http://www.ibm.com/xsp/core"
    xmlns:xc="http://www.ibm.com/xsp/custom">
    <xc:layoutContainer showLeftColumn="false" showRightColumn="true">
        <xp:this.facets>
            <xp:label id="label1" xp:key="leftColumnAreaFacet"
                value="Omega: Left Column Area">
            </xp:label>
            <xp:panel id="panel1" xp:key="contentAreaFacet">
                <xp:label value="Omega: Content Area"
                    id="label2"></xp:label>
                <xp:br></xp:br>
                <xp:link escape="true" text="Alpha" id="link2"
                    value="/alpha.xsp">
                </xp:link>
                <xp:br></xp:br>
                <xp:link escape="true" text="Beta" id="link3"
                    value="/beta.xsp">
                </xp:link>
            </xp:panel>
        </xp:this.facets>
    </xc:layoutContainer>
</xp:view>
```

Now, take the opportunity to preview the **alpha**, **beta**, and **omega** XPages. Select the alpha XPage in Domino Designer and choose to preview it either on the client or in a web browser. When opened, you see the XPage displays the **label1** and **panel1** controls in the **left ColumnAreaFacet** and **contentAreaFacet**—also shown in Figure 10.27.

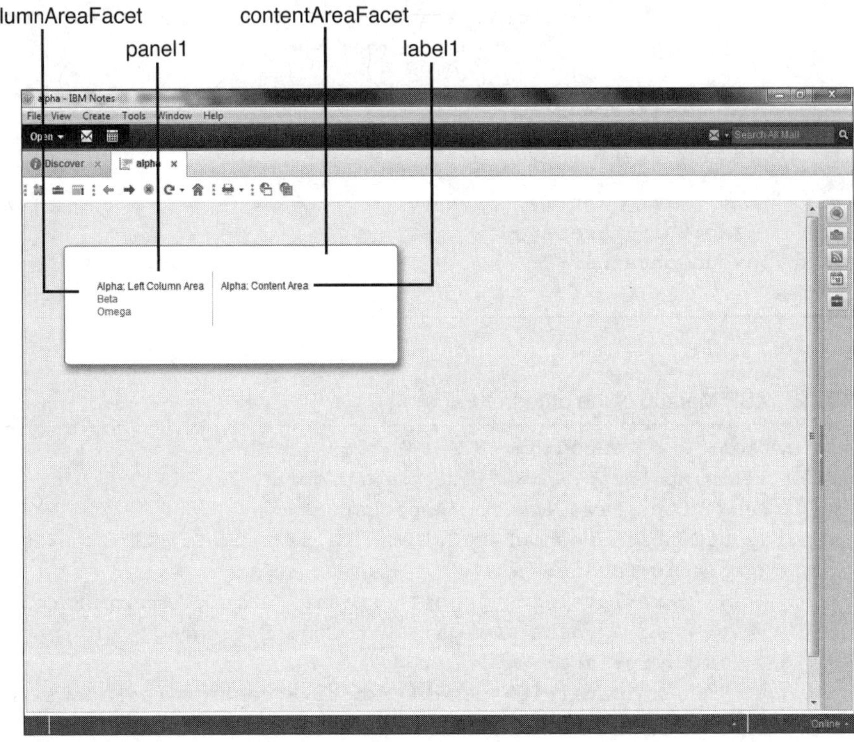

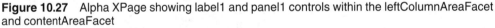

Figure 10.27 Alpha XPage showing label1 and panel1 controls within the leftColumnAreaFacet and contentAreaFacet

You can use the links to navigate to the **beta** and **omega** XPages. For each XPage, you see that the **layoutContainer** is correctly displaying the left column and content area, as per the settings of the `showLeftColumn` and `showRightColumn` custom properties.

This example outlines the fundamentals of the layout container design pattern. Basically, when you create a layout container, try to isolate all the commonly used structural layout elements, such as **Panels**, **Divs**, **Tables**, and even other nested Custom Controls. These are typically used to represent such things as title bars, action bars, and header/footer areas within an application. All can be abstracted into reusable artifacts. The more you can reduce the amount of duplicated code, the more you reduce the level of redundancy within your application, and this has a positive impact not only on maintenance tasks, but on the amount of memory used by your application on the server side within the XPages runtime—another way to make your application scale and perform better!

The other point to keep in mind is that a layout container can be made configurable by using custom properties, as you have seen here with the `showLeftColumn` and `showRightColumn` properties on the **layoutContainer** Custom Control. Consider the fact that a layout container might be used across several XPages, each requiring different values or items to appear within a title bar or menu bar for example. By exposing appropriate custom properties on the layout container, you can configure those on each XPage as required and further sustain the low maintenance cost objective within your XPages application. In Chapter 17, "Application Layout," you learn more about the layout and aggregate container design patterns as they are used by a dedicated control—the Application Layout control.

Conclusion

This concludes your lesson on Custom Controls. In Chapter 11, "Advanced Scripting," you learn about the capabilities that XPages gives you for programming on both the client-side and server-side of your application. This is a natural follow-up topic to Custom Controls and builds on the application customization techniques that you learned here.

CHAPTER 11

Advanced Scripting

This chapter builds on what you learned in Chapter 6, "Building XPages Application Logic," and Chapter 10, "Custom Controls." In those chapters, you learned about some of the fundamental principles of scripting in XPages. With this new knowledge safely under your belt, you are ready to learn how you can leverage advanced scripting techniques to further enhance your XPages applications. In this chapter, you improve your core skills by developing expertise in the following areas:

- AJAX and Partial Refresh
- Dojo integration
- Traditional Notes/Domino building blocks
- Creating and using Managed Beans
- Fulfilling a Customer Requirement—A practical field study

Before starting on the exercises within this chapter, download the two supporting applications **Chp11Ed2.nsf** and **Chp11Ed2b.nsf** from `www.ibmpressbooks.com/title/9780133373370`. Now, a brief summary of some fundamental underpinnings of the XPages runtime is required, some of which you will have already learned in Chapter 5, "XPages and JavaServer Faces," but nonetheless, a quick recap benefits your understanding of this chapter.

Application Frameworks

Some web application frameworks provide a *stateless* runtime environment. Effectively, this means that no information is maintained by the framework when a request is sent via a browser to the application; the request is simply processed and the resultant response is sent back to the user. In effect, each request is treated as a standalone stateless transaction. Other frameworks, such as JavaServer Faces (JSF), however, do support a *stateful* environment where special variables or buffers maintain session or environment details for the current application, request, or user. Thus, XPages is an example of a stateful application framework.

XPages maintains in-depth runtime state information so that you, the application developer, can exercise fine-grained granular control over the behavior of your apps. For any given XPage viewed in the browser, an in-memory, or serialized representation of that XPage, is maintained on the server-side. Of course, this can be a good thing or a bad thing, depending on the application scale and workload, but XPages provides features to control and tune the overhead associated with maintaining such a state. You learn about this in Chapter 19, "A First Look at Performance and Scalability" and Chapter 20, "Advanced Performance Topics." For now, just think about the power you have at your scripting fingertips with the XPages framework—not only can you script for the client-side of an application (as you would naturally assume), but you can script for the server-side stateful representation of it!

There are two interesting observations to make:

- XPages uses the JavaScript language as the default scripting language for both client-side and server-side programming. This benefits you, as the developer, in that you only need to know one language to script an application.
- There is direct correlation between what is emitted to the browser and what is maintained within the XPages runtime. Therefore, you need versatile ways to script functions on both the client-side and server-side of an application, and hence have a requirement for intermingling client-side and server-side code.

In summary, as a developer, you benefit not only from just needing to know about one language, but you can combine client-side and server-side code when you need to in order to get the job done!

Again, as you learned previously, one of the most fundamental characteristics of XPages is that it always ensures the uniqueness of component identifiers on both the client-side and server-side of an application. This guarantees that the elements within the client-side HTML DOM tree map to the server-side component tree, thus assisting the XPages runtime in maintaining a consistent current state of an application at all times. The XPages runtime then provides the `getComponent()`, `getClientId()` methods, and the `#{id:}` resolution operator, not only to resolve component identifiers, but to also intermingle client-side and server-side JavaScript code. All this makes for a powerful application-development platform using one common scripting language.

But, what about scripting with programmability paradigms, such as Asynchronous JavaScript and XML (AJAX) or dojo? Or what about interoperability with established Notes/Domino building blocks such as @Functions or agents? Not to worry, XPages provides you with all the programmability tooling you need to work with these features, and you learn about these in the upcoming sections.

AJAX and Partial Refresh

Partial refresh is the straightforward term that XPages uses to describe its AJAX interoperability feature. In essence, a partial refresh operation loads some designated part of an XPage in the browser without reloading the entire browser page. Unfortunately, if you were to implement AJAX directly in your XPages applications, you would need to develop a lot of infrastructural code before writing any application logic. XPages takes care of the AJAX infrastructure on your behalf and allows you to concentrate entirely on the application logic.

> **TIP**
>
> For more general information on AJAX and partial refresh, do some background reading at websites such as http://en.wikipedia.org/wiki/Ajax_(programming) and www.w3schools.com/Ajax/Default.Asp.

Partial Refresh: Out-of-the-Box Style!

Introducing partial refresh into your application is as simple as checking a radio button option and selecting a target component identifier from a list—all the supporting client-side framework code, resolution of client-side identifiers, and so forth is then automatically generated for you!

To see a worked example of this, open the **partialRefresh** XPage within the **Chp11Ed2.nsf** application. Once opened, select the **button1** control within the WYSIWYG editor to give it focus. Then, select the Events view below the WYSIWYG editor, as shown in Figure 11.1.

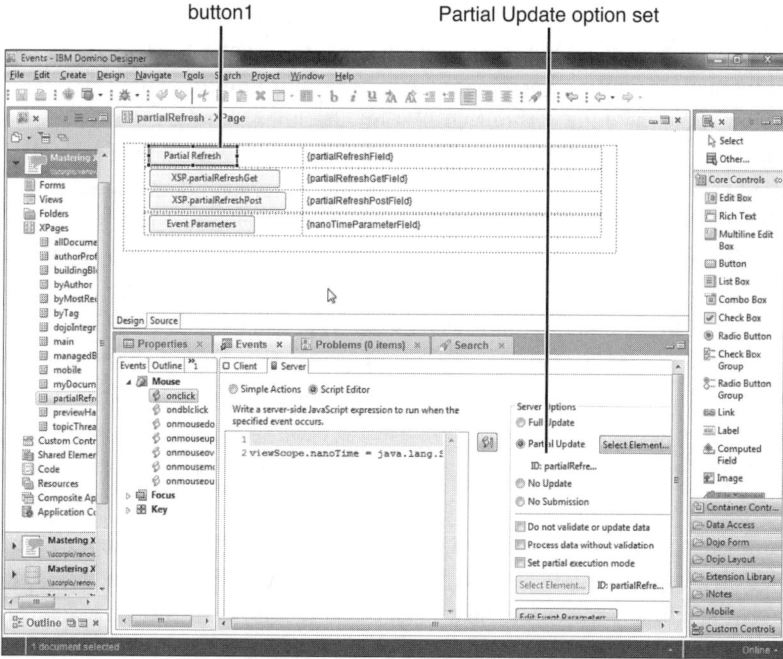

Figure 11.1 Selecting the Events view for the button1 control

As you already learned in Chapter 6, the **Events** view provides all the necessary settings and options that allow you to configure control events. One of the options that you have not yet learned about is **Server Options**. In Figure 11.1, this options group is shown on the right side of the **Events** panel and is only relevant to server-side events. This group is basically split into three distinct sections:

1. An update option section allows you to specify how an event updates the current XPage when triggered. The default for this option is **Full Update**. This means that the XPage will be entirely updated upon event invocation—in other words, the XPage is submitted and an entire reload occurs. On the other hand, the **Partial Update** option enables the event to be invoked, but subsequently only update a specified target element on the XPage when the response is received. The **No Update** option allows the server-side event to be invoked through a partial refresh call, but absolutely no refresh of the XPage occurs thereafter—this can be useful for certain application-specific use cases, such as sniffing information on events happening in the browser page. (For example, a user enters a value into an Edit Box and the value is sent to the server without reloading any of the browser page.) That value can then be processed on the server side. The **No Submission** option is more relevant to client-side events in that when this option is set, only client-side events can be invoked—no submission of the XPage is made regardless of whether associated server-side event code is specified on the event handler.
2. A validation and processing section allows you to configure two things: first, how an event submits data to participate within the validation phase of the XPages request lifecycle. (You learned about the XPages request lifecycle in Chapter 5.) This is configured using a mutually exclusive combination of the **Do not update or validate data** checkbox and the **Process data without validation** checkbox. You learn more on the ways you can configure validation later in this chapter. Second, by using the **Set partial execution mode** checkbox, you can control what degree of server-side component tree processing should occur when an event is invoked. By default, when a server-side event is invoked, the entire component tree of its parent XPage executes. When checked, this setting limits the processing of the component tree to only this event handler. There is also an additional `execId` property supported by an event handler that is now exposed in the Domino Designer UI in Notes/Domino 9.0.1 as previous releases only exposed this property in XSP markup. This property allows you to specify an execution target within the component tree. These settings are used to optimize an application and are not covered in this chapter. Instead, you learn more on the topic of partial execution in Chapter 19 and Chapter 20.
3. An event parameters section allows you to configure event specific parameters. These can be preset or computed when the event is invoked, and then subsequently read within the event-handling code on the server side. This provides a flexible mechanism

whereby you can pass dynamic parameter values into your event logic. You learn more on this in the section, "Event Parameters."

Referring to Figure 11.1 (alternatively, you can also view the **Events** view in the open application within Designer), you see that the update option is set to **Partial Update** in this case, and an element `id` of **partialRefreshField** is also specified. If you are in Designer, click the **Select Element** button. This opens a dialog that allows you to select a predefined element on the current XPage, or alternatively, you can specify statically, or by computing, an element `id`, as shown in Figure 11.2.

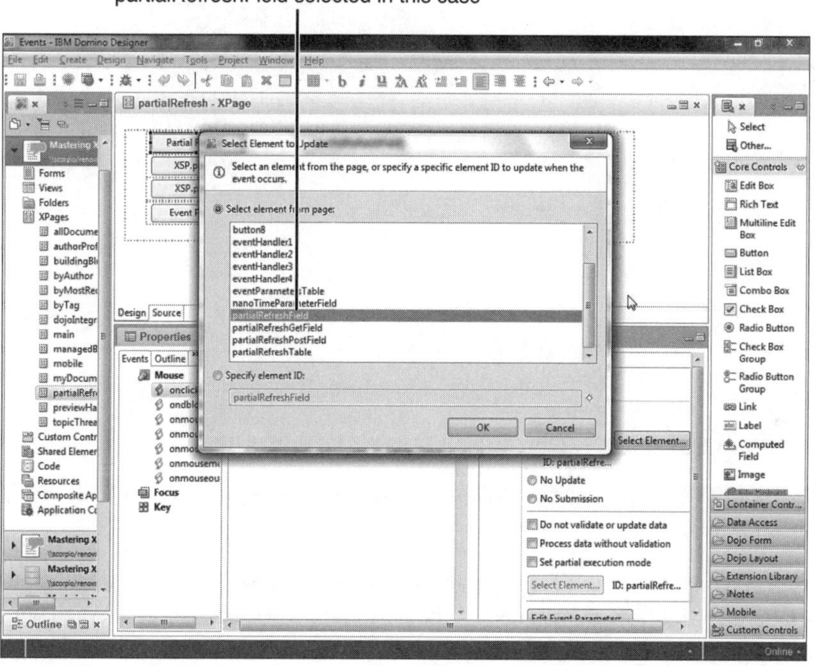

Figure 11.2 Select Element to Update dialog with the partialRefreshField element selected

In this case, the **partialRefreshField** element is already selected from the list of predefined elements within the current XPage (scroll down the list to find it). At this point, you should get an inkling as to what is actually happening with this example. In summary, the **button1** control is setup with an `onclick` server-side event. That event is configured to use the **Partial Update** option and has the **partialRefreshField** element specified as its update target. All of this results in a link that, when clicked, invokes its server-side event code and only updates the specified target within the XPage. You saw a similar example in Chapter 8, "Working with Domino Views."

Preview the **partialRefresh** XPage from Designer on the web or XPiNC client—your choice! Once launched, click on the Partial Refresh button, a partial refresh request is made, and the partialRefreshField HTML DOM element will be updated with the partial refresh response value. This is highlighted in Figure 11.3.

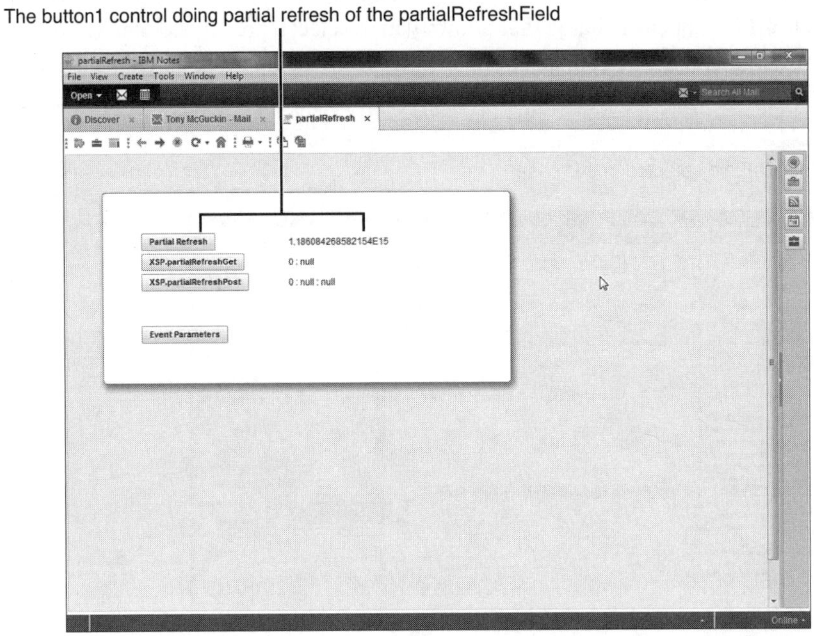

The button1 control doing partial refresh of the partialRefreshField

Figure 11.3 button1 and partialRefreshField working in tandem using partial refresh

In essence, this is an example of XPages enabling you to use AJAX capabilities without having to write a single line of AJAX-related code—the only code you should be concerned with is your application logic code! By simply creating a server-side event and setting it to use the **Partial Update** option, all the AJAX code is automatically managed by the XPages runtime, saving you precious development time.

Now explore this example plus other ways of doing partial refresh, by continuing to use the **partialRefresh** XPage. As you can see, there is a total of four button controls in the WYSIWYG editor for this XPage, as shown in Figure 11.4.

The first of these button controls is labeled **Partial Refresh** and, as already explained, is an example of doing a partial refresh without writing any supporting AJAX code. But let's now examine this example in greater detail. If you inspect the **Events** view for this button, you see that it has a server-side `onclick` event that is configured to partially refresh the `partialRefreshField` Computed Field control. It also contains one line of application logic code that simply assigns the system nanotime to the `viewScope.nanoTime` variable. If you now inspect the `partialRefreshField` Computed Field control's value panel, you see that it is bound to that particular variable, as shown in Figure 11.5.

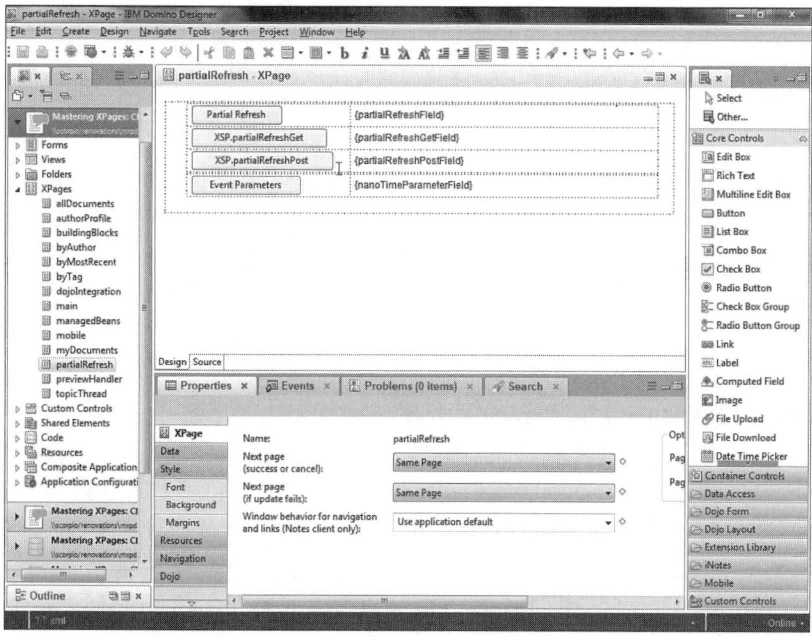

Figure 11.4 Four button controls on the partialRefresh XPage

> **TIP**
>
> For the examples of this section on partial refresh, you benefit most by previewing using an up-to-date version of the Firefox browser that also has the popular and cost-free Firebug plug-in installed. Alternatively, any other browser with a network sniffing plug-in or add-on installed, or any HTTP-sniffing application will suffice. This allows you to examine the partialRefresh XPage HTTP traffic that is transmitted over the network during partial refresh requests. Don't worry if you don't have Firefox or a HTTP-sniffing application installed, however—you can still proceed through this section.

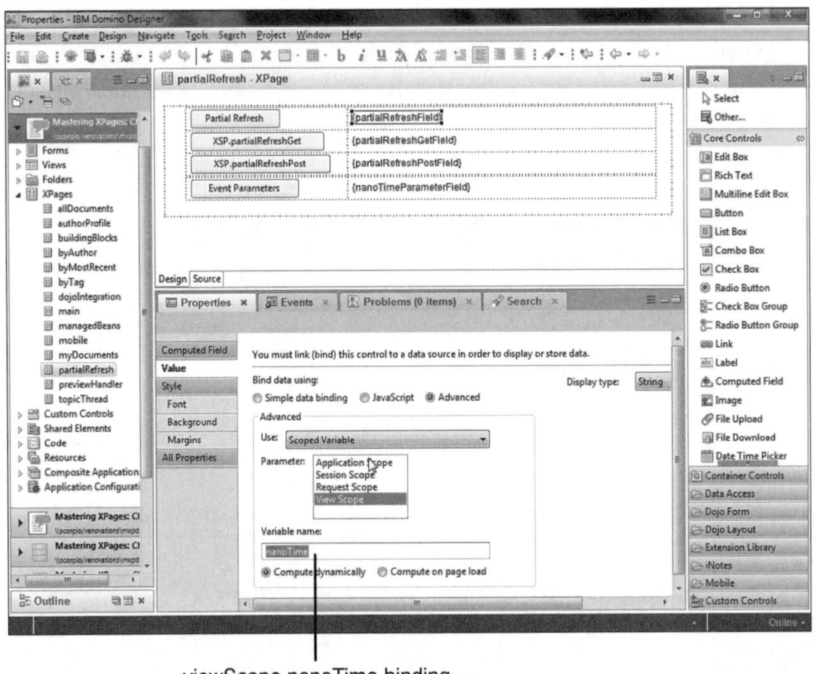

Figure 11.5 PartialRefreshField value bound to the viewScope.nanoTime variable

Now, preview this XPage using the **Preview in Web Browser** option in Designer. If you have Firefox installed, select it from the drop-down list of browser options, as shown in Figure 11.6.

After the XPage loads in the browser, enable Firebug or your HTTP-sniffing application and click the **Partial Refresh** button. This causes a request to be submitted to the XPages runtime that executes the associated server-side event handler. The result is the assignment of the system nanotime into the `viewScope.nanoTime` variable. Because this is a partial refresh request targeted at the `partialRefreshField` control, you now see the value of the `viewScope.nanoTime` variable within this control. Note the fact that the entire XPage does not reload when you click the **Partial Refresh** button. Also, at this point, examine the request/response data in debug utility program. As you will see, a POST-based request will have been sent from the browser, containing several important pieces of information.

First, the request querystring parameters contain a parameter named `$$ajaxid` with the client-side ID of the `partialRefreshField` control. XPages runtime uses this `$$ajaxid` as the target of the partial refresh request. This can be seen using Firebug in Figure 11.7.

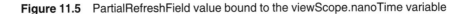

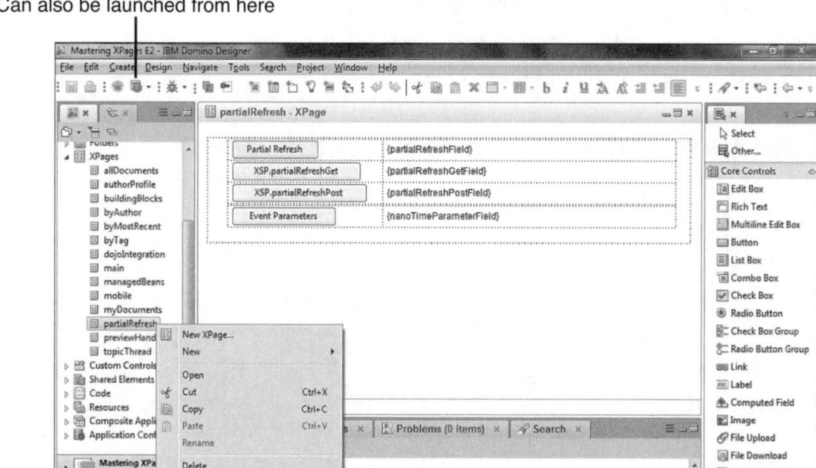

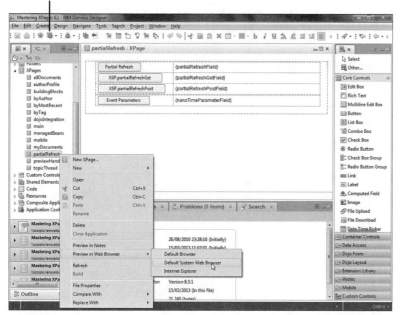

Figure 11.6 Preview in a web browser using Firefox option in Designer

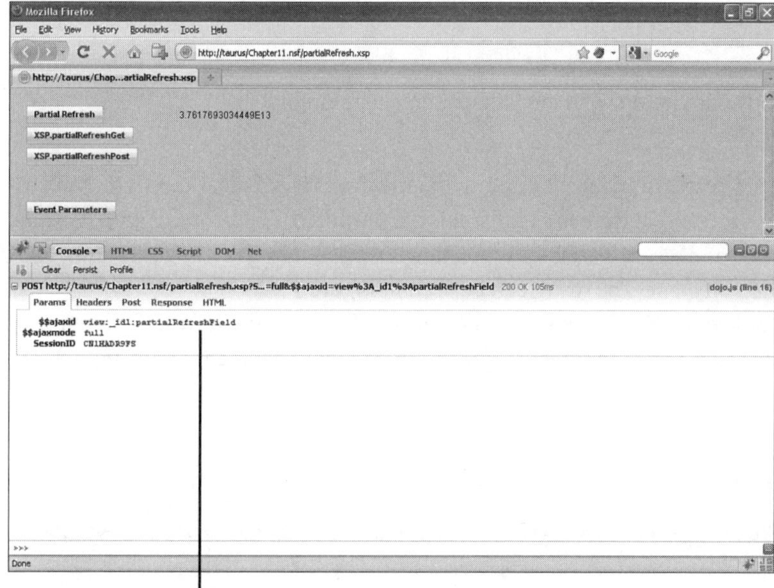

Figure 11.7 Request querystring parameters with the $$ajaxid parameter

Second, the POST body parameters also contain a parameter called `$$xspsubmitid`. The value of this parameter is the ID of the server-side event handler for the XPages runtime to execute. Again, this is shown using Firebug in Figure 11.8.

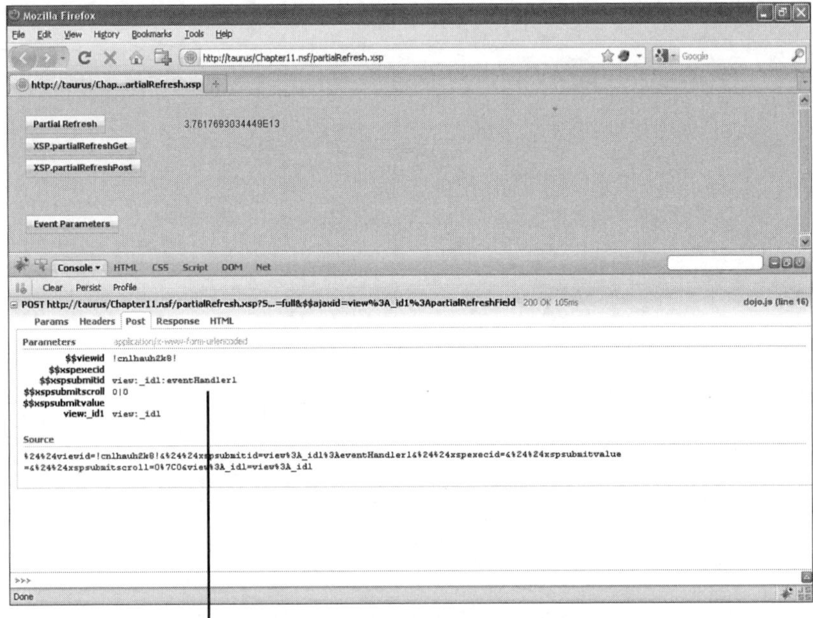

Figure 11.8 POST body parameters with the $$xspsubmitid parameter

If you examine the response data, you see a fragment of HTML markup, which represents the `partialRefreshField`. Remember that it is a **Computed Field** control with its value bound to the `viewScope.nanoTime` variable. When this is rendered by the XPages runtime, it is done so as a HTML `span` element. The result can be seen in Figure 11.9.

This simple example demonstrates just how powerful XPages partial refresh feature really is, and how it ultimately saves you a lot of development time without having to write any AJAX-related code!

TIP

Go to www.w3.org/2001/tag/doc/whenToUseGet.html for more information on GET- versus POST-based HTTP requests.

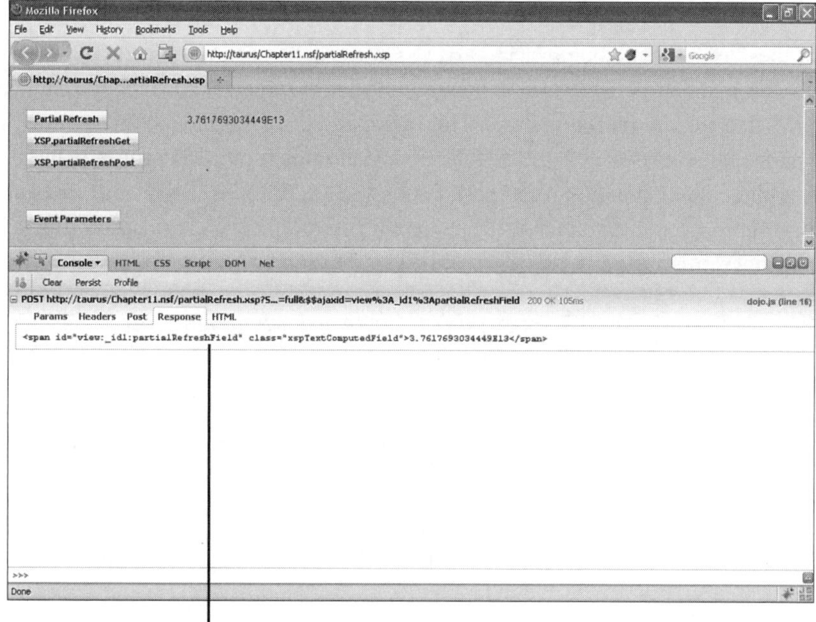

The updated <span> HTML response for the partialUpdateField

Figure 11.9 Response data containing the partialRefreshField HTML span element

Partial Refresh: Doing-It-My-Way Style!

As with just about everything else in XPages, you are also free to perform **partial refresh** manually using script. As you learned in Chapter 6, the client-side `XSP` scripting object exposes numerous XPages framework and utility functions. Two of these utility functions are detailed in Listing 11.1 and are used for partial refresh scripting.

Listing 11.1 Partial Refresh Utility Functions on the Client-Side XSP Object

```
XSP.partialRefreshGet(
    /*mandatory*/ refreshId,
    /*optional*/ options
)

XSP.partialRefreshPost(
    /*mandatory*/ refreshId,
    /*optional*/ options
)
```

partialRefreshGet Utility Function

The first of these two functions, `partialRefreshGet()`, is used to issue a GET-based AJAX call. It uses the mandatory `refreshId` parameter as the target element identifier within the HTML DOM tree for the partial refresh. The optional `options` parameter typically specifies additional parameters to send with the AJAX request through a `params` property, but it can also include up to three other function references for `onStart`, `onError`, and `onComplete` events. If supplied in the `options` parameter, these are triggered during the execution lifecycle of the associated partial refresh request, as shown in Listing 11.2.

Listing 11.2 Partial Refresh GET Example with Optional options Parameter

```
function prOnStart(){console.log("Started");}
function prOnError(){console.log("Error");}
function prOnComplete(){console.log("Completed");}

var prOptions = {"x" : 123.45, "y" : 678.90};

XSP.partialRefreshGet("#{id:prTargetId}",
    {
        params : prOptions,
        onStart : prOnStart,
        onError : prOnError,
        onComplete : prOnComplete
    }
);
```

You find a fully worked example of this on the `partialRefresh` XPage within the **Chp11Ed2.nsf** application. Focus on the second of the four button controls labeled *XSP.partialRefreshGet* in the WYSIWYG editor and look at the **Client** tab under **Events** view, as shown in Figure 11.10.

Remember that this is client-side JavaScript code. The only exception to this is the inclusion of the server-side client identifier binding `#{id:}` to resolve the fully expanded client-side identifier of the `partialRefreshGetField` target control. Basically, the call to `XSP.partialRefreshGet()` is given the target HTML DOM tree element identifier as its first parameter, and the second parameter is encapsulated within a JavaScript object notation (JSON) anonymous instance.

> **TIP**
>
> Learn about JSON at www.json.org and http://en.wikipedia.org/wiki/JSON.

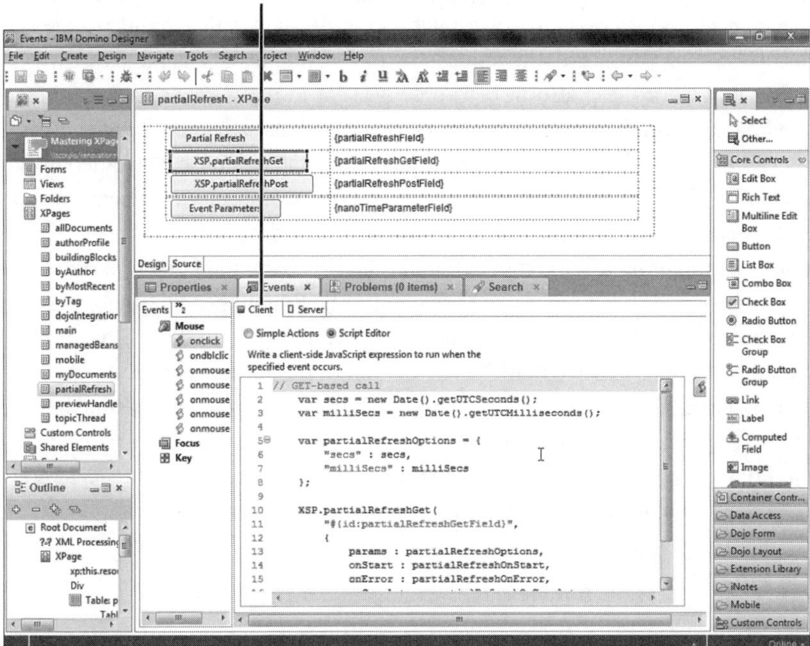

Figure 11.10 Client-side onclick code of the second button using XSP.partialRefreshGet

This second parameter contains the `params`, `onStart`, `onError`, and `onComplete` properties—the first pointing at the `partialRefreshOptions` JSON object, and the rest using the declared function references.

When this fragment of code is invoked, a background request is made by the platform (browser or client) using the underlying AJAX handler of that platform. This is typically the **XMLHttpRequest** object in Mozilla-based browsers and the **XMLHTTP** ActiveX® control in Microsoft-based browsers. Either way, XPages hides the complexities of the platform by bridging AJAX requests through the `dojo.xhr` API and exposing only the things you need via the `XSP` client-side object.

> **TIP**
>
> Learn about Dojo and dojo.xhr at www.dojotoolkit.org and www.dojotoolkit.org/reference-guide/dojo/xhr.html.

Therefore, by decorating the `dojo.xhr` API using the `XSP` client-side object, you get exactly what you need in terms of cross-platform interoperability and XPages integration for AJAX programmability. So, the background request in this example is channeled down to the underlying AJAX handler for the platform before being sent to the XPages runtime. Once received within the XPages runtime, the request must be processed and a response handed back to the AJAX handler. This is where the beauty lies within AJAX—the response is handled inline without reloading the entire XPage! Only the target element (and any of its child elements) specified by the `refreshId` get replaced with the response data.

So, at this point, you might be asking yourself about the `options` parameter, particularly around the `params` property and the JSON object assigned to it. Remember that the `options` parameter is optional, but is typically used to send additional parameters with the partial refresh request—so this example is doing exactly that! Under the hood, the `params` property actually gets expanded, encoded, and appended to the GET request URI that is invoked by the underlying AJAX handler. Therefore, you can retrieve whatever has been specified on the `params` property using the server-side JavaScript `param` object. So, for example, if you want to retrieve and concatenate the `x` and `y` property values from the params property on the server-side, simply access them as follows:

```
#{javascript:param.x + ' ' + param.y}
```

A fully worked example of this is shown in Figure 11.11 for the `partialRefreshGetField` Computed Field control of the `partialRefresh` XPage.

In this example, the `partialRefreshGetField` Computed Field is the target of the `XSP.partialRefreshGet()` request shown in Figure 11.10. Once invoked by the partial refresh request, it evaluates its value using the server-side expression shown in Figure 11.11.

As you can see, this uses the `param` object to access the `secs` and `milliSecs` properties that are available from the request data.

If you have not already done so, take this opportunity to click the **XSP.partialRefreshGet** button and, with your favorite debugging utility, examine the request/response data for this partial refresh request. Unlike the first **Partial Refresh** button example that sent a POST-based request when clicked, this request is GET based. Therefore, one key difference that you will see in the request data is the lack of a POST body section; therefore, no `$$xspsubmitid` parameter is required because no server-side event handler is needed this time. Also, notice that the `param` property is expanded into separate request `querystring` parameters. Therefore, the `secs` and `milliSecs` parameters appear on the GET URL, as shown using Firebug in Figure 11.12.

In this example, the response data carries the same HTML SPAN construct as shown in the first button example. This is the rendered markup that represents the evaluated **partialRefreshGetField** Computed Field control.

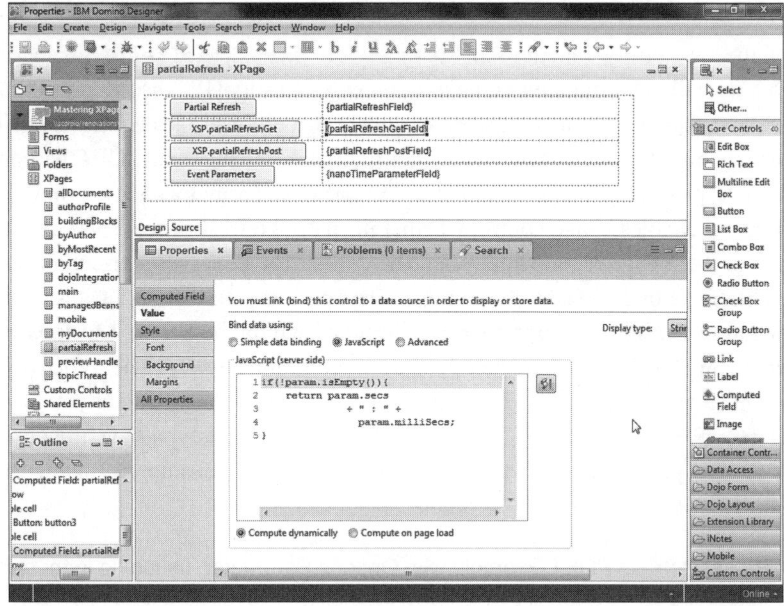

Figure 11.11 partialRefreshGetField value expression using the param object

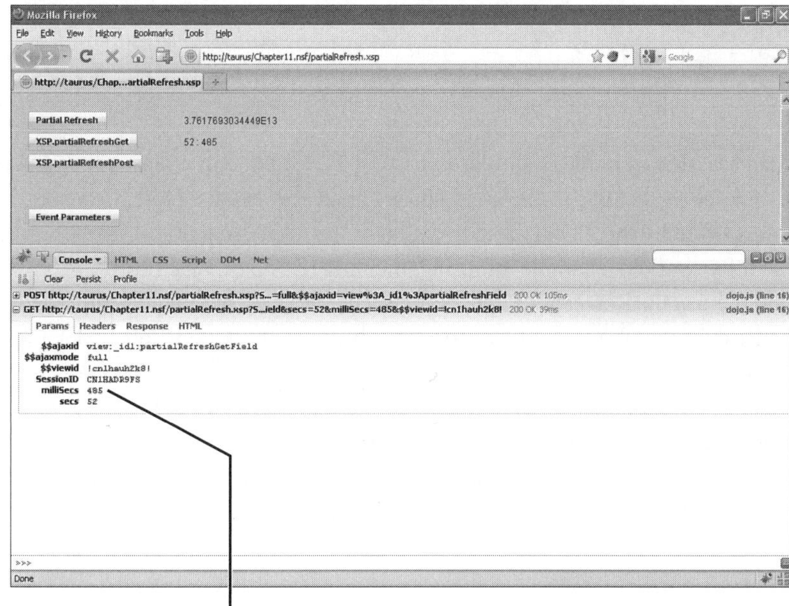

The milliSecs and secs option params in the querystring parameters

Figure 11.12 XSP.partialRefreshGet request data seen using Firebug

partialRefreshPost Utility Function

The second of the two utility functions in Listing 11.1, `partialRefreshPost()`, issues a POST-based AJAX call. The function signature is identical to its GET-based sibling in that it has a mandatory `refreshId` parameter and an optional `options` parameter. One key difference exists, however: The `options` parameter can be configured differently to the GET-based version with two additional properties being supported: the `immediate` and `execId` properties. The `immediate` property enables you to control whether the partial refresh request participates in the validation phase of the XPage request lifecycle. The default for all server-side submitting event handlers is to participate in this phase. Setting this script property, in fact, replicates checking or unchecking the **Do not validate or update data** checkbox within the **Server Options** group on the Events view within Designer—only here, you do it programmatically! The `execId` property is, as you might have guessed, related to the **Partial Execution** mode topic, and you learn about this in Chapter 16, "XPages Theming." For now, suffice it to say that you have the opportunity to control this feature programmatically. Listing 11.3 provides an example of using the `XSP.partialRefreshPost()` function.

Listing 11.3 Partial Refresh POST Example with Options Parameter, Including immediate Property

```
var prOptions = {"x" : 123.45, "z" : 678.90};

XSP.partialRefreshPost("#{id:prTargetId}",
    {params : prOptions,
     immediate : true}
);
```

As you can see, this example is similar to Listing 11.1, although it does not pass any function references for the `onStart`, `onError`, and `onComplete` events. Note, however, that this feature is also supported by this POST-based version of the utility function.

Again, a fully worked example of using the `XSP.partialRefreshPost()` function can be found on the **partialRefresh** XPage. Now, focus the third button control, labelled **XSP.partialRefreshPost** in the WYSIWYG editor, and examine the **Client** tab under the **Events** view, as shown in Figure 11.13.

Again, take the opportunity to click this button and use a debug utility program to examine the request/response data. In this `XSP.partialRefreshPost()` example, you see that the `options param` property also gets expanded, but unlike its GET-based sibling function, the items become POST body parameters, as shown in Figure 11.14.

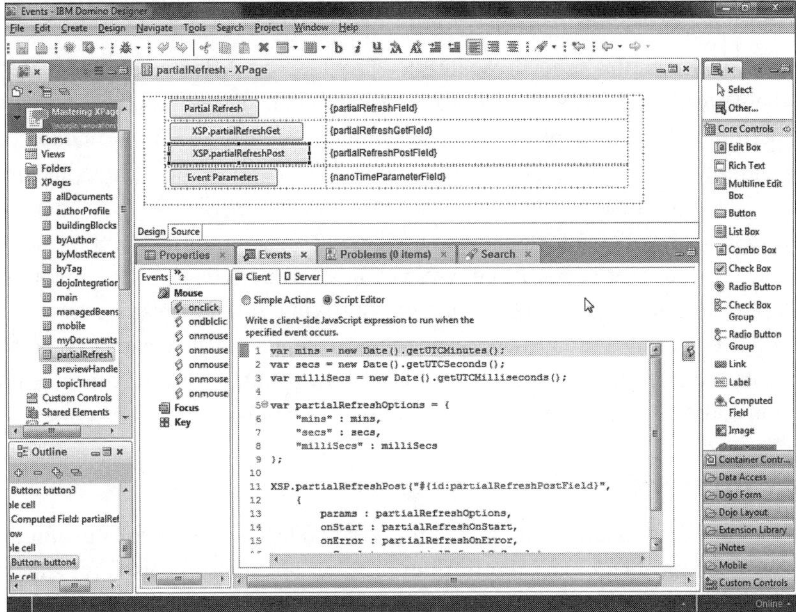

Figure 11.13 Client-side onclick code of the third button using XSP.partialRefreshPost

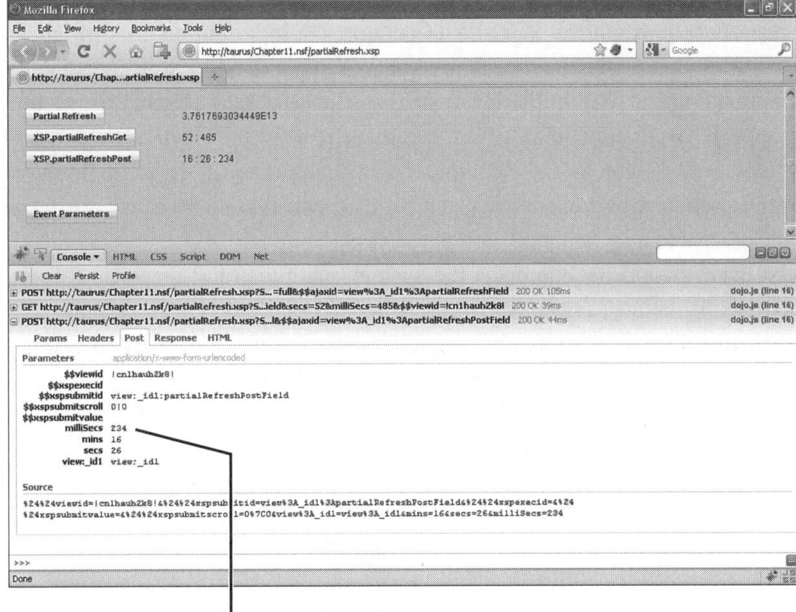

Figure 11.14 XSP.partialRefreshPost POST body parameters

Partial Refresh: A Low-Cost Performance Improvement

Appropriate use of the partial refresh capabilities provided by XPages can undoubtedly reap benefits for the performance and responsiveness of your applications. Applied correctly, it can improve the performance of an application by reducing the amount of HTML markup that must be processed and emitted as responses back to the client or browser. Hence, the application server uses less CPU cycles. This has a knock-on effect in that the responsiveness of an application is improved due to less network bandwidth being used to relay the response. Combine this with the fact that the client or browser is not actually reloading an entire XPage—only a part of it. This radically reduces the refresh time and gives a more satisfying visual display because of the lack of screen flicker seen during a full browser page reload. Chapter 19 and Chapter 20 both provide more detail on partial refresh. In particular, you learn how a partial refresh request is processed against the component tree and a way in which you can further optimize this process.

Event Parameters

A feature related to event handling that is also useful to understand is **Event Parameters**. This feature is not only applicable to partial refresh events, but it can also be used for standard full-page refresh events. This feature allows you to define parameters that can be used directly within the server-side JavaScript application logic of an event. Essentially, you have the ability to create parameterized event handlers.

To configure event parameters, you must use the same **Events** view used for the other partial refresh examples of this chapter. If it is closed, reopen the **partialRefresh** XPage within Designer. Once opened within the WYSIWYG editor, click the button control labeled **Event Parameter**. Now, click the **Events** view below the WYSIWYG editor to inspect the event handler for this button control. Within the **Events** view, click the **Edit Event Parameters** button, and a dialog appears. Within this dialog, you can manage a list of one or more event parameter names and values, both of which can be computed when necessary. In the example shown in Figure 11.15 for this particular button control event handler, two event parameters are defined. Each one has a static name and a dynamically computed value.

The first event parameter computes the system nanotime, and the second computes the milliseconds time. Both are named accordingly as `nanoTimeParameter` and `milliSecsParameter`. Listing 11.4 is a shortened version of the fragment of markup taken from the **partialRefresh** XPage related to the **Event Parameters** button.

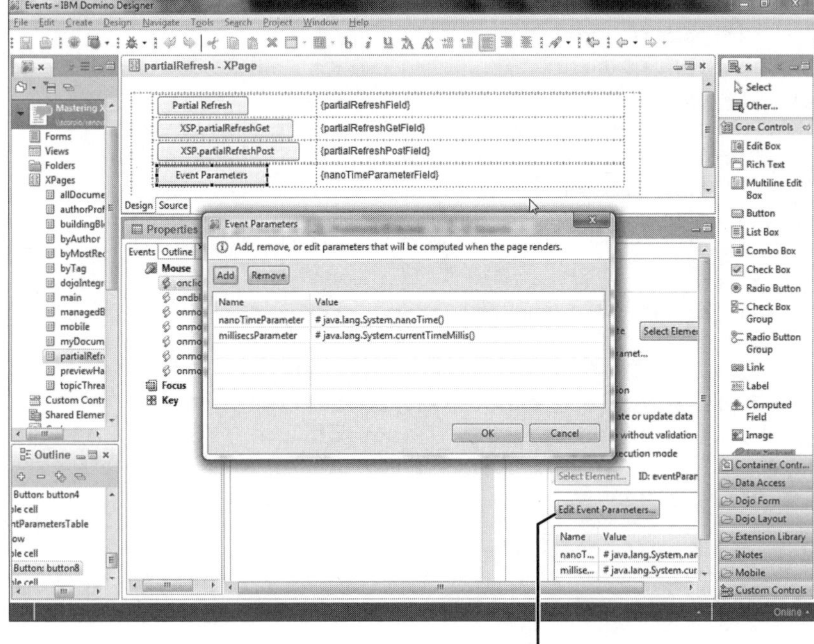
Click here to launch the Event Parameters editor

Figure 11.15 Event Parameters editor

Listing 11.4 Event Parameters Button and Related Code

```
<xp:table id="eventParametersTable">
    <xp:tr><xp:td>
    <xp:button value="Event Parameters">
        <xp:eventHandler event="onclick" submit="true"
            refreshMode="partial"
            refreshId="eventParametersTable">
            <xp:this.parameters>
                <xp:parameter
                    name="nanoTimeParameter"
                    value="#{javascript:java.lang.System.nanoTime()}">
                </xp:parameter>
                <xp:parameter
                    name="millisecsParameter"
                    value="#{javascript:// millisecs
```

```
                java.lang.System.currentTimeMillis()}">
            </xp:parameter>
        </xp:this.parameters>
        <xp:this.action><![CDATA[#{javascript:
            viewScope.nanoTimeParameter = nanoTimeParameter;
            viewScope.millisecsParameter = millisecsParameter;
        }]]></xp:this.action>
    </xp:eventHandler>
</xp:button>
</xp:td><xp:td>
<xp:text escape="true" id="nanoTimeParameterField">
    <xp:this.value><![CDATA[#{javascript:
        if(null != viewScope.nanoTimeParameter){
            return viewScope.nanoTimeParameter + " : " +
                viewScope.millisecsParameter;
        }
    }]]></xp:this.value>
</xp:text>
</xp:td></xp:tr>
</xp:table>
```

When an event handler is not configured for partial refresh, any associated event parameters are recomputed each time the event handler is reinvoked. Essentially, this means that any event parameters on an event handler will have their computed expressions reevaluated each time the parent XPage is reloaded in the browser or client. On the other hand, when an event handler is configured for partial refresh, any associated event parameters will only be computed when the entire XPage loads. This effectively means that, although the event handler will be executing a partial refresh request against a target element, the event parameters will not be recomputed during the partial refresh request. If you do require them to be recomputed, you must ensure that the event handler is included within the target partial refresh area of the component tree. This is shown in Listing 11.4, where `refreshId` for the **Event Parameters** button's event handler points at the enclosing `eventParametersTable` control. This table control actually encloses the button, its event handler, and the Computed Field that displays the event parameter values—therefore ensuring that the event handler is part of the partial refresh area of the component tree. If you try clicking this button in the browser, you see that the Computed Field does redisplay the recomputed `nanoTimeParameter` and `milliSecsParameter` time values.

In Listing 11.4, notice that the declared event parameters are accessed within the server-side JavaScript code directly by name. This makes it easy for you to work with event parameters within your code.

Dojo Integration

XPages supports the well-proven Dojo Toolkit as its JavaScript user interface library. If you are not familiar with Dojo, prime yourself by visiting `www.dojotoolkit.org` and `www.dojo-campus.org`. The Dojo Toolkit is an open source project supported by many industry leading companies, including IBM. In a nutshell, Dojo makes it easier to create dynamic, interactive, and cross-platform JavaScript-based web application user interfaces.

As previously mentioned, the `XSP` client-side JavaScript object actually decorates some of the Dojo API to provide a seamless integration between XPages and the Dojo Toolkit API. This is one of the great things about using XPages: You don't necessarily need to care about Dojo at all. The XPages runtime provides your applications with all the required Dojo resources without you writing a single line of code! Examples of XPages transparently providing and managing Dojo for you include the **Date Time Picker** and the **TypeAhead** controls. You simply drag-and-drop these to your XPage in Designer without providing any extra Dojo-related configuration or coding steps thereafter.

But, as always, some developers need to do special things with their applications—and Dojo integration does not get left out here. XPages provides a Dojo-integration mechanism that allows the standard library of XPages controls to be extended with Dojo widgets—both standard toolkit and custom-coded varieties for the die-hard Dojo developer. This can result in much richer user interfaces using Dojo widgets that still maintain the relationship between XPage control and server-side component tree.

If you include any of the Dojo-based XPages controls. such as the **Date Time Picker** or **TypeAhead**, on an XPage, a couple of steps take place behind the scenes when you view that XPage in a browser or client. First, the XPages runtime is notified by the control that it is a Dojo-based control. This means that the emitted markup for the XPage must include supporting Dojo code and resources for the control to initialize and render correctly as a Dojo widget. Therefore, as a second step, the Dojo Theme resources, the Dojo API resources, the Dojo Module resource, and Dojo Parser directive are included in the emitted XPage markup. The end result is an XPage in the browser or client with the Dojo-based control correctly loaded for you.

This is an example of XPages managing Dojo for you, but what about situations where you need to manage Dojo yourself? For this case, XPages provides you with a set of Dojo-related configuration properties and a resource tag.

dojoTheme and dojoParseOnLoad Properties

Both an XPage and a Custom Control support the `dojoTheme` and `dojoParseOnLoad` properties. Both properties can be set using the **All Properties** panel under the **Properties** view in Designer or alternatively in the editor panels where appropriate. Both are of boolean data type, so accept a `true` or `false` value. Note that the default for both is implicitly set to `false`.

When the `dojoParseOnLoad` property is set to `true`, the emitted HTML markup for the XPage includes a directive within the `djConfig` attribute instructing Dojo to parse the markup when loaded in the browser—this is the `parseOnLoad: true` directive shown in Listing 11.5. The Dojo Parser module is also included in the markup—the `dojo.require('dojo.parser')` script, which is also shown in Listing 11.5. The Dojo Parser ensures that Dojo widgets get initialized and rendered; without it, any widgets on the XPage would simply be broken.

When the `dojoTheme` property is set to `true`, the XPages runtime ensures that the Dojo Theme-related resources are emitted in the HTML markup. This is shown in Listing 11.5, where the link to `'.../tundra.css` is included, but the style class `tundra` is appended to the `body` tag's style `class` attribute.

Listing 11.5 Dojo Parser and Theme Resources Being Included in the Emitted HTML Markup

```
<head>
...
<script type="text/javascript"
    src="/domjs/dojo-1.8.3/dojo/dojo.js"
    djConfig="locale: 'en-gb', parseOnLoad: true"></script>
...
<script type="text/javascript">dojo.require('dojo.parser')</script>
...
<link rel="stylesheet" type="text/css"
    href="/domjs/dojo-1.8.3/dijit/themes/tundra/tundra.css">
...
<body class="xspView tundra">
...
</body>
```

dojoModule Resource

An XPage and Custom Control both support the `dojoModule` resource. For the automatically managed controls, such as the **Rich Text Editor**, the associated Dojo Module resource required expression is emitted to the browser or client for you. This is shown in Listing 11.6 where the `dojo.require('ibm.xsp.widget.layout.xspCKEditor')` script is included. This ensures that the required source code is loaded into the browser or client for that particular control.

Listing 11.6 dojo.require() Statement Being Emitted Based on the dojoModule Resources

```
<head>
...
<script type="text/javascript"
    src="/domjs/dojo-1.8.3/dojo/dojo.js"
    djConfig="locale: 'en-gb', parseOnLoad: true"></script>
...
<script type="text/javascript">dojo.require('dojo.parser')</script>
<script
type="text/javascript">dojo.require('ibm.xsp.widget.layout.
➥xspCKEditor')</script>
<script
type="text/javascript">dojo.require('dijit.form.Button')</script>
...
<link rel="stylesheet" type="text/css"
    href="/domjs/dojo-1.8.3/dijit/themes/tundra/tundra.css">
...
<body class="xspView tundra">
...
</body>
```

However, Listing 11.6 also shows a second instance of the `dojo.require()` statement in the `dojo.require('dijit.form.Button')` script. This instance is occurring in the emitted HTML markup, as it has been manually added to the XPage using the **Resources** panel under the **Properties** view in Designer. It has been added as required by the XPages button control that is being extended to leverage the Dojo `dijit.form.Button` widget, as shown in Listing 11.7.

Listing 11.7 XPage Markup Showing Extended Button Control

```
<?xml version="1.0" encoding="UTF-8"?>
<xp:view xmlns:xp="http://www.ibm.com/xsp/core" dojoParseOnLoad="true"
      dojoTheme="true">
      <xp:this.resources>
            <xp:dojoModule name="dijit.form.Button"></xp:dojoModule>
      </xp:this.resources>
      <xp:inputRichText id="inputRichText1"></xp:inputRichText>
      <xp:br></xp:br>
      <xp:button value="Cut" id="button2" dojoType="dijit.form.Button">
            <xp:this.dojoAttributes>
```

```
                <xp:dojoAttribute name="iconClass"
                    value="dijitEditorIcon dijitEditorIconCut">
                </xp:dojoAttribute>
                <xp:dojoAttribute name="showLabel" value="false">
                </xp:dojoAttribute>
            </xp:this.dojoAttributes>
        </xp:button>
</xp:view>
```

Note that the `dojoModule` resource tag supports the inclusion of a client-side conditional expression. This allows you to control the loading of a Dojo Module within the browser or client based on some client-side condition (such as checking the browser version number or checking for a specific locale). Therefore, by using the `dojoModule` resource, you can manage any Dojo Module source files required by your widgets or extended XPages controls with full control and flexibility.

dojoType and dojoAttributes Properties

You can see in Listing 11.7 that the extended button control makes use of the `dojoType` and `dojoAttributes` properties. The `dojoType` property declares the type of the widget, and this must match the associated `dojoModule` resource. You can use the `dojoAttributes` property to define a list of one or more special attributes supported by the widget. In the button example in Listing 11.7, the button `iconClass` and `showLabel` widget attributes are being managed using the `dojoAttributes` property. Both the `name` and `value` properties of a `dojoAttribute` can be computed when necessary.

On quick examination of the XPages controls, you see that most of the controls support the `dojoType` and `dojoAttributes` properties. This ensures that the Dojo integration mechanism can be leveraged across all the supporting XPages controls. Furthermore, you also find these Dojo-specific properties exposed on the Dojo Property panel within Designer to make it all the easier to manage.

Integrating Dojo Widgets and Extending the Dojo Class Path

In the **Chp11Ed2.nsf** application, find an XPage called **dojoIntegration** and open this in Designer. This XPage does several interesting things using Dojo to create a lightweight user interface that allows you to preview the `body` field of documents within this application. Preview this XPage using the Firefox browser option, because it is purposely designed to work with Firefox and not to work on the Notes client—an explanation why soon follows. Once launched, you see something like Figure 11.16.

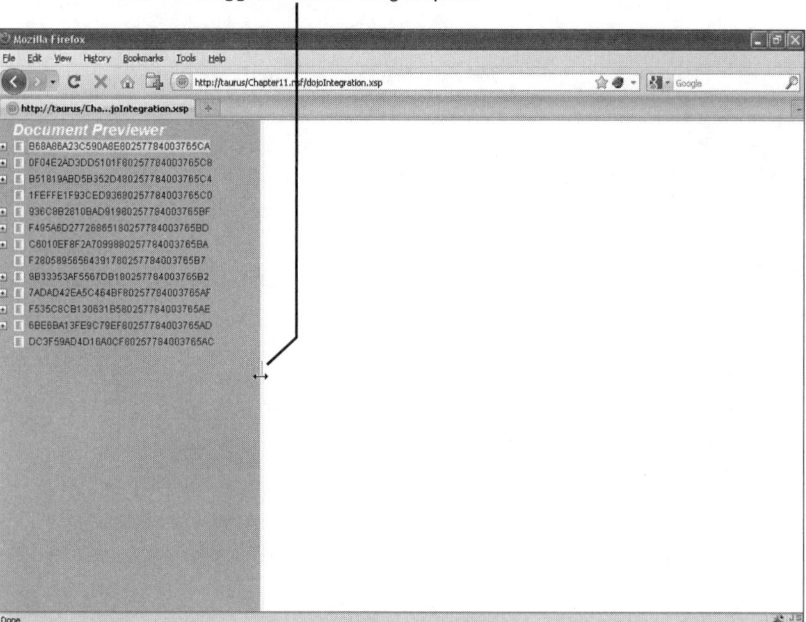

Figure 11.16 dojoIntegration XPage loaded in the browser

If you click any of the tree nodes within the left-side of the XPage, the contents of the target documents `body` field gets displayed in the right-side of the XPage, as shown in Figure 11.17.

Effectively, you are looking at an XPage composed of four Dojo widgets. First, there is a combination of two custom written widgets, one named `mxpd.ui.ViewTree` that extends the `dijit.Tree` widget. This provides the hierarchal tree of document IDs seen on the left side of the **dojoIntegration** XPage in Figure 11.16. The other one has been named `mxpd.data.ViewReadStore` and extends `dojo.data.ItemFileReadStore`. It provides the data for the tree widget by sending a partial refresh request against the Notes/Domino `ReadViewEntries` URL command—this is why this example only works against the in-built Domino preview server in your client or against a fully fledged Domino server, as a number of the classic Domino URL commands are not currently supported by XPages running in the client. This URL command returns all the view entries in the (`$xpAllDocuments`) view. Second, there is another combination of a `dijit.layout.ContentPane` and `dijit.layout.BorderPane` to provide a resizable, framed window.

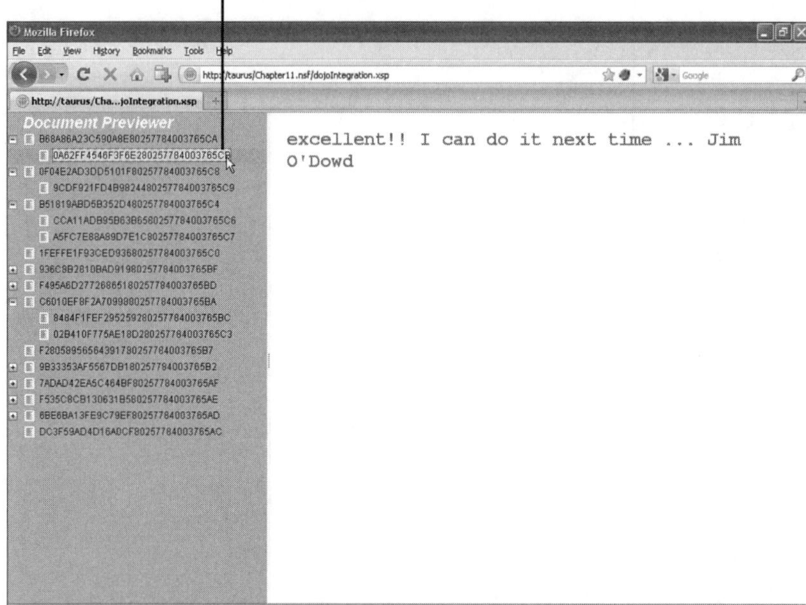

Figure 11.17 Body field content being displayed after clicking a tree node

When all this is put together, you are presented with an XPage that is a Dojo-based widget user interface. When you click the tree nodes in the left side, the contents of the related documents' `Body` field are displayed using partial refresh on the right side of the user interface. You are also able to drag the splitter pane. An examination of how this has been achieved is now in order.

Using Standard Dojo Widgets

As previously described, this XPage makes use of a combination of standard Dojo widgets and custom written widgets. In the case of standard Dojo widgets, all that is necessary to integrate these into an XPage is the declaration of the particular `dojoModule` and setting the `dojoType` on the bound control. Note/Domino 8.5 and upward ships with the Dojo Toolkit, so any required standard widget modules are already available to your application without you needing to perform any other deployment steps. Listing 11.8 is a fragment taken from the **dojoIntegration** XPage. It highlights the important things that enable the `dijit.layout.ContentPane` and `dijit.layout.BorderPane` to work correctly.

Listing 11.8 dojoIntegration XSP Markup Highlighting ContentPane and BorderPane Elements

```
<?xml version="1.0" encoding="UTF-8"?>
<xp:view xmlns:xp="http://www.ibm.com/xsp/core"
    dojoParseOnLoad="true"
    dojoTheme="true" ...>
    <xp:this.resources>
        ...
        <xp:dojoModule
            name="dijit.layout.BorderContainer"></xp:dojoModule>
        <xp:dojoModule
            name="dijit.layout.ContentPane"></xp:dojoModule>
    </xp:this.resources>
    <xp:div id="body" dojoType="dijit.layout.BorderContainer" ...>
        <xp:this.dojoAttributes>
            <xp:dojoAttribute
                name="persist"
                value="false">
            </xp:dojoAttribute>
            <xp:dojoAttribute
                name="gutters"
                value="false">
            </xp:dojoAttribute>
        </xp:this.dojoAttributes>
        <xp:div id="left" dojoType="dijit.layout.ContentPane" ...>
            <xp:this.dojoAttributes>
                <xp:dojoAttribute
                    name="region"
                    value="left">
                </xp:dojoAttribute>
                <xp:dojoAttribute
                    name="splitter"
                    value="true">
                </xp:dojoAttribute>
            </xp:this.dojoAttributes>
            ...
        </xp:div>
        <xp:div id="center" dojoType="dijit.layout.ContentPane" ...>
            <xp:this.dojoAttributes>
                <xp:dojoAttribute
                    name="region"
                    value="center">
```

```
                </xp:dojoAttribute>
            </xp:this.dojoAttributes>
        </xp:div>
    </xp:div>
</xp:view>
```

First, note the use of `dojoTheme` and `dojoParseOnLoad` on the XPage root tag. Because this example uses both standard toolkit and custom written Dojo widgets, the Dojo Theme and Dojo Parser must be made available. Remember that, for the automatically managed XPages controls, this step is done for you, but in a case like this, setting both of these properties to true is a configuration step that the developer must perform.

Second, note the inclusion of the two `dojoModule` resources, which point at the `dijit.layout.ContentPane` and `dijit.layout.BorderPane`, respectively. This is all that is required to ensure the underlying Dojo widget resources are included in the emitted XPage. As mentioned earlier, the actual Dojo standard toolkit widget resources are already shipped with Notes/Domino 8.5 and upward.

Finally, note the use of the `dojoType` and `dojoAbbributes` properties on the `<xp:div>` control tag. Essentially, this creates a binding between the HTML `DIV` tag and the Dojo widget instance when the Dojo Parser parses the emitted XPage in the browser or client.

Using Custom Dojo Widgets

As explained for the example in the previous section, the Dojo modules and other supporting resources are already deployed with Notes/Domino 8.5 and upward, so no further deployment steps are required to use these resources. The case for your own custom-coded widgets is slightly different in that you must ensure the widget source code files are deployed and available to your application. But, you must also ensure that the path to your widget code is registered with the Dojo framework. This allows Dojo to resolve any `dojoModule` references to your custom widget code.

It is important to explain the fact that the approach described in this section is one of several to integrate custom Dojo widgets within an XPage. It is a lightweight approach that involves deploying the custom widget source files from within the actual .NSF application file. Further optimizations could be employed to deploy from a global server location instead. The XPages Extensibility API is a separate XPages initiative that provides an extension and deployment mechanism for custom Dojo widgets. The approach used by that extension API is the best practice approach for production application use. The lightweight approach described in this example, however, teaches you the fundamentals of working with custom Dojo widgets in your XPages applications.

Listing 11.9 is a fragment taken from the **dojoIntegration** XPage, and it highlights the key elements of including custom-coded Dojo widgets in an XPage.

Listing 11.9 dojoIntegration XSP Markup Highlighting Key Custom Dojo Widget Elements

```
<?xml version="1.0" encoding="UTF-8"?>
<xp:view xmlns:xp="http://www.ibm.com/xsp/core"
    dojoParseOnLoad="true"
    dojoTheme="true" ...>
    <xp:this.resources>
        <xp:script src="/pathUtil.jss" clientSide="false"></xp:script>
        <xp:script clientSide="true">
            <xp:this.contents><![CDATA[
                var path = " ${javascript:getDatabasePath()} ".trim();
                dojo.registerModulePath("mxpd.ui", path+"mxpd/ui");
                dojo.registerModulePath("mxpd.data", path+"mxpd/data");
            ]]></xp:this.contents>
        </xp:script>
        <xp:dojoModule name="mxpd.ui.ViewTree"></xp:dojoModule>
        <xp:dojoModule
            name="mxpd.data.ViewReadStore">
        </xp:dojoModule>
    </xp:this.resources>
    <xp:div ...>
        <xp:div id="viewStore" style="visibility:hidden"
            dojoType="mxpd.data.ViewReadStore">
            <xp:this.dojoAttributes>
                <xp:dojoAttribute name="jsId"
                    value="allDocumentsReadStore">
                </xp:dojoAttribute>
                <xp:dojoAttribute name="url">
                    <xp:this.value>
                        <![CDATA[${javascript:
                            getDatabasePath() + "($xpAllDocuments)"
                        }]]>
                    </xp:this.value>
                </xp:dojoAttribute>
            </xp:this.dojoAttributes>
        </xp:div>
        <xp:div id="viewTree" dojoType="mxpd.ui.ViewTree">
            <xp:this.dojoAttributes>
                <xp:dojoAttribute name="store"
                    value="allDocumentsReadStore">
                </xp:dojoAttribute>
                <xp:dojoAttribute name="refreshId"
                    value="#{id:previewContainer}">
                </xp:dojoAttribute>
                <xp:dojoAttribute name="url"
```

```
44                      value="${javascript:getDatabasePath()}">
45                  </xp:dojoAttribute>
46                  <xp:dojoAttribute name="persist"
47                      value="false">
48                  </xp:dojoAttribute>
49              </xp:this.dojoAttributes>
50          </xp:div>
51      </xp:div>
52      ...
53 </xp:view>
```

To fully explain this markup, you also need to study Listing 11.10, which shows the code for the server-side `getDatabasePath()` function being using in Listing 11.9 on line 9. This function is held within the server-side JavaScript library, called `pathUtil.jss`, as declared in the resources for this XPage on line 6.

Listing 11.10 getDatabasePath() Function in the pathUtil.jss Server-Side JavaScript Library

```
function getDatabasePath(){
    var value = facesContext.getApplication()
                .getViewHandler().getResourceURL(facesContext, "/");
    value = facesContext.getExternalContext().encodeResourceURL(value);
    if(!value.endsWith("/")){
        value += "/";
    }
    return value;
}
```

As shown in Listing 11.9, for the XPage markup, the `pathUtil.jss` server-side Java Script library is included in the resources for the XPage. A second resource, which is a client-side piece of JavaScript, is coded directly within the resource declaration on line 7. This is done this way to allow the server-side `getDatabasePath()` call to be preprocessed before the XPage starts to emit HTML markup to the browser or client. This is one way to find out the full path to an .NSF application file, and it's demonstrated for you in this manner to simply highlight the intermingling of both server-side and client-side JavaScript. Therefore, this line of code gets preprocessed before delivery to the browser or client:

```
var path = " ${javascript:getDatabasePath()} ".trim();
```

It ends up looking like this when delivered to the browser or client:

```
var path = " /Chp11Ed2.nsf/ ".trim();
```

Lines 10 and 11, shown here, are where the actual paths to the custom-coded Dojo widget resources become registered with the Dojo framework:

```
dojo.registerModulePath("mxpd.ui", path + "mxpd/ui");
dojo.registerModulePath("mxpd.data", path + "mxpd/data");
```

The call to `dojo.registerModulePath()` is given two parameters. The first parameter is a Dojo package identifier. This is used as a prefix identifier to the widget class name, therefore resulting in the `dojoType` name for that widget. The second parameter is a physical path to the widget source code files. This enables the Dojo framework to resolve the Dojo package part of a `dojoType` attribute and `dojoModule` resource tag when initializing a rendered XPage. This registration step therefore allows the Dojo framework to load and initialize the module into the framework itself by using the special package/class name instead of using a URL based path name. So, in this particular example, two custom-coded Dojo modules are registered with the Dojo framework:

- `mxpd.ui` is resolvable at the location "`/Chp11Ed2.nsf/mxpd/ui`".
- `mxpd.data` is resolvable at the location "`/Chp11Ed2.nsf/mxpd/data`".

This of course implies that this subdirectory structure actually exists within the **Chp11Ed2.nsf** application. You can see that it does by examining the application using the Package Explorer view in Designer. To enable this view, select **Window > Show Eclipse Views > Other**. A dialog appears to assist you in selecting another view. Type the **Package Explorer** into the filter, as shown in Figure 11.18.

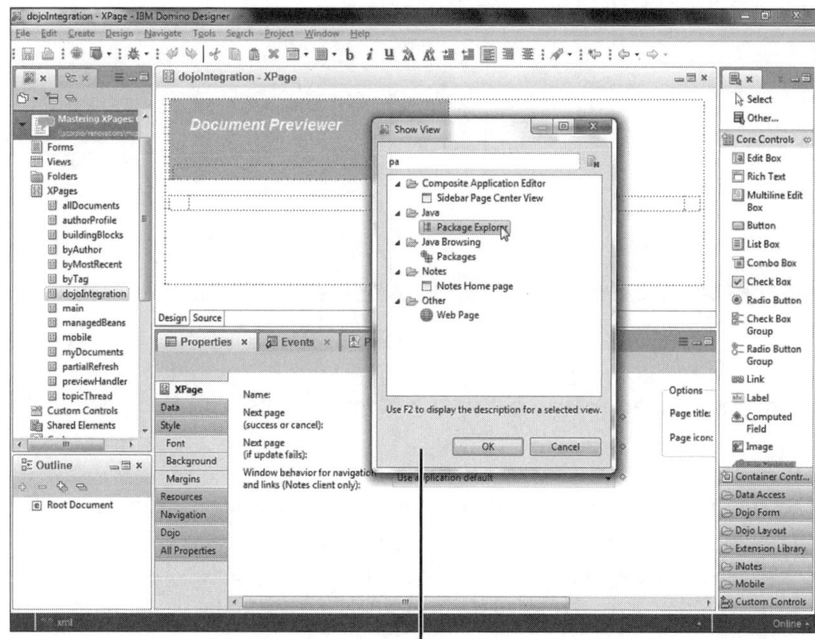

Window > Show Eclipse Views > Other...

Figure 11.18 Enabling the Package Explorer view in Designer

The **Package Explorer** view appears along the right side of Designer. It allows you to view an .NSF file as an Eclipse virtual file system. This means you can view the contents of the different design element folders within the .NSF file, but you can also manage content within the virtual file system. Now, expand the **Chp11Ed2.nsf** application within the **Package Explorer**. Among the virtual folders is a `WebContent` folder. Fully expand this folder and all of its subdirectories. This reveals numerous folders, including the `mxpd/ui` and `mxpd/data` subdirectories that contain the custom Dojo widget source files required by the **dojoIntegration** XPage, as shown in Figure 11.19.

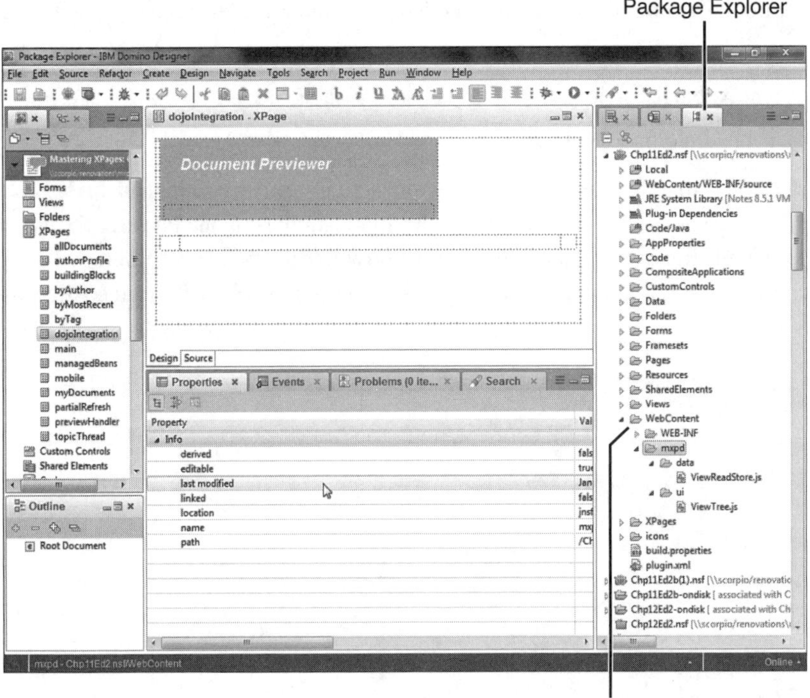

Figure 11.19 Examining the contents of the custom Dojo Module folders in the Package Explorer

You should be starting to understand how everything is tied together to integrate the custom Dojo widgets `mxpd.ui.ViewTree` and `mxpd.data.ViewReadStore` into the `dojoPartialRefresh` XPage. In Listing 11.9, you see two XPage `DIV` controls, both declaring the `dojoType` property. The first `<xp:div>` tag on lines 20-21 points to the `ViewReadStore` widget:

```
<xp:div id="viewStore" ... dojoType="mxpd.data.ViewReadStore">
```

The second `<xp:div>` tag on line 35 points at the `ViewTree` widget:

```
<xp:div id="viewTree" ... dojoType="mxpd.ui.ViewTree">
```

Now, double-click each custom-coded Dojo widget source file—`ViewTree.js` and `ViewReadStore.js`—within the **Package Explorer** to open them in Designer. Listing 11.11 shows the key pieces of code for the `ViewReadStore` widget. As you can see, the widget gets its full name from a combination of the registered module name and the filename of the actual JavaScript class. Hence, the `ViewReadStore` widget is formally declared and identified within the Dojo framework as `mxpd.data.ViewReadStore`. This same naming convention applies to the `ViewTree` widget, whereby it is formally declared and identified as the `mxpd.ui.ViewTree` widget.

Listing 11.11 Key Pieces of Code for the mxpd.data.ViewReadStore Custom Widget

```
dojo.provide("mxpd.data.ViewReadStore");
dojo.require("dojo.data.ItemFileReadStore");
dojo.declare("mxpd.data.ViewReadStore", [dojo.data.ItemFileReadStore],
{
    ...
    constructor: function ctor(keywordParameters){
        if(this._jsonFileUrl &&
            this._jsonFileUrl.indexOf("Expand") == -1){
                this._jsonFileUrl +=
                    ((this._jsonFileUrl.indexOf("?") == -1) ?
                        "?" : "&") +
                        "ReadViewEntries&OutputFormat=JSON&ExpandView";
        }
    },

    _getItemsFromLoadedData: function gifld(dataObject){
        ...
    }
});
```

The key to achieving successful integration of a custom Dojo widget is to ensure that the `dojoType` and `dojoModule` package and class name match the declared widget package and class name and that the physical path to the widget source files is resolvable and registered with the Dojo framework using the `dojo.registerModulePath()` function.

When Is an XPage Not an XPage?

Moving on from the integration topic, it is now worth explaining how this example actually retrieves the `Body` field contents. So, first, the interesting thing about the `mxpd.data.ViewReadStore` widget, as shown in Listing 11.11, is that it generates a URL in its constructor code. As previously described, this widget issues requests against the ReadViewEntries Notes/Domino URL command to retrieve view entry information. This information is parsed and reconstructed into a structure compatible for use by the mxpd.ui.ViewTree widget. This widget then displays this structure as a hierarchical tree. Listing 11.12 shows the key pieces of code for the mxpd.ui.ViewTree widget.

Listing 11.12 Key Pieces of Code for the mxpd.ui.ViewTree Custom Widget

```
dojo.provide("mxpd.ui.ViewTree");
dojo.require("dijit.Tree");
dojo.declare("mxpd.ui.ViewTree", [dijit.Tree],
{
    refreshId: "",
    url: "",

    loadHandler: function lh(response, ioArgs){
        var previewContainer = dojo.byId(this.refreshId);
        if(null != previewContainer){
            previewContainer.innerHTML = response;
        }
        return response;
    },

    onClick: function oc(item, node) {
        ...
        var position = this.store.getValue(item, "@position");
        ...
        var unid = this.store.getValue(item, "@unid");
        var loc = document.location.href;
        var actionURL = this.url +
                "previewHandler.xsp?" +
                    "action=openDocument&documentId=" + unid;
        dojo.xhrGet({
            url: actionURL,
            handleAs: "text",
            load: dojo.hitch(this, this.loadHandler)
        });
        ...
    },
    ...
});
```

Essentially, this widget renders itself as a hierarchal tree of document UNID nodes. On clicking a tree node, the contents of the target document's Body field is displayed using partial refresh. This is achieved via an AJAX GET-based request using the `dojo.xhrGet()` function, as shown in the `onClick` function in Listing 11.12. The target URL of this AJAX call is actually issued against another XPage, along with `action` and `documentId` querystring parameters. That target XPage is also inside the **Chp11Ed2.nsf** application and is named **previewHandler**. You can open this XPage in Designer and view its source code in the WYSIWYG editor. Listing 11.13 also details the XSP markup.

Listing 11.13 XSP Markup for the previewHandler XPage

```
<?xml version="1.0" encoding="UTF-8"?>
<xp:view xmlns:xp="http://www.ibm.com/xsp/core"
    rendered="false">
    <xp:this.afterRenderResponse>
        <![CDATA[#{javascript:
        var response = facesContext.getExternalContext().getResponse();
        var writer = facesContext.getResponseWriter();

        var unid = context.getUrlParameter("documentId");
        var responseContent = "<b>Document UNID is missing</b>";

        if(null != unid && unid.length > 0){
            var document = database.getDocumentByUNID(unid);
            var mimeEntity = document.getMIMEEntity("Body");
            if(null != mimeEntity){
                responseContent = mimeEntity.getContentAsText();
            }else{
                responseContent = document.getItemValueString("Body");
            }
            if(responseContent.equals("")){
                responseContent = "<b>No preview content available</b>";
            }
        }

        response.setContentType("text/html");
        writer.write(responseContent);
        writer.endDocument();}]]>
    </xp:this.afterRenderResponse>
</xp:view>
```

This is an example of using an XPage to generate a custom response. An XPage typically goes through the XPages execution lifecycle and finish by rendering a response to a browser or client. That response contains all the required HTML constructs, CSS, Dojo, and JavaScript resources to makeup the emitted XPage based on its XSP markup design. But as an alternative, you can also configure an XPage not to render by setting the `render` property on the `<xp:view>` tag to `false`. By then leveraging the `afterRenderResponse` XPage event as seen in Listing 11.13, you can access the XPages runtime `Response` and `ResponseWriter` objects to emit a custom response. In this particular example, the custom response is the content of the `Body` field within the target Notes Document. This content can be either MIME or CD record format, but either way this is written out as the response content when this XPage is requested. So, in this example, when you click a `mxpd.ui.ViewTree` node, this XPage is requested via an AJAX call. The response is then sent back to the AJAX handler, and the `mxpd.ui.ViewTree` partially updates the right-side of the XPage by assigning the response content to the `innerHTML` property of the `previewContainer` element shown in Listing 11.12.

The approach used here to retrieve a custom response is a very useful one. By using it, you can leverage the stateful XPages runtime of your application. You benefit from being able to access the XPages context and server-side API, but also in executing through the same security model as any other XPage. It is an approach that is not unlike using WebAgents written in either Java or LotusScript to return a custom response. The key difference is that WebAgents typically incur a large initialization time of up to 1.5 seconds when they are first requested. Whereas using an XPage in the manner described here, is several times faster to initialize and respond making it a better performing solution.

You have now learned a lot about XPages use of Dojo, but also about integrating your own custom Dojo widgets with XPages. And it is on this final topic about agents that you will learn more about, but also on working with other traditional Notes/Domino building blocks, such as @ Functions, and formula language in the next section of this chapter.

Working with Traditional Notes/Domino Building Blocks

Experienced Domino web-application developers undoubtedly assume certain things about XPages. That is, you most likely have an expectation that the way you did things for traditional Domino web-application development can still be done that way for the most part using XPages. The answer here is no for a few reasons—either XPages has a better way of doing it and the older way has been deprecated. Or in some cases, it simply has not been implemented in XPages yet (and we're working on it!)

The good news is that XPages, from Notes/Domino 8.5 onward, provides you with ways to work directly with @Functions in your server-side JavaScript code. You are also able to evaluate formula language and work with the scalar result directly in server-side JavaScript code. Of course, Java and LotusScript WebAgents can also be executed using server-side JavaScript code. New in Notes/Domino 8.5.2 onward, you can supply the current document context, or in-memory document, when running a WebAgent. This is in addition to the approach that has been there since Notes/Domino 8.5 of providing a parameter document ID. You learn more on these topics in the next three sections.

Working with @Functions, @Commands, and Formula Language

XPages provides you with 127 @Functions (this does not include the additional ones provided in the @FunctionsEx library). These are available through the server-side JavaScript @Function library, as shown in Figure 11.20. They are analogous to their Notes/Domino formula language siblings and make low-level calls on the same underlying backend @Function API.

Select the @Functions library from the dropdown list

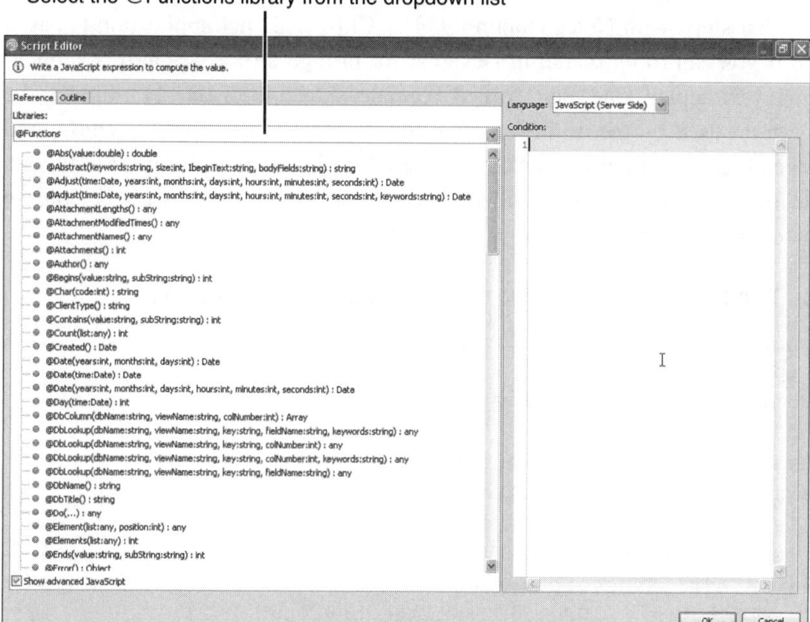

Figure 11.20 @Functions library within the Script Editor

Note that the same restrictions apply to the XPages implementation of these functions as those of their formula language siblings. (Refer to the in-built Domino Designer Help Index for details on Formula language restrictions.) One omission, for obvious reasons, is the `@Command` function. The `@Command` function cannot be run using a web application—its purpose is to execute Notes UI workspace actions. Leading on from this, certain other @Functions are not suitable for execution in the context of a web application, either. Of the 127 @Functions provided by XPages, the majority of these share functional parity with their formula language siblings. A small number that are available in the traditional formula language version have not been implemented in XPages, because there is another way to obtain the same information in the server-side JavaScript API, or they are candidates for future inclusion. The most notable examples that are not available in XPages are `@BrowserInfo`, `@URLOpen`, `@WebDbName`, and `@DbCommand`.

If you are already familiar with formula language @Functions, you may notice three key differences in the syntax used to invoke server-side JavaScript @Functions—firstly, you must use parentheses at the end of the @Function, secondly you must use a comma to separate parameters, not a semicolon, and finally, you need to quote special keywords such as [FailSilent] as strings like "[FailSilent]".

You can study several examples of server-side JavaScript @Functions at work within the Discussion template that ships with Notes/Domino 9. The **Chp11Ed2.nsf** application is based on this template, so if you can run a search in Designer for instances of `@` within this application, you can find many examples. One such worked example, shown in Listing 11.14, is for the **inputText2** input control used by the **mainTopic** Custom Control. This control is configured to perform a type-ahead search for entries in a target dataset, matching the word you are typing. In this example, the `@DbColumn` function provides the `xp:typeAhead` control with the column values from the first column in the `xpCategoryCloud` view.

Listing 11.14 inputText2 XSP Markup from the mainTopic Custom Control Using @DbColumn()

```
<xp:inputText id="inputText2"
    value="#{dominoDoc.WebCategories}"
    multipleSeparator=",">
    <xp:typeAhead mode="partial" ignoreCase="true"
        minChars="1" id="typeAhead1"
        valueListSeparator="," tokens=",">
        <xp:this.valueList>
            <![CDATA[#{javascript:
                @DbColumn(@DbName(), "xpCategoryCloud", 1)
            }]]>
        </xp:this.valueList>
    </xp:typeAhead>
</xp:inputText>
```

To study a second example, open the **buildingBlocks** XPage found within the **Chp11Ed2.nsf** application. You use this XPage for the remainder of this section, because it contains not only examples of working with @Functions, but examples of working with agents and evaluating formula language.

With the **buildingBlocks** XPage open in Designer, focus the button control labeled **Create** in the WYSIWYG editor. Using the **Events** view, open the **Script Editor** for this button's `onclick` server-side event. Listing 11.15 shows the key lines of code that use an @Function in this `onclick` server-side event.

Listing 11.15 onclick Server-Side Event Code for the Create Button Using @Random()

```
var document = database.createDocument();
if(null != document){
    document.appendItemValue("type", "jAgentDoc");
    document.appendItemValue("param1", @Random());
    document.appendItemValue("param2", @Random());
    ...
...
```

In this example, the `@Random()` function generates a randomized double number—note the use of the parenthesis! The returned random value is then appended as an item within the newly created document.

Moving onto another example within the **buildingBlocks** XPage, you should now select the link control labeled **subtract** within the WYSIWYG editor. Again, using the **Events** view, open the `onclick` server-side event in using the **Script Editor**. Listing 11.16 shows the key lines of code that make use of a @Function, but does so through an evaluated formula language expression.

Listing 11.16 onclick Event Code for the Subtract Link Using session.evaluate() and Formula

```
...
var result = session.evaluate("result - @Random", jAgentDoc);

if(!result.isEmpty()){
    jAgentDoc.replaceItemValue("result", result.firstElement());
    jAgentDoc.save();
}
...
```

In this case, the global `session` object is being used to evaluate a formula language expression using the `session.evaluate()` method. There are two variants of this method:

```
java.util.Vector session.evaluate("formula")
java.util.Vector session.evaluate("formula", document)
```

As you can see, both take a formula language expression as the first parameter. When a document object is supplied as the second parameter, the formula language parameter is executed under the context of that document. This allows you to run the given formula against a field within that document for instance. Both variants of this method return a `java.util.Vector` object. The first element in this vector contains a scalar result from the evaluation of the formula language expression. Note that you cannot make changes to the supplied document; you can only run an expression that returns a scalar result expression.

In Listing 11.16, you see that the two parameter version of `session.evaluate()` is being used. The first parameter, "`result - @Random`", is a formula language expression that subtracts a randomized double-number value from the result field using the `@Random` formula language @Function. Because a field name has been used in this expression, the second document parameter becomes mandatory. Therefore, the `jAgentDoc` name supplied is actually a reference to the current in-memory document. This document does, of course, contain a field named `result`. Listing 11.16 also shows how the scalar result is obtained from the `java.lang.Vector` result object, before being saved into the `jAgentDoc` document:

```
jAgentDoc.replaceItemValue("result", result.firstElement());
jAgentDoc.save();
```

Recall that you cannot make changes to a document using the formula language expression. Listing 11.16 is therefore making the change to the document's `result` field using the `document.replaceItemValue()` method, only after obtaining the formula language evaluation result.

These simple examples demonstrate not only how easy it is to leverage the @Function library, but to evaluate formula language expressions within your server-side JavaScript code. Before previewing the **buildingBlocks** XPage, read the next section, where you learn about working with agents expression.

Working with Agents, In-Memory Documents, and Profile Documents

A typical Notes/Domino application contains one or more agents. These artifacts are considered by many Notes/Domino developers as one of the most vital tools in their development arsenal. It, therefore, seems reasonable to expect XPages to be able to work with agents. Indeed, from Notes/Domino 8.5, XPages has provided the capability to run agents using server-side JavaScript by way of the following four methods:

```
Agent.run() / Agent.run(paramDocId)
Agent.runOnServer() / Agent.runOnServer(paramDocId)
```

The parameterized version of these methods takes a document Note ID, which can then be retrieved within the agent code through the `Agent.getParameterDocID()` method. This allows you to retrieve the associated document from the database, within the agent. You can then use this document in a read/write scenario before exiting the agent. On exiting the agent, your server-side JavaScript can then retrieve the document once more to further process against it.

TIP

A web application, either traditional Domino or XPages, can only ever run what is known as a WebAgent. This agent has its Run as web user option enabled to allow invocation by a web application. Note that, if an agent is written in LotusScript, it must not contain any of the NotesUI* classes. These include NotesUIWorkspace, NotesUIDatabase, NotesUIDocument, and NotesUIView, as these require special native client features that are not available in a web context.

The approach detailed in the preceding paragraphs has been considered cumbersome to effectively ensure the same document is used under the context of the server-side JavaScript, but also within the context of the agent. It is for this reason that XPages in Notes/Domino 8.5.2 and upward now provide two new methods for invoking and passing in an in-memory document to an agent. These two new methods are

```
agent.runWithDocumentContext(document)
agent.runWithDocumentContext(document, paramDocId)
```

To further examine these methods, reopen the **buildingBlocks** XPage in Designer if it is not already opened. This XPage contains four examples that demonstrate different ways you can run an agent from XPages server-side JavaScript code.

Once opened, click the button labeled **Create** in the WYSIWYG editor. Using the Events view, open the Script Editor for the **Create** button's `onclick` server-side event. You can either study the code in the Script Editor. (Listing 11.17 displays the same code.)

Listing 11.17 onclick Event Code for the Create Button Using agent.runWithDocumentContext()

```
var agent = database.getAgent("jAgent");
if(null != agent){
    var document = database.createDocument();
    if(null != document){
        document.appendItemValue("type", "jAgentDoc");
        document.appendItemValue("param1", @Random());
        document.appendItemValue("param2", @Random());
        try{
            agent.runWithDocumentContext(document);
        }catch(e){
            print("Error: " + e);
            return;
        }
        document.save();
    }
}
```

Listing 11.17 does many interesting things to make use of the new `Agent.runWithDocumentContext()` method. Listing 11.17 is explained as follows:

1. On line 1, a reference to the `jAgent` agent is retrieved from the database. (You see the code for this agent shortly.)
2. Having retrieved a reference to the `jAgent` agent, a new document is created on line 3.
3. Lines 5, 6, and 7 append three fields into the new document. The new document has not yet been saved, so is effectively an in-memory document.
4. The code on line 10 makes use of the new `agent.runWithDocumentContext()` method, passing in the in-memory document. At this point, control is handed to the `jAgent` agent. It processes against the in-memory document before handing control back to the server-side JavaScript event.
5. On successful running of the agent, line 10 attempts to save the in-memory document.

Take this opportunity to examine the `jAgent` agent in Designer. `jAgent` can be found under the **Code > Agents** design element in the **Applications** view, as displayed in Figure 11.21. Simply double-click `jAgent` to open it.

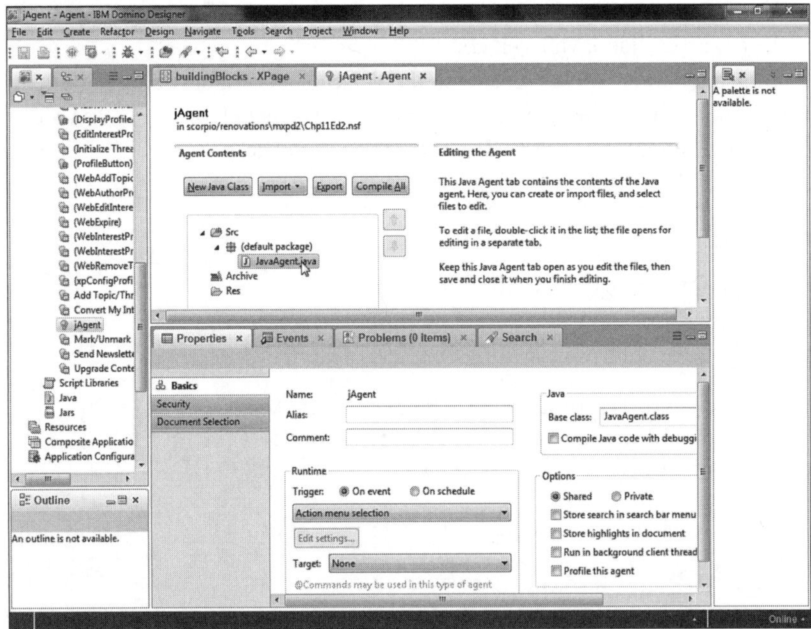

Figure 11.21 jAgent agent listed under Code > Agents in the Chp11Ed2.nsf application

Once opened, you are presented with the Java Agent tab page for this agent. This page enables you to configure the basic options, the security settings, and document selection criteria for an agent. This agent has been written in Java, so to view the source code, one more step is required: You must also double-click the `JavaAgent.java` entry, as shown in Figure 11.22. (Agents written in LotusScript open directly within the source code.) This extra double-click opens the Java agent source code, as a Java agent is a project unto itself with the capability to include other resources and reference other libraries; therefore, it's more than just simple Java source/class files.

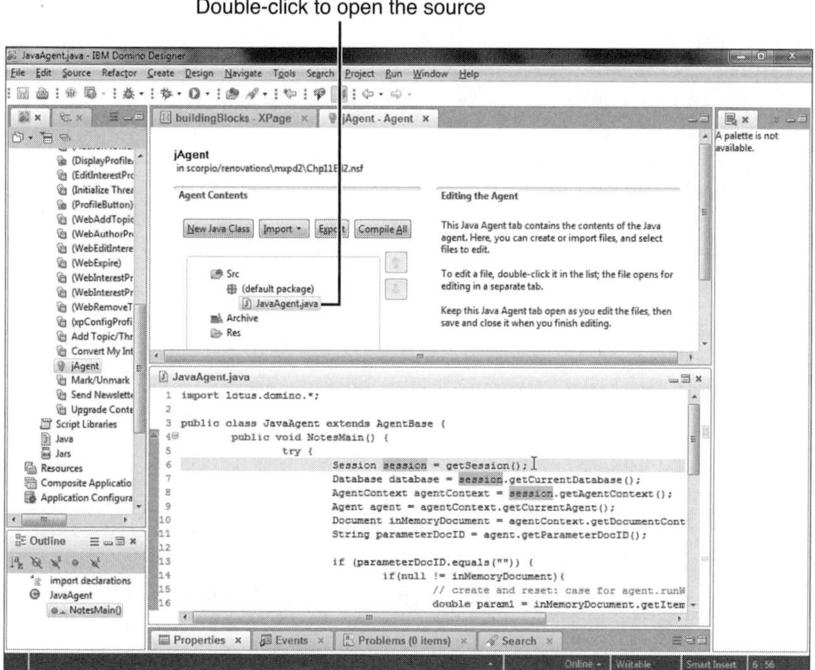

Figure 11.22 JavaAgent.java entry in the Java Agent tab page

Having double-clicked the `JavaAgent.java` entry, the Java source code for `jAgent` opens in Designer within the Java editor. A reduced code listing for this agent's `NotesMain` method is also provided in Listing 11.18.

Listing 11.18 Java Source Code for the jAgent Agent

```
...
public void NotesMain() {
    try {
        Session session = getSession();
        Database database = session.getCurrentDatabase();
        AgentContext agentContext = session.getAgentContext();
        Agent agent = agentContext.getCurrentAgent();
        Document inMemoryDocument = agentContext.getDocumentContext();
        String parameterDocID = agent.getParameterDocID();

        if(parameterDocID.equals("")){
            if(null != inMemoryDocument){
                // case: runWithDocumentContext(document)
                double param1 =
                    inMemoryDocument.getItemValueDouble("param1");
                double param2 =
                    inMemoryDocument.getItemValueDouble("param2");
                inMemoryDocument.replaceItemValue(
                    "result", Double.valueOf(param1 + param2)
                );
            }
        }else{
            Document parameterDoc =
                database.getDocumentByID(parameterDocID);
            if(null != parameterDoc){
                if(null != inMemoryDocument) {
                    // case: runWithDocumentContext(document, noteID)
                    double result =
                        inMemoryDocument.getItemValueDouble("result");
                    double addon =
                        parameterDoc.getItemValueDouble("addon");
                    inMemoryDocument.replaceItemValue(
                        "result", Double.valueOf(result + addon)
                    );
                }else{
                    // case: runOnServer(noteID)|agent.run(noteID)
                    double param1 =
                        parameterDoc.getItemValueDouble("param1");
                    double param2 =
                        parameterDoc.getItemValueDouble("param2");
                    double result =
                        parameterDoc.getItemValueDouble("result");
                    Document email = database.createDocument();
```

```
43                          email.replaceItemValue(
44                               "Subject", param1+" "+param2+" "+result
45                          );
46                          email.send(session.getUserName());
47                     }
48                }
49           }
50      }catch(Exception e){
51           e.printStackTrace();
52      }
...
```

The code for `jAgent` seen in Listing 11.18, and displayed within the Java editor in Designer, is designed to deal with three different running cases:

- `agent.runWithDocumentContext(document)`
- `agent.runWithDocumentContext(document, paramDocId)`
- `agent.run(paramDocId)` or `agent.runOnServer(paramDocId)`

The first thing done in the code for the agent, however, is initializing some important variables in lines 3 to 8 of the code. Lines 7 and 8 are the most notable of these assignments, in that the document context and the parameter document ID are both easily obtained:

```
7        Document inMemoryDocument = agentContext.getDocumentContext();
8        String parameterDocID = agent.getParameterDocID();
```

Referring to the **Create** button event of Listing 11.17, you can see that this particular "create" scenario is dealt with under the first of the three cases catered for by `jAgent`. Recall that an in-memory document is passed into the `jAgent` agent. Using Listing 11.18 as a reference, this case is then dealt with by lines 10 to 20 of the code. Line 7 has already obtained the in-memory document through the call to `agentContext.getDocumentContext()`, allowing lines 10 through 20 to work upon the in-memory document.

Take this opportunity to preview the **buildingBlocks** XPage using either the client or browser option. After the XPage launches, click the **Create** button a few times. This executes the `jAgent` agent, therefore creating a number of documents within the application. You see something similar to what's displayed in Figure 11.23.

The first of the three cases has now been explained. If you return to the **buildingBlocks** XPage in Designer, the remaining two cases can now be examined in turn. First, if you click the **addon** link within the WYSIWYG editor, using the **Events** view, open the **Script Editor** for this link's server-side `onclick` event. Listing 11.19 details the code of this event handler.

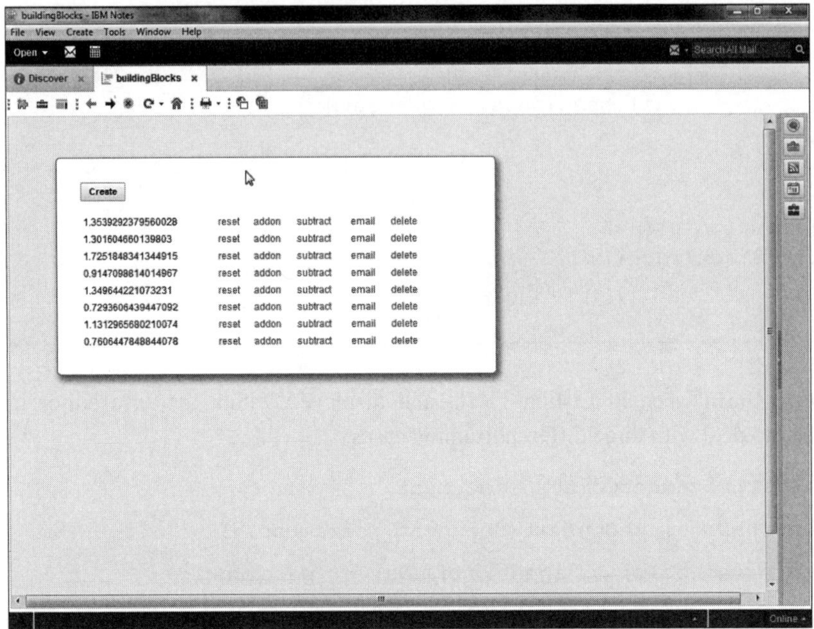

Figure 11.23 BuildingBlocks XPage being previewed

Listing 11.19 addon Link Event Using agent.runWithDocumentContext(document, paramDocId)

```
var agent = database.getAgent("jAgent");
if(null != agent){
    var profileDocument =
        database.getProfileDocument("jAgent", @UserName());
    if(null != profileDocument){
        profileDocument.appendItemValue("addon", @Random());
        profileDocument.save();
        try{
            agent.runWithDocumentContext(
                jAgentDoc, profileDocument.getNoteID()
            );
            jAgentDoc.save();
        }catch(e){
            print(e);
        }finally{
            profileDocument.removePermanently(true);
        }
    }
}
```

This code uses the `agent.runWithDocumentContext(document, paramDocId)` method, and the exact same `jAgent` agent is used to process against. The interesting thing about this example is the use of a secondary document. The document used for this is a special type of Notes Document called a *profile document*. Profile documents do not appear in views, nor do they get indexed, so they are a good solution for holding data, such as user-specific preferences and so forth. The profile document is created on line 3 of Listing 11.19. As you can see, it is created, and a field is immediately written into it before being saved. The call to run the agent is then given a reference to an already predefined document called `jAgentDoc` as its first parameter, and the `profileDocument.getNoteID` for its second parameter. You can see that using this version of the `agent.runWithDocumentContext()` method gives you a way to supply not only an in-memory document, but also a secondary document Note ID. This document Note ID can then be used to retrieve that document within the agent. This can be seen in Listing 11.18, where lines 22 through 33 take care of retrieving the profile document and work on the in-memory document.

The final scenario dealt with by the `jAgent` agent is the `agent.run(paramDocId)` or `agent.runOnServer(paramDocId)` case. This can be examined by looking at the *email* link's `onclick` server-side event handler code in the **Script Editor**. Listing 11.20 also shows this code for your convenience.

Listing 11.20 Code of the Email Link Using agent.runOnServer(paramDocId)

```
var agent = database.getAgent("jAgent");
if(null != agent){
    try{
        agent.runOnServer(jAgentDoc.getNoteID());
    }catch(e){
        print(e);
    }
}
```

The `jAgentDoc` reference is a predefined document. In this case, its Note ID is supplied as the parameter to the call on `agent.runOnServer(paramDocId)`. The `jAgent` agent is also used for this example, so referring to Listing 11.18 of the `jAgent` code, you see that lines 22 through 24 and 35 through 46 deal with retrieving the document using the parameter doc ID, and processing the email.

Now that you have learned about the different ways the `jAgent` agent is being used in the **buildingBlocks** XPage, spend some time previewing it and digesting what you covered in this section.

Managed Beans

In Notes/Domino 8.5.2 and upward, XPages provides support for managed beans. This feature is provided by the JSF framework, so it is essentially a Java technology. Note, however, that XPages makes it easy to develop an application using this feature—the **Chp11Ed2.nsf** application includes a managed bean to make the **managedBeans** XPage more interactive and efficient.

As the name implies, there is some degree of automated management involved, and this is certainly true. A managed bean has both an execution lifecycle, and a scope under which it lives. The "managed" part is related to the management of that lifecycle and scope. This makes it easy to develop managed beans, because all the infrastructural code is already in-place within the JSF layer. Where XPages lends a further helping hand is in its support for managed beans. This support provides a registration mechanism through the `faces-config.xml` file, but also in allowing you to work directly with managed beans in your server-side JavaScript code. You also do not have to worry about initializing or constructing any managed bean instances, because this is taken care of for you by the XPages runtime the first time you call a method on a managed bean in server-side JavaScript code.

Now, reopen the **Chp11Ed2.nsf** application in Designer if it is closed. The first thing to look at is the `faces-config.xml` file. Do this by opening it directly using the `Application Navigator > Faces Config` design element if you are using the XPages Perspective (new with Notes/Domino 9.0) or alternatively by opening it under `WebContent/WEB-INF/faces-config.xml` using the **Package Explorer** view. Listing 11.21 shows the content of this file.

Listing 11.21 Faces-config.xml from the Discussion Template and Chp11Ed2.nsf application

```
<?xml version="1.0" encoding="UTF-8"?>
<faces-config>
    <managed-bean>
        <managed-bean-name>previewBean</managed-bean-name>
        <managed-bean-class>
            com.ibm.xpages.beans.PreviewBean
        </managed-bean-class>
        <managed-bean-scope>view</managed-bean-scope>
    </managed-bean>
    <!--AUTOGEN-START-BUILDER: Automatically generated by
        IBM Domino Designer. Do not modify.-->
    <!--AUTOGEN-END-BUILDER: End of automatically generated section-->
</faces-config>
```

This is an XML-based file, and as you have already learned in Chapter 5, declares JSF-related items for an application. In this case, one managed bean is being declared as follows:

1. The `<managed-bean-name>` element declares the name that is used to reference the managed bean in server-side JavaScript or EL Language code.

2. The `<managed-bean-class>` element declares the implementation Java class.
3. The `<managed-bean-scope>` element declares under which scope the managed bean lives. Valid scopes are `application`, `session`, `request`, and `view`. These scopes are comparable to the XPages server-side JavaScript scopes detailed in Chapter 6.

You can declare as many managed beans as you need within each of the scopes using the `faces-config.xml` file. For example, you might require several different managed beans in your application, doing different things within the view scope, and perhaps another couple that work with the session scope.

Next, study the implementation Java class for this managed bean. As seen in Listing 11.21, the `<managed-bean-class>` element declares `com.ibm.xpages.beans.PreviewBean` to be the implementation Java class. In Designer, use the **Package Explorer** view to examine the **Build Path** for the **Chp11Ed2.nsf** application. This shows you that a directory named `source` has been configured to be included in the compilation build path for the application. This means that any `*.java` source files within that directory are automatically compiled. The compiled `*.class` files are then part of the executable application. Figure 11.24 shows the **Java Build Path** editor for the **Chp11Ed2.nsf** application.

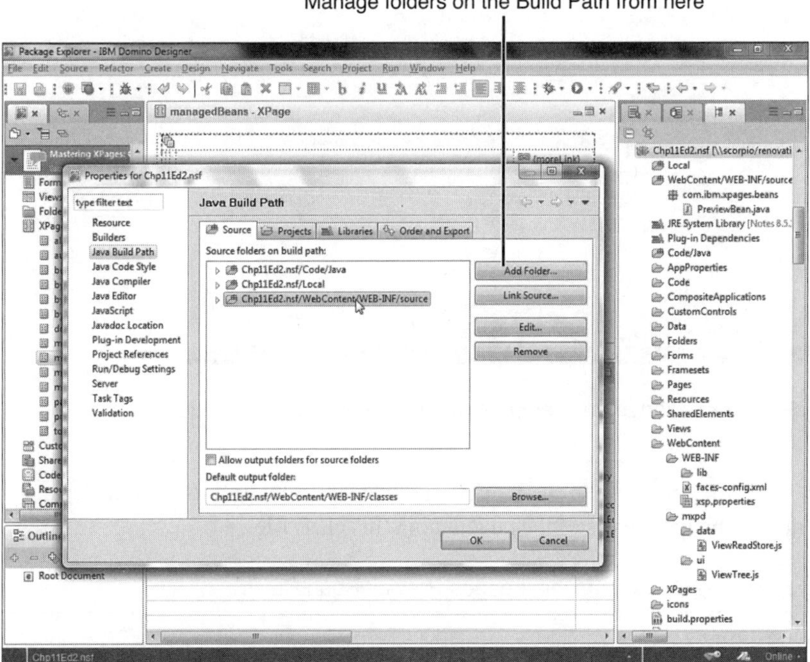

Figure 11.24 Java Build Path Editor

Using the **Java Build Path** editor, you can see that the `WebContent/WEB-INF/source` directory is on the build path. You are free to create directories under the `WebContent` folder as required—in this example, the *source* directory was created by me under the `WebContent/WEB-INF/` folder so that its content is not accessible using a web URL. Any content under the `WebContent/WEB-INF/` folder is protected from web URL access. Close the **Java Build Path** editor and return to the **Package Explorer** view, where you should fully expand the `WebContent/WEB-INF/source` Java folder. Inside, you find the declared managed bean implementation Java package and class file, as shown in Figure 11.25.

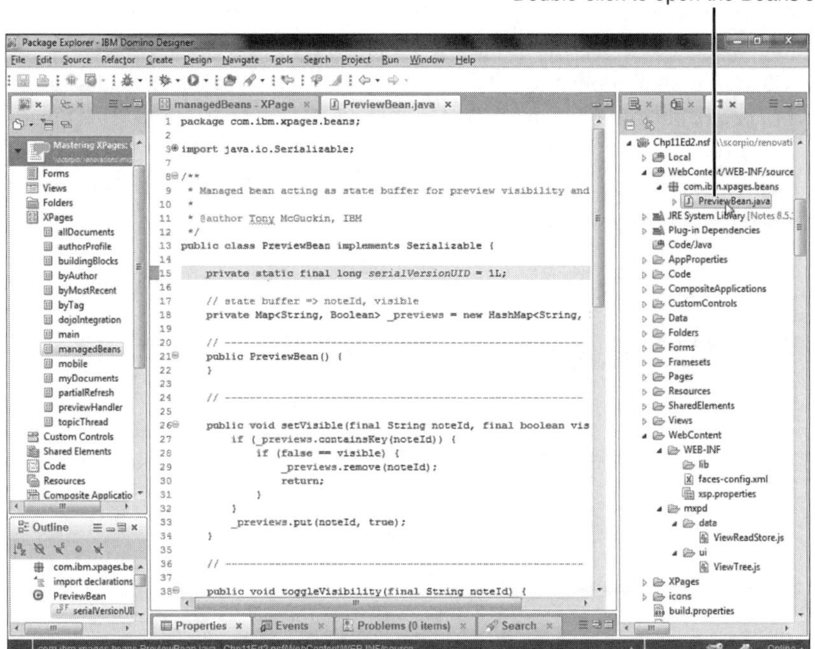
Double-click to open the Beans Java source

Figure 11.25 Declared managed bean implementation Java package and class

If you double-click the `PreviewBean.java` file, it opens in a Java editor within Designer. Listing 11.22 also details the main parts of the code within this class file.

Listing 11.22 Source Code for the com.ibm.xpages.PreviewBean Class

```
package com.ibm.xpages.beans;
...
public class PreviewBean implements Serializable {
    ...
```

```
private Map<String,Boolean> _previews=new HashMap<String,Boolean>();

public PreviewBean(){}

public void setVisible(final String noteId, final boolean visible) {
    if(_previews.containsKey(noteId)) {
        if (false == visible) {
            _previews.remove(noteId);
            return;
        }
    }
    _previews.put(noteId, true);
}

public void toggleVisibility(final String noteId) {
    if(_previews.containsKey(noteId)) {
        _previews.remove(noteId);
    }else{
        _previews.put(noteId, true);
    }
}

public boolean isVisible(final String noteId) {
    if(_previews.containsKey(noteId)) {
        return (_previews.get(noteId).booleanValue());
    }
    return (false);
}

public String getVisibilityText(
    final String noteId, final ResourceBundle resourceBundle) {
    String moreLinkText = "More";
    String hideLinkText = "Hide";

    if(null != resourceBundle){
        moreLinkText = resourceBundle.getString(
            "alldocuments.more.link"
        );
        hideLinkText = resourceBundle.getString(
            "alldocuments.hide.link"
        );
    }
    if(_previews.containsKey(noteId)) {
        return (hideLinkText);
    }
```

```
        return (moreLinkText);
    }

    public String getSelectedClassName(final String noteId) {
        if(_previews.containsKey(noteId)) {
            return ("xspHtmlTrViewSelected");
        }
        return ("xspHtmlTrView");
    }

    public String getVisibilityLinkStyle(final String noteId) {
        if(_previews.containsKey(noteId)) {
            return ("visibility:visible");
        }
        return ("visibility:hidden");
    }
}
```

The implementation class for this managed bean is not complex. It simply declares a number of public methods that are used by server-side JavaScript code in the **managedBeans** XPage, as you will see shortly. The main things to remember are that a managed bean should declare a public no-parameter constructor and should also implement the `java.io.Serializable` interface if the scope if anything other than **none** or **request**. This enables the managed bean to be serialized and deserialized between requests to an XPage that uses the managed bean. This supports the scope mechanism, without which the managed bean would not persist between requests, therefore invalidating the notion of the persisted scopes (that is, view, session, and application scopes).

The last thing to examine is the **managedBeans** XPage to see how server-side JavaScript code leverages this managed bean. Open this XPage in Designer, and within the WYSIWYG editor, click the link with the ID **moreLink**. Then, switch to the Source editor, where you see the full range of server-side JavaScript calls being used by this link control against the managed bean. Listing 11.23 shows the key lines of code in the XSP markup for the `moreLink` control.

Listing 11.23 XSP Markup for the moreLink Link in the allDocumentsView Custom Control

```
<xp:link id="moreLink"
text=
"#{javascript:previewBean.getVisibilityText(rowData.getNoteID(), res)}"
style=
"#{javascript:previewBean.getVisibilityLinkStyle(rowData.getNoteID())}">
    <xp:eventHandler event="onclick" submit="true" ...>
        <xp:this.action>
        <![CDATA[
```

```
        #{javascript:previewBean.toggleVisibility(rowData.getNoteID())}
        ]]>
        </xp:this.action>
    ...
    </xp:eventHandler>
</xp:link>
```

As you can see in Listing 11.23, and within the **managedBeans** XPage, if you have Designer opened, the **moreLink** is making extensive use of the managed bean. The interesting aspect to this is the direct reference to the managed bean name, `previewBean`, within the server-side JavaScript.

Now, take the opportunity to preview the **managedBeans** XPage. With this new knowledge about the how the **managedBeans** XPage is working, you should toggle the **moreLink** on different rows of the view, and also page back and forth through the view. Note how the `previewBean` is maintaining the state of expanded and collapsed rows for the **managedBeans** XPage, changing the style of the rows, and also changing the text of the moreLink for each row, as shown in Figure 11.26.

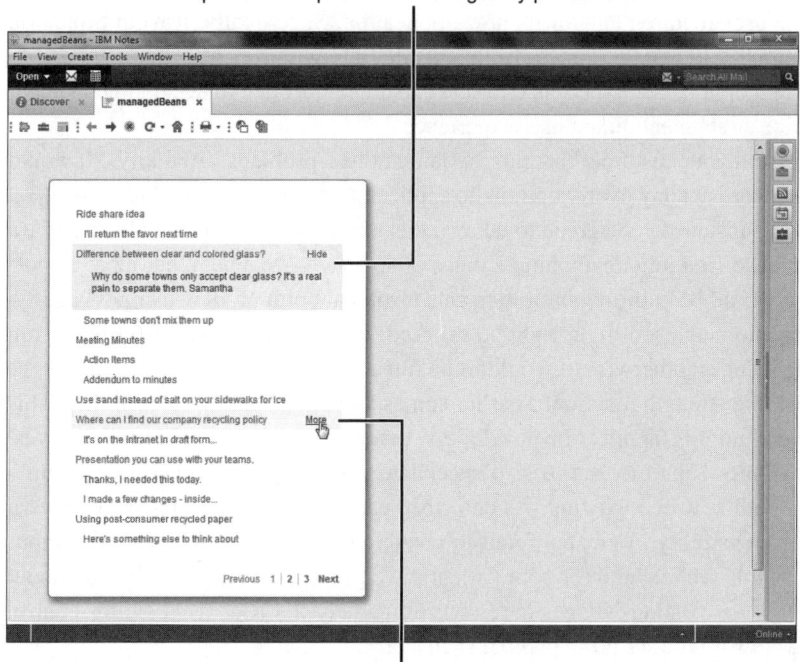

Figure 11.26 managedBeans XPage and previewBean in action

This is just one use case where the introduction of a managed bean provided a good solution. I'm sure that you can think of many use cases within your own applications that would benefit from a managed bean. The great thing is that XPages makes it so easy to develop them. So, what are you waiting for?

TIP

Learn more about using Managed Beans in a JavaServer Faces application at http://docs.oracle.com/javaee/6/tutorial/doc/bnaqm.html

Fulfilling a Customer Requirement: A Practical Field Study

One of the greatest strengths of XPages lies in its capability to be extended and adapted to the specific needs of an application. In Chapter 12, "XPages Extensibility," you learn all about this topic in great detail, particularly related to the common server-side aspects of this area.

For now, though, in this concluding section of Chapter 11 you examine a use case in which Acme Corporation (our fictitious customer) has tasked you to help develop its new XPages CRM application. It recently asked you to customize the existing Rich Text Editor control provided by XPages to suit the user requirements of its new application. Specifically, it would like you to provide a new capability to handle inline attachments directly within rich text content and to also present a consistent dialog user experience for the existing embedded image dialog so that it matches any new inline attachment dialog user experience.

You, of course, told your customer that this "would not be a problem." Actually, "It would be easy!" Famous last words of any overly optimistic application developer—you know who you are! Nonetheless, in this instance you agreed to take on this task because it sounded like "fun" (a good reason to jump head first into developing a piece of software—maybe?), but more important, you knew that it would be entirely possible from a technical point of view using XPages—no river too deep, no mountain too high, right? Yes! And, of course, it would be a lot of fun because you're using XPages; otherwise, it wouldn't be fun at all.

So this is where that strength mentioned earlier comes into play, namely extensibility. This strength allows us mere mortals (application developers) to not only extend and adapt the server-side aspects of the XPages Runtime, but to also specialize the client-side rendering and functionality of controls, both new and existing. As described earlier, in the next chapter you learn how to use XPages Extensibility in greater detail to create a brand new user interface component. Whereas, here in this section, and for your patiently waiting customer, you will learn about extending and adapting an existing XPages core control, namely the Rich Text Editor control with a little more bias toward the scripting parts of such a task.

In many ways, this can provide you with a gentle introduction to the next chapter, but it can also lead you into several distinctly different areas of the XPages Runtime. And this being the "Advanced Scripting" chapter, it can, of course, lean heavily toward script-centric types of operations, techniques, patterns, and mechanisms on the client-side and server-side. So the choice of an example for this section is quite deliberate on the author's part as a means of setting your mind thinking about the many-fold and wildly varied technical possibilities that could be achieved by harnessing the flexibility and strength of the XPages Extensibility model coupled with the extremely powerful client-side and server-side scripting model of the XPages Runtime. And where you perhaps will have the most fun is seeing how an implementation can be brought together full circle using both client-side and server-side technologies (and everything else in between) within the XPages Runtime to provide a seamless and highly integrated, reusable solution.

Before continuing with this section, you should ensure you have downloaded and opened the **Chp11Ed2b.nsf** application within Designer and signed it—the remainder of this section will be based upon this particular application.

Comparing Apples with Apples!

So, let's take a first look at the "runtime" end result of the **Chp11Ed2b.nsf** application and then reverse-engineer the pieces that make up the tailored solution for Acme Corporation. First, Figure 11.27 shows the standard, existing Rich Text Editor control in edit mode before any specialized extensions have been put in place. You can also view this on your own browser or Notes client by viewing the **standardRTE** XPage from the **Chp11Ed2b.nsf** application.

> **TIP**
>
> The XPages Rich Text Editor control in Notes/Domino 9.0.1 inherently uses the popular CKEditor rich text editing control, version 3.6.6.2. Therefore, ensure that you are viewing this sample using a CKEditor 3.6.6.2 compatible browser. For example, Microsoft Internet Explorer 11 is not compatible with this CKEditor version. Refer to the following CKEditor 3.6 compatibility documentation for further information: http://docs.cksource.com/CKEditor_3.x/Users_Guide/Compatibility

Now compare the Rich Text Editor in Figure 11.27 with that shown in Figure 11.28. Here, you need to look carefully at the toolbars for each. And again, you can also view this on your own browser or Notes client by viewing the **extendedRTE** XPage from the **Chp11Ed2b.nsf** application.

Essentially, Figure 11.28 shows the specialized version of the Rich Text Editor control whereby two new toolbar buttons have been provided—being more exact about that statement, one is a brand new Attach a file button, and the second is a replacement for the preexisting Embed an image button.

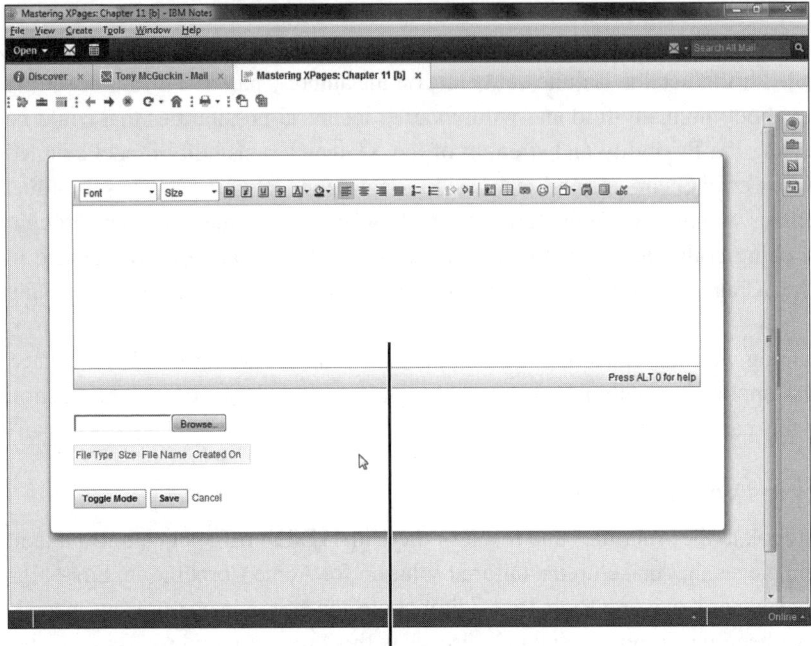

Figure 11.27 Rich Text Editor control in edit mode before specialized extensions are provided

Now continue with our comparison in which Figure 11.29 shows the brand new Attach a File dialog user experience when pressing the Attach a file toolbar button on the Rich Text Control in the **extendedRTE** XPage. As you can see, it's a straightforward dialog enabling you to choose a file from the local file system, and after pressing OK, you can attach the chosen file into the Rich Text Editor control—and therefore add the attachment into a DominoDocument RichTextField binding declared on the Rich Text Control (assuming that to be the type of binding used of course—for the most typical uses cases it will be the case).

After a file has been attached in edit mode, a link is then injected into the Rich Text Editor control at the current cursor position within the rich text content. This can be anywhere within the rich text content—before, between, or after text, images, or indeed any other inline attachment link, as shown in Figure 11.30.

Now turn your attention to the Embed an Image toolbar button. When this button is pressed in the existing standard Rich Text Control (important to note I said existing Rich Text Editor in this instance), a dialog is presented to the end user, as shown in Figure 11.31—this example is taken from the **standardRTE** XPage if you also want to compare it locally for yourself.

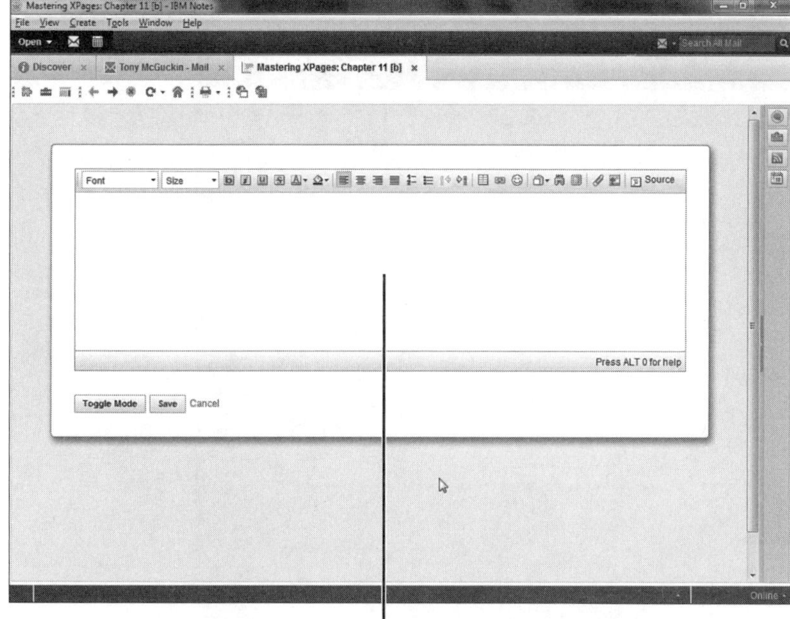

Specialized Rich Text Editor on the extendedRTE XPage

Figure 11.28 Rich Text Editor control in edit mode after specialized extensions are provided

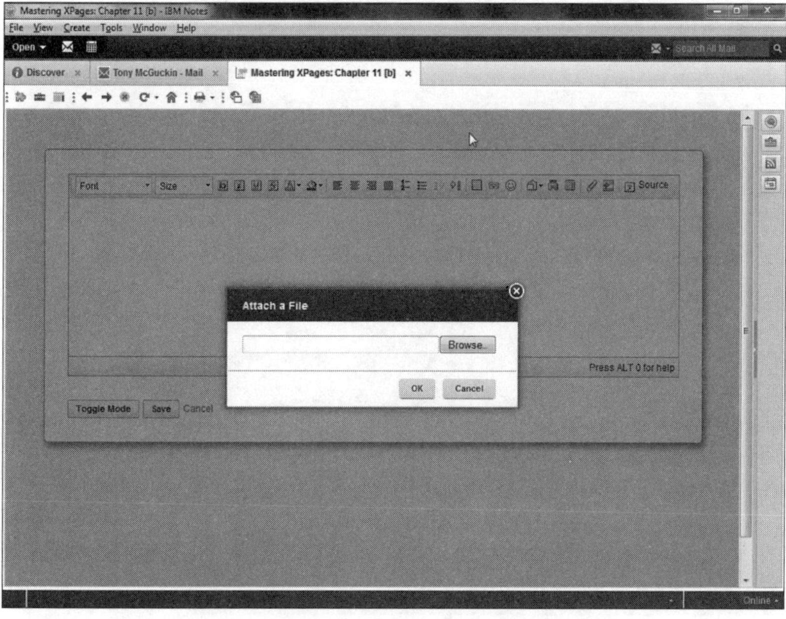

Figure 11.29 The new Attach a File dialog experience

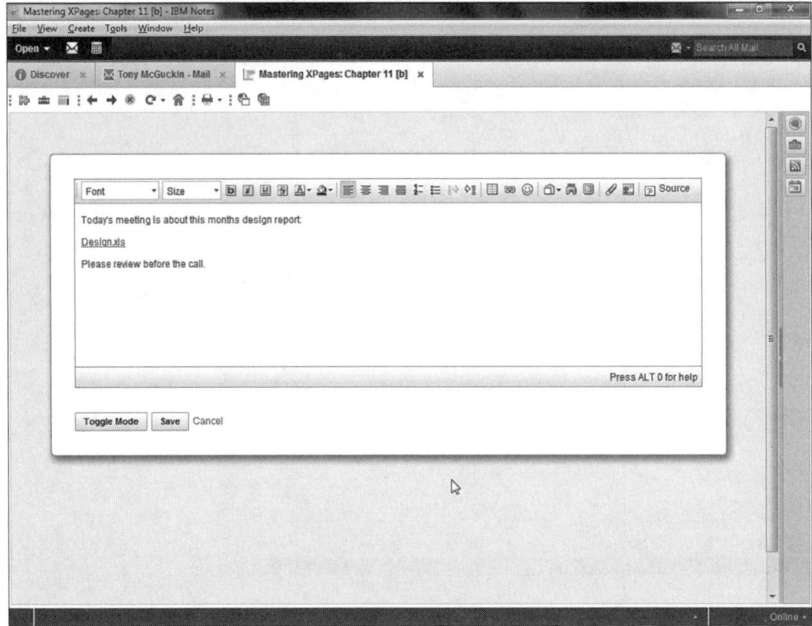

Figure 11.30 Rich text content including an inline attachment link in edit mode

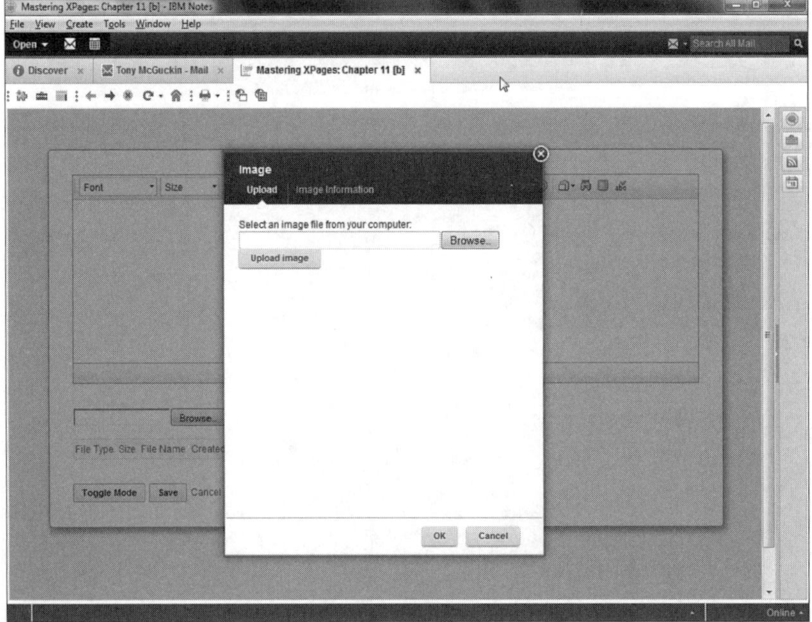

Figure 11.31 The existing Embed an Image dialog user experience before customization

However, according to the customer, Acme Corporation, this dialog provides what is arguably an inappropriate user experience because it is bloated and unnecessary under certain contexts—for instance, when running an application in the XPages in the Notes Client (See Chapter 13, "XPages in the Notes Client") or when rendering within a Mobile or Tablet device—all of which are platforms that Acme Corporations new CRM application will be used.

Therefore, this warrants a suitable alternative to satisfy the request from the customer to provide a consistent Attach a File and "Embed an Image" dialog user experience collectively. So, this particular dialog has been adapted to match the Attach a File dialog user experience, as shown in Figure 11.32. This example is taken from the **extendedRTE** XPage if you would like to view it for yourself locally.

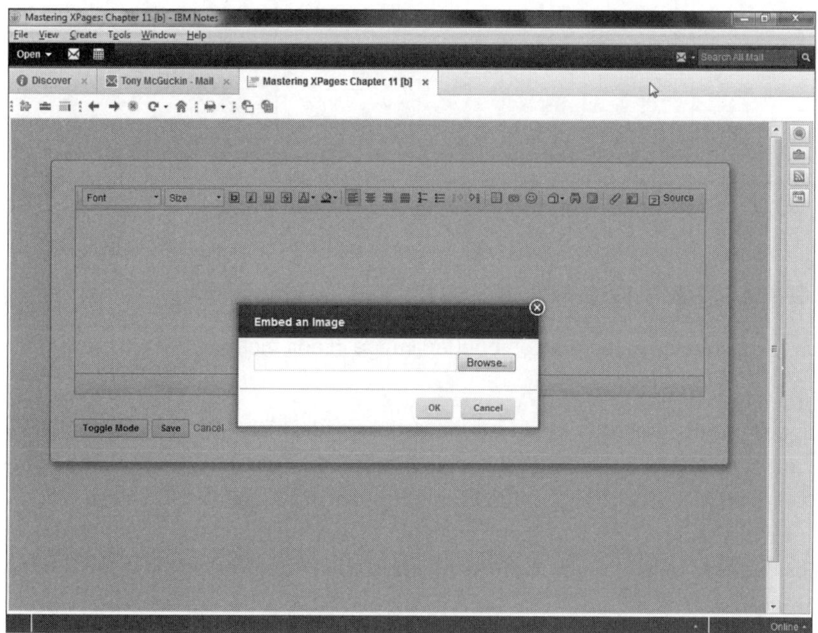

Figure 11.32 The new Embed an Image dialog user experience after customization

And in a similar manner to the Attach a File behavior, when an image has been chosen in the "Embed an Image" dialog in edit mode, the image is then injected into the Rich Text Editor control at the current cursor position within the rich text content. This can be anywhere within the rich text content—before, in between, or after text, inline attachments, or any other embedded images, as shown in Figure 11.33.

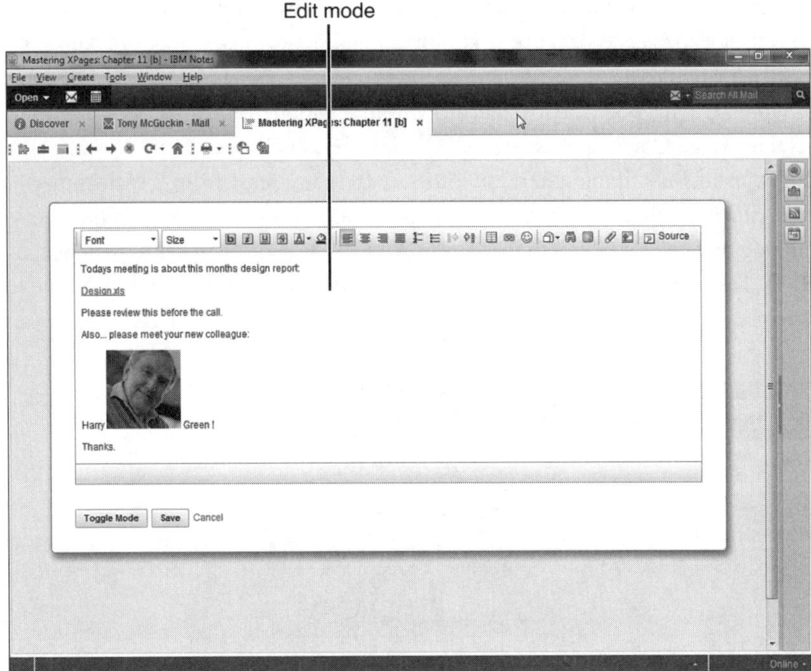

Figure 11.33 Rich text content including an embedded image in edit mode

And after the current document is saved by the end user, the rich text content, inclusive of any inline attachments and embedded images, is persisted within the underlying value binding (for example, DominoDocument RichTextField binding) for subsequent retrieval in read or edit mode at a later time. Figure 11.34 shows one example in which inline attachment links and embedded images can be seen in read mode in our specialized Rich Text Control on the **extended RTE** XPage at runtime.

Finally, also note that in read mode, each inline attachment link within the rich text content is a fully resolvable HTTP resource URI to the actual persisted attachment within the underlying value binding declared on the Rich Text Control—for the most typical use cases this will be a DominoDocument RichTextField binding. Therefore, when end users click an inline attachment link in read mode, they will be prompted for a location to save the attachment on their own local file system, as shown in Figure 11.35.

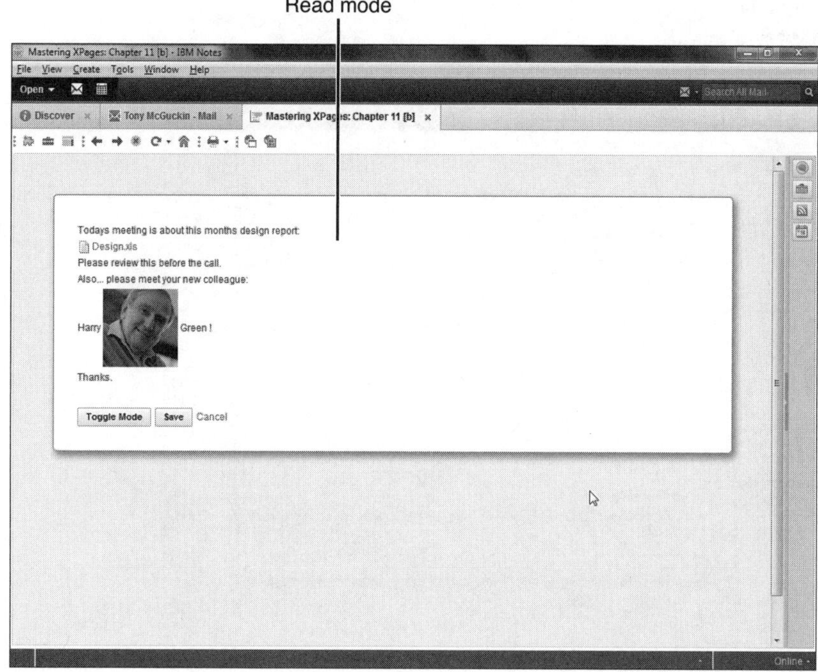

Figure 11.34 Rich text content containing an inline attachment and embedded image in read mode

Who, What, Where, and (More Important) How?

I hope you have been captivated by the brief introduction to the **Chp11Ed2b.nsf** application—obviously, this contains only the relevant pieces needed to demonstrate the specialized Rich Text Editor control and not the entire Acme Corporation CRM application. Nonetheless, it is a good example of demonstrating how to use the powerful client and server-side scripting models of the XPages Runtime, coupled with the XPages Extensibility model to create a highly specialized, reusable solution in XPages.

Now examine the most relevant parts that play a role in providing the extended and adapted Rich Text Editor control. Again, you can stick with the **Chp11Ed2b.nsf** application for the remainder of this section.

With the **Chp11Ed2b.nsf** application open in Designer, view the XSP source markup for the **standardRTE** XPage. This is also listed in its entirety in Listing 11.24 for your convenience.

Clicking inline attachment link causes prompt to Save As

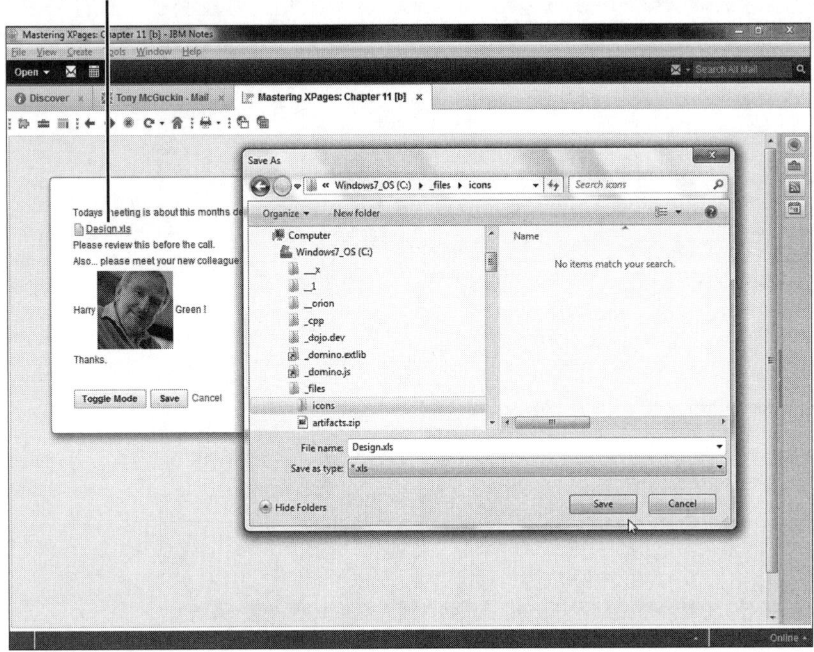

Figure 11.35 Prompting the end user to select a location to save the chosen inline attachment

Listing 11.24 standardRTE.xsp Source Markup

```
<?xml version="1.0" encoding="UTF-8"?>
<xp:view xmlns:xp="http://www.ibm.com/xsp/core"
    pageTitle="Mastering XPages: Chapter 11 [b]">
    <xp:this.data>
        <xp:dominoDocument var="document1"
            formName="myForm">
        </xp:dominoDocument>
    </xp:this.data>
    <xp:div themeId="container" style="width:900px">
        <xp:inputRichText id="inputRichText1"
            value="#{document1.Body1}">
        </xp:inputRichText>
        <xp:br></xp:br>
        <xp:br></xp:br>
        <xp:fileUpload id="fileUpload1" value="#{document1.Body1}">
            <xp:eventHandler event="onchange" submit="true"
                refreshMode="complete">
```

```
18              </xp:eventHandler>
19          </xp:fileUpload>
20          <xp:br></xp:br>
21          <xp:br></xp:br>
22          <xp:fileDownload rows="30" id="fileDownload1"
23              displayLastModified="false" value="#{document1.Body1}"
24              allowDelete="true">
25          </xp:fileDownload>
26          <xp:br></xp:br>
27          <xp:br></xp:br>
28          <xp:button value="Toggle Mode" id="button6">
29              <xp:eventHandler event="onclick" submit="true"
30                  refreshMode="complete">
31                  <xp:this.action>
32                      <xp:changeDocumentMode mode="toggle"
33                          var="document1">
34                      </xp:changeDocumentMode>
35                  </xp:this.action>
36              </xp:eventHandler>
37          </xp:button>
38          <xp:button value="Save" id="button2">
39              <xp:eventHandler event="onclick" submit="true"
40                  refreshMode="complete">
41                  <xp:this.action>
42                      <xp:save name="/index.xsp"></xp:save>
43                  </xp:this.action>
44              </xp:eventHandler>
45          </xp:button>
46          <xp:link escape="true" text="Cancel" id="link2"
47              value="/index.xsp">
48          </xp:link>
49      </xp:div>
50 </xp:view>
```

Note the presence of a standard Rich Text Editor control declared by the `<xp:inputRichText>` tag on lines 10, 11, and 12. To provide an end user with the ability to both select and attach a file to the underlying DominoDocument value binding as shown on line 11, the **standardRTE** XPage also includes two other core controls to support the Rich Text Editor, namely, the `<xp:fileUpload>` shown on lines 15–19 and also the `<xp:fileDownload>` declared on lines 22–25 in Listing 11.24. This means that three controls are required to provide a fairly basic file upload or download user experience and functionality. This also means that if multiple Rich Text Editor controls are required within a single XPage, each one also needs its own supporting duo of File Upload and File Download controls given the specific value bindings relative to each DominoDocument field.

So moving swiftly on, Listing 11.25 shows the alternative—the Acme Corporation alternative, that is. You can also find the full XSP source markup for the **extendedRTE** XPage within the **Chp11Ed2b.nsf** application if you want to view it locally in Designer. Otherwise, Listing 11.25 includes the entire source of this XPage for your convenience.

Listing 11.25 extendedRTE.xsp Source Markup

```
<?xml version="1.0" encoding="UTF-8"?>
<xp:view xmlns:xp="http://www.ibm.com/xsp/core"
    xmlns:mxpd2="http://www.ibm.com/xsp/mxpd2"
    xmlns:xe="http://www.ibm.com/xsp/coreex"
    pageTitle="Mastering XPages: Chapter 11 [b]">
    <xp:this.data>
        <xp:dominoDocument var="document1" formName="myForm">
        </xp:dominoDocument>
    </xp:this.data>
    <xp:this.resources>
        <xp:script clientSide="true" type="text/javascript">
            <xp:this.contents><![CDATA[
                // Note: important this is kept in the <head> otherwise
                // it's too late thereafter... used to intercept nsf
➥resource
                // requests and prevent ?t=timestamp being appended by
➥ckeditor
                window.CKEDITOR_GETURL = function(resourceRequest){
                    if(null != resourceRequest &&
                        resourceRequest.indexOf(".nsf") > -1){
                        return resourceRequest;
                    }
                }
            ]]></xp:this.contents>
        </xp:script>
    </xp:this.resources>
    <xp:scriptBlock id="scriptBlock3" defer="false">
        <xp:this.value><![CDATA[
            XSP.addOnLoad(function(){
                if(typeof CKEDITOR != "undefined"){
                    // TODO: add RTE id's to this list as required so
➥each
                    // instance has its own unique upload url targetted
                    // at its component tree object...
                    var ids = [ "#{id:inputRichText1}" ];

```

```
// calculate the relative path to this
➥application...
var path = "#{javascript:rteBean.
➥getDatabasePath()}";

// define the "Attach a file" action handler...
AttachmentHandler = function(editor){
    return new CKEDITOR.dialogCommand
➥("AttachmentDialog");
};

// define the "Embed an image" action handler...
ImageHandler = function(editor){
    return new CKEDITOR.
➥dialogCommand("ImageDialog");
};

// register the "Attach a file" extension...
CKEDITOR.plugins.add("AttachmentExtension", {
    init: function(editor){
        editor.on("pluginsLoaded", function(ev){
            if(!CKEDITOR.dialog.exists(
                "AttachmentDialog")
            ){
                CKEDITOR.dialog.add(
                    "AttachmentDialog",
                    path + "AttachmentDialog.js"
                );
            }
            editor.ui.addButton("Attachment", {
                label: "Attach a file...",
                command: "AttachmentHandler",
                icon: path + "iconAttachment.png"
            });
            editor.addCommand(
                "AttachmentHandler",
                AttachmentHandler(editor)
            );
        });
    }
});

// register the "Embed an image" extension...
CKEDITOR.plugins.add("ImageExtension", {
```

```
                        init: function(editor){
                            editor.on("pluginsLoaded", function(ev){
                                if(!CKEDITOR.dialog.
➥exists("ImageDialog")){
                                    CKEDITOR.dialog.add(
                                        "ImageDialog",
                                        path + "ImageDialog.js"
                                    );
                                }
                                editor.ui.addButton("ImageEx", {
                                    label: "Embed an image...",
                                    command: "ImageHandler",
                                    icon: path + "iconImage.gif"
                                });
                                editor.addCommand(
                                    "ImageHandler",
                                    ImageHandler(editor)
                                );
                            });
                        }
                    });

                    // set each RTE instance's upload url...
                    for(var x = 0; x < ids.length; x++){
                        var url = document.location.href.substring(
                            0, document.location.href.indexOf('?')
                        );
                        if(null != url){
                           url += "?$$axtarget=" + ids[x] +
➥"&$$viewid=" +
                                XSP.findForm(ids[x])["$$viewid"].value;
                        }
                        CKEDITOR.instances[ids[x]].config.axtargetUrl
➥= url;
                    }
                }
            });
        ]]></xp:this.value>
    </xp:scriptBlock>
    <xp:div themeId="container" style="width:900px">
        <mxpd2:inputRichText id="inputRichText1"
            value="#{rteBean['document1.Body1']}">
            <xp:this.converter>
                <xp:converter converterId="InputRichTextConverter">
```

```
                </xp:converter>
            </xp:this.converter>
            <xp:this.dojoAttributes>
                <xp:dojoAttribute name="extraPlugins"
                    value="AttachmentExtension,ImageExtension">
                </xp:dojoAttribute>
                <xp:dojoAttribute name="toolbar">
                    <xp:this.value><![CDATA[#{javascript:
                        var customToolbar = "[\n" +
                        // group 1
                        "['Font', 'FontSize', 'Bold', 'Italic',\n" +
                        " 'Underline', 'Strike', 'TextColor',
➥'BGColor'],\n" +
                        // group 2
                        "['JustifyLeft', 'JustifyCenter',
➥'JustifyRight',\n" +
                        " 'JustifyBlock', 'NumberedList',
'BulletedList',\n" +
                        " 'Outdent', 'Indent'],\n" +
                        // group 3
                        "['Table', 'Link', 'Smiley'],\n" +
                        // group 4
                        "['MenuPaste', 'Find', 'Maximize'],\n" +
                        // group 5
                        "['Attachment', 'ImageEx'],\n" +
                        // group 6
                        "['Source']\n" +
                        "]";
                        return customToolbar;
                    }]]></xp:this.value>
                </xp:dojoAttribute>
            </xp:this.dojoAttributes>
        </mxpd2:inputRichText>
        <xp:br></xp:br>
        <xp:br></xp:br>
        <xp:button value="Toggle Mode" id="button6">
            <xp:eventHandler event="onclick" submit="true"
                refreshMode="complete">
                <xp:this.action>
                    <xp:changeDocumentMode mode="toggle"
                        var="document1">
                    </xp:changeDocumentMode>
                </xp:this.action>
            </xp:eventHandler>
```

```
156         </xp:button>
157         <xp:button value="Save" id="button7">
158             <xp:eventHandler event="onclick" submit="true"
159                 refreshMode="complete">
160                 <xp:this.action>
161                     <xp:save name="/index.xsp"></xp:save>
162                 </xp:this.action>
163             </xp:eventHandler>
164         </xp:button>
165         <xp:link escape="true" text="Cancel" id="link2"
➥value="/index.xsp">
166         </xp:link>
167     </xp:div>
168 </xp:view>
```

As you can see, this XPage contains more lines of source code compared with that of the **standardRTE** XPage. For the most part, this is made up of client-side and server-side JavaScript but with similar XSP markup. The biggest difference between the **extendedRTE** XPage and the **standardRTE** XPage is that no File Upload or File Download controls are used, so this has reduced the number of controls on the XPage. Instead, the job of providing file upload and download functionality is provided directly by our new specialized Rich Text Editor control—by using the Attach a File dialog and inline attachment link coming from our new extension.

As you can see, our new control is declared by the `<mxpd2:inputRichText>` tag on lines 111–144 in Listing 11.25, and this is your first clue as to what has been done here to specialize the core Rich Text Editor. Got you thinking? Well, let me explain. You will have noticed the different tag namespace prefix for a start. Instead of the core tag namespace prefix `xp:` as shown on line 10 of Listing 11.24 for the **standardRTE** XPage, our specialized control tag is declared with the `mxpd2:` namespace on line 111 of Listing 11.25. The declaration for this namespace can also be seen on line 3 in Listing 11.25:

```
xmlns:mxpd2="http://www.ibm.com/xsp/mxpd2"
```

You should also note that there are basically three items that make up our special tag declaration. First, the value binding is of a particular format on line 112—not the normal format by any means. Second, there is a declaration for a **Converter** online 113–116. And third, there is a declaration for a collection of `dojoAttributes` on lines 117–143. You will come back to each of these three items in a moment, but let us first dig a little deeper into that `mxpd2:` namespace.

By using the Package Explorer view in Designer, look under the **Chp11Ed2b.nsf/WebContents/WEB-INF/** directory structure, as shown in Figure 11.36.

When you find this directory, open the **mxpd2.xsp-config** file in Designer by simply double-clicking it. Listing 11.26 also contains all the content for this file.

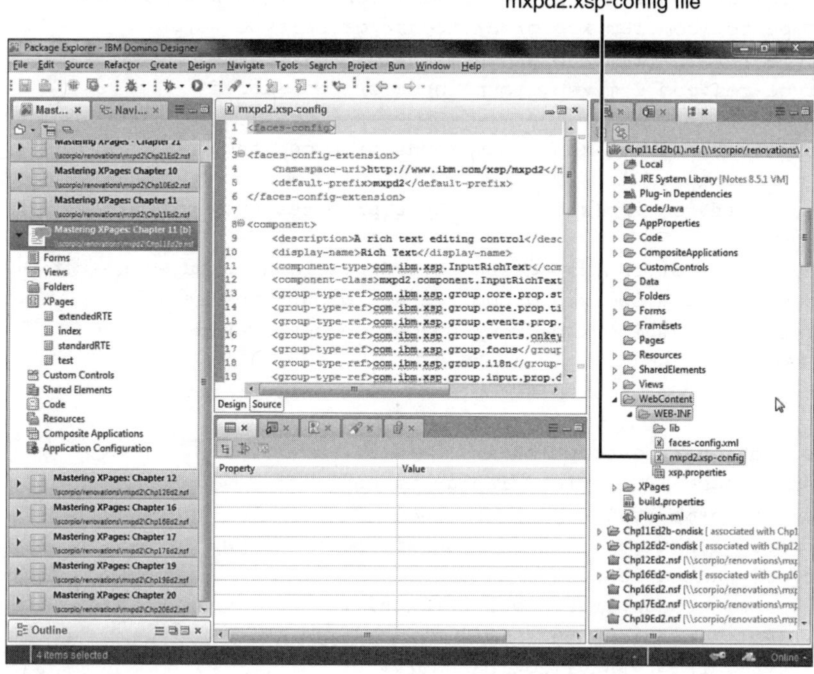

Figure 11.36 Chp11Ed2b.nsf/WebContents/WEB-INF directory in the Package Explorer

Listing 11.26 mxpd2.xsp-config Source

```
<faces-config>

<faces-config-extension>
    <namespace-uri>http://www.ibm.com/xsp/mxpd2</namespace-uri>
    <default-prefix>mxpd2</default-prefix>
</faces-config-extension>

<component>
    <description>A Rich Text Editor control for Acme
➥Corporation</description>
    <display-name>Rich Text</display-name>
    <component-type>com.ibm.xsp.InputRichText</component-type>
    <component-class>mxpd2.component.InputRichText</component-class>
    <group-type-ref>com.ibm.xsp.group.core.prop.styleClass
➥</group-type-ref>
    <group-type-ref>com.ibm.xsp.group.core.prop.title</group-type-ref>
    <group-type-ref>com.ibm.xsp.group.events.prop.onclick
➥ </group-type-ref>
```

```
    <group-type-ref>com.ibm.xsp.group.events.onkey</group-type-ref>
    <group-type-ref>com.ibm.xsp.group.focus</group-type-ref>
    <group-type-ref>com.ibm.xsp.group.i18n</group-type-ref>
    <group-type-ref>com.ibm.xsp.group.input.prop.disabled
➥</group-type-ref>
    <group-type-ref>com.ibm.xsp.group.input.prop.onchange
➥</group-type-ref>
    <group-type-ref>com.ibm.xsp.group.input.prop.readonly
➥</group-type-ref>
    <group-type-ref>com.ibm.xsp.group.outerStyleClass</group-type-ref>
    <group-type-ref>com.ibm.xsp.group.filter</group-type-ref>
    <group-type-ref>com.ibm.xsp.group.dojoUsage.deprecated
➥</group-type-ref>
    <group-type-ref>com.ibm.xsp.group.aria.role</group-type-ref>
    <property>
        <description></description>
        <display-name>CSS Style</display-name>
        <property-name>style</property-name>
        <property-class>java.lang.String</property-class>
        <property-extension>
            <pass-through>true</pass-through>
            <designer-extension>
                <category>styling</category>
                <editor>
                    com.ibm.workplace.designer.property.editors.
➥StylesEditor
                </editor>
                <styles-excluded>background, font</styles-excluded>
            </designer-extension>
        </property-extension>
    </property>
    <component-extension>
        <javadoc-description>
            <p>Rich Text Control</p>providing rich text editing
➥functionality
        </javadoc-description>
        <base-component-type>com.ibm.xsp.UIInputRichText
➥</base-component-type>
        <renderer-type>com.ibm.xsp.InputRichText</renderer-type>
        <tag-name>inputRichText</tag-name>
        <designer-extension>
            <category>Mastering XPages</category>
```

```
51          </designer-extension>
52      </component-extension>
53 </component>
54
55 </faces-config>
```

To summarize, what you are looking at within the `mxpd2.xsp-config` file is registration details for our extended Rich Text Editor control. I won't go into details here in this chapter about what an xsp-config is other than to say it is used to register extensions within the XPages Runtime registry; therefore giving you an all-important entry point—one of many I should state, provided by the powerful XPages Extensibility model. You will, of course, learn about xsp-config files in detail in the next chapter, but for the purposes of this particular example, let's deal with the most salient details of the `mxpd2.xsp-config` file. There are several points of interest (already marked in bold typeface) in Listing 11.26 of which to be aware:

- The `mxpd2` namespace and prefix is declared on lines 4 and 5, respectively. For the astute reader, you will notice these match exactly, the namespace and prefix declarations within the `extendedRTE` XPage for our `<mxpd2:inputRichText>` tag. So the `mxpd2.xsp-config` is the source of the registration of the `mxpd2` namespace in this case.
- The description, display name, and category for our extended Rich Text Editor control are all declared on lines 9, 10, and 50, respectively. These are used to expose the control within the Control Palette in Designer, as shown in Figure 11.37.
- To register a component within the XPage Runtime registry, there are three important component configuration settings required that define the type of the component, its ancestor type, and in most cases where a component requires rendering capabilities, its renderer type. These are details you will learn fully about in the next chapter. In `mxpd2.xsp-config`, we can see that our specialized Rich Text Editor has its `<component-type>` declared on line 11, `<base-component-type>` on line 46, and finally, its `<renderer-type>` on line 47. The `<component-type>` specifies what is effectively the exact same value used by the preexisting core Rich Text Editor, therefore you can see the same value being specified for the `<base-component-type>` setting. Furthermore, the `<renderer-type>` is exactly the same renderer type used by the preexisting core Rich Text Editor. The reason for this is to allow our specialized version of the Rich Text Editor to simply leverage the same renderer. There is essentially no need to provide any new rendering as such, as our extensions are performed against the client-side JavaScript widget toolbar, dialogs, and so on.

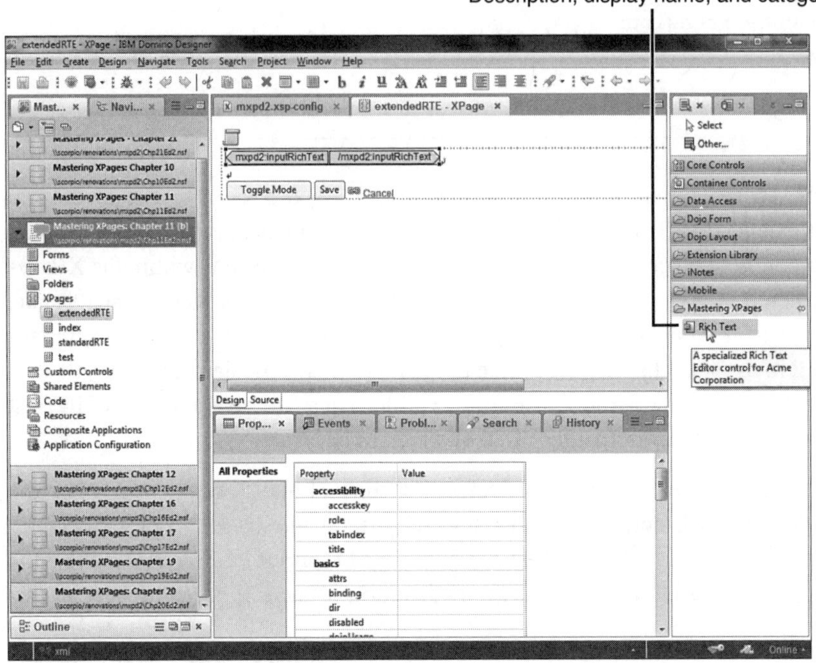

Figure 11.37 Description, display name, and category in Designer using the xsp-config values

- A vital configuration setting our specialized component registration could not be without is the `<component-class>` as listed on line 12 of Listing 11.26. As you might have already guessed, the `<component-class>` setting is used to specify the actual component Java class that will represent the server-side component. It is the central artifact that will be used to instantiate instances of the component. Hence if an XPage contains several instances of a particular control, there will be several corresponding server-side objects within the component tree for that XPage. In our case, the `<component-class>` specifies a class name of `mxpd2.component.InputRichText`, which is a Java class already defined within our **Chp11Ed2b.nsf** application. You will look at that in moment.
- Finally, the `<tag-name>` configuration setting on line 12 of Listing 11.26 is used by the XPage internal XPage page builders during page compilation and so on. For us mere mortals using Designer, it is the way to declare our intent to use a particular control within the XSP markup of an XPage. So essentially, this is the XSP markup tag. Thus, when an instance of our specialized Rich Text Editor is dragged onto the design editor or coded into the XSP markup of an XPage, a combination of namespace prefix and

`<tag-name>` is used to construct the entire tag element. Hence `<mxpd2:inputRichText>` appears in XSP markup based on the `mxpd2.xsp-config` values for the namespace prefix and `<tag-name>`.

Although the WYSIWYG design editor within Designer does not present a specific visualization for our extended Rich Text Editor control (and it can be done quite easily), a generic tag visualization is presented when a `<mxpd2:inputRichText>` tag exists within the XSP markup for an XPage. The valuable point to note though is that you can select the tag in design or source mode, and see all the properties within the All Properties editor for that control. In the case of our specialized Rich Text Editor control, you know it extends the preexisting, core Rich Text Editor, so therefore the All Properties editor now exposes all the core properties, events, and so on from the base class, as shown in Figure 11.38.

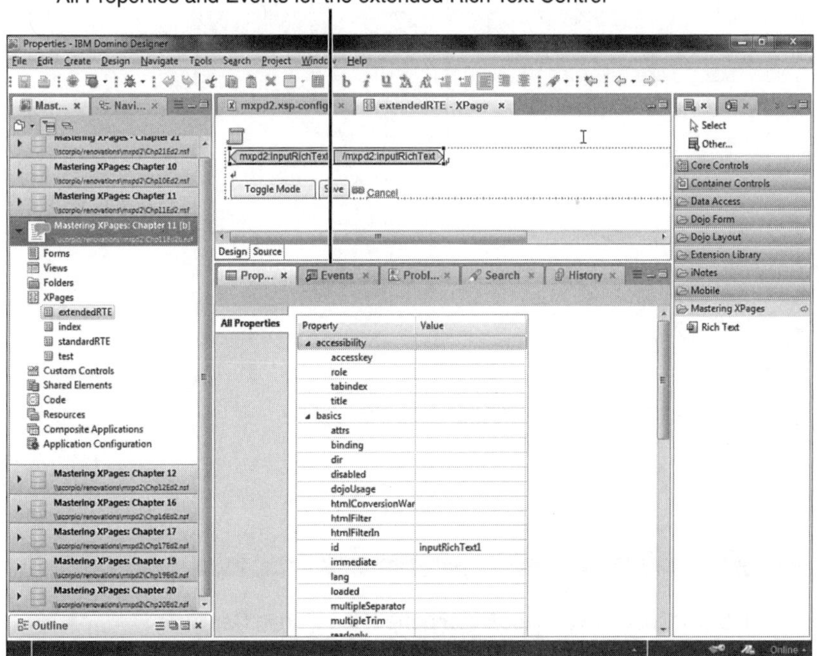

Figure 11.38 Core Rich Text Editor properties/events available for extended Rich Text Editor control

Just a quick explanation of where we're at to help keep you focused—I am leading you into our specialized Acme Corporation solution in a connect-the-dots manner whereby I want to unravel the different parts of the solution in a bottom-up manner in which the server-side parts are the "bottom" and this is where our current focus is at. You'll quickly surface up into the top-most parts over the next few pages—the client-side script and so on. This will allow you to then fully understand how the front, middle, and back-end parts of our specialized Rich Text Editor all play together to not only provide a solution for Acme Corporation, but to also form a good advanced scripting example with elements of server-side and client-side scripting and programming.

The next dot that needs to be joined up is that <component-class> declaration on line 12 of Listing 11.26 of the mxpd2.xsp-config file. Using Designer you can find and open the mxpd2.component.InputRichText class file from within the Chp11Ed2b.nsf/Code/Java/mxpd2/component location under the Package Explorer view or alternatively under the same location in the Application Navigator. Both options are shown in Figure 11.39.

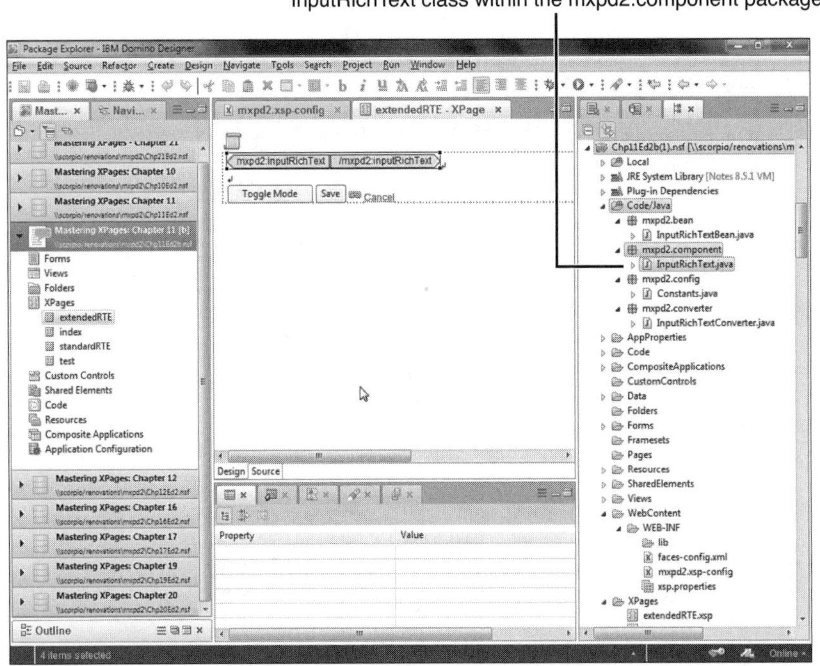

Figure 11.39 Chp11Ed2b.nsf/Code/Java/mxpd2/component location in Designer

We'll not drill too deep in the Java code within the mxpd2.component.InputRichText class at this point, but it is important for you to understand some of what it is providing for us and what it is capable of at runtime. At an abstract level, this class has been developed to extend the preexisting Rich Text Editor control, as shown on line 5 in Listing 11.27. In doing so, this provides the capability to attach a file inline within the rich text content of the Rich Text Editor, This has meant integrating our logic in a way that does not break the existing capability of this control to also handle embedded images, which is already coded within a related area of the parent class.

So with this in mind, there are two specific areas of the source code for the `mxpd2.component.InputRichText` class that you need to be aware of: first, the new inline attachment handling code, and second, the integration of the preexisting embedding image handling code. Listing 11.27 details the most relevant parts of the source code for you. At this time, I encourage you to take a few moments to review the entire source code file in Designer to absorb more of the meaning beyond the explanations given here because Listing 11.27 provides only a fragment of the actual source code.

Listing 11.27 Fragment of mxpd2.component.InputRichText.java Source

```
package mxpd2.component;

import ...

public class InputRichText extends XspInputRichText {

    public InputRichText()...

    // ------------------------------------------------------------

    public String getObjectBinding()...

    // ------------------------------------------------------------

    public String getPropertyBinding()...

    // ------------------------------------------------------------

    public void processAjaxRequest(...) ... {
        ...
        try {
            String objectBinding = getObjectBinding();
            String propertyBinding = getPropertyBinding();
            HttpServletRequestWrapper request = ...
            Object requestWrapper = request.getRequest();
            DominoDocument dominoDocument = ...
            InputRichTextBean rteBean =
➥InputRichTextBean.getInstance();
            ...
            if (...) {
                request = (FileUploadRequestWrapper)
➥requestWrapper;
                ...UploadedFile uploadedFile = ...get("upload");
                String actionType = ...get("actionType");
                if (null != actionType) {
```

```
                    if (actionType.equalsIgnoreCase
➥("inline-attachment")) {
                        ...
                        _processInlineAttachmentAjaxRequest(...);
                    } else if
➥(actionType.equalsIgnoreCase("embedded-image")) {
                        ...
                        _processEmbeddedImageAjaxRequest(...);
                    }
                }
            }
        } finally {
            boolean saveState = false;
            UIViewRoot root = context.getViewRoot();
            if (root instanceof UIViewRootEx) {
                saveState =
➥((UIViewRootEx) root).shouldSaveState(context);
            }
            if (saveState) {
                StateManager stateManager = ...getStateManager();
                StateManager.SerializedView state = ...
                TypedUtil.getRequestMap(...);
            }
        }
    }

    // -------------------------------------------------------------

    protected Boolean _processEmbeddedImageAjaxRequest(...) ... {
        ...
        HttpServletResponse response = ...
        response.setContentType("text/html; charset=utf-8");
        PrintWriter out =
➥new PrintWriter(response.getOutputStream());
        ...
        try {
            String imageName = uploadedFile.getClientFileName();
            String contentType = uploadedFile.getContentType();
            ...
            if (InputRichText.isValidImageType(contentType)) {
                EmbeddedImage embeddedImage = new
➥EmbeddedImage(...);
                if (null != embeddedImage) {
                    dominoDocument.setValue(propertyBinding,
➥embeddedImage);
```

```
                    ...
                    if (null != fileRowData) {
                        String imageSrc =
➥...getRequestContextPath() + "/xsp";
                        imageSrc += fileRowData.getHref();
                        ...
                        HashMap<String, String> map = ...
                        map.put("tag", "img");
                        map.put("src", imageSrc);
                        map.put("dataSrc", imageSrc);
                        map.put("statusMessage", "SUCCESS");
                        jsonResponse = JsonGenerator.toJson(
                            new JsonJavaFactory(), map
                        );
                        ...
                        out.println(
                            "<html><body><textarea>" +
                                jsonResponse +
                            "</textarea></body></html>"
                        );
                    }
                }
            }
            ...
        } catch (Throwable t) {
            ...
        } finally {
            out.close();
        }
        ...
        return status;
    }

    // ------------------------------------------------------------

    protected Boolean _processInlineAttachmentAjaxRequest(...) ... {
        ...
        HttpServletResponse response = ...
        response.setContentType("text/html; charset=utf-8");
        PrintWriter out =
➥new PrintWriter(response.getOutputStream());
        ...
        try {
```

```
            String attachmentName = uploadedFile.
➥getClientFileName();
            String contentType = uploadedFile.getContentType();
            UIFileuploadEx.UploadedFile attachment =
                new UIFileuploadEx.UploadedFile(
                    uploadedFile, attachmentName, contentType
            );
            dominoDocument.setValue(propertyBinding, attachment);
            ...
            if (null != fileRowData) {
                ...
                HashMap<String, String> map =
➥new HashMap<String, String>();
                map.put("tag", Constants.XSP_INLINE_ACTIVE_TAG);
                map.put("name", fileRowData.getName());
                map.put(
                    "href",
                    Constants.s_PROTOCOL_PREFIX +
➥fileRowData.getName()
                );
                ...
                map.put(
                   "clazz",
                   Constants.XSP_INLINE_ATTACHMENT_STYLECLASS + " "
➥+ type
                );
                map.put("statusMessage", "SUCCESS");
                jsonResponse = JsonGenerator.toJson(new
➥JsonJavaFactory(), map);
                ...
                out.println(
                   "<html><body><textarea>" +
                       jsonResponse +
                   "</textarea></body></html>"
                );
            }
            ...
        } catch (Throwable t) {
            ...
        } finally {
            out.close();
        }
        ...
        return status;
    }
```

```
155
156     // ----------------------------------------------------------------
157     ...
158 }
```

Drawing upon Listing 11.27, note that the InputRichText class extends the XspInputRichText class as defined on line 5. And for your interest, the XspInputRichText class is in actual fact the class used by the core XPages Runtime Rich Text Editor control.

```
public class InputRichText extends XspInputRichText
```

From an object-oriented perspective in Java, this means that our class will inherit from XspInputRichText class, therefore forming a base to subclass relationship. Furthermore, all public and protected methods and properties published by XspInputRichText can be overridden or overloaded by our new mxpd2.component.InputRichText subclass. And this is the exact reason for creating our extended subclass to enable our subclass to redefine the behavior of the XspInputRichText.processAjaxRequest(FacesContext) method, for it is this method that performs the default embedded image handling within the core Rich Text Editor control. The overridden version of the processAjaxRequest method can be seen on line 19 of Listing 11.27.

One important fact to highlight is that the processAjaxRequest method is exposed to implementers of the com.ibm.xsp.component.FacesAjaxComponent interface. So, naturally as XspInputRichText implements this interface, our mxpd2.component.InputRichText subclass also inherits the capability provided by its base class. But for us, it's a case of overriding the base class behavior to not only handle embedded images, but also inline attachments to fulfill the requirement for our customer, Acme Corporation.

As seen on lines 59 and 107, the _processEmbeddedImageAjaxRequest and _processInlineAttachmentAjaxRequest methods take care of processing an embedded image or inline attachment request, respectively. A similar pattern is used in either case whereby the file content within the AJAX POST body is extracted and assigned to either a UIFileUploadEx.UploadedFile or EmbeddedImage file object. Then the file object is applied to the value binding on the designated DominoDocument property as seen on lines 72 and 120 using the respective method calls of dominoDocument.setValue(propertyBinding, embeddedImage) for embedded images, and dominoDocument.setValue(propertyBinding, attachment) for inline attachments. After this setting of the underlying value binding, a response is then constructed as detailed on lines 83 and 138 in Listing 11.27. In both cases, the response is constructed to contain a simple HTML envelope that itself contains a JSON packet embedded within a <textarea> element as detailed in Listing 11.28 for an inline attachment response, and Listing 11.29 for an embedded image response.

Listing 11.28 Response HTML Envelope with JSON Packet for an Inline Attachment

```
<html>
    <body>
        <textarea>
            {
                "clazz": "xsp-inline-attachment application-octet-stream",
                "tag": "a",
                "href": "xsp:\/\/Project1.cpp",
                "name": "Project1.cpp",
                "statusMessage": "SUCCESS"
            }
        </textarea>
    </body>
</html>
```

Listing 11.29 Response HTML Envelope with JSON Packet for an Embedded Image

```
<html>
    <body>
        <textarea>
            {
                "tag": "img",
                "src": "/Chp11Ed2b.nsf/xsp/.../DominoDoc-NEW_2-Body/xyz.png",
                "dataSrc": "/Chp11Ed2b.nsf/xsp/.../DominoDoc-NEW_2-Body/
➥xyz.png",
                "statusMessage": "SUCCESS"
            }
        </textarea>
    </body>
</html>
```

At this point enough detail has been established to understand the Java side of this particular example. Sure enough there are other server-side Java artifacts that also contribute to the working of this example such as the `mxpd2.component.InputRichTextBean` and `mxpd2.component.InputRichTextConverter` classes, but I will refrain from delving into the mechanics of those at this point within this chapter. However, you can study those if you want to gain a deeper understanding of how URLs are processed for any persisted embedded images and inline attachments during the conversion processes of this example. Instead I want to continue concentrating on the scripting elements that are at play here.

So for your interest I will soon explain how the HTML/JSON envelope responses of Listing 11.28 and Listing 11.29 are handled within the client-side of our example. But first take a more detailed look at the `com.ibm.xsp.component.FacesAjaxComponent` interface because it is one of the most versatile interfaces available within the XPages Runtime for interacting with an XPage using advanced scripting techniques. As you have already seen in Listing 11.27, by providing a Java class that implements this interface (just like our `mxpd2.component.InputRichText` class), you are opening up the opportunity to interact with an object of that class via AJAX requests—both path-info and direct AJAX requests targeted against objects of that class within the component tree are catered for. The latter being the mechanism used by our specialized Rich Text Editor as it receives inline attachment files and embedded image files when client-side AJAX POST requests are invoked using the Attach a File and Embed an Image dialogs.

Listing 11.30 details the full declaration of the `com.ibm.xsp.component.FacesAjaxComponent` interface for your convenience.

Listing 11.30 FacesAjaxComponent Interface

```
package com.ibm.xsp.component;

/**
* Implemented by UIComponents which can handle Ajax requests and return
* a valid response.
* @ibm-api
*/
public interface FacesAjaxComponent {

    /**
    * Check if the pathinfo request is for this target ajax component
    *
    * @param context
    * @return true if request handler
    */
    public boolean handles(FacesContext context);

    /**
    * Process the request for this target ajax component
    *
    * @param context
    * @throws IOException
    */
    public void processAjaxRequest(FacesContext context) throws IOException;

}
```

As shown in Listing 11.30, there are two methods declared by this interface. The `handles` method allows implementers to process an AJAX request that satisfies a `path-info` condition. For example, if the AJAX request URL were as follows:

http://hello.com/world.nsf/foo.xsp**/bar**

where the `/bar` portion after the XPage page name represents the `path-info` part, then this could be dealt with by an implementer of `FacesAjaxComponent` that accepts /bar `path-info` requests.

However, the `processAjaxRequest` method allows implementers to process an AJAX request based upon the request being targeted directly at an instance of an object (aka component) within the corresponding XPage server-side component tree. This is exactly what is happening with our specialized Rich Text Editor solution for Acme Corporation in that when an inline attachment or embedded image request is issued against the current XPage, the request not only contains the actual file or image of interest within the POST body but it also contains the `$$ajaxtarget` and `$$viewid` request parameters. These are used by the XPages Runtime to determine which component tree to restore and execute against, based upon the `$$viewid` value, and which object to target within that component tree to process the incoming request, based upon the `$$axtarget` value. For example, if inputRichText1 is the ID of a Rich Text Editor control receiving an inline attachment for an Attach a file request, and the current `viewid` is `!dhmzk8ybs7!`, then the AJAX POST URL will be similar to the following, with the selected file included within the POST body of the request:

http://hello.com/world.nsf/foo.xsp**?$$axtarget=view:_id1:inputRichText1&**
$$viewid=!dhmzk8ybs7!

I encourage you to take another moment to revisit the last paragraph. Yes that is correct—support to execute AJAX POST requests directly against a discrete server-side object within the hierarchical component tree for the current XPage with which an end user is interacting. Furthermore, this type of request is executed without affecting the processing of any other component tree objects during in invocation, so the request is processed in a highly efficient manner. All this is made possible via the `FacesAjaxComponent` interface and utilized from client-side AJAX JavaScript requests.

Now return to Listing 11.28 and Listing 11.29 where you learned about the HTML/JSON envelope responses for both embedded image and inline attachment requests. Firstly, you should now open **AttachmentDialog.js** and **ImageDialog.js** from within the **Chp11Ed2b.nsf** application in Designer. You will find both of these files under the `Code/Script Libraries` design element category, as shown in Figure 11.40.

If you open each of these two files within Designer and study the code, you can quickly recognize a similar pattern used for both cases. As shown in both Listing 11.31 for the `AttachmentDialog.js` and Listing 11.32 for the `ImageDialog.js`, lLines 4 to 35 declare new dialog definitions within the `CKEDITOR` namespace registry. In each file lines 16 and 17 declare an `HTMLInputElement` element with a `name` defined as “upload” and a `type` as "file"—essentially creating an `<input name="upload" type="file/>` tag within the dialog contents.

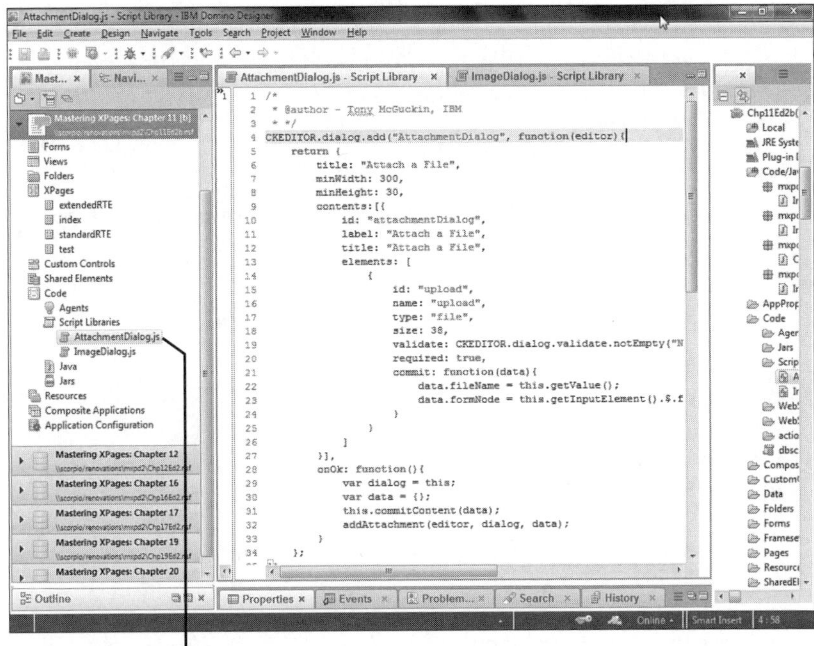

The two dialog JavaScript files

Figure 11.40 AttachmentDialog.js and ImageDialog.js in Designer

Listing 11.31 AttachmentDialog.js Source Code

```
/*
 * @author - Tony McGuckin, IBM
 * */
CKEDITOR.dialog.add("AttachmentDialog", function(editor){
    return {
        title: "Attach a File",
        minWidth: 300,
        minHeight: 30,
        contents:[{
            id: "attachmentDialog",
            label: "Attach a File",
            title: "Attach a File",
            elements: [
```

```
                {
                    id: "upload",
                    name: "upload",
                    type: "file",
                    size: 40,
                    validate: CKEDITOR.dialog.validate.notEmpty("No
➥attachment has been selected for inserting yet."),
                    required: true,
                    commit: function(data){
                        data.fileName = this.getValue();
                        data.formNode = this.getInputElement().$.form;
                    }
                }
            ]
        }],
        onOk: function(){
            var dialog = this;
            var data = {};
            this.commitContent(data);
            addAttachment(editor, dialog, data);
        }
    };
});

function addAttachment(editor, dialog, data){
    dojo.require("dojo.io.iframe");
    dojo.io.iframe.send({
        url: editor.config.axtargetUrl,
        method: "POST",
        form: data.formNode,
        content: {
            fileName: data.fileName,
            actionType: "inline-attachment"
        },
        handleAs: "html",
        load: function(response, ioArgs){
            // example expected successful response format:
            // <html><body><textarea>{"clazz":"xsp-inline-attachment
➥application-octet-stream","tag":"a","href":"xsp:\/\/Project1.
➥cpp","name":"Project1.cpp"}</textarea></body></html>
            try{
                var attachment = XSP.fromJson(response.documentElement.
➥childNodes[1].firstChild.innerHTML);
                if(null != attachment && attachment.statusMessage ==
➥"SUCCESS"){
```

```
                        var attachmentElement =
➥editor.document.createElement(attachment.tag);
                        attachmentElement.setAttribute("class",
➥attachment.clazz);
                        //>>decode
                        attachmentElement.setAttribute("href",
➥decodeURIComponent(attachment.href));
                        //<<decode
                        attachmentElement.setHtml(attachment.name);
                        editor.insertElement(attachmentElement);
                    }else{
                        if(null != attachment){
                            XSP.alert(attachment.statusMessage);
                        }else{
                            XSP.alert("A problem has occurred - please try
➥again.");
                        }
                    }
                }catch(e){
                    console.log(e);
                }
                return response;
            },
            error: function(response, ioArgs){
                XSP.alert(response.status);
                console.log(response);
                return response;
            }
        });
}
```

Furthermore, in both cases, line 23 assigns the dialog's embedded `<form>` element to a `data.formNode` variable. This is an important reference that is later used during the POST request processing when the `onOK` function, as shown on line 28, is invoked as a user selects OK within either dialog.

Listing 11.32 ImageDialog.js Source Code

```
1  /*
2   * @author - Tony McGuckin, IBM
3   * */
4  CKEDITOR.dialog.add("ImageDialog", function(editor){
5      return {
6          title: "Embed an Image",
7          minWidth: 300,
```

```
        minHeight: 30,
        contents:[{
            id: "imageDialog",
            label: "Embed an Image",
            title: "Embed an Image",
            elements: [
                {
                    id: "upload",
                    name: "upload",
                    type: "file",
                    size: 40,
                    validate: CKEDITOR.dialog.validate.notEmpty("No
➥image has been selected for embedding yet."),
                    required: true,
                    commit: function(data){
                        data.fileName = this.getValue();
                        data.formNode = this.getInputElement().$.form;
                    }
                }
            ]
        }],
        onOk: function(){
            var dialog = this;
            var data = {};
            this.commitContent(data);
            embedImage(editor, dialog, data);
        }
    };
});

function embedImage(editor, dialog, data){
    dojo.require("dojo.io.iframe");
    dojo.io.iframe.send({
        url: editor.config.axtargetUrl,
        method: "POST",
        form: data.formNode,
        content: {
            fileName: data.fileName,
            actionType: "embedded-image"
        },
        handleAs: "html",
        load: function(response, ioArgs){
            try{
                var embeddedImage = XSP.fromJson(response.
➥documentElement.childNodes[1].firstChild.innerHTML);
```

```
51                  if(null != embeddedImage &&
➥embeddedImage.statusMessage == "SUCCESS"){
52                      var imageElement = editor.document.
➥createElement(embeddedImage.tag);
53                      imageElement.setAttribute("src",
➥embeddedImage.src);
54                      imageElement.setAttribute("data-cke-saved-src",
➥embeddedImage.dataSrc);
55                      editor.insertElement(imageElement);
56                  }else{
57                      if(null != embeddedImage){
58                          XSP.alert(embeddedImage.statusMessage);
59                      }else{
60                          XSP.alert("A problem has occurred - please try
➥again.");
61                      }
62                  }
63              }catch(e){
64                  console.log(e);
65              }
66              return response;
67          },
68          error: function(response, ioArgs){
69              XSP.alert(response.status);
70              console.log(response);
71              return response;
72          }
73      });
74 }
```

So when the `onOK` function is invoked, the `data` variable is used to buffer the `fileName` and `formNode` references via the call on `this.commitContent(data)` on line 31, which is actually internally calling the `commit()` function on line 21 in each case. Following this, line 32 in each dialog implementation then invokes its `addAttachment(editor, dialog, data)` and `embedImage (editor, dialog, and data)` functions, respectively. In each case, three parameters are passed-by-reference; the `editor` parameter represents the owning CKEditor instance itself, the `dialog` parameter being the current dialog instance, and the `data` parameter being the data payload containing the `fileName` and `formNode` references as mentioned before.

So this is where the interaction between front-end client-side JavaScript and server-side Java object within the XPage component tree ties together. Within each of the two functions `addAttachment()` and `embedImage()`, there is use made of the `dojo.io.iframe` object as shown on lines 38 and 39 of both Listing 11.31 and Listing 11.32. This particular Dojo object provides functionality to perform complex I/O operations such as File upload under the context of an AJAX request—exactly the type of operation you are trying to perform here with the specialized Rich Text Editor use case. To tie everything together here, there are a number of properties set upon the `dojo.io.iframe` object to configure it to POST a request against the exact `FacesAjaxComponent` component along with the correct `<form>` body content containing the selected file or image of interest. This is shown on line 40 in each case where the `url` property is set to the predefined `editor.config.axtargetUrl` value. This property was already configured by the client-side JavaScript on the `extendedRTE` XPage, as shown on lines 95 to 105 of Listing 11.25. This is also shown here in Listing 11.33 as a convenient reminder for you where line 104 is of most interest.

Listing 11.33 Fragment Taken from extendedRTE.xsp Showing axtargetUrl Configuration

```
95  // set each RTE instance's upload url...
96  for(var x = 0; x < ids.length; x++){
97      var url = document.location.href.substring(
98          0, document.location.href.indexOf('?')
99      );
100     if(null != url){
101         url += "?$$axtarget=" + ids[x] + "&$$viewid=" +
102         XSP.findForm(ids[x])["$$viewid"].value;
103     }
104     CKEDITOR.instances[ids[x]].config.axtargetUrl = url;
105 }
```

Effectively, this fragment of client-side JavaScript in Listing 11.33 produces a URL like the following example whereby a Rich Text Editor control with an id of `inputRichText1` exists within the current XPage. The corresponding component tree for the current XPage has a server-side id of `!dhmzk8ybs7!`. Hence, the `axtargetUrl` property contains everything needed by the XPages Runtime to delegate the incoming request processing to the exact component within the specified component tree.

```
http://hello.com/world.nsf/foo.xsp?$$axtarget=view:_id1:
inputRichText1&$$viewid=!dhmzk8ybs7!
```

In our case this is an instance of our specialized Rich Text Editor component and its `projectAjaxRequest` method. Moving on, line 42 from Listing 11.31 and Listing 11.32 show the `data.formNode` reference being applied to the `dojo.io.iframe` object's `form` property. This ensures the POST request will be invoked against the target `url` using the content of the referenced formNode's `<form>` element—this is in effect the embedded `<form>` element within each of the two dialogs. This means that the file or image selected using either of the two dialogs will be included in the POST body content and therefore readily available to the targeted server-side component that has implemented the `FacesAjaxComponent` interface, through the `FacesContext` parameter of the `processAjaxRequest` method. This can be seen on lines 30 and

31 of Listing 11.27 taken from the mxpd2.component.InputRichText class where the HTML InputElement of "file" type with the name "upload" is extracted from the FacesContext object's request parameter map. This is the same <input type="file" name="upload"/> element defined in the AttachmentDialog.js and ImageDialog.js files for our custom dialogs.

With all the configuration in place, when the dojo.io.iframe.send() function has been invoked, the load function callback seen on line 48 of Listing 11.31 and Listing 11.32 will handle the asynchronous response from the targeted component. This is the response sent back from our specialized Rich Text Editor components processAjaxRequest method as already seen in Listing 11.27. Therefore, when an Add Attachment or Embed an Image request is successfully processed by the targeted component, the response parameter of the load function callback will contain the same HTML/JSON envelopes, as seen in Listing 11.28 for an inline attachment and Listing 11.29 for an embedded image.

Following the process of actually receiving a successful response, it is then simply a matter of extracting the relevant information from these "response" envelopes to compose the appropriate visual elements within the Rich Text Editor content to represent the action just performed—specifically a link in the case of an inline attachment that also has some complementary CSS styling to display a file type icon, and an image for an embedded image, of course. Examples of both are shown in Figure 11.41 where an image icon complements the .gif file attachment, a PDF icon complements the .pdf file attachment, and then the embedded image appears as-is.

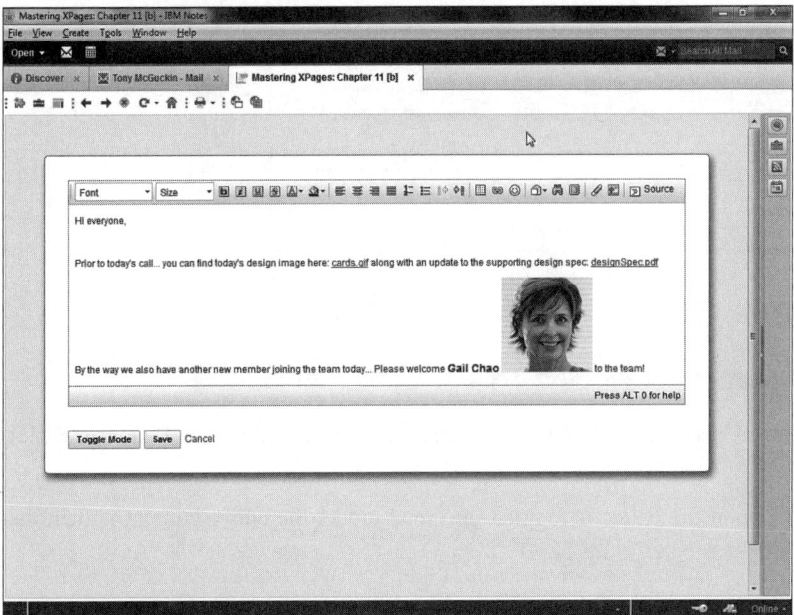

Figure 11.41 Examples of inline attachments and an embedded image within the Rich Text Editor

The client-side JavaScript code that performs this task can be seen on lines 52 to 60 of Listing 11.31 for the `AttachmentDialog.js` file. A similar pattern is also applied in the `ImageDialog.js` file as seen in Listing 11.32 on lines 50 to 55. Effectively both dialog implementations extract the JSON response packet from the HTML `<texarea>` envelope that is contained within the response parameter. This is then converted into a JSON object where the properties of the JSON object are then used to define the corresponding HTML DOM element that will be injected into the Rich Text Editor. This is done by making direct use of the `editor` reference to call the `insertElement()` function to inject the visual HTML DOM element at the current cursor position within the Rich Text Editor.

Note that the Source toolbar button can be used to toggle the Rich Text Editor from visual edit mode to source edit mode. This provides a clear way to view the HTML markup that is manipulated and injected into the editor. Figure 11.42 shows the source edit mode with two inline attachments and an embedded image within the editor's underlying HTML markup.

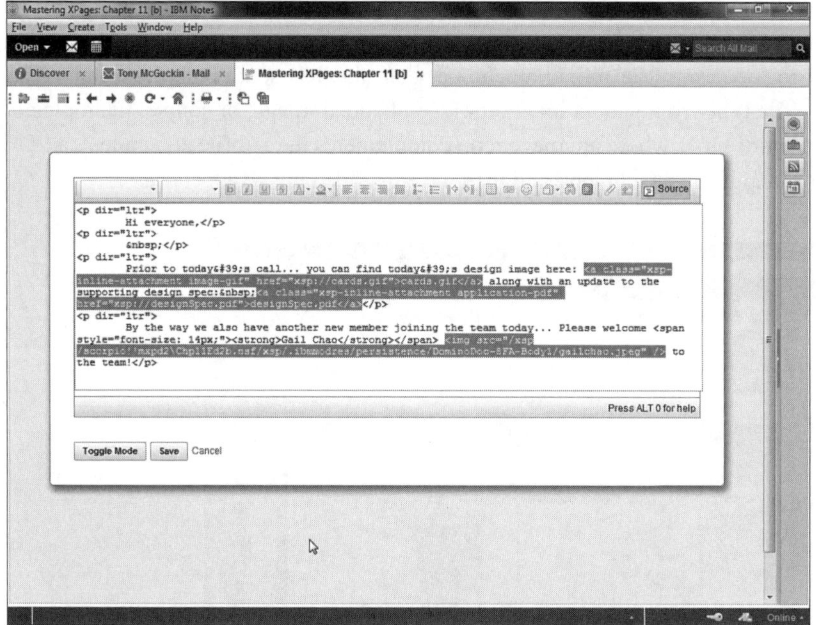

Figure 11.42 Source of inline attachments and an embedded image within the Rich Text Editor

And of course, when the editor is toggled into read-mode, the editor content is then displayed to the end user, as seen in Figure 11.43.

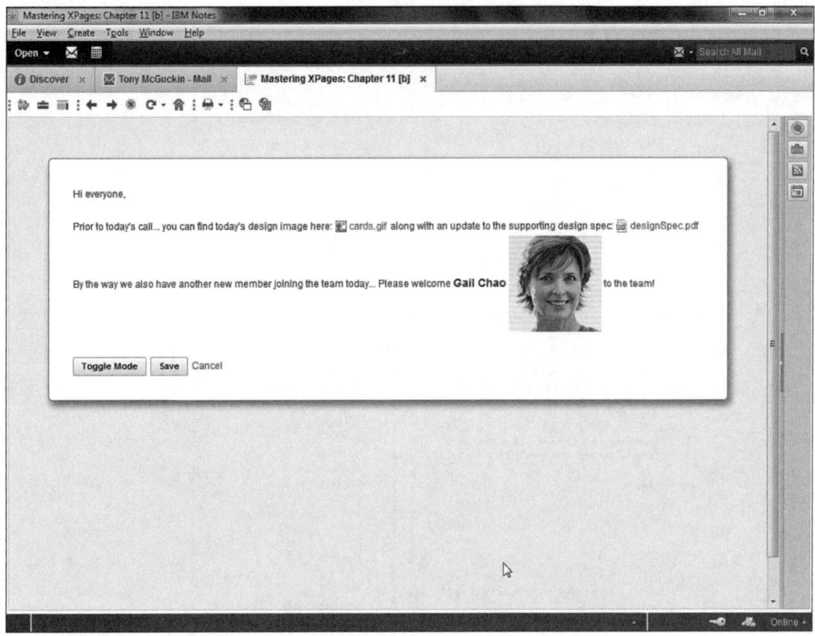

Figure 11.43 The same content toggled into read mode within the Rich Text Editor

In this case, the editor content is actually round-tripped with the server-side Rich Text Editor component, plus there is some other magic that happens here to perform conversion of the content. This conversion is necessary to transform edit-mode links such as `<a href="xsp://designSpec.pdf"/>`, which can be seen in Figure 11.42, into a fully resolvable read-mode URL such as `<a href=http://scorpio/mxpd2/Chp11Ed2b.nsf/xsp/.ibmmodres/domino/OpenAttachment/mxpd2/Chp11Ed2b.nsf/74AFA75CE2CB8C3080257B9F002ADCED/Body1/designSpec.pdf/>`. In Designer, you should take some time to read more into the code in this area to gain a deeper understanding of this functionality. In particular you should now open the `mxpd2.converter.InputRichTextConverter` Java class file, as seen in Figure 11.44.

If you examine lines 113 to 116 from Listing 11.25, again you will see that the `<mxpd2:inputRichText/>` instance declared in **extendedRTE** XPage also declares its intent to use our special `InputRichTextConverter` class. Listing 11.34 also shows the converter property configuration taken from the **extendedRTE** XPage for your convenience.

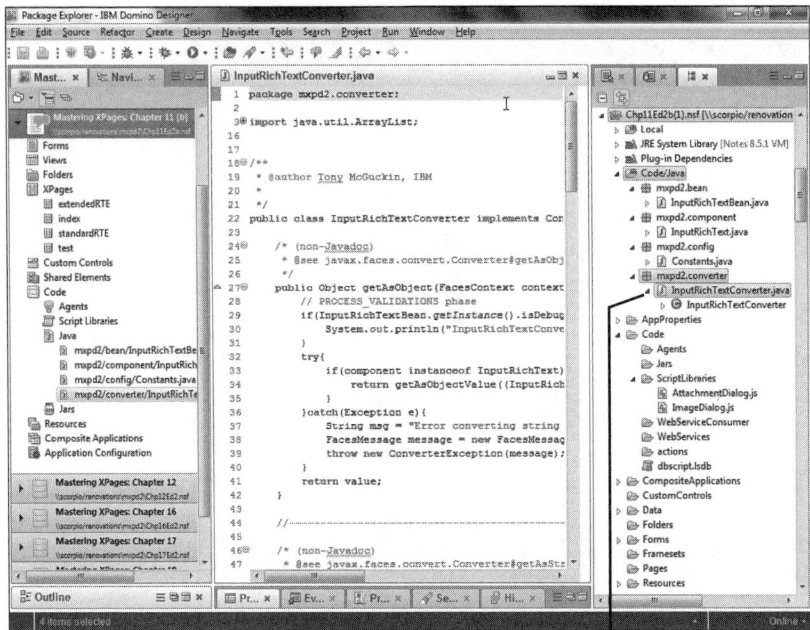

Figure 11.44 The mxpd2.converter.InputRichTextConverter class opened in Designer

Listing 11.34 Fragment Taken from extendedRTE.xsp Showing InputRichTextConverter Configuration

```
<xp:this.converter>
     <xp:converter converterId="InputRichTextConverter">
     </xp:converter>
</xp:this.converter>
```

For the astute reader delving around **Chp11Ed2b.nsf** using Designer, you will have noticed that the `InputRichTextConverter` has already been declared within the `face-config.xml` file for this application. This allows us to then reference it by the registered `converterId`, as seen in Listing 11.34 and Figure 11.45 for the `faces-config.xml` file.

The most interesting aspect of the `InputRichTextConverter` class lies in its capability to perform a conversion of the Rich Text Editor components content. This conversion happens on incoming editor content but also on outgoing editor content, in other words, for incoming POST request editor content, but also on response editor content during the rendering phase of the XPages Request Processing Lifecycle. The key point about this functionality is that it gives you, the developer, another great tool in your arsenal in that you can also manipulate the Rich Text Editor content in the server-side. You have already learned from the `AttachmentDialog.js` and `ImageDialog.js` files that you, of course, manipulate the editor content using client-side scripting, but as described here, you also have a similar capability on the server-side. As aforementioned, you should take time to read further into the `InputRichTextConverter` class to gain a deeper understanding of the functionality of this class. In particular, you should look at the `getAsObject() / getAsObjectValue()` and `getAsString() / getAsStringValue()` methods defined within this class. These methods will show you how to consume and manipulate the editor content directly on the server-side.

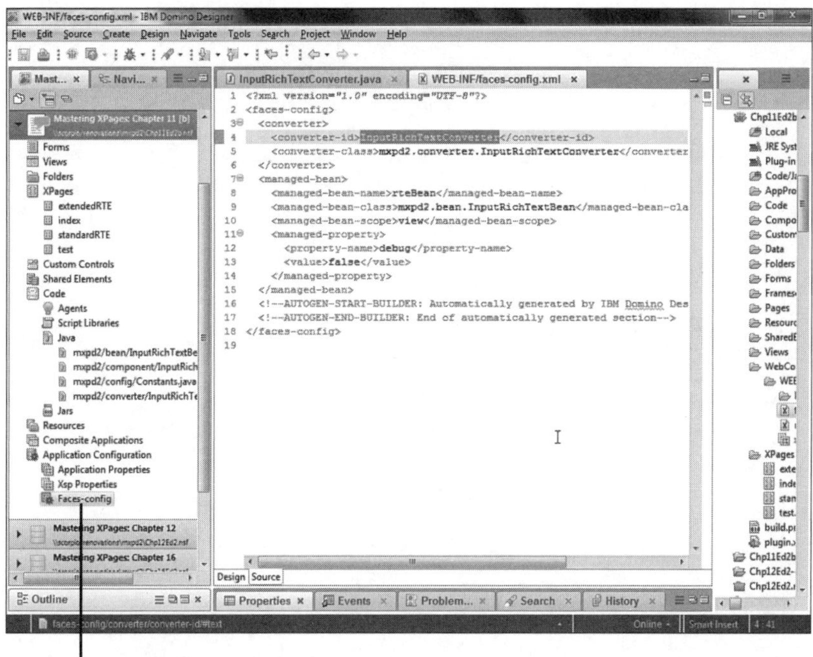

Figure 11.45 The faces-config.xml file showing the InputRichTextConverter registration

As you have learned from this section on tailoring a custom solution for the customer, Acme Corporation, there are some powerful and flexible mechanisms available within the XPages Runtime to complete the task at hand. Hopefully, this section has enlightened you into thinking about opportunities and solutions you, too, could create by using the flexibility and extensibility made available to you by XPages.

Conclusion

This chapter taught you about some of the key advanced scripting techniques that you can use with XPages. It by no means covers everything that you could classify as an "advanced scripting topic," but nonetheless, it teaches you some of the fundamentals. It also taught you about the FacesAjaxComponent interface. This is a versatile interface that can be used to create powerful server-side Java components that can be interacted with using client-side AJAX scripting. The next chapter deals with another advanced area of the XPages runtime: how to extend the XPages runtime using Java.

Chapter 12

XPages Extensibility

XPages provides a wide range of feature-rich components that enable you to build powerful Internet applications. These applications are more visually appealing than, and functionally superior to, similar applications created using traditional Notes/Domino developer tools.

However, there are limits to what is provided with XPages insofar as only so many components can be provided out-of-the-box. Although building Custom Controls is a powerful mechanism for developing reusable XPages artifacts with valuable functionality, it is inherently constrained to building on top of standard components or in combination with other Custom Controls. XPages extensibility provides a way for you to extend the XPages runtime framework to build your own user interface controls from the ground up, featuring their own behaviors and functionality that you and others can then consume within XPages applications. Writing your own user interface controls requires some Java programming skills, but this chapter guides you through the process.

In fact, there is a lot more to XPages extensibility than new user interface controls. There are many ways to extend XPages and the services that it provides. For example, creating versioned reusable libraries, developing custom NSF servlets, and building custom resource providers in an NSF are all (nonvisual) examples of how to extend the XPages framework. It is true to say that everything to do with XPages extensibility could probably fill an entire book by itself!

This chapter focuses on the framework and, in particular, the extensibility of user-interface components. XPages is a server-side component-based framework for creating web applications that run on the Domino server and locally in the Notes client. The XPages framework leverages and extends (and even enhances, in places) the JavaServer Faces framework. One of the key features that JSF provides is the capability to extend existing components to create your own user interface components. This chapter walks you through XPages extensibility and configuration mechanisms by building a simple number spinner user interface control that can be run from within an application NSF.

To see a fully working example of the exercises used in this chapter, download the **Chp12Ed2.nsf** file provided online for this book. You can access this file at `www.ibmpressbooks.com/title/9780133373370`.

> **TIP**
>
> To find out more about all the various XPages Extensibility mechanisms not covered in this chapter, visit the IBM Notes and Domino Application Development wiki (www-10.lotus.com/ldd/ddwiki.nsf) and look under the API documentation category.

How to Create a New User Interface Control

Creating a new user interface control using the XPages Extensibility mechanisms is a simple three-step process. The following steps provide a high-level overview of the process; each step is explored later in this chapter:

1. **Create a user interface (UI) component extension Java class**: This class implements the `UIComponent` interface (a JSF interface that all UI components must implement). It stores and manages the state of properties that support the functionality being provided by the component. Just like a standard JavaBean, the component exposes its properties via setter and getter methods. It also implements several other expected methods that are required to support the JSF request processing lifecycle upon which XPages is based; however, numerous classes already implement all of this required functionality. Your component can simply extend one of these classes, override one or two methods that identify the component, and focus on the properties it should manage.

> **TIP**
>
> Not familiar with JavaBeans? Wikipedia has a short and simple summary that can help you quickly get up to speed: http://en.wikipedia.org/wiki/JavaBean.

2. **Create an xsp-config configuration file**: This file essentially defines the tag that will be used in the XPages source XML markup and will tie it to the UI component extension class that Domino Designer will create for it when it builds the Java class for any XPage that consumes the component. In addition to defining the component in terms of a tag element, namespace, and attributes, it can also specify whether those attributes are required, if they must be specified explicitly, or if they can be computed dynamically. There will also be information specifically for Domino Designer, describing how the

property declarations should be manipulated and even information on how the component should be displayed in the **Controls** palette, what icons to use, and so on.

3. **Create a Java renderer class**: The role of the XPages renderer is to emit the HTML (or other markup) that provides the visualization of the component. It implements numerous methods that will be expected by the JSF request processing lifecycle, but its main two responsibilities are to capture any user input for the component (decode) and generate a representation of the component (encode) for the target platform based on the component properties. Although a component can generate its own HTML, it is useful to provide a separate renderer if the component is to be used on multiple platforms where the emitted markup may be different. If a separate renderer is used, it must be registered in the application `faces-config.xml` so that the XPages runtime knows this is the one to use for the component.

The `xsp-config` file, and the Domino Designer XPages registry that uses the `xsp-config` file, is the magic glue that pulls everything together. It defines the tag that is used in the source of an XPage, it enables Domino Designer to provide appropriate Property editors, and generates the appropriate component class when building the XPage that will use the XPages runtime framework.

Example Component

This section walks you through creating a simple UI component extension, the classic number spinner component. It is a simple component in terms of functionality. This chapter focuses on the extension mechanisms and does not get into the specific XPages framework classes and JavaScript development. Figure 12.1 shows the end result of the application that is created with the number spinner. The number spinner consists of an input text box and two buttons: one that increments and one that decrements the value in the input box. The increment size and the minimum and maximum values are all configurable as properties of the tag that represents the control. The buttons pick up the XPages theme that has been configured for the application. In the application, three number spinners are used to represent a date, day, month, and year, whose values are bound to a managed bean with session scope via value binding expressions. As the values are changed and saved to the bean, the application updates the number of changes by triggering a value change listener method that is bound to the control.

OK, it is not the most spectacular component in the world, but the focus is really on the steps, configuration, and coding required to create an XPages component that XPages can use. It is a good idea that you learn about the JavaServer Faces (JSF) lifecycle as the XPages framework is based on JSF (refer to Chapter 5, "XPages and JavaServer Faces") and borrows and shares many of the same concepts and processes. A complete understanding of JSF is not a prerequisite for reading this chapter; the only assumption is a bit of Java knowledge. If you follow the instructions and copy the code samples, you will be fine.

Figure 12.1 Custom XPages UI Component extension

Let's Get Started

Everything you need to create UI component extensions for XPages is available with Domino Designer. It provides an XPages development environment, a preview web server for testing the output, and Java editors and tooling support for building the Java component classes.

The steps in this section walk you through getting your Domino Designer development environment set up, which prepares you to progress to the next section, where you create some basic infrastructure classes and configuration files. Pretty quickly, you will have something up and running!

Create the Initial Application

Start by creating a blank new application based on the blank application template that ships with the Notes client and Domino server. From Domino Designer, follow these steps:

1. Choose **File > New > Application**.
2. In the New Application dialog (see Figure 12.2), select **Local** if you are just developing for the Notes client or your Domino server (in both the Specify New Application Name Location and Specify Template for New Application sections).
3. Enter a title for the application (for example, **Chp12Ed2**), which automatically generates the filename (for example, **Chp12Ed2.nsf**). Note that when you enter an application name, the filename is autogenerated (but only up to the first eight characters if you are storing the application on a Domino server).
4. Select **Blank** as the Template and choose **OK**.

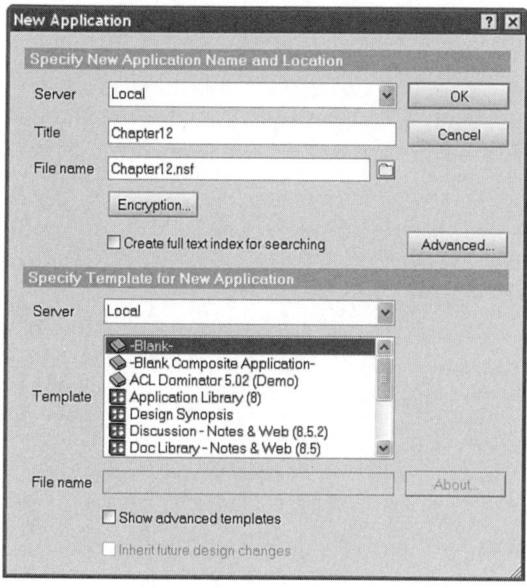

Figure 12.2 New Application dialog

Add Package Explorer to the Domino Designer Perspective

UI Component extensions are written in the Java programming language, so you need to open the Package Explorer in Domino Designer, which allows you to view the contents of the application NSF as a raw Java web-application archive (WAR) file system. Follow these steps:

1. Choose **Window > Show Eclipse Views > Other**.
2. In the **Show View** dialog (see Figure 12.3), under the Java directory, select **Package Explorer**.
3. Choose **OK**.

You now see the **Package Explorer** on the right-hand side of Domino Designer beside the **Controls** and **Data** palettes, as shown in Figure 12.4. With the **Package Explorer** view, Domino Designer gives you a file-system representation of the contents of your application NSF that you can easily navigate around and add your own Java source files that are compiled and added to the `WEB-INF\classes` directory under the `WebContent` folder.

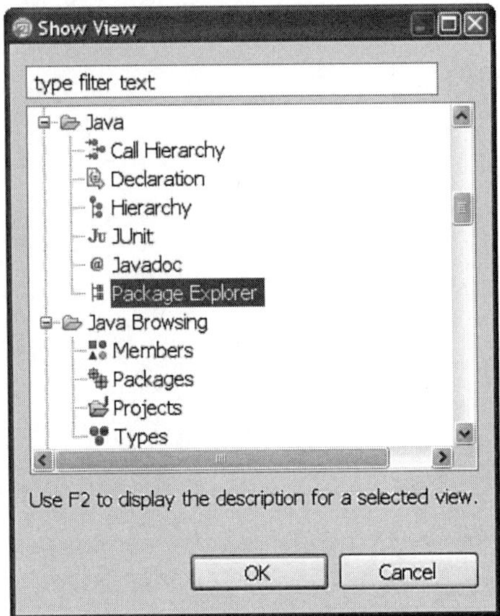

Figure 12.3 Show View dialog

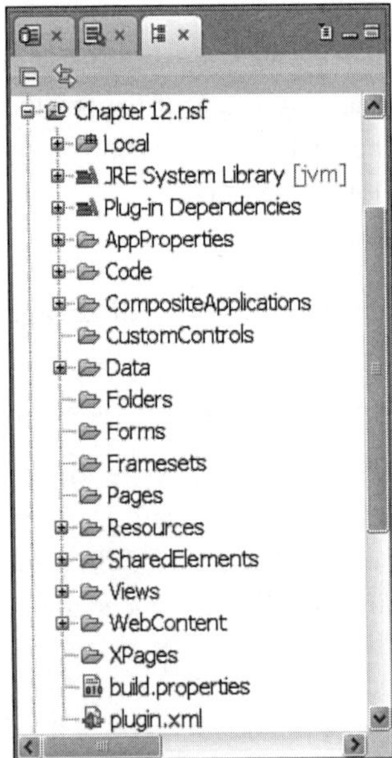

Figure 12.4 Domino Designer Java Package Explorer

Add a Java Source Code Folder

In the **Package Explorer**, create a new folder that will store the Java source files you create for the UI component extension. This folder has a little hash symbol on it to distinguish it from general folders. Follow these steps:

1. In the **Package Explorer**, select the top-level folder, **Chp12Ed2.nsf**.
2. Right-click and select **New > Other...**.
3. See the **New** dialog.
4. Under the **Java** folder, select **Source Folder**.
5. Choose **Next**.
6. See the New Source Folder dialog (see Figure 12.5). Enter `src` for the Folder Name field.
7. Choose **Finish**.

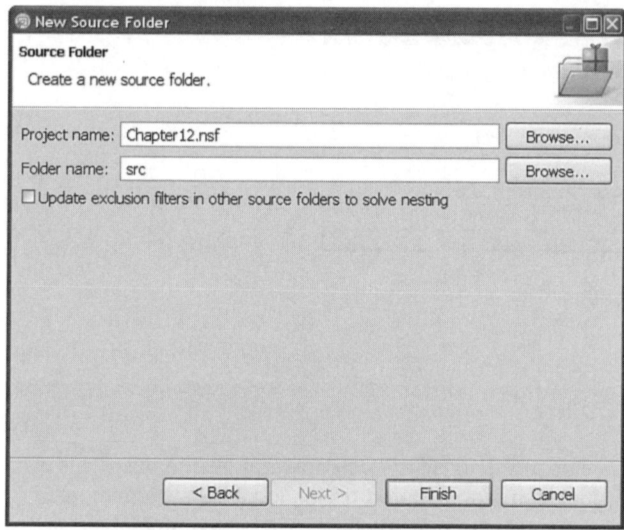

Figure 12.5 New Source Folder dialog

There is a new `src` folder (with a special hash icon to signify that it is a source folder and not a general file folder) under the top-level **Chp12Ed2.nsf** folder (see Figure 12.6).

The source folder has special properties, most notably defining where compiled Java classes from the source code in this folder are stored. For the XPages runtime to find the compiled classes, they need to be stored under the `WebContent/WEB-INF/classes` folder. You can verify this for the *`src`* folder by examining the Java Build Path properties. To do this, right-click the *src* folder in the **Package Explorer**, choose **Build Path > Configure Output Folder...**, and note the value of the project's default output folder; it should be `Chp12Ed2.nsf/WebContent/WEB-INF/classes`, as shown in Figure 12.7.

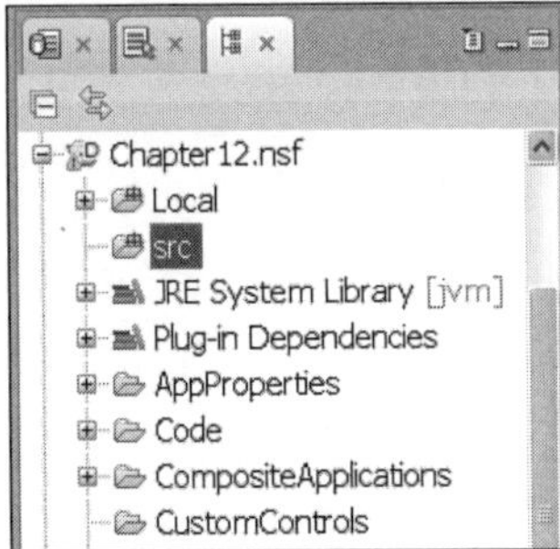

Figure 12.6 Java Source code folder

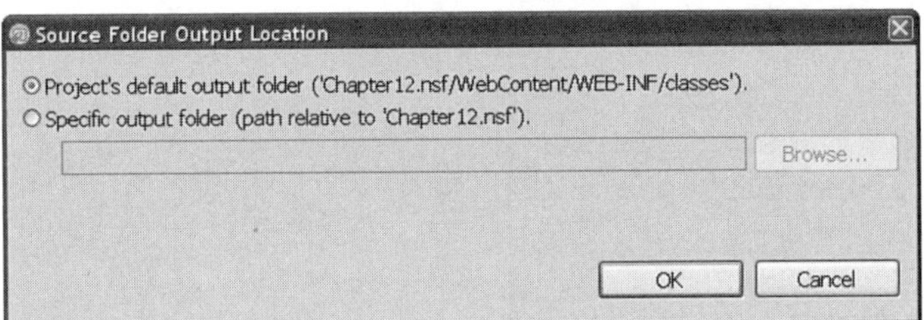

Figure 12.7 Source folder output location

> **NOTE**
>
> You should not create Java source files in the existing *Local* folder; Local in this context represents the Domino Designer workspace that is stored on the local file system of your workstation. Everything would work fine until you make a change—the incremental builder in Domino Designer would then flush the contents of the Local folder before recompiling all the XPages again. Your custom Java source files would be permanently deleted in this case. Furthermore, if you copied the NSF file somewhere else, the original source also would not be included.

Building a Component

This section follows the three steps for extending the XPages framework with custom UI component extensions that were outlined at the beginning of this chapter. There is a sprinkle of JSF theory, just enough to provide some context.

1. Create a UI Component Extension class that implements `UIComponent`.
2. Create an `xsp-config` file that defines the tag and properties of the component.
3. Create a renderer that emits the HTML to provide a realization of the component.

Create a UI Component Extension Class

Now, it's time to create the Java class that represents the number spinner component. The class extends an existing JSF class, `javax.faces.component.UIInput`, because the number spinner is a control that accepts user input (whose value can be manipulated by the associated buttons).

JSF provides a component model that is based on the composite pattern. The composite pattern defines a whole-part hierarchy where all components implement a common interface. This means that all components, either container or individual components, can be treated equally. In JSF, the `UIComponent` interface specifies the common behaviors that all components must have to support and function correctly within the JSF request-processing lifecycle. This also holds true for XPages components. `UIComponent` specifies a large set of behaviors; however, to ease development, JSF provides the `UIComponentBase` class. This is a concrete implementation of all the `UIComponent` methods except one, `getFamily()`, a method that returns the component's family identifier which, along with a render type identifier, can be used to associate a specific renderer with the component. You could start from the `UIComponentBase` class, but you would have to provide much more functionality to do something interesting or useful. Standard JSF components extend this base class (`UIOutput`, for example). `UIOutput` provides the capability to display data, read only, that is read from a data model. `UIInput`, in turn, extends `UIOutput` to provide the capability to edit the displayed data and save it back to the data model. Custom classes can, of course, extend the standard components. That is one of the main goals of JSF: to provide an easy-to-use, reusable, and extensible user interface component framework for building web-based applications.

XPages extends the standard JSF components. For example, `com.ibm.xsp.component.UIInputEx` extends `UIInput` and provides extra Notes/Domino functionality, such as the capability to deal with multivalue items, XPage themes and styling, and filtering of data for harmful script code.

For now, keep it simple, and just work off the standard JSF `UIInput` component. To create the `UISpinner` class, follow these steps:

1. In **Package Explorer**, select the `src` folder.
2. Right-click and select **New** > **Other...**.
3. See the **New** dialog.
4. Under the **Java** folder, select **Class**.
5. Choose **Next**.

6. See the **New Java Class** dialog.
7. Enter `mxpd.component` for the Package field.
8. Enter `UISpinner` for the Name field.
9. Enter `javax.faces.component.UIInput` for the Superclass field. Note that you can also type `Ctrl+Space` here to have the super class name suggested.
10. Your dialog should be populated, as shown in Figure 12.8.
11. Choose **Finish**.

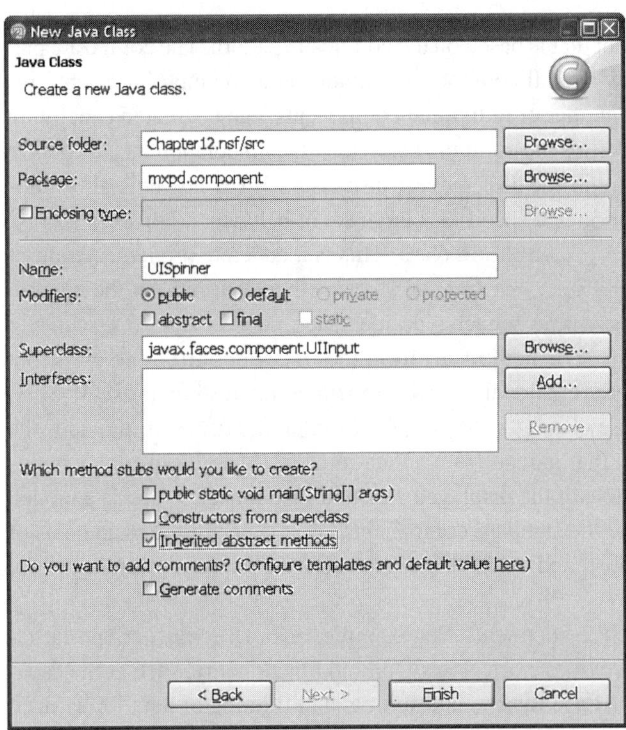

Figure 12.8 New Java class for the UI component extension

Completing these steps gives you an empty class file. There is nothing to implement, because `UIInput` has implemented everything from the `UIComponent` interface. However, there are couple of methods to override and add, namely, `getFamily()`, and the constructor to set the render type. Shortly, you will see these two identifiers (family and renderer type) used in the `faces-config.xml` application configuration file to associate a specific renderer class with this component. Every component can render itself, and this is the default behavior for components. Specifying `null` as a parameter to the `setRendererType()` method instructs the component to render itself rather than delegate to an associated renderer. You could override the rendering methods within the component itself to produce the HTML output. This is often a good approach when starting to learn about this topic. It reduces some of the initial complexity of requiring additional renderer classes and having to register them. However, this example extends `UIInput` and certain behaviors are inherited. One of these behaviors is that it expects rendering to be delegated to a separate renderer class, and this is the approach followed in the example.

Listing 12.1 shows the updates. Make these changes and save the file.

Listing 12.1 Implement Standard Methods

```
package mxpd.component;

import javax.faces.component.UIInput;

public class UISpinner extends UIInput {

    public static final String COMPONENT_FAMILY =
                                    "mxpd.component.UISpinner";
    public static final String RENDERER_TYPE =
                                "mxpd.renderer.UISpinnerRenderer";

    public UISpinner() {
        super();
        setRendererType(RENDERER_TYPE);
    }

    @Override
    public String getFamily() {
        return COMPONENT_FAMILY;
    }
}
```

Create Tag Specificaton (.xsp-config) for the UI Component Extension

To use the new UI component in XPages, you need to extend the current set of XPages control tags. To do this, specify a new tag name as part of a component definition in an `xsp-config` file. Then, when Domino Designer comes across a reference to the component extension tag in an XPage, it generates Java code to create a new instance of the custom UI component extension as part of the XPage component tree. To create an `xsp-config` file, follow these steps:

1. In **Package Explorer**, select the `WebContent/WEB-INF` folder.
2. Right-click and select **New > Other...**.

3. See the **New** dialog.
4. Under the **General** folder, select **File**.
5. Choose **Next**.
6. See the **New File** dialog. In the **File Name:** field, specify the `.xsp-config` file by calling it the name `uispinner.xsp-config`.
7. Choose **Finish**.
8. Add the configuration information in Listing 12.2 and save the file.

Listing 12.2 Initial xsp-config File for the Tag Specification

```
<faces-config>

    <faces-config-extension>
        <namespace-uri>http://mxpd/xsp/control
        </namespace-uri>
        <default-prefix>mx</default-prefix>
    </faces-config-extension>

    <component>

        <description>MXPD Spinner Example</description>

        <display-name>MXPD Spinner</display-name>

        <component-type>mxpd.component.UISpinner
        </component-type>
        <component-class>mxpd.component.UISpinner
        </component-class>

        <component-extension>
            <tag-name>uiSpinner</tag-name>
            <component-family>mxpd.component.UISpinner
            </component-family>
        </component-extension>

    </component>

</faces-config>
```

Although the `xsp-config` file is proprietary to XPages, the syntax and tags specification are very much based on JSF with the XPages enhancements and additions typically found in the `<something-extension>` tags. The extension tags are a JSF mechanism that is typically used by development tools to implement additional functionality. They are heavily used and extended by XPages and Domino Designer. If you are familiar with writing custom JSF components for JavaServer Pages (JSP), you would typically specify the Java component extension class in the `faces-config` file and the tag namespace and description in a separate tag library definition file (`.tld`). Although JSF integrates well with JSP, they are separate technologies and have separate extension mechanisms. XPages has just one, the xsp-config file where both the Java component extension is registered, along with the tags, properties, and attributes for the component, which will be used in XPages XML source code. Table 12.1 describes the basic `xsp-config` tag elements. Note that the `xsp-config` file also defines Custom Controls within XPages.

Table 12.1 XPages xsp-config Tags

Tag	Description
`<faces-config>`	Outer tag element for the configuration file.
`<faces-config-extension>`	XPages-specific extensions for declaring the tag namespace.
`<namespace-uri>`	The XPages namespace for the custom component. There need not be anything at the URL. The default prefix is `xp`. This namespace is, as are all namespaces beginning with http://www.ibm.com/xsp, reserved for use by IBM. When you need to define your own namespace, the convention is to use a URL that starts with your company's web address to ensure that there are no collisions.
`<default-prefix>`	The XPages tag prefix used to denote your namespace.
`<component>`	Register a component extension with XPages.
`<description>`	A text description of the component.
`<display-name>`	A name used by Domino Designer when displaying the component in a palette or selector.
`<component-type>`	A unique name for the component typically uses a qualified name prefix. com.ibm.xsp is used for XPages components, `com.ibm.xsp.InputText`, for example.
`<component-class>`	The fully qualified Java class name for the component that implements the `UIComponent` interface or extends some class that does.
`<component-extension>`	Domino Designer uses configuration information supplied in here.
`<tag-name>`	Tag name for the component to be used in XPages XML source.
`<component-family>`	The component family identifier.

At this point, create an XPage and add your new control by following these steps:

1. From the **Application Navigator**, select the **XPages** folder.
2. Right-click and select **New XPage**.

3. See the **New XPage** dialog.
4. Name the XPage `xpBasicTest`.
5. Choose **OK**.
6. Select a point on the XPage.
7. From the **control palette**, select **Other... > Other Controls**.
8. See the **Create Control** dialog (shown in Figure 12.9) and select **MXPD Spinner**.

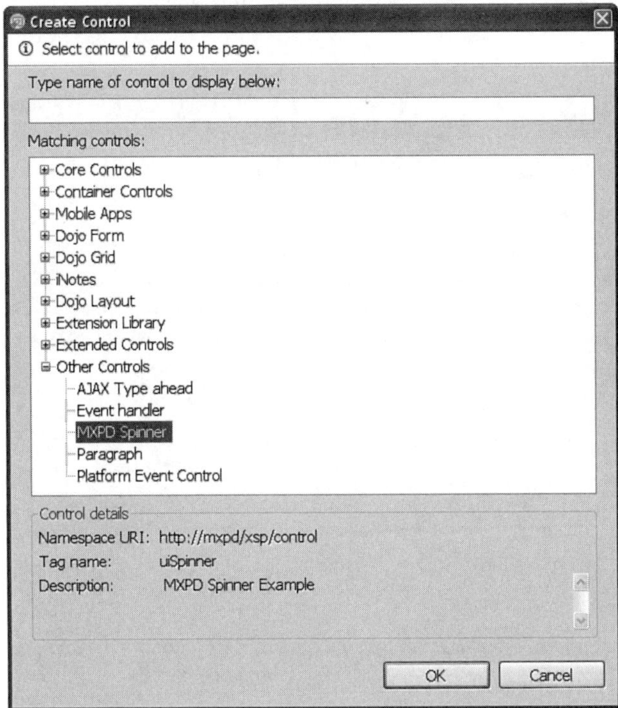

Figure 12.9 Create Control dialog

9. Choose **OK**.
10. The tag that presents the UISpinner control appears on the XPages Design canvas (see Figure 12.10).

Figure 12.10 also shows the default properties XPages creates for a component. There is no point in running the XPage in a web browser; it does not do anything right now, because there is no renderer to generate the appropriate HTML for the component.

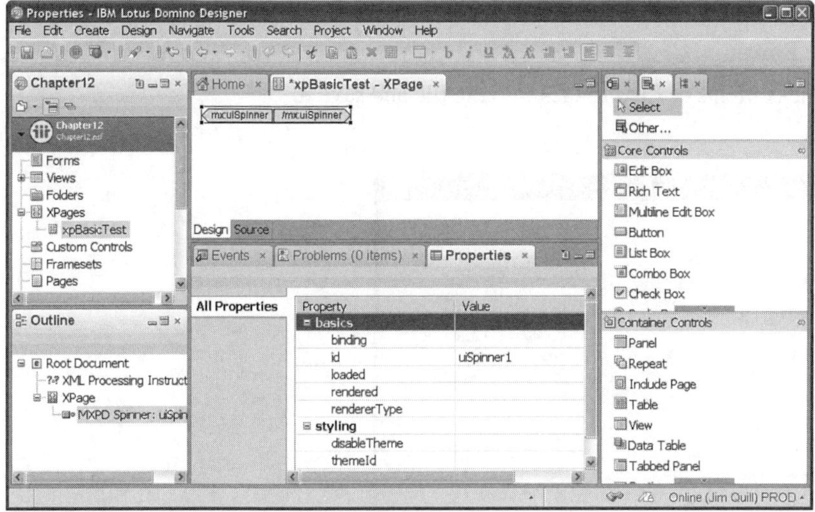

Figure 12.10 Default mx:uispinner representation

Create a Renderer and Register It in the Application Configuration (faces-config.xml)

A UI component must implement the required JSF methods to retrieve user input for the component in the request and emit the appropriate HTML to represent the component in a web browser. The JSF request-processing lifecycle implemented by the XPages runtime invokes these methods at the appropriate time. Most components typically delegate these responsibilities to a specific renderer class that implements the required methods by extending the abstract class `javax.faces.render.Renderer`.

To create a Java class for the renderer, follow these steps:

1. In **Package Explorer**, select the `src` folder.
2. Right-click and select **New** > **Other**…
3. See the **New** dialog.
4. Under the **Java** folder, select **Class**.
5. Choose **Next**.
6. See the **New Java Class** dialog.
7. Enter `mxpd.renderer` component for the **Package** field.
8. Enter `UISpinnerRenderer` for the **Name** field.
9. Enter `javax.faces.render.Renderer` for the **Superclass** field.

10. Your dialog should be filled, as shown in Figure 12.11.
11. Choose **Finish**.
12. Copy the contents of Listing 12.3 into the file and save it.

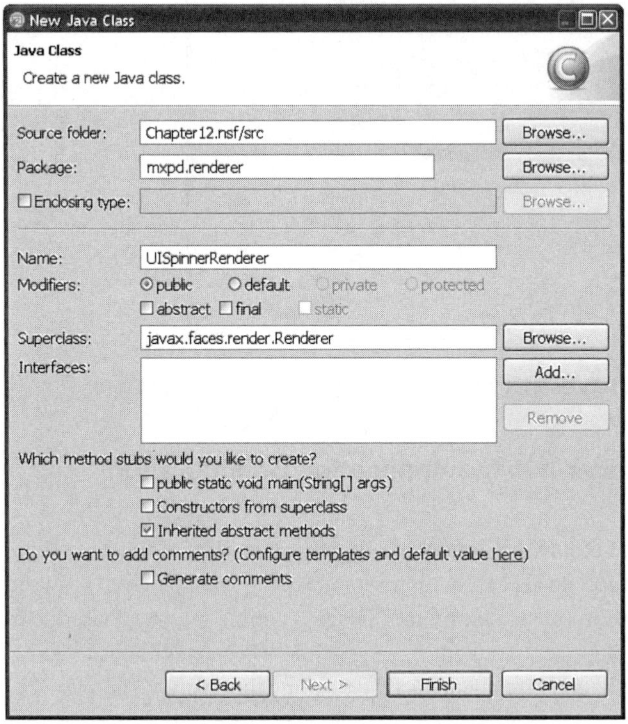

Figure 12.11 New Java Class dialog

Listing 12.3 Simple Renderer Implementation

```
package mxpd.renderer;

import java.io.IOException;

import javax.faces.component.UIComponent;
import javax.faces.context.FacesContext;
import javax.faces.context.ResponseWriter;
import javax.faces.render.Renderer;
```

```
public class UISpinnerRenderer extends Renderer {

    @Override
    public void encodeEnd(FacesContext context, UIComponent component)
            throws IOException {
        ResponseWriter rw = context.getResponseWriter();
        rw.startElement("input", component);
        rw.writeAttribute("type", "button", "type");
        rw.writeAttribute("style", "border:orange solid thin", null);
        rw.writeAttribute("value", "Hello World!", "value");
        rw.endElement("input");
        super.encodeEnd(context, component);
    }
}
```

Note that `javax.faces.render.Renderer` implementations are stateless; only one instance is created irrespective of the number of components on the page. (The component class is the one responsible for managing state; more on that in the next section.) Now that a renderer has been created, you need to register it as the renderer to be used by XPages runtime to create the HTML representation of the `mxpd.component.UISpinner` component family. Follow these steps:

1. In Package Explorer, open the `WebContent/WEB-INF` folder.
2. Select the `faces-config` file and open it.
3. Replace the contents with the configuration information shown in Listing 12.4.
4. **Save** the file.

Listing 12.4 Register Renderer for UI Component Extension in faces-config.xml

```
<?xml version="1.0" encoding="UTF-8"?>
<faces-config>
  <render-kit>
    <renderer>
      <component-family> mxpd.component.UISpinner </component-family>
      <renderer-type> mxpd.renderer.UISpinnerRenderer </renderer-type>
      <renderer-class> mxpd.renderer.UISpinnerRenderer </renderer-class>
    </renderer>
  </render-kit>
</faces-config>
```

Quick Test Application to Verify Everything Is OK So Far

Now that everything is in place, you can test out the new UI component extension by adding it to an XPage and running it in the preview web engine. The XPage does not do much. It just simply displays a button with an orange border, but at least you have successfully created a custom XPages UI component extension.

To create a new XPage and add the UISpinner control, follow these steps:

1. From the **Application Navigator**, select the **XPages** folder.
2. Right-click and select **New XPage**.
3. See the **New XPage** dialog.
4. Name the XPage `xpQuickTest`.
5. Choose **OK**.
6. Select a point on the XPage.
7. From the control palette, select **Other... > Other Controls > MXPD Spinner**.
8. Choose **OK**.
9. See the tag that represents the UISpinner control appear on the XPages Design canvas.

The XPage should look similar to the one created for the previous basic test (refer to Figure 12.10). In fact, if you run xpBasicText.xsp now, you get the same output, as shown in Figure 12.12, because the `mx:uispinner` tag now has a renderer for creating output associated with its component.

Figure 12.12 Test run for mx:uispinner configuration

Before running the XPages application using the preview web server, add the Anonymous user to the application access control list (ACL) with at least author access and the ability to create documents.

Select the XPage and save the contents if necessary. To see the result of the test page (shown in Figure 12.12), select **Design > Preview in Web Browser > Default System Web Browser**. When the browser opens up, you should see the button created from the HTML the renderer was coded to emit.

That should all be working nicely. Now, it is time to implement the number spinner.

Working with Component Properties

Most of the files needed to complete the number spinner are now in place, and their role in developing a control should be clear. They just need some editing, and for any new files that need to be created, particularly Java classes, the processes should be familiar now.

Component Properties and Attributes

The characteristics of a component that give it certain behavior and state when loaded, irrespective of the type of renderer producing the visualization of the component, are usually called *properties* (or render-independent properties). They are generally represented as JavaBean component properties with getter and setter methods. Properties represent the state of a component, a value entered by a user that needs to be maintained between requests until it is saved to the data model, for example. XPages, through the JSF request processing lifecycle, supports state management between requests. There is more on state management in the section, "State Holder: Saving State Between Requests."

Attributes of a component tend to be of interest to the renderer of a component. They are not managed directly by the component itself, but via a `Map` that is accessed using the `getAttributes()` method. For example:

```
component.getAttributes().get("styleClass")
```

In the XPages `xsp-config` file, both properties and attributes associated with a component are specified as properties using the `<property>` tag. When XPages generate the code for a component that has a value specified in a tag attribute, it can introspect the component associated with the tag to see whether it should generate setter code or store the property value in the generic attribute map. If a **set** method exists in the component class for the property, it is called passing the value as a parameter. Otherwise, a call to **put** the value into the attribute map for the component is generated. If you really want to specifically designate an attribute, use the `<attribute>` tag instead.

One interesting thing about the implementation of the attribute map in JSF is that it supports attribute-property transparency. This means that, when the attribute map is requested to get or set a value, the attribute map first tries to find a property setter or getter on the component, wrapping primitive types in their equivalent object representations, if necessary.

XPages supports both simple properties that are based on a single datatype (a string or integer, for example), and complex properties that are based on an object type. Complex properties are usually called *complex types*. A complex type is an object representation of a piece of data that is the property of a component. In JSF, converters and validators are specific cases of complex types; however, XPages provides support for the general case of declaring any object as a property of a component.

Adding a Property to a Component

The sequence of steps for adding properties and attributes to a tag is to

1. Specify the `<property>` tag in the xsp-config file for the `<component>`. Only this step is needed for attributes. In fact, you can specifically use the `<attribute>` tag for generic attributes of the component.
2. In the UI input component class, implement the setter and getters methods for the components properties (if it is not an attribute of the component).
3. If the property should maintain state (it's not an attribute), override or extend the `saveState()` and `restoreState()` methods that implement the StateHolder interface.

All the `<property>` and `<attribute>` tags specified for the component appear in All Properties section on the Properties tab for the component in Domino Designer. When a value for a property is specified, Domino Designer adds the appropriate component tag attribute and value in the XPage XML source.

State Holder: Saving State Between Requests

StateHolder is a JSF interface that must be implemented by components that need to save their state between requests. Note that both the `saveState()` and `restoreState()` methods must be implemented and equally reflect each other's content. The same data must be saved and restored in the same component class.

If the component that implements the StateHolder interface also has references to objects that implement StateHolder (complex properties, for example) the `saveState()` and `restoreState()` methods of the component must call the respective `saveState()` or `restoreState()` of the complex property.

Saving and restoring the state of a component object is done as a serializable object, and any class implementing the StateHolder interface must have a public no-args constructor. If a component does not implement save and restore state for its properties correctly, the first time the XPage with the component is referenced, the properties are set initially when the XPages view component tree is first constructed. On subsequent postbacks to the same XPage, the view component tree is restored—restoring the view is the first phase, Restore View, of the JSF request processing lifecycle (see Chapter 5 for more details on the request processing lifecycle)—using the no-arg constructor to create the instance. Its properties are then set via the `restoreState()` method. If you neglect to implement the appropriate save/restore, your user interface components appear with blank values on subsequent reloads.

See Listing 12.8 in the section, "Inheriting xsp-config Properties," for an example of the `saveState()` and `restoreState()` methods.

Specifying Simple Properties

The behavior of a component can be altered by changing its properties in the tag. To get a list of all the properties and attributes associated with a particular tag:

1. Select the component on the XPage.
2. Select the **All Properties** section from the Properties tab.

All the properties for a tag are listed in this section and reflect the properties as specified in the xsp-config file for the tag. They are also organized per the categories assigned. If no category is assigned to a property, it is assigned the default category `others`. The base set of categories are as follows:

- **Basics**: General category of properties
- **Styling**: Properties that control the visual appearance of the component

More complete components would have Events and Data categories. To add a simple property to the UISpinner control, first specify the property definition in the `uispinner.xsp-config` file. Listing 12.5 shows an example specification for a simple property.

Listing 12.5 Example Specification of a Simple Property

```
<faces-config>
...
  <component>
  ...
    <property>
      <description>Value</description>
      <display-name>value</display-name>
      <property-name>value</property-name>
      <property-class>int</property-class>
      <property-extension>
        <designer-extension>
            <category>spinner</category>
        </designer-extension>
    </property-extension>
</property>
```

When you save the configuration file, the new property shows up in the All Properties section of the Properties tab for the component. The next step is to implement the property in the component class file. Because the `UISpinner` component inherits from `UIInput` (which extends `UIOutput` and implements the `ValueHolder` interface), the component class inherits the `getValue()` and `setValue()` methods, so there is no need to implement them (or the `saveState()` and `restoreState()` methods for the property). The next section shows an example, Listing 12.8, where the property getter and setters and state management are implemented for properties specific to the UISpinner component.

Inheriting xsp-config Properties

You are not limited to one xsp-config file; there may be several, and all the definitions in their content are stored in the XPages registry, which is a catalog that Domino Designer uses to define controls in the controls palette and fill out all the component properties in the All Properties section of an XPages component Properties tab.

An interesting feature of XPages component definitions is their capability to inherit other xsp-config artifacts and definitions. This avoids duplication and reduces development time, maintenance, and mistakes when developing new XPages components. It also helps promote reuse at the component configuration level.

This allows you to define a hierarchy of XPages UI component extension classes and interfaces and have an equivalent set of XPages xsp-config files that mirrors that hierarchy.

For example, take a component that should work like a UIInput component, which accepts a value, but also supports minimum and maximum values declaratively as a tag property so that an XPages developer using the component would not have to add a validator.

The minimum and maximum properties can be defined as a group. See the xsp-config configuration snippet shown in Listing 12.6.

Listing 12.6 <group> Snippet from base.xsp-config

```
<faces-config>
...
    <group>
        <group-type>mxpd.component.group.minmaxpair</group-type>
        <property>
            <description>Minimum value allowed</description>
            <display-name>min</display-name>
            <property-name>min</property-name>
            <property-class>int</property-class>
            <property-extension>
              <designer-extension>
                <category>spinner-base</category>
              </designer-extension>
            </property-extension>
        </property>
        <property>
            <description>Maximum value allowed</description>
            <display-name>max</display-name>
            <property-name>max</property-name>
            <property-class>int</property-class>
            <property-extension>
```

```
                <designer-extension>
                  <category>spinner-base</category>
                </designer-extension>
              </property-extension>
          </property>
      </group>
...
</faces-config>
```

Table 12.2 details the group- and property-related `xsp-config` tags.

Table 12.2 XPages Group and Property xsp-config Tags

Tag	Description
`<group>`	Specifies a group of related properties.
`<group-type>`	An identifier for the group.
`<group-type-ref>`	Includes predefined groups in another group or component by specifying the target `<group-type>` identifier in the body of the tag.
`<property>`	Specifies an individual property.
`<description>`	Description of the property that appears in Domino Designer.
`<display-name>`	A name used by Domino Designer when displaying the property.
`<property-name>`	Name of the property.
`<property-class>`	Datatype that represents the property.
`<property-extension>`	Domino Designer-specific information is supplied in here.
`<designer-extension>`	Domino Designer uses property information supplied in here.
`<category>`	Groups properties under headings to appear in the All Properties property tab in Domino Designer.

With the group defined, any other component can include the properties. In the `uispinner.xsp-config`, as shown in Listing 12.7, the predefined group of properties are referenced using the `<group-type-ref>` tag, and they are added to the components properties in the XPages registry. The is no need to reference the actual `xsp-config` filename, all the `xsp-config` files get loaded into the XPages registry, which makes all the types and properties available for reference.

Listing 12.7 <group-type-ref> Snippet from uispinner.xsp-config

```
<component>
...
    <group-type-ref>mxpd.component.group.minmaxpair</group-type-ref>
...
</component>
```

A component class that supports a specific component definition should define the properties, implement the property setters and getters, and handle the state management. Listing 12.8 shows the `UISpinner` class that defines a component with two properties. The setter and getter follow standard JavaBean conventions and the class implements the required `StateHolder` interface methods so that the data that represents this component is preserved correctly as the component tree is saved and restored.

Listing 12.8 MinMaxInput Snippet

```
public class UISpinner extends UIInput implements StateHolder {

    int min = Integer.MIN_VALUE;
    int max = Integer.MAX_VALUE;
    private boolean transientFlag = false;

    public UISpinner() {  super();  }

    public int getMin() {
        if (min != Integer.MIN_VALUE) {return min;}
        ValueBinding vb = getValueBinding("min");
        if (vb != null){
            Object value = vb.getValue(getFacesContext()) ;
            if (value != null){
                return ((Number)value).intValue();
            }else {
                return Integer.MIN_VALUE;
            }
        } else {
            return Integer.MIN_VALUE;
        }
    }

    public void setMin(int min) {  this.min = min;  }

    public int getMax() {
        if (max != Integer.MAX_VALUE) {return max;}
        ValueBinding vb = getValueBinding("max");
```

```
        if (vb != null){
            Object value = vb.getValue(getFacesContext()) ;
            if (value != null){
                return ((Number)value).intValue();
            }else {
                return Integer.MAX_VALUE;
            }
        } else {
            return Integer.MAX_VALUE;
        }
    }

    public void setMax(int max) {  this.max = max;  }


    public boolean isTransient() {  return transientFlag;  }
    public void setTransient(boolean transientFlag) {
        this.transientFlag = transientFlag;
    }

    public void restoreState(FacesContext context, Object state) {
        Object values[] = (Object[]) state;
        super.restoreState(context, values[0]);
        this.min = ((Integer) values[1]).intValue();
        this.max = ((Integer) values[2]).intValue();
    }

    public Object saveState(FacesContext context) {
        Object values[] = new Object[3];
        values[0] = super.saveState(context);
        values[1] = new Integer(this.min);
        values[2] = new Integer(this.max);
        return values;
    }
}
```

NOTE

In Listing 12.8, because the property types are a primitive type, int, they need to be changed to Integer objects to support serialization. In the case where the min and max properties allow runtime binding (they are a computed value), there is support for getting the values from a ValueBinding. Normally, with primitive types, you also have to manage the case where the property was never set (because a primitive type cannot be null) using an appropriate value that is **boxed** and **unboxed** based using a boolean to track if the value was ever set directly. However, in this case, a default value is set and used so it is never unset.

The declaration of the `group-type` named `mxpd.component.group.minmaxpair` in `base.xsp-config`, and the definition of the `UISpinner` class encourages reuse. This means that, if there was a requirement to implement a component that allowed a user input a value which should have a configurable minimum and maximum value, the new component could extend `UISpinner` class, and the `xsp-config` definition for the component tag could reference the `mxpd.component.group.minmaxpair` property group definition. Note that the `UISpinner` class is just used as an example and is not used in the `UISpinner` component example.

Create the Initial xsp-config Definitions

As just described, XPages provided support for creating certain definitions, like a property group, that can be referenced and reused in another xsp-config file. The next section walks through creating `base.xsp-config`, which contains definitions to be used in the main component configuration file, `uispinner.xsp-config`. This base configuration file contains a definition for a complex type. Complex types were briefly mentioned earlier in this chapter, but they are covered in more detail in the next section.

Create base.xsp-config

The UISpinner class example already extends UIInput, so it cannot extend another class. However, it can implement an interface and still leverage the predefined `mxpd.component.group.minmaxpair` property group.

Follow these instructions to create another xsp-config file, `base.xsp-config`. It contains definitions of a property group and complex types that are referenced by the `uispinner.xsp-config` configuration file. It simply shows how an interface can be used, and the all component and complex-type definitions can be referenced between `xsp-config` files:

1. In **Package Explorer**, select the `WebContent/WEB-INF folder`.
2. Right-click and select **New** > **Other...**.
3. See the **New** dialog.
4. Under the **General** folder, select **File**.
5. Choose **Next**.
6. See the **New File** dialog. In the File Name field, specify the `xsp-config` file by calling it the name `base.xsp-config`.

7. Choose **Finish**.
8. Enter the faces-config information shown in Listing 12.9 into `base.xsp-config` and save it. Note that `base.xsp-config` is not a special name; it can be anything.

Don't worry about the complex-type definitions for now; we will return to them later.

Listing 12.9 base.xsp-config

```
<faces-config>

    <faces-config-extension>
        <namespace-uri>http://mxpd/xsp/control
        </namespace-uri>
        <default-prefix>mx</default-prefix>
    </faces-config-extension>

    <complex-type>
        <complex-id>mxpd.component.step.LargeSmallStepInterface
        </complex-id>
        <complex-class>mxpd.component.step.LargeSmallStepInterface
        </complex-class>
    </complex-type>

    <complex-type>
        <description>Large and Small Step Size</description>
        <display-name>largeSmallStepSize</display-name>
        <complex-id>mxpd.component.step.LargeSmallStepImpl
        </complex-id>
        <complex-class>mxpd.component.step.LargeSmallStepImpl
        </complex-class>
        <property>
            <description>Large and Small Step Size</description>
            <display-name>small</display-name>
            <property-name>smallStep</property-name>
            <property-class>int</property-class>
            <property-extension>
                <required>false</required>
                <allow-run-time-binding>true</allow-run-time-binding>
            </property-extension>
        </property>
        <property>
            <description> Large and Small Step Size </description>
            <display-name>large</display-name>
            <property-name>largeStep</property-name>
            <property-class>int</property-class>
```

```
        <property-extension>
            <required>false</required>
            <allow-run-time-binding>true</allow-run-time-binding>
        </property-extension>
    </property>
    <complex-extension>
        <tag-name>largeSmallStep</tag-name>
        <base-complex-id>mxpd.component.step.LargeSmallStepInterface
        </base-complex-id>
    </complex-extension>
</complex-type>

<complex-type>
    <description>Large and Small Step Size</description>
    <display-name>largeSmallStepSize</display-name>
    <complex-id>mxpd.component.step.DummyStepImpl
    </complex-id>
    <complex-class>mxpd.component.step.DummyStepImpl
    </complex-class>
    <property>
        <description> Large Small Step Size </description>
        <display-name>small</display-name>
        <property-name>smallStep</property-name>
        <property-class>int</property-class>
        <property-extension>
            <allow-run-time-binding>false</allow-run-time-binding>
        </property-extension>
    </property>
    <property>
        <description>Step Size for Large Small</description>
        <display-name>large</display-name>
        <property-name>largeStep</property-name>
        <property-class>int</property-class>
        <property-extension>
            <required>true</required>
            <allow-run-time-binding>false</allow-run-time-binding>
        </property-extension>
    </property>
    <complex-extension>
        <tag-name>dummyStep</tag-name>
        <base-complex-id>mxpd.component.step.LargeSmallStepInterface
        </base-complex-id>
    </complex-extension>
</complex-type>
```

```
    <group>
        <group-type>mxpd.component.group.minmaxpair</group-type>
        <property>
            <description>Minimum value allowed</description>
            <display-name>min</display-name>
            <property-name>min</property-name>
            <property-class>int</property-class>
            <property-extension>
              <designer-extension>
                <category>spinner-base</category>
              </designer-extension>
            </property-extension>
        </property>
        <property>
            <description>Maximum value allowed</description>
            <display-name>max</display-name>
            <property-name>max</property-name>
            <property-class>int</property-class>
            <property-extension>
              <designer-extension>
                <category>spinner-base</category>
              </designer-extension>
            </property-extension>
        </property>
    </group>

</faces-config>
```

TIP

The xsp-config file definitions use many different tags that have special meaning and purpose for XPages and the XPages registry in Domino Designer. Many of the tag meanings are obvious by inspection, and some are explained in this chapter as appropriate. The "XPages Extensibility API Developers Guide" contains extensive reference material covering all the xsp-config tag formats and meaning. This reference material is highly recommended reading. A reference to this guide is given at the end of this chapter.

Create an Interface to Match the Group Property Definition in base.xsp-config

Now that `base.xsp-config` defines a specific group of properties, create a Java interface that specifies the setters and getters for the `min` and `max` properties. The `UISpinner` component class implements this interface. The `min` and `max` properties are used to allow a user of the spinner to restrict the minimum and maximum values allowed by clicking on the increment and decrement buttons of the spinner control. To create the interface, follow these steps:

1. In **Package Explorer**, select the *src* folder.
2. Right-click and select **New** > **Other....**
3. See the **New** dialog.
4. Under the **Java** folder, select **Interface**.
5. Choose **Next**.
6. See the **New Java Interface** dialog.
7. Enter `mxpd.component.group` for the **Package** field.
8. Enter `MinMaxPair` for the **Name** field.
9. Choose **Finish**.
10. Add the four method declarations to the interface, as shown in Listing 12.10 and save the file.

Listing 12.10 MinMaxPair.java

```
package mxpd.component.group;

public interface MinMaxPair {

    public void setMin(int min);
    public int  getMin();
    public void setMax(int max);
    public int  getMax();

}
```

The next step is to update `uispinner.xsp-config` (under the **Chp12Ed2.nsf\WebContent\WEB-INF** folder) to include a reference that includes the `mxpd.component.group.minmaxpair` property group and a simple `value` property. The modified section to add is highlighted in bold, as shown in Listing 12.11. Note that, although the property group name is identical to the package hierarchy used for the `mxpd.component.group.MinMaxPair` interface, the naming is done purely from an organizational clarity point of view and implies no special implementation meaning. Only the `<component-class>` declaration in an `xsp-config` file actually ties an implementation to a property or type declaration.

Listing 12.11 uispinner.xsp-config

```
<faces-config>

      <faces-config-extension>
            <namespace-uri>http://mxpd/xsp/control
            </namespace-uri>
            <default-prefix>mx</default-prefix>
      </faces-config-extension>

      <component>

            <description>MXPD Spinner</description>

            <display-name>MXPD Spinner</display-name>

            <component-type>mxpd.component.UISpinner
            </component-type>
            <component-class>mxpd.component.UISpinner
            </component-class>

        <component-extension>
            <tag-name>uiSpinner</tag-name>
            <component-family>mxpd.component.UISpinner
            </component-family>


        </component-extension>

        <group-type-ref>mxpd.component.group.minmaxpair</group-type-ref>

        <property>
            <description>Value</description>
            <display-name>value</display-name>
            <property-name>value</property-name>
            <property-class>int</property-class>
            <property-extension>
                <designer-extension>
                    <category>spinner</category>
                </designer-extension>
            </property-extension>
        </property>    </component>
</faces-config>
```

Revisit the Component Properties in Domino Designer

Now, go back to the test XPage with the single `UISpinner` control (or simply create a new XPage and, from the **controls palette**, select **Other... > Other Controls > MXPD Spinner** and choose **OK**). On the Domino Designer XPage design canvas, select the `UISpinner` control and open the Properties tab. There, you see the component properties, as shown in Figure 12.13.

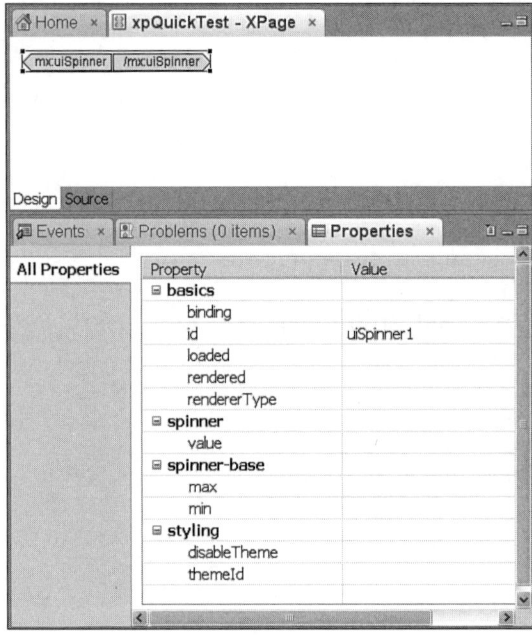

Figure 12.13 Properties for the mx:uiSpinner control showing inherited properties

Notice that there is now a `value` property under the `spinner` category and that the `min` and `max` properties inherited from the `<group>` definition can be found under the `spinner-base` category.

Specifying Complex Properties

So far, the component tag properties and attributes have been primitive data types, strings, and integers, and so on, but not all properties of a component need necessarily be primitive types. Non-primitive properties are referred to as *complex properties*. Complex properties are represented as their own tags. Listing 12.12 shows an example XPage source code snippet for a `<mx:uiSpinner>` control that includes a `complex-type` property using `mx:this` syntax.

Listing 12.12 Complex Property Referenced Using the mx:this. Syntax

```
<mx:uiSpinner id="uiSpinner1" size="2" value="#{spinnerBean.day}"
              min="1" max="31">
    <mx:this.stepSizes>
        <mx:largeSmallStep largeStep="10" smallStep="1">
        </mx:largeSmallStep>
    </mx:this.stepSizes>
</mx:uiSpinner>
```

The `<mx:uiSpinner>` control has a property, `stepSizes`, that references a complex type. The complex type is represented by its own tag, `<mx:largeSmallStep>`, which has two properties that are set using attributes of the tag element.

A complex property is defined in a component just like any other property; however, the `<property-class>` tag specifies an object (a class name or an interface name that is implemented by a class) rather than a basic data type. Listing 12.13 shows an example of setting a `complex-type` property for a control tag in an `xsp-config` file. Note that Listing 12.13 specifies an interface called `mxpd.component.step.LargeSmallStepInterface`, which is implemented later in this section.

Listing 12.13 Setting a Complex-Type Property

```
<faces-config>
...
  <component>
  ...
    <property>
        <description>The big increment value</description>
        <display-name>Big increment</display-name>
        <property-name>stepSizes</property-name>
        <property-class>mxpd.component.step.LargeSmallStepInterface
        </property-class>
        <property-extension>
            <designer-extension>
                <category>spinner</category>
            </designer-extension>
        </property-extension>
    </property>
```

The significance of specifying interface for a complex type is that the Domino Designer registry automatically detects any classes that implement the interface and offers a choice of complex-type classes when setting the complex property. To demonstrate this, you need to add the following Java interface and two Java classes that implement the interface to the application.

TIP

The XPages registry in Domino Designer is where all the components, groups, types, and properties that have been declared in various `xsp-config` files get stored for reference. This enables types and components to easily reference each other. In addition, Domino Designer also uses the registry to associate feature-rich property editors with different XPages components (for example, the XPage and View property editors, which provide a better and richer design time experience than the standard "All Properties" editor that is available for every XPages component).

To create a Java interface that specifies the behavior of a component that supports incrementing a value in small or large steps, follow these steps:

1. In **Package Explorer**, select the `src` folder.
2. Right-click and select **New > Other....**
3. See the **New** dialog.
4. Under the **Java** folder, select **Interface**.
5. Choose **Next**.
6. See the **New Java Interface** dialog.
7. Enter `mxpd.component.step` for the **Package** field.
8. Enter `LargeSmallStepInterface` for the **Name** field, as shown in Figure 12.14.
9. Choose **Finish**.
10. Add the code to the interface, as shown in Listing 12.14, and save the file.

Listing 12.14 LargeSmallStepInterface.java

```
package mxpd.component.step;

public interface LargeSmallStepInterface {

    public void setSmallStep(int smallStep);
    public int  getSmallStep();
    public void setLargeStep(int largeStep);
    public int  getLargeStep();
}
```

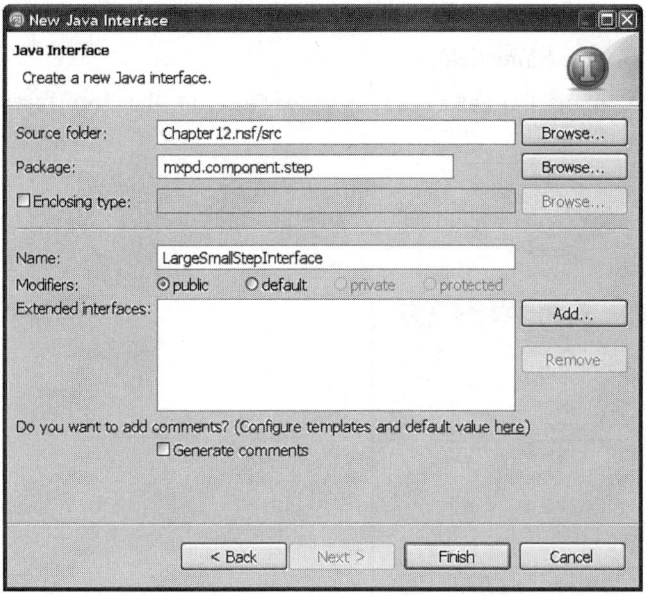

Figure 12.14 New Java Interface dialog

Now, create the first of two classes that implements the interface. The first is a dummy class that does nothing and is not used in the `UISpinner` example. Having the second class helps demonstrate the capability of the Domino XPages registry to detect classes that implement a certain interface that has been specified as the `<property-class>` of a `complex-type`. In the final version of the `UISpinner` control, when you select the `stepSizes` property, Domino Designer displays a little Add button that, when selected, pops up a list of available `complex-type` tags for the property. The list includes the tags for the two complex types whose `<complex-class>` classes have implemented the interface that was specified as the `<property-class>` for the `stepSizes` property. The interesting thing about this is that the control property class could be a data source interface, and the complex type classes could implement the interface but provide the data in different formats, depending on what the XPages designer required.

To create the dummy class, follow these steps:

1. In **Package Explorer**, select the `src` folder.
2. Right-click and select **New** > **Other...**.
3. See the **New** dialog.
4. Under the **Java** folder, select **Class**.
5. Choose **Next**.
6. See the **New Java Class** dialog.

7. Enter `mxpd.component.step` for the **Package** field.
8. Enter `DummyStepImpl` for the **Name** field.
9. Add `mxpd.component.step.LargeSmallStepInterface` to the **Interfaces** field, as shown in Figure 12.15.
10. Choose **Finish**.
11. Add the code to the interface, as shown in Listing 12.15, and save the file.

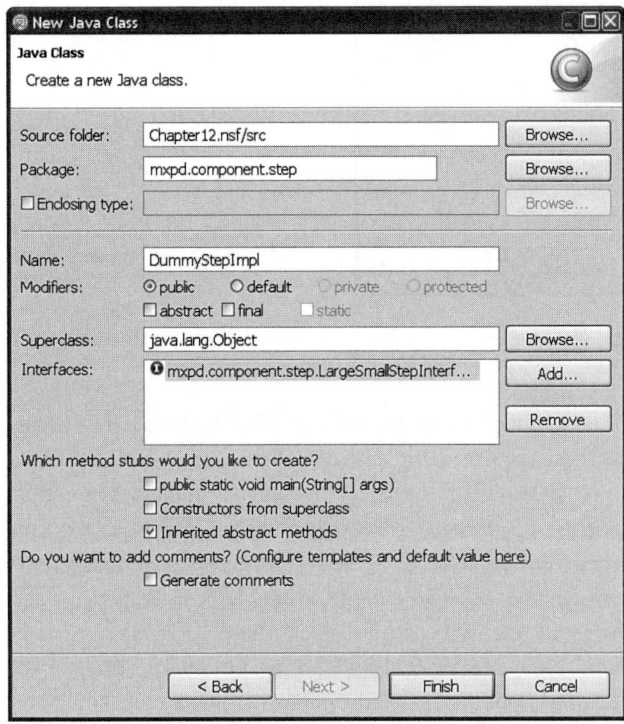

Figure 12.15 New Java Class dialog

Listing 12.15 Complex Property Referenced Using the mx:this Syntax

```
package mxpd.component.step;

public class DummyStepImpl implements LargeSmallStepInterface {
    private int smallStep;
    private int largeStep;

    public int getLargeStep() {  return largeStep;  }
```

```
    public int getSmallStep() {  return smallStep;  }
    public void setLargeStep(int largeStep) {
                    this.largeStep = largeStep;  }
    public void setSmallStep(int smallStep) {
                    this.smallStep = smallStep;  }
}
```

Now, create another Java class that implements the `LargeSmallStepInterface`. This class is used for the `complex-class` property for the `UISpinner` component. Follow these steps:

1. In **Package Explorer**, select the `src` folder.
2. Right-click and select **New** > **Other**...
3. See the **New** dialog.
4. Under the **Java** folder, select **Class**.
5. Choose **Next**.
6. See the **New Java Class** dialog, as shown in Figure 12.16.

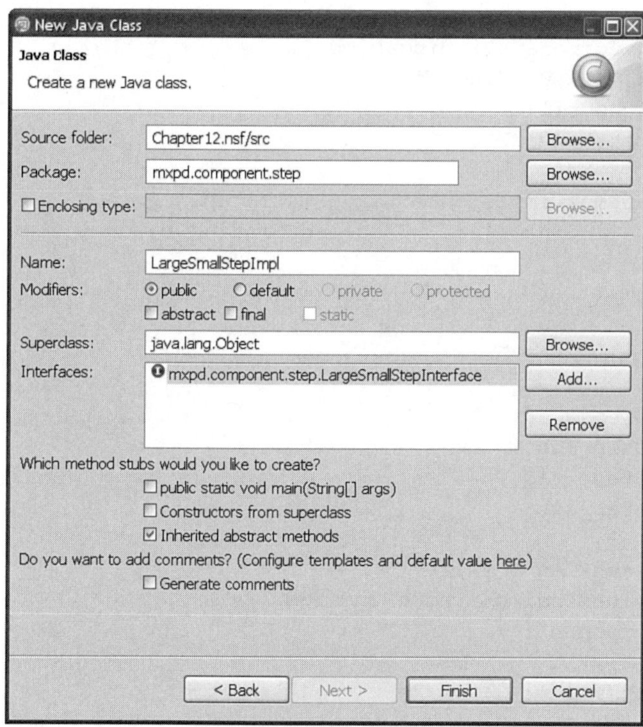

Figure 12.16 New Java Class dialog

7. Enter `mxpd.component.step` for the **Package:** field.
8. Enter `LargeSmallStepImpl` for the **Name:** field.
9. Add `mxpd.component.step.LargeSmallStepInterface` to the **Interfaces** field (by selecting the **Add** button). Note that the Implemented Interface Selection dialog automatically suggests the interface as you type `mxpd`.
10. Choose **Finish**.
11. Add the code to the class, as shown in Listing 12.16, and save the file.

Listing 12.16 LargeSmallStepImpl.java

```
package mxpd.component.step;

import java.util.HashMap;
import java.util.Map;

import javax.faces.component.StateHolder;
import javax.faces.component.UIComponent;
import javax.faces.context.FacesContext;
import javax.faces.el.ValueBinding;

import com.ibm.xsp.binding.ComponentBindingObject;
import com.ibm.xsp.complex.ValueBindingObject;
import com.ibm.xsp.util.FacesUtil;
import com.ibm.xsp.util.StateHolderUtil;

public class LargeSmallStepImpl implements LargeSmallStepInterface
        , StateHolder, ValueBindingObject, ComponentBindingObject {

    public LargeSmallStepImpl() {
        super();
    }

    private int     smallStep = 1;
    private boolean smallStep_set ;
    private int     largeStep = 10;
    private boolean largeStep_set;

    private boolean transientFlag = false;
    private Map<String, ValueBinding> valueBindings;
    private UIComponent component;

    public int getSmallStep() {
        if (this.smallStep_set) {
```

```
            return this.smallStep;
        }
        ValueBinding vb = getValueBinding("smallStep");
        if (vb != null) {
            FacesContext context = FacesContext.getCurrentInstance();
            Object value = vb.getValue(context);
            if (value == null) {
                return smallStep; // default
            } else {
                return ((Number)value).intValue();
            }
        } else {
            return this.smallStep;
        }
    }

    public int getLargeStep() {
        if (this.largeStep_set) {
            return this.largeStep;
        }
        ValueBinding vb = getValueBinding("largeStep");
        if (vb != null) {
            FacesContext context = FacesContext.getCurrentInstance();
            Object value = vb.getValue(context);
            if (value == null) {
                return largeStep; //default
            } else {
                return ((Number)value).intValue();
            }
        } else {
            return this.largeStep;
        }
    }

    public void setLargeStep(int largeStep) {
        this.largeStep = largeStep;
        this.largeStep_set = true;
    }

    public void setSmallStep(int smallStep) {
        this.smallStep = smallStep;
        this.smallStep_set = true;
    }
```

```
public boolean isTransient() {
    return transientFlag;
}

public void restoreState(FacesContext context, Object state) {
    Object values[] = (Object[]) state;
    this.valueBindings =
      StateHolderUtil.restoreValueBindings(
                           context, component, values[0]);
    this.component =
      FacesUtil.findRestoreComponent(context, (String)values[1]);
    this.smallStep = ((Integer) values[2]).intValue();
    this.smallStep_set = ((Boolean) values[3]).booleanValue();
    this.largeStep = ((Integer) values[4]).intValue();
    this.largeStep_set = ((Boolean) values[5]).booleanValue();
}

public Object saveState(FacesContext context) {
    Object values[] = new Object[6];
    values[0] = StateHolderUtil.saveValueBindings(
                                   context, valueBindings);
    values[1] = FacesUtil.getRestoreId(context, component);
    values[2] = new Integer(this.smallStep);
    values[3] = this.smallStep_set ? Boolean.TRUE : Boolean.FALSE;
    values[4] = new Integer(this.largeStep);
    values[5] = this.largeStep_set ? Boolean.TRUE : Boolean.FALSE;
    return values;
}

public void setTransient(boolean transientFlag) {
    this.transientFlag = transientFlag;
}

public ValueBinding getValueBinding(String name) {
    if( null == valueBindings){
        return null;
    }
    return valueBindings.get(name);
}

public void setValueBinding(String name, ValueBinding binding) {
    if( null == valueBindings){
        valueBindings = new HashMap<String, ValueBinding>(4);
    }
    valueBindings.put(name, binding);
}
```

```
    // Implement ComponentBindingObject Interface
    public void setComponent(UIComponent component) {
        this.component = component;
    }


    public UIComponent getComponent() {
        return this.component;
    }

}
```

Before moving on to the final version of uispinner.xsp-config, a couple of things are worthwhile to highlight from Listing 12.16.

The `LargeSmallStepImpl` class not only implements the `LargeSmallStepInterface` interface, it also implements three other interfaces: `StateHolder`, `ValueBindingObject`, and `ComponentBindingObject` as repeated here:

```
public class LargeSmallStepImpl implements LargeSmallStepInterface
      , StateHolder, ValueBindingObject, ComponentBindingObject {
```

Table 12.3 describes these interfaces.

Table 12.3 Key XPages Interfaces for Complex Types

Interface	Description
`StateHolder`	Component classes that need to save their state between requests implement the `javax.faces.component.StateHolder` interface.
`ValueBindingObject`	Properties that can be computed dynamically must implement the `com.ibm.xsp.complex.ValueBindingObject` interface. For properties that are specifically designed not to have computed values (that is, the xsp-config), the `<property>` has a `<property-extension>` configured to `<allow-run-time-bindings>` to be false. Any attempt to set dynamically computed values cause a design-time error.
`ComponentBindingObject`	The `com.ibm.xsp.binding.ComponentBindingObject` interface must be implemented by complex types that need to know the `UIComponent` instance that they are added to.
`ValueBindingObjectImpl`	The class `com.ibm.xsp.complex.ValueBindingObjectImpl` provides a base implementation for complex-type classes that need to support computed expressions to extend.

A class used for a `complex-type` does not extend or implement `UIComponentBase`, and therefore would not implement the behaviors that other `UIComponent` subclasses would have. However, if the complex-type class is intended to be used to store computed values (which are maintained in `ValueBinding` objects) it needs to provide the expected methods for storing and retrieving `ValueBinding instances` and support state management.

The process for saving and restoring state for value bindings and component bindings is a bit more complex than primitive data types. The XPages framework provides numerous utility classes, `StateHolderUtil` and `FacesUtil`, for example (note that the JARs containing these classes are automatically part of the Java build path for every NSF application) to support these common operations:

```
    public void restoreState(FacesContext context, Object state) {
        Object values[] = (Object[]) state;
        this.valueBindings =
          StateHolderUtil.restoreValueBindings(
                              context, component, values[0]);
        this.component =
          FacesUtil.findRestoreComponent(context, (String)values[1]);
...

    public Object saveState(FacesContext context) {
        Object values[] = new Object[6];
        values[0] = StateHolderUtil.saveValueBindings(
                                    context, valueBindings);
        values[1] = FacesUtil.getRestoreId(context, component);
```

Also note the property getters. Because the properties have been specified to allow literal values and computed values, the getters must support getting the data from a value binding. The general syntax follows. If a literal value has not been set to the property, try to retrieve a value binding. If neither are set, this property returns a default value:

```
public int getSmallStep() {
    if (this.smallStep_set) {
        return this.smallStep;
    }
    ValueBinding vb = getValueBinding("smallStep");
    if (vb != null) {
        FacesContext context = FacesContext.getCurrentInstance();
        Object value = vb.getValue(context);
        if (value == null) {
            return smallStep; // default
        } else {
            return ((Number)value).intValue();
        }
    } else {
```

```
            return this.smallStep;
        }
}
```

This getter pattern for properties that support computed values applies to components and complex types.

Complete the xsp-config for the UISpinner Component

This section finishes off `uispinner.xsp-config`, the XPages component configuration file for the `UISpinner` component. All the properties that should be associated with the component are specified, and several `<designer-extension>` have been added. They are explained shortly, but first update the `uispinner.xsp-config` configuration file that was started earlier in this chapter. From the Package Explorer,

1. Open the `WebContent/WEB-INF` folder.
2. Select the `uispinner.xsp-config` file.
3. Right-click and choose **Open**.
4. Replace the contents of `uispinner.xsp-config` with the configuration information specified in Listing 12.17.

Listing 12.17 uispinner.xsp-config (Final)

```
<faces-config>

    <faces-config-extension>
        <namespace-uri>http://mxpd/xsp/control
        </namespace-uri>
        <default-prefix>mx</default-prefix>
    </faces-config-extension>

    <component>

        <description>MXPD Spinner</description>

        <display-name>MXPD Spinner</display-name>

        <component-type>mxpd.component.UISpinner
            </component-type>
            <component-class>mxpd.component.UISpinner
        </component-class>
```

```
<component-extension>
    <tag-name>uiSpinner</tag-name>
    <component-family>mxpd.component.UISpinner
    </component-family>

    <designer-extension>
        <in-palette>true</in-palette>
        <category>MXPD</category>
        <render-markup>
            &lt;?xml version="1.0"
            encoding="UTF-8"?&gt;&#xd; &lt;xp:view
            xmlns:xp="http://www.ibm.com/xsp/core"&gt;&#xd;
         &lt;xp:inputText size="5"
   value="&lt;%=this.value?this.value:'spin'%&gt;"&gt;&#xd;
         &lt;xp:this.converter&gt;&#xd;
         &lt;xp:convertNumber
           type="number"&gt;&lt;/xp:convertNumber&gt;&#xd;
         &lt;/xp:this.converter&gt;&#xd;
         &lt;/xp:inputText &gt;&#xd;
         &lt;xp:button value=" - " &gt;&#xd;
         &lt;/xp:button&gt;&#xd;
         &lt;xp:button value=" + " &gt;&#xd;
         &lt;/xp:button&gt;&#xd;
         &lt;/xp:view&gt;&#xd;
       </render-markup>
    </designer-extension>

</component-extension>

<group-type-ref>mxpd.component.group.minmaxpair
</group-type-ref>

<property>
    <description>Value</description>
    <display-name>value</display-name>
    <property-name>value</property-name>
    <property-class>int</property-class>
    <property-extension>
        <designer-extension>
            <category>spinner</category>
        </designer-extension>
    </property-extension>
</property>
```

```
        <property>
            <description>Number of visible digits</description>
            <display-name>size</display-name>
            <property-name>size</property-name>
            <property-class>int</property-class>
            <property-extension>
                <designer-extension>
                    <category>spinner</category>
                    <editor>
    com.ibm.workplace.designer.property.editors.comboParameterEditor
                    </editor>
                    <editor-parameter>
                        1
                        2
                        3
                        4
                        5
                    </editor-parameter>
                </designer-extension>
            </property-extension>
        </property>

        <property>
            <description>The big increment value</description>
            <display-name>Big increment</display-name>
            <property-name>stepSizes</property-name>
            <property-class>mxpd.component.step.LargeSmallStepInterface
            </property-class>
            <property-extension>
                <designer-extension>
                    <category>spinner</category>
                </designer-extension>
            </property-extension>
        </property>

        <property>
            <description>Example Method Binding</description>
            <display-name>ExampleMethodBinding</display-name>
            <property-name>valueChangeListener
            </property-name>
            <property-class>javax.faces.el.MethodBinding
            </property-class>
            <property-extension>
                <required>false</required>
```

```
                <designer-extension>
                    <category>spinner</category>
                </designer-extension>
                <method-binding-property>true</method-binding-property>
                <method-param>
                    <method-param-name>event</method-param-name>
                    <method-param-class>
                        javax.faces.event.ValueChangeEvent
                    </method-param-class>
                </method-param>
            </property-extension>
        </property>

        <property>
            <description>style</description>
            <display-name>style</display-name>
            <property-name>style</property-name>
            <property-class>string</property-class>
            <property-extension>
                <designer-extension>
                    <category>styling</category>
                </designer-extension>
            </property-extension>
        </property>

        <property>
            <description>styleClass</description>
            <display-name>styleClass</display-name>
            <property-name>styleClass</property-name>
            <property-class>string</property-class>
            <property-extension>
                <designer-extension>
                    <category>styling</category>
                </designer-extension>
            </property-extension>
        </property>

    </component>

</faces-config>
```

Many interesting `xsp-config` `<designer-extension>` tags are used in Listing 12.17. The relevant section is reproduced here:

```
 <designer-extension>
      <in-palette>true</in-palette>
      <category>MXPD</category>
      <render-markup>
          &lt;?xml version="1.0"
          encoding="UTF-8"?&gt;&#xd; &lt;xp:view
          xmlns:xp="http://www.ibm.com/xsp/core"&gt;&#xd;
       &lt;xp:inputText size="5"
value="&lt;%=this.value?this.value:'spin'%&gt;"&gt;&#xd;
       &lt;xp:this.converter&gt;&#xd;
       &lt;xp:convertNumber
         type="number"&gt;&lt;/xp:convertNumber&gt;&#xd;
       &lt;/xp:this.converter&gt;&#xd;
       &lt;/xp:inputText &gt;&#xd;
       &lt;xp:button value=" - " &gt;&#xd;
       &lt;/xp:button&gt;&#xd;
       &lt;xp:button value=" + " &gt;&#xd;
       &lt;/xp:button&gt;&#xd;
       &lt;/xp:view&gt;&#xd;
     </render-markup>
 </designer-extension>
```

Table 12.4 details the highlighted tags from the code section.

Table 12.4 More xsp-config <designer-extension> Tags

Tag	Description
`<in-palette>`	The `<in-palette>` tag enables you to have your control appear in Domino Designers Controls palette.
`<category>`	The `<category>` tag allows you to specify a category under which your control appears in the Controls palette.
`<render-markup>`	The `<render-markup>` tag enables you to specify an XSP description of how you want your control to appear visually on the XPage Design canvas. Note that you can even embed JavaScript scriptlets to dynamically generate content in the visualization, and even better, you can use the `this` notation to access the values of control attributes.

TIP

For more information on visualizing XPages components, see the "Native and Custom Control Custom Visualization Best Practices" article on the IBM Notes and Domino Application Development Wiki: www-10.lotus.com/ldd/ddwiki.nsf/dx/Native_and_Custom_Control_Custom_Visualization_Best_Practices.

For a property that should be restricted to a certain set of options, you can specify a designer `<editor>`. For example, the `comboParameterEditor` can specify a set of options that are listed using the `<editor-parameter>` tag:

```
            <designer-extension>
                ...
                <editor>
com.ibm.workplace.designer.property.editors.comboParameterEditor
                </editor>
                <editor-parameter>
                    1
                    2
                    3
```

Table 12.5 contains a subset of the available editors.

Table 12.5 Available Editors for the <editor> Tag

Editor	Functionality
Access Key Validator `com.ibm.workplace.designer.property.editors.accessKeyValidator`	Specifies a number in the range 0–9
Boolean Check Box `com.ibm.std.BooleanCheckBox`	Displays a checkbox for the value
Boolean Value `com.ibm.std.Boolean`	Drop-down list of true and false
Character Set Type Picker `com.ibm.workplace.designer.property.editors.charSetPicker`	Drop-down list of several prepopulated character sets (ISO-8859-1, UTF-8, and so on)
Client Side Event Editor `com.ibm.workplace.designer.ide.xfaces.internal.editors.ClientSideEventEditor`	Pop-up JavaScript editor
Client Side Script Editor `com.ibm.designer.domino.client.script.editor`	Pop-up JavaScript editor
Combo Box `com.ibm.workplace.designer.property.editors.comboParameterEditor`	Drop-down list of values populated from line items specified in `<editor-parameter>` tag

Editor	Functionality
Content Type Picker `com.ibm.workplace.designer.property.editors.contentPicker`	Drop-down list of HTML content types (text/html, image/png, and so on)
Control Picker `com.ibm.workplace.designer.property.editors.controlPicker`	Pop-up select control dialog
Data Source Picker `com.ibm.workplace.designer.property.editors.dataSourcePicker`	Drop-down list of data sources
DoubleValue `com.ibm.std.Double`	Only allows double values to be entered
Generic File Picker `com.ibm.workplace.designer.ide.xfaces.internal.editors.FilePicker`	Pop-up file system browser for selecting a filename
Image File Picker `com.ibm.workplace.designer.property.editors.ImagePicker`	Pop-up image picker with previewer
Integer Value `com.ibm.std.Integer`	Only allows integer values to be entered
Language Direction Picker `com.ibm.workplace.designer.property.editors.dirAttrPicker`	Drop-down list (left to right, right to left)
Language Picker `com.ibm.workplace.designer.property.editors.langPicker`	Drop-down list of world languages
MIME Image Type Picker `com.ibm.workplace.designer.property.editors.imageMIMEPicker`	Drop-down list of common MIME image formats (audio/mpeg, image/gif, and so on)
Method Binding Editor `com.ibm.workplace.designer.ide.xfaces.internal.editors.MethodBindingEditor`	Pop-up JavaScript and Expression Language (EL) editor
Multiline Text `com.ibm.std.MultiLine`	Pop-up multiline editor

Editor	Functionality
Number Format Editor com.ibm.workplace.designer.property.editors.numberFormatPicker	Pop-up editor to specify a number with decimal places, currency symbol, or percent
Password Value com.ibm.std.Password	Entered characters appear as dots
Regular Expression Editor com.ibm.workplace.designer.property.editors.regExpression	Specifies a regular expression
Release Line Picker com.ibm.workplace.designer.property.editors.relPicker	Alternate, style sheet, Start, Next, Previous, Contents, Index, glossary, Contents, and so on
Shape Type Picker com.ibm.workplace.designer.property.editors.shapePicker	Drop-down list of shapes (Default, Circle, Rectangle, Polygon)
String Value com.ibm.std.String	Specifies a String value
Style Class Editor com.ibm.workplace.designer.property.editors.StyleClassEditor	Pop-up editor to specify style classes and/or themes
Style Editor com.ibm.workplace.designer.property.editors.StylesEditor	Pop-up editor to specify height, width, font background, and margin sizes
Time Zone Picker com.ibm.workplace.designer.property.editors.timeZonePicker	Drop-down list of standard time-zone abbreviations
XSP Document Action Picker com.ibm.workplace.designer.property.editors.XSPDocumentActionPickerEditor	Drop-down list of available document actions (openDocument, editDocument, newDocument)
XSP Page Picker com.ibm.workplace.designer.property.editors.PagePicker	Creates a drop-down list of XPages available in the application

Specifying javax.faces.el.MethodBinding as a <property-class> with <method-binding-property> set to true causes Domino Designer to enable a button for the property.

When clicked, this button launches a Script Editor for the property that allows the designer to specify an EL reference value for the method binding:

```
<property-class>javax.faces.el.MethodBinding
</property-class>
<property-extension>
    <required>false</required>
    <designer-extension>
        <category>spinner</category>
    </designer-extension>
    <method-binding-property>true</method-binding-property>
    <method-param>
        <method-param-name>event</method-param-name>
        <method-param-class>
            javax.faces.event.ValueChangeEvent
        </method-param-class>
    </method-param>
</property-extension>
```

As mentioned earlier, you can specify a property in the xsp-config file that does not correspond to any property managed by the component, and it is treated as an attribute of the component, which is typically of interest to renderers.

The `styleClass` attribute demonstrates this feature:

```
<property>
    <description>styleClass</description>
    <display-name>styleClass</display-name>
    <property-name>styleClass</property-name>
    <property-class>string</property-class>
    <property-extension>
        <designer-extension>
            <category>styling</category>
        </designer-extension>
    </property-extension>
</property>
```

If `styleClass` is set, the final renderer implementation for the `UISpinner` uses the value of the `styleClass` property as the value for the `class` attribute in the HTML elements used to render the `UISpinner` control. In addition, if you want your component to support XPages themes, you need to specify this attribute and implement the `ThemeControl` interface. It is easy to add an XPages theme to a custom UI component extension and the next section shows you how to do that.

Complete the UI Component Extension, UISpinner

In this section, you complete the implementation of the UI component extension class. Points of interest in the code for this class are discussed throughout this section.

To complete the implementation, follow these steps:

1. From the **Package Explorer**, open the `src` folder.
2. Select the `UISpinner.java` file.
3. Right-click and choose **Open**.
4. Replace the contents of `UISpinner.java` with the Java code specified in Listing 12.18.

Listing 12.18 UISpinner .java

```
package mxpd.component;

import javax.faces.component.UIInput;
import javax.faces.context.FacesContext;
import javax.faces.convert.IntegerConverter;
import javax.faces.el.ValueBinding;
import javax.faces.validator.Validator;
import javax.faces.validator.LengthValidator;

import mxpd.component.group.MinMaxPair;
import mxpd.component.step.LargeSmallStepInterface;

import com.ibm.xsp.stylekit.ThemeControl;
import com.ibm.xsp.util.StateHolderUtil;


public class UISpinner extends UIInput
                        implements MinMaxPair, ThemeControl {

    public static final String COMPONENT_FAMILY =
                                "mxpd.component.UISpinner";
    public static final String RENDERER_TYPE =
                                "mxpd.renderer.UISpinnerRenderer";

    LargeSmallStepInterface stepSizes;

    int min = Integer.MIN_VALUE;
    int max = Integer.MAX_VALUE;
```

```
public UISpinner() {
    super();
    setConverter(new IntegerConverter());

    Validator v = new LengthValidator();
    ((LengthValidator)v).setMaximum(4);
    ((LengthValidator)v).setMinimum(1);
    addValidator(v);

    this.setRendererType(RENDERER_TYPE);
}


@Override
public String getFamily() {
    return COMPONENT_FAMILY;
}

public LargeSmallStepInterface getStepSizes() {
    return stepSizes;
}

public void setStepSizes(LargeSmallStepInterface stepSizes) {
    this.stepSizes = stepSizes;
}

public int getMin() {
    if (min != Integer.MIN_VALUE) {return min;}
    ValueBinding vb = getValueBinding("min");
    if (vb != null){
        Object value = vb.getValue(getFacesContext()) ;
        if (value != null){
            return ((Number)value).intValue();
        } else {
            return Integer.MIN_VALUE;
        }
  } else {
        return Integer.MIN_VALUE;
    }
}

public void setMin(int min) {
    this.min = min;
}
public int getMax() {
```

```
    if (max != Integer.MAX_VALUE) {return max;}
        ValueBinding vb = getValueBinding("max");
        if (vb != null){
            Object value = vb.getValue(getFacesContext()) ;
            if (value != null){
                return ((Number)value).intValue();
            }else {
                return Integer.MAX_VALUE;
            }
        } else {
            return Integer.MAX_VALUE;
        }
    }

    public void setMax(int max) {
        this.max = max;
    }

    // StateHolder Interface
    public void restoreState(FacesContext context, Object state) {
        Object values[] = (Object[]) state;
        super.restoreState(context, values[0]);
        this.stepSizes =
      (LargeSmallStepInterface) StateHolderUtil.restoreObjectState(
                                          context, this, values[1]);
        this.min = ((Integer) values[2]).intValue();
        this.max = ((Integer) values[3]).intValue();
    }

    public Object saveState(FacesContext context) {
        Object values[] = new Object[4];
        values[0] = super.saveState(context);
        values[1] = StateHolderUtil.saveObjectState(context,
➥stepSizes);
        values[2] = new Integer(this.min);
        values[3] = new Integer(this.max);
        return values;
    }

    public String getStyleKitFamily() {
        return "Button.Command";
    }

}
```

A couple of things about the UI component class from Listing 12.18 are worth highlighting. The `com.ibm.xsp.stylekit.ThemeControl` interface is implemented. All that is required is to implement the `getStyleKitFamily()` method to return a theme identifier (see Chapter 16, "XPages Theming," for details about XPages themes):

```
public class UISpinner extends UIInput
                       implements MinMaxPair, ThemeControl {
...
    public String getStyleKitFamily() {
        return "Button.Command";
    }
```

Then, depending on what XPages theme has been set for the application, the style class that is associated with the theme ID returned by the component's `getStyleKitFamily()` method is set automatically by the XPages runtime as the value for the `styleClass` attribute of the component. If the renderer set for the component supports the `styleClass` attribute, the rendered control has the appropriate XPages theme styling applied.

Simply for convenience, the component explicitly sets its own Converter and `Validator`:

```
setConverter(new IntegerConverter());

Validator v =
        new LengthValidator();
((LengthValidator)v).setMaximum(4);
((LengthValidator)v).setMinimum(1);
addValidator(v);
```

Complete the Renderer UISpinnerRenderer

The third and final step in the process for creating a custom UI component extension is to implement the renderer. A simple renderer was created earlier in this chapter. However, you now update that renderer to implement the expected behavior for the UISpinner control.

Follow these steps:

1. From the Package Explorer, open the `src` folder.
2. Expand the `mxpd.renderer` package.
3. Select the `UISpinnerRenderer.java` file.
4. Right-click and choose **Open**.
5. Replace the contents of `UISpinnerRenderer.java` with the configuration information specified in Listing 12.19 and save.

NOTE

For a good article that describes building custom JSF components and implementing a separate renderer, see "JSF for nonbelievers: JSF component development" on the IBM developerWorks website (www.ibm.com/developerworks/java/library/j-jsf4/).

Listing 12.19 UISpinnerRenderer.java

```
package mxpd.renderer;

import java.io.IOException;
import java.util.Map;

import javax.faces.component.UIComponent;
import javax.faces.component.UIInput;
import javax.faces.component.ValueHolder;
import javax.faces.context.FacesContext;
import javax.faces.context.ResponseWriter;
import javax.faces.convert.Converter;
import javax.faces.convert.ConverterException;
import javax.faces.render.Renderer;

import mxpd.component.UISpinner;

public class UISpinnerRenderer extends Renderer {

    private static final String SMALL_INCR = ".smlincr";
    private static final String SMALL_DECR = ".smldecr";

    @Override
    public void encodeBegin(FacesContext context,
                UIComponent component) throws IOException {

        ResponseWriter rw = context.getResponseWriter();
        String clientId = component.getClientId(context);

        int smallStep = 1;
        int largeStep = 10;

        if (!(component instanceof UISpinner)){
            return;
        }
        UISpinner s = (UISpinner)component;
```

```
        encodeInputText(rw, clientId, component, context);

        if (s.getStepSizes() != null){
            smallStep = s.getStepSizes().getSmallStep();
            largeStep = s.getStepSizes().getLargeStep();
        }

        encodeButton(rw, clientId, s, SMALL_DECR, "<",
                                (smallStep*-1), (largeStep*-1));
        encodeButton(rw, clientId, s, SMALL_INCR, ">",
                                smallStep, largeStep);
    }

    @Override
    public void encodeEnd(FacesContext context, UIComponent component)
        throws IOException {

        ResponseWriter rw = context.getResponseWriter();
        StringBuffer sb = new StringBuffer();
        sb.append(" <script type=\"text/javascript\"> ");
        sb.append("   function spin(target, increment, clkEvent,
                                        minVal, maxVal) { ");
        sb.append("     var newValue; ");
        sb.append("     if (increment > 0) { ");
        sb.append("         newValue = Math.min(maxVal,
                         Number(target.value) + (increment)); ");
        sb.append("     } else { ");
        sb.append("         newValue = Math.max(minVal,
                         Number(target.value) + (increment)); ");
        sb.append("     } ");
        sb.append("     target.value = newValue; ");
        sb.append("   } ");
        sb.append(" </script> ");

        rw.write(sb.toString());
    }

    @Override
    public void decode(FacesContext context, UIComponent component) {

        String clientId = null;
        if (!(component instanceof UISpinner)) {
            return;
        }
```

```
        clientId = component.getClientId(context);

        Map<?, ?> requestMap = context.getExternalContext()
                                        .getRequestParameterMap();

        String newValue = (String)requestMap.get(clientId);

        if (newValue != null) {
            ((UIInput) component).setSubmittedValue(newValue);;
        }
    }


    protected Object getValue(UIComponent component) {

        if (component instanceof ValueHolder) {
            Object value = ((ValueHolder) component).getValue();
            return value;
        }
        return null;
    }


    protected String getCurrentValue(FacesContext context,
                                      UIComponent component) {

        if (component instanceof UIInput) {
            Object submittedValue =
                        ((UIInput) component).getSubmittedValue();
            if (submittedValue != null) {
                return submittedValue.toString();
            }
        }
        String currentValue = null;
        Object currentObject = getValue(component);

        if (currentObject != null) {
            Converter c = ((ValueHolder)component).getConverter();
            if (c != null) {
                currentValue = c.getAsString(context, component,
                                              currentObject);
            } else {
                currentValue = currentObject.toString();
            }
        }
```

```
        return currentValue;
    }

    @Override
    public Object getConvertedValue(FacesContext context,
                      UIComponent component, Object submittedValue)
        throws ConverterException {

        Converter converter = ((UIInput)component).getConverter();
        if (converter != null) {
            Object result = converter.getAsObject(context, component,
                                                   (String)submittedValue);
            return result;
        }
        return submittedValue;
    }

    protected void encodeInputText(ResponseWriter rw, String clientId,
                       UIComponent component, FacesContext context)
        throws IOException {

        rw.startElement("input", component);
        rw.writeAttribute("type", "text", null);
        rw.writeAttribute("id", clientId, null);

        rw.writeAttribute("name", clientId, null);

        String currentValue = getCurrentValue(context, component);

        if (currentValue!=null){
            rw.writeAttribute("value", currentValue, "value");
      }

        Integer s = (Integer)component.getAttributes().get("size");
        if (s != null){
            rw.writeAttribute("size", s, "size");
        }
        rw.endElement("input");
    }


    protected void encodeButton(ResponseWriter rw, String clientId,
            UISpinner component, String idSuffix, String buttonLabel,
            int smallStep, int largeStep) throws IOException {
```

```
        rw.startElement("button", component);
        rw.writeAttribute("type", "button", null);
        rw.writeAttribute("id", clientId + idSuffix, "id");

        if (null != component.getAttributes().get("style")) {
            rw.writeAttribute("style",
                  component.getAttributes().get("style"), "style");
        }
        if (null != component.getAttributes().get("styleClass")) {
            rw.writeAttribute("class",
                   component.getAttributes().get("styleClass"),
                              "styleClass");
        }

        rw.writeAttribute("name", clientId + idSuffix, null);
        rw.writeAttribute("onclick", "return spin("
            + "document.getElementById('" + clientId + "')," +
➥smallStep
            + "," + "'SGL'" + "," + component.getMin() + ","
            + component.getMax() + ")", null);
        rw.writeAttribute("ondblclick", "return spin("
            + "document.getElementById('" + clientId + "'),"
            + (largeStep - (2 * smallStep)) + "," + "'DBL'" + ","
            + component.getMin() + "," + component.getMax()
            + ")", null);
        rw.write(buttonLabel);
        rw.endElement("button");
    }

}
```

In Listing 12.19, note the three key renderer methods and the `ValueHolder` interface:

- **`encodeBegin()`**: Renders the component to the output stream associated with the response.
- **`encodeEnd()`**: Renders the component to the output stream associated with the response after any children of the component need to be rendered.
- **`decode()`**: Extracts (decodes) submitted values from the request and stores them in the component.
- **`ValueHolder`**: Components that store a local value and support conversion between String and the values native datatype should implement the ValueHolder interface.

Chapter 5 offers more information on the three key renderer methods.

Create a Sample Application Using the UISpinner Component

At last! The custom UI component extension is complete and ready to use. This section creates the test application that was shown at the start of this chapter in Figure 12.1 to demonstrate the capabilities of the component. But first, let's quickly try out the new UI component.

Take Your New UI Component Extension for a Test Drive

Create a test application that exercises the properties and behaviors of the UISpinner control. To create a new XPage, follow these steps:

1. From the application navigator, select the **XPages** folder.
2. Right-click and select **New XPage**.
3. See the New XPage dialog.
4. Name the XPage `xpSpinnerTest`.
5. Choose **OK**.
6. From the controls palette, drag your MXPD Spinner control onto the design canvas.
7. Open the Properties tab and set minimum (min) and maximum (max) values under the `spinner-base` category.
8. Add a new `stepSizes` complex property and override the default smallStep and largeStep step sizes, as shown in Figure 12.17.
9. **Save** the XPage and preview it in a web browser.

Initially, the spinner is blank; there is no data bound to the control. Enter in any numeric value and click and double-click the spinner buttons to see the value change as expected and stop at the limits specified.

The final sections create a slightly more complex example that tests more of the component's properties.

Create a Backing Bean

To finish the final application, first create a backing bean for the XPage that the day, month, and year UISpinner components to which they are bound. A backing bean is another name for a managed bean that is used to manage data that appears in a control in a user interface. This example uses a bean to store the data instead of a Domino Document. See the section, "Creating and Using Managed Beans" in Chapter 11, "Advanced Scripting," for details on creating and using managed beans. When the XPage is submitted, the beans properties are updated with the values entered (provided they converted correctly and passed validation, of course).

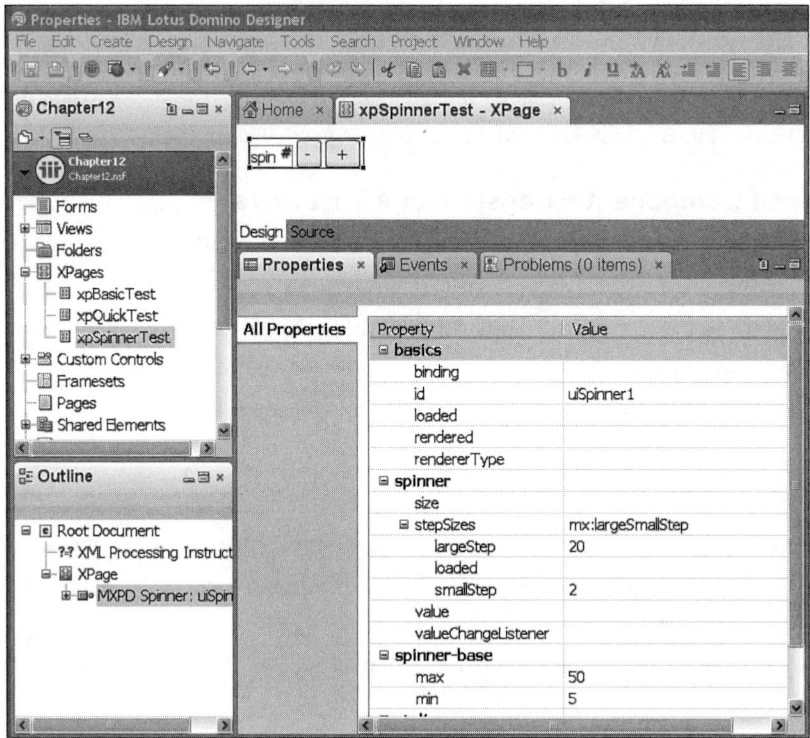

Figure 12.17 Test Drive the new UI Component

To create the backing bean, follow these steps:

1. In **Package Explorer**, select the `src` folder.
2. Right-click and select **New** > **Other....**
3. See the New dialog.
4. Under the **Java** folder, select **Class**.
5. Choose **Next**.
6. See the New Java Class dialog.
7. Enter `mxpd.bean` for the **Package** field.
8. Enter `SpinnerBean` for the **Name** field.
9. Choose **Finish**.
10. Add the code shown Listing 12.20 to the SpinnerBean class and save the file.

Listing 12.20 SpinnerBean.java

```
package mxpd.bean;

import java.util.Date;

import javax.faces.event.ValueChangeEvent;

public class SpinnerBean {

    private int day;
    private int month;
    private int year;
    private int dateChangeCount;

    @SuppressWarnings("deprecation")
    public SpinnerBean() {
        Date d = new Date();
        setDay(d.getDate());
        setMonth(d.getMonth()+1);
        setYear(d.getYear()+1900);
    }

    public int getDay() {  return day;  }
    public void setDay(int day) {  this.day = day;  }
    public int getMonth() {  return month;  }
    public void setMonth(int month) {  this.month = month; }
    public int getYear() {  return year;  }
    public void setYear(int year) {  this.year = year;  }

    public void dateChangeListener(ValueChangeEvent e){
        dateChangeCount++;
    }

    public int getDateChangeCount() {
        return dateChangeCount;
    }

    public void setDateChangeCount(int dateChangeCount) {
        this.dateChangeCount = dateChangeCount;
    }
}
```

Register the Backing Bean

Follow these steps to register the backing bean with `faces-config.xml`:

1. In **Package Explorer**, open the `WebContent/WEB-INF` folder.
2. Select `faces-config.xml`, right-click, and select **Open**.
3. Add the code to the SpinnerBean, as shown in Listing 12.21, and save the file.

Listing 12.21 Updated faces-config.xml with Managed Bean

```
<?xml version="1.0" encoding="UTF-8"?>
<faces-config>
  <render-kit>
    <renderer>
      <component-family> mxpd.component.UISpinner </component-family>
      <renderer-type> mxpd.renderer.UISpinnerRenderer </renderer-type>
      <renderer-class> mxpd.renderer.UISpinnerRenderer
      </renderer-class>
    </renderer>
  </render-kit>
  <managed-bean>
    <managed-bean-name> spinnerBean </managed-bean-name>
    <managed-bean-class> mxpd.bean.SpinnerBean </managed-bean-class>
    <managed-bean-scope> session </managed-bean-scope>
  </managed-bean>
</faces-config>
```

Create the Final Test Application

Create a test application that exercises all the properties and behaviors of the UISpinner control, the computed properties, complex types, and method bindings. To create the test XPage, follow these steps:

1. From the application navigator, select the **XPages** folder.
2. Open the XPage `xpSpinnerTest`.
3. Open the Source tab for the XPage and replace it with the contents of Listing 12.22 and save.

Listing 12.22 xpSpinnerTest.xsp

```
<?xml version="1.0" encoding="UTF-8"?>
<xp:view xmlns:xp="http://www.ibm.com/xsp/core"
         xmlns:mx="http://mxpd/xsp/control">
```

```
    <xp:label value="UISpinner Example" id="label4"
        style="font-weight:bold;font-size:14pt"></xp:label>

    <xp:br></xp:br>

    <xp:table border="1" style="width:800.0px">
        <xp:tr>
            <xp:td style="width:50.0px">
                <xp:label id="label1" value="Day"></xp:label>
            </xp:td>
            <xp:td style="width:200px">
                <mx:uiSpinner id="uiSpinner1" size="2"
                    value="#{spinnerBean.day}"
            valueChangeListener="#{spinnerBean.dateChangeListener}"
                    max="31" min="1">
                    <mx:this.stepSizes>
                        <mx:largeSmallStep largeStep="10"
➥ smallStep="1">
                        </mx:largeSmallStep>
                    </mx:this.stepSizes>
                </mx:uiSpinner>
            </xp:td>
            <xp:td>
                <xp:message id="message1" for="uiSpinner1">
➥</xp:message>
            </xp:td>
        </xp:tr>
        <xp:tr>
            <xp:td>
                <xp:label value="Month" id="label2"></xp:label>
            </xp:td>
            <xp:td>
                <mx:uiSpinner id="uiSpinner2" size="2"
                    value="#{spinnerBean.month}"
            valueChangeListener="#{spinnerBean.dateChangeListener}"
                    max="#{javascript:return 12}"
                    min="#{javascript:return 1*1}">
                </mx:uiSpinner>
            </xp:td>
            <xp:td>
                <xp:message id="message2" for="uiSpinner2">
➥</xp:message>
            </xp:td>
        </xp:tr>
        <xp:tr>
```

```
            <xp:td>
                <xp:label value="Year" id="label3"></xp:label>
            </xp:td>
            <xp:td>
                <mx:uiSpinner id="uiSpinner3"
                    value="#{spinnerBean.year}" size="4"
            valueChangeListener="#{spinnerBean.dateChangeListener}">
                    <mx:this.stepSizes>
                        <mx:largeSmallStep
                            largeStep="#{javascript:return (10*10)}"
                            smallStep="#{javascript:return (1*1*1)}">
                        </mx:largeSmallStep>
                    </mx:this.stepSizes>
                </mx:uiSpinner>
            </xp:td>
            <xp:td>
                <xp:message id="message3" for="uiSpinner3"></xp:message>
            </xp:td>
        </xp:tr>
        <xp:tr>
            <xp:td></xp:td>
            <xp:td>
                <xp:button value="Save" id="button1"
                            disableTheme="false"
                themeId="Button.command">

                    <xp:eventHandler event="onclick" submit="true"
                        refreshMode="complete" immediate="false"
                        save="true">
                        <xp:this.action>
                            <![CDATA[#{javascript:var
            computedField1:com.ibm.xsp.component.xp.XspOutputText =
                                getComponent("computedField1");

var uiSpinner1:mxpd.component.UISpinner = getComponent("uiSpinner1");
var uiSpinner2:mxpd.component.UISpinner = getComponent("uiSpinner2");
var uiSpinner3:mxpd.component.UISpinner = getComponent("uiSpinner3");


var dd = uiSpinner1.getValue();
var mm = uiSpinner2.getValue();
var yy = uiSpinner3.getValue();
y = (yy > 1900) ? yy-1900 : yy;
```

```
var someTime    = new java.util.Date(y, mm-1, dd);
var currentTime = new java.util.Date();

var oneDay=1000*60*60*24; //1 day in milliseconds
diff = (Math.floor((currentTime.getTime()-someTime.getTime())/oneDay));

var days = (Math.abs(diff) == 1 ? " day" : " days");
var togo = (diff <= 0 ? " to go." : " ago.");

computedField1.setValue(Math.abs(diff) + days + togo + ((true) ? "
("+dd+"/"+mm+"/"+yy+")" : ""));

}]]></xp:this.action>
                    </xp:eventHandler>
                </xp:button>
            </xp:td>
            <xp:td>
                <xp:table border="0" style="width:200.0px">
                    <xp:tr>
                        <xp:td>
                            <xp:text escape="true" id="computedField1"
                             value="Select a date and click Save.">
                            </xp:text>
                        </xp:td>
                    </xp:tr>
                    <xp:tr>
                        <xp:td>

                            <xp:text escape="true" id="computedField2">
                                <xp:this.value>
<![CDATA[#{javascript:spinnerBean.dateChangeCount + " changes.";}]]>
                                </xp:this.value>
                            </xp:text>
                        </xp:td>
                    </xp:tr>
                </xp:table>

            </xp:td>
        </xp:tr>
    </xp:table>

    <xp:br></xp:br>

</xp:view>
```

Figure 12.18 illustrates how the design of the test application should look. Notice that the `UISpinner` control looks like how it will be rendered, rather than the plain test default tag representation.

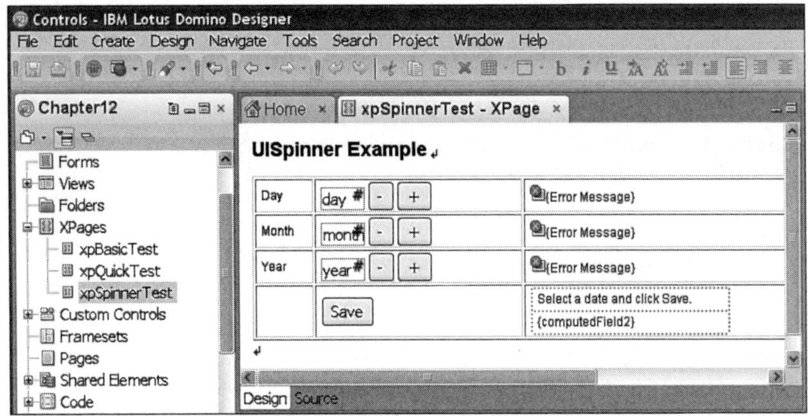

Figure 12.18 XPage design for the application to test the new mx:uiSpinner control

Nice Look and Feel

The final step is to provide a nice look and feel by specifying the IBM `OneUI` theme for the application. Follow these steps to set it:

1. From the **application navigator**, select the application.
2. Right-click and choose **XSP Properties**.
3. Open the **General** tab.
4. Specify `oneuiv2.1` in the **Application theme:** field (if not already specified).
5. Select **File > Save**.
6. Close the **Properties** file.

Test to Ensure That It All Works!

Return to the XPage `xpSpinnerTest` and run it by selecting **Design > Preview in Web Browser > Default System Web Browser**.

Use a spinner control to set a date, check to see how many days until Christmas, or enter junk dates to see the converter and validator in action, as shown in Figure 12.19. Have fun with it!

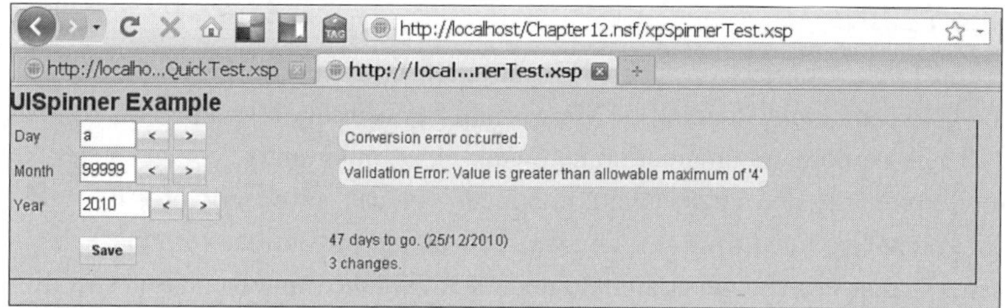

Figure 12.19 mx:uiSpinner control in action showing conversion and validation errors

Where to Go from Here

This chapter has only scratched the surface of what is possible with XPages extensibility. Many excellent resources are available on the Internet to help you build on what you have learned here in this chapter. Hopefully, this chapter got the basics out of the way and enables you to tackle more complex XPages extensibility challenges and projects.

XPages Extensibility API Developers Guide

The "XPages Extensibility API Developers Guide" is part of the IBM Notes and Domino application development wiki. It is the place to go for more information about XPages extensibility. There is a wide range of information here to help you with your XPages development and answers what are probably your next two questions:

- How do I build my component as an XPages library as a plug-in so it can be distributed and shared?
- How to deploy your plug-in to Domino Designer, Domino Server, and the Notes client?

Although this chapter focused on the XPages extension mechanisms and the aspects of JSF that are important for XPages extension development, it did not cover the details and specifics of the XPages framework classes and interface. That would be a huge documentation effort, and thankfully, it has already been done:

> **Javadoc for the XPages framework programmatic and extensibility APIs**: www-10.lotus.com/ldd/ddwiki.nsf/dx/Master_Table_of_Contents_for_XPages_Extensibility_APIs_Developer_Guide
>
> Here, you can learn about the XPages classes you may want to extend that already provide XPages specific integration. The Javadoc APIs in conjunction with articles on the "XPages Extensibility Developers Guide" is a useful resource to get to the next level in XPages component development.

XPages Extension Library

The XPages Extension Library project on OpenNTF (http://extlib.openntf.org/) is a great way to deepen your knowledge and understanding of XPages and extensibility by seeing lots of real-world components. There is more documentation here and, most importantly, you get access to the source code. So, if you really like a particular component, you can see exactly how it is built. With the knowledge you have gained from this chapter, you should be familiar with the XPages extension mechanisms so that you can get straight to understanding the implementation specifics of the UI component extension.

IBM developerWorks

To learn more about JSF, visit the Java technology section of the IBM developerWorks website and search for JSF. You can find many useful articles on the technology and architecture: `www.ibm.com/developerworks/java/`.

Conclusion

This concludes your lesson on XPages extensibility. Up to now, the fact that XPages is based on JSF will have been largely hidden in your daily XPages development. Going under the hood into the JSF internals is a big step, especially considering the simplicity of mainstream XPages application development. However, the XPages extensibility model opens up all sorts of new horizons for you as a software developer. Effectively, you no longer depend on the primary technology provider to supply the components that you need for a particular app! You now have the option of building any component yourself, obtaining it from a third-party provider or perhaps just downloading it for free from community resources, such as OpenNTF.org. The potential benefits of this completely outweigh the incremental complexity involved in dabbling in a little Java programming. Hopefully, this chapter taught you how to harness some of that power for your own applications and that you will go on to provide and consume XPages components to the benefit of yourself and the broader community.

CHAPTER 13

XPages in the Notes Client

No sooner was XPages released on the Domino server in version 8.5 than requests flooded in from business partners and customers alike to have this technology running in the Notes client. The primary reason, of course, was so that XPages web applications could be taken offline. NSF data replication and synchronization has always been a key core asset of Notes/Domino, so leveraging its power for XPages applications was, not surprisingly, the next big customer use case.

Despite the ubiquity of broadband services nowadays, it is often useful to be able to make an exact replica of an application locally on your personal computer and work with it in isolation for a period of time. This can be handy in a read-only context (for example, if you just want to browse application data while disconnected from the network) or if you want to make changes and post these updates at a later point once connected again. Through the years, local replicas of mail and other corporate applications have made many a long-haul flight a more productive experience for the traveling Notes user. There was no question that XPages applications needed to take advantage of this powerful feature as early as possible in its own product development lifecycle.

Apart altogether from scenarios where offline application access is a key requirement, other important factors also made XPages in the Notes client an important strategic move. For example, many organizations have a non-homogeneous end-user mix (such as external clients and internal employees who need access to the same application data). The former might need to access the application over the web, whereas the latter might have the Notes client installed across the corporate desktops with no (or restricted) browser access. In this situation, the ideal solution is a single application that can execute in both environments—something XPages could not offer until such time as it ran in the Notes client.

However, it is to some extent "old hat" to enumerate the motivating factors behind the decision to "port" XPages to the client, because they are much the same imperatives that drove traditional Notes apps to run on the web back in 1996. Clearly, there are many advantages to having a cross-platform runtime capability, so the question shifts to how well and how quickly

XPages could support the Notes client platform. When initially introduced to the application development community, XPages was heralded as a "write-once run-anywhere" technology and, in Notes V8.5.1, it was time to see just how well it could deliver on that promise.

As usual, before you get started download the sample application, **Chp13ed2.nsf**, from this website: `www.ibmpressbooks.com/title/9780133373370`.

Think Inside the Box

At first, you might have a difficult time conceiving just how XPages could run in a Notes client environment. After all, it is a Java technology that requires a web-application server, a Java virtual machine, and an HTML browser as fundamental components to function. On second thought, however, the Notes client has all these components embedded within it...maybe all XPages has to do is use them!

In Notes version 8.0, the Notes standard edition moved to an Eclipse-based platform known as Expeditor (often referred to as XPD). XPD includes a web container based on IBM WebSphere Application Server (WAS) technologies. In simple terms, a web container provides the runtime environment for Java web applications. The XPages runtime requires a web container that supports the Java Servlet 2.4 specification, which the XPD web container does. This requirement also exists on the server side, so the Domino web engine needed to be upgraded in version 8.5 to support the 2.4-specification level in that environment at the time.

The Notes client has been shipping an embedded browser in various shapes and forms for a long time. In fact on Windows platforms, Notes ships two browsers and provides an embedded version of Internet Explorer® (IE) as the default. On Macintosh and Linux, where IE is not an option, Notes provides an embedded browser based on a Mozilla runtime technology known as XULRunner (pronounced "ZoolRunner"). Although XULRunner itself is not a browser, it provides the underlying browser engine required to render HTML and can execute rich cross-platform applications based on a programming language known as XML User Interface Language (XUL). The Mozilla Firefox browser is based on XULRunner, as are many other rich client applications. XPD provides a browser component based on XULRunner, and this is the browser that XPages uses when running in the Notes client across *all* client platforms.

The reasons for choosing XULRunner were twofold. First, a single common browser greatly simplifies development—for both the XPages runtime development team, and you, the XPages application developer. Cross-browser rendering inconsistencies test the patience and sanity of web developers on a continual basis! The richer and more sophisticated the runtime application, the more likely it is to have bugs across different browsers because of variances in the implementation and support of the core technologies (HTML, CSS, and JavaScript). XULRunner is now automatically included in the Notes installation packages on Windows platforms. Prior to version 8.5.1, XULRunner was an available option that, if required, needed to be explicitly installed as a supplementary package. This default installation of XULRunner and related browsing components does not, however, impact the regular web-browsing experience of the Notes user. Internet Explorer is still used for this purpose in the same way as before.

The XPages runtime, on the other hand, explicitly instantiates the XULRunner-based embedded browser when an XPages application is run in the Notes client.

The second reason for choosing XULRunner was made with a view to the future. Although the XPages Notes user experience at this point in time is similar to that of XPages on the web, a XULRunner-based browser offers more options for a richer client offering down the road. Part II, "XPages Development: First Principles," explained the concept of JSF renderkits (a renderkit is a library of Java classes, commonly referred to as *renderers*, which are responsible for displaying components on a given runtime platform). Although XPages uses its own Rich Client Platform (RCP) renderkit when running on the Notes client, it is almost identical to the web renderkit. That is, the RCP renderkit extends the default web renderkit and overrides its rendering behavior in a *very* limited number of cases. The end result is that the XPages markup emitted for the Notes client and the web browser are about 99 percent the same! This, however, is a point-in-time statement. As already briefly mentioned, the XULRunner runtime is capable of rendering XUL markup that can build rich client user interfaces. Why not modify the RCP renderkit in a future release to emit XUL rather than dynamic HTML on the client platform? Having this option available, whether ever exercised in the future or not, was another compelling reason to opt for XULRunner as the client rendering engine.

XULRunner V1.8.1.3 was shipped with Notes V8.5.1, which is the version on which Firefox V2.x is based. In Notes V8.5.2, the embedded XULRunner runtime was upgraded to V1.9.1.3, which is the version on which Firefox V3.5 is based. XULRunner 1.9.2.10, the base for Firefox 3.6.2, arrived with Notes V8.5.3. No upgrade occurred with Notes 9.0, but the 9.0.1 release saw the inclusion of XULRunner 10.0.6 in 2013. It is worth mentioning that XULRunner's version numbering system was rebased in the intervening time between the 8.5.3 and 9.0.1 releases—it now matches the Firefox versioning system, which accounts for the massive leap from 1.9.2.10 to 10.0.6. Nonetheless, this upgrade brings a lot of benefit to the XPages experience in Notes as applications can leverage the underlying browser improvements in areas such as performance, security, and support for HTML5.

TIP

If you want to check out the version of XULRunner installed with your Notes client in the future, first locate the XULRunner plug-in in the Notes installation. For example, on Windows in Notes 9, you can find it under the Notes framework folder, like this:

```
<notes_root_install_dir>\framework\rcp\eclipse\plugins\com.ibm.
rcp.xulrunner.runtime.win32.x86_9.x.x.yyyymmdd-hhmm
```

If you then move to the `xulrunner` subfolder and execute the command `xulrunner.exe /v`, a dialog box displays the version of XULRunner installed with Notes. Figure 13.1 shows an example.

Figure 13.1 XULRunner version dialog

Getting Started with XPages in the Notes Client

If you are new to XPages in a Notes client environment, but you have Notes V8.5.1 or later, it is easy to get started with XPages applications and get a sense of how it works in that environment. The standard Notes Discussion template application contains a lot of ready-made examples of XPages client features, as does the Teamroom template if you use Notes V8.5.3 or later. In any event, you can start by creating a new instance of the Discussion app. To do this, simply select the **File > New** menu option or type **Ctrl-N** and create a new application like what's shown in Figure 13.2.

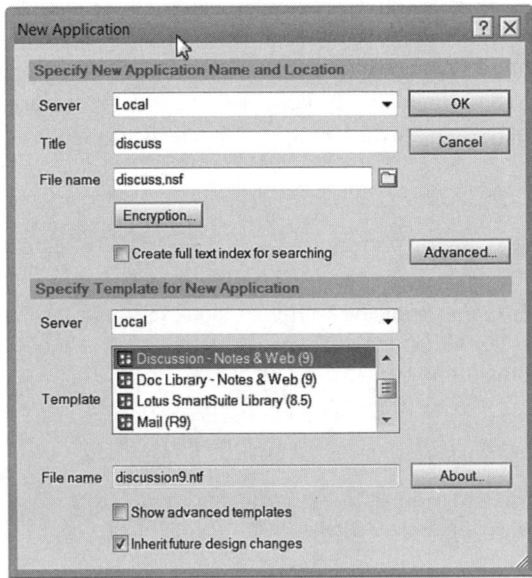

Figure 13.2 New local discussion application for Notes client

When the application opens in Notes, it does not feature an XPages interface by default but, in fact, is the same good ol' Notes Discussion application. This is because the default client launch option is still configured to open the application using the conventional Notes frameset.

To run the application using XPages you must therefore change the application launch option, which you can do immediately by opening up the infobox properties for the database and completing these steps:

1. Type **Alt-Enter** anywhere in the application to open the infobox.
2. Switch the top combo box to Database (if not already selected).
3. Pick the **Launch** tab.
4. Change the Notes client launch property to match the option already chosen for the browser at the bottom of the same panel (**main.xsp** for Notes 9 or **allDocuments.xsp** in earlier releases).

Figure 13.3 shows the required settings. Note that XPages is the default interface for the Discussion app when run on the web, but not so when run on the client.

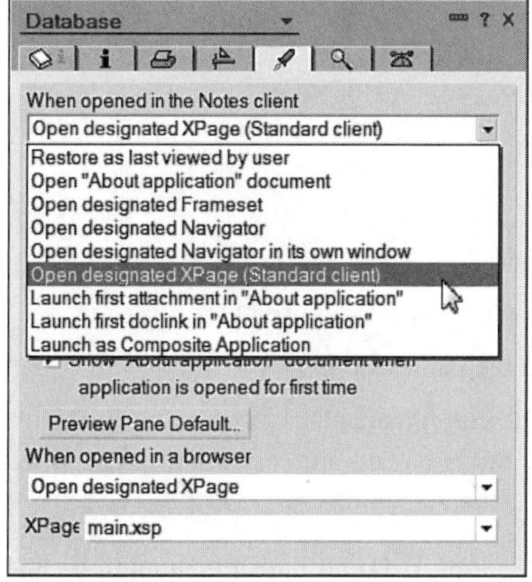

Figure 13.3 XPages application launch options

After your new selections are completed, close the Discussion app and reopen it to see the XPages interface presented in the client. Note that if you happen to have any other live XPages web applications, you could also change their launch properties and run them in the Notes client in the manner just described.

TIP

If you are launching a new third-party XPiNC application in Notes/Domino 9.0.1 or later, you may be challenged with an Execution Control List (ECL) dialog to trust the signer of the application. This is because a new Load Java code permission was created in the 9.0.1 release, effectively disabling Java programs (such as XPages applications) in the Notes client as a protection mechanism against Java JVM vulnerabilities. Customers must explicitly trust the signers of such applications to run them in Notes.

3, 2, 1...Lift Off

So, what exactly happens when you change those launch options and invoke the application in Notes? As a first step, the Notes core inspects the properties, identifies them as XPages launch options, builds an XPages client URL internally, and passes it to the XPages client container. For an arbitrary Discussion application instance, the launch URL looks like this:

```
notes:///discuss.nsf/allDocuments.xsp?OpenXPage
```

This complies with the following canonical form:

```
protocol://serverName/dbName.nsf/XPageName.xsp?OpenCmd
```

where:

- `notes` is the URL protocol.
- The database is local, so no server name is supplied.
- `discuss.nsf` is the database name. The replica ID can also be used here.
- `allDocuments.xsp` is the XPage specified in the launch options.
- `?OpenXPage` is a new Notes client 8.5.1 URL command, just like `?OpenForm`. This parameter is not used by XPages on the web, but it has no side effects if it is applied there.

Internally, the XPages client container reconstructs the URL into a form suitable for the XPD web container. The new internal URL would look something like this:

```
http://127.0.0.1:1234/xsp/discuss.nsf/allDocuments.xsp?OpenXPage
```

where:

- The standard http request/response protocol is used to interact with the local XPD web container.
- `127.0.0.1` is the standard IP address used for the local host (this computer). The next four digits, say "1234" as shown here, represent the port number and are randomly generated at runtime for security reasons.

- /xsp is the servlet alias used to identify XPages requests to the web container.
- If the NSF was located on a server, named "bigIron" for example, the database segment of the URL would be bigIron!!discuss.nsf.

The remainder of the URL remains as before.

The XPages runtime instantiates the XPD web container if it is not already running. It then creates an instance of the XULRunner-based browser in a new tab in the Notes client and sets the new URL as its content. Thus, the XPD web container is fed the request from the browser instance and recognizes it as an XPages request. The XPages runtime is bootstrapped if this is the first XPages application to be opened in the current Notes session (you no doubt notice a delay while opening the first app of a session), and the request is then processed by the XPages runtime. From that point on, everything works as it does when running on the Domino web server. That is, a component tree is constructed for the nominated launch page and the appropriate (RCP) renderers emit HTML markup back to the (XULRunner) browser. And—presto!—an XPage duly appears in a new tab in the Notes client. Figure 13.4 summarizes this process.

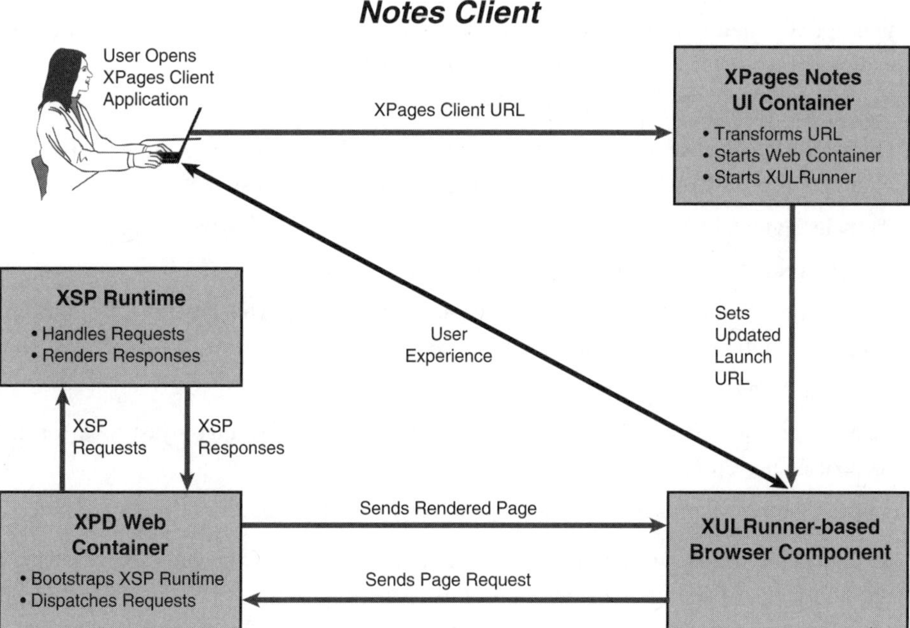

Figure 13.4 XPages in the Notes client

With this model, all application processing occurs locally on your personal computer, regardless of whether the Notes application resides there or on a remote Domino server. In remote mode, all the application's Java class files, Domino document data, and resources need to be retrieved across the network from the Domino server, but the local XPD web container and XPages runtime do all the processing.

In terms of performance, the cost of the initial bootstrapping of the XPages runtime classes together with the extra network overhead associated with running remote applications can be expensive. Steps were taken in both the Notes 8.5.3 and 9.x releases to mitigate this situation, full details of which are described in a later section in this chapter, titled "Optimizing XPages for Notes."

Bookmarks

Although the launch page represents the entry point nominated by the application developer, it is not the only way to bring up an XPages app in Notes. A client URL, like the one built on-the-fly by Notes at launch time, can also be stored as a bookmark and used as an alternative entry point by the end user.

Suppose, for example, that you are an active user of an XPages Discussion application, but you find that you predominantly use the **By Author** view and **By Category** views. It might be convenient for you, in this scenario, to simply bookmark these pages so that you can open the application directly inside these views with a one-mouse click.

This can be achieved by following these steps:

1. Open an XPages Discussion application instance in the Notes (for example, perform a client preview of **Chp13ed2.nsf > allDocuments.xsp** from Designer).
2. Activate a view, like **By Author**, by selecting it in the Discussion navigator.
3. Select **Create > Bookmark** from the Notes main menu.
4. Accept the default options in the **Add Bookmarks** dialog. This creates a **By Author** bookmark in the **Favorite Bookmarks** space.
5. Close the XPages application.
6. Select **Open** > **Favorite Bookmarks** and click your XPages entry—just look for the name used in step 4.
7. Verify that the XPages application is opened using the By Author as the entry point.

As an interesting follow-up exercise, copy (via right mouse menu on the bookmark entry) and paste the bookmark to your desktop and look at its properties. Figure 13.5 shows the desktop properties in a Windows environment (the simple URL format described earlier).

Of course, you can customize this bookmark in clever ways to really refine your entry point to the XPages application. For example, suppose you are interested in the contents of a particular topic in a hypothetical Discussion application (for example, all documents relating to XPages in the Notes client that happen to be have been categorized using an XPiNC tag). Simply create a new bookmark entry or edit an existing entry to read as follows:

```
notes:///discuss.nsf/byTag.xsp?OpenXPage&categoryFilter=XPiNC
```

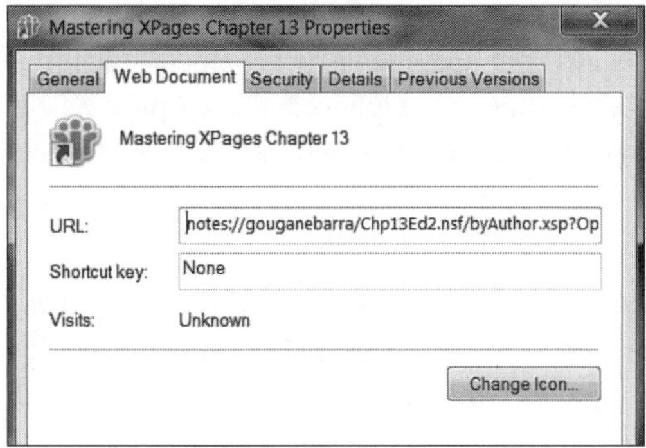

Figure 13.5 XPages bookmark

As shown in Chapter 8, "Working with Domino Views," the `categoryFilter` is simply applied to the view data source on the specified XPage. So here, your bookmark essentially executes a query while launching the Notes XPages application and thus reduces, or even eliminates, unnecessary navigations that you would otherwise have to perform after opening the NSF.

The new `?OpenXPage` URL command also ensures that XPages applications go through the traditional Notes failover procedure when invoked from the Notes workspace. That is, should a specific application instance be unavailable when clicked (such as when a server is down or a database has been deleted), any known replicas are looked up and the next available replica, if any, is launched in its place. For this reason, it is regarded as a best practice to include the `?OpenXPage` command when constructing URLs for the client, although it's not always strictly required for the link to be successfully resolved.

Apart from bookmarks and HTML links, these URLs can also be invoked directly from the Notes toolbar (see Figure 13.6), the OS desktop, the client browser, and so forth.

Figure 13.6 XPages URL in Notes Address toolbar

Furthermore, they can be used programmatically as a means of integrating XPages applications with traditional Notes design elements. For example, enveloping an XPages Notes URL in an `@Function` means that you can launch an XPage from a form, frameset, and so on. For example:

```
@URLOpen("notes:///discuss.nsf/byAuthor.xsp?OpenXPage")
```

This means that XPages can be plugged into existing client applications, so XPages can be incrementally adopted on a piecemeal basis if that suits your application development strategy.

Remember that Chapter 9, "Beyond the View Basics," explained the Display XPage Instead form property, which provides another alternative means of launching XPages.

Working Offline

Working with your XPages web applications offline is a snap, thanks to the simplicity of the replication and sync process. An example of how this works is again best illustrated using the standard Notes Discussion application. If you want to step through this section in concert with the text, you need access to a Domino server.

The exercise can be summarized as follows:

1. Create a Discussion application on a Domino server from the Notes client.

   Use the same process as shown in Figure 13.2, except specify a server. Call the application **OfflineSample**.

2. Change the Notes client launch options to XPages, and reopen the application.

3. Use the **New Topic** button to create the first document.

4. Create a local replica of the application.

Use the **File > Replication > New Replica** menu, as shown in Figure 13.7 and Figure 13.8.

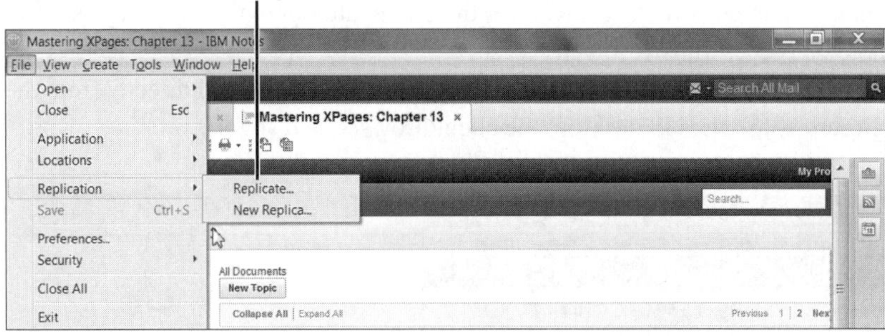

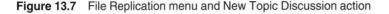

Figure 13.7 File Replication menu and New Topic Discussion action

5. Open the server instance of the application in a web browser and create a response to the first topic.

   Your browser URL will be http://*<servername>*/OfflineS.nsf.

6. Revert to the Notes client and verify that the response can be seen on the server copy, as shown in Figure 13.9.

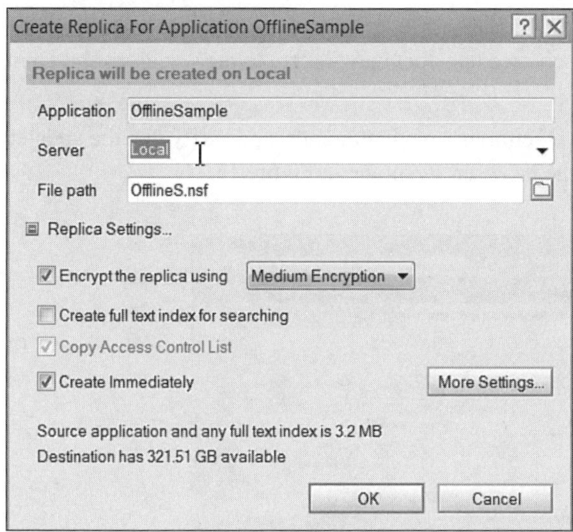

Figure 13.8 File New Replica dialog

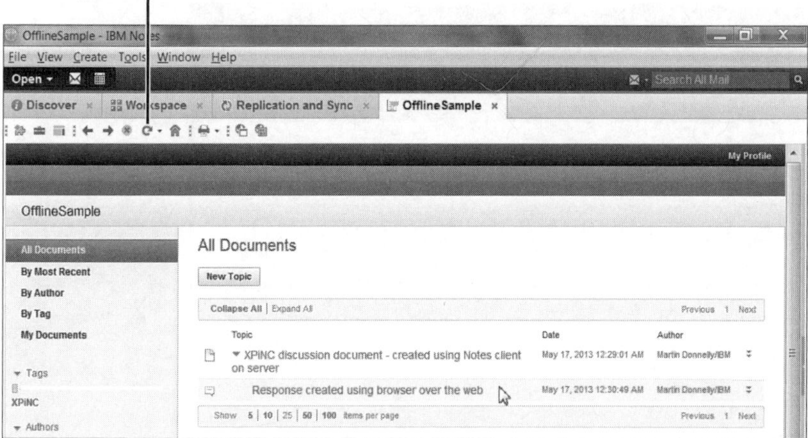

Figure 13.9 OfflineSample in Notes client on server

7. Open the local replica and verify that the response *cannot* be seen there.
8. Execute a replication task via **Open > Replication and Sync** or simply select **File > Replication > Replicate** from the main menu.
9. Verify that the web response document is now visible in the local replica.

10. Create another response document locally.
11. Execute a replication task again; you see one document is sent to the server, as shown in Figure 13.10.
12. In the web browser, click the **All Documents** navigator entry and verify that the updates from the local replica appear in the browser, as shown in Figure 13.11.

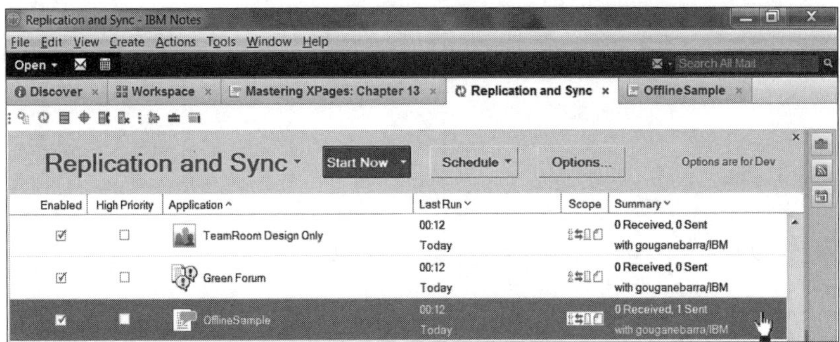

Figure 13.10 Notes Replication and Sync page

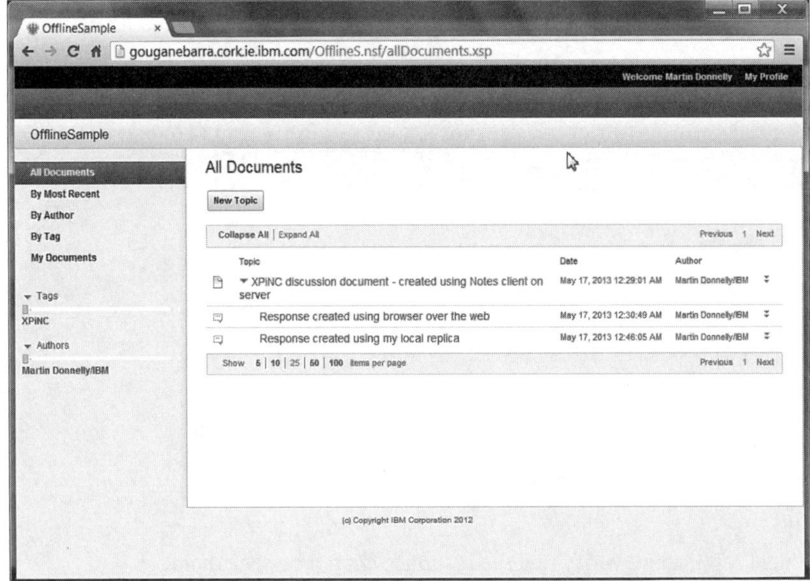

Figure 13.11 Discussion application viewed on the web after replication

Some additional points are worth noting in regards to the preceding exercise. First, unless you grant anonymous access to the Discussion application via the Notes access control list (ACL), your credentials will be challenged on the web. If so, simply use your Domino Internet ID and password.

Second, if you are using Notes version 8.5.1, you see that the **File > Replication** menu is disabled at step 4. As part of some XPages client-integration work done in Notes version 8.5.2, that menu is now enabled. Readers using version 8.5.1 can access the replication menu by moving to the Notes workspace and using the right-mouse menu on the **OfflineSample.nsf** entry.

At step 5, if no XPage is specified as part of the browser URL, the Domino web engine looks up the launch page and retrieves the default setting. Figure 13.9 shows the server instance of the application in the Notes client after a response has been created on the web. You need to force a refresh of the XPage before that web document appears.

The Notes Replication and Sync page, which was shown in Figure 13.10, can be accessed by choosing the Replication and Sync entry from the Open drop-down button in the Notes workspace.

Figure 13.11 shows the end result: Three documents all created in different ways, but ultimately located in a single NSF repository. Note that when a new replica is created, both the document *data and design* elements are copied to the new NSF instance by default. This allows you to execute the Discussion application in splendid isolation on your local computer—if you have a wired network connection, you can remove the cable just before step 10 and reconnect it immediately afterward to fully verify that activity.

One of These Things Is Not Like the Other

Compare the tab window shown in Figure 13.9 to that in Figure 13.11. Okay, so the latter has an extra document, but concern yourself more with application structure than content...do you notice anything different?

The perceptive reader has no doubt observed that the banner area featured in the top-right corner of the application has one less entry when displayed in the client. That is, the web has a **Welcome Martin Donnelly** entry while the Notes version does not. Perhaps now is a good time to revisit those earlier statements that claimed that application rendering is virtually identical on both the Notes client and the web. Well, it is...unless you choose it not to be!

For this particular application, what relevance does a **Welcome** entry have in the Notes client? The answer is none at all. After all, Notes establishes the user's identity at startup or whenever an ID switch occurs, and only one user can be active at any one time during a given Notes session. The web, of course, is a more stateless anonymous environment, so it is appropriate for the Discussion banner to adopt different behavior in that context. The web behavior, in fact, identifies authenticated users in the manner shown in Figure 13.11 and presents a **My Profile** option so that personal information can be entered or updated. If anonymous access is allowed for the application, however, a **login** action is displayed instead, because anonymous users have no profile information. Figure 13.12 shows the banner area configuration for an anonymous user.

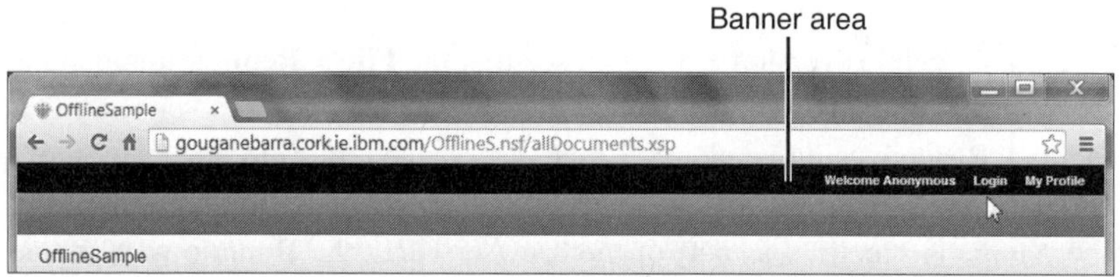

Figure 13.12 Discussion application banner area for anonymous users

Of more interest to you, of course, is the manner in which this conditional behavior is achieved. All the Notes 8.5 versions of the Discussion template achieved this using renderkit-specific properties. Even though the sample application created for this chapter is based on the 9.0.1 Discussion template, the original custom control has been re-inserted for illustrative purposes. (It is no longer used.) Open Domino Designer and inspect the Custom Control named **banner.xsp**. Listing 13.1 shows the relevant markup snippet.

Listing 13.1 Renderkit-Specific Properties

```
<xp:label value="Welcome " id="labelWelcome">
      <xp:label.rcp rendered="false">
      </xp:label.rcp>
</xp:label>
<xp:text escape="true" id="cfUserName"
      value="#{javascript:sessionScope.commonUserName;}">
      <xp:text.rcp rendered="false">
      </xp:text.rcp>
</xp:text>
```

You can see special `rcp` qualifiers being applied in this snippet, such as `label.rcp`, `text.rcp`. The `rcp` qualifier is a renderkit identifier and, as previously mentioned, the Notes renderkit is named `rcp` for Rich Client Platform. So, as the markup indicates, the text and label components in this snippet are not rendered by the Notes renderkit, and thus they do not appear when the XPage is displayed in the client because `rendered="false"`.

This feature is similar in concept to the Hide/When logic used in conventional Notes applications, and you might find it useful if the applications you are building have more than one target platform to support.

TIP

If you need to detect programmatically in XPages whether you are running on the web or in the Notes client—say that you want to build some platform-specific behaviors or logic—the @ClientType @Function can be used; it returns "Web" and "Notes", respectively. More variations on this topic are discussed later in the section "Optimizing XPages for Notes."

Other Subtle Differences

If you continue to explore the Discussion application on both the client and the web, other subtle differences become apparent. For example, if you go to the Notes client and delete the response document created using the local replica, and then use a web browser to delete the other response document, you can compare the warning dialogs presented in each case. Figure 13.13 and Figure 13.14 show the client and web dialogs, respectively. Note that the web warning dialog will vary depending on the browser used.

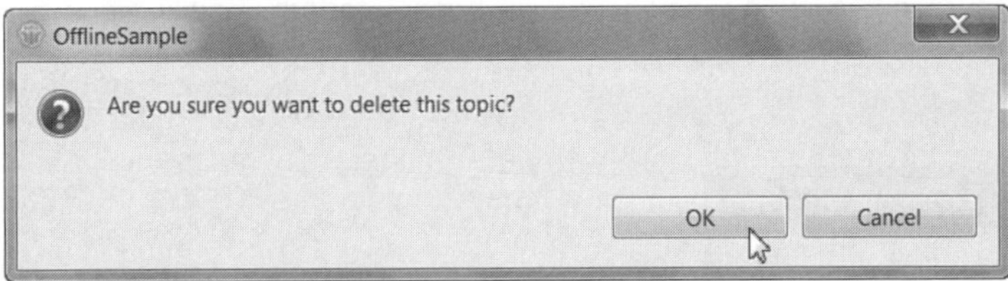

Figure 13.13 XPages Notes warning dialog

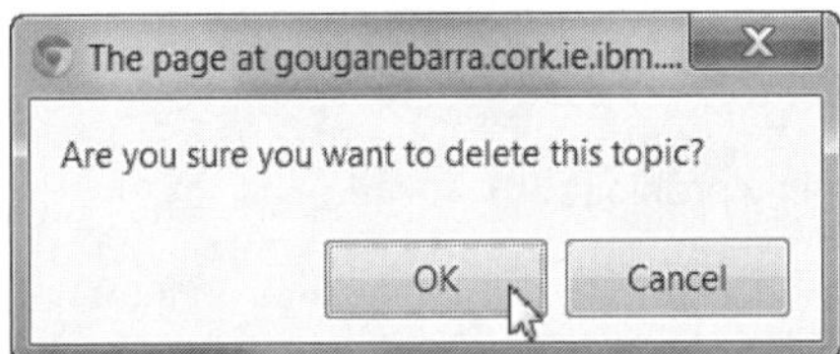

Figure 13.14 XPages web warning dialog

Because you now know that XPages in the client runs in an embedded browser, and you have seen the internal URL that is passed to the web container, you might question why Figure 13.14 does not read as follows:

```
"The page at http://127.0.0.1 says"
```

In fact, in the early days of XPiNC internal development, that's exactly how it did read! Because this looks out of place in the Notes client, even for an offline web application, there was some work done in the XPages client runtime to make sure that the standard Notes dialogs are automatically presented to the user in such scenarios. Typically with JavaScript, UI dialogs are handled using the `alert()`, `confirm()`, and `prompt()` functions. These native function calls are overridden by the XPages runtime in the client so that a proper Notes caption is provided. The `XSP` JavaScript object also provides implementations for these as illustrated in Figures 13.15 through 13.18, and included in the **csJavaScriptAPIs.xsp** in **Chp13ed2.nsf**.

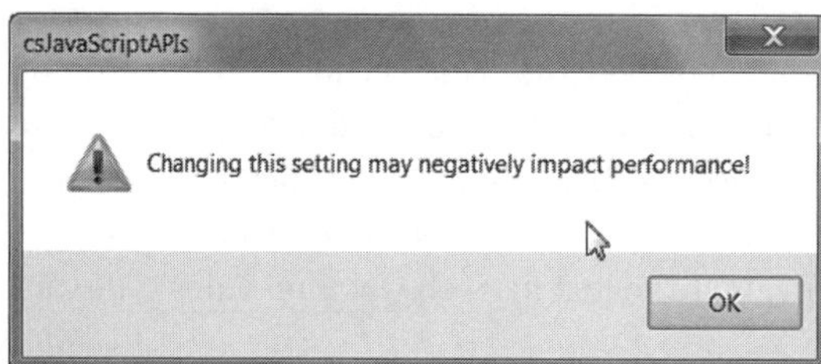

Figure 13.15 XSP.alert ("Changing this setting may negatively impact performance!")

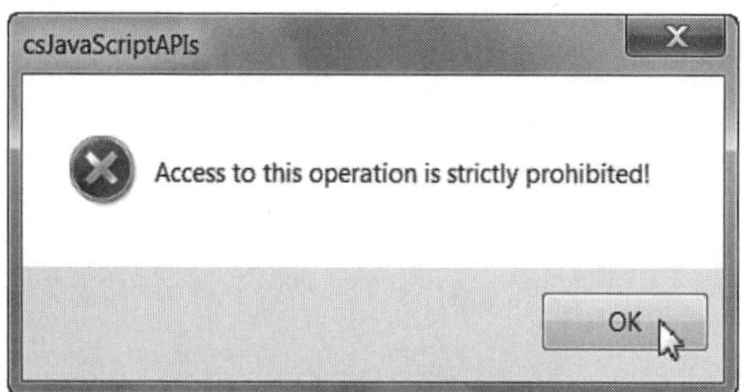

Figure 13.16 XSP.error ("Access to this operation is strictly prohibited!")

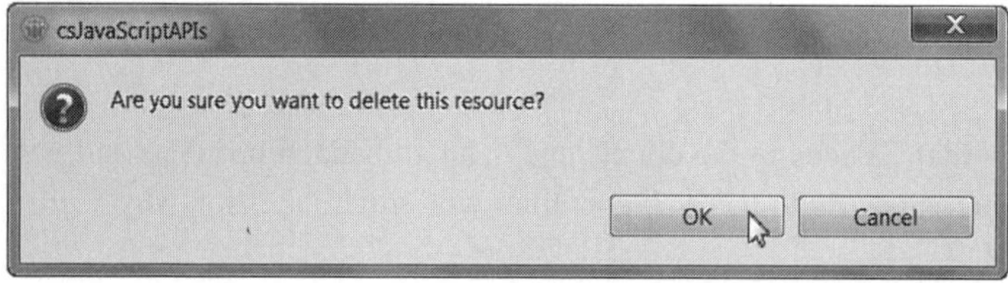

Figure 13.17 XSP.confirm ("Are you sure you want to delete this resource?")

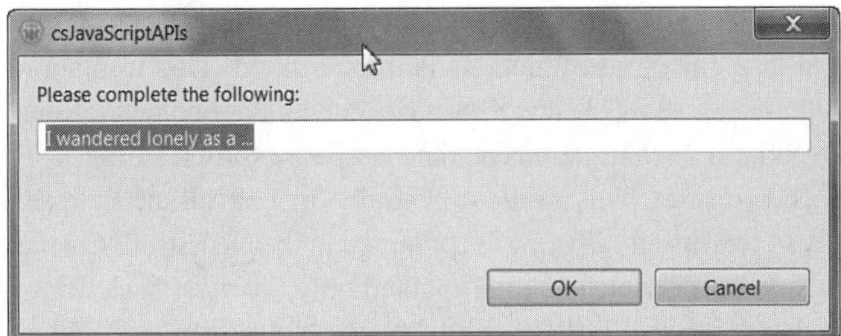

Figure 13.18 XSP.prompt ("Please complete the following," "I wandered lonely as a....")

In all cases, the dialog caption is the name of the XPages application containing the executable JavaScript code—this is automatically set for you by the XPages runtime code. The behavior of `XSP.alert()` and `XSP.error()` is similar, insofar as they both issue informational warnings to the user (along with a beep)—the latter is simply more severe than the former in terms of the harshness of the beep emitted and the iconography employed. The next two solicit a response from the user, which can then be processed by the application. `XSP.confirm()` is used to pose questions where a boolean `true` or `false` response is required, whereas `XSP.prompt()` is used to gather arbitrary end-user input. Listing 13.2 shows a snippet where `XSP.prompt()` poses a question and tweaks the XPage UI based on the user's response—when executed, the dialog prompt text is highlighted in advance and the user is supposed to overwrite it by simply typing the answer. A standalone snippet has been created for you in **qzWordsworth.xsp** in **Chp13ed2.nsf**.

Listing 13.2 Wordsworth Quiz

```
var answer = XSP.prompt("Please complete the following:",
             "I wandered lonely as a ...")
var button = document.getElementById("#{id:button1}");
if (null != button && null != answer) {
      if (answer == "cow" || answer == "cloud")
            button.innerHTML = "Correct 8-)";
      else
            button.innerHTML = "Incorrect :'-("
}
```

In any case, Eclipse Java developers will no doubt recognize the XSP user dialogs as Standard Widget Toolkit (SWT) controls. The XSP JavaScript functions are mapped to the appropriate Java UI classes (for example, `org.eclipse.swt.widgets.Messagebox`) by the XPages RCP runtime. On the web, they are mapped to the standard browser dialog functions.

Other functions are provided by the XSP JavaScript object; for example, later you use the `XSP.publishEvent()` function when working with XPages in Notes composite applications.

However, compared to the amount of client-side functions available via the Notes LotusScript UI classes, the standard set of client-side JavaScript functions is quite limited. This limitation was imposed in the initial XPiNC release (Notes 8.5.1) due to security concerns. If no restrictions applied, then it would be possible to call *any* Java functions on the classpath exposed by the NSF application in which the JavaScript code resides. This would potentially open up all the Eclipse/Expeditor APIs and Notes Java APIs as well as any Java code contained in the NSF itself. On the other hand, the limited set of client-side JavaScript functions enabled only the most basic functions, meaning that the application developer had little control over the Notes front-end. What to do?

Extended Client-Side JavaScript Commands

Notes 9 introduced a new feature aimed at enabling powerful XPages programming capabilities in the Notes front-end while maintaining the integrity of the XPiNC security model. These conflicting goals are achieved by providing a new generic XSP client-side JavaScript (CSJS) command that enables front-end Java classes to be called—as long as the classes in question have been explicitly added to the Notes framework as one or more plug-ins that implement a new XPages Eclipse extension point. If this sounds complicated, then this section should prove to you that it is not.

The new XSP CSJS command is named `XSP.executeCommand()` and it takes the following form:

```
XSP.executeCommand(String commandName, Object commandArgs)
```

For example, a command enabling an XPiNC application to dynamically update the Notes status bar could be provided like this:

```
XSP.executeCommand("com.whatever.xsp.ext.cmds.UpdateStatusBar", "Hello")
```

This makes for a simple and uniform scripting interface in XPages—all that remains is for you, the developer, to provide a Java implementation of the command. At a macro level, you need to do five things:

1. Create and configure a plug-in project in Domino Designer.
2. Implement the extended command in Java.
3. Create a feature and an update site project for your plug-in.
4. Install the update site into Notes.
5. Call the extended command for CSJS code in your XPages applications.

These steps will now be expanded upon in full detail. To complete the first step, open the Java perspective from Domino Designer by selecting the **Window > Open Perspective > Java** menu. Then create a new plug-in project by selecting **File > New Project > Plug-in Development > Plug-in Project**. This brings up a wizard dialog that steps you through the process. On the first screen you need to enter only a project name—for example, `com.whatever.xsp.ext.cmds`—and accept all the other defaults by clicking **Next**. On the second screen, you should set the execution environment to J2SE-1.5 and click **Finish**. Your plug-in project is then created and just needs a little more configuration before it is useful. This work is carried out by editing the **MANIFEST.MF** file. You can find this in the **META-INF** folder in the Package Explorer pane.

Start by configuring your plug-in to depend on some other Notes plug-ins so that it can use the Java code contained within them. For the purposes of our sample extended commands, you just need to add four dependencies, which you can do by clicking the **Dependencies** tab and clicking the **Add** button:

- `com.ibm.rcp.ui`
- `com.ibm.notes.java.ui`
- `com.ibm.notes.client`
- `com.ibm.xsp.rcp`

Before finishing with step 1, you must declare that your plug-in implements a new extension point service—one that was added by XPages in Notes 9.0. An extension point is a mechanism that a plug-in uses to declare that it implements a particular service, like extended XPages commands in this case. When an extended command is called from CSJS within an XPages application, the extension point declaration enables the XPages runtime to retrieve a list of plug-ins that purport to contribute extended commands. (There could be several.) It then looks up the Java class within the plug-in that claims to provide the extended command implementation. List 13.3 shows the extension point service markup. You must include such a declaration in any custom plug-in you provide by typing similar markup in the **plugin.xml** tab in the Manifest editor.

Listing 13.3 XPages Extended Command Extension Point Service Declaration

```
<plugin>
       <extension
            point="com.ibm.commons.Extension">
         <service
            type="com.ibm.xsp.rcp.ExtendedCommands"
            class="com.whatever.xsp.ext.cmds.CommandHandler" />
   </extension>
</plugin>
```

For step 2, you can create the Java class by selecting **File > New > Class** from the main menu. In the resulting dialog enter `CommandHandler` as the class name, and click the **Add** button so that the class implements the XPages `IExtendedCommand` interface. A Java interface simply defines one or more programming methods that a class must implement to support an abstract conceptual object. In this case, for your Java class to become the concrete embodiment of an XSP extended command, it needs to implement two methods, namely `getCommandList()`

and `executeCommand()`. The former means that your class must return a list of commands that it supports. This is necessary as the XPages runtime needs to execute arbitrary commands and needs to query the extended command contributors to see if they provide the required implementation for a given command id. A match is established as soon as a Java class returns a list containing an entry equal to the command id used in the CSJS code. It is a good practice to namespace the command ids so that various contributors do not cause a conflict by using common short names. The foregoing namespaced example is a good one: `"com.whatever.xsp.ext.cmds.UpdateStatusBar"`

Figure 13.19 shows the completed dialog used to create the `CommandHandler` Java class.

Figure 13.19 Java New Class Dialog

The `CommandHandler` class needs to implement the `IExtendedCommand` interface and provide implementations for whatever extended commands it declares—two in this instance. Study the Java code shown in Listing 13.4 to see if you can understand what the four required methods are doing.

Listing 13.4 XPages Extended Command Extension Point Service Declaration

```
package com.whatever.xsp.ext.cmds;
import java.util.ArrayList;
import java.util.HashMap;
import java.util.List;
import lotus.domino.NotesException;
import org.eclipse.jface.action.IStatusLineManager;
import com.ibm.notes.java.api.data.NotesDatabaseData;
import com.ibm.notes.java.ui.NotesUIWorkspace;
import com.ibm.xsp.rcp.IExtendedCommands;
import com.ibm.xsp.rcp.IRcpContext;
import com.ibm.xsp.rcp.XspViewPart;

public class CommandHandler implements IExtendedCommands {
       public static final String UpdateStatusBar  =
"com.whatever.xsp.ext.cmds.UpdateNotesStatusBar";
       public static final String AddDbToWorkspace =
"com.whatever.xsp.ext.cmds.AddDbToWorkspace";
       // execute the commands we support
       public Object executeCommand(IRcpContext rcpContext,
                                String command, List<?> params) {
              if (command.equalsIgnoreCase(UpdateStatusBar)) {
                    updateNotesStatusBar(rcpContext,params);
              } else if (command.equalsIgnoreCase(AddDbToWorkspace)) {
                     addDbToWorkspace(rcpContext,params);
              }
              return null;
       }
       // list the commands we support...
       public List<String> getCommandList() {
              ArrayList<String> cmdList = new ArrayList<String>();
              cmdList.add(UpdateStatusBar);
              cmdList.add(AddDbToWorkspace);
              return cmdList;
       }
       // UpdateStatusBar Command (Print a message on the Notes status bar)
       private Object updateNotesStatusBar(IRcpContext context, List<?>
➥params) {
              XspViewPart xvp = (XspViewPart)context.getViewPart();
              IStatusLineManager statusManager =
                      xvp.getViewSite().getActionBars().
➥getStatusLineManager();
              Object arg1 = params.get(0);
              if (arg1 instanceof HashMap) {
                       HashMap map = (HashMap)arg1;
                         String txt = (String)map.get("message");
```

```
                        if(statusManager != null){
                              statusManager.setErrorMessage(txt);
                        }
                }
                return null;
        }
        // AddDbToWorkspace Command (Add a database to the Notes workspace)
        private Object addDbToWorkspace(IRcpContext context, List<?> params) {
                NotesUIWorkspace ws=new NotesUIWorkspace();
                try {
                        Object arg1 = params.get(0);
                        if (arg1 instanceof HashMap) {
                              HashMap map = (HashMap)arg1;
                              String server = (String)map.get("server");
                              String database = (String)map.get("db");
                              if (server != null && database != null) {
                                      NotesDatabaseData dbData =
                                              new NotesDatabaseData(server,
➥ database);
                                      ws.addDatabase(dbData);
                              }
                        }
                } catch (NotesException e) {
                        e.printStackTrace();
                }
                return null;
        }
        // etc.
}
```

The package and import statements are just standard Java constructs that organize the code and pull in dependencies. In the body of the class itself, you can see that two command ids are declared—the short form being `UpdateStatusBar` and `AddDbToWorkspace`. When this class is called upon to declare its commands, it simply constructs a list object, populates it with both command ids, and then returns the list. When the class is called to execute a command, it simply attempts to match the input command id with its own ids. When there is a match, the method implementing the command is called. Simple enough?

Interestingly, the `executeCommand` call passes in an `IRcpContext` object that represents the XPiNC container from which the command originated. This object gives access to the view part for the running application and can be queried in various useful ways. For instance, the `UpdateNotesStatusBar` method uses it to get a reference to the object managing the Notes status bar, which thus enables it to post message updates. The message content is passed in as a parameter. The contents of the params object will vary from one command to the next—it is a contract between the

CSJS side and the Java side. If the JavaScript code inserts server and database strings into the object, that is what *must* be extracted on the Java side. You can see how these values are used in the `AddDbToWorkspace` method to call Notes Java APIs. This is how the JavaScript and Java objects communicate.

Now that the development work is complete, your thoughts should turn to step 3, which entails packaging up the Java code and deploying it to Notes for testing. This is a two-part process. First, you need to make a feature project to contain the plug-in project, and second create an update site so that the projects can be deployed. This may seem like overkill, but typically this packaging process is dealing with much larger projects than this small sample, in which case it works well for keeping things organized and manageable.

To create the feature, select **File > New Project > Plug-in Development > Feature Project** from the main menu. In the dialog you need to enter a project name; for example, `com.whatever.xsp.ext.cmds.feature`. The other fields are filled in with default values, which you can accept—although you may want to assign something more meaningful as the feature name; for example, Extended Commands Feature. Click **Next** to move to the next page of the wizard dialog. This is where you can select the plug-ins that comprise the project. In this case there is but one, so just select `com.whatever.xsp.ext.cmds` from the list and click **Finish**. Depending on how thorough you want to be at this stage, you can fill out other properties of the feature.xml file in the newly created project, like the feature description, copyright text, and so on, but it is functional in its current form. Figure 13.20 shows the dialog used to create the Feature project.

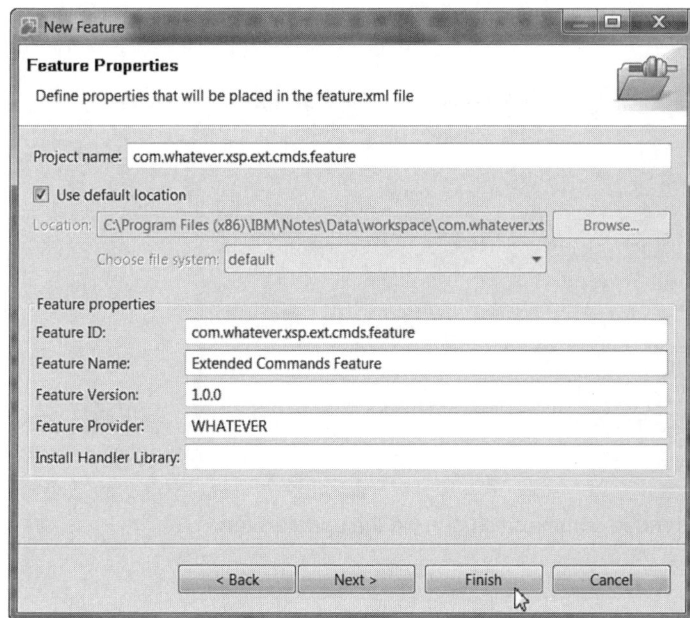

Figure 13.20 Creating the Feature project

To create the update site, you basically follow the same pattern as has gone before: Select **File > New Project > Plug-in Development > Update Site Project** from the main menu. Pick a project name, such as Extended Commands Site, and click **Finish**. To complete the task, double-click the site.xml file, click **Add Feature,** and then select `com.whatever.xsp.ext.cmds.feature`. You should save the file using **Ctrl-S** and then click **Build All** to create the update site artifacts. You now have an update site ready for installation. You should make a note of the update site location because you will need it later when installing. Simply right-click the project and select the **Properties** context menu. By default, the update site is laid down under your workspace folder, which would read like this with a typical installation:

```
C:\Program Files (x86)\IBM\Notes\Data\workspace\Extended Commands Site
```

Step 4 is the installation of the update site—a topic previously discussed in Chapter 2, "Getting Everything You Need." It is actually easiest to use Domino Designer to install the update site to the Notes client; although, there are various installation mechanisms. Remember that Domino Designer and Notes share the same Eclipse infrastructure, so installing plug-ins into Domino Designer means that they are also installed into the Notes client. To recap, in Domino Designer select **File > Application > Install > Search for new features to install > Add Folder Location**. This is where you need the update site location shown previously. Simply enter the location and click **OK**. After the update site appears in the **Applications Locations** list, click **Finish**. You need to step through the next dialogs, accepting the license and so forth until the plug-in is ready to be installed. Most important, note that the default option is set *not* to install the plug-in, so you must explicitly choose to do so when prompted. Figure 13.21 shows the relevant dialog.

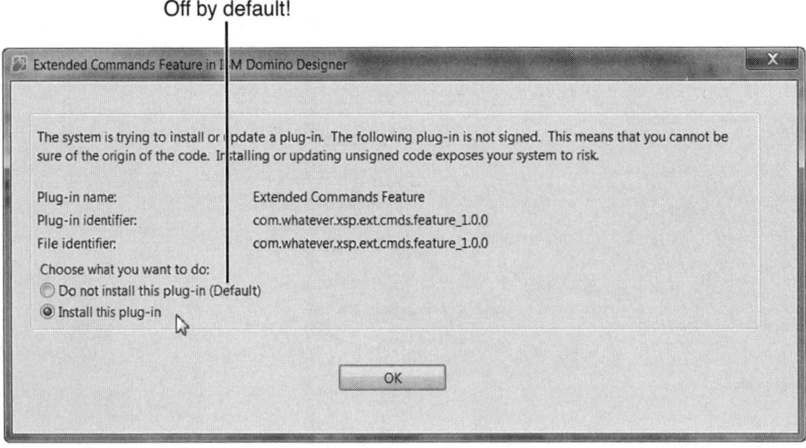

Figure 13.21 Installing the extended command plug-in via the update site

On completion of the installation, Domino Designer (and Notes if running) must be restarted. When it restarts you should double-check that the plug-in is installed. One simple means of doing so is to select **Help > About > Plug-in Details** and sort the plug-ins by id in the resulting dialog. You can then scroll the list of plug-ins and verify that `com.whatever.xsp.ext.cmds` is included, as shown in Figure 13.22.

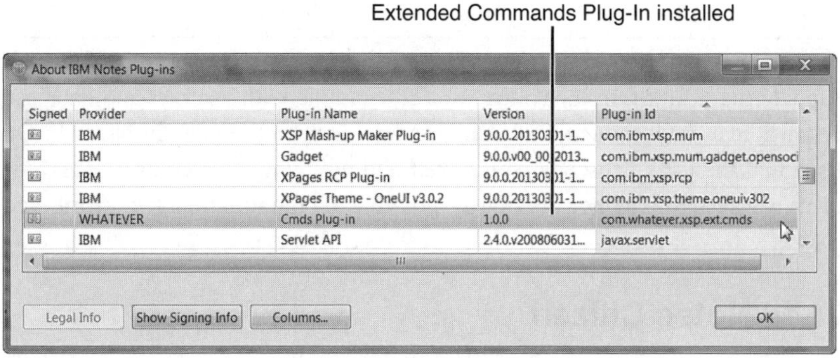

Extended Commands Plug-In installed

Figure 13.22 Your new plug-in installed in Notes/Designer

All that remains now is to exercise the commands from an XPage. The sample application contains an XPage named **myExtCmd.xsp**, which calls both of the extended commands from JavaScript, as demonstrated in Listing 13.5.

Listing 13.5 Extended Commands Called from an XPage Using CSJS

```
<xp:button id="button4" value="Update Notes Status Bar">
       <xp:eventHandler event="onclick" submit="false">
              <xp:this.script><![CDATA[var text = XSP.prompt("Enter
➥some text", "Update Status Bar");
var myParams = new Object();
myParams.message=text;
XSP.executeCommand("com.whatever.xsp.ext.cmds.UpdateNotesStatusBar",
➥myParams);
]]></xp:this.script>
       </xp:eventHandler>
</xp:button>


<xp:button id="button6" value="Add DB To Notes Workspace">
       <xp:eventHandler event="onclick" submit="false">
              <xp:this.script><![CDATA[
// Add app Ch13 1st edition Notes workspace or activate chiclet if
➥already there
```

```
var myParams = new Object();
myParams.server="ballybeg"; // your server name here
myParams.db="chp13ed1";
XSP.executeCommand("com.ibm.xsp.rcp.ext.sample.AddDatabaseToWorkspace",
➥myParams);
]]></xp:this.script>
        </xp:eventHandler>
</xp:button>
```

You should update the `AddDatabaseToWorkspace` example with a server and database appropriate to your particular environment, and then preview or open the page in Notes 9. On doing so you will see that the extended code works well and now you have control over your Notes environment in a way that was not previously possible. Congratulations—go forth and extend!

XPages: A Good Notes Citizen

Although the native dialogs, custom commands, and renderkit-specific properties certainly help XPages applications blend more seamlessly into the Notes client environment, XPages had to adopt new behaviors to qualify as a model citizen. For example, how do you make sure that document updates are not gratuitously lost when a user, inadvertently or otherwise, closes an XPages window in Notes that contains unsaved data? Remember that as far as the Notes client is concerned, that tab window just contains an embedded browser instance and, thus, it has no inherent knowledge regarding the state of the window's content. Allowing an XPages window to simply close might result in lost data, but how do XPages and the Notes core communicate to prevent this scenario?

Again, you need look no further than the Discussion template to see the correct XPages client behavior in action and learn how to apply this to your own applications. To work through this section, open the sample application in the Notes client and create a new topic.

Before entering any data, there's something you must observe: The **File > Save** menu is initially not enabled. Pressing **Esc** at this point simply closes the window because no data has been entered in the document. Enter some arbitrary data into a few fields and check the **File > Save** menu once more. On this occasion, you can see that it is enabled, so selecting the menu item or typing **Ctrl+S** saves your document.

The important point, however, is that Notes is obviously aware of when the XPages document is "dirty" (has unsaved modifications) and when it is not dirty. This behavior is easy to implement, but it is not automatic—that is, you, as the developer, need to explicitly enable your application to take advantage of these advanced document save features.

But, there are more aspects to this feature that you need to first examine before diving into the code. You have seen that explicit save operations are enabled at the right times and execute successfully. Also, XPages and Notes need to handle a window close event on a dirty document and give the user the option of saving the updates. This can occur when a user chooses **File > Close**, types **Esc**, or uses the window tab's **Close** button. Figure 13.23 shows the **Save Resource** dialog that is used to prompt the user under any of those conditions.

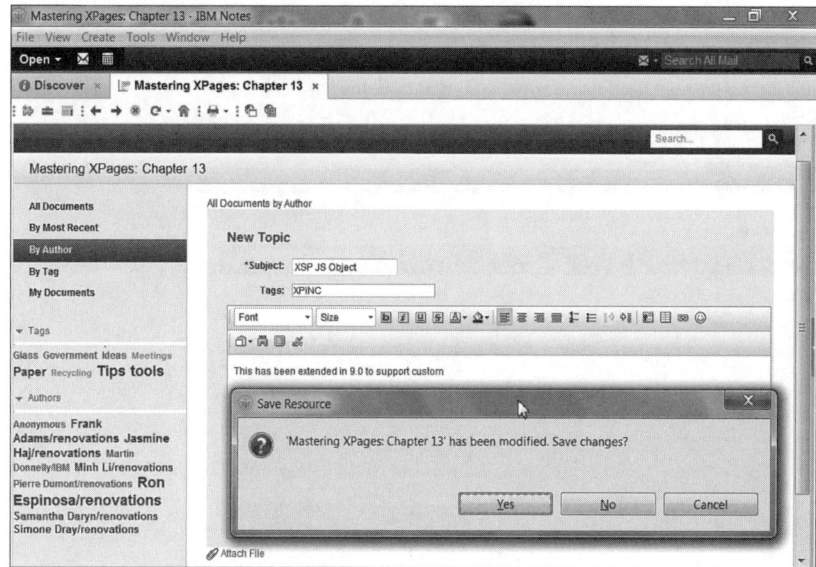

Figure 13.23 XPages Save dialog for dirty documents

There are still more conditions to account for, however. Given that the entire Discussion application is contained within the tab window (an artifact of being designed for web), it is possible to a have a topic document open in edit mode and still click a navigator link that causes the active page to be replaced. For example, create a new topic, enter some data, and click the **By Tag** link. If updates in the current page are not saved at this point, they are lost after **byTag.xsp** loads and the current page is discarded. This is similar to, but not exactly the same as, the previous use case. Figure 13.24 shows that the condition is trapped and the user is given the option of continuing or cancelling the page navigation. If important data really needs to be saved, the user can cancel the operation and perform a deliberate save and then repeat the original navigation.

Of course, you must consider the case where the data entered on a page simply is not important. If, for example, you click the **New Topic** button, enter some text box in the **Search** box, and close the window—what do you expect to happen?

Well, the XPiNC behavior is that window is simply closed and the user is not prompted to save anything. This is based on the fact that the search text is transient data and, even though it is on the same page as the other input controls, it is not saved under normal circumstances when a document itself is saved. Thus, the Discussion application is configured such that entering text in the **Search** field does not dirty the document, but entering data in **Subject**, **Tags**, or **Body** fields does. This makes sense from an application standpoint, so clearly, there is a way for the developer to distinguish between required data and temporary data in XPages applications and enforcing the correct application behavior in all cases. It's finally time to go to Designer and understand how this is achieved!

Navigation forced by selecting a link while editing a document

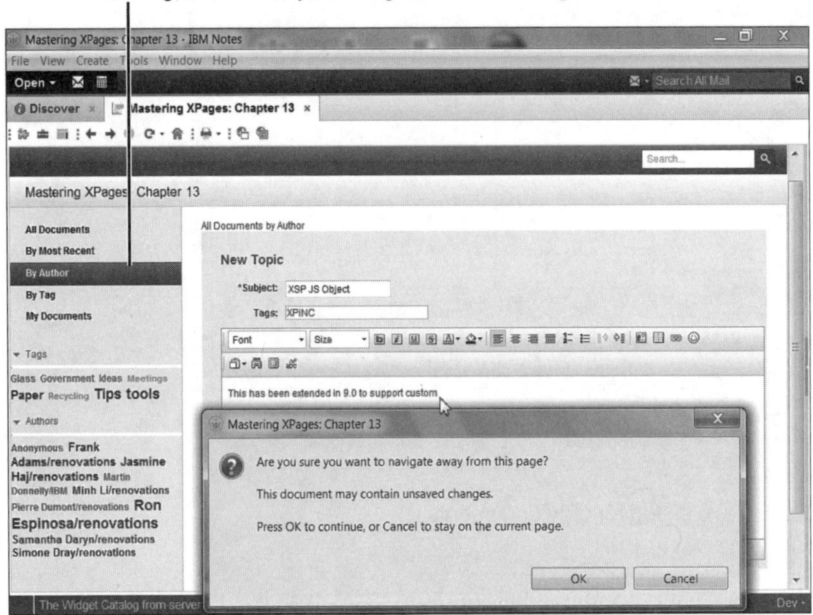

Figure 13.24 XPages preemptive dialog for navigations from dirty documents

Introducing enableModifiedFlag and disableModifiedFlag

If you've been following the previous use cases in a Discussion application in the Notes client and want to quickly open this app in Designer, simply right-click the tab window and select the **Open In Designer** context menu. The main reason for pointing this out is that this menu was not provided for XPages applications in version 8.5.1, but was among the features added in version 8.5.2 to better integrate XPages to the client environment.

In any case, after you open the Discussion application in Designer, you need to search the design elements for references to an **enableModifiedFlag** string. The **Search** dialog can be launched from the main menu (**Search > Search**), the toolbar, or by typing the **Ctrl+H** keyboard accelerator. Figure 13.25 shows the **Search** dialog with the required search string and scope restrictions.

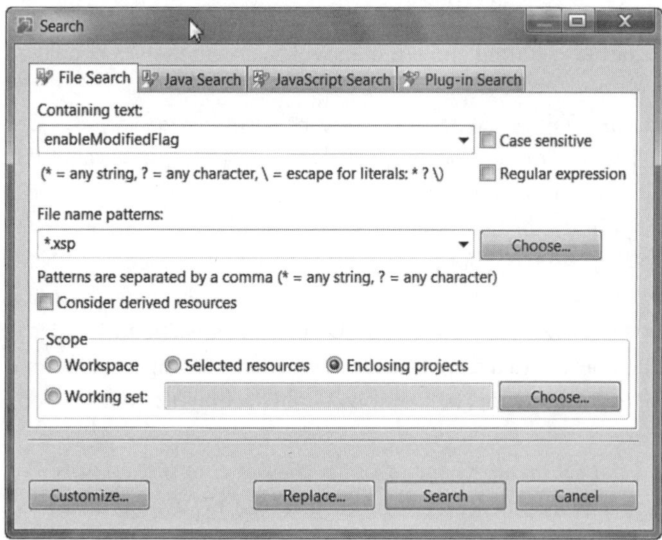

Figure 13.25 Search dialog for enableModifiedFlag

As shown in Table 13.1, the search results in just four hits, all of which are custom controls.

Table 13.1 Search Results for enableModifiedFlag

Custom Control	Purpose	Hits
`authorProfileForm.xsp`	Creates/edits profile information	1 – top level `<xp:view>` tag
`mainTopic.xsp`	Creates/edits top-level discussion documents	1 – top level `<xp:view>` tag
`viewTopic.xsp`	Edits a topic thread	1 – top level `<xp:view>` tag
`viewTopic2.xsp`	Edits a topic thread (mobile)	1 – top level `<xp:view>` tag

All four custom controls use the `enableModifiedFlag` property in much the same way—as a property value set on the custom control itself:

```
<xp:view ...  enableModifiedFlag="true">
```

In two cases, the boolean property value is computed depending on whether the app is mobile, in this way:

```
<xp:view ...  enableModifiedFlag"#{javascript:!isMobile()}">
```

Mobile versions of web or RCP applications generally aim to support a different set of use cases, typically enabling users to read content and take actions, and are less concerned with editing content. In the previous instances, the `enableModifiedFlag` property is enabled only when the application is not mobile because editing and pre-emptively saving inputs is not a concern in these particular scenarios.

Therefore, when applied at the XPages view level, `enableModifiedFlag="true"` means all input controls contained within the custom control are participating in a game that entails raising a "modified" flag if a user types something into any of them. Input controls can be edit boxes, rich text controls, multiline edit fields, and so on—basically, anything on a page that can be updated by user input. Thus, all the input controls on the four custom controls listed here set a dirty flag for a given document after any update is performed. The dirty notification is done transparently via some under-the-covers XSP client-side JavaScript calls, but this underlying implementation is not really that relevant to the application developer. The important point is that your XPage or custom control can acquire this behavior by simply setting this one property value.

If `enableModifiedFlag` is not set on an XPage or on its custom controls, no dirty flag is set when fields are updated; so, it is assumed that unsaved data can always be discarded. After `enableModifiedFlag` is set, the opposite behavior occurs. As usual, reality is most likely somewhere between these two extremes. When a field needs a way of opting out of the `enableModifiedFlag` scheme and it can do so by using a property called `disableModifiedFlag`, this property denotes an exception to the general rule. An example would be as follows:

```
<xp:inputText id="transientText" ... disableModifiedFlag="true">
```

Thus, using a combination of these two properties, you should be able to build the required behaviors into your own application. There is no specialized support in Designer for this feature, so you need to work with the All Properties panel or directly in the XSP Source pane, as shown here.

At this point, you may wonder how all this works when combined with page validation. For example, a user closes a Notes window containing a dirty document and is prompted with a save option because the XPage has `enableModifiedFlag="true"`. The user chooses to save the document, so the request to do so is sent off to Notes and the window is closed. What happens if the document fails server-side validation? If this occurs, the document cannot be saved, so the window had better not close in the meantime! It's easy to try this use case because the **Subject** field on **mainTopic.xsp** has a server-side `required` validator. In other words, when the page is submitted, the **Subject** field is tested for a null value, and the save operation fails if the field is empty. Create a new topic and simply enter data into the other fields, leaving **Subject** empty and close the window. As you can see from Figure 13.26, if server-side validation fails, the window is not closed and the validation error is displayed in the proper way.

Client-side validation is also handled, although that it is the simpler use case because the client-side validator executes *before* the page is submitted, so no call back from the server side is necessary to prevent the window from closing if validation fails. If you are interested in this scenario, simply add a `required` validator to the **Tags** field, preview **allDocuments.xsp** in the

Notes client, and repeat the previous test (leaving **Tags** empty in this case). Remember that validators are client-side by default unless explicitly disabled in favor of server-side validation, as is the case with the **Subject** field. The bottom line is that you do not need to do any extra development work to get validation to work with the `enableModifiedFlag` feature.

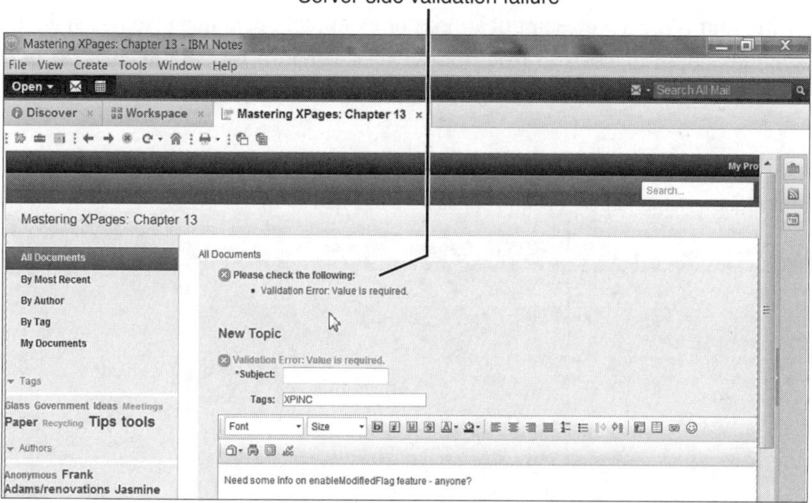

Figure 13.26 enableModifiedFlag and server-side validation

> **TIP**
>
> The enabledModifiedFlag value can also be set at an application-wide level using Themes. An example of this is provided in Chapter 16, "XPages Theming."

Finally, all this behavior is supported, albeit to a slightly lesser extent, on the web. That is, when closing a browser or browser tab window or navigating to another page when a document is dirty, a preemptive dialog box, similar to Figure 13.24, is displayed. The option to instantly save is not available, but accidental data loss is preempted. There are more use cases to support on the Notes client and more control over the window management APIs in that environment, so it was both necessary and feasible to provide a more sophisticated solution there.

Keeping Tabs on Your Client Apps

As fleetingly mentioned earlier, the XPages Discussion app executes within the confines of its own tab window. That is, when a new page is loaded, it replaces the current page in the active window tab instead of opening in a new tab window. This design paradigm emanates from the web where, until recently, some browsers did not support tab windowing well and, more importantly, where it's not possible to reliably identify the particular tab windows that belong to a given application. The upshot of this is that sharing application session data across a multitabbed application is not feasible on the web and, thus, applications are typically constructed for a single window runtime context.

Contrast this with your typical Notes application. For example, opening a discussion document in the regular Notes client discussion (the non-XPages version) by default does so in a new tab window. The default behavior is actually set by a client-wide preference, as shown in Figure 13.27.

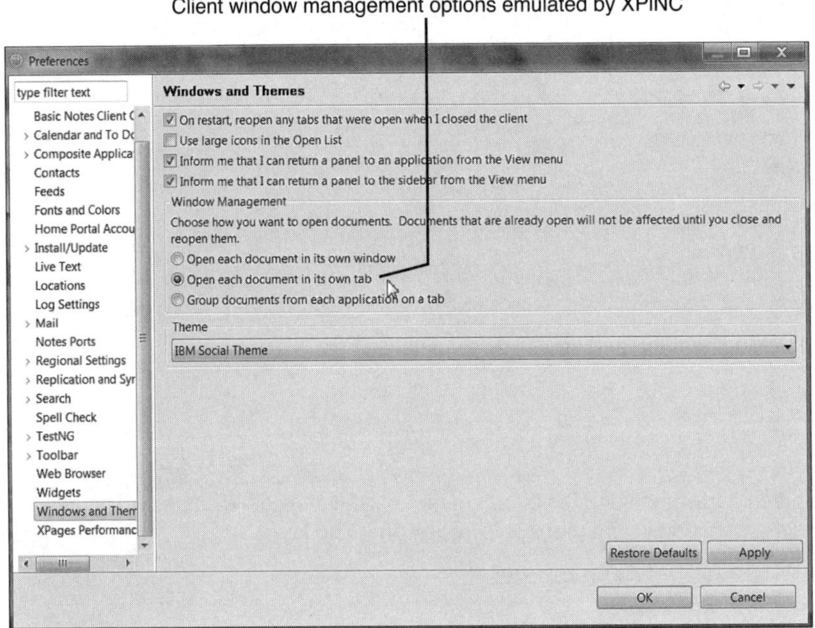

Figure 13.27 Notes window management preferences

It was deemed important for XPages applications to support the client application windowing model, so from Notes version 8.5.2 onward, you can build this tabbing behavior into your client apps. This is achieved by using a combination of some XPages properties and extending the behavior of a preexisting HTML property. Table 13.2 displays a summary.

Table 13.2 Tab Management Property Summary

Container	Property	Value
<xp:link>	target	_self, _blank values determine if link opens in same page on new tab.
<xp:viewPanel>	target	Uses same values to define link behavior for all columns in the view.
<xp:view>	defaultLinkTarget	Uses same values to define default behavior for all links on the page.
xsp.properties	xsp.default.link.target	Uses same values to define default behavior for all links in the application.

A quick glance at the property table indicates that a hierarchical model similar to that used in the implementation of the enableModifiedFlag feature has been applied in this instance. For example, if you set _blank as the value for the target property on a link control, your link target opens in a new tab window. If you want to apply this default behavior to all links on a given XPage, apply this same property at the root <xp:view> level, and it is applied to all links on the page, *except* where individual links contain an alternative setting. You can go a step further and assign default link target behavior for the entire application by assigning the same values in the **Xsp Properties > General** sheet in Designer.

As usual, an example paints a thousand of words. Listing 13.6 shows a link snippet taken from preview **tabManagement.xsp** in the sample NSF for this chapter. Click the link after the containing XPage is loaded in Notes and observe that the profile page is loaded in a new tab window. Then load the same page in a web browser and you see that both the link text and link behavior are different. This is achieved using a little of the knowledge gleaned earlier— namely, applying the target setting only to the rcp renderkit.

Bear in mind that the target="_blank" attribute on a Link control actually works on the web because it is a native HTML feature. That is, a new tab *will* be opened by the browser; however, this does *not* mean that application session data is maintained for the application on the web—it is not! This is why you might want to suppress the target attribute on that platform. The tab behavior for the View control and XPage itself is under the full control of the XPages runtime, so the tab management feature is only honored in the Notes client for those controls.

Listing 13.6 Link Target Property for Notes and Web

```
<xp:link escape="true"
    text="Author Profile - Same Tab"
    value="/authorProfile.xsp">
        <xp:link.rcp
```

```
            target="_blank"
            text="Author Profile - New Tab">
        </xp:link.rcp>
</xp:link>
```

The `target` property on the link control is not new—it's been there since the first release of XPages and is a standard HTML link attribute. The target behavior on the client, however, is new to version 8.5.2, because not only are tab windows supported, but session data can be properly managed across all tabs in any given application. The View control (`<xp:viewPanel>`) acquired a new target property in version 8.5.2 so that the same behaviors could be easily applied to links contained in any of the view columns. It is left to you to temporarily modify the behavior of one or more of the view controls in the Discussion app in the same manner as done previously for the profile link. For example, look in the **byTagViewCc** custom control, which is used by the **byTagViewPanel** XPage in the sample application. Designer provides some special UI assistance with this feature, as shown in Figure 13.28.

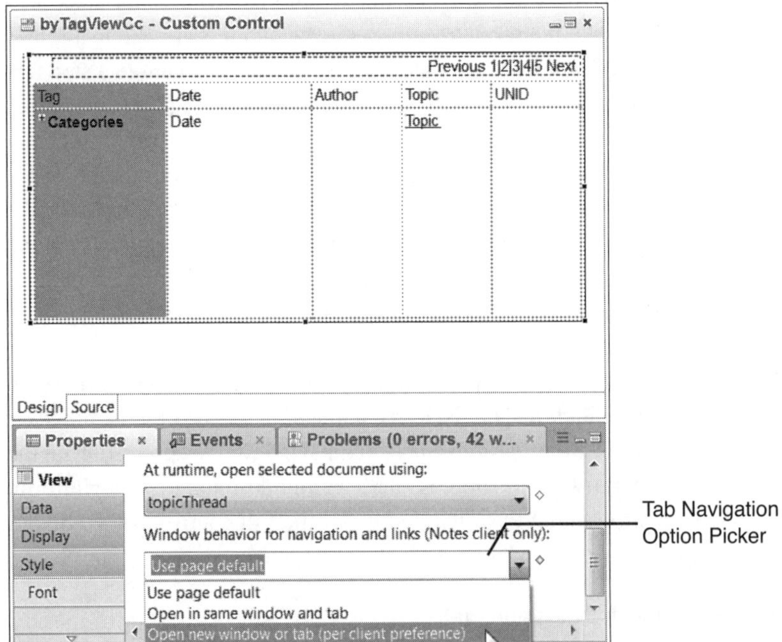

Figure 13.28 View control link behavior options in Designer

This same property is available for the XPage itself on the main XPage property sheet. The **Use page default** option, if selected, means that the View control's behavior is determined by the target setting on the page itself. Finally, to apply the setting as an application-wide preference, you need to make the appropriate selection in the XPages pane in **Xsp Properties Editor**, as shown in Figure 13.29. Note that all properties on this page are written to an `xsp.properties` text file.

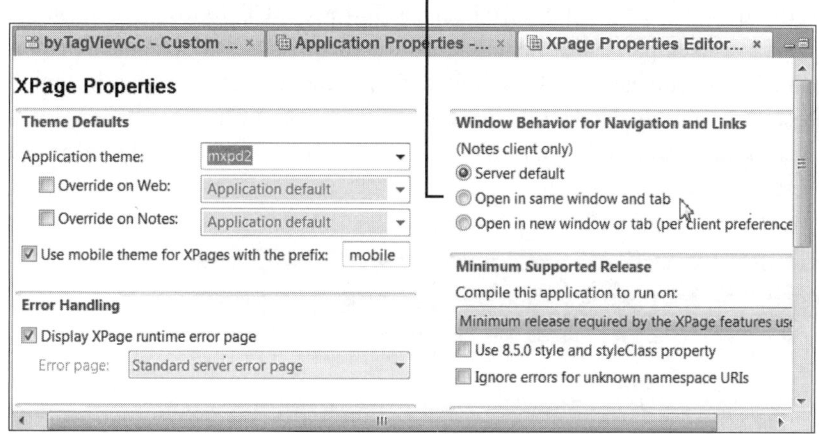

Figure 13.29 Application settings for link and navigation behavior

Notes Links Versus Domino Links

This section is important for anyone providing an XPages interface to an existing application that already contains documents created using the regular Notes client or the traditional Domino web engine. To ensure smooth integration, you need to be aware of incompatibility issues that can arise when older documents of different formats are surfaced in XPages and what best practices you can adopt to deal with such occurrences.

The first issue stems from the fact that there is not one, but two, data formats used in Notes/Domino to manage rich text content. Documents containing rich text fields created in the standard Notes client are stored natively as composite data/compound data (CD) records. Rich content in documents created on the web is stored using MIME format. The MIME acronym stands for Multipurpose Internet Mail Extensions, but, at this point, that description might be considered dated because, today, MIME represents content types in a general context, rather than anything specific to mail per se. MIME can descriptively encapsulate fancy HTML content, such as text fonts and styles, inline images, tables, and attachments, so that content can be reliably stored, retrieved, and exchanged.

In XPages, whether your application is running in the Notes client, on the web, or in both environments, any rich content is always saved in MIME format. Traditional Domino web applications use MIME format to store rich content. Thus, if your XPages application is new (contains no old data of a different format), you will not have any incompatibility issues that result from data format conversions. It might well be, however, that many or all documents in your XPages application were created using the native Notes client and must, therefore, go through a CD-to-MIME conversion when surfaced in XPages. The conversion process can be lossy in certain circumstances, because not all CD objects map identically to equivalent MIME entities.

To make this discussion more practical, you can easily force a CD-to-MIME conversion scenario in your client. For example, using the regular Notes client, create a document that contains three links, namely a document link, view link, and application link, as shown in Figure 13.30. To create these links, use the Notes **Edit > Copy As** main menu when you have a document open, when you have a view active, and when you have a database icon selected in the Notes workspace, respectively.

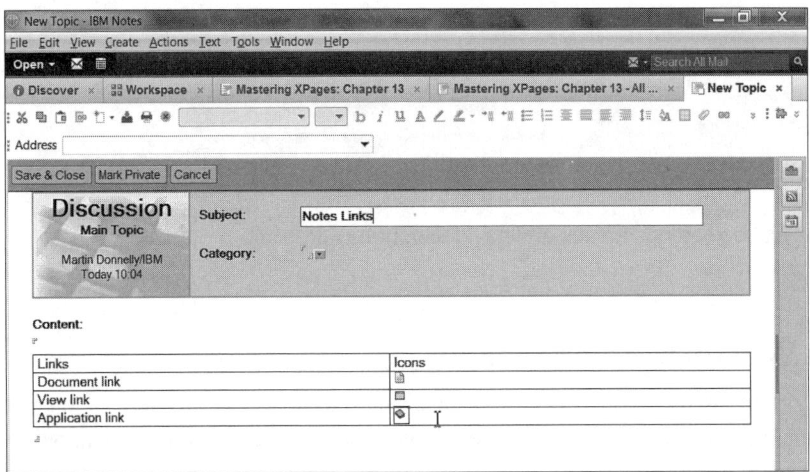

Figure 13.30 Document, View, and Application links in Notes

Change the application's launch options to XPages, restart the application, and open the document. The native Notes document goes through a data format conversion in this process, and the links are correctly displayed for use in XPages, as shown in Figure 13.31. The link icons are provided by the XPages runtime and, if you click these links, you can also observe the correct link behavior.

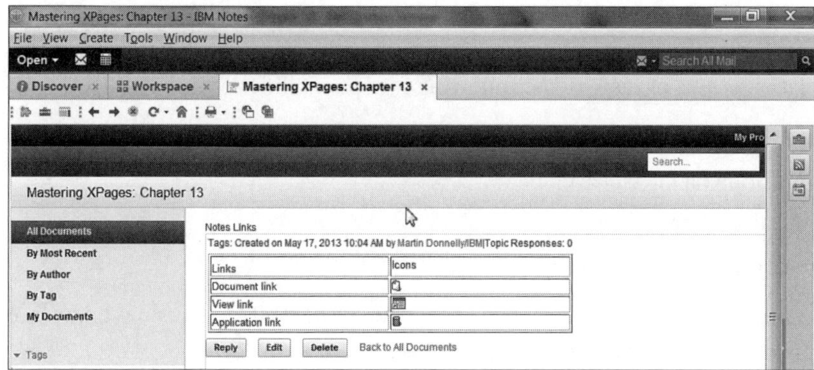

Figure 13.31 Document, View, and Application links in XPiNC

Editing and saving this document in XPages, however, rewrites the rich text content in MIME format. XPages recognizes that a data format conversion is about to take place when the save event occurs and duly warns the user as to the potential loss of formatting, as shown in Figure 13.32.

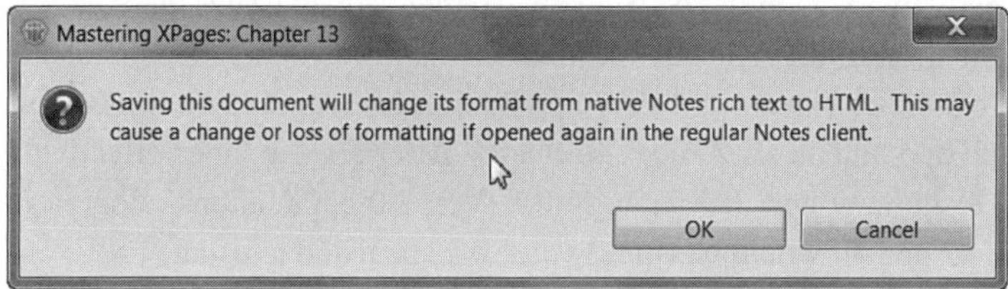

Figure 13.32 Warning dialog on data format Conversion

Until the advent of XPages in the Notes client, MIME format in Notes/Domino was synonymous with the web. In other words, it was assumed that a CD-to-MIME conversion always meant that someone was accessing a native Notes document from the web (as opposed to an XPages user accessing the document in the client). As part of the CD record to MIME entity conversion, Notes links are transformed into Domino links, and these two sets of links are often not compatible. Although one-off conversions tended to work reasonably well, round tripping documents between CD and MIME formats tended to break down. In Notes version 8.5.1, for example, links became unusable in this to-and-from scenario because the image icon used to display a document link could not be resolved on a MIME-converted document that was reopened in the native client. From version 8.5.2 onward, icons are no longer embedded in document links contained in MIME-converted documents to prevent this error.

In Notes 8.5.2, the application developer was granted control over the type of link used when saving rich text content in XPages. If your application is used in a mixed runtime environment, it is a combination of two or more of the following four possibilities:

- XPages application on the web
- XPages application on the Notes client
- Native application Notes client
- Classic Domino web application

In the first two instances, there is no problem because no CD/MIME conversions take place among XPages applications running on different platforms.

If your application runs natively on the Notes client and you have some combination of the first two possibilities, you should not encounter any link issues as long as your links are always saved in XPages as Notes links. Why? Because the XPages runtime can handle converted Notes links both on the web and on the client and, obviously, the Notes client can handle its own links.

If you have a traditional Domino web application and you have some combination of the first two possibilities, you should not encounter any broken links as long as your links are stored in Domino format when saved using XPages. Again, this is because the XPages runtime can handle Domino links when running on the client. When running XPages on the web, the Domino links are actually handled directly by the Domino web engine, so there are no issues there.

If you have some combination of all four possibilities, this is problematic. This is also a highly unusual scenario. For example, why would your application be available on the web as both a traditional Domino web app and as an XPages web app? After all, the latter effectively *replaced* the former as part of the new app-dev strategy for Web 2.0 applications adopted in V8.5. A direct combination of #2 and #4 would be equally problematical and unusual.

Thus, the vast majority of link compatibility issues can be resolved by simply choosing the link format that is most appropriate to your mix of runtime environments. You can do this at both the document data source level (for any given document that you save links in a particular format) and as an application-wide preference. The latter is more likely to be the more popular setting. Figure 13.33 shows how to set the `saveLinkAs` property on the document data source via the **All Properties** sheet in Designer.

The application-wide link format preference is stored in the `xsp.properties` file, and you can access it in Designer via **Xsp Properties > Page Generation > Rich Text Options**, as shown in Figure 13.34. You can view the raw properties file directly via the **Source** tab—observe that the web format option sets the following `xsp.save.links=UseWeb` entry. This specifies the default link behavior for the application as a whole. If nothing is specified here or on the relevant document data sources, the Notes link format is assumed by default. Be aware that the default runtime behavior in Notes 8.5.1 was to use web links.

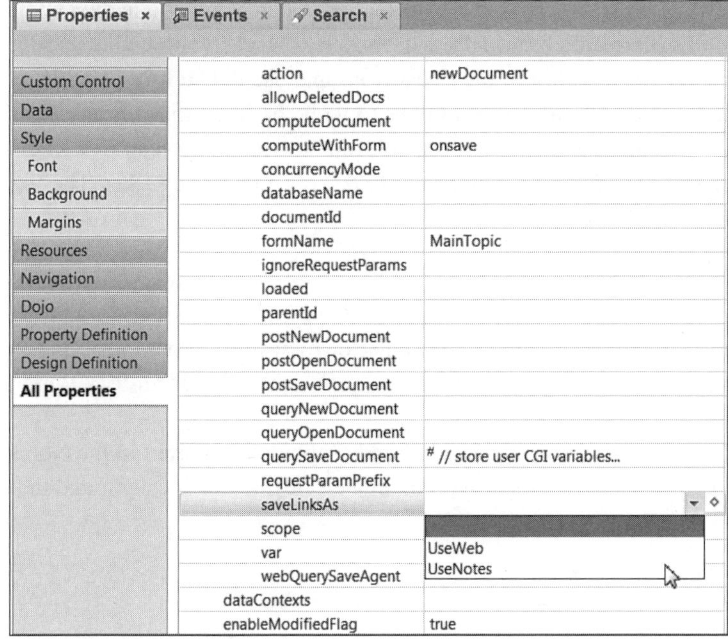

Figure 13.33 saveLinkAs property on Domino Document data source

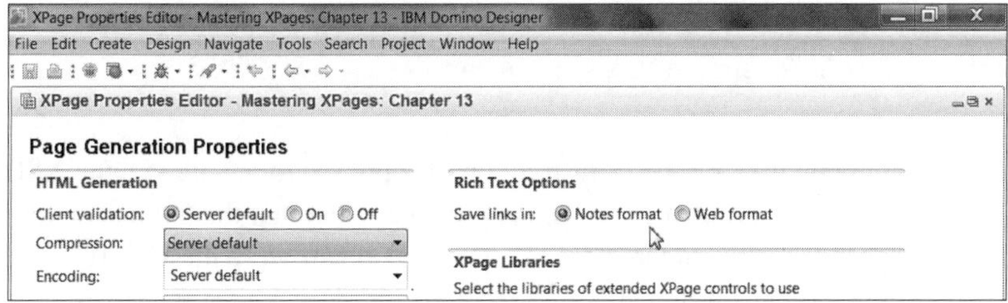

Figure 13.34 xsp.properties preference setting for link format

Some XPiNC Debugging Tips

At this point, it should be clear that you can build a lot of cool stuff using XPages in the Notes client. It's probably appropriate, therefore, at this juncture to impart some tips on what to do when you're getting hot under the collar trying to build all that cool stuff! This section provides miscellaneous tips and tricks to employ when your code is not fully cooperating with your ideas.

The first step is knowing where to look for information when your application malfunctions. If your application fails to load or loads with an error stack, you should inspect some logs clues as to what went wrong. Start in the client itself and use the **Help > Support > View Log** or **Help > Support > View Trace** menu options to view the latest logs for any error information that may be related to the problem. If nothing relevant is evident, you can look in the `IBM_TECHNICAL_SUPPORT` folder under your Notes data folder for XPages log files. The log file names of interest to you are of the form:

```
xpages_yyyy_mm_dd@hh_mm_ss.log
```

If the stack information shown in the logs doesn't help you resolve the issue, it might be useful if you need to revert to a technical support specialist or to search the various XPages forums on the web—refer to Appendix C, "Useful XPages Sites on the Net," for a list of great online resources.

Any client side JavaScript errors that occur in your code should be reported in the Notes status bar. For example, in Figure 13.35, a simple typo in an alert instruction is caught and displayed at runtime.

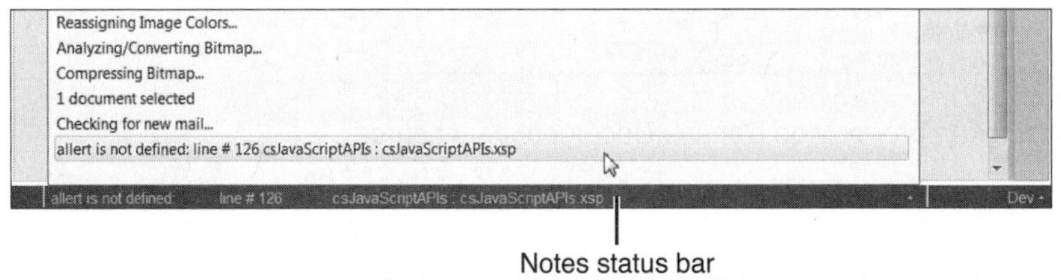

Figure 13.35 Client-side JavaScript error in Notes status bar

This command shows the faulty `allert()` instruction (as opposed to `alert()`), the XSP page on which it is located, and line number in the rendered page. Note that this is not the line number in the source XPage but in the rendered HTML page. You can view the HTML page source using the XPages client toolbar, as shown in Figure 13.36.

Apart from the standard navigation and print functions, the toolbar has some handy utilities to aid with debugging. In particular, the **Clear Private Data** button is handy in overcoming stubbornly cached resources (such as CSS or JavaScript) that have been updated in the application design and need to be replaced in the client browser.

View Page Source is handy when you need to see the HTML markup that has been generated for your XPage, and **View Browser Configuration** may also help you tweak some application settings that affect caching, character sets handling, and so forth—although it is strongly suggested that you know exactly what you're doing before you venture into this domain. Both options are only displayed when Domino Designer has been included as part of the Notes client installation and thus are not available to "mere mortals"!

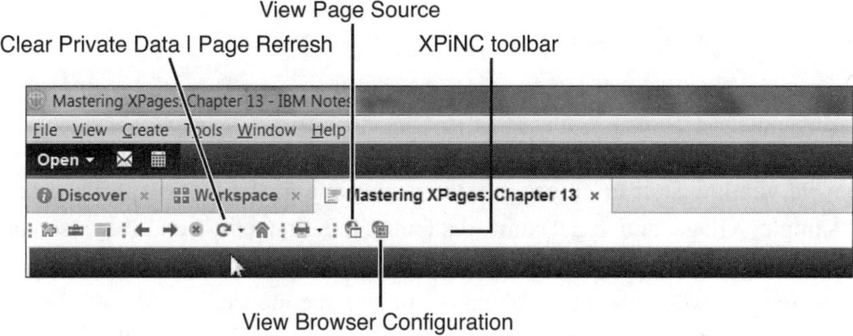

Figure 13.36 XPages client toolbar

For Server-Side JavaScript debugging, the `print()` and `_dump()` utility functions provided by the XPages runtime can help you out by simply displaying the real value of variables and other objects. On the Domino server, the output of these commands is obviously directed to the server console, but you might well wonder where the client console is. The answer is that the Notes client console is turned off by default and needs to be explicitly invoked when the client starts up. This can be achieved by adding `-RPARAMS -console` to your startup command. In a Windows environment, your revised desktop target properties might read like this:

```
"C:\Notes\notes.exe" "=C:\Notes\notes.ini" -RPARAMS -console
```

To see how this works, create an XPage in Designer based on the markup shown in Listing 13.7 and restart the Notes client as previously shown. For your convenience, **printConsole.xsp** in the sample application contains the listed code.

Listing 13.7 Client Print-to-Console Debugging Sample

```
<?xml version="1.0" encoding="UTF-8"?>
<xp:view xmlns:xp="http://www.ibm.com/xsp/core">
    <xp:inputText id="inputText1" password="true">
        <xp:eventHandler
            event="onblur"
            submit="true"
            refreshMode="complete">
            <xp:this.action><![CDATA[#{javascript:
                var c1 = getComponent("inputText1");
                var c2 = getComponent("inputText2");
                var hiddenText = c1.getValue();
                print (hiddenText);
                c2.setValue(hiddenText);
            }]]></xp:this.action>
        </xp:eventHandler>
```

```
    </xp:inputText>
    <xp:inputText id="inputText2">
    </xp:inputText>
</xp:view>
```

Observe a console window start up at roughly the same time as the Notes splash screen appears. Open the sample XPage and type some data into the first edit box. Because the `password="true"` property has been applied to this control, any text entered is obscured as you type. Then, move focus to the next edit box by tabbing or clicking the mouse.

As you can see, the "hidden" text content is displayed in the adjoining field, in the console, and in the trace window (**Help > Support > View Trace**). Note that `print()` and `_dump()` output will always appear in the view trace log regardless of whether the `-RPARAMS -console` is used. It's also interesting to see that hidden input is only as hidden as the application developer wants it to be. Chapter 21, "Security," covers trusting XPages code created by other people in more depth.

The final tip shows how to integrate Firebug Lite into the embedded XULRunner-based browser component. Many web developers will no doubt be familiar with the Mozilla Firebug add-on for the Firefox browser and its various tools for inspecting, debugging, and editing the DOM, CSS, JavaScript, and so on. Some of these tools are dependent on Firefox-specific features, but the Lite version is more generic and runs successfully within Notes. To enable Firebug Lite, all you need to do is to include one JavaScript resource in your XPage. This can be done by entering the tag (as shown in Listing 13.8) directly into the XPages source or by adding the `src` portion of the tag as the link value for a JavaScript library resource in the Designer **Resources** property sheet. If pasting the tags manually, look for a `<xp:this.resources>` section in the XPage and paste the script tag within that section. If no such section exists, surround the markup shown in Listing 13.8 with the `<xp:this.resources> </xp:this.resources>` tags and paste this block anywhere on the page.

Listing 13.8 Firebug Lite Tag for XPiNC Applications

```
<xp:script
    src="http:// getfirebug.com/firebug-lite.js" clientSide="true">
</xp:script>
```

Figure 13.37 shows how this renders using the Discussion application as an example. After an XPage with Firebug Lite enabled is rendered, you can use function key **F12** to bring up and dismiss the debugger window. (This is true on Windows; other platforms may have different key bindings.) Alternatively, for Notes/Domino 8.5.3 UP1 onward, there is a Firebug Lite control in the **Extension Library** drawer of the control palette, and this can be simply dragged and dropped on to any XPage to achieve the same outcome.

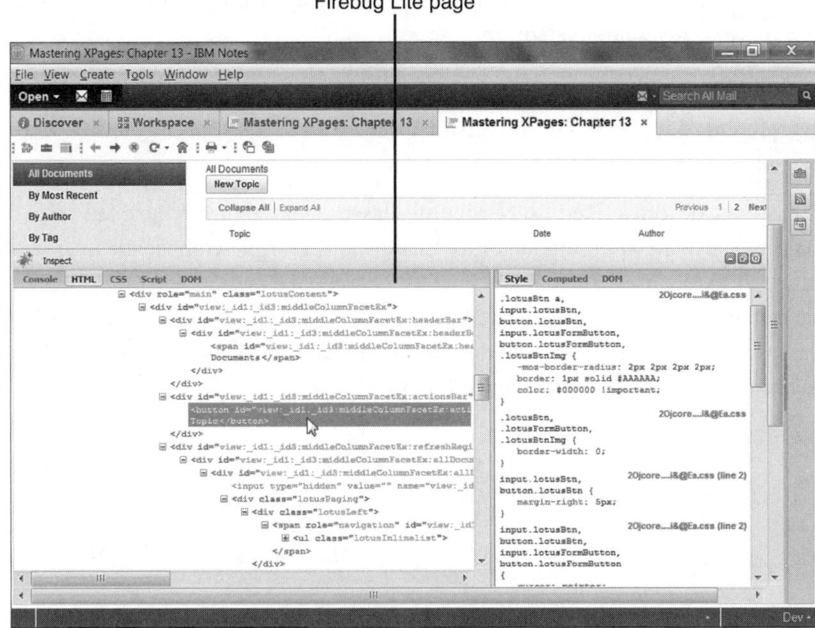

Figure 13.37 Firebug Lite running in XPiNC

Optimizing XPages for Notes

As previously discussed, opening the first XPages application in a Notes session can take a number of seconds, even for a local application. Profiling the startup code showed that the bulk of the processing time was spent loading the XPages runtime Java classes, followed by the Java classes needed by the application itself. Remember that all your XPages and custom controls end up as Java classes at runtime and thus must be loaded by the Java classloader for the page to be run. The runtime class count alone amounted to 465 objects in Notes V853. Thus the burden of loading several hundred Java classes when a user first opens an XPiNC application became the immediate performance challenge to resolve on the road to delivering a responsive user experience.

The initial remedy was introduced in V8.5.3, with two new NOTES.INI variables that enabled XPages Java classes to be preloaded when the Notes client started up. These variables took the following form:

```
XPagesPreload=1
XPagesPreloadDB=db.nsf/xpage.xsp,server!!remoteDb.nsf/somePage.xsp
```

When set to 1, the `XPagesPreload` variable causes the XPages Java *runtime* classes to load. Two distinct groups of classes are loaded:

- Java classes from the XPages runtime plug-ins (`com.ibm.xsp.core` and so on)
- Java classes referenced in the `*-faces-config.xml` files in the core plug-ins (`core-faces-config.xml`, `extsn-faces-config.xml`, and so on)

The first group is loaded from a fixed list of runtime classes, not only from the `core com.ibm.xsp.*` plug-ins, but also from common utility classes, JavaScript wrapper classes, and underlying JSF runtime classes.

In the second instance, all the `faces-config.xml` files in the following core plug-ins are read, and the classes declared inside them are then loaded in a batch. These mostly consist of XPages control renderers, data sources, and complex types.

- `com.ibm.xsp.core`
- `com.ibm.xsp.extsn`
- `com.ibm.xsp.designer`
- `com.ibm.xsp.domino`
- `com.ibm.xsp.rcp`

Note that preload works on both the Notes client and Domino server (`com.ibm.xsp.rcp` is a Notes client-only plug-in, however) and that both groups of classes are loaded simultaneously on separate threads. Also, unless these preload variables are set in NOTES.INI, no XPages class loading of any description is performed before the first XPages application is opened in a given client or server session.

Although the `XPagesPreload` variable is concerned with loading critical pieces of the core runtime platform, the `XPagesPreloadDB` is concerned with the application layer. The `XPagesPreloadDB` variable points to one or more NSF applications, which, as shown in the sample at the beginning of this section, can be local to the client or server or on a remote server. The XPages .xsp filename is optional.

In the normal course of events, when an end user from a browser loads an XPages application, the XPages runtime loads the NSF as a virtual web application module. The concept behind preloading is to load the web application module into memory at startup time in the same way it would occur normally if a real user had submitted an actual application load request. Thus, the XPages runtime fakes a real request for each argument in the `XPagesPreloadDB` comma-separated list. This means that an XPages URL is constructed for each argument and sent to the web application server. The web application server loads the application module, caches it, and renders back markup if an XPages file is specified. The XPages runtime then simply throws away the response from the web application server, but the module has been loaded into memory and will be available instantly for the next real user request.

In Notes 9.0 SE, the preload feature was promoted from its lowly INI variable status to that of official Notes preference. If you bring up the preferences dialog (**File > Preferences**) you will see a newly added **XPages Performance** page, as shown in Figure 13.38.

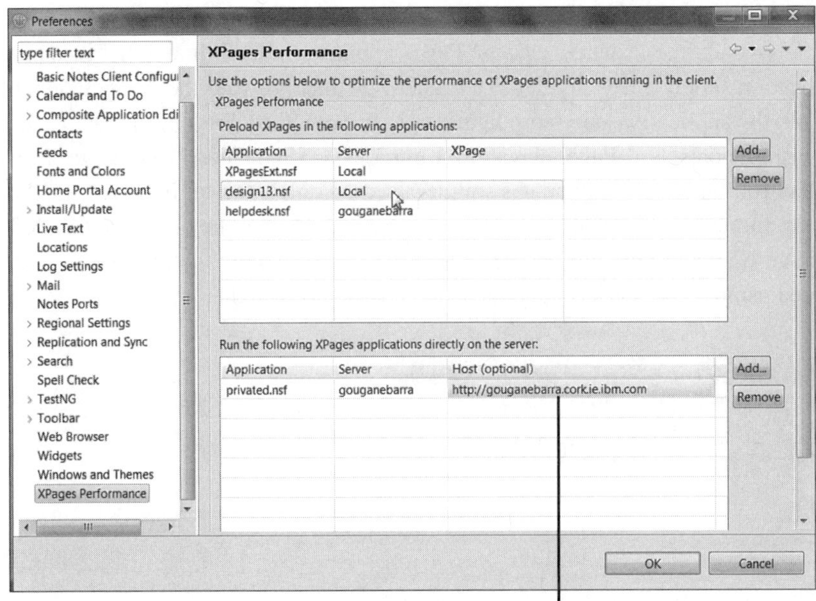

Figure 13.38 Setting XPages Performance Preferences in Notes 9

Applications can be added to or removed from the preload list directly via the UI, assuming the user has sufficient privilege to update Notes preferences. Alternatively, such preferences can be provisioned by policy just like any other Notes preference. Any preload applications present in NOTES.INI will not appear in the preference dialog, but all such requests will continue to be honored by the XPages runtime on client startup. No administrative UI exists to preload XPages web apps on the Domino server, so the NOTES.INI declarations continue to be the modus operandi in that context. And on the subject of preloading web apps on the server, you should set default access in the ACL to read level at a minimum for applications you plan to preload (assuming that is compatible with your security policy). This is to ensure that any XPages nominated for preloading can be accessed and read when the server starts up—otherwise preload will fail.

Although the preload options certainly help address application startup performance in general, not all use cases are accounted for as yet. For instance, what if you need to run many instances of the same application on an on-going basis? A service engineer may, for example, maintain a site management application on a separate-instance-per-customer basis. It doesn't make sense to constantly manage a long list of applications for preloading purposes. A more efficient solution is needed.

Single Copy XPages Design Meets Preload

Single Copy XPages Design (SCXD) was introduced in V8.5.2 to enable XPages design resources to be shared by different runtime instances of an XPages application. Each individual instance of a particular application simply needs to refer to a master NSF that provides the XPages design resources. As a result, the applications are more lightweight because they don't need to carry the extra bloat of the custom controls, XPages, JavaScript libraries, CSS resources, and so forth. It also makes the task of rolling out design updates simpler because only a master NSF needs to be updated and not a multitude of individual application instances. Note that the nominated SCXD application must be an NSF and *not* an NTF file. Figure 13.39 shows how the reference to the SCXD NSF is created using the XPages Properties panel in Domino Designer.

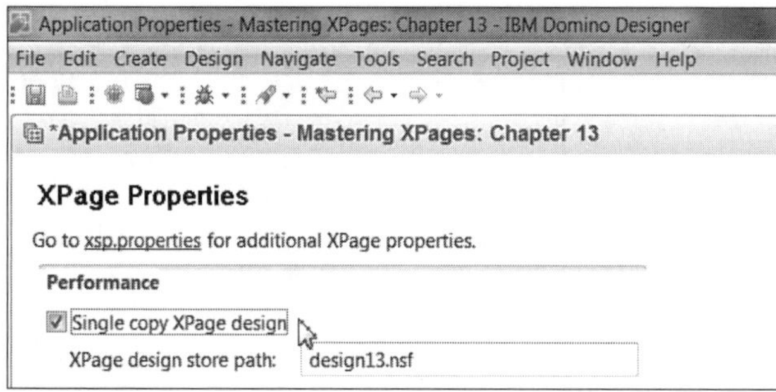

Figure 13.39 Setting the Single Copy XPage Design Property in Domino Designer 9.0

When building the 9.0 release, it was realized that this SXCD feature could benefit XPiNC when running applications on a remote server. How? Because if all the design resources could be loaded from a local design-only application, then that amounts to one less network transaction for each resource loaded...and network transactions between Notes and the remote server are the single biggest factors affecting XPiNC performance. Unfortunately, in XPiNC for 8.5.2 and 8.5.3, an SCXD reference contained in a remote application was resolved on the same remote server. That is, if no server reference were contained in the SXCD path, the runtime sought to resolve the master design NSF on the same server on which the remote application resided. Experiments showed that significant performance improvements were achieved by using a *local* SCXD application, so the decision was taken to modify the SXCD pattern for remote XPiNC applications, as follows:

1. Attempt to resolve simple SCXD NSF references on the local client first.
2. If no local copy is found, attempt to locate the master NSF on the remote server.

3. If no server copy is found, revert to the application itself to load the design resources.
4. If you need to use a remote SXCD NSF, provide an explicit server reference, like this:

```
serverName!!scxdDb.nsf
```

Creating a design-only copy of an application to serve as the SCXD NSF is easy. Simply select **File > Application > New Copy**, and then choose the **Application design only** option from the dialog, as shown in Figure 13.40.

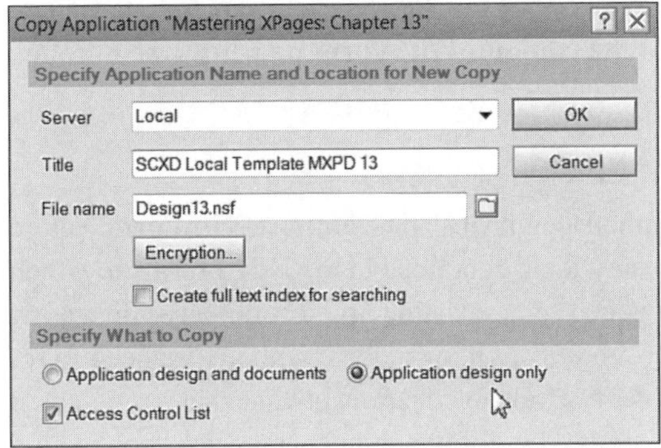

Figure 13.40 Creating a design-only NSF for use as a Single Copy XPage Design application

If you have access to a remote server, it would be a worthwhile exercise for you to experiment with this feature in Notes 9. You could perform the following exercise using the **Chp13ed2.nsf** sample application.

1. Open **Chp13ed2.nsf** in Domino Designer on the remote server.
2. Create a local design-only copy, **design13.nsf**, using **File > Application > New Copy**.
3. Open in **design13.nsf** Designer and change its theme from **oneuiv2_1_blue** to **oneuiv2_1_green (Application Configuration > Xsp Properties > General)** and save these settings.
4. Back in **Chp13ed2.nsf** set its SXCD property to **design13.nsf**.
5. Add to **design13.nsf** to the list of preload applications for the Notes client using **File > Preferences > XPages Performance** (select **main.xsp** as the XPage to preload).
6. Shutdown Designer (and Notes if running) and launch a new instance of Notes.
7. Open **Chp13ed2.nsf** in Notes on the remote server.

When complete, you should notice two things. First, the application has opened faster. Second, the application looks different. The latter is a visual proof point that the design resources are loaded from the local design-only NSF—remember that you set its theme to **oneuiv2_1_green**. If you view the source of the page, you can see resource references pointing to like this:

```
<img src="/xsp/design13.nsf/xpPostUnread.gif" ...>
```

The double-whammy here is that the Java classes are preloaded from the design-only application upon Notes startup and then the web resources (JavaScript, CSS, and so on) are fetched locally when the application is run. Also, only the SCXD application needs to be preloaded, and not each individual application.

There is one other important benefit that arises when this SCXD/Preload pattern is applied on XPiNC, and this pertains to the behavior of the **computeWithForm** property when dealing with Domino documents.

A Second Look at computeWithForm for XPiNC

As described in Chapter 7, "Working with Domino Documents," the **computeWithForm** feature can be used by XPages applications to execute any logic contained in the Notes forms to which an XPages is bound. Thus, where XPages are added to an existing application, any application logic already in place can be executed without modification, or indeed, without the need to re-create the same logic in XPages. This is undoubtedly a valuable feature, but one that has potential performance implications and thus should not simply by glibly applied across your application design.

The reason for this is that the form *and all its resources must be loaded* for **compute WithForm** to execute. These resources include any subforms, shared fields, background bitmaps, and so forth. Bearing in mind that XPages uses forms purely as a metadata document schema, a lot of the content of the traditional Notes form is often irrelevant to XPages. If you compute forms that happen to also contain many other resources, then, when running this application on a remote server, the form and all its constituent parts must be copied from the remote server to the local Notes web container for processing. Should the form contain heavyweight objects, the sheer network overhead imposed on the application to open or update a document can be a performance nightmare.

This performance issue can be demonstrated outside of XPages by simply using a Java agent to reproduce the use case. Listing 13.9 shows a Java agent that creates a new document, computes its form, and saves the document.

Listing 13.9 Java Agent Exercising computeWithForm in a Local and Remote Scenario

```
import lotus.domino.*;

public class JavaAgent extends AgentBase {

    public void NotesMain() {

        try {
```

```
            Session session = getSession();
            AgentContext agentContext = session.getAgentContext();

            String server = ""; // Run blank (local) and with servername
            Database app = session.getDatabase(server, "testApp");
            Document doc = app.createDocument();
            doc.replaceItemValue("Form", "MainTopic");
            doc.replaceItemValue("Subject", "computeWithForm operation)");
            doc.replaceItemValue("Categories", "Performance");
            doc.replaceItemValue("Body", "Text ... ...");
            // log time before computeWithForm operation
            long startTs = System.currentTimeMillis();
            if (doc.computeWithForm(false, false)) {
                 // log time after computeWithForm operation
                 String testType = (server.equals("")) ?
                    "local: " : "remote: ";
                 long endTs = System.currentTimeMillis();
                 System.out.println(testType +
                    Long.toString(endTs - startTs) +
                        " millisecs (local)");
                 doc.save(true, true);
                 System.out.println("document saved");
            }

        } catch (Exception e) {
            e.printStackTrace();
        }
    }
}
```

This agent was run on a real-world application containing large forms, first using a local instance, and then rerun using a remote server across a high-latency network. The results, as shown in Figure 13.41 were startling. A transaction that completed in 15 milliseconds locally took a whopping 50,484 milliseconds when running remotely...the difference is off the scale.

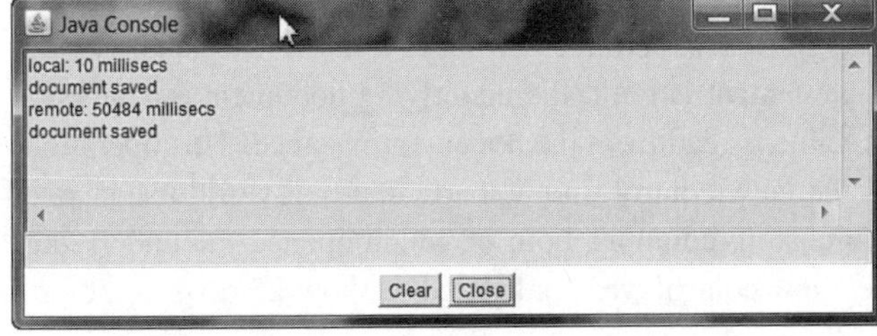

Figure 13.41 Results of a computeWithForm performance experiment

The good news from 9.0 onward is that when the SCXD feature is applied on XPiNC, then with a local design copy of the application in place, the form is loaded from the local NSF—thus avoiding the network transaction and a potentially significant download. If you are not using Notes 9 or the SXCD XPiNC pattern described here, then you would be well advised to look at your application's usage of the **computeWithForm** feature. If the forms referenced are lightweight in nature, you probably have no issue to deal with because performance should not be noticeably impacted. However, if the forms involved contain heavyweight objects, it would be worth considering the creation of new forms for XPages that simply serve as lightweight document data schemas. Even if you need to re-create some application logic in XPages, the performance benefit may be worth the extra effort.

Other Performance Gotchas

You will notice that a big focus area for XPiNC performance improvements so far have concentrated on the reduction of network transactions. The runtime has been enhanced to avoid costly network chit-chat where possible, but now it's your turn. As an application developer you should also look at the design of your application through the same lens. Does your application code create unnecessary network I/O? The answer may not be gapingly obvious because some coding practices that appear to work fine when running on the web then perform poorly when that application runs in remote mode on the Notes client. One common bad practice appears again and again in situations in which customers report a performance issue in XPiNC. The use case pertains to customizing views and can be explained as follows.

XPages makes it easy to access and display view data using container controls such as the View panel, Repeat control, Data Table, or DataView. These controls attach to a Domino view via a data source and display its content by iterating though the view entries, accessing the row data, and formatting it for display according to various design-time parameters. The controls offer the powerful capability of adding customized view columns to the output, which often transform back-end view data or compute new values based on Domino view data for display purposes. However, there are efficient and inefficient ways of customizing view column data. The egregious offender is the column value computation that uses Server Side JavaScript code to do something like this:

```
return tagRow.getDocument().getItemValueString("Abstract");
```

Here, `tagRow` is the sample variable name parameter on the container control (that is, the name assigned to the `var` property) that gives access to the current row in the view as it is read and rendered at runtime. When the page content is built, the underlying document for the current view entry is opened, and an item value is read from the document instance. This operation is repeated for every row displayed in the view control. In one particular real-world instance, a View control was configured with two custom columns, both of which opened the underlying document to extract item data, and the View control was configured to show 25 rows at a time.

Thus, in one swoop, 50 extra and expensive network transactions had to be carried out for this page when this NSF was run as a remote application on the Notes client. Ouch!

When custom columns are required, it is always best to work with columns that are already defined in the back-end Domino view and then retrieve the column content for custom computation using either the `getColumnValue()` API call on the `NotesXspViewEntry` JavaScript class or an EL expression. If the required column does not exist in the back-end Domino view, add it if you have sufficient design privilege, but do not open the underlying document to read the item and then have this bad practice repeated iteratively for every view entry to be displayed.

XPages RunOnServer

One final option is available that may be useful if a particular application runs slowly in remote mode and where it is not practical to apply the aforementioned XPiNC optimizations. This feature, known as XPiNC Run On Server, was introduced in Notes 9.0 and enables the application to be run on the server and simply render inside the XPages Notes container. A number of conditions must be met for this option to be feasible, namely:

1. The server must be running the HTTP task.
2. The user must have a Notes account in place to connect to the Domino http server.
3. The Notes launch properties for the remote app must have the Run On Server option selected.
4. A Notes preference must identify the HTTP server hostname if different to the Notes server name.

For the first point, it is important to understand that no http communication takes place between the Notes client and Domino server when remote XPages applications run in the client. Forgetting about the Run On Server feature for a moment and just focusing on native XPiNC, all HTTP communication takes place between the Notes embedded browser (XULRunner) and the embedded web container. When the application is remote, data and resources are fetched from the server by the XPages runtime using Notes APIs. If your XPages environment includes a Domino server, you can prove this point to yourself by shutting down the http task on the server, and then, in the client, open a remote XPages application residing on that same server and watch it run. The Run On Server feature however reverts to the simple web model—it runs on the Domino server over HTTP, and thus requires XPages to be installed on the server and to have the HTTP task running. If you are supporting web access to your applications, however, then this condition is already in place.

The second point pertains to the Notes accounts framework. Notes accounts are used to provide the information necessary to connect to server-based services. You may already have some Notes accounts defined on your local client—select the **File > Preferences > Accounts** menu to view the list. To run XPages on the server, you need to have an http account in place.

This account stores the user authentication information needed to connect automatically to the remote server. That is, any http requests to the nominated server will have the authentication information automatically passed to the server by the Notes embedded browser. The goal here is that Notes users should not be reprompted for their Internet credentials when using the XPiNC Run On Server feature, as long as the Notes account for that server is properly set up. Figure 13.42 shows a sample HTTP account set up to support XPiNC Run On Server.

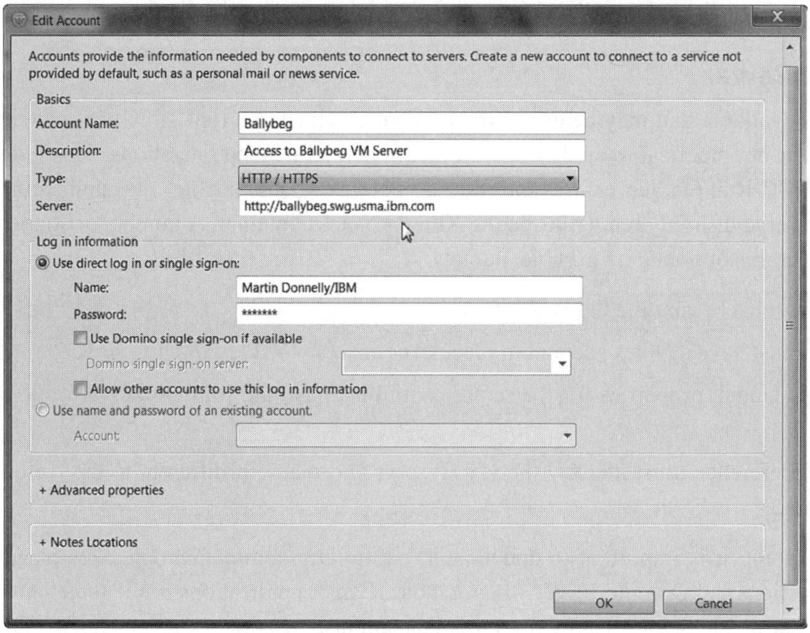

Figure 13.42 Notes HTTP Account Details

A Notes account can use different means of authentication with Domino. Domino single sign-on (SSO) if enabled supports Notes users automatically authenticating with the web container on that server. The details of configuring SSO are out of the scope of this chapter, but suffice to say that the Notes account framework with the embedded browsers can automatically pass the required LPTA tokens to Domino and silently authenticate with the web server. This facilitates a more seamless user experience, uninterrupted with extra login prompts. It is also possible to provide basic authentication information in the account, as in the user's Domino Internet user name and password. Accounts can be created using this dialog as long as the user has sufficient permission to update the account preferences locally, or more commonly, the account details can be provisioned down to the client from the server and can appear in the dialog as read-only entries.

The accounts framework is a Notes feature leveraged by XPages to support Run On Server, and it is important to verify that the account is functional before proceeding any further. This can and should be done independently of XPages. Take the server details entered in your account information and enter them into the Notes URL address bar along with any other details needed to complete a valid URL. This can be an XPages URL or a traditional Domino web URL. At the same time, do the same thing in a fresh instance of a standalone web browser. If your account details are set up correctly, the URL should be resolved without an authentication challenge in Notes, whereas you should be prompted for a username and password in the standalone browser. This exercise assumes that the NSF in question does *not* permit anonymous access and that you have ACL access to the application. Figure 13.43 shows a sample URL entered in the Notes URL address bar and the application loading correctly in the Notes embedded browser.

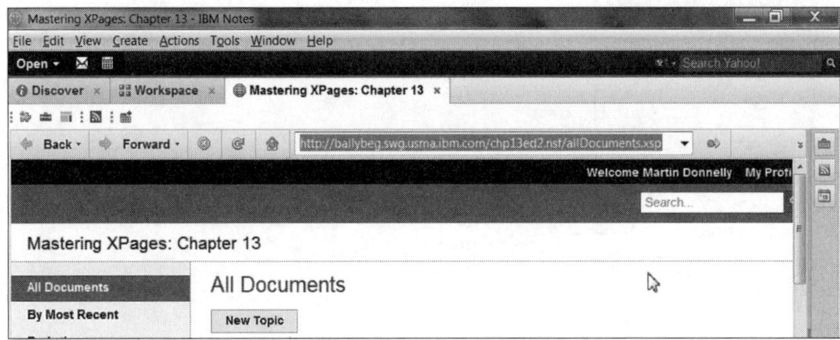

Figure 13.43 Testing a Notes Account via the Notes address bar

If your Notes account is not set up correctly, then you will be prompted for login details, as shown in Figure 13.44. One reason that this can occur is if using SSO that the server name saved in the account does not exactly match the server name saved in the Domino Web SSO document stored on the server. They must match exactly. For example, you cannot use a fully qualified server name in the Domino SSO configuration document and then use an abbreviated server name in the Notes account. Also, if a hostname is provided in the Run On Server preferences page shown previously in Figure 13.38, this must match the server name provided in the Notes account used to support running the application on the server.

After you verify that the Notes/Domino configuration is correctly in place, you can set up the XPages details. In Notes 9.0, the remote XPages application has a new launch parameter that is used to indicate whether the application should be executed in the Notes client (the default) or on the Domino http server. This option can be selected via Domino Designer or in the Notes client. With the former, a check box option is available on the **Launch** tab in the **Application Properties** panel, whereas the latter uses a new option on the **Launch** tab of the Notes infobox, as shown in Figure 13.45

Figure 13.44 Domino Login page displayed when authentication fails

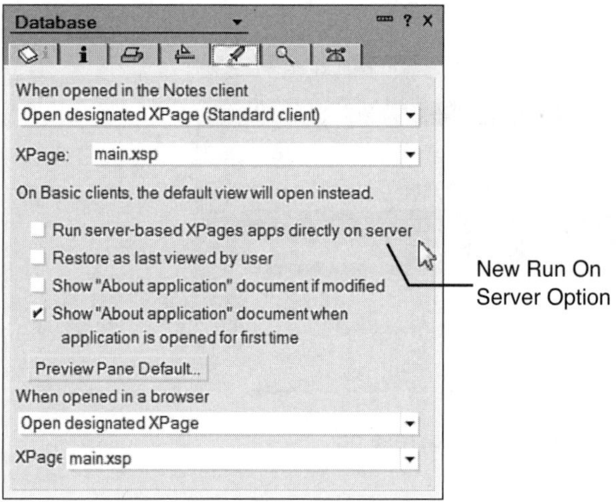

Figure 13.45 The XPiNC Run On Server Infobox option

When this option is set, a **RunOnServer** URL parameter is passed through to the XPages runtime when the application is opened in the Notes client. On seeing this parameter, XPages then creates a Domino HTTP URL from the Notes launch URL and sends it directly to the Domino server. Identifying the Domino server to which to send the request is the key part of the process. By default, XPages will use the server name on the Notes launch URL, which is normally the short name (for example simply "ballybeg" in Figure 13.42). It is a common practice, however, for administrators to map other hostnames to the Domino server using the website configuration document. Thus if a hostname such as xpages.ibm.com has been mapped to the Domino server, this needs to be accounted for when transforming the Domino HTTP URL. Otherwise, the computed HTTP request will fail.

Because it is not possible for the XPages runtime to reliably derive a mapped hostname, it needs a hint as to what it is. At this point you should refer to the **XPages Performance**

Preference dialog shown in Figure 13.38. The bottom panel of the dialog lists the XPages applications selected to run on the server and includes the option to specify an optional hostname. Wherever an optional hostname is specified, it is substituted for the Domino server name in the final computed HTTP URL. Effectively, this is a local override of the default Domino server name. Thus, a Notes URL that starts out like this:

```
notes://gouganebarra/privated.nsf/main.xsp?OpenXPage&runOnServer
```

is converted to a simple Domino web URL if no alternative hostname is provided, like so:

```
http://gouganebarra/privated.nsf/main.xsp?xspRunningContext=Notes
```

or to this, when an optional hostname preference is specified:

```
http://xpages.ibm.com/privated.nsf/main.xsp?xspRunningContext=Notes
```

Earlier in the chapter the topic of renderkits was discussed, and you saw how to customize XPages code for the Notes client using renderkit-specific properties. What is interesting to note at this juncture is that although an XPages application using the Run On Server feature appears to be running in Notes, it is actually running on the server. Therefore, the renderkit in use is no longer RCP but is actually the web HTML renderkit. If your application contains hide/show logic based on RCP renderkit properties, it may not function properly in this mode. There are alternative coding means at your disposal to account for Notes applications running in this remote mode. You can notice in the computed URLs shown here that an `xspRunningContext=Notes` parameter is provided to the Domino server when a Notes application is redirected. Thus, the XPages runtime on the server knows that Notes is the client when it sees this running context value and can adapt its behavior accordingly in terms of what it serves up.

Listing 13.10 is an interesting example of how you can programmatically detect the runtime platform, using three different mechanisms, namely the renderkit-specific properties logic, the `@ClientType()` function, and `SSJS context.isRunningContext("Notes")` API. This code is contained in **whatPlatform.xsp** in the sample application for this chapter.

Listing 13.10 Logic to Compute the Runtime Platform

```
<xp:table>
     <xp:tr>
          <xp:td>
               <xp:label id="label5" value="Logic Method"
                    style="font-weight:bold"></xp:label>
          </xp:td><xp:td>
               <xp:label value="Platform Id" id="label4"
                    style="font-weight:bold"></xp:label>
          </xp:td>
     </xp:tr><xp:tr>
          <xp:td>
```

```
            <xp:label id="label1"
                value="RenderKit Properties ">
            </xp:label>
        </xp:td><xp:td>
            <xp:text escape="true" id="computedField1">
                <xp:this.value>
                    <![CDATA[#{javascript:return "Web"}]]>
                </xp:this.value>
                <xp:text.rcp>
                <xp:this.value>
                    <![CDATA[#{javascript:return "Notes"}]]>
                </xp:this.value>
                </xp:text.rcp>
            </xp:text>
            </xp:td>
        </xp:tr><xp:tr>
            <xp:td>
                <xp:label value="@ClientType()" id="label2">
                </xp:label>
            </xp:td><xp:td>
                <xp:text escape="true" id="computedField2"
                    value="#{javascript:return @ClientType()}">
                </xp:text>
            </xp:td>
        </xp:tr><xp:tr>
            <xp:td>
                <xp:label id="label3"
                    value="SSJS: context.isRunningContext(arg)">
                </xp:label>
            </xp:td><xp:td>
                <xp:text escape="true" id="computedField3">
                    <xp:this.value>
                       <![CDATA[#{javascript:
                    if (context.isRunningContext("Notes")) {
                       return "Notes";
                    } else {
                       return "Web";
                    }}]]>
                    </xp:this.value>
                </xp:text>
            </xp:td>
        </xp:tr>
</xp:table>}
```

Notice that when this code is run as a native XPiNC app that all the computed platform ids are returned as "Notes". Similarly, when run on the web, all platform ids are returned as in the browser as "Web". However when the page is opened in Notes when the application is launched using the hybrid Run On Server mode, you see that the SSJS `context.isRunningContext("Notes")` API returns "Notes", whereas the others return "Web". Figure 13.46 illustrates this result. The key point is that these various programming methods can be used in combination to detect exactly what your runtime environment is, which will give you precise control over the look, feel, and behavior of multiplatform applications.

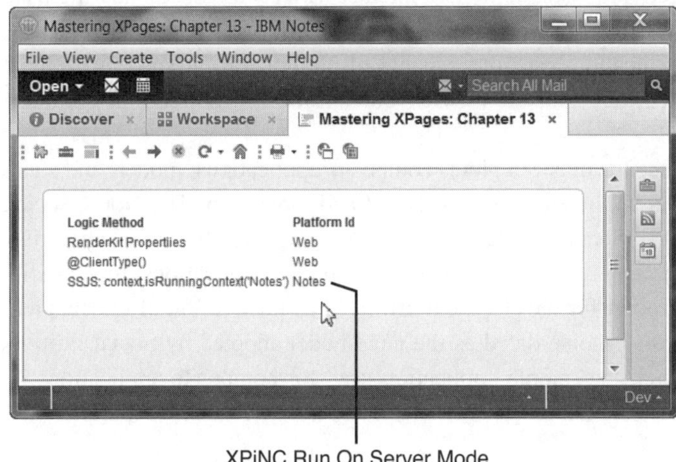

Figure 13.46 whatPlaform.xsp open in Notes in Run On Server mode

> **TIP**
>
> XPages falls back gracefully from Run On Server mode to regular XPiNC mode if the http server refuses to allow a connection, if the hostname cannot be resolved, and so forth. Should this occur, a warning will be posted to the Notes status bar and to the XPages log file, but the application will launch as it would if Run On Server mode had not been requested on the launch options.

As a result of this, almost all the cool adapted XPages client behaviors continue to work well in the Notes client when Run On Server mode is in use. Features such as bookmarking, `enableModifedFlag`, extended client-side JavaScript functions, Notes context menu customization, and so forth are all supported. The one exception pertains to composite applications. When executing in Run On Server mode, XPages applications can be included in a composite application but cannot communicate with other components using the property broker for security reasons. What are composite applications you may well ask? Well, you are about to find out.

XPages and Composite Applications

Composite applications were introduced to Notes when the client was rebased to the Eclipse RCP platform in Notes 8.0, which was released in 2007. The idea was to further enhance the collaborative nature of Notes through interapplication communication and aggregation. In other words, applications, such as team rooms, calendaring, mail, and other ad-hoc components, could be loosely assembled into a larger composite entity and interact with each other by sharing data using a common event model. When XPiNC was released in 2009, it was seen as strategically important that XPages client applications be fully capable of participating in any such client aggregation, so additional features were added to the XSP client runtime to support the composite application model.

In the intervening years since the debut of Notes composite applications, models and standards for collaborative and social applications have evolved and moved on. The Notes Social Edition now puts forward the OpenSocial standard as the new component-based collaborative framework, as does IBM Connections. As a consequence, composite applications, though still supported, are no longer a focal point for development effort. Thus this section of the chapter, although entirely valid, is likely to become dated as the new model adopted by Social Edition becomes the standard. To this end, the sample application used for composite applications in this section remains based on the V8.5 Discussion template, and is provided as a separate NSF, namely **Chp13ed1.nsf.**

Making a Component of an XPages Application

To be part of a composite application, any participant must acquire the social capability of both listening and talking to its neighbors. In XPages, this is achieved through the use of an independent "component," which is literally a component design element (introduced in V8.5.1) that allows send and receive events to be defined and associated with one or more XPages.

In this section, you implement a simple comp app use case by extending the search facility of the Discussion template so that its internal search queries are also relayed to a third-party search engine. You need to ensure that the Composite Applications Editor is included in your Notes installation because it is an optional component. Also, be aware that you need a full text-indexed sample application because this use case depends on the capability to search the application. You can verify that **Chp13ed1.nsf** is full-text indexed by looking ahead to Figure 13.54 and making sure that the search bar displayed in the top-right corner of the diagram is also visible in your local application instance. If not, for whatever reason, you need to create a full-text index, and full details for performing that task are provided in Chapter 8 in the section, "View Data Source Filters."

Chp13ed1.nsf has a **search** component defined that contains a **searchQuery** publish event that passes the search text to another component in a composite application. The component design element is located under Composite Applications in the Designer navigator, as shown in Figure 13.47, along with the details of the **searchQuery** event.

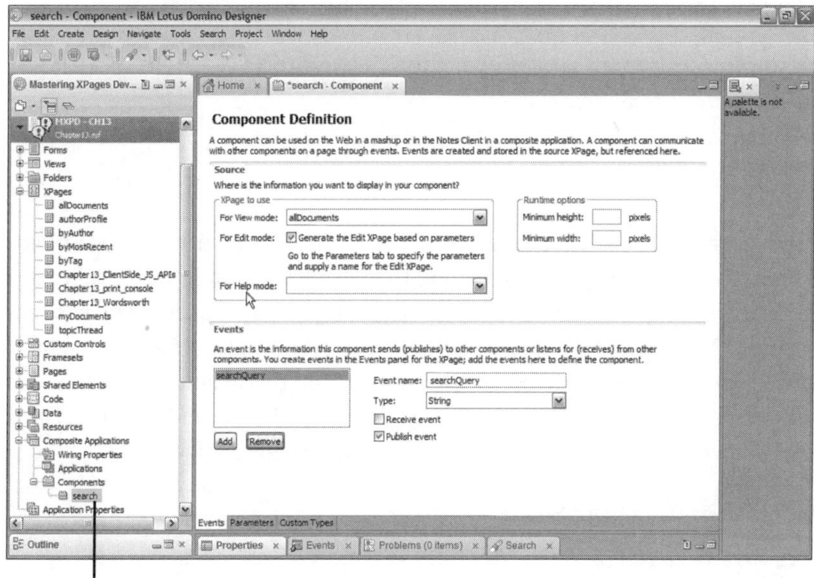

Figure 13.47 Component design element with sample search component

When you create a component, you also need to provide the name of an XPage to open when this component is added to a composite application. In this particular example, the main page of the application, **allDocuments.xsp**, is used because it contains the search text control. In fact, the search text control is defined in a custom control named **titleBar.xsp**, and this in turn is included in **allDocuments.xsp** and other pages. Thus, any modifications you make here to **titleBar.xsp** bleeds through to the rest of the application, just as you would want!

To extend the current custom control logic, you need to open **titleBar.xsp** custom control in Designer and move to the Events panel. Notice that the **linkSubmit** control adjacent to the search edit box already has a server-side simple action attached to it, and if you inspect the source markup you will see the simple action shown in Listing 13.11.

Listing 13.11 Simple Action for Search Control

```
<xp:actionGroup>
    <xp:openPage>
        <xp:this.name>
            <![CDATA[#{javascript:
                "/allDocuments.xsp?vm=0&searchValue=" +
                viewScope.searchValue;
            }]]>
        </xp:this.name>
    </xp:openPage>
</xp:actionGroup>
```

Simply put, the search query, once entered in the edit box, is stored in a scoped variable called **searchValue**. When the user clicks the link to execute the search, the default page (**allDocuments.xsp**) is reopened, but its contents are filtered with the user's query, which is provided as a **searchValue** URL parameter. You need to leave this server-side logic intact and add some *client-side* JavaScript code to publish the search Value. To do this, activate the **Client** tab on the **Events** panel, select the `onclick` event, and click the **Script Editor** radio button. Enter the JavaScript snippet shown in Listing 13.12 into the editor and save the XPage.

Listing 13.12 Client-Side JavaScript for Search Control

```
// find the searchText edit box in the client DOM
var searchCtl = document.getElementById("#{id:searchText}");
// copy whatever text it contains in searchTxt
var searchTxt = searchCtl.value;
// if there is a non-blank search query, publish it
if (searchTxt != null && searchTxt != "") {
    XSP.publishEvent("searchQuery", searchTxt, "string");
}
```

Earlier in this chapter, you were promised an introduction to the `XSP.publishEvent()` client–side JavaScript function, so here it is. It captures whatever value is typed into the search edit box and then passes this on to any component that might be listening. Note that you have combined both client-side JavaScript and server-side Simple Actions on the same event, `onclick`, for the search link. The client-side JavaScript is executed first, followed by the simple action after the XPage is submitted.

Is Anyone Out There? Creating a Component that Listens to Your XPages Component

The listener in this scenario is any other component that is wired to the **searchQuery** publish event using the Composite Applications Editor. The listening component could be a Notes mail component, a browser instance, a Notes widget, a Notes plug-in, another XPage, and so on. In this particular use case, you use a Notes widget (widgets are small, specialized applications that enable users to leverage existing services or resources) to manage a web browser instance configured to give access to the Google search engine.

To create a Google search widget, you need to first enable the widget toolbar via Notes preferences (select **File > Preferences > Widgets**), and then select the **Show Widget Toolbar** checkbox. Once this setting is applied, you can launch a Widget wizard from the Notes toolbar icon, from the side panel link or from the **Tools > Widgets > Getting Started with Widgets** main menu. Clicking any selection causes the dialog shown in Figure 13.48 to launch.

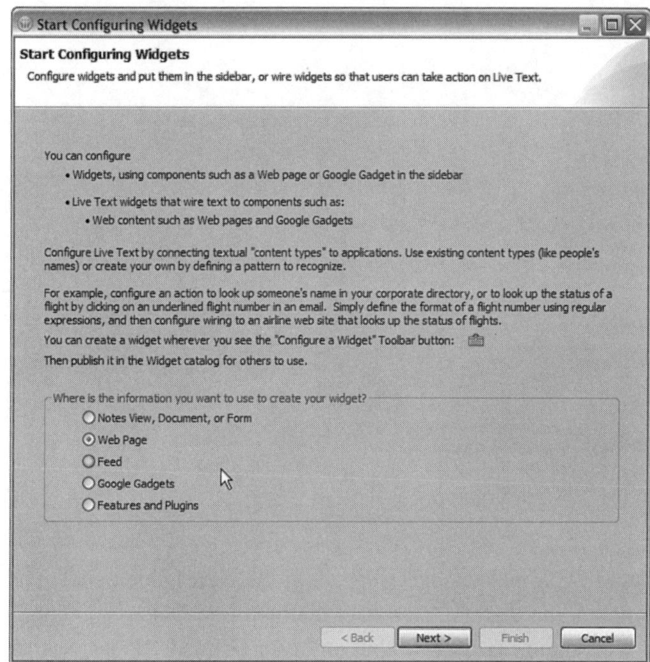

Figure 13.48 Start Configuring Widgets Wizard dialog: Initial page

You need to navigate through the wizard dialog screens, making the following options in the same sequence as shown here:

1. Click the **Web Page** radio button as the source for the widget.
2. Choose **Web Page by URL** and enter `http://www.google.com` as the URL.
3. Choose the **Form** option to use HTTP POST requests when working with the widget.
4. Click **Form Google Search** in the **Form** group box.

5. Select the **Advanced** tab and click the **Configure** checkbox on the final screen, as shown in Figure 13.49.

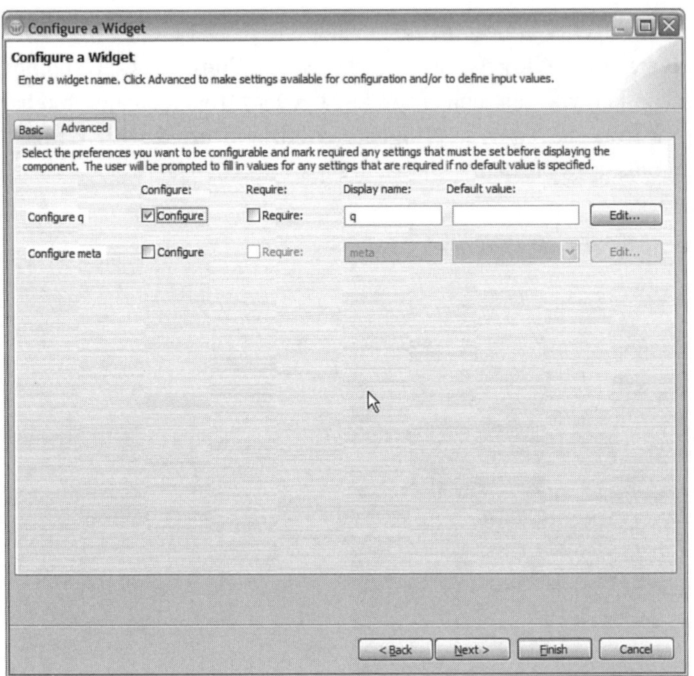

Figure 13.49 Start Configuring Widgets Wizard dialog: Final page

After you click the **Finish** button, a Google widget appears in the Notes side panel. The next step is to create a composite application that contains both the modified Discussion application and the Google widget and wire them together so that any user-defined XPages search applies to both components.

Assembling a Composite Application: Aggregating the XPages Discussion Component and Notes Google Widget

Create a new Notes application based on the Blank Composite Application template, for example, **DiscExtn.nsf**, as shorthand for an extended Discussion application. This creates a shell application that contains no components by default. Components are added using the Composite Application Editor (CAE), as shown in Figure 13.50, which can be invoked via **Action > Edit Application** from the Notes main menu.

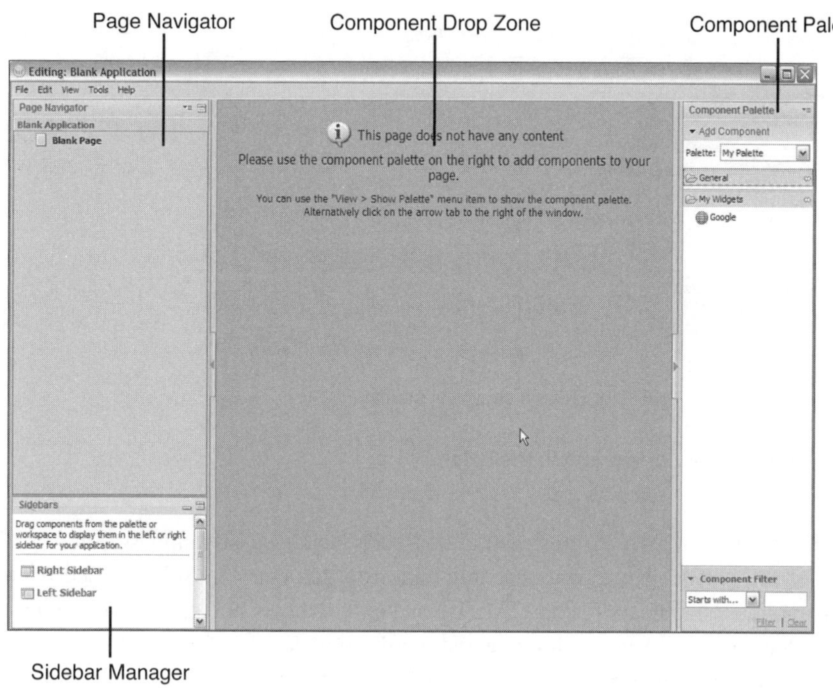

Figure 13.50 Composite Application Editor

Figure 13.50 shows Composite Application Editor (CAE) in its initial state. The middle pane is the drop zone for components, and components can be chosen from the palette on the right-hand side. Here, by right-clicking, you find the **Add Component** drop-down menu. You should choose the **Add NSF Component** submenu so that you can add the Discussion application to the palette. In the resulting dialog box, click the **Browse** button adjacent to the **Notes URL** text box so that the **search** component created earlier can be located and selected. Figure 13.51 shows both dialogs with the appropriate selections.

Note that the Notes URL generated is of the form:

```
notes:///replicaId/name.component
```

When an XPage application is launched as a composite application, the startup URL contains a component reference rather than the name of an XSP page.

> **TIP**
>
> If you are building an NTF template that will be used to create NSF application instances, use the replica ID rather than the database name as the startup URL. This means that the launch property for any and every NSF created from the NTF will not need to be manually updated.

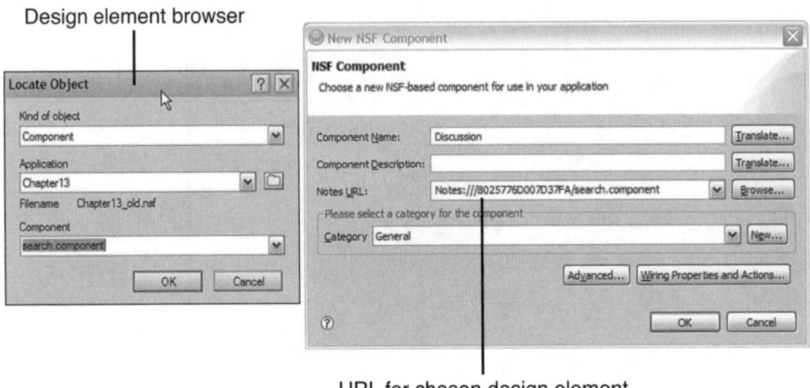

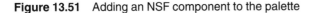

Figure 13.51 Adding an NSF component to the palette

Clicking OK on the **New NSF** Component dialog adds the Discussion application to the General category of the palette. Now, you can drag-and-drop this entry into the middle pane and—voilà!—the application appears live in CAE. Be aware that this is not a mock-up preview approximation, but the component is running live and is fully functional in CAE at this point. It is in dire need of some companionship, however, so add the Google widget next. This component can be found in the **My Widgets** category of the palette and can be dragged and dropped on the middle pane just as before. Try to place this component so that it shares the lower half of the middle pane with the Discussion component (the screen is split in half horizontally). If you hover over the lower region of the middle pane, almost to the bottom, in fact, while dragging the component, CAE outlines the drop area in shadow form, which allows you to release once the lower rectangle is outlined.

Figure 13.52 shows both components in their assembled positions. It also shows an activated context menu in Page Navigator on the left-hand side of the screen. You should follow suit and choose the **Wiring** menu item by right-clicking in this space. On the resulting Wiring tab, simply use the mouse to drag a connection from the Discussion **searchQuery** event to the Google **q** property. This gesture wires the components together; the value of a **searchQuery** event will be published across a virtual wire to the Google widget as a search engine query. After the wire is graphically represented, as shown in Figure 13.53, click the **Apply** button and terminate CAE by closing its window.

You are prompted to save your application on exit, which, of course, you should do. The regular Notes client window is reactivated, and your composite application is refreshed to include your two new components. To test your new feature, simply type some text into the Discussion search box and see how it is applied in the usual way in XPages, but also passed to the Google search engine in the bottom half of the screen. Figure 13.54 shows a sample result.

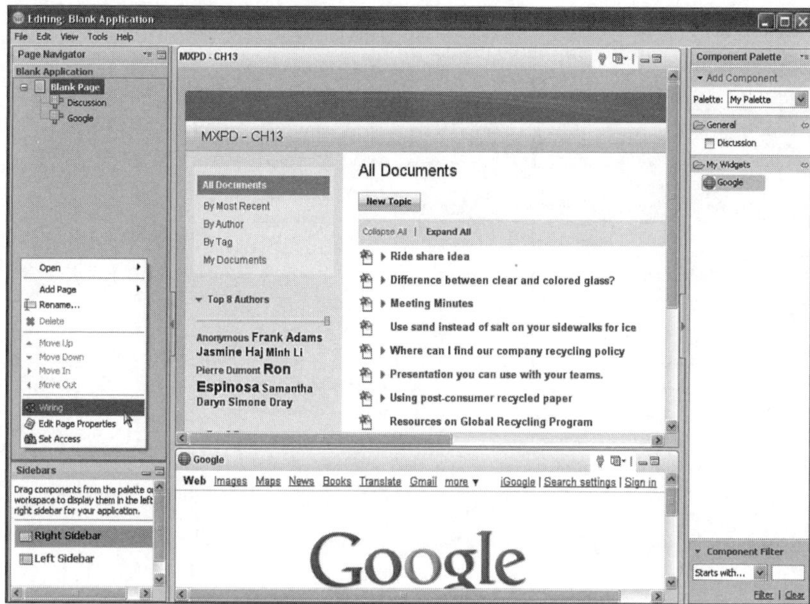

Figure 13.52 Two components aggregated in the CAE

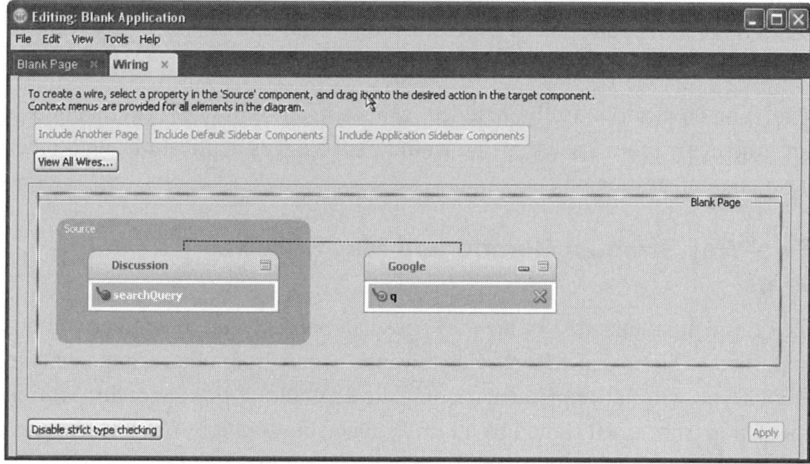

Figure 13.53 Wiring components in CAE

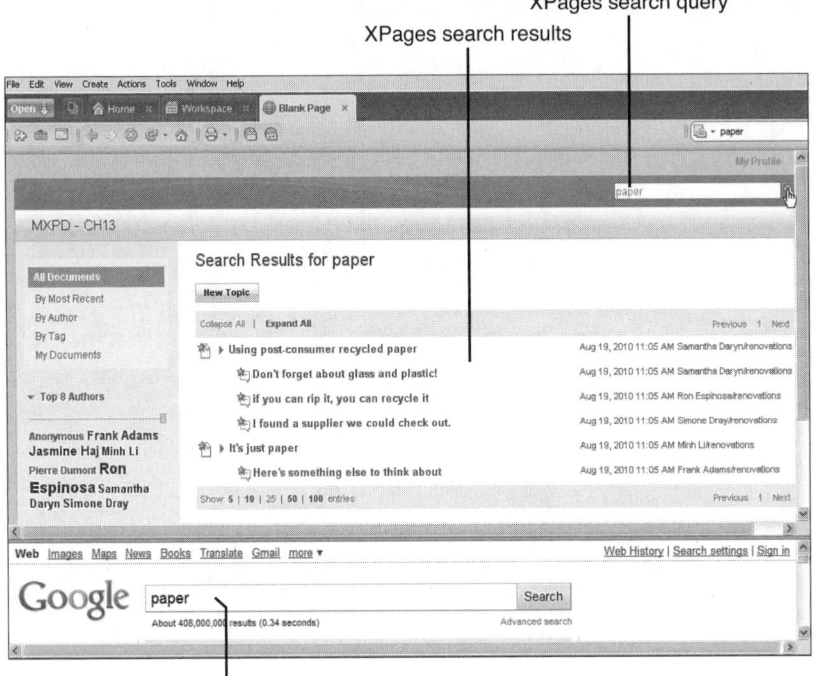

Figure 13.54 Integrated search results

Congratulations! You have successfully included XPages in a useful client aggregation—you can probably imagine many other use cases that would bind XPages applications with other components to achieve cool integration points.

Hey, This Is a Two-Way Street. A Component May Receive and Publish Events

Although you worked through an example of how XPages can publish data to another component, it is equally important to know that XPages can consume events from other components in the same way. Although you will not implement a complete example of that here, this section explains the implementation path, and it should be intuitive to you because it is, for the most part, a mirror image of what you just completed with the **searchQuery** publish event.

The steps are as follows:

1. Define a receive event (see Listing 13.13).
2. Add a handler for the receive event (see Listing 13.14).
3. Add your components to a composite application in CAE as before.

4. Wire a publish event of another component to your receive event.
5. Save your composite and test as before.

The receive event is defined in the same way as the publish event (just an event name, type, and identifier). In Figure 13.55, a **viewFilter** receive event is defined, which enables an external component to provide a text value that the Discussion application can use to refine its current view, such as a view category filter or a full text query.

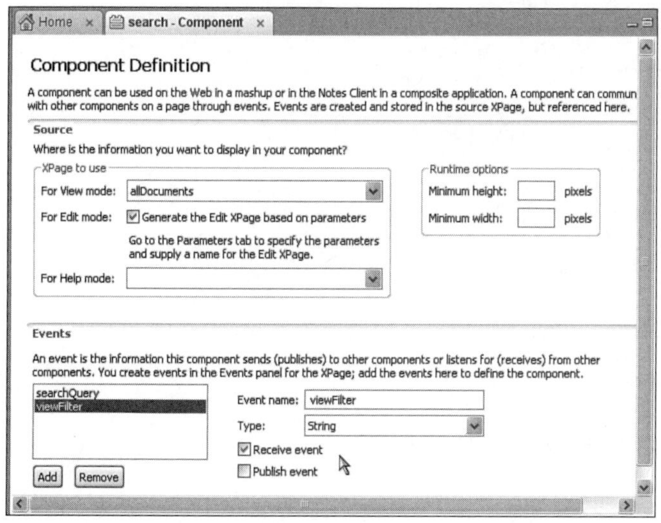

Figure 13.55 Simple action receive event

Handling the receive event, on the other hand, is different. In Designer, you must activate the XPage itself, say **allDocuments.xsp**, and select the **Events** tab. A `Components (Receive)` event is listed in the panel and, by double-clicking the `New Event` subentry, you can provide a handler. Note that the name you provide here must match the name of the receive event *exactly*, (**viewFilter** in this example). Figure 13.56 shows a simple action defined as the handler for the **viewFilter** receive event.

This is where the example explained in Listing 13.11 comes in handy (how the regular full-text search box submits a search query). You can apply the same logic here. In other words, when a **viewFilter** event is received from another component, capture the value and apply it as a full-text search query in the same way as what's done when the end user enters one directly. Thus, the `Target Document` of the `Open Page` simple action can execute similar server-side JavaScript to that described earlier, as shown in Listing 13.13.

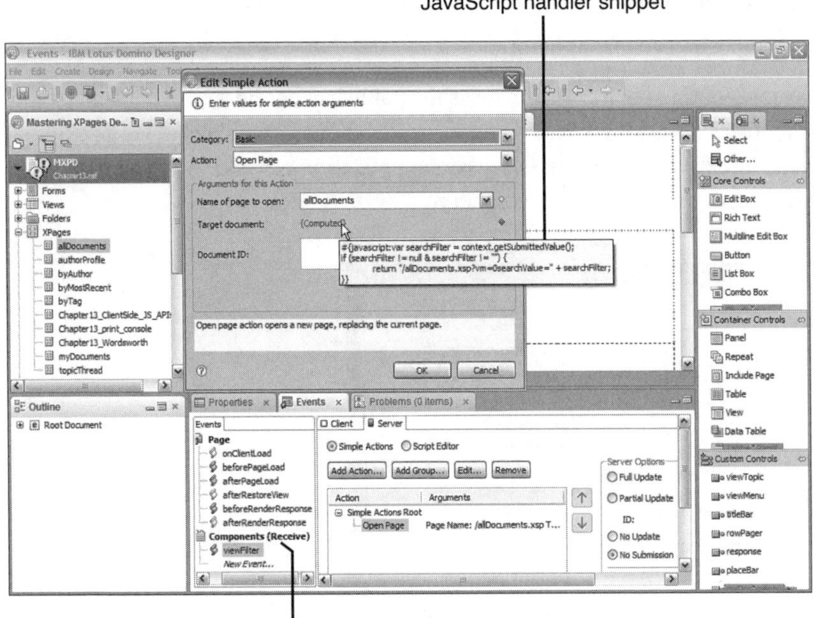

Figure 13.56 Creating simple action receive event handler

Listing 13.13 JavaScript to Compute a Target Document Based on a Receive Event

```
var searchFilter = context.getSubmittedValue();
if (searchFilter != null && searchFilter != "") {
   return "/allDocuments.xsp?vm=0&searchValue=" + searchFilter;
}
```

This means that just the first line needs some explanation. The `context.getSubmittedValue()` function does exactly as the name suggests—it returns the value submitted for the current page. If a value has been submitted, it is applied as a full-text filter in the usual way. What is perhaps not obvious is why the handler is looking for a submitted value in the first place. How does this receive event value end up as the submitted page value?

To understand this, first preview a page containing a receive event and then view the HTML source. You see that the renderer for the receive event has inserted an invisible `<div>` element into the rendered page, something like what Listing 13.14 demonstrates. It is not visible because of the inline `"display:none"` style rule that is applied.

Listing 13.14 HTML Markup Emitted for the Receive Event

```
<div id="view:_id1:platformEvent1"
    class="XspHandler-viewFilter"
    onclick="XSP.fireEvent(arguments[0],
        "view:_id1:_id21",
        "view:_id1:platformEvent1", null, true, 2, null);"
    style="display:none">
</div>
```

TIP

If you are building a receive event into an XPage, the logic needs to be on every application page that should handle the event. Thus, it probably make sense for you to define your receive event handler in a custom control and include that in the appropriate XPages.

When an XPage is launched with a component URL (refer to Figure 13.51 if necessary), as opposed to a regular XSP URL, the XPages client container reads and registers the properties declared in the component, and provides a Java handler for any receive events that happen to exist—this is all done automatically by the XPages runtime. Once another component publishes data across a virtual wire to XPages, that Java handler is notified, reads the published data, and dispatches it by dynamically injecting some JavaScript into the XPages client browser. The dynamic JavaScript looks for a well-known element on the page (the `<div>` element shown in Listing 13.14) and calls its `onclick` event passing along the original data. As you can see in Listing 13.14 the `<div>` element has a `class` attribute whose value can be deduced based on a combination of a descriptor (**XspHandler**) and the receive event name (**viewFilter**). This allows the element to be deterministically located in the DOM and calling its `onclick` code causes the XPage to be submitted. Thus, the receive event handler can read the submitted value and thereby obtain the receive event data on the server side. Nothing like a little indirection to whet the curiosity of a software engineer—hope you enjoyed that!

Further Adventures with Composite Applications

This book does not assume that you have a fully functional Notes client complete with mail and so on. The minimal requirement is simply the no-charge download of Domino Designer. This limits the components that can be guaranteed to be in your workspace and, thus, the types of component interaction that that can be explored in this chapter. However the XPages runtime team has posted a highly informative online video on the subject of XPages in composite applications. The video walks through the integration of the XPages Discussion, Notes mail, and widgets in great depth. It is highly recommended if you want to explore this topic.

The video comes in two parts, and the URLs are as follows:

```
http://tinyurl.com/XPagesCompAppsPart1
http://tinyurl.com/XPagesCompAppsPart2
```

This section concludes the discussion of XPages in the Notes client.. Hopefully, no stone has been left unturned in our explorations of all things XPiNC.

CHAPTER 14

XPages Mobile Application Development

The mobile features from the XPages Extension Library were promoted into the core XPages runtime in Domino 9.0. This reflects the importance of mobile support in application development as mobile devices (phones and tablets) move to outsell desktop systems and are becoming the norm for how people access web applications. XPages has implemented a Mobile Web Development strategy—that is, it uses web technologies to provide mobile access to your applications. Mobile devices feature powerful web browsers; however, the web interface you have built for desktop clients just won't cut it for mobile clients. If you have ever accessed the full version of a website from a mobile device, you will have experienced first-hand the type of problems encountered when there is no mobile version of a site. These include

- **Limited resources:** Device processor power, memory, and network bandwidth all tend to be limited on a mobile device.
- **User experience:** Users have particular expectations when using a mobile device—for example, fast response times, navigation to most important features, minimal data entry, UI adapts to device orientation, and many more.
- **Limited functionality:** Users typically need only a subset of functionality and expect applications to reuse functionality from other applications on their mobile device.

The *XPages Extension Library* book provides an introductory description of the XPages mobile controls and the pattern to be used to develop a Create, Read, Update, Delete (CRUD) mobile sample application. The approach this chapter takes is to focus on best practices and design patterns for XPages Mobile Application Development. So even if you are familiar with building mobile applications with XPages, this chapter contains some discussion that you will find interesting. While writing the second edition of this book, Domino 9.0.1 had just been released. It includes some important enhancements for mobile developers, which will be covered in this chapter. For an excellent description of the best practices for Mobile Web Applications, visit `www.w3.org/TR/mwabp/`. Some of the best practices outlined in this document are referred to later in the chapter. Be sure to download the **chp14ed2.nsf** file provided online for this book to run through the exercises throughout this chapter. You can access these files at `www.ibmpressbooks.com/title/9780133373370`.

> **TIP**
>
> There is also an introductory tutorial available at www-10.lotus.com/ldd/ddwiki.nsf/dx/XPages_Mobile_Controls_Tutorial.

Getting Started with Mobile Application Development

Start with a simple XPage that displays the browser User Agent string. This enables you to detect which device is accessing your application. When you preview the XPage shown in Listing 14.1 in a browser, it displays the User Agent string for your browser, which for Firefox version 18.02 is Mozilla/5.0 (Windows NT 6.1; WOW64; rv:18.0) Gecko/20100101 Firefox/18.0.

Listing 14.1 Display User Agent

```
<?xml version="1.0" encoding="UTF-8"?>
<xp:view xmlns:xp="http://www.ibm.com/xsp/core"
        style="padding-top:20.0px;padding-right:10.0px;padding-left:20.0px">
        <h3>Mobile XPages Applications</h3>
        <xp:br></xp:br>
        User Agent: 
        <xp:text escape="true" id="computedField1"
                value="#{javascript:context.getUserAgent().getUserAgent()}"
                style="color:rgb(128,0,0)">
        </xp:text>
</xp:view>
```

As I write this, I'm using my home wireless network—so now I can enter the URL for this page into the Safari browser on my iPhone, and I can see the page rendered there. The User Agent string displayed is

```
Mozilla/5.0 (iPhone; CPU iPhone OS 6_1 like Mac OS X) AppleWeb-
Kit/536.26 (KHTML, like Gecko) Version/6.0 Mobile/
10B143 Safari/8536.25
```

Figure 14.1 shows how the page displays on an iPhone.

Figure 14.1 iPhone User Agent

Straight away I can see problems:

- Typing a URL on my iPhone is painful; I don't want to have to do a lot of typing using this device.
- I need to pinch and zoom to see the text in the browser. By default I'm seeing the full page with some tiny text at the top, which is not readable.
- This is going to slow down my development if I have to keep switching between my development machine and device to test my changes.
- What if I don't have an iPhone, an iPad, or an Android device?

The first thing to know is that you don't need a device to get started with Mobile Application Development. There are a number of alternative options to testing on a real device:

- Using a device emulator, these are typically part of a mobile platform SDK and are available for Mac, Android, Microsoft, and Blackberry devices.
- You can modify the User Agent in your desktop browser.

Most of the demonstrations in this chapter use the technique of overriding the User Agent your desktop browser sends with each request. User Agent spoofing doesn't provide 100 percent fidelity with the actual device but is a quick way to get your application built before you begin testing on real devices. The remainder of this chapter uses the Safari and Chrome browsers to emulate Apple and Android devices, respectively.

Safari Browser

The Windows versions of the Safari browser are available from the Apple support site. The WebKit engine used by the Safari for Windows browser is similar to the one on the Apple iPhone and iPad, so this browser is a good option for basic emulation of the Apple mobile devices. Use the following steps to override the User Agent string sent by the browser:

1. If you do not have menus enabled by default, do so via the Show Menu Bar from the General Safari Settings toolbar drop-down.
2. Open **Preferences** and go to the **Advanced** tab.
3. Select the option to **Show Develop menu in menu bar**.
4. Select the User Agent override you want to use from the **Develop -> User Agent** menu.

Figure 14.2 shows the Safari User Agent choices. You can now select one of these. If you access the XPage in the Safari browser, the page displays the appropriate User Agent string.

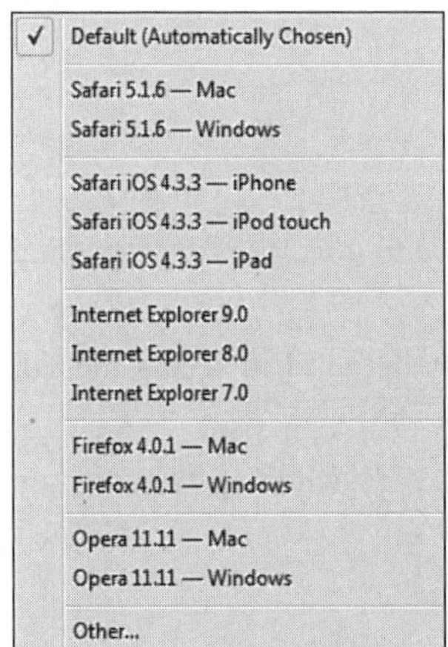

Figure 14.2 Safari User Agent choices

For example, I selected Safari iOS 4.3.3—iPhone, and the XPage displayed the following User Agent:

```
Mozilla/5.0 (iPhone; U; CPU iPhone OS 4_3_3 like Mac OS X; en-us)
AppleWebKit/533.17.9 (KHTML, like Gecko) Version/5.0.2 Mobile/
8J2 Safari/6533.18.5
```

Chrome Browser

The Chrome browser provides similar functionality as follows:

1. Go to the **Tools** menu and select **Developer tools**.
2. Select the **Settings** (cogged wheel) icon in the bottom-right corner of the **Developer tools** panel.
3. Select the **Overrides** tab.

Figure 14.3 shows the Chrome developer tools Overrides tab. You can override the User Agent and also other settings like the device metrics and orientation. The device metrics and orientation and useful for giving you that immediate feedback on how your page will be rendered on the device.

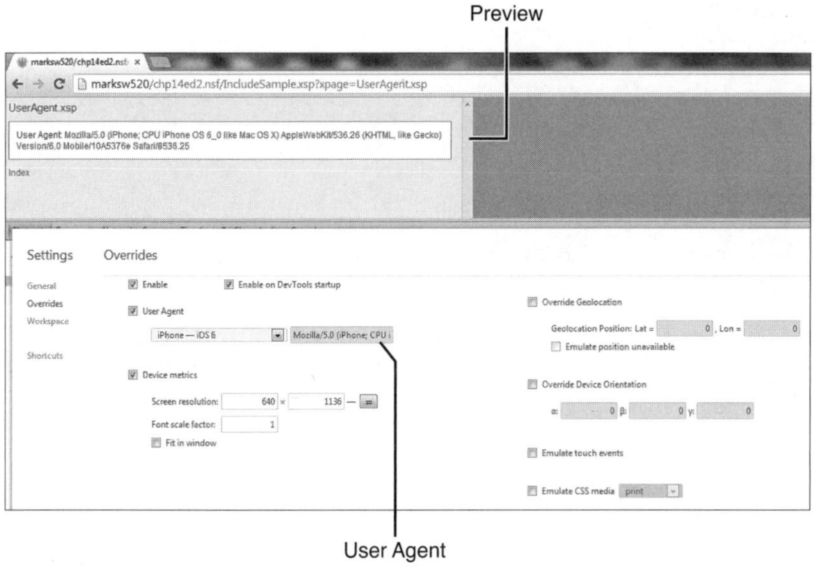

Figure 14.3 Chrome Developer tools Overrides tab

Firefox Browser

There is an add-on for FireFox called User Agent Switcher (addons.mozilla.org/en-US/firefox/addon/user-agent-switcher/), which provides the equivalent functionality. One nice feature of this add-on includes the capability to define your own User Agent string.

User Agent Device Detection

Detecting that your application is being accessed using a mobile device is important because it allows you to use server-side logic to adapt the content for the requesting client. It is preferable to do the adaptation on the server-side because this will improve the user experience and prevent the transfer of unnecessary data. The User Agent is typically used to detect the device in use. Listing 14.2 shows an example of how to detect if the device is an iPhone, iPad, Android, or BlackBerry device.

Listing 14.2 User Agent Device Detection

```
<?xml version="1.0" encoding="UTF-8"?>
<xp:view xmlns:xp="http://www.ibm.com/xsp/core"
       style="padding-top:20.0px;padding-right:10.0px;padding-
➥left:20.0px">
       <h3>Mobile XPages Applications</h3>
       <xp:br></xp:br>
       User Agent: 
       <xp:text escape="true" id="computedField1"
              value="#{javascript:context.getUserAgent().getUserAgent()}"
              style="color:rgb(128,0,0)">
       </xp:text>
       <xp:br></xp:br>
       Device: 
       <xp:text escape="true" id="computedField2"
              style="color:rgb(128,0,0)">
              <xp:this.value>
<![CDATA[#{javascript:var ua = context.getUserAgent().getUserAgent();
if (ua.indexOf("iPhone") > -1) {
       return "iPhone";
} else if (ua.indexOf("iPad") > -1) {
       return "iPad";
} else if (ua.indexOf("Android") > -1) {
       return "Android";
} else if (ua.indexOf("BlackBerry") > -1) {
       return "BlackBerry";
} else {
```

```
        return "Unknown";
}}]]>
                </xp:this.value>
        </xp:text>
</xp:view>
```

Given the large number of devices in use and that new devices come to the market frequently, this type of coding can become complex. The best practice for mobile applications is to use broader device classification to simplify the process of adapting your content. For example, you might want to generate different content for mobile phones versus tablet devices. In Domino 9.0.1, a new managed bean called the `deviceBean` has been added to the XPages runtime to simplify this process and allow you to implement a device classification strategy.

Device Bean

The Device Bean is used to identify the most common mobile and tablet devices—that is, Android; Apple iPhone or iPad; Blackberry; or Windows Mobile devices. The heavy lifting of parsing the User Agent string is handled for you. The most commonly used methods are `deviceBean.isMobile()` and `deviceBean.isTablet()`. For tablet devices, the method `deviceBean.isMobile()` returns false, which means you often see the two values being OR'd to determine if any mobile device is used. Listing 14.3 shows a list of the values available from the Device Bean.

Listing 14.3 DeviceBean

```
<?xml version="1.0" encoding="UTF-8"?>
<xp:view xmlns:xp="http://www.ibm.com/xsp/core">
<style>.desc{position:absolute;left:20em;color:blue;}</style>

<h3>DeviceBean Properties</h3>
deviceBean.isMobile=<xp:text value="#{javascript:deviceBean.
isMobile()}"/>

<span class="desc">Identifies a device as a mobile device.</span><br/>
deviceBean.isTablet=<xp:text value="#{javascript:deviceBean.
isTablet()}"/>

<span class="desc">Identifies a device as a tablet device.</span><br/>
deviceBean.isIphone=<xp:text value="#{javascript:deviceBean.
isIphone()}"/>

<span class="desc">Identifies a device as an iPhone.</span><br/>
deviceBean.isIpad=<xp:text value="#{javascript:deviceBean.isIpad()}"/>
```

```
<span class="desc">Identifies a device as an iPad.</span><br/>
deviceBean.getVersion('ipad')=<xp:text value="#{javascript:deviceBean.
getVersion('ipad')}"/>

<span class="desc">Version of iPad.</span><br/>
deviceBean.isAndroid=<xp:text value="#{javascript:deviceBean.
isAndroid()}"/>

<span class="desc">Identifies a device as an Android device.
</span><br/>
deviceBean.isBlackberry=<xp:text value="#{javascript:deviceBean.
isBlackberry()}"/>

<span class="desc">Identifies a device as a Blackberry device.
</span><br/>
deviceBean.isWindows=<xp:text value="#{javascript:deviceBean.
isWindows()}"/>

<span class="desc">Identifies a device as a Windows Mobile device.
</span><br/>

</xp:view>
```

Figure 14.4 shows the values that are displayed when accessing this page with the User Agent set to that of an iPad.

DeviceBeanTable.xsp

DeviceBean Properties

Property	Value	Description
deviceBean.isMobile	false	Identifies a device as a mobile device.
deviceBean.isTablet	true	Identifies a device as a tablet.
deviceBean.isIphone	false	Identifies a device as an iPhone.
deviceBean.isIpad	true	Identifies a device as an iPad.
deviceBean.getVersion('ipad')	4	Version of iPad.
deviceBean.isAndroid	false	Identifies a device as an Android device.
deviceBean.isBlackberry	false	Identifies a device as a Blackberry device.
deviceBean.isWindows	false	Identifies a device as a Windows Mobile device.

Figure 14.4 iPad Device Bean Values

Now we have an easy to use technique to identify that a mobile or tablet device is accessing our application we can use this information to adapt the presentation of our application to a form that is suitable for the device being used. The design pattern used to present content suitable for use in mobile applications is the Single Page Application pattern and this is the topic for the next section.

TIP

The device bean is cached for the lifetime of a user session, which means if you are using a browser plug-in to change the user agent *Agent* you actually need to restart the browser for a change to take effect. Starting in Domino 9.0.1 there is a new mobile property in the Xsp properties called *Debug user agent*. This allows you to specify either an iOS or Android User Agent, and the change will take effect the next time you load a page from that application.

Single Page Application Design Pattern

The Single Page Application design pattern was created to address a number of Mobile Application Development best practices related to the conservative use of resources and improving user experience. Consider the following best practices that aim to improve the user experience:

- Bandwidth is typically more constrained on mobile networks; therefore, fewer but larger requests are recommended.
- Application start-time needs to be optimized.
- View switching must be fast and must support bookmarking and back button navigation.

One way to support these best practices is to load the application views either statically or dynamically without requiring a full page reload. Loading additional views is recommended to reduce the number of requests and provide for fast view switching. Associate fragment identifiers with each view, and use these for navigation and bookmarking. XPages includes the Single Page Application Control (`xe:singlePageApp`), which encapsulates all this functionality for you and provides the standard XPages declarative interface to allow you to configure and control its behavior. This and the other XPages mobile controls are available in their own category—that is, Mobile, within the Controls Palette. Figure 14.5 shows the Mobile controls category.

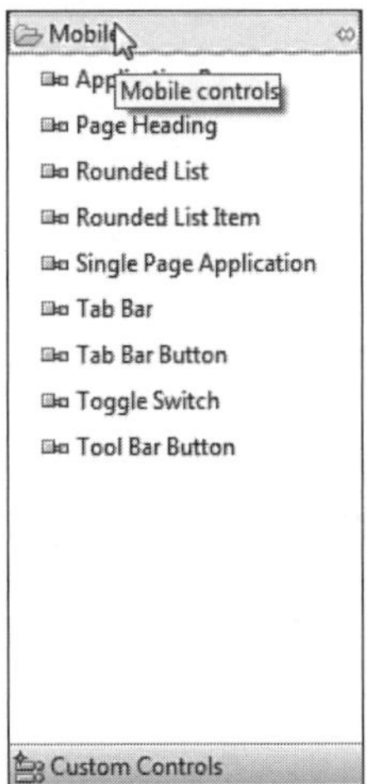

Figure 14.5 Mobile controls

Before creating any XPages that use the Mobile controls, there is some configuration required to get the pages to render correctly.

Mobile XPage Properties

There is a specific theme for use in mobile XPages. This theme is required for the Mobile controls to render with the correct device look and feel. This can be enabled automatically by specifying a prefix for XPages that should use the mobile theme. The standard prefix is `m_` but you can specify your own—for example, `mobile_` is used in the Discussion template. To enable the mobile theme based on a page prefix, use these steps:

1. Go to **Application Configuration > Xsp Properties**.
2. Select the option to **Use mobile theme for XPages with the prefix**.
3. Optionally specify the prefix to use.

Figure 14.6 shows the Mobile XPage properties.

Mobile theme setting

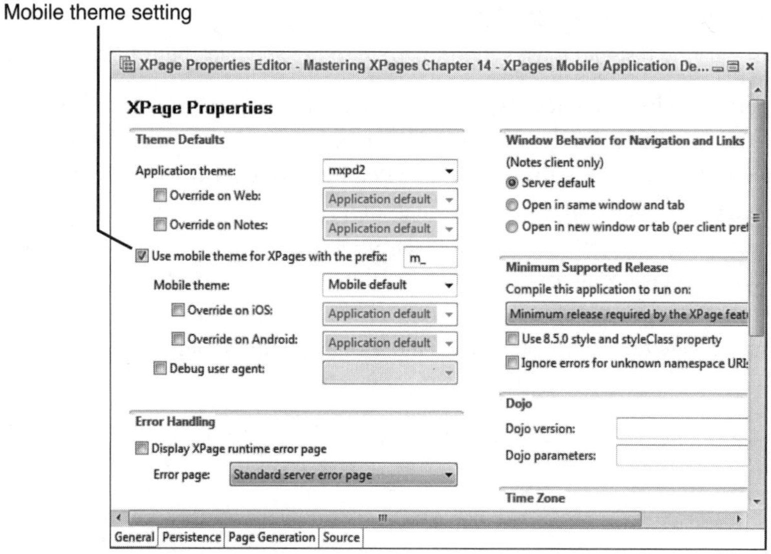

Figure 14.6 Mobile XPage properties

All mobile pages must have the prefix you specified; otherwise, they will include the default theme and won't render with the device look and feel. Mobile themes will be explored later in this chapter in the section, "Mobile Themes."

In addition to the mobile theme prefix setting, there are additional mobile properties that can be configured:

- **Mobile theme:** Enables you to specify the mobile theme to use if you want to change from the Mobile default theme.
- **Override on iOS:** Enables users to specify a specific theme for iOS devices.
- **Override on Android:** Enables users to specify a specific theme for Android devices.
- **Debug user agent:** Enables users to override mobile device detection behavior and force all mobile pages to render as either iOS or Android.

Now you are ready to create some mobile specific XPages.

Single Page Application Control (xe:singlePageApp)

The Single Page Application Control enables you to define your entire application behavior within a single XPage. The control contains a collection of views that can either be loaded as part of the initial page request or can be dynamically retrieved as needed. Listing 14.4 shows the XPages markup for a mobile page using the Single Page Application control.

Listing 14.4 Mobile XPage

```
<?xml version="1.0" encoding="UTF-8"?>
<?xml version="1.0" encoding="UTF-8"?>
<xp:view xmlns:xp="http://www.ibm.com/xsp/core"
       xmlns:xe="http://www.ibm.com/xsp/coreex"
       xmlns:xc="http://www.ibm.com/xsp/custom">
       <xe:singlePageApp id="singlePageApp1" selectedPageName="appPage1">
              <xe:appPage id="appPage1" pageName="appPage1">
                     <xe:djxmHeading id="djxmHeading1">
                            <xe:this.label>Page 1</xe:this.label>
                     </xe:djxmHeading>
                     <xe:djxmLineItem id="djxmLineItem1" label="Go to Page 2"
                            moveTo="appPage2">
                     </xe:djxmLineItem>
              </xe:appPage>
              <xe:appPage id="appPage2" pageName="appPage2">
                     <xc:mobile_appPage2></xc:mobile_appPage2>
              </xe:appPage>
       </xe:singlePageApp>
</xp:view>
```

This XPage includes two Application Pages (`xe:appPage`), the first of which is included inline in the page. The second Application Page is included via a custom control and this is the recommended pattern to use. The XPage that includes the Single Page Application control can quickly become complex and difficult to maintain if all the pages are included inline. If you look in the Discussion template at the `mobile.xsp` XPage, you can see another example of this pattern being used. The sample in Listing 14.4 is available in the database that accompanies this chapter in two XPage design elements, one named `m_SinglePageApplicationControl` and one named `SinglePageApplicationControl`. If you run these samples, only the one with the `m_` prefix will display correctly with the mobile theme.

> **TIP**
>
> The id parameter is required on each Application Page (`xe:appPage`) control because the default behavior is to dynamically load each page when it is displayed. You can use the preload property to have a page load when its parent is being loaded. This will improve performance for page transition at the cost of a larger initial download.

Figure 14.7 shows the sample running with the mobile theme on an iPhone.

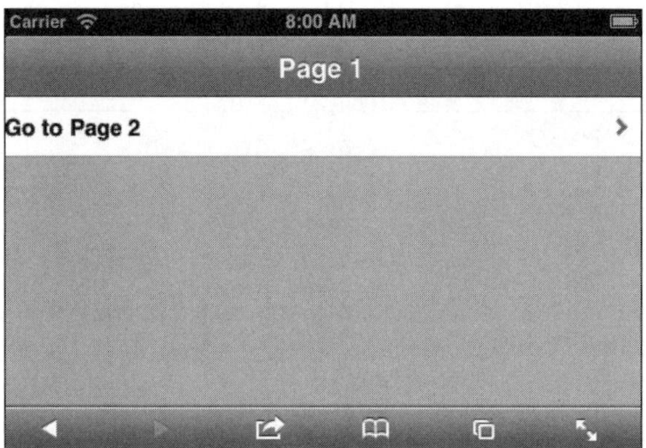

Figure 14.7 Single Page Application Control on iPhone

It is recommended you review the user interface guidelines for the devices you are targeting to ensure your application fits in on that device. These guidelines provide some basic principles for any mobile application and also specific details on designing for a specific version of a mobile operating system. The next section looks at how the XPages Mobile Controls enable you to build an application that adheres to the best practices in Mobile Application Navigation.

Mobile Application Navigation

Users should always know where they are within your application and how to get back to where they have just come from. The views in your application can be organized in different ways. For example, you could implement a navigator that allows the user to jump straight to a particular place in the application. This is best-suited where the application views are organized in a simple flat list. In a mobile application you may not have the luxury of displaying the navigator all the time, so the ability to quickly get back to the main navigator is important. Another common approach is to use a menu-like hierarchical navigation scheme in which users select different options to navigate through the hierarchy. When using a hierarchical scheme, a Back button is important to allow users to quickly retrace their steps. The final approach you look at is providing context-sensitive navigation options. In this case, users will be provided with the navigation options that logically make sense based on where they are and what they are doing within the application.

You saw an example of how to do navigation using the Rounded List Item (`xe:djxmLineItem`) control earlier in this chapter in Listing 14.4. The Rounded List Item control enables you to specify the page name to move to but also the transition type to use. The valid types of transition are

- **`slide`:** New pages moves in from the side to cover the old page. This is the default.
- **`fade`:** The old page fades out while the new page fades in.
- **`flip`:** The old page flips over to display the new page as if the new page were printed on the back of the old page.
- **`none`:** The new page appears immediately without any transition effect.

Listing 14.5 shows how to specify the transition type that will be used when a user changes the Application Page.

Listing 14.5 Application Page Transitions

```
<?xml version="1.0" encoding="UTF-8"?>
<xp:view xmlns:xp="http://www.ibm.com/xsp/core"
  xmlns:xe="http://www.ibm.com/xsp/coreex"
  xmlns:xc="http://www.ibm.com/xsp/custom">
  <xe:singlePageApp id="singlePageApp1" selectedPageName="appPage1">
    <xe:appPage id="appPage1" pageName="appPage1">
      <xe:djxmHeading id="djxmHeading1">
        <xe:this.label>Page 1</xe:this.label>
      </xe:djxmHeading>
      <xe:djxmLineItem id="djxmLineItem1" label="Fade to Page 2"
        moveTo="appPage2" transition="fade">
      </xe:djxmLineItem>
    </xe:appPage>
    <xe:appPage id="appPage2" pageName="appPage2">
      <xe:djxmHeading id="djxmHeading2">
        <xe:this.label>Page 2</xe:this.label>
      </xe:djxmHeading>
      <xe:djxmLineItem id="djxmLineItem2" label="Flip to Page 1"
```

```
        moveTo="appPage1" transition="flip">
      </xe:djxmLineItem>
    </xe:appPage>
  </xe:singlePageApp>
</xp:view>
```

Navigator

To implement a basic navigator, you need to use the Page Heading (`xe:djxmHeading`) and Rounded List Item (`xe:djxmLineItem`) controls. Listing 14.6 shows an XPage that provides a basic navigator. The Page Heading shows users where they are within the application at all times. Each Page Heading includes two additional attributes:

- **`back:`** Label for the back button
- **`moveTo:`** Page to move to when the Back button is selected

The combination of these two parameters adds a Back button to each page, which allows users to return to the Home page, which includes the Navigator with a single-click. The main Navigator displays on its own Application Page to optimize real estate on the device.

Listing 14.6 Navigator XPage

```
<?xml version="1.0" encoding="UTF-8"?>
<xp:view xmlns:xp="http://www.ibm.com/xsp/core"
       xmlns:xe="http://www.ibm.com/xsp/coreex"
       xmlns:xc="http://www.ibm.com/xsp/custom">
       <xe:singlePageApp id="navigationApp" selectedPageName="homePage">
              <xe:appPage id="homePage" pageName="homePage">
                     <xe:djxmHeading id="djxmHeading1">
                            <xe:this.label>Home</xe:this.label>
                     </xe:djxmHeading>
                     <xe:djxmLineItem label="Visitor Info"
                                   moveTo="visitorPage"/>
                     <xe:djxmLineItem label="Conservation"
                                   moveTo="conservePage"/>
                     <xe:djxmLineItem label="Education"
                                   moveTo="educatePage"/>
                     <xe:djxmLineItem label="Get Involved"
                                   moveTo="involvePage"/>
                     <xe:djxmLineItem label="Shop" moveTo="shopPage"/>
              </xe:appPage>
              <xe:appPage id="visitorPage" pageName="visitorPage">
                     <xe:djxmHeading back="Home" moveTo="homePage">
                            <xe:this.label>Visitor Info</xe:this.label>
```

```
                </xe:djxmHeading>
            </xe:appPage>
            <xe:appPage id="conservePage" pageName="conservePage">
                <xe:djxmHeading back="Home" moveTo="homePage">
                    <xe:this.label>Conservation</xe:this.label>
                </xe:djxmHeading>
            </xe:appPage>
            <xe:appPage id="educatePage" pageName="educatePage">
                <xe:djxmHeading back="Home" moveTo="homePage">
                    <xe:this.label>Education</xe:this.label>
                </xe:djxmHeading>
            </xe:appPage>
            <xe:appPage id="involvePage" pageName="involvePage">
                <xe:djxmHeading back="Home" moveTo="homePage">
                    <xe:this.label>Get Involved</xe:this.label>
                </xe:djxmHeading>
            </xe:appPage>
            <xe:appPage id="shopPage" pageName="shopPage">
                <xe:djxmHeading back="Home" moveTo="homePage">
                    <xe:this.label>Shop</xe:this.label>
                </xe:djxmHeading>
            </xe:appPage>
        </xe:singlePageApp>
</xp:view>
```

Figures 14.8 and 14.9 show the Home page with the XPages Navigator and also an Application Page, which includes a Page Heading with an integrated Back button to return to the Home page.

Figure 14.8 Mobile Navigator

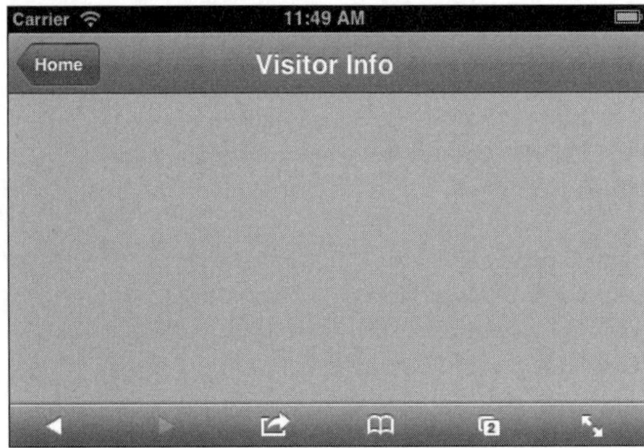

Figure 14.9 Page Heading with Back button

Hierarchical Navigation

Hierarchical navigation can be implemented with the Outline (`xe:outline`) and associated Node (`xe:basicContainerNode and xe:basicLeafNode`) controls. Listing 14.7 shows a custom control that supports hierarchical navigation for a Single Page Application. The Outline has a collection of Container Nodes, which in turn have a collection of children that are Basic Nodes and represents the leaves in the tree structure. Selecting one of the Basic Nodes will trigger navigation to the associated Application Page within the Single Page Application.

Listing 14.7 Outline Custom Control

```
<?xml version="1.0" encoding="UTF-8"?>
<xp:view xmlns:xp="http://www.ibm.com/xsp/core"
  xmlns:xe="http://www.ibm.com/xsp/coreex">
  <xe:outline id="outline1">
    <xe:this.treeNodes>
      <xe:basicContainerNode label="Services">
        <xe:this.children>
          <xe:basicLeafNode label="Business" href="#businessPage">
          </xe:basicLeafNode>
          <xe:basicLeafNode label="Training" href="#trainingPage">
          </xe:basicLeafNode>
        </xe:this.children>
      </xe:basicContainerNode>
      <xe:basicContainerNode label="Products">
        <xe:this.children>
          <xe:basicLeafNode label="Software" href="#softwarePage">
          </xe:basicLeafNode>
```

```
            <xe:basicLeafNode label="Systems" href="#systemsPage">
            </xe:basicLeafNode>
          </xe:this.children>
        </xe:basicContainerNode>
        <xe:basicContainerNode label="Support">
          <xe:this.children>
            <xe:basicLeafNode label="Downloads" href="#downloadsPage">
            </xe:basicLeafNode>
          </xe:this.children>
        </xe:basicContainerNode>
      </xe:this.treeNodes>
  </xe:outline>
</xp:view>
```

Listing 14.8 shows the Single Page Application that uses the Outline custom control.

Listing 14.8 Hierarchical Navigation XPage

```
<?xml version="1.0" encoding="UTF-8"?>
<xp:view xmlns:xp="http://www.ibm.com/xsp/core"
  xmlns:xe="http://www.ibm.com/xsp/coreex"
  xmlns:xc="http://www.ibm.com/xsp/custom">
  <xe:singlePageApp id="navigationApp" selectedPageName="outlinePage">
    <xe:appPage id="outlinePage" pageName="outlinePage">
      <xc:Outline></xc:Outline>
    </xe:appPage>
    <xe:appPage id="businessPage" pageName="businessPage">
      <xe:djxmHeading back="Services" moveTo="outlinePage">
        <xe:this.label>Business</xe:this.label>
      </xe:djxmHeading>
    </xe:appPage>
    <xe:appPage id="trainingPage" pageName="trainingPage">
      <xe:djxmHeading back="Services" moveTo="outlinePage">
        <xe:this.label>Training</xe:this.label>
      </xe:djxmHeading>
    </xe:appPage>
    <xe:appPage id="softwarePage" pageName="softwarePage">
      <xe:djxmHeading back="Products" moveTo="outlinePage">
        <xe:this.label>Software</xe:this.label>
      </xe:djxmHeading>
    </xe:appPage>
    <xe:appPage id="systemsPage" pageName="systemsPage">
      <xe:djxmHeading back="Products" moveTo="outlinePage">
        <xe:this.label>Systems</xe:this.label>
      </xe:djxmHeading>
```

```
    </xe:appPage>
    <xe:appPage id="downloadsPage" pageName="#downloadsPage">
      <xe:djxmHeading back="Support" moveTo="outlinePage">
        <xe:this.label>Downloads</xe:this.label>
      </xe:djxmHeading>
    </xe:appPage>
  </xe:singlePageApp>
</xp:view>
```

Context-Sensitive Navigation

Context-sensitive navigation means that your application provides users with the navigation options that represent the next logical steps within the application. It is important not to overload users with too many navigation options because this can make your application difficult to use, and mobile application users have a very low tolerance for difficult-to-use applications.

Listing 14.9 shows a mobile XPage with four application pages used for home, start, settings, and advanced functionality. In this scenario, the advanced functionality is only accessible from the Settings page. The intention here is to hide complexity, but another reason to do this is that it might only make sense to make screens available after another operation—for example, after the start functionality.

Listing 14.9 Context-Sensitive Navigation XPage

```
<?xml version="1.0" encoding="UTF-8"?>
<xp:view xmlns:xp="http://www.ibm.com/xsp/core"
       xmlns:xe="http://www.ibm.com/xsp/coreex"
       xmlns:xc="http://www.ibm.com/xsp/custom">
       <xe:singlePageApp id="contextSensitiveApp"
➥selectedPageName="homePage">
              <xe:appPage id="homePage" pageName="homePage">
                     <xc:TabBar pageName="home"></xc:TabBar>
                     Home Page
              </xe:appPage>
              <xe:appPage id="startPage" pageName="startPage">
                     <xc:TabBar pageName="start"></xc:TabBar>
                     Start Page
              </xe:appPage>
              <xe:appPage id="settingsPage" pageName="settingsPage">
                     <xc:TabBar pageName="settings"></xc:TabBar>
                     Settings Page
              </xe:appPage>
              <xe:appPage id="advancedPage" pageName="advancedPage">
                     <xc:TabBar pageName="advanced"></xc:TabBar>
                     Advanced Page
```

```
            </xe:appPage>
        </xe:singlePageApp>
</xp:view>
```

The navigation for this application is implemented in the page heading using a segmented button list, as shown in Figure 14.10.

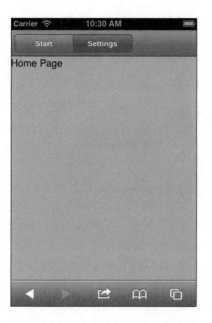

Figure 14.10 Heading with segmented buttons

The functionality is encapsulated in a custom control, the code for which is demonstrated in Listing 14.10. A Page Heading with a nested Tab Bar is used to implement this navigation strategy. The custom control takes a single parameter that is the name of the page currently displayed. Each Tab Bar button uses a computed rendered property to determine if it should display. The button for the advanced screen displays only when the Settings screen is active.

Listing 14.10 Context-Sensitive Navigation Custom Control

```
<?xml version="1.0" encoding="UTF-8"?>
<xp:view xmlns:xp="http://www.ibm.com/xsp/core"
  xmlns:xe="http://www.ibm.com/xsp/coreex">
  <xe:djxmHeading>
    <xe:tabBar id="tabBar1"
      style="background-color:rgb(255,255,255);width:100%;"
```

```
      barType="segmentedControl">
      <xe:tabBarButton id="homeButton" label="Home"
        rendered="#{javascript:compositeData.pageName!='home'}"
        onClick="location.hash='#homePage';">
      </xe:tabBarButton>
      <xe:tabBarButton id="startButton" label="Start"
        onClick="location.hash='#startPage';">
        <xe:this.rendered>
        <![CDATA[#{javascript:compositeData.pageName!='start' &&
compositeData.pageName!='advanced'}]]>
        </xe:this.rendered>
      </xe:tabBarButton>
      <xe:tabBarButton id="settingsButton" label="Settings"
        rendered="#{javascript:compositeData.pageName!='settings'}"
        onClick="location.hash='#settingsPage';">
      </xe:tabBarButton>
      <xe:tabBarButton id="advancedButton" label="Advanced"
        onClick="location.hash='#advancedPage';">
        <xe:this.rendered>
        <![CDATA[#{javascript:compositeData.pageName!='home' &&
          compositeData.pageName!='start' &&
          compositeData.pageName!='advanced'}]]>
        </xe:this.rendered>
      </xe:tabBarButton>
    </xe:tabBar>
  </xe:djxmHeading>
</xp:view>
```

Another commonly used way to implement this pattern is to use a Tab Bar with a list of icons for navigation displayed at the bottom of the screen.

Now you have seen how to navigate around your application using a number of commonly used patterns. There may be times in which you need to write script that responds to transition events—for example, to prompt the user to perform some action with values entered on the current page. Starting in the 9.0.1 release, XPages also supports new touch-based events:

- `onBeforeTransitionIn`: Triggered before transitioning into a page
- `onAfterTransitionIn`: Triggered after transitioning into a page
- `onBeforeTransitionOut`: Triggered before transitioning out of a page
- `onAfterTransitionOut`: Triggered after transitioning out of a page

The XPage in Listing 14.11 shows how to block transition out of a page.

Listing 14.11 onBeforeTransitionOut Sample XPage

```
<?xml version="1.0" encoding="UTF-8"?>
<xp:view xmlns:xp="http://www.ibm.com/xsp/core"
xmlns:xe="http://www.ibm.com/xsp/coreex">
  <xe:singlePageApp selectedPageName="firstPage">
    <xe:appPage id="transitionPage" pageName="firstPage">
      <xp:eventHandler event="onBeforeTransitionOut"
        submit="false">
        <xe:this.script>
<![CDATA[
alert("Leaving First page!");
]]>
        </xe:this.script>
      </xp:eventHandler>
      <xe:djxmHeading id="djxmHeading3">
        <xe:this.label>First</xe:this.label>
      </xe:djxmHeading>
      <xe:djxmLineItem label="Second Page" moveTo="secondPage"/>
    </xe:appPage>
    <xe:appPage id="secondPage" pageName="secondPage">
      <xe:djxmHeading id="djxmHeading1">
        <xe:this.label>Second</xe:this.label>
      </xe:djxmHeading>
      <xe:djxmLineItem label="First Page" moveTo="firstPage"/>
    </xe:appPage>
  </xe:singlePageApp>
</xp:view>
```

Interacting with a Mobile Application

Mobile devices introduce some new interaction methods that you need to consider during the development of your application. XPages provides additional mobile events to support the following mobile specific interaction methods:

- Orientation-based
- Touch-based
- Multitouch-based

Orientation-Based Interaction

The optimum layout of the UI can vary depending on the device orientation. Your application should respond to orientation change events and adapt the UI accordingly. If this is not possible, the UI should be designed to provide a good user experience for each orientation. CSS provides functionality that allows you to control the presentation based on the media type; the `@media` rule can be used to optionally hide content depending on the orientation. Listing 14.12 shows some CSS that defines a style class that enables you to hide elements in portrait orientation. The `@media` rule is used to define different values for the style class based on the current orientation, which hides it when in portrait mode.

Listing 14.12 Landscape-Only Display

```
@media only screen and (orientation:portrait) {
  .landscape-only {
    display: none;
  }
}
@media only screen and (orientation:landscape) {
  .landscape-only {
    display: block;
  }
}
```

Listing 14.13 shows an XPage that uses the CSS in Listing 14.12. The Application Page has a control that displays only in landscape orientation. When you run this sample and switch the device orientation, the Optional Stuff shows or hides automatically.

Listing 14.13 Landscape-Only Display Using CSS

```
<?xml version="1.0" encoding="UTF-8"?>
<xp:view xmlns:xp="http://www.ibm.com/xsp/core"
  xmlns:xe="http://www.ibm.com/xsp/coreex">
  <xp:this.resources>
    <xp:styleSheet href="/orientation.css"></xp:styleSheet>
  </xp:this.resources>
  <xe:singlePageApp selectedPageName="orientationPage">
    <xe:appPage id="orientationPage" pageName="orientationPage">
      <xe:djxmHeading id="djxmHeading3">
        <xe:this.label>Orientation</xe:this.label>
      </xe:djxmHeading>
      <xe:djxmRoundRectList id="djxmRoundRectList1">
        Required Stuff
      </xe:djxmRoundRectList>
      <xe:djxmRoundRectList id="djxmRoundRectList2"
        styleClass="landscape-only">
        Optional Stuff
```

```
      </xe:djxmRoundRectList>
    </xe:appPage>
  </xe:singlePageApp>
</xp:view>
```

Listing 14.14 shows a further refinement on this technique to define separate style sheets for each orientation and then uses the media attribute on the `xp:styleSheet` tag to determine which style sheet is used.

Listing 14.14 Landscape-Only Display Using Style Sheets

```
<?xml version="1.0" encoding="UTF-8"?>
<?xml version="1.0" encoding="UTF-8"?>
<xp:view xmlns:xp="http://www.ibm.com/xsp/core"
  xmlns:xe="http://www.ibm.com/xsp/coreex">
  <xp:this.resources>
    <xp:styleSheet media="only screen and (orientation:portrait)"
href="/portrait.css"></xp:styleSheet>
    <xp:styleSheet media="only screen and (orientation:landscape)"
href="/lanscape.css"></xp:styleSheet>
  </xp:this.resources>
  <xe:singlePageApp selectedPageName="orientationPage">
    <xe:appPage id="orientationPage" pageName="orientationPage">
      <xe:djxmHeading id="djxmHeading3">
        <xe:this.label>Orientation</xe:this.label>

      </xe:djxmHeading>
      <xe:djxmRoundRectList id="djxmRoundRectList1">
        Required Stuff
      </xe:djxmRoundRectList>
      <xe:djxmRoundRectList id="djxmRoundRectList2"
        styleClass="landscape-only">
        Optional Stuff
      </xe:djxmRoundRectList>
    </xe:appPage>
  </xe:singlePageApp>
</xp:view>
```

Starting with the 9.0.1 release XPages now includes an `onOrientationChange` event on the Single Page Application control. You can write client-side application logic, which is executed when the user changes the device orientation. Listing 14.15 shows some client-side JavaScript, which is called in response to an orientation change. The `orientation` property can have the following values:

- 0: Portrait mode
- 90: Landscape mode with the screen turned to the left
- -90: Landscape mode with the screen turned to the right
- 180: Portrait mode with the screen upside down

Not all devices support all the modes, for example, iOS devices do not support 180. Also notice in this sample that the initial value is set to Unknown. It is not possible to write a server-side computed expression that computes the current orientation. Because of network latency, the user could have changed the device orientation between requesting the page and it displaying. Therefore, client-side computations need to be used when developing orientation-based logic.

Listing 14.15 onOrientation Change Event

```
<?xml version="1.0" encoding="UTF-8"?>
<xp:view xmlns:xp="http://www.ibm.com/xsp/core"
xmlns:xe="http://www.ibm.com/xsp/coreex">
  <xe:singlePageApp selectedPageName="orientationChangePage"
    id="singlePageApp1">
    <xe:appPage id="orientationChangePage"
➥pageName="orientationChangePage">
      <xe:djxmHeading id="djxmHeading3">
        <xe:this.label>OnOrientationChange</xe:this.label>
      </xe:djxmHeading>
      <xp:label value="Unknown" id="label1"></xp:label>
    </xe:appPage>
    <xp:eventHandler event="onOrientationChange" submit="false">
      <xe:this.script>
<![CDATA[
var label = document.getElementById("view:_id1:orientationChangePage_
content:label1");
if ( orientation == 0 ) {
    label.innerHTML = "Portrait Mode {orientation=0}";
}
else if ( orientation == 90 ) {
    label.innerHTML = "Landscape Mode {orientation=90}";
}
else if ( orientation == -90 ) {
    label.innerHTML = "Landscape Mode {orientation=-90}";
}
else if ( orientation == 180 ) {
    label.innerHTML = "Portrait Mode {orientation=180}";
}
]]>
```

```
      </xe:this.script>
    </xp:eventHandler>
  </xe:singlePageApp>
</xp:view>
```

Touch-Based Interaction

Most mobile devices now support the ability for users to interact using a finger or stylus. When designing a UI for a touch-based interaction, controls should be positioned and sized so users can individually select them. Controls that can be selected need to be large enough so that they can be easily selected and it is clear which item is currently selected. Remember part of the screen may be obscured by users' fingers as they select items, so you need to make sure that you provide feedback (for example, use roll-overs) to indicate what item is currently selected. Also, you need to avoid frustrating users if they cannot easily select a particular option. Listing 14.16 shows an example of interacting with touch-based events when using the mobile switch.

Listing 14.16 onTouchStart and onTouchEnd Events

```
<?xml version="1.0" encoding="UTF-8"?>
<xp:view xmlns:xp="http://www.ibm.com/xsp/core"
xmlns:xe="http://www.ibm.com/xsp/coreex">
  <xe:singlePageApp selectedPageName="transitionPage">
    <xe:appPage id="transitionPage" pageName="transitionPage">
      <xe:djxmHeading id="djxmHeading3">
        <xe:this.label>Transition</xe:this.label>
      </xe:djxmHeading>
      <xp:label value="Swipe Me: " id="label1"></xp:label>
      <xe:djxmSwitch leftLabel="ON" rightLabel="OFF" id="djxmSwitch1">
      <xp:eventHandler event="onTouchStart" submit="false">
        <xe:this.script>
<![CDATA[
var label1Id = '#{javascript:getClientId("label1")}';
var label1 = document.getElementById(label1Id);
label1.innerHTML = "--- Swiping ---";
]]>
        </xe:this.script>
      </xp:eventHandler>
      <xp:eventHandler event="onTouchEnd" submit="false">
        <xe:this.script>
<![CDATA[
var label1Id = '#{javascript:getClientId("label1")}';
var label1 = document.getElementById(label1Id);
```

```
label1.innerHTML = "Swiped Me: ";
]]>
        </xe:this.script>
      </xp:eventHandler>
      </xe:djxmSwitch>
    </xe:appPage>
  </xe:singlePageApp>
</xp:view>
```

Multitouch-Based Interaction

A multitouch interaction is the ability of the touch screen to detect the presence of multiple points of contact. One of the most common multitouch gestures is pinch-to-zoom, which allows the user to zoom in and out. When designing an XPage that will be accessed on a mobile device, you must take care to ensure users don't need to zoom when they first view the page. You may have some XPages that you don't want to or have time to convert to a mobile design, but you can still improve the experience for mobile users by making sure the pages render with the optimum zoom when accessed with a mobile device. The way you do this is to use the viewport meta tag. Listing 14.17 shows how to set the viewport for an XPage using the `xp:metaData` tag with a width of 500. (A further enhancement would be to compute this value based on the specific device.)

Listing 14.17 Viewport Meta Tag

```
<?xml version="1.0" encoding="UTF-8"?>
<xp:view xmlns:xp="http://www.ibm.com/xsp/core">
  <xp:this.resources>
    <xp:metaData name="viewport" content="width=500">
    </xp:metaData>
  </xp:this.resources>
<h1>Mobile XPages Applications</h1>
...
</xp:view>
```

Take, for example, the launch page (`index.xsp`) for this chapter's sample database. Figure 14.11 shows how the page will display first with the default viewport width (which is 980 for an iPhone) and then with the viewport set as shown in Listing 14.17. The XPage is displayed in a more readable and usable manner by changing the width.

The viewport meta tag supports some other attributes that allow you to control how your XPages displays:

- **`width:`** Viewport width, that is, the width of the page a user sees.
- **`height:`** Viewport height, that is, the height of the page a user sees.

- **`initial-scale:`** Initial zoom scale of the viewport.
- **`maximum-scale:`** Maximum view scale of the view port.
- **`minimum-scale:`** Minimum view scale of the view port.
- **`user-scalable:`** Determines if the user is allowed to zoom in and out of the viewport.

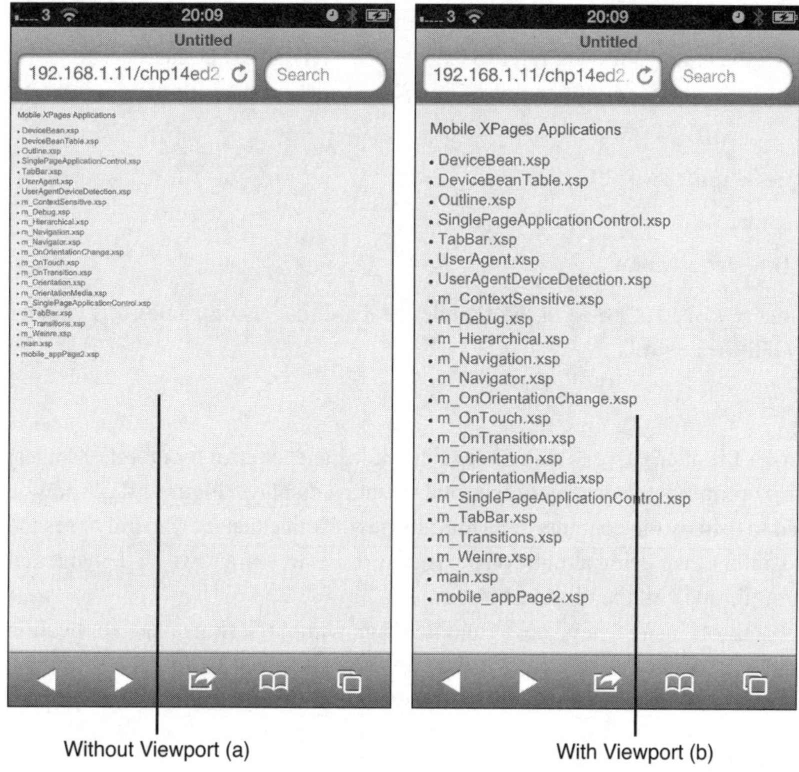

Figure 14.11 With and without viewport

Mobile Themes

XPages comes with mobile theme support for iOS and Android devices. As explained earlier, you can configure a mobile theme for use with your mobile XPages by identifying those pages using a special prefix (typically `m_`). The default mobile theme is called Mobile default. When this option is selected, the appropriate theme is automatically selected for you, that is, the theme named iPhone (because of historical reasons) for iOS device or the theme named Android for Android devices. Each theme can cause mobile styles to be applied to selected controls, which give them a native look and feel when they are rendered on a mobile device. You can select an alternative theme for mobile pages—for example, selecting the OneUI IDX v1.3 mobile theme provides a consistent look and feel between all mobile devices accessing your application. You can also define your own mobile theme; if, for example, you wanted to have you own look and feel irrespective of the mobile device. You can also specify separate themes for iOS and Android devices; again, this flexibility works if your application has its own branding. If you want to switch the style based on the device, you need to add logic within the theme. This is how the One UI theme works, and this will be further explored later in this section. For more detailed information on themes and how to create your own, refer to Chapter 16, "XPages Theming."

Mobile styling is provided for all the mobile XPages controls and the following Extension Library controls:

- Data View (`xe:dataView`)
- Outline (`xe:outline`)
- Form Table (`xe:formTable`)

The XPage name `m_mobileTheme` in the sample database that accompanies this chapter includes pages with all these controls.

Data View

The Data View control is the alternative to using a regular View Panel control for mobile XPages. The Data View control optimizes the display of the rows of data it displays. Figure 14.12 shows a Data View configured to display the contents of a Domino view. Notice that it efficiently uses the available space. Also, rather than using a traditional pager, it retrieves extra rows on demand and allows the user to scroll through all the retrieved rows.

The Data View control can also navigate to another page within the singe page application to display the document associated with a row in the view. As shown in Listing 14.18, this is achieved by setting the `pageName` property to the hash tag value of the application page to open.

Listing 14.18 Data View Application Page

```
<xe:appPage id="dataViewPage" pageName="dataViewPage">
  <xe:djxmHeading back="Home" moveTo="controlsPage">
    <xe:this.label>Data View</xe:this.label>
  </xe:djxmHeading>
  <xe:dataView id="dataView1" rows="10"
    pageName="#formTablePage">
    <xe:this.data>
      <xp:dominoView var="view1" viewName="CarMakes">
      </xp:dominoView>
    </xe:this.data>
    <xp:this.facets>
      <xp:link text="Show More" escape="true"
        xp:key="pagerBottom" id="link1">
```

```
        <xp:eventHandler event="onclick"
          submit="false">
          <xp:this.script>
            <xe:addRows for="dataView1"
              rowCount="10">
            </xe:addRows>
          </xp:this.script>
        </xp:eventHandler>
      </xp:link>
    </xp:this.facets>
    <xe:this.summaryColumn>
      <xe:viewSummaryColumn columnName="CarMake">
      </xe:viewSummaryColumn>
    </xe:this.summaryColumn>
  </xe:dataView>
</xe:appPage>
```

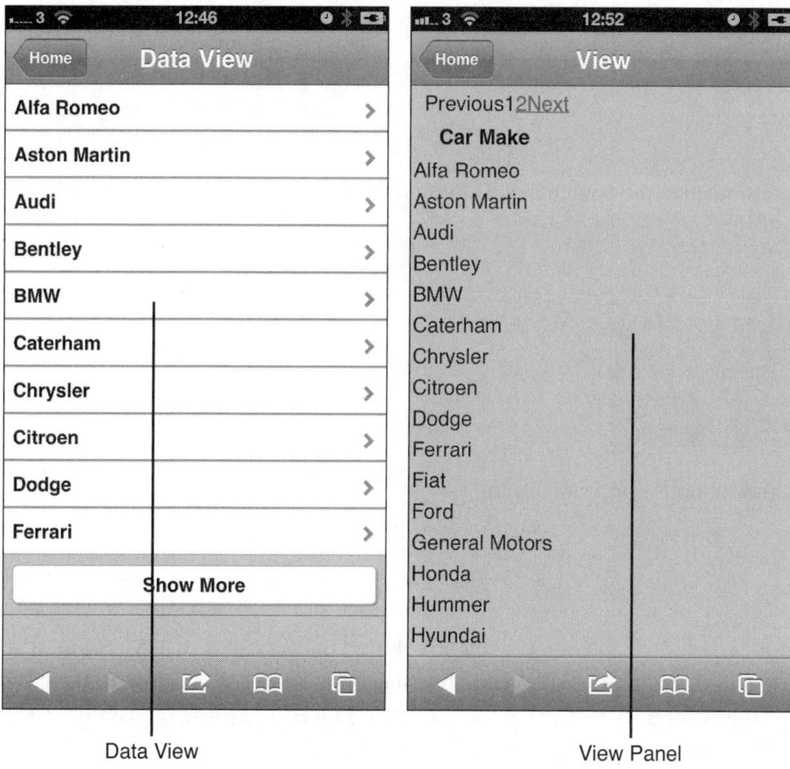

Figure 14.12 Data View versus View Panel

Outline

The Outline control was introduced earlier in the chapter as a way to provide navigation within your Mobile application. Figure 14.13 shows the difference between the mobile and web styling. When used in a mobile XPage, the Outline control supports expanding and collapsing of nodes, which makes it suitable providing an application menu.

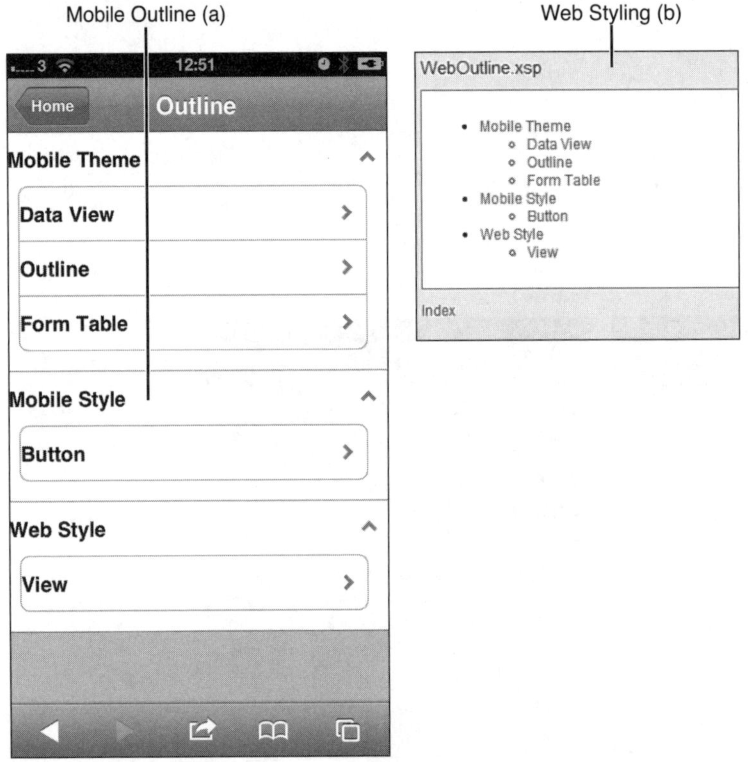

Figure 14.13 Outline with mobile and web styling

Form Table

The Form Table control is a useful container when you design data entry or display forms. The Form Table has a title and description displayed above the rows of data. Each row in the table has a label and one or more controls to display the row data. Figure 14.14 shows the difference in how the Form Table is styled for a mobile device or desktop web browser. If you inspect the

DOM for the two pages, you'll notice that for a desktop web browser a table is used, but for a mobile browser, the Form Table Rows are created as div elements with appropriate styling. HTML tables are not a good choice for laying out content when you have limited screen real estate and should be avoided. The common problem when using HTML tables on mobile devices is that they result in excess whitespace, which wastes the valuable device real estate.

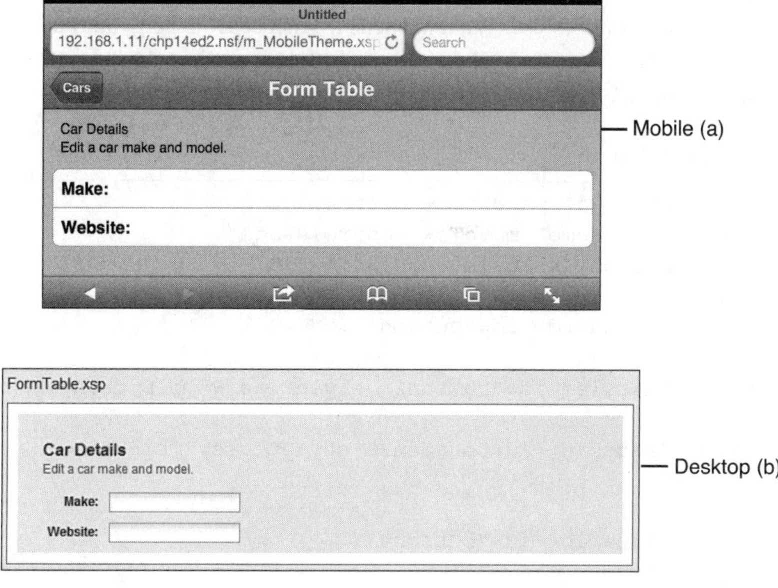

Figure 14.14 Form Table with mobile and web styling

So now you've seen what you get for free for the default mobile themes, but what about the rest of the controls? The next section looks at the options for styling XPages controls.

Styling XPages Controls for Mobile Applications

Standard XPages controls don't automatically change their styling when displayed as part of a mobile page using the standard mobile themes. So how do you style a standard XPages control so that it appears well on a mobile device? There are a number of approaches you can use. Take a button as an example use case and explore these options. Listing 14.19 shows an application page with five buttons, and Figure 14.15 shows how they display on a mobile device. The first button (lines 5 through 6) has no styling applied, and if you look at how this is displayed, you'll see it's not a good fit for what you would expect on a mobile device. That is, it's too small and the styling looks out of place. The second button (lines 7 through 8) has the `styleClass` set to `mblButton`, and this causes it to display well on a mobile device. This is a style class that is provided by the mobile theme. Ideally, this is all you would have to do, but unfortunately this is not the case because the style class is different between iOS and Android devices. The third button (lines 9 through 10) shows how to use the Android version of the mobile button style class. So what if you target multiple devices? One option, which is shown in the fourth button (lines 1 through 15) is to compute the appropriate style class to use based on the information from the device bean. This works but is awkward to use. What happens if you use Dojo and your buttons have a `dojoType` attribute set? This use case is shown in the fifth button (lines 16 through 17) and again no styling is applied so you have work to do, or do you?

Listing 14.19 Button Mobile Styling

```
1.  <xe:appPage id="buttonPage" pageName="buttonPage">
2.    <xe:djxmHeading back="Home" moveTo="controlsPage">
3.      <xe:this.label>Button</xe:this.label>
4.    </xe:djxmHeading>
5.    <xp:button value="Standard" id="button1">
6.    </xp:button>
7.    <xp:button value="Mobile" id="button2" styleClass="mblButton">
8.    </xp:button>
9.    <xp:button value="Android" id="button3" styleClass="mblButton_
android">
10.   </xp:button>
11.   <xp:button value="Dynamic" id="button4">
12.     <xp:this.styleClass>
13. <![CATA[#{javascript:deviceBean.isAndroid() ? "mblButton_android" :
"mblButton" }]]>
14.     </xp:this.styleClass>
15.   </xp:button>
16.   <xp:button value="Dojo" id="button5" dojoType="dijit.form.
Button">
17.   </xp:button>
18.   <br />
19.   deviceBean.isIphone=
20.   <xp:text value="#{javascript:deviceBean.isIphone()}" />
21.   <br />
22.   deviceBean.isAndroid=
23.   <xp:text value="#{javascript:deviceBean.isAndroid()}" />
24.   <br />
25. </xe:appPage>
```

Figure 14.15 Buttons with mobile styling

If instead of using the default mobile theme, you switch to using One UI the situation changes. Figure 14.16 shows how the same five buttons display when the One UI theme is selected as the mobile them in the XPages Properties. So now things look much better; the standard and Dojo buttons both display well without having had to make any changes. This is the ideal situation; you can just add standard XPages controls and have them display well on mobile devices automatically.

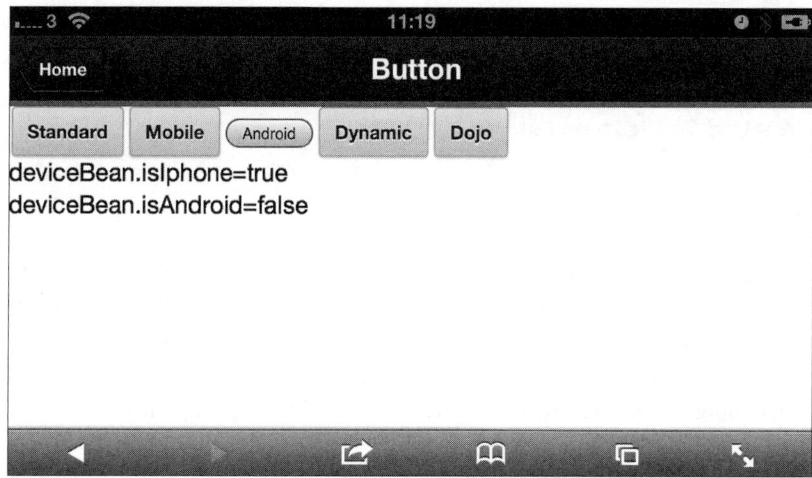

Figure 14.16 Buttons with mobile styling using One UI

So how does this work? If you inspect the DOM of the mobile page, you can notice that the standard and Dojo buttons are rendered in the page with the style class set to `mblButton mblPrimaryButton`. So these style classes are added automatically to all buttons that are rendered when the One UI theme is used. Listing 14.20 shows an extract from the One UI theme file (`oneui_idx_v1.3.theme`). You can see the One UI theme specifies the `lotusBtn` style class is specified for buttons.

Listing 14.20 One UI Button Theme

```
<!-- Basic Button -->
<control>
  <name>Button</name>
  <property>
    <name>styleClass</name>
    <value>lotusBtn</value>
  </property>
</control>
```

However, this isn't the full story. There is another theme file used by One UI that is associated with the mobile renderers; this file is called `oneui_idx_v1.3_mobile_renderers_fragment.theme`. If you look at the contents of this file, you will see additional styling configuration, and it is here you see the mobile style classes applied, as demonstrated in Listing 14.21.

Listing 14.21 One UI Button Mobile Theme

```
<!-- Command Button -->
<control>
  <name>Button.Command</name>
  <property>
    <name>styleClass</name>
    <value> mblButton mblPrimaryButton</value>
  </property>
</control>
```

Using One UI is a good option if you want to have your applications display with a consistent look and feel and to automatically display well on mobile devices. It is recommended that you consider using OneUI by default when developing mobile applications, or indeed create your own theme in preference to adding lots of conditional styling logic within your XPages. Next, look at what to do when things go wrong when you develop a Mobile XPages application.

Debugging Mobile XPages

When something goes wrong with your mobile XPages, you need to debug them to diagnose the problem and figure out how to resolve the problem. For client debugging you will likely have used a browser debugging tool like Firebug for Firefox or Web Inspector for Safari. In this section, you learn about two techniques you can use to debug Mobile XPages. There are other options, for example, there is a recently released Firebug Lite Bookmarklet for iPad, but these techniques described here are the ones favored by the book authors when debugging their Mobile XPages. There are two approaches described in the following sections, both of which rely on viewing the DOM hierarchy for your mobile XPage in real time on another device. The first approach is targeted at iOS mobile development, and the second approach is a more generic solution, which works irrespective of the mobile device you target.

Debugging XPages on iOS

If you have a Mac, you can use it to debug your Mobile XPages. The procedure is straightforward using the following steps:

1. Enable the Develop menu in the Advanced preferences.
2. Connect your mobile device to the Mac with a USB cable.
3. A new menu item appears in the Develop menu that enables you to inspect a page on your mobile device.

Figure 14.17 shows an example of the type of menu item that displays if you had an iPhone connected to your Mac.

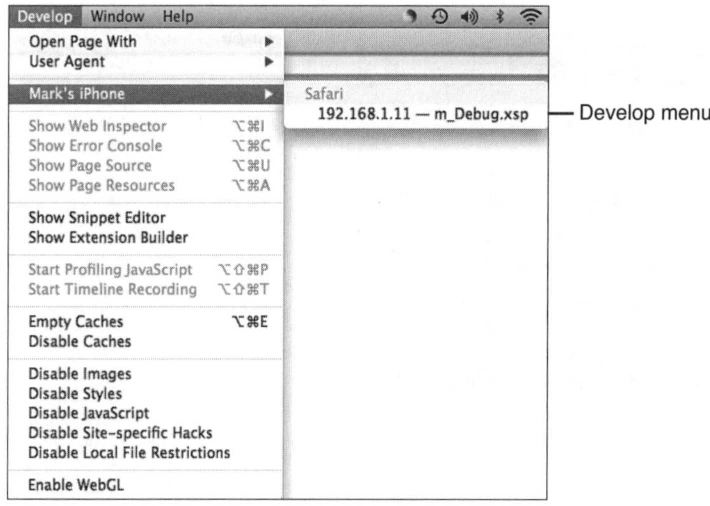

Figure 14.17 Develop menu item

When you select the menu item, the Web Inspector opens. The Web Inspector can be used to view the DOM of the page, which displays within the browser on the iPhone. Figure 14.18 shows the DOM for the **m_Debug.xsp** page.

Figure 14.18 Web Inspector

As you select elements from within the DOM in Web Inspector, the equivalent element within the browser is highlighted. For example, if you select the span element that corresponds to the Toolbar button, the button is highlighted on the device, as shown in Figure 14.19.

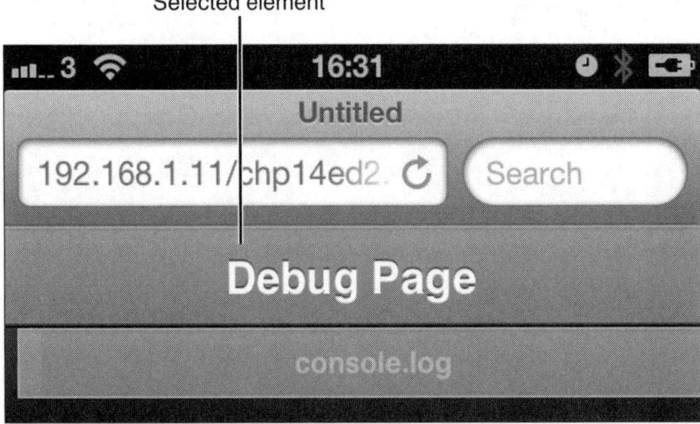

Figure 14.19 Selected element

In addition to viewing the DOM, you can also display a JavaScript console. Any logging statements that are output using the console JavaScript class can be viewed within Web Inspector. Figure 14.20 shows the JavaScript console with some text that was output when the Toolbar Button in the **m_Debug.xsp** XPage was clicked.

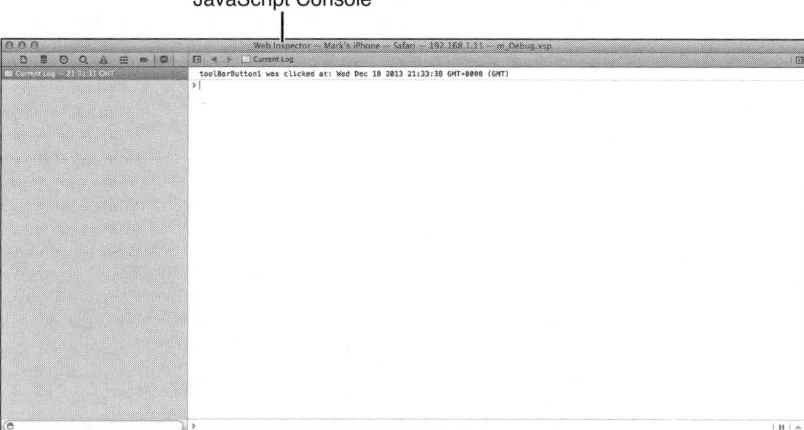

Figure 14.20 JavaScript console

For more information on the Web Inspector, visit the iOS Developer Library at `https://developer.apple.com/library/ios/navigation/`.

Debugging XPages with Web Inspector Remote (aka weinre)

If you don't have a Mac or if you need to debug XPages on an Android or other non-iOS-based device, you can use weinre. The weinre debugger is run as a node.js application, so you need to download and install node.js first. To get the setup to start debugging with weinre, follow these steps:

1. Download and install node (see `http://nodejs.org/download/`).
2. Install the weinre npm package (use **npm -g install weinre**).
3. Execute the following command to run weinre: **weinre --httpPort <port> --boundHost -all-**
4. Add a client-side script tag to each XPage you want to debug; the script tag must load the weinre target script from the server where weinre is running (see Listing 14.22 where weinre is running on a server with ip address 192.168.1.11).
5. Open the weinre client from your desktop browser using the url: `http://<host>:<port>/client/`.
6. Open the XPage that includes the weinre target script in your mobile browser.
7. Now refresh the weinre client in your desktop browser, and you should see the mobile target listed (as shown in Figure 14.21).

Listing 14.22 Script Tag for weinre Target Script

```
<xp:script type="test/javascript"
      src="http://192.168.1.11:8090/target/target-script-min.js"
      clientSide="true">
</xp:script>
```

TIP

Select a port for weinre to use that doesn't conflict with any other server you may be running on the same machine. Also specify either -all- or a specific ip address/hostname as the bound host. Using localhost isn't sufficient unless the browser you are debugging is running on the same localhost.

Figure 14.21 weinre client

Figure 14.22 shows the DOM for the **m_Weinre.xsp** page.

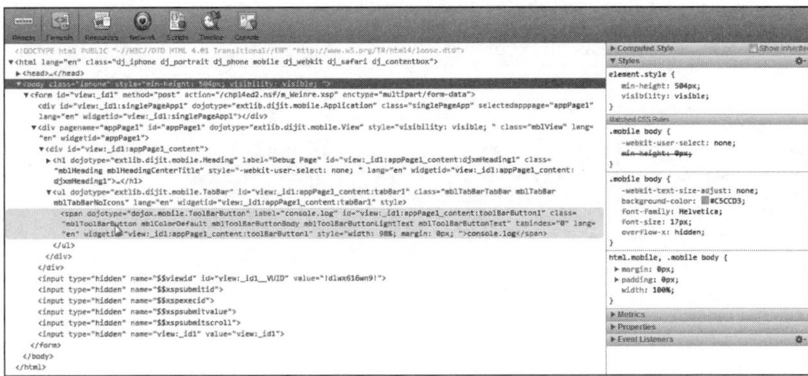

Figure 14.22 Web Inspector

The Element tab in the weinre client enables you to view the DOM of the page you are debugging. As you select elements from within the DOM in the weinre client, the equivalent element within the browser is highlighted. For example, if you select the `span` element that corresponds to the Toolbar button, the button itself is highlighted on the device, as shown in Figure 14.23.

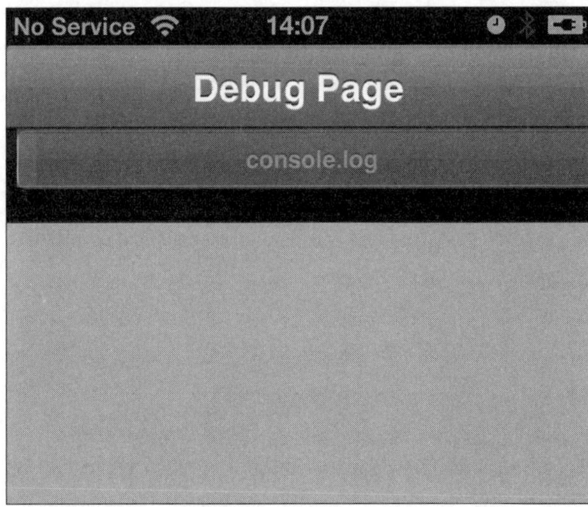

Figure 14.23 Selected element

In addition to viewing the DOM, you can also display a JavaScript console. So any logging statements that are output using the console JavaScript class can be viewed within Web Inspector. Figure 14.24 shows the JavaScript console with some text that was output when the Toolbar button in the `m_Weinre.xsp` XPage was clicked.

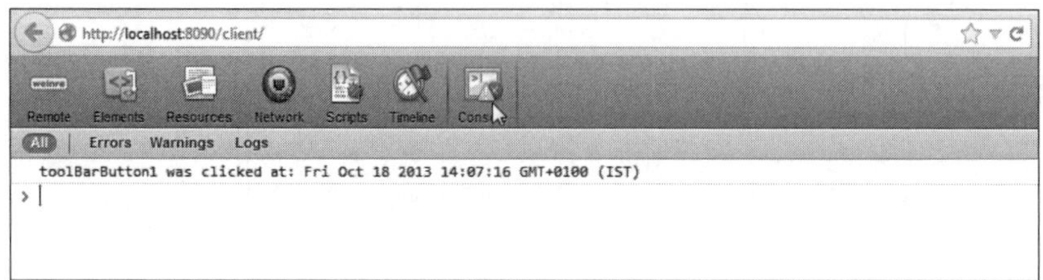

Figure 14.24 JavaScript console

For more information on weinre, visit the documentation pages at `http://people.apache.org/~pmuellr/weinre/docs/latest/`.

XPages Mobile Extensions

As mentioned earlier, at the time of writing, Domino 9.0.1 has just been released and includes many new mobile features. Also included in this release is a series of extension points within the XPages runtime and Domino Designer to enable new mobile features to be delivered outside of the normal Domino release cycle. The Extension Library project on OpenNTF is used as a vehicle to allow new features to be delivered on a continuous basis. These features include enhancements to the XPages runtime—for example, support for new properties or events and also features within Domino Designer to simplify the development of mobile applications. For example, within 6 weeks of the delivery of Domino 9.0.1, a new Extension Library release is available that includes two new features for mobile application development:

- Addition of the `infiniteScroll` property to the Data View (`xe:dataView`) control
- Addition of the Single Page Application Wizard

> **TIP**
>
> To use Infinite Scroll and the Single Page Application Wizard you need to install the XPages Extension Library version 901v00_02.x (or higher). The XPages Extension Library is available for free download at http://extlib.openntf.org/.

> **TIP**
>
> The samples in this section depend on having these new features so they are included in a separate database called chp14ed2ext.nsf.

Infinite Scrolling

A new property called `infiniteScroll` has been added to the Data View control for use only in mobile XPages. When infinite scrolling is enabled, as the user scrolls through rows in the Data View control, additional rows will be automatically loaded. Rows are prefetched and added directly to the Data View.

Property:

`infiniteScroll`

Values:

- **`enable:`** Enable infinite scrolling in the Data View control. (This overrides the application default.)
- **`disable:`** Disable infinite scrolling in the Data View control. (This overrides the application default.)
- **`auto:`** Uses the application setting xsp.progressive.enhancement=[enable|disable]. (This is the default value.)

Listing 14.23 shows a page containing two Data View controls, both of which have infinite scrolling enabled. Each Data View control has 1,000 rows, and when you open the page on a mobile device, you can keep scrolling down, and pages are automatically loaded for you. The sample shows that two data views can be used on the sample page, each with infinite scrolling enabled.

Listing 14.23 Stacked Data Views with Infinite Scrolling

```
<?xml version="1.0" encoding="UTF-8"?>
<?xml version="1.0" encoding="UTF-8"?>
<xp:view xmlns:xp="http://www.ibm.com/xsp/core"
      xmlns:xe="http://www.ibm.com/xsp/coreex"
      xmlns:xc="http://www.ibm.com/xsp/custom">
      <xp:label value="First Data View" id="label1"></xp:label>
      <xe:dataView id="dataView1" var="viewEntry"
            collapsibleCategory="false" collapsibleDetail="false"
➥rows="20"
            collapsibleRows="false"
            style="height:200px; border:2px solid blue; margin: 5px"
```

```
            summary="Activity" infiniteScroll="enable"
            value="#{javascript:1000}">
            <xe:this.summaryColumn>
                  <xe:viewSummaryColumn
                        value="#{javascript:'First Data View -
➥'+viewEntry}">
                  </xe:viewSummaryColumn>
            </xe:this.summaryColumn>
      </xe:dataView>
      <xp:label value="Second Data View" id="label2"></xp:label>
      <xe:dataView id="dataView2" var="viewEntry" collapsibleRows="true"
            collapsibleDetail="true" columnTitles="true"
            rows="20" showCheckbox="false"
            style="height:200px; border:2px solid #008abf; margin: 5px;"
            infiniteScroll="enable" value="#{javascript:1000}">
            <xe:this.summaryColumn>
                  <xe:viewSummaryColumn
                        value="#{javascript:'Second Data View -
➥'+viewEntry}">
                  </xe:viewSummaryColumn>
            </xe:this.summaryColumn>
      </xe:dataView>
      <xe:tabBar id="tabBar1">Mastering XPages</xe:tabBar>
</xp:view>
```

TIP

Refer to the release notes for the Extension Library version you have installed for details of any limitations associated with new mobile features. For example, at the time of writing, infinite scrolling works only with mobile views, and it is necessary to disable this for a web view.

Single Page Application Wizard

This is a new Domino Designer feature that has been delivered as part of the Extension Library. The feature provides a wizard that can guide you through the process of adding a Single Page Application (`xe:singlePageApp`) control to an XPage. The wizard automatically opens every time you add the Single Page Application control to a page. By default the wizard enforces the best practice of having a custom control for each Application Page you need to create. The wizard also enables you to specify how to navigate between the Application pages.

TIP

Make sure you have installed the Designer extensions from the updateSiteOpenNTF-designer site that comes with the Extension Library to use this feature.

To start using this new wizard, you need to drop a Single Page Application control on to an XPage. Figure 14.25 shows the Single Page Application Wizard.

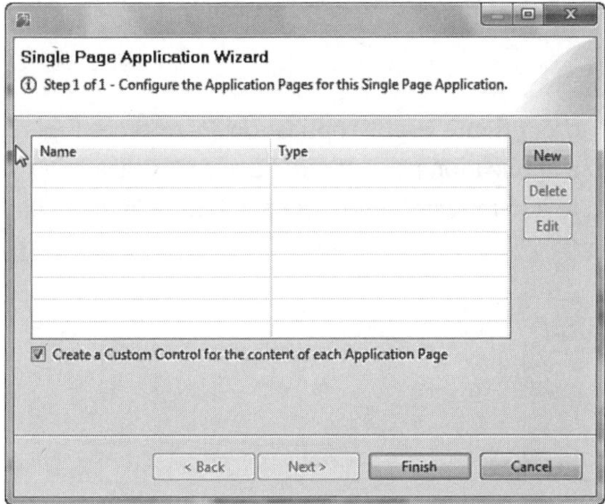

Figure 14.25 Single Page Application Wizard

The wizard has an option to create a custom control for the content of each application page. This is the recommended approach because it helps reduce the complexity of the single page application XPage and results in a more maintainable design. Occasionally, having a custom control per application page can be overkill, so you can turn off this option. The start screen of the wizard also enables you to add the application page by selecting the New button. Figure 14.26 shows the New Application Page dialog, which enables you to create different types of templated application pages.

The following Application Page types are supported:

- General
- Application Navigator
- Document Collection
- Document Viewer

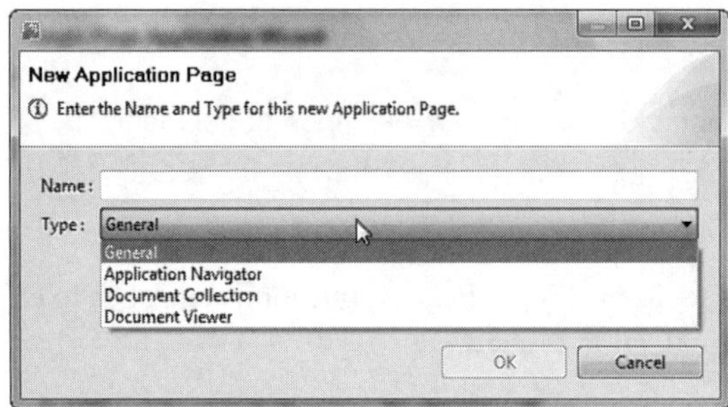

Figure 14.26 New Application Page dialog

The wizard provides different options to configure each Application Page type. Figure 14.27 shows the general options available for an application page. It will have a page heading by default, and you can optionally use the wizard to add toolbar buttons, a back button, and tab bar buttons.

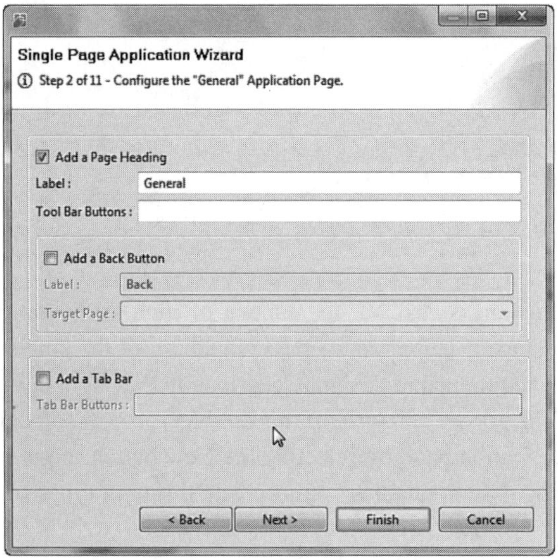

Figure 14.27 General Application Page options

An application navigator application is a special type of page used to navigate around the single page application. You can configure the same options that are supported by a general page. Figure 14.28 shows the options available for an application navigator page; you can create a set of links that allow users to navigate around the application.

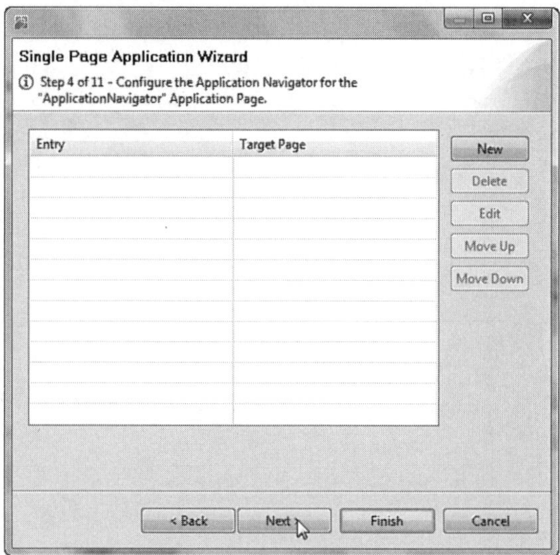

Figure 14.28 Application Navigator Page options

For a document collection application page, the wizard guides you through the process of creating a data source to retrieve the document collection and a data view to display the data. Figure 14.29 shows the options to configure the data source for a document collection page.

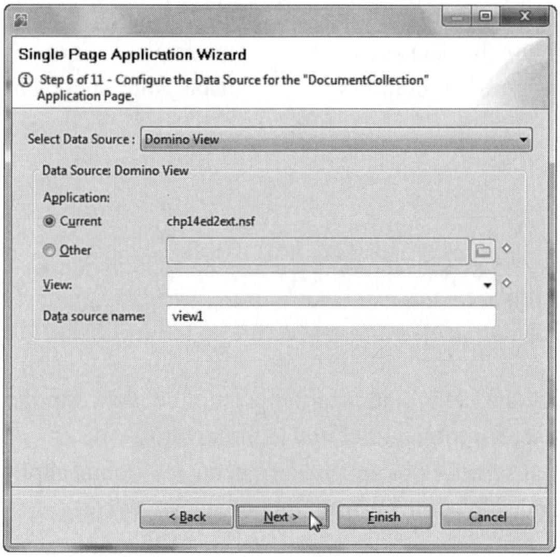

Figure 14.29 Document collection data source configuration

Figure 14.30 shows the options to configure the data view used to display the document collection (including an option to enable infinite scrolling).

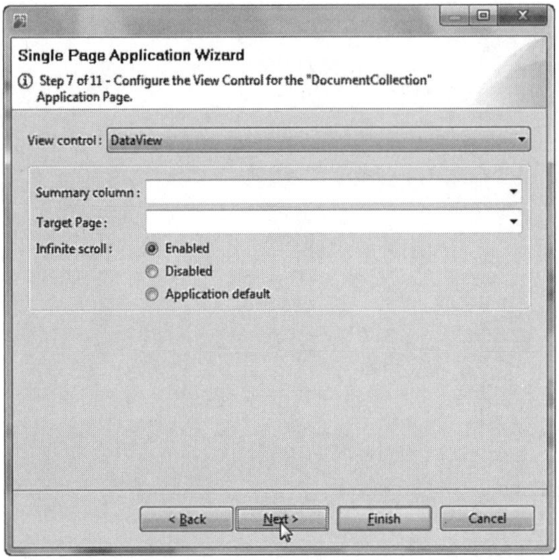

Figure 14.30 Document collection Data View configuration

For a document viewer application page, the wizard guides you through the process of creating a data source to retrieve the document and a set of controls to view the fields of the document. Figure 14.31 shows the options to configure the data source for a document viewer page.

Figure 14.32 shows the options to configure the controls used to display the document fields.

> **TIP**
>
> At the time of writing, there was no support in the wizard for creating a page to support document editing, but this is something that is planned for the Extension Library.

The final step in the wizard is to specify the default application page to be shown in the single page application. Figure 14.33 shows a screen for the final step in the wizard.

You can see from these two examples that some important enhancements for mobile application development are being made available outside of the normal Domino release cycle.

Figure 14.31 Document Viewer data source configuration

Figure 14.32 Document Viewer Fields configuration

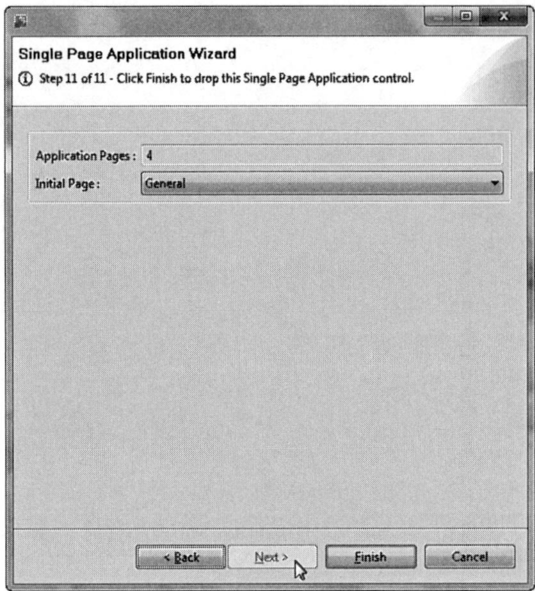

Figure 14.33 Finish Single Application Page Wizard

Summary

This concludes the chapter on XPages mobile application development. So what does the future hold? Responsive web design is emerging as a new approach for building web interfaces with an optimal viewing experience across mobile and desktop browsers and beyond. Bootstrap for XPages is already available as an extension Library, and this provides functionality to allow you to build responsive user interfaces. For more information on using Bootstrap with XPages, visit: `http://bootstrap4xpages.com/`. One UI is expected to also evolve in this direction. So in the future (if you are not already there) the lines between developing for the desktop and developing for mobile will blur, and the techniques you will use now for building Mobile XPages applications will become the mainstream techniques you will use.

CHAPTER 15

XPages Unplugged and Debugged

A dedicated chapter on debugging is perhaps the most fitting way to conclude this section on programmability. After all, you are now well versed with the XPages programming model and have worked through many practical development examples using the XSP markup language, JavaScript, Java, agents, and so forth. Now is the perfect time to learn what to do when things are not working out according to plan.

Because XPages is a server-side application development framework with JavaScript as its default programming language, it makes sense to start these debugging excursions with server-side JavaScript (SSJS). You then move from debugging JavaScript to debugging Java, and finally move to the flip-side of the equation with a section on debugging client-side JavaScript (CSJS)—by which time it is hoped that you will have learned a lot. The good news is that there are a whole slew of tools and techniques at your disposal for figuring out the daily puzzles that application development tends to send your way. These range from the simple (basic print statements) to the superlative (a fully fledged JavaScript debugger) and everything in between. As usual, all debugging capabilities will be explained by way of examples, so you need to work along with the sample application provided for this chapter, namely **Chp15ed2.nsf**, which is part of the download zip file available from the publisher's website: `www.ibmpressbooks.com/title/9780133373370`.

Although this is a general-purpose chapter focusing on common debugging tools and techniques, you should note that some other chapters in the book provide more specialized debugging treatment. For instance, Chapter 13, "XPages in the Notes Client," includes a section titled "Some XPiNC Debugging Tips," aimed at dealing with debugging topics unique to the Notes platform. Similarly, Chapter 14, "XPages Mobile Application Development," has a debugging section pertaining to the issues peculiar to mobile platforms, namely "Debugging Mobile XPages." Finally, Chapter 19, "A First Look at Performance and Scalability," and Chapter 20, "Advanced Performance Topics," focus on application performance, so if you need to debug issues relating to performance or scalability, as opposed to general function or design, then those chapters will most likely provide the answers you seek. This chapter is a general debugging primer, however, and should be read as a prerequisite to Chapters 19 and 20.

Debugging XPages Apps on the Server Side

Mr. Brian Kernighan (well-known co-author of *The C Programming Language*, amongst other things) once stated:

> The most effective debugging tool is still careful thought, coupled with judiciously placed print statements.

Although an undeniably primitive and patently obvious technique, writing out the value of some variable or other is almost always the first port of call when ostensibly simple code yields an unanticipated outcome. (Okay, this may sometimes be due to a lack of "careful thought.")

Printing, Dumping, and Logging

Now there's a heading that should strike fear into the heart of any self-respecting environmentalist. But you can relax; this is not about clearing ancient forests to feed your insatiable printers and creating barren wastelands to consume your unwanted trash. It's far more important than that. This is all about recording information that helps developers figure out how an XPages application is behaving (or misbehaving) at runtime. In SSJS, there are a few different ways to print the state of scalar or complex objects or emit useful error debug information, namely:

- `print(message)` prints the message to the platform console.
- `_dump(object)` prints the details of the object to the platform console.
- Extend an XPages Java logger to print context information to a platform log file.

The workings of the first command should contain no surprises for anyone. That is, if you insert `print("Hello World!")` as SSJS code into an XPage, then the specified message will be output to the Domino server console when the page is opened on the web and that particular piece of script is run. Although that is an intentionally trivial example, you can quickly start to apply this command in more useful contexts in real-world development. Take a look at the Discussion template, and you can quickly imagine how the `print()` command would have been useful when almost any of the XPages were under development. Listing 15.1 contains a snippet extracted from the **authorProfileForm.xsp** custom control, which is used to add or edit the details of registered participants in a discussion application. Three `print` statements, highlighted in **bold**, have been added to the mix, and if you are looking in the custom control, this snippet begins on line number 9:

Listing 15.1 Use of print Statements in SSJS Code

```
<xp:this.documentId>
  <![CDATA[#{javascript:// obtain the document id if it exists...
    var db:NotesDatabase = database;
    var vw:NotesView = db.getView("xpAuthorProfiles");
    var ve:NotesViewEntry = vw.getEntryByKey(userBean.canonicalName,
true);
    var unid = null;

    if (null != ve) {
      print(userBean.canonicalName + " found!");
       unid = ve.getUniversalID();
    } else {
       print(userBean.canonicalName + " NOT found!");
       print(vw.getColumnValues(0));
    }
    return(unid);}]]>
</xp:this.documentId>
```

To exercise this code snippet, just load the sample application in a browser, and click the **My Profile** link on the toolbar. This SSJS code looks up the name of the current user in the **xpAuthorProfiles** view and returns the unique id of the view entry when a match is found; otherwise, a null value is assigned to the document id. When creating code like this, the application developer initially may often insert `print` statements like those shown here to validate what is going on. When an empty profile document is displayed, the developer can quickly verify that the user was not found in the view lookup by glancing at the console.

Listing 15.2 shows the output of the insert `print` statements in the Domino console in a scenario in which some simple smoke tests end up failing:

Listing 15.2 Output of print Statements on Domino Server Console

```
CN=Gail Chao/O=IBM NOT found!
[CN=Frank Adams/O=IRL, CN=Ron Espinosa/O=IRL, CN=Samantha Daryn/O=IRL]
CN=Samantha Daryn/O=IBM NOT found!
[CN=Frank Adams/O=IRL, CN=Ron Espinosa/O=IRL, CN=Samantha Daryn/O=IRL]
```

Interestingly, the two cases in Listing 15.2 are printed for different reasons. When logged in as test user Gail Chao, no profile document existed in the view, so no profile document could be resolved. However, a mismatch also occurred when logged in as Samantha Daryn because the test id used did not match the id used to create the sample data—the organization part of the canonical names differ (IBM versus IRL). You get the idea.

It is worth noting that the "message" passed into the `print()` command does not necessarily have to be a String type. As long as the parameter value can be coerced or cast to a String, then the command works. For example, in the previous sample you could also successfully pass in arbitrary objects like the NotesDatabase instance because the `print()` command implementation simply calls the `toString()` method on the object. Thus `print(database)` actually emits the name of the current database because that is the behavior of the `toString()` method. Native scalar types are also fully supported, so `print("1 + 1 = " + (1+1))` is perfectly valid.

When dealing with complex objects, however, you will often be better off using the `_dump()` command because it is designed to work with compound objects, arrays, and so forth. Some simple examples can illustrate the difference. You can experiment by declaring a simple JSON object and attempting to write its contents to the console. Listing 15.3 shows such a snippet.

Listing 15.3 Snippet Writing a JSON Object to the Console

```
// Create a simple JSON object and write it to the console
var jsonObject = {"firstName" : "Samantha", "lastName" : "Daryn",
"department" : "Sales"};
_dump(jsonObject);
print("*************");
print(jsonObject);
```

The output of the `_dump()` and `print()` statements are shown in a snapshot of the Domino server console in Figure 15.1. You can see that the former captures all the detail of the JSON object, whereas the latter is basically useless: "`[object Object]`".

Listing 15.4 performs a similar exercise using a JavaScript array. Although the `print()` statement does marginally better with this example compared to the last, it still succeeds only in writing out *summary* array data, whereas the output of the `_dump()` statement explodes all the detail for each entry.

Listing 15.4 Snippet Writing a JavaScript Array to the Console

```
// Create a simple array to capture basic staff details
// FirstName, LastName, Dept, StartDate
var staff = [
    ['Frank','Adams','HR',new Date(2008, 0, 1)], //note: months are
➥zero-based!
    ['Ron','Espinosa','Support',new Date(2001, 7, 26)],
    ['Samantha','Daryn','Sales',new Date(1999, 10, 11)]
];
_dump(staff);
print("*************");
print(staff);
```

```
Select gouganebarra/IBM: IBM Domino Server (64 Bit)
[2CB0:000A-2EF8] 13/12/2013 01:24:14   HTTP JVM: Object
[2CB0:000A-2EF8] 13/12/2013 01:24:14   HTTP JVM: =
[2CB0:000A-2EF8] 13/12/2013 01:24:14   HTTP JVM: [object Object]
[2CB0:000A-2EF8] 13/12/2013 01:24:14   HTTP JVM:
[2CB0:000A-2EF8] 13/12/2013 01:24:14   HTTP JVM: +-
[2CB0:000A-2EF8] 13/12/2013 01:24:14   HTTP JVM: department
[2CB0:000A-2EF8] 13/12/2013 01:24:14   HTTP JVM: :
[2CB0:000A-2EF8] 13/12/2013 01:24:14   HTTP JVM: string
[2CB0:000A-2EF8] 13/12/2013 01:24:14   HTTP JVM: =
[2CB0:000A-2EF8] 13/12/2013 01:24:14   HTTP JVM: Sales
[2CB0:000A-2EF8] 13/12/2013 01:24:14   HTTP JVM:
[2CB0:000A-2EF8] 13/12/2013 01:24:14   HTTP JVM: +-
[2CB0:000A-2EF8] 13/12/2013 01:24:14   HTTP JVM: lastName
[2CB0:000A-2EF8] 13/12/2013 01:24:14   HTTP JVM: :
[2CB0:000A-2EF8] 13/12/2013 01:24:14   HTTP JVM: string
[2CB0:000A-2EF8] 13/12/2013 01:24:14   HTTP JVM: =
[2CB0:000A-2EF8] 13/12/2013 01:24:14   HTTP JVM: Daryn
[2CB0:000A-2EF8] 13/12/2013 01:24:14   HTTP JVM:
[2CB0:000A-2EF8] 13/12/2013 01:24:14   HTTP JVM: +-
[2CB0:000A-2EF8] 13/12/2013 01:24:14   HTTP JVM: firstName
[2CB0:000A-2EF8] 13/12/2013 01:24:14   HTTP JVM: :
[2CB0:000A-2EF8] 13/12/2013 01:24:14   HTTP JVM: string
[2CB0:000A-2EF8] 13/12/2013 01:24:14   HTTP JVM: =
[2CB0:000A-2EF8] 13/12/2013 01:24:14   HTTP JVM: Samantha
[2CB0:000A-2EF8] 13/12/2013 01:24:14   HTTP JVM: **************
[2CB0:000A-2EF8] 13/12/2013 01:24:14   HTTP JVM: [object Object]
```

Figure 15.1 The output of _dump() and `print()` statements on the Domino console

The output of the `_dump()` statement is quite verbose, so it is left to the reader to run this snippet and view the output. All the examples from this section are included in the **PrintDump-Log.xsp** page in the sample chapter, which should make that task easy for you—just open the XPage, click the buttons, and view the console.

try / catch / finally

Although you can happily use `_dump()` and `print()` statements to help decipher unanticipated behavior in your XPages SSJS code, you need also to protect your code against potential exceptions that can occur when the code executes at runtime. Calling the Java backend classes from JavaScript is probably the most common programming pattern used in XPages. The vast majority of Notes Java APIs throw an exception if the procedure cannot execute successfully. For example, examine the signatures of the methods of the `View` and `Document` Java classes by perusing the help documentation on the backend classes provided in Domino Designer—practically every one can throw an exception, like this (taking an arbitrary example from the `Document` class, for example):

```
public String getItemValueString(String name) throws NotesException
```

When there is a chance that making a Java call via SSJS will cause an exception to be thrown, then it is best practice to surround such code in a `try` / `catch` / `finally` block so that the error can be caught and handled gracefully. Java and JavaScript developers should be familiar with this exception handling construct. In brief, you should execute the code in question within the `try` block, handle any potential exceptions with the `catch` block, and perform any necessary clean up in the `finally` block. Be aware that the `finally` block is always executed, regardless of whether an exception is thrown, or whether the `try` block is exited using a `return` statement or some such break.

Examples of this practice can be seen in the XPages Teamroom and Discussion application templates. (For instance, just search these applications for occurrences of a `"try{"` string.) The **viewTopic** custom control contains a good example, which is outlined in Listing 15.5. Extra code has been added to the original snippet to leverage the `_dump()` and `print()` statements, and a `finally` block has been added to enhance the sample. These lines are highlighted in **bold** font.

Listing 15.5 postOpenDocument SSJS Event Handler

```
<xp:this.postOpenDocument>
 <![CDATA[#{javascript:// get the main topic details...
  print("BEGIN viewTopic>postOpenDocument ...");
  var parentDoc = true;
  viewScope.mainUNID = dominoDoc.getItemValueString("mainID");
  if("" != viewScope.mainUNID){
    var mainTopic:NotesDocument = null;
      try{
        // try to locate parent topic...
        mainTopic = database.getDocumentByUNID(viewScope.mainUNID);
        if(null != mainTopic){
          viewScope.mainID = mainTopic.getNoteID();
          viewScope.mainSubject =
➥mainTopic.getItemValueString("Subject");
          viewScope.mainCreated =
➥mainTopic.getCreated().toJavaDate();
          viewScope.mainFrom = mainTopic.getItemValueString("From");
          viewScope.mainAbstract =
➥mainTopic.getItemValueString("Abstract");
        }
      }catch(e){
         // if non-existent, then use current document...
         parentDoc = false;
         mainTopic = dominoDoc;
        if(null != mainTopic){
          viewScope.mainID = mainTopic.getNoteID();
          viewScope.mainSubject =
➥mainTopic.getItemValueString("Subject");
          viewScope.mainCreated =
             mainTopic.getDocument().getCreated().toJavaDate();
          viewScope.mainFrom = mainTopic.getItemValueString("From");
```

```
            viewScope.mainAbstract = mainTopic.
➥getItemValueString("Abstract");
         }
      } finally {
      if (parentDoc) {
          print("... using parent doc...");
      } else {
          print(".. using current doc...");
      }
        _dump(viewScope); // dump the object details regardless
        print("... viewTopic>postOpenDocument END");
   }
}}]]></xp:this.postOpenDocument>
```

The postOpenDocument event runs after the Domino document has been loaded by the XPage and the SSJS code in this handler seeks to store the values of various document fields in the viewScope map because they will be used when displaying the view topic thread to the user. For any document in a given thread, the UNID of the root document is used to resolve the main topic and fish out the required items. If a document cannot be resolved for a particular UNID, however, a NotesException will be thrown—this is the specified behavior of the getDocumentByUNID method. If this exception is not handled, a bad user experience is the inevitable outcome, manifesting in the form of an exception and stack trace in the browser window. In this snippet, however, you can see that the code can recover by reverting to the current document and using that instead. Thus, the viewScope variables will be assigned values one way or the other.

If you want to see the values of the viewScope variables and ensure they are all properly assigned, you can use the _dump() statement to conveniently print *all* the map variables in one fell swoop (as opposed to a bunch of individual print() statements). Furthermore, by calling the _dump() statement within the newly added finally block, you are guaranteed that the viewScope variables have been assigned in either the try or catch block by that point, so that helps to confine the call to just one path. On top of that, print() statements have been used (judiciously) to record whichever code path is taken.

To experiment with this code, open the sample application in a browser, and select various topics in the **All Documents** page. You see the full debug details written to the Domino console, as demonstrated in Figure 15.2

The use cases examined thus far are typical of the type of debugging a developer would usually do in the early stages of developing an application, particularly when engaged in getting basic functionality to work. When an application is deployed, however, you do not want print() and _dump() statements spewing miscellaneous development information willy-nilly to the console. Not only should the application be sufficiently robust to make such output unnecessary, but it also is *not* best practice to overload the console with application runtime information in any case. Nonetheless there will always be cases even with deployed applications in which you need to collect application information in the event that something goes wrong. This is where logging comes in.

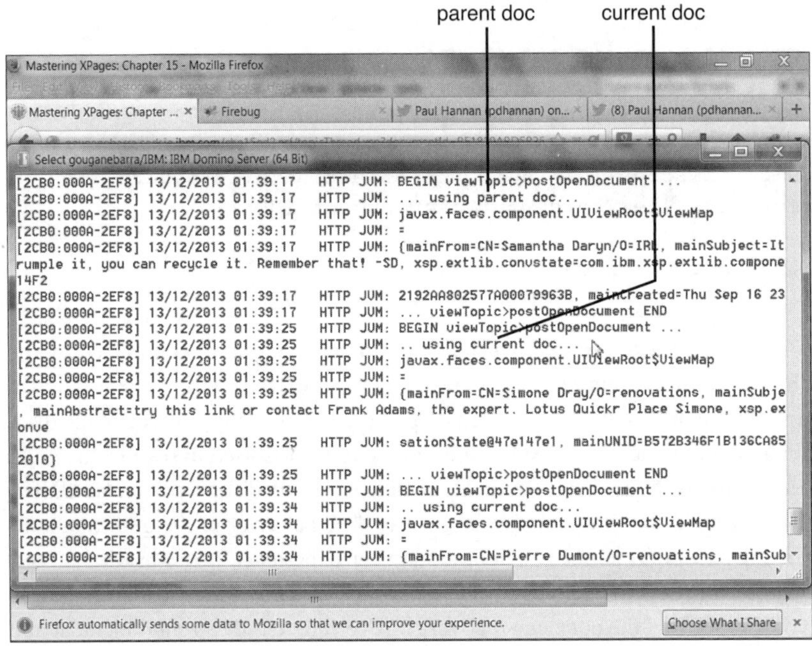

Figure 15.2 viewTopic.xsp with some debug information written to the Domino console

You can add a logging facility to your application that enables you to capture runtime context information and save it to a log file for examination at some future point in the event of unforeseen problems. The XPages runtime itself and all other Notes/Domino components also have built-in logging code that can be turned on for client serviceability—more on this later. What's important now is for you to know that you can extend the XPages logging service to silently record information when your application is rolled out and used in the real world.

You can create a Java logger by tapping into the runtime classes used by the XPages runtime for logging as these are callable from SSJS. A simple custom logger has been created in the sample application. It is trivial in nature, as shown in Listing 15.6:

Listing 15.6 postOpenDocument SSJS event handler

```
package com.me.log;

import com.ibm.commons.log.Log;
import com.ibm.commons.log.LogMgr;
```

```
// Logger class leveraging some common utility classes in XPages runtime

public class MyLogger extends Log {
    // Create a log manager instance for this app
    public static LogMgr MYAPP  = load("com.me.log.myapp");
}
```

The Java code just creates a logger class called MyLogger, which extends the XPages runtime Log class. The runtime Log class can be treated as a black box and just leveraged for the logging facilities it provides—no need to look inside the implementation to see what it does. Within your extended class, a log manager instance called MYAPP is created and assigned a unique id, namely **com.me.log.myapp**. The MYAPP object can then be called within SSJS to manage the logging of debug information, as demonstrated in Listing 15.7.

Listing 15.7 Using Java Logging via SSJS

```
var logger = com.me.log.MyLogger.MYAPP;
var logArgs = new java.util.ArrayList();
logArgs.add(@UserName());
var canDelete= (userBean.accessLevel>=lotus.domino.Database.
➥ DBACL_DELETE_DOCS);

if (!canDelete) {
       if (logger.isWarnEnabled()) {
              logger.warnp("PrintDumpLog.xsp", "Delete Profile",
             "ACL restriction for {1}: user cannot delete documents",
              logArgs.toArray());
       }
} else {
      var db:NotesDatabase        = database;
      var vw:NotesView = db.getView("xpAuthorProfiles");
      var ve:NotesViewEntry = vw.getEntryByKey(userBean.canonicalName,
➥ true);
      if (ve != null) {
             ve.getDocument().remove(true);
             if (logger.isWarnEnabled()) {
                    logArgs.add(ve.getUniversalID());
                    logger.warnp("PrintDumpLog.xsp",
                         "Delete Profile",
                         "Profile document {1} for user {0} deleted! ",
                         logArgs.toArray());
             }
      } else {
              if (logger.isWarnEnabled()) {
```

```
                logger.warnp("PrintDumpLog.xsp", "Delete Profile",
                "Delete failed - no profile document exists for user
➥{0}",
                logArgs.toArray());
            }
        }
}
```

From the listing you can see that the static logger created in the Java class is assigned to the SSJS `logger` variable and then used throughout the snippet to write warnings to the log file so that the behavior of the code can be tracked. A strong benefit of logging is that it can be enabled at different levels: `trace`, `info`, `warn`, and `error` (in increasing order of severity). Notes or Domino typically have `warn` level enabled by default. Thus, if you execute this snippet of code, which is available on the **Delete Profile** button in the sample **PrintDumpLog.xsp** page, you will find warnings are written to the `console.log` file located in the `IBM_TECHNICAL_SUPPORT` folder under the data folder in Notes/Domino.

The sample code is straightforward. The logger object provides extensive APIs to control what is written to the log and under what conditions. In this snippet the logging code is exercised only when warn level is enabled, but similar APIs are available for each log level—`isInfoEnabled()`,`isErrorEnabled()`, and such. This enables you, the developer, to qualify your log output based on your perception of the potential severity in any given use case.

The `warnp()` method, and its equivalents at the other log levels, takes four parameters. In Java, the first two identify the class file and method that emits the log output, so in SSJS in this instance you can map these to the name of the XPage and the event that is called—the **PrintDumpLog.xsp** XPage and the `Delete Profile` button, respectively. The third parameter is the log message you want to record, which can have an arbitrary number of variables embedded within it, `{0}`,`{1}` through `{n}`. The indices inside the curly braces point to a slot position in an array of parameter data, logArgs, in this example. The `logArgs` object is a Java `ArrayList`, which is used to store context information like the username and note id of the profile document, and this is cast to a Java array when passed to the `warnp()` method. Note that the logger output methods expect a Java array here and *not* a JavaScript array, which is why the Java `ArrayList` object is used. For full details on all the logger methods available, refer to the Javadoc for the XPages LogMgr interface: `http://tinyurl.com/XPagesLogMgrAPI`.

Figure 15.3 shows a snapshot of the console.log file after the **Delete Profile** button has been clicked twice. The first click removes the user profile document and the second click attempts to do so but fails because the profile document no longer exists. This activity is clear from reading the log file, so it gives an insight into the value of good logging code when you need to figure out what an application is doing after it is released in the field.

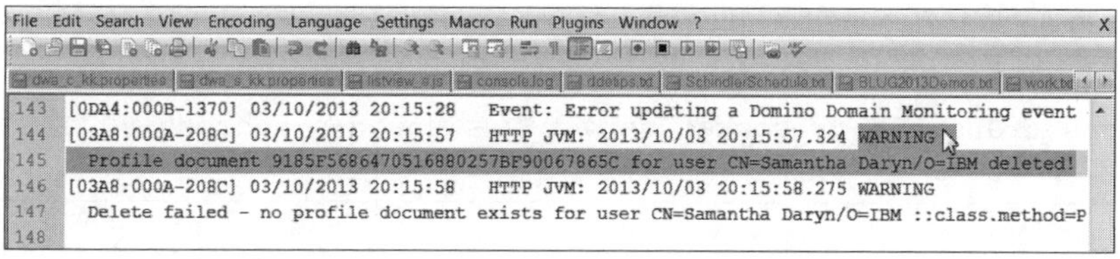

Figure 15.3 console.log with logging information written from an XPages application via SSJS

Note that your `print()` and `_dump()` statements are also written to the console log file *but* they are also automatically written to the console itself, and, unlike logging, you do not have granular control over when output should be emitted.

> **TIP**
>
> If you want to see log messages written to the console, which can be useful when actively working on a debug issue, you can enable this by setting `HTTP_OSGI_ENABLE_CONSOLE_LOGGING=1` in `notes.ini` on the Domino server. Of course, then you will see *all* logging messages from any services running under the HTTP task and not just your own loggers. You must also remember to restart the Domino server or the http task if you apply this setting when the server is already running.

The subject of logging will be revisited later in the chapter when you look at how the XPages runtime manages this task in the section entitled "Enabling XPages Java Logging."

Introducing the SSJS Debugger

Domino Designer 9.0 saw the arrival of the SSJS debugger. If you are not yet using a 9.x release of Domino Designer, then upgrade, quick—if only to use this feature. Although the preceding sections are all good for basic debugging, you will eventually need a full-fledged debugger to get to the bottom of more complex issues. According to Mr. Kernighan, debugging is a formidable task:

> Debugging is twice as hard as writing the code in the first place. Therefore, if you write the code as cleverly as possible, you are, by definition, not smart enough to debug it.

Getting Started

The three lines shown in Listing 15.8 need to be included in the `notes.ini` file for your client or server. You can run the SSJS debugger when previewing applications from within Domino Designer or when running on a Domino server. For convenience, this section concentrates on the latter.

Listing 15.8 Debug Settings Required in notes.ini

```
JavaEnableDebug=1
JavaDebugOptions=transport=dt_socket,server=y,suspend=n,address=8000
JavascriptEnableDebug=1
```

When the settings have been applied, you need to restart your server or the http task. Note that the `JavascriptEnableDebug` setting is case-sensitive, so be sure to apply it exactly as spelled out here. (You might be inclined to enter `JavaScriptEnableDebug`, as I did, but resist that temptation and save yourself a minor headache.) In any case these three lines are conveniently provided for you in a debugger dialog that you will need shortly (see Figure 15.4), so you can copy and paste them from there. If you have debugged Java code on the Domino server before, you will recognize the first two settings in Listing 15.8 as they are required for Java debugging. You need them for SSJS debugging because the JavaScript debugger piggy-backs on top of the Eclipse Java debugging system.

On startup, the Domino server will confirm that it is running in debug mode and inform you that this can potentially degrade server performance and negatively impact security. These are two good reasons not to do this on a production server, unless absolutely necessary, and then only for the minimum time required to resolve the issue under investigation.

The next step is to launch Domino Designer and to connect to the Domino server so that a debugging session can be initiated. As is the norm when debugging in Eclipse, you need to create a debug configuration file before establishing a debug connection with the Domino server. The configuration simply stores the details needed to connect to the server, the hostname, and port number of the server and such. You enter these details by selecting the **Tools > Debug Server-Side JavaScript > Manage Debug Configurations** menu and filling in the fields in the resulting dialog box, as shown in Figure 15.4.

The same menu dialog may be invoked via the Domino Designer toolbar using the blue bug drop-down button. From within the dialog navigator, create a new configuration by selecting **Domino Designer JavaScript > New** using the right mouse menu. When the configuration name (any meaningful text), hostname, and port number are provided, then you can click the **Debug** button to set up a debug connection with the Domino server. If your configuration is valid and your server is up and running, you should see a message confirming that the debug connection has been established in the status bar. For this particular configuration, the message for a successful connection would read like this: `Debug connection successfully created using localhost on port 8000`. If your attempt to connect fails, you will get an error message, as shown in Figure 15.5.

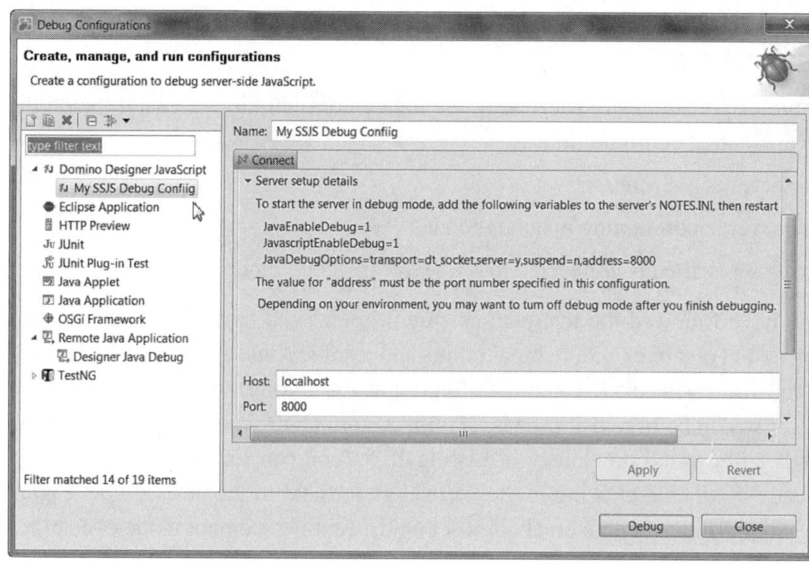

Figure 15.4 The Debug Configurations dialog with some sample data

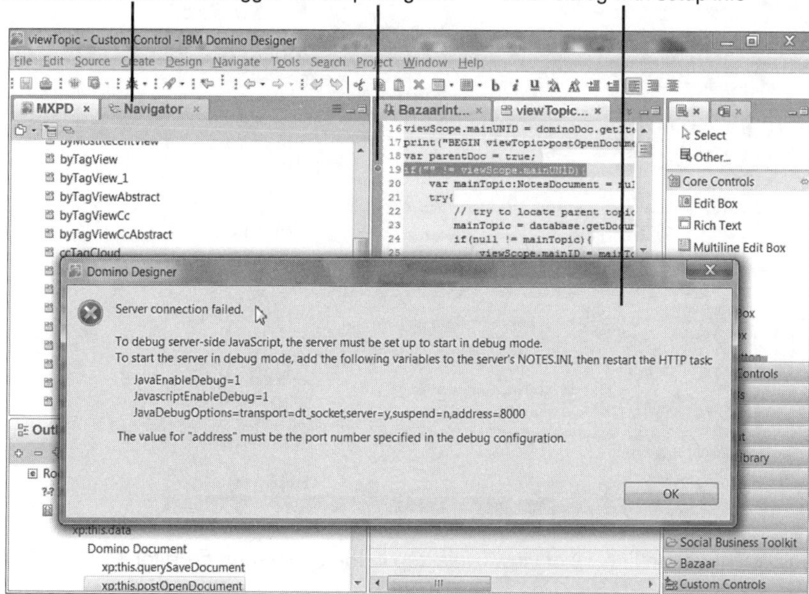

Figure 15.5 Error dialog shown when a debug session with the Domino Server is not established

A failure to establish a debug connection typically is the result of one of the following conditions (I know; I've done them all):

- The hostname or port number specified in the debug configuration does not match the remote server's actual configuration.
- The remote server is not running.
- The remote server is not running in debug mode.
- Domino Designer is already connected to the server in debug mode.

Assuming you have followed the instructions carefully and you have Designer in debug mode, the next thing to do is set one or more breakpoints and resolve some annoying SSJS puzzle that's been "bugging" you for weeks! A good starting point for getting to grips with the rudiments of the debugger would be to revisit the **viewTopic** custom control and set a breakpoint in the SSJS event handler illustrated previously in Listing 15.5. You can set a breakpoint on any executable line of code by double-clicking in the vertical gutter next to the desired line. Figure 15.6 shows the XSP source editor with a breakpoint set on the first if statement in the code block (line 19).

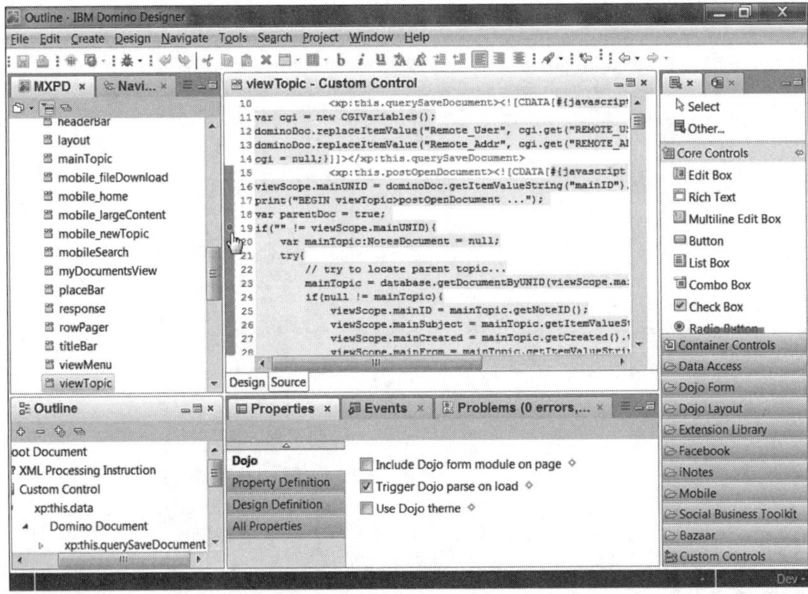

Figure 15.6 Breakpoint set on line 19 of viewTopic.xsp in the XSP Source Editor

Before invoking the debugger you should switch to the debug perspective by selecting the **Window > Open Perspective > Debug** item off the main menu. You then need to cause the SSJS event handler to be executed on the server, so open the **allDocuments.xsp** page in a browser and click one of the document links in the **All Documents** section. For example, if you select the "It's just paper" entry, then you should immediately see that that Domino Designer is activated because the loading of the page stopped when the breakpoint in the SSJS code is reached. You can step through the code using the debug toolbar (or function key `F6` from 9.0.1 onward) and observe the code path taken, as well as the values assigned to each variable en route. This makes the `print` and `_dump` debugging of the same code in the previous section seem primitive.

TIP

Before long you may become weary of constantly switching perspectives from Domino Designer to Debug and back again. To make life easier you can customize any perspective and add in views to suit the job at hand. For example, you could add the Applications navigator from the Domino Designer perspective to the Debug perspective, which would enable you to open design elements from within the Debug perspective—thus avoiding a lot of switching. To do so, select **Window > Show Eclipse Views > Other** from the main menu within the Debug perspective. Then expand the **Domino Designer** entry and select **Applications**. Simple.

The **Variables** tab allows you to inspect the state of all variables in scope at each step of code execution. Much of the time you will be interested in the contents of the **Global Variables** entry because all the XPages scope variables and implicit objects (`currentDocument`, `database`, and such) are contained within. While stepping through this code, you can expand the **Global Variables** entry and click individual entries of interest to inspect state. For instance, you can see all the `viewScope` variables being manipulated at each step in code—a significantly more dynamic experience than the `_dump(viewScope)` technique. Figure 15.7 shows a snapshot taken while stepping through the code, with annotations highlighting useful debug features.

Common Debugger Actions

Table 15.1 summarizes the main debug actions at your disposal.

Table 15.1 Developer Data Definition

Name	Description
`Step Into`	Dives into an SSSJ method or function on the active line of code. The shortcut is `F5`.
`Step Over`	Executes the current statement and moves to the next line in the current code block. The shortcut is `F6`.
`Step Return`	Completes execution of the current method and steps back to the calling method. The shortcut is `F7`.

Name	Description
`Suspend`	Suspends or pauses execution of the active thread allowing the developer the opportunity of inspecting the current state of the application.
`Resume`	Resumes execution of the application, which will suspend again if another breakpoint is hit. The shortcut is `F8`.
`Terminate`	Ends the current debug session and disconnects the debug connection with the server. The shortcut key is `Control+F2`
`Toggle Breakpoint`	Creates or deletes a breakpoint on the current line in the SSJS code block. The shortcut is `Control+Shift+B`.
`Enable/Disable Breakpoint`	Leaves a breakpoint in place but arms or disarms it depending on its current state.

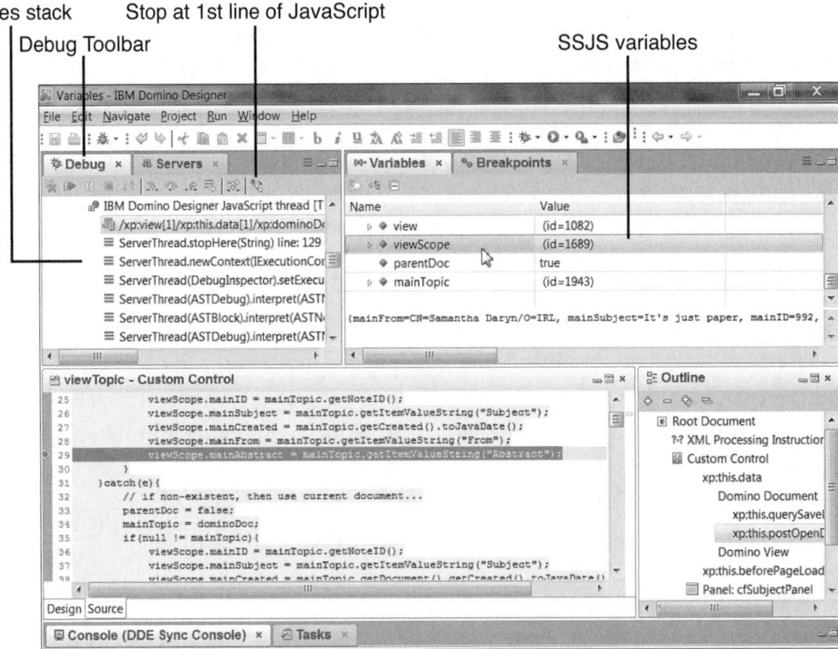

Figure 15.7 Using the SSJS debugger to step through the postOpenDocument event handler

In general, all the debug actions summarized here can be invoked from the debug toolbar, right mouse menus, or the Domino Designer main menu. Some improvements in 9.0.1 mean that the function key bindings are also operational from that release forward.

Interesting Debug Features

There are a few things to note for breakpoints in Domino Designer. First, even though you can double-click in the gutter of the XSP source editor in practically any location and have a breakpoint symbol appear, breakpoints are applied only at runtime to executable lines of SSJS code. Breakpoints on XSP markup, SSJS comments, blank lines, and such are ignored. Second, any valid breakpoints you do create are persisted in your workspace and reappear after you shut down and restart Domino Designer. It is not possible, however, to export or transfer these breakpoints to another workspace, and sometimes developers want to do this type of thing in a team development situation. For example, Tom wants to pass an NSF on to Anne with breakpoints set on particular lines of code because he discovered problems in those areas and wants to have the application automatically suspend at those exact points when run in debug mode. Even though the breakpoint won't accompany the application on its travels, there is another solution.

The debugger Statement

From Domino Designer 9.0 onward, you can insert the `debugger` keyword into your SSJS code and have it behave for all intents and purposes as a breakpoint. For example, the breakpoint shown in Figure 15.5 could also have been achieved by inserting a new `debugger` statement after line 19, as shown in the snippet featured in Listing 15.9:

Listing 15.9 postOpenDocument SSJS Event Handler

```
1  <xp:this.postOpenDocument>
2  <![CDATA[#{javascript:// get the main topic details...
3   print("BEGIN viewTopic>postOpenDocument ...");
4   var parentDoc = true;
5   viewScope.mainUNID = dominoDoc.getItemValueString("mainID");
6   if("" != viewScope.mainUNID){
7     debugger; // break here !!!
8     var mainTopic:NotesDocument = null;
9
10       try{ // ... code continues as shown in previous listing ...
```

The `debugger` statement on line 7 effectively resolves the aforementioned use case to do with sharing breakpoints—Tom can insert `debugger` statements where needed in the SSJS code and then pass the application to another team member. Be careful, however, not to run such applications on versions of Notes or Domino earlier than 9.0 because the `debugger` statement will not be understood in those releases and will cause errors. Also remember to remove any `debugger` statements from your code when doing production builds.

Stop at the First Line of Server-Side JavaScript

Eventually, as your work as an XPages developer, you will run into unexpected JavaScript errors and have a hard time finding the offending code in the application. If this has already been your experience, you may wonder why the code referenced in the error stack in your browser cannot be found when you search through all the JavaScript and XSP resources in the NSF. One plausible explanation is that the code is not actually coming from within the XPages themselves or the SSJS libraries that they load, but actually is executing from within a theme that is activated when the application is loaded. A good way to bring an end to such mysteries is to take advantage of the Stop at First Line of server-side JavaScript feature.

This is presented as a check box option in the **Debug Configuration** dialog box. If selected, it means that the application will suspend after the first line of SSJS executes in the application on the remote server after you have established your debug connection. It continues to stop at each subsequent block of SSJS code. If indeed you have code emanating from mysterious sources, then this is a good way to track it down. In other words, open the offending application, break at the first line of SSJS, and walk through the code until you hit the problem. If you want to debug only SSJS code contained within XPages, custom controls, or SSJS libraries, the dialog allows you to choose to stop at the first line of server-side JavaScript only in design elements. This option is also available from the debug toolbar so that the setting can be toggled dynamically during the debug session. Refer to the relevant icon highlighted in Figure 15.7.

Conditional Breakpoints

When you get the hang of the SSJS debugger, you'll probably quickly end up in a situation in which you want breakpoints only to take effect only when a particular condition is true. Typically, this occurs when you are debugging a problem that occurs within a loop or some iterative form of code. For example, if you are building a Repeat control and happen to notice that the 20th row displays properly, it would be preferable not to have to pause and resume application execution 19 times before breaking on the required line. Similarly, if you are processing a large collection of documents and encounter a problem with a particular one, then it would be great to set a breakpoint to pause the code when and only when the offending document is being processed, and not also for all its predecessors in the collection. Thus being able to attach conditions to breakpoints so that they kick in only when, for example, a Repeat row index is 20 or a document note id is 0FA2, is a valuable feature. The good news is that you have that ability.

You can right-click any given breakpoint in the XSP source editor and select the **Breakpoint Properties** context menu. This displays a dialog, as shown previously in Figure 15.7, which allows you to select an **Enable Condition** dialog check box. Doing so exposes a text editor in the dialog into which you can enter any JavaScript expression that evaluates to a boolean type. At runtime, if the expression evaluates to `true`, then the breakpoint is applied; if not, it is skipped. To experiment with this feature in a simple way, a snippet of SSJS has been included in the **PrintDumpLog.xsp** page, under the **Update Image** button. This snippet computes the URL used for an image control and is outlined in Listing 15.10:

Listing 15.10 SSJS Snippet to Compute a Random Resource URL

```
var randomNum = (viewScope.randomNumber == null) ? 0 : viewScope.
➥randomNumber;
var randomUrl = "/" + randomNum.toPrecision(0) + ".gif";
if (randomNum > 9) {
       randomUrl = "/" + "ellipsis" + ".gif";
}
return randomUrl;
```

The image control sits between a button and a computed field on the sample page. When the button is clicked, two things happen:

- A random number between 1 and 10 is generated and stored as a `viewScope` variable.
- The neighboring image and computed field controls are partially refreshed.

When the image control is refreshed, the SSJS code in Listing 15.10 is executed. This reads the random number and generates a URL to a gif image resource, which happens to reside within the NSF, namely `/0.gif`, `/1.gif`, and so on. If the random number exceeds 9, a `/ellipsis.gif` URL is created. The adjacent computed field just reads and displays the same random number. Loading the XPage and clicking under the **Update Image** button should thus cause a random number and corresponding image to display. You should verify that this snippet works as described at this juncture.

Next, you should set a breakpoint on the final line of Listing 15.10 where the `randomUrl` variable is returned, and then bring up the dialog box for conditional breakpoints (by right-clicking the breakpoint within the editor and selecting **Breakpoint Properties**) and set a condition using an SSJS expression. The example shown in Figure 15.8 is `randomNum > 5`.

In debug mode, reload the XPage and click the **Update Image** button again a number of times. Observe that the debugger kicks in only when the random number condition is met, so you play a guessing game with yourself as to what will happen when you click the button. Figure 15.9 shows a snapshot of Domino Designer when the random number satisfies the condition.

Be aware also that you can change the value of any variable shown in the **Variables** pane at this point. Simply double-click the value for the variable or right mouse click and choose from the **Change Value...** context menu. For example, you can change the URL value that is returned in this snippet. Figure 15.10 shows the result of such a change.

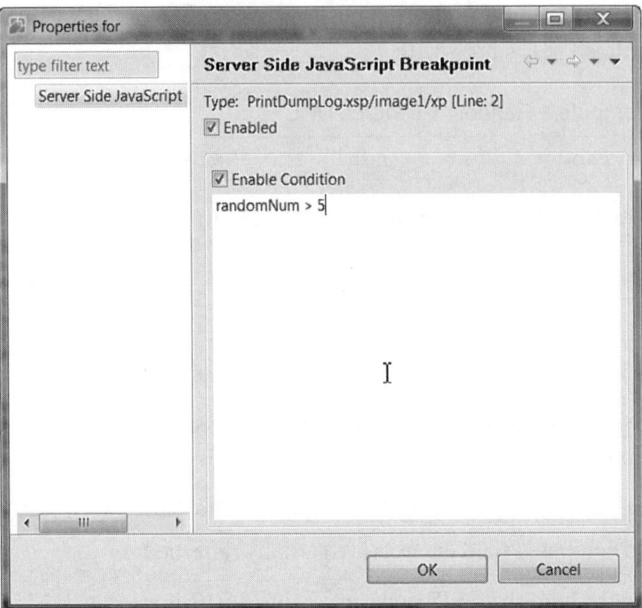

Figure 15.8 SSJS Conditional Breakpoint option

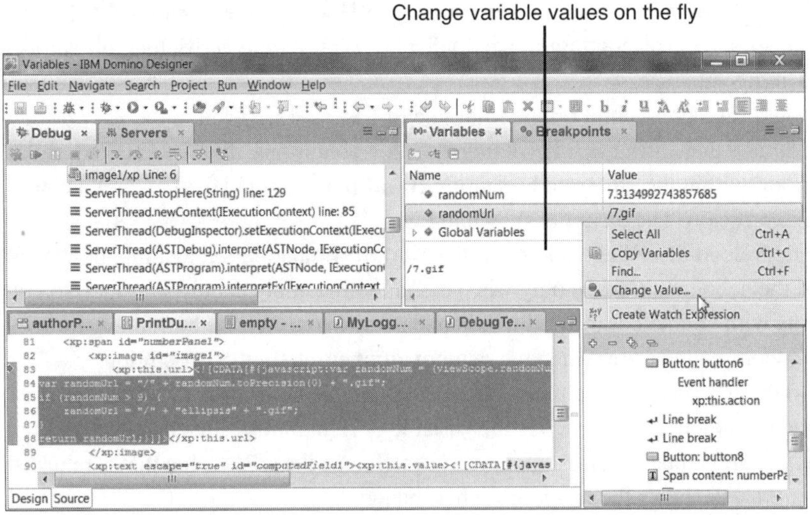

Change variable values on the fly

Figure 15.9 Designer paused in debug mode on a conditional breakpoint

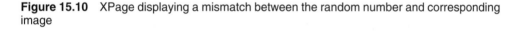

Figure 15.10 XPage displaying a mismatch between the random number and corresponding image

Although the example is trivial and just a bit of fun, the use case should be clear. Use conditional breakpoints to reduce hits in repetitive code because this will save you time when debugging. Be aware that you can alter variable values on-the-fly in the debugger, which can also help you dynamically and interactively validate code. Very powerful!

Java Breakpoints

Yes, you read that title correctly. Even though you are running the SSJS debugger, you are also, by default, running a Java debugger, so you can also set Java breakpoints here. Remember that the SSJS debugger piggy-backs on top of the Java debugger, and this can actually be quite useful in certain circumstances. Take, for example, a case in which you are calling some Java code from SSJS and an exception is thrown in the Java code. You may or may not have the Java code in question. The problem may be in Java code you have written and included in your NSF, or lie somewhere deep within a jar or plug-in that your application is consuming. If you have the Java source, then you can add Java breakpoints to it in the same way you added SSJS breakpoints to XPages earlier. That is, open the Java class and double-click in the editor gutter for the line on which you want to break—try this in the Java class shown in Listing 15.10. And even if you do not have the Java source code, you can still add a Java exception breakpoint, which can help resolve problems.

For simplicity, take the case in which you have a Java class in your application that is misbehaving under certain conditions. The sample application has such a class, which can be found under **Code > Java > DebugTest.java** in the Domino Designer navigator. Listing 15.11 outlines the source code of this class.

Listing 15.11 Java Class with Poorly Written xprint() Method

```
package com.me.test;
// Trivial class for demonstrating some debugger capabilities
public class DebugTest {
        // just pass param through to Java print func
        public void print(String out) {
                System.out.println(out);
        }
        // print a string but limit size to 25 chars
        public void xprint(String out) {
                // NOT checking for null before calling length()
                // => possible NPE!
                if (out.length() > 25) {
                        out = out.substring(0, 25);
                }
                System.out.println(out);
        }
         public String getInterestingString() {
                return null; // TODO implement this one of these fine
days
        }
}
```

The code in the class is purely for demonstrative purposes. The Java class provides a `print()` and `xprint()` method, where the latter limits the length of the text string to be printed to a maximum of 25 characters. Unfortunately, the code does not check for null input strings before calling methods on the input object, leaving it vulnerable to null pointer exceptions. The **NPE Test** button in **PrintDumpLog.xsp** will exercise this contrived use case. Listing 15.12 shows the snippet for that event handler.

Listing 15.12 SSJS Event Handler Testing for Null Pointer Exceptions

```
var dbgTest = new com.me.test.DebugTest();
// xprint limits the print buffer to 25 chars
dbgTest.xprint("abcdefghijklmnopqrstuvwxyz");

// xprint does not check for null (tutt,tutt)
var interestingString = dbgTest.getInterestingString();
dbgTest.xprint(interestingString);
```

Before running this snippet, switch to the Debugger perspective in Domino Designer and activate the Breakpoints panel. On the breakpoint toolbar, select the **Add Java Exception Breakpoint** option, and select the `NullPointerException` breakpoint in the resulting dialog, as shown in Figure 15.11.

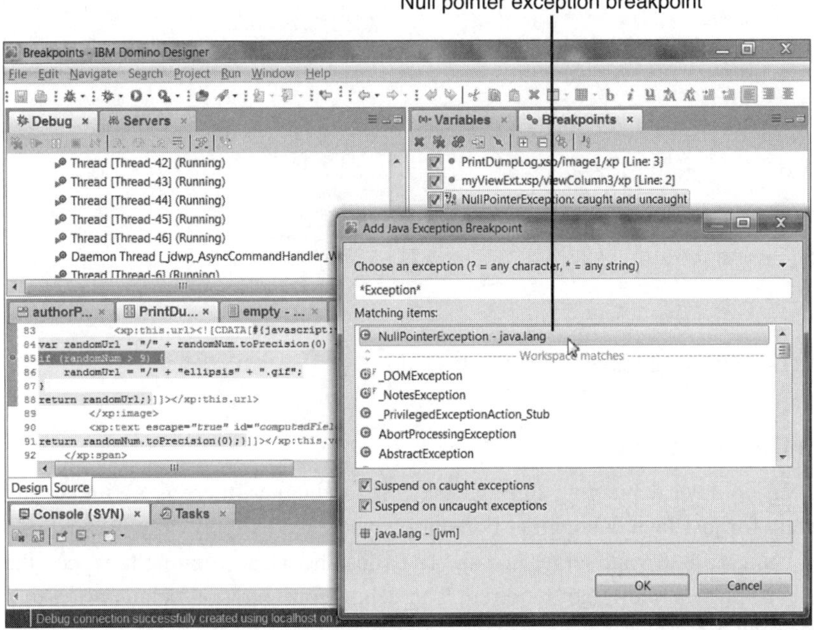

Figure 15.11 Selecting an exception in the Java Exceptions Breakpoints dialog

You could, of course, pick any Java exception class. When the breakpoint is set, then load the XPage, and click the **NPE Test** button. The initial `xprint()` call works well, printing all characters of the alphabet up to but not including z. The next `xprint()` call is contrived to fail because the `getInterestingString()` method sneakily returns null. (This is a lesson for us all—beware of any Java code you consume.) With the exception breakpoint in place, the debugger conveniently pauses at the point where the NPE is encountered, showing exactly the point in the Java code where the exception occurs and the values of the relevant variables at that moment in time. Figure 15.12 captures this.

This technique may prove useful to you in situations in which you are consuming opaque Java libraries in your application, and somewhere deep in the bowels of it all, an exception is thrown. Try it out.

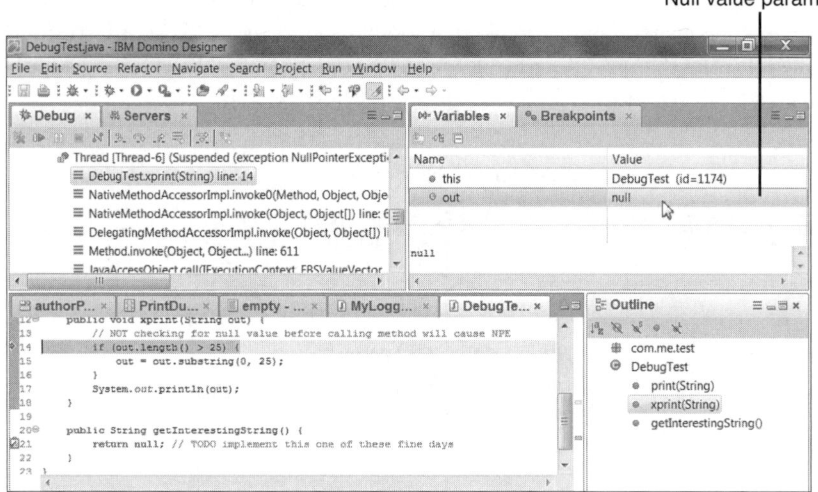

Figure 15.12 Breaking on a NullPointerException in SSJS

Using the Java Debugger

Even though you can do Java debugging through the SSJS debugger, there is a similar and slightly simpler set up for just Java debugging. For starters you need to apply only the first two settings shown in Listing 15.8 to your server `notes.ini` file. That is, as you might expect, the `JavascriptEnableDebug=1` line is not required. The debug configuration details are also a little simpler. In the dialog box you need to create only a new `Remote Java Application` configuration, and set the name, host, and port details (using the same values as for the SSJS configuration). Then when the server http task is running you can run the debug configuration to establish a Java debug session.

> **TIP**
>
> The `suspend` parameter specified in the `JavaDebugOptions` setting is turned off by default but can come in handy if you try to debug Java code that runs when the server is starting up. Take for example a scenario in which you use the XPages preload feature to auto-load applications on startup and that app runs some Java initialization code that you need to debug. Because the preloaded applications are tagged on to the XPages server bootstrap process, the code may already have executed *before* you get a chance to establish a debug connection in Domino Designer. By setting `suspend=y` as a debug option, you are instructing the server to wait for a debug connection request after the JVM is loaded. This allows you to establish a debug session before any Java code runs. Otherwise, you end up playing a catch-me-if-you-can game with the server to see if you can time your debug connection request such that it is honored by the JVM before the preloaded application kicks off.

As discussed in the previous section, you can set a breakpoint on any Java element within your application and debug that code. In the same way, you can debug any managed beans in your application. This all works the same regardless of whether you deal with Java or SSJS code. Less obvious perhaps is the fact that you can debug any custom XPages library installed on your server from inside any application that uses it. Suppose that you install a third-party XPages library to make use of extended functionality in your application. All is going well initially, but then you notice some unexpected behavior in your application—can you debug what's going on? Absolutely! An example of this is up next.

First, you need a sample XPages extension library to use in this experiment—one has been provided in the archive file supplied with this book, namely **exampleLibraryFiles.zip**. This is also available as a downloadable attachment from the following page on the Domino Development wiki: `www.tinyurl.com/CreateAnXPagesLibrary`.

After you obtain the zip file, you should expand it in a local folder and install the update site contained within. Installing update sites has been covered in "Working with the XPages Extension Library" section of Chapter 2, "Getting Everything You Need," and the "Extended Client Side JavaScript Commands" section of Chapter 13, so it should be old hat to you at this stage. (Hint: Start by selecting **File > Application > Install > Search for new features to install > Add Folder Location** in Domino Designer.) For this particular library, the install process should locate the **Example XSP** feature shown in Figure 15.13, and after all the steps are completed you must restart Domino Designer before you can use the new library.

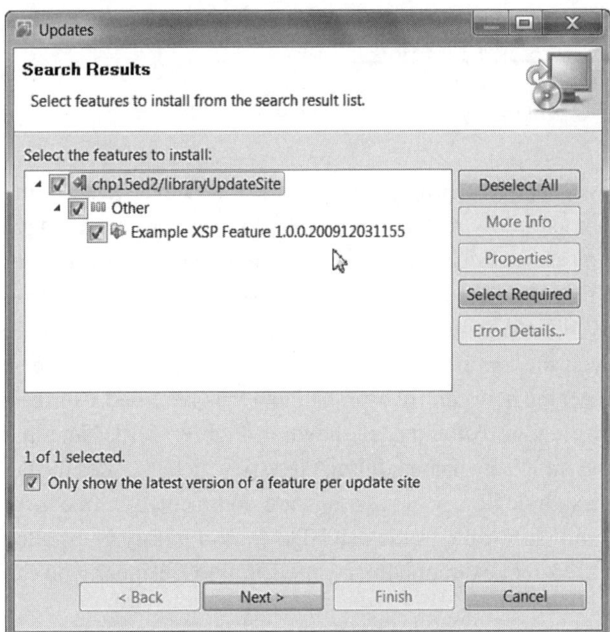

Figure 15.13 Installing a simple XPages Library via Domino Designer

Even though the library is successfully installed, you must make an explicit reference to it in your application to use it. This is done in the **XPage Libraries** user interface in Domino Designer, which you can locate by selecting **Application Configuration > Xsp Properties > Page Generation > Library ID** list box. You can see the new com.example.library entry in the list, and you must enable it by clicking the adjacent check box. Figure 15.14 shows a snapshot of a list of libraries that includes this sample (com.example.library).

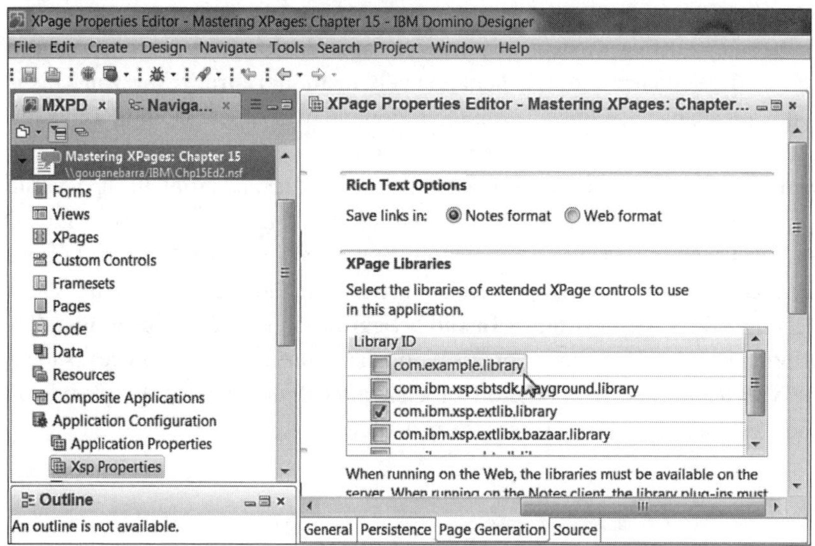

Figure 15.14 XPages libraries available for use by applications in Domino Designer

Next, you can create a new XPage, such as **debugMe.xsp**, and use whatever features the new library provides, in this case just a harmless rectangular display object...but from a Java debugging perspective, this suits our purposes quite well. In other words the functionality of the library is irrelevant, and you don't need to be distracted by it—the object of the exercise is to learn how to debug a third-party library. You can find the sample control by dragging and dropping from the **Other** category at the top of the XPages control palette. This invokes a **Create Control** dialog, and you can select the new control by expanding the **Extended Controls** sections and double-clicking the **Example Control** entry, as shown in Figure 15.15. Note that your sample application already contains an XPage named **debugMe.xsp**, which includes the tag markup for the test control from com.example.library. These tags are commented out because Domino Designer will report an error until such time as the extended control library is installed and registered. Now that you have installed com.example.library into Domino Designer, you can uncomment these tags and remain error free.

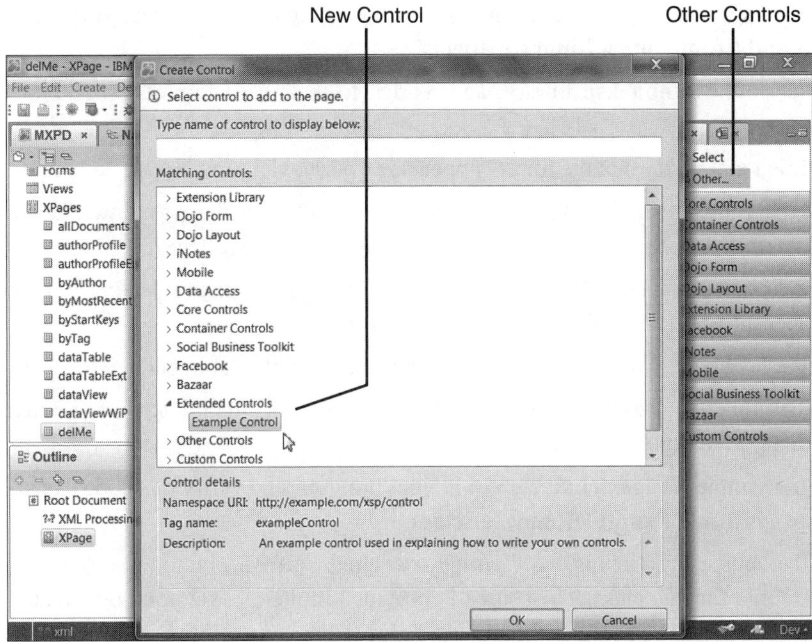

Figure 15.15 Inserting an extended control into an XPage

You can preview the XPage immediately in the Notes client because installing the update site for Domino Designer automatically means that the new library is also available to the Notes client. To run this sample XPage on the Domino server, however, you must first ensure that the sample extension library is also installed there. There are various ways of doing this, but one of the quickest is to simply copy the library that you have just installed into Domino Designer over to the Domino server (assuming you have a Domino server for development purposes under your full control). You can locate the library as follows:

```
<notes_root_dir>\data\workspace\applications\eclipse\plugins\
com.example.xsp_1.0.0.200912031155.jar
```

You need to copy this jar to the equivalent folder in your Domino server root folder (as follows) and then restart the server or the http task:

```
<domino_root_dir>\data\domino\workspace\applications\eclipse\plugins\
com.example.xsp_1.0.0.200912031155.jar
```

The sample page will now run when you load **debugMe.xsp** in a browser. The results are unremarkable, just some text surrounded by an orange colored rectangle. The goal now is to debug this third-party library, and to do so, follow these steps in Domino Designer:

1. Switch to the Java perspective, right-click in the navigator, and select **Import > Plug-ins and Fragments > Binary Projects**.
2. Select the **com.example.xsp** library, and **Add** it to the list of imports (see Figure 15.16).
3. Click **Finish** and verify that the library appears in your navigator window.
4. Expand the **Referenced Libraries** in the navigator entry all the way down to the methods within the **ExampleRenderer** class, as shown in Figure 15.17.
5. Set a breakpoint in the **encodeBegin** method by clicking it and then selecting **Toggle Method Breakpoint** from the right-mouse context menu.
6. Invoke the Java debug launch configuration and switch to the Debugger perspective.
7. Verify that the debug session is established and that you see the breakpoint you just created in the **Breakpoints** view.
8. Reload the sample XPage **debugMe.xsp** in your browser, and verify that code execution suspends inside **ExampleRenderer.class**.
9. Attach the source by clicking the **Change Attached Source...** button and pointing to Java source for this class. The source is provided in the zip file you downloaded and expanded prior to installing the library. Point to the source folder wherever you expanded the zip: `<expanded_zip_folder>/com.example.xsp/src` (see Figure 15.18).
10. Debug the code using the techniques learned earlier in the chapter.

So these ten steps covered a multitude. To understand the process as a whole, it's best to break them into subgroups. Steps 1–3 describe how to get the extended library into your Domino Designer workspace. As a general rule, projects need to be in your workspace before they can be debugged. Note that the import dialog shown in Figure 15.16 displays *all* the plug-ins visible to Designer (and there are several hundred of these) so it can help to use the filter field to cut down the list and, as it were, to remove the background noise from the conversation. For instance, just type `com.ex` into the filter field, and the plug-in you wanted is isolated immediately.

Steps 4 and 5 show you how to enable a breakpoint in a Java class when you don't have access to the source code. The jar file can be introspected from the navigator so that the classes and method names are exposed. A method breakpoint can then be set on any given method, which, in a similar way to the exception breakpoints discussed earlier, causes code execution to suspend after the nominated method is called.

Steps 6–8 focus on invoking the debugger on a particular method within the extended control, using some of the techniques learned earlier in the chapter when working with the SSJS debugger. When these are complete you should arrive at the point where you can hit the method you want to debug, but you cannot actually see the code, as shown in Figure 15.17.

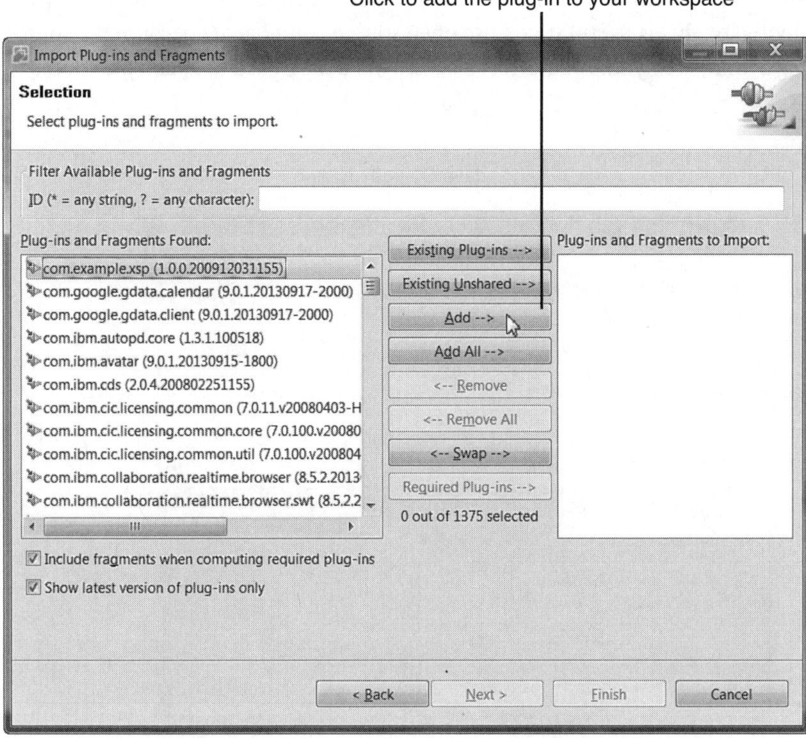

Figure 15.16 Importing a plug-in into Domino Designer

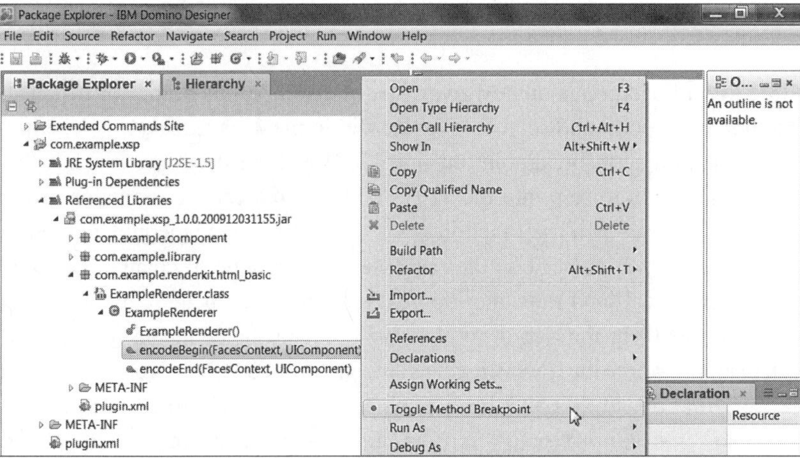

Figure 15.17 Debugging a binary plug-in inside Domino Designer

Steps 9 and 10 enable you to import the source code for the Java classes contained in the extended library. Obviously, this is useful if you use open source components because the source code, by definition, is available to you. Figure 15.18 shows the dialog used to attach the source to the binary Java class.

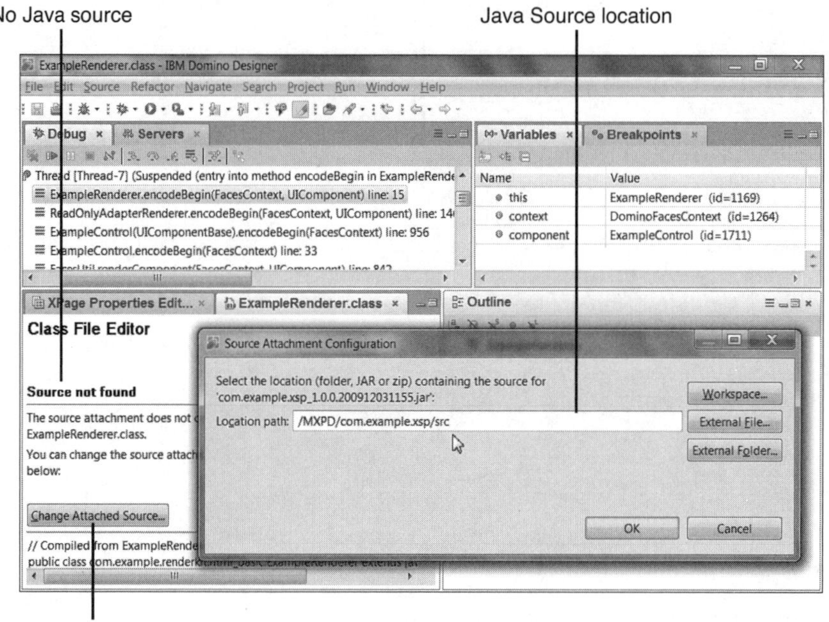

Figure 15.18 Importing source code for a binary plug-in

You are now free to set breakpoints on any given line of code. At this point, for instance, you can delete the method breakpoint and set a breakpoint within the `encodeBegin()` method on any given line. Suppose you set a breakpoint on line 17. When the debugger reaches this code, you can use function key `F5` to step into the `writer` object and change the value of the string parameter passed in. You can then use function key `F7` to complete the method and return back up the stack from whence you came. Use the same `F5/F7` technique to change the value of text used in the next method call and thus alter the text emitted to the page. Obviously, the same actions can be performed via the debug toolbar, so use whichever means you prefer. Figure 15.19 shows an example where the CSS string was changed from `border:orange solid thin` to `border:green dotted thick` and the display text was changed from `This is an ExampleControl using the renderer` to `This is an ExampleControl altered in the debugger`.

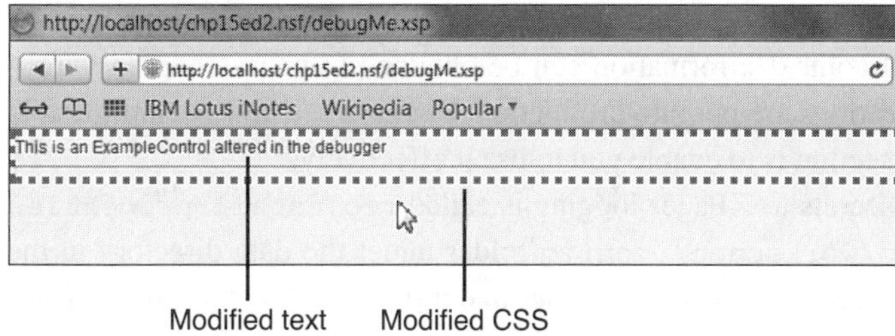

Figure 15.19 Example Control modified via Java Debugger

Mission accomplished. You have successfully debugged into a third-party extended library, attached the Java source code, stepped through it, and even dynamically changed its behavior. This is a vital skill to acquire if you are considering extending your application's capabilities through the use of open source XPages libraries.

> **TIP**
>
> What works for a little toy XPages library like this one will also work for big industrial libraries. For example, all the source code for the plug-ins that originated from the XPages Extension Library can be debugged in the same way as just shown here. That source code ships as a plug-in that is installed with Domino Designer. For 9.0.1 the name of the jar file is of the form **com.ibm.xsp.extlib.feature.source_9.0.1.v00_00_yyyymmdd-hhmm.jar** and you can find it in the **/framework/shared/eclipse/plugins** folder under the Notes root directory. You need to first unpack this archive on disk before you can attach the source code contained within to any of the XPages Extension Library plug-ins, like mobile, iNotes controls, and such.

Before wrapping up this section, just a word to the wise that the full Eclipse Java debugging capability is at your fingertips here in Domino Designer. You can customize the Java and Debug perspectives to enhance productivity and add more views to take advantage of even more advanced features. For instance the Display view available under the Debug category (**Window > Show Eclipse Views > Other > Debug**) enables you to do all sorts of dynamic interactive code manipulations at debug time. It would be well worth your time to explore these options after you have mastered the material covered here.

Enabling XPages Java Logging

Earlier in the chapter you learned how to extend the XPages logging classes to create a logger of your own using SSJS. Although it may be handy to leverage the XPages loggers via JavaScript, it is far more likely that you will need to enable XPages Java runtime logging classes at some point to generate clues for a problem whose cause is unclear. The XPages runtime uses Java logging extensively to ensure that useful context information can be obtained to help debug any problems that may occur when applications are put into production. Logging is a highly configurable mechanism, and the goal of this section is to enable you to use it effectively.

The file that holds all the secrets to XPages logging is called `rcpinstall.properties` and it is located in the `/domino/workspace/.config` folder under the data directory in the Domino server or under the `/workspace/.config` folder under the data directory in the Notes client. You should locate and inspect the contents of this file, but be careful not to make inadvertent modifications because logging can impact runtime performance. (Gathering runtime information and writing it to a log file does not come for free.)

Much of the file content may come across as gobbledygook and is not directly relevant to your needs. To help you navigate the content in double quick time, you can use two search terms to jump directly to the sections of the file likely to be of most interest, namely `JSR47` and `.xsp`. Listing 15.13 shows an abbreviated version of the `rcpinstall.properties` file based on the content located by these terms, as follows:

Listing 15.13 rcpinstall.properties Content for XPages Fans

```
# JSR47 Logging Configuration
handlers=com.ibm.domino.osgi.core.adaptor.DominoConsoleHandler com.ibm.
rcp.core.internal.logger.boot.RCPLogHandler com.ibm.rcp.core.internal.
logger.boot.RCPTraceHandler
com.ibm.rcp.core.internal.logger.boot.RCPLogHandler.encoding=UTF-8
com.ibm.rcp.core.internal.logger.boot.RCPTraceHandler.encoding=UTF-8
.level=WARNING
SystemOut.level=INFO
SystemErr.level=INFO

#To enable logging groups, uncomment and modify the commented line
appropriately
#com.ibm.xsp.adapter.level=FINEST
#com.ibm.xsp.adapter.env.level=FINEST
#com.ibm.xsp.adapter.servlet.level=FINEST
#com.ibm.xsp.adapter.servlet.wrapper.level=FINEST
#com.ibm.xsp.adapter.servlet.mime.level=FINEST
#com.ibm.xsp.adapter.notescontext.level=FINEST
#com.ibm.xsp.adapter.notesurl.level=FINEST
#com.ibm.xsp.adapter.module.level=FINEST
#com.ibm.xsp.adapter.module.timeout.level=FINEST
#com.ibm.xsp.adapter.module.classloader.level=FINEST
#com.ibm.xsp.adapter.preload.level=FINEST
#com.ibm.domino.xsp.bridge.websrv.level=FINEST
#com.ibm.domino.xsp.bridge.websrv.dispatcher.level=FINEST
#com.ibm.domino.xsp.bridge.websrv.servlet.level=FINEST
```

```
#com.ibm.xsp.core.level=FINEST
#com.ibm.xsp.core.component.level=FINEST
#com.ibm.xsp.core.validation.level=FINEST
#com.ibm.xsp.config.level=FINEST
#com.ibm.xsp.core.page.compiled.level=FINEST
#com.ibm.xsp.theme.level=FINEST
#com.ibm.xsp.user.timezone.level=FINEST
#com.ibm.xsp.designer.level=FINEST
#com.ibm.xsp.designer.application.level=FINEST
#com.ibm.xsp.domino.level=FINEST
#com.ibm.xsp.domino.view.level=FINEST
#com.ibm.xsp.domino.document.level=FINEST
#com.ibm.xsp.domino.richtext.level=FINEST
#com.ibm.xsp.domino.filesystem.level=FINEST
#com.ibm.xsp.domino.app.tagcloud.level=FINEST
#com.ibm.xsp.domino.provisioning.level=FINEST
#com.ibm.xsp.extsn.level=FINEST
#com.ibm.xsp.extsn.component.level=FINEST
#com.ibm.xsp.extsn.state.level=FINEST
#com.ibm.xsp.rcp.level=FINEST
#com.ibm.xsp.rcp.preload=FINEST
#com.ibm.xsp.rcp.level=FINEST
```

JSR47 refers to the official Java logging API specification, which XPages adheres to. The section under this comment declares three log handlers that "handle" the output of log messages. The log handlers provided are for the Domino console, a log file, and a trace file. You have already seen how log messages can be directed to the Domino console. In Chapter 13, you were also introduced to some Notes client facilities that display the contents of the system log and trace files—**Help > Support > View Log** and **Help > Support View Trace**. The log files are written in XML format and these menu options help present the content in a reader-friendly manner. This is done with the aid of an XSL viewer, which is also provided by the Domino server and used whenever a log file is opened in a browser. Note also that the trace and log files are encoded as UTF-8, so internationalization is supported, whereas the console handler will use the encoding method in force on the platform in question.

The `.level=WARNING` statement sets the default logging level for all loggers that do not explicitly set their own level—note that Listing 15.12 shows a long list of XPages loggers, all of which are recognizable due to the `.xsp` identifier in the name, with a `FINEST` level assigned to each. To enable any such logger, simply uncomment the statement by removing the # symbol at the start of the line, and restart the http task. You saw in the SSJS sample earlier in the chapter how a logger can emit log information at different levels of granularity (for example, `logger.isWarnEnabled()`) and this is where you can affect the required logging levels at runtime. Table 15.2 outlines a full list of logging levels.

Table 15.2 XPages Runtime Logging Levels

Level Name	Definition
ALL	This is the most verbose level available. Tells the logger framework that all logged events should be reported to the log file.
OFF	This level tells the logger framework that no logged events should be reported to the log file.
SEVERE	This is the least verbose of the logging levels that allows for log messages to be output. This level is reserved for all severe system events, typically events that prevent the system from continuing to function normally. This level normally has an exception associated with it, as in `Failed to open database test.nsf, could not find file on server serverA/ibm`.
WARNING	A little more verbose than SEVERE, this level is reserved for system events that are of interest to end users and system administrators. The events reported at this level report potential problems, but problems that do not prevent the system from functioning. An example is `Failed to connect to server serverA/ibm, failed over to serverB/IBM`.
INFO	Reserved for events that may be of interest to end users but that do not inhibit system function. Typically, messages at this level report successful events/operations, as in `created database test.nsf at 11:45AM`.
CONFIG	This level is normally used to provide static configuration information generated by the system. Typically used to provide OS, system version, memory info, and so The three levels—FINE, FINER, and FINEST—are meant to be relative levels. FINEST is the most verbose level, and FINE the least verbose. The FINE level is normally used to log information that is interesting to developers debugging the system. The FINER level is normally reserved for granular tracing events. Events logged at this level should provide a clear indication of the code path within the system—for example, `entering method xyz`. The FINEST level tells the logger to output even the most detailed messages and is rarely needed. It is usually thought of as developer or debug tracing. This level is sometimes used during development to track the behavior of the system at a fine level or when trying to diagnose difficult issues.

Finally, you can now see that it is possible to turn on logging for different parts of the XPages runtime *and* to set different levels for each log group. There are 36 different `.xsp` log groups called out in Listing 15.12, and for the most part, the names are fairly self-explanatory, identifying the runtime component involved. Table 15.2 then lists eight different levels of logging. All in all this combination should give you the power to get the debug information you need when it comes time to track down a problem in this way. It is recommended that you turn on loggers *selectively* when debugging problems. Turning on all the loggers will result in a flood of XPages system logging, and more often than not this drowns out the nuggets of information that the relevant loggers produce. Instead you should make an educated guess at which loggers should be enabled, and run the system with just those loggers turned on to see if the generated information identifies the issue at hand. If not then it's time to disable some more loggers and enable some others—rinse and repeat until successful!

Debugging XPages Apps on the Client Side

The virtues of printing, dumping, and logging were extolled at the beginning of the chapter as key debugging aids for SSJS. This principle holds equally true on the client side and equivalent utilities are available for that purpose. Chief among these are

- `alert(object)`: Displays a text representation of an object in a browser dialog
- `console.log(object)`: Prints a text representation of an object in the browser console
- `XSP.log(message)`: Prints the message in a separate browser window
- `XSP.dumpObject(object)`: Returns a text representation of an object for debugging

Each of these utilities achieve much the same thing in slightly different ways and thus one may be more suitable than another in a given debug situation. Just like the **PrintDumpLog.xsp** XPage provided examples in an SSJS debug context, an analogous **AlertDumpLog.xsp** XPage is contained in the sample NSF to provide examples for CSJS debugging.

The `alert()` statement is where most web developers started when some simple script code needed debugging. It provided a simple way to display the value of a variable or expression in a dialog box. The modal nature of the dialog, however, can negatively impact the debug use case, perhaps by interrupting a flow of events or causing a time out to occur. As a result, it might be more effective to simply print such values to a console window and inspect them after the use case has completed—this is where `console.log()` comes in handy because it will do just that and seems to be supported in all modern browsers. The `XSP.log()` function provides a similar printing solution but is provided as part of the XPages runtime and seeks to avoid any dependency on cross-browser console implementations by sending its output to an independent browser window (see Figure 15.20). Note, however, that it does not always do a great job of expanding complex objects. For instance, compare and contrast the difference in output from `console.log()` and `XSP.log()` when printing a simple JSON object in **AlertDumpLog.xsp**. For this reason, it is often used in combination with `XSP.dumpObject()` whose purpose in bytes is to "stringify" objects so that they are readable by mere humans. The content in Figure 15.20 is textual representations of a JavaScript JSON object and a DOM object.

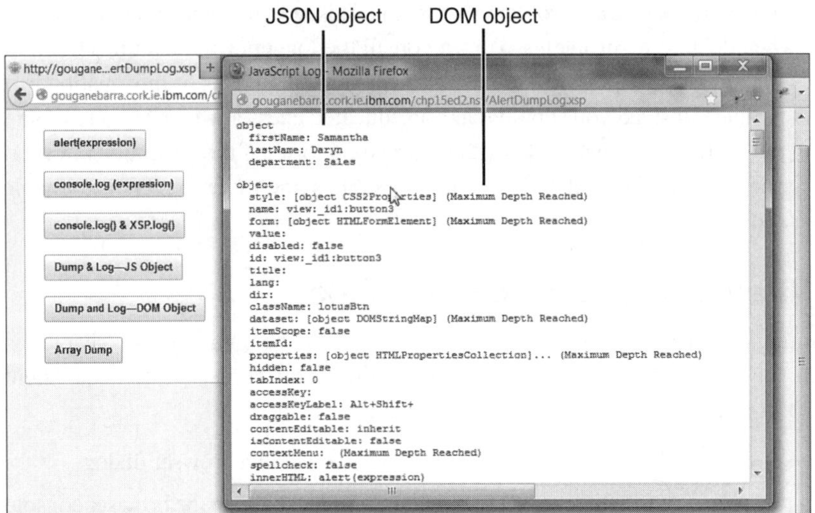

Figure 15.20 Browser window opened and populated by the XSP.log() command

The `XSP.dumpObject()` also can take arguments such as a `name` for the String object it returns and the `depth` to dive into the object at hand. Given that objects may have child objects composed of an arbitrary number of layers, the `depth` parameter is important from the point of view of performance. The various examples in **AlertDumpLog.xsp** should cover the pros and cons of these debug utilities adequately, and you should experiment with these when debugging CSJS issues.

CSJS Debuggers

All the main web browser vendors today provide debug facilities either directly built-in to the out-of-the-box browser or an installable plug-in that can be added on to the base browser installation. The Firebug add-on for Firefox is an example of the latter.

On most browsers the debugger can be pressed into action and discarded from view by toggling function key `F12`. (On Windows at least—be aware that key bindings on other platforms may differ.) When activated, the tooling typically provides a full suite of services such as a JavaScript code debugger, CSS viewers and editor, DOM inspector, console, logger, profiler, network transaction monitor, and so forth. This area has grown much richer in recent years.

For example, invoke Firebug in Firefox by pressing function key `F12` when the **AlertDumpLog.xsp** XPage is loaded. A lower portion of the browser screen is taken over by the debugger, which provides a tabbed toolbar and display panes for various different services. You can, for example, choose the console and view the output of the `console.log()` commands exercised by various buttons on the page. At the bottom a console command line is provided for dynamic interaction with the active page, and an extensive command-line API ensures that the utilities you need are at your fingertips. For example, type `help()` to see all the available commands. As well as the listed commands, you can execute *any* valid JavaScript expression from here. All objects in the current DOM are also instantly accessible. For instance, the client-side XSP object is loaded for every XPage, so you can simply type `XSP` followed by a period character (.) to invoke the type ahead on its available methods. These methods can be run interactively from the console command line for any XPage at any time—Figure 15.21 shows an example of console usage.

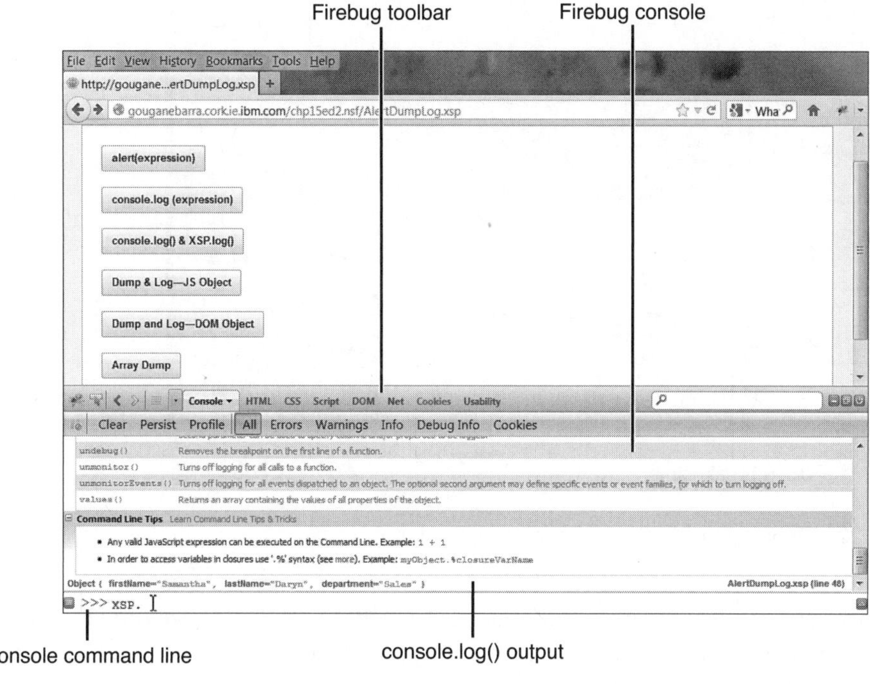

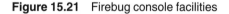

Figure 15.21 Firebug console facilities

Switching to Internet Explorer, you can invoke its debugger with the same function key `F12`. You can debug some JavaScript on the sample XPage by selecting the **Script** tab, which displays all the HTML page source in an editor window. Locate some JavaScript source code within the page, and you can set a breakpoint by double-clicking in the gutter—just like in the SSJS debugger. You should then click the **Start Debugging** button to load the debugger and use the XPage in the browser to invoke the code of interest. Figure 15.22 shows what happens when a breakpoint is set in the **Dump & Log JS Object** button. The code pauses at that line of code (line 57) and you are free to step or resume as one would expect in any debugger. The adjacent **Locals** window shows the values assigned to the `options` and `jsonObject` variables, which can be explored and edited. Basically this is close to a full-fledged Java debugger experience.

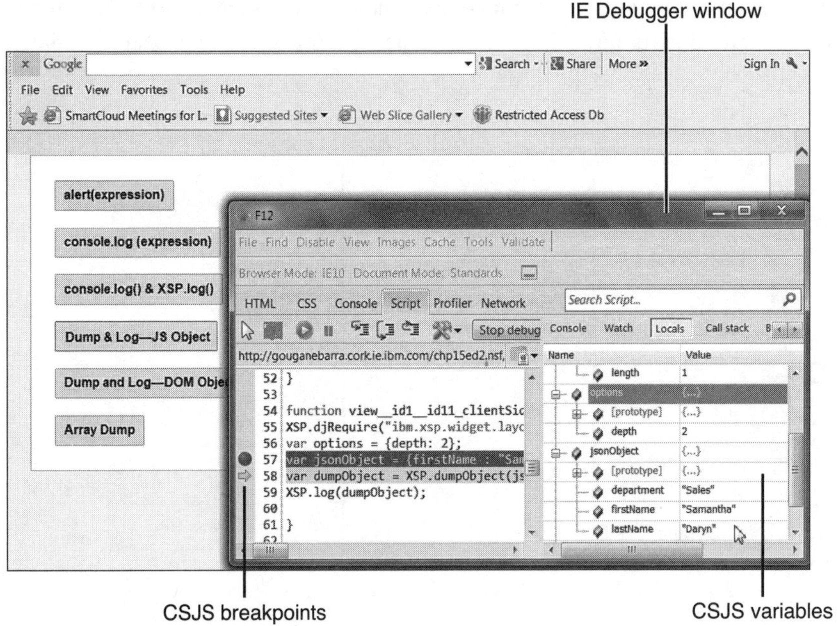

Figure 15.22 Debugging CSJS code in Internet Explorer

With a little experience you can find your way around the debugging tools provided by the individual browser vendors without too much difficulty because they all have a lot in common. One useful website that explores all the major browser debugging tools is `debugbrowser.com`. This should assist you to get up to speed with all the features and foibles of the main players.

Debugging Dojo

The XPages framework uses the Dojo client-side JavaScript library extensively. Although other libraries such as JQuery can also be used as part of an XPages application, Dojo is a key integrated component and at this point regarded as an inseparable part of the core runtime.

Up to the Notes and Domino 8.5.3 release, the Dojo libraries shipped and used by XPages were simply laid down on the file system of the Notes client and Domino server. From 8.5.3 forward they are packaged in a plug-in and installed as a zipped jar file in the `osgi/shared/eclipse/plugins` folder under the Notes/Domino root directory. Although this is a more efficient way to package and deploy the Dojo resources, it became a hindrance in terms of debugging. Why? Because being part of a compressed archive makes the source code difficult to access for the debugger. They need to be unplugged before they can be debugged.

An additional complication was added by the fact that much of the Dojo JavaScript source files are aggregated by the runtime when served up, thus drastically reducing the number of resource requests from the browser and delivering better performance as a result. Again however, aggregations make it difficult to locate the JavaScript source code you want to debug, as individual JS files may no longer be identifiable at runtime given that they could have been rolled up into a larger aggregated resource. Figure 15.23 shows a list of Dojo JS resources served up to the browser when rendering the **allDocuments.xsp** page within the sample Discussion application, including an aggregated JS resource with an unintelligible name.

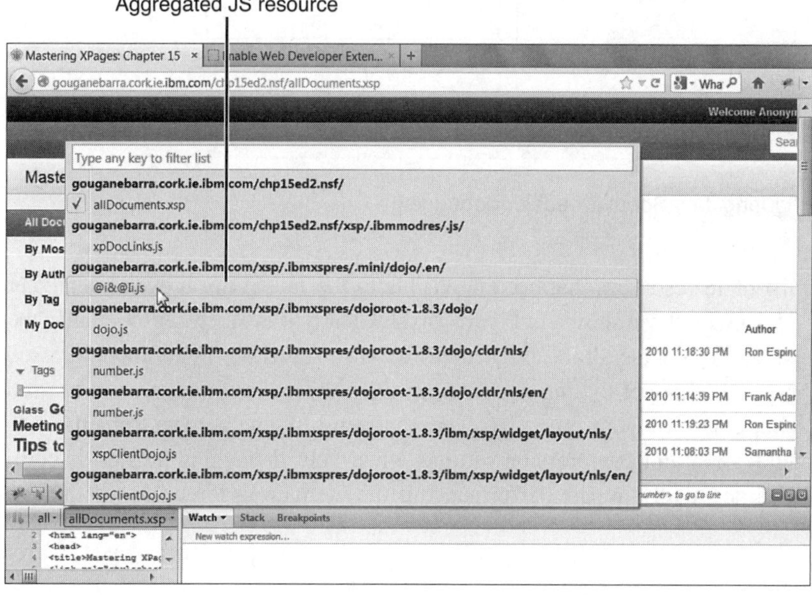

Figure 15.23 Aggregated JS resources used when serving an XPage

The 9.0 release delivered a solution. A new check box was added to the **Application Configuration > Xsp Properties > Persistence > Performance Properties > Options** that enabled developers to opt for uncompressed resource files (CSS & Dojo). This meant that the uncompressed JS and CSS resources contained in the Dojo plug-in were served up—not the obfuscated or gzipped versions that are used by default. If the developer enabled this option and at the same time disabled the neighboring **Use runtime optimized JavaScript and CSS resources** check box, not only were the uncompressed versions used, but aggregation was also turned off. Result: Developer-friendly JS source code served up in their original files—a much easier debugging experience. Figure 15.24 shows the options in question, with the debug-friendly settings in place.

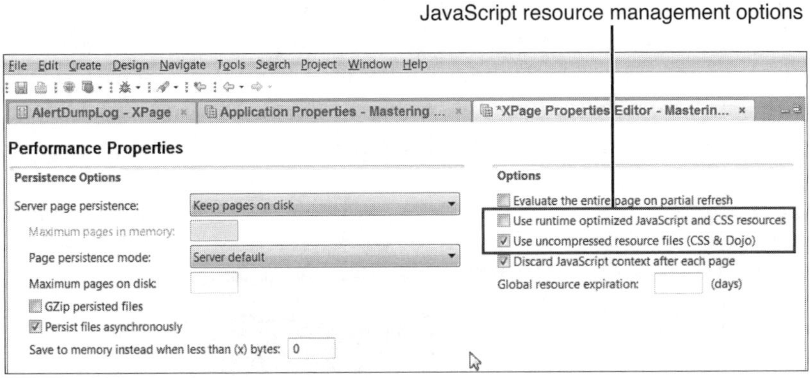

Figure 15.24 Configuring JavaScript for easier debugging

Compare the list of JS resources that become visible to the JavaScript browser debugger as shown in Figure 15.25 with those shown in Figure 15.23. Clearly it is far easier to identify the JS resource you need, and of course all these resources are also served up in an uncompressed fashion. Thus the browser debugger tooling discussed in the previous section can now be used to good effect in debugging any Dojo issues you may happen to come across. Remember to revert both these aggregation and compression settings when your debugging session is complete because they will negatively impact performance if they remain in force in a production environment.

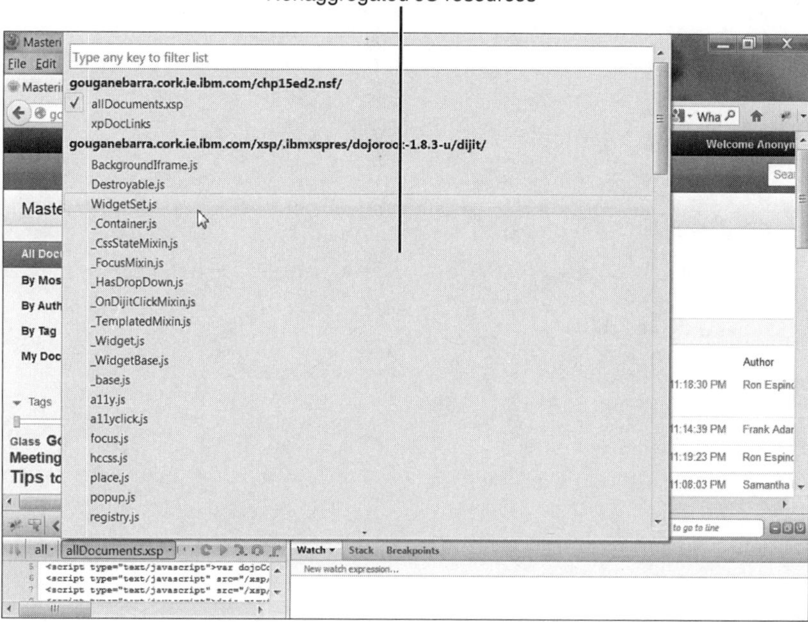

Figure 15.25 Unaggregated and uncompressed JS resources listed in the JS debugger

Conclusion

This concludes this chapter on XPages debugging. Hopefully, you have learned a range of skills across the entire gamut of application debugging—everything from emitting useful context information that helps decipher issues, to JavaScript debugging on the client and server side, to advanced Java debugging. If so you will be well equipped to deal with most problems that come your way in the course of creating and deploying XPages applications. May all your bugs be small ones!

PART V

Application User Experience

CHAPTER 16

XPages Theming

User-interface design and frontend engineering are well-established disciplines in today's software development industry. It is now commonplace to have dedicated UI designers and frontend developers on a development team. The need for these specialists is due to the fact that a well-constructed and robust application can ultimately fail because of a badly designed or poorly performing user interface.

If you have ever done any Domino web-application development, you are familiar with the practice of embedding pass-through web browser presentation code into forms, providing styling information within views, and so on. These practices make it difficult to maintain the presentation logic of an application. This is mainly because there is no clear separation between application and presentation logic, with the two entities heavily intertwined across the various design elements of an application. XPages alleviates this problem by providing dedicated design elements and features to loosely couple presentation logic from application logic.

This chapter explains the design elements and features provided by XPages that can help you develop well-constructed user interfaces and deliver a visually consistent user experience. Before you start into the exercises of this chapter, be sure to download the **Chp16Ed2.nsf** application provided online for this book. You can access this file at `www.ibmpressbooks.com/title/9780133373371`. Once downloaded, open in Domino Designer and sign it.

It Used to Be Like That...But Not Anymore

Web application user interfaces have come a long way since the inception of HTML in the early 1990s. At that time, the choice of browsers was limited, with the rendering of an HTML page left much to the vagaries of a vendor's browser-specific behavior. Prior to this, user interface design and frontend engineering were not even recognized disciplines, or even requirements in those early years.

Over time, major advancements have been made in client-tier and server-tier technologies to assist user-interface development and support efficient delivery of presentation logic to the end user. The concept of a web application has become ever more prominent, both culturally and commercially, all but displacing client application architectures. Web-based programming languages and standards have also flourished. This cohort of programming languages and standards, each staking their own claim on providing the perfect solution or specification for some key aspect of web-application development, are manifold and constantly evolving. But, it is true to say, without exception, that only one language and standard remains the pillar-post for aesthetic web-application development: Cascading Style Sheets (CSS). In its most elementary form, CSS style rules can be statically embedded within a HTML page to define the look of that page once rendered in a web browser, mobile device, printer, or some other form of media. Equally, in its most complicated form, CSS style rules and classes can be contained within separate files, and dynamically injected or removed from the HTML page's Document Object Model (DOM) using JavaScript. This can be further enhanced with CSS pseudo-events triggered by a user-input device, such as a mouse, touch-screen, or speech tool, interacting to provide a degree of feel within the page.

Domino web-application development has, up to the introduction of XPages in version 8.5, relied heavily on tightly coupled techniques for providing the look and feel of a web application—for example, embedding pass-through HTML constructs, conditional statements controlling display of web constructs, distributed setting of styles within views, and so on! All of this makes the task of maintaining, or revamping, an out-of-date application a daunting and costly development job when it shouldn't be.

XPages does things differently. One of the primary objectives of XPages is to provide a clean separation between data, structure, and presentation. This is evident in many ways:

- An XPage doesn't need to bind itself directly to fields in the way a traditional form does.
- An XPage supports the inclusion of different types of resources, even conditionally if necessary.
- An XPage supports the use of Custom Controls and nested XPages, which gives you a flexible and dynamic development and runtime environment for Notes/Domino application development.

The end result is that an application can be cleanly separated into specific parts. You have already seen that the data model can be developed separately from the structure. You now learn that the same is true for application look and feel; that is, it can be developed separately from both the data model and structure. All in all, this gives you, the developer, the greatest degree of flexibility to create great Notes/Domino web applications that you can come back to, time and time again, to modernize without restriction.

In the first practical section, "Styling with Style," you learn how to use inline styles within an XPage. This is the most basic technique that can be used to create a visual appearance for an XPage using CSS. The following section, "Styling with Class," teaches you about incorporating

CSS resources within your XPages, and using CSS style classes. The final section, "Theming on Steroids!" teaches you about the XPages Theme design element.

> **TIP**
>
> If you are unfamiliar with CSS, or want a refresher, you might find it beneficial to read some of the following resources before continuing with the rest of this chapter: `www.w3.org/Style/CSS/` and `www.w3schools.com/css/`

Styling with Style

In this section, you learn how to use inline CSS styles within an XPage—this is a technique commonly known as *inline styling*. This is the most basic technique you can use to alter the visual appearance of an XPage and its controls. Domino Designer helps by providing a **Style** properties panel. This assists you by generating the CSS code required to support the format selections made within the **Style** properties panel. Therefore, without having any CSS knowledge, you can still create visually appealing XPages.

On the **Style** properties panel, you can change three groups of style formatting using child panels located within this panel. The first group is related to **Font** settings, as shown in Figure 16.1.

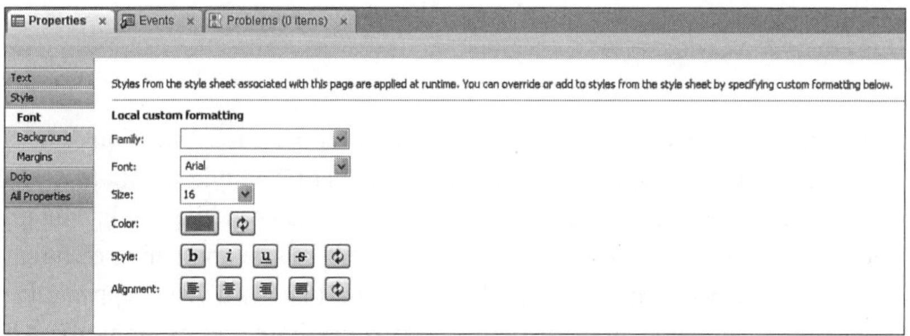

Figure 16.1 Font tab on the Style properties panel

The second tab contains the **Background** group of settings. These settings can alter the background appearance, such as background image or color, and so on, as shown in Figure 16.2.

The third and final styling tab contains the **Margins** group of settings. You can use this tab to alter the padding and margin settings, as shown in Figure 16.3.

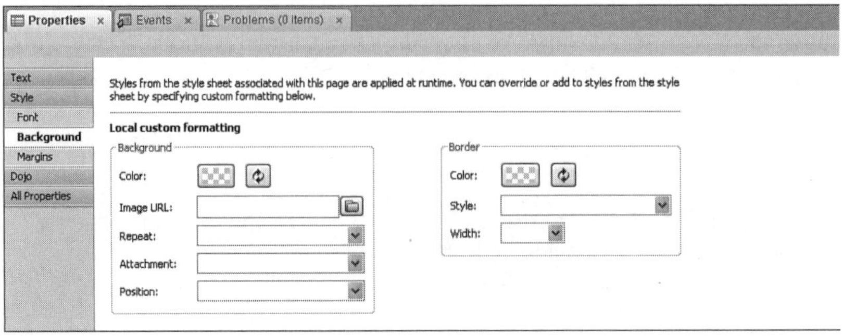

Figure 16.2 Background tab on the Style properties panel

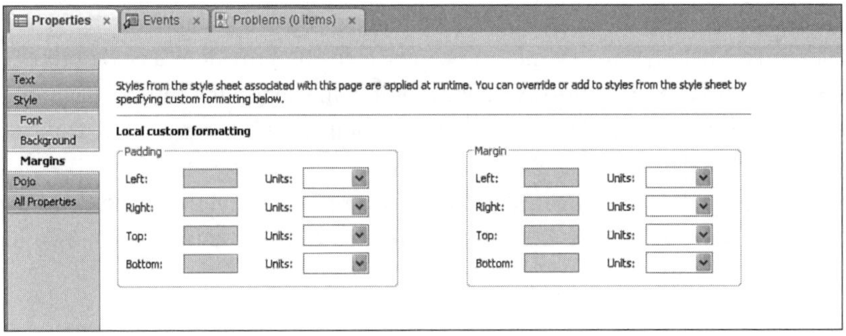

Figure 16.3 Margins tab on the Style properties panel

If you are familiar with creating CSS styles, you undoubtedly come across situations where the three **Style** properties panel groups do not expose some particular CSS style setting that you might need. This is expected, of course, as the three groups of style-related settings only contain some of the most frequently used CSS style settings; therefore, you can do something different by using the `style` property directly. Almost every XPages control that has a visual appearance supports the `style` property. Take any control from the **control palette** and examine the **All Properties** panel—there, you find the `style` property listed, as shown in Figure 16.4.

You can set the `style` property with a static string value that contains any CSS style rules. Equally, you can also specify a computed value. Note that whenever you use the three **Style** properties panel editors to specify stylistic settings, the values get joined together to form a single string value containing CSS style rules code. This CSS style rules value is then written into the `style` property within the XSP markup.

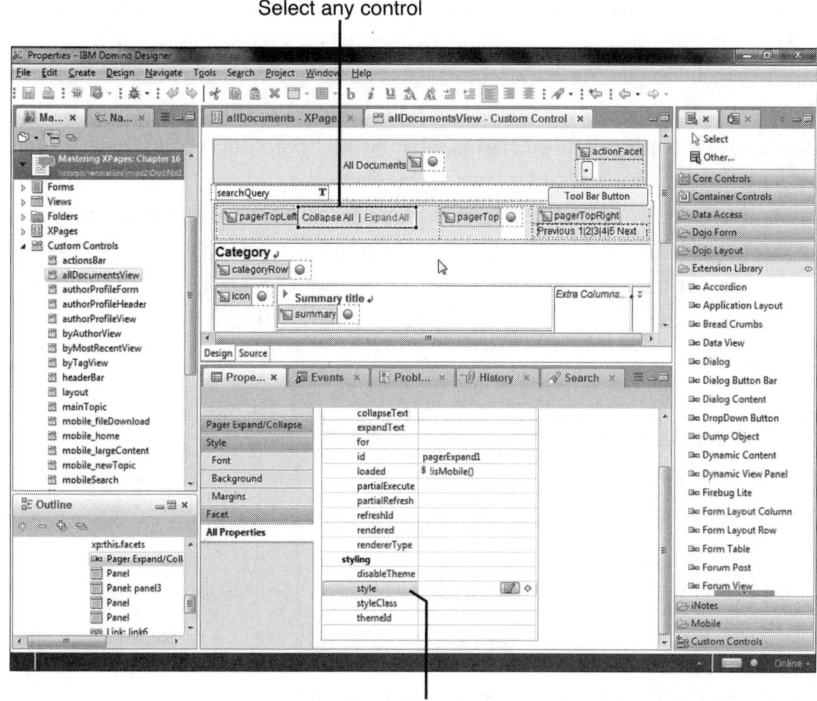

Figure 16.4 style property listed in the All Properties panel

Now, you try out the **Style** properties panel and `style` property in Domino Designer. With Designer open, open the **Chp16Ed2.nsf** application. Then, create a new XPage called **styling**. On the WYSIWYG editor for this XPage, type an arbitrary sentence and press the **Enter** key a couple of times to put in two carriage returns. Now, drag-and-drop a **Button** control on to the XPage. Create two more carriage returns just after the **Button** control, drag-and-drop a **Label** control on to the XPage. You should have something similar to Figure 16.5.

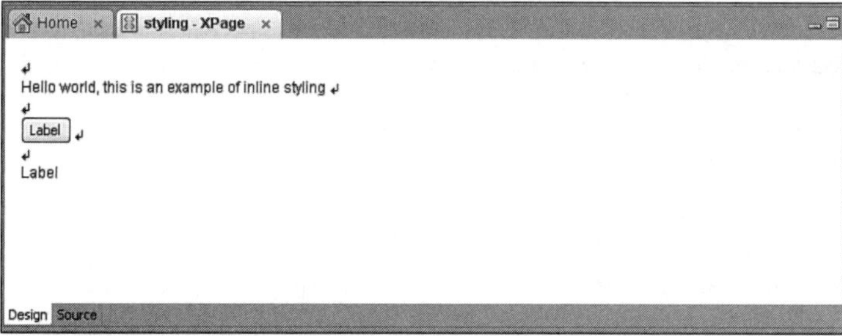

Figure 16.5 Sample styling XPage with the typed sentence, the Button, and Label controls

Now, highlight one or all words within the sentence you typed earlier. In the Style properties editor, click the **Font** tab. On this tab, select some font settings for the sentence, such as font, size, color, and so on. Also, select settings from the **Background** and **Margins** tabs. After you finish styling the sentence, select the Button control and go through the same process of setting its style using the **Font**, **Background**, and **Margins** tabs. At this point, do not give the **Label** control any styling details—you come back to it later in this section.

As you already noticed, the WYSIWYG editor displays the visual changes you have made. This editor does support the visualization of CSS, but there are some CSS style rules that it does not support. However, for the vast majority of use cases, it does a good job of giving you a design-time visualization of the CSS used by an XPage for the **styling** XPage, as shown in Figure 16.6.

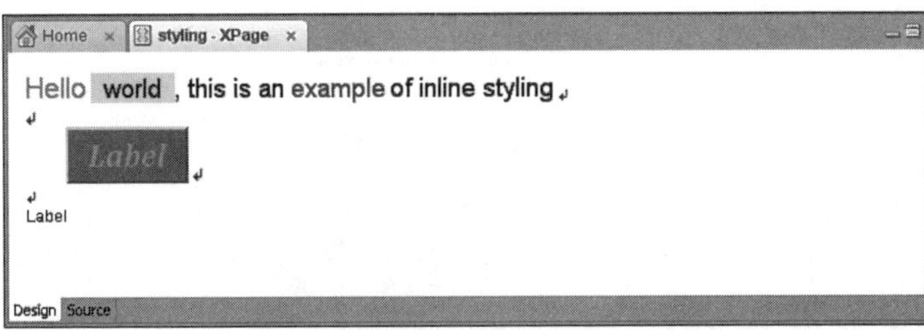

Figure 16.6 Styling XPage in Designer with the style changes applied

Now, examine the XSP source markup for your **styling** XPage. Simply select the **Source** panel in the WYSIWYG editor. In the markup, you see a number of `style` properties have been generated on the words of the sentence and the **Button** control. These `style` properties now contain CSS style rules code that is similar to Listing 16.1.

Listing 16.1 XSP Markup for the Styling XPage, Including Generated style Properties

```
<?xml version="1.0" encoding="UTF-8"?>
<xp:view xmlns:xp="http://www.ibm.com/xsp/core">
      <xp:spanstyle="font-family:Arial;font-
size:16pt;color:rgb(255,0,0)">Hello</xp:span>
      <xp:span style="font-family:Arial;font-size:14pt;background-
color:rgb(0,255,255);padding-left:10px;padding-right:10px">world
</xp:span><xp:span
style="font-family:Arial;font-size:14pt">,
this is an </xp:span>
      <xp:span style="font-family:Arial;font-
size:14pt;color:rgb(0,0,255)">example</xp:span>
      <xp:span style="font-family:Arial;font-size:14pt"> of inline
styling</xp:span>
```

```
        <xp:br></xp:br>
        <xp:br></xp:br>
        <xp:button value="Label" id="button1" style="font-
family:Cambria;font-
size:18pt;color:rgb(255,128,255);font-weight:bold;font-
style:italic;background-
color:rgb(128,128,0);margin-left:30px"></xp:button>
        <xp:br></xp:br>
        <xp:br></xp:br>
        <xp:label value="Label" id="label1"></xp:label>
</xp:view>
```

Having saved your changes to the **styling** XPage, preview your artistic masterpiece. You might have something like that seen in Figure 16.7.

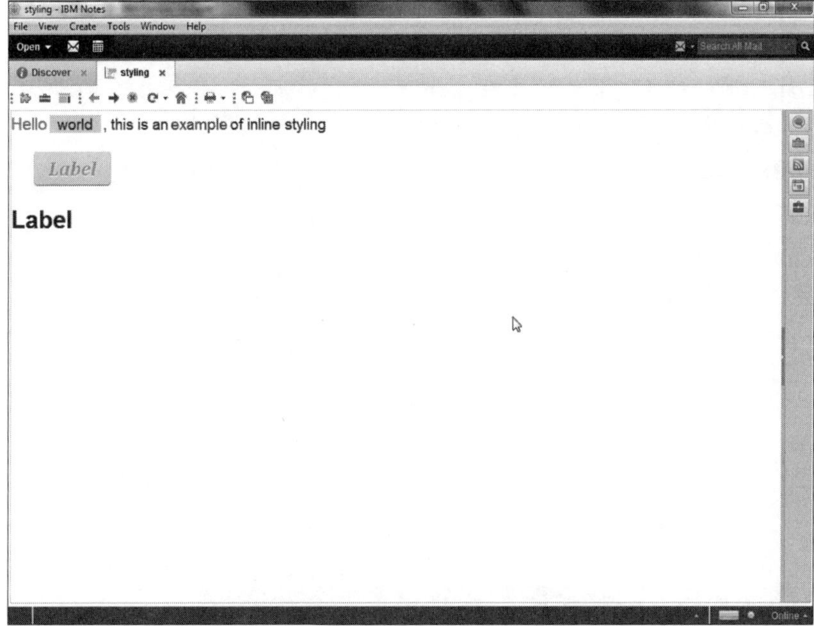

Figure 16.7 Styling XPage in the Notes client with changes to the sentence and button control

So, without writing a single line of CSS code, you styled your XPage controls using the built-in features of Domino Designer. This is a straightforward example of applying styling details to an XPage. You should now revisit your **styling** XPage in Designer to learn about using the `style` property directly for situations where you need more than the built-in styling editors of Designer.

Setting the Style Property Manually

On the **styling** XPage, select the **Label** control in the WYSIWYG editor in Designer. Now, click the **All Properties** panel in the **Properties** view. Scroll through the list of properties, and you see a **styling** category that contains four properties, one of which is the `style` property. (You learn all about the other three later in this chapter.) Select the `style` property by clicking in its value editor and typing some CSS style rules into it, such as the following:

```
font-weight:bold;font-size:30px;
```

You should see something similar to that of Figure 16.8, where the **Label** control is selected in the WYSIWYG editor, and the `style` property has the suggested CSS style rules typed directly into its value editor.

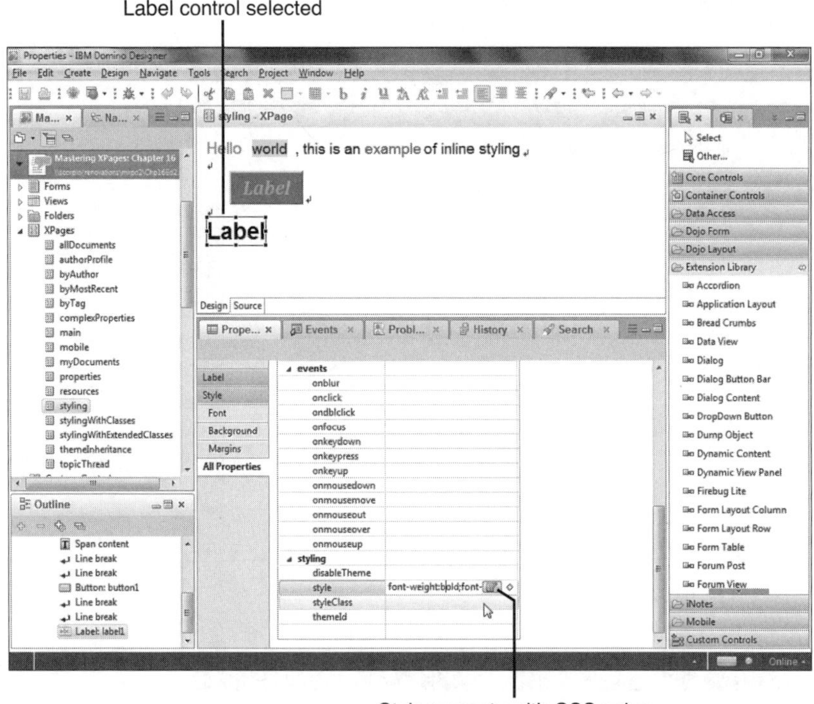

Figure 16.8 All Properties panel showing the style property of the Label control with CSS typed into it

Having set the `style` property, examine the XSP markup for the **Label** control using the **Source** panel in the WYSIWYG editor. You see that the CSS code you typed into the `style` property has been written into the XSP markup of the `<xp:label>` tag, as shown here in Listing 16.2.

Listing 16.2 XSP Markup Fragment Showing the Manually Added Style Property on the Label Control

```
<?xml version="1.0" encoding="UTF-8"?>
<xp:view xmlns:xp="http://www.ibm.com/xsp/core">
      ...
      <xp:label value="Label" id="label1"
            style="font-weight:bold;font-size:30px"></xp:label>
</xp:view>
```

Understanding How the Style Property Is Used

Again, preview your **styling** XPage. This time around, view the emitted HTML source of the XPage. This task makes you aware of how the `style` property and its CSS style rules value are used by a browser or client.

In the emitted HTML source, or alternatively also shown here as a fragment in Listing 16.3, you see several instances of the `style` attribute on the HTML elements. The value for each contains the same values you set within Designer for the sentence and each of the XPages controls.

Listing 16.3 Emitted HTML Source Fragment Showing the Inline Style Attributes and CSS Values

```
<?xml version="1.0" encoding="UTF-8"?>
<!DOCTYPE HTML PUBLIC ...
<html lang="en">
...
<body ...>
...
<span style="font-family:Arial;font-size:16pt;color:rgb(255,0,0)">
➥Hello</span>
<span style="font-family:Arial;font-size:14pt;background-color:
➥rgb(0,255,255);padding-left:10px;padding-right:10px">world</span>
<span style="font-family:Arial;font-size:14pt">, this is an</span>
<span style="font-family:Arial;font-size:14pt;color:rgb(0,0,255)">
➥example</span>
<span style="font-family:Arial;font-size:14pt">of inline styling</span>
<br>
```

```
<br>
<button style="font-family:Cambria;font-size:18pt;color:rgb(255,128,
➥255);font-
weight:bold;font-style:italic;background-color:rgb(128,128,0);margin-
left:30px" ...  type="button" name="view:_id1:button1"
id="view:_id1:button1">Label</button><br>
<br>
<span id="view:_id1:label1" style="font-weight:bold;font-size:30px;"
...>Label</span>
...
</body>
</html>
```

Note that CSS is a technology used to alter the presentation of HTML, XML, and other types of document elements. The parsing and visualization process of CSS takes place in the client-side browser. This process does not occur until the emitted HTML markup has been received by the browser or client, and must then complete before presenting the resultant HTML page to the user. Therefore, when you specify CSS style rules using the `style` property on an XPage and its controls, these are basically written directly into the emitted HTML markup as `style` attributes on the associated HTML tags, as shown in Listing 16.3. It is then the responsibility of the receiving browser or client to parse the `style` attribute values accordingly for presentation to the user.

Computing the Style Property

You might have noticed that the `style` property supports computed values also. The examples explained so far in this section have been focused on using static values. To see a worked example of a computed `style` property value, you should open the **Chp16Ed2.nsf** application in Designer. Once launched, open the **viewTopic** Custom Control. Then, use the **Source** view to locate and select the Panel control on line 621. Having selected this control in the **Source** view, click the **All Properties** panel under the **Properties** view, and scroll to the `style` property. You see that this property indicates it has a computed value—denoted by the blue diamond icon in the value editor. Click the blue diamond and select **Compute Value** from the pop-up menu to open the **Script Editor**. In this editor, you see that the computed value expression contains code to calculate the CSS background color style rule, as shown in Figure 16.9.

This example calculates the background color that should be applied to the current topic's HTML DIV element. This is a great example of dynamically computing some CSS style rule and applying it directly to the `style` property. This gives you a flexible mechanism to manipulate the presentation of an XPage and its controls.

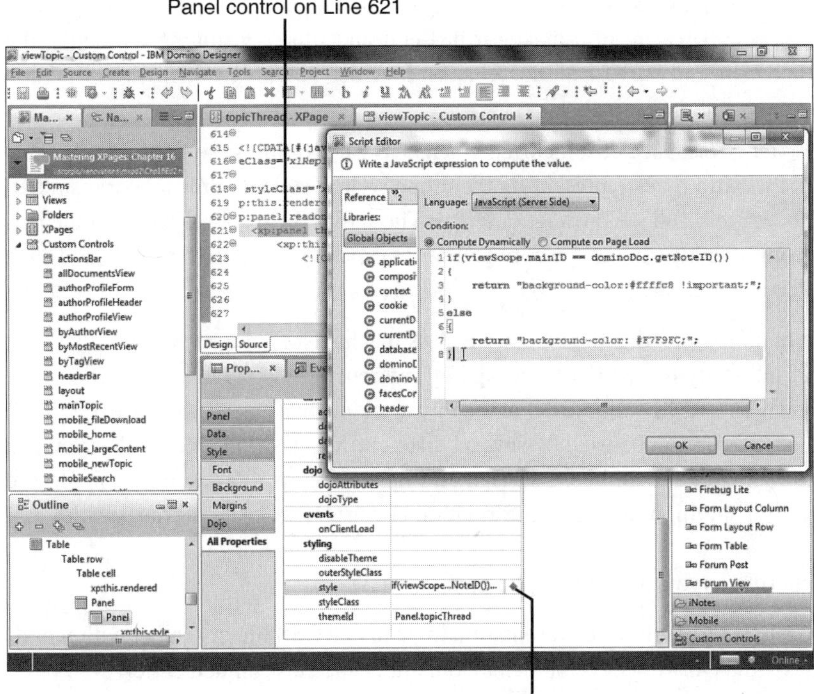

Figure 16.9 Computed style value for the Panel control in the viewTopic Custom Control

Styling with Class

This section teaches you how to adopt a slightly more advanced approach to styling an XPage. This approach involves using another CSS construct known as a *style class*. A CSS style class is used as a means of referencing CSS style rules stored in a separate file, from within a web page. Typically, this mechanism is supported by most browser implementations for HTML, XML, and several other types of documents containing presentation markup. As an XPage is ultimately rendered as a HTML document, using and understanding how CSS style classes work is therefore important.

Getting Something for Nothing

In the last section, you learned all about XPages support for inline styling using the `style` property and should now understand its benefits. But, take a minute to consider what negative aspects might be introduced by inline styling across an application containing many XPages:

- A lot of redundancy exists across all the XPages due to many instances of duplicated CSS styling code. This, in turn, makes it difficult and time consuming to change the presentation consistently across all the XPages. It is also equally as difficult to find and correct any presentation anomalies.
- There is also a performance cost incurred when heavy use of inline styling is made. This is due to all the extra bytes representing the inline styling code that must be transmitted over the network to reach the browser or client. This slows the responsiveness of the network and, consequently, that of the application. This process must also be repeated each time an XPage is requested.

It is for these main reasons that the CSS style class mechanism is important. It effectively allows you to avoid inline styling within an XPage by referencing a style class definition kept in a linked file known as a CSS file. An XPage can use more than one CSS file if required. Conversely, a single CSS file can be used by several different XPages. This means that you can declare all the CSS styling code within a CSS file, and link as many XPages to this single file as needed. You are then sharing the styling information consistently across all the XPages that use it.

This reaps benefits for you and your application in two ways:

- You can consistently change the presentation logic in one CSS file instead of within multiple XPages—thus making development and maintenance tasks much easier.
- The performance of your application is boosted by the fact that the number of bytes transmitted over the network is radically reduced. This is streamlined by the fact that the first time an XPage is requested, the emitted HTML is loaded into the browser or client along with any linked CSS and JavaScript files. These are then typically saved into the browser or client cache to avoid retransmitting them over the network in subsequent XPage requests. The style classes within the emitted HTML document then simply reference the linked CSS file that is cached, for the complete CSS style rule definition.

Now, reopen the **Chp16Ed2.nsf** application in Designer if it has been closed. Once opened, bring up the **stylingWithClasses** XPage. This XPage might look familiar to you in the sense that it is similar to the **styling** XPage you created in the last section. This is intentional, and you learn the reason for this soon—Figure 16.10 shows the **stylingWithClasses** XPage previewed in the Notes client.

Note the similarity to the styling XPage

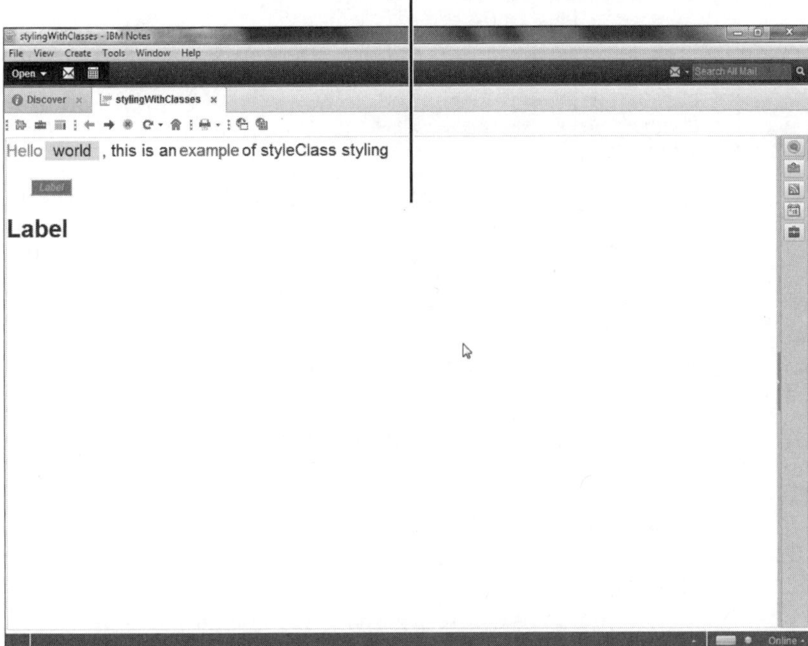

Figure 16.10 stylingWithClasses XPage previewed in the Notes client

Returning to Designer, you need to examine the **Resources** panel under the **Properties** view for the **stylingWithClasses** XPage. You see that one Style Sheet resource called `classes.css` is listed (see Figure 16.11).

You learned about the **Resources** panel in Chapter 4, "Anatomy of an XPage," so you should already understand that it is used to attach different types of resources to an XPage. CSS style sheets are one of those resource types. In this example, the `classes.css` style sheet has been created, coded, and attached to the **stylingWithClasses** XPage for your convenience. You should now open it in Designer by expanding the **Resources > Style Sheets** design element in the **Navigator** view, and double-clicking `classes.css`, as shown in Figure 16.12.

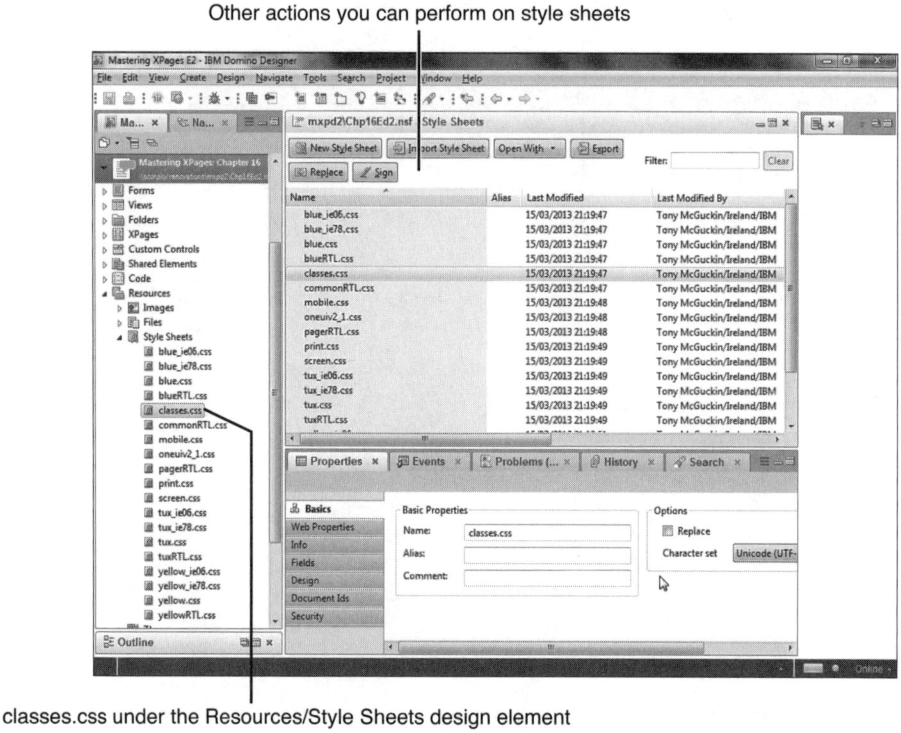

Other actions you can perform on style sheets

classes.css under the Resources/Style Sheets design element

Figure 16.11 classes.css Style Sheet resource listed in the Resources panel

It is important for you to remember that you manage CSS style sheets under the **Resources > Style Sheets** design element, as shown in Figure 16.11. Therefore, any time you need to create a style sheet, you do so by right-clicking this design element and selecting **New Style Sheet**. You then are prompted to name the newly created file. Once created, it can be attached using the **Resources** panel of any XPage.

With the style sheet `classes.css` now open in Designer's CSS editor, you can see that it contains several style class declarations, each with their own associated style rule definitions. These are also detailed in Listing 16.4.

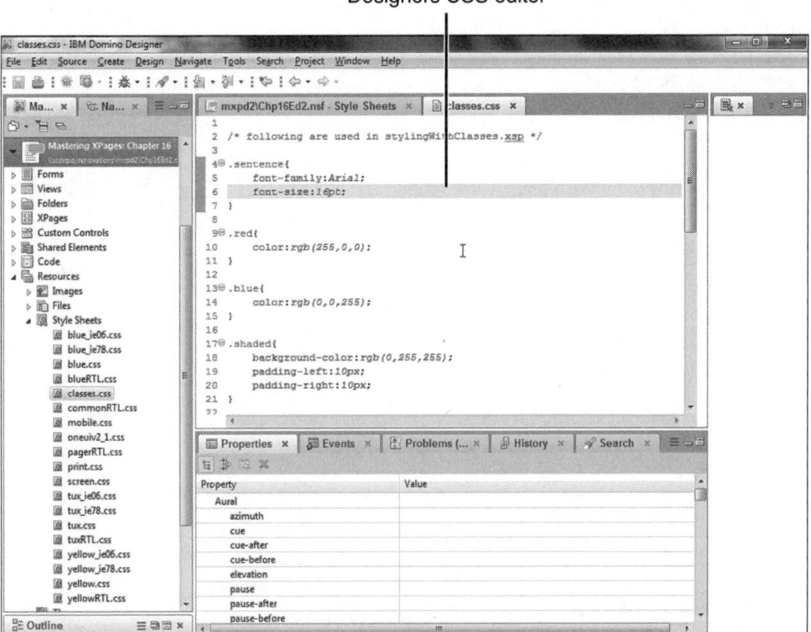

Figure 16.12 Resources > Style Sheets design element containing classes.css

Listing 16.4 CSS Style Class Declarations and Style Rule Definitions Within classes.css

```
.sentence{
    font-family:Arial;
    font-size:16pt;
}

.red{
    color:rgb(255,0,0);
}

.blue{
    color:rgb(0,0,255);
}

.shaded{
    background-color:rgb(0,255,255);
    padding-left:10px;
    padding-right:10px;
}
```

```
.button{
    font-family:Cambria;
    font-size:18pt;
    color:rgb(255,128,255);
    font-weight:bold;
    font-style:italic;
    background-color:rgb(128,128,0);
    margin-left:30px;
}

.label{
    font-weight:bold;
    font-size:30px;
}

.h3OuterClass{
    margin:50px;
}

.orange{
    font-size:30px !important;
    font-family:arial;
    color:orange;
}

.odd{background-color:AliceBlue;}
.even{background-color:Cornsilk;}

.captionStyleClass{font-weight:bold;font-size:30px;}
```

These style classes contain the same style rule settings selected using the three different groups of style-related settings on the **Style** properties panel in Listing 16.1 and typed directly into the `style` property in Listing 16.2. In this case, the CSS styling code is contained within this single style sheet file, with each set of style rules wrapped into a style class that is identifiable by its class name.

If you now look at the XSP markup for the **stylingWithClasses** XPage in Designer, you see that the text, the **Button** control, and the **Label** control all have references to the style class names within `classes.css` by way of the `styleClass` property. This is also shown in Listing 16.5.

Listing 16.5 styleClass Properties Referencing the Style Classes Within classes.css

```
<?xml version="1.0" encoding="UTF-8"?>
<xp:view xmlns:xp="http://www.ibm.com/xsp/core">
    <xp:this.resources>
        <xp:styleSheet href="/classes.css"></xp:styleSheet>
    </xp:this.resources>
    <xp:span styleClass="sentence red">Hello</xp:span>
    <xp:span styleClass="sentence shaded">world</xp:span>
    <xp:span styleClass="sentence">, this is an</xp:span>
    <xp:span styleClass="sentence blue">example</xp:span>
    <xp:span styleClass="sentence">of styleClass styling</xp:span>
    <xp:br></xp:br>
    <xp:br></xp:br>
    <xp:button value="Label" id="button1" styleClass="button">
    </xp:button>
    <xp:br></xp:br>
    <xp:br></xp:br>
    <xp:label value="Label" id="label1" styleClass="label"></xp:label>
</xp:view>
```

Take this opportunity to compare the XSP markup of the **styling** XPage, detailed in Listing 16.1, which uses inline styling, to that of the **stylingWithClasses** XPage, detailed in Listing 16.5, which uses style classes and a style sheet. I am sure that you will agree that the latter is much easier to read and comprehend—never mind the inherent benefits it now bestows by using the style class technique.

In the previous section, you learned about the three different groups of style-related settings on the **Style** properties panel. You did not, however, learn about the main **Style** properties panel itself. You use the **Style** properties panel to effectively set the `styleClass` property on a control, from whatever CSS style sheets are attached to the current XPage. Figure 16.13 shows an example for the **Button** control on the **stylingWithClasses** XPage, where you can see the `.button` style class has been selected from the available list of style classes in the `classes.css` style sheet.

Understanding How the styleClass Property Is Used

Take a moment to preview the **stylingWithClasses** XPage. When opened, view the emitted HTML source of the XPage. This task makes you aware of how the `styleClass` property is used by a browser or client and highlights the performance benefit explained earlier.

In the emitted HTML source, or alternatively shown as a fragment in Listing 16.6, you can see several instances of the `class` attribute on the different HTML elements. Each one contains a class name that is contained within the `classes.css` style sheet linked in the head section of the HTML source.

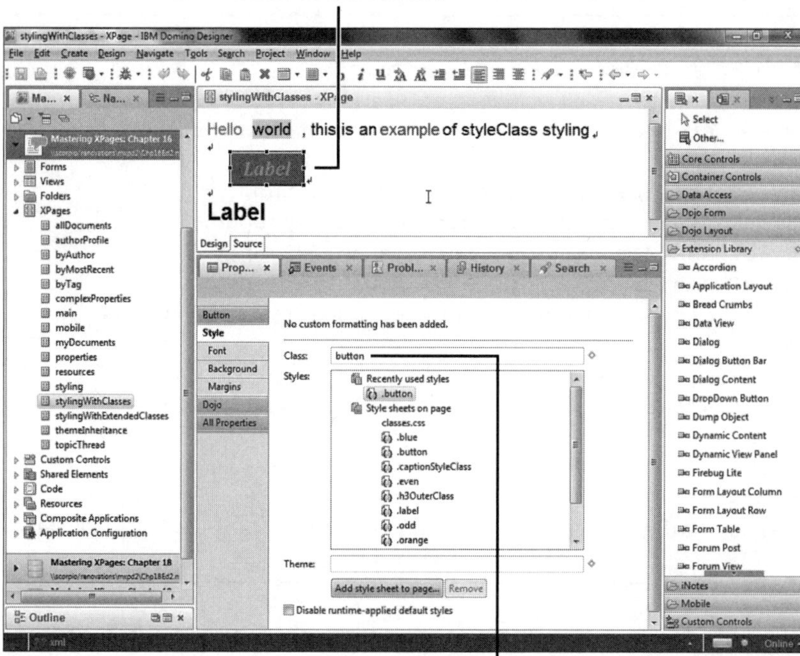

Figure 16.13 Style properties panel for the Button control

Listing 16.6 Emitted HTML Source Fragment Showing the Style class Attributes

```
<?xml version="1.0" encoding="UTF-8"?>
<!DOCTYPE HTML PUBLIC ...
<html lang="en">
<head>
    ...
    <link rel="stylesheet" type="text/css"
        href="/xsp/taurus!!Chp16Ed2.nsf/xsp/classes.css">
</head>
<body ...>
    ...
    <span class="sentence red">Hello</span>
    <span class="sentence shaded">world</span>
    <span class="sentence">, this is an</span>
    <span class="sentence blue">example</span>
    <span class="sentence">of  styleClass styling</span>
    <br>
```

```
    <br>
    <button class="button" type="button" name="view:_id1:button1"
        id="view:_id1:button1">Label</button>
    <br>
    <br>
    <span id="view:_id1:label1" class="label">Label</span>
    ...
</body>
</html>
```

When the browser or client receives this HTML markup, it needs to do a couple of things. First, if caching is enabled, check the local cache to see if the `classes.css` file is already stored there from a previous request. If not, it is downloaded at this point, cached for subsequent requests, and made available to the HTML document. Otherwise, a comparison of the last modification or expiry timestamps in the request headers against the cached version is calculated to ascertain if the cached version should be updated with a more recent version. After this process completes, the cached version, updated or not, is made available to the HTML document.

TIP

The default cache expiration date for resources emitted for an XPages request is 10 days from the time of the first request. You can, however, change this period of time using the Custom Browser Cache Expiration (days) settings for JavaScript, style sheet files, and image files—each independent of one another. You can find this group of settings on the Basics tab of the Application Properties panel. It is recommended that production-ready applications should have the cache expiration durations set far into the future (for example, 365 days) to reduce unnecessary workload on the server. Any resource changes you might make within this period will still be picked up by browsers as they perform a cache-to-remote resource last modified timestamp comparison.

Second, the browser or client must then resolve any `class` attributes on elements within the HTML document. These attribute references are resolved against the style classes within the currently loaded style sheet files.

Earlier, the point was made about gaining a performance benefit using the style class technique. This is evident here in the reduced amount of emitted HTML markup in Listing 16.6; therefore, radically reducing the number of bytes being transmitted over the network.

The final thing to say about this example hearkens back to the observation that the **styling** and **stylingWithClasses** XPages both look remarkably similar. This is intentional, of course, because it simply shows that you can achieve an identical presentation using style classes and a style sheet instead of inline styling and gain all the benefits of style classes at the same time!

Computing the styleClass Property

The `styleClass` property can also be computed in the same way as the `style` property. The examples in the **stylingWithClasses** XPage all used static `styleClass` values, but you can examine a worked example in the **Chp16Ed2.nsf** application by opening the **viewTopic** Custom Control. Select the **Source** panel for this Custom Control, and you can see an `<xp:button>` tag on line 442 that has a computed `styleClass` property. Listing 16.7 shows this as a fragment of XSP markup from that Custom Control.

Listing 16.7 Computed styleClass Property in the viewTopic Custom Control

```
...
<xp:button value="Reply" id="replyButton">
    <xp:this.styleClass><![CDATA[#{javascript:
        if(isMobile())
        {
            return "mblSmallFormFooterButton";
        }
        else
        {
            return "lotusFormButton"
        }
    }]]></xp:this.styleClass>
    ...
</xp:button>
...
```

Note that, for any XPages control that supports the `styleClass` property, you can specify a computed value expression by selecting the **All Properties** panel under the **Properties** view, and scrolling to the `styleClass` property in the same way you did for the `style` property. The `styleClass` property is the second of the four properties under the **styling** category you have now learned about. In the same manner, as you also did for the `style` property, you need to click the blue diamond icon in the value editor and select **Compute Value** from the pop-up menu to open the **Script Editor**. Alternatively, as shown in Figure 16.14, you can double-click the `{Computed}` link on the **Style** properties panel. Using the **Script Editor**, you can then specify the computed value expression to calculate the `styleClass` value.

Listing 16.7's example dynamically computes the `styleClass` name for the Reply Button. The end result is shown in Figure 16.15, where the presentation of both the web and mobile renderings is shown.

Listing 16.8 shows the dynamically computed CSS style class names in a fragment of the emitted HTML markup for the tag cloud in Figure 16.15.

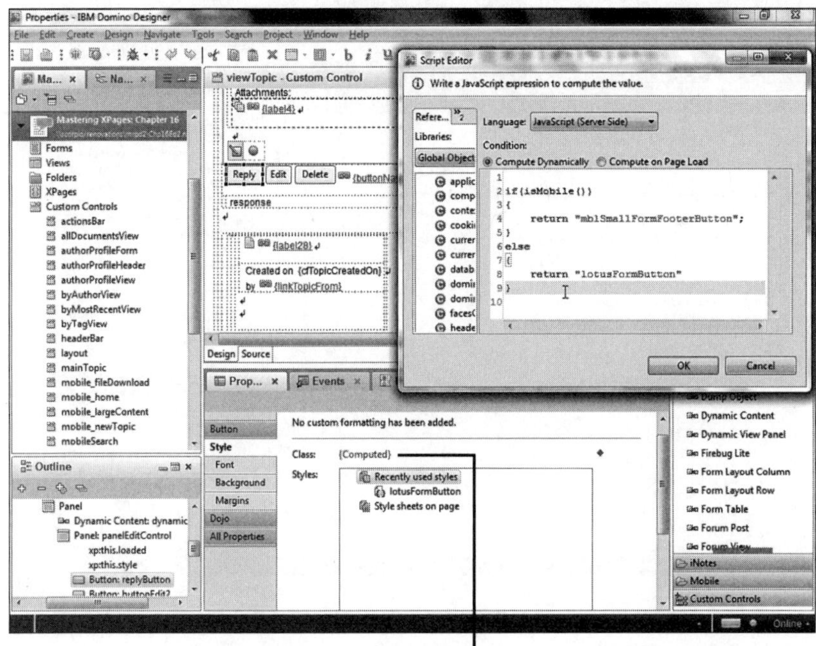

Figure 16.14 Reply Button's computed value expression for its styleClass property

Listing 16.8 Emitted HTML Fragment for the Reply Button Showing Dynamically Computed styleClass Names Dependent on Web and Mobile Conditions

```
...
<!- - mobile condition - - >
<div ...>
    <button class="mblSmallFormFooterButton" ...</button>
</div>
<!- - web condition - - >
<div ...>
    <button class="lotusFormButton" ...</button>
</div>

...
```

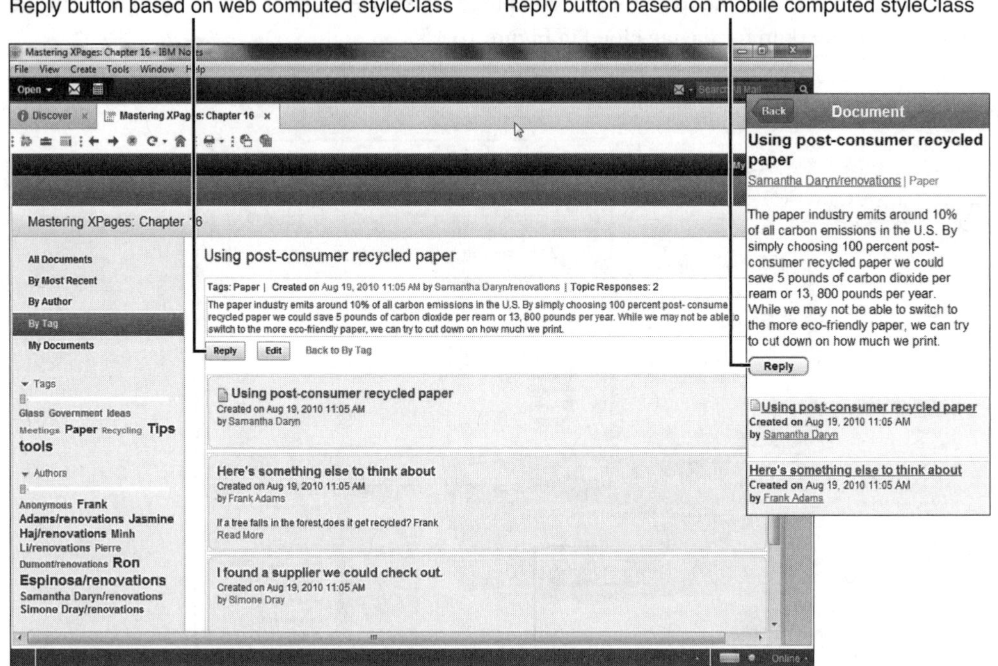

Figure 16.15 Reply button at runtime presented using a dynamically computed style class

Working with Extended styleClass and style Properties

So far, you learned how to use both the `style` and `styleClass` properties. You can, however, use a set of extended `styleClass` and `style` properties to enhance the presentation of your XPages. They are typically used to apply `styleClass` and `style` values to specific areas of a control composed of several parts—cases where a single `styleClass` or `style` property would not be enough to customize the appearance of that control. Therefore, different extended `style` and `styleClass` properties are supported by various controls.

From the **Chp16Ed2.nsf** application, open the **stylingWithExtendedClasses** XPage in Designer. This XPage contains a **Computed Field** control and a **View Panel** control, both of which expose different extended `styleClass` and `style` properties. These extended properties can be found by inspecting the properties within the **styling** category in the **All Properties** view for each of these two controls. Figure 16.16 shows the **styling** category for the Computed Field control.

You might notice the inclusion of a second `styleClass` property called `outer StyleClass`. This property can be used to specify an additional CSS class for the **Computed Field** that is applied to an enclosing HTML SPAN element. This element effectively wraps the generated HTML element that contains the value of the Computed Field, therefore creating a pair of nested tags. If the `outerStyleClass` is not specified, no enclosing element is generated.

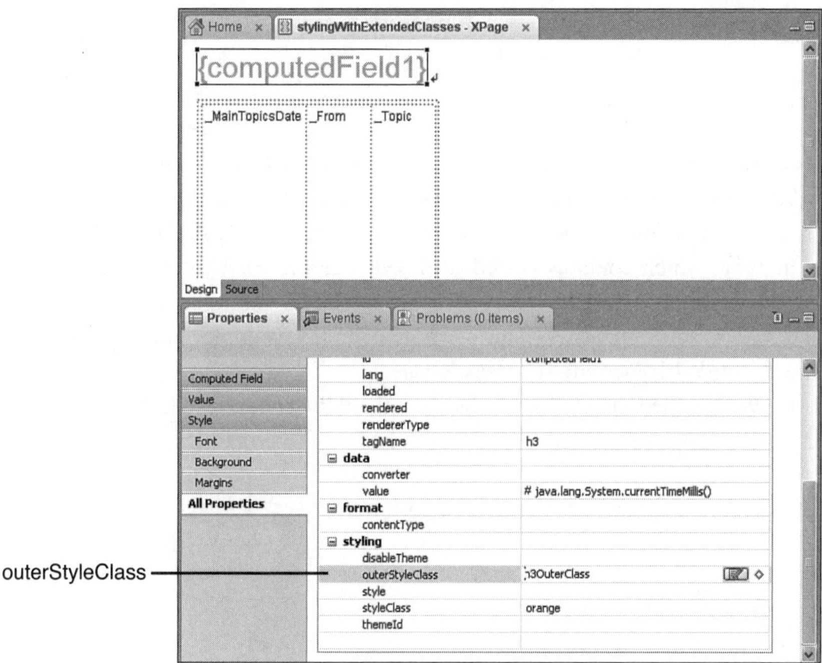

Figure 16.16 outerStyleClass property supported by the Computed Field control

Examine the XSP markup of the **Computed Field** control using the **Source** editor in Designer. Listing 16.9 shows a fragment of XSP markup for this.

Listing 16.9 XSP Markup for the Computed Field Control with the outerStyleClass Property Set

```
...
<xp:text escape="false" id="computedField1" tagName="h3"
    value="#{javascript:java.lang.System.currentTimeMillis()}"
    outerStyleClass="h3OuterClass" styleClass="orange">
</xp:text>
...
```

As you can see, both the `outerStyleClass` and `styleClass` properties are both set. The result of which can then be seen in Listing 16.10, where the emitted HTML markup contains a pair of nested tags representing the value of the **Computed Field** control.

Listing 16.10 HTML Markup for the Computed Field Represented as a Pair of Nested Tags

```
...
<span class="h3OuterClass">
<h3 id="view:_id1:computedField1" class="orange">1.284413698328E12</h3>
</span>
...
```

This simple example shows a convenient way to generate container elements that wrap some computed value without the need to create extra tags in the XSP markup to achieve the same thing. This is convenient for situations where you might be using CSS from a library or toolkit not of your making, which contains nested CSS style class rules. This is not an uncommon occurrence, and the `outerStyleClass` property saves you having to generate the nested structures to fulfill the CSS requirements. To study a more complex example, examine the **View Panel** control on the **stylingWithExtendedClasses** XPage.

In Figure 16.17, you can see the **styling** category in the **All Properties** view for the **View Panel** control. This shows several extended `styleClass` and `style` properties.

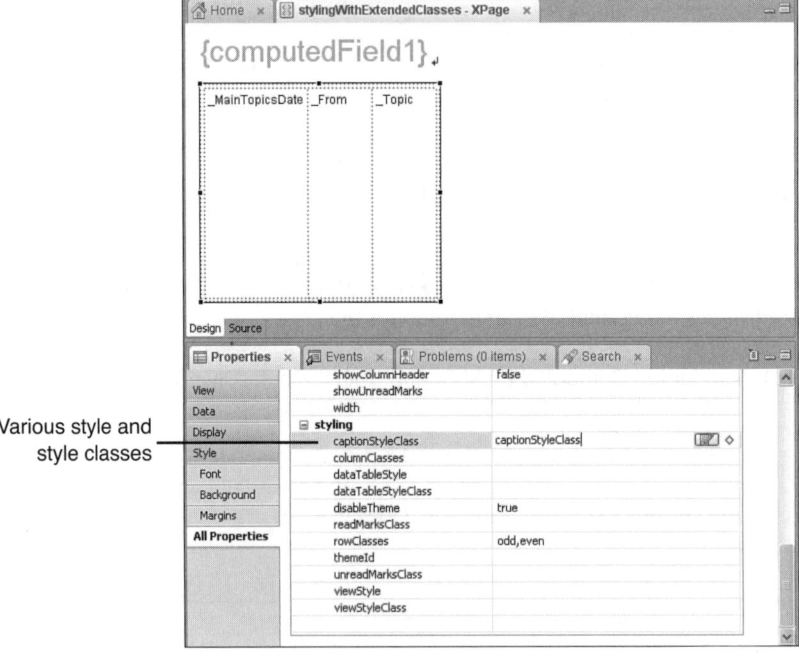

Figure 16.17 Various styleClass and style properties supported by the View Panel control

As you can see in Figure 16.17, only two of these are set. The first of these two is the `captionStyleClass`. This is used to apply a CSS class name to any caption declared on the **View Panel**. The second is the `rowClasses` property. This comma-separated list of CSS class names get applied sequentially to the rows within the View Panel. This can provide alternate styling of the rows, so providing a minimum of two different CSS class names achieve this. Table 16.1 lists all the `styleClass` and `style` properties supported by the View Panel control.

Table 16.1 styleClass and Style Properties Supported by the View Panel Control

Property	Description
`captionStyleClass`	A single CSS class or space-separated list of CSS classes applied to the View Panel caption.
`columnClasses`	A comma-separated list of CSS classes applied to View Panel columns sequentially in the order specified.
`rowClasses`	A comma-separated list of CSS classes applied to View Panel rows sequentially in the order specified.
`dataTableStyle`	CSS style rules applied to the data table within the View Panel
`dataTableStyleClass`	A single CSS class or space-separated list of CSS classes applied to the data table within the View Panel.
`readMarksClass`	A single CSS class or space-separated list of CSS classes applied to the first column within the View Panel indicating the read status of the view entry. If specified, this overrides the default `readMarksClass.`
`unreadMarksClass`	A single CSS class, or space-separated list of CSS classes applied to the first column within the View Panel indicating the unread -status of the view entry. If specified, this overrides the default `unreadMarksClass.`
`dataTableStyle`	CSS style rules applied to the data table within the View Panel structure.
`viewStyleClass`	A single CSS class or space-separated list of CSS classes applied to the overall View Panel structure.

Now, take a moment to preview the **stylingWithExtendedClasses** XPage to see both the `captionStyleClass` and `rowClasses` being applied to the View Panel. Figure 16.18 shows the XPage being previewed in the Notes client.

This concludes this section on styling an application using the `styleClass` property and **Style Sheet** resource. The next section examines a feature introduced by XPages in Notes/Domino 8.5 called the **Theme** design element.

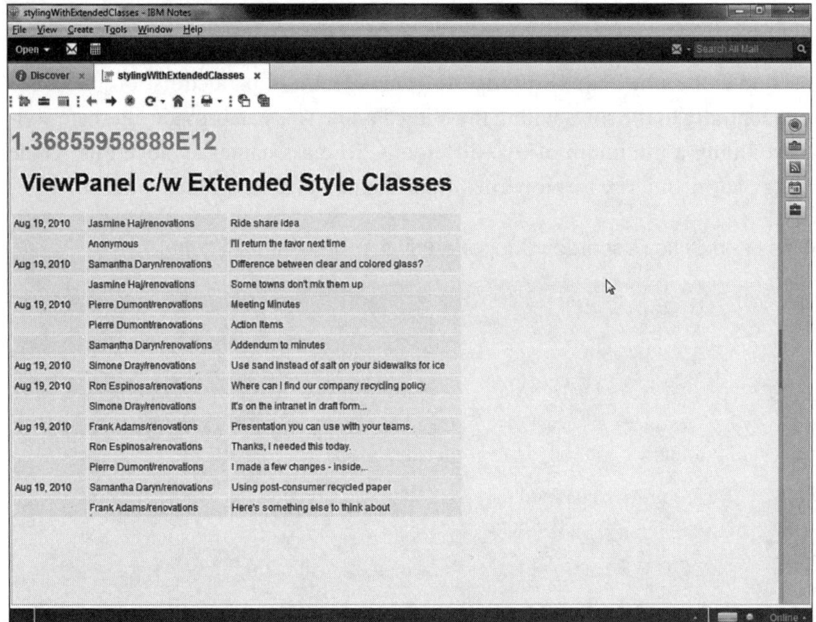

Figure 16.18 stylingWithExtendedClasses XPage being previewed in the Notes client

Theming on Steroids!

Along with the introduction of XPages in Notes/Domino 8.5 came a new design element called a *theme*. This design element is specific to XPages applications and can be used for numerous good reasons, as you learn in this section.

At this point, it is important to explain that you can style an XPages application solely using inline styling and/or style classes, as you have learned in the previous two sections of this chapter. A *theme* is simply another great feature provided by XPages to help you further abstract and separate the presentation logic of an application away from its underlying application logic. The result of which is much cleaner application code that can also lead to an improvement in the performance of an application. This also helps make the task of user interface development and maintenance a much easier one to undertake.

What Is a Theme?

To give a sound explanation of this feature, it is important to first define the concept of a *theme* so you understand the intent and scope of this when using a theme. First, the intent of a theme is to describe not only how an application appears visually, but also to describe any code or resources that affect the behavior of its visual appearance, otherwise known as presentation logic. Therefore, a theme should only be used to describe the look of an application and any logic or resources that contribute to the feel of an application. The scope of a theme is, therefore, bound to anything that is user interface related.

In the previous section, you already learned how CSS style classes and style sheets help you abstract inline CSS code out of an XPage and into manageable files. A theme can be used to achieve the same purpose with the `style` and `styleClass` properties, along with other control properties, and even style sheet and JavaScript resources declared within an XPage. This means that a lot of declarative XSP markup related to presentation logic can be removed from within all the XPages of an application and contained within a theme. You can then manage the look and feel of an entire XPages application, or any number of applications that are using that theme, from a single descriptive resource.

What Can You Do with a Theme?

Within any XPages application, you can create a theme or use any preexisting theme. This allows you to not only change the visual appearance of your application, but reduce or remove any presentation logic from within the XPages of that application. You can do this for example, by using any of the preconfigured OneUI themes in Notes/Domino 9 to make your XPages application look like an IBM Collaboration Solutions OneUI web application, as shown in the examples in Figure 16.19.

Alternatively, you can also extend any of the Notes/Domino 9 themes when creating your own themes as a way of establishing a baseline to work from. Either way, using the preexisting themes like this saves you a lot of development time when creating a user interface.

You can also create several themes that can be used by the same XPages application, or indeed any number of applications, as you learn later in this section, where each one describes totally different visual appearances and presentation behaviors. A good example of this is a use case where several different themes are used by an XPages application in a large multinational corporation. Depending on which geography a user logs in from, that user is presented with a totally different user interface for the same application.

A theme can also be used to set the values of custom properties on a Custom Control—therefore enabling different behaviors for Custom Controls, depending on which theme is currently being used by an application.

You can also use a theme to manage the look and feel in the context of specific browser, mobile device, or locale requests. This makes it easier to develop and maintain an application that serves multiple browser and mobile device types or bidirectional content.

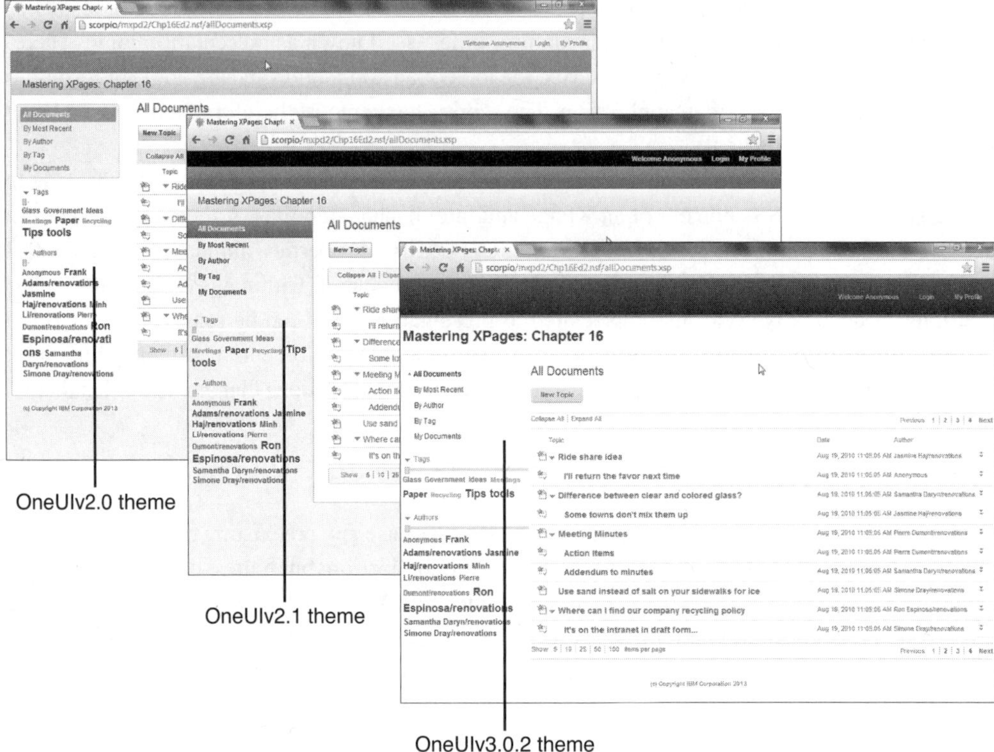

Figure 16.19 Examples of an XPages application using three different Notes/Domino 9 themes

Understanding Theme Architecture and Inheritance

A structural design, or architecture, is supported by the theme mechanism in XPages. The architecture is equally applicable to XPages applications running on either a Domino server or in a Notes client. As of Notes/Domino 8.5.2 and upward, the architecture supports eight different possible theme configurations. Note that a theme configuration is different from a theme in that the former is an architectural layout for a theme to run against—only eight different theme configurations are possible, whereas any number of themes can be created and run in this architecture. These exist to cater to the different use cases that can be encountered when developing themes for XPages applications that run on multiple platforms.

Out of the eight theme configurations, five are made possible by an inheritance mechanism. This means that the XPages runtime allows a theme to inherit from another one to provide extended presentation logic or even override existing presentation logic from an ancestor. As of Notes/Domino 8.5.2 and upward, single inheritance is supported, allowing up to five levels of inheritance to be achieved. Circular references to the same theme are not permitted.

The theme architecture has two levels:

- **Platform Level:** Represents the Domino server environment or equally the Notes client environment
- **Application Level:** Represents one or more applications running in the context of the Platform Level

Platform Level Default Theme Versus an Application Level Theme

As mentioned earlier, Notes/Domino 9 ships with a number of preconfigured themes. Of these, several reside in the Platform Level, with several more residing inside the *Discussion 9* and *TeamRoom 9 templates* that ship with Notes/Domino 9. Therefore, if you create an application based on either of these templates, or indeed replace the design of an existing application, your application will then contain several Application Level themes of its own. The interesting thing here is that all these Application Level themes directly inherit from several Platform Level themes!

Note that Notes/Domino 9 is preconfigured to use one of the Platform Level themes as a Platform Level default—out-of-the-box that default is the *webstandard* theme, but you can change this to one of the other preconfigured Platform Level themes or one of your own making in the case of having your own corporate theme. Having a Platform Level default is important for new XPages applications that get created because that is the default setting for new applications and ensures that even a new blank application gains some degree of presentation logic. Equally, it is also important for working XPages applications that depend on the Platform Level default theme. XPages applications can be configured to use their own themes, too. This means using a theme within the Application Level—just like the Discussion Template example. You learn how to specify and change the Platform Level default theme and an Application Level theme later in this section.

Theme Configuration #1

If you study Figure 16.20, you see that it depicts the most basic of the eight theme configurations supported by XPages.

This configuration enables an XPages application to directly use a Platform Level theme. For example, when you create a new XPages application and do not specify which theme to use, the application automatically uses the Platform Level default theme. Figure 16.20 shows this, where applications **W.NSF**, and **X.NSF**, both use the Platform Level default (which is set to theme **B** in the Platform Level). Applications **Y.NSF** and **Z.NSF**, on the other hand, specify that they use theme **C** in the Platform Level.

This configuration should be used when you do not want any presentation logic or resources to reside inside an .NSF application file. Everything the application needs for its presentation logic and resources should be available in the Platform Level.

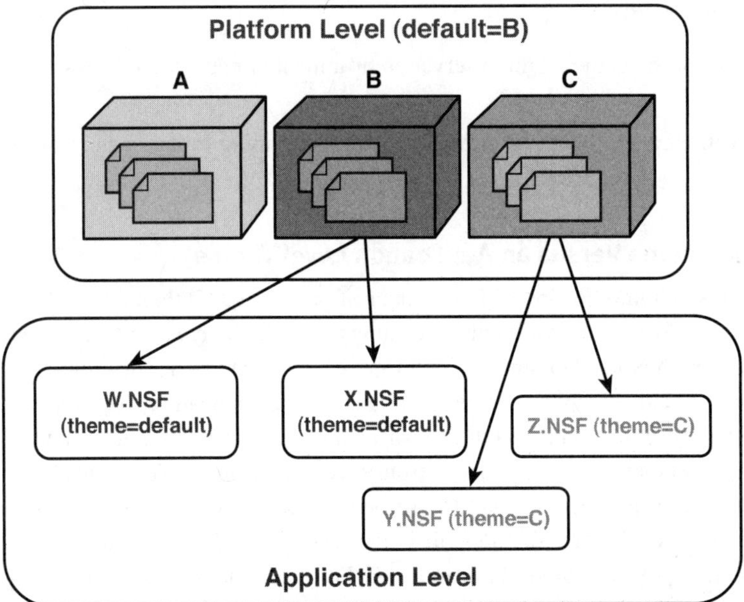

Figure 16.20 Theme configuration #1

Theme Configuration #2

Figure 16.21 details the most commonly used theme configuration for a typical XPages application. In this figure, application **W.NSF** no longer depends on the Platform Level default theme, but specifies that it uses its own Application Level theme.

You can see that application **W.NSF** inherits from a Platform Level theme. In this case, application **W.NSF** has its own Application Level theme called **B1** that inherits from Platform Level theme **B**.

The Discussion template actually uses this configuration for each of the themes residing inside that template. This configuration should be used when you want an application to benefit from using the preexisting Platform Level themes that ship with Notes/Domino 9, or one of your own Platform Level themes, but you also need to provide application-specific presentation logic and/or resources within that application.

Theme Configuration #3

Similar to Theme Configuration #2, Figure 16.22 shows how the same application goes one step further to provide a second Application Level theme within itself.

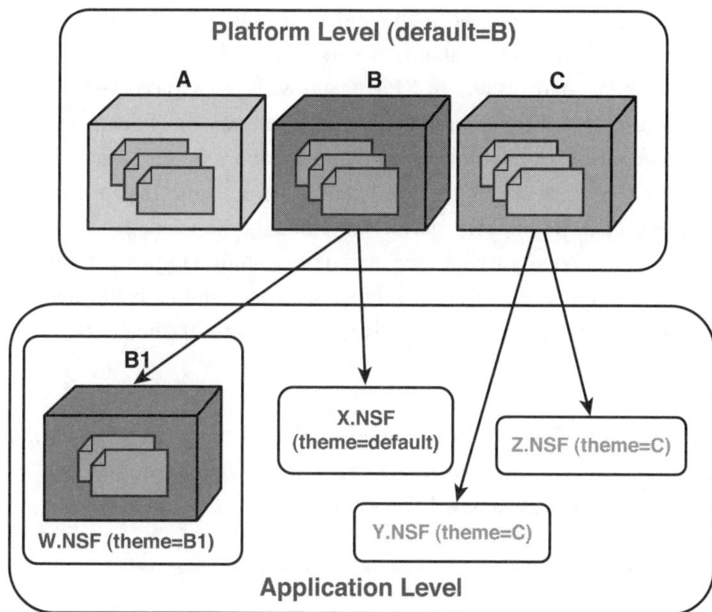

Figure 16.21 Theme configuration #2

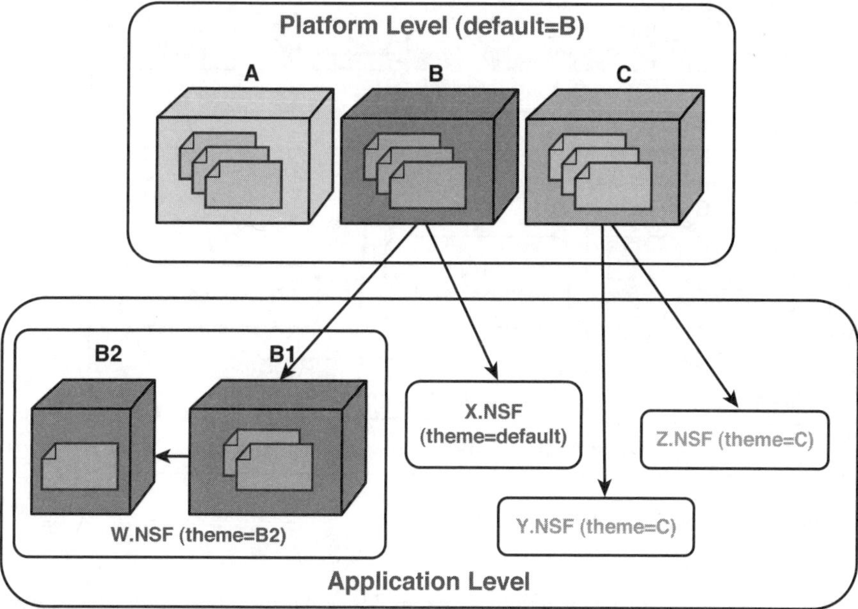

Figure 16.22 Theme configuration #3

The interesting aspect to this is that the second theme called **B2** inherits from theme **B1**. Therefore, enabling application **W.NSF** to provide another theme that builds upon the original one. As mentioned earlier, the theme mechanism within XPages allows up to a maximum of five levels of inheritance, and circular references to the same theme are not permitted. Therefore, this configuration allows a total of three more Application Level themes that are on the same inheritance path to Platform Level theme **B** to exist within this application. As a result, this application could potentially also contain themes **B3**, **B4**, and **B5**, all on the same inheritance path.

Use this configuration when you need to provide specialized presentation logic or resources to that already defined by any of the other Application Level themes (for example, handling logins from different geographies to provide different user interfaces to the same application).

Theme Configuration #4

In Figure 16.23, application **Z.NSF** specifies that it uses Platform Level theme **C**. Essentially, it uses the Theme Configuration #1. But, for this fourth architectural configuration, you can see that application **Z.NSF** has been changed to use a new Platform Level theme called **D**.

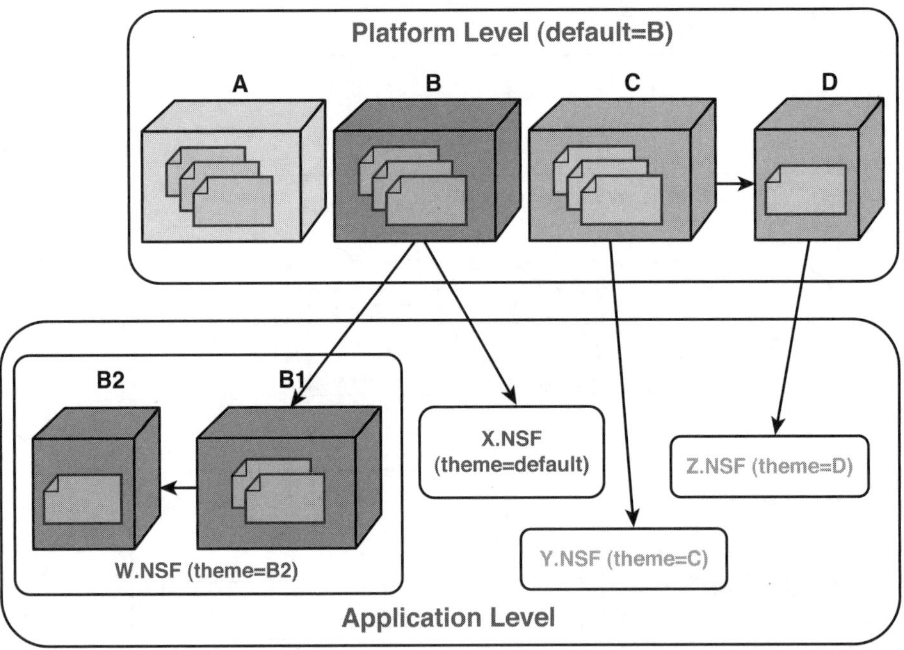

Figure 16.23 Theme configuration #4

You learned about theme inheritance and saw examples of it within the Application Level themes in the previous configuration, but this is an example of theme inheritance occurring in the Platform Level.

This configuration is actually used in Notes/Domino 9 within a number of the Platform Level themes. Basically, one of the Platform Level themes you get with Notes/Domino 9 is based on the IBM **OneUIv2.1** Stylekit. This is then extended by themes **OneUIv2.1_Gold**, **OneUIv2.1_Green**, **OneUIv2.1_Metal**, and **OneUIv2.1_Red**, and so on to provide the number of variants of the **OneUIv2.1** theme within the Platform Level.

Theme Configuration #5

Figure 16.24 shows application **Z.NSF** and Platform Level theme **D** being used again in a different configuration.

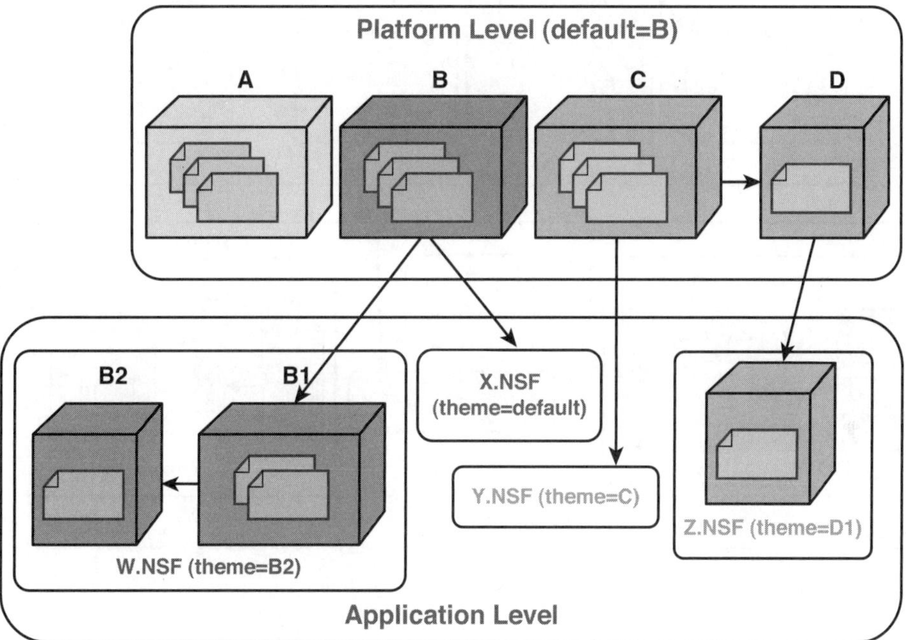

Figure 16.24 Theme configuration #5

In this configuration, application **Z.NSF** now has its own Application Level theme called **D1** that inherits from Platform Level theme **D**. This configuration demonstrates the flexibility of the different possible theme configurations.

Note that this configuration has been employed within the Discussion Template by a number of the Application Level themes within this template. These include the `oneuiv2.x` variants, `gold`, `green`, `metal`, and `red` themes, and so on that all inherit from Platform Level themes.

Theme Configuration #6

Figure 16.25 shows that this configuration is essentially a mix of configurations.

If you study the figure carefully around application **Z.NSF**, you can establish the fact this is an example of using all the configurations you've learned about so far. It demonstrates the use of Platform Level and Application Level theme inheritance, and is the most complex of all the possible configurations.

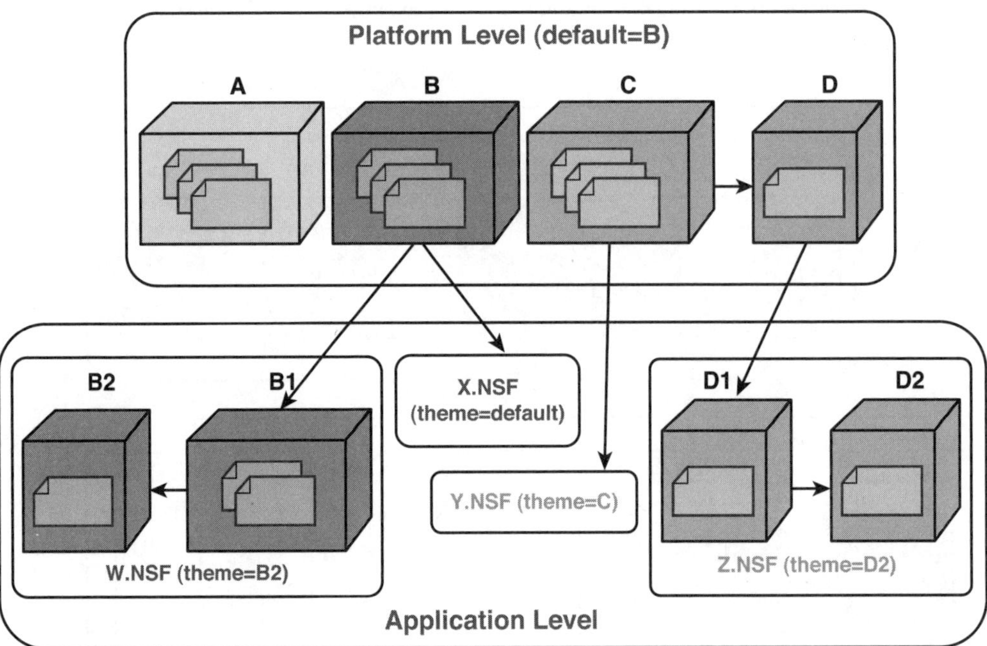

Figure 16.25 Theme configuration #6

Theme Configuration #7

Figure 16.26 shows the penultimate configuration supported by the theme mechanism in XPages. Examine the change to application **X.NSF** and how it no longer depends on the Platform Level for any presentation logic; it now specifies its own theme that is completely independent of the Platform Level.

To apply this configuration correctly requires detailed knowledge of the underlying Platform Level themes. If incorrectly configured, you will undoubtedly break your application. This can be caused by unresolved CSS or JavaScript resources, or even missing Dojo CSS style class information used by the core XPages controls. When an application uses any of the other configurations, a dependency on the Platform Level exists either directly or by inheritance. Presuming you are using or inheriting from a valid Platform Level theme, your application is then receiving all the necessary core XPages controls presentation logic and resources to function correctly.

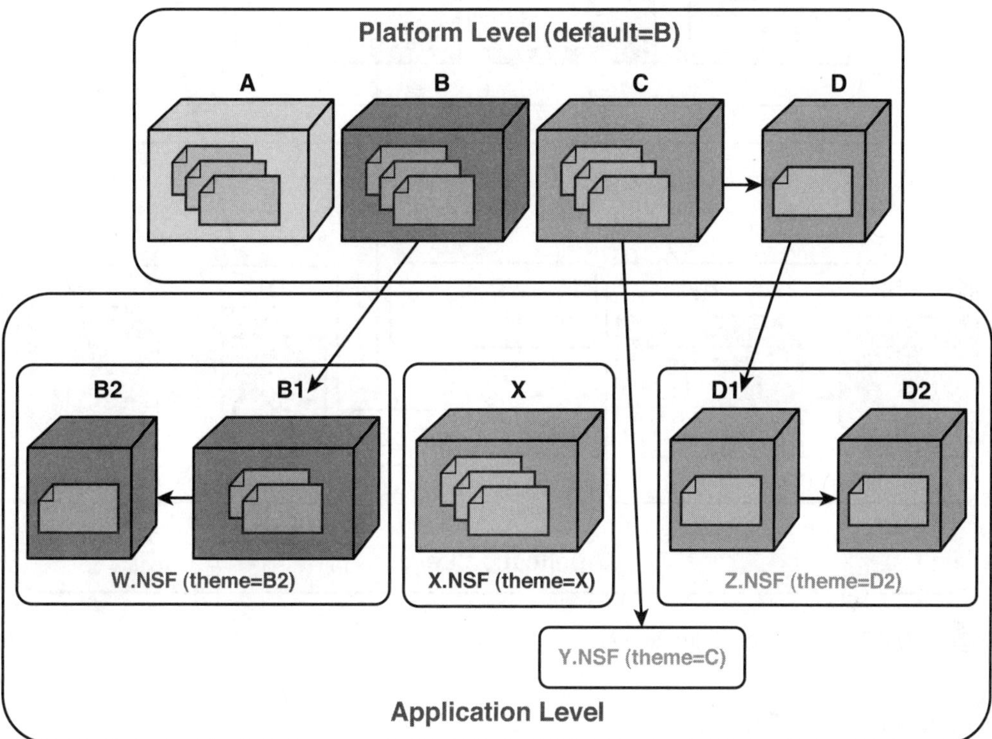

Figure 16.26 Theme configuration #7

Theme Configuration #8

Figure 16.27 shows the final possible configuration supported by the **theme** mechanism in XPages. Examine the change to application **X.NSF** in that it now specifies the `<empty>` theme.

The `<empty>` theme is a virtual theme that does not provide any presentation logic or resources to an application. It is important to note that emitted XPages coming from an application using this pseudo-theme lack any stylistic or structural presentation logic normally included by either direct or inherited use of a Platform Level theme. Therefore, this particular configuration should only be used when an application provides all of its own presentation logic for not only its own content, but also for the core XPages controls and Dojo.

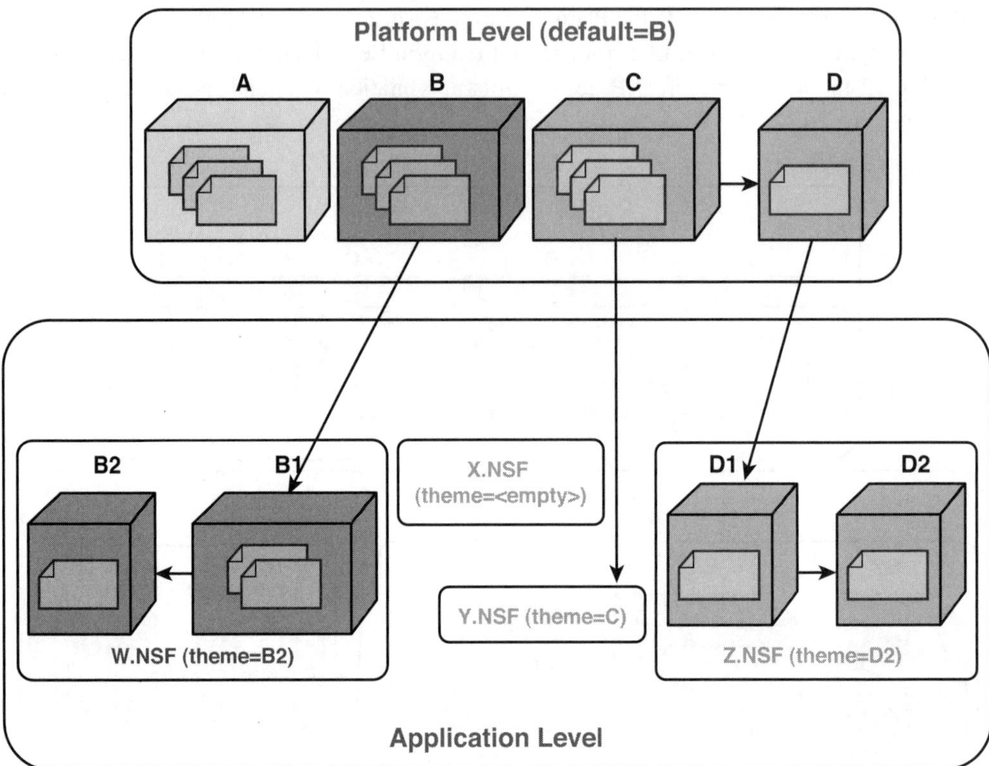

Figure 16.27 Theme configuration #8

Working with a Theme

At this point, you learned about the purpose of a theme and the different configurations supported by the theme architecture. Understanding these aspects is important for creating good themes. This means you are now ready to start working with a theme.

Creating a Theme

First, a theme design element can be created within an application, or as you learned about in the theme configurations, can reside within the Notes client or Domino server installation itself. To fully understand this, reopen the **Chp16Ed2.nsf** application in Designer (if it is closed). Once open, in the **Navigator**, expand the **Resources > Themes** design element. You see many themes already contained within this design element. Now, double-click the **Themes** design element to open the **Themes** viewer, as shown in Figure 16.28.

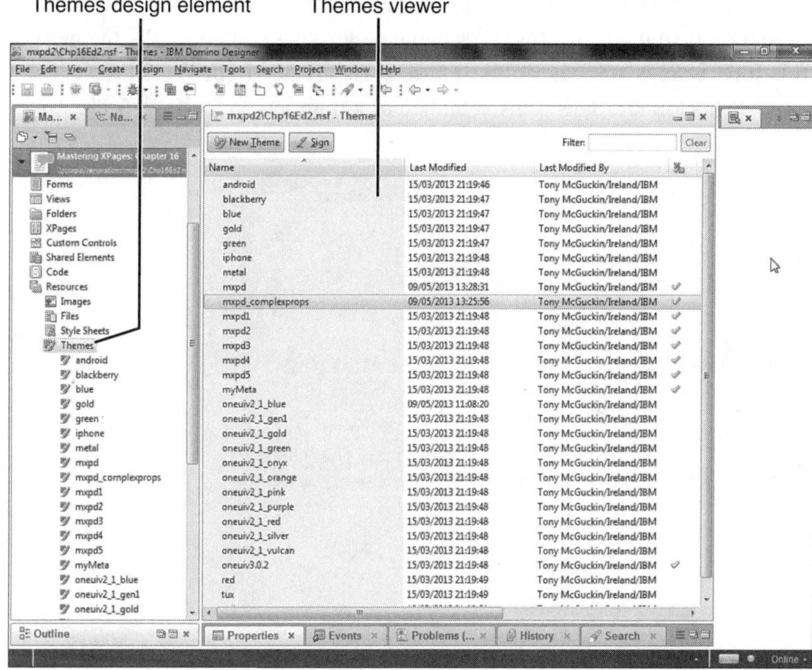

Figure 16.28 Resources > Themes and Themes viewer in Designer

There are four ways to create a new theme:

- Click the **New Theme** button at the top of the **Themes** viewer.
- Right-click the **Themes** design element in the **Navigator** and select the **New Theme** option from the right-click context menu.
- Select **Create > New > Theme** from the main Designer menu.
- Select **File > New > Theme** from the main Designer menu.

Whichever way you choose opens the **New Theme** dialog, as shown in Figure 16.29.

Having named your new theme with a name of your own choosing (*helloWorld*, for example) you should click the **OK** button. The *helloWorld* **theme** is now created and appears within the **Themes** viewer and **Themes** design element in the **Navigator**. It also automatically opens in the **Themes** editor, as shown in Figure 16.30 in **Source** mode. This is either Design or Source mode, depending on the format you selected during your last viewing of a theme file.

Similar to the XPages WYSIWYG editor, the Themes editor has a Design and a Source editor. The main difference between the two is the fact that a theme file does not have any visual presentation like the XPages WYSIWYG editor, so its Design editor simply displays the contents of the theme file in a hierarchical manner. This reflects the underlying content of the theme file, which as mentioned before, is an XML-based file. In the newly created **helloWorld** theme file, you see a preconfigured `<theme>` tag. This is also detailed as a fragment in Listing 16.11.

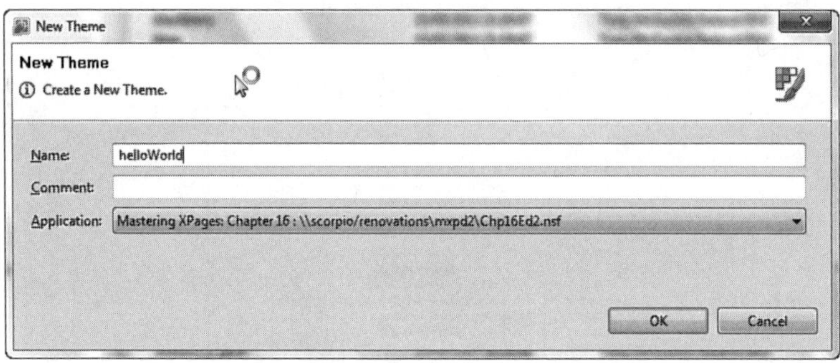

Figure 16.29 New Theme dialog

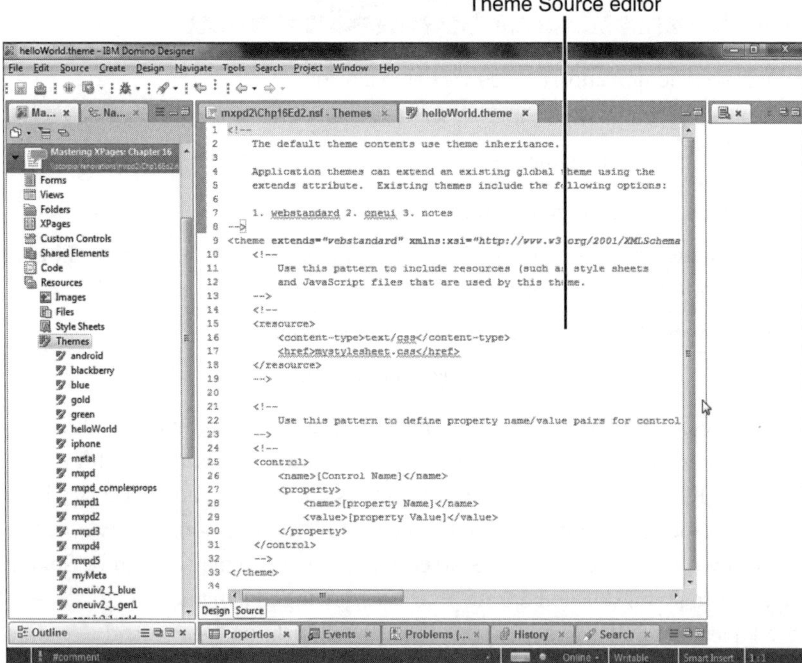

Figure 16.30 Newly created helloWorld theme file in Source mode

Listing 16.11 Fragment of the helloWorld Theme Detailing the Preconfigured <theme> Tag

```
...
<!--
      Application themes can extend an existing global theme using the
      extends attribute.  Existing themes include the following
      options:

      1. webstandard 2. oneui 3. notes
-->
<theme extends="webstandard">
...
```

This `<theme>` tag indicates that this new **theme** actually inherits from the *webstandard* theme. As shown in the comment in Listing 16.11, two other options can also be used, all of which are Platform Level themes residing in the Notes client and Domino server installations. Because of this preconfigured setting, when you create a new **theme**, by default, all newly created themes inherit a degree of presentation logic and resources from the *webstandard* theme. You can also see numerous other comments populated into a newly created **theme** file. These simply assist you with the task of creating the content for the theme. At this point, don't worry about these comments; you learn all about their meaning later.

You can close the theme you just created (save your changes). You now learn how to set or change a theme for your XPages applications.

Setting a Theme

You can configure an application to use a specific theme in many ways using the **Application Properties** editor or in a slightly more indirect manner using XSP properties. If you open the **Application Properties** editor for the **Chp16Ed2.nsf** application, you see several tabs across the bottom of this editor. One of these tabs is **XPages**. If you select this particular tab, you are presented with various XPages specific settings, as shown in Figure 16.31.

As you can see in Figure 16.31, there is a **Theme Defaults** group of settings. The interesting thing about this group is that it allows you to set the application theme in three different ways. This accommodates the possibility of an application running in different platforms, namely a Notes client or Domino server, and requires different themes for each. You can also use this group of settings to specify a single theme for use in all platforms—this being the most common case. This is done by not specifying any **Override on Web** or **Override on Notes** settings, therefore allowing the **theme** specified for the **Application Theme** setting to be the one that is used regardless of the running environment. Also, note that setting either of the two override settings makes the Application Theme setting redundant on that platform.

You should now examine the themes listed within the **Application Theme** drop-down combo box. Note the presence of the **helloWorld** theme you just created among several other themes within the **Chp16Ed2.nsf** application. Now, select `mxpd` from this list to set the **Application Theme**. Also, select `oneuiv2.1_red` for the **Override on Web** setting and `oneuiv2.1_vulcan` for the **Override on Notes** setting. Save your changes, and then preview the **allDocuments** XPage in both the web browser and Notes client.

Theme Defaults group of settings

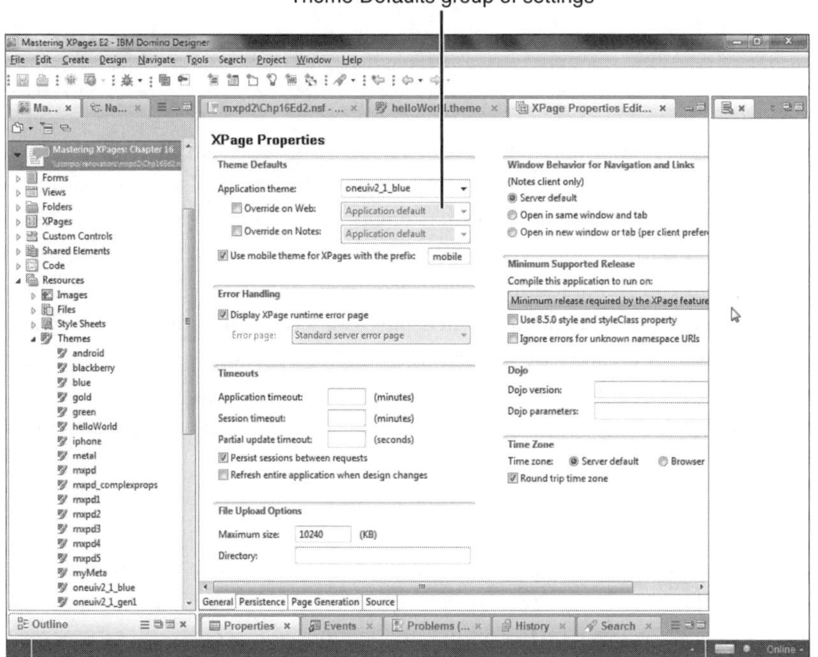

Figure 16.31 XPages Properties editor

When launched in preview mode, you can see subtle differences in the color scheme applied in the two different platforms. This is, of course, a consequence of the theme override settings being applied to the application in the context of the running environment. After previewing in the two different platforms, close the browser and Notes client and return to Designer, where you should now open the `xsp.properties` editor within the **Chp16Ed2.nsf** application. Alternatively, use the **Package Explorer** view to navigate to this file at `Chp16Ed2.nsf/WebContent/WEB-INF/xsp.properties`.

> **TIP**
>
> As an alternative means of opening a resource within an application, the key combination of *Ctrl* + *Shift* + *R* brings up the Open Resource dialog. This allows you to do a simple type-ahead search for any resource within the currently opened applications in the Designer workspace.

You see that the following XSP properties in Listing 16.12 have been written into the `xsp.properties` file for the **Chp16Ed2.nsf** application based on the settings you selected in the **Application Properties** editor.

Listing 16.12 XSP Properties for Theme Settings Within the xsp.properties File

```
...
xsp.theme=mxpd.theme
xsp.theme.web=oneuiv2.1_red.theme
xsp.theme.notes=oneuiv2.1_vulcan.theme
...
```

Had you not selected the **Override on Web** and **Override on Notes** settings, with only the **Application Theme** configured to `mxpd`, only the `xsp.theme` property would have been written into the `xsp.properties` file.

Also, note that when no **Application Theme** setting is configured, the value of *Server Default* appears within the drop-down combo box for this setting in Designer. (This relates to the Platform Level default you learned about earlier in the architecture section.) When **Server Default** is selected, no XSP properties are written into the `xsp.properties` file. Instead, the XPages runtime uses the Platform Level default as specified by the `xsp.theme` property defined within the XPages runtime or, alternatively, if declared in a special global `xsp.properties` file if it exists. This file does not exist unless you explicitly create it. Out of the box, Notes/Domino 9 is configured to use the *webstandard* theme as the Platform Level default. This default setting is held in-memory by the XPages runtime, but can be changed using the special global `xsp.properties` file. When created, this file must reside within the `<Notes/Domino>/data/properties` directory. A new installation of Notes/Domino does not have this file, but instead has an `xsp.properties.sample` file within this directory as a reference resource should you need to create your own. If you do, you can simply make a copy of this file, renaming it to `xsp.properties`. If you open this file in a text editor, you see a range of XSP properties that can be used to change all sorts of settings. One group of properties relates to global **Theme** settings, as shown in Listing 16.13.

Listing 16.13 Fragment of xsp.properties.sample File Showing Theme-Related Properties

```
...
# ##########################################
# THEME
# ##########################################

# Name of the XSP theme to use
#xsp.theme=webstandard

# Name of the XSP theme to use when running on the web
# If this property is not defined, the xsp.theme is used
#xsp.theme.web=

# Name of the XSP theme to use when running on the notes client
# If this property is not defined, the xsp.theme is used
#xsp.theme.notes=
```

As the comments suggest, if either `xsp.theme.web` or `xsp.theme.notes` are not defined, `xsp.theme` is used. (Note that comments are denoted by the # character by removing this character from a property enables that property.) You can, therefore, configure the default theme for a Notes client or Domino server using these settings; these are the Platform settings, and affect all new or existing applications that do not specify their own theme. However, applications can then override these settings using their own `xsp.properties` settings—these are the Application Level settings.

More on the <empty> Theme

As you learned earlier, the `<empty>` theme is a special pseudo theme. It does not provide any associated theme or resources on disk for an application. This, in effect, means that no Platform or Application Level theme resources are applied to an application using this virtual theme. A minimum set of client-side JavaScript resources are, however, included by the XPages runtime within the emitted HTML markup. These resources are required by the core XPages controls to ensure client-side JavaScript event handlers still function correctly—it is just a case of the visual appearance being diminished.

Now, preview the **allDocuments** XPage within the **Chp16Ed2.nsf** application. As you learned earlier, this application is using the `oneuiv2_1_blue` theme. Listing 16.14 shows a fragment of emitted HTML markup for the **allDocuments** XPage when using that theme. This theme inherits several OneUIv2.1 and XSP CSS style sheet resources from a Platform Level theme. It also declares two CSS style sheets of its own, called `blue.css` and `oneuiv2_1.css`. Hence, the markup you see in this example contains several different CSS style sheets, and most of the HTML tags have CSS class attributes.

Listing 16.14 Emitted HTML Markup for the allDocuments XPage Using the oneuiv2_1_blue Theme

```
...
<head>
    <title></title>
    <script type="text/javascript"
        src="/domjs/dojo-1.8.3/dojo/dojo.js"
        djConfig="locale: 'en-gb'">
    </script>
    <script type="text/javascript"
        src="/domjs/dojo-1.8.3/ibm/xsp/widget/layout/xspClientDojo.js">
    </script>
    <link rel="stylesheet" type="text/css"
        href="/oneuiv2.1/base/core.css">
    <link rel="stylesheet" type="text/css"
        href="/oneuiv2.1/blueTheme/blueTheme.css">
    <link rel="stylesheet" type="text/css"
        href="/domjava/xsp/theme/oneuiv2.1/xsp.css">
    <link rel="stylesheet" type="text/css"
        href="/domjava/xsp/theme/oneuiv2.1/xspLTR.css">
    <link rel="stylesheet" type="text/css"
        href="/domjava/xsp/theme/oneuiv2.1/xspFF.css">
    <link rel="stylesheet" type="text/css"
        href="/Chp16Ed2.nsf/blue.css">
    <link rel="stylesheet" type="text/css"
        href="/Chp16Ed2.nsf/oneuiv2_1.css">
</head>
<body class="xsp lotusui lotusSpritesOn tundra">
    <form id="view:_id1" class="lotusForm" ...>
...
```

Listing 16.15, on the other hand, lists a fragment of emitted HTML markup for the same **allDocuments** XPage when the **Chp16Ed2.nsf** application has its **Application Properties** theme set to the `<empty>` theme. If you now compare Listing 16.14 with that of Listing 16.15, notice two key differences:

- Several CSS style sheet resources are no longer included in the markup.
- Most of the HTML tags have no CSS class attributes set.

Listing 16.15 Emitted HTML Markup Fragment for the allDocuments XPage Using the <empty> Theme

```
...
<head>
    <title></title>
    <script type="text/javascript"
        src="/domjs/dojo-1.8.3/dojo/dojo.js"
        djConfig="locale: 'en-gb'">
    </script>
    <script type="text/javascript"
        src="/domjs/dojo-1.8.3/ibm/xsp/widget/layout/xspClientDojo.js">
    </script>
</head>
<body>
    <form id="view:_id1" ...>
...
```

Obviously, the emitted HTML markup and number of supporting resources is reduced in Listing 16.15 by using the `<empty>` theme, but the visual appearance of the emitted **allDocuments** XPage has now been totally diminished, as shown in Figure 16.32.

This virtual theme should, therefore, only be used for situations that require an application to provide all of its own presentation logic and supporting resources. This should also include presentation logic and resources for the core XPages controls.

More on the Five Levels of Theme Inheritance

As previously mentioned, the XPages runtime supports up to five levels of inheritance. This is a built-in safety measure within the XPages runtime to eliminate the possibility of infinite looping occurring because of a circular reference in a **theme**. It is also an optimal maximum number of inheritance levels for the XPages runtime to process and still provide excellent page loading performance.

To experience an example of the **theme** inheritance levels limit being exceeded, open the **XSP Properties** editor for the **Chp16Ed2.nsf** application in Designer. On the General tab, expand the **Application Theme** combo box. This contains a number of themes, including `mxpd`, `mxpd1`, `mxpd2`, `mxpd3`, `mxpd4`, and `mxpd5`. These all share the same inheritance path, with `mxpd` being the base ancestor. Change the current **theme** from its current value to `mxpd` and save this change before previewing the **themeInheritance** XPage. You then see the following information being displayed in the emitted XPage:

```
Theme: mxpd -> Level: 1
```

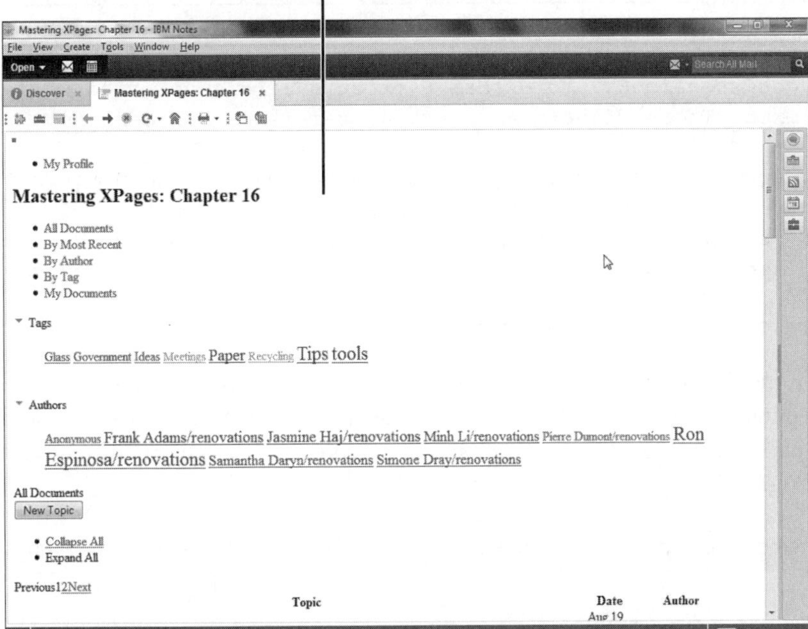

Figure 16.32 allDocuments XPage with diminished visual appearance due to using the <empty> theme

Now, repeat these steps by changing the theme to `mxpd1`, `mxpd2`, `mxpd3`, `mxpd4` and previewing the **themeInheritance** XPage between each change. Each time you preview, the information displayed changes, as follows:

```
Theme: mxpd1 -> Level: 2
Theme: mxpd2 -> Level: 3
Theme: mxpd3 -> Level: 4
Theme: mxpd4 -> Level: 5
```

As you can see, the information changes with each theme change. If you now reset the theme for a final time to `mxpd5`, preview again, you see something different this time. An exception occurs as the `mxpd5` theme has exceeded the maximum number of inheritance levels. If you select **Help > Support > View Trace**, you see an exception logged that's similar to Listing 16.16.

Listing 16.16 Exception Logged When Maximum Number of Inheritance Levels Is Exceeded

```
...
CLFAD0151E: Error while loading theme mxpd5
com.ibm.xsp.FacesExceptionEx: More than 5 extends levels detected while
loading theme mxpd. There might be a circular reference between the
themes
at com.ibm.xsp.application.ApplicationExImpl._loadTheme(Unknown Source)
at com.ibm.xsp.stylekit.StyleKitImpl.loadParent(Unknown Source)
at com.ibm.xsp.stylekit.StyleKitImpl._parseTheme(Unknown Source)
at com.ibm.xsp.application.ApplicationExImpl._loadTheme(Unknown Source)
...
```

Consequently, the XPage is not rendered because of this exception. To fully understand the reason for this exception, examine the contents of each of the `mxpd*` theme files by opening them in Designer. For your convenience, Listing 16.17 shows the root `<theme>` element from each one of these theme files.

Listing 16.17 <theme> Element from the mxpd* Theme Files Describing the Inheritance Path

```
mxpd  == <theme>
mxpd1 == <theme extends="mxpd">
mxpd2 == <theme extends="mxpd1">
mxpd3 == <theme extends="mxpd2">
mxpd4 == <theme extends="mxpd3">
mxpd5 == <theme extends="mxpd4">
```

Essentially, theme inheritance is established by using the `extends` attribute on the `<theme>` tag. The value for this is the name of the theme being extended, or inherited from. In this particular example, you can see that `mxpd` is the base level theme, with `mxpd1`, `mxpd2`, `mxpd3`, `mxpd4`, and finally `mxpd5` inheriting from it in that order to establish an inheritance path among these themes. As a result, `mxpd5` is the sixth theme to exist within the inheritance path of these themes and, therefore, exceeds the maximum number of inheritance levels that can be loaded.

Theme Resources

One of the primary tasks of a theme is to manage application resources. In a typical working web application, the resources required by each web page are declared in the source markup for each web page. This means that a degree of redundancy exists within the application code as some if not all declared resources are commonly used across all the web pages. A theme can, therefore, negate this redundancy by acting as a descriptor for commonly used resources across an application. Furthermore, a Platform Level theme can act as a descriptor for resources used across all applications running on that platform.

Sure enough, there are cases where a specific resource is perhaps infrequently used or should not be emitted with every XPage within an application. This is not a problem, because that resource can simply be enlisted in the Resources for that particular XPage itself, not within the list of theme resources.

In addition to managing collective lists of resources, a theme also supports a mechanism for detecting the type of requesting browser (aka User Agent), platform, locale, and bidirectional requests. This enables you to easily provide targeted resources for specific locales, browsers, and devices all from one well-defined, manageable place.

So, as you can now begin to understand, a theme is essentially providing a way for you to decouple presentation logic resources away from application logic within the XPages. This is analogous to a JavaScript library or a CSS file; instead of having inline JavaScript snippets or inline CSS rules within an XPage, you store these in manageable, separated files. The upshot here is a cleaner separation of source code and an easier to maintain application.

Many different resource types are supported by a theme, as shown in Table 16.2. Note that this list of resource types is exactly the same as that supported directly on an XPage when you use the Resources panel in Designer.

Table 16.2 Resource Types Supported by a Theme

Type	Description
`Cascading Style Sheet`	A CSS resource used for styling on the client side
`JavaScript`	A JavaScript code file executed on the client side
`Dojo Module`	A Dojo module identified by its full dijit package and used on the client side
`Link`	Any arbitrary file resource used on the client side
`META Data`	Provides a way to specify any meta tag information for use on the client side
`Server-side JavaScript`	A server-side JavaScript file executed within the XPages runtime
`Property Bundle`	A property bundle file referenced within the server side

The range of different resources supported by a theme cover the most commonly used resources you need.

Now, ensure that the `mxpd` theme is set in the **Application Properties** editor for the **Chp16Ed2.nsf** application. Also, open the `mxpd` theme for this application in Designer by double-clicking it under the Themes design element. Once opened, select the Source editor and scroll to the first of the `<resource>` elements within this theme file, as shown in Listing 16.18.

Listing 16.18 <resource> Elements Within the mxpd Theme

```
...
<resource target="xsp">
    <content-type>text/css</content-type>
    <href>screen.css</href>
    <media>screen,handheld,tv</media>
</resource>
<resource target="xsp">
    <content-type>text/css</content-type>
    <href>print.css</href>
    <media>print</media>
</resource>
<resource target="xsp">
    <content-type>application/x-javascript</content-type>
    <href>mxpd.js</href>
</resource>
```

These `<resource>` elements define three different resources that get emitted to the client-side. The first two are CSS resources. The last one is a client-side JavaScript resource. As you can see in Listing 16.18, each of the `<resource>` elements contains child elements. These are detailed in Table 16.3.

Table 16.3 Child Elements Supported by the <resource> Element

<resource> Child Element	Description
`<content-type>`	Can be either text/css or application/x-javascript.
`<href>`	Specifies either an absolute or relative path to the resource.
`<media>`	Only applicable to CSS type resources. Specifies the device context for the CSS. For a full list of supported CSS media types, see www.w3.org/TR/CSS2/media.html. Common media types are: screen, print, handheld, TV, and speech.

You also probably noticed the presence of the `target` attribute on the `<resource>` tag. It marks certain resources and other types of elements within a theme file for use by different target environments. As of Notes/Domino 8.5.2 and later, this attribute is only used by the XPages runtime, hence the declaration of `target="xsp"`. Perhaps in the future, this attribute might be used by other environments that are also built to leverage a theme, therefore allowing targeted use of elements within a theme file for any given environment (imagine `target="notes.mobile"` or `target="domino.classic"` for theme elements). Note, however, that this attribute is completely optional, so it can be left out of any theme file you create. The **Chp16Ed2.nsf** `mxpd` theme is simply making explicit use of it for your benefit.

A final point to make about the `<resource>` element is that it is used solely to declare client-side CSS and JavaScript resources. No other type of resource, client-side or server-side, can be declared using the `<resource>` element. To do that, you need to use a different sort of theme element, namely the `<resources>` element that you learn about next.

If you now scroll through the `mxpd` theme file, you find a `<resources>` element, as shown in Listing 16.19.

Listing 16.19 <resources> Element Within the mxpd Theme

```
...
<resources>
    <bundle target="xsp" src="foo.properties"
        var="foo" loaded="true" rendered="true">
    </bundle>
    <dojoModule target="xsp" condition="dojo.isFF"
        name="dijit.form.Form">
    </dojoModule>
    <script target="xsp" src="/xpServerSide.jss"
        clientSide="false" type="text/javascript">
    </script>
    <script target="xsp" src="/xpClientSide.js"
        clientSide="true" type="text/javascript">
    </script>
    <styleSheet target="xsp"
        contents=".foo{font-family:arial;}" media="screen">
    </styleSheet>
    <linkResource target="xsp" charset="UTF-8"
        dir="ltr" media="screen" type="image/png" href="foo.gif">
    </linkResource>
    <metaData target="xsp" name="viewport"
        content="initial-scale=1.0;maximum-scale=1.0">
    </metaData>
    <metaData target="xsp" httpEquiv="Content-Type"
        content="text/xsp">
    </metaData>
    <metaData target="xsp" name="date"
        content="2010-10-10" scheme="YYYY-MM-DD">
    </metaData>
</resources>
...
```

This element is a container for several different types of resource. Unlike the `<resource>` element, both client-side and server-side resources can be specified. The `<resources>` element is more powerful than its `<resource>` ancestor, and should be used in preference to it. Table 16.4 outlines a full list of resource types supported by the `<resources>` element.

Table 16.4 Resource Types Supported by the <resources> Element

Resource Type	Description	Execution Context
`<bundle>`	Properties file	Server side
`<dojoModule>`	Dojo module	Client side
`<script>`	JavaScript file	Client side and server side
`<styleSheet>`	CSS file	Client side
`<linkResource>`	Arbitrary file	Client side
`<metadata>`	Meta tag	Client side

As you can see from this list, a wide range of resource types are available using the `<resources>` element. This gives you lots of flexibility to create rich themes that describe not only client-side, but also server-side presentation logic.

The following set of tables detail the properties available on each of the resource types supported by the `<resources>` element.

<bundle> Resource

The `<bundle>` resource element declares a properties bundle resource within a theme file. This resource contains name/value properties that are accessed using server-side JavaScript. The most common use case is for retrieving localized property bundle strings for user-interface presentation as you learn in Chapter 18, "Internationalization." Table 16.5 lists the properties supported by this element.

Table 16.5 Properties Supported by the <bundle> Element

Property	Description
`target`	For targeting different environments. "xsp" is the default environment.
`loaded`	Controls loading of this resource into the server-side XPage component tree.
`rendered`	Controls rendering of this resource to the client-side handler (Notes or browser).
`src`	The absolute or relative path to the bundle resource file (required).
`var`	The name used to reference the bundle in server-side JavaScript (required).

<dojoModule> Resource

The `<dojoModule>` resource element declares a dojo module for the client-side XPage within a theme file. Table 16.6 lists the properties supported by this element.

Table 16.6 Properties Supported by the <dojoModule> Element

Property	Description
`target`	For targeting different environments. "xsp" is the default environment.
`loaded`	Controls loading of this resource into the server-side XPage component tree.
`rendered`	Controls rendering of this resource to the client-side handler (Notes or browser).
`name`	The full Dojo module package and widget name (required).
`condition`	A client-side condition that controls loaded of the Dojo module.

<script> Resource

The `<script>` resource element declares a client-side or server-side JavaScript resource within a theme file. Table 16.7 lists the properties supported by this element.

Table 16.7 Properties Supported by the <script> Element

Property	Description
`target`	For targeting different environments. "xsp" is the default environment.
`loaded`	Controls loading of this resource into the server-side XPage component tree.
`rendered`	Controls rendering of this resource to the client-side handler (Notes or browser).
`charset`	Defines the character encoding of the script designated by the emitted script tag.
`clientSide`	Indicates if this script is client side or server side. The default is server.side.
`contents`	Defines the script contents when the src is not specified (required if no `src`).
`src`	Defines an absolute or relative path to a script resource file (required if no `contents`).
`type`	Defines the scripting language to be used; text/javascript is the default.

<styleSheet> Resource

The `<styleSheet>` resource element declares a CSS resource within a theme file. Table 16.8 lists the properties supported by this element.

Table 16.8 Properties Supported by the <styleSheet> Element

Property	Description
target	For targeting different environments. "xsp" is the default environment.
loaded	Controls loading of this resource into the server-side XPage component tree.
rendered	Controls rendering of this resource to the client-side handler (Notes or browser).
href	Defines an absolute or relative path to a style sheet resource file (required if no contents).
media	Defines the media type for the style sheet resource. (See www.w3.org/TR/CSS2/media.html for full specification.)
contents	Defines the contents of the style sheet resource when the href is not specified (required if no href).

<linkResource> Resource

The `<linkResource>` resource element can also declare a CSS resource within a theme file. The main difference between this resource element and the `<styleSheet>` element is the fact that this one supports the full range of HTML LINK tag attributes. Table 16.9 lists the properties supported by this element.

Table 16.9 Properties Supported by the <linkResource> Element

Property	Description
target	For targeting different environments. "xsp" is the default environment.
loaded	Controls loading of this resource into the server-side XPage component tree.
rendered	Controls rendering of this resource to the client-side handler (Notes or browser).
charset	Defines the character encoding of the linked resource.
dir	Specifies the direction for text that does not inherit a direction.
href	Defines an absolute or relative path to the linked resource file (required).
hreflang	Specifies the language code of the linked resource.
media	Specifies which device displays the linked resource.
rel	Specifies the relationship between the current document and the anchor referenced by the control.
rev	Specifies a reverse link from the anchor referenced by the control in the current document.
style	Defines any CSS style rules to be applied to the rendered link resource.

Property	Description
styleClass	Defines any CSS style classes to be applied to the rendered link resource.
target	Specifies the target frame to load the link resource into.
title	Defines title information for the link resource.
type	Specifies the MIME type of the link resource file.

<metaData> Resource

The <metaData> resource element declares HTML meta tags in the header section of the emitted XPage. Table 16.10 lists the properties supported by this element.

Now, open the **resources** XPage from the **Chp16Ed2.nsf** application and examine its XSP markup. Listing 16.20 details the entire XSP markup for this XPage for your convenience.

Table 16.10 Properties Supported by the <metaData> Element

Property	Description
target	For targeting different environments. "xsp" is the default environment.
loaded	Controls loading of this resource into the server-side XPage component tree.
rendered	Controls rendering of this resource to the client-side handler (Notes or browser).
content	Defines the metadata entry value (required).
httpEquiv	Can be used in place of the name attribute to set a HTTP header when the name is not specified.
name	Defines the metadata entry name.
scheme	Defines a scheme to be used to interpret the entry value.

Listing 16.20 XSP Markup for the Resources XPage

```
<?xml version="1.0" encoding="UTF-8"?>
<xp:view xmlns:xp="http://www.ibm.com/xsp/core">
    <xp:dataTable id="dataTable1" rows="30" var="resource"
        value="${javascript:facesContext.getViewRoot().getResources()}">
        <xp:column id="column1">
            <xp:text escape="true" id="computedField1"
                value="#{javascript:typeof resource}">
            </xp:text>
        </xp:column>
        <xp:column id="column2">
            <xp:text escape="true" id="computedField2">
                <xp:this.value><![CDATA[#{javascript:
```

```
                var resourceDetails = "";
                switch(typeof resource){
                case "com.ibm.xsp.resource.StyleSheetResource" : {
                    if(resource.getHref() == null){
                        resourceDetails = "media=" +
                            resource.getMedia() +
                            " contents=" + resource.getContents();
                    }else{
                        resourceDetails = resource.getHref();
                    }
                    break;
                }
                case "com.ibm.xsp.resource.ScriptResource" : {
                    resourceDetails = resource.getSrc();
                    break;
                }
                case "com.ibm.xsp.resource.BundleResource" : {
                    resourceDetails = resource.getSrc();
                    break;
                }
                case "com.ibm.xsp.resource.DojoModuleResource" : {
                    resourceDetails = resource.getName();
                    break;
                }
                case "com.ibm.xsp.resource.LinkResource" : {
                    resourceDetails = resource.getHref();
                    break;
                }
                case "com.ibm.xsp.resource.MetaDataResource" : {
                    resourceDetails = "http-equiv=" +
                        resource.getHttpEquiv() +
                        " name=" + resource.getName() +
                        " content=" + resource.getContent() +
                        " scheme=" + resource.getScheme();
                    break;
                }}
                return resourceDetails;
                }]]></xp:this.value>
            </xp:text>
        </xp:column>
    </xp:dataTable>
</xp:view>
```

As you can see in Listing 16.20, the `<xp:dataTable>` control on the third line obtains a list of all the resources on the **resources** XPage. Note that the `var` property is given a reference name of "resource." This simply acts as a scripting reference to the current resource object that is iterated over from the call to `getResources()` in the value property:

```
<xp:dataTable ... var="resource"
value="${javascript:facesContext.getViewRoot().getResources()}">
```

This control then iterates over this list to display the resource names and their contents. The point here is that this list of resources is actually specified within the `mxpd` theme. You saw this in Listing 16.18 by the `<resource>` elements and Listing 16.19 by the `<resources>` elements. Therefore, no resources are declared on the **resources** XPage itself. You should now ensure that the `mxpd` theme is the currently set theme on the **Chp16Ed2.nsf** application before previewing the **resources** XPage in the Notes client, as shown in Figure 16.33.

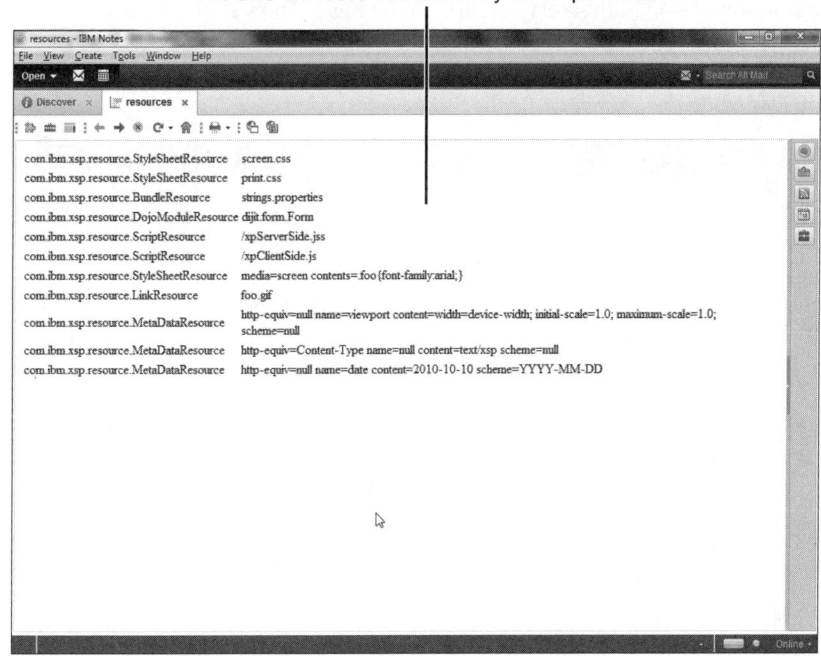

Figure 16.33 Previewing the resources XPage in the Notes client

As you can see in Figure 16.33 or in preview mode, the full list of `<resource>` and `<resources>` elements have been loaded based on the declarations in the `mxpd` theme file and are being used by the **resources** XPage.

Resource Paths

Up to this point, you have learned about declaring resources within a theme. These resources have been using relative paths to resources that reside within the **Chp16Ed2.nsf** application itself. But, how do you declare resources within a theme that reside outside of an application such as Notes/Domino 9 Platform Level theme resources, or even the OneUI style library resources? Not to worry, because the XPages runtime provides you with a special resource handling service known as the XPages Resource Servlet. This servlet understands how to retrieve and serve resources from a number of special dedicated global locations using specially registered path aliases. You can use these aliases whenever you need to use resources from the Notes client or Domino server platforms, as the XPages Resource Servlet ensures they are correctly resolved regardless of whichever platform your application is currently running in. The following subsections provide you with information on what is available by using this special servlet.

HTML Directory

To access the Notes/Domino HMTL directory, use the following XPages Resource Servlet path alias, as shown Table 16.11.

Table 16.11 HTML Directory

Path Alias	Physical Location	Server HTTP Location
`/.ibmxspres/domino`	`<Notes/Domino>/data/domino/html/`	`http://<server>/`

The HTML directory on Notes/Domino 9 contains amongst several other things, a full copy of the OneUIv2.0 and OneUIv2.1 style libraries. Listing 16.21 shows an example theme resource element that is declaring use of a CSS file in the OneUIv2.1 style library.

Listing 16.21 <resource> Using a CSS File in the HTML Directory

```
...
<resource>
    <content-type>text/css</content-type>
    <href>/.ibmxspres/domino/oneuiv2.1/base/core.css</href>
</resource>
...
```

When this `<resource>` element is loaded, its `href` property is resolved to the following location on a Domino server:

```
http://<server>/oneuiv2.1/base/core.css
```

Likewise, on a Notes client, it is resolved to the following relative location:

```
/xsp/.ibmxspres/domino/oneuiv2.1/base/core.css
```

Therefore, the resolved URL is translated appropriately by the XPages Resource servlet for the Notes client or Domino server automatically for you based on the running platform.

XPages Global Directory

In Notes/Domino 9, there is a dedicated directory used for XPages resources. This directory is known as the XPages Global directory. It contains all the Platform Level **theme** resources along with images used by the core XPages controls. Table 16.12 details the path alias to this directory.

Table 16.12 XPages Global Directory

Path Alias	Physical Location	Server HTTP Location
`/.ibmxspres/global`	`<Notes/Domino>/data/domino/java/xsp/`	`http://<server>/domjava/xsp/`

This directory location contains a `theme` subdirectory. Inside this directory, you find several subdirectories, each containing CSS and image resources for the different Platform Level themes. Appendix B, "XSP Style Class Reference," gives you details on the main CSS files and CSS style classes within these files, which can be found in the XPages Global Directory theme subdirectories. Listing 16.22 shows an example theme resource element that is declaring use of a CSS file in the *webstandard* theme resource location.

Listing 16.22 <resource> Using a CSS File in the XPages Global Directory

```
...
<resource>
    <content-type>text/css</content-type>
    <href>/.ibmxspres/global/theme/webstandard/xsp.css</href>
</resource>
...
```

When this `<resource>` element is loaded, its `href` property is resolved to the following location on a Domino server:

```
http://<server>/domjava/xsp/theme/webstandard/xsp.css
```

Likewise, on a Notes client, it is resolved to the following relative location:

```
/xsp/.ibmxspres/global/theme/webstandard/xsp.css
```

Again, the resolved URL is translated appropriately by the XPages Resource Servlet for the Notes client or Domino server automatically for you based on the running platform. It is important to know about the XPages Global Directory if you need to create and manage your own Platform Level theme.

Also note that this location can be changed using the `xsp.resources.location` XSP property in the `xsp.properties` file you learned about earlier.

Dojo Plug-in

In Notes/Domino 9, there is also a dedicated OSGi plug-in for Dojo resources. This plug-in contains a full copy of the Dojo 1.8.3 library, but also all the XPages Dojo modules and extensions. Table 16.13 details the path alias to this plug-in.

Table 16.13 Dojo Directory

Path Alias	Physical Location	Server HTTP Location
`/.ibmxspres/dojoroot`	`<Notes/Domino>/data/domino/js/dojo-1.8.3/`	`http://<server>/domjs/dojo-1.8.3/`

Listing 16.23 shows an example **theme** resource element that is declaring use of a JavaScript file in the Dojo plug-in.

Listing 16.23 <resource> Using a Client-Side JavaScript File in the Dojo Directory

```
...
<resource dojoTheme="true">
    <content-type>application/x-javascript</content-type>
    <href>
        /.ibmxspres/dojoroot/ibm/xsp/widget/layout/xspClientDojo.js
    </href>
</resource>
...
```

When this `<resource>` element is loaded, its `href` property is resolved to the following location on a Domino server that is then proxied into the Dojo OSGi plug-in automatically by the XPages Runtime:

```
http://<server>/domjs/dojo-1.8.3/ibm/xsp/widget/layout/xspClientDojo.js
```

Likewise, on a Notes client, it is resolved to the following relative location:

```
/xsp/.ibmxspres/dojoroot/ibm/xsp/widget/layout/xspClientDojo.js
```

Again, the resolved URL is translated appropriately by the XPages Resource Servlet for the Notes client or Domino server automatically for you based on the running platform from its virtual path used by the XPages Resource servlet into a HTTP URL path, that maps to the relevant OSGi plug-in within the Notes client or Domino server.

dojoTheme Property

You may have noticed the inclusion of a `dojoTheme` property on the `<resource>` element in Listing 16.23. This declares that a resource should only be included on an XPage that has Dojo controls. For example, if you drag-and-drop a Date Time Picker or Type-Ahead control onto an XPage, the dojoTheme property for that XPage is automatically set to true for you. When the XPage is then run, any theme `<resource>` elements that has an explicit dojoTheme property set to true, is included in the emitted HTML markup for that XPage. Otherwise, they are ignored.

User Agent Resources

One of the most common problems encountered by modern day web applications is serving specific content to different end-user browsers and devices. This problem is further complicated by different versions of end-user browsers and devices that have compatibility issues and so on. This is an area that a **theme** makes a lot easier to manage by providing a server-side JavaScript API for identifying a wide range of end-user browsers, versions, and devices.

In the following location, where `<Notes/Domino>` represents the install location of your Notes client, or Domino server, you find the `oneuiv2.1` theme:

```
<Notes/Domino>/xsp/nsf/themes/oneuiv2.1.theme
```

Listing 16.24 shows a fragment taken from the `oneuiv2.1` theme file that details some of the `<resource>` elements using the server-side JavaScript API to detect the end-user browser.

Listing 16.24 Some of the <resource> Elements in the oneuiv2.1 Theme Detecting the End User Browser

```
...
<!-- iehacks == if IE6 -->
<resource rendered="#{javascript:context.getUserAgent().isIE(6,6)}">
    <content-type>application/x-javascript</content-type>
    <href>/.ibmxspres/global/theme/oneuiv2.1/js/ie6.js</href>
</resource>
<!-- iehacks == if IE7 -->
<resource rendered="#{javascript:context.getUserAgent().isIE(7,7)}">
    <content-type>application/x-javascript</content-type>
    <href>/.ibmxspres/global/theme/oneuiv2.1/js/ie7.js</href>
</resource>
<!-- FireFox Specific -->
<resource rendered="#{javascript:context.getUserAgent().isFirefox()}">
    <content-type>text/css</content-type>
    <href>/.ibmxspres/global/theme/oneuiv2.1/xspFF.css</href>
</resource>
<!-- Safari Specific -->
<resource rendered="#{javascript:context.getUserAgent().isSafari()}">
    <content-type>text/css</content-type>
```

```
    <href>/.ibmxspres/global/theme/oneuiv2.1/xspSF.css</href>
</resource>
<!-- IE Specific -->
<resource rendered="#{javascript:context.getUserAgent().isIE(0,6)}">
    <content-type>text/css</content-type>
    <href>/.ibmxspres/global/theme/oneuiv2.1/xspIE06.css</href>
</resource>
<resource rendered="#{javascript:context.getUserAgent().isIE(7,8)}">
    <content-type>text/css</content-type>
    <href>/.ibmxspres/global/theme/oneuiv2.1/xspIE78.css</href>
</resource>
...
```

As you can see, there is a varied range of end-user browsers and versions being detected in Listing 16.24 mostly focusing on Microsoft Internet Explorer and Mozilla Firefox. You can also see that the `rendered` property is used to control whether or not to emit each resource in the final HTML markup. Furthermore, the API to detect the end-user browser is accessible from the global `context` object by calling the `getUserAgent()` method. This method returns an object of class type `com.ibm.xsp.designer.context.XSPUserAgent`. Table 16.14 lists all the methods supported by this class.

Table 16.14 API Provided by the com.ibm.xsp.designer.context.XSPUserAgent Class

Method	Description
`getBrowser() : String`	Returns a string that represents the browser common name. It analyses the browser based on the user-agent variable and currently recognizes: Firefox, IE, Opera, and Safari. For other browsers or devices, you should analyze the user-agent string.
`getBrowserVersion() : String`	Returns the version number as a string. This works if the browser has been properly identified by the class. Returns the version number or an empty string if not applicable.
`getBrowserVersionNumber() : double`	Returns the version number converted as a double. This works if the browser has been properly identified by the class. The number is converted to a double from the string, and every digit located after the second decimal point is ignored (for example, 3.0.1 becomes 3.0). Returns the version number or 0 if not applicable.
`getUserAgent() : String`	Get the USER-AGENT string. This method grabs the user-agent value from the request header variable named "user-agent." This string identifies the browser, operating system, and so on.

Method	Description
`getVersion(String) : String`	Get the version for a particular entry. This function scans the user agent and returns the version number immediately following the entry (in this case, the Version/VersionNumber entry).
`getVersionNumber(String) : double`	Get the number version for a particular entry. This function converts the version string to a version number by converting to a double. If the actual version string contains more than one decimal point (for example, 3.0.1), it ignores the digits after the second decimal point (for example, 3.0).
`hasEntry(String) : Boolean`	Check if an entry is available in the user agent.
`isChrome() : boolean`	Check if the user-agent is a Google Chrome browser.
`isChrome(double,double) : boolean`	Check if the user-agent is a Google Chrome browser within the given range (inclusive of given min and max range).
`isFireFox() : boolean`	Check if the user-agent is a Mozilla Firefox browser.
`isFireFox(double,double) : boolean`	Check if the user-agent is a Mozilla Firefox browser within the given range (inclusive of given min and max range).
`isIE() : boolean`	Check if the user-agent is a Microsoft Internet Explorer browser.
`isIE(double,double) : boolean`	Check if the user-agent is a Microsoft Internet Explorer browser within the given range (inclusive of given min and max range).
`isOpera() : boolean`	Check if the user-agent is an Opera browser.
`isOpera(double,double) : boolean`	Check if the user-agent is an Opera browser within the given range (inclusive of given min and max range).
`isSafari() : boolean`	Check if the user-agent is an Apple Safari browser.
`isSafari(double,double) : boolean`	Check if the user-agent is an Apple Safari browser within the given range (inclusive of given min and max range).
`parseVersion(int) : String`	This utility function extracts a version number located at a particular position. This function ignores all the letters, spaces, and slashes.

Currently, this API is heavily focused toward the five main browsers, namely Mozilla Firefox, Google Chrome, Microsoft Internet Explorer, Opera, and Apple Safari. This, however, does not limit you to detecting this range, as you can use the API to detect any device based on its

USER-AGENT string. Listing 16.25 shows you an example of a theme <resource> element that is only rendered when the end-user device is an Apple iPhone.

Listing 16.25 <resource> Element That Is Only Rendered to an Apple iPhone

```
...
<resource rendered="#{javascript:context.getUserAgent().
                        getUserAgent().indexOf('iPhone')>-1}">
    <content-type>application/x-javascript</content-type>
    <href>/.ibmxspres/global/iphone/screen.js</href>
</resource>
...
```

In this example, the call on context.getUserAgent().getUserAgent()typically returns a USER-AGENT string similar to

```
Mozilla/5.0 (iPhone; U; CPU like Mac OS X; en) AppleWebKit/420+ (KHTML,
like Gecko) Version/3.0 Mobile/1C25 Safari/419.3
```

It is then a case of parsing whatever relevant piece of the USER-AGENT string that is necessary to identify the end-user browser or device. In this example, the word iPhone appears in the string making it easy to identify the Apple iPhone as the requesting user-agent.

A related method that can be used to detect the current platform can be found on the context global server-side JavaScript object. Table 16.15 details this method.

Table 16.15 API Provided by the Context Global Object for Detecting the Current Platform

Method	Description
isRunningContext(String) : boolean	Check if the application is running under the given platform. Valid platforms are "Notes" and "Domino."

Listing 16.26 shows an example taken from the oneuiv2.1 theme. This example shows a theme resource element that is only rendered when the current application is running on the Notes client.

Listing 16.26 <resource> Element That Is Only Rendered When Running in the Notes Client

```
...
<!-- RCP Specific -->
<resource rendered="#{javascript:context.isRunningContext('Notes')}">
    <content-type>text/css</content-type>
    <href>/.ibmxspres/global/theme/oneuiv2.1/xspRCP.css</href>
</resource>
...
```

This is different to the user-agent related methods you have just learned about in that it can only be used to identify either a "Notes" or a "Domino" platform.

Bidirectional Resources

To assist you creating internationalized applications where reading direction is right-to-left in some countries, you can use two other methods that are also available on the global context object. Table 16.16 details both of these methods.

Table 16.16 API Provided by the Context Global Object Detecting Reading Direction

Method	Description
`isDirectionLTR() : boolean`	Checks if the reading direction is left to right
`isDirectionRTL() : boolean`	Checks if the reading direction is right to left

If you again examine the `oneuiv2.1` theme, you see several occurrences of both these methods, as shown in the fragment taken from this theme file in Listing 16.27.

Listing 16.27 Some of the <resource> Elements in the oneuiv2 Theme Detecting Reading Direction

```
...
<resource rendered="#{javascript:context.isDirectionLTR()}">
    <content-type>text/css</content-type>
    <href>/.ibmxspres/domino/oneuiv2.1/base/core.css</href>
</resource>
<resource rendered="#{javascript:context.isDirectionRTL()}">
    <content-type>text/css</content-type>
    <href>/.ibmxspres/domino/oneuiv2.1/base/coreRTL.css</href>
</resource>
<resource rendered="#{javascript:context.isDirectionLTR()}">
    <content-type>text/css</content-type>
    <href>
        /.ibmxspres/domino/oneuiv2.1/defaultTheme/defaultTheme.css
    </href>
</resource>
<resource rendered="#{javascript:context.isDirectionRTL()}">
    <content-type>text/css</content-type>
    <href>
        /.ibmxspres/domino/oneuiv2.1/defaultTheme/defaultThemeRTL.css
    </href>
</resource>
<resource rendered="#{javascript:(context.isDirectionLTR())}">
    <content-type>text/css</content-type>
    <href>/.ibmxspres/global/theme/oneuiv2.1/xspLTR.css</href>
</resource>
```

```
<resource rendered="#{javascript:context.isDirectionRTL()}">
    <content-type>text/css</content-type>
    <href>/.ibmxspres/global/theme/oneuiv2.1/xspRTL.css</href>
</resource>
<resource rendered="#{javascript:(context.isDirectionRTL()
                        &amp;&amp; context.getUserAgent().isIE())}">
    <content-type>text/css</content-type>
    <href>/.ibmxspres/global/theme/oneuiv2.1/xspIERTL.css</href>
</resource>
...
```

One of the most interesting uses of the both the user-agent and bidirectional methods can be seen in the last `<resource>` element in Listing 16.27. Here, a server-side JavaScript expression uses a combination of the two types of methods to detect right-to-left reading direction and a Microsoft Internet Explorer browser. It is important to note the encoding of the double-ampersand to maintain the validity of the theme XML file structure.

Theme Properties, themeId, Control Definitions, and Control Properties

As a descriptor of presentation logic and resources for an XPages application, a theme should naturally support more than just the inclusion of different resource types. This fulfills its requirements to also be a descriptor for presentation logic. Therefore, a theme supports a range of other features, namely theme properties, control definitions, and control properties.

These features allow you to declare the presentation logic for your application in a name/value property-based manner and through the theme inheritance mechanism you learned about earlier in this chapter. This mechanism is leveraged to enable control property definitions to be defined within a theme for any given control, and extended or overridden across themes as and when required.

This is a powerful mechanism, so let's begin with an explanation of theme properties.

Theme Properties

From the **Chp16Ed2.nsf** application, reopen the `mxpd` theme in Designer (if it is closed). Once open in the theme **Source** editor, scroll to the three instances of the `<property>` element. Listing 16.28 details these `<property>` elements for your convenience.

Listing 16.28 Three <property> Elements Within the mxpd Theme File

```
...
<property target="xsp">
    <name>mxpd.theme.info</name>
    <value>Theme: mxpd -> Level: 1</value>
</property>
<property target="xsp">
```

```
    <name>mxpd.panel.width</name>
    <value>14</value>
</property>
<property target="xsp">
    <name>mxpd.chapter.number</name>
    <value>14</value>
</property>
...
```

Here, you see how you can declare name/value properties for use in an application. The `<property>` element itself supports the optional `target` attribute (in the same way the `<resource>` element does), but also `<name>` and `<value>` child elements, as shown in Listing 16.28. Note, however, that both the `<name>` and `<value>` child elements cannot be dynamically computed using a server-side JavaScript or EL expression. Only static values are available.

If you now open each of the other `mxpd*` theme files in Designer, you see that the first of these properties, the one with the name `mxpd.theme.info`, is repeated within each of the other themes. By way of repeating the declaration of a property in an extended theme, implicitly overrides the parent version of that property. Listing 16.29 describes the content of each of the other four `mxpd*` themes.

Listing 16.29 Four Other mxpd* Theme Files Showing the Overridden mxpd.theme.info Property

```
...
<!-- mxpd1 -->
<theme extends="mxpd">
    <property>
        <name>mxpd.theme.info</name>
        <value>Theme: mxpd1 -> Level: 2</value>
    </property>
</theme>
...
<!-- mxpd2 -->
<theme extends="mxpd1">
    <property>
        <name>mxpd.theme.info</name>
        <value>Theme: mxpd2 -> Level: 3</value>
    </property>
</theme>
...
<!-- mxpd3 -->
<theme extends="mxpd2">
    <property>
        <name>mxpd.theme.info</name>
```

```
        <value>Theme: mxpd3 -> Level: 4</value>
    </property>
</theme>
...
<!-- mxpd4 -->
<theme extends="mxpd3">
    <property>
        <name>mxpd.theme.info</name>
        <value>Theme: mxpd4 -> Level: 5</value>
    </property>
</theme>
...
<!-- mxpd5 -->
<theme extends="mxpd4">
    <property>
        <name>mxpd.theme.info</name>
        <value>Theme: mxpd5 -> Level: 6</value>
    </property>
</theme>
...
```

Therefore, in this example, the `mxpd.theme.info` theme property is being overridden in each of the extended themes. You should now examine the XSP markup for the **properties** XPage in Designer. Listing 16.30 lists a fragment of XSP markup for the Computed Field control on the **properties** XPage.

Listing 16.30 XSP Markup for the Computed Field on the Properties XPage

```
...
<xp:text escape="true" id="computedField4" themeId="mxpd.text.control">
    <xp:this.value>
        <![CDATA[#{javascript:context.getProperty("mxpd.theme.
➥info")}]]>
    </xp:this.value>
</xp:text>
...
```

The interesting point here is the way in which the `mxpd.theme.info` theme property is retrieved by the Computed Field control using the `context.getProperty()` method. This means that theme properties are loaded into the XPage runtime and made available to an application from the runtime.

Now, ensure the `mxpd` theme is the currently set **theme** for the **Chp16Ed2.nsf** application. Then, preview the **properties** XPage in the Notes client where you see something similar to Figure 16.34.

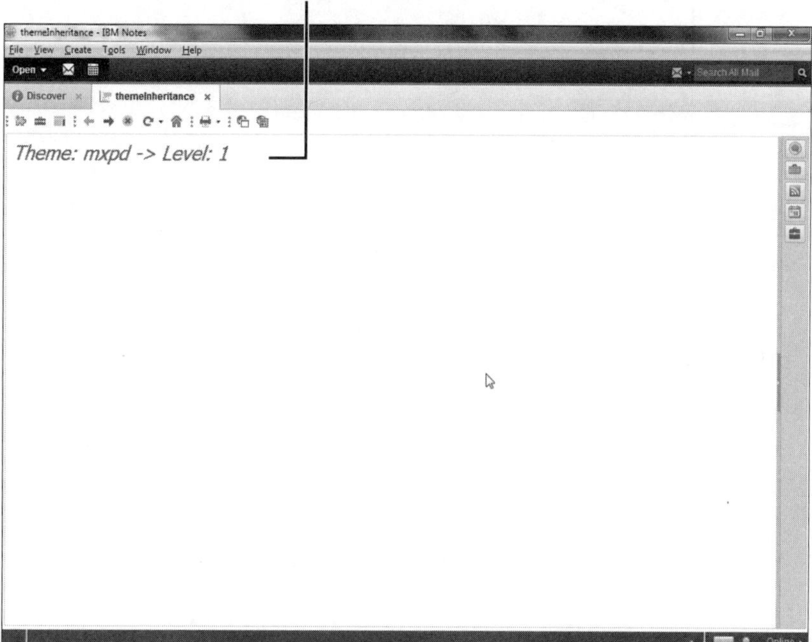

Figure 16.34 Previewing the properties XPage in the Notes client using the mxpd theme

In Figure 16.34, you can see the `mxpd.theme.info` property value has been displayed by the Computed Field control. Now, close the Notes client, reset the current theme to `mxpd1`, save your changes, and choose to preview in the Notes client again. On this occasion, as you might expect, the Computed Field displays the overridden `mxpd.theme.info` property value from the extended `mxpd1` theme, as shown in Figure 16.35.

If you repeatedly reset the current theme to each of the other `mxpd*` themes, previewing the properties XPage in between, you see the same behavior being applied each time.

themeId Property

Building on the concept of theme properties, a theme also supports controls and control properties. This feature allows you to associate an XPage control to a control definition within a theme. Furthermore, a control definition allows you to manage the actual property values that are supported by the associated XPage control. In essence, this is how a theme totally removes presentation logic from within an XPage, away from its application logic, into a loosely coupled and easy-to-manage theme file.

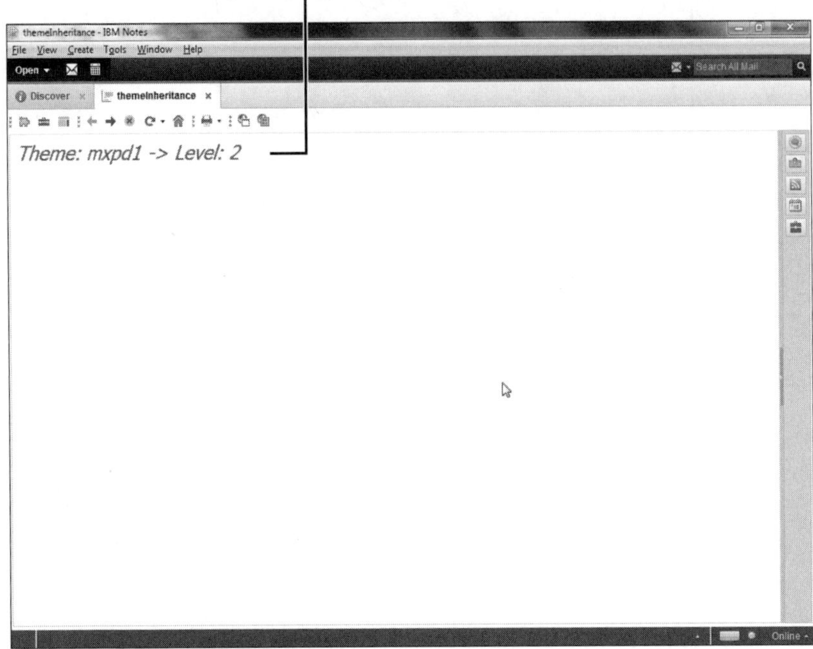

Figure 16.35 Previewing the properties XPage in the Notes client using the mxpd1 theme

You may have noticed the `themeId` property on the `<xp:text>` element in Listing 16.30. This property is the glue between an XPage control and a control definition in a theme. It achieves this by acting as a reference to a **Control** element within a **theme**. You can set the `themeId` property using the **All Properties** panel or the **Style** panel for any given XPages control. Figure 16.36 shows the Theme edit box on the Style panel used to specify the `themeId` for the `<xp:text>` control.

To fully understand this relationship, examine the `mxpd` theme in Designer. In this theme, you can find many `<control>` elements declared, one of which is shown in Listing 16.31 with the name `mxpd.text.control`.

Listing 16.31 mxpd.text.control <control> Element Within the mxpd Theme

```
...
<control>
    <name>mxpd.text.control</name>
    <property>
        <name>styleClass</name>
        <value>text</value>
    </property>
```

```
    <property>
        <name>tagName</name>
        <value>h1</value>
    </property>
</control>
...
```

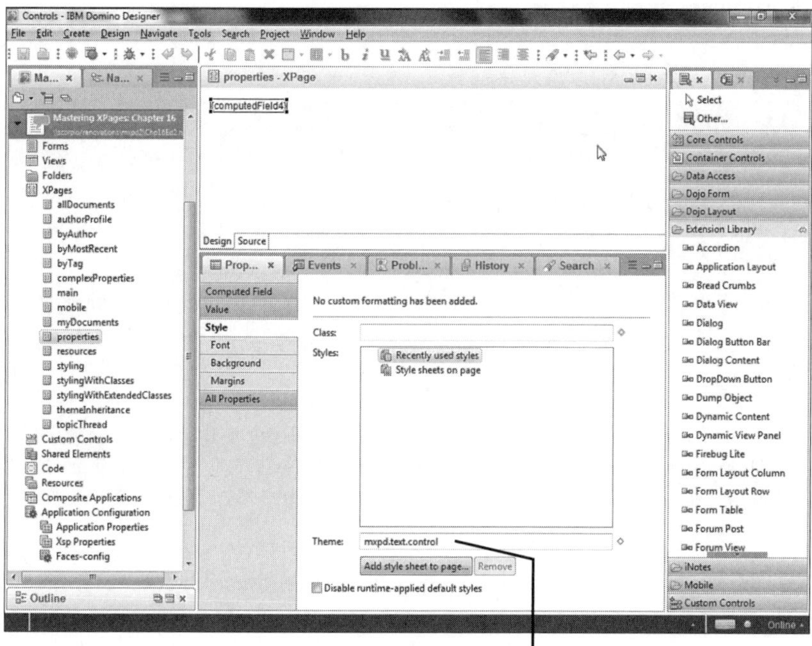

Figure 16.36 Style panel with the Theme edit box where you specify the themeId property

The `themeId` property shown in Listing 16.30, or on the **properties** XPage if you have it open in Designer, specifies the `<name>` element value of the `<control>` element as its value in the XSP markup:

```
<xp:text ... themeId="mxpd.text.control">
```

Because this `themeId` matches the `<control>` element with the name `mxpd.text.control`, a binding between the `<xp:text>` control and the control definition in the theme is established. Therefore, when the theme is loaded and this binding is established, any control properties declared on the control definition are applied to the XPages control. In the case of the properties XPage, the `styleClass` property of the `<xp:text>` control is set using the `styleClass` control property value from the `mxpd.text.control` in the `mxpd` theme.

Control Definitions

Themes go even further by supporting control definition inheritance when you are extending a theme. This allows a control definition in an extending theme to either override or merge the control definition from its parent theme. This is achieved by specifying the `override` property on the `<control>` element. The default behavior is to merge control definitions or, in other words, `<control override="false">`. Table 16.17 outlines what happens when you set the `<control>` override to either `true` or `false`.

Table 16.17 <control> Override Behaviors

What Happens with <control override="false">	What Happens with <control override="true">
An inherited control property that is redefined in an extending `theme` control definition is overridden by the redefined version.	An inherited control property that is redefined in an extending `theme` control definition is overridden by the redefined version.
An inherited control property that is not redefined in an extending `theme` control merges with the extended control definition.	An inherited control property that is not redefined in an extending `theme` control is ignored and, therefore, `NOT` included in the extended control definition.
Newly defined control properties that do not exist on the parent control definition are merged with the extended control definition.	Newly defined control properties that do not exist on the parent control definition merge with the extended control definition.

As you can see, the second item is where the key difference between the two `override` settings comes into play.

An example of using the `override` property can be seen by examining the `mxpd1` theme in Designer. Listing 16.32 shows a fragment from the `mxpd1` theme file containing an extended version of the `mxpd.text.control` control definition.

Listing 16.32 Extended mxpd.text.control Control Definition Within the mxpd1 Theme

```
...
<control override="true">
    <name>mxpd.text.control</name>
    <property>
        <name>styleClass</name>
        <value>bigText</value>
    </property>
    <property>
        <name>style</name>
```

```
        <value>text-decoration:underline;</value>
    </property>
</control>
...
```

This extended control definition has its `override` property set to `true`. The base version of this control definition, declared in the `mxpd` theme, defines a `tagName` property with the value of `h1` as seen in Listing 16.31. But, because `override` is set to `true` in the `mxpd1` extended control definition, the `tagName` property is ignored and not be merged into the extended control definition. Likewise, the `mxpd1` extended control definition declares a `style` property that is not declared on the base `mxpd` control definition. This new property is included in the extended control definition. The emitted HTML markup is as follows:

```
<span class="bigText" style="text-decoration: underline;"
id="view:_id1:computedField4">Theme: mxpd1 -> Level: 2</span>
```

On the other hand, if the `override` property were set to `false` in the `mxpd1` extended control definition for the `mxpd.text.control`, things would be slightly different. The `tagName` property coming from the base control definition would be included in the extended control definition. Likewise, the new `style` property definition would also be included. The base control definition `styleClass` property would be overridden by the extended version. The emitted HTML markup is as follows:

```
<h1 class="bigText" style="text-decoration: underline;"
id="view:_id1:computedField4">Theme: mxpd1 -> Level: 2</h1>
```

Ensure that the mxpd1 theme is set before previewing the **properties** XPage in the Notes client. Toggle the value of the `override` property for each case, `true` and `false`, and examine the change to the Computed Field control when you preview.

Control Properties

Control definitions are not just about the `<control>` element and its capability to use the `override` property. A control property itself also supports a similar capability to either override or concatenate its value with that defined in the XSP markup for an XPage control. A third option is available and is actually the default behavior that allows the value defined in the XSP markup to take precedence over a control property specified in a theme. Furthermore, unlike theme properties, control properties do support computable values using server-side JavaScript or EL expressions.

To understand these features, open the `mxpd2` theme in Designer. Listing 16.33 details the `mxpd.text.control` control definition in this theme.

Listing 16.33 Extended mxpd.text.control Control Definition Within the mxpd2 Theme

```
...
<control>
    <name>mxpd.text.control</name>
    <property mode="concat">
        <name>style</name>
        <value>text-decoration:underline;</value>
    </property>
    ...
</control>
...
```

In this version of the control definition, the `style` property now declares `mode="concat"` on itself. This specifies that its `style` property value should be concatenated to any value specified in the `style` property for the associated XPage control in the XSP markup.

If you do not specify the `mode` attribute on a control property, the default behavior applies whereby whatever value is specified for that property in the XSP markup takes precedence. Valid values for the `mode` attribute are `concat` to concatenate, and `override` to override whatever value is specified within the XSP markup for that property.

You now must format the `style` of the Computed Field control in the **properties** XPage by adding the following attribute and value to the `<xp:text>` element:

```
style="border:1px solid blue;"
```

Listing 16.34 shows the modified Computed Field control in the **properties** XPage with its `style` property specified.

Listing 16.34 Modified Computed Field Control with Its Style Property Specified

```
...
<xp:text escape="true" id="computedField4" themeId="mxpd.text.control"
    style="border:1px solid blue;">
    <xp:this.value>
        <![CDATA[#{javascript:context.getProperty("mxpd.theme.
➥info")}]]>
    </xp:this.value>
</xp:text>
...
```

You need to reset the current theme to be `mxpd2` in the **Application Properties** for the **Chp16Ed2.nsf** application, having saved all of your changes, preview the **properties** XPage once more in the Notes client. This time around, if you view the emitted HTML source for the XPage, you see something similar to the following for the Computed Field control:

```
<span dir="ltr" class="bigText" style="border: 1px solid blue; text-
decoration: underline;" id="view:_id1:computedField4">Theme: mxpd2 ->
Level: 3</span>
```

Note the fact that the `style` property value from the XSP markup and that of the **Theme** control definition have indeed been concatenated together within the emitted HTML markup.

Likewise, if you change the `mode` attribute on the `style` control property in the `mxpd2` theme to `mode="override"`, you see something similar to the following:

```
<span dir="ltr" class="bigText" style="text-decoration: underline;"
id="view:_id1:computedField4">Theme: mxpd2 -> Level: 3</span>
```

In this case, the `style` property value specified in the XSP markup has been completely ignored and not included in the emitted HTML markup.

The last available configuration is to modify the `mxpd2` control definition once more by removing the `mode` attribute from the `style` control property. If you examined the emitted HTML source for the Computed Field control, you see something similar to the following:

```
<span dir="ltr" class="bigText" style="border:1px solid blue;"
id="view:_id1:computedField4">Theme: mxpd2 -> Level: 3</span>
```

This time around, the `style` property value from the XSP markup takes precedence over the `style` control property value.

Computing Control Property Values As mentioned earlier, control properties support computed values using server-side JavaScript or EL language expressions. Listing 16.35 lists the dir control property shown in the previous examples and its computed value expression.

Listing 16.35 dir Control Property Using Server-Side JavaScript to Computes Its Value

```
...
<control>
    <name>mxpd.text.control</name>
    ...
    <property>
        <name>dir</name>
        <value>
            #{javascript:context.isDirectionLTR()?'ltr':'rtl'}
        </value>
    </property>
</control>
...
```

This is, of course, a trivial example, but nonetheless demonstrates the dynamic nature of a theme file for creating and enabling presentation logic.

Setting Properties on the XPages Core Controls You can also set the properties of the XPages Core Controls using a theme file. For example, you might want all submit type Button controls in your application to have the same textual label, such as OK, and all cancel type Button controls to have a label such as Cancel. You might also want to have the Modified Flag feature enabled for all XPages in your application. All of these use cases can easily be achieved by setting the appropriate control properties in a theme file, as shown in Listing 16.36.

Listing 16.36 Setting Submit and Cancel Type Button Control Labels and Enabling the Modified Flag on the View Control

```
...
<control>
    <name>Button.Submit</name>
    <property>
        <name>value</name>
        <value>OK</value>
    </property>
</control>

<control>
    <name>Button.Cancel</name>
    <property>
        <name>value</name>
        <value>Cancel</value>
    </property>
</control>

<control>
    <name>ViewRoot</name>
    <property>
        <name>enableModifiedFlag</name>
        <value>true</value>
    </property>
</control>
...
```

As you can see in Listing 16.36, each control has a specific `<name>` element. As you learned earlier, this corresponds to being the `themeId` for the control, and every XPage core control also obeys the rules of the `themeId` mechanism. This means you can interoperate with the core controls and provide your own specific settings. The secret is knowing what the implicit `themeId` values are for each XPages core control; Table 16.18 gives you that information.

Table 16.18 themeId values for the XPages Core Controls

Control	themeId
View	`ViewRoot`
Form	`Form`
Computed Field	`Text.ComputedField`
Label	`Text.Label`
Edit Box	`InputField.EditBox`
Edit Box [password = true]	`InputField.Secret`
Date Time Picker	`InputField.DateTimePicker`
Multiline Edit Box	`InputField.TextArea`
Rich Text	`InputField.RichText`
File Upload	`InputField.FileUpload`
File Download	`DataTable.FileDownload`
File Download Link	`Link.FileDownload`
Link	`Link`
Button	`Button.Command`
Button [type = submit]	`Button.Submit`
Button [type = cancel]	`Button.Cancel`
Check Box	`CheckBox`
Radio Button	`RadioButton`
List Box	`ListBox`
Combo Box	`ComboBox`
Image	`Image`
Error Message	`Message`
Error Messages	`Message.List`
Panel	`Panel`
Section	`Section`
Tabbed Panel	`TabbedPanel`
Tabbed Panel Tab	`Tab.TabbedPanel`
Data Table	`DataTable`
View Panel	`DataTable.ViewPanel`
View Panel Title	`Text.ViewTitle`

Control	themeId
View Panel Column	Column.View
View Panel Column Text	Text.ViewColumn
View Panel Computed Column Text	Text.ViewColumnComputed
View Panel Column Link	Link.ViewColumn
View Panel Column Image	Image.ViewColumn
View Panel Column Check Box	CheckBox.ViewColumn
View Panel Column Header	Panel.ViewColumnHeader
View Panel Column Header Text	Text.ViewColumnHeader
View Panel Column Header Link	Link.ViewColumnHeader
View Panel Column Header Check Box	CheckBox.ViewColumnHeader
View Panel Column Header Icon	Image.ViewColumnHeader
View Panel Column Header Sort Image	Image.ViewColumnHeaderSort
View Panel Column Header Image	Image.ViewColumnHeader
Pager	Pager
Pager Control	PagerControl
Pager First	PagerControl.Pager.First
Pager Previous	PagerControl.Pager.Previous
Pager Next	PagerControl.Pager.Next
Pager Last	PagerControl.Pager.Last
Pager Group	PagerControl.Pager.Group
Pager Status	PagerControl.Pager.Status
Pager Goto	PagerControl.Pager.Goto
Pager Separator	PagerControl.Pager.Separator

Control Property Types Another feature of control properties for you to learn about is support for data-types. In the `mxpd` theme, you can find a control definition for the `mxpd.types.control` control. Listing 16.37 also details this control definition for your convenience.

Listing 16.37 mxpd.types.control Control Definition Showing the Different Supported Data Types

```
...
<control>
    <name>mxpd.types.control</name>
    <property type="char">
```

```
        <name>charProp</name>
        <value>#{javascript:java.lang.Character.MAX_VALUE}</value>
    </property>
    <property type="byte">
        <name>byteProp</name>
        <value>#{javascript:java.lang.Byte.MAX_VALUE}</value>
    </property>
    <property type="short">
        <name>shortProp</name>
        <value>#{javascript:java.lang.Short.MAX_VALUE}</value>
    </property>
    <property type="int">
        <name>intProp</name>
        <value>#{javascript:java.lang.Integer.MAX_VALUE}</value>
    </property>
    <property type="long">
        <name>longProp</name>
        <value>#{javascript:java.lang.Long.MAX_VALUE}</value>
    </property>
    <property type="float">
        <name>floatProp</name>
        <value>#{javascript:java.lang.Float.MAX_VALUE}</value>
    </property>
    <property type="double">
        <name>doubleProp</name>
        <value>#{javascript:java.lang.Double.MAX_VALUE}</value>
    </property>
    <property type="boolean">
        <name>booleanProp</name>
        <value>#{javascript:java.lang.Boolean.TRUE}</value>
    </property>
    <property type="string">
        <name>stringProp</name>
        <value>#{javascript:"String value!"}</value>
    </property>
</control>
...
```

A total of nine different data types can be specified on a control property. If unspecified, the default type is assumed to be `string`. Use cases for using property types can be varied, but one useful case is to provide a control definition within a theme for a Custom Control and its properties. By doing so, you can drive the values of a Custom Control's custom properties using a theme file and ensure that the expected data types are being loaded into the Custom Control.

Complex Properties A final feature of control properties for you to understand is support for Complex Properties. In the `mxpd_complexprops` theme, you can find a control definition for the `mxpd.number.spinner` control. Listing 16.38 also details this control definition for your convenience.

Listing 16.38 mxpd.number.spinner Complex Properties

```
...
<control>
    <name>mxpd.number.spinner</name>
    <property>
        <name>dojoType</name>
        <value>dijit.form.NumberSpinner</value>
    </property>
    <property>
        <name>dojoAttributes</name>
        <complex type="xp_dojoAttribute">
            <property>
                <name>name</name>
                <value>value</value>
            </property>
            <property>
                <name>value</name>
                <value>5</value>
            </property>
        </complex>
        <complex type="xp_dojoAttribute">
            <property>
                <name>name</name>
                <value>valuemax</value>
            </property>
            <property>
                <name>value</name>
                <value>10</value>
            </property>
        </complex>
        <complex type="xp_dojoAttribute">
            <property>
                <name>name</name>
                <value>valuemin</value>
            </property>
            <property>
                <name>value</name>
                <value>1</value>
            </property>
```

```
        </complex>
    </property>
    <property>
        <name>attrs</name>
        <complex type="xp_attr">
            <property>
                <name>name</name>
                <value>largeDelta</value>
            </property>
            <property>
                <name>value</name>
                <value>0.5</value>
            </property>
        </complex>
    </property>
</control>
...
```

As shown in Listing 16.38, Complex Properties can be declared on a Control by specifying the type of property. Currently, two complex types are supported: `xp_dojoAttribute` and `xp_attr`. These types map directly to the `dojoAttribute` and `attrs` Complex Properties found on many of the XPages controls. These are recognized as Complex Properties because they support special object types such as Collections or Objects as values. Both supported types are Lists containing one or more property instances declared using the special property/name/value format, as shown in Listing 16.38. Listing 16.39 demonstrates how a simple `<xp:div>` element is bound to the mxpd.number.spinner theme element using the `themeId` property. At runtime this causes the `<xp:div>` element to be configured according to the mxpd.number.spinner configuration within the `mxpd_complexprops.theme` file. You will find this XSP markup within the **complex Properties** XPage within the **Chp16Ed2.nsf** application.

Listing 16.39 styleClass Properties Referencing the Style Classes Within classes.css

```
<?xml version="1.0" encoding="UTF-8"?>
<xp:view xmlns:xp="http://www.ibm.com/xsp/core">

    <xp:div id="inputText2" themeId="mxpd.number.spinner"></xp:div>

</xp:view>
```

Listing 16.40 shows the resultant HTML markup that is then emitted for the **complex-Properties** XPage. As seen, each of the two `dojoAttributes` and the single `attr` complex properties are bound to the generated `<div>` element.

Listing 16.40 complexProperties Emitted HTML Markup

```
...
<div dojoType="dijit.form.NumberSpinner" value="5" valuemax="10"
valuemin="1"
id="view:_id1:inputText2" largeDelta="0.5"></div>
...
```

Conclusion

This concludes this chapter on XPages theming. In this chapter, you learned a lot about the different ways you can use the features that XPages provides to create and manage presentation logic. Techniques that support inline styling, style classes, and themes all provide different levels of efficiency, productivity, consistency, and flexibility to you, as the developer, when developing and maintaining the look and feel of an application. You now have a better understanding of the benefits and most suitable use cases for employing each available technique.

CHAPTER 17

Application Layout

This chapter takes its lead from the learning material covered in the closing sections of Chapter 10, "Custom Controls," where you learned about the Layout Container and Aggregate Container design patterns. Both of these design patterns are typically used by many XPages developers when constructing an XPages application and are also inherently supported by a number of out-of-the-box controls, particularly the Application Layout control. In this chapter, you learn more about this particular control so that you can fully utilize it for your everyday XPages development.

Before starting on the exercises within this chapter, you are encouraged to download, install, sign, and open the supporting **Chp17Ed2.nsf** application from `www.ibmpressbooks.com/title/9780133373370` within Domino Designer.

Divide and Conquer

Chapter 10 closed by looking at two design patterns, namely the Layout Container design pattern and the Aggregate Container design pattern. These two design patterns lend themselves well to Custom Control construction and reuse tasks within an XPages application design.

But the story about design patterns does not stop there. Indeed, with careful examination, it is easy to recognize many different design patterns that are used within many XPages applications or indeed by some of the XPages controls themselves such as the **Application Layout** control, for example. Even the XPages Runtime is strongly designed and built upon the concepts of the popular Model View Controller or MVC in its acronym form, design pattern.

You look deeper at the Application Layout control shortly, of course, but also be aware that the opposite of a design pattern also exists and is indeed commonly entangled within the design of many XPages applications.

In this case, there is a high degree of poor design and implementation at play that results in extra redundancy and inefficiency within an application. It is essentially what is known as the antipattern. And with careful consideration of the requirements of the use case, a good design pattern can be employed to eliminate the antipattern.

TIP

For more general information on software design patterns, refer to the "Design Patterns: Elements of Reusable Object-Oriented Software," by Erich Gamma, Richard Helm, Ralph Johnson, and John Vlissides (1995). *Design Patterns: Elements of Reusable Object-Oriented Software*. Addison-Wesley. ISBN 0-201-63361-2.

One of the greatest strengths of a design pattern is in introducing formality into the design of an application. The degree of formality can have some degree of flexibility in its implementation of course, but nonetheless the important point to note is that when a developer studies over the source code of an implementation that honors one or more design patterns, it inevitably makes the task of software enhancement and maintenance so much easier. Almost similar to the way in which a software API specification outlines the boundaries of that API, a design pattern establishes certain expectations, knowns, and limitations about the design and implementation of an application, and its software components.

A big part of good application design is all about finding and identifying decomposition within an application design so that it can be broken down into smaller, more manageable parts or units. These smaller units or parts of an application should ideally reflect a high degree of loose coupling to ideally form the basis of the reusable components of the application—in the same way you learned about how the Layout Container and Aggregate Container design patterns support this concept of loose coupling when building Custom Controls. Essentially, good application design and implementation is a game of "divide and conquer" that can be made more productive and maintainable when best practice design patterns are employed.

Application Layout: One Easy Way

Chapter 10 taught you about applying the Layout Container and Aggregate Container design patterns when building Custom Controls. This was very much based upon a ground-up approach that can be quite involved depending on the requirements of your application layout design. However, to make life a little simpler, XPages provides you with the Application Layout control.

The Application Layout is a control that encapsulates a common application layout along with a varied array of computable properties to configure the layout to suit your own application requirements. Within this application layout you can find a range of common layout areas such as a **banner**, **title bar**, **place bar**, **middle**, **footer**, and **legal** areas. All areas are exposed by the control through combinations of properties and **facets** in a similar manner to the **Editable Areas** exposed by a Custom Control honoring the Layout Container design pattern.

This control was added to the XPages Runtime control library based upon the Layout Container and Aggregate Container design patterns—effectively, the XPages team identified the commonality that existed within an application layout during the construction of a particular

XPages template and used that understanding as the basis and inspiration for the **Application Layout** control. This is also true of the **DataView** and **Form Table** controls whereby similar use of the Layout Container and Aggregate Container design patterns using Custom Control implementations within early Discussion and TeamRoom template versions inspired the design and implementation of these dedicated controls. Therefore, this makes it easier for developers to incorporate and build XPages applications based on these design patterns.

Now take a deeper look at the **Application Layout** control. Using Domino Designer, you should create two new XPages within the **Chp17Ed2.nsf** application. You can name these two XPages whatever you like, but for the purposes of this exercise, I am using **appLayout1** and **appLayout2**, respectively, for each XPage. Note that **Chp17Ed2.nsf** already contains a completed version of the **appLayout1** and **appLayout2** XPages for your reference should you want to review the final result of this particular exercise. Next, you can find the **Application Layout** control nestled among the Extension Library category within the Control palette, as shown here in Figure 17.1.

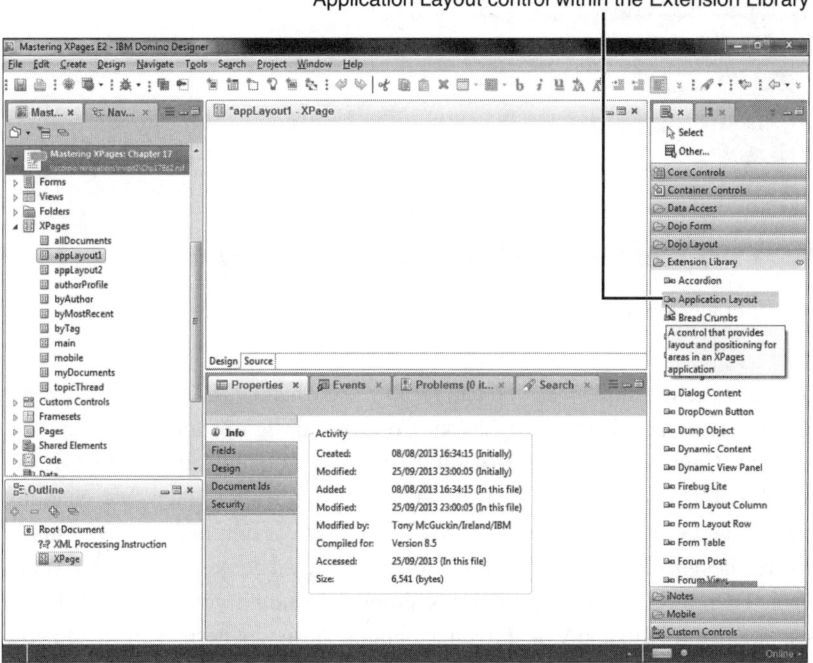

Figure 17.1 The Application Layout control within the Extension Library category

Drag and drop or simply double-click this control to include an instance of it within only one of the two XPages you have newly created. As you do this, you find Domino Designer prompting you that you are attempting to include this control on a top-level XPage, as shown in Figure 17.2.

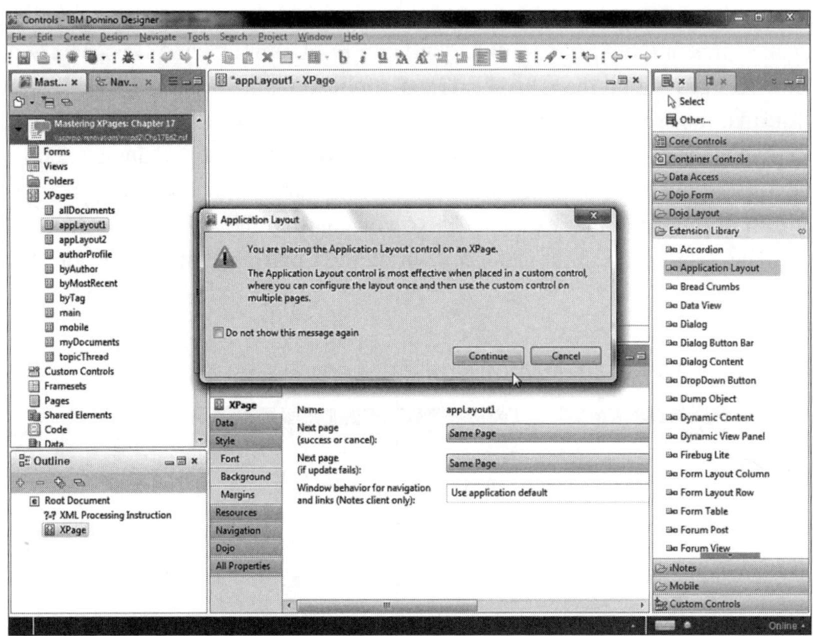

Figure 17.2 Prompt about including the Application Layout control on a top-level XPage

The reason for this is quite simple—as you can recall from Chapter 10, where you learned about the Layout Container design pattern, the Layout Container design pattern is best applied by using a single Custom Control to hold the structural layout of the application. This Custom Control is then shared among one or more XPages within the application, therefore enabling reduction of redundancy and ease of maintenance as the structural design and layout is stored within one single, shared design element. So this is no different when it comes to using the Application Layout control. Therefore, Domino Designer is simply reminding you about this design decision and the best practice way to apply the Layout Container design pattern. You should now cancel including the Application Layout control on your chosen XPage, and instead proceed to create a new Custom Control. Again, the naming is entirely up to you, but I have chosen **layout Container** for the purposes of this exercise, and a completed version of this Custom Control is also included within the **Chp17Ed2.nsf** application for your convenience.

Now you should attempt to include an instance of the Application Layout control on your newly created Custom Control. As you do this, you will notice Domino Designer does not prompt you with the same dialog as it did before. Actually, this time a useful Configuration Wizard dialog appears. This enables you to configure several different areas within the Application Layout control such as the banner, title bar, place bar, middle, footer, and legal areas. In addition, you can also use this wizard to set the application theme that will be used as demonstrated in Figure 17.3.

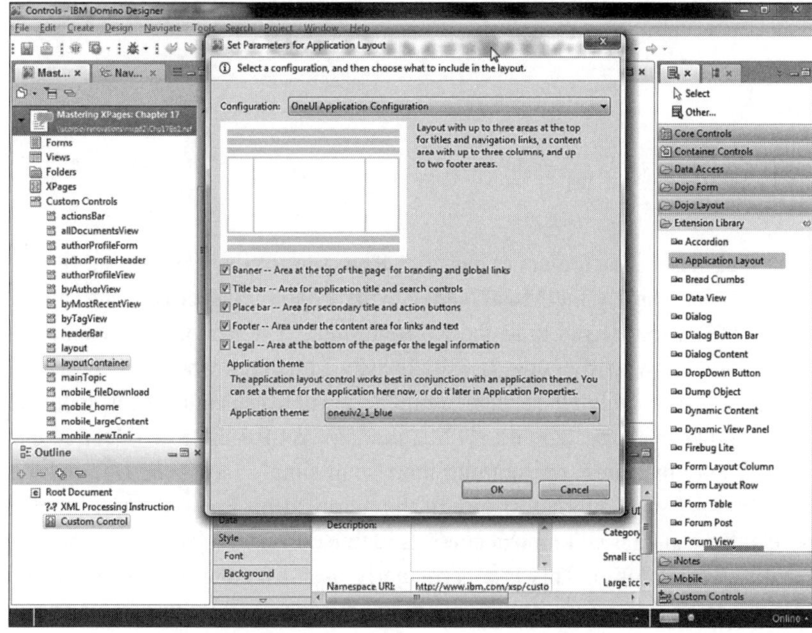

Figure 17.3 Configuration Wizard dialog when including the Application Layout control

In summary, the options within this wizard can be divided into three main sections. The first section enables you to select the configuration of the application layout. Basically, the Application Layout control provides two possible configurations:

- **A Basic Application configuration:** This configuration provides you with a basic grid structure for your application layout. Within this grid structure, there are three possible header areas, two columns for left and right areas, respectively, and two footer areas. All of which can be included within an application layout optionally, and each can have a number of different computable properties and property collections such as drop-down menu options, titles, legal text labels, and so on.

- **A OneUI Application configuration:** This configuration builds upon the basic configuration to provide an IBM OneUI-specific application layout. This ensures that all control renderers that exist within an XPage using this configuration emit HTML and CSS markup based upon the OneUI v2.1 or v3.0.1 specifications, along with the applicable resources, depending on which application theme you select.

The second section enables you to select which areas within the supported grid structure should be included within the application layout. By using this Configuration Wizard dialog, you can include or exclude five different areas based on your requirements:

- Banner
- Title Bar
- Place Bar
- Footer
- Legal

You should note that these areas are not exhaustive. The Application Layout control also supports four additional areas, namely the **MastHeader**, **MastFooter**, **SearchBar**, and a special **Middle** area (sometimes also referred to as the **Content** area). The Middle area cannot be controlled via the Configuration Wizard dialog. It will always be rendered when any child controls exist within this special area. Only when there are no child controls available for inclusion in this area will it be omitted from the emitted HTML markup. As for the **MastHeader** and **MastFooter**, you should note that these are nothing more than simple facets (or **callbacks** if you prefer that terminology). This is another feature of the **Application Layout** control in that it exposes several facets that can be used to inject controls within designated facet areas (or drop targets if you prefer that terminology). This is a particularly useful feature and demonstrated quite well by the **Middle** area. This area is effectively divided into three columns, each having its own facet exposed. There is the **LeftColumn** facet, the **RightColumn** facet, and the unnamed central facet. The reason it is unnamed is to allow it to act as a "collect all" area. That is to say that for any child controls included within an **Application Layout** control as direct children of the control itself, and without any xp:key property binding them to one of the other specific named facets, they will simply be collected and included within the unnamed **Middle** facet area. More on these particular facet areas in a moment, but first here's an explanation of the third and final section within the Configuration Wizard dialog.

The third section enables you to select an XPages Theme that will be used by your application. You can set this option using the wizard dialog at this point, or alternatively you can always visit the **Application Properties > XSP Properties > General > Application Theme** section to do so at a later time. As the label for the Application Theme drop-down combo-box in Figure 17.4 explains, the Application Layout control works best with an XPages Theme. This is due to some of the interdependencies provided by the underlying OneUI themes within the XPages runtime such as resources and **rendererType** settings for controls. This implies that if you are creating a new application theme of your own, you should at least extend one of either the OneUI v2.1 or OneUI v3.0.1 versions to ensure correct rendering of the XPages controls.

For now, you can just leave all the settings as they are within each of the three sections, and select the **OK** button. Having done this, Domino Designer will place an instance of the Application Layout control within your Custom Control. As always is the case when creating XPages and Custom Controls in Domino Designer, it is interesting to view both the Design and Source panes within the WYSIWYG editor. Figure 17.4 shows the Design pane and Listing 17.1 details the underlying XSP markup within the Source pane.

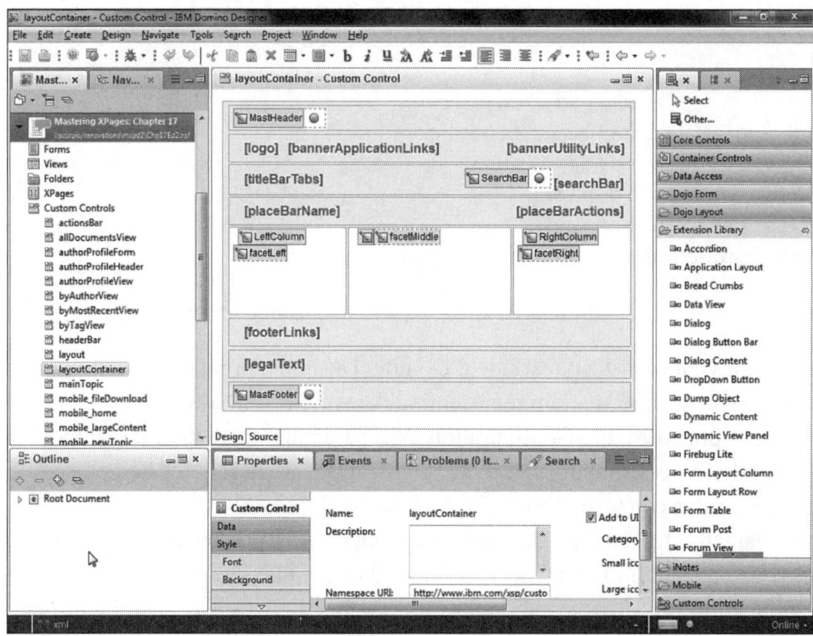

Figure 17.4 layoutContainer Design pane with an instance of the Application Layout control

Listing 17.1 XSP Source Markup for the layoutContainer XPage

```
<?xml version="1.0" encoding="UTF-8"?>
<xp:view xmlns:xp="http://www.ibm.com/xsp/core"
    xmlns:xe="http://www.ibm.com/xsp/coreex">
    <xe:applicationLayout id="applicationLayout1">
        <xe:this.configuration>
            <xe:oneuiApplication>
                <xe:this.footerLinks>
                    <xe:basicContainerNode label="Container 1">
```

```
                    <xe:this.children>
                        <xe:basicLeafNode label="Link 1"
                            href="/"></xe:basicLeafNode>
                        <xe:basicLeafNode label="Link 2"
                            href="/"></xe:basicLeafNode>
                    </xe:this.children>
                </xe:basicContainerNode>
                <xe:basicContainerNode label="Container 2">
                    <xe:this.children>
                        <xe:basicLeafNode label="Link 1"
                            href="/"></xe:basicLeafNode>
                        <xe:basicLeafNode label="Link 2"
                            href="/"></xe:basicLeafNode>
                    </xe:this.children>
                </xe:basicContainerNode>
            </xe:this.footerLinks>
        </xe:oneuiApplication>
    </xe:this.configuration>
  </xe:applicationLayout>
</xp:view>
```

As you can see from your own XSP markup in Domino Designer, or indeed within Listing 17.1, there is now some skeletal XSP markup representing the Application Layout control based upon the default settings applied by the Configuration Wizard dialog. Also note the automatic inclusion of some example **footerLinks** for the footer area—these are purely for demonstration purposes and can be removed if you want during production development.

This is by no means the finished product though—indeed it is just the beginning of the process of defining your application layout. Rest assured, though, that the process to continue fleshing out your application layout from this point onward is relatively easy compared with constructing a layout from scratch using multiple Custom Controls and applying the Layout Container and Aggregate Container design patterns. This is because the process of further describing and enhancing the application layout is down to *property-driven* development. This means that you can use the various Properties editors and All Properties editor for the Application Layout control to quite rapidly and easily further configure the application layout. And as you would naturally expect with XPages, almost all the applicable properties can be either statically defined or computed using EL or ServerSide JavaScript expressions.

Figure 17.5 shows the various Properties editors for the Application Layout control in Domino Designer. These are divided into six distinctly different categories—there is one high-level Application Layout category containing options to include and exclude the different Middle area facets as described earlier—and more on this still to come. This category is then followed by five other categories, one for each of the main areas that are listed in the second section of the Configuration Wizard dialog. And finally, there is the all-encompassing All Properties category.

Now take a moment to look through each of these categories of properties within Domino Designer to become familiarize with the wide range of configuration options.

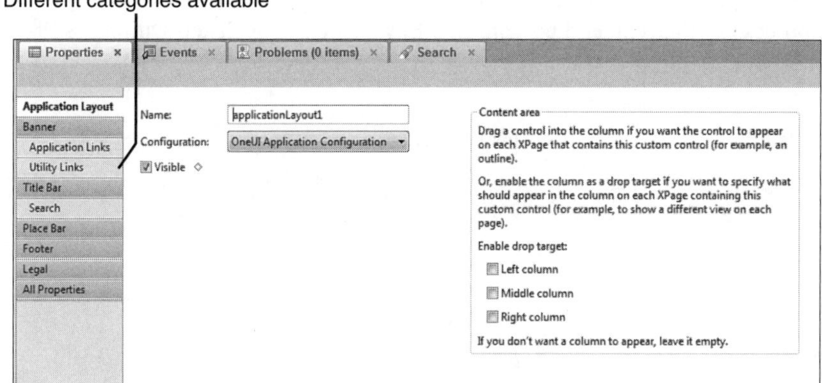

Figure 17.5 The various Properties editors for the Application Layout control

If you take a moment to review the different Properties editors for the Application Layout control, you will undoubtedly realize that there are quite a number of options available to you. Now take a look at a couple of examples. First, click the **Place Bar** properties editor tab, and then add a **Place name** such as "My App" Layout into the edit box. Then click the **Add Item** button, which causes a pop-up menu to appear listing various types of items, as shown in Figure 17.6.

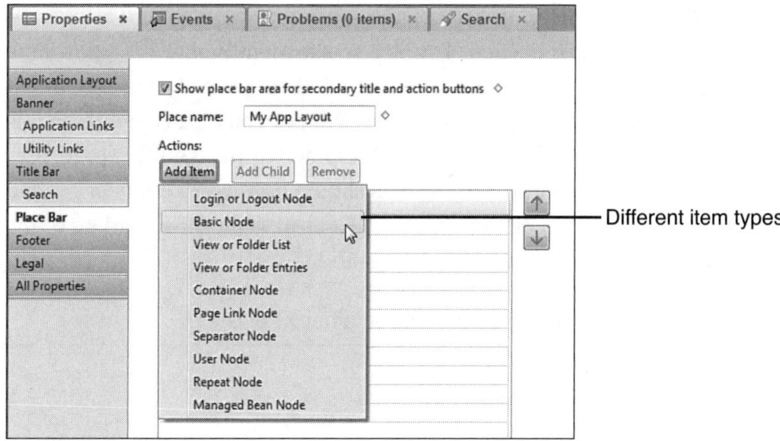

Figure 17.6 Adding a Place name and the list of various item types available

As you can see in Figure 17.6, there are many different item types available, all serving different purposes, of course. Essentially, these encapsulate different behaviors and renderings depending on where they are included within a control tree hierarchy (such as in the banner versus the footer). In this particular example, you should select the **Basic Node** item type. You should repeat the process so that you end up with two Basic Node items listed within the Place Bar actions list, as shown in Figure 17.7.

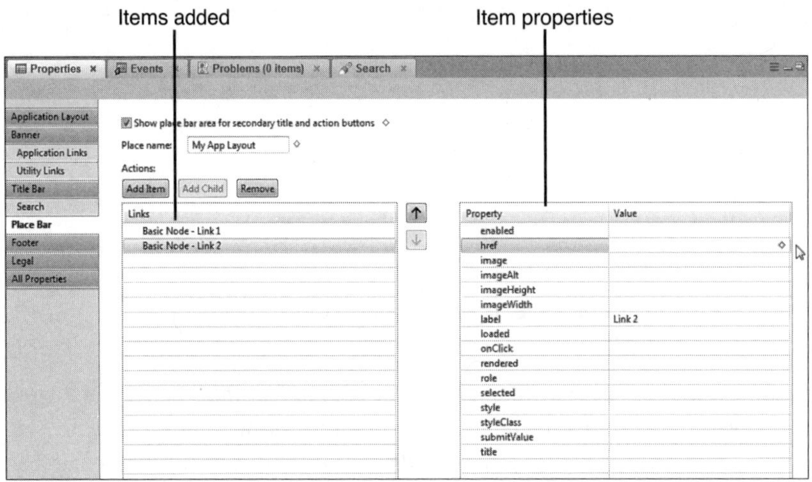

Figure 17.7 Adding two Basic Node items to the Place Bar actions list

After you have done that, you then see an extensive list of properties that are also available for the Basic Node items you have just created. This is also shown in Figure 17.7, down the right side of the figure. So in this instance, you should now set the **href** property for each of the two items you have just created to match the names of the two XPages you created earlier in this exercise. For example, in my case I am setting **appLayout1.xsp** and **appLayout2.xsp**, respectively, for each of the Basic Node items **href** properties. You should now save your changes and have something similar in your own layout container Custom Control to the XSP markup of the **layoutContainer** Custom Control, as detailed here in Listing 17.2.

Listing 17.2 Updated XSP Source Markup for the layoutContainer XPage

```
<?xml version="1.0" encoding="UTF-8"?>
<xp:view xmlns:xp="http://www.ibm.com/xsp/core"
    xmlns:xe="http://www.ibm.com/xsp/coreex">
    <xe:applicationLayout id="applicationLayout1">
        <xe:this.configuration>
            <xe:oneuiApplication>
                <xe:this.footerLinks>
```

```
                    <xe:basicContainerNode label="Container 1">
                        <xe:this.children>
                            <xe:basicLeafNode label="Link 1"
                                href="/"></xe:basicLeafNode>
                            <xe:basicLeafNode label="Link 2"
                                href="/"></xe:basicLeafNode>
                        </xe:this.children>
                    </xe:basicContainerNode>
                    <xe:basicContainerNode label="Container 2">
                        <xe:this.children>
                            <xe:basicLeafNode label="Link 1"
                                href="/"></xe:basicLeafNode>
                            <xe:basicLeafNode label="Link 2"
                                href="/"></xe:basicLeafNode>
                        </xe:this.children>
                    </xe:basicContainerNode>
                </xe:this.footerLinks>
                <xe:this.placeBarActions>
                    <xe:basicLeafNode label="Link 1"
                        href="appLayout1.xsp">
                    </xe:basicLeafNode>
                    <xe:basicLeafNode label="Link 2"
                        href="appLayout2.xsp">
                    </xe:basicLeafNode>
                </xe:this.placeBarActions>
            </xe:oneuiApplication>
        </xe:this.configuration>
    </xe:applicationLayout>
</xp:view>
```

Now go back to each of the two XPages you created earlier and either drag and drop, click-drop, or double-click your application layout container Custom Control onto each XPage. Again in my case, I include the **layoutContainer** Custom Control on **appLayout1** and **appLayout2** XPages before saving my changes to each XPage. If you view the XSP markup for each XPage, you should see something similar to that of Listing 17.3 for the **appLayout1** XPage, bar the change of layout container Custom Control tag-name you may have chosen.

Listing 17.3 XSP source markup for the appLayout1 XPage

```
<?xml version="1.0" encoding="UTF-8"?>
<xp:view xmlns:xp="http://www.ibm.com/xsp/core"
    xmlns:xp="http://www.ibm.com/xsp/custom">
    <xc:layoutContainer></xc:layoutContainer>
</xp:view>
```

So as you can see in Listing 17.3, there is nothing surprising about the XSP markup—it simply defines a basic XPage that now contains a single Custom Control. With these changes in place and saved, you should now proceed to preview or view the newly created XPages that are harnessing the application layout container Custom Control using the XPiNC browser or your own preferred browsing experience. An example of this for the **appLayout1** XPage can be seen in Figure 17.8.

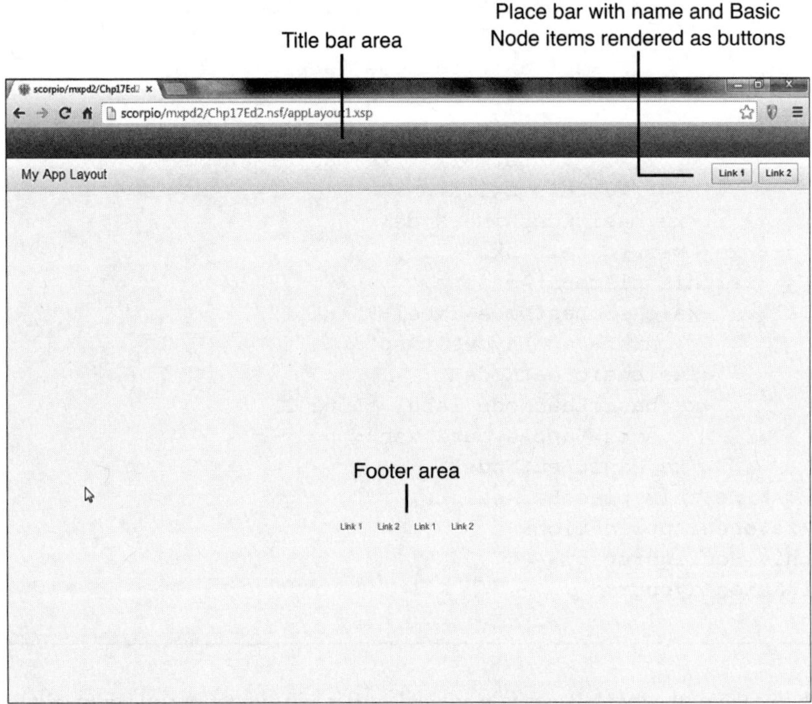

Figure 17.8 The appLayout1 XPage previewed in a browser

When you preview, you should note how the different areas of the application layout have been rendered to display only the **title bar**, **place bar**, and **footer** areas as also seen in Figure 17.8—no other areas appear at this time because there is either no content or properties configured within those areas to warrant emitting HTML markup for them. For instance, because we did not configure any properties for the **legal** area, it simply does not get rendered. Likewise at this point, there is no Middle (or Content) area being rendered because we did not declare any content for it either—we will in a few moments, though.

You can now take this opportunity to test out the two Basic Node items that appear within the Place Bar by clicking on either of these. If you have configured the **href** property correctly for each of them, you should find yourself navigating between the two XPages you created earlier in this exercise. The interesting point to note here is how these Basic Node items have been rendered contextually to appear as Buttons within the Place Bar area—this is something that is being taken care of automatically for you by the underlying Application Layout renderers. In fact, if you try setting the same Basic Node items within the Banner area, they will be rendered automatically to appear as Links in that area—further demonstrating the convenience afforded to you by the Application Layout control to make you more productive when it comes to creating an application layout. Hence, you are freed up to concentrate more on the all important logic of an application instead of lower level rendering details within the application presentation logic.

In summary at this point, there is one single Custom Control that now contains the application layout, and this is shared across two individual XPages. This now allows you to make changes to the underlying application layout using a property-driven approach as used earlier in this exercise, and to see those changes immediately reflected across both XPages. Therefore, this provides you with a low-maintenance, easy way to enhance your application. In essence this demonstrates the benefits of applying the Layout Container design pattern within an application. But what about adding specific content for each individual XPage when using the Application Layout control approach? Well, that is where the Aggregate Container design pattern can also be used to complement the abilities of your application layout Custom Control, and this is done by using some of those facets mentioned earlier.

So you should now go back to your application layout container Custom Control in Domino Designer. And in this instance, you should go to the Application Layout properties editor tab, and check all three of the drop target check boxes within the Content area pane, as shown here in Figure 17.9.

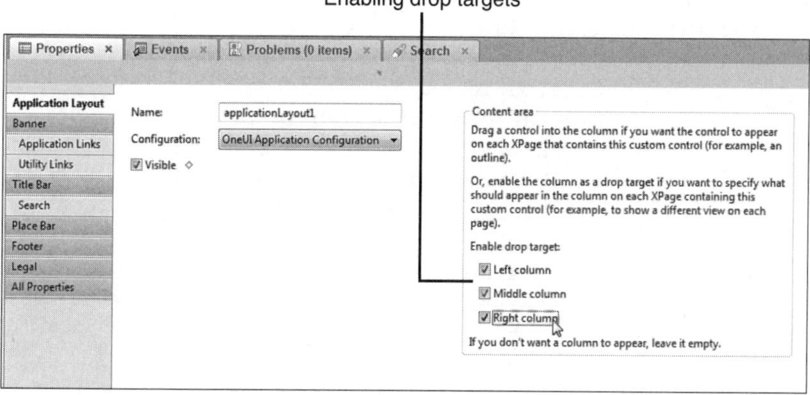

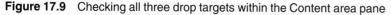

Figure 17.9 Checking all three drop targets within the Content area pane

The net result of checking each of these check boxes results in nine new lines of XSP markup being injected into the Application Layout control instance, as detailed in Listing 17.4. Effectively, this new XSP source markup declares three new facets (or callbacks) named **facetMiddle**, **facetLeft**, and **facetRight** that are now exposed by the Application Layout instance. This, of course, means that within each of the two XPages currently dependant upon the **layoutContainer** Custom Control, they can now avail of these new drop target areas. Therefore, additional controls and/or other Custom Controls can be included independently into the application layout within each individual XPage.

Listing 17.4 Updated XSP Source Markup for the layoutContainer XPage with Drop Targets Included

```
<?xml version="1.0" encoding="UTF-8"?>
<xp:view xmlns:xp="http://www.ibm.com/xsp/core"
    xmlns:xe="http://www.ibm.com/xsp/coreex">
    <xe:applicationLayout id="applicationLayout1">
        <xp:callback facetName="facetMiddle"
➥id="facetMiddle"></xp:callback>
        <xe:this.facets>
            <xp:callback facetName="facetRight" id="facetRight"
                xp:key="RightColumn">
            </xp:callback>
            <xp:callback facetName="facetLeft" id="facetLeft"
                xp:key="LeftColumn">
            </xp:callback>
        </xe:this.facets>
        <xe:this.configuration>
            <xe:oneuiApplication>
                <xe:this.footerLinks>
                    <xe:basicContainerNode label="Container 1">
                        <xe:this.children>
                            <xe:basicLeafNode label="Link 1"
                                href="/"></xe:basicLeafNode>
                            <xe:basicLeafNode label="Link 2"
                                href="/"></xe:basicLeafNode>
                        </xe:this.children>
                    </xe:basicContainerNode>
                    <xe:basicContainerNode label="Container 2">
                        <xe:this.children>
                            <xe:basicLeafNode label="Link 1"
                                href="/"></xe:basicLeafNode>
                            <xe:basicLeafNode label="Link 2"
                                href="/"></xe:basicLeafNode>
```

```
                        </xe:this.children>
                    </xe:basicContainerNode>
                </xe:this.footerLinks>
                <xe:this.placeBarActions>
                    <xe:basicLeafNode label="Link 1"
                        href="appLayout1.xsp">
                    </xe:basicLeafNode>
                    <xe:basicLeafNode label="Link 2"
                        href="appLayout2.xsp">
                    </xe:basicLeafNode>
                </xe:this.placeBarActions>
            </xe:oneuiApplication>
        </xe:this.configuration>
    </xe:applicationLayout>
</xp:view>
```

The difference this makes can also be seen within the Design pane for either of the XPages that depend upon the application layout container Custom Control by comparing the visual WYSIWYG design of the latest versions of these XPages with that of Figure 17.4 from earlier in this exercise. In this case, the Application Layout control in Figure 17.4 does not include the three new facets as exposed in the latest updated version of the same XPage. The significance of this means there is no way to include custom content within the application layout structure in the earlier versions of each XPage. Whereas in the latest version that does expose the drop targets, there are named facet areas visible within the Design pane, and these contain all-important small green circles. These small green circles denote the presence of available drop target areas.

Using each of the two XPages, you should now add Label controls into each drop target area. In doing so, you should set the Label value to be indicative of its owning XPage and drop target area names (for example, appLayout1 - facetLeft). When you next preview your changes, this will help to demonstrate how each XPage and drop target uses custom content accordingly to inject that content into the intended area within the overall application layout for each individual XPage. After making these changes to your own XPages, you should have XSP markup similar to my **appLayout1** and **appLayout2** XPages as detailed here for **appLayout1.xsp** in Listing 17.5.

Listing 17.5 XSP Source Markup for the appLayout1 XPage Using Drop Target Areas

```
<?xml version="1.0" encoding="UTF-8"?>
<xp:view xmlns:xp="http://www.ibm.com/xsp/core"
    xmlns:xp="http://www.ibm.com/xsp/custom">
    <xc:layoutContainer>
        <xp:this.facets>
```

```
            <xp:label id="label3" xp:key="facetRight"
                value="appLayout1 - facetRight"></xp:label>
            <xp:label id="label2" xp:key="facetMiddle"
                value="appLayout1 - facetMiddle"></xp:label>
            <xp:label id="label1" xp:key="facetLeft"
                value="appLayout1 - facetLeft">
            </xp:label>
        </xp:this.facets>
    </xc:layoutContainer>
</xp:view>
```

You should now proceed to preview the two XPages again. This time around you should see the Middle content area being rendered along with each of the indicative Label controls. Figure 17.10 shows an example of this for the **appLayout1** XPage.

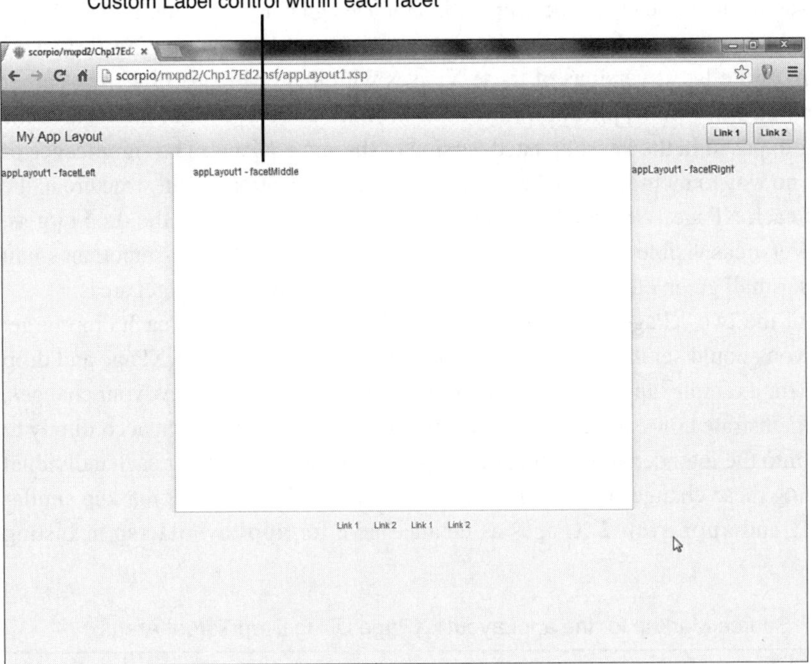

Figure 17.10 Preview of the appLayout1 XPage including three drop targets and label contents

The use of Label controls in this exercise is purely for simplicity. In a production development scenario, it would be more typical to add Custom Controls into these facet areas. Such

Custom Controls would be encapsulations of different functional elements within the application layout structure (for example, Profile Viewer, Calendar, Mini-Form, TagCloud, and so on)—all honoring the Aggregate Container design pattern. And it is also important to realize that the possibilities for further definition and exposure of additional facet areas (or drop targets), is always possible even within nested Custom Controls in this scenario by using the Editable Area control (**<xp:callback/>**). Therefore, you are not bounded by the predefined set of drop targets already available on the Application Layout control should you have requirements to go beyond this.

Application Layout: Customizing the Content Area

Now move away now from the previous exercise to look at a more advanced use of the content area within the Application Layout control. For this examination exercise, you should open the **allDocuments** and **byMostRecent** XPages and the layout Custom Control from the **Chp17Ed2.nsf** application, inside Domino Designer. All three of these design elements are based upon their respective Discussion 9.0.1 template definitions and illustrate a worked example of using the Application Layout control. You should also take a moment to preview these XPages.

For the benefit of the reader without preview access at this point, Figure 17.11 shows the **allDocuments** XPage, and Figure 17.12 shows the **byMostRecent** XPage. These figures show the Content area for each rendered XPage.

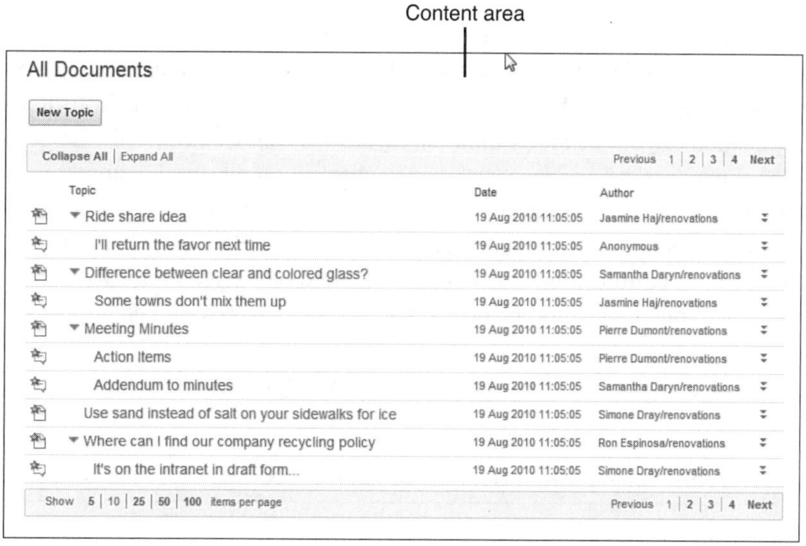

Figure 17.11 Preview of the allDocuments XPage containing the Content area

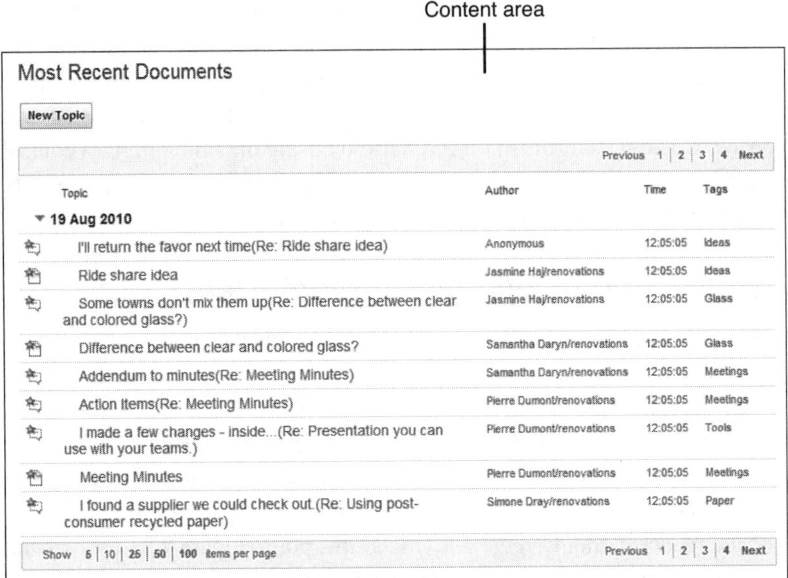

Figure 17.12 Preview of the byMostRecent XPage containing the Content area

Note that the same design pattern has been used here, in that a single Custom Control holds the application layout logic and is shared across several XPages within the application. The key difference, however, is in the way in which the existing and newly defined additional facets have been used on the Application Layout control within the **layout** Custom Control. This use goes beyond just having the three drop target area check boxes checked on the Application Layout property editor tab to provide custom content within each of the Middle (or Content) areas at the Application Layout control level but furthermore, also within each individual XPage. Therefore, allowing augmentation of custom content at both levels based on the requirements of each individual XPage and the overall application layout design. How this works is explained in the remainder of this section.

Listing 17.6 details a fragment of XSP source markup taken from the `allDocuments` XPage.

Listing 17.6 Fragment of XSP Source Markup for the allDocuments XPage

```
<?xml version="1.0" encoding="UTF-8"?>
<xp:view xmlns:xp="http://www.ibm.com/xsp/core"
    xmlns:xp="http://www.ibm.com/xsp/custom" ...
    <xc:layout navigationPath="/allDocuments.xsp">
        <xc:headerBar id="headerBar"
            displayType="#{javascript:DISPLAY_ALL_DOCUMENTS}">
        </xc:headerBar>
```

```
        <xc:actionsBar id="actionsBar"></xc:actionsBar>
        <xp:panel id="refreshRegion">
            <xc:mainTopic id="mainTopic" gotoPage="/allDocuments.xsp"
                loaded="${javascript:getDisplayFormType() == 1}">
            </xc:mainTopic>
            <xc:allDocumentsView id="allDocumentsView"
                refreshId="refreshRegion"
                loaded="${javascript:getDisplayFormType() == null}" ...>
            </xc:allDocumentsView>
        </xp:panel>
    </xc:layout>
</xp:view>
```

In Listing 17.6, note that no facets are utilized on the <xc:layout/> element even though it does have child elements nested within it such as the <xc:headerBar/>, <xc:actionsBar/>, and so on. To further illustrate this, also review the fragment of XSP source markup taken from the **byMostRecent** XPage in Listing 17.7.

Listing 17.7 Fragment of XSP Source Markup for the byMostRecent XPage

```
<?xml version="1.0" encoding="UTF-8"?>
<xp:view xmlns:xp="http://www.ibm.com/xsp/core"
    xmlns:xp="http://www.ibm.com/xsp/custom" ...
    <xc:layout navigationPath="/byMostRecent.xsp">
        <xc:headerBar id="headerBar"
            displayType="#{javascript:DISPLAY_BY_MOST_RECENT}">
        </xc:headerBar>
        <xc:actionsBar id="actionsBar"></xc:actionsBar>
        <xp:panel id="refreshRegion">
            <xc:mainTopic id="mainTopic" gotoPage="/byMostRecent.xsp"
                loaded="${javascript:getDisplayFormType() == 1}">
            </xc:mainTopic>
            <xc:byMostRecentView id="byMostRecentView"
                loaded="${javascript:getDisplayFormType() == null}" ...>
            </xc:byMostRecentView>
        </xp:panel>
    </xc:layout>
</xp:view>
```

Again, in Listing 17.7, we can see that the **byMostRecent** XPage also uses the **<xc:layout/>** application layout Custom Control, but there is also no utilization of facets on the <xc:layout/> element, even though it does have child elements nested within it. If you recall from our previous exercise, we checked all three of the drop target area check boxes to expose the **facetMiddle**,

facetLeft, and **facetRight** areas on our application layout Custom Control. This allowed us to then add custom Label controls into each area independently for each XPage. As a reminder of this, Listing 17.4 details the XSP source markup complete with the defined facets on the **layoutContainer** Custom Control. In addition, Listing 17.5 details the XSP source markup of the **appLayout1** XPage—this clearly shows how the facets are used within the XPage to associate content with the different drop target areas.

So why does the **<xc:layout/>** application layout Custom Control not use these same facets within the **allDocuments** and **byMostRecent** XPages, yet custom child content is nested within the element? Well, the answer for this lies within the **layout** Custom Control itself and has already been alluded to earlier in this chapter when a description of the second section within the Configuration Wizard dialog was given. This described how the special "unnamed" area can automatically collect child elements for inclusion within the content area. Now look a little deeper at this within the **layout** Custom Control in Domino Designer. Listing 17.8 also contains a fragment of XSP source markup that illustrates this for your convenience.

Listing 17.8 Fragment of XSP Source Markup for the Layout Custom Control

```
<?xml version="1.0" encoding="UTF-8"?>
<xp:view xmlns:xp="http://www.ibm.com/xsp/core"...
    ...
    <xe:applicationLayout id="oneUILayout1">
        <xe:this.configuration>
            <xe:oneuiApplication ...>
                ...
            </xe:oneuiApplication>
        </xe:this.configuration>
        <xe:this.facets>
            <xp:div xp:key="LeftColumn">
                <xc:viewMenu id="viewMenu"></xc:viewMenu>
                <xp:panel styleClass="layoutPanel">
                    <xp:section id="tagCloudSection" ...>
                        <xe:tagCloud alternateText="{0} documents"
➥id="tagCloud"
                            ...
                        </xe:tagCloud>
                    </xp:section>
                    <xp:br></xp:br>
                    <xp:section id="authorCloudSection" ...>
                        <xe:tagCloud alternateText="{0} documents"
➥id="authorCloud"
                            ...
                        </xe:tagCloud>
                    </xp:section>
                </xp:panel>
```

```
                <xp:callback id="leftColumnFacetEx"
                    facetName="LeftColumn">
                </xp:callback>
            </xp:div>
            <xp:callback id="rightColumnFacetEx" xp:key="RightColumn"
                facetName="RightColumn">
            </xp:callback>
        </xe:this.facets>
        <xp:callback id="middleColumnFacetEx"
➥xp:key="MiddleColumn"></xp:callback>
    </xe:applicationLayout>
    ...
</xp:view>
```

So if you study Listing 17.8, or the actual XSP source markup for the **layout** Custom Control within Domino Designer, you can see that an instance of the Application Layout control is defined. This control also defines its <xe:this.facets/> collection that ultimately declares each of the facets that are utilized by this control.

As seen in the XSP source markup, the first child element within the facets collection is the <xp:div xp:key="LeftColumn"/> element. Effectively, this is stipulating that a **<xp:div/>** control is bound to the **LeftColumn** facet area. Being an **<xp:div/>** element, of course, means that it can wrap other content and act as a container as such. This is exactly what it is doing as this element itself has a number of child elements including the **<xc:viewMenu/>** Custom Control, an **<xp:panel/>** control that holds two **TagCloud** controls, and finally another **<xp:callback/>** (or Editable Area) of its own. And as you can see in Listing 17.8, this Editable Area exposes itself with the same name, "`LeftColumn`", as the current facet.

In effect, this demonstrates an overriding capability whereby you can extend a facet directly on the Application Layout control but still hook in another Editable Area to allow further customization at the XPage level. The **RightColumn** facet is not providing any overriding or customization at the Application Layout level; it is simply exposing the **RightColumn** facet to individual XPages should they require it.

And finally, you can see the last **<xp:callback/>** declared within Listing 17.8 for the **MiddleColumn** facet. This is the "collect all" facet that allows the **allDocuments** and **byMostRecent** XPages to simply nest child content directly into the **<xp:layout/>** application layout Custom Control without the explicit need to bind to any particular facet. If you compare Listing 17.5 for the **layoutContainer** Custom Control in the previous exercise, or indeed review the smaller fragment for the same, in Listing 17.9, you should note the presence of the **facetName** property on the Editable Area tag.

Listing 17.9 Fragment of XSP Markup for the facetMiddle <xp:callback/> in layoutContainer.xsp

```
<?xml version="1.0" encoding="UTF-8"?>
    ...
    <xp:callback facetName="facetMiddle" ...></xp:callback>
    ...
</xp:view>
```

And if you compare this with the **MiddleColumn** facet declared in Listing 17.8, or here in a smaller fragment for the same, in Listing 17.10, you can see that it does not declare the **facetName** property but instead binds itself to the **MiddleColumn** facet explicitly using the special **xp:key** attribute. If you try to configure callback facets like this, you should use only the XSP Source pane as the Design pane will not support you in creating this level of indirection. This in turns allows the **MiddleColumn** to then act as a facet within the Middle (or Content) area that will consume any child elements of the application layout container that are not already directly bound to any other specific facet.

Listing 17.10 Fragment of XSP Markup for the MiddleColumn <xp:callback/> in layout.xsp

```
<?xml version="1.0" encoding="UTF-8"?>
    ...
    <xp:callback xp:key="MiddleColumn" ...></xp:callback>
    ...
</xp:view>
```

You should now appreciate that the Application Layout control is quite a powerful and extensive control. It provides a wide range of properties and features out-of-the-box but in turn also supports the idea of further extension by way of drop target areas and custom facets.

This examination of the Application Layout control has by no means covered all the available configuration options of this control. Therefore, you are strongly encouraged to take your lead from this initial study to further investigate and prototype with it to broaden your understanding of it. As a further sideline activity, you should also review how it is used within the corresponding TeamRoom 9.0.1 template that comes out-of-the-box with a Notes/Domino 9.0.1 installation.

Conclusion

This concludes your lesson on Application Layout and some of the design patterns that are useful to everyday XPages development. In the next chapter, Chapter 18, "Internationalization," you learn about the capabilities that XPages provides you with for building localized applications that are ready to serve diverse international end users. This will then conclude the chapters within Part V, "Application User Experience," of this book.

CHAPTER 18

Internationalization

Internationalization refers to the process whereby you prepare your application for users from varied geographies. There are two parts to this:

1. Localization
2. International enablement

The need for localization is obvious; a German user wants to see an application in German and a French user in French, and so on. Localization involves making different language versions of all the application's user interface available and ensuring the correct strings are used based on user preferences. Some programming models require that you think about localization upfront and instead of just inserting strings directly into your application, you must instead enter keys that reference the actual strings from a separate resource file. In this chapter, you see that XPages provides a mechanism that allows you to create your application in your native language and then translate it later. This mechanism covers everything you might need to translate so you also learn how to handle some of the more complex translation requirements.

International enablement on the other hand can be more subtle—different geographies have their own locale specific conventions, such as how dates and numbers are displayed. You might also need to change page layout, such as right to left versus left to right and even images/colors as part of your international enablement. This chapter deals with both the translation and international enablement of XPages. You learn how to use the features provided by Domino Designer to translate your XPages and how to ensure your XPages application is fully internationalized. Be sure to download the .nsf file provided online for this book to run through the exercises throughout the chapter. There are two .nsf files for this chapter: **Chp18Ed2.nsf** and **Chp18Ed2_untranslated.nsf**. If you want to follow along and perform the steps outlined in this chapter, use the untranslated version; if you want to see the end results, use the translated version. You can access these files at `www.ibmpressbooks.com/title/9780133373370`.

Using Localization Options

The starting point for this section is where you have an application containing some XPages in which you have entered all the labels, messages, and other UI elements in your native language, such as English. This is a natural way to create your application and allows you to make a lot of progress quickly. Figure 18.1 shows a sample XPage, and you can see that the labels are all English strings. If you are following along with the accompanying .nsf files, refer to the untranslated version, **Chp18Ed2_untranslated.nsf**.

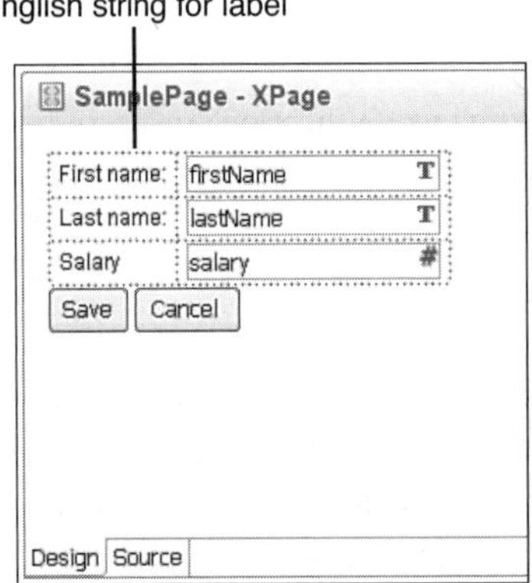

Figure 18.1 Sample XPage

If you use the Package Explorer view to look at the associated Java file (for example, SamplePage.java), you see that the English strings are hard-coded into the Java code. Figure 18.2 shows the string "First name:" being set for one of the labels.

Now, you want to provide translations for these pages to support some other countries, such as Arabic, Chinese, and German. The procedure to add support for additional languages is as follows:

1. Edit the application's **Localization Options** to specify the languages your application supports; go to **Application Configuration > Application Properties > XPages > Localization Options**. Refer to the translated version of the accompanying .nsf file, **Chp18Ed2.nsf**.
2. Optionally, you can now generate a pseudo translation of your application for testing purposes by choosing **Project** > **Clean** and rebuilding the project. The properties files are generated in the XPages folder and can be seen when you view the project in the **Package Explorer**. A property file is generated from each language selected in the **Application Properties**.

3. Export a set of property bundles containing the source strings that need to be translated and send out for translation.
4. Import the translated property bundles and test the translated version of your application.

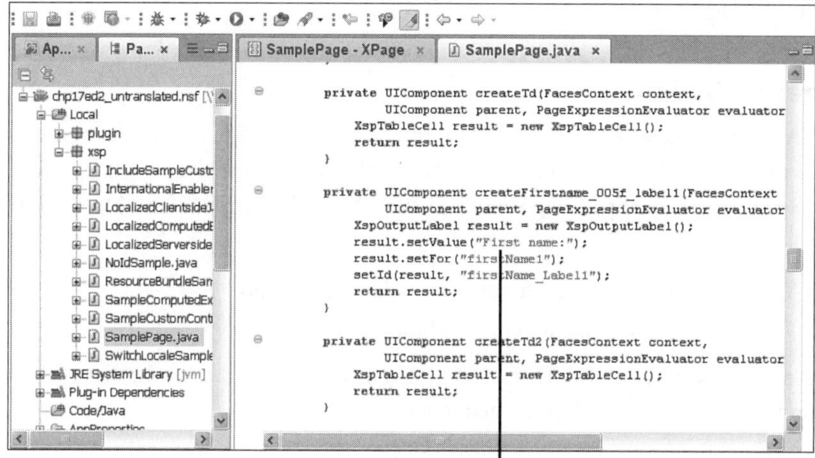

Figure 18.2 Hardcoded English string

Localization with Resource Bundle Files

XPages uses resource bundle files for managing the translated strings for each language, so all the strings for a particular language are stored in its own resource bundle file. A resource bundle file is a text file with the extension `.properties`, where each line is either:

- A key/value pair in the format `<key>=<value>`.
- Blank lines, which are ignored.
- A comment, which are lines starting with the '#' character.

The Java programming language also uses resource bundles to handle translations, and a full description of this mechanism can be found by searching the web for the article, "Java Internationalization: Localization with Resource Bundles" (see `www.ibm.com/developerworks/java/tutorials/j-i18n/section5.html`).

Each language has its own resource bundle file and a special naming convention identifies the correct file to load: `<base file name>_<locale identifier>`. In XPages, the resource bundle file has the same name as its corresponding XPage so the French translations for a page called `SamplePage.xsp` is stored in `SamplePage_fr.properties`. A locale identifier can specify more than just the language (for example, there are two variations of Portuguese spoken in the world, one in Portugal and one Brazil). To distinguish between these two variations, the following locale identifiers are used:

- **Portuguese (Brazil):** pt_BR
- **Portuguese (Portugal):** pt_PT

Setting Localization Options

To add support for Arabic, Chinese, and German in addition to the language the application was written in (English, in this example), you must edit the Application Properties as follows (use the untranslated version of the accompanying sample [**Chp18Ed2_untranslated.nsf**] when performing these steps):

1. Open the Application Properties editor and go to the **XPages** tab.
2. Select the checkbox to enable localization for your application.
3. Use the **Add** button to add Arabic, Chinese, English, and German to the list of languages for which property bundles are generated.
4. Select the source language, which is the language you are using when creating your application, in this case English.
5. Leave the language as being the source language in this case. Note that if you create your application in a language that is not intended as the default, you can set the default language here.

The default language is the one that is used if the user's preferred locale cannot be determined or is a locale that is not supported by the application. For example, if a French user tries to access this application, she sees English strings. Figure 18.3 shows the localization options as they should appear when you complete these steps.

To get the new localization options to take effect, you must clean and rebuild the project, as follows:

1. Select the **Project > Clean** option.
2. In the **Clean** dialog, select the option to **Clean projects selected below** and select your application, as shown in Figure 18.4.
3. Selecting **OK** causes the project-derived artifacts to be removed and rebuilt.

Cleaning the project causes the property bundle files required for translation to be created. It also causes all the XPages and Custom Controls to be resigned.

After the clean and rebuild process completes, the application contains resource bundle files for each of the languages you configured in the localization options. The resource bundle file names for the language versions are constructed as follows: `<XPage base file name>_<locale identifier>.properties`. The resource bundle filename for the default language is simply `<XPage base file name>.properties`. The generated resource bundle files are in the same directory as the associated XPage, and you can use the Package Explorer view to see them.

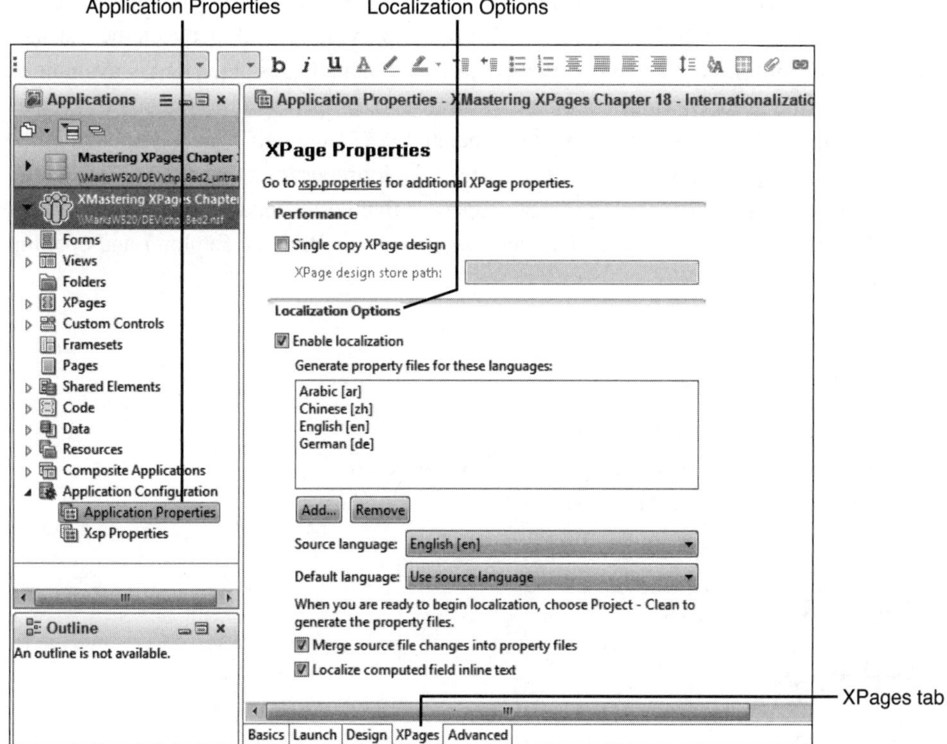

Figure 18.3 Localization options

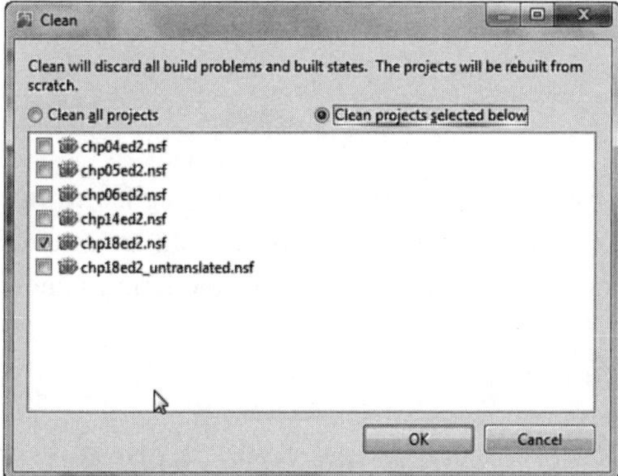

Figure 18.4 Cleaning the project

Figure 18.5 shows the resource bundle files for the sample XPage shown earlier and the contents of the default language file. You can see that the keys are generated from a combination of the control ID and the property name for which the string applies. If the control does not have an ID and the control contains translatable attributes, the builder still adds keys to the properties file for those controls, and an XPath expression is used to provide the link between the translatable string and the control. For each property associated with an XPages tag, a flag is maintained to specify whether the property value should be localized. All property values that are flagged as localizable automatically are extracted and an associated key/value pair is added to each property resource bundle. Unfortunately, no list specifies which properties support localization and which don't. The general rule of thumb is that properties that correspond to user visible strings are extracted. You can find the resource bundles by going to the Package Explorer and opening the XPages folder.

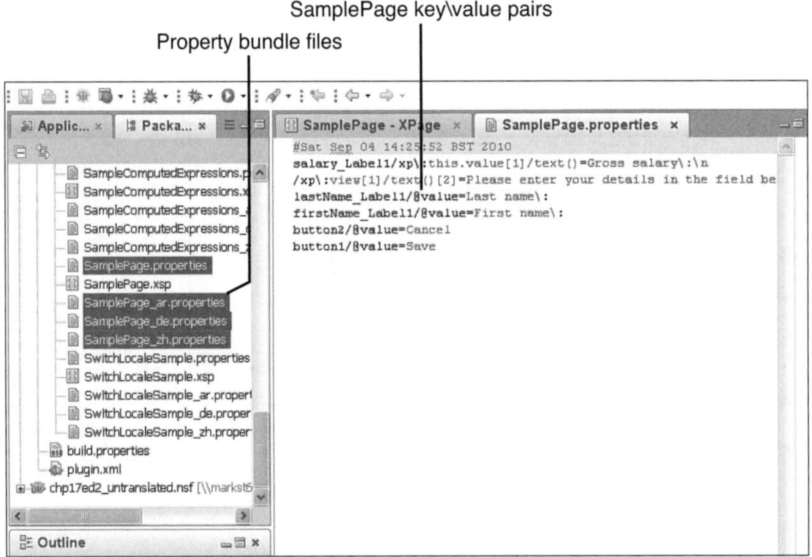

Figure 18.5 Resource bundle files

Now, if you look at the associated Java file for the XPage, you see that the English strings are no longer hardcoded into the Java code. Instead, each string is referenced from an array of strings that contain the translations for the current locale. Figure 18.6 shows the string is now being set for the label you looked at earlier.

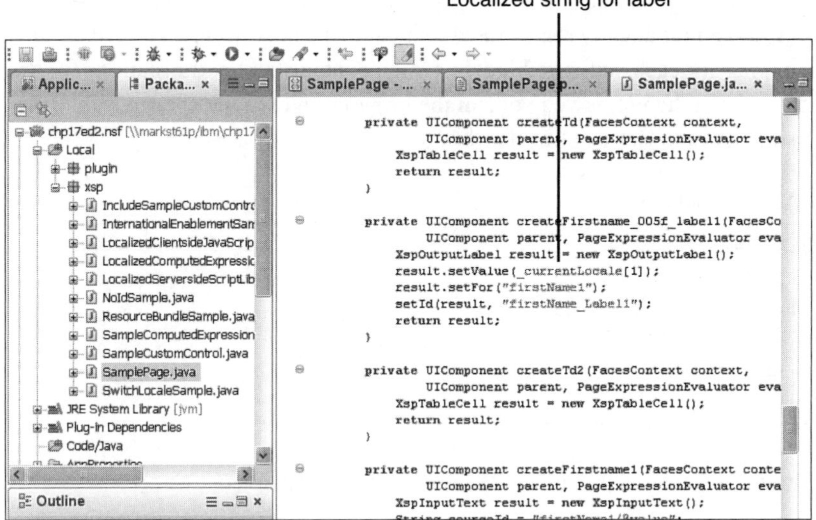

Figure 18.6 Localized string

Testing a Localized Application

The resource bundle files for the non-source languages contain pseudo translations in the format `"[[locale identifier]| [original source string]]"`. This allows you to test the internationalization support in your application. You can preview the application in a browser that is configured to use one of the supported languages and the XPages appear with the pseudo translations (see Figure 18.7). If there are parts of your application where the automatic string extraction has not been able to locate a string that needs to be localized, you see this in the preview. This can happen when using Custom Controls or when computing labels using JavaScript.

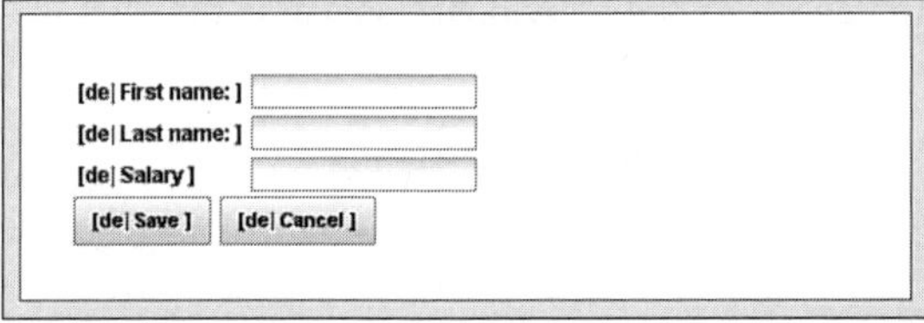

Figure 18.7 Browser preview with psuedo translations

You can edit the resource bundle file for a particular language and, when you save the file, the XPage Java file is automatically regenerated to include the new strings. The XPage Java file contains a string array for each supported locale, which contains all the translations for that locale. Then, you can refresh the previewed page in the browser and see the change right away. Listing 18.1 shows some sample German translations.

Listing 18.1 German Translations

```
#Fri Mar 15 10:44:44 GMT 2013
firstName_Label1/@value=Vorname:
lastName_Label1/@value=Nachname:
button1/@value=Speichern
button2/@value=Abbrechen
salary_Label1/@value=Gehalt:
```

Figure 18.8 shows the updated preview with the German translations.

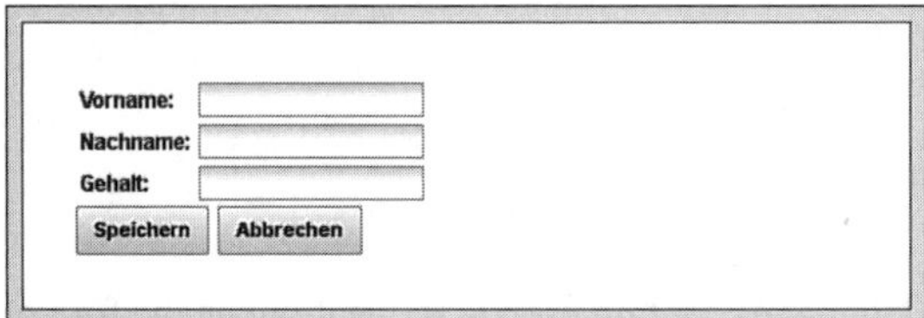

Figure 18.8 Browser preview with German translations

Working with Translators

If you are doing all the translations yourself, editing the resource bundle files within Domino Designer is probably going to be just fine. More likely is that you are dealing with individual translators or a translation agency who in turn deals with the individual translators for each language. The recommended approach now is that you do the following:

1. Export all the resource bundle files and send them out for translation.
2. Import the translated resource bundle files and test your application.

Exporting Resource Bundle Files

There is an export feature available using the Package Explorer view. Switch to this view and follow these steps:

1. Right-click the root element of the project and then select **Export**.
2. Expand the **General** option, select **File System**, and click **Next**.

3. Select the **Filter Types** button, select the ***.properties** option, and click **OK**.
4. All the folders that contain files with a `.properties` extension remain selected. There are some `.properties` files you should not send to the translators: `build. properties` in the root folder, `xsp.properties` in the `\WebContent\WEB-INF` folder, and `database.properties`, `xspdesign.properties` in the `\App Properties` folder. Deselect both of these.
5. Specify the directory to export to in the **To directory** edit control.
6. Select the **Create directory structure for files** option and select **Finish** to export the files.

Figure 18.9 shows the Export dialog and the files which should be exported to do the translations of `SamplePage.xsp`.

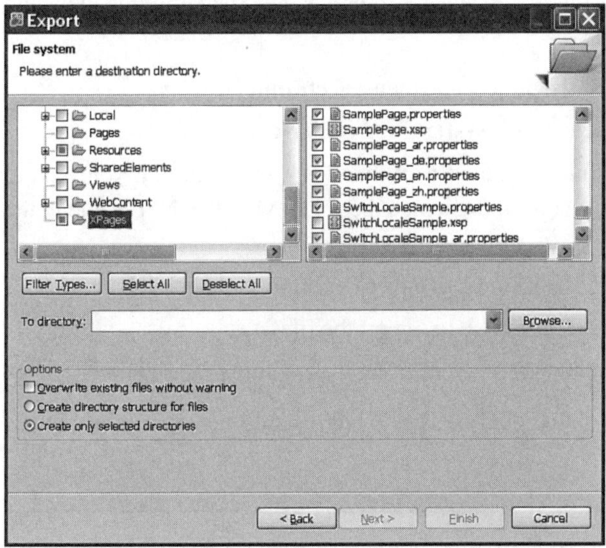

Figure 18.9 Resource Bundle Export using Package Explorer

The contents of the exported folder are now ready to be sent out from translation. It is important that you maintain this directory structure as it is needed for the import procedure to work correctly.

One more thing about property bundle files that you need to understand is that they should only contain ASCII and/or Unicode escape sequences to represent Unicode characters. This is because there is no way to specify the character set being used in the file. Many JVMs ship with a tool called **native2ascii.exe**. This tool will convert all non-ASCII characters to their Unicode code points using the specified locale. So, for the preceding sample, the translated resource bundle file for Chinese looks something like the translations shown in Listing 18.2. These are some free translations I looked up on the web, so please excuse any inaccuracies.

Listing 18.2 Chinese Translations

```
#Fri Mar 15 10:44:44 GMT 2013
firstName_Label1/@value=\u7B2C\u4E00\u540D\u79F0\uFF1A
lastName_Label1/@value=\u59D3\u6C0F\uFF1A
button1/@value=\u4FDD\u5B58
button2/@value=\u53D6\u6D88
salary_Label1/@value=\u85AA\u916C\uFF1A
```

Importing Resource Bundle Files

There is an import feature available using the Package Explorer view. Switch to this view and follow these steps:

1. Right-click the root element of the project and then select **Import**.
2. Expand the **General** option, select **File System**, and click **Next**.
3. Specify the directory to import from in the **From directory** edit control. If you want to use the same location earlier, you need to include the folder with the .NSF name in the path.
4. Select the **Filter Types** button, select the ***.properties** option, and click **OK**.
5. Select the **XPages** folder and select **Finish** to import the files.
6. Select **Yes To All** when prompted about overwriting the existing property files.

Figure 18.10 shows the Import dialog and the files which should be exported to do the translations of `SamplePage.xsp`.

Importing Resource Bundles in Domino Designer 8.5

Domino Designer introduces a new feature, which is the ability to merge source file changes into property files. This feature was not available in 8.5, so before importing, go to Application Properties, select the XPages tab and, in the Localization Options section, check the option for "Do not modify Existing Properties Files." This prevents Domino Designer from overwriting your translations. You can do the same in Domino Designer 8.5.1 by deselecting the option to "Merge source file changes into property files." If you do this in Designer 8.5.1, you start to see warnings that the XPages localization property files are out of date if you change the associated XPages.

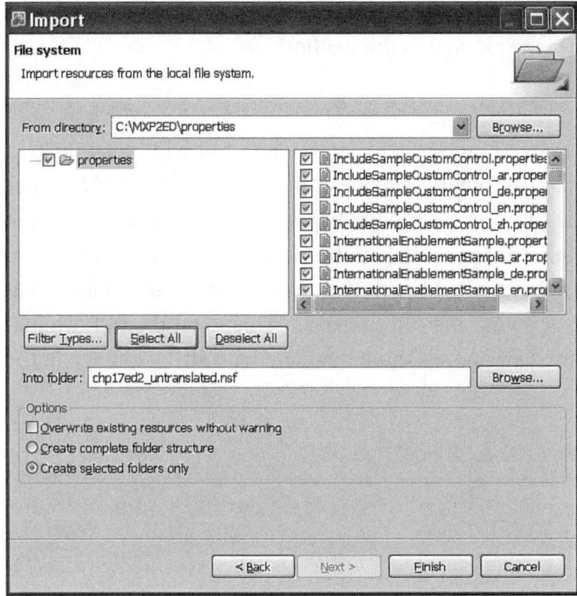

Figure 18.10 Resource Bundle Import using Package Explorer

Figure 18.11 shows the updated preview with the Chinese translations.

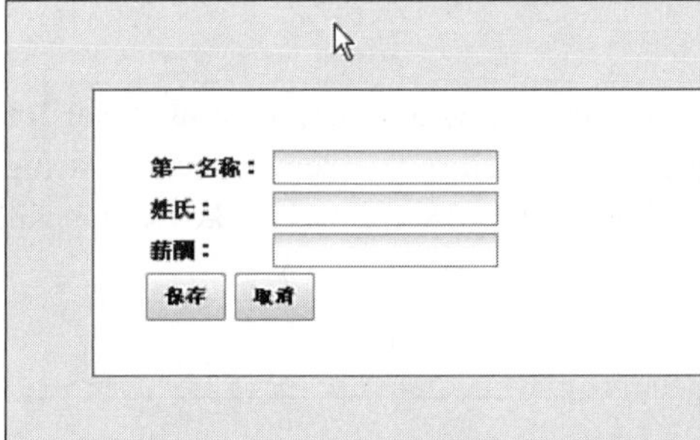

Figure 18.11 Browser preview with Chinese translations

Merging XPage Changes

You need to make updates to your XPages either while the resource bundle files are out from translation or after they are returned. There is an option to merge XPage changes into the property files, which automates the process of keeping the resource bundle files up to date. The behavior for string changes, additions, and deletions is explained in this section.

Changing a String

When you modify a string, the default resource bundle file is simply updated with the new key/value pair; however, the resource bundle files for other languages get a special update if Designer detects a translation exists for the changed file. Consider what happens if the "Salary:" string is changed to "Gross salary:". If you make this change and open the German resource bundle, you see that the value associated with this string is updated with the default pseudo translation, but a comment is added to the top of the file showing the old translated value and the old original value. Listing 18.3 shows the changes in the German resource bundle after a string change in the associated XPage.

Listing 18.3 Translated Resource Bundle After a String Change

```
#-----
# key: salary_Label1/@value
# src: Salary:
# nls: Gehalt:
#-----
#Sat Sep 04 14:01:32 BST 2010
salary_Label1/xp\:this.value[1]/text()=[de| Gross salary\:\n ]
...
```

Adding a String

When you add a string, all the resource bundle files are updated with a new key/value pair for the new string. The existing translations are preserved and translators can identify the new string because it is in the form of the standard pseudo translation. Listing 18.4 shows the key/value pair that is inserted if you type some text directly into the XPage.

Listing 18.4 Resource Bundle Adding a String

```
#-----
# key: salary_Label1/@value
# src: Salary:
# nls: Gehalt:
#-----
#Sat Sep 04 14:15:53 BST 2010
salary_Label1/xp\:this.value[1]/text()=[de| Gross salary\:\n ]
/xp\:view[1]/text()[2]=[de| Please enter your details in the field below. ]
```

Removing a String

When you remove a string, the default resource bundle file is simply updated to remove the existing key/value pair, but the resource bundle files for other languages get another special update. The key/value pair gets deleted from these files also, but additionally, a comment is added to the top of the file showing the old translation. If you delete the Cancel button from the sample XPage, the German resource bundle file ends up looking like Listing 18.5.

Listing 18.5 Resource Bundle Removing a String

```
#-----
# key: salary_Label1/@value
# src: Salary:
# nls: Gehalt:
#-----
# key: button2/@value
# src: Cancel
# nls: Abbrechen
#-----
#Sat Sep 04 14:21:16 BST 2010
salary_Label1/xp\:this.value[1]/text()=[de| Gross salary\:\n ]
/xp\:view[1]/text()[2]=[de| Please enter your details in the field below. ]
firstName_Label1/@value=Vorname\:
lastName_Label1/@value=Nachname\:
button1/@value=Speichern
```

If you add the Cancel button back in, Designer does not automatically revert to the old translation; this is something you have to do manually.

> **BACKUP TRANSLATIONS!**
>
> Translation is a costly process, so we strongly advise you to back up your translations. Don't just rely on the copy stored in the Domino database.

Gotchas!

The process for localizing XPages fits well with how the application developer would naturally work, meaning that you can create XPages using your native language and then automatically extract the strings that need to be translated without having to change the design of the XPage. The responsibility for dealing with the translated resource bundles resides with the XPages runtime and the XPage Java files. So far, so good, but there are some gotchas that you need to be aware of:

- Control IDs are required.
- Custom Control properties must be flagged as being localizable
- Computed values and client-side JavaScript are not handled.

Computed values and JavaScript are handled in the next section.

Control IDs

The key value that is used in the resource bundle file is derived from the control ID and the property name in the format `[control id]/@[property name]`. So, what happens if you don't specify an ID? XPages derives an ID for the component based on its location within the component hierarchy. Consider the XPage shown in Listing 18.6.

Listing 18.6 Label Without ID

```
<?xml version="1.0" encoding="UTF-8"?>
<xp:view xmlns:xp="http://www.ibm.com/xsp/core">
      <xp:label value="First Label">
      </xp:label>
</xp:view>
```

The resource bundle entry for the string associated with this label looks like this:

```
/xp\:view[1]/xp\:label[1]/@value=First Label
```

The key can be interpreted as the first `xp:label` tag inside the first `xp:view` tag (of which there can only ever be one). If you now insert another label before the first one, the key changes to:

```
/xp\:view[1]/xp\:label[2]/@value=First Label
```

The problem gets worse if the new label doesn't have an ID either, as shown in Listing 18.7.

Listing 18.7 Two Labels Without IDs

```
<?xml version="1.0" encoding="UTF-8"?>
<xp:view xmlns:xp="http://www.ibm.com/xsp/core">
      <xp:label value="Another Label">
      </xp:label>
      <xp:label value="First Label">
      </xp:label>
</xp:view>
```

The associated resource bundle looks like Listing 18.8.

Listing 18.8 Resource Bundle for Two Labels Without IDs

```
#Sat Sep 04 15:21:56 BST 2010
/xp\:view[1]/xp\:label[2]/@value=First Label
/xp\:view[1]/xp\:label[1]/@value=Another Label
```

So, for controls with no IDs, moving the controls is going to cause updates to the keys in the resource bundle file, which causes problems with translations. The prime case where this happens is if you use pass-through text. The associated components implicitly have no IDs, so the use of pass-though text is discouraged; if you are going to be translating the application, use a label or span control instead.

Custom Control Properties

You saw earlier that certain properties of the standard controls are flagged as containing localizable strings and Domino Designer automatically generates an entry in the language resource bundles when a string value is set for one of these properties. So, what happens when you create a Custom Control and define custom properties for use with that control? In this case, what you can do is flag that the property value is a localizable string, and Domino Designer treats it in the same way as it treats localizable property values for the standard controls.

Consider the following example of a Custom Control, which has a single property called label. The property is defined using the **Property** definition tab in the Custom Controls properties panel. The type of the property can be set to Localizable String. Figure 18.12 shows the property definition property sheet for such an example. Now, when you include this Custom Control in an XPage where localization options are enabled, an entry is created in the associated resource bundle file like this:

```
custom1/@label=Hello World
```

Localizing Computed Expressions and JavaScript

The localization mechanism outlined in the previous sections works fine when the property is flagged as being a localizable string and the value is not being computed. Computed expressions can also include strings that need to be localized, as can client-side JavaScript. In this section, you learn how to handle these elements of your application.

Consider the XPage shown in Listing 18.9. In this sample, the label value property (which we know is a localizable string) is being computed in the first case using a combination of static text and a computed expression and, in the second case, using a server-side JavaScript expression. Also, a client-side JavaScript expression includes a string that should be localized. If you look at the associated resource bundle file, you see that it is empty. (Domino Designer has detected these are all cases it cannot handle.)

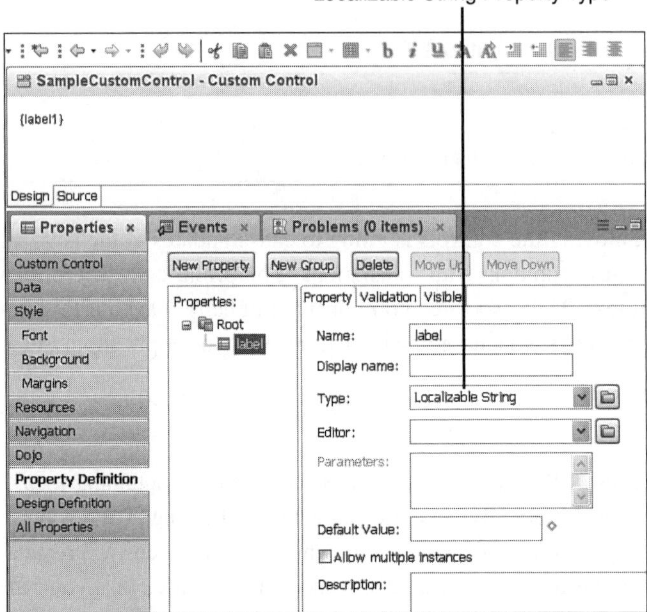

Figure 18.12 Localizable string custom property type

Listing 18.9 XPage with Computed Expressions and JavaScript

```
<?xml version="1.0" encoding="UTF-8"?>
<xp:view xmlns:xp="http://www.ibm.com/xsp/core">
      <xp:label value="Hello #{session.commonUserName}" id="label1">
      </xp:label>
      <xp:br></xp:br>
      <xp:label id="label2">
            <xp:this.value>
<![CDATA[#{javascript:"Hello " + session.getCommonUserName()}]]>
            </xp:this.value>
      </xp:label>
      <xp:br></xp:br>
      <xp:label id="label3" value="Click Here
#{session.commonUserName}"> // is this right?
            <xp:eventHandler event="onclick" submit="false">
                  <xp:this.script><![CDATA[alert("Hello
World");]]></xp:this.script>
            </xp:eventHandler>
      </xp:label>
</xp:view>
```

AVOID STRING CONCATENATION

Listing 18.9 uses string concatenation to build the labels that is displayed to the user. This is something you need to avoid in a real application. The assumption here is that the convention of a greeting followed by a person's name applies everywhere. This may not always be the case. Instead of using string concatenation, your strings need to contain placeholders that indicate where the value(s) should be inserted. The translator can then move the placeholders to the appropriate position in the translated string.

Localizing these strings involves the following tasks:

1. Adding a resource bundle to the XPage that contains the translated strings.
2. Modifying the computed expressions to reference the resource bundle.
3. Modifying the client-side JavaScript to reference the resource bundle.

Adding a Resource Bundle

A resource bundle is one of the resource types that you can add to an XPage. Follow these steps to add a resource bundle to your XPage:

1. Create a new file in your application (select **File** > **New** > **File**) with the extension `.properties` (see Figure 18.13).

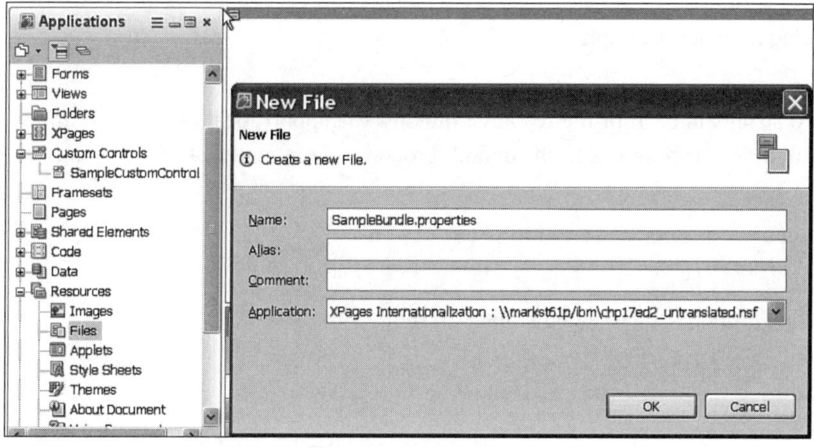

Figure 18.13 Adding a property file

2. Create a second file for the German translations using the same filename, but with the `_de` suffix.

3. Add a resource of type **Resource Bundle** using **Resources** tab in the XPage properties sheet, which references the property file you have just added (see Figure 18.14).

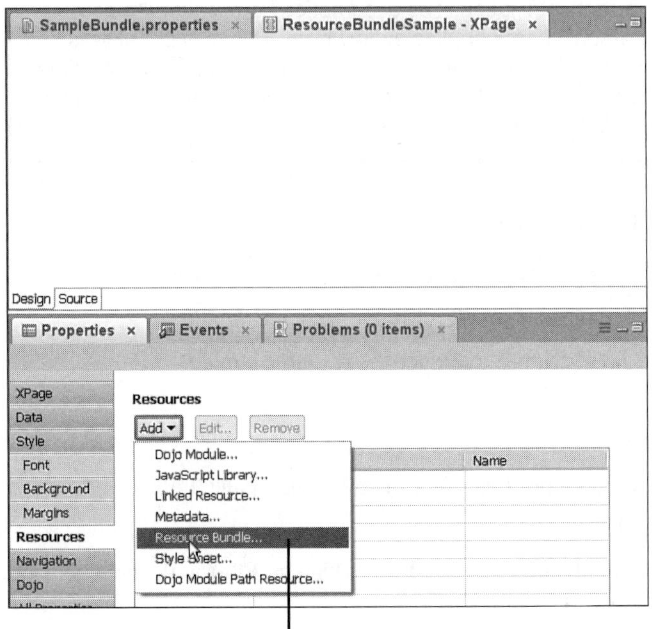

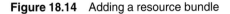

Figure 18.14 Adding a resource bundle

You need two strings in each of the resource bundles to support localizing the computed expression and client-side JavaScript. Edit the default property file to include the following key/value pair:

```
greeting=Hello {0}. Current language is {1}.
clickHere=Click Here {0}
```

Edit the German property file to include this key/value pair:

```
greeting=Hallo {0}. Aktuelle Sprache ist {1}.
clickHere=Klicken Sie Hier {0}
helloWorld=Hallo Welt
```

Note that the strings added to the property bundle are written to include a placeholder, such as `{0}` for the text that needs to be inserted. This placeholder can be moved by the translators if a specific locale convention requires.

Localizing Computed Expressions

After you add a resource bundle to an XPage, you can reference those strings from your computed expressions. The following code shows the updated computed expression that now references the localized string from the resource bundle (refer to the XPage named **LocalizedComputedExpression**). It also uses the `I18n.format()` method to insert the parameters into the localized string:

```
var message = sampleBundle["greeting"];
return I18n.format(message, session.getCommonUserName(),
context.getLocaleString());
```

Figure 18.15 show a preview of the page using a browser with a German locale configured.

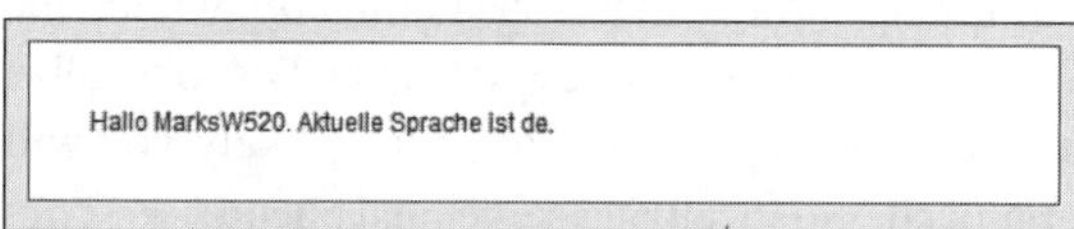
Hallo MarksW520. Aktuelle Sprache ist de.

Figure 18.15 Preview of a computed expression

I18n is one of a collection of runtime classes that supports internationalization. I18n is a shorthand way of writing "internationalization." The class provides methods to perform locale specific operations, such as the following:

- Building strings to display to the end user
- Comparing strings
- Parsing a number and date values to and from string values
- Converting date values to different time zones

The other XPages runtime classes provided for internationalization support are `Locale` and `TimeZone`. A `Locale` object represents a specific geographical or cultural region and helps process data in a region-specific manner, such as displaying a date using a regional convention. A `TimeZone` object represents the time zone offset.

Refer to the IBM Domino Designer XPages Reference help pages for more information on these classes.

Localizing Client-Side JavaScript

You can localize inline client-side JavaScript by using a computed expression within the script. This computed expression references the value from the resource bundle that your client-side script needs to use. Listing 18.10 shows an example of how to reference a localized string from some inline client-side script.

Listing 18.10 Using a Resource Bundle from Client-Side Script

```
<xp:label id="label1" value="Click Me">
      <xp:eventHandler event="onclick" submit="false">
            <xp:this.script>
<![CDATA[alert("#{javascript:sampleBundle['helloWorld']}");]]>
            </xp:this.script>
      </xp:eventHandler>
</xp:label>
```

Localizing Script Libraries

The built-in localization support handles localizing strings that appear directly within the XPage, like control labels and such, and you have seen how to use resources bundles to localize JavaScript that appears in the XPage. For more complex application logic, it is likely you will use script libraries. In this section, you learn approaches to localizing server and client-side script libraries.

Server-Side Script Libraries

You can use resource bundles from within your server-side JavaScript libraries by programmatically loading the bundle and then referencing the associated localized strings. Listing 18.11 shows you how to programmatically load a resource bundle. Here is what it does:

1. Retrieve the locale object from the current view instance so you know what language version of the string to load.
2. The code is caching the loaded resource bundle so it checks to see if the strings already been loaded for this locale.
3. Create an instance of `com.ibm.xsp.resource.BundleResource` and set the `src` property to the resource bundle file to use and the `component` property to the current view instance.
4. Cache the loaded strings in application scope so they can be reused later. (The code to create the map, which contains to cached resources, is synchronized to make sure it's only done once.)

Listing 18.11 Programatically Loading a Resource Bundle

```
function greeting() {
  var message = sampleBundle()["greeting"];
  var name = session.getCommonUserName();
  var lang = context.getLocaleString()
  return I18n.format(message, name, lang);
}
```

```
function sampleBundle() {
  var locale = view.getLocale();

  if (applicationScope.sampleBundle) {
     var strings = applicationScope.sampleBundle[locale];
     if (strings) {
       return strings;
     }
  }

  var resource = new com.ibm.xsp.resource.BundleResource();
  resource.src = "/SampleBundle.properties";
  resource.component = view;

  var strings = resource.contents;

  synchronized(applicationScope) {
    if (!applicationScope.sampleBundle) {
      applicationScope.sampleBundle = new java.util.HashMap();
    }
    applicationScope.sampleBundle[locale] = strings;
  }

  return strings;
}
```

Elsewhere in the same script library, the resource bundle can be referenced by invoking the `sampleBundle()` method, as shown in Listing 18.12.

Listing 18.12 Referencing the Loaded Resource Bundle

```
function greeting() {
  var message = sampleBundle()["greeting"];
  var name = session.getCommonUserName();
  var lang = context.getLocaleString()
  return I18n.format(message, name, lang);
}
```

Client-Side Script Libraries

One additional technique you can use to localize client-side JavaScript is to dynamically generate a client-side JavaScript object that contains the localized strings you need to use in your XPage. Here is how you can do this:

1. Create a server-side JavaScript library with a method to programmatically load the resource bundle you want to use (as shown previously).
2. Create a new method that creates a JavaScript object representation of the resource bundle.
3. Add a client-side script library to your XPage, whose contents are computed using the method from the previous step.

Listing 18.13 shows an example of how to generate a JavaScript class representation of a resource bundle.

Listing 18.13 JavaScript Class Representation of a Resource Bundle

```
function sampleBundleAsClass() {
      var bundle = sampleBundle();
      var keys = bundle.getKeys();
      var asClass = "var sampleBundle = { ";
      while (keys.hasMoreElements()) {
            var key = keys.nextElement();
            asClass += key + ": '" + bundle.getString(key) + "'";
            if (keys.hasMoreElements()) {
                  asClass += ", ";
            }
      }
      asClass += "}";
      return asClass;
}
```

Listing 18.14 shows an XPage that uses this technique. The contents for the client-side script library are computed at page load time using the method defined in the server-side JavaScript library. This causes a script block to be included in the generated HTML, which declares a class called `sampleBundle`, which can be referenced later. The JavaScript code associated with the label control is referencing the `sampleBundle` class to get the hello world string with the correct translation.

Listing 18.14 Using JavaScript Class Representation of a Resource Bundle

```
<?xml version="1.0" encoding="UTF-8"?>
<xp:view xmlns:xp="http://www.ibm.com/xsp/core">
      <xp:this.resources>
            <xp:script src="/SampleBundleScriptLibrary.jss"
                  clientSide="false">
            </xp:script>
            <xp:script clientSide="true"
                  contents="${javascript:sampleBundleAsClass()}">
```

```
            </xp:script>
      </xp:this.resources>
      <xp:label id="label1" value="Click Me">
            <xp:eventHandler event="onclick" submit="false"
                  script="alert(sampleBundle.helloWorld)">
            </xp:eventHandler>
      </xp:label>
</xp:view>
```

International Enablement

The good news is that XPages is fully internationalized, so it provides a lot of built-in functionality, as described here:

- **Built-in Translations for XPages Runtime:** XPages comes with built-in translations for the strings that it includes in the user interface. For example, the column headers in the File Download control are already translated, so you don't need to translate them in every application that uses the control. Similarly, if you choose to make a field required and do not provide your own error message, a translated message is provided by default. The context locale is used to determine which translation of the message is displayed. Additional translations are provided by the Domino Server Language Pack installers, which need to be installed onto your Domino server.
- **Loading the Correct Application Translations:** The XPages runtime loads the correct translations for your XPages once the appropriate resource bundles exist or reverts to the default language. You have seen examples of this earlier in this chapter.
- **Handling Locale-Sensitive Data Correctly:** The converters provided as part of the XPages runtime correctly converts to and from different data types (numbers and dates in a locale-sensitive manner). This means that, when you need to display a date or allow the user to input such data, you don't need to worry about the locale issues, because this is handled by the converters.
- **Built-in Translations for Dojo:** The translated strings for Dojo toolkit JavaScript library are provided by default. This means that controls that depend on Dojo (such as the Rich Text Editor) work correctly across multiple locales. The Dojo translations are always included in the server, even when the Language Packs are not installed. The Dojo locale is usually the same as the context locale, except for the deprecated locales listed next.
- **Computing the Correct Page `dir` and `lang` Property Values:** The XPage view tag supports the `dir` and `lang` properties, and these can be manually configured in your XPages. The `dir` property is the direction (left to right or right to left) for the page. The

`lang` property is the language for the page. If these properties are not explicitly set, they are computed based on the context locale.

- **Loading the Correct Bundle Resources:** If you include resource bundles to translate text in your application's server JavaScript libraries, the XPages runtime loads the correct translations based on the current locale. Again, this topic was covered earlier.
- **Library of Internationalization Classes:** The Runtime library provide an asset of classes for performing locale sensitive operations, such as manipulating dates, numbers, and strings that are presented to the user. Always use these methods within your server-side JavaScript to ensure your application logic is correctly internationally enabled.

Locales in XPages

The locale for an XPage is computed using a combination of what the user has configured and what is supported by the application. The user's browser or Notes client contains a configuration which lists the users preferred locales in order. This information is sent to the server when the user requests an XPages to be displayed. The following algorithm is used to compute the locale for the XPage:

1. If the localization options are configured for the application, the user's first preferred locale is used.
2. If the first browser locale is a Norwegian language, the special rules for Norwegian are used (see the section, "Deprecated Locale Codes").
3. If the localization options are configured for the application, a best-match locale is computed by comparing the user's preferences in order against the list of supported locales.
4. If no best match can be established, the default locale for the application is used or the server locale (if the default is not available).

The locale for a page can be programmatically set if, for example, you want to allow the user to manually switch between the available language versions of your application. Listing 18.15 shows an XPage that uses this technique to allow the user to select what language version of the page they want to view. Four links are displayed at the top of the page, and clicking a link

1. Changes the page locale using `context.setLocaleString()`
2. Reloads the page using `context.reloadPage()`

Listing 18.15 Switching Locale Programmatically

```
<?xml version="1.0" encoding="UTF-8"?>
<xp:view xmlns:xp="http://www.ibm.com/xsp/core">
    <xp:link escape="true" text="Arabic" id="link1">
```

```
        <xp:eventHandler event="onclick" submit="true"
              refreshMode="complete">
              <xp:this.action><![CDATA[#{javascript:
                    context.setLocaleString("ar");
                    context.reloadPage();}]]>
              </xp:this.action>
        </xp:eventHandler>
    </xp:link>
    <xp:link escape="true" text="Chinese" id="link2">
        <xp:eventHandler event="onclick" submit="true"
              refreshMode="complete">
              <xp:this.action><![CDATA[#{javascript:
                    context.setLocaleString("zh");
                    context.reloadPage();}]]>
              </xp:this.action>
        </xp:eventHandler>
    </xp:link>
    <xp:link escape="true" text="English" id="link3">
        <xp:eventHandler event="onclick" submit="true"
              refreshMode="complete">
              <xp:this.action><![CDATA[#{javascript:
                    context.setLocaleString("en");
                    context.reloadPage();}]]>
              </xp:this.action>
        </xp:eventHandler>
    </xp:link>
    <xp:link escape="true" text="German" id="link4">
        <xp:eventHandler event="onclick" submit="true"
              refreshMode="complete">
              <xp:this.action><![CDATA[#{javascript:
                    context.setLocaleString("de");
                    context.reloadPage();}]]>
              </xp:this.action>
        </xp:eventHandler>
    </xp:link>
    <xp:br></xp:br>
    <xp:label id="label1"
        value="This is the English version of this page">
    </xp:label>
</xp:view>
```

When this page is initially viewed, the locale of the user (if supported) is used. Figure 18.16 shows the German version of the page.

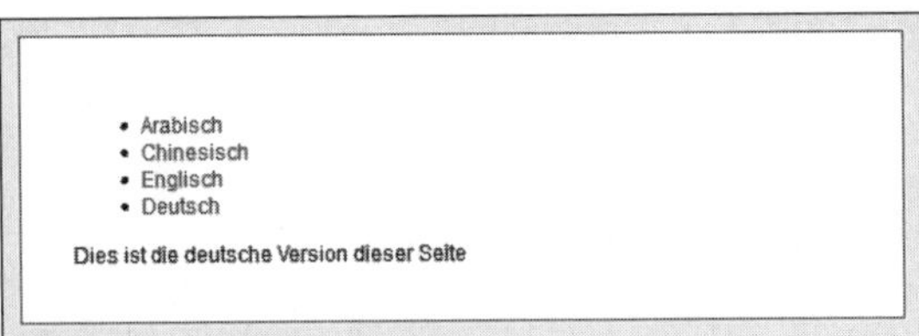

Figure 18.16 German page

If the first link on the page is selected, the page is reloaded, and the Arabic version is displayed. Loading the Arabic version of the page not only changes the language, but also changes the layout to right to left, which is the locale convention as demonstrated in Figure 18.17. If you view the page source, you see that the generated HTML tag includes the direction and language attributes like this: <html dir="rtl" lang="ar">.

Figure 18.17 Arabic page

The final example shows you the default behavior for locale-sensitive data conversion and how to override this behavior.

Looking at Listing 18.16, notice that the converter in the first row of the table has no locale configured, so it defaults to the locale of the page. The page contains a repeat, which loops over all the available locales. Inside the repeat is a converter, which uses a specified locale so in this case the locale of the page is ignored.

Listing 18.16 Arabic Page

```
<?xml version="1.0" encoding="UTF-8"?>
<xp:view xmlns:xp="http://www.ibm.com/xsp/core">
    <xp:table>
        <xp:tr style="background-color:rgb(187,255,187)">
            <xp:td>
                <xp:text escape="true" id="computedField1"
                    value="${view.locale}">
                </xp:text>
            </xp:td>
```

```
                <xp:td>
                    <xp:text escape="true" id="computedField2"
                        value="#{javascript:new Date()}">
                        <xp:this.converter>
                            <xp:convertDateTime type="both"
                                dateStyle="full"
                                timeStyle="full">
                            </xp:convertDateTime>
                        </xp:this.converter>
                    </xp:text>
                </xp:td>
            </xp:tr>
            <xp:repeat id="repeat1" rows="30"
                value="${javascript:Locale.getAvailableLocales()}"
                var="locale" repeatControls="true">
                <xp:tr>
                    <xp:td>
                        <xp:text escape="true" id="computedField3"
                            value="${locale}">
                        </xp:text>
                    </xp:td>
                    <xp:td>
                        <xp:text escape="true" id="computedField4"
                            value="#{javascript:new Date()}">
                            <xp:this.converter>
                                <xp:convertDateTime
                                     type="both"
                                    dateStyle="full"
                                    timeStyle="full"
                                    locale="${locale}">
                                </xp:convertDateTime>
                            </xp:this.converter>
                        </xp:text>
                    </xp:td>
                </xp:tr>
            </xp:repeat>
        </xp:table>
</xp:view>
```

As shown in Figure 18.18, the first row of the table displays the default locale and the full representation of the current date and time according to the conventions of this locale. The following rows of the table show all the available locales and the corresponding representation of the current date and time. Notice that all the strings are already translated.

en	Friday, March 15, 2013 3:03:04 PM United Kingdom Time
zh	2013年3月15日星期五 下午03时03分04秒 英国
th	วันศุกร์ที่ 15 มีนาคม ค.ศ. 2013, 15 นาฬิกา 3 นาที 04 วินาที สหราชอาณาจักร
ko	2013년 3월 15일 금요일 오후 03시 03분 04초 영국
iw	יום שישי 15 מרץ 2013 15:03:04 שעון GB
uk	П'ятниця, 15 березня 2013 р. 15:03:05 Великобританія
tr	15 Mart 2013 Cuma 15:03:05 Birleşik Krallık Saati
sq	e premte, 15 mars 2013 3.03.05.MD Mbretëria e Bashkuar
sk	Piatok, 15. marec 2013 15:03:05 Spojené kráľovstvo
pt	sexta-feira, 15 de março de 2013 15h03min05s Horário Reino Unido
pl	piątek, 15 marca 2013 15:03:05 Wielka Brytania
nl	vrijdag 15 maart 2013 15:03:06 Verenigd Koninkrijk
ms	Jumaat, 2013 Mac 15 15:03:06 United Kingdom
mk	петок, 15 март 2013 15:03:06 Велика Британија
lv	piektdiena, 2013. gada 15. marts 15:03:06 Lielbritānija
lt	2013 m. kovo 15 d.,penktadienis 15:03:06 Didžioji Britanija
kk	жұма, 15 наурыз 2013 ж. 15:03:06 GB
is	föstudagur, 15. mars 2013 15:03:06 Bretland
hr	petak, 15 ožujka 2013. 15:03:06 Ujedinjena Kraljevina
gu	શુક્રવાર, ૨૦૧૩ માર્ચ ૧૫ ૧૫:૦૩:૦૭ GB
ga	Dé hAoine, 2013 Márta 15 15:03:07 An Ríocht Aontaithe
fr	vendredi 15 mars 2013 15:03:07 Royaume-Uni
es	viernes 15 de marzo de 2013 03:03:07 p.m. Reino Unido
cs	pátek, 15. března 2013 15:03:07 Velká Británie
ca	divendres 15 de març de 2013 15:03:07 Regne Unit
es_PR	viernes 15 de marzo de 2013 03:03:08 p.m. Reino Unido
en_HK	Friday, 15 March 2013 3:03:08 PM United Kingdom Time
pt_PT	sexta-feira, 15 de Março de 2013 15H03m08s Horário Reino Unido
es_PY	viernes 15 de marzo de 2013 03:03:08 p.m. Reino Unido
ar_YE	الجمعة، ١٥ مارس، ٢٠١٣ المملكة المتحدة ٣:٠٣:٠٨ م
hu_HU	2013. március 15. 15:03:09 Egyesült Királyság

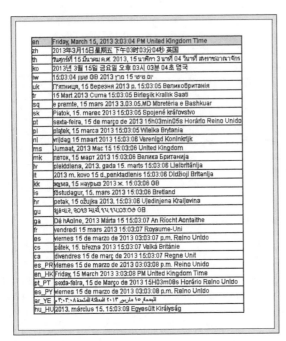

Figure 18.18 Default and available locales

Deprecated Locale Codes

Table 18.1 lists four language codes that are deprecated and their replacement codes. The XPages runtime still uses the old codes, but the Dojo toolkit uses the new codes.

As explained earlier, XPages uses the Dojo toolkit for some controls, such as the Rich Text Editor. The Dojo Toolkit includes some translated strings. When Dojo is included in the output from an XPage, it outputs the locale it's using into the markup of the generated HTML page. The Dojo locale differs from the XPage locale for the deprecated languages listed in Table 18.1.

Table 18.1 Deprecated Language Codes

Language	Deprecated Code	New Code
Yiddish	ji	yi
Hebrew	Iw	he
Indonesian	In	id
Norwegian (Bokmål)	no	nb

One exception to this behavior is Norwegian, which has some special handling.

Because there are two different Norwegian languages—Norwegian (Bokmål) and Norwegian (Nynorsk)—the old Norwegian language code "no" has been deprecated and replaced by two codes. Norwegian (Bokmål) uses the code "nb" and Norwegian (Nynorsk) uses "nn." Strings that were previously translated to the single Norwegian "no" locale are in fact Norwegian (Bokmål). So, "nn" can be considered the replacement for "no." Some browsers still use the old "no" code.

Table 18.2 describes the behavior of the different parts of your application depending on the locale sent by the browser and whether or not you have localization enabled.

Table 18.2 Default and Available Locales

Locale Usage	Browser Locale		
	no	nb	nn
If Localization Is Disabled			
Context Locale	no	no	no
Server Strings	no	no	no
Application Strings	-	-	-
Dojo Locale (8.5)	no		no
Dojo Locale (8.5.1 or higher)	nb	nb	nb
If Localization Is Enabled			
Context Locale	no	nb else no	no
Server Strings	no	no	no
Application Strings	no	nb else no	no
Dojo Locale (8.5)	no	no	no
Dojo Locale (8.5.1 or higher)	nb	nb	nb

The XPages runtime contains property bundles with the "no" suffix and, if the page locale is set to either "nb" or "nn" languages, the "no" strings are used. When localization is disabled, application strings are not translated so the source language is displayed. When localization is enabled, you can choose between using the "no" or "nb" language code, but whichever you choose, it must still match the other code if that's what the browser specifies. For example, if you choose to use "nb" and the browser requests "no," the "nb" translations are still used and vice versa. The localization options do not list the "nn" language code.

In the 8.5 release, the Dojo strings used the "no" language code. This changed for 8.5.1 and higher to use the "nb" language code.

Localizing Computed Fields

Prior to Notes 8.5.3, the value of a computed field was included by default for localization. This caused problems because frequently computed fields were used to compute non-localizable text, for example, HTML. In Notes 8.5.3, a new localization option was introduced to control how computed fields are handled during the localization process, as shown in Figure 18.19. The default option is not to treat a computed field's value as being localizable, and these values will not be extracted for translation. This change does introduce a risk of regression if your application were relying on the old behavior. The quick solution is to re-enable the old behavior. A good practice is to use labels for text that needs to be translated and computed fields for text that does not need to be translated.

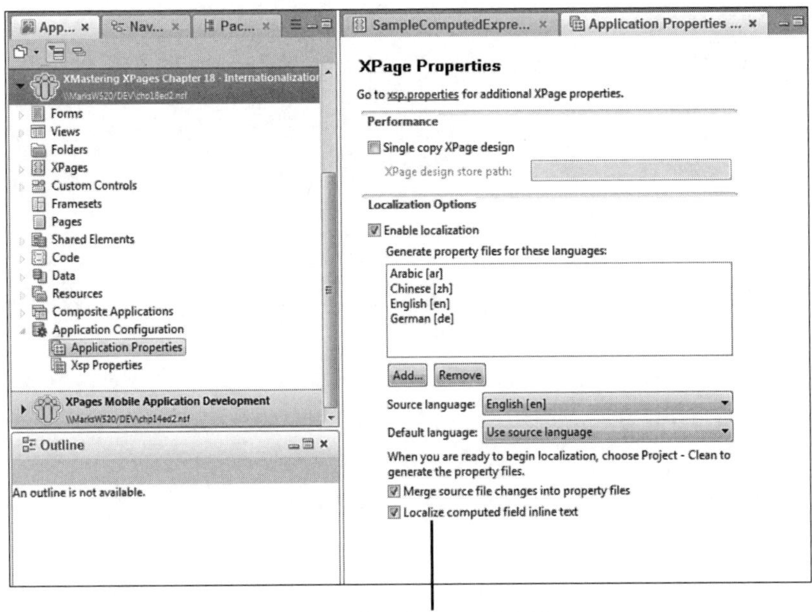

Figure 18.19 Localize computed field inline text

Conclusion

This chapter taught you techniques that allow you to localize your XPages applications. You saw how XPages provides a natural localization model where the normal controls automatically handle geographic conventions and where you can create your applications in your own language and translate to other languages later with relative ease. You also learned some techniques to allow you to localize your application logic. This completes the Application User Experience section of the book and now you can move on to examining the topics of performance, scalability, and security.

Part VI

Performance, Scalability, and Security

CHAPTER 19

A First Look at Performance and Scalability

Your XPages journey thus far has covered a lot of ground. Assuming that you worked your way to this point from the beginning of the book, you have learned how to construct XPages and Custom Controls, interpret XSP tag syntax, manage data sources, build application logic, style a cool UI, internationalize apps, and even contribute your own custom components. With all this knowledge, you can build sophisticated dynamic applications that impress customers and end users alike...well, almost.

No matter how slick your application, it is absolutely essential for its success that it performs and scales well. Large development projects typically have metrics defined from the outset that define the viability of an application in hard numbers, such as transactions per second, minimum number of concurrent users, and so forth. Even when such metrics are not formally applied, users and customers tend to become increasingly dissatisfied when it comes to sites with slow response times and unresponsive pages, so these apps quickly drop in the popularity stakes and are eventually used only grudgingly in cases of necessity. This chapter and the next try to make sure that such a fate does not happen to you.

XPages has a lot of magic levers and special tools that can be applied to ensure your application meets acceptable performance and scalability standards. It must be understood, however, that performance and scalability objectives can often work against each other—for instance, allocating lots of memory to each user session can certainly work wonders for performance when there are a small number of users but also kill your application as the number of concurrent users begins to scale upward. Thus, any set of performance and scalability requirements must be analyzed in context, with each stipulation understood in its own right, but with due consideration also given to how individual requirements can impact each other. It is then and only then that the appropriate tweaks can be applied to the XPages runtime so that an optimal and well-balanced application tuning can be achieved.

Golden Rules

Notes/Domino 9.0.1 comes with numerous performance enhancements within the XPages core runtime. Some of these are automatically applied to XPages applications running in Notes/Domino 9.0.1; so by installing or upgrading to Notes/Domino 9.0.1 will improve the performance and scalability of your XPages applications. In special cases, however, you need to configure your applications to benefit from some of the performance and scalability related features. In essence, these changes and features aim to optimize central processing unit (CPU) and random access memory (RAM) utilization under different workloads and environments for an application.

Before examining the ways in which you can configure your XPages applications to improve performance and scalability, you should take into account these 10 golden rules when developing an XPages application:

1. Try to use partial refresh whenever possible. You learned about the different ways you can use partial refresh in Chapter 11, "Advanced Scripting," and should now understand the benefits of this feature. Therefore, you should be prepared to learn about its powerful sibling, partial execution, in the introductory material in this chapter, but more important in the next chapter, Chapter 20, "Advanced Performance Topics."
2. Try to use GET-based requests whenever possible (for example, like those issued by links) instead of POST-based requests (for example, like those issued by event handlers to execute server-side logic such as invoking the Open Page simple action). In this context, not all cases to open a link require a POST-based redirect, for example.
3. Try to use the `readonly` property on container type controls when no processing is required by any controls within the container, such as a panel containing a list of Computed Field controls; therefore, nothing is editable, and no server-side event handlers need to be executed.
4. Try to limit server-side execution of an XPage to only the required part of that XPage for any given request or action within the user interface. This is known as `partial execution mode`. You were introduced to this feature in Chapter 11 and will learn about it in greater detail in Chapter 20. It is similar to partial refresh in that it refreshes only a designated part of the user interface but is instead used to control execution of parts of the XPage component tree on the server side.
5. Try to use the `dataCache` property on the Domino View data source appropriately. You were introduced to this property in Chapter 8, "Working with Domino Views," in the section titled "Caching View Data." When ID is used for this property, less memory is consumed in the server-side component tree representing the Domino View data source.
6. Try to use the `viewScope` object to maintain lightweight server-side primitive data type variables for an XPage instead of the heavier-weight scopes, like `sessionScope` and `applicationScope`. This reduces the amount of memory consumed

during the life of an application. Try to avoid buffering SSJS Objects defined within SSJS Libraries into the viewScope because these cannot be serialized when using disk persistence. Instead, for more complex use cases, consider using Managed Bean objects that are scoped into the view scope level. Managed Beans also give you the greatest degree of flexibility and capability for utilizing the *XPages State Management Layer* (aka Persistence Options) for an application. You will learn about the XPages State Management Layer in Chapter 20.

7. Try to avoid using the computed rendered property expressions to show or hide controls because it is a special property in a JavaServer Faces context and is calculated up to four times during the processing of an XPages POST type request. Instead, you should favor using computed loaded property expressions where possible. This approach is most effective when used alongside the Dynamic Content control, as you will learn in Chapter 20.
8. Avoid using the Notes/Domino backend `getDocument()` API methods (that is, `getDocument()`, `getDocumentByKey()`, `getDocumentByUNID()`, and such) in computed expressions that are within repeated areas and controls for example, a computed field in a DataView column calling `viewEntry.getDocument().getItemValueString("xyz")`. In this scenario, the associated backend document will be opened for each view entry to extract a string field value from its document. A leaner, more efficient solution involves including another column in the underlying Domino view and using the column value directly within the computed expression using `viewEntry.getColumnValue("xyz")`. This eliminates having to open the underlying document, therefore reducing CPU and system I/O cost.
9. Favor disk persistence for the Server Page Persistence mode whenever possible. This ensures that XPages applications make minimal JVM heapspace memory usage. You will learn much more on this particular aspect in the next chapter.
10. Always enable Resource Aggregation and long browser cache expiration values before deploying an application into a production environment.

The next section examines the underlying XPages Request Processing Lifecycle and how it relates to the JavaServer Faces Lifecycle. Having a clear understanding of the XPages Request Processing Lifecycle is necessary to make the most of the XPages performance and scalability features. The sections that then follow teach you about a number of more general day-to-day features that can help application performance and scalability, and how you can apply them.

Before proceeding, you need to download the **Chp19Ed2.nsf** application provided online for this book to run through the exercises in this chapter. You can access this file at `www.ibmpressbooks.com/title/9780133373370`. When downloaded, open it in Designer and sign it.

Understanding the XPages Request Processing Lifecycle

In Chapter 5, "XPages and JavaServer Faces," you learned that XPages is built on the JSF 1.1 framework and, therefore, utilizes the JSF Request Processing Lifecycle. If you are serious about application performance and scalability, then having a good understanding of the XPages Request Processing Lifecycle is necessary to get the most out of the XPages performance and scalability features. Having this understanding also helps you design, implement, and profile your XPages applications with performance and scalability factored in from the start of your application development and performance testing cycles. This means you massively reduce the risk of introducing performance bottlenecks and can therefore potentially eradicate the need for costly redevelopment work after production deployment.

The HTTP protocol supports a set of commands for retrieving and sending data. Two of the most frequently used of those commands for XPages requests are GET and POST:

- **GET-based request:** This type of request is typically sent from a browser when a user enters a URL in a browser address bar or navigates from one web page to another using a standard HTML link. When this type of request is issued, the browser discards any information pertaining to the currently loaded web page before retrieving the next web page. Browsers typically cache web pages retrieved using a GET request and are bookmarkable and linkable.
- **POST-based request:** This type of request is issued by a browser when the <form> contents of the currently loaded web page are submitted as part of the request information to the server. Typically, this is done when submitting an online order form (for example, using a Submit button). The server then processes the incoming data and then either redisplays the same web page updated with the new data or redirects to another page. Browsers typically do not cache POST-based web pages due to the risk of persisting sensitive data within the cached copy of the web page. Web pages retrieved using a POST request are not bookmarkable or linkable in the same manner as GET-based web pages. This type of request is executed each time an XPages server-side simple action or server-side JavaScript event handler is triggered—regardless of whether it is partial refresh, or complete refresh, enabled.

So, this is where the understanding of the XPages Request Processing Lifecycle becomes important when you want to optimize your applications. When processing a request, the XPages runtime executes a six-phase lifecycle that governs processing of the request and its data. This lifecycle ensures that XPages requests are processed in a reliable, integral, consistent, and efficient manner. Figure 19.1 shows a diagram of the XPages Request Processing Lifecycle.

> **TIP**
>
> You can find further information on GET-based versus POST-based requests at www.w3.org/2001/tag/doc/whenToUseGet-20040321.

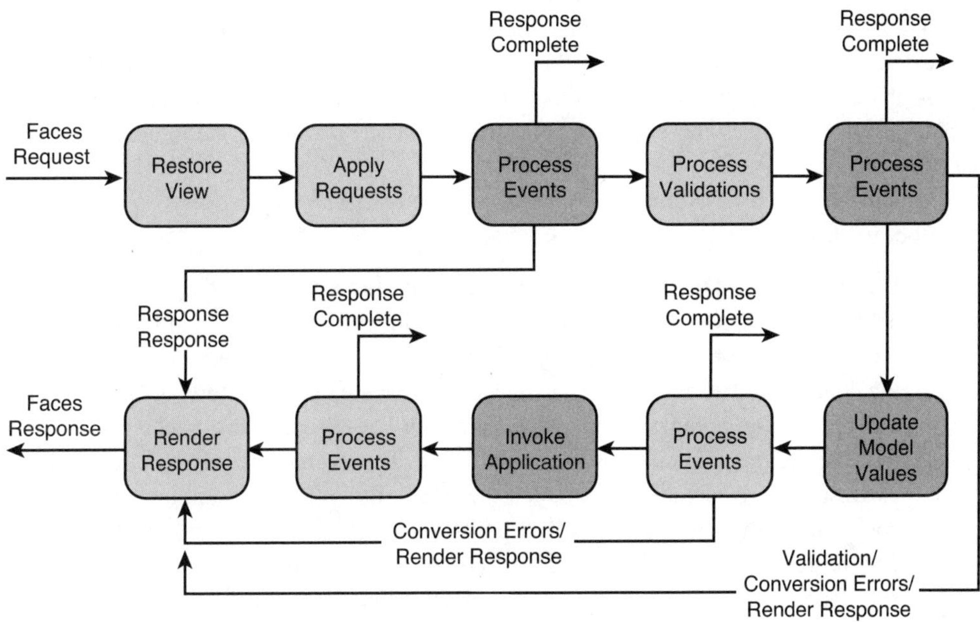

Figure 19.1 The XPages Request Processing Lifecycle

Note, however, that not all the six phases need to be executed for every XPage request. In certain circumstances, you can omit certain phases of the lifecycle depending on the type of the request, GET versus POST, and the requirements of the request data, such as validation requirements, and so on. The following sections explain how the XPages Request Processing Lifecycle applies to GET-based and POST-based HTTP requests.

GET-Based Requests and the XPages Request Processing Lifecycle

A GET-based HTTP request goes through a maximum of two of the six possible lifecycle phases; therefore making this type of request inherently more efficient than its POST-based alternative. The reason I say "a maximum of two" is because for the most typical use case of a plain GET-based request such as clicking a link or entering a URL in the address bar of a browser, only the final life-cycle phase is executed. However, if an AJAX GET-based request is received by the XPages runtime, the first and final phases are executed (Restore View and Render Response, to give the phases their formal names as shown in Figure 19.1).

The semantics behind this difference is because for a plain GET-based request, a component tree will not already exist in the XPages runtime and therefore must be created. This occurs as part of the processing of the request before entering the sixth phase, the Render Response phase where the HTML markup is generated and sent back to the requesting browser. For an AJAX GET-based request, the assumption is that a component tree will already exist because it is a request targeted at a specific element within the web page. Therefore, it makes sense to execute the first phase (the Restore View phase) to quite literally restore the serialized component tree state before further processing occurs to generate the HTML markup in the Render Response phase.

This is the reason for recommending as much use of GET-based requests as possible, as one of the "golden rules":

1. **Lifecycle Phase One: Restore View:** The request is received by the XPages runtime. Two courses of action can then happen, depending on the existence of the component tree in-memory or in-disk persistence. If the request is an initial call for a given XPage, the component tree for that XPage does not already exist. Therefore, the runtime creates the corresponding component tree in memory by executing the precompiled XPage .class file from within the associated .NSF file. This is an extremely efficient process, as Designer has already precompiled the .class file with highly optimized Java byte code when the application was first built using Designer. When executed, the component tree is then added to a cache of component trees under the current context for subsequent retrieval as the user uses the application. Should the user revisit an XPage that is in the component tree cache, that component tree can be restored directly at this point, therefore avoiding the need to restore from the precompiled .class file within the .NSF file.
2. **Lifecycle Phase Six: Render Response:** Every object within the restored component tree is then recursed over by the XPages runtime. During this process, the renderers of each control object in the component tree are called upon to emit the relevant HTML markup for their controls back to the requesting browser.

POST-Based Requests and the XPages Request Processing Lifecycle

Because of the formalities of dealing with a POST-based HTTP request that contains FORM field data that can potentially be sensitive, this type of request must go through up to a maximum of all six of the XPages Request Processing Lifecycle phases. This can be streamlined to create efficiencies, however. You, as the XPages developer, can therefore tailor the actions of your application appropriately to fulfill its requirements and still improve performance where possible:

1. **Lifecycle Phase One: Restore View:** The XPages request is received by the XPages runtime. Then, similar to a GET-based request, the runtime simply restores the associated XPage based on its state, from either disk persistence or from the in-memory component tree for that XPage. This incurs minimal processing cost to the XPages runtime as the XPage has been previously created through an initial GET-based request.
2. **Lifecycle Phase Two: Apply Request Values:** The XPages runtime extracts the request data, including POST content (such as form data) sent by the browser and assigns the values to the corresponding control objects in the restored component tree. It is important to note that the incoming request data is known as the "submitted value." This is a temporary buffer for the incoming data and is not applied directly to the "real" value of any control until the next two phases of the lifecycle are successfully processed. At this point, the event handler that should be used as the invocation target of the POST submission is identified from within the component tree objects. Any processing failure during this phase automatically causes the lifecycle to jump to the Render Response phase, where the XPage will then get rendered as is, and no underlying data will have been modified or events triggered against the component tree.
3. **Lifecycle Phase Three: Process Validations:** At this point, all the XPage component tree control and event handler objects use the "submitted value" assigned to them during the execution of any associated validators or convertors to ensure the temporarily assigned data values fulfill the stipulations of the any validators or convertors on the XPage. Any failure during this phase causes the next two phases to be entirely passed over because error messages must be displayed to the end user without saving any of the assigned data values. Any error messages or error messages controls on the XPage display such queued error messages during the Render Response phase.
4. **Lifecycle Phase Four: Update Model Values:** If the previous phase has successfully passed any validation or convertor checks, the XPages runtime applies the assigned values for each component tree control object to the associated controls and underlying data model. This is typically a Domino Document with its fields bound to the edit box, rich text controls, and so on. The submitted value buffer of any control that has had its real value changed during this request is also reset to null in preparation for any future requests.
5. **Lifecycle Phase Five: Invoke Application:** For the normal POST lifecycle invocation use case, the event handler that was identified in the Apply Request Values phase is executed against the component tree at this point. Note, however, if `immediate="true"` were specified on the event handler, then the invocation of the event handler would actually be brought forward to occur within the second life-cycle phase. This allows any application logic defined for that event handler to execute against the updated and validated data model values.

6. **Lifecycle Phase Six: Render Response:** This final phase sees each of the XPage component tree control objects have their associated renderer objects invoked. These renderer objects generate the HTML markup that is then sent to the requesting browser. Finally, the current state of the component tree is saved to the in-memory or disk cache for subsequent retrieval should the user request the same XPage during that user session again.

It is clear to see that a POST-based request is more expensive in terms of processing compared with a GET-based request. Also note that every phase, except for Phase One: Restore View, entails a complete recursion through the XPage component tree control objects. This in itself can potentially be expensive for a large, complex XPage. Therefore, you need to gain a good understanding of the XPages Request Processing Lifecycle so that you can fully optimize your applications to avoid unnecessary execution and processing within the first five phases of this lifecycle. Chapter 20 contains a section, "Making Efficient XPages Requests," that goes into great detail on this topic.

Reducing CPU Utilization

You can apply several optimizations to your XPages applications that inevitably reduce the amount of CPU processing required. This is important because the amount of CPU cycle capacity determines the speed at which an application request gets executed. Ultimately, this heavily influences the performance metrics for response times of an application. Other factors, such as network latency and bandwidth, will have an influence, of course, and also need to be factored in.

In the following sections, you learn more about GET-based and POST-based HTTP requests and the read-only and immediate properties in terms of their impact on CPU usage. In Chapter 11, you learned how to leverage partial refresh, but this section also teaches you why using it can reduce CPU usage. Finally, you learn about a complementary feature of partial refresh called partial execution mode that enables you to fine-tune your applications and radically reduce CPU usage.

GET-Based Versus POST-Based Requests

As explained in the preceding section, GET-based requests cost less in terms of server-side processing. Therefore, try to use GET-based requests where applicable and possible—especially for link controls. One of the most common mistakes in a lot of XPages applications is the assignment of an **Open Page** simple action to a **link** control without any associated server-side JavaScript application logic. Effectively, this wastes server-processing time in that a POST-based request is sent to the server, the server sends back a client-side redirect response to the browser, and finally the browser executes against the client-side redirect to send back a GET-based request to the server for the target of the **Open Page** simple action. In effect, two requests are required, the first is a POST request and the second is a GET, in order to simply navigate from one XPage to another while not executing any server-side application logic in between.

All this can be done simply by just assigning a value to the **link** control for the target page, resulting in a single GET-based request. Furthermore, if query string parameters need to be sent with the request, the **link** control supports a **Parameters** complex property. This can be found under the **All Properties** panel for a **link** control, as shown in Figure 19.2.

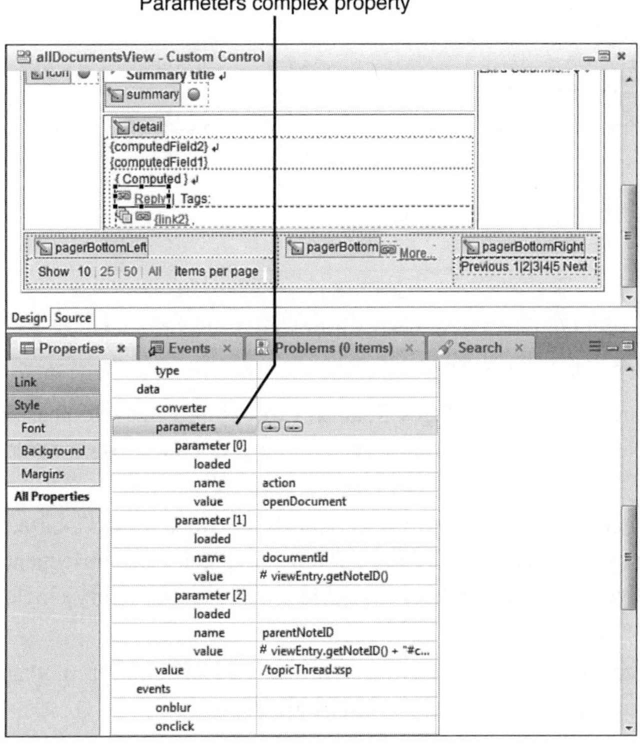

Figure 19.2 The parameters complex property of a link control

Figure 19.2 is taken from the Notes/Domino 9.0.1 Discussion template. If you open the **Chp19Ed2.nsf** application in Domino Designer and then open the **allDocumentsView** Custom Control, you can see this by examining the `linkReply` **link** control's **All Properties** panel, or alternatively viewing the XSP markup, as shown in Listing 19.1.

Listing 19.1 XSP Markup Fragment for the linkReply Link Control with Parameters

```
...
<xp:link text="Reply" id="linkReply"
    value="/topicThread.xsp">
    <xp:this.rendered>
```

```
        <![CDATA[#{javascript(userBean.accessLevel >= lotus.domino.ACL.
➥LEVEL...}]]>
    </xp:this.rendered>
    <xp:this.parameters>
        <xp:parameter name="action" value="openDocument">
        </xp:parameter>
        <xp:parameter value="#{javascript:viewEntry.getNoteID()}"
            name="documentId">
        </xp:parameter>
        <xp:parameter name="parentNoteID">
            <xp:this.value><![CDATA[#{...}]]></xp:this.value>
        </xp:parameter>
    </xp:this.parameters>
</xp:link>
...
```

In summary, the benefits of using GET-based requests for link controls, or indeed for any other navigation type scenario, in this way is three-fold:

- As a plain GET-based request is issued, XPages Request Processing Lifecycle phases one through five are completely avoided, therefore reducing the amount of server-side CPU processing incurred.
- It eliminates the double-request scenario described previously in which a POST-based request is issued, followed by a client-side HTTP 302 redirect that causes a subsequent GET-based request; effectively, a server utilizes the CPU twice over for every single Link/Open Page simple action request.
- The requesting browser caches the retrieved XPage for subsequent requests of that XPage. This also means a large reduction of CPU usage on the server.

Using the readonly Property

Another way to omit processing of XPages Request Processing Lifecycle phases two through five is by using the `readonly` property on container type controls. When a Panel control, an XPage, or even a Custom Control does not contain any controls that need server-side JavaScript or simple action processing to occur in a POST-back request, setting the `readonly` property to `true` prevents life-cycle phases two through five from being processed on those containers and their child controls. Figure 19.3 shows you where to find this property within the **All Properties** panel.

You can find an example of this in the **viewTopic** Custom Control from the **Chp19Ed2.nsf** application, shown in the XSP markup fragment of Listing 19.2.

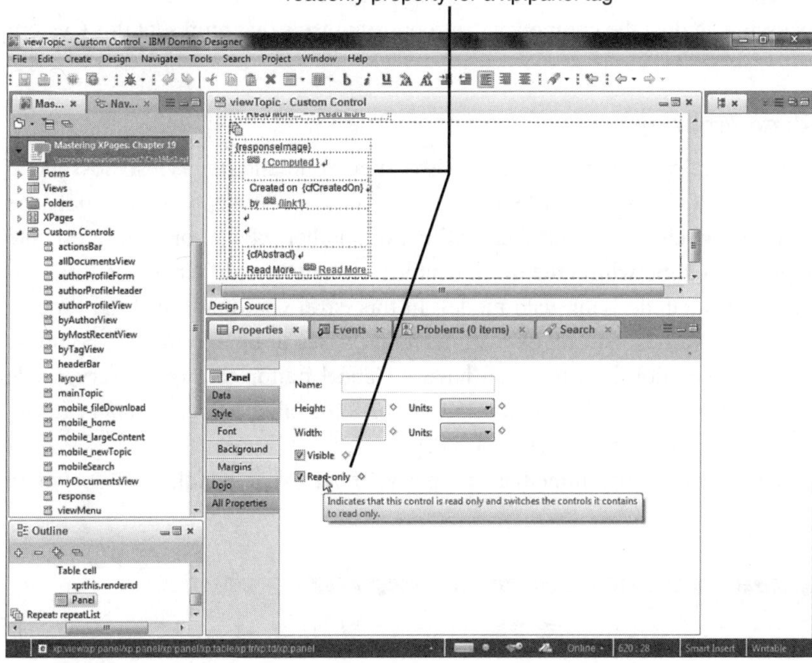

Figure 19.3 The readonly property within the All Properties panel

Listing 19.2 XSP Markup Fragment for the viewTopic Custom Control

```
<?xml version="1.0" encoding="UTF-8"?>
...
    <xp:table styleClass="xlReplyTable">
        <xp:tr>
            <xp:td styleClass="xlReplyBorder">
                <xp:this.rendered><![CDATA[#{javascript:...]]>
</xp:this.rendered>
                <xp:panel readonly="true">
                    <xp:panel themeId="Panel.topicThread">
                        <xp:this.style>
                            <![CDATA[#{javascript: ...
...
</xp:view>
```

This Custom Control contains only link controls and other controls with no server-side processing requirements during a POST-back request. It doesn't contain any user entry controls, such as edit boxes, so it doesn't need to have XPages Request Processing Lifecycle phases two through five processed against it. Therefore, setting `readonly` to `true` in this case reduces the amount of CPU processing against the component tree control objects that represent this Custom Control.

Using the immediate Property

Eliminating XPages Request Processing Lifecycle phases three, four, and five is also possible to reduce CPU utilization for POST-based HTTP requests. In some situations, you need only the triggered event handler to be identified and then redirect to another XPage, or simply execute some server-side application logic within the event handler without any further server-side processing happening against the underlying data model. In this case, you don't need the Process Validations, Update Model Values, and Invoke Application phases to be executed. A common example of this type of interaction is where you have a Cancel button that resets server-side scoped variables and then navigates to the previous XPage or some other XPage without causing any validation or saving to occur within the current XPage.

This is achieved by using the immediate property of an event handler, as shown in Figure 19.4.

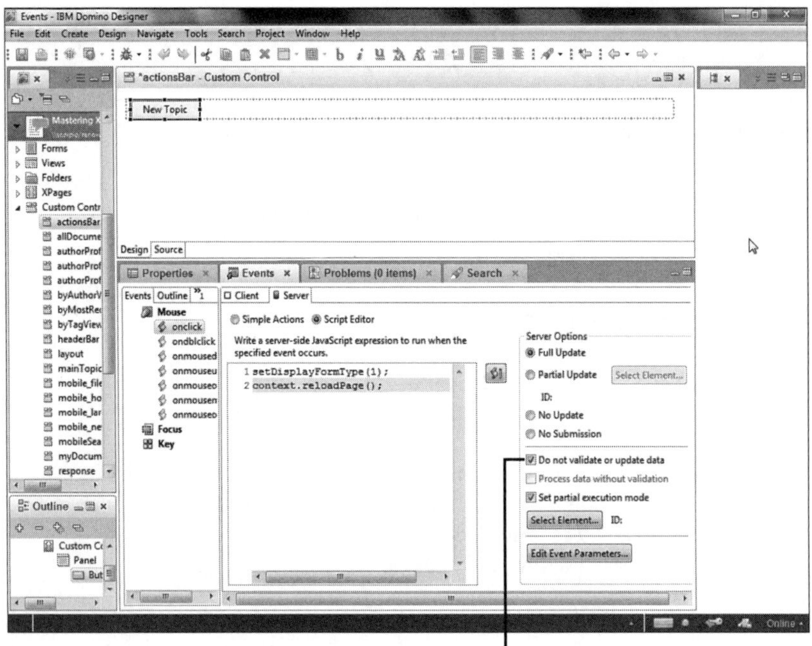

Figure 19.4 The immediate property of an event handler

As just explained, with this option set, XPages Request Processing Lifecycle phases three, four, and five are ignored during server-side processing of the POST-back request. You should use this option when you have an event handler that needs to execute server-side application logic and possibly redirect to a different XPage afterward without an express need to execute validation or save any data sources within the current XPage.

An example of using the `immediate` property can be seen in the XSP markup of Listing 19.3, taken from the `actionsBar` Custom Control in the **Chp19Ed2.nsf** application.

Listing 19.3 XSP Markup Fragment for the buttonNewTopic Control with an Immediate Property

```
...
<xp:button value="New Topic" id="buttonNewTopic">
    ...
    <xp:eventHandler event="onclick" submit="true"
        refreshMode="complete" execMode="partial" immediate="true">
        <xp:this.action>
            <![CDATA[#{javascript:setDisplayFormType(1);
                context.reloadPage();}]]>
        </xp:this.action>
    </xp:eventHandler>
</xp:button>
...
```

Essentially, the button in Listing 19.3 triggers a server-side onclick action that executes some server-side JavaScript and reloads the current XPage in the browser. It does so without processing XPages Request Processing Lifecycle phases three, four, and five, so reducing CPU utilization simply with the `immediate` property set on the button controls the event handler.

Partial Refresh

Appropriate use of the partial refresh capabilities provided by XPages undoubtedly reaps benefits for the performance and responsiveness of your applications. It improves the performance of an application by reducing the amount of HTML markup that must be processed and emitted in a response back to the client or browser; hence, the application server is utilizing less CPU cycles. This has a knock-on effect in that the responsiveness of an application is improved because of less network bandwidth used to relay the response. Combine this with the fact that the client or browser is not actually reloading an entire XPage, only a part of it. This radically reduces the refresh time and gives a much more satisfying visual display due to the elimination of any screen flicker that can occur during a full web page reload.

Using partial refresh results in XPages Request Processing Lifecycle phase six being much more efficient regardless of the HTTP request being GET-based or POST-based. This is due to several reasons, as explained in the following sections.

Only the Selected Branch of the Component Tree Is Processed

This designated branch is defined by setting the `refreshId` property on an event handler to the `id` of a target control (as you learned in Chapter 11). Thereafter, during the Render Response phase, only the renderers of the target refresh control, and its child controls are invoked to emit their HTML markup. Therefore, this partial rendering processes only the controls that need to be rendered during the Render Response phase instead of the whole component tree.

This behavior was different in Notes/Domino 8.5, whereby the entire component tree was rendered during the Render Response phase. This was further complicated by the fact that HTML markup generated by nontarget controls of the partial refresh was discarded before a response was sent to the browser. Obviously, this meant CPU cycles were consumed unnecessarily.

The current behavior in Notes/Domino 9.0.1 has been optimized to avoid the unnecessary invocation of nontarget refresh control renderers; however, this can present an uncommon side effect in an XPage. If some server-side JavaScript is evaluating some expression outside of the target refresh area and is used within the target refresh area (on repeated requests to partially refresh the target area), the value used by the dependent control does not get updated. This is generally easy to fix within an application, but if you require the previous behavior, an XSP property can be set to revert the behavior accordingly:

```
xsp.ajax.renderwholetree=true | false (default false in N/D8.5.2)
```

If you need to use this, you can simply add the `xsp.ajax.renderwholetree` property to the `xsp.properties`. You can find an example of this in the **Chp19Ed2.nsf** application, as shown in Figure 19.5.

HTML Markup for the Response Is Reduced

Because of the targeted invocation of component tree control renderers, a partial refresh request results in less HTML markup being emitted in a response. This means your application requires less CPU cycles on the server and receiving browser, and inherently uses less network bandwidth to transfer the response data.

Browser Processing Is Faster

When an XPage is rendered for the first time, all the JavaScript and CSS files are downloaded, parsed, and executed by the browser. Although today's leading browsers are highly optimized to process web page markup, the delay in processing the incoming markup for a web page can result in a delay of some number of milliseconds, or seconds in poorly developed situations, which can be noticeable by an end user.

When using partial refresh, the XPage is not entirely reloaded by the browser as you now understand, but instead only a designated target area is refreshed. As a direct result, any JavaScript and CSS resources used by the web page do not need to be reloaded from the browser cache or from the web server and reprocessed for each partial refresh request. The end result is a more responsive user interface and less CPU utilization within the end users' client machine.

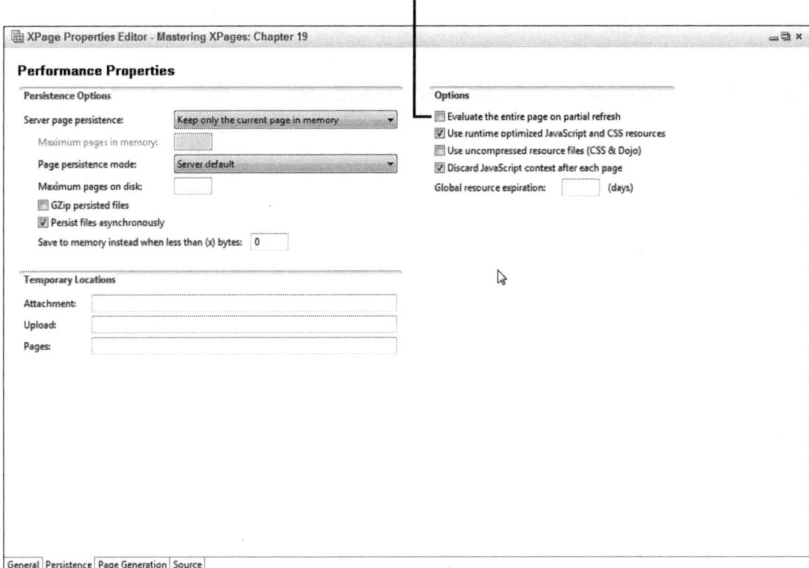

Figure 19.5 The xsp.ajax.renderwholetree property

Partial Execution Mode

Partial execution mode is similar to partial refresh; however, instead of being an optimization for just the Render Response phase of the XPages Request Processing Lifecycle, it allows you to control the amount of component tree processing that occurs during phases two through five of the lifecycle. Also, unlike partial refresh, which affects the requesting browser through the amount of emitted HTML markup received, partial execution mode is purely a server-side optimization. Also note that the two do not depend on each other—you can leverage partial execution mode even for actions that do not use partial refresh, therefore still providing you with a mechanism to optimize the amount of server-side processing performed by an XPages application.

To explain it simply, if only a portion of an XPage should be updated and processed, the event handler control has an `execMode` property that accepts the values of either `complete` or `partial`. By default, this property is set to `complete`. When `partial` mode is specified, only the associated component tree control, and its children, referenced by the event handler is processed through the XPages Request Processing Lifecycle—all other component tree controls for a given XPage are ignored. This is a powerful and efficient feature that can also manage component tree controls held within a Repeat control or other iterable control, such as a Repeat, Data Table, DataView, or View Panel. In such a scenario, the iterator is not re-executed during the invocation of a child event handler, therefore streamlining the amount of CPU usage to a minimum.

Domino Designer makes this feature available to you on the **Server Options** section of the **Events** panel, as shown in Figure 19.6.

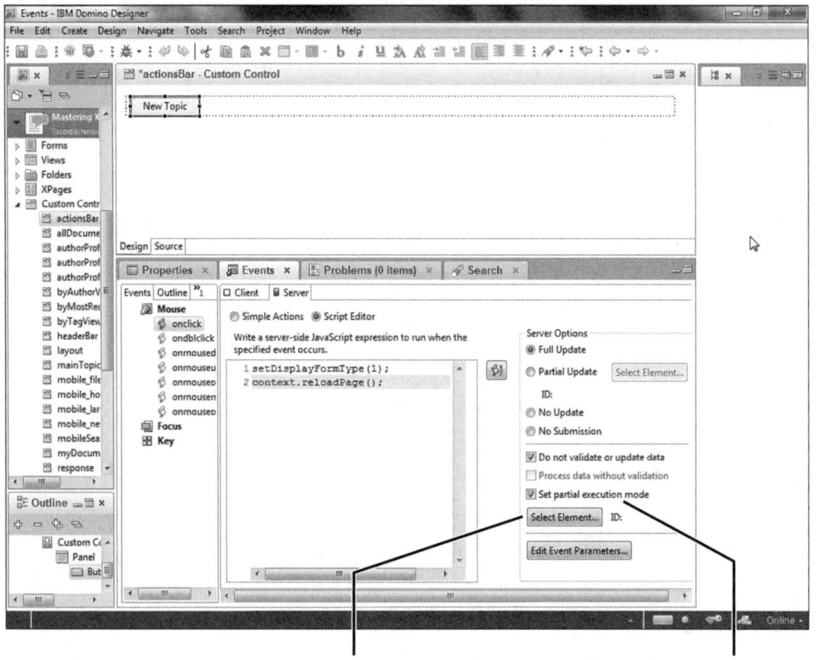

Figure 19.6 Partial Execution Mode and Execution ID options on the Event panel

By simply selecting the **Set partial execution mode** check box, you enable partial execution mode on the event handler of the associated control. This can be taken further, of course, in that you can also set a designated target for partial execution processing instead of the current control and its event handler. This is similar to the way you specify a `refreshId` property for a partial refresh target control. Basically, it allows you to perform targeted partial execution of a portion of an XPage from a control that is not the parent of that target area. This is done by specifying an `execId` property on an event handler with the `id` of the target control. You can set this property in three ways, either adding it directly in the XSP markup for an event handler tag, by using the Execution ID editor, as shown in Figure 19.6, or by using the **All Properties** panel for an event handler, as shown in Figure 19.7.

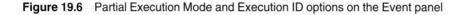

The execId property for the buttonSave Event Handler

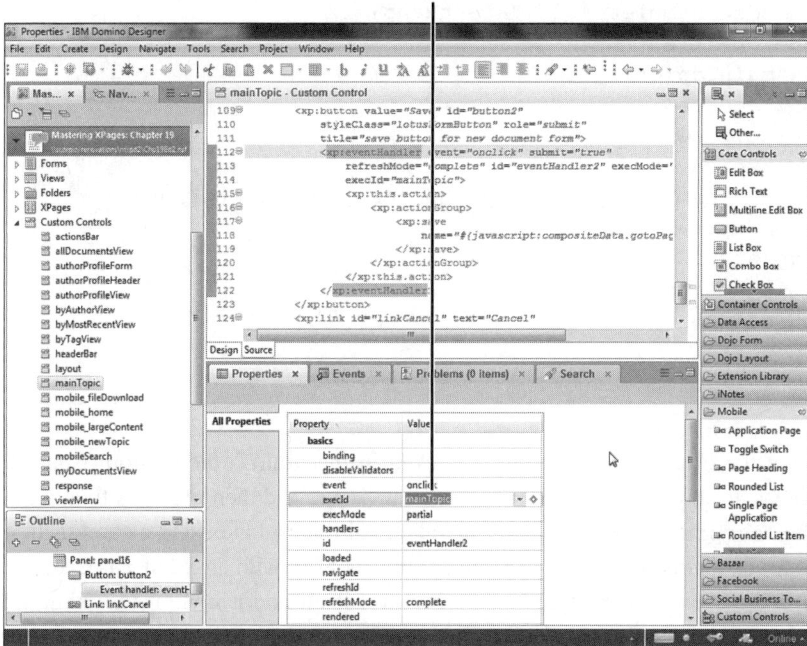

Figure 19.7 execId property exposed in the All Properties of an event handler

You can find an example of using `execMode` and `execId` in tandem in the **Chp19Ed2.nsf** application within the **mainTopic** Custom Control. For your convenience, Listing 19.4 shows the relevant XSP markup for you.

Listing 19.4 XSP Markup Fragment for buttonSave in mainTopic.xsp and allDocuments.xsp

```
...
<!-- allDocuments.xsp -->
<xc:mainTopic
    id="mainTopic"
    gotoPage="/allDocuments.xsp">
</xc:mainTopic>
...
...
<!-- mainTopic.xsp -->
<xp:button value="Save" id="buttonSave">
```

```
    <xp:eventHandler event="onclick" submit="true"
        refreshMode="complete" id="eventHandler2"
        execMode="partial"
        execId="mainTopic">
        <xp:this.action>
            <xp:actionGroup>
                <xp:save
                    name="#{javascript:compositeData.gotoPage}">
                </xp:save>
            </xp:actionGroup>
        </xp:this.action>
    </xp:eventHandler>
</xp:button>
...
```

Basically, when the **buttonSave** button is clicked in the **mainTopic** Custom Control, a Save simple action saves any data sources on the current XPage and then redirects to a target XPage defined by the `compositeData.gotoPage` value. All this is done using a combination of partial execution mode that is targeted to execute only the control with an `id` of `mainTopic`. This target control is the actual **mainTopic** Custom Control itself and is contained within the **allDocuments** XPage. This means that only the Custom Control and all its child controls get executed through the XPages Request Processing Lifecycle when the **allDocuments** XPage is submitted to save data held on the **mainTopic** Custom Control, thus minimizing the amount of CPU utilization needed in this case.

Using the immediate Property with Partial Execution Mode

In some cases, it makes perfect sense to combine the use of both the `immediate` property and partial execution mode, typically for a Cancel button, but also for actions that do not require the data in the current XPage to be processed during a POST-back request. For example, when clicking a Pager control bound to some iterator, such as a View Panel, or when selecting actions within a custom built Repeat view, such as More/Hide. In effect, this combination of settings allows a POST-based HTTP request to not only avoid XPages Request Processing Lifecycle phases three, four, and five, but to also leverage the power of a targeted partial execution for a branch of the component tree.

Some of the XPage Core Controls support a `partialExecute` property to make it easy for you to use this combination of immediate and partial execution features. If you examine the properties of a Pager or View Panel control, you see this property listed among its **All Properties**, as shown in Figure 19.8 for the Pager control.

Note that both the Pager and the View Panel controls (used for its category row collapse/expand actions) have their `partialExecute` property set to true by default.

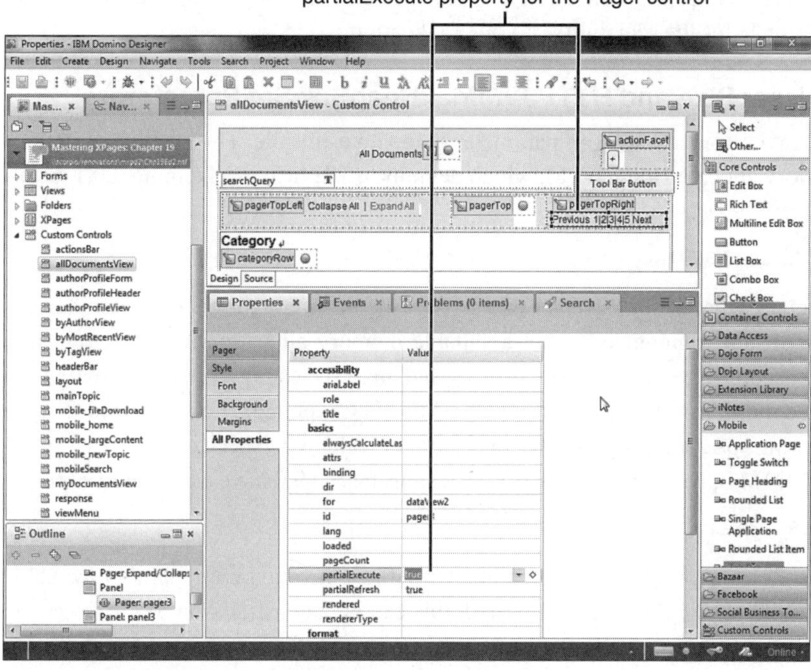

Figure 19.8 The partialExecute property for the Pager control

Reducing Memory Utilization

The XPages runtime persists (or serializes, depending on whichever terminology you prefer) a predefined number of component tree state representations for the XPages requested by users during their sessions using an application. A standard JavaServer Faces application can be configured to save the state of a component tree on the client or server, but XPages does it specifically on the server. Therefore, it is important to minimize the amount of information that is persisted into the component tree state to avoid unnecessary degradation of server performance and potential scalability. The smaller it is kept allows a server to manage more users with the same amount of JVM memory. You need to be aware of a few things in this area:

- `HTTPJVMMaxHeapSize` and `HTTPJVMMaxHeapSizeSet` parameters
- `xsp.persistence.*` properties
- `dataCache` property

The following sections describe these features so that you gain an understanding of the ways in which you can optimize the amount of memory consumed by your XPages applications. The biggest impact of memory is in enabling an application to scale to larger numbers of users and requests. Where reducing CPU utilization helps the performance of your application, reducing memory utilization helps the scalability of your application.

HTTPJVMMaxHeapSize and HTTPJVMMaxHeapSizeSet Parameters

You can find the `HTTPJVMMaxHeapSize` parameter in the notes.ini file. This parameter defines the maximum memory allocated to the JVM, which defaults to 1024Mb in a Domino 9.0.1 installation, as shown here:

```
HTTPJVMMaxHeapSize=1024M
```

The more memory that is allocated for this setting, the more concurrent users can be supported by a server. It is recommended to set a suitable memory allocation to this setting in a production server based on careful memory profiling and analysis testing of potential maximum expected workload conditions—you will learn more on this in Chapter 20. You also need to specify the `HTTPJVMMaxHeapSizeSet` parameter to ensure the value you specify is not reset to the system default of 1024M in Notes/Domino 9.0.1. (Versions before 9.0 have a default of 64M.)

```
HTTPJVMMaxHeapSizeSet=1
```

Although the `HTTPJVMMaxHeapSize` parameter defines the maximum memory available to the JVM and not the physical memory allocated, this can be a constraint on 32-bit operating systems, such as some versions of Windows. In this case, a contiguous range of addressable memory is reserved for the operating system address space, therefore reducing the total space made available for other processes such as the Java Virtual Machine. This impacts applications and services as it reduces the amount of memory available for normal running use—hence, less memory for the HTTP server itself. Note that, on 64-bit systems, this is typically not a problem, and this parameter should be set to a higher value relative to the total available physical memory of the server hardware.

It is important to note that just by setting a higher JVM heapspace memory allocation does not mean a server will be optimally tuned—indeed it is fair to say that there is no "silver bullet" in terms of a perfect JVM heapspace memory size that will fit all demands for any given server. Just by setting a higher value relative to the amount of available memory space on a system is only a starting point to achieving highly optimized usage of JVM heapspace memory. To reach this goal requires a deeper understanding of the XPages applications within a server. In some instances, XPages applications may be putting little demand on memory usage, versus others that may be completely and unnecessarily hogging JVM heapspace memory. This can boil down to such things as suboptimal server-side Java, Managed Bean, or server-side JavaScript cluttering JVM memory with scoped variables and large objects, and further compounded by improper use of the XPages State Management Layer.

You will read about Server Page Persistence in the next section, but over and above this you will learn in great detail much more on this feature along with how you can profile and monitor JVM heapspace memory usage of your XPages Applications in Chapter 20.

xsp.persistence.* Properties

The underlying XPages JSF framework persists a predefined maximum number of component tree state representations for XPages requested by users during their session using an application. This process happens to allow a component tree to be restored with its previous state as users navigate their way back and forward through an application. It also helps to improve the performance of the Restore View phase of the XPages Request Processing Lifecycle when reconstructing a component tree.

To cater for differing application workloads that require a balancing of scalability and performance capabilities, XPages supports three different persistence modes. This feature is known as Server Page Persistence and can be configured using the XPages tab of the **Application Properties** editor, as shown in Figure 19.9. (Note that the term `page` is used in this context to refer to a component tree state representation.)

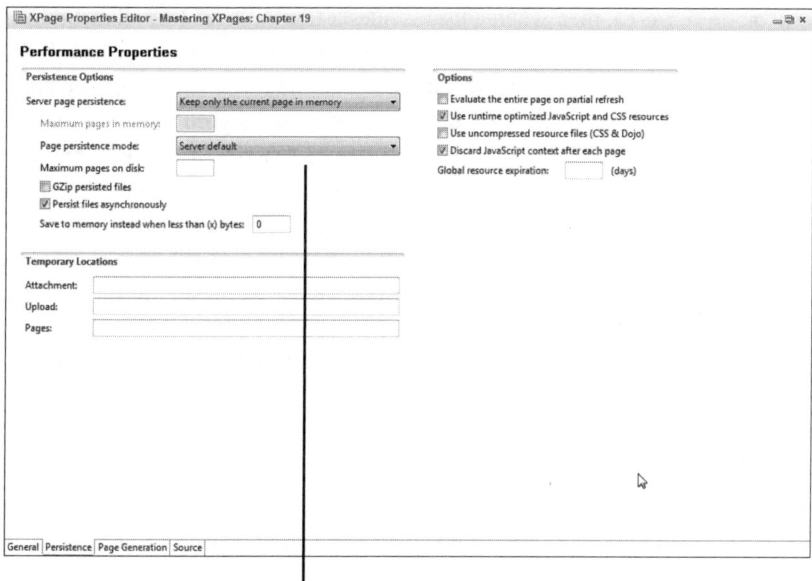

Persistence Options including Server Page Persistence and others

Figure 19.9 The Server Page Persistence options

The three different modes enable you to optimize the component tree state persistence process as follows:

- **`basic`:** Keeps all pages in memory (performs well)
- **`file`:** Keeps all pages on disk (scales well—default setting in Notes/Domino 9.0.1)
- **`fileex`:** Keeps only the current page in memory (scales and performs well)

As mentioned previously, you can configure Server Page Persistence using the XPages tab of the **Application Properties** editor since Notes/Domino 9.0. By doing so, the `xsp.persistence.mode` property is written into the `xsp.properties` file of an application like the following example:

```
xsp.persistence.mode=fileex
```

By default, the number of component tree state representations persisted is limited to 4 when the `xsp.persistence.mode` property is set to `basic`. Otherwise, when `xsp.persistence.mode` is set to either `file` or `fileex`, it is limited to 16. Two properties are used to configure these limits under each context, like so:

```
xsp.persistence.tree.maxviews=4  (for basic mode)
xsp.persistence.file.maxviews=16 (for file and fileex mode)
```

For example, this means that if an application is configured to Keep all pages in memory (`xsp.persistence.mode=basic`), then when a user requests four XPages from that application, the maximum number of persisted component trees and their state has been reached. If the user then requests a fifth XPage from the same application, one of the preexisting persisted component trees are discarded from the cache based on a most recently used algorithm.

Therefore, these properties enable you to establish a balance between faster component tree restoration and minimizing the amount of memory used to maintain the persisted component tree state representations based on the application workload. The default limits for persisted pages under each mode is adequate for most of the common use cases, but as mentioned previously, if you need to reconfigure these properties, you can do so by setting them in the `xsp.properties` file of an application. Alternatively, they can also be specified in the global `xsp.properties` file of a server to reset any applications running in that server that do not provide their own specific overriding values.

dataCache Property

You were first introduced to this property in Chapter 8, in the section "Caching View Data." A fully worked example is detailed in that section, so it is worth revisiting if you've not done so, or need a quick recap.

The `dataCache` property optimizes the amount of component tree data persisted when an XPage containing a Domino View data source is requested. When an `xp:dominoView` data source is included on an XPage, the XPages runtime needs to persist the view-related values displayed by the XPage in the event that a POST-back submission of the same XPage might occur. This mechanism ensures that the same view-related data is available for processing during the Apply Request Values phase and subsequent phases of the XPages Request Processing Lifecycle for the POST-back request regardless of any changes that may have occurred to the underlying view data within the database. However, this mechanism introduces two costly side effects:

- The persisted view-related data for the Domino View data source can consume a large amount of JVM memory.
- Not all the objects within the view-related data can be easily persisted or restored, if at all in some cases, such as Domino backend Java objects. Therefore, some level of transformation or representation is required that can consume more memory and CPU cycles.

Therefore, you can optimize the Domino View data source based on its requirements to be more memory and CPU efficient using the `dataCache` property. Basically, the rules here are that, if the view-related data is not required during a POST-back request by any server-side JavaScript code, a subset of scalar type view-related data need only be persisted. This scalar data includes the `id` of the XPages view row entry and its `position`—essentially, just enough information to reconstruct the Domino View-related data during normal pagination or category row expand/collapse requests.

Figure 19.10 shows where you can find the `dataCache` property within Domino Designer when working with the Domino View data source.

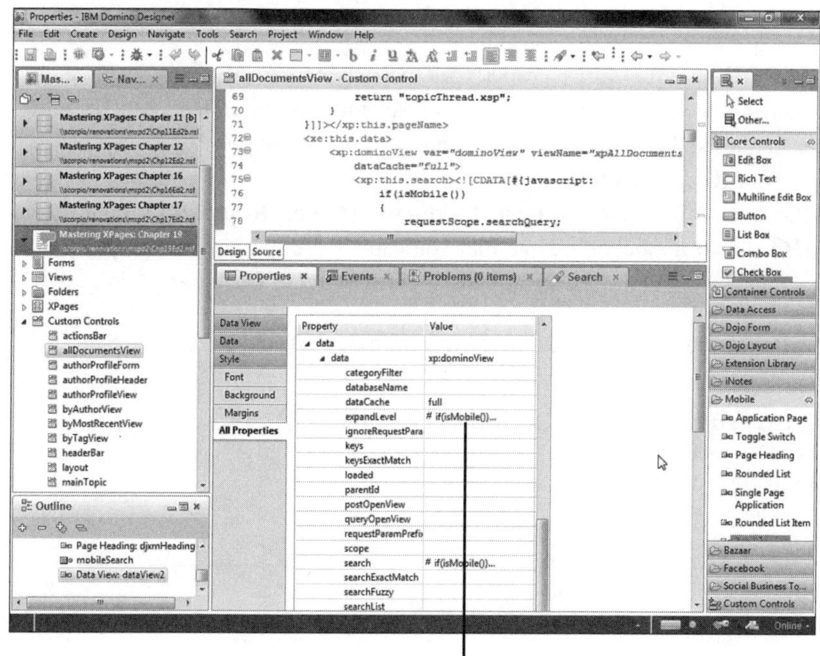

Figure 19.10 The dataCache property within the Domino View data source properties

Three different values are supported by the `dataCache` property:

- **full [default]:** The entire view-related data is persisted after a request. This can reduce the amount of CPU processing required to reconstruct the Domino View data source during a subsequent request for the same XPage. Access to the column values is possible during a POST-back request by server-side JavaScript code. This option consumes the most memory and CPU utilization of these three options.
- **id:** Only a minimum amount of scalar type view-related data, such as `id` and `position`, is persisted after a request. Access to the column values is not possible during a POST-back request by server-side JavaScript code. This option uses the least amount of CPU utilization and an optimized amount of memory consumption of these three options.
- **none:** No view-related data is persisted after a request. More CPU processing is required on a subsequent request for the same XPage as the Domino View data source needs to be fully reconstructed. Access to the column values is possible during a POST-back request by server-side JavaScript code as the view-related data has been fully reconstructed. This option uses the least amount of memory of the three options but requires the most CPU utilization.

As you can see, with the `dataCache` property set to `id`, a Domino View data source uses less CPU utilization and reduces the amount of memory consumption needed to restore the view-related data between requests. Therefore, try to use this option for Domino View data sources whenever possible in your XPages applications.

Listing 19.5 shows an XSP markup fragment taken from the **allDocumentsView** Custom Control in the **Chp16Ed2.nsf** application. Note that you can set the `dataCache` property on a Domino View data source by using the **All Properties > Data panel in Designer**.

Listing 19.5 XSP Markup Fragment for a Domino View Data Source with dataCache Set

```
...
<xp:dominoView var="dominoView"
    viewName="xpAllDocuments"
    dataCache="full">
    ...
</xp:dominoView>
```

Conclusion

This concludes this introductory chapter on application performance and scalability. You learned about a wide range of features and practices that you can leverage to help optimize your XPages applications to reduce the amount of CPU and memory used. You gained an understanding of the XPages Request Processing Lifecycle and the ways in which you can use partial refresh and partial execution to streamline execution of the lifecycle. This has given you a vital skill in knowing when to apply these features within your application so that every XPage request is tailored to be fast and efficient. You also gained an understanding of the ways in which you can increase the amount of allocated JVM memory but also how to help your application use less of it. In essence, this enables your application to process more users and requests.

You should now appreciate that, by spending time during your development cycles to focus on reducing utilization of CPU and memory, you help your XPages applications perform faster, serve more users and requests, and thereby keep your application users and customers satisfied.

In Chapter 20, you learn more about performance and scalability and the ways in which you can profile an XPages application and then interpret and analyze such information. This enables you to unravel the inner workings of an XPages application so that you can gain deeper insight into how it is functioning and performing under stress-loaded conditions. In turn, you can progressively and systematically identify and eradicate performance and scalability bottlenecks from an XPages application.

CHAPTER 20

Advanced Performance Topics

The time has finally arrived to deep dive into more complex performance topics. In this chapter, you learn how to investigate the performance behavior of XPages applications using profilers, memory analyzers, as well as some other interesting tools and techniques. This enables you not only to pinpoint performance bottlenecks, but also to provide remedies using field-tested best practices for each use case.

Unless you are an experienced XPages developer, it is not recommended that you jump in here without first reading Chapter 19, "A First Look at Performance and Scalability," as an absolute prerequisite. You do need to understand the JSF request processing lifecycle, to have a basic competence in Java programming, and to be comfortable with concepts like threading and so forth to get the most out of this chapter. Also, you need full administrative access to a Domino server including the ability to modify security settings to take full advantage of some of the topics discussed.

The performance material covered here has been developed over several years based on lessons learned from real-world scenarios. Some of the content was first delivered as part of a series of XPages Performance Master Classes that received a terrific response from the community. It has since been honed further, and this is the first opportunity to encapsulate all the content concisely in a single place. **Chp20ed2.nsf** contains the worked examples that you need to experiment with and can be downloaded from this website: `www.ibmpressbooks.com/title/9780133373370`. Note that you also need to install and sign another Domino application **XPagesToolbox.nsf** because this is used as an important profiling tool throughout this chapter—starting now.

Making Efficient XPages Requests

A key factor in ensuring that an XPages application is both performant and robust is the efficiency and scalability of its request/response cycle. These challenges are dealt with separately. This section explores the various tools and techniques that can be exploited to deliver efficiency.

Scalability impediments and solutions are dealt with later in the section, "Making Scalable XPages Requests."

Profiling XPages Applications

A *profiler* is a tool used to measure program performance by analyzing things like the duration and frequency of the procedures called from within your application. When a performance problem is reported with a particular XPages application, as an XPages developer, you usually have some intuition as to what the source of the underlying problem might be based on the symptoms described. It is surprising how often these inklings are wrong—not to mention the time wasted investigating non-offending code and features! The value of a good profiling tool is that it can take all the guesswork out of identifying the cause of a given performance issue and help you to speedily get to the problem at the heart of the matter. The XPages Toolbox does exactly that.

Toolbox Setup

The XPages Toolbox is a prime example of yet another great OpenNTF.org project. It was contributed by Philippe Riand (IBM) in 2010 and has more than 2,000 downloads at the time of this writing. To install the latest release of the toolbox, you need to download the latest release from OpenNTF at `www.openntf.org/projects/pmt.nsf/ProjectLookup/XPages%20 Toolbox`.

Figure 20.1 displays the project's content when you expand the toolbox zip file locally after completing the download.

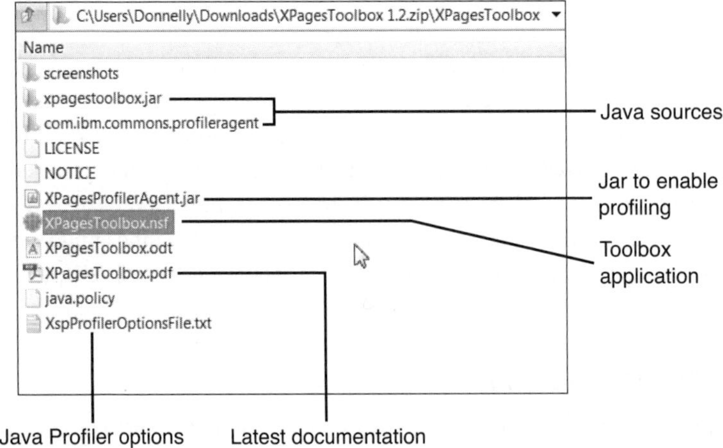

Figure 20.1 XPages Toolbox project artifacts

Next, you need to carry out the following steps to get the toolbox up and running on the Domino server:

1. Copy **XPagesToolbox.nsf** to the data folder of the Domino server.
2. Sign the NSF using Domino Designer or the Domino Administrator program.
3. Copy **XPagesProfileAgent.jar** to the `xsp` folder under the root directory of the Domino server.
4. Copy **XPagesProfilerOptionsFile.txt** to the same `xsp` folder and then update the **javaagent:** property within this file to match the file path to **XPagesProfileAgent.jar** in step 3.
5. Add this new line

   ```
   "JavaOptionsFile=C:\Domino\xsp\XspProfilerOptionsFile.txt"
   ```

   to your **notes.ini** file where the path should also match the file path to the **XPages ProfilerOptionsFile.txt** file in step 4.
6. Modify the **java.policy** file in the `jvm/lib/security` folder under the Domino root directory to contain the entry shown in Listing 20.1.
7. Restart the Domino server, and keep a watch out for this message in the console:

   ```
   *** Activating IBM XPages profiler agent
   ```

8. Restart the Domino server and load **XPagesToolbox.nsf** application in a browser.

If you have completed these eight steps successfully, the toolbox application will open at its home page, as shown later in Figure 20.3.

Listing 20.1 Permission Grant for the Toolbox Application to Run the Java Code

```
grant codeBase "xspnsf://server:0/xpagestoolbox.nsf/script/-" {
   permission  com.ibm.designer.runtime.domino.adapter.security.
AdminPermission "AdminPermission.debug";
};
```

Suffice to say that the code in Listing 20.1 grants special permission to the **XPagesToolbox.nsf** application, and only that application, to have the elevated administrative debug privileges needed to profile applications. In Figure 20.1 you saw a source folder for **XPagesToolbox.jar** but no actual jar file. That is because the jar file is contained within **XPagesToolbox.nsf** (as shown in Figure 20.2) and loaded and run from there—hence the need to grant permission to that application. More detailed information on security topics like this is discussed in Chapter 21 "Security." The section "Troubleshooting XPages Java Security Exceptions" deals with granting permissions just like this one.

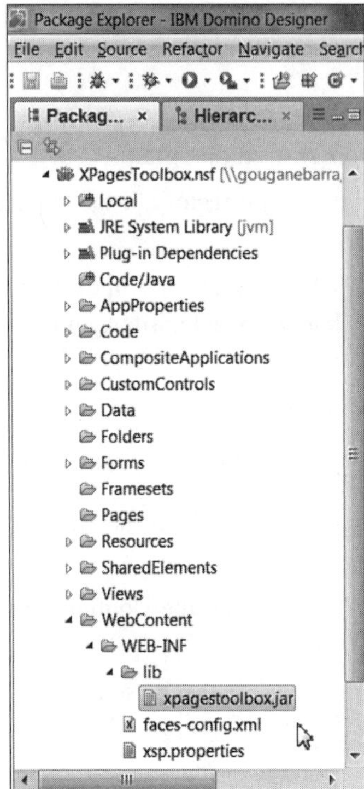

Figure 20.2 XPagesToolbox.jar located within XPagesToolbox.nsf

A word to the wise: It should be apparent, due to the security adjustments you have to make, that this tool should not be run on production servers. The toolbox requires some invasive powers to analyze the behavior of an XPages application, inspect session data, and so forth. As a consequence, this can potentially compromise the security of your Notes/Domino runtime installation and you are thus advised to use this tool only in a private development environment. If you must use it in a production environment to resolve a problem, you should do so expediently, protect the access to **XPagesToolbox.nsf** via its ACL, and remember to disable the toolbox when your profiling investigations are complete.

In the event that the XPage Toolbox has not loaded properly, you may want to consult the following checklist to ensure that you avoid some common errors:

- **XPagesToolbox.nsf** has not been signed with the appropriate id.
- You are attempting to use the toolbox on an older version of Notes/Domino. (8.5.2 is the minimum version required.)

- **XPagesToolbox.nsf** has not been installed into the default data folder. Installing into a subfolder means that permission granted in Step 8 needs to be updated to reflect the correct NSF path.
- Verify that there are no typos in your new **notes.ini** entry.

> **TIP**
>
> Although we have described the setup of the toolbox using the Domino server, the application also runs in the Notes client. Follow the same instructions outlined previously *except* for those pertaining to the profiler configuration, as described in steps 4 and 5. Instead you need to update the <notes_root_dir>\framework\rcp\deploy\jvm.properties file and add this line:
>
> ```
> vmarg.javaagent=-javaagent:c:/Notes85/xsp/XPagesProfilerAgent.jar
> ```

The XPages Toolbox project, although unlikely to undergo *radical* change in the future, will continue to improve and evolve on OpenNTF.org. Remember that the documentation provided with the project, as highlighted in Figure 20.1, will always have the latest and greatest information on the setup and features of the toolbox—so it a good idea to check there periodically and make sure you are up to date. In any case, it's now time to start profiling.

Using the XPages Toolbox

The tabbed UI displayed in Figure 20.3 shows seven different categorizations of tooling, from CPU profiling to logging. This section concentrates on the **CPU Profiler** and **Backend Profiler** tabs, in that order.

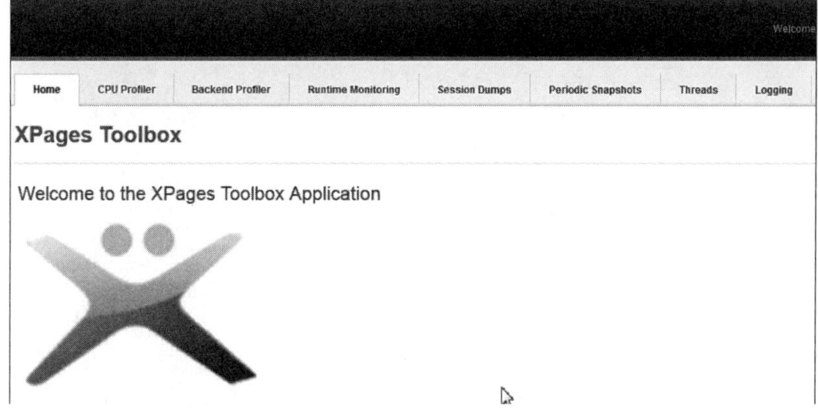

Figure 20.3 XPagesToolbox.nsf when first loaded in a browser

CPU Profiler

The title of this tab tells only one-half of the story in terms of what it offers because the profiling options available here can measure the time your computer system spends running your application (CPU time) *and/or* the real-world time taken to run your application (wall clock time). The former encompasses all the processing time spent actively running your code plus any OS level functions it invokes. The latter reflects what the user experiences, literally the time taken to run the program according to the clock on the wall. This measurement can be strongly affected by third-party noise like network activity, unrelated background processes, and such. Nonetheless wall clock time can be a useful metric—just that you must be aware that the results can be skewed by factors of circumstance, such as those already mentioned.

The sample application provided with this chapter provides good examples that you can use for both cpu profiling and wall clock profiling. Open **Chp20ed2.nsf** in Domino Designer and look at the **testCPUvsWallTime** XPage. It contains three snippets of interest from a profiling perspective, the first of which is illustrated in Listing 20.2.

Listing 20.2 SSJS Code Performing a CPU-Intensive Task

```
<xp:button value="Run CPU Intensive Task (clocking 'CPU Time')"
id="button1">
    <xp:eventHandler event="onclick" submit="true"
        refreshMode="complete">
        <xp:this.action>
            <![CDATA[#{javascript:
                println("Performing CPU intensive operation...");
                var i = java.lang.System.currentTimeMillis();
                var t = i + 10000, r = 0;
                for(var c = i;
                       c < t;
                       c = java.lang.System.currentTimeMillis()){
                      r += 14562 / 38344;
                      r += 45645 / 45455;
                      r += 96279 / 34278;
                      r += 99059 / 64493;
                      r += 99059 / 64492;
                      r += 32655 / 42039;
                      r += 15299 / 67838;
                      r += 86785 / 80672;
                      r += 16768 / 93296;
                      r += 47892 / 13403;
                      r += 37801 / 70415;
                      r += 48427 / 28505;
                }
                println("Finished CPU intensive operation!");
            }]]>
```

```
        </xp:this.action>
    </xp:eventHandler>
</xp:button>
```

A quick inspection of the code snippet indicates that it performs long division operations over the course of 10 seconds—an operation that should keep your CPU reasonably well occupied for the duration of the `for` loop. This will serve you well as a trial use case for the CPU profiler. Given that you know what the code is doing, then profiling this operation using the XPages Toolbox should both affirm the expected results as well as enable you to get familiar with the reporting mechanism it uses.

A good practice here would be to open the **testCPUvsWallTime** XPage in an adjacent browser tab to the toolbox application. This can enable you to quickly flip from the profiler to the test application, which you need to do to run and measure the test operations. When both applications are open side by side, activate the **XPages Toolbox** and select the **CPU Profiler tab**. You will see an XPage similar to that shown in Figure 20.4.

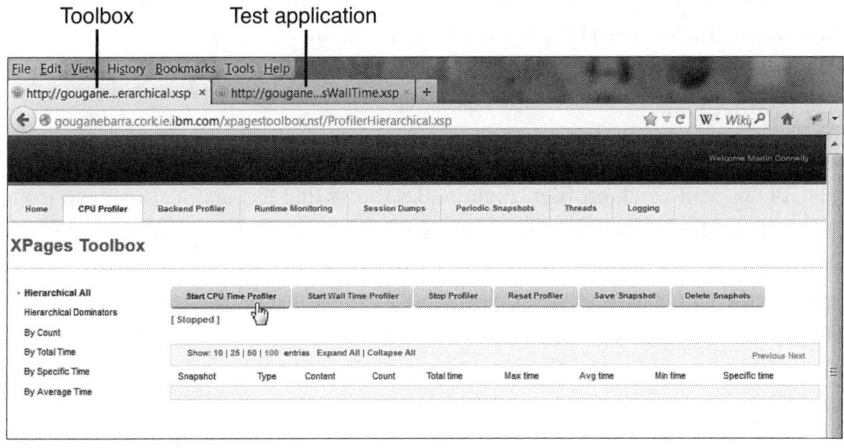

Figure 20.4 XPagesToolbox.nsf with the CPU Profiler ready to go

Effectively, the toolbox gives you a bunch of different views stacked vertically in the left navigator and an array of actions aligned horizontally across the top of the page. To profile the CPU-intensive use case, you should carry out the following steps:

1. Click the **Start CPU Time Profiler** button.
2. Switch to the adjacent tab containing the sample application, and click the **Run CPU Intensive Task (clocking 'CPU time')** button, as shown in Figure 20.5.
3. When this operation completes, revert to the toolbox, and click the **Stop Profiler** button.

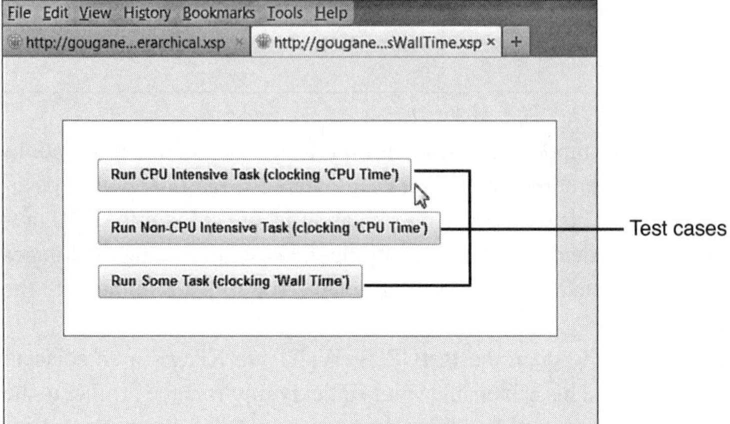

Figure 20.5 Chp20ed2.nsf with the test testCPUvsWallTime page open and ready for testing

4. Click the **100 entries** option when a report for the profiling operation you just completed appears in the XPage. This should happen immediately.
5. If you do not want to continue from this point to measure other related operations, click the **Reset Profiler** button.

These five steps represent a common repeatable pattern used to profile an operation, whether using the CPU or wall clock profiler. Figure 20.5 shows that test application page from the sample chapter displayed in a browser—that is, the page that you should have open in the tab adjoining the toolbox tab.

After completing the CPU profiling steps, you should expand the profiler report and examine its results. The report title is effectively a timestamp representing the absolute time at which the operation was run. Next to it lies the **Type** column that classifies the kind of operation that was run (like a JavaScript expression, for example) and the phase of the JSF lifecycle in which it was executed. Given that these tests are submitted as post requests, this means that all six phases of the JSF lifecycle feature in the report, as you can see. The **Content** column provides some specific detail for each operation carried out in the particular test case, for instance, the actual JavaScript code executed, or as much of the code as can be squeezed into the column space. The **Count** column is potentially interesting because it shows the number of times a particular piece of code was called. Because performance bottlenecks are commonly caused by large iterative repetitive execution of some code block, this is a column you will learn to look at immediately when deciphering issues. Finally, there is an array of time value columns, all recorded in milliseconds, giving the max/min, average, and total times associated with each line item and also the cumulative times when several operations occur within a group, as you will see in later examples. The profiler report for a sample run of the code shown in Listing 20.2 is displayed in full in Figure 20.6.

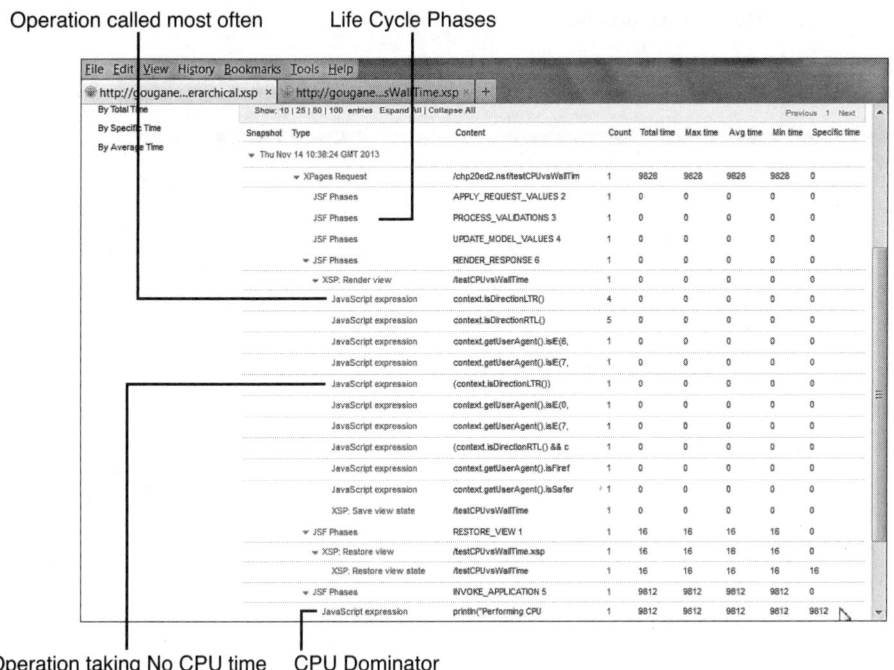

Figure 20.6 CPU Profiler report for a sample CPU-intensive operation

As you would expect, the overall CPU time taken to run the operation should be in the region of 10 seconds. In this instance, the overall time taken is 9,828 milliseconds, or 9.828 seconds, so it is pretty much as you would expect. Why not exactly 10 seconds you may well ask, because the code was set up to loop for that precise duration? The answer is that 10 seconds is the wall time assigned to the loop operation. In other words, the loop is structured to fire long division operations at the CPU for 10 seconds, but inevitably there must be some overhead time associated with the loop code itself, so the actual CPU time spent executing the instructions will always be that little bit less than the time assigned to code that wraps it.

Another observation to make on the data presented in Figure 20.6 is that a lot of the operations featured in the report took virtually no CPU time at all. There are 16 rows with a total time of zero milliseconds. This can be because the operation was lightweight or possibly able to take advantage of the runtime computed expression cache. To remove this noise from the report, you can click the **Hierarchical Dominators** link in the toolbox navigator. This is just a fancy way of saying that you want to see only the total time taken for operations above zero CPU time, or only entries that have influenced or perhaps dominated the outcome. Figure 20.7 shows the same profile run displayed after **Hierarchical Dominators** has been selected.

Option to filter out zero total time operations

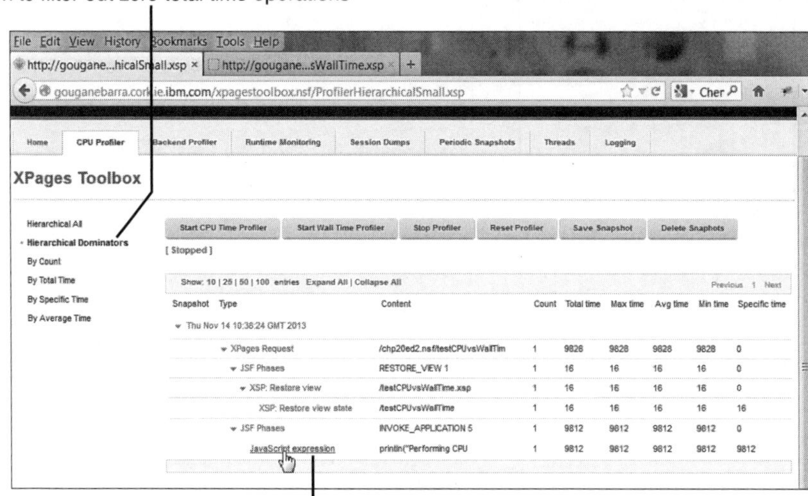

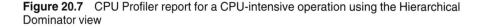

Links to deep dive on underlying code

Figure 20.7 CPU Profiler report for a CPU-intensive operation using the Hierarchical Dominator view

With the report reduced to just six lines, it becomes much easier to see the important aspects of it. A powerful feature of the profiler is that it allows you to dive on the code behind any of the operations reported on a given row. So, after you have studied the reduced data set presented in Figure 20.7 and now that you know how to interpret it, you can quickly home in on the bottom line—the single operation that took practically all the CPU time (9,812 milliseconds). By clicking the JavaScript expression link for that entry, as highlighted in Figure 20.7, you can expose the culprit. You should expect in this use case that you will be taken to the long division code you first saw in Listing 20.2, and so you are. Figure 20.8 illustrates the actual information displayed by the toolbox.

The capability of the profiler to pinpoint issues in this way is powerful. The navigator provides several other options that present the profile data from different perspectives; for example, sorted highest to lowest by count (number of times an operation was called), specific times for reported entries, and so forth. You need to experiment with these options to see how each one can offer different insights into what's happening in your application.

Now it's time to look at another example. This sample takes approximately the same length of time to run as the previous one (from an end user perspective) but consume virtually no CPU cycles. Listing 20.3 shows the SSJS code for this example.

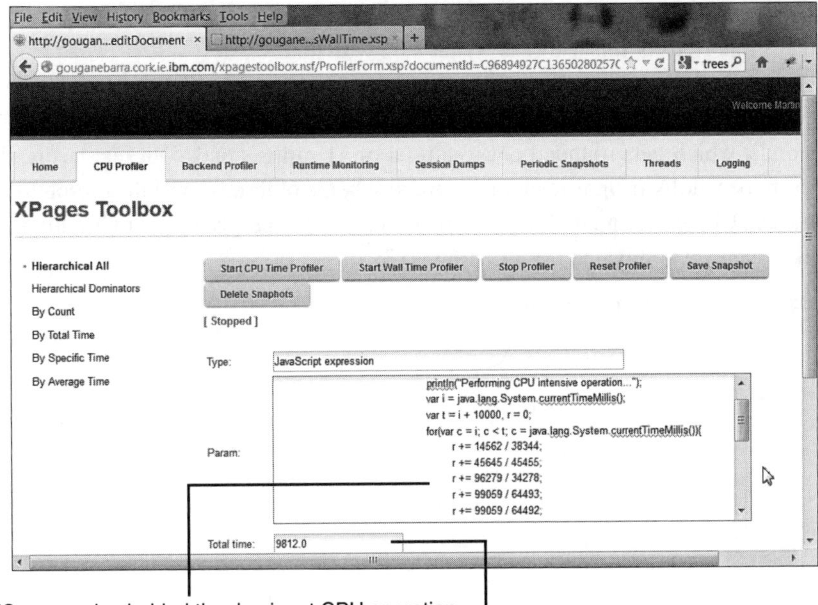

Figure 20.8 CPU Profiler deep dive on the JavaScript expression behind a particular entry

Listing 20.3 SSJS Code Performing a Non-CPU-Intensive Task

```
<xp:button value="Run non-CPU Intensive Task (clocking 'CPU Time')"
id="button3">
   <xp:eventHandler event="onclick" submit="true"
      refreshMode="complete">
      <xp:this.action>
         <![CDATA[#{javascript:
            println("Performing Non-CPU intensive operation...");
            java.lang.Thread.sleep(10000);
            println("Finished Non-CPU intensive operation!");
         }]]>
      </xp:this.action>
   </xp:eventHandler>
</xp:button>
```

To run this code through the CPU profiler, do as you did as the last time, but click the **Run Non-CPU Intensive Task (clocking 'CPU time')** button instead. This will generate a new profiler report. The critical point to notice is that although roughly the same real-world time elapsed when running this latest test, the CPU takes a different view of things. A meager 31 milliseconds of CPU time is reported for this use case. What's up with that?

As shown in Figure 20.9, the CPU profiler reports only two flimsy lifecycle events, `Restore View` and `Render View`, as those taking any CPU cycles. Both are logged as taking 16 milliseconds, which gets rounded out to a total of 31 milliseconds—in real terms, this is so negligible as to be wholly insignificant in the grand scheme of things. And the reason for this disconnect between CPU time and real-world time is because the program spent virtually all its time sleeping, as evidenced in this line from Listing 20.3:

```
java.lang.Thread.sleep(10000);
```

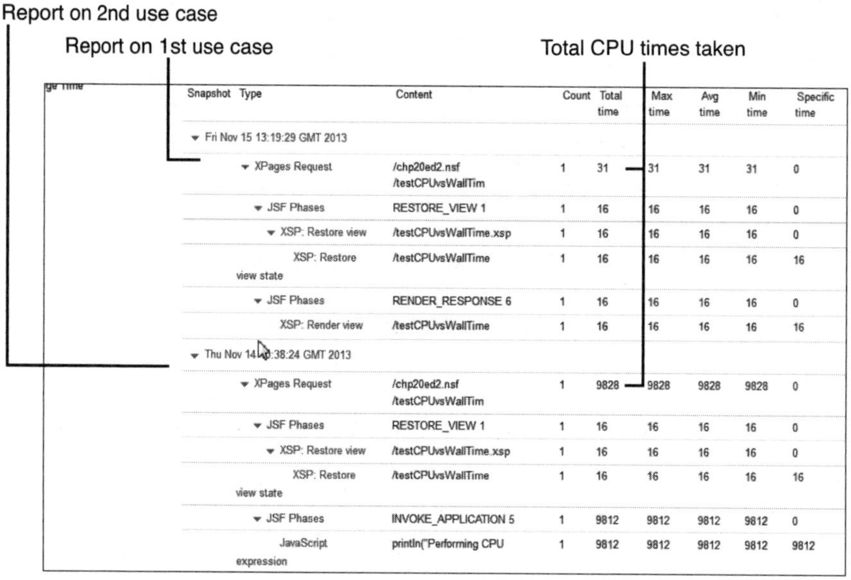

Report on 2nd use case

Report on 1st use case

Total CPU times taken

Snapshot Type	Content	Count	Total time	Max time	Avg time	Min time	Specific time
▾ Fri Nov 15 13:19:29 GMT 2013							
▾ XPages Request	/chp20ed2.nsf /testCPUvsWallTim	1	31	31	31	31	0
▾ JSF Phases	RESTORE_VIEW 1	1	16	16	16	16	0
▾ XSP: Restore view	/testCPUvsWallTime.xsp	1	16	16	16	16	0
XSP: Restore view state	/testCPUvsWallTime	1	16	16	16	16	16
▾ JSF Phases	RENDER_RESPONSE 6	1	16	16	16	16	0
XSP: Render view	/testCPUvsWallTime	1	16	16	16	16	16
▾ Thu Nov 14 1[illegible]:38:24 GMT 2013							
▾ XPages Request	/chp20ed2.nsf /testCPUvsWallTim	1	9828	9828	9828	9828	0
▾ JSF Phases	RESTORE_VIEW 1	1	16	16	16	16	0
▾ XSP: Restore view	/testCPUvsWallTime.xsp	1	16	16	16	16	0
XSP: Restore view state	/testCPUvsWallTime	1	16	16	16	16	16
▾ JSF Phases	INVOKE_APPLICATION 5	1	9812	9812	9812	9812	0
JavaScript expression	println("Performing CPU	1	9812	9812	9812	9812	9812

Figure 20.9 CPU Profiler reports for CPU-intensive and non-CPU-intensive use cases

The message to the developer from this use case is that even though the program takes more than 10 seconds to run, the profile indicates that it is not spending any time of note in the CPU. So, if a program is not hogging the CPU but still taking a considerable time to run, what other avenues can be explored to track down the offender? Elementary, my dear Watson (apologies for any perceived IBM humor)—the wall time profiler is the way to go now!

Wall Time Profiler

To dive straight in, rerun the previous test using the wall time profiler rather than the CPU profiler. You follow the same five steps as before, but just starting with the **Start Wall Time**

Profiler button. When the operation is complete, click the **Hierarchical Dominators** link, and expand the report. The results, shown in Figure 20.10, are more in line with what you may have expected on the previous run.

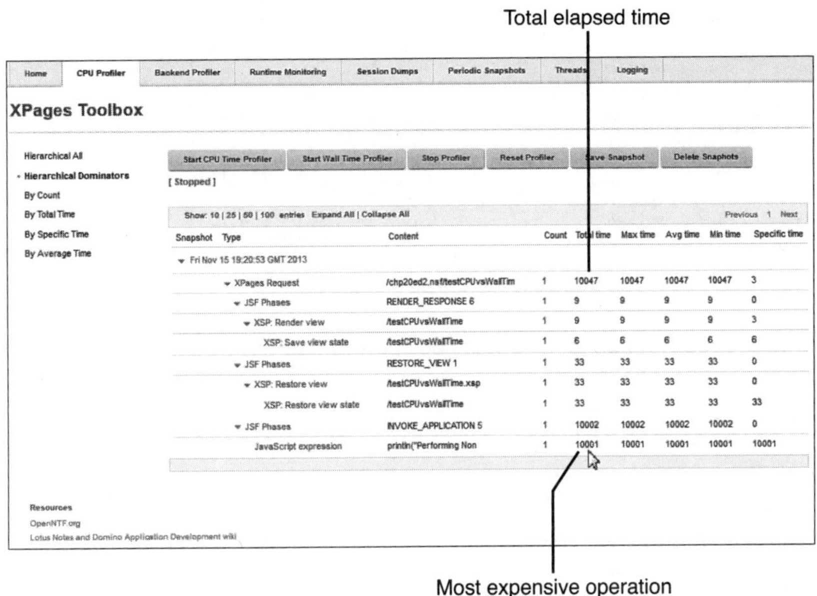

Figure 20.10 Wall Time Profiler reports for non-CPU-intensive use cases

As you can see, the total time taken is just over the sleep time set in the SSJS code, which, given that the code snippet does nothing else of substance, is the expected result. You can validate that the offending code is also pinpointed by clicking the JavaScript expression on the bottom line of the report. As you might expect, this displays the code block containing the `sleep` instruction. These are simple examples that validate straightforward use cases, but things can get a little more complicated than this, as the next example shows.

The **testCPUvsWallTime** XPage has a third and final button labeled **Run Some Task (clocking 'Wall Time')**. You should profile this operation using the wall time profiler by following what can now be described as the usual pattern. When completed, you will see a report similar to that displayed in Figure 20.11.

The **Hierarchical Dominators** view again quickly shows you that the bulk of the total time (27,117 milliseconds) is consumed by an `executeBackendLogic` operation whose specific time is 26,937 milliseconds. The stack is interesting, though. If you dive into the JavaScript expression that ultimately calls the dominating code, you can see some SSJS code that in itself takes virtually no time to execute—just 1 millisecond! That code snippet is illustrated in Listing 20.4.

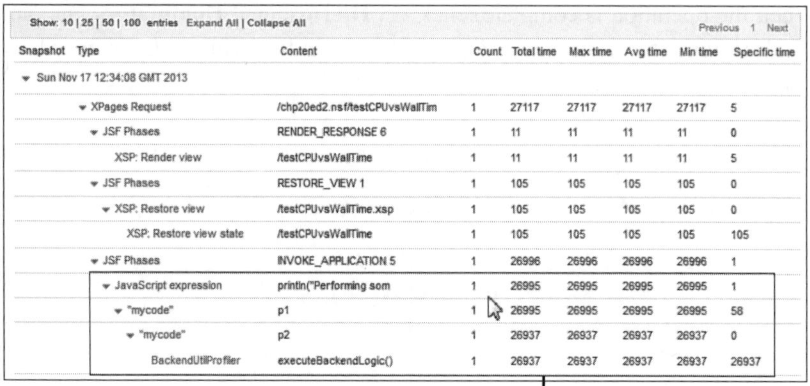

Show: 10 | 25 | 50 | 100 entries Expand All | Collapse All Previous 1 Next

Snapshot	Type	Content	Count	Total time	Max time	Avg time	Min time	Specific time
▾ Sun Nov 17 12:34:08 GMT 2013								
	▾ XPages Request	/chp20ed2.nsf/testCPUvsWallTim	1	27117	27117	27117	27117	5
	▾ JSF Phases	RENDER_RESPONSE 6	1	11	11	11	11	0
	XSP: Render view	/testCPUvsWallTime	1	11	11	11	11	5
	▾ JSF Phases	RESTORE_VIEW 1	1	105	105	105	105	0
	▾ XSP: Restore view	/testCPUvsWallTime.xsp	1	105	105	105	105	0
	XSP: Restore view state	/testCPUvsWallTime	1	105	105	105	105	105
	▾ JSF Phases	INVOKE_APPLICATION 5	1	26996	26996	26996	26996	1
	▾ JavaScript expression	println("Performing som	1	26995	26995	26995	26995	1
	▾ "mycode"	p1	1	26995	26995	26995	26995	58
	▾ "mycode"	p2	1	26937	26937	26937	26937	0
	BackendUtilProfiler	executeBackendLogic()	1	26937	26937	26937	26937	26937

Relevant profile stack

Figure 20.11 Wall Time Profiler report for an undefined operation

Listing 20.4 SSJS Code Calling an Arbitrary Backend Utility Function

```
println("Performing some operation...");
__profile("mycode", "p1"){
      importPackage(com.ibm.xsp.masterclass.utils);
      var backendUtil = new BackendUtil();
      if(null != backendUtil){
            __profile("mycode", "p2"){
                  backendUtil.executeBackendLogic();
            }
      }
}
println("Finished some operation!");
```

You can relate this code directly back to the profile stack displayed in Figure 20.11, and even if the semantics of the code are not clear at this point (which will more often than not be the case anyway when you are profiling third-party applications), the structure is the important thing from a profiling perspective. The profiler stack in Figure 20.11 shows you that an SSJS expression calls a `"p1"` code block that takes 58 milliseconds, which in turn calls a `"p2"` code block, which takes no time, which finally calls a backend utility operation, which takes practically all the time.

The `"p1"` and `"p2"` entries in the stack have something in common: they both call a `__profile()` function. These are what are known as profile blocks and, as you can see in Figure 20.11, anything wrapped inside a profile block is measured and reported as a separate operation by the profiler. When you dig into the backend code shortly, you can see that it also makes use of a profile block to ensure that its operations can be monitored by the profiler. Thus, rather than seeing that just one single blob of code takes 26,996 milliseconds, you get a far more granular view of what has taken place. That is, four logical operations with specific times, namely 1 ms, 58 ms, 0 ms, and 26,937 ms. From a performance analysis perspective, this allows you to focus solely on line 7 from Listing 20.4, as this is where the time is being spent. The profile blocks show that the specific times taken by the other lines of code are not significant. This in itself can be useful in terms of eliminating irrelevancies from a profiling examination, and you will learn shortly how to create profile blocks for your own code so that you, too, can make use of this feature in the future.

To finish out the investigation of this use case, however, you first need to open the sample application in Domino Designer and drill into the identified function. After you have opened **Chp20Ed2.nsf**, type **Control-Shift-R** to open the Java class identified in Listing 20.4; then type `BackendUtil` and click **OK**. This is the Java code that sucks up all the wall clock time, and it is included in Listing 20.5.

Listing 20.5 Java Class Performing Arbitrary View, Document, and Agent Operations

```
public class BackendUtil {
    private static final ProfilerType pt = new
                      ProfilerType("BackendUtilProfiler");
    public BackendUtil() {}

    private void _executeBackendLogic() {
       Database database = ExtLibUtil.getCurrentDatabase();
       if (null != database) {
           try {
               // step 1...
               Document doc;
               long i = System.currentTimeMillis();
               long t = i + 5000;
               for (long c = i, r = 1;
                  c < t; c = System.currentTimeMillis(), r++) {
                   doc = database.createDocument();
                   doc.replaceItemValue("field1", String.valueOf(r));
                   doc.replaceItemValue("field2", String.valueOf(c));
                   doc.save();
                   doc.recycle();
                   doc = null;
               }
               View view = database.getView("myView");
               System.out.println("ec1: " + view.getEntryCount());
               view.getAllEntries().removeAll(true);
               System.out.println("ec2: " + view.getEntryCount());

```

```
27              // step 2...
28              Agent agent = database.getAgent("myBackendAgent");
29              if (null != agent) {
30                  agent.run();
31              }
32          } catch (NotesException e) {
33              e.printStackTrace();
34          }
35      }
36  }
37
38  public void executeBackendLogic() {
39      if (Profiler.isEnabled()) {
40          ProfilerAggregator pa =
Profiler.startProfileBlock(pt, "executeBackendLogic()");
41          long startTime = Profiler.getCurrentTime();
42          try {
43              _executeBackendLogic(); // call private version of method
44          } finally {
45              Profiler.endProfileBlock(pa, startTime);
46          }
47      } else {
48          _executeBackendLogic();
49      }
50  }
```

As previously stated, line 7 in Listing 20.4 (`backendUtil.executeBackendLogic`) is the expensive wrongdoer in this use case. That line of SSJS code calls directly into the public class method starting at Line 38 in Listing 20.5, which as you can see, wraps a Java-style profile block around a call to a private method on line 43. The private method (defined on lines 6 through 36) is the work horse: It performs all sorts of arbitrary Java backend operations, including creating documents, removing documents, running agents, and so forth. For the wall time profiler, this is where the investigative path ends. It has demonstrated beyond any doubt that the program spends all its time doing document and agent operations via the Java backend classes. This may be all you need to know, or you may need to drill down further into the backend classes themselves. To delve into the Java backend classes, you need to use the Backend profiler.

Backend Profiler

The Backend Profiler feature makes use of the profiling capabilities built into the Java backend classes and can give a granular account of where the wall time is being spent in the individual backend operations. It works in much the same way as the two other profilers used thus far;

although, the output format it uses is a little different. To profile the backend operations detailed in Listing 20.4, follow these steps:

1. Select the **Backend Profiler** tab in the toolbox, and click the **Start Profiler** button.
2. Switch to the adjacent tab containing the sample application, and click the **Run Some Task (clocking 'Wall time')** button, as shown in Figure 20.5.
3. When this operation completes, revert to the toolbox, and click the **Stop Profiler** button.

A profile report is generated, and a sample run for this use case is shown in Figure 20.12. The report is simple to interpret. Basically, it includes the wall time spent in each method call on any backend Java classes that are used, how many times that method was called, and the cumulative elapsed times are sorted in descending order (meaning that the most expensive operations are at the top of the list). Thus, you can see at a glance in Figure 20.12 that the main culprit in this example is the Java agent, as this in itself takes just more than 15 seconds, well ahead of all other backend operations in the code.

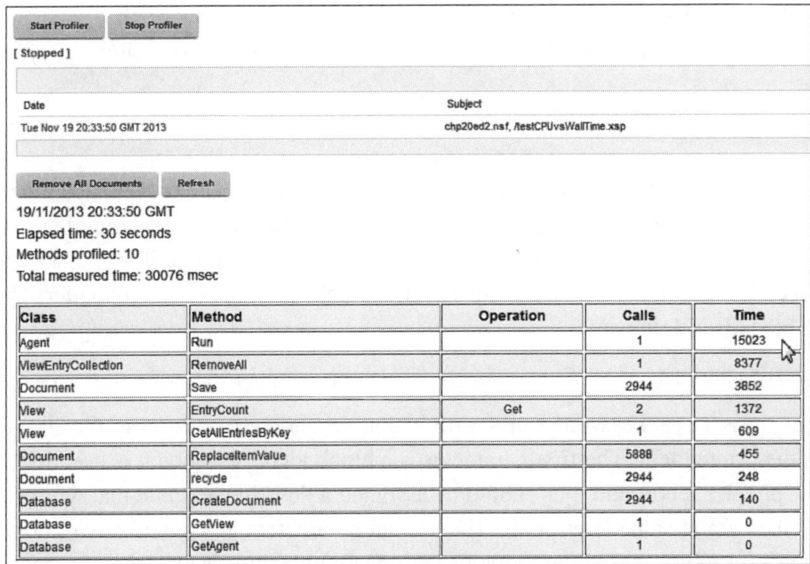

Class	Method	Operation	Calls	Time
Agent	Run		1	15023
ViewEntryCollection	RemoveAll		1	8377
Document	Save		2944	3852
View	EntryCount	Get	2	1372
View	GetAllEntriesByKey		1	609
Document	ReplaceItemValue		5888	455
Document	recycle		2944	248
Database	CreateDocument		2944	140
Database	GetView		1	0
Database	GetAgent		1	0

Figure 20.12 Backend Profiler report for arbitrary backend operations

To investigate why the agent is so costly in terms of wall clock time, you should open it in Domino Designer. Listing 20.6 shows the Java agent code that is displayed when you select **Code > Agents > myBackendAgent** from the design element navigator.

Listing 20.6 Java Agent Called from XPages SSJS Code

```
1       import lotus.domino.*;
2
3       public class JavaAgent extends AgentBase {
4                  public void NotesMain() {
5              try {
6                  java.lang.Thread.sleep(15000);
7              } catch (Exception e) {
8                  e.printStackTrace();
10              }
11          }
12      }
```

Line 6 in Listing 20.6 exposes why the agent is the dastardly offender on this occasion—in fact, the Java code does nothing except sleep the thread for 15 seconds! Nevertheless, the key point here is how the wall time profiler and backend profiler were instrumental in hunting down the source of the bottleneck.

Now that you have used all three profilers in the toolbox, you should ensure that your own SSJS and Java code is profiler-friendly. You can do this by introducing profile blocks to your source code.

Profile Blocks

As already established, profile blocks are used to wrap logical sections of code (or perhaps illogical sections of code, depending on how the results come out) so that they can be measured as discrete operations by the profiler. Refer to Listing 20.4 to see an example of how profiler blocks can be included in SSJS code. As you can see, inserting a profile block is a simple enough matter. The generic form of the block is as follows:

```
__profile("blockId", "optionalInformation) { //wrap required code here ... }
```

Note that the `__profile` keyword starts with a double underscore, in case that is not entirely clear from the printed text. The first parameter is a block identifier, which is used in the **Type** column of the profiler report and thus should be assigned a descriptive name that will help the reader interpret the data at some later point. The second parameter can contain any optional information that you want to use within the scope of your profile block. It is also surfaced in the **Content** column of the report. You should also observe from Listing 20.4 that profile blocks can be nested, which means you can generate granular profile analysis. This can be particularly useful for iterative code such as `for` or `while` loop code where some conditional logic nested within the iterative block is invoked during one or more iterations and potentially causing bottlenecks. By way of nesting profile blocks in this situation, you can obtain deeper insight into the root cause of any issue.

Adding profile blocks to Java code is done a little differently, but again, a full example is provided in Listing 20.5 and the pattern can be explained as follows:

1. Add a static `ProfilerType` member to your Java class, as shown in line 2 of the listing, and instantiate this class with some descriptive text.
2. For each class method you want to profile, create a public and private implementation. The latter must have a modified name, so adding an underscore prefix is the convention used here.
3. The public method then wraps a profile block around the private method, as shown in lines 39 through 49.
4. The logic of the profile block implementation is to first check if profiling is turned on. If not, the private method is called without further ado.
5. To actually do the profiling, a `ProfilerAggregator` class must be instantiated to manage the time measurement and so forth. A time stamp is taken and then the private method is called within a `try` block. It is imperative that the `endProfileBlock` method call is performed within the `finally` clause of the `try` block.

This is a repeatable pattern that could and should be applied to your new and existing Java classes, and doing so will ensure that any performance issues that may arise at some future stage can be easily tracked down with some help from the XPages Toolbox. Be aware also that enabling profiling in this way has no negative impact on your code when the profiler is not turned on. And even when profiling is enabled, the profiling hooks are noninvasive from a performance perspective—so everything to gain and nothing to be lost. This brings the subject of profiling to a close—hopefully it is one that will prove to be of great benefit to you from here on out. Right now, however, it's time to move this discussion to a whole new phase.

Introspecting XPages Requests Using a PhaseListener

In Chapter 5, "XPages and JavaServer Faces," you learned about how XPages is built upon the JavaServer Faces framework and therefore provides support for the JSF Request Processing Lifecycle. In Chapter 19, you also learned that XPages extends the JSF framework to provide optimal request processing behavior via features like Partial Refresh and Partial Execution. (These extensions and optimizations effectively mean that there is an *XPages* Request Processing Lifecycle.) More recently in this chapter, you learned about the merits of using the XPages Toolbox to profile XPages applications. And now, just when you thought you'd seen it all, you learn that there's still more to come. Although much of the content within the following sections will continue to use the XPages Toolbox, it will introduce a more primitive but insightful method of profiling—one that is less commonly used by the development community at large and known to the XPages development team as "XPages Request Introspection."

This primitive profiling method differs from the XPages Toolbox profilers in that it gives you a "real-time" view into the processing of an XPages request relative to the XPages Request Processing Lifecycle and other code invocations that occur during the processing of an XPages request. When used together with the XPages Toolbox, you truly have no excuses for being unable to perform detailed and thorough problem detection and resolution analysis for the majority of performance bottlenecks. In fact, the authors would go further to say that both the XPages Toolbox and the XPages Request Introspection technique should be used in tandem during normal development iterations—that is, over the *full* course of the software development lifecycle of an XPages application and not just for post-deployment performance problem identification and resolution.

To get going, ensure the **index** XPage of the **Chp20Ed2.nsf** application is open in Domino Designer. Within the WYSIWYG editor, you should scroll down the page to find the **debug checkbox**, and highlight it as shown in Figure 20.13.

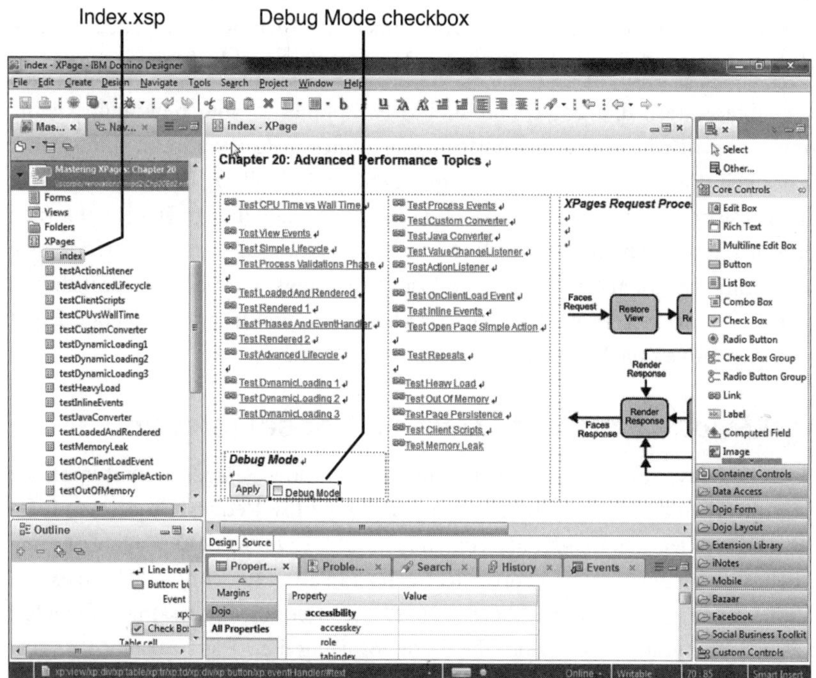

Figure 20.13 index.xsp open in Designer showing the debug check box

Notice that the **Checked by default** option is a computed value for the **debug checkbox**. If you simply double-click the **{Computed}** element within the properties panel for this option, you can see the actual computed expression used for this within the Script Editor, as shown in Figure 20.14.

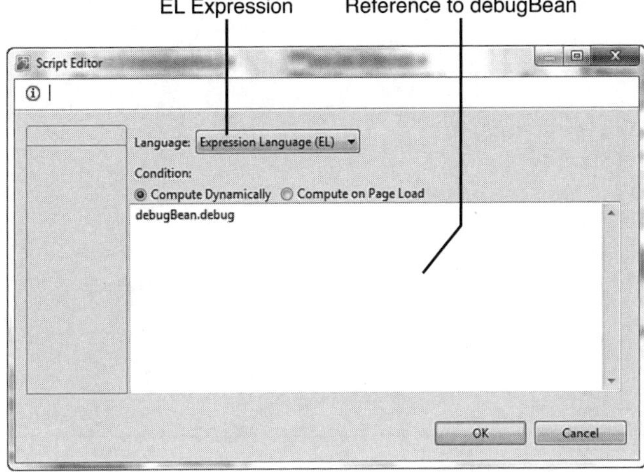

Figure 20.14 The {Computed} expression in the Script Editor for the debug check box

As you can see, it's Expression Language (EL) code that references the `debugBean` object and the `debug` property of the same object. In effect, this means that when the **debug checkbox** is rendered at runtime, the default state of this control is assigned from the `debugBean.debug` property. Next, you should also look at the **Apply** button that is defined just before the **debug checkbox** within the XSP markup of the **index** XPage. This button is effectively the glue between the **debug checkbox** and the `debugBean` as it has an SSJS event handler to apply debug mode within the application by setting the current **debug checkbox** value to the `debugBean.setDebug()` method. Listing 20.7 contains the XSP markup and SSJS snippet from the **Apply** button for your convenience.

Listing 20.7 "Apply" Button XSP Markup and ServerSide JavaScript Code

```
<xp:button value="Apply" id="button1">
    <xp:eventHandler event="onclick" submit="true"
        refreshMode="partial" refreshId="dvManageDebugMode"
➥execMode="partial"
        execId="dvManageDebugMode" disableValidators="true">
        <xp:this.action>
            <![CDATA[#{javascript:
                try{
                    println(" ");println(" ");
                    println("XPages Request Introspection");
                    println(" ");
                    println("Setting Debug Mode:");
                    var b = getComponent("cbxDebugMode").getValue();
                    if(b && b == "false"){
```

```
                        println("Turning Debug Off...");
                    }else{
                        println("Turning Debug On...");
                    }
                    debugBean.setDebug(b);
                    println("Done.");
                    println(" ");
                }catch(e){
                    println(e);
                }
            }]]>
        </xp:this.action>
    </xp:eventHandler>
</xp:button>
```

This now gives you a cue for the next piece of the XPages Request Introspection puzzle. If you now open the **faces-config.xml** file by using the keystroke **Ctrl+Shift+R** in Domino Designer, type in **faces-config.xml,** and open it up, you can find a declaration for the `debugBean` listed near the top of this file. You should also take note of the `<phase-listener>` declaration just before it that is referring to the `DebugBeanPhaseListener` Java class file. Both of these **faces-config.xml** declarations are also listed in the XSP markup fragment in Listing 20.8 for your convenience.

Listing 20.8 faces-config.xml Fragment Detailing debugBean/DebugBeanPhaseListener

```
<lifecycle>
    <phase-listener>
        com.ibm.xsp.masterclass.lifecycle.DebugBeanPhaseListener
    </phase-listener>
</lifecycle>
<managed-bean>
    <managed-bean-name>debugBean</managed-bean-name>
    <managed-bean-class>com.ibm.xsp.masterclass.beans.DebugBean
➥</managed-bean-class>
    <managed-bean-scope>session</managed-bean-scope>
    <managed-property>
        <property-name>debug</property-name>
        <value>false</value>
    </managed-property>
</managed-bean>
```

Before looking at either of the two referred Java class files, namely `DebugBean` and `DebugBeanPhaseListener`, respectively, you should note the `<managed-property>` that is declared on the `DebugBean`. Yes, that is correct—it's the same `debug` property that is referenced by the **Checked by default** option on the **debug checkbox** back in the **index** XPage. In this particular case, the **debug checkbox** will initially take on the value of **false**, and hence, not be checked by default. It is then up to the application end user to manually toggle the **debug checkbox** to also set the `debugBean.debug` property value over to a **true** state.

And with that said, it is now an appropriate time to open both the `DebugBean` and `DebugBeanPhaseListener` Java classes within Domino Designer. As already explained in several other places throughout this book, and indeed, as you might have come to expect, there are a number of ways in which you could open both of these Java class files. Again, using the keystroke **Ctrl+Shift+R** will provide you with the **Open Resource** dialog where you can simply type in the filenames and select your target file. Or alternatively, you can expand the **Code/Java** design elements in the Application Navigator for the **Chp20Ed2.nsf** application within Domino Designer and double-click each of the files of interest, as shown in Figure 20.15.

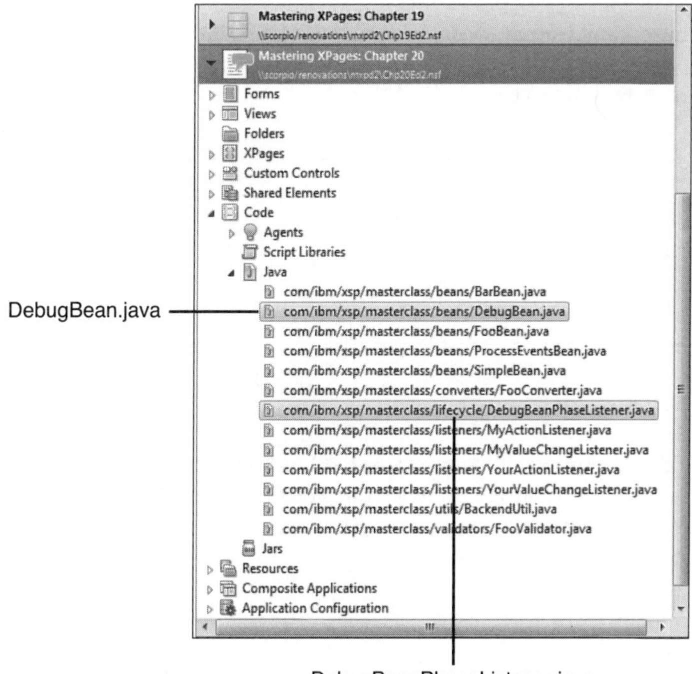

Figure 20.15 Opening DebugBean and DebugBeanPhaseListener using the Code/Java section

After you have opened each of these Java class files, you should take a moment to study the source code within each. Listing 20.9 details the source code within the **DebugBean.java** class file, and Listing 20.10 details the source code within the **DebugBeanPhaseListener.java** class file, for your convenience.

Listing 20.9 DebugBean.java Source Code

```
package com.ibm.xsp.masterclass.beans;
import java.io.Serializable;
import javax.faces.context.FacesContext;
import com.ibm.xsp.masterclass.lifecycle.DebugBeanPhaseListener;

public class DebugBean implements Serializable {

    private static final long serialVersionUID =
➥-1698889483899280998L;

    public static final String BEAN_NAME = "debugBean";

    public static DebugBean instance;

    protected boolean debug = false;

    // ---------------------------------------------------------------

    public DebugBean() {
        instance = this;
    }

    // ---------------------------------------------------------------

    public static DebugBean getInstance() {
        if (null == instance) {
            FacesContext context = FacesContext.getCurrentInstance();
            instance = (DebugBean) context.getApplication()
                .getVariableResolver().resolveVariable(
                    context, BEAN_NAME
            );
        }
        return instance;
    }

    // ---------------------------------------------------------------

    public boolean isDebug() {
        return debug;
    }
```

```

    public void setDebug(boolean debug) {
        this.debug = debug;
    }

    public void setDebug(String debug) {
        this.debug = Boolean.parseBoolean(debug);
    }

    // ------------------------------------------------------------

    public boolean isRestoreViewPhase(){
        DebugBeanPhaseListener listener =
➥DebugBeanPhaseListener.getInstance();
        return (null != listener && listener.isRestoreViewPhase());
    }

    public boolean isApplyRequestValuesPhase(){
        DebugBeanPhaseListener listener =
➥DebugBeanPhaseListener.getInstance();
        return (null != listener &&
➥listener.isApplyRequestValuesPhase());
    }

    public boolean isProcessValidationsPhase(){
        DebugBeanPhaseListener listener = DebugBeanPhaseListener.
➥ getInstance();
        return (null != listener &&
➥listener.isProcessValidationsPhase());
    }

    public boolean isUpdateModelValuesPhase(){
        DebugBeanPhaseListener listener =
➥DebugBeanPhaseListener.getInstance();
        return (null != listener &&
➥listener.isUpdateModelValuesPhase());
    }

    public boolean isInvokeApplicationPhase(){
        DebugBeanPhaseListener listener =
➥DebugBeanPhaseListener.getInstance();
        return (null != listener &&
➥listener.isInvokeApplicationPhase());
    }

    public boolean isRenderResponsePhase(){
```

```
        DebugBeanPhaseListener listener =
➥DebugBeanPhaseListener.getInstance();
        return (null != listener &&
➥listener.isRenderResponsePhase());
    }
} // end DebugBean
```

Listing 20.10 DebugBeanPhaseListener.java Source Code

```
package com.ibm.xsp.masterclass.lifecycle;
import javax.faces.event.PhaseEvent;
import javax.faces.event.PhaseId;
import com.ibm.xsp.masterclass.beans.DebugBean;

public class DebugBeanPhaseListener implements
➥javax.faces.event.PhaseListener {

    private static final long serialVersionUID = 1L;

    private static DebugBeanPhaseListener instance;

    private PhaseId phaseId;

    public DebugBeanPhaseListener(){
        instance = this;
    }

    // --------------------------------------------------------------------

    public static DebugBeanPhaseListener getInstance(){
        if(null == instance){
            instance = new DebugBeanPhaseListener();
        }
        return instance;
    }

    // --------------------------------------------------------------------

    public boolean isRestoreViewPhase(){
        return (null != phaseId && phaseId.equals(PhaseId.RESTORE_VIEW));
    }

    public boolean isApplyRequestValuesPhase(){
```

```
        return (null != phaseId && phaseId.equals(PhaseId.APPLY_REQUEST_VALUES));
    }

    public boolean isProcessValidationsPhase(){
        return (null != phaseId && phaseId.equals(PhaseId.PROCESS_VALIDATIONS));
    }

    public boolean isUpdateModelValuesPhase(){
        return (null != phaseId && phaseId.equals(PhaseId.UPDATE_MODEL_VALUES));
    }

    public boolean isInvokeApplicationPhase(){
        return (null != phaseId && phaseId.equals(PhaseId.INVOKE_APPLICATION));
    }

    public boolean isRenderResponsePhase(){
        return (null != phaseId && phaseId.equals(PhaseId.RENDER_RESPONSE));
    }

    public PhaseId getPhaseId() {
        return PhaseId.ANY_PHASE;
    }

    // -------------------------------------------------------------------

    public void beforePhase(PhaseEvent event) {
        try {
            phaseId = event.getPhaseId();
            if (DebugBean.getInstance().isDebug()) {
                if (event.getPhaseId().equals(PhaseId.RESTORE_VIEW)) {
                    System.out.println(" ");
                    System.out.println("Request:\tStarted...");
                }
                System.out.println(" ");
                System.out.println(
                    "Lifecycle:\tBefore Phase: " + event.getPhaseId()
                );
            }
        } catch (Exception e) {
            e.printStackTrace();
```

```
74          }
75      }
76
77      // ---------------------------------------------------------------
78
79      public void afterPhase(PhaseEvent event) {
80          try {
81              phaseId = event.getPhaseId();
82              if (DebugBean.getInstance().isDebug()) {
83                  System.out.println(
84                      "Lifecycle:\tAfter Phase: " + event.getPhaseId()
85                  );
86                  System.out.println(" ");
87                  if (event.getPhaseId().equals(PhaseId.RENDER_RESPONSE))
{
88                      System.out.println("Request:\tCompleted.");
89                      System.out.println(" ");
90                  }
91              }
92          } catch (Exception e) {
93              e.printStackTrace();
94          }
95      }
96 } // end DebugBeanPhaseListener
```

What you should immediately realize is the interdependency between the two classes. This is a two-way relationship. First, the `DebugBean` depends on the `DebugBeanPhaseListener` to expose details on the status of each lifecycle phase—specifically a boolean test of whether any given phase is the currently executing phase, as shown in Listing 20.9 on lines 51 through to 79. Second, the `DebugBeanPhaseListener` depends on the `DebugBean` within its `beforePhase()` and `afterPhase()` methods, as shown in Listing 20.10 on lines 62 and 82, respectively. This dependency is based on the `DebugBeanPhaseListener` using the `debugBean.debug` property value as a means of either activating or deactivating console debug information. And it is via the manual toggling of the **debug checkbox** and pressing of the **Apply** button at runtime by the end user that this activation/deactivation of the console debug information occurs.

At this point, you may be wondering why you should be concerned with all this because it appears to be nothing more than a rudimentary technique to emit console log information based on the value of a boolean property. Well, the answer is relatively simple and is better illustrated by following through with a couple of simple demonstrations. You now perform three tasks against three different XPages—namely the **index** XPage that you have already learned about and the **testPhasesAndEventHandler** and **testAdvancedLifecycle** XPages. But before performing the upcoming three tasks, ensure you have access to and can view your Domino server console either in the Domino Administrator client or directly on a desktop, as shown in Figure 20.16.

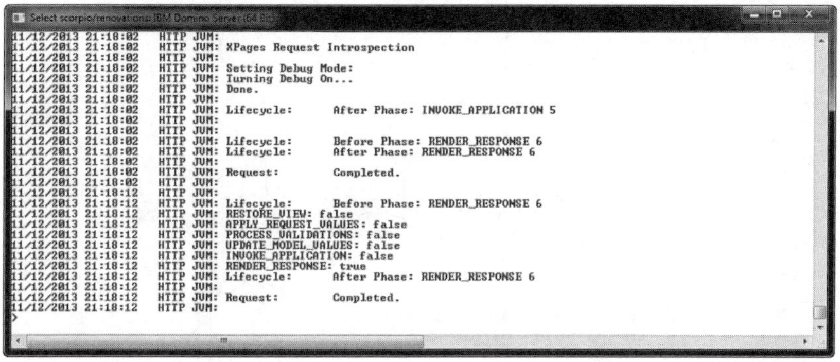

```
11/12/2013 21:18:02   HTTP JVM:
11/12/2013 21:18:02   HTTP JVM: XPages Request Introspection
11/12/2013 21:18:02   HTTP JVM:
11/12/2013 21:18:02   HTTP JVM: Setting Debug Mode:
11/12/2013 21:18:02   HTTP JVM: Turning Debug On...
11/12/2013 21:18:02   HTTP JVM: Done.
11/12/2013 21:18:02   HTTP JVM:
11/12/2013 21:18:02   HTTP JVM: Lifecycle:      After Phase: INVOKE_APPLICATION 5
11/12/2013 21:18:02   HTTP JVM:
11/12/2013 21:18:02   HTTP JVM:
11/12/2013 21:18:02   HTTP JVM: Lifecycle:      Before Phase: RENDER_RESPONSE 6
11/12/2013 21:18:02   HTTP JVM: Lifecycle:      After Phase: RENDER_RESPONSE 6
11/12/2013 21:18:02   HTTP JVM:
11/12/2013 21:18:02   HTTP JVM: Request:        Completed.
11/12/2013 21:18:02   HTTP JVM:
11/12/2013 21:18:12   HTTP JVM:
11/12/2013 21:18:12   HTTP JVM: Lifecycle:      Before Phase: RENDER_RESPONSE 6
11/12/2013 21:18:12   HTTP JVM: RESTORE_VIEW: false
11/12/2013 21:18:12   HTTP JVM: APPLY_REQUEST_VALUES: false
11/12/2013 21:18:12   HTTP JVM: PROCESS_VALIDATIONS: false
11/12/2013 21:18:12   HTTP JVM: UPDATE_MODEL_VALUES: false
11/12/2013 21:18:12   HTTP JVM: INVOKE_APPLICATION: false
11/12/2013 21:18:12   HTTP JVM: RENDER_RESPONSE: true
11/12/2013 21:18:12   HTTP JVM: Lifecycle:      After Phase: RENDER_RESPONSE 6
11/12/2013 21:18:12   HTTP JVM:
11/12/2013 21:18:12   HTTP JVM: Request:        Completed.
11/12/2013 21:18:12   HTTP JVM:
>
```

Figure 20.16 Viewing the Domino server console on a desktop

So your first task is to now open the **index** XPage in a browser. When this XPage has opened, check the **Debug Mode** check box and press the **Apply** button. Visually there won't be any change to the **index** XPage within the browser other than the debug mode check box becoming checked. But the interesting aspect about this change can be seen in the Domino server console. You should see something similar to that of Figure 20.17 where the SSJS `println()` strings from the event handler of the **Apply** button have been written to the console log. In effect, these strings confirm that debug mode is now turned on.

You can also note the presence of other console log strings that have not come from the SSJS `println()` calls within the **Apply** button event handler. For instance, in Figure 20.17 the following additional messages can also be seen:

```
Lifecycle: After Phase: INVOKE_APPLICATION 5
Lifecycle: Before Phase: RENDER_RESPONSE 6
Lifecycle: After Phase: RENDER_RESPONSE 6
```

These are the `System.out.println()` strings coming from the `DebugBeanPhaseListener` Java class, which can be seen in Listing 20.10 on lines 64 through 69 and again from lines 83 through 89.

This is where things can start to get interesting in terms of introspection of any given XPage request. This particular example demonstrates a blend of SSJS code invocation and XPages Request Processing Lifecycle invocation through the emission of console log messages that allow you to visually recognize *where* code is called during the processing of an XPage request. The important aspect and benefit of this lies in the fact that it is now possible for you as an XPages developer to implant SSJS `println()` or Java `System.out.println()` statements within your application code and monitor the live, real-time invocation of the associated code blocks, functions, and objects within the actual lifecycle phase in which they are contained.

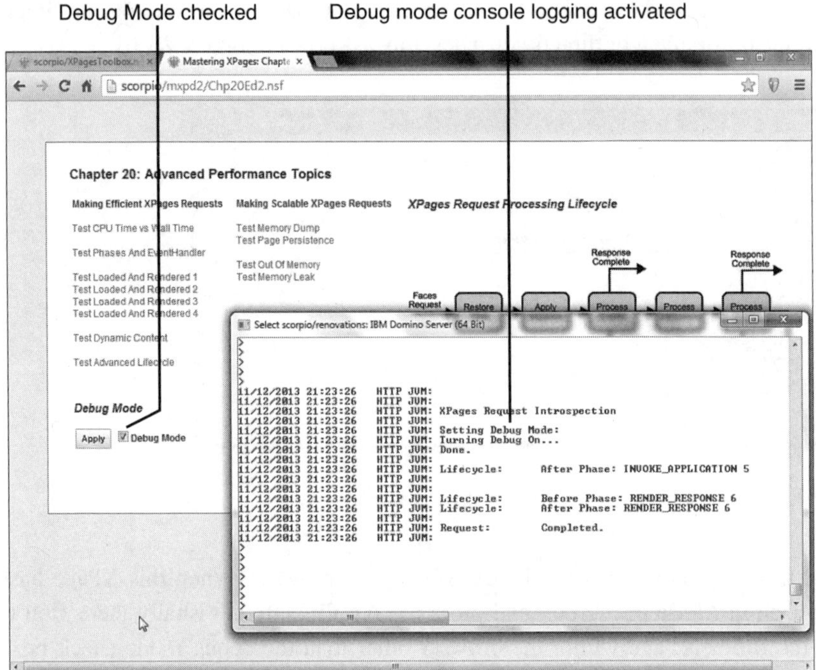

Figure 20.17 The Domino server console output after pressing the Apply button

It's time to take this a little further by completing the final two of the three tasks mentioned earlier. So you should now open both the **testPhasesAndEventHandler** and **testAdvancedLifecycle** XPages in Domino Designer. First, switch over to source mode within the WYSIWYG editor for each of these two XPages. Listing 20.11 contains the source code for the **test PhasesAndEventHandler** XPage.

Listing 20.11 The Source of the testPhasesAndEventHandler XPage

```
<?xml version="1.0" encoding="UTF-8"?>
<xp:view xmlns:xp="http://www.ibm.com/xsp/core">
    <xp:this.afterRestoreView>
        <![CDATA[#{javascript:println("RESTORE_VIEW: " +
            debugBean.isRestoreViewPhase());
        }]]>
    </xp:this.afterRestoreView>
    <xp:button value="Test Phases" id="button1">
      <xp:this.rendered><![CDATA[#{javascript:
      println("RESTORE_VIEW: " + debugBean.isRestoreViewPhase());
```

```
        println("APPLY_REQUEST_VALUES: " +
➥debugBean.isApplyRequestValuesPhase());
        println("PROCESS_VALIDATIONS: " +
➥debugBean.isProcessValidationsPhase());
        println("UPDATE_MODEL_VALUES: " +
➥debugBean.isUpdateModelValuesPhase());
        println("INVOKE_APPLICATION: " +
➥debugBean.isInvokeApplicationPhase());
        println("RENDER_RESPONSE: " +
➥debugBean.isRenderResponsePhase());
        return true;}]]>
        </xp:this.rendered>
          <xp:eventHandler event="onclick" submit="true"
              refreshMode="complete">
              <xp:this.action>
                  <![CDATA[#{javascript:
                      println("INVOKE_APPLICATION: " +
                          debugBean.isInvokeApplicationPhase()
                      );
                  }]]>
              </xp:this.action>
          </xp:eventHandler>
      </xp:button>
</xp:view>
```

As you can see in Listing 20.11, there is a single button with an event handler calling what is effectively one line of SSJS code. This button also has a computed rendered property that is calling an SSJS code block. And finally the XPage has an `afterRestoreView` event defined. This is also calling a single line of SSJS. What you can note, however, is the commonality among all the SSJS code—it is all based around calling `println()` to emit console log messages. Those messages are all using the `debugBean` and the methods exposed on it to ascertain which lifecycle phase is currently invoked. To fully understand this simple example, you should now open this XPage in a browser, and ensuring that you have debug mode activated, press the **Test Phases** button. Having done this you should see similar Domino server console output to that in Figure 20.18.

You should now be seeing at least some of the potential value of this simple profiling technique. As clearly shown in Figure 20.18, the `println()` statements have been emitted relative to each lifecycle phase invocation, thus allowing you to see exactly where the various lines of SSJS logic executed as the XPage request was processed. It should be noted that in this particular example, explicit use was made of the special rendered property to gain deeper level insight into the invocation of some of the lifecycle phases. You can learn more about this special property and its close cousin, the loaded property, in the upcoming sections of this chapter. Nonetheless, it is easy to see in the server output that the `afterRestoreView` XPage event was invoked during the `RESTORE_VIEW` lifecycle phase and that the Test Phases button event handler was invoked during the `INVOKE_APPLICATION` phase due to the “true” result of the corresponding `println()` statements within each of those code blocks. Meanwhile, in relation to the computed rendered property invocations, it is also easy to see where each test has returned a result of “true” relative to the current lifecycle phase invocation.

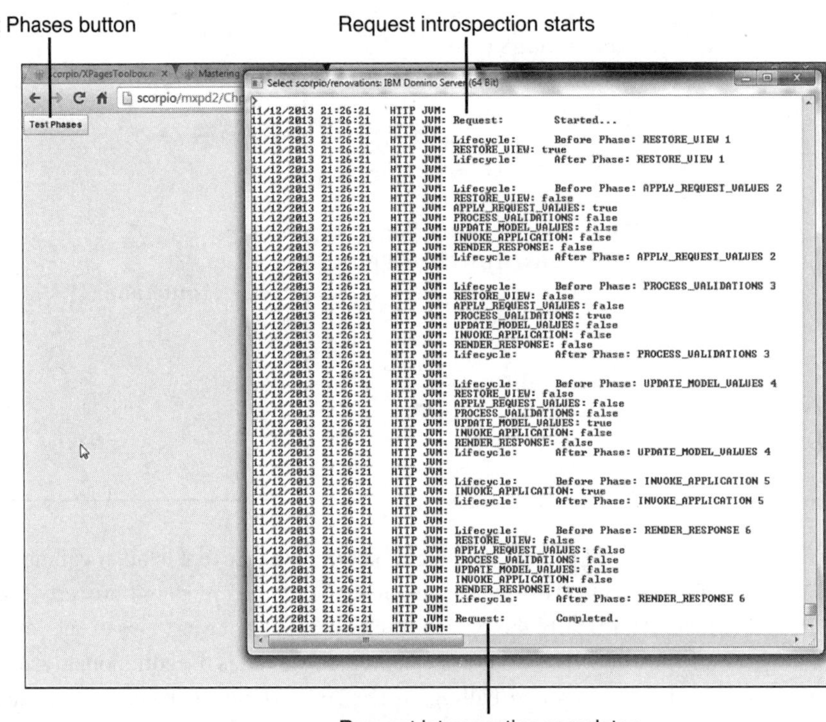

Figure 20.18 The Domino server console output after pressing the Test Phases button

Finally, you should now perform the third task for this particular section. If you review the XSP markup and SSJS code within the **testAdvancedLifecycle** XPage in Domino Designer, you will quickly recognize that it is heavily peppered with `debugBean.isDebug()` and `println()` statements. This is done as a means of extending the XPages Request Introspection technique so that the various `println()` and/or `System.out.println()` statements that may be embedded within an application’s logic are emitted only when the debug mode is true. Combining this “shield” around such statements, along with the use of a PhaseListener allows you to incorporate noninvasive XPages Request Introspection monitoring logic into an XPages application that can be utilized for future development, maintenance, or problem resolution tasks—in effect you do not need to rip out your embedded monitoring code. To gain a sense of this, you should now also open the **testAdvancedLifecycle** XPage in a browser, and ensure debug mode is activated before experimenting with any of the various buttons you may freely choose within the rendered XPage. What is important to remember here is that as you press the buttons and interact with the XPage, you should also review the live monitoring information that is emitted to the Domino server console.

To give you some sense of what to expect and look for in this example, Figure 20.19 shows an example whereby the **p2 Std** button has been pressed, but the input field on the XPage has been left blank. In this case, the input field is marked as a required field and therefore is expecting a value. Given that a value has not been supplied, when the **p2 Std** button event handler is invoked, the XPages Request Processing Lifecycle has processed only lifecycle phases 1, 2, 3, and 6, therefore bypassing lifecycle phases 4 and 5. This is because lifecycle phase 3 is the **PROCESS_VALIDATIONS** phase, and in this case, the required validator on the input field has failed and caused the bypass of the **UPDATE_MODEL_VALUES** and **INVOKE_APPLICATION** phases to occur.

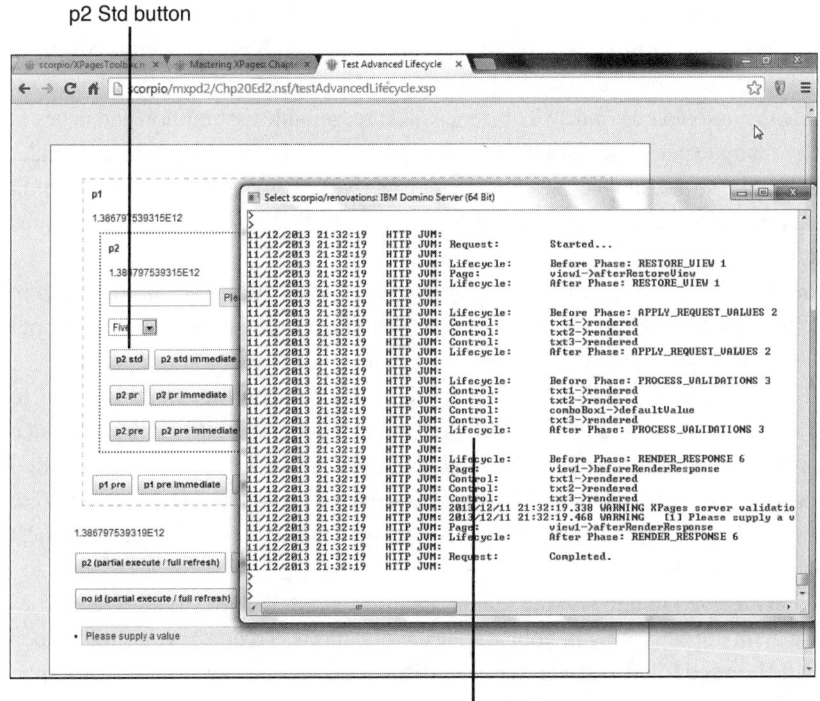

Figure 20.19 The Domino server console output after pressing the p2 Std button

At this point, you should take time to try the different examples on this XPage and see if you can work out and come to understand what is happening with each. Don't worry, though, if you don't work them all out. This particular XPage will be used and explained in an upcoming section within this chapter.

You should now hopefully understand the importance of the XPages Request Introspection technique and also recognize that it is a vital tool in your XPages arsenal to help you both develop and debug XPages applications. It is not suitable for all problem identification and resolution tasks that you may encounter, but when combined with the use of the XPages Toolbox and a thorough understanding of the mechanics of the XPages Request Processing Lifecycle, it certainly can prove invaluable to you going forward. For the upcoming sections in this chapter, you will use both the XPages Toolbox and the XPages Request Introspection technique interchangeably as you work your way through more performance-related worked examples and tasks.

The Myths and Realities of the Rendered and Loaded Properties

The previous section alluded to the special nature of the **rendered** and **loaded** properties. For the inquisitive reader, there are a number of unanswered questions about these properties, particularly if you consider the request introspection information in the previous section within Figure 20.18. In this example, the **rendered** property was used on the "**Test Phases**" button to execute an SSJS computed expression. Ordinarily, you might expect the **rendered** property to simply evaluate a computed expression *once* during the processing of a request and then use that result to either show or hide the associated control. This feels like a reasonable assumption and is based upon expectations by many experienced Notes/Domino developers who have implemented hide/when logic into their applications. In fact, the **rendered** property is even labeled as *Visible* within the Domino Designer property editing panels, as shown in Figure 20.20. However, the reality is somewhat different.

The typical outcome of using the rendered property for this hide/when scenario is seen in Figure 20.18 where the computed expression `println()` statements are emitted within four out of six lifecycle phases—indicating *four* evaluations of the same code within a single request.

Obviously, there is more at play here than you might innocently expect, and it is fair to say that for a production-level application that has performance and scalability demands, such extra request processing logic could prove to be fatal if the hide/when logic within the **loaded** or **rendered** properties is doing any "heavy lifting." Therefore, it is imperative to have a solid understanding of the mechanics behind these two special properties and how the XPages Request Processing Lifecycle is affected by them.

The time has duly arrived to uncover the reality about the **rendered** and **loaded** properties and thus learn to use them appropriately in your XPages applications. To do so, you should open the **testRenderedAndLoaded1** and **testRenderedAndLoaded2** XPages in Domino Designer. In addition, you should prime the XPages Toolbox to the **Wall Time** CPU profile and also ready request introspection using the **Debug Mode** facility within the **Chp20Ed2.nsf** application. Then you should examine the **testRenderedAndLoaded1** XPage, as detailed in Listing 20.12.

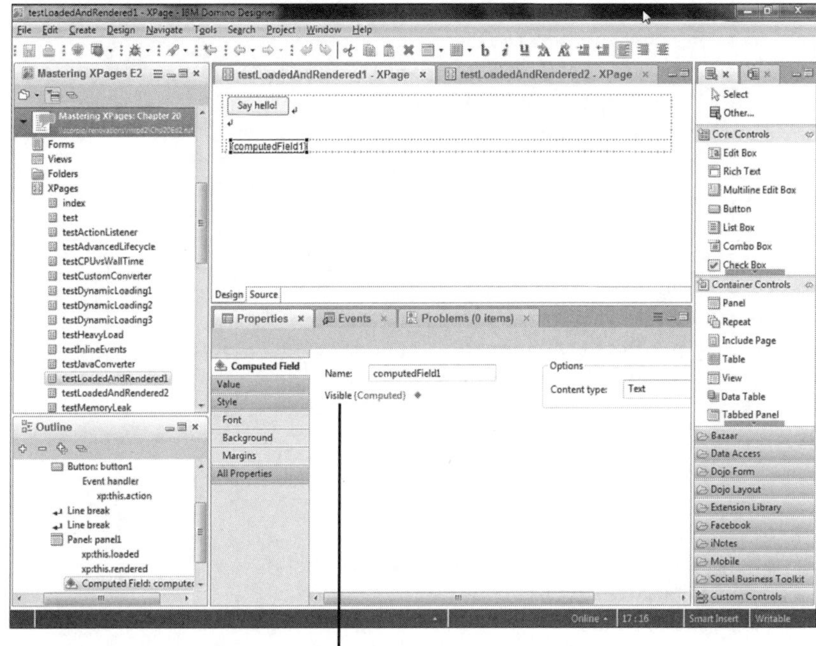

Rendered property represented as the Visible UI element

Figure 20.20 The rendered property as it appears in the property panels within Domino Designer

Listing 20.12 The Source of the testRenderedAndLoaded1 XPage

```
<?xml version="1.0" encoding="UTF-8"?>
<xp:view xmlns:xp="http://www.ibm.com/xsp/core"
    pageTitle="Test Loaded &amp; Rendered 1">
    <xp:div themeId="container">
        <xp:button value="Say hello!" id="button1">
            <xp:eventHandler event="onclick" submit="true"
                refreshMode="complete">
                <xp:this.action>
                    <![CDATA[#{javascript:
                        println("button 'Say hello!' triggered...");
                        viewScope.foo = "foo says hello!";
                    }]]>
                </xp:this.action>
            </xp:eventHandler>
        </xp:button>
        <xp:br></xp:br>
        <xp:br></xp:br>
        <xp:panel id="panel1">
```

```
            <xp:this.loaded>
                <![CDATA[${javascript:
                    __profile("Loaded", "panel1:loaded") {
                        println("panel1 loaded");
                        java.lang.Thread.sleep(2000);
                        return true;
                    }
                }]]>
            </xp:this.loaded>
            <xp:this.rendered>
                <![CDATA[#{javascript:
                    __profile("Rendered", "panel1:rendered") {
                        println("panel1 rendered");
                        java.lang.Thread.sleep(2000);
                        return true;
                    }
                }]]>
            </xp:this.rendered>
            <xp:text escape="true" id="computedField1"
                value="#{viewScope.foo}">
                <xp:this.loaded>
                    <![CDATA[${javascript:
                        __profile("Loaded", "computedField1:loaded") {
                            println("computedField1 loaded");
                            java.lang.Thread.sleep(2000);
                            return true;
                        }
                    }]]>
                </xp:this.loaded>
                <xp:this.rendered>
                    <![CDATA[#{javascript:
                        __profile("Rendered", "computedField1:rendered") {
                            println("computedField1 rendered");
                            java.lang.Thread.sleep(2000);
                            return true;
                        }
                    }]]>
                </xp:this.rendered>
            </xp:text>
        </xp:panel>
    </xp:div>
</xp:view>
```

As you can see in Listing 20.12, there is basically a button, a panel, and a computed field. The important thing to note is that the panel and computed field both have computed **loaded** and

rendered properties. For the panel, these are declared on lines 18 through 36 and for the computed field on lines 40 through 57. In each case, you can see that profile blocks (`__profile()`) have been specified to highlight each particular segment of code as the XPage is profiled using the XPages Toolbox. Furthermore `println()` statements have also been embedded within each profile block to mark the execution of code segments during the processing of the lifecycle phases. You should now open both the XPages Toolbox and the **testRenderedAndLoaded1** XPage in a browser.

Within the XPages Toolbox you should prepare to perform a "wall time" profile of this particular XPage—to do this just make sure you have clicked **Reset Profiler** on the CPU Profiler tab, but don't start the wall time profiler just yet. Before doing that, you should also ensure that debug mode is enabled within the **Chp20Ed2.nsf** application by checking the check box and pressing the **Apply** button on the **index** XPage. After you have enabled debug mode, go into the XPages Toolbox, and then click the **Start Wall Time Profiler** button. You now have both the XPages Toolbox and XPages Request Introspection mechanism primed to profile the processing of the **testRenderedAndLoaded1** XPage. Now select the **Test Loaded And Rendered 1** link from the **Chp20Ed2.nsf** to launch this XPage in a new tab, as shown in Figure 20.21. Remember that all you need to do is simply click the highlighted link because a new tab or window will be opened automatically for you when you do this.

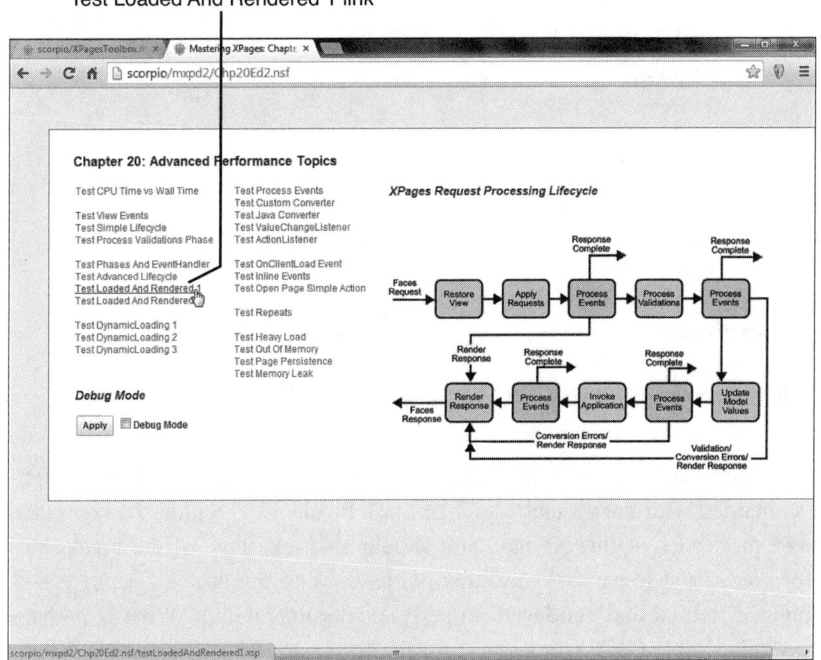

Figure 20.21 The Test Loaded And Rendered 1 link on the index XPage

When the new tab or window opens, a **GET** type request is sent to the XPages runtime for the **testLoadedAndRendered1** XPage. And because both the XPages Toolbox and XPages Request Introspection mechanism are enabled, they automatically profile and listen to the request. When the **testLoadedAndRendered1** XPage finishes loading in your browser, you can then return to the XPages Toolbox and select **Stop Profiler**. A new profiling snapshot now appears within the view. This contains all the relevant profiling information for the previously processed request, as shown in Figure 20.22.

Total time: 8005 milliseconds (ie: > 8 seconds)

Snapshot Type	Content	Count	Total time	Max time	Avg time	Min time	Specific time
▾ Thu Nov 28 10:00:10 GMT 2013							
▾ XPages Request	/mxpd2/Chp20Ed2.nsf/testLoaded	1	8005	8005	8005	8005	1
▾ JSF Phases	RENDER_RESPONSE 6	1	4002	4002	4002	4002	0
▾ XSP: Render view	/testLoadedAndRendered1	1	4002	4002	4002	4002	2
JavaScript expression	context.isDirectionLTR()	4	0	0	0	0	0
JavaScript expression	context.isDirectionRTL()	5	0	0	0	0	0
JavaScript expression	context.getUserAgent().isIE(6,	1	0	0	0	0	0
JavaScript expression	context.getUserAgent().isIE(7,	1	0	0	0	0	0
JavaScript expression	(context.isDirectionLTR())	1	0	0	0	0	0
JavaScript expression	context.getUserAgent().isIE(0,	1	0	0	0	0	0
JavaScript expression	context.getUserAgent().isIE(7,	1	0	0	0	0	0
JavaScript expression	(context.isDirectionRTL() && c	1	0	0	0	0	0
JavaScript expression	context.getUserAgent().isFiref	1	0	0	0	0	0
JavaScript expression	context.getUserAgent().isSafar	1	0	0	0	0	0
▾ JavaScript expression	__profile("Rendered", "p	1	2000	2000	2000	2000	0
"Rendered"	panel1:rendered	1	2000	2000	2000	2000	2000
▾ JavaScript expression	__profile("Rendered", "	1	2000	2000	2000	2000	0
"Rendered"	computedField1:rendered	1	2000	2000	2000	2000	2000
XSP: Save view state	/testLoadedAndRendered1	1	1	1	1	1	1
XSP: apply styles		1	1	1	1	1	1
▾ XSP: Create view root	/testLoadedAndRendered1	1	4001	4001	4001	4001	1
▾ JavaScript expression	__profile("Loaded", "pan	1	2000	2000	2000	2000	0
"Loaded"	panel1:loaded	1	2000	2000	2000	2000	2000
▾ JavaScript expression	__profile("Loaded", "co	1	2000	2000	2000	2000	0
"Loaded"	computedField1:loaded	1	2000	2000	2000	2000	2000

Loaded and rendered profile blocks

Figure 20.22 A profile snapshot of the testLoadedAndRendered1 XPage

The interesting aspects of the wall time profiling snapshot of the **testLoadedAndRendered1** XPage are contained with the special `__profile()` blocks used within the computed **loaded** and **rendered** properties of this XPage. You should also take note of the breakdown of time involved to process the request. Again, this points back to the special `_profile()` blocks and the computed **loaded** and **rendered** property expressions within. What is perhaps most surprising about this simple **GET** type request for the **testLoadedAndRendered1** XPage is highlighted by the total time taken to process the request and not necessarily the count of times the computed loaded and rendered property expressions have actually been invoked. If you have successfully profiled this XPage, you should also see a total time of approximately 8 seconds or above for the wall time. The other thing to check is the XPages Request Introspection console output, as shown in Figure 20.23.

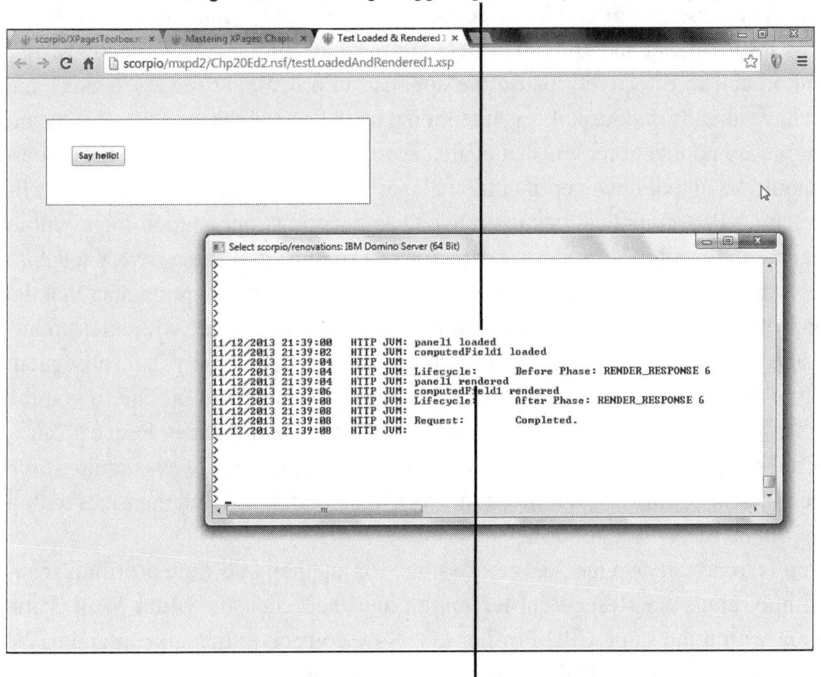

Figure 20.23 The XPages Request Introspection console output for testLoadedAndRendered1

By using the introspection console output, you can notice that the computed **loaded** property expressions for both the **panel1** and **computedField1** controls are executed first, followed by the computed **rendered** properties. The interesting thing about this is that the computed **loaded** properties do not occur within a lifecycle phase—instead they appear to occur before the **RENDER_RESPONSE** phase is executed, as shown in Figure 20.23. This is because the request for the **testLoadedAndRendered1** XPage was a simple **GET** type request. Therefore, only lifecycle phases **RESTORE_VIEW** (1) and/or **RENDER_RESPONSE** (6) will be executed depending on whether the request is a simple **GET** or an AJAX **GET**, respectively. In this particular example, the request is a simple **GET**, which means that the page-loading event is triggered when the request is received by the XPages runtime. This page-loading event, in turn, causes the invocation of **loaded** properties within an XPage and the `beforePageLoad` and `afterPageLoad` methods if they are defined. Following this step you can then see in Figure 20.23 that the **RENDER_RESPONSE** phase is entered and the computed **rendered** properties of the **panel1** and **computedField1** controls are invoked before this phase exits.

As previously mentioned, this particular request ends up taking 8 seconds or more to complete server-side processing, as shown in the XPages Toolbox profiling and XPages Request Introspection results. This time is artificial in the sense that the computed **loaded** and **rendered** property expressions for the panel and computed field all make use of a `java.lang.Thread.sleep(2000)` method call to effectively pause the application processing for 2 seconds each time. As you might have already deduced, this is intentional on the part of the author and is meant to represent some arbitrary application logic that evaluates to the hide/when result for the associated controls—it should be noted, however, that the XPages team have come across many well-presented and powerful XPages applications that have "heavy-lifting" application logic within such hide/when **loaded** and **rendered** property expressions. The impact of these is very much to the detriment of performance, as you learn in a moment. It is important to also remember that the results taken when profiling the **testLoadedAndRendered1** example are done without accounting for any client-side waiting for the normal request/response network activity and subsequent browser processing of the HTML, CSS, and JavaScript markup. This should outline to you the fact that the activities you perform here using the XPages Toolbox and XPages Request Introspection technique are purely server side. The task of tuning any application always requires *both* server-side and client-side profiling and optimization work to be performed, but the focus within this section remains on the server side for now.

Your next step is to now rearm the XPages Toolbox for another wall time profiling snapshot. To do this simply click the **Reset Profiler** button and then click the **Start Wall Time Profiler** button again within the same CPU Profiler tab. Now go back to the tab containing the **testLoadedAndRendered1** XPage and this time click on the **Say hello!** button. You should now wait for the request to complete—when this has happened, you should see a message appearing below the button saying **foo says hello!**, as shown here in Figure 20.24.

Now return to the XPages Toolbox, and click **Stop Profiler** to end the profiling session and have the wall time snapshot created. This snapshot appears within 1 to 2 seconds and also highlights to you just how effective this particular tool is for identifying performance bottlenecks. In this particular example you should see that the request took 16 seconds or longer to complete. Obviously, this is an unacceptable time for a response to complete, especially when you consider the trivial demands of the Say hello! button. To remind yourself of this, refer to Listing 20.12 for the full XSP markup of the **testLoadedAndRendered1** XPage. Alternatively, view the actual XSP markup in Domino Designer or indeed review the XSP fragment in Listing 20.13 that is also provided here for your convenience.

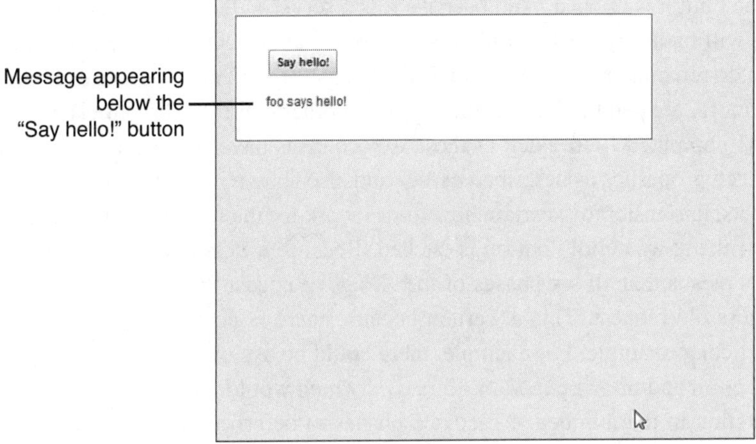

Figure 20.24 The message below the button after the "Say hello!" request is completed

Listing 20.13 The Source of the Say hello! Button

```
<xp:button value="Say hello!" id="button1">
    <xp:eventHandler event="onclick" submit="true"
        refreshMode="complete">
        <xp:this.action>
            <![CDATA[#{javascript:
                println("button 'Say hello!' triggered...");
                viewScope.foo = "foo says hello!";
            }]]>
        </xp:this.action>
    </xp:eventHandler>
</xp:button>
```

As you can see in Listing 20.13, the "**Say hello!**" button is extremely trivial and undemanding. You would not expect this server-side event handler to put the XPages runtime under any degree of stress, yet it took 16 seconds or more to complete processing of this particular action. And this is where the insight that can be gleaned from the XPages Toolbox snapshot and the XPages Request Introspection console output becomes invaluable. By reviewing these along with applying your knowledge and understanding of the XPages Request Processing Lifecycle, it will become clear as to what is actually happening here.

Take a brief moment now to establish some important facts about the **testLoadedAndRendered1** XPage. There is the "**Say hello!**" button, which has an associated server-side event handler. This event handler invokes two lines of simple SSJS. The event handler causes a full-page refresh to occur when the button is clicked. And because it is a server-side event handler action that is being invoked, it will naturally cause a **POST** type request to be sent to the XPages runtime—and it is important to remember this is NOT a **GET** request like the initial request example profiled earlier! Furthermore, also on the XPage, there are two other controls: the **panel1** panel and the **computedField1** computed field. Each of these two controls have corresponding computed **loaded** and **rendered** properties as described earlier and also shown in Listing 20.12.

So given all the facts, it is easier to ascertain how things work for the **testLoadedAndRendered1** XPage whenever the "**Say hello!**" button is clicked. Because a POST request is sent to the XPages runtime, this means that all six phases of the XPages Request Processing Lifecycle will be invoked to process the request. This is certain because there is no optimization of the event handler in this particular example. For example, there could be use made of `No Validation`, or `Partial Refresh` and/or `Partial Execution`, which would all be beneficial here and because of the reduction in the number of lifecycle phases to be processed along with the reduced amount of server-side component tree processing that occurs. You will be glad to hear that these features of the XPages runtime will be described in the next section of this chapter. But for now it is known that the "**Say hello!**" button event handler is simply causing a full-page refresh to happen and therefore six phases of the lifecycle will be invoked during the processing of a request. It is also known that two other controls on the XPage have computed **loaded** and **rendered** properties, namely the **panel1** panel and the **computedField1** computed field. And as already seen in the previous exercise of profiling the "**Test Phases**" example and Figure 20.18, the computed **rendered** properties have also been executed multiple times within four out of six lifecycle phases for a single request. This is because of the special nature of the **rendered** property itself, which now deserves an explanation.

Because XPages is built upon and extends the JavaServer Faces framework, the **rendered** property is a feature, along with associated behavior, that is inherited from JSF. However, it should be noted that the XPages runtime does optimize the way in which the **rendered** property is executed in comparison to how JSF treats it. Nonetheless it is a unique property within the XPages runtime (or within the JSF for that matter) in the sense that it is executed during lifecycle phases 2, 3, 4, and 6. Therefore, the **rendered** property must be given special consideration during your XPages development endeavors to ensure appropriate and efficient use of it. In summary, the effect of the **rendered** property for an XPage request using the two most common HTTP protocol action types of **GET** and **POST** is as follows:

- For a **GET** request, a **rendered** property is invoked only during the **RENDER_RESPONSE** phase (6).
- For a **POST** request, a **rendered** property is invoked during the **PROCESS_VALIDATIONS** (2), **APPLY_REQUEST_VALUES** (3), **UPDATE_MODEL_VALUES** (4), and **RENDER_RESPONSE** (6) lifecycle phases.

Technically, there are sound reasons for this behavior that effectively enable and support the notion of executable subparts, or branches, of the corresponding server-side component tree for an XPage during request processing, particularly when coupled with Partial Refresh and/or Partial Execution type request processing. For example, you might have editable controls on an XPage such as Edit Boxes that may be in read-only or edit-mode depending on some particular workflow logic at a given point in time within the application. As the end user interacts with the XPage, there are Partial Refresh and Partial Execution requests being issued to dynamically update and change the User Interface, such as toggling an Edit Box from read-only into edit-mode. During these requests the XPages runtime can determine which branches within the corresponding server-side component tree should be processed based on the **rendered** property value of each control within that hierarchical component tree. Hence, if some control and its children should be processed during the processing of a given request, it is due to the **rendered** property evaluating to **true**, versus some other control within the same server-side component tree having its own **rendered** property evaluating to **false**.

As mentioned earlier, there is more on Partial Refresh and Partial Execution in the next section. For now, know that there are special technical requirements underlying the **rendered** property that enable efficient server-side component tree processing. And conversely if the **rendered** property is not used in an appropriate manner, all kinds of inverse performance problems will be introduced into an XPages application, just like the examples being looked at here within the **testLoadedAndRendered1** XPage.

With all that said, it should go a long way toward helping you understand why there are multiple invocations of the same computed **rendered** property expressions during a single request made against the **testLoadedAndRendered1** XPage. To conclude this particular example, you should now review the XPages Toolbox snapshot and XPages Request Introspection console output for the "**Say hello!**" button click. Figure 20.25 shows the "**Say hello!**" button click wall time profiling snapshot described earlier.

As shown in Figure 20.25, the `__profile()` block "Rendered" statements appear exclusively within lifecycle phases 2, 3, 4, and 6. This is consistent with the explanation given earlier. You should note that through regular use of the XPages Toolbox, you can quickly deduce a lot of information about a request just by looking at a profiling snapshot without actually looking at the underlying XSP markup. In this particular example, it is clearly a **POST** request given all six lifecycle phases have been collated in the snapshot. For completeness, Figure 20.26 shows the request introspection console output that also reaffirms the way in which the various loaded and rendered statements are being emitted as the lifecycle phases are processed.

Total time: 16039 milliseconds (ie: > 16 seconds)

▾ XPages Request	/mxpd2/Chp20Ed2.nsf/testLoaded	1	16039	16039	16039	16039	7
▾ JSF Phases	RESTORE_VIEW 1	1	28	28	28	28	0
▾ XSP: Restore view	/testLoadedAndRendered1.xsp	1	28	28	28	28	0
XSP: Restore view state	/testLoadedAndRendered1	1	28	28	28	28	28
▾ JSF Phases	UPDATE_MODEL_VALUES 4	1	4000	4000	4000	4000	0
▾ JavaScript expression	__profile("Rendered", "p	1	2000	2000	2000	2000	0
"Rendered"	panel1:rendered	1	2000	2000	2000	2000	2000
▾ JavaScript expression	__profile("Rendered", "	1	2000	2000	2000	2000	0
"Rendered"	computedField1:rendered	1	2000	2000	2000	2000	2000
▾ JSF Phases	APPLY_REQUEST_VALUES 2	1	4001	4001	4001	4001	0
▾ JavaScript expression	__profile("Rendered", "p	1	2000	2000	2000	2000	0
"Rendered"	panel1:rendered	1	2000	2000	2000	2000	2000
▾ JavaScript expression	__profile("Rendered", "	1	2000	2000	2000	2000	0
"Rendered"	computedField1:rendered	1	2000	2000	2000	2000	2000
▾ JSF Phases	PROCESS_VALIDATIONS 3	1	4002	4002	4002	4002	0
▾ JavaScript expression	__profile("Rendered", "p	1	2001	2001	2001	2001	0
"Rendered"	panel1:rendered	1	2001	2001	2001	2001	2001
▾ JavaScript expression	__profile("Rendered", "	1	2001	2001	2001	2001	0
"Rendered"	computedField1:rendered	1	2001	2001	2001	2001	2001
▾ JSF Phases	RENDER_RESPONSE 6	1	4002	4002	4002	4002	0
▾ XSP: Render view	/testLoadedAndRendered1	1	4002	4002	4002	4002	1
▾ JavaScript expression	__profile("Rendered", "p	1	2000	2000	2000	2000	0
"Rendered"	panel1:rendered	1	2000	2000	2000	2000	2000
▾ JavaScript expression	__profile("Rendered", "	1	2000	2000	2000	2000	0
"Rendered"	computedField1:rendered	1	2000	2000	2000	2000	2000

Figure 20.25 The "Say hello!" button click wall time profiling snapshot

You should also note the absence of any of the `__profile()` block "Loaded" statements. This also clearly indicates that it is a **POST** request issued against an already loaded XPage and not using any special "reload" techniques such as `context.reloadPage()` or the **Dynamic Content** control, for example. And this is important because it also affirms the explanation given earlier about the **loaded** property in that this property is executed only once during the special page-loading event and subsequent triggering of the `beforePageLoad` and `afterPageLoad` events. In this particular "**Say hello!**" example, the XPage had already been loaded during the initial request when you clicked the **"Test Loaded And Rendered 1"** link from the **index** XPage. And therefore, the "**Say hello!**" request was actually a second request in a sense being issued against an already existent XPage server-side component tree, hence no reinvocation of the computed **loaded** properties within the XPage.

This is one advantage of the **loaded** property over the **rendered** property in that it is only evaluated during the initial XPage load, but it also means it is inflexible because it requires a `context.reloadPage()` to actually cause a reevaluation of the **loaded** property to occur because a normal **POST** Complete or Partial Refresh request will not cause this. You may now want to use the loaded property more predominantly within your own XPages applications to dynamically hide or display controls within an XPage based on workflow logic (just like the example described earlier) but you should note that this requires use of the **Dynamic Content** control to overcome the **loaded** property limitation—you will learn more about this shortly.

It's now time to move onto a second example to further bolster your understanding of the **loaded** and **rendered** properties. You should now open the **testLoadedAndRendered2** XPage within Domino Designer and review the XSP markup using the Source editor. Listing 20.14 contains all XSP source markup for this particular XPage.

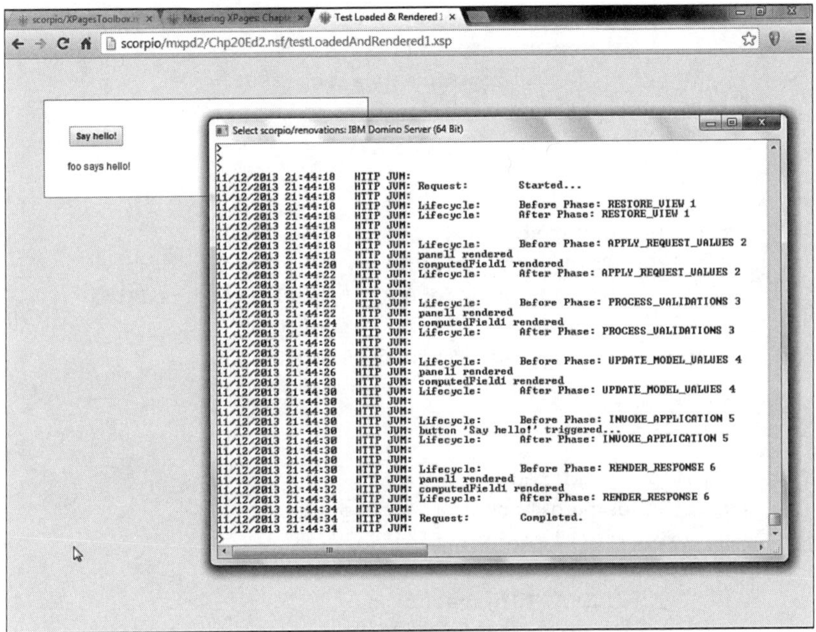

Figure 20.26 The "Say hello!" button click request introspection output

Listing 20.14 The Source of the testRenderedAndLoaded2 XPage

```
<?xml version="1.0" encoding="UTF-8"?>
<xp:view xmlns:xp="http://www.ibm.com/xsp/core"
    pageTitle="Test Loaded &amp; Rendered 2">
    <xp:div themeId="container">
        <xp:button value="Say hello again!" id="button1">
            <xp:eventHandler event="onclick" submit="true"
                refreshMode="complete">
                <xp:this.action>
                    <![CDATA[#{javascript:
                        println("button 'Say hello again!' triggered...");
                        viewScope.foo = "foo says hello again!";
```

```
              }]]>
            </xp:this.action>
          </xp:eventHandler>
        </xp:button>
        <xp:br></xp:br>
        <xp:repeat id="r1" value="#{javascript:5}" repeatControls="true">
          <xp:panel id="panel1">
            <xp:this.loaded>
              <![CDATA[${javascript:
                __profile("Loaded", "panel1:loaded") {
                  println("panel1 loaded");
                  java.lang.Thread.sleep(2000);
                  return true;
                }
              }]]>
            </xp:this.loaded>
            <xp:this.rendered>
              <![CDATA[#{javascript:
                __profile("Rendered", "panel1:rendered") {
                  println("panel1 rendered");
                  java.lang.Thread.sleep(2000);
                  return true;
                }
              }]]>
            </xp:this.rendered>
            <xp:text escape="true" id="computedField1"
              value="#{viewScope.foo}">
              <xp:this.loaded>
                <![CDATA[${javascript:
                 __profile("Loaded", "computedField1:loaded") {
                   println("computedField1 loaded");
                   java.lang.Thread.sleep(2000);
                   return true;
                 }
                }]]>
              </xp:this.loaded>
              <xp:this.rendered>
                <![CDATA[#{javascript:
                 __profile("Rendered",
➥"computedField1:rendered") {
                   println("computedField1 rendered");
                   java.lang.Thread.sleep(2000);
                   return true;
                 }
                }]]>
```

```
57                      </xp:this.rendered>
58                  </xp:text>
59              </xp:panel>
60          </xp:repeat>
61      </xp:div>
62 </xp:view>
```

If you have not already noticed it, you should be aware that the **testLoadedAndRendered2** XPage is similar to the **testLoadedAndRendered1** XPage. Actually, the only difference is on two lines of XSP source markup, specifically lines 17 and 60, that declare an `<xp:repeat>` and then close it with `</xp:repeat>`. This **Repeat** control has been introduced to further highlight the effects of the **loaded** and **rendered** properties within an area of an XPage that is created by iteration. Examples of this type can go far beyond just using a **Repeat** control, but nonetheless the same principles apply for custom "detail" facet content within a DataView, or computed column content within a View Panel, and so forth—effectively all the custom type XSP programming you might do within a "view" as such. In these use cases, it is not uncommon for XPages developers to innocently use computed **rendered** properties on the content within such iterable areas that end up either showing or hiding controls depending on values within the current row of the underlying data model. And the **testLoadedAndRendered2** helps to demonstrate this quite succinctly.

Therefore again, rearm the XPages Toolbox for another wall time profiling snapshot, not forgetting to click the **Reset Profiler** button and also ensure the XPages Request Introspection mechanism is enabled. Having done this, you should now click the **Test Loaded And Rendered 2** link from the **index** XPage. This opens a new tab and sends a request to the XPages runtime for the **testLoadedAndRendered2** XPage. When this completes, you should return to the XPages Toolbox and stop the profiler to have the wall time profiling snapshot created for you. But before reviewing this information, you need to take a brief moment to review the XPages Request Introspection console output for the request that has just completed. You should see information similar to that shown in Figure 20.27.

As you can see in Figure 20.28, the same lifecycle phases are invoked as previously for the **testLoadedAndRendered1** XPage. However, because there is now a **Repeat** control wrapping the **panel1** and **computedField1** controls, there is additional overhead to process both the **loaded** and **rendered** properties for each of these two controls as the **Repeat** iterates over the data model. In effect, there has been a significant increase in the total amount of time taken to process the initial simple **GET** request of the **testLoadedAndRendered2** XPage in comparison to the already rather dismal 8 seconds taken to process the same operation against the **testLoadedAndRendered1** XPage. You should now review the wall time profiling snapshot information. Again you should see something similar to Figure 20.28.

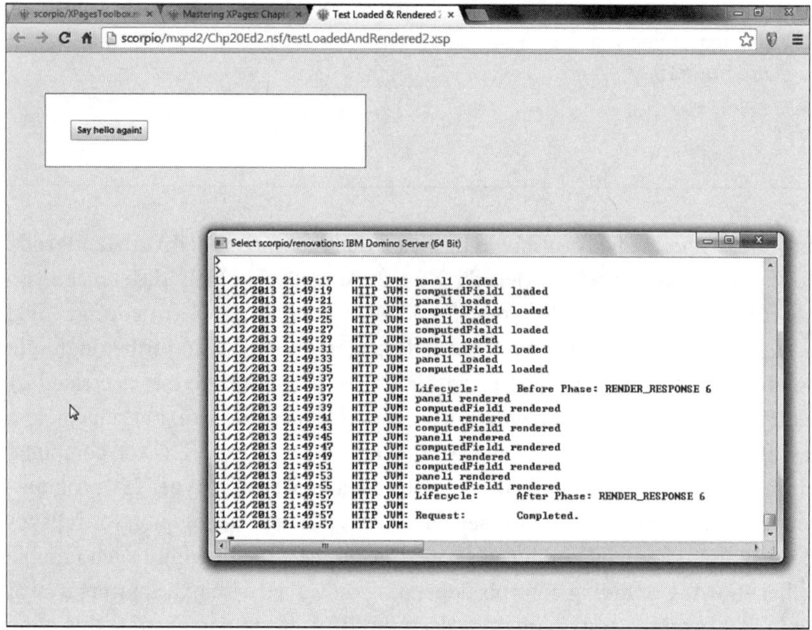

Figure 20.27 The request introspection details of the testLoadedAndRendered2 XPage

As you can see in Figure 20.28, the total processing time has now jumped to just more than 40 seconds for this initial simple **GET** type request—many end users would have already navigated away or simply closed this particular XPages application. You should also notice the way in which the snapshot is now littered with `__profile()` block "Rendered" statements. This is obviously a result of the iteration occurring over the underlying data model of the **Repeat** control that subsequently creates new corresponding controls for the current iteration row.

Take this a stage further now and perform the same "**Say hello!**" button test as done against the **testLoadedAndRendered1** XPage, with the only difference being that for this particular example, it is called the "**Say hello again!**" button. So before clicking this button, don't forget to go back to the XPages Toolbox and ensure you have clicked the **"Reset Profiler"** button before clicking **"Start Wall Time Profiler"** once more. Having done all that, you should now go back to the **testLoadedAndRendered2** XPage and click the **"Say hello again!"** button. As you can see in the XSP source markup for this button, it is performing the exact same operations as the **"Say hello!"** button described in the earlier example. All the same mechanics are utilized, such as a **POST** type request that causes a full refresh and so on. You will notice that this request will take a considerable amount of time to complete—this is further exacerbated by the 2-second sleep "heavy lifting" delay that is used for each **loaded** and **rendered** invocation. Nonetheless, it elaborates the point being made here about the inappropriate use of computed **loaded** and **rendered** properties—particularly the latter. As the request is processed, it is interesting to watch the Server console where you see the live processing occur via the XPages Request Introspection output that is generated. When the request finishes, you should go directly back to the XPages Toolbox and click the **"Stop Profiler"** button. And if you then review the XPages Request Introspection console output, you should see something similar to Figure 20.29.

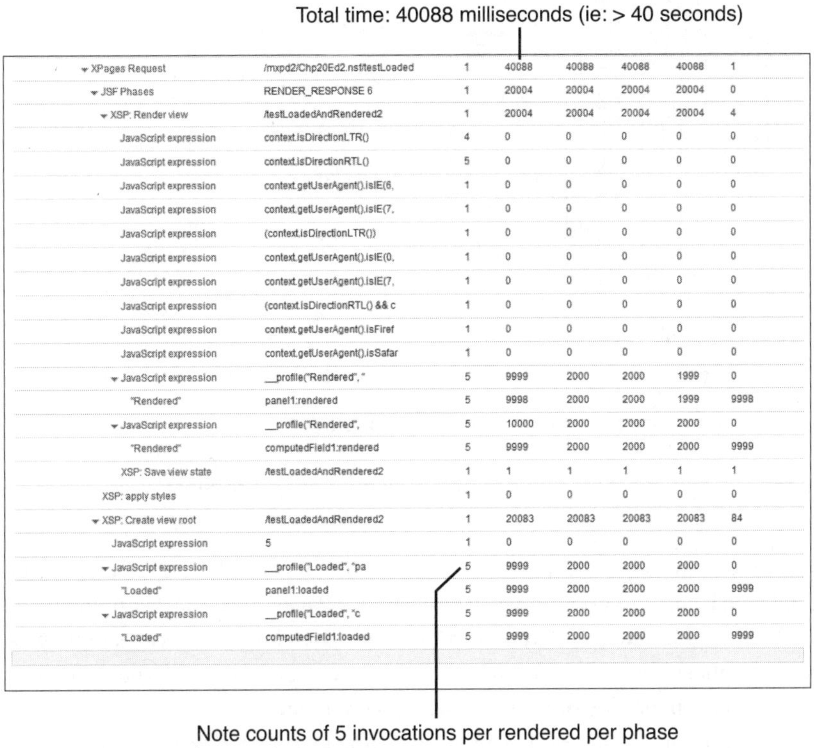

Total time: 40088 milliseconds (ie: > 40 seconds)

▾ XPages Request	/mxpd2/Chp20Ed2.nsf/testLoaded	1	40088	40088	40088	40088	1
▾ JSF Phases	RENDER_RESPONSE 6	1	20004	20004	20004	20004	0
▾ XSP: Render view	/testLoadedAndRendered2	1	20004	20004	20004	20004	4
JavaScript expression	context.isDirectionLTR()	4	0	0	0	0	0
JavaScript expression	context.isDirectionRTL()	5	0	0	0	0	0
JavaScript expression	context.getUserAgent().isIE(6,	1	0	0	0	0	0
JavaScript expression	context.getUserAgent().isIE(7,	1	0	0	0	0	0
JavaScript expression	(context.isDirectionLTR())	1	0	0	0	0	0
JavaScript expression	context.getUserAgent().isIE(0,	1	0	0	0	0	0
JavaScript expression	context.getUserAgent().isIE(7,	1	0	0	0	0	0
JavaScript expression	(context.isDirectionRTL() && c	1	0	0	0	0	0
JavaScript expression	context.getUserAgent().isFiref	1	0	0	0	0	0
JavaScript expression	context.getUserAgent().isSafar	1	0	0	0	0	0
▾ JavaScript expression	__profile("Rendered", "	5	9999	2000	2000	1999	0
"Rendered"	panel1:rendered	5	9998	2000	2000	1999	9998
▾ JavaScript expression	__profile("Rendered",	5	10000	2000	2000	2000	0
"Rendered"	computedField1:rendered	5	9999	2000	2000	2000	9999
XSP: Save view state	/testLoadedAndRendered2	1	1	1	1	1	1
XSP: apply styles		1	0	0	0	0	0
▾ XSP: Create view root	/testLoadedAndRendered2	1	20083	20083	20083	20083	84
JavaScript expression	5	1	0	0	0	0	0
▾ JavaScript expression	__profile("Loaded", "pa	5	9999	2000	2000	2000	0
"Loaded"	panel1:loaded	5	9999	2000	2000	2000	9999
▾ JavaScript expression	__profile("Loaded", "c	5	9999	2000	2000	2000	0
"Loaded"	computedField1:loaded	5	9999	2000	2000	2000	9999

Note counts of 5 invocations per rendered per phase

Figure 20.28 The wall time profiling snapshot of the testLoadedAndRendered2 GET request

Again, it is evident from the request introspection output what is happening during the processing of the **"Say hello again!"** request. The biggest consumer of processing time and count of times executed is the computed **rendered** properties on the two controls nested within the **Repeat** control. By reviewing the wall time profiling snapshot, you can also see that the entire request has taken more than 80 seconds to complete, which is completely unacceptable. As a comparable example, you should see something similar to that of Figure 20.30, which shows the "**Say hello again!**" wall time profiling snapshot.

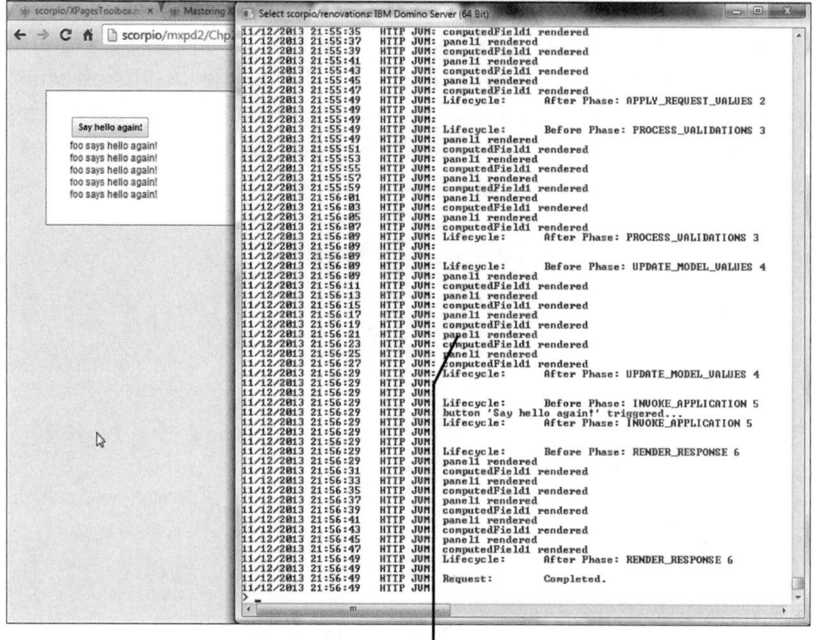

Figure 20.29 The request introspection output for the "Say hello again!" request

By working your way through the profiling and request introspection exercises of the **testLoadedAndRendered1** and **testLoadedAndRendered2** XPages, you can learn about the real technicalities of both the **loaded** and **rendered** properties. More important, you should now recognize the adverse implications of inappropriately using these properties in your everyday XPages development and err on the side of caution if you do use them.

The next section builds upon this by teaching you XPages runtime features that enable you to not only write code that will have minimal server-side component tree processing cost, but also to reduce the amount of response output generated. Specifically, you learn how to use `Partial Refresh` and `Partial Execution` effectively, plus other aspects of controlling and optimizing the XPages Request Processing Lifecycle by using features such as `No Validation` and the Dynamic Content control.

Total time: 80018 milliseconds (ie: > 80 seconds)

▾ XPages Request	/mxpd2/Chp20Ed2.nsf/testLoaded	1	80018	80018	80018	80018	4
▾ JSF Phases	RESTORE_VIEW 1	1	8	8	8	8	0
▾ XSP: Restore view	/testLoadedAndRendered2.xsp	1	8	8	8	8	0
XSP: Restore view state	/testLoadedAndRendered2	1	8	8	8	8	8
▾ JSF Phases	PROCESS_VALIDATIONS 3	1	20000	20000	20000	20000	1
▾ JavaScript expression	__profile("Rendered", "	5	9999	2000	2000	2000	0
"Rendered"	panel1:rendered	5	9999	2000	2000	2000	9999
▾ JavaScript expression	__profile("Rendered",	5	10000	2000	2000	2000	0
"Rendered"	computedField1:rendered	5	10000	2000	2000	2000	10000
▾ JSF Phases	UPDATE_MODEL_VALUES 4	1	20000	20000	20000	20000	1
▾ JavaScript expression	__profile("Rendered", "	5	9999	2000	2000	2000	0
"Rendered"	panel1:rendered	5	9999	2000	2000	2000	9999
▾ JavaScript expression	__profile("Rendered",	5	10000	2000	2000	2000	0
"Rendered"	computedField1:rendered	5	10000	2000	2000	2000	10000
▾ JSF Phases	APPLY_REQUEST_VALUES 2	1	20001	20001	20001	20001	2
▾ JavaScript expression	__profile("Rendered", "	5	9999	2000	2000	2000	0
"Rendered"	panel1:rendered	5	9999	2000	2000	2000	9999
▾ JavaScript expression	__profile("Rendered",	5	10000	2000	2000	2000	0
"Rendered"	computedField1:rendered	5	10000	2000	2000	2000	10000
▾ JSF Phases	RENDER_RESPONSE 6	1	20005	20005	20005	20005	0
▾ XSP: Render view	/testLoadedAndRendered2	1	20005	20005	20005	20005	5
▾ JavaScript expression	__profile("Rendered", "	5	9999	2000	2000	2000	0
"Rendered"	panel1:rendered	5	9999	2000	2000	2000	9999
▾ JavaScript expression	__profile("Rendered",	5	9999	2000	2000	2000	0
"Rendered"	computedField1:rendered	5	9999	2000	2000	2000	9999

Note counts of 5 invocations per rendered per phase

Figure 20.30 The wall time profiling snapshot for the "Say hello again!" request

Using Partial Refresh, Partial Execution, and Dynamic Content

In the previous section, you learned about two relatively simple boolean properties available on almost every control within the XPages runtime—the **loaded** and **rendered** properties. You also worked through two worked XPage samples to gain a deeper understanding of the importance and inherent implications of using these two properties relative to the processing of a request by the XPages Request Processing Lifecycle. The benefit of this understanding is that you should now question and analyze the possibilities and limitations of developing optimal (and suboptimal) XSP code within your XPages applications with a certain level of awareness and consideration of the server-side processing cost involved.

One thing you should immediately be asking yourself is about ways in which you could potentially streamline the server-side processing cost of requests to your applications. Furthermore, following the explanations given in the previous section about the **loaded** and **rendered** properties, you should also be wondering to yourself how you could still continue to leverage these two properties when the need arises but in a technically efficient and robust way. And if you are asking yourself these questions, then you are definitely thinking in the right direction, and this section aims to answer those questions for you.

To begin, you can start by dividing the server-side processing of an XPages request into two fundamental lifecycle stages: *Inbound* and *Outbound*. This is a rudimentary division of the processing of an XPages request, and again, just like the previous sections, it focuses solely on the server-side component tree processing cost (without consideration for what else might be occurring on the network and the requesting browser or device itself). Now, take a look at the principles behind this.

First, the *Inbound* stage is most typically concerned with phases 1 through 5 of the XPages Request Processing Lifecycle (that is, **RESTORE_VIEW** through to **INVOKE_APPLICATION**). Second, the *Outbound* stage is ordinarily involved with just the *last* phase, the **RENDER_RESPONSE** phase. Obviously, this broad division of the processing of a request is only a semantic overlay of the real underlying six phase lifecycle, but it's enough to know to start optimizing this processing.

Using Partial Refresh

Perhaps rather oddly, this examination begins by looking at the last stage first—that is, the *Outbound* stage of a request. The reason for this decision is because it typically involves one of the most commonly used features available within XPages, namely `Partial Refresh`. It is assumed that readers understand the details of `Partial Refresh`—if not then you should refer to Chapter 11, "Advanced Scripting," and specifically to the section titled "AJAX and Partial Refresh" for a deep-dive on how to use this feature.

Partial Refresh is a powerful mechanism within XPages that allows targeted HTML DOM interactions and updates to occur without refreshing the entire HTML Document. As you can appreciate, this is a highly desirable behavior for any modern-day web, mobile web, or XPiNC application because it can smooth out the interaction and transition model for an end user, resulting in a much superior user experience. But it also provides performance benefits to the requesting client and processing server in that only a reduced amount of response data is required within the eventual response payload. Obviously, the processing server has less work to do because it needs to collect only the targeted fragment of response data and stream this out over the network. In turn the requesting client also has less processing to perform because it accepts a smaller response payload that it in turn dynamically injects directly into the current HTML DOM within the predefined target refresh area. A win-win all round you might think, but how much benefit are you actually getting? A deeper look at the mechanics of this operation relative to the processing of the XPages Request Processing Lifecycle phases can help measure this.

You know that XPages function as a server-side web application. Within this runtime, there is a mechanism to manage a server-side component tree representation of an XPage—and this mechanism is also responsible for the management of multiple XPages, XPages applications, and end users. Furthermore, you also know that within this runtime there is a request processing lifecycle that governs the processing of a component tree when a request is received. But questions remain about how `Partial Refresh` is applied within this model, for instance:

- Do all lifecycle phases automatically process less of the corresponding component tree?
- Do less lifecycle phases become involved, hence reducing the processing cost?

All perfectly valid questions, but the technical fact behind this feature is that *only the very last request processing lifecycle phase becomes leaner.* Just in case you think that is a typing error, it is not and to restate it in other words, only the **RENDER_RESPONSE** (6) phase processes a reduced component tree for a given request—and all the other lifecycle phases are still processed in the same manner as a standard complete refresh request.

Think back to the previous section about the **loaded** and **rendered** properties where both samples demonstrated multiple invocations of the same computed **rendered** property expressions within lifecycle phases 2, 3, 4, and 6. If you can now imagine setting `refreshMode="partial"` and `refreshId="button1"` on the **"Say hello!"** button event handler of the **testLoaded AndRendered1** XPage. This enables Partial Refresh requests to target only the button control; then believe it or not, you still see multiple computed **rendered** expression invocations still occurring during lifecycle phases 2, 3, and 4 for both the **panel1** and **computedField1** controls—but not in phase 6. Instead within lifecycle phase 6, you will not see any computed rendered statements appear at all in profiling and/or request introspection results. This is because the button is the designated refresh target, and it doesn't have any computed rendered property containing `println()` statements specified—the **panel1** and **computedField1** controls are effectively excluded from processing within this final lifecycle phase.

This may sound slightly odd to you, but should be examined using a sample. So you should now open the **testLoadedAndRendered3** XPage in Domino Designer and study the XSP source markup, particularly for the **"Say hello once more!"** button. Listing 20.15 contains the XSP source markup for the **"Say hello once more!"** button for your convenience.

Listing 20.15 The Source of the "Say hello once more!" Button

```
<xp:button value="Say hello once more!" id="button1">
    <xp:eventHandler event="onclick" submit="true"
        refreshMode="partial" refreshId="computedField1">
        <xp:this.action>
            <![CDATA[#{javascript:
```

```
                println("button 'Say hello once more!' triggered...");
                viewScope.foo = "foo says hello once more!";
            }]]>
        </xp:this.action>
    </xp:eventHandler>
    <xp:this.rendered>
        <![CDATA[#{javascript:
            __profile("Rendered", "button1:rendered") {
                println("button1 rendered");
                return true;
            }
        }]]>
    </xp:this.rendered>
</xp:button>
```

You may have already noticed that the **refreshMode** and **refreshId** properties for the button's event handler, along with the inclusion of a computed **rendered** property, are the only differences on this XPage when compared to the **testLoadedAndRendered1** XPage used in the previous section. The computed rendered property has been introduced on the button simply to give insight into the execution of this control during lifecycle processing. You will also notice that this expression does not call the `sleep(2000)` function, so in effect no wall clock time will be used by this expression. If you recall, when the **testLoadedAndRendered1** example was profiled using the XPages Toolbox, a click on the **"Say hello!"** button took more than 16 seconds to complete. Furthermore, the request introspection console output for that example showed multiple computed **rendered** property expression invocations in lifecycle phases 2, 3, 4, and 6 for both the **panel1** and **computedField1** controls (refer to Figures 20.25 and 20.26 for a reminder of this).

So the interesting thing to do now with the **testLoadedAndRendered3** XPage is to perform the same type of button click profiling and request introspection tests. To do this, you should prepare the XPages Toolbox for a wall time profiling snapshot. You also need to launch the **testLoadedAndRendered3** XPage so that it is ready for you to click the **"Say hello once more!"** button. When you have the XPage ready, remember to go back to the XPages Toolbox and click the **Start Wall Time Profiler** button before clicking the **"Say hello once more!"** button. Finally, on request completion remember to also click the **Stop Profiler** button in the XPages Toolbox to generate the wall time profiling snapshot. If you have profiled this example for yourself, you should see profiling snapshot results similar to that of Figure 20.31 and request introspection console output similar to that of Figure 20.32.

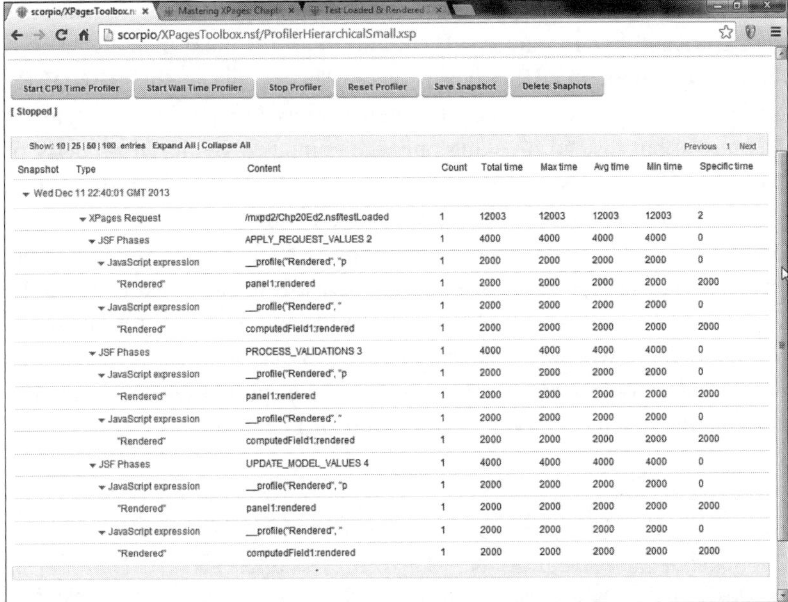

Figure 20.31 The wall time profiling snapshot for the "Say hello once more!" request

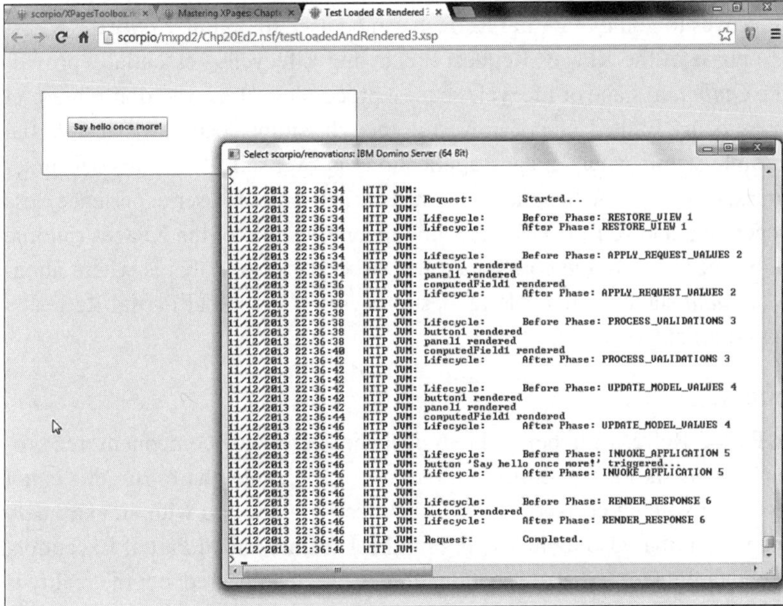

Figure 20.32 The request introspection output for the "Say hello once more!" request

As you can clearly see in Figure 20.31, this request has taken approximately 4 seconds less than its **testLoadedAndRendered1** counterpart, coming in at just more than 12 seconds versus 16 seconds for the **testLoadedAndRendered1** case. This is due to the **RENDER_RESPONSE** (6) lifecycle phase not processing the computed **rendered** properties of the **panel1** and **computedField1** controls, but instead invoking only the computed **rendered** property of the **button1** control because it is the designated refresh target of the Partial Refresh (that is, `refreshId="button1"`). Hence, a reduction of 4 seconds due to not executing the two computed **rendered** expression's `sleep(2000)` delay in the final lifecycle phase. The remaining processing time is, however, used up by the other lifecycle phases, 2, 3, and 4, as shown in the snapshot information in Figure 20.31. You can also see this reflected in the request introspection console output in Figure 20.32 whereby lifecycle phases 2, 3, and 4 all show the emitted **rendered** statements for all three controls (**button1, panel1**, and **computedField1**), but the last lifecycle phase contains only the statement produced by the **button1** control.

TIP

In the event that you might have modified the Chp20Ed2.nsf application in Designer between debugging runs, you should ensure that the debug mode option is rechecked before attempting a new debugging cycle. This is due to the application having the Refresh on Design Change option enabled.

This experiment proves to you that Partial Refresh can be used to optimize *only* the **RENDER_RESPONSE** (6) phase of the XPages Request Processing Lifecycle—essentially providing optimization for the *Outbound* stage of lifecycle request processing. However, don't interpret this runtime behavior as being limited or not powerful enough, simply because using Partial Refresh whenever possible within your XPages applications is by itself always a good practice and strongly encouraged due to the benefits explained earlier (smooth user experience, less response data, less processing, and so forth). But it is not the only feature of the XPages runtime you can leverage to minimize server-side component tree processing. And this is where attention now turns to the *Inbound* stage of lifecycle request processing to look at Partial Refresh's complementary sibling—Partial Execution.

Using Partial Execution

You have learned that Partial Refresh can be used to reduce the server-side component tree processing cost that occurs during the final `RENDER_RESPONSE` (6) lifecycle phase. But this is not enough I hear you say—and you are correct! As ever, XPages provides you with an extremely powerful development arsenal that also includes another great feature called Partial Execution. This may sound slightly daunting or perhaps something that is over-engineered, but the reality is a simple one: If you understand Partial Refresh, then you will naturally understand Partial Execution. In effect it's a feature that can and should be used to complement event handlers that also uses Partial Refresh. Although, it should be noted that this is not a prerequisite because Partial Execution can be used by itself without any Partial Refresh configuration in place on an event handler, but greater benefits can be had by using the two features in unison. If you can, think of it as "server-side partial refresh" of a component tree that is being processed during XPages Request Processing Lifecycle phases 2, 3, 4, 5, but not phase 6 because this is governed by the *Outward* stage Partial Refresh capabilities, then this goes someway to establishing an analogy for you to conceptualize. In essence, it allows you as the developer to fine-tune request processing during the *Inward* stage of the request processing lifecycle.

You should now open the **testLoadedAndRendered4** XPage in Domino Designer and select the **"Say hello one last time!"** button that you see in the WYSIWYG editor—also shown in Figure 20.33. Select the **Events** tab so that you clearly see the **Server Options** group, as shown in Figure 20.33.

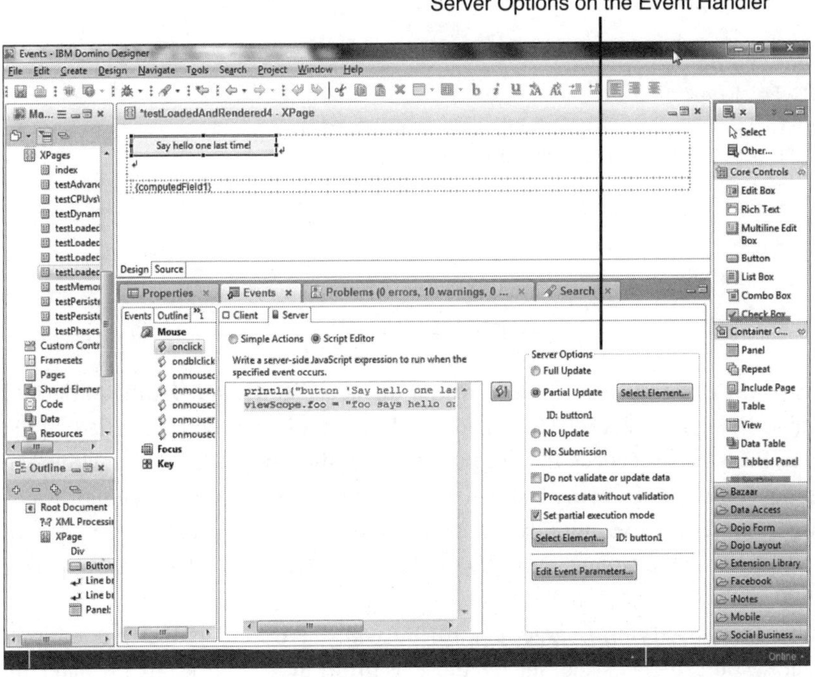

Figure 20.33 The Say hello one last time! button selected in the WYSIWYG editor

The important aspect to note about the **Server Options** is that not only is Partial Refresh enabled along with a refresh target of **button1**, but Partial Execution is also enabled and also targeting **button1**. For your interest, the **Select Element** button and associated control picker were both added into the **Server Options** group for an event handler in Notes/Domino 9.0. This makes it easy and intuitive for you to configure Partial Execution, effectively following the same path as you do for Partial Refresh. And just for completeness, Listing 20.16 contains the XSP source markup for the "Say hello one last time!" button for your convenience.

Listing 20.16 The Source of the "Say hello one last time!" Button

```
<xp:button value="Say hello one last time!" id="button1">
    <xp:eventHandler event="onclick" submit="true"
        refreshMode="partial" refreshId="button1"
        execMode="partial" execId="button1">
        <xp:this.action>
            <![CDATA[#{javascript:
                println("button 'Say hello one last time!' triggered...");
                viewScope.foo = "foo says hello one last time!";
            }]]>
        </xp:this.action>
    </xp:eventHandler>
    <xp:this.rendered>
        <![CDATA[#{javascript:
            __profile("Rendered", "button1:rendered") {
                println("button1 rendered");
                return true;
            }
        }]]>
    </xp:this.rendered>
</xp:button>
```

As you can see in Listing 20.16 or indeed within the actual **testLoadedAndRendered4** XPage within Domino Designer, the **execMode** and **execId** properties are both specified on the button event handler. So when you check the **Set partial execution mode** check box within the **Server Options** group, `execMode="partial"` will be written onto the event handler. Similarly, if you choose to target the execution by choosing **Select Element**, a control picker will appear enabling you to choose the target control ID for the Partial Execution. This control picker is shown in Figure 20.34.

Also remember that specifying a target control ID with the **execId** property is entirely optional. For instance, you can check the **Set partial execution mode** check box or manually write `execMode="partial"` onto any event handler to enable this feature without actually selecting a target control ID. In terms of XPages runtime behavior, this translates to execution only of that specific event handler in absolute isolation to everything else contained within the component tree. It is the most minimalist form of processing available within the *Inbound* stage for an event handler. And conversely you can select any target control ID within the current XPage—either as listed within the control picker or a computed ID if you so choose. The only requirement to take account of when computing the target control ID is to ensure that it will resolve to some "real" control within the current server-side component tree at runtime; otherwise a runtime exception will be raised.

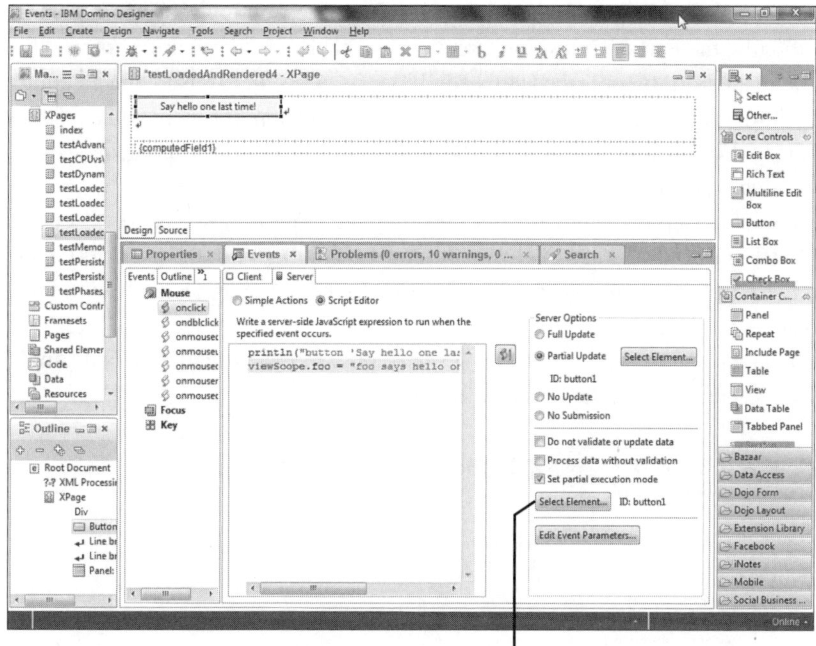

Figure 20.34 The Partial Execution control picker

If you take a moment to reflect over the last paragraph, you should start to realize the potential flexibility and power being afforded to you as a developer when using Partial Execution. This feature on its own obviously gives you an ability to either "broaden" or "narrow" the scope of server-side component tree execution. And as you have learned, this applies to the *Inbound* stage lifecycle phases (2, 3, 4, and 5). But now think about the benefits of a "dual relationship" formed by coupling Partial Refresh with Partial Execution so that the *Outbound* stage lifecycle phase (6) also gets similar treatment. In this scenario, you also then either "broaden" or "narrow" the scope of server-side component tree execution to either match or suit that of the Partial Execution scope. Obviously, this means you can potentially execute a broader chunk of the server-side component tree during the *Inbound* stage and then render back a narrower chunk during the *Outbound* stage. Or you could also do the complete opposite.

The important thing to be aware of is that you always ensure an appropriate offset between the two so that any variable or control dependencies are valid at the point of execution. For example, if you were receiving an updated edit box value that will be used within the

RENDER_RESPONSE phase by a computed field but the Partial Execution scope was too narrow to actually consume the incoming edit box value during the *Inbound* stage in the first place, then obviously, the computed field will not have the latest value during the *Outbound* stage. In this situation, the offset between the *Inbound* and *Outbound* stage execution scopes needs to be reconfigured. Specifically, the Partial Execution target control ID needs to specify a control that is either the parent or an ancestor of, or is the actual edit box control itself, to ensure the incoming value is consumed within the server-side component tree processing appropriately—this ensures any new value input by the end user will actually be applied into the updated component tree. Otherwise, the new value is simply lost.

This is a good point to step back into another profiling and request introspection test cycle of the **testLoadedAndRendered4** XPage. You should now be familiar with the usual test cycle process to perform these tasks. If not, you should refer back to the previous sections within this chapter to remind yourself.

After you have taken a new wall time profiling snapshot of the **"Say hello one last time!"** button, you should see something similar to Figure 20.35.

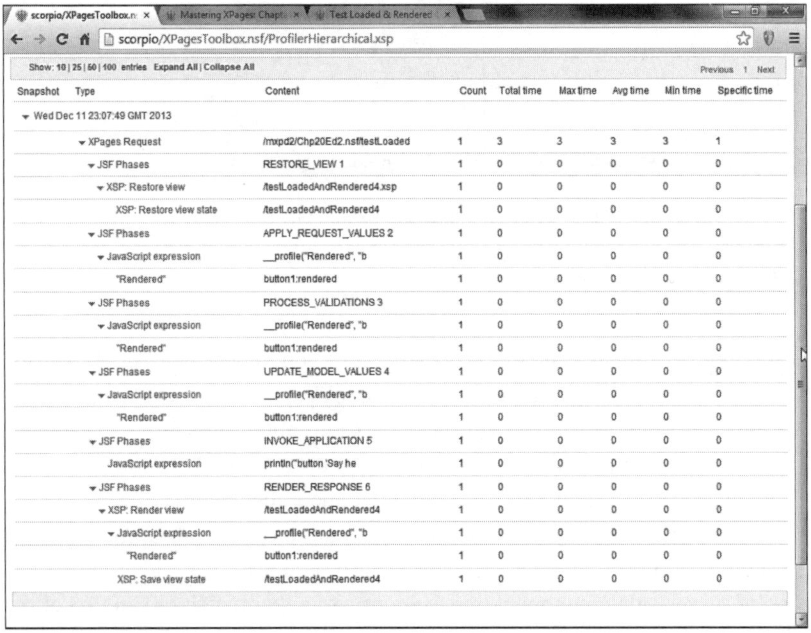
scorpio/XPagesToolbox.nsf/ProfilerHierarchical.xsp
Show: 10 | 25 | 50 | 100 entries Expand All | Collapse All
Previous 1 Next
Snapshot Type Content Count Total time Max time Avg time Min time Specific time
Wed Dec 11 23:07:49 GMT 2013
XPages Request /mxpd2/Chp20Ed2.nsf/testLoaded 1 3 3 3 3 1
JSF Phases RESTORE_VIEW 1 1 0 0 0 0 0
XSP: Restore view /testLoadedAndRendered4.xsp 1 0 0 0 0 0
XSP: Restore view state /testLoadedAndRendered4 1 0 0 0 0 0
JSF Phases APPLY_REQUEST_VALUES 2 1 0 0 0 0 0
JavaScript expression __profile("Rendered", "b 1 0 0 0 0 0
"Rendered" button1:rendered 1 0 0 0 0 0
JSF Phases PROCESS_VALIDATIONS 3 1 0 0 0 0 0
JavaScript expression __profile("Rendered", "b 1 0 0 0 0 0
"Rendered" button1:rendered 1 0 0 0 0 0
JSF Phases UPDATE_MODEL_VALUES 4 1 0 0 0 0 0
JavaScript expression __profile("Rendered", "b 1 0 0 0 0 0
"Rendered" button1:rendered 1 0 0 0 0 0
JSF Phases INVOKE_APPLICATION 5 1 0 0 0 0 0
JavaScript expression println("button 'Say he 1 0 0 0 0 0
JSF Phases RENDER_RESPONSE 6 1 0 0 0 0 0
XSP: Render view /testLoadedAndRendered4 1 0 0 0 0 0
JavaScript expression __profile("Rendered", "b 1 0 0 0 0 0
"Rendered" button1:rendered 1 0 0 0 0 0
XSP: Save view state /testLoadedAndRendered4 1 0 0 0 0 0

Figure 20.35 The wall time profiling snapshot for the "Say hello one last time!" request

As you can see in the wall time profiling snapshot of Figure 20.35, the entire **"Say hello one last time!"** request has now taken only a fraction of a second. This is in complete contrast to the previous examples that were taking more than 16 seconds in some cases. But why has there been such a radical reduction in the processing time? To explain the mechanics behind this time saving, first take a brief look at the request introspection console output. You should also see similar results to that in Figure 20.36.

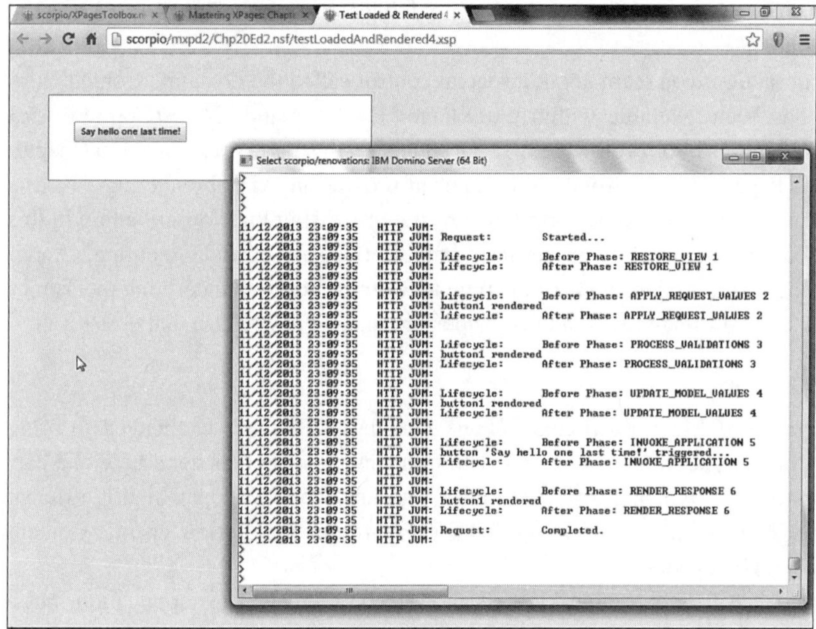

Figure 20.36 The request introspection output for the "Say hello one last time!" request

The reason for the reduction in processing time should be quite evident to you when you look at the request introspection console output. The key clue lies in the absence of the computed **rendered** expression statements for the **panel1** and **computedField1** controls within each of the lifecycle phases. Instead, the only computed **rendered** expression statement that is present within the request introspection console output is the one emitted by the **button1** control. This is due to the `execMode="partial"` and `execId="button1"` properties that are defined on the **button1** event handler. Therefore, succinctly demonstrating and proving to you how effective Partial Execution is in terms of being able to control and influence the amount of server-side component tree execution that occurs during lifecycle phase processing.

You may now be excited by the prospect of leveraging Partial Refresh and Partial Execution together and already foresee opportunities to combine these two powerful features. Or indeed, you may be slightly daunted by the idea —don't be. In any case, there is nothing like a little practice to make improve your skills. And the author strongly encourages you to do just that: Create a test harness XPage and play around with these two features together before enhancing your production applications. And when you do get to enhance your production applications, always profile your code using the XPages Toolbox and/or XPages Request Introspection technique so that you have complete clarity on what you are doing along with scientific results on the gains you are introducing.

In the next subsection, you learn about a special control called the Dynamic Content control. This control has been available within the XPages Runtime since Notes/Domino 8.5.3 Upgrade Pack 1. Within this book, you were first introduced to this particular control in Chapter 4, "Anatomy of an XPage." This control does not in itself provide any visual rendering—its true power though lies in its capability to perform much of the processing logic described up to this point in relation to loaded and rendered properties, Partial Refresh and Partial Execution. (And it does so in a smart and discrete manner.) It's now time to examine how the underlying mechanics of this control work and how its use will impact the performance of any XPage that uses it.

Using Dynamic Content

In this closing section on "Making Efficient XPages Requests," you are challenged to bring together all the learning material covered so far within this chapter to understand how one particular XPages control, the Dynamic Content control, can help you develop a highly efficient XPages application. You should refer to Chapter 4 for an introduction to the Dynamic Content control if you have not already done so.

It must be said that it is one thing knowing how to build an XPages application, but a completely different thing knowing how to build a highly performant and scalable XPages application. XPages as an out-of-the-box technology provides you with a base level of inherent performance and scalability capabilities, but it is then up to you as the developer to extrapolate the requirements of your application into real technical solutions that are adequate and robust enough to efficiently process and manage the particular performance and scalability demands expected by the requirements. In implementation terms, this is typically achieved by custom developer coding that also leverages inbuilt system features and API that are already known to be or stated as highly performant and scalable. Therefore, it is typically both useful and productive to harness any available inbuilt controls or functions of a system that promise the absolute maximum benefits to gain the most from that system. In this case, the Dynamic Content control fits that bill on many fronts where efficient loading and rendering of XPages controls is paramount. Another valuable and useful benefit gained from the Dynamic Content control is that it also provides the capability to support URL context reading/writing and bookmark restoration of dynamically generated content. Effectively, this gives your application end users the flexibility to save bookmarks for dynamically generated AJAX/Partial Refresh content that they can obviously share with others or revisit at a later point in time. In Chapter 4, you also learned about the Search Engine Robot compatibility feature that is also built into this control as of Notes/Domino 9.0.1. Given that Search Engine Robots cannot execute JavaScript as they "crawl" the source markup of web pages, this feature still enables reading and indexing to occur of what is normally dynamically generated content by the Dynamic Content control.

As mentioned in the closing paragraph of the last subsection on Partial Execution, the Dynamic Content control became officially available in Notes/Domino 8.5.3 Upgrade Pack 1. For some XPages Developers, it is the "silver bullet" when it comes to creating a highly interactive, smoothly transitioning user experience for an XPage. For others, they simply have not discovered its prowess yet. This closing subsection aims to teach you about the mechanics of this particular control relative to XPages Request Processing Lifecycle processing. Therefore, regardless of which side of the XPages Developer camp you fall into, you will be fully aware of the benefits to be gained when using it.

Ultimately, you should think of the Dynamic Content control as a structural element that provides scaffolding for you to "hang your artwork" onto—the artwork in this sense being your Custom Controls or other XSP markup for the user interface. And at any given point in time, this structural element allows only one piece of artwork to be made visible to the naked eye through a "viewing gallery." In doing so, it completely discards any currently loaded piece of artwork from the viewing gallery and then loads the newly requested piece of artwork into the viewing gallery in its place. And this process is repeated each time another piece of artwork is requested. Therefore, the scaffolding is never overloaded by carrying all pieces of artwork within the exhibition. It simply has designated placeholders for each piece and dynamically retrieves and discards each piece as needed.

If you now try to translate this analogy into the technical workings of the Dynamic Content control and also consider the role of the XPages Request Processing Lifecycle within this context, then it should be relatively easy for you to work out what is happening to each "piece of artwork" as an end user of your application interacts with an XPage using this control.

At this point, you should open the **testDynamicContent** XPage in Domino Designer. You should also have the **Chp20Ed2.nsf** application open in a browser and ensure *Debug Mode* is enabled to capture request introspection console output. Now also open the **testDynamicContent** XPage in your browser. You can do this by clicking the **"Test Dynamic Content"** link on the **index** XPage of **Chp20Ed2.nsf**. After you have done this, you will see the XPage, as shown in Figure 20.37. This XPage demonstrates an extensive range of available methods used to interact with a Dynamic Content control using either HTTP **GET** or **POST** action types. Table 20.1 describes summary information for each available method of interaction.

Table 20.1 Available Dynamic Content Control Interaction Methods

Method	Properties
`#content=facetName{¶m=value, ...}`	URL Fragment / AJAX / HTTP GET
`XSP.showContent(id, facetName, {params})`	CSJS Function / AJAX / HTTP GET
`component.show(facetName, {params})`	SSJS Method / HTTP POST
`changeDynamicContentAction[for, facetName, {params}]`	Simple Action / HTTP POST

All these methods are typically used by the Link or Button control client and/or server-side event handlers depending on the type of method being used.

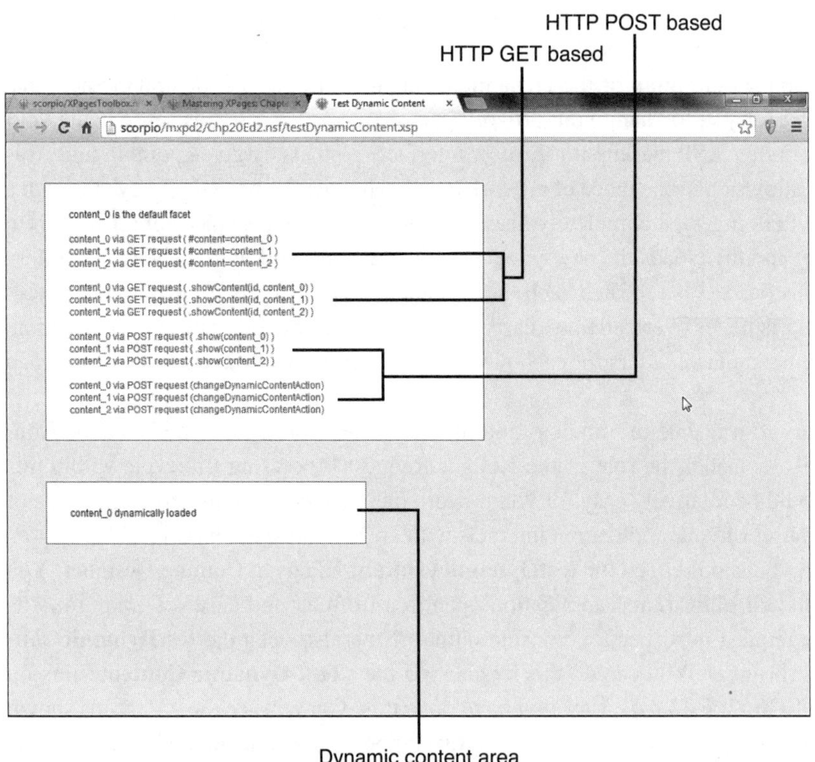

Figure 20.37 The testDynamicContent XPage at Runtime

Because the XPages Request Introspection technique is being used here, you should also see console output similar to Figure 20.38 after opening the **testDynamicContent** XPage. Obviously, this request introspection output is for the initial request for this particular XPage. Effectively only the *page load time event* and last XPages Request Processing Lifecycle phase (`RENDER_RESPONSE`) are executed for this `GET` request scenario. This results in the computed `loaded` and `rendered` properties being evaluated, but more interestingly the Dynamic Content control's `beforeContentLoad` and `afterContentLoad` events are also triggered as seen within the request introspection console output in Figure 20.38. You will come back to study this request introspection console output and other examples later in this subsection. For now, you just need to be aware that request introspection will be an important part of understanding the mechanics of the Dynamic Control as you progress through this subsection.

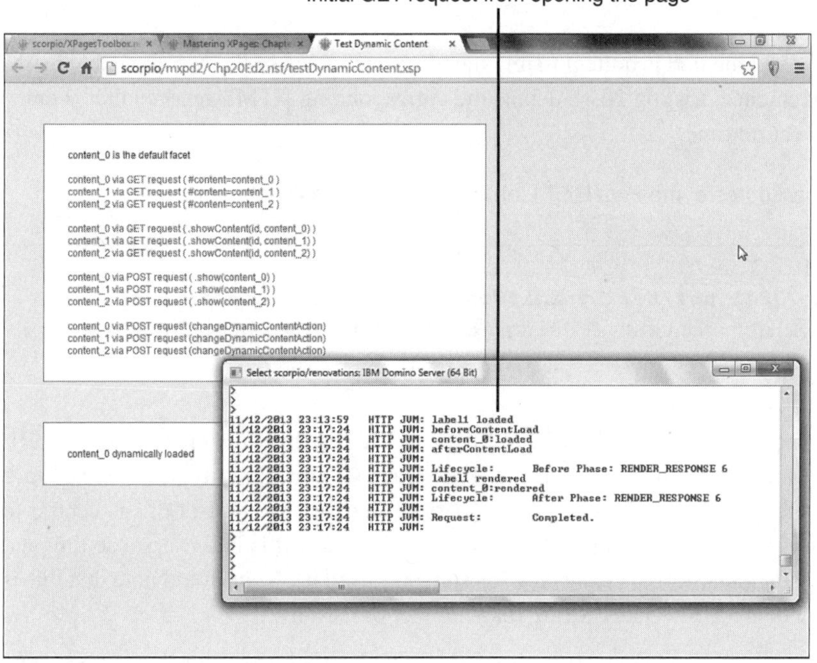

Figure 20.38 The initial testDynamicContent XPage request introspection console output

Coming back to the range of methods available to interact with the Dynamic Content control, specifically there are four methods available, two of which are `GET`-based and two `POST`-based as you can deduce from Table 20.1. If you study the XSP source markup within the **testDynamicContent** XPage, you can identify the method used by each of the Link controls and event handlers based on the textual values declared on each, as indicated in Figure 20.37. For the purposes of this chapter, though, only one of the GET-based and one of the POST-based methods will be covered in detail. This will sufficiently explain the essence of the workings of the Dynamic Content control under each HTTP protocol action type. By gaining an understanding of just two out of the four possible interaction methods, you can understand how the other GET-based and POST-based methods function as the underlying principles are all similar.

To begin, the XSP source markup for one of the **GET**-based methods is illustrated in Listing 20.17, which you will also find within the **testDynamicContent** XPage.

Listing 20.17 The XSP Source Markup of the First GET-Based Method

```
<xp:link escape="true" id="link0"
    text="content_0 via GET request ( #content=content_0 )"
    value="/testDynamicContent.xsp#content=content_0">
</xp:link>
```

This example and method is quite possibly the most interesting of the four available methods. For your convenience, Listing 20.18 details the corresponding HTML markup that is emitted by this example at runtime.

Listing 20.18 The Source of the First GET Link in the Emitted testDynamicContent HTML Markup

```
<a id="view:_id1:link0"
    href="/Chp20Ed2.nsf/testDynamicContent.xsp#content=content_0"
    class="xspLink">content_0 using GET request ( #content=content_0 )
</a>
```

As you can see in both Listing 20.17 and Listing 20.18, the **href** rather oddly has a URL that contains a # symbol after the XPage name. This is where you might typically expect a ? symbol to appear along with an arbitrary list of Query String parameters. But this is central to the mechanical workings of the Dynamic Content control because it is based upon setting and resetting the URL Fragment (or the "*hash part*" as some refers to it). You should note that this is somewhat different than a URL Query String for a number of reasons:

- A URL Fragment is denoted by the # symbol, whereas a URL Query String is denoted by the ? symbol.
- A URL Fragment is not actually sent as part of the request data (that is, within any HTTP Request Headers or Body data), whereas a URL Query String is.
- A URL Fragment can be directly manipulated within a browser using client-side JavaScript without it actually causing a browser reload or refresh of the current page to occur.

You should also be aware that a URL Query String and Fragment can coexist within the same URL. Therefore, a URL can be resolved by using a URL Query String initially and subsequent interaction with the retrieved page can then lead to further addition and/or manipulation of the URL Fragment part. For the astute reader, you will recognize the URL Fragment as being commonly used for everyday "anchoring" within a HTML page, for example as "*Move to bottom*" or "*Back to top*" links within a web page (for example, `href="#top"` | `href="#bottom"`) that allow you to easily move to specific locations within the current page without actually causing a reload or refresh to occur. And when you would click an anchor link like the examples given here, you would see the browser's URL address being updated to reflect the change of `#anchor` name along with the browser automatically scrolling to that location within the document. This then allows you to bookmark the updated link if you so want for future reference. Subsequently, if you did revisit that bookmark, the browser would request the URL and upon receiving the response, then attempt to locate and move (scroll) to the `#anchor` within the content automatically for you. Conversely, if the named `#anchor` no longer existed within the received response content, the browser would simply not find it and quietly ignore it without retrying or resending a follow-up request.

For the Dynamic Content control, the mechanics that deal with URL Fragment processing and manipulation are hidden from the end user and XPages developer alike to keep things relatively simple when using this control. However, as an XPages developer, it is certainly beneficial for you to be aware of the way in which the URL Fragment is used by this control. Other than that, this control allows you to be productive when you need to create a highly responsive user interface as a lot of the request lifecycle processing, **rendered** property, and **loaded** property processing, and URL manipulation are handled for you automatically. Nonetheless, it is beneficial for an XPages developer to understand the inner workings to a certain degree to eke out the most performance and scalability from an XPage using this control.

Returning to the description of the URL Fragment in relation to the Dynamic Content control, this special part of a URL is used to manage both the wanted facet name for the actual content, but also any required additional contextual information about the state of an XPage that is going to be or is already loaded within a browser. This means that instead of appending or manipulating Query String parameters within the URL, the URL Fragment is used instead for any adding or manipulating of contextual parameters as an end user interacts with the associated XPage—such end user interactions in this case are Partial Refresh-based. And it is important to note that you can create an ampersand delimited list of URL Fragment parameters that are appended after the # in more or less the exact same format you would typically use for a URL Query String. In fact, Listing 20.17 describes an example where one URL Fragment parameter exists, namely parameter "*content*" with a value of "*content_0*":

```
#content=content_0
```

This could just as well be something more extensive with several parameters coming after the initial # marker, and important, being delimited by the ampersand character:

```
#content=content_0&foo=bar&x=y
```

The interesting aspect about the Dynamic Content control mechanism lies in the way that unlike the default browser behavior of simply trying to scroll to the named **#anchor** position, the XPage actually listens for changes to the URL Fragment using a client-side JavaScript handler via the XSP client-side JavaScript object. When a URL Fragment change is detected by the XSP client-side object listener, it follows up by making a Partial Refresh request targeted at the associated Dynamic Content control within the server-side component tree. One important part of this process is that it collects all available URL Fragment parameters and adds them into the HTTP **GET** request headers. This means that any contextual URL Fragment parameters are then transported with the request data and made available within the server-side component tree.

Following the introduction to the Dynamic Content control in Chapter 4, you should already understand the significance of the URL Fragment parameter called *content*. If not, this is a special parameter used by the Dynamic Content control to switch between the available named facets contained within it—typically one of these will be preselected as the initial "default facet." Specifically, the value of the *content* parameter should equate to one of the available facet names that are predefined within the Dynamic Content control; otherwise the fallback will be to use the default facet when a given named facet does not exist. Therefore, you should ensure that this special parameter is used by any links or actions within an XPage that should cause requests to a Dynamic Content control within the component tree. Otherwise, the URL Fragment will be ignored by the XSP client-side JavaScript object and instead treated by the browser as normal "anchor" links.

You should now ensure that *Debug Mode* is still enabled within the **Chp20Ed2.nsf** application as request introspection console output is especially important for the next couple of exercises. With this done and the **testDynamicContent** XPage ready, you should also open your browser's developer tools or debugging utility. Firefox has Firebug, Chrome has Developer Tools, and so forth—regardless of whichever browser you use, the Network tab is what you need for the following exercises. Just to explain the reason for this, armed with your browser network sniffing utility and the request introspection console output, you can capture detailed information about requests you are about to send to the Dynamic Content control within the **testDynamic Content** XPage in both the client-side browser and server-side XPages runtime.

In its initial state, the **testDynamicContent** XPage uses and renders the named **content_0** facet content. This is predefined within the XSP source markup where the `defaultFacet` property is set on the Dynamic Content control (that is, `defaultFacet="content_0"`). Refer to the XPage source in Domino Designer to view this. This has also previously been highlighted in Figure 20.37. You are now going to change this to the **content_1** facet and in doing so inspect the *Network* tab and also the request introspection console output. This will give you deep insight into what is happening as you interact with the Dynamic Content control within this XPage. To do this, you should now click the second link within the XPage that is titled "*content_1 via GET request (#content=content_1)*". After you have done this, the *Network* tab within your browser should have captured details of a **GET** request similar to Figure 20.39.

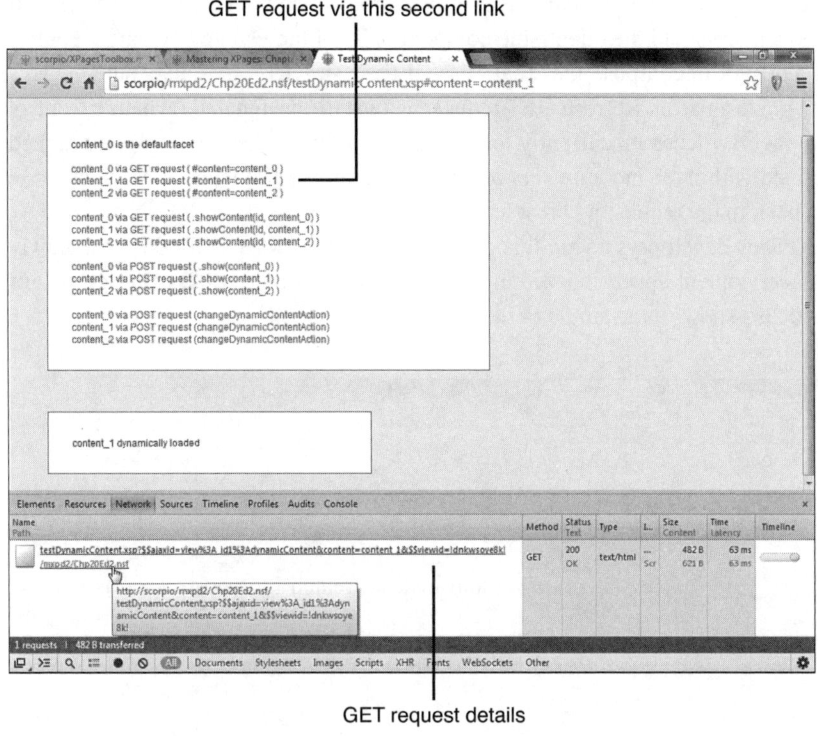

Figure 20.39 The GET request captured in Chrome Developer Tools Network tab

So the interesting aspect of this **GET** request is highlighted by the way in which the link that was clicked had a **href** value of:

```
http://scorpio/mxpd2/Chp20Ed2.nsf/testDynamicContent.
xsp#content=content_1
```

Yet the **GET** request that was captured in the browser network sniffing utility and sent to the XPages Runtime has a value of:

```
http://scorpio/mxpd2/Chp20Ed2.nsf/testDynamicContent.
xsp?$$ajaxid=view%3A_id1%3AdynamicContent&content=content_
1&$$viewid=!dncos3nny0!
```

This relates to and confirms the description given earlier about the XSP client-side JavaScript object listener reacting to changes of the URL Fragment and issuing a Partial Refresh request back against the target Dynamic Content control in the server-side component tree. Basically, the XSP listener has reacted to the URL Fragment being changed from the default facet state of `#content=content_0` to the wanted `#content=content_1` when you clicked the second link. It then collected the URL Fragment parameter information, along with the current **$$viewid** of the XPage component tree, and the client-side component ID of the Dynamic Content control for use in the **$$ajaxid**; all to compose the "real" Partial Refresh URL previously shown. This URL is then used to make a Partial Refresh GET request against the designated Dynamic Control instance. It, in turn, then switches its currently loaded facet content to the newly wanted named facet content as defined within the incoming *content* URL Fragment parameter before a response is collated and sent back to the requesting browser again.

Eagle-eyed XPages developers trying this out in their own browser will notice the newly loaded **content_1** facet content appearing within the bottom panel in the **testDynamicContent** XPage. Figure 20.40 also shows an example of this for your convenience.

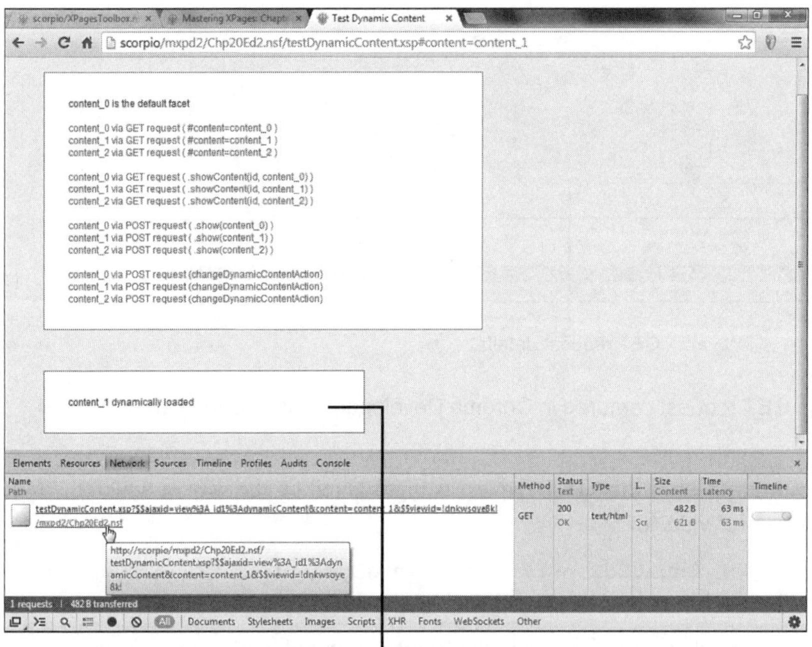

Figure 20.40 The newly loaded content_1 facet content after the request

Now you can turn your focus on the XPages Request Introspection console output also captured for the same request. You should have request introspection console output similar to that of Figure 20.41.

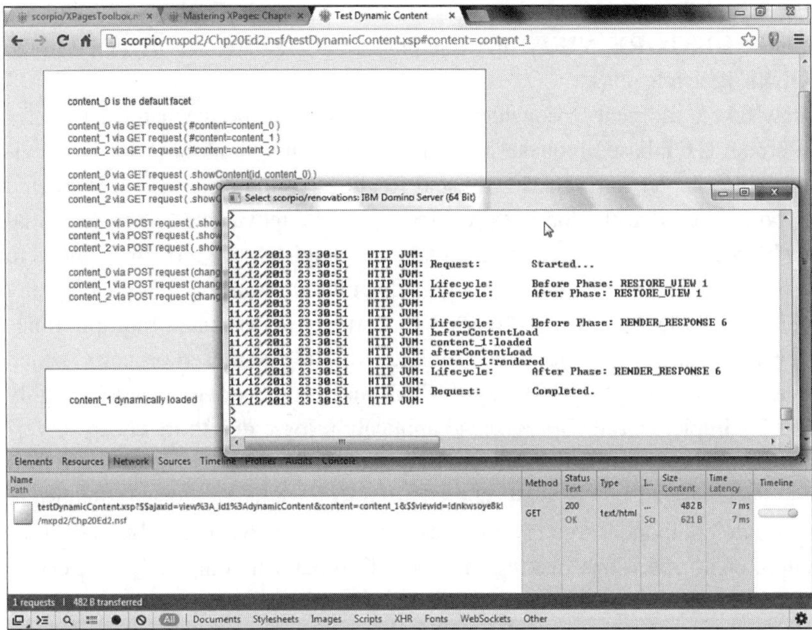

Figure 20.41 The GET request introspection console output for the content_1 request

If you compare this request introspection output with the first initial request (refer to Figure 20.38), you can see a couple of subtle differences. Essentially both requests are **GET**-based. But the initial request was a simple **GET** request to retrieve the entire **testDynamicContent** XPage contents, whereas this latest request is an AJAX **GET** request indirectly sent by the XSP client-side JavaScript object in reaction to an end user forced change to the URL Fragment. The differences are evident in the request introspection console output as the initial request has computed **loaded** evaluations occurring during the *page load time event* followed by the **RENDER_RESPONSE** lifecycle phase processing. In contrast, the AJAX **GET** request sent by the XSP client-side JavaScript object listener first invokes the **RESTORE_VIEW** lifecycle phase, which is then followed by the **RENDER_RESPONSE** lifecycle phase processing. This is the expected of behavior for an AJAX/Partial Refresh **GET** request, and also the justification for including the **$$viewid** and **$$ajaxid** request parameters within the request URL. Effectively, these parameters are used by the XPages Runtime to ensure the correct server-side component tree is restored, and component instance within this is correctly used. However, the interesting aspect of this relates to the mechanics that are worked within the Dynamic Content control during the lifecycle phase processing of this second request. This appears in the request introspection console output in Figure 20.41, whereby the computed **loaded** property evaluations and `beforeContentLoad`/`afterContentLoad` events of the Dynamic Content control are not triggered by the *page load time event* like in the initial request example shown in Figure 20.38, nor are they triggered within the **RESTORE_VIEW** lifecycle phase, but they are now triggered in the **RENDER_RESPONSE** lifecycle phase.

You should now take a moment to consider the ramification of the mechanical flow for this AJAX/Partial Refresh **GET** based request. To help you with this, think back to the previous subsection within this chapter, on "The Myths and Realities of the Loaded and Rendered Properties," where you learned that the **loaded** property cannot be reevaluated after the initial *page load time event* has been triggered. In essence, it takes a complete page refresh or reload to do this which is costly and does not provide an integrated, smoothly transitioning page by any means. Furthermore, you also learned that the **loaded** property is *not* executed multiple times within different lifecycle phases for a single request, unlike its sibling **rendered** property, which is executed up to four times for a single **POST** request. This makes the **loaded** property a highly attractive proposition for implementing "*hide when*" application logic due to its cheap server-side processing cost. But you also learned in that same subsection that because of the page load time event triggering of the **loaded** property all AJAX/Partial Refresh based requests against an already loaded server-side component tree cannot cause the reevaluation of any **loaded** properties within that component tree. Thus making the **loaded** property a completely ineffective programming pattern to use when implementing "*hide when*" application logic within a highly interactive and responsive AJAX/Partial Refresh enabled XPage.

But having just learned about and seen evidence of how the Dynamic Content control does indeed actually cause a reevaluation of the **loaded** property during a Partial Refresh **GET** request, the establishment is then upturned. So the next thing to learn about here involves introspecting one of the two possible HTTP **POST** based methods of interacting with the Dynamic Content control to further validate the lean capabilities of this control. For this, you should now click on the content_2 via POST request (.show(content_2)) link within the **testDynamic Content** XPage. After this, you should have request introspection console output, as shown in Figure 20.42.

Referring to Figure 20.42, you can see that the Dynamic Content control also demonstrates its capability to efficiently load and discard content on demand even for a HTTP **POST** type request against an XPage. The main point of this example is illustrated within the request introspection console output whereby again the computed **loaded** properties within the target facet and the `beforeContentLoad` and `afterContentLoad` events of the Dynamic Content control are all triggered again for this AJAX/Partial Refresh POST request.

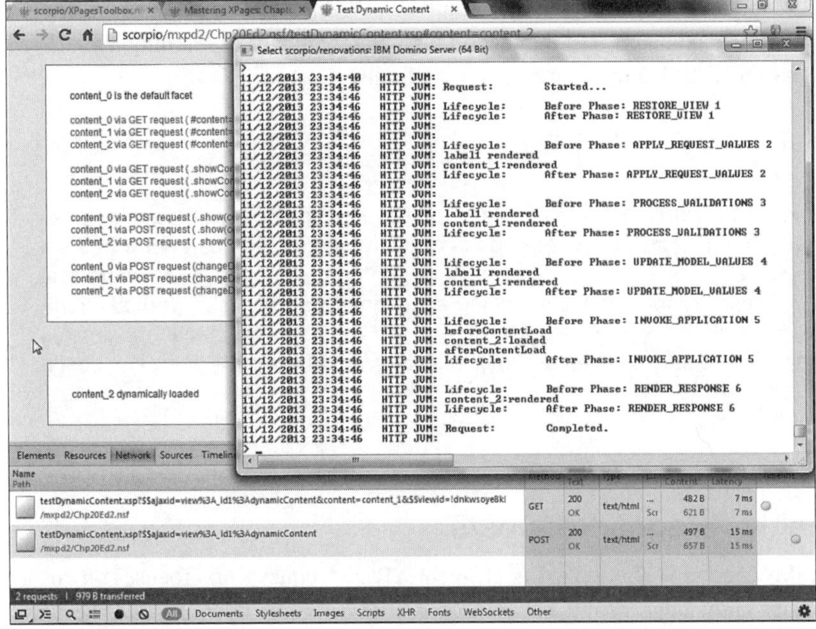

Figure 20.42 The POST request introspection console output for the content_2 request

Therefore, this approach effectively demonstrates that using a combination of a Dynamic Content control and computed **loaded** properties is an efficient way to implement "*hide when*" logic within an XPages application that results in minimal processing overhead, especially when compared to a computed **rendered** property equivalent. Specifically, the benefit is twofold as there is minimal server-side processing cost coupled with reduced memory usage. This is because only those exact branches and components of a server-side component tree are loaded and resident within memory at any point in time—instead of every component within an XPage always being loaded—hence, resident in memory and using CPU cycles but just not rendering under certain conditions. As an end user interacts with the XPage in a browser, device, or XPiNC client, highly responsive AJAX/Partial Refresh requests will be used to update and navigate within the application, which in turn results in a smoothly transitioning, highly interactive, and performant user experience.

At this point if you were to analyze a JVM Heap Dump or Session XML Dump of the **testDynamicContent** component tree, you would find all the hierarchical objects in-place as you would expect, but more interesting you would find the Dynamic Content control present with only the subcomponent object structure of the "*content_1*" facet resident in memory. All the other facets and their associated content defined within the XSP source markup would not be resident within the component tree, including the default facet "*content_0*" because it was simply discarded from memory when you clicked the second link. Note you will be learning about JVM Heap Dumps and Session XML Dumps in the next part of this chapter.

> **TIP**
>
> If you are interested in further learning material about how to make efficient XPages requests and the XPages Request Processing Lifecycle in general, you can get a free set of videos and supporting application at http://www.openntf.org/p/xpages%20masterclass. Within this project, there are four videos spanning approximately 4 hours of worked examples with explanations of underlying theory, profiling, and request introspection examples that all complement the content covered within the "Making Efficient XPages Requests" section of this chapter.

Making Scalable XPages Requests

The first section of this chapter is about making efficient XPages requests and focuses on ensuring you have adequate knowledge of the *XPages Request Processing Lifecycle* and the ways in which it governs the processing of an XPage request. It also teaches you about certain features, properties, and controls that you, as the XPages developer, can use to positively influence minimal request processing and remove redundancy from this cost. This enables you to then gain maximum processing efficiencies from your XSP code during request lifecycle processing, thus reducing the amount of Central Processing Unit (CPU) cycles used by a server.

Therefore, the learning material in the first part of this chapter is critical to developing a highly performant XPages application that uses a minimal amount of CPU cycles on a server. But what should you know about and understand to develop a highly scalable XPages application? This is where the second part of this chapter comes to the foreground and teaches you about the ingredients needed to support and process high scalability. Needless to say, minimizing usage of virtual and physical memory (RAM/disk) is one of the biggest factors in achieving this goal.

You should therefore consider the first part of this chapter as dealing with the "vertical" capability and cost of an XPage where the primary focus is on minimizing the actual processing cost on the CPU and secondarily on reducing the memory consumption of a single XPage on RAM/disk. And consider the second part of this chapter as dealing with the "horizontal" capability and cost of an XPages application where the primary focus is on reducing the memory consumption of an XPage and/or XPages application on RAM/disk and secondarily on reducing the processing cost on the CPU. Effectively, this requires you, as the XPages developer, to establish the *optimum scalability configuration* for a given XPages application so that it can support the upper limits of the anticipated end user load relative to the demands of each XPage within that application and still function and serve the end users within a reasonable amount of time.

However, to establish the *optimum scalability configuration* for an XPages application requires you to first have some understanding of the host environment and its memory management model—namely the *XPages State Management Layer*—also sometimes referred to as the *XPages Persistence Layer*. In addition, similar to using the XPages Toolbox and the XPages Request Introspection technique to gain deep insight into the "vertical" capability and cost of an XPage request, there are tools and techniques that you also need to become familiar with to gain deep insight into the "horizontal" capability and cost of an XPage and/or XPages application.

You learn about all these scalability aspects in the upcoming sections. Ultimately, you should come away from reading this chapter understanding that achieving the best possible "vertical" cost for an XPage along with the best possible "horizontal" cost for an XPages application, means you have set a model in place that supports high performance and scalability for that application based on the specifications and requirements, and expectations of it.

Understanding the XPages Memory Model

Before you can effectively analyze and optimize your XPages applications for scalability, you must first understand the memory model within the XPages Runtime. Only then can you effectively analyze memory and make decisions about the way your XPages applications should use memory. As mentioned within the introduction to this part of the chapter, developing for scalability in XPages is primarily focused on good memory usage, which can be virtual and/or physical—virtual memory being random access memory (RAM) and physical memory being disk allocated storage space. (You learn more about RAM later in the RAM and disk persistence subsection. For now, it is sufficient to be aware that RAM is effectively the *JVM Heapspace* allocated within the system.) The XPages Runtime makes use of both of these memory locations and provides you, the XPages developer, with settings to configure and use these locations appropriately for each of your XPages applications—more on this coming up soon.

At the core of the XPages Runtime, there are two mainstays within the architecture that are critical to the functioning of the runtime:

- XPages Request Processing Lifecycle
- XPages State Management Layer

You should already be aware of the XPages Request Processing Lifecycle after reading the first part of this chapter. But for many readers, this will probably be the first introduction to the *XPages State Management Layer* within this book or elsewhere. In its most basic form, the *XPages State Management Layer* is responsible for saving and restoring the state of a server-side component tree during normal execution of the *XPages Request Processing Lifecycle*. In a more complete form, it is also responsible for managing many of the other *context* specific objects and caches you will undoubtedly have used or will use in the future, such as the scoped variables (**requestScope**, **viewScope**, **sessionScope**, and **applicationScope**) among other things such as the current user object, Managed Beans, and so forth. And it is also important to realize that the responsibility of the XPages State Management Layer is exponential because it functions not just for a single XPage component tree in isolation, but for many component trees within many XPages applications that are potentially being used by many end user sessions all at the same time. Figure 20.43 shows a diagram that depicts the main components within the XPages Runtime architecture including the two mainstays previously described.

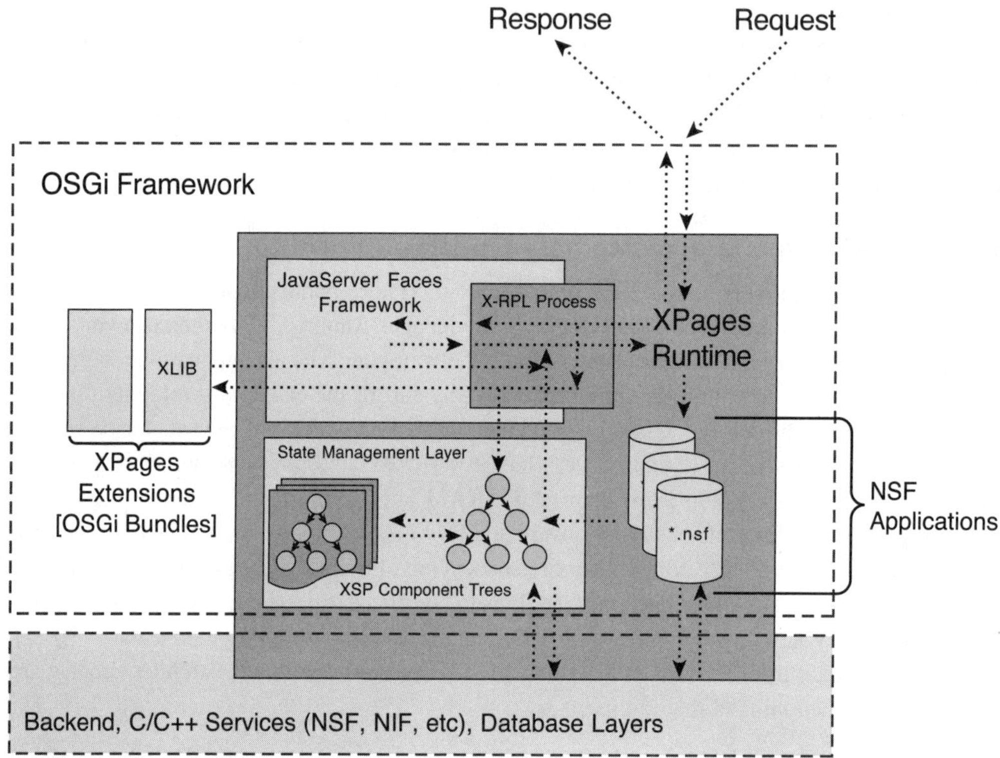

Figure 20.43 The main components within the XPages Runtime Architecture

In terms of the basic function of the state management layer, the processing that is involved entails the execution of special methods during the **RESTORE_VIEW** and/or **RENDER_RESPONSE** lifecycle phases for every XPage request. These methods are called `restoreState()` and `saveState()` and are implemented by every XPages component that needs to have state persisted in between each end user request during that user session. This mechanism is obviously a critical feature that enables the XPages Runtime to work as a powerful, stateful web application framework. This effectively means that stateless HTTP requests can be received and are then executed against a stateful server-side representation of an XPage (aka component-tree) for the specific requesting end user for as long as the associated user session exists. And this concept is the same regardless of the number of end users and applications being served and hosted by any given XPages server.

So obviously, all this state management is extremely important but also has an inherent cost involved. Memory is the currency most heavily traded in relation to scalability, but also CPU to a lesser extent. Therefore, careful consideration must be given to the upper limit demands of an application relative to the boundaries of the underlying XPages memory model and processing power.

The actual processing involved with state management is for the most part hidden from you and happens automatically based on a default configuration. As an XPages developer, this means you are freed up to concentrate on developing the logic of the application. This also means that the XPages application you develop is then hosted and executed using the default *state management layer* configuration. Technically this may not be the optimum scalability configuration for that application. This is because the optimum scalability configuration is a subjective thing and specific to the needs of any given XPages application based on the unique requirements and expectations imposed upon it.

For example, one application might be a complex online scientific processing engine that has low end user and concurrency demands, but high demand for CPU processing cycles. Therefore, state management using RAM persistence exclusively could potentially provide greater performance benefits for this type of application because scalability is not necessarily the real demand, but speed and capacity of execution is. Whereas another application might be a relatively simple online data entry application with very high user and concurrency demands. Therefore, state management using a blend of RAM and Disk persistence could potentially provide a good balance of performance and scalability for this particular application. This is provided the custom logic of the application is both efficient, and this is where your knowledge of and ability to apply the principles taught in the first part of this chapter on developing efficient XPage requests benefit your efforts here, and robust enough to cope with high concurrency. Note you will be introduced to setting the memory options for RAM and Disk persistence (formally known as the *Persistence Options*) for an application in the coming material and then study these in more detail within the next subsection on establishing the optimal scalability configuration.

To establish the optimal scalability configuration for your XPages application, you need to monitor and analyze memory usage to truly understand the horizontal cost for any given XPages application. From your analysis activities, you may also uncover bottlenecks that require vertical correction to unblock horizontal capability and cost. Therefore, you should realize that your efforts to identify and correct "vertical" issues using the XPages Toolbox CPU Profiler and the XPages Request Introspection technique are only one-half of a bigger effort that also requires "horizontal" analysis and corrective measures to take place in an iterative manner.

One final thing to also remember during efforts to ascertain the best scalability configuration and most performant application code: You should also look for evidence of the underlying host hardware simply being inadequate for the upper limit demands of your application requirements. Having a finely tuned, efficient XPages application and well-configured XPages State

Management Layer will not unleash the full potential for that application to fulfill its upper-limit demands if the underlying hardware is maxing out on CPU and available memory just because it is not powerful enough. Therefore, you may also need to either revise the upper limits expected from an application to suit the maximum capabilities of the underlying hardware. Or alternatively you may need to invest in more powerful hardware, memory, and/or CPU processing power.

Ultimately, Performance and Scalability tuning is very much about finding an acceptable balance between time, cost, and quality—where time equals responsiveness, cost equals memory and processing cost, and quality equals functional capability.

Analyzing XPages Memory Usage

You now learn how to analyze XPages memory usage by first taking a look at the XPages Toolbox again, followed by a third-party tool called the Eclipse Memory Analyzer. In the first part of this chapter, you used the CPU Profiler and Backend Profiler tabs within this application to identify performance issues and reduce vertical cost. Now you learn about the Session Dumps tab, which can help you analyze the horizontal cost of an application.

You should now open the XPages Toolbox in a browser, and click the **Session Dumps** tab if you have not already done so. Figure 20.44 shows how the content appears within this tab.

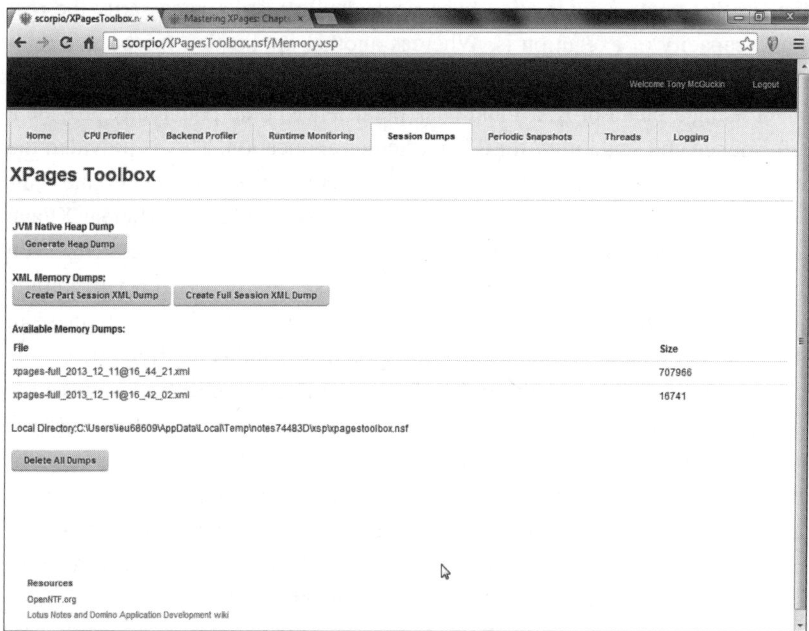

Figure 20.44 The Session Dumps tab within the XPages Toolbox

In addition, you should also have the **Chp20Ed2.nsf** application open in Domino Designer. And just to confirm to you at this point, the **Chp20Ed2.nsf** application should be using RAM persistence exclusively—you can confirm this by looking at the **Persistence > Persistence Options > Server page persistence** option under the **XSP Properties** of this application. This should be set to **"Keep pages in memory"**. If it is not, then you should reset it to this value, save the change, and then restart the HTTP task before proceeding because all the exercises that you carry out within this particular subsection are based on this persistence configuration. You learn about this area in greater detail and its effects within the next subsection.

Next, you should open and review the XSP source markup of the **testMemoryDump** XPage. Listing 20.19 also contains the XSP source markup for your convenience.

Listing 20.19 The XSP Source Markup for the testMemoryDump XPage

```
<?xml version="1.0" encoding="UTF-8"?>
<xp:view xmlns:xp="http://www.ibm.com/xsp/core">
    <xp:text escape="true" id="myGreetingField">
        <xp:this.value>
            <![CDATA[#{javascript:"Hello from " + userBean.commonName}]]>
        </xp:this.value>
    </xp:text>
</xp:view>
```

The **testMemoryDump** XPage of Listing 20.19 contains only one single Computed Field control, which has **id** of **myGreetingField**. It is certainly not a complex XPage by any stretch of the imagination. Nonetheless, you can use it to become familiar with the utilities available under the **Session Dumps** tab of the XPages Toolbox.

As you can see referring to Figure 20.44, within the Session Dumps tab there are three options available that all invariably generate a file containing details of the current state of memory within the underlying XPages Runtime and Java Virtual Machine (JVM). As you can also see in Figure 20.44 or indeed within your own browser, you can Generate Heap Dump, Create Part Session XML Dump, or Create Full Session XML Dump. You can click any one of these three buttons at any time while a server is running. As mentioned before, the outcome is similar for each one because they all dynamically produce a memory dump file, albeit in different formats and levels of detail.

Before going any further, you should now open the **testMemoryDump** XPage in a browser, as shown in Figure 20.45.

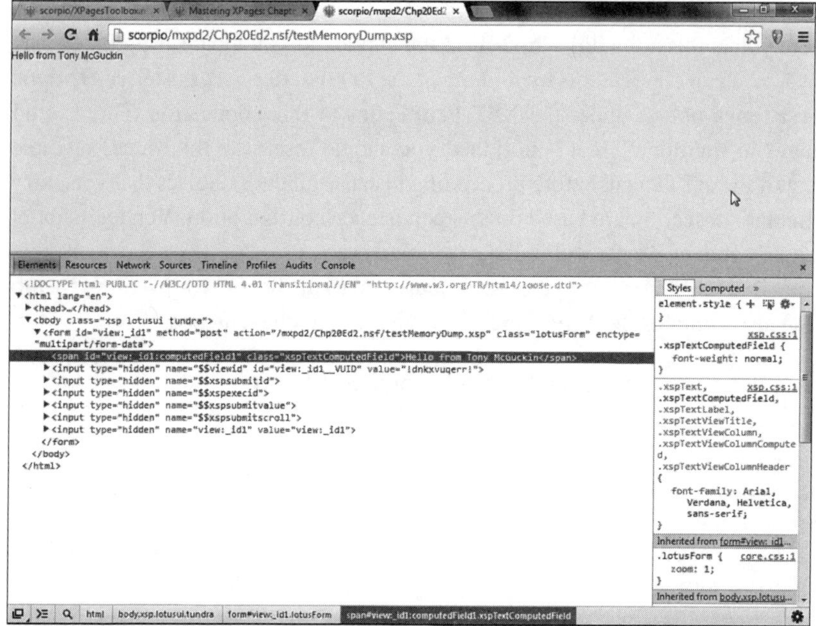

Figure 20.45 The testMemoryDump XPage at runtime in a browser

Now return to the XPages Toolbox Session Dumps tab and click the first of the three buttons titled **Generate Heap Dump**. The XPages Runtime then delegates execution to the underlying JVM to dynamically generate what is commonly known as a JVM Heap Dump. If you bring your Domino server console to the foreground on your desktop, you see a JVM message emitted to confirm the generation of the heap dump file. You should see something similar to that in Figure 20.46.

As shown in Figure 20.46, the emitted message confirms that a Heap Dump has been generated along with the absolute Operating System file path to the newly generated heap dump file. There is also a second way to perform this same operation, so you should perform that action at this point so that you are familiar with it. To do this, you should also ensure your Domino server console is in the foreground on your desktop. Then within your Domino server console, type the following command and then press the **Enter** key:

```
tell http xsp heapdump
```

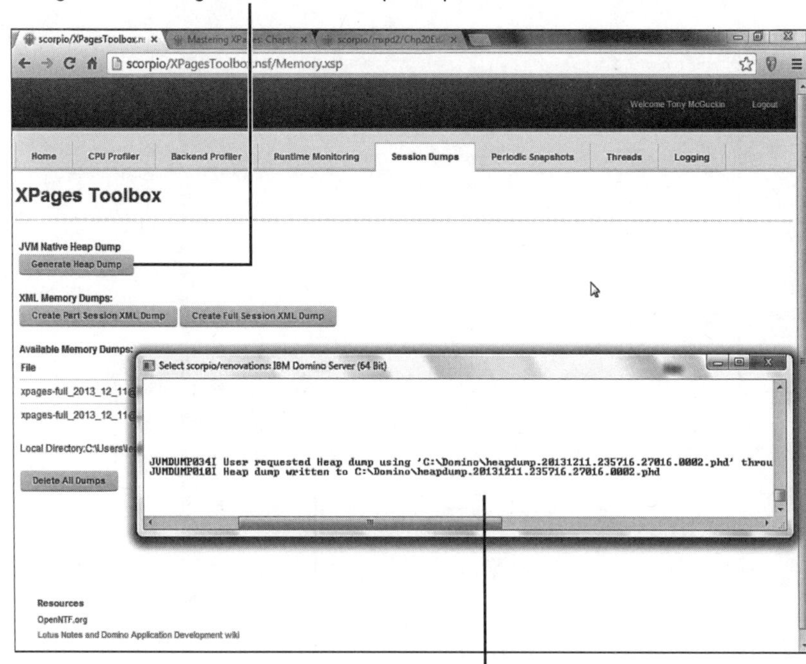

Figure 20.46 The JVM Heap Dump message on the Domino server console

Again, you see a similar message emitted on the Domino server console as the XPages Runtime requests the underlying JVM to generate a JVM Heap Dump for you. Obviously, at this point you have created two JVM Heap Dump files. But before progressing to read and understand the contents within these files, you should now also click both of the other two buttons within the **Session Dumps** tab. After you have done so, you should see XML file links appearing within this tab, as shown in Figure 20.47.

Now you have four different memory dump files at your disposal: a single Part Session XML Dump file, a single Full Session XML Dump, and two JVM Heap Dump files. You can discount one of the two JVM Heap Dump files at this time because they will both effectively contain the same information given the short duration of time taken in between generating them both. So now open these valuable resources to understand what sort of information you can glean from each of them.

First, start by clicking the link for the **Part Session XML Dump** file. This will be the link with the smaller file size indicated in the **Size** column under the **Session Dumps** tab. You should see XML output within your browser similar to Figure 20.48.

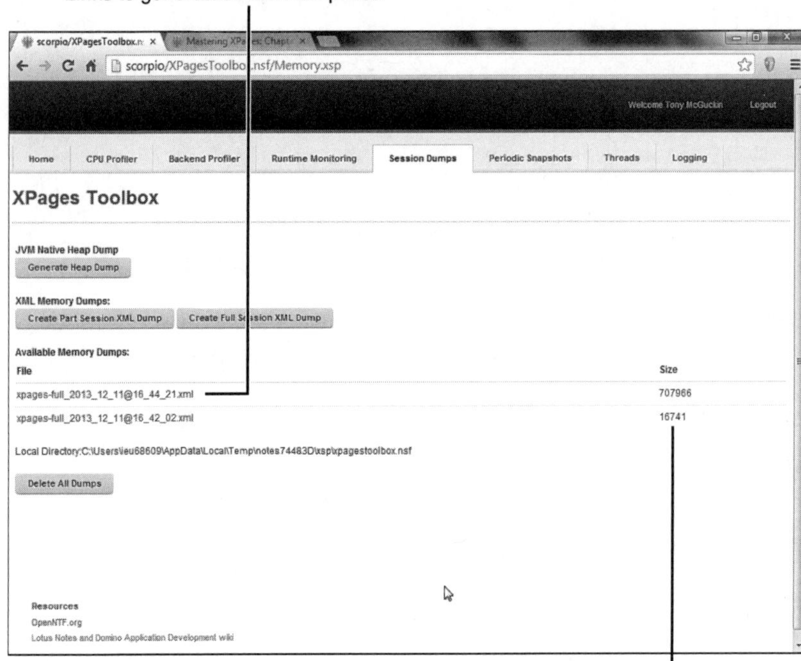

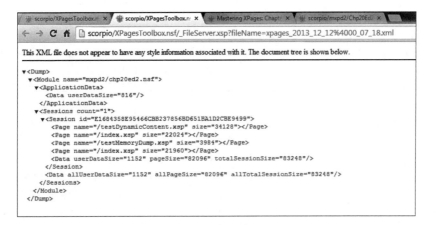

Figure 20.47 The newly generated XML Memory Dump file links in the Session Dumps tab

scorpio/XPagesToolbox.nsf/_FileServer.xsp?fileName=xpages_2013_12_12%4000_07_18.xml

This XML file does not appear to have any style information associated with it. The document tree is shown below.

```
▼<Dump>
  ▼<Module name="mxpd2/chp20ed2.nsf">
    ▼<ApplicationData>
       <Data userDataSize="816"/>
     </ApplicationData>
    ▼<Sessions count="1">
      ▼<Session id="E1684358E95466CBB237856BD651BA1D2CBE9499">
         <Page name="/testDynamicContent.xsp" size="34128"></Page>
         <Page name="/index.xsp" size="22024"></Page>
         <Page name="/testMemoryDump.xsp" size="3984"></Page>
         <Page name="/index.xsp" size="21960"></Page>
         <Data userDataSize="1152" pageSize="82096" totalSessionSize="83248"/>
       </Session>
       <Data allUserDataSize="1152" allPageSize="82096" allTotalSessionSize="83248"/>
     </Sessions>
   </Module>
 </Dump>
```

Figure 20.48 The Part Session XML Dump file

As shown in Figure 20.48, this particular type of memory dump file contains only high-level details on the currently loaded applications such as application name, sessions within each application, and names and sizes of XPages (aka component trees) that are also open within each session. Note that all sizes are given as bytes. Albeit only the **Chp20Ed2.nsf** application is listed in this particular instance, but if you try this on your own system with multiple XPages applications open, you will see information collected on each individual application within the Part Session XML Dump file. Notably, you will not find details collected about the XPages Toolbox application itself because this would be surplus to requirements.

Now you should click the **Full Session XML Dump** file link. In this instance, you can see a lot more information displayed within this file, as shown in Figure 20.49.

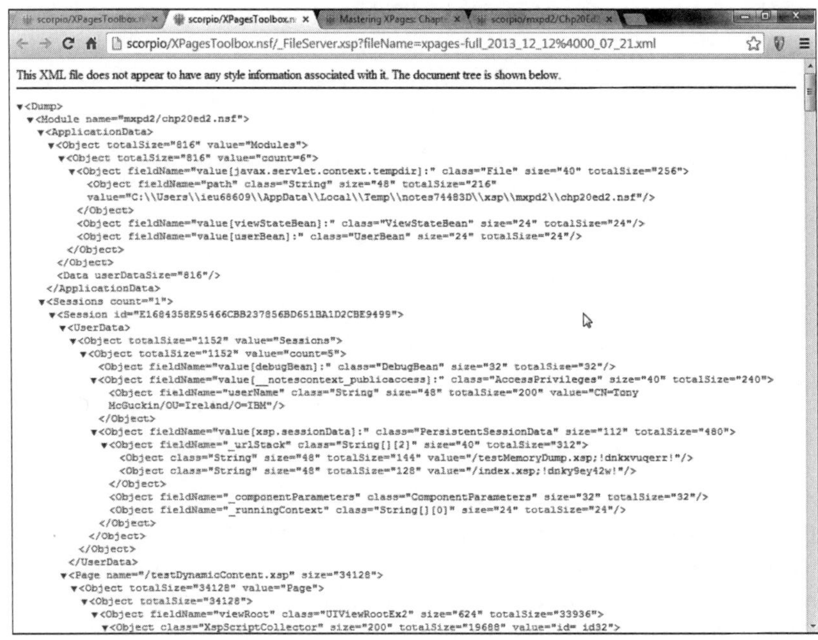

Figure 20.49 The Full Session XML Dump file

Unlike the previous XML Dump example, you can clearly see some interesting details listed within the Full Session XML Dump in Figure 20.49. This type of memory dump file collects detailed information not only on the items described previously for a Part Session XML Dump, but also goes much deeper into the memory state to collect a substantial amount of information from the underlying XPages State Management Layer about the currently loaded applications, caches, objects, user sessions, and component trees within each of these. To demonstrate the point, you can even see the component tree structure of the **testMemoryDump** XPage encapsulated within the fragment of XML taken from the Full Session XML Dump, as shown in Figure 20.50. Notably the **myGreetingField** object has also been highlighted within Figure 20.50 so you can see the level of detail available in this type of memory dump file.

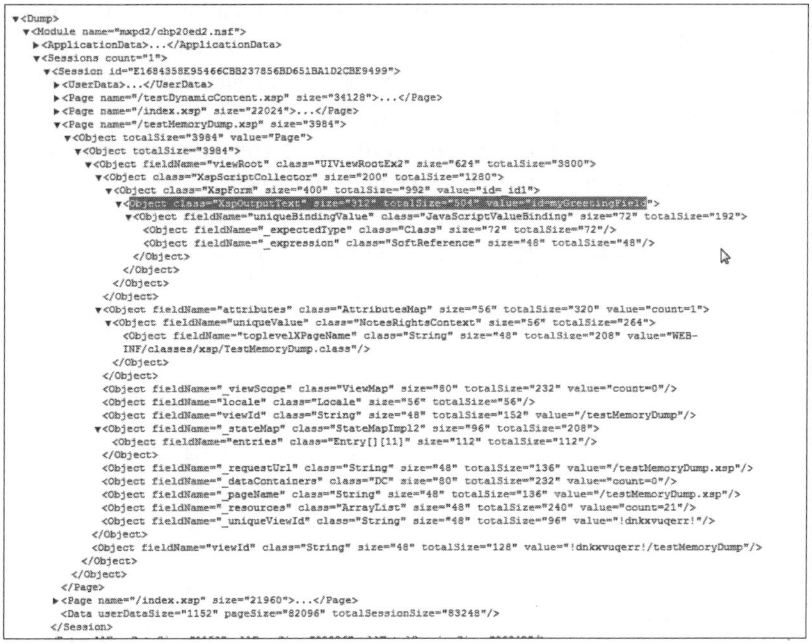

```
▼<Dump>
 ▼<Module name="mxpd2/chp20ed2.nsf">
  ▶<ApplicationData>...</ApplicationData>
  ▼<Sessions count="1">
   ▼<Session id="E1684358E95466CBB237856BD651BA1D2CBE9499">
    ▶<UserData>...</UserData>
    ▶<Page name="/testDynamicContent.xsp" size="34128">...</Page>
    ▶<Page name="/index.xsp" size="22024">...</Page>
    ▼<Page name="/testMemoryDump.xsp" size="3984">
     ▼<Object totalSize="3984" value="Page">
      ▼<Object totalSize="3984">
       ▼<Object fieldName="viewRoot" class="UIViewRootEx2" size="624" totalSize="3800">
        ▼<Object class="XspScriptCollector" size="200" totalSize="1280">
         ▼<Object class="XspForm" size="400" totalSize="992" value="id= id1">
          ▼<Object class="XspOutputText" size="312" totalSize="504" value="id=myGreetingField">
           ▼<Object fieldName="uniqueBindingValue" class="JavaScriptValueBinding" size="72" totalSize="192">
             <Object fieldName="_expectedType" class="Class" size="72" totalSize="72"/>
             <Object fieldName="_expression" class="SoftReference" size="48" totalSize="48"/>
           </Object>
          </Object>
         </Object>
        </Object>
        ▼<Object fieldName="attributes" class="AttributesMap" size="56" totalSize="320" value="count=1">
         ▼<Object fieldName="uniqueValue" class="NotesRightsContext" size="56" totalSize="264">
           <Object fieldName="toplevelXPageName" class="String" size="48" totalSize="208" value="WEB-
           INF/classes/xsp/TestMemoryDump.class"/>
         </Object>
        </Object>
        <Object fieldName="_viewScope" class="ViewMap" size="80" totalSize="232" value="count=0"/>
        <Object fieldName="locale" class="Locale" size="56" totalSize="56"/>
        <Object fieldName="viewId" class="String" size="48" totalSize="152" value="/testMemoryDump"/>
        ▼<Object fieldName="_stateMap" class="StateMapImpl2" size="96" totalSize="208">
          <Object fieldName="entries" class="Entry[][11]" size="112" totalSize="112"/>
        </Object>
        <Object fieldName="_requestUrl" class="String" size="48" totalSize="136" value="/testMemoryDump.xsp"/>
        <Object fieldName="_dataContainers" class="DC" size="80" totalSize="232" value="count=0"/>
        <Object fieldName="_pageName" class="String" size="48" totalSize="136" value="/testMemoryDump.xsp"/>
        <Object fieldName="_resources" class="ArrayList" size="48" totalSize="240" value="count=21"/>
        <Object fieldName="_uniqueViewId" class="String" size="48" totalSize="96" value="!dnkxvuqerr!"/>
       </Object>
       <Object fieldName="viewId" class="String" size="48" totalSize="128" value="!dnkxvuqerr!/testMemoryDump"/>
      </Object>
     </Object>
    </Page>
    ▶<Page name="/index.xsp" size="21960">...</Page>
    <Data userDataSize="1152" pageSize="82096" totalSessionSize="83248"/>
   </Session>
```


Figure 20.50 The testMemoryDump fragment within the Full Session XML Dump file

Finally, to open and read the JVM Heap Dump files generated earlier requires the use of a special third-party tool that can process and understand the Portable Heap Dump (.phd) file format. For the purposes of this discussion, the author explains this task by using a freely available, open source tool called the Eclipse Memory Analyzer.

Tip

You can download the Eclipse Memory Analyzer from http://www.eclipse.org/mat/ for free. In addition, you also need to install an Eclipse extension into the Eclipse Memory Analyzer called the IBM Diagnostic Tool Framework for Java Version 1.1 to allow the Eclipse Memory Analyzer to understand the Portable Heap Dump (.phd) file format. You can find this extension at the following IBM developerWorks URL: http://www.ibm.com/developerworks/java/jdk/tools/dtfj.html.

When the last of the two JVM Heap Dump Files is then opened in Eclipse Memory Analyzer tool, you can search within the data and find instances of the objects that exist within the XPages State Management Layer. For example, captured within the data you can find the actual application objects that were running when the memory dump was generated as **NSFComponentModule** instances, or individual XPage instances as **UIViewRootEx2** instances, and so forth. For your interest, the **myGreetingField** Computed Field control used within the **testMemoryDump** XPage can be found nestled within the owning **UIViewRootEx2** parent component tree structure as an **XspOutputText** instance, as shown in Figure 20.51.

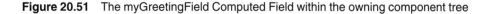

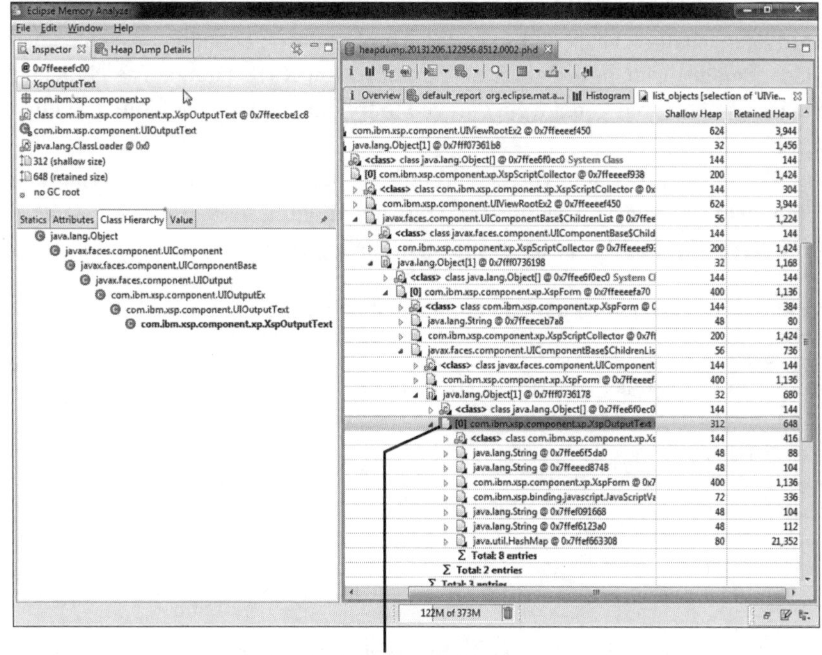

Figure 20.51 The myGreetingField Computed Field within the owning component tree

> **TIP**
>
> It is outside the scope of this book to teach you about using the Eclipse Memory Analyzer, but you should investigate the Object Query Language (OQL) editor and viewer within this tool. This feature enables you to query heap dumps using OQL statements. For example, to drill down into all instances of UIViewRootEx2 within a heap dump, you can issue the following OQL statement: select * from com.ibm.xsp.component.UIViewRootEx2.

Figure 20.51 illustrates some similarity to the structure and level of information already captured in the Full Session XML Dump taken previously and shown in Figure 20.50. So you have two similar ways in which you can interrogate the XPages Runtime memory model—one approach as valuable as the other. By using the **Full Session XML Dump** generation option within the XPages Toolbox, you get a quick-and-easy way to generate, view, and revisit previous XML memory dumps. The data captured within is detailed and relevant to the running XPages environment at the point in time of generation. If you then compare the JVM Heap Dump approach, first, it requires a special third-party tool to both open and parse the generated binary file. Second, it can be difficult to navigate within the data and find exactly what you are looking for as it is a complete snapshot of the JVM memory state at the point in time of generation (all JVM objects, retained heap, shallow heap, and so forth). Third, it doesn't contain the same level of XPages State Management Layer information as a Full Session XML Dump. The choice of approach and tool to use is yours, but you are encouraged to try out and become familiar with at least one approach.

As your next task in this subsection, you should now go back into Domino Designer and modify the **testMemoryDump** XPage. Specifically, you should add a **loaded** property with a value of **false** to the **myGreetingField** control, as shown in Listing 20.20.

Listing 20.20 The Modified XSP Source Markup for the testMemoryDump XPage

```
<?xml version="1.0" encoding="UTF-8"?>
<xp:view xmlns:xp="http://www.ibm.com/xsp/core">
    <xp:text escape="true" id="myGreetingField" loaded="false">
        <xp:this.value>
            <![CDATA[#{javascript:"Hello from " + userBean.commonName}]]>
        </xp:this.value>
    </xp:text>
</xp:view>
```

After you make this change and save it, return to the browser and refresh the **testMemoryDump** XPage. Then return to the **Session Dumps** tab of the XPages Toolbox and generate a new Full Session XML Dump file. When the file is generated, click the link that appears within the list of available XML memory dumps. Figure 20.52 shows the impact on the component tree structure for this XPage after making this change for your convenience.

As you can see in the Full Session XML Dump shown in Figure 20.52, the **myGreetingField** no longer exists within the component tree structure of the **testMemoryDump** component tree. Therefore, it no longer is resident in memory.

This is a trivial example of removing part of a component tree branch and actually getting to see the impact on the memory being used. So if you take this thought and also consider the learning material already covered in the previous sections of this chapter, particularly the "Using Dynamic Content" section, you should then quite easily imagine what the impact of dynamically loading and unloading facets, Custom Controls, and other large branches of a component tree can potentially have on memory usage. You now have a tool that can give you deep insight into this factor of horizontal cost.

myGreetingField no longer exists in the component tree viewRoot

Figure 20.52 The impact of loaded=false on the myGreetingField in the testMemoryDump XPage

As a final task for this subsection, you should now change the **loaded** property value to **true** and then introduce a **rendered** property with its value set to **false**, as shown in Listing 20.21.

Listing 20.21 The Modified XSP Source Markup for the testMemoryDump XPage with rendered=false

```
<?xml version="1.0" encoding="UTF-8"?>
<xp:view xmlns:xp="http://www.ibm.com/xsp/core">
    <xp:text escape="true" id="myGreetingField" loaded="true"
➥rendered="false">
        <xp:this.value>
            <![CDATA[#{javascript:"Hello from " + userBean.commonName}]]>
        </xp:this.value>
    </xp:text>
</xp:view>
```

After making this small update and saving your change, you should proceed to generate another Full Session XML Dump. Continue to then open this latest memory dump to analyze the impact of your change. You should see results similar to Figure 20.53 whereby the **myGreetingField** instance is now nestled within the **testMemoryDump** component tree structure.

Figure 20.53 The myGreetingField control resident in memory but not rendering

The interesting aspect to this change can be seen (or unseen perhaps) when you view the XPage output in your browser. Figure 20.54 shows the result of this change whereby the **myGreetingField** is no longer visible within the XPage—you should compare this to Figure 20.45 from earlier to see the difference. In addition, it does not even exist within the emitted HTML markup if you care to check it in your own browser.

So again, you can see just how powerful this analysis technique for generating live memory dump information is in terms of giving you deep insight into the micro-level component tree structure of an XPage and the memory usage involved at this level. In the next subsection, you learn more about this area and the overarching XPages State Management Layer. You also learn how you can configure this mainstay of the XPages Runtime to cope with the specific scalability demands of your XPages applications.

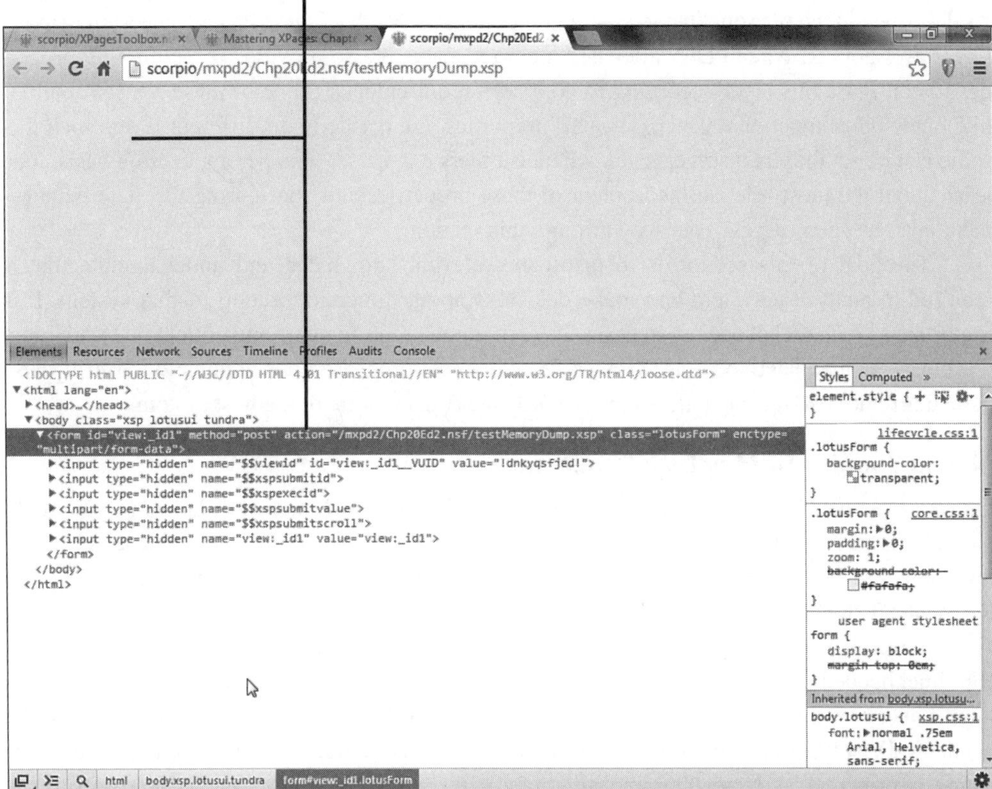

Figure 20.54 The testMemoryDump XPage not rendering the myGreetingField control

> **TIP**
>
> The Eclipse Memory Analyzer is just one example of many third-party profiling and memory analysis tools. You can also look at the IBM Health Center (www.ibm.com/developerworks/java/jdk/tools/healthcenter/) and YourKit (www.yourkit.com/) tools as possible alternatives. Furthermore, if you are interested in scalability testing, you should look at IBM Rational Performance Tester (www-03.ibm.com/software/products/en/performance/) and HTTP Grinder (http://grinder.sourceforge.net/). Both of these tools enable you to mimic scalability scenarios in which sequences of multiple user requests can be executed against an application simultaneously with performance and profiling results automatically collected into reports for your analysis.

Establishing the Optimal Scalability Configuration

As described in the section, "Understanding the Memory Model," the XPages State Management Layer uses both RAM and Disk allocated memory space. It also provides you with XSP properties to configure this layer according to your own requirements. Some of these XSP properties, like many other functional groups of XSP properties, are divided into different levels such that some can be set only at a server level, whereas others can be set on a per application basis. You learn about the most relevant and potent of these properties and configuring the state management layer as you progress your way through this section.

The goal of this section is to instill the relevant knowledge and understanding that is required to analyze a system and make decisions about the configuration of that system. It is important to realize that each system has its own unique requirements and anticipated maximum workload. Your objective as an XPages Developer is to ensure your applications fulfill these demands relative to the capabilities of the hardware and software of the host system.

Should You Use RAM or Disk Persistence?

Given the XPages Runtime is built upon JSF and Eclipse OSGi technology platforms, you might naturally assume it is also a Java-based platform. And you are correct. At a deeper technical level, this use of Java technology lends itself to the XPages State Management Layer for both RAM and Disk allocated storage—aka RAM and Disk persistence.

In relation to RAM persistence, this is by way of the underlying JVM hosting the XPages Runtime, hence hosting your applications, too. Consequently, when the XPages State Management Layer is using RAM persistence, XPage component trees then end up residing within the available JVM heapspace memory that is allocated on that system. And although a default allocation is provided by Notes/Domino, this may still require fine-tuning in the field to suit the demands of your applications.

However, if Disk persistence is used, XPage component trees end up being *serialized* to the disk after the **saveState()** method processing and *deserialized* before the **restoreState()** method processing on the associated component tree. Obviously, this latter option entails heavier integration and dependency on the underlying operating system (OS) environment to perform the necessary file input/output operations on the resultant serialized file, but one benefit of this approach is the removal of the dependency upon RAM persistence.

By considering the pros and cons of each can certainly help establish a foundation to build upon when looking to ascertain the optimal scalability configuration for your own server and applications hosted within that environment. When a foundation is established, this can be fine-tuned on a per application basis by using the appropriate application level XSP properties. And it is advisable to be as scientific in your approach during this fine-tuning effort as possible to come to a well-founded and proven conclusion. There is no "silver bullet" in terms of an optimum scalability configuration that "fits all"; it is established following iterations of careful analysis and testing based on the unique demands of each application or set of applications on a given server. This means using all the insightful tools and techniques that are already at your disposal such as the XPages Toolbox, XPages Request Introspection technique, and memory profiling using XPages XML Session Dumps and/or JVM Heapdumps.

RAM Persistence

RAM is a finite resource on any given system. It has always been and still remains to be one of the most expensive computer hardware components to purchase, so it is available at a premium for purchase but also for software execution. Technically, this means that all the software components that need to execute within an OS must compete and contend for use of RAM. The JVM and XPages Runtime are no different in this regard.

The JVM within Notes/Domino has a specially designated block of memory commonly known as the JVM *heapspace*. This is essentially a block of RAM assigned to the JVM for applications and processes running within the JVM. Out-of-the-box Notes/Domino 9.0.1 provides a 1024 Megabyte (MB) default allocation of JVM heapspace. You can reconfigure this allocation if necessary by using the special **notes.ini HTTPJVMMaxHeapSize** and **HTTPJVMMax HeapSizeSet** variables.

It is important to note that this "block" is typically allocated by the hosting OS using a lazy-load/preemptive algorithm such that the allocation is provided in chunks up to the maximum allocated amount. In a situation where the maximum allocation should become exhausted, the JVM throws a **java.lang.OutOfMemoryError** that indicates that no more JVM heapspace memory can be obtained because the maximum allocation has been reached, and furthermore, because the JVM Garbage Collector cannot release any of the already used RAM storage.

Tip

An important side effect of a java.lang.OutOfMemoryError occurrence is that a JVM Heapdump file is automatically generated by the system. This file is then available within the root of the Notes client or Domino server directory depending on whether it has occurred within the XPiNC client or on the server. You should refer to the previous section on analyzing XPages memory usage to review how to open and read this type of file. Needless to say, a JVM Heapdump file automatically generated on the basis of the JVM being out of memory is an invaluable resource because it contains a snapshot of the entire JVM memory state at that point in time. You can use the Eclipse Memory Analyzer to identify the offending objects easily by using the Memory Leak Suspects report within this particular tool.

For the astute reader or experienced developer, you can note that the object thrown is an *Error* type and not an *Exception* type—the upshot of this means that a JVM can unwind the current execution stack without actually crashing or going into an unstable condition. Subsequently, it is a matter of the JVM then waiting for the Garbage Collector to eventually find JVM heapspace memory that is marked for release before any further objects can be allocated and executed within the allocated JVM heapspace.

The greatest benefit of RAM is the speed of execution it bears on application code. This is due to tightly integrated hardware/software technicalities between this component and the CPU of a system. At a basic level, file input/output to disk is eliminated during the execution of application code because instead it is transferred directly through RAM/CPU memory registers, buffers, and so forth. Needless to say this is an area beyond the scope of this particular book, but nonetheless it is important to be aware of the inherent benefit of using RAM persistence. You can find the RAM persistence option within the **Application Properties > Persistence Options > Server page persistence** setting of any application, as shown in Figure 20.55.

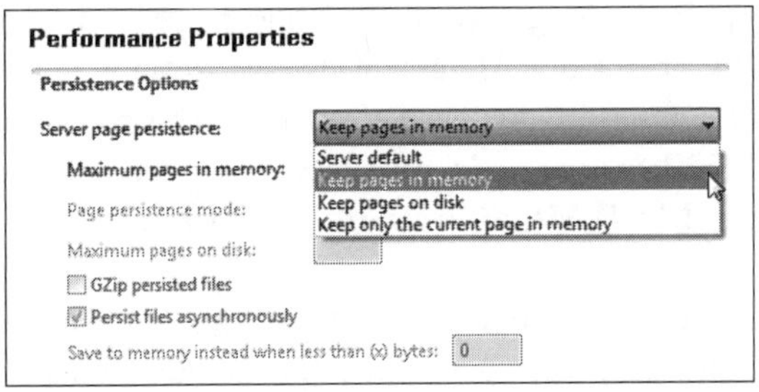

Figure 20.55 The "Keep pages in memory" RAM persistence setting

This setting appears in the list of options with the textual description "Keep pages in memory." As far as the XPages developer should be concerned, using RAM persistence means that a component tree is in "pole position" as such. When end users interact with the corresponding XPage in their browser, after the request is received by the server-side runtime, it is executed almost instantaneously against the in-memory component tree. All the **restoreState() / saveState()** and XPages Request Processing Lifecycle work is done against the in-memory hierarchy of objects representing that XPage. This shaves precious time off the overall processing time and also reduces execution cycles within the CPU.

As described earlier, the downside to using RAM persistence is the finite amount of it that is available on any given system. Therefore, there may not be enough JVM heapspace either allocated or physically available to actually cope with the maximum horizontal cost of a particular application or set of applications (also commonly referred to as the *working set*). And that is where Disk persistence comes into play.

Disk Persistence

This is actually the default persistence mode of the XPages State Management Layer in Notes/Domino 9.0.1. You can find the Disk persistence option in the **Application Properties > Persistence Options > Server page persistence** setting of any new application you create in Notes/Domino 9.0.1 by default or by simply selecting it within a preexisting application. This is highlighted in Figure 20.56 where the textual description for this option appears as "Keep pages on disk" within the list of available options.

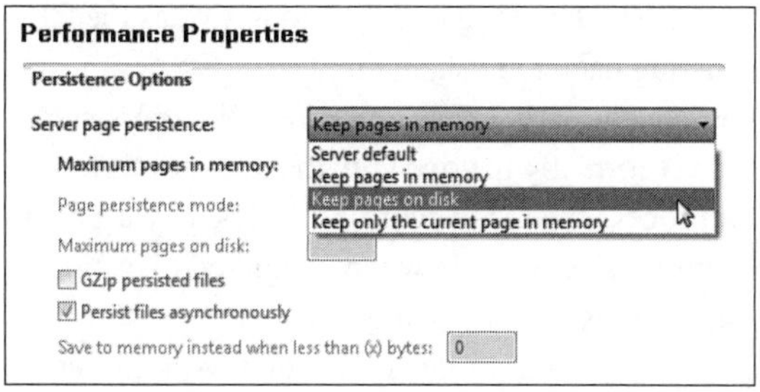

Figure 20.56 The "Keep pages on disk" Disk persistence setting

Unlike RAM persistence, Disk persistence can provide much larger storage space for component trees. In fact, it can be as large as the available amount of disk space within the designated temporary "pages" disk location. The XPages Runtime defaults this special location to the **/xspstate** subdirectory within the system user temporary directory. However, you should note that there is a server level XSP property available that allows you to configure this location as detailed in Listing 20.22—you can find this property in the global **xsp.properties** file within a Domino server.

Listing 20.22 The Temporary Pages Location, Server Level XSP Property

```
# Define the directory where the JSF pages are persisted
# defaults to <tempdir>/xspstate
#xsp.persistence.dir.xspstate=
```

You could, for example, set the temporary disk persistence "pages" location to point at *Network Assigned Storage* (*NAS*) or a *Solid State Drive* (*SSD*). The NAS/SSD could have an incredibly large amount of disk storage—perhaps hundreds of gigabytes or terabytes, for example. Obviously, this opens up huge scalability opportunities for an XPages Runtime instance that goes way beyond the limits of even the biggest possible RAM configurations.

However, there is slightly more to achieving high-end scalability. If you are looking for high-end scalability, it is important to ensure the application working set is as *vertically* efficient as possible. (Refer to the first part of this chapter to remind yourself about vertical efficiency.) This is always a prerequisite to achieving high-end scalability, simply because CPU power becomes a critical factor within the configuration. This is due to the higher level of file input/output that occurs during serialization and deserialization of disk persisted component trees.

Ultimately, it is all about trying to free up CPU power as much as possible, so it can perform "quality" minimal processing of component trees that must first be deserialized into the

JVM heapspace before normal lifecycle processing occurs, followed by serialization back to disk storage. This, in turn, enables a higher throughput of end user requests to be processed at any given point in time by the CPU—ensuring a faster turnaround of serialized/deserialized component trees as these artifacts make the journey from Disk, then temporarily into RAM, as the CPU then executes the object code within, before persisting back to Disk again.

In essence slightly longer response times are the side effect of using Disk persistence exclusively. Nonetheless, if the system is configured correctly to cope with the upper limits of the expected workload, it will continually serve and process the load accordingly. The key aspect to this persistence configuration is that higher scalability is achievable when compared to exclusive use of RAM persistence, with a measured increase in request processing time.

However, under certain conditions in which the demands of the application working set are suitable, it is also possible to consider a blend of both RAM and Disk persistence to provide a balance of speed of execution and scalability.

RAM and Disk Persistence

It is also possible to configure the XPages State Management Layer to use a blend of RAM and Disk persistence. The goal of this feature is to provide a balance of faster in-memory component tree processing along with a relatively higher level of scalability, though not as high as the pure "Keep pages on disk" option. Similar to the options for setting RAM and Disk persistence, this option can be set using the **XSP Properties > Persistence Options > Server page persistence** option, as shown in Figure 20.57.

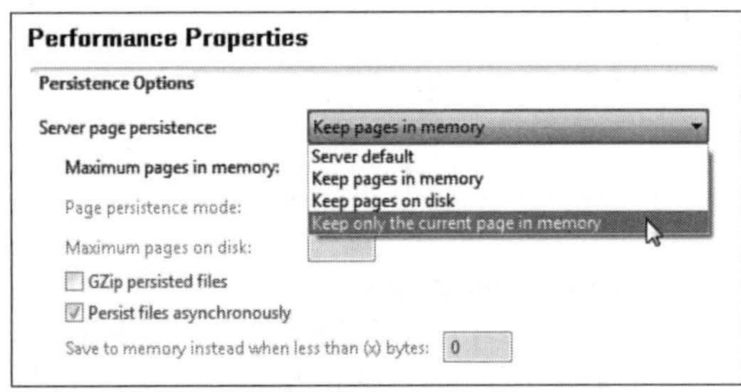

Figure 20.57 The "Keep only the current page in memory" RAM/Disk persistence setting

The interesting aspect to this particular option is that it persists only the current component tree in memory—the other "pages" (aka component trees) are persisted to disk. To understand this particular treatment of component trees requires a deeper explanation of the way in which component trees are managed during a user session as a user interacts and navigates around an application.

To explain this, consider that when an end user initially enters an application, there is a unique session object assigned to that user within the state management layer—even an anonymous user gets one of these. Then as the user interacts and navigates within the application, there is a component tree created for each XPage visited during that session up to a predefined limit depending on the type of persistence mode being used. These persisted component trees are then used to aid "back" navigation and/or multitab navigation against previously viewed XPages and also post-back operations against the currently viewed XPage within a browser. The predefined limits can be configured by using two different XSP properties, both of which can be set at the server level or on a per application level using the **xsp.properties** file for each, respectively. One applies to RAM persistence, whereas the other applies to Disk persistence. Both of these properties are detailed in Listing 20.23.

Listing 20.23 The Server and Application Level XSP Properties for Maximum Views

```
# Defines the number of pages persisted on disk, when "file" is defined
➥(MRU algorithm)
#xsp.persistence.file.maxviews=16

# Defines the number of pages persisted when in memory (MRU algorithm)
#xsp.persistence.tree.maxviews=4
```

Listing 20.23 also shows the default values for each of these properties. Taking the first of these two, the `xsp.persistence.file.maxviews` property by default limits the XPages State Management Layer to persisting up to 16 component trees on disk within a user session. If an end user navigates around an application such that more than 16 component trees are created, then the least recently used component tree is discarded from Disk persistence. This behavior then ensures that there is never more than the predefined maximum number of component trees actually persisted to disk and that only the most recently used are kept.

The second of the two XSP properties in Listing 20.23 is the `xsp.persistence.tree.maxviews` property. By default, this property assumes a value of 4. This is a reflection of the smaller finite nature of RAM so therefore reduces the potential burden placed on RAM persistence for each user. This value also means that more concurrent users can be catered for within the available JVM heapspace as less component trees are persisted for each user—so obviously a lower number is preferable for this setting.

Therefore, having the option to use both RAM and Disk persistence is a certainly a viable one and suitable under certain conditions. You should not expect the same degree of horizontal scale with this option, though. This is due to the increase in use of the JVM heapspace to persist all the component trees being viewed by all concurrent end users of a system.

Given this factor, possible memory outage is something you must give particular consideration to in a similar manner to the "Keep pages in memory" option—simply because only a finite number of "current" component trees will fit within the allocated JVM heapspace at any given time.

The upshot is that this option enables faster component tree processing to occur because there is no file input/output overhead involved to serialize/deserialize the current component tree. And just to reiterate the point made earlier—vertical efficiency is critical to the success of this option also because an overloaded CPU that is wasting cycles on suboptimal application code will impede the possibility of providing a balanced speed gain and good request throughput under this context.

Compression

It is a good point within this reading material to also make you aware of the GZip persisted files option. This is because of the understanding you now have about Disk persistence and its increased use of CPU power to perform file input/output on serialized component tree files. Similarly, the GZip compression option also has a direct bearing on CPU power when using Disk persistence. Figure 20.58 shows you the **XSP Properties > Persistence > Persistence Options** group with the GZip persisted files check box highlighted for your convenience.

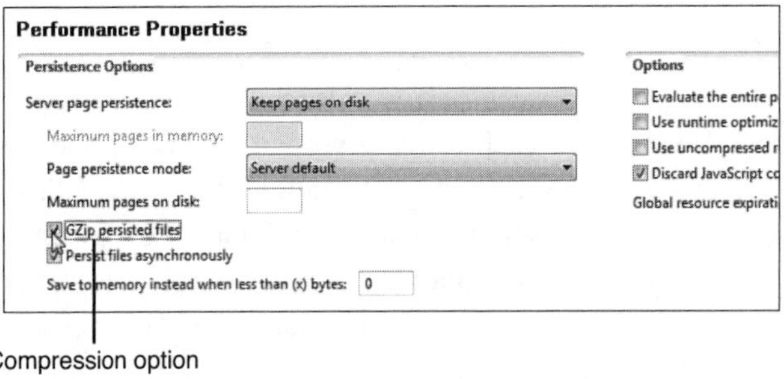

Compression option

Figure 20.58 The GZip persisted files option

When using Disk persistence, you should give careful consideration with regard to using or not using this option depending on certain factors. This option is not enabled by default, which means that disk persisted component trees are not GZip compressed. The consequence is slightly larger **.ser** (this is the extension of a serialized component tree file) files being saved into the "Pages" temporary location when compared with having this option enabled. But like many other features related to performance, there is an inherent cost involved to reap the benefit.

In this case, the cost involves a degree of extra CPU processing to not only generate a compressed disk persistence file during component tree serialization, but to also decompress it during component tree deserialization. A compressed disk persistence file is simply a **.zip** file containing the actual **.ser** file. The benefit in this case is a reduction in the size of the disk persistence file, which obviously means space-saving within the designated disk persistence location.

The decision to use this option should therefore be well thought out by performing analysis and testing with and without it. In particular, measurements of CPU usage should be monitored with and without this option enabled and preferably under maximum expected upper workload conditions.

Serialization

When using RAM persistence, serialization of objects is generally not something you need to code for or deal with in any specific way within your XPages applications. However, the same is not true when using Disk persistence or the combined RAM/Disk persistence configurations. When using either of these two configurations, you as the XPages developer must ensure that any objects referenced within custom application code, or objects provided by you or a third party such as custom Java classes or Managed Bean classes, are *serializable* if they are expected to persist between requests. You should also be aware that custom SSJS objects cannot be serialized using Disk persistence. In such circumstances, you should consider using custom Java classes or Managed Beans to perform the operations of the custom SSJS object instead. Effectively, custom SSJS objects can be managed only within RAM persistence and therefore can be costly resources when scalability is a key requirement of an application.

You should also note that the Notes/Domino Backend Java classes are not serializable. Therefore, under the constraints of Disk persistence, you cannot buffer an instance of a Backend class into a scoped variable, or assign a Backend class as a custom Java class or Managed Bean class member, for example. And just for your interest, this is not something specific to the Notes/Domino Backend Java classes as you may encounter the same aspect with other third-party Java libraries that you might use at some point in the future.

Generally, this means that such Java classes implement the **java.io.Serializable** interface. Furthermore, you should ensure class members are equally serializable. Alternatively, you can consider declaring any class member that doesn't need to be persisted as **transient**—this eliminates such a class member from being included in the serialization/deserialization processing that occurs for Disk persistence and hence reduces CPU workload a little bit.

Configuring the XPages State Management Layer

You have now learned about the three main persistence options available within the XPages State Management Layer, namely RAM, Disk, and a RAM/Disk persistence combination, along with other important features and aspects such as compression and serialization. Therefore, it is now a good time to review and learn about the range of persistence-related XSP properties at your disposal.

The introduction to this section of the chapter briefly described that a range of server and application level persistence-related XSP properties are available, and indeed you have already learned about three of them (that is, temporary page location, maximum number of trees in-memory, and maximum number of trees persisted on disk). The purpose of this group of XSP properties is to provide an XPages developer, or indeed a Notes/Domino administrator, with a mechanism to reconfigure the XPages State Management Layer. This is needed because every application working set has its own unique requirements and expected workload. Indeed even at a finer-grained level each application within a working set will typically have its own specific requirements and expected work load. So the intent of providing both server and application level persistence related XSP properties is to give a high degree of flexibility to fine-tune a system at these two distinct levels of operation.

Table 20.2 lists the relevant XSP properties and the respective level of where you can configure each. As you can see in Table 20.2, only one of the properties is server level. This means it can be reconfigured only within the Notes/Domino **xsp.properties** file. If you set it within the application **xsp.properties** file, your setting will be ignored and the server level setting will still apply.

Table 20.2 Relevant State Management Layer XSP Properties

Property	Level
xsp.persistence.mode	Server and Application
xsp.persistence.viewstate	Server and Application
xsp.persistence.tree.maxviews	Server and Application
xsp.persistence.file.maxviews	Server and Application
xsp.persistence.file.gzip	Server and Application
xsp.persistence.file.async	Server and Application
xsp.persistence.file.threshold	Server and Application
xsp.persistence.dir.xspstate	Server Only

If you make any changes to the persistence-related XSP properties within either the system or application **xsp.properties** files, you need to restart the HTTP task or server. Typically, you can make live changes to the **xsp.properties** file within an application and then simply refresh the application to see those changes in effect. But for the persistence-related XSP properties, this is not the case—a restart is required to reset the underlying XPages State Management Layer.

You should now undertake a small exercise that involves taking a couple Full Session XML Dumps, followed by changing one of the XSP persistence properties and then retaking another Full Session XML Dump on two worked example XPages. The main purpose of this exercise is to give you some insight and hands-on experience of making a change to the configuration of the state management layer. More important, it also shows you how to use the XPages Toolbox to see the effect of your change in a scientific, measurable manner.

First, ensure you have the XPages Toolbox primed and ready on the **Session Dumps** tab. Second, open the **testPersistence1** XPage from within the **Chp20Ed2.nsf** application in your browser. Listing 20.24 contains the XSP source markup from this XPage for your convenience.

Listing 20.24 The XSP Source Markup of the testPersistence1 XPage

```
<?xml version="1.0" encoding="UTF-8"?>
<xp:view xmlns:xp="http://www.ibm.com/xsp/core">
    <xp:inputText id="inputText1" value="hello world"></xp:inputText>
</xp:view>
```

As you can see in Listing 20.24, there is only one single Edit Box control nestled with the design of the **testPersistence1** XPage. When ready you should then press the **Full Session XML Dump** button within the XPages Toolbox. After the dump file is generated, open the link in a new tab and review the content within. You should see something similar to Figure 20.59.

The important point to note about this first session dump of the **testPersistence1** XPage is that it has been generated with the **Chp20Ed2.nsf** application configured to use RAM persistence: Keep pages in memory. This is evident from looking at the **XSP Properties > Persistence > Persistence Options > Server page persistence** setting or the underlying **xsp.persistence.mode** property, which is set to **basic**. Alternatively, you can ascertain this by simply looking at the contents within the generated session dump. How can you tell? The answer is simple. There are details about the in-memory component tree structure, values, sizes, and so forth listed directly within the session dump. (In a moment, you will understand this better when you make a change to the state management layer.)

And just as a matter of interest, by reviewing the information from the **testPersistence1** XPage session dump in Figure 20.59, you can easily see that it consumes 15,800 bytes (or 15.43 kilobytes) of JVM heapspace for this single, simple XPage.

For the next step of this exercise, you should open the **testPersistence2** XPage in your browser. Listing 20.25 contains the source markup for this XPage where you can see that it is also a relatively simple XPage that will iterate using Repeat control to create 1,000 Edit Box instances.

Listing 20.25 The XSP Source Markup of the testPersistence2 XPage

```
<?xml version="1.0" encoding="UTF-8"?>
<xp:view xmlns:xp="http://www.ibm.com/xsp/core">
    <xp:repeat id="repeat1" repeatControls="true"
value="#{javascript:1000}">
        <xp:inputText id="inputText1" value="hello world"></
xp:inputText>
    </xp:repeat>
</xp:view>
```

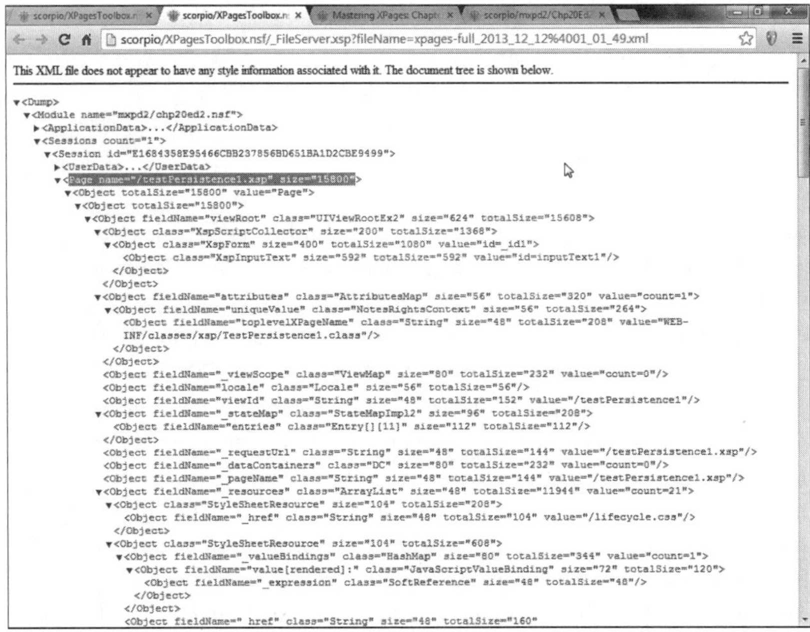

Figure 20.59 The testPersistence1 session dump information using RAM persistence

When this XPage is finished loading, you should use the XPages Toolbox to generate another Full Session XML Dump. This time drill-down into the session dump information to find the information of the **testPersistence2** XPage. Again, you should see something similar to Figure 20.60.

Again it is evident from reading the newly generated session dump information that RAM persistence is still used. And again, one of the most interesting aspects of the data collected is that this XPage component tree uses 1,155,976 bytes of JVM heapspace. Or in other metrics this equates to 1128.88 kilobytes or 1.10 megabytes of RAM memory usage for this single XPage.

Just as a side note, even though this exercise is run against a single XPage test case, it should be relatively easy for you to start thinking more "horizontally" in this case. For example, what would the horizontal memory cost be if the requirements stipulated an expected maximum concurrent user workload of 2,000 end users against this particular XPage? Could RAM persistence cope with the memory consumption demands of this workload based on the host server having only 1 gigabyte of RAM assigned to the Domino server JVM heapspace? These are the sort of questions you should be starting to ask along with using the XPages Toolbox to scientifically measure the results of your analyses as you iteratively improve upon the scalability configuration of a system.

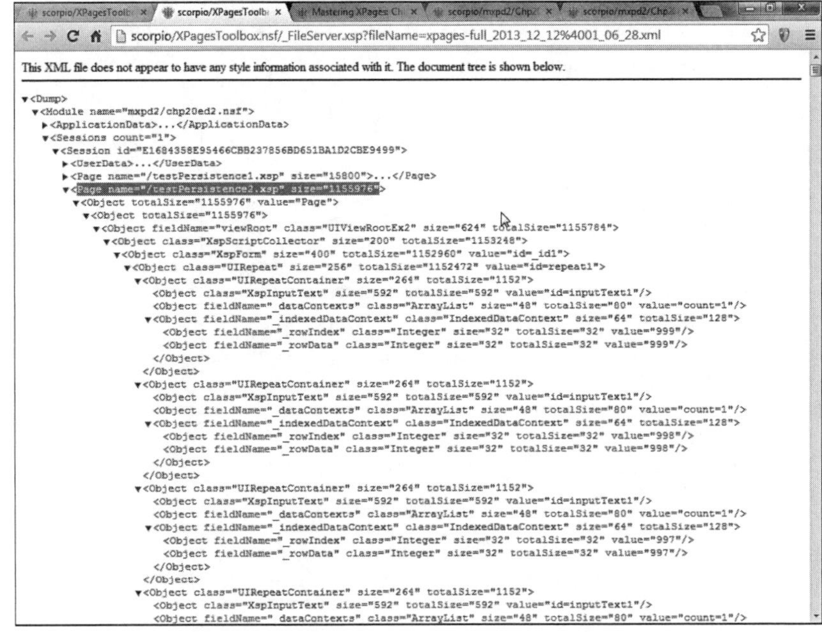

Figure 20.60 The testPersistence2 session dump information using RAM persistence

For the next step, you should open the **XSP Properties > Persistence > Persistence Options** of the **Chp20Ed2.nsf** application and change the **Server page persistence** setting to the **Keep pages on disk** option. Having saved your change, you should then restart the HTTP task by typing the following command on the server console and pressing the enter key:

```
restart task http
```

When the HTTP is available again, reload the XPages Toolbox and the **testPersistence2** XPage in your browser. When ready, generate a new Full Session XML Dump again. Figure 20.61 shows an example of the result of this.

Unlike the previous session dump that was taken using RAM persistence, you can now see that your change to the `xsp.persistence.mode` property, which now has a value of **file**, has had a direct effect on the data collected within this latest session dump. As a consequence, there is now no component tree structure and related data captured within the session dump file. Instead there is now a temporary page location path to the associated serialized **.ser** file within disk persistence. Effectively, your change has caused the **testPersistence2** component tree and its associated state to be serialized and saved to disk allocated storage, therefore, having an immediate effect on the amount of RAM used by this particular XPage. Would you like to recalculate your estimates for the horizontal cost again based on this reduced usage of JVM heapspace and increased volume of available disk storage space?

Figure 20.61 The testPersistence2 session dump information using Disk persistence

As further tasks to this exercise, you should explore the third "Keep only the current page in memory" option—don't forget to restart the HTTP task after making the change. You could also analyze memory usage for some of your own XPages applications if you want to expand upon your experience with using this tool. Regardless, it should be apparent to you just how important it is to ensure an XPage is both efficient and lean to get the best possible scalability out of an XPages application.

Variances of a Theme

When using RAM and Disk persistence, the state management layer serializes the entire component tree structure and state of the data within this by default. You should however be aware of the different ways in which this serialization process is configured. This relates directly to the server and application level `xsp.persistence.viewstate` XSP property as listed earlier in Table 20.2. There are exactly four different values that can be applied to this property. Out-of-the-box Notes/Domino 9.0.1 is configured to use the `fulltree` option by default—you have already seen the effects of this by working through the previous exercise in this section. Table 20.3 details all the possible values that can be applied to this particular XSP property.

Table 20.3 The xsp.persistence.viewstate XSP Property

Value	Effect
fulltree	`Entire tree and state persisted (`**`default`**`)`
nostate	`No tree or state persisted`
delta	`Initial tree and updates to state after`
deltaex	`No tree but only state`

As you can see in Table 20.3, there are four different possible values of which the **fulltree** option is the default. When using the default setting, the XPages State Management Layer always persists the entire component tree structure plus all the associated state within that structure during the **saveSave()** processing. Subsequently, during the **restoreState()** processing, the runtime has no need to refetch the original **.class** file for a component tree because it simply reuses the already persisted version. This option also always ensures a true reflection of the component tree structure is always persisted for every request. This is important when a given XPage uses such controls as the **Dynamic Content** control such that the component tree structure is of a volatile nature. Therefore, the persisted representation must be kept up to date at all times.

You also have the option of specifying absolutely no tree or state saving by using the **nostate** option. This is only useful for pure read-only XPages as you might imagine; therefore, using this option at a server or application level would be abnormal. Instead, for your interest, you can also find a **viewState** property exposed on the **viewRoot** of an XPage and Custom Control. This can be used to specify **nostate** for any particular XPage in isolation of all others within an application.

The **delta** and **deltaex** options are advanced options that need to be used with careful consideration. Furthermore, they are only applicable when using RAM persistence exclusively. Going back to the explanation given earlier about the volatile nature of some XPages that use Dynamic Content, for example, means that the fulltree option is the best option for this particular use case.

Conversely though, if you have an XPage where the integral component tree structure is not going to alter over the course of its runtime lifetime, then the **delta** option is a viable option while under RAM persistence. Effectively this option will persist the first impression of the component tree and for all subsequent user requests posted back against that component tree, only the changes in the actual state of the data will be updated back into the already persisted component tree. Obviously, if newly injected dynamic content were introduced into the XPage at runtime, this would be lost during any further post-back requests against the associated component tree when using this option.

Finally, as already mentioned, the **deltaex** option also needs to be used with careful consideration. In fact, it is only viable for extreme use cases that require advanced per component self-setting of state. Technically this means that the components on an XPage must individually deal with setting their own state. This is done programmatically using a **setControlState()** method available on components. In terms of the type of data that is persisted, only the changes to the state made by components contributing to the overall page state are persisted. Absolutely no component tree structure is used or persisted while using this option. Needless to say, if an XPage is not coded robustly using this approach, then there is a high chance of data loss at runtime. Furthermore, the code maintenance cost is relatively high when trying to implement and maintain an XPage using this option.

Conclusion

This chapter focused on two key aspects of XPages development that underpin good performance and higher scalability, specifically efficient memory and processing power usage. Essentially the content attempts to make you think more about the consequences of the way you have coded something or thought about it relative to two fundamental components within the XPages Runtime, namely the XPages Request Processing Lifecycle and the XPages State Management Layer.

Throughout this chapter, you have also been introduced to a range of insightful tools and techniques that should be used in an ongoing basis for your everyday XPages development projects to ensure acceptable levels of performance and scalability are built-in from the start, not just as an afterthought or critical fix during post-deployment into a production environment—prevention is always better and cheaper than the cure.

CHAPTER 21

Security

Notes/Domino has always delivered, and continues to deliver, a robust and powerful security solution in terms of the protections it provides and its ease of administration. XPages maintains this long tradition by leveraging and enforcing the existing security model for document security, access control, and code execution. Wheter XPages is run on Domino server or in the Notes client, the XPages security model tightly integrates and extends the platform's existing administration and control mechanisms to provide an experience that will be both familiar to and easily understood by administrator, application developer, and end user alike.

Notes/Domino provides several layers of security with each layer gradually refining the level of access and controlling the ability to perform certain functions. This chapter covers the security mechanisms that XPages provides in the various layers to control access to design elements and data and to restrict what code can execute.

> **BEFORE YOU START**
>
> To follow the examples in this chapter, you must have administrator access to a Domino server where you can create applications, modify the server configuration document, and register users. Be sure to download the **Chp21Ed2.nsf** file provided online for this book in order to run through the exercises throughout this chapter. You can access this file at `www.ibmpressbooks.com/title/9780133373370`.

Notes/Domino Security and XPages

Notes/Domino provides several security mechanisms to protect your applications and the data stored within them. The security model can be viewed as several layers working from the outside in. Starting from the Domino server hosting the applications and working toward the documents stored inside applications, each layer gradually refines the access and authority a user has to execute certain operations.

- **Server:** Controls access to the Domino server.
- **Application:** Controls privileges within applications.
- **Design Element:** Controls access to parts of an application.
- **Document:** Controls who can read and edit documents.
- **Workstation ECL:** Controls what can execute on a user's workstation.

The following sections outline the key Notes/Domino layers of security and how they apply to XPages.

Server Layer of Security

This layer has several functions. It determines the set of users allowed to access the Domino server through the use of server access lists and by performing user authentication. It also restricts the set of users allowed to create or sign any design elements that the Domino server allows to execute.

There is a definite distinction between a user who requests an XPage and a user who is the creator of an XPages design element, both of whom are governed by orthogonal aspects of XPages and Notes/Domino security.

The server security layer identifies those users allowed to create XPages that run on the server and controls the methods and functions that the XPage application is allowed to execute. The application and document security layers, on the other hand, control which document related tasks (such as create/read/edit/delete) the XPage requestor can perform and the data that they are allowed to access. Both aspects are discussed briefly here and are examined later in this chapter.

The creator, or indeed the last user to modify an XPage design element, is called the signer of the XPage, or simply the signer. For an XPage to be allowed to execute, the signer of the XPage—or a group to which the signer belongs—must be granted the right to run XPages. The Domino server administrator grants this right in the **Security > Programmability Restrictions** section of the Domino server configuration document. Peek ahead to Figure 21.8 if you want to see how this is managed in the Domino Administrator UI.

Any end user requesting an XPage is only asked for a name and password by the Domino server when the web browser tries to access a protected resource. Initially, when a user requests an XPage and no HTTP session has been established, the Domino server creates an anonymous session for the web browser. If the application access control allows Anonymous access, the XPage is then opened. If not, a no access signal is thrown, and the Domino server causes the web browser to prompt (assuming basic authentication is configured) for a username and password.

If valid, these are then used to create an authenticated session. Note that an Internet password must be set in the Person document on the Domino server for the user for basic authentication to succeed.

Name-and-Password Authentication

Domino provides two Internet name-and-password authentication methods: basic and session. Basic authentication is not very secure; name and password details are transmitted unencrypted with each request and should be used on a secure sockets layer (SSL) port for better protection. Session authentication only transmits credentials once, uses a cookie to identify the session, and offers more features, such as session to timeout after a set period and for the user to log out without having to close the web browser.

The Domino session, meaning the connection from the XPages runtime thread to the Domino server, is created based on the current server ID. This is an internal Domino session object, which includes the identity of the authenticated web user. Therefore, when it comes to application access control and document security, an XPages application is effectively **Run as Web user**. Checking the invoker's rights can provide more security as it is this authenticated web username (or anonymous, as the case may be) that is used for any application, design element, and document security checks. Notice that, when an XPage executes, querying some of the session user information can return the Domino server name, while at the same time, querying the effective user name for the session returns the web user.

Note

The phrase "Run as Web user" is more often associated with traditional Notes/Domino web agents and describes a security setting on the agent that instructs Domino to check the invoker's rights to access the database instead of the agent signer's rights.

Application Layer of Security

A Domino administrator controls the list of users who have access to the server. An access control list (ACL) controls those who have access to an application and the operations and tasks the user is allowed to perform. Every application has an ACL. Table 21.1 lists the ACL access levels and describes the permissions each access level grants.

Table 21.1 ACL Access Levels

Access Level	Description
MANAGER	This is the highest access level. Users granted this access level can edit the ACL, perform encryption and replication operations on the application, and delete the application. The MANAGER level access includes all permissions granted to the other lower access levels.
DESIGNER	Users granted this level of access can edit design elements and create a full-text index. The DESIGNER level access includes all permissions granted to the other lower access levels.
EDITOR	EDITORs can create new documents and read and edit all other existing documents. To be able to edit a document, an EDITOR must have read access to the document (which could be prevented by the user not being listed in the Readers field on the document).
AUTHOR	Despite the name AUTHOR, users granted this level of access must also be granted the Create Documents privilege if they are to create documents. AUTHORs can edit documents where the user is specified in the Authors field of a document, and they can read all documents (unless the document has a Readers field and the user is not included in the list).
READER	Users granted this level of access only have the permission to read documents. Note that if the document has a Readers field, the user can only read that document if they are listed in that field.
DEPOSITOR	DEPOSITORs only have the permission to create documents. They do not have the ability to read their own or any other documents (unless they are marked for public access).
NO ACCESS	This is the lowest level of access. Users with this level of access can only read or create public-access documents.

Any web user allowed to access the server can open an XPage in a Domino application if they have at least DEPOSITOR level access to the application, unless of course there are further access restrictions applied at the application and design element layers.

Applications hosted on a Domino server are governed by an access control list (ACL), which is stored and managed within each application. The ACL specifies the access level (READER, AUTHOR, EDITOR, and so on) granted to users and controls who can access the application, the type of tasks they are entitled to perform, and the access privileges (privileges that govern the ability to perform specific types of operations, such as create and delete documents) they have been granted.

The application ACL is one of the fundamental building blocks for Notes/Domino application security and is fully supported, enforced, and leveraged by XPages.

ACL Maximum Internet Name and Password

XPages applications on a Domino server accessed via a web browser connection use an Internet name and password. The access level given to Internet users is limited to a maximum level, irrespective of the access level directly assigned to the user in the ACL. The default setting is Editor. To view or change the current setting from Domino Designer, select your application, choose File > Application > Access Control..., open the Advanced tab, and for the Maximum Internet name and password field, choose the required level, as shown in Figure 21.1.

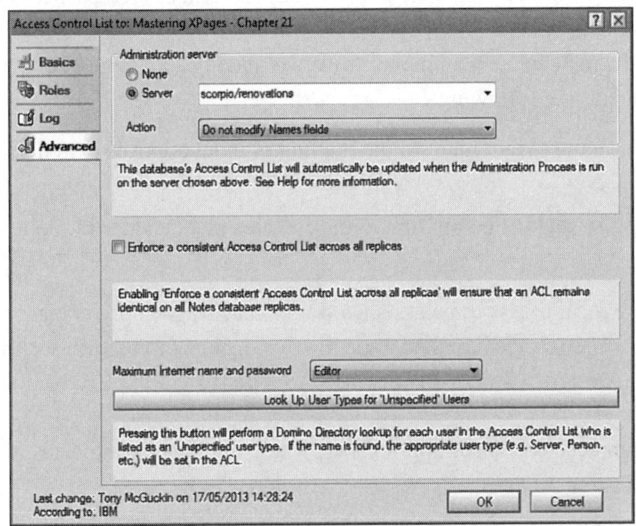

Figure 21.1 Application ACL Advanced tab

Roles provide a handy way to group a number of users together and help simplify administration. Security can be applied to a role and users that belong to that role receive the privilege or have the restriction applied. The role artifact is supported and can be used in XPages applications.

Design Element Layer of Security

Form, view, and XPage design elements have many security mechanisms associated with them. The key point to note from this section is that, although an XPage is typically based on and associated with a form, none of the form design element security features automatically apply to documents created with XPage. The XPage Domino Document data source property `computeWithForm` should be used to associate any hidden security related fields with documents created by the XPage so that any default setting stored with the form would populate their initial value. You set the `computeWithForm` property of a Domino Document data source by navigating to **XPage > All Properties > data > data > dominoDocument[0] > computeWithFrom** and selecting either `onload`, `onsave`, or `both`, depending on whether you require the computation to occur as the document is read, saved, or for both read and save events.

XPages and Form Access Control Options

In traditional Notes/Domino application development, presentation (forms for entering and displaying information) and data (documents for storing the information) are tightly integrated. Form access control security settings can be configured so that any document created with that form inherits those access control settings.

XPages does not require a form to create documents; however, having an XPage bound to a form provides many benefits, such as the following:

- Acting as a type of data schema to facilitate simple binding of input controls to items in a document.
- Executing application logic, such as computing default values associated with items in the documents.

Although you can specify a form that is to be associated with an XPage and you can configure a Domino Document data source that is based on a specific form, none of the form security access control options (**Menu > Design > Form Properties > Security**) get applied to documents created by XPages.

The following lists the form access control options and, where applicable, indicates how similar security may be achieved using XPages:

- **Default read access for documents created with this form:** By default, users with `Reader` access and above can read documents created with a form. This option enables the application designer to create a form reader access list, a subset of users who populate the document reader access list field (`$Readers`) for documents created with this form. This form security option has no effect for XPages applications, and there is no equivalent. Although new documents created with an XPage do not have a `$Readers` field, existing documents and new documents created with the form in a traditional Notes/Domino application have the `$Readers` field, and Notes/Domino enforces the document level security. Therefore, care needs to be taken in mixed environments because authorized web users may not have the same access to documents via XPages if this form security option is used.
- **Who can create documents with this form:** By default, only users with `Author` access and above can access the form to create documents. This option enables an application designer to further restrict who can use this form to a subset of users. With XPages, the default is that any authorized web user with access to the application can open an XPage.

Note that if the XPage is managing a document data source, the user must also have the appropriate access level in the application ACL to open, edit, or create a document. The loading of an XPage can be restricted using the loaded and rendered properties with a programmatic expression that evaluates to true or false based on some aspect of the user credentials. An easier and more declarative way to limit specific XPages access to just a subset of users is to create a list of ACL entries for the XPage, and only those users gain access at the specified level.

- **Default encryption keys:** XPages does not currently support field encryption.
- **Disable printing/forwarding/copying to the clipboard:** Does not apply to XPages.
- **Available to Public Access users:** Setting this option gives users with `No Access` to the application the ability to view and modify specific documents created with this form. Documents to be made available to a `Public Access` user must have a field called `$PublicAccess`, which is of type text and has a default value of 1. This form security option has no effect on XPages applications. See the section, "XPages and Public Access Users," for more details on adding `Public Access` support to XPages applications.

Notes/Domino forms also provide a feature (**Menu > Design > Form Properties > Form Info > Options > Anonymous form**) whereby users who edit a document with the form are not tracked in any `$UpdatedBy` field. This type of capability is not supported by XPages.

XPages and View Access Control Options

The Domino View is the other important XPages data source and is based on the Domino view design element. The following two view security options (**Menu > Design > View Properties > Security**) are available to control access to the view by users listed in the application ACL and affect XPages applications. Note that these options only control access to the view and not the underlying documents:

- **Who may use this view:** By default, all readers and above can use a view. This option can be changed to only allow a subset of users in the application ACL to access this view. Because a View Panel control in an XPage uses a Domino view as data source, Notes/Domino will enforce this access control. An authorized web user accessing an XPage with a View Panel who has not been granted permission to use the view will not see any data returned from the view.
- **Available to Public Access users:** Setting this option gives users with No Access to the application the privilege to access the view if it is included in an XPage that also has Public Access enabled. If an XPage has been made available to Public Access users but the view used as a data source for the XPage View Panel has not, and then the View Panel pager and column headings display, but no data entries are displayed. See the section, "XPages and Public Access Users," for details on adding Public Access support to XPages applications.

The web user must still have `Reader` access to the documents contained in the view. If they do not, no entries are displayed and an empty View Panel with view pager and column headers are simply displayed.

Similarly, if the web user has no access to the Domino view that has been defined as a data source for a View Panel, no data is returned, so no entries are displayed either, and the view pager and column headers still appear.

To visually distinguish between users who do not have access to the view and users who simply do no have access to any documents currently contained in the view, the View Panel can be prevented from appearing when the user has no access to the underlying view. Set the View Panel **Properties > View > Visible property** (which can also be accessed via **Properties > All Properties > basics > rendered > Compute value...**) with a computed value to control whether the View Panel is displayed, depending on the web user's ability to access the view that is used as a data source. Listing 21.1 shows how to determine if a user has access to the view that is the basis of an XPages Domino View data source.

Listing 21.1 Check Access to Underlying View

```
var viewPanel1:com.ibm.xsp.component.xp.XspViewPanel =
        getComponent("viewPanel1");
var dataSource:com.ibm.xsp.model.DataSource =
        viewPanel1.getDataSource();

if (typeof(dataSource) != "undefined" && dataSource != null){
    var dominoView:lotus.domino.View = dataSource.getView();
    if (dominoView != null){
        return true;
    } else {
        return false;
    }
} else {
    return false;
}
```

XPage Access Control

The XPage design element provides the ability to restrict who can access and run specific individual XPages. This is controlled using the `acl` property. Listing 21.2 shows the syntax for the `<xp:acl>` tag.

Listing 21.2 XPages acl and aclEntry Syntax

```
<xp:acl loaded="true|false">
      <xp:this.entries>
            <xp:aclEntry fullName="common name" name="canonical name"
                  right="NOACCESS|READER|EDITOR"
                  type="USER|GROUP|ROLE|DEFAULT|ANONYMOUS"
                  loaded="true|false">
            </xp:aclEntry>
      </xp:this.entries>
</xp:acl>
```

Watch out for a couple of things when creating an `<xp:aclEntry>`:

- XPages 8.5.2 and earlier include the options `ORGUNIT` and `ORGROLE` for the `type` attribute. Do not use these values for `type` as they are deprecated and have no function.
- Do not use the `fullName` attribute in XPages 8.5.2 and earlier; it has no function. Use the `name` attribute and supply a canonical name if the `type` attribute is set to `USER`.

Table 21.2 describes the `<xp:acl>` tag attributes.

Table 21.2 acl Attributes and Properties

Property	Values	Description
`entries`	Zero or more occurrences of an `<xp:aclEntry>` tag	If there are multiple ACL entries, the first entry that matches the user, the user's group, or the user's role, is the level of access is enforced. If no aclEntry matches the user, group, or role of the user, the user has no access to the XPage and a no-access signal is thrown, which causes the web browser to prompt the user to log in. If the ACL is loaded, but there are no entries, the aclEntry Editor right is assigned by default.
`loaded`	`true or false`	Default is `true`. If `loaded` is `false`, the ACL is never evaluated and applied to the user.

Table 21.3 describes the `<xp:aclEntry>` tag attributes.

Table 21.3 AclEntry Attributes and Properties

Property	Values	Description
`name`		Enter the name of the user, group, or role to which this access should apply. Ensure that the type attribute is set appropriately to identify the name correctly. Note: If the type is user, ensure that the name specified uses the canonical form; for example, CN=Web User/O=MyOrg.

`type`	`USER`
	`GROUP`
	`ROLE`
	`DEFAULT`
	`ANONYMOUS`
		If name is specified, set type to `USER`, `GROUP`, or `ROLE` to identify the type of name.
		`DEFAULT` applies to any user not specified directly by name. It also applies to anonymous user if there is no other aclEntry for `ANONYMOUS`.
		`ANONYMOUS` restricts the right specified to anonymous users.

`right`	`NOACCESS`
	`READER`
	`EDITOR`
		`NOACCESS` prevents access.
		`READER` and `EDITOR` correspond to whether the components on an XPages are read only or editable, respectively.
		Granting `EDITOR` access to a user who has only `READER` access specified in the application ACL doesn't escalate the privilege, the user continues to have `READER` only access to the XPages.
		Although a user may have a right to edit a document, if the XPages ACL access restricts them to READER, the XPage is opened in read-only mode. Although the user may programmatically modify the fields, when the page is submitted, it does not go thorough validate and update model phases; therefore, any updates to the fields on the XPage are not saved.

`loaded`	`true or false`	Default is `true`. If loaded, is set to `false`, and then the specific ACL entry is never evaluated and applied to the user.

Listing 21.3 shows an `<xp:acl>` that is associated with an XPage that prevents any users who belong to the `[WebUser]` role accessing the XPages. However, the user Web Developer can load the XPages, even though they belong to the `[WebUser]` role, because the Web Developer user entry is positioned before the `[WebUser]` role entry.

Listing 21.3 XPages acl Property Example

```
<xp:acl loaded="true">
      <xp:this.entries>
            <xp:aclEntry right="EDITOR" type="USER"
```

```
                              name="CN=Web Developer/O=IBM"
                              loaded="true">
              </xp:aclEntry>
              <xp:aclEntry right="NOACCESS" type="ROLE" loaded="true">
                  <xp:this.name><![CDATA[[WebUser]]]></xp:this.name>
              </xp:aclEntry>
          </xp:this.entries>
</xp:acl>
```

Other XPages controls that support the <xp:acl> tag include the following:

- **Panel container control:** Enables large subsections of an XPage to be optionally loaded depending on the user currently accessing the XPage.
- **Include Page:** Enables an entire XPage to be optionally included in another XPage depending on the user currently accessing the XPage.

XPages loaded, rendered, and readonly Properties

Every control in XPages includes two particular properties: `loaded` (**Properties > All Properties > basics > loaded**) and `rendered` (**Properties > All Properties > basics > rendered**). The `rendered` property is often labeled *Visible* in the control section of the properties tab.

`loaded` specifies whether the control should be instantiated when the server-side component tree is first created. Whereas `rendered` indicates whether a control that has already been loaded should also display to the end user in the first instance of a request to the parent XPage. Thereafter, it is used to determine if a control should be processed during POST back requests to the same parent XPage and subsequently to have that control HTML markup emitted in the response.

For an XPage, if the `loaded` property evaluates to `false`, the XPage returns an error. If `rendered` evaluates to `false`, an empty HTML page is returned. For all other controls contained in an XPage, a `false` value for either `loaded` or `rendered` property prevents the control from being displayed.

The `readonly` property for an XPage (**Properties > All Properties > data > readonly**) indicates that the XPage is read-only and switches any controls it contains to also be read-only. The XPage, Panel, and Include Page controls all have a `readonly` property in their **All Properties > data** section that effects the read-only property of any controls they contain.

Input controls that have their `readonly` property set to `true` render in the web browser as a read-only feature. A related property, the `disabled` property (**Properties > All Properties > basic > disabled**) indicates that a control prohibits changes by the user and is similar to the `readonly` property, the difference being that a read-only control can still receive focus unless it has also been set to `disabled`. In addition, the value of a disabled field is not sent to the server when the enclosing form is submitted.

The `readonly`, `rendered`, and `loaded` properties can be set to a value that is appropriate for certain security conditions and can be used to control the appearance of the user interface, depending on what information you want to communicate to the end user. For example, if you want a component to be loaded or rendered only if the web user has been granted Editor ACL level access, you can use the code snippet shown in Listing 21.4 to perform this security check.

Listing 21.4 Check ACL Access Level

```
database.queryAccess( session.getEffectiveUserName() )
                              >= NotesACL.LEVEL_EDITOR ? true : false
```

If the control is available for the user, but a certain set of conditions has not been met, you could set disabled to `true` so that the control remains visible, but ineffective, until the required conditions are met.

Document Layer of Security

Full document security, enforced via Readers and Authors fields, is fully supported and respected in XPages.

To create and edit documents, a user typically needs the right combination of ACL access level privileges and document level security. This means the user must have at least Author access level with the create documents privilege and not be restricted from editing the document. If a document has an Authors field, modifying the Authors field can restrict who can edit the document after it has been created to the list of specified users, or to users that belong to one of the groups or roles specified. Similarly, if a document has a Readers field, specifying users, roles, and groups in the Readers field can restrict who can subsequently read the document after it has been created.

This is a core Notes/Domino security feature and is managed in the form properties security settings. The Notes/Domino backend classes used by XPages enforce security for existing documents with this information. However, for new documents you need to be careful and use the computeWithForm property to ensure the same security settings in the form properties are added to the same documents. Although forms provide a useful data schema template for creating a data entry XPage, by default only those fields that are bound to the Domino Document data source are created and stored. Because document security fields are not something you typically present to the end user to edit and configure, they need to be set programmatically or by using the computeWithForm property to pick up default values from the base form.

The next four sections discuss traditional Notes/Domino document level security mechanisms and how they apply to XPages.

Reader Access List

In XPages, there is no way to specify a default reader access list that is to be inherited by documents created via a Domino Document data source. If an existing document has been created with a document reader access list, those restrictions are honored in an XPages application.

Authors and Readers Fields and the XPages computeWithForm Property

For XPages Domino Document data sources, if `computeWithForm` is set, all fields specified in the form are appended to the document that is being created. Any formulas used to calculate default values are executed and the result stored in corresponding field. This is important for Readers and Authors fields and any other fields that provide document security, for example `$PublicAccess`, where you want to maintain the existing document security settings.

If the Domino Document data source used by an XPage is based on an existing form that is also used by traditional Notes applications where documents inherit security setting from the form, review the XPages `computeWithForm` property setting and the default form security settings to ensure that the resulting document level security is the same through both interfaces. Figure 21.2 shows how you can examine and set the value of the `computeWithForm` property for a data source on an XPage.

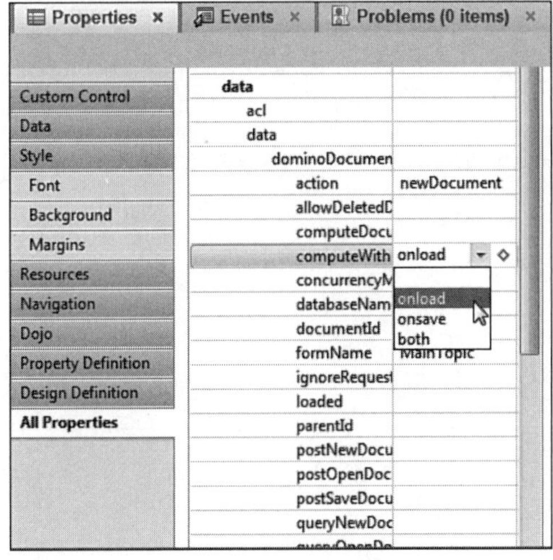

Figure 21.2 XPage computeWithForm property

Sections, Paragraphs, and Layout Regions

Traditional Notes/Domino document area-control mechanisms, such as sections, paragraphs, and layout regions, which can be hidden from viewing based on, for example, a user's current mode or a formula, do not apply to XPages. However, a similar effect can be achieved in XPages through the panel container control that can hide areas of an XPage based on a computed formula or JavaScript expression. Note that these types of area control mechanisms are not true document security. Listing 21.5 shows how to use a JavaScript expression in the `loaded` property of an `<xp:panel>` container control to determine if the current user has the HR role, and, only if this is true, the section of the XPage with the salary information will be loaded and displayed.

Listing 21.5 Using a Panel Container Control to Hide Sections of an XPage

```
<xp:panel>
  <xp:this.loaded><![CDATA[${javascript:
    var db1:NotesDatabase = session.getCurrentDatabase()
    var acl1:NotesACL = db1.getACL()

    var aclEntry = acl1.getEntry(session.getEffectiveUserName())
    if (aclEntry == null){
      aclEntry = acl1.getEntry("-Default-");
    }

    return aclEntry.isRoleEnabled("HR")}]]>
  </xp:this.loaded>
  <xp:br></xp:br>
  <xp:label value="Salary Details" id="label2"></xp:label>
  <xp:table>
    <xp:tr>
      <xp:td>
        <xp:label value="Salary:" id="salary_Label1" for="salary1">
        </xp:label> </xp:td>
      <xp:td>
        <xp:inputText value="#{document1.salary}" id="salary1">
        </xp:inputText> </xp:td>
    </xp:tr>
  </xp:table>
</xp:panel>
```

Field Encryption and Document Signing

Field encryption and signing are not supported or applicable in XPages applications.

Workstation ECL Layer of Security

Much of the discussion so far focused on Notes/Domino security on a Domino server with XPages applications being opened in a web browser. XPages also runs in the Notes client, and although there is no control over which signers can run XPages on the Notes client, the end user can still control which operations, methods, and tasks that embedded code created by specific signers within an XPages application may execute. This is achieved by means of a workstation execution control list (ECL), which limits access to workstation functions and local applications. Any attempt by embedded code in an XPages application to execute a protected operation or task causes the end user to be warned via an execution security alert (ESA). The ESA dialog provides the ability to prevent the operation, allow it to proceed, or to always trust the signer to perform the operation, which results in the workstation ECL being updated with the signer being granted the permission. To see an example of an ECL, peek ahead to Figure 21.9, where the workstation ECL is covered as part of the section, "XPages Security in the Notes Client."

Useful Resources

Although a little old, Overview of Notes/Domino security gives a good concise and complete overview of Notes/Domino security:

`https://www.ibm.com/developerworks/lotus/library/ls-security_overview/`

For more detailed and up-to-date information on Notes/Domino security, see the IBM Notes and Domino Information Centre documentation at http://tinyurl.com/DominoInfoCentre.

Now Get Started

As you saw in the previous section, Notes/Domino is, by default, initially very open and as you work through the layers, security, and access control becomes more and more restricted and granular.

In a similar fashion, a new XPages application based on the Discussion–Notes & Web application template can run without requiring any signature to be added to the security tab in the server configuration document. This provides a quick and easy way for users to get started with Notes/Domino applications. Subsequent sections demonstrate how to restrict access using many of the various access control mechanisms already discussed.

Creating the Initial Application

The first step is to create a new application based on the Discussion application template that ships with the Domino server. In Domino Designer,

1. Choose **File > New > Application**.
2. In the New Application dialog (shown in Figure 21.3), select your Domino server (in both the Specify Application and Specify Template sections). Remember, you need a Domino Server to be able to follow these steps. You cannot use the local Domino Designer Web Preview to follow these examples.
3. Enter a title for the application (for example, **Chapter 21**) and a filename (for example, **Chp21Ed2.nsf**).
4. Select **Discussion—Notes & Web (9)** as the Template, and choose **OK**.

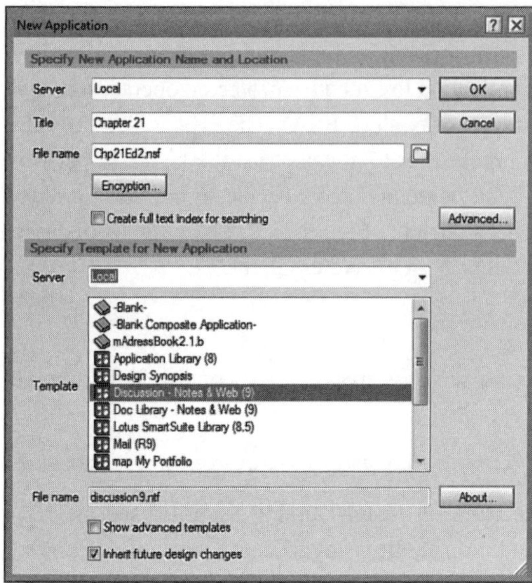

Figure 21.3 New Application dialog

The Chapter 21 application is ready to run. Select the Chapter 21 application in the application navigator and choose **Design > Preview in Web Browser > Default System Web Browser** to launch the application in a web browser. You are prompted with a login dialog. Supply the username and password of a registered user on your server who has an Internet password, and the application opens with the allDocuments.xsp page. Note that this application ran out of the box. You have not had to perform any security configuration or add users to the application ACL. How come?

In the application navigator, expand the Chapter 21 application and double-click the XPages tree item to list all the XPage design elements (see Figure 21.4).

Notice that the Lotus Notes Template Development/Lotus Notes signature was the last signature to modify all the XPage design elements.

Lotus Notes Template Development/Lotus Notes

The application templates supplied with IBM Notes and Domino are all signed with Lotus Notes Template Development ID file. This signature (along with the server's signature on Domino server) is trusted implicitly by Notes/Domino and does not require security access to be specified either in the server configuration on Domino server or the workstation ECL on the Notes client.

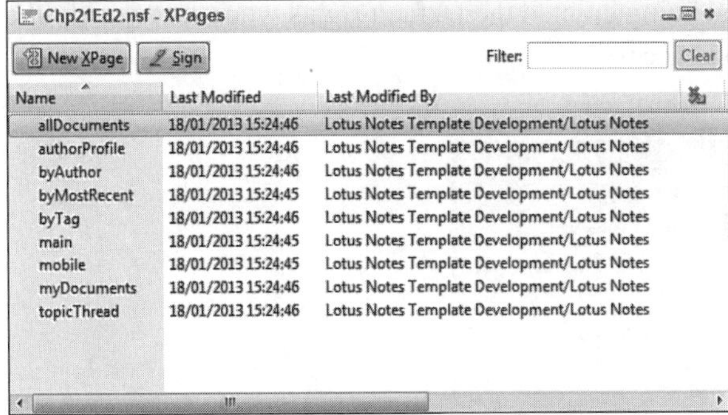

Figure 21.4 XPage design elements

Signatures

When a user creates or modifies an XPage design element, his signature is stored with the XPage in the $UpdatedBy item and anyone else who subsequently modifies the XPages is also tracked. The signer of an XPage is the last person to have updated and XPage design element. This is the same for any other XPages-related design element, Custom Controls, server-side JavaScript libraries, and Java code (classes and JARs). Security for XPages is based on controlling the privileges granted to signers of an XPage and XPages components.

Implementing ACLs

The other security aspect enabling the end user to run the application is the access control list (ACL). The ACL controls access to the application and what operations users can perform, for example read and create documents, and modify the application design. Choose **File > Application > Access Control...** to see the application ACL (see in Figure 21.5).

Examine the ACL and notice that it contains two special names, Anonymous and Default, with Anonymous having No Access, and Default having Author-level access. When the XPage is requested, anonymous access is attempted first. That fails, throws a no access signal, and causes the Domino server to prompt for a valid username and password. After authenticated, the application ACL is again checked—this time to see if the username is listed as an entry. Because it is not, the rights associated with the Default entry, Author, are granted, and the XPage is loaded successfully.

Special Names

The Anonymous name governs what access rights are granted to unauthenticated users. The Default user (every ACL must have a Default name) governs which access rights are given to authenticated users who are not explicitly listed in the ACL (and unauthenticated users if the Anonymous user is not listed). The Anonymous user is optional. To prevent unauthenticated users from accessing the applications and being granted the Default rights, you must specify the Anonymous user with the No Access-level access.

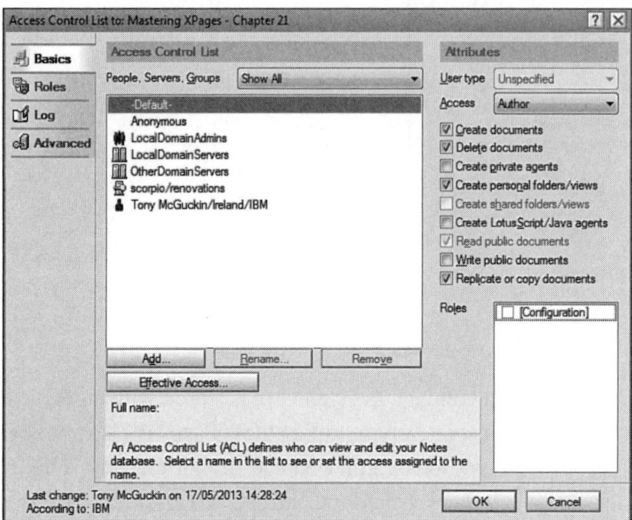

Figure 21.5 Access control list

Sign the XPages with Your Signature

To update the existing XPage design elements with your signature, you can modify and save each XPage. However, Domino Designer provides a useful button that does the same job. From Domino Designer, open the list of XPages (double-click the XPages tree item in the application navigator), select them all, and click the Sign button. Notice that the Last Modified By column (see Figure 21.6) now contains the signature of the user currently logged into Domino Designer.

mxpd2\Chp21Ed2.nsf - XPages

New XPage | Sign | Filter: | Clear

Name	Last Modified	Last Modified By
allDocuments	17/05/2013 14:23:04	Tony McGuckin/Ireland/IBM
authorProfile	17/05/2013 14:23:04	Tony McGuckin/Ireland/IBM
byAuthor	17/05/2013 14:23:04	Tony McGuckin/Ireland/IBM
byMostRecent	17/05/2013 14:23:04	Tony McGuckin/Ireland/IBM
byTag	17/05/2013 14:23:04	Tony McGuckin/Ireland/IBM
main	17/05/2013 14:26:13	Tony McGuckin/Ireland/IBM
mobile	17/05/2013 14:26:13	Tony McGuckin/Ireland/IBM
myDocuments	17/05/2013 14:23:03	Tony McGuckin/Ireland/IBM
topicThread	17/05/2013 14:23:03	Tony McGuckin/Ireland/IBM
xpNetworkTest	17/05/2013 14:31:27	Tony McGuckin/Ireland/IBM

Figure 21.6 Last Modified By list of XPages

Reload the XPage and notice that, this time, the web browser displays an error, as shown in Figure 21.7, which indicates a permission problem. As expected, the signer of the XPage design elements does not have the right to sign XPages that are permitted to run on the Domino server (this assumes that no changes have been made to the default Domino server configuration document).

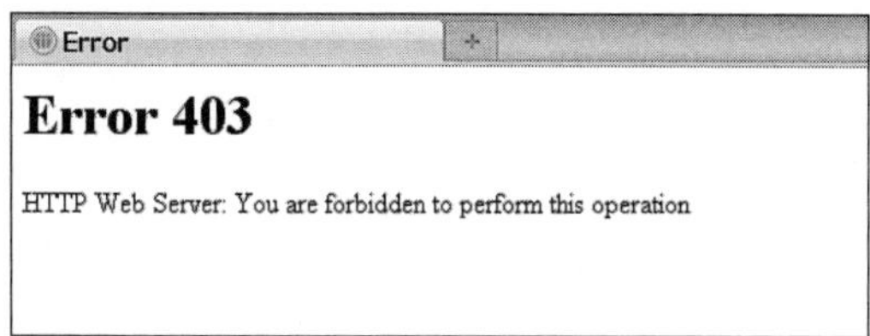

Figure 21.7 Error 403 HTTP Web Server

To fix this, the signer needs to be added to the Programmability Restrictions sections under the Security tab of the server configuration document.

Programmability Restrictions

Because XPages are executable code, similar to agents, authorization for who can create and modify XPages that run on the server is controlled by the server configuration.

To view and edit the programmability restrictions,

1. From Domino Administrator, log in as an administrator.
2. Connect to your Domino server (**File > Open Server...**).
3. Open the **Security** tab of the Server Configuration document (**Server > Current Server Document > Configuration > Security**).
4. Navigate to the **Programmability Restrictions** section, as shown in Figure 21.8, and add your user to the Sign agents or XPages to run on behalf of the invoker field.

Reload the web browser page again with the application and this time notice that the XPages application is now displayed.

The Programmability Restrictions section in the Security tab of the Server Configuration document controls which users can sign XPages applications that run on the Domino server and what privileges they have.

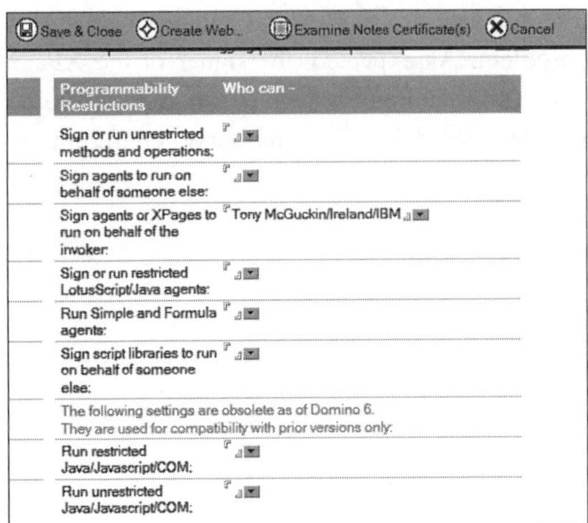

Figure 21.8 Domino server programmability restrictions

Note that, when talking about signing an XPages design element, the security and programmability restrictions also apply to XPages-related design elements that can be contained in an XPage. This includes:

- Custom Controls
- Server-side JavaScript libraries
- Java classes
- JAR files

The following sections detail the relevant Programmability Restrictions fields for XPages.

Sign or Run Unrestricted Methods and Operations

In this field, enter the name of users or groups who have the ability to sign XPages that run unrestricted. On Domino server, design elements that execute embedded code, such as LotusScript/Java agents and XPages, have two modes of operation: restricted and unrestricted. Running restricted prevents a signer from using protected operations, such as network access and file I/O, while running unrestricted allows all those protected operations to succeed.

Leaving this section blank means no user is granted this ability (except for the current server and Notes Template developers who are granted unrestricted access by default).

Any users who have been specified in the Full Access Administrator field (also under the Security tab of the server configuration document) also have the ability to run XPages with unrestricted rights. Note that XPages do not execute with full administration rights.

Any users granted this right also gains the following rights:

- Sign agents to run on behalf of someone else
- Sign agents or XPages to run on behalf of the invoker
- Sign or run restricted LotusScript/Java agents
- Run Simple and Formula agents

Sign Agents to Run on Behalf of Someone Else

In this field, enter the names of user and groups who are allowed to sign agents that are executed on anyone else's behalf.

Leaving this section blank means no user is granted this ability (except for the current server and Notes Template developers who are granted this right by default).

Any users granted this right also gain the following rights:

- Sign agents or XPages to run on behalf of the invoker
- Sign or run restricted LotusScript/Java agents
- Run Simple and Formula agents

Although this right provides no specific XPages privilege, it is significant for XPages applications because any user or group listed here also includes the right to sign agents or XPages to run on behalf of the invoker.

Sign Agents or XPages to Run on Behalf of the Invoker

In this field, enter the names of user and groups who are allowed to sign agents or XPages that are executed on behalf of the invoker.

Leaving this section blank means no user is granted this ability (except for the current server and Notes Template developers who are granted unrestricted access by default). Therefore, any users you want to have the ability to run XPages must be specified here (or be part of a group that is specified here).

This security right reflects the typical XPages configuration, where an XPage is created by one user but runs as the web user who authenticated with the server and was granted access to the XPages application.

Any users granted this right also gain the following rights:

- Sign or run restricted LotusScript/Java agents
- Run Simple and Formula agents

Sign Script Libraries to Run on Behalf of Someone Else

In this field, enter the names of users who are allowed to sign script libraries and/or agents or XPages executed by someone else. A script library is a design element for storing code that can be shared by other design elements. Server-side JavaScript libraries are a type of script library and are specific to XPages.

Leaving this section blank means everybody is granted this right. Therefore, add the names of user or groups here so that only trusted users have this capability.

As usual, the current server and Notes Template developers are granted this right by default.

If is a signer name is specified (or is part of a group specified here), that signer name must also be specified in one of the preceding fields.

Restricted Operation

Create a new XPage that has two inputs (two Edit Box controls, named `networkHost` and `networkPort`, for specifying a hostname and port), a status output (a Computed Field control named `networkStatus`, to display the result), and a button (named `Test`) that executes the server-side JavaScript code shown in Listing 21.6 when clicked.

Listing 21.6 Code Snippet That Executes a Restricted Network Operation

```
var h = getComponent("networkHost").getValue();
var p = getComponent("networkPort").getValue();

var errmsg = "Exception: ";
var statuscomp = getComponent("networkStatus");

try {
    var s:java.net.Socket = new java.net.Socket(h, parseInt(p));
    if (s != null) {
        s.close();
    }

    statuscomp.setValue("OK: ");
} catch (e) {
    var msg = e.getMessage();
    if (msg == null){
        var e2 = e.getCause();
        msg = e2.getMessage();

        if (msg == null || msg.equalsIgnoreCase(h)){
            msg = e2.getClass().getName();
        }
    }
    statuscomp.setValue(errmsg + msg);
}
```

When you run the XPage, enter the hostname of your Domino server and 80 as the port number. When you click the **Test** button, you get an error similar to the following.

```
Exception: not allowed to make a socket connection to jquill-laptop,-1
```

Now, as Domino administrator, in the Programmability Restrictions, add your user signature to the **Sign or run unrestricted methods and operations** field and save the changes.

Rerun the test application and this time notice that the network status output is simply

```
OK:
```

Now that the XPages signer has the right to run unrestricted methods, the socket connection in the example code is successful.

XPages Security Checking

Each request for an XPage creates a security context that performs two things:

- Verifies that all the signers of the design elements that comprise the XPages are valid.
- Determines the level of execution privileges (unrestricted or restricted) to be associated with the security context based on all the design element signers.

For an XPage to execute, all the signers must have at least been granted the ability to run XPages on behalf of the invoker.

The following lists the design elements that can comprise an XPages application. The signers of these design elements are verified and, together, they collectively set the execution privilege level for an XPage:

- XPage
- Custom Control
- Server-side JavaScript library
- Java Design Element/Java class (stored in WEB-INF/classes)
- JAR Design Element/JAR (Java Archive File stored in WEB-INF/lib)

Because the XPage design element is the one that is a *container* for all the other XPages-related design elements, the signer of the XPage is known as the *top-level signer*.

In order for the XPages security manager to allow any design element to execute restricted operations contained in embedded Java code, all the signers of the XPages design elements must have the ability to sign or run unrestricted methods and operations. Initially, the security context assumes unrestricted. Then, as each signer is checked, once one signer does not have the unrestricted right, the XPages security context for the request is downgraded to restricted.

When any embedded user-defined Java code subsequently executes a protected operation, the security context is referenced to see if the operation should be allowed to proceed. If the security context is restricted, then a security exception is thrown.

Most of the design elements are verified and checked at start of the request. The Java class files stored in the NSF are only checked when they are loaded.

For safety, security context information is not maintained between requests. When the request is complete, the security context is discarded and recalculated for the next request.

NSF ClassLoader Bridge

XPages has its own classloader for reading XPages, user-defined Java classes, and JARs stored within the application's NSF. Because this NSF classloader is used to load the initial XPage, any subsequent reference to a class always looks to use this classloader first, which checks the NSF first and doesn't delegate to its parent until it cannot find the class. The parent of the NSF class loader provides a bridge between the NSF and the classloader hierarchy of the platform running XPages (OSGi on Domino server and Eclipse on Notes client) and prevents any code from within the NSF accessing external classes that XPages wants to restrict on security grounds. For example, classes in the following two packages, `org.osgi.*` and `org.eclipse.*`, and several internal packages (such as `com.ibm.*` and `com.ibm.xsp.*)` are not accessible from classes in the NSF, because they could potentially be used to access information and code outside the current application that is not fully managed by the XPages security manager.

XPages Security in the Notes Client

On the Notes client, workstation execution control lists (ECLs) restrict which tasks and operations embedded code in an application can perform based on who the application signers are. XPages security on the Notes client is integrated with the workstation ECLs to prevent XPages applications from running security sensitive operations where the user has not explicitly trusted all the signers.

XPages security in the Notes client also enforces many other restrictions that do not apply for XPages applications on Domino server:

- The embedded XULRunner browser that is used to run XPages applications in the Notes client can only access the application for which it was invoked. Because the user is already authenticated on the Notes client and has unrestricted access to data in the local applications, this restriction prevents any malicious code in one application from simply redirecting the XULRunner browser to another application and accessing the data. It is still possible to access data from other applications through the programmatic interfaces. These methods check the workstation ECL to ensure the application signers have been authorized by the user to access data from other applications.
- An XPages application cannot be invoked from an external web browser, HTTP session information is stored with the XPages runtime, and when the embedded XULRunner is closed, any subsequent request is rejected. Also, the port number for which the embedded web application container listens for HTTP requests is random and changes each time it is instantiated.

- By default, there is no access to Java from client-side JavaScript within the XULRunner browser. However, the XPages Runtime supports a limited set of Notes client platform capabilities that provide a richer user experience (for example, native dialogs instead of standard web browser dialogs for alerts) that are available to JavaScript within an XPages application. This functionality is provided though the XPages Client-Side Java Script functions, `XSP.alert`, `XSP.error`, `XSP.confirm`, and `XSP.publishEvent`. In addition, you can also extend the client-side JavaScript to Java capabilities within the XPiNC client via the XSP.executeCommand bridge. This enables you, as the XPages Developer, to create custom client-side JavaScript API within an XPages application that can invoke underlying Java code within the Notes client. This is explained in detail in Chapter 13, "XPages in the Notes Client," in the "Extended Client-Side JavaScript Commands" section.
- The ECL controls the ability to load Java in the Notes client. As of release 9.0.1 Java is disabled by default in the Notes and Domino Designer clients. You must therefore enable the ability to run Java code for a given ECL named entry. This is done by checking the **Load Java code** check box under the **File > Security > User Security > What Others Do > Using Workstation** dialog or alternatively by accepting a prompt from the Notes client itself to trust an application to Load Java code when the application is being opened. You can read more about this in the next section of this chapter.
- The ECL also controls the capability for an XPages application to perform Property Broker access. (Property Broker is the underlying technology for publishing events when running XPages as a Composite Application in the Notes client.)

Execution Control List (ECL)

The Notes client workstation ECL is a more granular approach to security than Unrestricted/Restricted signer on Domino server. Instead of just specifying if a signer can perform protected operations, a signer may be allowed to perform some protected operations but not others.

The ECL maintains a list of names (signers) and the operations they are allowed to perform. XPages uses the capabilities granted under the **Using Workstation** tab for User Security to grant/deny permission to signers of XPages applications. To examine the ECL that controls XPages applications in the Notes client, select **File > Security > User Security... > What Others Do > Using Workstation**. Figure 21.9 shows an example.

This is the same ECL that controls Java agents on the Notes client. Java agents called synchronously from an XPages application has the same ECL restrictions enforced by the agent security manager.

You should note the presence of the new **Load Java code** check box as highlighted in Figure 21.9. The ability to load Java code with release 9.0.1 is disabled by default in the Notes and Domino Designer clients following a security review. Therefore, you must explicitly enable the ability to load Java code by checking this option under named ECL entries (on an entry-by-entry case) using the **File > Security > User Security > What Others Do > Using Workstation** dialog, or by accepting the **Execution Security Alert** prompt to trust an application to load Java code at runtime, as shown in Figure 21.10.

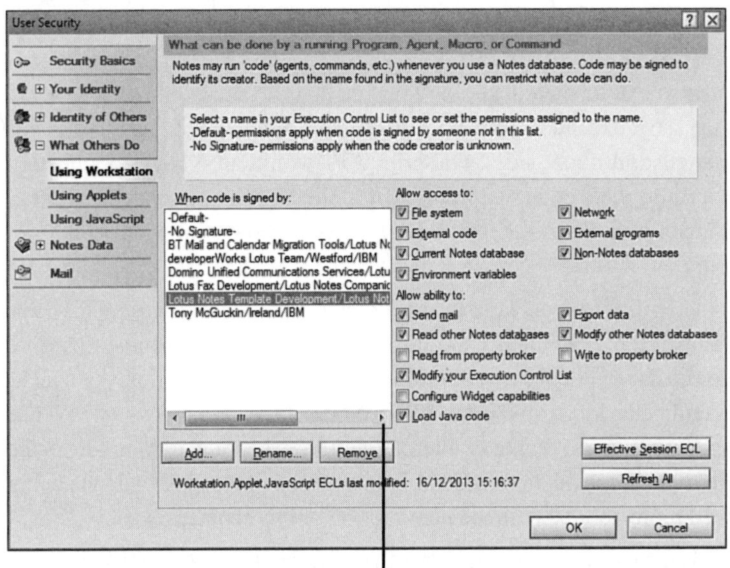

Figure 21.9 Notes client ECL security settings

Note that "Lotus Notes Template Development/Lotus Notes" signature has full access and the ability to Load Java code by default.

The Notes/Domino backend classes called from an XPages application perform the appropriate security check directly with the Notes Client ECL.

Any embedded Java code in an XPages application that calls a security-sensitive operation (such as file IO or network IO) triggers a Java permission check. XPages in the Notes client supplies an implementation of a Java Security Manager that maps Java permissions to ECL access rights and passes the required security contexts and signer information to the Notes client ECL for permission checking to determine if the Java operation should be allowed.

If all the XPages design element signers are listed the ECL and have been granted access to the particular operation, the execution continues.

If any of the signers are not listed, or are not allowed perform the operation, an Execution Security Alert (ESA), detailing the operation that is being attempted and the signer of the code who does not have the permission, is displayed to the user. For example, if you run the network test XPages application that you created based on the code snippet in Listing 21.6, when you first open the application in the client, you are presented with an Execution Security Alert asking you to accept the request to load Java code, similar to the one shown in Figure 21.10.

Type of security operation being performed – Load Java code in this example

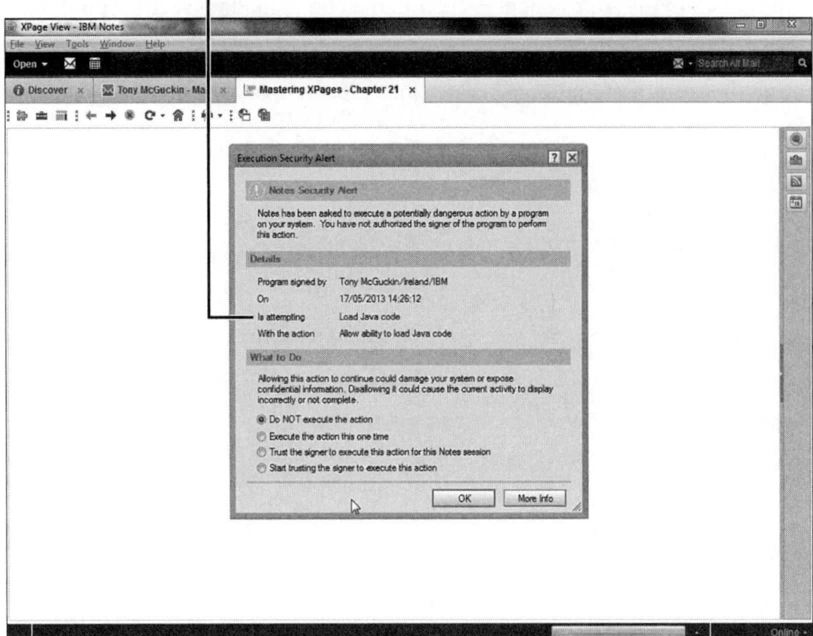

Figure 21.10 Notes client Exception Security Alert

From the ESA dialog, a Notes client user can then choose to allow the operation and optionally add the signer name to the ECL so the signer has permission to perform that operation in future.

If the user does not allow the signer to perform the operation, a security exception is raised and the request is ended unless the exception is handled in the application code.

The ESA options are

- **Do NOT execute the action:** Prevents the operation from executing and raises security exception that should be caught by the calling code so the user experience is handled appropriately.
- **Execute the action this one time:** Allows the operation to proceed. The next time the same operation is executed, the user is again prompted.

- **Trust the signer to execute this action for this Notes session:** This option is not supported in XPages. It allows the operation to proceed and behavior is similar to choosing execute the action this one time.
- **Start trusting the signer to execute this action:** Allows the operation to proceed and add the signer to the Notes client ECL with the corresponding access option granted.

Table 21.4 lists the ECL access options that apply to Java code embedded in an XPages applications and the corresponding Java permissions that are managed by the XPages Java security manager.

Table 21.4 Notes Client ECL Access Options for XPages

ECL Access Option	Java Permission Mapping
File system	FilePermission (read, write, delete)
Network	SocketPermission, NetworkPermission
External code	RuntimePermission (loadLibrary.{library name})
External programs	FilePermission (execute)
Environment variables	PropertyPermission

Note: Several Java runtime permissions, for example RuntimePermission (exitVM), are never allowed by the XPages Java security manager.

Active Content Filtering

Active Content Filtering (ACF) can remove potentially malicious active content from data that has just been entered before it is saved to the application, or as application data is retrieved and before it is returned to the web browser, where it may be interpreted and executed. ACF helps prevent the type of attack where one user tries to enter malicious code as input to an application in an effort to have another user unwittingly upload and execute that code in their web browser.

Several XPages input controls (for example, InputText, InputTextArea, and InputRichText) include two properties (under **All Properties** > **basics**) that support ACF:

- **htmlFilter:** Defines the ACF engine to use when the control sends data to the client.
- **htmlFilterIn:** Defines the engine to use when the control receives input from the client.

These properties can be set explicitly in the Properties section of the control or by using themes.

The output controls (for example, Input Text, Text Area, Rich Text editor Computed Field, Link, and Label) just use the `htmlFilter` property to filter the value emitted by the control.

Also, the following View Panel components can have their content displayed as HTML and also support the `htmlFilter` property:

- View Title
- View Column Header
- View Column.

Four ACF engines are available for XPages applications:

- **acf:** Parses the HTML text and filters out the unsafe constructs. The filter used is based on a default configuration shipped with the XPages runtime. The default configuration can be over-ridden by specifying a custom `acf-config.xml` configuration file in your Notes/Domino `data/properties` directory.
- **striptags:** Removes all the tags using a regular expression:

```
'replaceAll("\\<.*?>","")'
```

- **identity:** Does nothing but return the original string. This option is useful if you have the engine set to `acf` and you want to override this setting for one particular control.
- **empty:** Removes everything and returns an empty string.

The Rich Text Editor control is a special case, because it can allow HTML to be directly entered and displays its content as HTML by default. There are two global properties with the following default values:

```
xsp.richtext.default.htmlfilter=acf
xsp.richtext.default.htmlfilterin=
```

This means that the content for any Rich Text Editor control is, by default, filtered when the HTML data is emitted from the RichTextEditor control but not when input from a web browser.

Note that these default ACF properties can be overridden in the Notes/Domino `data/properties/xsp.properties` file. If this file does not exist, make a copy of the supplied `xsp.properties.sample` file and rename it `xsp.properties`.

To create a custom configuration file for the ACF filter engine, specify the configuration file to use in Notes/Domino `data/properties/xsp.properties` by adding (or uncomment) the line:

```
xsp.htmlfilter.acf.config=acf-config.xml
```

In the `data/properties` directory, make a copy of `acf-config.xml.sample` in the same folder and use this file as the basis for your extended or enhanced ACF rules. Listing 21.7 shows an example `acf-config.xml` file with some filter rules.

Listing 21.7 Sample ACF Custom Configuration

```
<?xml version="1.0"?>
<config>

    <filter-chain>
        <filter name='base'
                class='com.ibm.trl.acf.impl.html.basefilter.BaseFilter'
                verbose-output='false' use-annotation='false' />
    </filter-chain>

    <filter-rule id='base'>
        <target scope=''>
            <!— C14N rules —>
            <rule c14n='true' all='true' />

            <!— Base rules —>
            <rule attribute='on' attribute-criterion='starts-with'
                  action='remove-attribute-value' />
            <rule attribute='${' attribute-criterion='starts-with'
                  action='remove-attribute-value' />
            <rule attribute='href' value='javascript:'
                  value-criterion='contains'
                  action='remove-attribute-value' />
            <rule attribute='style' action='remove-attribute-value' />

            <rule tag='script' action='remove-tag' />
            <rule tag='style' action='remove-tag' />
        </target>
    </filter-rule>
</config>
```

The best way to learn is to look at the sample configuration file where most of the keywords are self-explanatory. For example:

```
<rule attribute='on' attribute-criterion='starts-with' action='remove-
attribute-value' />
```

This rule means remove attributes that start with the sequence of letters 'on'. If the input contains any tag attributes, such as onmouseover or onclick, these are removed, while still leaving the enclosing tag. If you want to strip out the complete tag, use a rule similar to the following:

```
<rule tag='script' action='remove-tag' />
```

This rule removes all the '`script`' tags.

One important thing to remember with ACF filtering is that it is based on a "blacklist" approach. This means that everything is allowed, and only code matching the specified patterns are removed. As new vulnerabilities are discovered, the blacklist needs to be updated.

ACF filtering can also be applied programmatically. The XPages server-side JavaScript context global object provides two methods:

```
filterHTML(html:String, processor: String) : String
filterHTML(html:String) : String
```

The methods accept a string of markup that is filtered using the specified engine and return the processed string as a result. If no engine is specified, `acf` is used. A typical use case might be where you want to verify that the result of several input fields do not form a string with malicious content when concatenated.

Public Access

Public Access is supported in XPages from release 8.5.2 onward. Public Access enables users to view, create, and edit documents they would not normally have access to. In the application Access Control List (ACL), the `Anonymous` user, for example, can have a level of `No Access` that, by default, gives the user no access privileges at all. You can then optionally grant the `Read public documents` and/or `Write public documents` privileges to `Anonymous`, which allows the `Anonymous` user to view, create, and edit certain documents in the application that have been marked for public access.

Any documents that should be accessible to Public Access users must contain a field called `$PublicAccess`, which is a text field with a default value of 1. After the user has the ACL privilege to `Read public documents` or `Write public documents`, they can access the document accordingly.

As previously mentioned, although XPages are typically associated with forms, it is not necessary to have the `Available to Public Access users` attribute set in the Security tab of the Forms Properties box to enable public access for XPages.

Views also have a public access property and this is enforced in an XPages application. Typically, users who are not on the view Readers list do not see the contents of a view. If the view has the `Available to Public Access User` property set in the access control options for the view, those documents that are available to Public Access users appear in the view. On an XPage, if the view defined as the data source for a View Panel component does not make its data available to Public Access users, the View Panel does not display any data—only the column headers and pagers.

Setting Public Access for XPages

To make an XPage available to Public Access users, enable the `Available to Public Access users` property in the Security section of the Properties tab for the XPages design element. To access the design element properties, ensure the XPages design element is selected, not the actual XPage open in the design canvas.

If a user is a Public Access user and the XPage is not available for Public Access users, a `NoAccessSignal` exception is thrown, which causes the web browser to prompt the user to authenticate.

For XPages in the Notes Client, if a user does not have access to a particular XPage, a security exception is thrown instead of a `NoAccessSignal`; therefore, the user is not prompted to log in again. They see a default error page or other appropriate page that the application presents if it catches and handles the security exception.

Checking for Public Access in XPages

Only the XPage is checked for Public Access. All the other design elements and controls are not checked. A Public Access user that only has the `Write public documents` access level privilege does not get access to a Public Access XPage. The user must have at least the `Read public documents` privilege.

If a Public Access user without the `Write public documents` access level privilege tries to open an XPage that is available to Public Access users to create a new document, the XPages runtime raises a `NoAccessSignal` exception that causes the web browser to prompt the user to authenticate as a user who has the appropriate privileges. If they cannot, permission to open the XPage is denied. If the same user tries to edit an existing public access document, XPages shows the data but opens the XPage in read-only mode.

A Public Access user may try to open an XPage, either programmatically via an Open Page Server Side Simple Action, or via a URL. For example:

```
http:servexpages.nsf/xPerson.xsp?action=readDocument
```

The XPages runtime checks for a document ID. If no document ID is specified, even though the requested mode was readDocument, XPages attempts to create a new document. Because the Public Access user does not have the privilege to create documents, a `NoAccessSignal` is thrown, and the web browser prompts the user to log in as a user with the appropriate access level privilege.

A Public Access user may try to view a document by entering a URL directly into the web browser. For example:

```
http://server/xpages.nsf/myXPage.xsp?documentId=ABCD44ABC2F008C68025776
E00450E1A&action=readDocument
```

The request is prevented, and the application raises a `NotesException: Invalid universal id`.

SessionAsSigner

At the start of this chapter, it was pointed out that there are two orthogonal security aspects to XPages. The first controls which users can sign XPages that are allowed run on the Domino server. The second controls the tasks and operations the authenticated web user is allowed to perform, as specified in the application ACL and document security. When an XPage is invoked, security checking is applied using the invoker name (the web user).

There are some scenarios where you want security checking applied to the creator, the signer of the XPage. For example, you might want a web user to be able to add comments to a discussion thread as a response document. However, you might not want them to be able to edit the original parent document, but you do want the application, after they added their comment, to increment and update the comment count item in the parent document. Because the XPage runs in the security context of the web user, this operation would be prevented, even though the signer of the XPages would have the required application ACL permissions.

From XPages 8.5.2 onward, there are two server-side JavaScript objects to support this scenario where the application can execute in the security context of the XPage signer, as opposed to the web user. The two objects, listed in Table 21.5, are `sessionAsSigner`, which opens a session using the signer rights, and `sessionAsSignerWithFullAccess`, which opens a session using the signer rights, while giving it full access to document data. The signer credential used for the session is the top level XPage signer.

Table 21.5 sessionAsSigner Server-Side JavaScript

Server Side JavaScript Object Name	Comment
`sessionAsSigner`	Opens a session based on the signer of the XPages design element. The session is restricted by the application's ACL and the Security tab of the server's Domino Directory entry.
`sessionAsSignerWithFullAccess`	Opens a session based on the signer of the XPages design element and allows full administrative access to the application's data. A Readers field in a document does not restrict full access. The signer must have the appropriate right to full access or the session is not created.

Listing 21.8 shows how to obtain a sessionAsSigner session. When run, the snippet can be used to show how the effective user is different from the current session using credentials of the web user and the sessionAsSigner that uses the credentials of the XPage signer.

Listing 21.8 Using sessionAsSigner

```
<xp:inputText id="inputText1"
    value="#{javascript:session.getEffectiveUserName()}">
</xp:inputText>

<xp:inputText id="inputText2"
value="#{javascript:sessionAsSigner.getEffectiveUserName();}">
</xp:inputText>

<xp:inputText id="inputText3">
<xp:this.value><![CDATA[#{javascript:var sess:NotesSession =
                                                        sessionAsSigner;
var result = "";
var dbname = "TestCase01"
if (sess != null) {
    var db:NotesDatabase = sess.getDatabase(null, dbname, false);
    if (db != null) {
        result += "Using Application ("+db.getFileName()+") ";
        if (sess.isOnServer()) {
            result += "running on Server ("+sess.getServerName()+").";
        } else {
            result += " running locally.";
        }
    } else {
        result = "database is NULL";
    }
}
else {
    return "sessionAsSigner is NULL";
}
return result;}]]>
</xp:this.value>
</xp:inputText>
```

After the server-side JavaScript code has a reference to the session that runs as the signer, it can, based on the application ACL restrictions for the signer, get the database and read, create, or edit documents and perform whatever tasks are required that the web user who invoked the XPage is prevented from doing.

Note that for XPages in the Notes client, this functionality is not supported and these Java Script objects return the current session for the user logged into the Notes client.

Enabling Extended Java Code with the java.policy File

Another configuration file to know about is the java.policy file. The XPages Java Security Manager uses this file to determine what classes are trusted in the XPages runtime environment of the Notes client and Domino server. It is located in the `jvm\lib\security` folder under the Notes/Domino root installation directory. The Notes client has an additional java.policy file in its root directory. This is done to support the Mac platform. The content of both files is effectively concatenated as one by the security manager on the Notes client. Listing 21.9 shows a snippet from the java.policy file on a Domino 9.0.1 server.

Listing 21.9 Sample Snippet from a Domino 9 Server java.policy Configuration File

```
// Standard extensions get all permissions by default

grant codeBase "file:${java.home}/lib/ext/*" {
    permission java.security.AllPermission;
};

// default permissions granted to all domains

grant {
    // Allows any thread to stop itself
    // using the java.lang.Thread.stop()
    // method that takes no argument.
    // Note that this permission is granted by default only to remain
    // backwards compatible.
    // It is strongly recommended that
    // you either remove this permission
    // from this policy file or further restrict it to code sources
    // that you specify, because Thread.stop() is potentially unsafe.
    // See "http://java.sun.com/notes" for more information.
    permission java.lang.RuntimePermission "stopThread";

    // allows anyone to listen on un-privileged ports
    permission java.net.SocketPermission "localhost:1024-", "listen";

    // "standard" properties that can be read by anyone

    permission java.util.PropertyPermission "java.version", "read";
    permission java.util.PropertyPermission "java.vendor", "read";
    permission java.util.PropertyPermission "java.vendor.url", "read";
    "java.vm.specification.name", "read";
    permission java.util.PropertyPermission "java.vm.version", "read";
    // etc ...
    permission java.util.PropertyPermission "java.vm.vendor", "read";
```

```
    permission java.util.PropertyPermission "java.vm.name", "read";
    permission java.util.PropertyPermission "javax.realtime.version",
➥"read";
};

// Notes java code gets all permissions

grant codeBase "file:${notes.binary}/*" {
    permission java.security.AllPermission;
};

grant codeBase "file:${notes.binary}/rjext/*" {
    permission java.security.AllPermission;
};

grant codeBase "file:${notes.binary}/ndext/*" {
    permission java.security.AllPermission;
};

grant codeBase "file:${notes.binary}/xsp/-" {
    permission java.security.AllPermission;
};

grant codeBase "file:${notes.binary}/osgi/-" {
    permission java.security.AllPermission;
};
```

The first grant statement in Listing 21.9 declares that the security manager trusts any Java JAR files located in the `jvm\lib\ext` folder under the root Notes/Domino directory. This means that you could drop your own custom Java libraries into this location, and they would be included in the class path and trusted by the security manager at runtime. This is not a recommended practice, however, because the location is intended for global system libraries, hence including private custom libraries in this location could potentially compromise the security model if not managed properly. With that said, if you have a Java library that should be usable by both the XPages Runtime and the Java Agent Manager, then this location will allow that library to be visible for each case.

At the bottom of the listing are some other locations that are also granted all permissions by the security manager. Shaded in gray is the xsp subfolder; you can include your own custom Java libraries at this location (for example, by including a JAR file in the `xsp\shared` folder). This is no longer a recommended practice, but it is still supported for historical reasons. You can also encapsulate your custom Java classes in a plug-in and place them in the OSGi location (the last entry in the listing), to ensure that your classes are successfully loaded. However, this is also not recommended because the upgrade installer removes everything under the osgi folder whenever the server is next upgraded. The recommended way is to deploy custom plug-ins in the workspace subfolder path under the server data directory (`domino\workspace\applications\eclipse\plugins`). This location automatically inherits all Java 2 security settings of the OSGi directory, and contents are preserved in the event of an upgrade.

If you want to include custom Java code in an NSF and reuse it in other XPages applications, you must add a grant declaration, such as that shown in Listing 21.10.

Listing 21.10 A Grant Declaration for XPages Java Code Contained in an NSF Application

```
grant codeBase "xspnsf://server:0/xsp85code.nsf/-" {
    permission java.security.AllPermission;
};
```

The xspnsf protocol identifies the code source as coming from XPages in an NSF file. The server, port, and actual NSF file are then specified in the remaining part of the URL. You can refine the scope of the approved code source by further modifying the URL. For example, to allow only Java code called via server-side JavaScript to execute, add a script path identifier. Listing 21.11 shows the modified grant declaration.

Listing 21.11 A Grant Declaration for XPages Java Called Via SSJS in an NSF Application

```
grant codeBase "xspnsf://server:0/xsp85code.nsf/script/-" {
    permission java.security.AllPermission;
};
```

Note also that some URLs are suffixed with an asterisk character (*), whereas others end with a hyphen (-). The former includes all files in the designated location; the latter is recursive, meaning it also includes any libraries found in subfolders of the location.

The other entries in the java.policy file may be vaguely interesting to you. For example, you can see where the other standard Java components, such as Notes/Domino extensions (ndext), are declared. There is also a collection of individual permission declarations:

```
permission java.util.PropertyPermission "java.version", "read";
```

This simply means that anyone is allowed to read the version of Java running on Notes/Domino. The other individual statements are equally straightforward.

Conclusion

There are many aspects to XPages security, but at its core, it builds on the existing Notes/Domino security mechanisms and honors and enforces both document security and ACL access—two cornerstones of Notes/Domino security. XPages are run as compiled Java code and may contain embedded user-defined Java code. The XPages runtime must protect the server and client platforms from any potential malicious code that might be contained within the application NSF. It leverages the Java security architecture to provide tight control while endeavoring to keep XPages as flexible and powerful as possible. This chapter should help you, as an application developer, build XPages applications that provide all the necessary functionality in a secure and reliable way.

PART VII

Appendixes

APPENDIX A

XSP Programming Reference

Over the course of this book, you learned to build a host of XPages samples using the XSP tag language, JavaScript, and Java. Although all the various examples and exercises covered most of the mainstream XSP tags and programming classes, you need a complete reference guide at your finger tips to get the most out of XPages application development. This appendix provides access to these resources, which can be broken into four main categories:

- XSP tags that comprise markup language
- XSP Java classes that comprise XPages Java API
- Notes/Domino Java API classes
- JavaScript pseudo classes that map to the XSP and Notes/Domino APIs

The reference documentation for these resources is available from various different sources, and access to them is explained in the following sections.

XSP Tag Reference

The help documentation in Notes/Domino 9.0.1 has matured a lot since the early 8.5 releases and provides a full description of all standard XSP component tags, including all tags introduced to the XPages runtime from the XPages Extension Library. It is probably easiest for you to access this information via Domino Designer. To do so, invoke the **Help > Help Contents** main menu, choose the **IBM Domino Designer User Guide** from the content navigator, and open the **Designing XPages applications** section. Here you should explore both the **Adding controls** and **Control reference** topics from the XPages Extension Library links. Figure A.1 shows sample content.

This information has also been published on the web and can be found on the IBM developerWorks site (and possibly others):

`www.ibm.com/developerworks/lotus/documentation/dominodesigner/.`

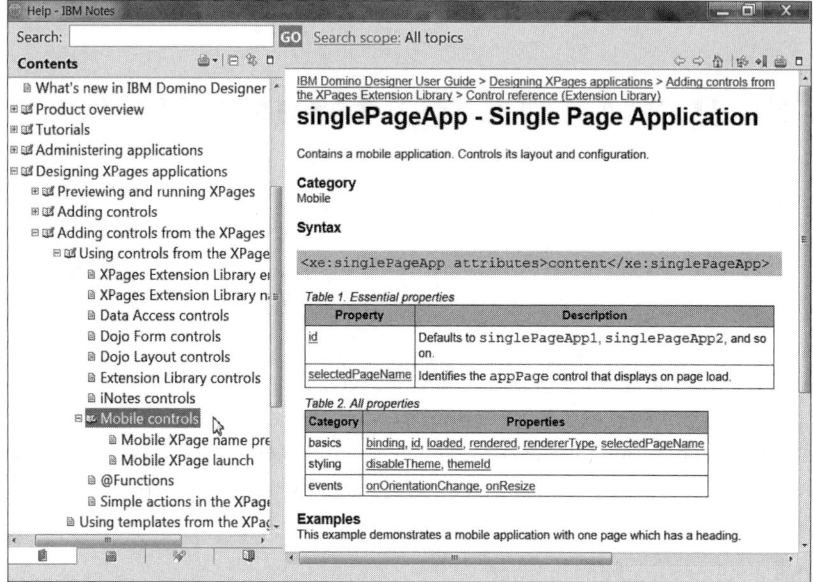

Figure A.1 XSP tag reference guide

XSP Java Classes

The XSP Java classes are described in Javadoc format and are available for you to download from IBM Press website:

```
www.ibmpressbooks.com/title/9780133373370/XPages_JavaDoc_901.zip
```

After you download the zip file to your local computer or server, unzip the archive to a folder so that you can access its contents using a web browser. For example, if you choose an installation folder named XPages-Doc, your top-level directories should look like this:

```
Directory of <root_installation_dir>\XPages-Doc\9.0.1\
com
resources
allclasses-frame.html
allclasses-noframe.html
constant-values.html
contents.out
deprecated-list.html
help-doc.html
index-all.html
index.html
overview-frame.html
overview-summary.html
```

```
overview-tree.html
package-list
serialized-form.html
stylesheet.css
version
```

You need to open index.html, which is highlighted in the previous code, in your browser, because this is the main entry point to the Javadoc library. Figure A.2 shows that page.

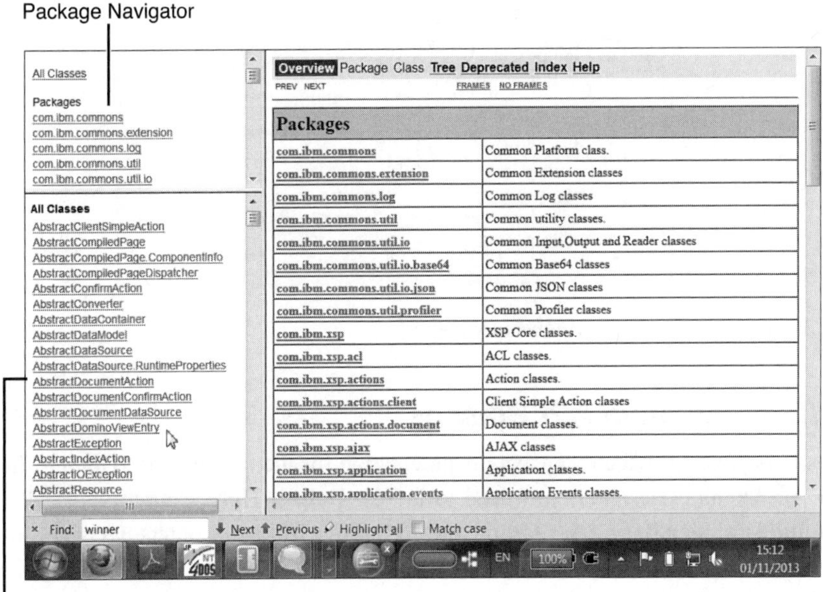

Figure A.2 Javadoc for XPages Java classes

In keeping with standard Javadoc format, classes are organized by package and class listings in the frames on the left side of the screen, and detailed content is displayed in the main frame. You can navigate to any particular Java package or class and select it for display. After you select a class, a summary of its member variables, methods, and other details are provided in the main window. Figure A.3 shows the `DominoViewEntry` class, which was used extensively in various chapters, particularly those in Part III, "Data Binding."

If you want to browse the Javadoc online rather than downloading the archive locally, the documentation is also available on the Domino Designer wiki at this location: `www-10.lotus.com/ldd/ddwiki.nsf/dx/XPages_Extensibility_API_Documentation`.

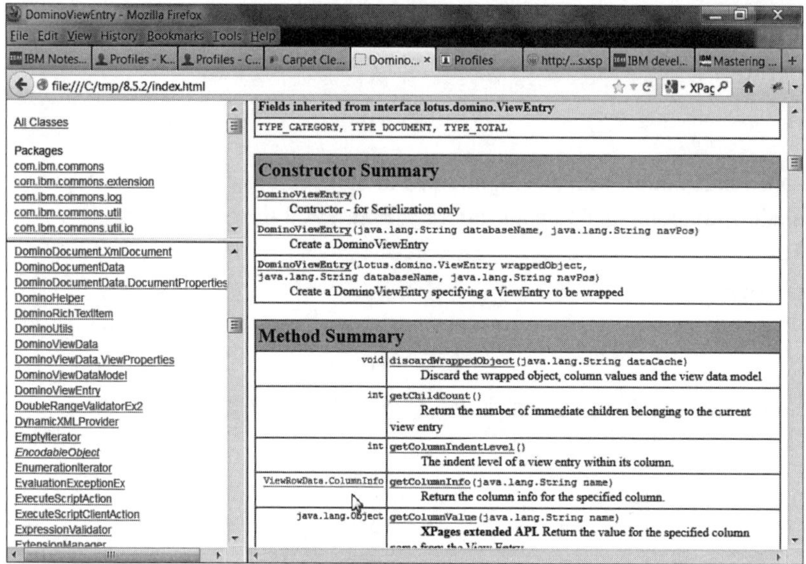

Figure A.3 Javadoc for DominoViewEntry class

Notes/Domino Java API Classes

The Notes help pages provide extensive documentation for the native Notes/Domino Java API classes. From Domino Designer, you need to invoke **Help > Help Contents** and choose the **IBM Domino Designer Basic User Guide and Reference** from the content navigator in the left frame. Expand the **Java/CORBA Classes > Java Classes A –Z** section for full details of all Java classes. Figure A.4 shows a sample help page:

XSP JavaScript Pseudo Classes

Both the XSP and Notes/Domino Java API classes can be called directly from JavaScript in XPages. To do so, you need to always use the fully qualified class name, which can prove awkward for an application developer. A library of XSP JavaScript pseudo classes has been provided to make this task easier. For example, the `NotesViewEntry` JavaScript class provides script access to the Notes/Domino `ViewEntry` class, but it removes the need to know and types out the full package name of the underlying class. It also offers useful features, such as predictive method name type ahead and so forth.

In certain instances, some XSP Java classes also wrap Notes/Domino Java API (for example, `DominoViewEntry` wraps `ViewEntry`, `DominoDocument` wraps `Document`, and so on). The XSP wrapper classes manage and adapt the native Notes/Domino classes so that they function properly in an XPages runtime context. These XSP wrapper classes ensure, for example, that object data contained in the native classes is kept in scope for the duration of the XPages request processing lifecycle. The wrapper classes sometimes offer supplemental methods to enhance XPages programmability or remove access to some native methods that cannot always be guaranteed to work in an XPages context. Script access to the XSP wrapper classes is also provided via the library of JavaScript pseudo classes. For example, the JavaScript `NotesXspViewEntry` class is to the XSP `DominoViewEntry` Java class what JavaScript `NotesViewEntry` class is to the Notes `ViewEntry` class, `NotesXspDocument` is to `DominoDocument` what `NotesDocument` is to `Document`, and so on. As you can see, the pattern is to prefix the JavaScript classes that map to the XSP Java class as `NotesXspXxx`, while the `NotesXxx` JavaScript classes target the regular Notes/Domino Java API classes.

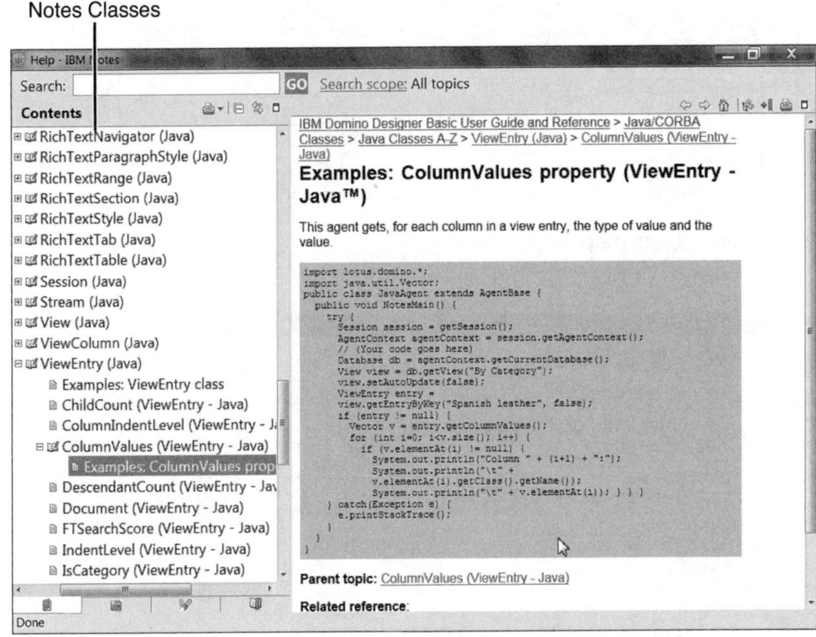

Figure A.4 Help pages for Notes/Domino Java API classes

A map of all these JavaScript classes is available on the Domino Designer wiki. Selecting any object in the map allows you navigate to its associated reference documentation. This works as a handy quick reference for you: `www-10.lotus.com/ldd/ddwiki.nsf/dx/XPages_Domino_Object_map_8.5.2`. This object map is still valid today for Notes/Domino 9.0.1.

Figure A.5 shows the object map.

The class documentation that the object map targets is also available as part of the Notes/Domino help pages. Invoke the **Help > Help Contents** main menu, choose the **IBM Domino Designer XPages Reference Guide** from the content navigator, and open the **Domino** section. Figure A.6 shows sample content.

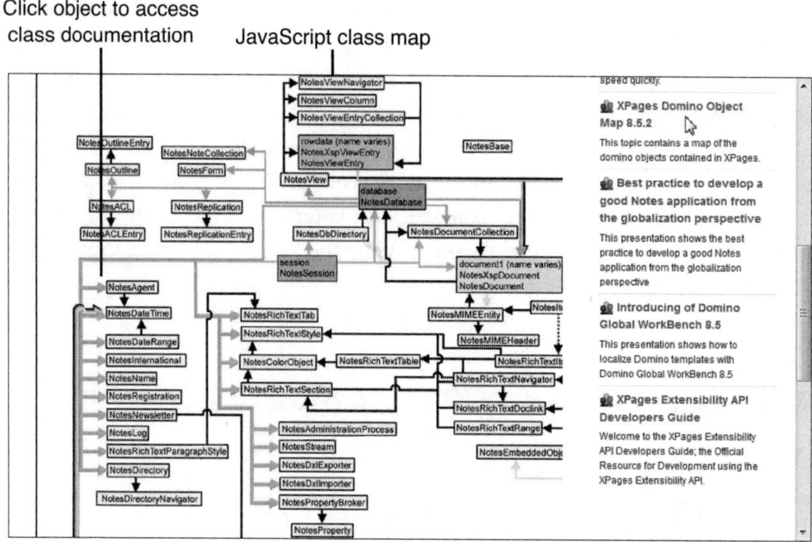

Figure A.5 XPages Domino object map

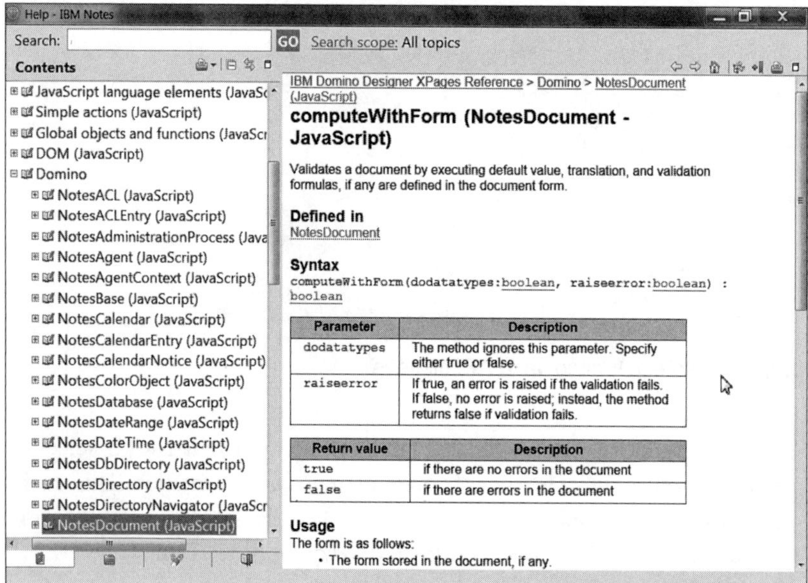

Figure A.6 XPages Domino JavaScript class reference

APPENDIX B

XSP Style Class Reference

For each of the themes provided by XPages in a Notes/Domino 9.0.1 installation, there are several XPages-specific CSS files included over and above those that are specific to the theme. Each of these CSS files is prefixed with `xsp` to denote its special use by the XPages runtime. Subsequently, each CSS style class within these CSS files is also prefixed with `xsp` to denote its relationship to XPages. This appendix describes both the XPages CSS files and style classes. In addition, the closing section of this appendix also describes information about the IBM OneUI specific style classes and where to find the public documentation about this styling toolkit.

XSP CSS Files

As Table B.1 shows, there are ten different XPages CSS files. You can find these within your Notes/Domino 9.0.1 installation within the following location:

```
<Notes/Domino>\data\domino\java\xsp\theme\<Theme>
```

Note that only a subset of these gets emitted when an XPage is requested. This is calculated based on the type of requesting browser and required language direction for the request locale. This is managed by the underlying Theme resource declarations and conditions, as detailed in Chapter 16, "XPages Theming." However, the xsp.css file is regarded as the base CSS file and is always emitted for every XPage. The other CSS files then build upon its contents based on target browser and locale requirements using server-side responsive resource management.

Table B.1 The XPages Specific CSS Files Found Within Each Theme

CSS Filename	Description
`xsp.css`	Base CSS file used by all emitted XPages
`xspLTR.css`	Used by XPages in a left-to-right direction
`xspRTL.css`	Used by XPages in a right-to-left direction

CSS Filename	Description
xspIE.css	Used by XPages in any version of a Microsoft IE browser
xspIERTL.css	Used by XPages in any version of an Microsoft IE browser in a right-to-left direction
xspIE06.css	Used by XPages in a Microsoft IE version 6 browser
xspIE78.css	Used by XPages in a Microsoft IE version 7 or 8 browser
xspFF.css	Used by XPages in any version of a Firefox browser
xspSF.css	Used by XPages in any version of a Safari browser
xspRCP.css	Used by XPages in the Notes client

XSP Style Classes

Table B.2 contains a list of the top-level XPages style classes. All these can be found in the `xsp.css` file within any of the Themes. You will also find a subset of overridden versions within each of the other XPages CSS files that fulfill the needs of their respective target browser and locale requirements. Table B.2 gives you the style class name, a brief description of what XPages control uses it, and to what type of HTML tag it gets applied. If you require more information on any of these style classes, examine the contents of the XPages CSS files, where you see the actual style rules of each of these style classes.

Table B.2 Style Classes Found Within Each of the XPages-Specific CSS Files

Style Class	Description	HTML Tag
xspView	Applied to the emitted body of an XPage	<BODY>
xspForm	Applied to the emitted form of an XPage	<FORM>
xspTextComputedField	Applied to a Computed Field	<SPAN>
xspTextLabel	Applied to a label	<SPAN>
xspTextViewTitle	Applied to a view panel title	<SPAN>
xspTextViewColumn	Applied to a view panel column text value	<SPAN>
xspTextViewColumnComputed	Applied to a view panel column computed value	<SPAN>
xspTextViewColumnHeader	Applied to a view panel column header	<SPAN>
xspInputFieldDateTimePicker	Applied to a Date Time Picker icon	<INPUT>
xspInputFieldDateTimePicker Icon	Applied to a Date Time Picker icon	<SPAN>

Style Class	Description	HTML Tag
xspInputFieldDatePickerIcon	Applied to a Date Picker icon	<SPAN>
xspInputFieldTimePickerIcon	Applied to a Time Picker icon	<SPAN>
xspInputFieldEditBox	Applied to an edit box	<INPUT>
xspInputFieldSecret	Applied to an edit box with password set	<INPUT>
xspInputFieldTextArea	Applied to a multiline edit box	<TEXTAREA>
xspInputFieldRichText	Applied to a rich text	<DIV>
xspInputFieldFileUpload	Applied to a file upload	<INPUT>
xspLink	Applied to a link	<A>
xspLinkFileDownload	Applied to a file download column link	<A>
xspLinkViewColumn	Applied to a view panel column link	<A>
xspLinkViewColumnImage	Applied to a view panel column link image	<IMG>
xspButtonCommand	Applied to a button	<BUTTON>
xspButtonSubmit	Applied to a button with type set to Submit	<BUTTON>
xspButtonCancel	Applied to a button with type set to Cancel	<BUTTON>
xspCheckBox	Applied to a checkbox	<INPUT>
xspCheckBoxViewColumn	Applied to a view panel column checkbox	<INPUT>
xspCheckBoxViewColumnHeader	Applied to a view panel header checkbox	<INPUT>
xspRadioButton	Applied to a radio button	<INPUT>
xspListBox	Applied to a listbox	<SELECT>
xspComboBox	Applied to a combo box	<SELECT>
xspImage	Applied to an image	<IMG>
xspImageViewColumn	Applied to a view panel column image	<IMG>
xspImageViewColumnHeader	Applied to a view panel column header image	<IMG>
xspImageViewColumnHeaderSort	Applied to a view panel column header sort image	<IMG>
xspMessage	Applied to an error message	<SPAN>
xspMessages	Applied to error messages	<SPAN>
xspSection	Applied to a section	<DIV>
xspSection-header	Applied to a section header	<DIV>
xspSection-header-underline	Applied to a section header, underline type	<DIV>

Style Class	Description	HTML Tag
xspSection-wide-header	Applied to a section header, wide type	<DIV>
xspSection-box-header	Applied to a section header, box type	<DIV>
xspSection-tab-header	Applied to a section header, tab type	<DIV>
xspSection-tab-header-layout	Applied to a section header, tab layout container	<DIV>
xspSection-tab-header-layout-underline	Applied to a section header, tab layout underline	<DIV>
xspSection-body	Applied to a section body	<DIV>
xspTabbedPanelOuter	Applied to a tabbed panel outer container	<DIV>
xspTabbedPanelContainer	Applied to a tabbed panel container	<DIV>
xspTabbedPanelTabs	Applied to a tabbed panel tabs container	<UL>
xspSelectedTab	Applied to a tabbed panel selected tab	<LI>
xspTabbedPanelContent Separator	Applied to a tabbed panel content separator	<DIV>
xspTabTabbedPanel	Applied to a tabbed panel tab content container	<DIV>
xspUnselectedTab	Applied to a tabbed panel unselected tab	<LI>
xspStartTab	Applied to a tabbed panel leading tab	<LI>
xspMiddleTab	Applied to all tabbed panel middle tabs	<LI>
xspEndTab	Applied to a tabbed panel trailing tab	<LI>
xspDataTableFileDownload	Applied to a file download	<TABLE>
xspDataTableFileDownloadType	Applied to a file download Type column header	<TH>
xspDataTableFileDownloadSize	Applied to a file download Size column header	<TH>
xspDataTableFileDownloadName	Applied to a file download Name column header	<TH>
xspDataTableFileDownload Created	Applied to a file download Created column header	<TH>
xspDataTableFileDownload Modified	Applied to a file download Modified column header	<TH>
xspDataTableFileDownload Delete	Applied to a file download Delete column header	<TH>

Style Class	Description	HTML Tag
xspDataTableFileDownload Caption	Applied to a file download caption	<CAPTION>
xspDataTableCaption	Applied to a data table caption	<CAPTION>
xspDataTable	Applied to a data table	<TABLE>
xspDataTableRowUnread	Applied to a data table unread row	<TR>
xspDataTableRowRead	Applied to a data table read row	<TR>
xspColumnRead	Applied to a view panel read row cell	<TD>
xspColumnUnread	Applied to a view panel unread row cell	<TD>
xspDataTableViewPanel	Applied to a view panel	<TABLE>
xspDataTableViewPanelHeader	Applied to a view panel header region	<TH>
xspDataTableViewPanelFooter	Applied to a view panel footer region	<TD>
xspDataTableViewPanelBody	Applied to a view panel body region	<TABLE>
xspDataTableViewPanel HeaderStart	Applied to a view panel leading column header	<TH>
xspDataTableViewPanel HeaderMiddle	Applied to all view panel middle column headers	<TH>
xspDataTableViewPanel HeaderEnd	Applied to a view panel trailing column header	<TH>
xspDataTableViewPanel FooterStart	Applied to a view panel leading column footer	<TD>
xspDataTableViewPanel FooterMiddle	Applied to all view panel middle column footers	<TD>
xspDataTableViewPanel FooterEnd	Applied to a view panel trailing column footer	<TD>
xspDataTableViewPanelCaption	Applied to a view panel caption	<CAPTION>
xspPanel	Applied to a panel	<DIV>
xspPanelViewColumnHeader	Applied to a view panel column header	<SPAN>
xspColumnViewStart	Applied to a view panel leading column	<TD>
xspColumnViewMiddle	Applied to all view panel middle columns	<TD>
xspColumnViewEnd	Applied to a view panel trailing column	<TD>
xspLeft	Utility style class used to left float a block container	<DIV>

Style Class	Description	HTML Tag
xspRight	Utility style class used to right float a block container	<DIV>
xspPagerContainer	Applied to a pager container	<DIV>
xspPager	Applied to a pager	<DIV>
xspPagerLeft	Applied to a pager to left float within a view panel	<DIV>
xspPagerRight	Applied to a pager to right float within a view panel	<DIV>
xspPagerNav	Applied to a pager link	<SPAN> <A>
xspStatus	Applied to a pager page number status item	<SPAN>
xspSeparator	Applied to a pager separator item	<SPAN>
xspGroup	Applied to a pager page number links group	<SPAN>
xspFirst	Applied to a pager first page link	<SPAN> <A>
xspPrevious	Applied to a pager previous page link	<SPAN> <A>
xspNext	Applied to a pager next page link	<SPAN> <A>
xspLast	Applied to a pager last page link	<SPAN> <A>
xspCurrentItem	Applied to a pager current page number item	<SPAN>

IBM OneUI Themes and Documentation

Notes/Domino 9.0.1 comes with a number of IBM OneUI themes that are readily available for use within XPages applications. In fact, both the TeamRoom and Discussion templates already make extensive use of these themes. In addition, there are a number of different versions also available within Notes/Domino 9.0.1, such as IBM OneUI v2.0, v2.1, and v3.0.2. However, in terms of supporting documentation for these particular flavors of themes, you must visit the corresponding publically available IBM OneUI documentation websites as detailed here:

IBM OneUI v2 Documentation: `www-12.lotus.com/ldd/doc/oneuidoc/docpublic/index.htm`

IBM OneUI v3 Documentation: `infolib.lotus.com/resources/oneui/3.0/docPublic/index.htm`

These documentation sites make for very valuable and interesting reading both in terms of technical detail and recommended usage patterns when using the IBM OneUI themes.

Appendix C

Useful XPages Sites on the Net

There are some great XPages resources out there on the web, and the list is growing as XPages adoption moves onward and upward. Table C.1 provides a snapshot of some of the authors' favorites—sorry if we missed your site!

Table C.1 Useful XPages Sites

Name	URL
XPages.info	xpages.info/XPagesHome.nsf/Resources.xsp
IQJam	iqjam.net/iqjam/iqjam.nsf/home.xsp?iqspace=Domino+Development%7EXPages
Stack Overflow	stackoverflow.com/questions/tagged/xpages
dominoGuru.com	www.dominoguru.com/
Matt White's Blog	mattwhite.me
XPages101 Video Training	xpages101.net
Notes/Domino 8.5 Forum	www-10.lotus.com/ldd/nd85forum.nsf/Dateallthreadedweb?OpenView
Notes/Domino Application Development wiki	www-10.lotus.com/ldd/ddwiki.nsf
NotesIn9 Screencast	notesin9.com
OpenNTF	www.openntf.org
OpenNTF Blog	www.openntf.org/blogs/openntf.nsf/FullArchive?openview
Planet Lotus	planetlotus.org/search.php?search=xpages&sort=1
Taking Notes Podcast	takingnotespodcast.com
XPages.TV	xpages.tv
XPages101 Video Training	xpages101.net
YouAtNotes XPages wiki	xpageswiki.com

Index

SYMBOLS

A

B

E

F

G

H

J

M

P

Q

R

S

T

U

V

W

Z

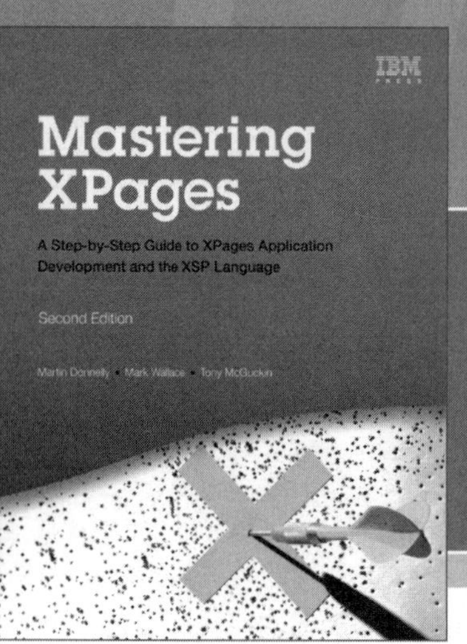

FREE Online Edition

Safari Books Online

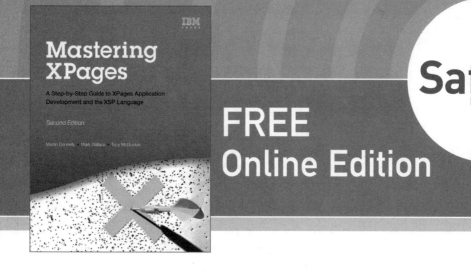

Your purchase of ***Mastering XPages: A Step-by-Step Guide to XPages Application Development and the XSP Language, Second Edition,*** includes access to a free online edition for 45 days through the **Safari Books Online** subscription service. Nearly every IBM Press book is available online through **Safari Books Online**, along with thousands of books and videos from publishers such as Addison-Wesley Professional, Cisco Press, Exam Cram, O'Reilly Media, Prentice Hall, Que, Sams, and VMware Press.

Safari Books Online is a digital library providing searchable, on-demand access to thousands of technology, digital media, and professional development books and videos from leading publishers. With one monthly or yearly subscription price, you get unlimited access to learning tools and information on topics including mobile app and software development, tips and tricks on using your favorite gadgets, networking, project management, graphic design, and much more.

Activate your FREE Online Edition at informit.com/safarifree

STEP 1: Enter the coupon code: QECQGBI.

STEP 2: New Safari users, complete the brief registration form. Safari subscribers, just log in.

If you have difficulty registering on Safari or accessing the online edition, please e-mail customer-service@safaribooksonline.com

AdobePress

Cisco Press